■ THE RESOURCE FOR THE INDEPENDENT TRAVELER

"The guides are aimed not only at young budget travelers but at the indepedent traveler; a sort of streetwise cookbook for traveling alone."

—The New York Times

"Unbeatable; good sight-seeing advice; up-to-date info on restaurants, hotels, and inns; a commitment to money-saving travel; and a wry style that brightens nearly every page."

—The Washington Post

"Lighthearted and sophisticated, informative and fun to read. [Let's Go] helps the novice traveler navigate like a knowledgeable old hand."

—Atlanta Journal-Constitution

"A world-wise traveling companion—always ready with friendly advice and helpful hints, all sprinkled with a bit of wit."

—The Philadelphia Inquirer

■ THE BEST TRAVEL BARGAINS IN YOUR PRICE RANGE

"All the dirt, dirt cheap."

—People

"Anything you need to know about budget traveling is detailed in this book."

—The Chicago Sun-Times

"Let's Go follows the creed that you don't have to toss your life's savings to the wind to travel—unless you want to."

—The Salt Lake Tribune

■ REAL ADVICE FOR REAL EXPERIENCES

"The writers seem to have experienced every rooster-packed bus and lunar-surfaced mattress about which they write."

—The New York Times

"A guide should tell you what to expect from a destination. Here Let's Go shines."

—The Chicago Tribune

LET'S GO PUBLICATIONS

TRAVEL GUIDES

Alaska & the Pacific Northwest 2003
Australia 2003
Austria & Switzerland 2003
Britain & Ireland 2003
California 2003
Central America 8th edition
Chile 1st edition **NEW TITLE**
China 4th edition
Costa Rica 1st edition **NEW TITLE**
Eastern Europe 2003
Egypt 2nd edition
Europe 2003
France 2003
Germany 2003
Greece 2003
Hawaii 2003 **NEW TITLE**
India & Nepal 7th edition
Ireland 2003
Israel 4th edition
Italy 2003
Mexico 19th edition
Middle East 4th edition
New Zealand 6th edition
Peru, Ecuador & Bolivia 3rd edition
South Africa 5th edition
Southeast Asia 8th edition
Southwest USA 2003
Spain & Portugal 2003
Thailand 1st edition **NEW TITLE**
Turkey 5th edition
USA 2003
Western Europe 2003

CITY GUIDES

Amsterdam 2003
Barcelona 2003
Boston 2003
London 2003
New York City 2003
Paris 2003
Rome 2003
San Francisco 2003
Washington, D.C. 2003

MAP GUIDES

Amsterdam
Berlin
Boston
Chicago
Dublin
Florence
Hong Kong
London
Los Angeles
Madrid
New Orleans
New York City
Paris
Prague
Rome
San Francisco
Seattle
Sydney
Venice
Washington, D.C.

CHINA

ELIZABETH LITTLE EDITOR
JING LIN ASSOCIATE EDITOR
ANGIE SUN ASSOCIATE EDITOR
KAITLIN SOLIMINE UPDATE EDITOR

RESEARCHER-WRITERS

EMILY BINKLEY
CHERYL CHAN
BARTLOMIEJ CZECH
RAN LI
ANDOR MESZAROS
EMMA NOTHMANN
CHRIS PARLATO
MICHELLE SULLIVAN
TANNA TANLAMAI
JULIE WECSIER
ALICE YANG

ANDY POON MAP EDITOR
KATHARINE HOLT MANAGING EDITOR
ALEX LEICHTMAN MANAGING EDITOR
DAVID MUEHLKE TYPESETTER

MACMILLAN

HELPING LET'S GO

If you want to share your discoveries, suggestions, or corrections, please drop us a line. We read every piece of correspondence, whether a postcard, a 10-page email, or a coconut. Please note that mail received after May 2003 may be too late for the 2004 book, but will be kept for future editions. **Address mail to:**

Let's Go: China
67 Mount Auburn Street
Cambridge, MA 02138
USA

Visit Let's Go at **http://www.letsgo.com,** or send email to:

feedback@letsgo.com
Subject: "Let's Go: China"

In addition to the invaluable travel advice our readers share with us, many are kind enough to offer their services as researchers or editors. Unfortunately, our charter enables us to employ only currently enrolled Harvard students.

Published in Great Britain 2003 by Macmillan, an imprint of Pan Macmillan Ltd.
20 New Wharf Road, London N1 9RR
Basingstoke and Oxford
Associated companies throughout the world
www.panmacmillan.com

Published in the United States of America by St. Martin's Press.

ISBN: 1-4050-0062 7
First edition
10 9 8 7 6 5 4 3 2 1

Let's Go: China is written by Let's Go Publications, 67 Mount Auburn Street, Cambridge, MA 02138, USA.

ADVERTISING DISCLAIMER

All advertisements appearing in Let's Go publications are sold by an independent agency not affiliated with the editorial production of the guides. Advertisers are never given preferential treatment, and the guides are researched, written, and published independent of advertising. Advertisements do not imply endorsement of products or services by Let's Go, and Let's Go does not vouch for the accuracy of information provided in advertisements.

If you are interested in purchasing advertising space in a Let's Go publication, contact: Let's Go Advertising Sales, 67 Mount Auburn St., Cambridge, MA 02138, USA.

CONTENTS

HOW TO USE THIS BOOK

Congratulations on discovering *Let's Go: China.* Our researchers have compiled a list of China's most fascinating features, with 800 pages of spectacular sights, history, and useful information.

INTRODUCTORY MATERIALS. The first chapter, **Discover China,** offers a broad introduction to China's most famous sights; the **Suggested Itineraries** give you an idea of what not to miss and how not to miss it. The **Life and Times** chapter provides an overview of Chinese history, art, and culture, as well some useless information purely for entertainment purposes. The **Essentials** section outlines the practical information that you will need before and during your trip.

COVERAGE. The book is divided into 11 main chapters; coverage generally moves east to west, beginning in Beijing and ending in Tibet. Within each region, cities are usually ordered as they would appear clockwise on a map. The **black tabs** in the margins will help you navigate between chapters quickly and easily.

APPENDIX. The appendix contains a **glossary** of words and phrases that may not be fully explained in the text. There's also a **pronunciation guide** and some useful **conversion** tables for those of you who opted out of the metric system. A comprehensive **phrasebook** lists useful Chinese phrases and a few choice words in Cantonese, Tibetan, and Uighur. The appendix also includes a diagram of a Chinese train ticket to help you get a handle on China's complex transportation system.

PHONE CODES AND TELEPHONE NUMBERS. The **phone code** for each region, city, or town appears next to the name of that region, city, or town, and is denoted by the ☎ icon. **Phone numbers** in text are also preceded by the ☎ icon.

THINK INSIDE THE BOX. Grayboxes feature short stories or cultural commentary that are usually amusing and are definitely informative. **Whiteboxes** provide important practical information on warnings (**!**), helpful hints and further resources (**i**), and border crossing information (**⊞**).

CHINESE CHARACTERS. Nearly every listing in this book includes Chinese **characters** and a **romanization;** even if you can't pronounce Chinese to save your life, you can at least point to the characters in the text to help you get around China.

PRICE RANGES AND RANKINGS. Our researchers list establishments in order of value from best to worst. Our absolute favorites are denoted by the Let's Go thumbs-up (☒). Since the best value does not always mean the cheapest price, we have incorporated a system of price ranges in the guide. The table below lists how prices fall within each bracket.

CHINA	❶	❷	❸	❹	❺
ACCOMMODATIONS	Y1-80	Y81-160	Y161-240	Y241-320	Y321-up
FOOD	Y1-15	Y16-30	Y31-50	Y51-100	Y101-up

A NOTE TO OUR READERS The information for this book was gathered by *Let's Go* researchers from May through August of 2001. Each listing is based on one researcher's opinion, formed during his or her visit at a particular time. Those traveling at other times may have different experiences since prices, dates, hours, and conditions are always subject to change. You are urged to check the facts presented in this book beforehand to avoid inconvenience and surprises.

RESEARCHER-WRITERS

Emily Binkley

From Beijing, Emily headed west to Wutaishan mountain and exchanged greetings with friendly monks before continuing to the Mu Us Desert. In Yulin, she sent back clean, beautiful copy and sparkling new coverage of the Great Wall (not to mention candy and Mao souvenirs for her attention-starved editors). She forged westward and gazed upon the mighty Terracotta Warriors in Xi'an; then, she trekked to Zhongwei to surf down sand dunes. Her quick pen and incredible determination were second only to her positive attitude and stellar writing; Emily was indeed a model researcher.

Cheryl Chan

Cheryl was renowned in the office for her sharp wit and scathing honesty. Cheryl threatened to overdose on mountains, visiting Jiahuashan, Huangshan, Lushan, and Wuyishan. She captured the gorgeous alpine sunrises with wistfully beautiful prose, the ease and grace of her writing amazing even the most hardened editor. Her journey then took her to China's most culinarily rich cities, where Cheryl composed some of her most jealousy-inducing prose. Her keen eye for detail contributed immeasurably to the book. But it was Cheryl's sense of humor and irreverent writing style that made her a such a superb addition to the *Let's Go: China* team.

Bartlomiej Czech

Master of languages and king of the outdoors, Bartlomiej visited the spectacular Summer Palace in Chengde before heading northeast to Changchun. At Dog Meat Village, he savored fresh-out-of-the-cage puppies. Whether in Qiqihar or elsewhere, he always kept an eye out for hilarious graybox ideas. His charm came in handy at the North Korean border, where he convinced the PSB border officials to pose for pictures. His amazing grasp of the English language often sent his editors scurrying to the dictionary, and his playful sense of humor added the perfect touch to his already remarkable copy. Bartek thanks Stella Christie for all her help.

Ran Li

Ran took on her lengthy itinerary with ease. She dove into Shanghai for an exploration of the city and its nightlife, and then meandered eastward to relax in Suzhou's peaceful gardens, where she accepted dinner invitations from besotted locals. After crossing the Grand Canal to Wuxi and staring dumbstruck at the kitschy Dragon Light Cave, she accepted a few more dinner invitations. Following the canal northeast to Zhenjiang for tasty pickled goods and dumplings, Ran then headed to Nanjing to revel in city life. There, she accepted even more dinner invitations, and topped off her itinerary with a cold bottle of Tsingtao beer. Hilarious anecdotes are proof of her amazing ability to adapt to any environment. Note to Wall Street: prepare to be dazzled.

Andor Mezaros

Lamb kebab connoisseur extraordinaire, Andor arrived in Beijing and flew to Lanzhou, where he braved the thick layers of pollution in order to send back immaculate copy. Next, he headed northwest, imbibed local spirits, and discovered a deep love for meat on a stick. Andor ventured toward Ürümqi and relaxed at Tianchi

Lake before heading to a minority village near Yining; once there, he had a nice chat with the PSB, where he honed his skills of persuasion and self-criticism. His unwitting charm never failed him throughout his unbelievable misadventures. Entertaining stories and flawless copy are the order of the day for this truly outstanding researcher.

Emma Nothmann

An editor of *Let's Go: Southeast Asia 2003*, Emma delivered irreverance with a precise combination of outrageous wit and properly placed expletives. From Chengdu, Emma headed to Moxi and Hailuogou Glacier Park, where she wrote amazingly clear copy from scratch. Making her way to Tiger Leaping Gorge, she indulged in fabulous hiking before heading south to Dali for good beer and a true Oklahoma experience. Sweet and street savvy, Emma tackled the Southwest with easy grace and good humor, weathering a blistering sunburn and resisting Dali's siren song in the process.

Chris Parlato

Chris blazes trails with reckless abandon; this trip was no exception. After sifting through the dinosaur bones and bamboo forests near Chongqing, Chris headed to the spectacular Emeishan Mountain where he composed flawless, achingly well-written copy. After sampling the cosmopolitan delights of Chengdu, he journeyed westward to Lhasa where he encountered first-hand the trials and tribulations of travel in Tibet. Along the way, however, Chris still managed to produce some of *Let's Go: China*'s most comprehensive and thoughtful coverage. This outstanding two-time researcher possesses the sense of adventure and keen observational skills that make a truly great travel writer.

Michelle Sullivan

Upon arrival in Hong Kong, she immediately began researching Guilin, exploring the surrounding minority villages, and sending back perfect copy that exceeded her editors' wildest expectations. And trust us, expectations were certainly high enough for this former *Let's Go* Publishing Director. After conquering Guangxi and Guizhou, Michelle headed north to Chongqing and took a magnificent cruise through the Three Gorges. Patient, inquisitive, and genuinely fascinated with her surroundings, Michelle found the beauty in everything; suffice it to say, we had no trouble finding the beauty in her work.

Tanna Tanlamai

Tanna gracefully fended off crowds of admiring males during her sojourn in China. She began in Qufu, the former home of Confucius. When a slightly less-than-reputable taxi driver left her in the middle of nowhere, our Tanna was able to charm her way back to civilization by hitching a ride on a passing oil tanker (despite *Let's Go*'s instruction to the contrary). In Beijing, Tanna hit the clubs and pubs and sampled the city's culinary offerings. While there, she also celebrated Beijing's winning Olympic bid in Tiananmen Square with hundreds of thousands of her closest friends. Cheerfully ignoring all mishaps and misfortune, Tanna turned in upbeat, amazingly thorough copy and kept us entertained all summer long.

Julie Wecsler

Julie stunned us with her shopping expertise and extensive knowledge of Cantonese pop culture; who would have thought that this sweet and articulate art student could tackle the crazed urbanity of Hong Kong with such ease? Julie started her travels in Zhangjiajie, where she got some fresh air before heading south to Changsha. Throughout Hunan province, she pushed patiently through the maddening crowds, emerging with heaps of thorough, accurate copy. In Guangzhou she indulged in the cosmopolitan delights of night clubs and shopping, stopping in Shenzhen to rediscover her love for kitsch. Julie's extensive knowledge of China and impeccable sense of direction helped her successfully navigate the urban jungles of Hong Kong and compose clear, eminently readable prose.

Alice Yang

Alice sent back the meticulous and thorough coverage typical of a true perfectionist. From Hong Kong, she headed to the tropical beaches on beautiful Hainan Island. Despite the less-than-inspiring city of Haikou, she pushed forward and wrote blissfully elegant copy. She basked in the sun at Sanya, met delightful and unabashedly helpful locals, avoided the unnerving chattering noises at Monkey Island, and burned her leg on a motorcycle's exceptionally poorly designed exhaust pipe. Then, she continued to research despite her painful third-degree burn, sending back miraculously pristine copy. Alice's beautiful copy and good humor remained intact, as does her reputation as an exemplary RW.

CONTRIBUTING WRITERS

Bernard Chang

Bernard is a graduate student at Harvard University and an avid fly fisher. He serves as a regional fly-fishing guide in New York and is the author of *Fly-fishing in the Middle Kingdom*, to be published in 2003.

Victoria Drake

Victoria's experience in China began 14 years ago, when she conducted research on endangered gibbons on Hainan Island. In 2002, she returned to China to devise a management plan for a new national park in Yunnan. Previously, she worked for the Smithsonian Institute and The Great Lakes Conservation Fund; started IUCN-US in Washington, DC; and was the first program director for Global Alliance for Africa in Chicago.

Alice Kung

Alice Kung is a business development consultant in Hong Kong, helping high-tech startups from Silicon Valley sell their products in Asia.

Josh Levin

Josh graduated from Harvard in 2002 and is a Let's Go veteran. He has traveled extensively throughout China, connecting with locals and getting to the heart of Chinese culture.

ACKNOWLEDGMENTS

TEAM CHINA THANKS: Our brilliant, hard-working RWs; our fabulous managing editor; our outstanding map editor; and all our typists and proofers for taking the time to make this book possible. To the women of PEB for late-night laughter, to Jen and Caleb for their help and patience, and to 7-Eleven for sweet sustenance.

ELIZABETH THANKS: Angie for her wit and friendship. Jing for her intelligence and kindness. Amélie for knowing when to help and when to humor me. Michelle for inspiration. Dan for uncommonly good conversation. Carolyn Thomas for my command of the English language. Sheila for sanity. Jason for laughter. Ellen for existing. And finally and most importantly, my parents for that whole procreation, making-me-everything-I-am thing.

JING THANKS: 爸爸妈妈 for their tender love and care; 外公外婆 for their loving support through the years. 林薇 for being my best friend; Jorge for being my best pika; Maureen for simply being the best. Angie for her great humor, Liz for her amazing leadership. 韩文爷爷 and 慧中奶奶 for the cozy Saturday afternoons. Alisha, Wuzhen, Shaz, Jinger, Gloria, 莉莉, 晓林, and 晓中 for their enduring friendships. Nicholas Tse for great music. Thanks guys; you keep me from feeling lonely.

ANGIE THANKS: Mom for passing on good advice and ■ good looks, Liz for her mischievous antics and capacity for understanding, Jing for her easy laughter and quirky humor, Amélie and PEB for being beautiful in every way, Angie M., Lil, Ria, and Shelby for laughs and good times, Sarah for being you, G for baked goods, my Mather boys, 黄老师 for being an amazing (and forgiving) teacher, Dad for your support, m-w.com for being my brain, romance novels, Starbucks, and the Afroman.

KAITLIN THANKS: Mom, Dad, A.J., and Buster, for keeping me closer to sane, Joey for always being my better (read: sexier) half, Alex for keeping this masterpiece intact, Ankur for all the cat chow mein, Harold Sheedy and Dibble for finding the Harry in me, Siggy for email therapy, Qian for sharing a bed, and China for all the dumplings I could ever eat.

Editor Elizabeth Little
Associate Editors Jing Lin, Angie Sun
Update Editor Kaitlin Solimine
Managing Editors Katharine Holt, Alex Leichtman
Map Editor Andy Poon

Publishing Director
Matthew Gibson
Editor-in-Chief
Brian R. Walsh
Production Manager
C. Winslow Clayton
Cartography Manager
Julie Stephens
Design Manager
Amy Cain
Editorial Managers
Christopher Blazejewski, Abigail Burger, D. Cody Dydek, Harriett Green, Angela Mi Young Hur, Marla Kaplan, Celeste Ng
Financial Manager
Noah Askin
Marketing & Publicity Managers
Michelle Bowman, Adam M. Grant
New Media Managers
Jesse Tov, Kevin Yip
Online Manager
Amélie Cherlin
Personnel Managers
Alex Leichtman, Owen Robinson
Production Associates
Caleb Epps, David Muehlke
Network Administrators
Steven Aponte, Eduardo Montoya
Design Associate
Juice Fong
Financial Assistant
Suzanne Siu
Office Coordinators
Alex Ewing, Adam Kline, Efrat Kussell

Director of Advertising Sales
Erik Patton
Senior Advertising Associates
Patrick Donovan, Barbara Eghan, Fernanda Winthrop
Advertising Artwork Editor
Leif Holtzman
Cover Photo Research
Laura Wyss

President
Bradley J. Olson
General Manager
Robert B. Rombauer
Assistant General Manager
Anne E. Chisholm

RUSSIA
KAZAKHSTAN
Lake Balkhash
Alma-Ata
Bishkek
KYRGYZSTAN
Yining
Ürümqi
Kuqa
TAJIKISTAN
Kashgar
XINJIANG
AFGHANISTAN
Dunhuang
GANSU
Jiayuguan
Great Wall
MON
Claimed by India, controlled by China
PAKISTAN
Golmud
QINGHAI
TIBET
Claimed by China, controlled by India
Delhi
NEPAL
Yarlung Zanbo (Brahmaputra)
Lhasa
Shigatse
Nu (Salween)
Yangzi
Claimed by China, controlled by India
Kathmandu
Mt. Everest (8848m)
Thimphu
BHUTAN
Kangding
Mekong
Lijiang
Dali
Kunmin
Baoshan
BANGLA-DESH
Dhaka
INDIA
YUN
XISHUANGBANN
MYANMAR
LAOS
Bay of Bengal
0
400 miles
0
400 kilometers
THAILAND
LG

Lake Baikal
Mohe
RUSSIA
HEILONGJIANG
Qiqihar
Ulaanbaatar
Harbin
Mudanjiang
OLIA
INNER MONGOLIA
Jilin
Changchun
JILIN
LIAONING
NORTH KOREA
Shenyang
Hohhot
Chengde
Dandong
Great Wall
Baotou
P'yongyang
Beijing
Datong
BEIJING
Tianjin
TIANJIN
Dalian
Seoul
HEBEI
Weihai
Yinchuan
Great Wall
Taiyuan
Shijazhuang
Yantai
SOUTH KOREA
Yellow (Huang)
Yellow Sea
Yanan
SHANXI
Jinan
Qingdao
NINGXIA
Yellow
SHANDONG
Anyang
Zhengzhou
Xian
Luoyang
Kaifeng
JIANGSU
JAPAN
Tianshui
SHAANXI
HENAN
ANHUI
Yangzhou
Zhenjiang
Suzhou
Nanjing
Shanghai
Hefei
Wuxi
SHANGHAI
HUBEI
Chengdu
Wuhan
Hangzhou
Ningbo
East China Sea
Yichang
Yangzi
Jiujiang
ZHEJIANG
Chongqing
CHONGQING
Yueyang
Leshan
Nanchang
Changsha
Zunyi
HUNAN
JIANGXI
FUJIAN
GUIZHOU
Fuzhou
Guiyang
Hengyang
Taipei
Anshun
Quanzhou
Guilin
TAIWAN R.O.C
Xiamen
Shaoguan
GUANGXI
GUANGDONG
Shantou
Guangzhou
Nanning
HONG KONG SAR
MACAU SAR
South China Sea
Hanoi
Haikou
HAINAN
Sanya
People's Republic of China

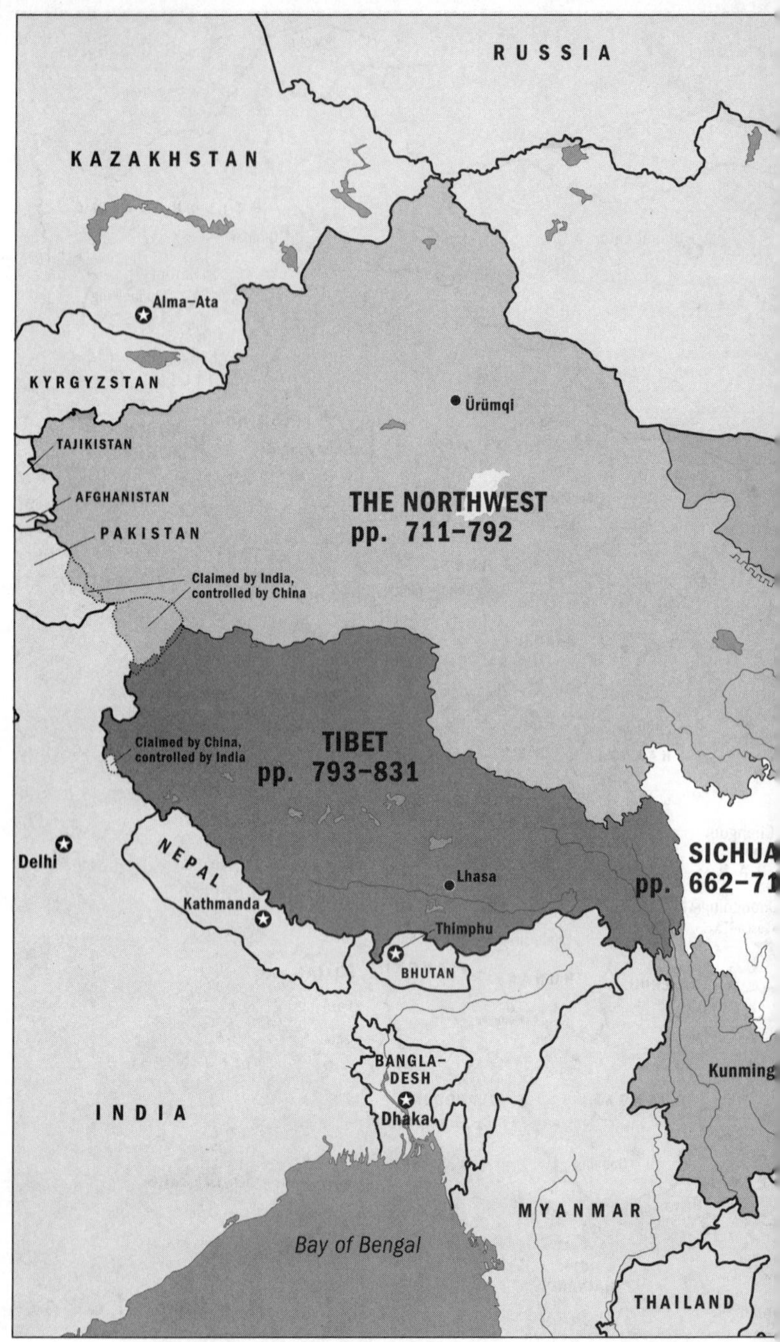
RUSSIA
KAZAKHSTAN
Alma-Ata
KYRGYZSTAN
Ürümqi
TAJIKISTAN
AFGHANISTAN
PAKISTAN
THE NORTHWEST
pp. 711–792
Claimed by India,
controlled by China
TIBET
pp. 793–831
Claimed by China,
controlled by India
Delhi
NEPAL
Kathmanda
Lhasa
Thimphu
BHUTAN
SICHUA
pp. 662–71
BANGLA-
DESH
Dhaka
Kunming
INDIA
MYANMAR
Bay of Bengal
THAILAND

RUSSIA
THE NORTHEAST
pp. 203–244
Harbin
Changchun
Ulaanbaatar
MONGOLIA
NORTH
KOREA
Shenyang
Great Wall
Hohhot
Beijing
P'yŏngyang
CENTRAL CHINA
pp. 245–312
Tianjin
Seoul
BEIJING AND
THE NORTH COAST
pp. 112–202
Taiyuan
SOUTH
KOREA
Yellow
Sea
Qingdao
JAPAN
Xi'an
Nanjing
Hefei
Shanghai
Chengdu
Wuhan
Hangzhou
SHANGHAI AND
THE YANGZI DELTA
pp. 313–396
Chongqing
East China
Sea
THE YANGZI BASIN
pp. 397–456
Guiyang
THE
SOUTH
COAST
pp. 457–520
T'aipei
TAIWAN
THE SOUTHWEST
pp. 571–661
Guangzhou
VIETNAM
Hanoi
HONG KONG
AND MACAU
pp. 521–570
South China
Sea
Haikou
0
400 miles
0
400 kilometers
China: Chapters

DISCOVER CHINA

China is in the midst of a slow explosion. Five thousand years of history and not yet anywhere near past its prime, China today is very much under construction. Chinese history is a staggeringly long tale of civilzation, conquest, and expansion, and this particular moment in time is no exception. Everywhere, old buildings, roads, traditions, and ideas are being torn down as new frameworks are erected, some making careful use of the past, others branching out in new directions altogether. China is dynamic and exciting, with sprawling, sophisticated cities. It is diverse, with dozens of minority nationalities, cuisines, and cultures. It is a place of tremendous natural beauty, with vast, fertile plains and expansive mountain panoramas. Don't let the world's most populous country intimidate you, however: Jump into this guide and get to know the people, places, and pleasures of the real China, an experience that will surpass all of your expectations.

WHEN TO GO

Even the best-laid travel plans are no match for the monsoons, typhoons, snowstorms, and heavy floods that periodically close China's roads, rails, and airports, sometimes making whole areas seasonally inaccessible. In general, **summer** is hot almost everywhere (except at high altitudes), and rainy and very humid south of the Yangzi River; **winters** range from extremely cold in the far north (especially north of Beijing) to extremely mild in the south. **Late spring** and **early autumn** are usually the best times to travel.

Although most of the country is temperate, southern Yunnan, Guangxi, and Guangdong provinces, as well as Hong Kong, Macau, and Hainan Island, lie in the tropics. Travelers in the summer should watch out for summer **monsoons**, which originate in the South Pacific and can carry rain as far as Mongolia; as a result, rainfall is generally greatest in the southeast, least in the northwest, and heaviest in the summer. **Typhoons** (tropical cyclones) occur year-round in coastal China, but are strongest in late summer and early autumn. Many of China's rivers, particularly the Yellow and the Yangzi, are prone to seasonal **flooding**, especially in June, July, and August. Frequent floods, landslides, and mudslides caused by heavy summer rains can make land travel treacherous, particularly in

CHINA FACTS AND FIGURES

POPULATION: 1.3 billion

LAND AREA: 9.5 million km^2

POP. DENSITY: 127.9 people per km^2

TOTAL NUMBER OF CHICKENS IN CHINA: 3 billion

EGGS LAID PER YEAR: 278.6 trillion

AMOUNT OF TEA CONSUMED PER YEAR: 17.4 billion liters

AMOUNT OF BEER PRODUCED PER YEAR: 20.9 billion tons

NUMBER OF PEOPLE PER YEAR INJURED BY EXPLODING BEER BOTTLES: 470

areas with dirt roads, rickety bridges, and otherwise poor infrastructure. For temperature and rainfall charts, see **Climate**, p. 845.

China's many **festivals** and **national holidays** can both attract and deter travelers. Traveling during the holidays is fraught with hassels—train and bus tickets are usually harder to come by, and hotels are often booked. Visiting during **Chinese New Year** (February 1, 2003) is only for the most determined of festival-goers; travel is extremely difficult all through the week surrounding that date. For a list of the major festivals in China, see p. 44.

THINGS TO DO

From temple-hopping to bar-hopping, there is a great deal of everything in China. Those with specialized interests can indulge to their hearts' content; those without will find no better opportunity to develop them. China's neon-lit cities, fascinating age-old customs, incredible sense of history, and gorgeous sights will quench the soul of even the most travel-thirsty explorer. For more specific regional attractions, see the **Highlights of the Region** section at the beginning of each chapter.

THE BACKPACKER SCENE

You've seen them here, you've smelled them there, backpackers turn up in every corner of the globe, weathered and stinky. And yet you find their lack of hygiene strangely appealing. Story-rich but currency-poor, backpackers flock to cheap and scenic towns everywhere, and China is no exception. The typical backpacker town has a handful of Western cafes, lots of cheap beer, and crowds of idle, amiable travelers who sit around, talk, and have little inclination to do much else. **Yangshuo** (p. 583), in Guilin province, and **Dali** (p. 602), in Yunnan province are China's archetypical backpacker towns. Each is blessed with natural splendor, a mild climate, friendly residents, and few oft-used showers in sight. The desert oasis of **Dunhuang** (p. 746), in Gansu province, is coming to enjoy almost the same reputation for a laid-back atmosphere and clean-free policy. Shanghai's **Nanjing Xi Lu** and **French Concession** (p. 328), Beijing's **Sanlitun** (p. 144), Hong Kong's **Lan Kwai Fong** (p. 542), and much of **Guangdong province** (p. 480) welcome more permanent foreign vagabonds, cleanliness optional.

... AND HOW TO AVOID IT

The backpacker scene does have its drawbacks, namely, other bodies crowding your elbow room. Other Westerners can doubtless insulate you from the very culture that you traveled thousands of miles to experience; and they probably smell, too (see above). Fortunately, a few regions have features (including cheap accommodations, cultural diversity, and striking topography) that *should* attract hordes of backpackers—but don't, at least not yet. The remote **Kaili** (p. 651) region of Guizhou province is filled with tiny Miao, Dong, and other minority villages set amid breathtaking scenery. Much of northwestern China, especially the Silk Road towns of **Kashgar** (p. 777) and **Kuqa** (p. 774), the Tibetan-style village of **Xiahe** (p. 731), and the **Yili River** region (p. 764) to the far north, presents a vastly different portrait of China, sans conversation-prone tourists. In Sichuan, the small towns of **Moxi** (p. 686), **Kangding** (p. 688), and **Songpan** (p. 693) tempt travelers with lush, untrampled scenery and exciting outdoor activities. In the southeast, venture to Fujian's **Wuyishan** (p. 464) or the rural areas of **Guangdong**

(p. 508) for a glimpse of rice and tea plantations, craggy peaks, and traditional villages left virtually untouched by the region's recent economic success, not to mention by the grubby hands of chatty backpackers.

URBAN LEGENDS

More than 100 Chinese cities have over one million inhabitants, and almost each one is on the bumpy road to modernization. Take your time to ogle at and explore the sumptuous streets of these busy cities: **Hong Kong** (p. 525), crowned with cosmopolitan nightlife and ambrosial shopping; **Beijing** (p. 112), with its imperial palaces and luxurious hotels; **Shanghai** (p. 313), a gathering place for Western nightclubs and shopping complexes; in Liaoning province, the fresh-faced and bustling harbor of **Dalian** (p. 239), known as "Hong Kong of the North"; the ancient dynastic capital of **Nanjing** (p. 338), now replete with decadent high-rises; and flower-bedecked **Kunming** (p. 591), the fragrant capital of Yunnan province, now a lively inland commercial center.

NATURAL WONDERS

Indulge in a rendezvous with China's vast natural scenery of luscious valleys, undulating lakes, rock-hard mountains, and huge trees, all of which have inspired ecstatic literary praise for thousands of years. Needless to say, countless tour groups swarm to China's hotspots every day, and it's near impossible to get any time alone with the more experienced topographic delights. But if you can't avoid the throngs of camera-clickers and you find them tolerable, then by all means, join them. The most famous of China's natural reserves, **Zhangjiajie** (p. 440) in Hunan province boasts thundering rapids and virile stalagtites alongside soothing mountain pools and deep underground rivers. Those with a flare for the exotic can look farther east in Yunnan province to the lush rain forests, tropical plants, and—mmm—botanical gardens of **Xishuangbanna** (p. 631). But if all that luscious nature is a bit much, head north for the quiet splendor of the alpine mountains, nestled in Sichuan's remote **Jiuzhaigou** nature reserve (p. 689). Or perhaps you'd like to get a piece of **Inner Mongolia**'s (p. 300) vast, grasslands, best experienced by horse, camel, or sand ski. Near Ürümqi, the lake of **Tianchi** (p. 758) sparkles within verdant mountain ranges high above sea level, where many nature-lovers get their fix of tantalizing alpine hiking trails and soulful star-gazing. And, finally, although the towering **Mt. Everest** (p. 828) seems to offer only size, its sweeping magnificence is enough eye-candy to satisfy even those with the highest panoramic standards.

SPIRITUAL SIGHTS

The most revered **Daoist temple structures** in China are located near five different mountain ranges. These majestic peaks sit in seas of swirling mist and eerie atmospheres that often seem to convey the presence of supernatural forces. Visit **Taishan** (Dongyue; p. 183) in Shandong province, **Huashan** (Xiyue; p. 256) in Shaanxi province, **Songshan** (Zhongyue; p. 265) in Henan province, **Hengshan** (Beiyue; p. 294) in Shanxi province, and **Hengshan** (Nanyue; p. 436) in Hunan province.

Buddhist grottoes, temples, and **chapels** are also found near gorgeous mountains, whose beauty inspires peace and serenity. The most popular Buddhist pilgrimages include **Jiuhuashan** (p. 413) in Anhui province, **Emeishan** (p. 680) in Sichuan province, **Putuoshan** (p. 390) in Zhejiang province, and **Wutaishan** (p.

LET'S GO PICKS

BEST PLACES TO GET HIGH: Marvel at the pristine alpine forests and snow-capped peaks outside **Yining** (p. 764) or **Ürümqi** (p. 754). Scramble up the stairs in **Shanghai**'s annual race up one of its tallest skyscrapers (p. 313). Parachute off the enormous Singing Sand Dunes of **Dunhuang** (p. 746). Hang out at **Everest Base Camp** (p. 828) and gaze at the world's highest mountain.

BEST PLACES TO FEEL LOW: In the **Turpan Depression,** the second-lowest point in the world. In any of China's innumerable karaoke bars, when you realize that you're actually enjoying yourself while singing to Céline Dion.

BEST WAYS TO START THE MORNING: Climb up **Taishan** (p. 183) at midnight to arrive in time for its famed sunrise. Emerge from a yurt to watch the sun rise over the gently sloping grasslands of **Inner Mongolia** (p. 300). Gaze in anticipation at the Beihai sunrise from one of **Huangshan**'s lookouts (p. 403). Stand with crowds of camera-toting tourists and PLA soldiers at the daily flag-raising ceremony in Beijing's **Tiananmen Square** (p. 132).

BEST WAYS TO END THE DAY: Sip brandy in **Tunxi** (p. 405)—just avoid the dead snake at the bottom of the bottle. Guzzle Tsingtao beer straight from the source at the famous brewery in **Qingdao** (p. 189). Risk liver failure with a taste of China's alarmingly potent grain beverage, *máotái*.

BEST FOOD: Plow into a plate full of heaven at **Kaifeng**'s No. 1 Dumpling Restaurant (p. 274) or **Shanghai**'s Chang'an Dumpling Restaurant (p. 327). Feast on delicious spieced lamb kebabs in the night markets of **Ürümqi** (p. 754). Indulge in Peking duck at **Beijing**'s famous Quanjude Roast Duck Restaurant (p. 128).

BEST DRINK: Indulge yourself amid the lush hills and sprawling terraced fields of **Longjing tea plantations,** west of Hangzhou (p. 381). Sip some "silver needle" tea while batting away thirsty monkeys on Yueyang's **Junshan Island** (p. 440). Enjoy a delicious cup of Eight Treasure Tea while gazing at the steep, rocky landscape of **Lanzhou** (p. 723). Whip out the *mahjong* tiles and sit back in a bamboo chair in one of **Chengdu**'s many tea gardens (p. 670). Inhale the pungent scent of yak-butter tea wafting through the alleyways in **Lhasa** (p. 803).

BEST PLACES TO FIGHT: Go face to face, arm to arm, and flying kneecap to muscular abdomen as you master the art of *wǔshù* on the practice fields of Henan's **Shaolin Monastery** (p. 265). Discover your inner Jet Li among the Daoist temples and misty trails of **Wudangshan** (p. 453).

BEST PLACES TO SHOP: Charm your way to lower prices at the famed Kashgar **Sunday Bazaar** (p. 780), Lhasa's **Barkhor Market** (p. 811), and Beijing's **Pajiayuan Flea Market** (p. 143).

286), in Shanxi province. Grottoes house some of the best-preserved Buddhist art, including statues and religious murals, plus really big Buddhas. In the Northwest, visit the massive **Xumishan Grottoes** (p. 723) near Guyuan, the spectacular **Mogao Grottoes** (p. 749) clustered in the desert around Dunhuang, and the intricately-carved **Maijishan Grottoes** (p. 737) near Tianshui. The **Yungang Grottoes** (p. 293) near Datong, in Shanxi, and the riverside **Longmen Grottoes** (p. 269), outside Luoyang in Henan province, round out the magnificent array.

SUGGESTED ITINERARIES

BEST OF CHINA (2½-3 WEEKS) The capital city of **Beijing** (p. 112) is the perfect starting point for a whirlwind tour of the best sights in China. Beijing's Forbidden City (p. 133) is a treasure trove of dynastic history. Just opposite is Tiananmen Square (p. 132), the largest public gathering space in the world and the site of the 1989 student protests (see p. 20). Of course, no trip to China would be complete without a glimpse of the Great Wall (p. 150), the only man-made structure visible from space. Board a train to **Xi'an** and visit the famous Terracotta Warriors (p. 253), 7000 clay soldiers in battle formation that have been called the "eighth wonder of the world." Leave imperial ostentation behind and head to hilly **Chongqing** (p. 699), the starting point for a two-day boat tour through the soon-to-be-submerged Three Gorges (p. 705). Disembark at **Yichang,** catch a bus to Wuhan, and travel to the story-book scenery of **Guilin** (p. 578). After relaxing amidst some of China's most beautiful scenery, mosey on over to eye-popping, exhilarating **Hong Kong** (p. 525). Dance until the wee hours of the morning in the Lan Kwai Fong area (p. 549), shop the "Golden Mile" (p. 540), and indulge in *dim sum* (p. 538). Then, swing north to **Shanghai** (p. 313) for whispers of China's colonial past and a stroll down the fantastic waterfront promenade. Finish up in the earthly paradise of **Hangzhou** (p. 374), and indulge in some of China's most delicious cuisine.

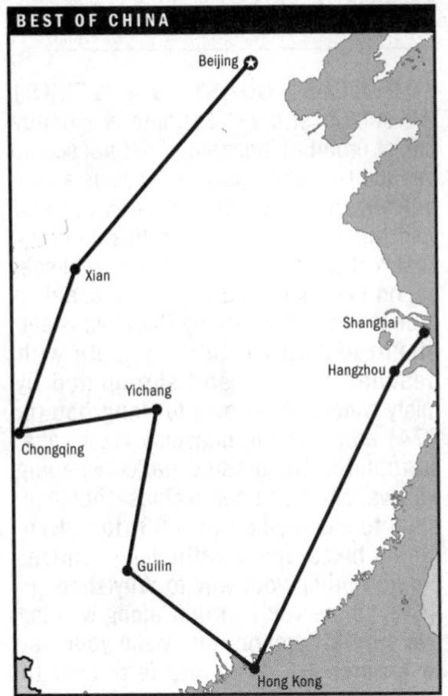

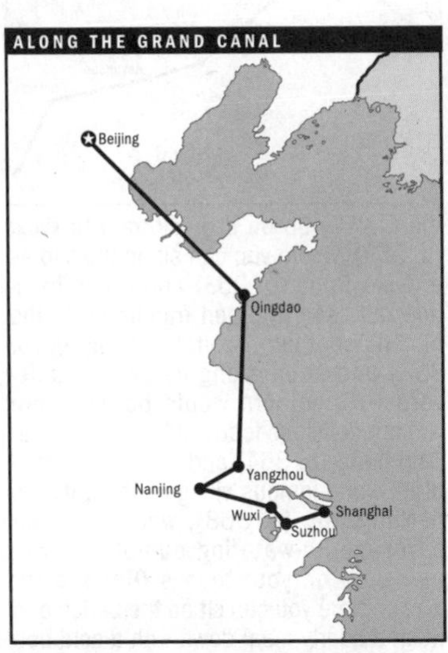

ALONG THE GRAND CANAL (3 WEEKS) Built in the Sui dynasty, the 1600km-long Grand Canal links China's two great waterways, the Yellow and Yangzi Rivers. A trip along the canal and to the sights along its banks can be particularly rewarding, especially for history buffs. Start your trip in **Shanghai** (p. 313) and visit the Bund's concession-era architecture; or, do what everyone else does in Shanghai: shop. Then trace the canal as it meanders past the classical gardens of **Suzhou** (p. 349), dubbed the "Venice of

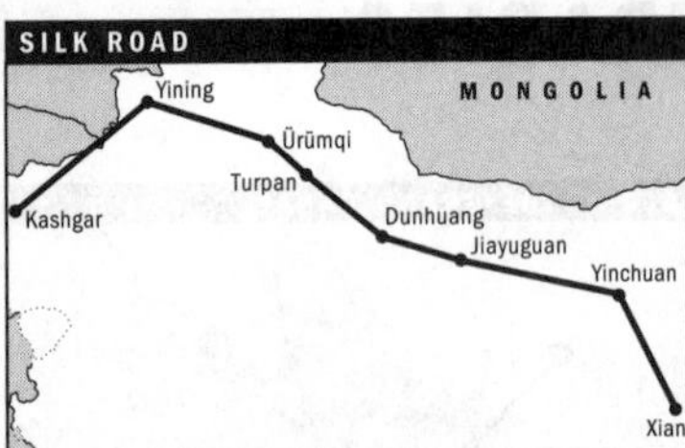

the East." Hop on a quick train to **Wuxi** (p. 359), where you can sit on the shores of Lake Taihu (p. 363) and watch bamboo rafts sail by. Then trundle on to the historic southern capital of **Nanjing** (p. 338) and stroll along its broad boulevards. No sojourn would be complete without delicious food, so board a train to **Zhenjiang** (p. 364) and pick up a bottle of its world-famous vinegar. Then, it's on to **Yangzhou** (p. 368), where you can savor mouth-watering dumplings. The next stop on your tour is **Qingdao** (p. 189), where you can sit on the beach and wash a hearty meal down with a cold bottle of beer. Finally, finish up your trip in **Beijing** (p. 112), the sprawling seat of imperial splendor.

SILK ROAD (1 MONTH) This journey takes you down the fabled Silk Road, a 2000-year-old trade route that moved the ancient world's most treasured commodity between Asia and Europe. Start in **Xi'an,** once the home of imperial silk factories, and visit the mighty Terracotta Warriors (p. 253). Continue on to **Yinchuan** (p. 714) to peek at the eerie tombs of forgotten kings. Then forge westward to **Jiayuguan** (p. 739), and climb the Great Wall's most famous pass, which marks the end of the 2000km-long architectural marvel. Press on to **Dunhuang** (p. 746) for a glimpse of the Buddhist art of the Mogao Grottoes, then go paragliding or tobogganing in the Singing Sand Dunes (p. 750) of the Gobi Desert. As you chug into Xinjiang, the barren desert gives way to the rocky Taklimakan, "desert of no return." But why return when sweet hami melons and grapevine-laced trellises await you in **Turpan** (p. 754)?

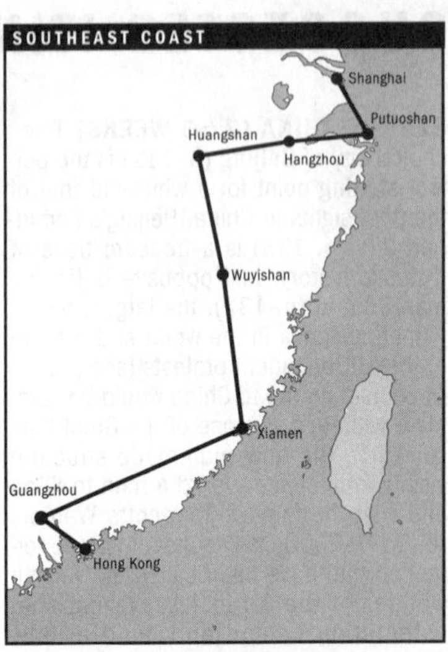

When weary of the barren scenery, head north to **Tianchi** (p. 758), a heavenly lake near Ürümqi, or explore the area near **Yining** (p. 764), home to Kazakh minorities and spectacular alpine vistas. Finally, loop back down along the Tarim Basin's northern rim to the Sunday Bazaar of **Kashgar** (p. 777).

SOUTHEAST COAST (3-4 WEEKS) The southeast coast of China is a happy mix of urban affluence and natural scenic beauty. Use **Shanghai** (p. 313) as a central base from which to branch out and visit the first few sights on this itinerary. First rest up with shopping and sight-seeing on the Bund (p. 313) before boarding a boat to the enchanting Buddhist island of **Putuoshan** (p. 390), replete with peaceful temples and surrounded by misty waters. Wind over to **Hangzhou** (p. 374) and visit the heavenly West Lake, surrounded by forested parks, weeping willows, and perfumed orchids. Then continue to **Huangshan** (p. 403) for adventurous hikes and breathtaking sunrises before finding your way to **Wuyishan** (p. 464), where you can drift along winding rivers on a bamboo raft. Make your way to **Xiamen** (p. 469) and ferry over to Gulangyu, an island renowned for its surreal setting, colonial architecture, shimmering sunsets, and pristine ocean views. Then, head over to **Guangzhou** (p. 480) and **Hong Kong** (p. 525) to finish off your trip with some cosmopolitan excitement.

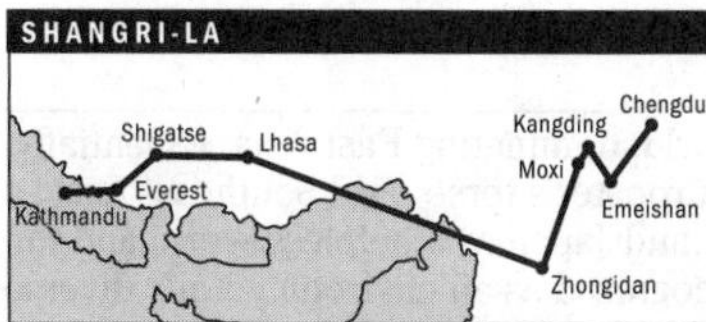

SHANGRI-LA (3 WEEKS) This karma-cleansing itinerary includes sights that are guaranteed to bring you peace and enlightenment. **Chengdu** (p. 662) is the perfect jumping-off point from which to visit the nearby heaven-on-earth mountain range of **Emeishan** (p. 680) and the beautiful city of **Kangding** (p. 688). Hop on a train to Luding, where you can take a taxi to **Moxi** (p. 686) and visit the nearby Hailuogou Glacier Park for misty views of the massive Gonggashan Mountain. Then continue to **Zhongdian** (p. 619) and explore the beautiful surrounding sights. Next, head to Tibet, the "Roof of the World." Enter **Lhasa** (p. 803) and visit the Potala Palace, the former home of the Dalai Lama. Then, board a bus to **Shigatse** (p. 823) and Tashilhunpo, the home of Tibetan Buddhism's second-in-command, the Panchen Lama. To finish, careen down the Friendship Highway and gaze at the snow-capped peak of **Mt. Everest** (p. 828).

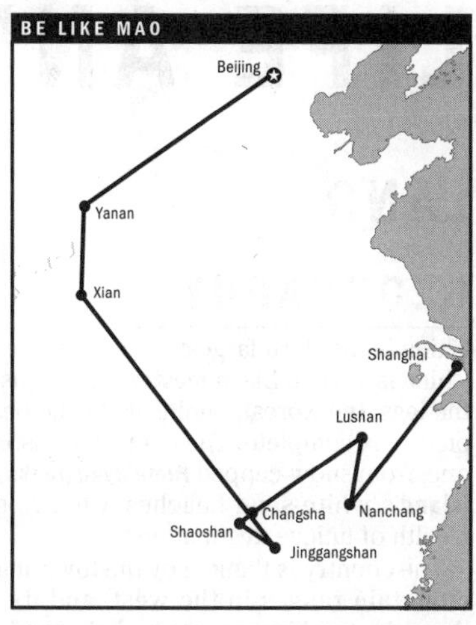

BE LIKE MAO (3 WEEKS) Start your socialist sojourn in **Shanghai** (p. 313), the home of the first national congress of the CCP. Board a train to **Nanchang** (p. 416), where the Communists got their military start. Indulge in a daytrip to **Lushan** (p. 422), a gorgeous scenic area where Mao held conferences, purged political rivals, drew up plans for the Great Leap Forward, and took a relaxing vacation or two. Next, return to Nanchang and board a bus to **Jingangshan** (p. 427), where, early in his career, Mao united his forces with other Communist troops. Continue to **Changsha** (p. 430), where Mao spent his early revolutionary years; then visit **Shaoshan** (p. 434), his birthplace and childhood home. Head to **Yan'an** (p. 259; via Wuhan), the birthplace of the Communist Revolution and once the home of the CCP headquarters. Finally, end your Mao pilgrimage in **Beijing** (p. 112), and marvel at the wonders of formaldehyde when you pay a visit to Mao's Mausoleum in Tiananmen Square.

LIFE AND TIMES

CHINA

LAND

GEOGRAPHY

China is the third-largest country in the world, dominating East Asia. Essentially, China is shaped like a **rooster.** Or, at least, a rooster's torso. Add Southeast Asia as the legs, the Korean peninsula as the beak, and Japan as a helpless worm and the picture is complete. The country is also recognized as an environmentally diverse one; from snow-capped **Himalayan peaks** and lush oases in the **Tarim Basin** to **Hainan Island**'s white-sand beaches, China's geographic landscape offers travelers a wealth of unique destinations.

The country is flanked by the towering Himalayan, Pamir, Kunlun, and Tianshan mountain ranges in the west, and its elevation gradually descends eastward through stair-like mountain chains and basins. In the north, the **Takla Makan** and **Gobi** deserts separate China from Central and North Asia. Beyond China's historic northeastern boundary, the **Great Wall,** is the region formerly known as Manchuria, now simply referred to as *dōngbêi* (东北; the Northeast). In Central China, sealed between these two highland areas, is the flat and lush **Sichuan Basin,** a historically isolated but prosperous region.

Rivers wind through the landscape of Southeast China. The **Yangzi River** or *cháng jiâng* (长江; literally "Long River") is 6500 km long, the longest in China and the third longest in the world. The Yangzi flows from Tibet into Sichuan, curving through the scenic **Three Gorges** to the **East China Sea.** It is China's most navigable river and serves the industrial centers of Shanghai, Chongqing, Wuhan, and Nanjing. The **Yellow River** is China's second longest (5464 km) and the world's most heavily sedimented. It roars through the **Loess Plateau,** carrying away 1.6 billion tons of yellow, powdery soil every year. Although the catastrophic floods caused by the river have earned it the title "China's Sorrow," the Yellow River Valley is still regarded as the cradle of Chinese civilization.

Officially, China's main island is **Taiwan,** but if you use the commonly accepted definition of "possession," China's largest offshore territory is actually **Hainan Island,** south of Guangdong province. China's semantic difficulties extend beyond Taiwan; its territorial claims in the **South China Sea** also include hundreds of tiny, uninhabitable, and disputed rocks and reefs.

FLORA AND FAUNA

China's highly varied topography and climate makes it home to many rare plants and animals. The district of **Xishuangbanna** in southern Yunnan province harbors most of China's tropical flora and fauna, including the **white-cheeked gibbon,** the **Asiatic elephant,** and the **flying frog,** as well as medicinal plants like the **Japanese snowbell** and the **sandal tree.** Farther north, the **giant panda** (see p. 675) feasts on bamboo in the more temperate forests of Sichuan, Gansu, and Shaanxi provinces, sharing its distinctive habitat with the **golden snub-nosed monkey, takin, Asiatic black bear,** and **golden pheasant.** The Tibetan Plateau in far west China houses **snow leopards** and **wild yaks** (see p. 808), while the far north functions as a breeding ground for many of China's distinctive **crane** species. **Chinese alligators, Chinese river dol-**

phins, and **South China tigers** are thinly scattered throughout the Yangzi River basin.

Rapid economic development and population growth threatens much of China's natural wealth, and nearly all of these animals are currently on the long list of endangered species. In recent years, the government has imposed steep penalties on **poachers** (the primary cause of the decimation of the panda and tiger populations). The government has also created a network of **nature reserves.** These reserves are typically open to the public and many, like **Wolong** (see p. 674), **Jiuzhaigou** (see p. 689), **Zhangjiajie** (see p. 440), **Wudalianchi** (see p. 214), **Zhalong** (see p. 213), and **Changbaishan** (see p. 228), are prime spots to admire scenery and wildlife.

HISTORY

No matter where you travel in China, one thing will be abundantly clear: China is old. China's recorded history alone spans almost 5000 years, long enough to make Britain's civilization look like an impertinent upstart and the US's like a toddler in a wading pool. What follows is a relatively short, sweet, and simplified rundown of China's illustrious past.

For more on the history of Tibet (as well as China's influence there), see **Tibet: History,** p. 797.

ca. 3000 BC
The beginning of the Bronze Age. Another important discovery: recreational drugs.

2698
The Chinese calendar is invented; Feb. 12, 2002 will usher in year 4700 on the Chinese calendar.

2137
The first eclipse is recorded. Two royal astronomers are executed for failing to predict it.

ONCE UPON A TIME IN CHINA

Civilization didn't quite get started until 2000 BC when, according to legend, the **Xia dynasty** was founded. The Xia and the following two dynasties, the **Shang** (ca. 1600) and the **Zhou** (ca. 1050), left little hard archaeological evidence; the exploits of the ancient kings and their peoples are remembered in story, myth, and potsherds.

EGG: 1, CHICKEN: 0 Every civilization has its creation myth, and China is no exception. According to legend, the world was once entirely contained in an **egg.** Inside this egg grew a giant, **Pangu,** who grew for 18,000 years before he emerged. With a hammer and chisel, he separated heaven and earth and created the world as we know it. Some versions of the story claim that Pangu carved out the sun and the moons, the ocean and the grass; others point to Pangu's decomposing body as the source of such scenic features. Nearly everyone agrees on one thing, however: humans and animals were made with Pangu's lice.

CLASSICAL CHINA

THE BIRTH OF A NATION

From Qin (spelled Ch'in in the Wade-Giles romanization) comes China. The highly centralized and martial bureaucracy of the **Qin Dynasty** (221-207 BC) transformed an isolated Shaanxi kingdom into a powerful military state with a common currency, a written language, and a standardized administration system that lasted for 2000 years. After the death of Qin Shihuang, the founding emperor, deep-rooted popular discontent grew into open rebellion. One villager Liu Bang, known posthumously as **Han Gaozu,** proclaimed the **Han dynasty** (206 BC-AD 220), modeling his rule on Confucian ideals (see p. 27) and the practices of the ancient Zhou dynasty. The Han was not entirely short-lived, but in AD 9 **Wang Mang,** the regent of emperor Ping (1 BC-AD 6), mounted the throne and proclaimed his own **Xin dynasty.** Natural disaster aggravated the disruptive outcomes of Wang Mang's policy decisions, however, and Xin China soon collapsed into civil war. The frustrated populace joined anti-dynastic movements that eventually gave way to a period of division by AD 220.

THE WAY OF THE WEI

Although China was briefly unified again under the **Jin dynasty** (265-316), the area soon dissolved into wary factions. In the south, five successive dynasties existed between 316 and 589 and in the north, foreign invaders sacked the Jin court at Luoyang in 311. In 386 the foreign **Xianbei** tribe forged the **Northern Wei.** The Northern Wei successfully implemented the equal-field system, which granted parcels of farm land to individual peasants for the duration of their lifetimes. The regime also sponsored Buddhist scholarship and art; the cave temples of Longmen Grottoes (see p. 269) stand out among its legacies. In 589, the Xianbei rulers fell from power when their compatriots at the frontier garrisons turned against them.

A REBIRTH OF SORTS

In 589, **Yang Jian,** a prominent northern general of mixed Chinese and Turkish ancestry, ousted the Northern Zhou and conquered the Chen dynasty in the south, ending 300 years of political division. The **Sui dynasty** (581-618) reinstated a highly centralized bureaucratic state, established a lasting legal code, boosted agricultural output, restored the Great Wall, and built the **Grand Canal.** But all good things must come to an end, and costly campaigns against Korea drained resources and prompted yet another cycle of repressive taxation, unrest, and rebellion.

THE TANG SOLUTION

When the dust settled in 617, **Li Yuan** (Emperor Gaozu) emerged victorious and founded the **Tang dynasty** (618-907). Early emperors were skilled tacticians, savvy diplomats, and fearless commanders who built a swift strike force that could contend with the armies of Central Asia. At the height of Tang power in the 7th century, Tang military protectorates extended from western Iran to Vietnam and Tang diplomats forged alliances with the Uighurs and Tibetans.

The following years brought about a swift downturn in dynastic greatness. **An Lushan** fomented a palace coup in 755 that dragged on for a decade, leaving much of northern China in

213
Emperor Qin Shihuang burns all Confucian works except for one copy, which is kept in the Imperial Library.

ca. 100 BC
Chinese astronomers propose a theory of a round earth; Buddhism arrives in China.

AD 265-617
The Three Kingdoms Period; three separate kingdoms fight for Han territory.

ca. 300
The Chinese first begin to make paper, using rags, bark, hemp, and other fabric.

ca. 600
Liu Zhuo (544-610) publishes the Imperial Standard Calendar; Chinese mathematicians have discovered algebra, estimated the first 7 digits of pi, and learned to use trigonometry.

635
The first Christian missionary arrives in Chang'an (modern-day Xi'an).

690-705
Wu Zetian, a former imperial concubine, rules as empress.

ruins. Defeat on foreign battlegrounds effectively ended Tang dominance in Central Asia, and the Tibetan sacking of Chang'an in 763 further weakened the dynasty. By the time order was restored, a weak Tang court was unable to reign over fractious warlords and starving peasants, and China again splintered into warring factions.

THE SONG

In 960, General **Zhao Kuangyin** (Emperor **Taizu**) reunified much of China and founded the **Northern Song dynasty.** The Song rulers concentrated on preserving traditional Confucian culture and introduced a meritocratic civil service examination system, a welfare system, and paper money. Song cities, fueled by high agricultural yields, supported booming commerce and iron industries. Vernacular lyric poetry (see **Literature,** p. 36) and landscape painting (see **Painting,** p. 40) grew in popularity, and the growth of Buddhism resulted in the construction of numerous temples and pagodas, including the Iron Pagoda in present-day **Kaifeng** (see p. 271).

Despite significant reforms and cultural developments at home, the Song dynasty was constantly harassed and threatened by the "barbarians" from the north. Shortly after the founding of the Song, **Khitan** nomads from Mongolia conquered Beijing, secured the Great Wall, and founded the **Liao** dynasty (c. 916-1125). Too weak to drive out the Liao and unwilling to pay tribute, the Song court collaborated with another rising tribe, the **Jurchens** of Manchuria, who swept south and conquered the Liao before pressing on to the Song capital in 1126, where they established the **Jin dynasty** (1115-1234).

Remnants of the Song, led by Emperor **Gaozong**, established the **Southern Song** capital in the present-day city of **Hangzhou** (see p. 374). Cultural achievements continued, but foreign affairs grew increasingly strained, and the court became hopelessly corrupt. Unable to contend with the expansionist Jin, the Song courtiers eagerly forged an alliance with another powerful nomadic nation to the far north: the Mongols.

THE MIGHTY KHAN

Before the 13th century, the Mongols were a nomadic people composed of dispersed, roving clans. In 1205, **Genghis Khan** unified these clans and stormed across Eurasia, sacking Baghdad, trampling Moscow, and pounding on the gates of Vienna. Genghis died fighting against the Western Xia in 1227, but his sons and grandsons finished the job, conquering all of China by 1279.

Kublai Khan's **Yuan dynasty** court hosted guests including Italian explorer **Marco Polo** and also tackled major projects like Beijing's **Beihai Park** (see p. 134), Zhongnanhai Compound (now the residence of top CCP leaders), a stately pleasure dome in Xanadu, and an expanded Grand Canal system. To keep the vast Chinese populace under control, the Mongols employed harsh measures. Instead of pacifying the people, however, the Mongols' widespread discrimination only encouraged the Chinese to dream of a Song restoration.

751
Tang forces are defeated at the Battle at Talas River in modern Kyrgyzstan.

1024
The Song rulers issue the world's first paper currency.

1041
The first moveable-type printing system is developed.

ca. 1138
The Song name Hangzhou their capital.

ca. 1150
The Chinese begin to use explosive powder in their weaponry.

1163
The emperor allows a Jewish synagogue to be built in Kaifeng (see p. 271).

1167
Temujin, the man who would be Khan, is born.

ca. 1200
The Chinese develop and use a crude vaccine for smallpox.

1293
The Grand Canal is completed, running 1600km from the Yangzi to the Yellow River.

1344
China sees its first outbreak of the Bubonic plague.

ca. 1340
150,000 civilians and 20,000 troops work to build a channel to divert Yellow River flooding.

1417
Ming explorers reach the African coast.

1421
The Ming dynasty moves the capital to Beijing and begins construction of the Forbidden City (see p. 133).

1645
Dorgon, the regent for the young Kangxi emperor, captures Nanjing. He then orders all men to shave their foreheads and wear their hair in a queue (ponytail).

1662
Anti-Qing forces expel the Dutch from Taiwan. Manchu forces prevail in 1683.

1689
China agrees to sign the Treaty of Nerchinsk, which settles border disputes with Russia.

1699
The British East India Company establishes a trading post in Guangdong province.

1720
Tibet becomes a part of the Qing empire.

While the Mongols supported Tibetan Lamaism, much of the Chinese populace joined cult-like societies like the **White Lotus Society.** In 1352, the **Red Turban Society** (named for the headgear worn by its followers) launched a rebellion that engulfed most of the south for the next three years. Although the Mongols crushed the rebellion, clan member **Zhu Yuanzhang** (posthumously known as Ming Taizu) formed another rebel group that eventually toppled the Yuan in 1368.

THE MING

Founding emperor **Ming Taizu** (r. 1368-1398) established an autocratic and stable government, initiating extensive tax, labor, and education reforms. His son **Yongle** (r. 1402-24) oversaw ambitious public works programs, including the production of a comprehensive literary canon. The Ming dynasty, with imperialistic glee, expanded into Turkestan, Korea, Mongolia, Vietnam, and Myanmar, while **sea expeditions** brought Chinese ships, people, and goods as far afield as Madagascar.

As time went on, fewer capable leaders came to power. High inflation and constant fighting with Manchu and Mongol armies furthered dissention, and soon disgruntled commoners and officials began to stage small-scale rebellions.

LATE IMPERIAL CHINA: THE QING

ATTACK OF THE DISGRUNTLED POSTAL WORKER

In 1644, a former postal official, **Li Zicheng,** led a brutal but efficient rebel attack on Beijing. The last Ming emperor hanged himself in present-day **Jingshan Park** (see p. 135), and the rebel army easily passed through the city gates. In a last-ditch attempt to save the dynasty, loyalist general **Wu Sangui** allowed Manchu armies into Beijing, hoping they would help quell Li's rebellion. The Manchus succeeded, but characteristic of victorious armies, they had little inclination to part with the wine and women of China's capital city. Of course, the Manchus' desire to rule all of China also inspired their stay.

Declaring Beijing the capital of their new dynasty, the **Qing** (Chinese for "pure") became the first dynasty of Manchu rule. Yet the Qing emperors relied heavily on Chinese tradition, upholding the examination system, patronizing Chinese art and literature, and continuing to appoint their Chinese counterparts to official posts. Most importantly, they used Confucianism as a way to build and maintain political authority.

Emperor **Kangxi** (r. 1668-1722), famous for his personal inspection tours and ascetic habits, oversaw distant military campaigns in Russia, Mongolia, and Tibet. Turmoil over Kangxi's successor ended with the reign of **Yongzheng** (r. 1723-1735), an efficient, tough, but ultimately short-lived ruler. Emperor **Qianlong** (r. 1736-1796), widely regarded as one of the greatest rulers in Chinese history, presided over a period of unprecedented wealth, territorial, and population expansion.

By the end of Qianlong's reign, however, expensive military campaigns had depleted imperial coffers and corruption once again plagued the government. The developing conflict over foreign intrusion exacerbated these problems.

CRUEL BRITTANIA

Although maritime trade was essential for southeastern communities, Qing emperors remained wary of overseas commerce. The Qianlong emperor forced all foreign traders to remain in the vicinity of Guangzhou (Canton) province. This so-called **Canton system** (1760-1842) required all commercial transactions to go through a select group of Chinese merchants who had been granted a monopoly on foreign trade.

Despite the restrictions of the Canton system, the British had a compelling reason to maintain trade with China: **tea** (see p. 36). The balance of trade was tilted heavily in China's favor until the introduction of **opium,** a highly addictive narcotic. By the 1820s, vast quantities of silver flowed out of China to pay for the opium, turning a public health issue into a financial crisis. In 1836, Emperor Daoguang decided to make a vigorous attempt to stamp out opium once and for all. Dealers and users were imprisoned or executed, and demand for opium plummeted. A few years later, the hardnosed official **Lin Zexu** suspended all trade, blockaded factories, held 250 foreigners hostage, and demanded that the British relinquish their opium. The Chinese court was pleased with Lin's apparent success, but the British were not about to forgo their favorite afternoon beverage; Britain decided that the only appropriate response to China's behavior was war.

The **Opium War** (1840-1842) began when British warships blockaded Guangzhou and moved north toward Xiamen (see p. 469). After several military conflicts and failed negotiations, the Chinese finally consented to the stipulations imposed by Britain's **Treaty of Nanjing,** the first in a long series of humiliating concessions that has led to perennially tense foreign relations. Five ports were opened to Western trade and the Canton system was abolished. The British also demanded the right to set tariff rates and obtained most-favored-nation status, and used claims of extraterritoriality to restrict the authority of the Chinese legal system over British subjects. There was no mention, however, of the very controversy that had sparked the war or its subsequent events, and traders continued to import opium into China until 1917.

AND WORSE STILL

After 1850, floods, famine, and overpopulation combined with governmental neglect and corruption to further domestic unrest. Armed uprisings broke out around the country, the most notorious of which was the **Taiping Rebellion.** The leader of the rebellion, **Hong Xiuquan,** a militant evangelist, claimed to be God's *other* son, having been driven a bit batty after failing his fourth civil service exam. Nonetheless, over 20,000 discontented Chinese responded to Hong's call to arms. This formidable army captured the capital city of Nanjing in 1853 and

1729
The sale and production of opium is banned in China.

1796-1804
Fed up with Qing corruption, peasants flock to the White Lotus society, which promises a Ming restoration. Widespread riots ensue.

1821
The British establish a port in Hong Kong.

1834
The British government abolishes the British East India Company's monopoly on trade with China.

1856
The Chinese government arrests twelve sailors on *The Arrow,* accusing them of piracy. The British retaliate by seizing Guangdong province.

1860
China cedes its lands north of the Amur River to the Russians. The Russians found Vladivostok, "Ruler of the East."

1870
In Tianjin, the French consul and 20 other foreigners are killed by a mob after rumors spread that Catholic nuns are kidnapping Chinese orphans.

1894-95
Sino-Japanese War. China loses, cedes Taiwan to Japan, and borrows heavily from foreign nations to pay the indemnity.

1902
The Empress Dowager issues a decree banning foot binding.

1910
A couple, aged 8 and 9, have a baby, making them the youngest parents in history.

1914
Japan seizes German concessions in Shandong Province.

1915
Japan makes its "21 Demands." China refuses to become a Japanese protectorate, but yields parts of Shandong province, Inner Mongolia, and Manchuria to the Japanese.

1917
China severs diplomatic relations with Germany. Five months later, it declares war on Germany.

1919
As a condition of the Treaty of Versailles, Japan receives former German concessions in Shandong province. China never signs the treaty.

eventually numbered over one million. In 1864, loyalist armies led by **Zeng Guofan** finally defeated the rebels.

TIME FOR A CHANGE

The suppression of the Taiping rebellion gave the Qing dynasty one last chance to consolidate its power. During the **Tongzhi period** (1862-1874), the government reformed the examination system, tried to eliminate corruption, and established a foreign affairs office to deal with Western powers. Supporters of the **Self-Strengthening Movement** (1874-1894) promoted Western science and technology and the retention of traditional Chinese values and morals. China's humiliating defeat in the Sino-Japanese war of 1894 inspired the short-lived **Hundred Days of Reform,** during which Emperor **Guangxu** finally broke free of the iron grip of his mother, the Empress Dowager, and fought for fundamental political reform.

Intellectuals and the ruling elite weren't alone in their desire for change. In response to the humiliating concessions demanded by foreign powers, Chinese peasants formed **secret societies** and vowed to pick Britain last in international games of kickball. One society was slightly more serious. The **Society of Righteous and Harmonious Fists** vowed to "Protect the Qing, destroy the Foreigners," while also practicing martial arts and shadow boxing, earning them the title of "Boxers." The Boxers attacked and looted Beijing in 1898, killing foreign and Chinese Christians. This inflamed foreign imperial powers, who exacted a hefty settlement and the right to station troops in the capital. As China neared the turn of the century, the failure of the Boxers and China's inability to stand up to foreign powers were indications that Qing rule had fallen on hard times.

THE REPUBLICAN ERA

REVOLUTION

As the Qing languished, dissident groups and their leaders debated the future of the country. **Dr. Sun Yat-sen,** who believed that the ruling tradition could not be preserved in a traditional monarchy, eventually prevailed. Sun organized the **Tong Meng Hui** (United League), and aimed to overthrow the Qing regime with support from abroad. Meanwhile, league members in present-day Wuhan (see p. 443) pulled off a successful armed uprising on October 10, 1911. The **Xinhai Revolution** spread like wildfire, and in 1912, Sun Yat-sen was inaugurated as the first president of the **Republic of China,** and six-year-old **Henry Pu Yi,** the **last emperor,** abdicated. The Tong Meng Hui became known as the **Nationalist Party** or **Guomindang (GMD),** and October 10 became a national holiday; it is still celebrated in Taiwan.

Despite the revolution's nominal success, it barely altered China's power structure. Real political clout remained in the hands of **Yuan Shikai,** a cunning warlord who exploited the confusion and chaos of the time. First, the former Qing general turned on the boy emperor. Then, he persuaded Sun to yield the presidency to him. It was not long before Yuan had a key GMD leader assassinated. He then dissolved the legislature, and, in 1916, declared himself emperor. A fresh round of rebellions commenced, culminating in Yuan's death.

POWER IN NUMBERS

On May 4, 1919, 3000 students marched on Tiananmen Square to protest the terms of the Treaty of Versailles, denouncing imperialism and China's weak international standing. Although the warlord government jailed more than 1000 students, the **May Fourth Movement** still spread. In Shanghai, sympathetic workers went on strike and merchants closed their shops while publications criticized nearly every aspect of Chinese culture. Even arranged marriages were protested by young citizens.

Chinese intellectuals quickly turned their attention to another vehicle for rapid social change: **Communism.** In 1921, 11 delegates, including **Mao Zedong,** attended the First Party Congress in Shanghai (see p. 331). Police raids forced the meeting to relocate to a boat on a lake in Zhejiang province, but could not prevent the establishment of the Chinese Communist Party (CCP) on July 1st of that year.

Meanwhile, Sun Yat-sen was busy trying to revitalize the nationalist cause. With the help of Soviet advisors, Sun streamlined the GMD and learned Bolshevik methods of party organization and propaganda dissemination. Sun then established the **Huangpu Military Academy** in Guangzhou in order to build the army he would need to wrest power from the warlords. His brother-in-law **Chiang Kai-shek,** fresh from training in Moscow, became the first commandant, and **Zhou Enlai,** a capable young Communist, served as the political commissar. Sun did not live to see the fruits of his labor, however, dying of cancer in 1925. To this day, he remains a national hero.

THE LONG AND WINDING ROAD

In 1926, Generalissimo Chiang Kai-shek led the joint forces of the GMD and the CCP on a military campaign against the warlords. In less than a year, the forces had defeated or subjugated all warlords south of the Yangzi River. But as Chiang's forces approached Shanghai, Communist forces led by Zhou Enlai seized control of the city. In retaliation, the Generalissimo unleashed a bloody campaign that killed and jailed thousands of Communists and suspected sympathizers. Chiang's regime in Nanjing took control, conquering Beijing in 1928.

The shock of Chiang's sudden purges left the Communist movement in disarray. When the CCP's morale hit an all-time low in 1928, the tattered forces of Mao Zedong and Zhu De established a guerrilla base on **Jinggangshan** (see p. 427) in Jiangxi province, where the **Red Army** grew strong enough to fend off four **Guerrilla Extermination Campaigns** led by the illustrious Chiang Kai-shek.

However, soon enough the CCP was thrown into confusion by leadership changes and poor decision-making. The under-equipped Red Army was eventually overwhelmed by the 700,000 member-strong GMD and, in 1934, forced to flee on the infamous **Long March.** The ragged guerrillas limped into the

1921-22
Nine countries meet at the Washington Conference to discuss the future of East Asia after WWI. Meanwhile, modern China's peasant uprising is led by Peng Bai.

1925
In Shanghai, Chinese labor demonstrators fire on the international settlement, killing 10.

1927
Chiang Kai-shek executes labor and Communist Party leaders; anti-imperialist mobs attack foreigners and raid theirs homes and businesses.

1931
A bomb explodes on a railway track near Shenyang; the Japanese blame the Chinese and attack the Chinese garrison stationed nearby. In the end, China loses Manchuria to Japan.

1932
The Japanese establish a puppet state, naming the last emperor, Henry Pu Yi ruler of Manchuria. Soon thereafter, Manchuria declares its "independence" from China.

1938
Japanese prime minister Prince Konoe Fumimaro decides that Chiang Kai-shek's regime is illegitimate and announces Japan's intention to invade China.

1945
US General George Marshall travels to China in an attempt to mediate a peace settlement between the GMD and CCP; under the Yalta agreement, China regains sovereignty over Taiwan.

1947
Anti-GMD riots break out in Taiwan; tens of thousands of people are killed.

1950
China signs the Sino-Soviet pact as Chinese troops enter Korea and halt plans to invade Taiwan.

1951
The PLA takes control of Tibet; the UN institutes trade embargoes against China.

town of **Zunyi** (see p. 659) in Guizhou, where top CCP leaders convened to decide on the future of the movement. After three days of bitter arguments, Mao Zedong emerged as the undisputed leader of the CCP. Mao and his army of 90,000 followers continued on their epic journey across 8000km of China's most rugged terrain, which included 18 mountain ranges and 23 major rivers. A year later, fewer than 8000 of the original marchers finally reached **Yan'an** (see p. 259).

THE WORLD AT WAR

Japan didn't waste any time capitalizing on the chaos in China. Despite national outrage at Japanese aggression, Chiang insisted that internal unity must come before resistance to foreign powers. Although Mao declared his willingness to unite with the GMD against the Japanese, Chiang preferred instead to exterminate the CCP. Mao's offer did appeal to Manchurian general **Zhang Xueliang;** he kidnapped Chiang Kai-shek in what is known as the **Xi'an Incident.** The Generalissimo was eventually released, but only after the GMD agreed to put aside the civil war to concentrate on the fight against Japan.

WWII began in China on July 7, 1937, when Japanese troops clashed with Chinese guards on the **Marco Polo Bridge** outside Beijing (see p. 149). The Japanese launched an all-out offensive and took eastern China by storm. Chinese forces retreated into Sichuan while the Japanese slaughtered thousands of surrendered soldiers and civilians and raped at least 20,000 women in the capital city of Nanjing (see p. 338).

In the midst of all the chaos, Communist guerrillas took control of rural areas, recruiting volunteers and carrying out small-scale raids against the Japanese and pro-Japanese militias. In 1941, Chiang Kai-shek, once again threatened by the Communists' burgeoning power, rescinded his promise of a United Front and attacked the Communist forces in southern China.

Once Japan surrendered to the Allied forces, the two factions rushed to reclaim former Japanese territories. Despite efforts by the US to negotiate a settlement, full-scale civil war broke out in 1947. Eventually, the Nationalist cause, overwrought with inflation and corruption, gave way to Mao's prevailing **People's Liberation Army (PLA).** Chiang Kai-shek and the Nationalists fled to **Taiwan** where they continued to administer the **Republic of China (ROC).** On October 1, 1949, Chairman Mao stood on the rostrum of the Gate of Heavenly Peace (see p. 132) and formally established the **People's Republic of China (PRC).**

THE COMMUNIST ERA

After winning power in 1949, the PRC faced the daunting task of transforming a war-torn and bankrupt country into a Communist state. In the early years of the PRC, Chairman Mao ruled along with the collective leadership of his comrades-in-arms, who included **Zhou Enlai, Liu Shaoqi,** and **Deng Xiaoping.** During this so-called "Camelot Period" (1949-57), the CCP made impressive gains both at home and abroad.

Due in part to the insistence of most Western powers that the exhiled ROC government in Taiwan was the legitimate government of all of China, Mao adopted the **Lean to One Side Policy,** which forged close ties with the Soviet Union. Mao's policy had both pros and cons; Soviet policy advisors flowed into the country, but Stalinist architecture spread throughout Chinese cities like a concrete-block infection.

The party leadership initiated a series of campaigns to solidify their hold on Chinese society. In the countryside, **land reform** diminished the power of the gentry and increased peasant political participation while **collectivization** transferred private lands to public ownership. In urban areas, workers were organized into **work units** (see p. 32), which provided lifetime employment, housing, food allotments, schooling for children, health care, and retirement pensions.

THE FALL OF INTELLECTUALISM

In the early 1950s, the consolidation of economic power proceeded fairly smoothly. Reining in those pesky free-thinking intellectuals proved to be much more difficult. Despite the objections of his second-in-command, Mao Zedong decided to let intellectuals offer the party leadership suggestions and participate in the party-led socialist transformation. This was known as the **Hundred Flowers Movement,** after Mao's statement: "Let a hundred flowers bloom, and a hundred schools contend." Of course, by "a hundred" Mao meant "party-supporting." When the intellectuals challenged the legitimacy of party dictatorship, criticized the bureaucracy, and called for open elections (allowing for opposition parties) Mao was very displeased.

His **Anti-Rightist Campaign** of 1957-58 moved swiftly to crush dissent. Hundreds of thousands of intellectuals and dissidents were rounded up and sent to labor camps for a hearty dose of "thought reform." The Anti-Rightist Campaign was one of the first—but by no means one of the last—times that intellectuals were persecuted by the PRC's reigning government.

THE GREAT LEAP BACKWARD

By 1958, agricultural output was unable to keep up with population growth, and Mao was growing impatient with the slow pace of industrialization. Instead of advocating technological improvements, as many advisors suggested, Mao turned to his favorite strategy: mass mobilization. As part of his **Great Leap Forward** (1958-1960), he ordered massive labor-intensive public works projects and organized enormous **People's Communes,** which housed as many as 1000 farmers and replaced smaller cooperatives.

In the end, the Great Leap Forward, combined with a run of bad weather, led only to disaster: between 28 and 40 million people in the countryside starved to death in what has become known as the greatest man-made catastrophe in history.

COMRADES NO MORE

Since the 1950s, Russian leader Nikita Khrushchev had sneered at Mao's fanatical programs. Mao, a bit put off, accused Khrush-

1951-52
The "Three-Anti Campaign" targets corruption, waste, and bureaucracy; the "Five-Anti Campaign" cracks down on private businesses.

1953
China institutes its first Five-Year Plan.

1954
Communist forces shell the ROC-controlled islands of Quemoy and Matsu. US forces arrive in support of the ROC, with plans to use nuclear weapons on China if necessary; China adopts its first state constitution.

1958
The government initiates its second Five-Year Plan; Mao steps down as chairman of the PRC with Liu Shaoqi taking his place.

1959
China suppresses a revolt in Tibet; the Dalai Lama flees to India.

1962
China and India, still touchy after the emigration of the Dalai Lama, fight a short-lived border war. As a result, China allies itself with Pakistan.

1963
China designs its first nuclear bomb. It is successfully detonated a year later.

1966
The PLA transports more than 10 million students to Beijing to hold mass rallies.

1967
China's nuclear weapons program culminates with the successful detonation of its first hydrogen bomb on June 17; meanwhile, Red Guards seize control of the government, throwing officials out of their offices and burning their papers.

1968
Mao formally disbands the Red Guards.

1969
The Chinese army ambushes Soviet Troops stationed near Damansky Island, located in the Amur River; the Soviets work to reinforce border security and the Chinese turn to the US for assistance.

1970
Chinese universities, many of which were closed due to the Cultural Revolution, reopen.

chev of tampering with Marxist-Leninist doctrine and cuddling up to the US. This ideological clash led to the **Sino-Soviet Split** of 1960 when diplomatic and economic ties between the two countries were severed. In 1962, Mao was forced to hand over his position as head of state to second-in-command **Liu Shaoqi,** who, along with **Deng Xiaoping,** set about reviving China's dying economy and reversing the policies of the Great Leap Forward. This new change of events was unacceptable to Mao, and so he turned to **Jiang Qing,** his wife, and **Lin Biao,** the head of the PLA, to help him bolster support and regain power. While Lin rallied his soldiers with copies of *The Quotations of Chairman Mao* (also called the **Little Red Book**), Jiang spearheaded Mao's cultural reforms and tapped into a network of radical intellectuals from Shanghai. All the Chairman was hoping for was another surge of public enthusiasm to jump-start his next mass mobilization campaign.

A RED TIDE ENGULFS THE NATION

Having already conquered landlords, capitalists, and intellectuals in his rise to power, Mao turned his attention to party rivals. In 1966, Mao ordered Liu Shaoqi to cleanse the party bureaucracy of corruption, but provided no further instructions. When subversive posters appeared on the campus of Beijing University, a confused Liu sent party inspection teams to the campus to suppress student activities. Meanwhile, propagandists spread rumors that corrupt government forces were trying to overthrow the Chairman, and as a result, radical students organized **Red Guard** groups to protect him. Within a few short months, millions of youths heeded Mao's call to "bombard the headquarters" of party "capitalists" and "revisionists." Simultaneously, Mao turned against his comrades in arms, accusing Liu of suppressing the voice of the people and diverting China onto a capitalist path. Liu was tried on trumped-up charges and eventually tortured to death; Deng Xiaoping was condemned to manual labor. Thousands of other cadres were purged and sent to hard labor camps.

When he launched the **Great Proletariat Cultural Revolution** (1966-69), Mao hoped to train a new generation of socialist visionaries. The Red Guards were instructed to purge Chinese culture of the **Four Olds:** old culture, old customs, old habits, and old ideas. Traditional books were burned and countless historical sites and temples were ransacked and destroyed. Academics and teachers were humiliated in public, and hundreds committed suicide. By 1967, the violence had veered out of control and the Red Guards had fallen into fractious infighting. Chinese cities turned into war zones; militant Red Guard factions fought street battles using tanks and missiles looted from arms shipments intended for Vietnam. After shutting down schools, Mao transported youth to China's vast countryside, where they were instructed to undergo re-education by the peasantry. In 1968, some 15 million youths left the cities to live on impoverished farms.

With the CCP in tatters from repeated purges, the PLA moved to fill the power vacuum. By 1969, the PLA dominated the Party

Congress, and Lin Biao was affirmed as Mao's chosen successor. After Lin staged a coup and subsequently died in a suspiciously convenient plane crash, Deng Xiaoping and Zhou Enlai reemerged in the forefront of Chinese politics.

THE POST-MAO ERA

The Mao era didn't officially end until the Chairman's death in 1976. After the death of Lin Biao in 1971, however, the country—partially due to influence of Zhou Enlai—pursued a more moderate political and economic course that was markedly different from that of the past two decades.

WITH FRIENDS LIKE THESE...

For his part, Zhou played an instrumental role in advancing **Sino-American relations.** Practical politics had overcome ideological differences as a series of unofficial cultural and athletic contacts known as **Ping Pong Politics** (see **Sports,** p. 42) paved the way for official agreements. After Secretary of State **Henry Kissinger**'s secret visit to China, **Richard Nixon** (see p. 42) stunned the world by exchanging toasts with Chairman Mao in 1972. The two leaders drafted the **Shanghai Communique,** which stipulated that the US would recognize the mainland government (and not the Taiwanese regime) as the true government of China.

THREE'S COMPANY, FOUR'S A CROWD

As Zhou guided China toward political moderation, Jiang Qing and her zealous cohorts, known as the **Gang of Four,** sought to keep the flames of the Cultural Revolution alive. After Zhou's death from cancer in early 1976, they denounced his policies and banned official mourning. Nevertheless, during the Qing Ming Festival in early April, thousands of mourners gathered in Tiananmen Square to remember the beloved premier and to vent anger at radical leaders. In a sentimental move, the Gang of Four called in militant thugs to break up the demonstration. In the aftermath of the **April Fifth Incident,** Deng Xiaoping was again purged and went into hiding. The Gang of Four could not, however, hold onto power; on September 9, 1976, the Great Helmsman, Chairman Mao, passed away at the ripe old age of 83 and a month later, the Gang of Four was arrested.

THE MORE THINGS CHANGE...

Hua Guofeng emerged as China's new leader. The conservative Hua followed the policy of **Two Whatevers:** "whatever Mao said and whatever Mao did." The Chinese population was not quite as politically dogmatic, however, and political posters sprang up on public bulletin boards in Beijing, in what came to be known as the **Democracy Wall Movement.** Deng Xiaoping, on the final upswing of his roller-coaster-like political career, rode a surge of popular support and quickly used his old connections to oust Hua and take control of the country.

With Deng in control, reform and not revolution was the path of progress. He pursued Zhou Enlai's policy of **Four Mod-**

1971
The PRC replaces the ROC in the UN.

1975
Chiang Kai-shek dies. His body is kept in his family's living room in preparation for the fall of the Communists and its triumphant return to the mainland.

1976
An 8.0 earthquake in Tangshan and a lunar eclipse precede the death of Mao Zedong.

1977
The Gang of Four is charged with framing and persecuting more than 700,000 people.

1979
The US and the PRC establish diplomatic relations.

1981
Jiang Qing and another leader of the Gang of Four are sentenced to death. Later, their sentence is commuted to life in prison.

1983
Deng Xiaoping finishes de-collectivizing nearly all of the nation's communes in an effort to raise standards of living in the country.

1986
Student protests erupt at the University of Science and Technology in Hefei.

1987
Pro-independence rallies in Lhasa draw the government's ire; martial law in Taiwan is lifted.

1988
Tenzin Gyatso, the 14th Dalai Lama, receives the Nobel Peace Prize.

June 4, 1989
Over 1000 people are killed and between 10,000 and 30,000 are arrested in the Tiananmen Square uprising.

1991
92 restaurants in Luoyang are shut down after inspectors discover dishes spiked with opium in order to addict customers.

1992
Deng Xiaoping embarks on a "southern tour," hoping to boost the economy and development. Beijing also makes a bid to host the 2000 Olympic Games; Sydney, Australia wins by two votes, angering well over a billion people.

ernizations, focusing on improvements in industry, agriculture, science, and defense. The speed and scope of liberalization quickly became a topic of national debate: while conservative hardliners urged the maintenance of state control, Democracy Wall activists advocated the implementation of a fifth modernization: democracy. Deng jailed key activists, outlawed the Democracy Wall Movement, and started a campaign against "spiritual pollution" from the West. It soon became clear that China's liberalization would be restricted to the economic sphere.

The government did, however, relax cultural restrictions. Western fashions replaced Mao suits and the domestic travel industry revived. Foreign products invaded the mainland and celebrities like Michael Jackson and Michael Jordan became familiar names and faces to most Chinese citizens.

THE MORE THEY STAY THE SAME?

In the late 1980s, the Chinese economy slumped as soaring inflation eroded consumer savings and undermined public confidence. Moreover, the economic boom had created great disparities in wealth unheard of in the egalitarian Maoist era.

As the public simmered, party chief **Hu Yaobang** was fired for being too liberal and permissive. While in power, Hu was dismissed by college students as a ranting liberal buffoon, but after his death on April 15, 1989, he was eulogized as a shining progressive leader cut down by other party members. As a result, thousands of college students marched to Tiananmen Square (see p. 132) in memory of Hu. They called on the party to grant freedom of the press and freedom of speech, root out corruption, and institute open elections. The number of protestors in Beijing ballooned to over one million by May 20th, upstaging a summit meeting between Deng and Soviet leader Mikhail Gorbachev. In fact, international journalists in town to cover the summit found themselves in the midst of a revolution, their presence furthering international attention of the events unfolding. Attempts at negotiation failed and the PLA was called in to disperse the demonstrators, resulting in the **Tiananmen Square massacre** that lasted from June 3 to 4. Western television audiences watched as some 350,000 PLA soldiers poured into Beijing, guns firing as tanks and troops plowed through the streets. Although it did little to change daily life in China, the Tiananmen Square Democracy Movement paved the way for a series of anti-Communist demonstrations in Eastern Europe and alerted the West to China's human rights violations (see **Human Rights,** p. 32).

ALL FOR ONE AND ONE FOR ALL

At the start of the 1990s, China began to focus more and more attention on the "rogue province," Taiwan. In 1991, Lee Teng-hui, the president of Taiwan, forced former GMD officials to retire and embarked on a series of reforms, instituting free elections and freedom of the press. Previously, the Taiwanese government had spent much of its time sulking and weakly vowing to retake the mainland. As mainland support for democratic movements grew, however, the government saw a very real problem with Taiwan's increasing liberalization. The Chinese government continued to promise to bring Taiwan into line and pressured foreign governments not to support the ROC. In 1996, tensions escalated when, during a Taiwanese presidential election, the PRC held a series of war games and blasted missiles a mere 25km from the coast of Taiwan. The US sent aircraft carriers, and the Taiwanese rallied behind their president; China, however, held fast to its **One-China policy.**

1996
Inventor Pu Danming creates the "healthy cigarette," a tube of herbs with a glowing light that simulates burning ash.

THE LATE 90'S

After Deng Xiaoping's death in 1997, the transfer of power to current president **Jiang Zemin** proceeded without incident, and Jiang has stayed loyal to Deng's pledge to allow controlled market reforms. Hong Kong and Macau returned to Chinese hands in 1999 without major disturbances and the economy continued to expand at a dizzying pace, maintaining a double digit GDP growth rate for much of the 90s before the **Asian financial crisis** of 1997 slowed things down. Nevertheless, the government continued to push for economic reform while consolidating political control. Today, the government continues to encourage development with almost reckless abandon, eager to make China one of the world's foremost economic and political powers.

TODAY

China is now emerging onto the international spectrum in a major way, most notably with its recent admission into the World Trade Organization in December of 2001. The long-awaited and debated admission has rapidly progressed China's integration into the world economy. Membership in the WTO will increase China's exports to the US, EU and Japan, boosting the economy while opening up several Chinese economic sectors to foreign competitors.

Meanwhile, Beijing is currently preparing to host the **2008 Summer Olympic Games** as the city undergoes huge reforms. Beijing has vowed to hold a "Green Olympics" and has already taken aggressive steps to mitigate the city's coal-smoke pollution problem with the construction of a natural-gas pipeline. By 2007, most Beijing buses and taxis will operate only off natural gas energy, and the city is working to make itself 40% "green" in its massive plantation of forests, trees and grass on exposed land. Beijing is also undergoing improvement in its infrastructure, with the addition of five new subway lines and the extensive expansion of the expressway.

Diplomatic relations with the US were strained when on April 1, 2001, a US EP-3 spy plane collided with a Chinese fighter plane over the South China Sea. The US plane was able to make an emergency landing on Hainan island; the Chinese pilot's plane crashed into the ocean. The two countries immediately went into diplomatic overdrive, throwing accusations, making demands, and stirring up nationalistic sentiment. The US crew was eventually released.

Jan. 1, 2001
A Taiwanese boat crosses to the Chinese mainland legally for the first time since the establishment of the PRC.

Feb. 16, 2001
Members of Falun Gong, a group targeted by the Chinese government, set themselves on fire in Tiananmen Square, protesting the government's harsh treatment of their movement.

Mar. 24, 2001 Taiwan elects a new president, Chen Shui-bian, a member of the Democratic Progressive Party and a supporter of an independent Taiwan.

Relations with Taiwan continue to be a point of contention between China and the US, although no major conflicts have occurred. Efforts were severely strained by US President George W. Bush's decision to sell four naval destroyers to Taiwan. The Chinese government, for its part, arrested three US-based Chinese scholars on charges of spying for Taiwan. Two were released in time for US Secretary of State Colin Powell's visit to China in July of 2001, prompting him to comment that relations between the two countries were on an "upswing." In May 2002, then Vice-President Hu Jintao visited the US, discouraged US interference in Taiwan, and reasserted the Chinese government's "one country, two systems" policy.

PEOPLE

China estimates that its population will increase to 1.4 billion by the year 2010. By 2050, that number will peak at 1.6 billion.

Over 100 Chinese cities have over 1 million residents.

China is mostly rural. Only 30% of the country is considered urbanized, but that figure is likely to double in the next 30 years.

Today, China has approximately 1.28 billion people in an area only slightly larger than the US. If you squish three-quarters of China's population into less than half of its land mass, you have a rough idea of the population density in the east. Sound a bit crowded? Things are only getting worse. Almost 100 million peasants float in and out of China's major cities in search of work. City dwellers blame migrants for all sorts of urban social problems, including rising crime rates and disease outbreaks (not to mention longer bathroom lines and overcrowded karaoke bars).

The increase in migrant workers is just one consequence of China's economic transition. In order to stimulate economic growth, the government is moving away from its Communist roots and building a more market-driven economy. The adoption of Western capitalist ideas has only served to highlight the contrast between modern materialism and independence and the Communist ideals that have only recently fallen out of favor.

POPULATION GROWTH

Census-taking began in China in AD 4 for the purpose of tax-collection. At the time, Imperial accountants recorded 69 million inhabitants.

In April 2000, China released the *White Paper* discussing China's progress with human rights, and making it legal for couples who are both only children to have 2 children.

Every year China grows by about 14 million people, approximately the entire population of Shanghai. When he first founded the People's Republic in 1949, Mao Zedong was all for Stalin's "the more, the merrier" approach to baby-making. Mothers who gave birth to five or more children were honored as "Revolutionary Mothers" and awarded government subsidies. Mao loved mass mobilization, even if it extended to the bedroom, and with some help from health care and food production, the population ballooned from 550 million in 1950 to an out-of-control 900 million near the end of the 70s.

In 1978, China instituted its **One-child Policy,** implementing new regulations and propaganda campaigns that urged parents to use family planning. Posters of smiling mothers and cherubic babies proclaimed, "Mama only had me; having one is good." Today, population control is one of China's top priorities, with the notion that the country cannot hope to tackle environmental issues without first controlling its ballooning population.

SEX AND THE SINGLE GUY China's one-child policy and traditional preference for baby boys has led to an overabundance of mate-able males. Chinese parents often abort, don't report, or even abandon their baby girls, resulting in a gender imbalance significantly more severe than the world-wide average. As a result, the marriage pool has become quite a frightening place for most single men. One survey claims that never-married men aged 20 to 44 outnumber single females 2 to 1 and for every 4 men aged 25 to 39, only one will find a bride. At this rate, by 2020 roughly 1 million "excess" males *per year* will enter the marriage market (also known as "the bottomless pit of failure").

ETHNIC COMPOSITION

Most of what is considered to be Chinese culture comes from the Han Chinese, who trace their ancestry back to the Han dynasty (see **The Birth of a Nation,** p. 9). During the Republican Era, Sun Yat-sen envisioned a nationalist state ruled by China's five main ethnic groups: the Han, Manchu, Tibetan, Mongolian, and Uighur peoples. That failed (see **You Say You Want a Revolution,** p. 14). When Mao took over, he followed Stalin's model and decided to offer minority groups significant autonomy. As long as each minority accepted the Communist government, it would be allowed semi-self-rule. Those who rebelled faced the massive strength of the PLA, which routinely squelched ethnic rebellion. Not surprisingly, there have been relatively few dissenters. Han Chinese migration into minority areas, both government-sanctioned and spontaneous, has further marginalized minorities in their homelands and contributed to ethnic tension.

China's population is 91% Han Chinese; the 55 other officially recognized ethnic groups (the remaining 9%) number approximately 108 million people. National minorities receive some special government benefits, including exemption from the one-child policy, tax breaks, and subsidies. In general, Han Chinese relations tend to be better with groups that have assimilated (Manchu, Zhuang, Korean) and worse with those that have not (Tibetan, Uighur, Xinjiang).

MINORITY NATIONALITIES

NORTHEASTERN MINORITIES

The **Manchus** (numbering 10 million) were once the kings of the Northeast (see p. 12). Due to the popular and political strength of the Han majority and the political machinations of the Qing emperors, Han Chinese influence eventually took its toll on the Manchu culture. Even though there are many Manchus in Liaoning province and Beijing, today their language is virtually extinct, and as a people they are almost indistinguishable from the Han.

Regardless of government policy, women in China have on average 2 children each; there are 350 million women in their childbearing years.

Certain government regulations require that women in China use birth control. After many women have their first child, they are forced to use birth control or, if they become pregnant again, abort.

Kidnapping is a growing problem in China. Due to the relative scarcity of women, many men have resorted to buying wives from kidnapping rings. Other women are forced into prostitution. Last year, over 6000 women were reported missing.

In recognition of China's minority languages, examples of major non-Chinese scripts appear on Chinese paper currency.

China's flag is a red field with five gold stars. The largest symbolizes the Han Chinese, while the four smaller ones Tibetan, Manchu, Hui, and Mongol minorities.

At Manchu courts, Pekingese dogs were prized. Some dogs had bodyguards, private palaces, and even human wet nurses.

In 2000, China began to deport illegal immigrants from North Korea, numbering as many as 200,000.

The Hui, Muslim minorities, do not drink alcohol or eat pork, the favorite meat of the Han Chinese, which is forbidden by the Koran.

The Mongol Yuan dynasty reopened trade routes between China and the West and was documented in Marco Polo's memoirs.

In Xinjiang, young men and women play the game "Catch the Maiden," where men on horseback try to steal kisses from girls. If they succeed, the girls run after them with riding crops.

In Uighur towns, conservative Muslim women still wear veils in public.

A large number of **Koreans** live in eastern Jilin, Liaoning, and Heilongjiang provinces along the Yalu River (see **The Northeast,** p. 203). Most are descendants of those who fled when the Japanese annexed the Korean peninsula in 1895. The Koreans have lived peacefully and prosperously and share strong cultural ties with the Chinese. Since the mid 90s, thousands of North Koreans have fled to the Chinese-Korean communities to escape devastating famines in their homeland, putting even more strain on China's resources.

NORTHERN MINORITIES

The **Hui,** or Chinese Muslims, are found throughout China but are most heavily concentrated in Ningxia province, Beijing, and Shanghai. Most Hui are farmers, but urban Hui are often active merchants and craftsmen. During Mao's guerrilla war in Yan'an, many Hui locals joined the Communist cause, eventually rising to power with the establishment of the Ningxia Hui Autonomous Region in 1956. Although the Hui and Han usually coexist peacefully, religious differences still cause strife.

Like their 12th-century leader Genghis Khan, the **Mongols** are often viewed as hardy, horse-loving, yurt-dwelling people who follow their grazing herds across the steppes of Central Asia. In their heyday, the Mongols ruled much of Asia. Today, Mongols in China live mostly in the northern section of the country, stretching from Xinjiang to Heilongjiang. Although many Mongols have become sedentary farmers or city dwellers, many clans still live in yurts and maintain age-old traditions.

NORTHWESTERN MINORITIES

The northwestern minorities share something other than their hard-to-pronounce monikers: the Uighur, Kazakh, Tatar, Tajik, Uzbek, and Kyrgyz peoples also share a common religion and home. They reside in Xinjiang, a land dominated by **Islam** (see p. 30). The **Uighur**, eight million strong, are by far the most numerous. Many depend on irrigation agriculture, building elaborate underground channels and planting their crops in the desert.

Since 1949, the percentage of Han Chinese in the Northwest has risen from 3.7% to more than 50% of the total. This huge demographic shift has led to a good deal of conflict. In the 1950s, the PLA executed thousands of separatists, GMD sympathizers, and nomads. Ethnic tensions during the Great Leap Forward (see p. 17) led to the exodus of 20,000 Uighurs to the Soviet Union. In 1997, riots broke out in Yining (see p. 764). Today, Uighur separatists are notorious for terrorist activities and are closely watched by government officials. The Chinese government has succeeded in securing pledges from Central Asian neighbors to deny support to Uighur separatists.

SOUTHWESTERN MINORITIES

Over three dozen minority groups live in the mountains of southwest China. For centuries, many of these people lived in familial clans, planting rice and raising livestock. Most of these minority groups originally lived in the lower Yangzi valley, but Han expansion forced them into their present mountain homes.

The relationship between these minorities and their Han neighbors varies widely. The **Zhuang,** China's largest ethnic minority with over 17 million people, live mainly in Guangxi province. The Zhuang speak Mandarin dialects, study classical Chinese literature, and are almost indistinguishable from the Han. The **Yi,** who are more resistant to Han influence, have worked hard to uphold their traditions, but their habit of enslaving Han captives has been officially outlawed.

The **Dai** in Yunnan (see **Xishuangbanna,** p. 631) share a language and cultural kinship with the peoples of Thailand, Lao, and Myanmar, while the **Naxi** (see **Lijiang,** p. 611) belong to both Tibetan Buddhist sects and cults of supernatural spirits. Western influence has reached Guizhou province, where a considerable number of **Miao** and **Yao** Christians live.

The **Li** minority on Hainan Island are famed for their knowledge of medicinal and practical herb use. Women chew the Arica herb to dye their lips red.

Before 1949, the **Yi** would stage bridal kidnappings in which the bridegroom's family would pretend to attack the bride's family before whisking the bride away on a horse.

LANGUAGE

The official language of the People's Republic is **Mandarin Chinese** (pûtõnghuà; 普通话; "common language"), which is based on the Beijing dialect. Unofficially, there are an astonishing number of different forms of Chinese. The Han, Hui, and Manchu speak about eight different dialects; the remaining minority groups each have their own spoken language. Twenty-three have their own written ones.

Mandarin is spoken in most parts of China, even if it isn't the predominant language. In Hong Kong, **Cantonese,** which is approximately as close to Mandarin as French is to Italian, is the dominant spoken dialect (see p. 524). In the west, especially in rural areas, local languages like Uighur, Tibetan, and Kazakh are widely spoken and often more welcome than Mandarin.

Even a minimal knowledge of Mandarin makes a visit to China much easier and more rewarding. Although English is increasingly popular among language students in China, outside of major cities few Chinese speak fluently enough to be of use to travelers. If you need the assistance of an English speaker, your best bet is to ask a young student or urban professional. *Let's Go: China* gives the pronunciation and characters for most Chinese establishment and place names; if no one can understand you, you can always point at the Chinese characters and gesture to convey your meaning. See also the phrasebook (p. 833) in the **Appendix** for help.

The Defense Language Institute in Monterey, CA estimates that at least 1320 hours of instruction are necessary in order to be moderately proficient in Chinese.

China's languages represent four major language families: Sino-Tibetan (Chinese and Tibetan), Altaic (Manchu, Uighur, and Mongolian), Indo-European (Tajik, in Xinjiang province), and Austroasiatic (Kawa, in Yunnan province).

TONES

Chinese words are all assigned certain **tones.** The number of tones varies; Mandarin only has five, but Cantonese has a mind-boggling, tongue-twisting seven or more (depending on whom you ask). Sometimes Chinese-speakers play it fast and loose with tones, depending on the dialect, but most should understand the standard pronunciation. For more information on **pronunciation,** see the pronunciation guide in the **Appendix** (p. 833).

There are 6000 Chinese surnames, but 87% of the population uses only 100. The top 10 surnames are used by 40% of the Chinese.

Only five surnames have more than one syllable: Ouyang, Sima, Moqi, Tantai, and Puyang.

Tones can drastically change the meaning of a syllable. For example, *mã* (妈) means "mom," *má* (麻) "sesame," *mǎ* (马) "horse," mà (骂) "to scold," and *ma* (吗) is a word that changes a sentence into a question.

Some dialects vary from Mandarin Chinese only by tone (e.g., assigning the 3rd tone to Mandarin's 1st tone words and vice versa gives you the Nanjing dialect).

Grammar is essentially the same throughout the different dialects. Some follow a slightly different word order; for example, Shanghainese often uses a subject, object, verb order.

Chinese characters first appeared as logographs (symbols representing entire words) on Shang dynasty oracle bones 4000 years ago. A picture of a mother and child was the character for "love."

TONE	PINYIN	PRONUNCIATION
First	ā	A doctor tells you to say "AHHH."
Second	á	A confused "huh?"
Third	ǎ	Inviting further explanation: "Go on..."
Fourth	à	"[Insert the expletive of your choice]!"
Neutral	a	A thoughtful "hm."

GRAMMAR

Compared to its pronunciation, Chinese grammar is remarkably simple. You don't have to conjugate verbs or decline nouns or adjectives. Word order is usually fixed: usually **subject, time, verb, object.** This is not to say, however, that Chinese is a flat, simple language consisting entirely of dull Tarzan-like sayings ("Me on branch want swing"). Though efficient, the language is far from inelegant. Proverbs or idioms are often expressed with **four-character phrases,** which convey a wealth of meaning—sometimes entire stories—in only four words.

WRITING

MONKEY...SECOND MONKEY Since there is no general stock of Chinese Johns and Janes, parents create proper names out of character combinations that sound pleasant, lucky, and beautiful and that encourage moral and scholastic achievement. Former favorites often involved mythological creatures ("Dragon Power" or "Phoenix Beauty") but are now widely considered to be old-fashioned and hokey. In large farm families, children are often enumerated "Big Dog," "Second Monkey," (the hard to believe but true) "Third Shit," and so on. Superstitious peasants who fear that the gods might take their children choose these simpler names so that the gods mistake their children for common animals and move on. Communist ideological fervor brought about a flurry of "Resist Americans," "Learn from the Peasants" and "Victory for Mao." Even today, "May the Country be Mighty" is a favorite pick among patriotic parents.

Perhaps the greatest uniting factor of China today (apart from a predilection for sentimental pop songs) is its written language. Regardless of the spoken dialect, all Chinese is expressed with one common written language. Unfortunately, its universality is the only convenient thing about it. The non-alphabetic **Chinese writing system** includes 40,000 to 70,000 characters, torturing earnest language students who spend years acquiring fluency.

Chinese characters first appeared as pictographs 4000 years ago. Because of the system's long history, the pictographic derivations of many characters are completely unidentifiable. Of course, for some words, any idiot can see the relationship between character and meaning. Take, for instance: 串 (kebab), 山 (mountain), 口 (mouth), and 磷 (phosphorus).

The ancient Chinese sometimes used the same character to represent different words with similar pronunciations. Not surprisingly, this led to confusion and some serious strife between long-distance penpals. To resolve the homonym horror, extra characters called **radicals** were added to each word. Today about 90% of today's Chinese characters have two parts: the radical, which helps clarify the meaning, and the original character, which indicates the pronunciation. For example, many words that have to do with manual actions include the hand radical (手): pull (拉), hold back (拦), arrange (排). Because spoken Chinese has changed so drastically over the centuries, characters that today share a phonetic radical are not always pronounced the same way.

Until 1949, the Chinese writing system was basically the same as 2000 years before: confusing as all hell. In order to simplify the written language and increase literacy rates, the CCP reduced the number of strokes in each character. They instituted **simplified characters** (jiǎntǐzì; 简体) written with fewer strokes than **traditional characters** (fántǐzì; 繁体) for many commonly used characters. The government also established the **pinyin romanization system** (拼音) as a more accurate way to write Chinese sounds with the Roman alphabet. It replaced the somewhat puzzling **Wade-Giles romanization system** (from which we get "Peking" for Beijing).

In order to read a Chinese newspaper, one needs to know at least 3000 characters. An educated Chinese speaker can recognize about 6000 characters.

Until the 18th century, half of all the world's books had been written in Chinese.

CHINA

RELIGION AND PHILOSOPHY

Until the Communists arrived, China was dominated by three major faiths: Confucianism, Daoism, and Buddhism. These faiths coexisted rather peacefully and it was not uncommon for one person to feel some affinity with more than one of these faiths. In addition, Islam, Christianity, and Judaism have a number of followers in China.

CONFUCIANISM. Scholars often dispute the characterization of Confucianism as a religion, arguing that it should instead be considered a philosophy. Although Confucianists don't necessarily believe in an otherworldly power, Confucianism has inspired the creation of temples and shrines and has reached a much vaster audience than most purely philosophical systems. This position between religion and philosophy is unique in world history.

Semantics aside, Confucianism all started with the birth of the man himself, **Confucius.** Born in 551 BC in the city of **Qufu** (see p. 185), Confucious initially wanted to attain public office and gain the confidence of a major ruler, but he never succeeded. After years of wandering from kingdom to kingdom searching for a ruler who would respect his ideas, he gave up, settled down, and devoted himself to teaching. After Confucius's death in 479 BC, his pupils compiled the **Analects,** a loose and disjointed collection of his oral teachings. Confucius himself is not known to have written a single word.

China is officially atheist; nevertheless, an estimated 20% of the population is Confucian, 6% Buddhist, 2% Daoist, 2% Muslim, and 1% Christian.

Confucian ideals have spread throughout the world, most notably to Japan, Korea, and Vietnam.

Confucius (kǒngfūzi; 孔夫子) literally means "Master Kong." Kong was his surname; his proper name was Qiu (Çǒ), which means "mound" because he was born with a mound-like head.

Confucius didn't believe that everyone could reach perfection; only the educated and morally upright could find the way and, later, guide the masses.

In the centuries after Confucius's death, other thinkers, most notably **Mencius (Mengzi)** and **Xunzi,** made further contributions to Confucian doctrine.

During the Song dynasty, **Neo-Confucianism** adapted Confucian ideals to the behavior of rulers and political leaders and also applied them to everyday family decisions.

Many scholars believe that the *Dao De Jing* was written as a response to Confucianism around 300 BC.

According to legend, Laozi, the author of the *Dao De Jing,* was fathered by a shooting star and gestated for 82 years so that when he was born, he was already a wise old man.

Laozi is the quintessential grandfather who gives incomprehensible advice. One of his best quotes: "Be still like a mountain and flow like a great river."

According to Confucius, **sacred ritual** and **ceremony** play an important role in government and society. Societal hierarchies are also extremely important; sons should obey fathers, wives should obey husbands, and subjects should obey their ruler. **Filial piety,** a favorite Confucianist catchphrase, is a necessary condition for social harmony, which is considered to be more important than the needs of individuals. **Self-cultivation** and **right behavior,** not noble birth, determine one's status as a gentleman. **Benevolence** is one of the most fundamental of all virtues.

Confucianism evolved into arguably the single most important institution in China. The educational and examination systems focused almost exclusively on the **Confucian classics,** a selection of works on topics ranging from poetry to history that had been compiled and edited by Confucius and his followers. By the end of the 19th century, Chinese intellectuals had rejected Confucianism in favor of more modern, Western ideologies. Communist leaders also initially criticized Confucianism as a nepotistic political philosophy that legitimized the domination of the ruling class at the expense of the proletariat. But the effects of Confucian thought on Chinese culture lingered, often unacknowledged, throughout the 20th century. In recent years, scholars have suggested that the ability of certain East Asian societies to adapt to the demands of modern society is due at least in part to the region's Confucian heritage.

DAOISM. In contrast to Confucianism's overwhelming emphasis on social relations, Daoism focuses on the individual's relation to nature and metaphysical reality. In other words, Daoism is a wee bit confusing. It dates back to the 3rd century BC, when the **Dao De Jing** (or Tao Te Ching) is thought to have been written. Its clearer assertions concern the inadequacy of language and the power of the *Dao*, an all-encompassing force that guides the workings of the world. Of course, it cannot be defined sufficiently in words. In Daoism, everything is relative, and binary distinctions are moot, making it difficult to describe, much less make any sort of qualitative comparison.

As with Confucianism, many scholars draw a distinction between the philosophical and religious aspects of Daoism. The distinction, however, is a bit blurry, and the ideas of the former are closely bound to the practices of the latter. Philosophical Daoism is based on a tradition of intellectual exploration and occasional forays into mystical and alchemical practices; this is the Daoism of philosophers, monks, and nuns.

Religious Daoism is the Daoism of the common people. It has little explicit connection with the ideas contained in the philosophical texts. Instead, it is oriented toward the supernatural and draws a number of its elements from age-old Chinese folk beliefs. A belief in various gods and spirits, fortune-telling, magic, and alchemy are all associated with popular Daoism. Other elements of Chinese culture that predated Daoism have since been incorporated into popular practice, including ideas about man's relationship to nature and the importance of ancestor worship. For many, the language and practices of

Daoism also mixed easily with those of Buddhism, forming the base of Chinese popular religion.

Daoism may never have enjoyed the state patronage that Confucianism did, but its influence on Chinese culture was immense nonetheless. The experiments in alchemy prompted by Daoist searches for immortality did much to advance early Chinese science. Daoist conceptions of man's relation to nature also influenced generations of landscape painters, and Daoist ideals informed many of the philosophical and personal expressions found in China's classical poetry.

BUDDHISM. Unlike Confucianism and Daoism, Buddhism originated outside China. **Siddhartha Gautama,** the one who would come to be called **The Buddha** (Enlightened One), was born around 560 BC in Lumbini, just within the modern borders of Nepal. As a prince, Gautama was lavished with creature comforts, preventing him from experiencing the life of a normal man. But one day, Siddhartha got his first glimpses of the outside world. He went on four outings and saw a sick man, an old man, a corpse, and a beggar. Siddhartha realized that he could no longer be satisfied by the Hindu explanation for worldly suffering, so he fled his posh life as a prince at the age of 29 to wander the forests of India as an ascetic. Eventually, he gave up extreme asceticism, and chose a more moderate path of meditation. In this way, he was able to achieve **nirvana** (enlightenment), and he set off to preach about his discoveries.

The Buddha advocated total detachment from the world. Desire for physical and mental things and the corresponding belief in an individual existence are only fleeting illusions, he said, and bring only suffering. One can end suffering by ending desire and entering a state of nirvana. According to the Buddha, right understanding, thought, speech, action, livelihood, effort, mindfulness, and concentration (the **Eightfold Path**) are the keys to reaching nirvana. He also preserved Hindu's doctrines of *karma* and reincarnation, in which an individual's actions in one life determine their position in the next, hence advocating universal non-violence.

Chinese Buddhism is part of the **Mahayana** ("Great Vehicle") school, which differs in many ways from the **Hinayana** ("Small Vehicle") school that dominates most of Southeast Asia. The Mahayana school developed as a popular sect around the first century AD and became predominant in most of Northeast Asia and Vietnam. Its doctrines argue that the quest for nirvana is one undertaken by all of society, not by individuals (as the Hinayana school professes). It also stresses the importance of compassion for others.

Buddhism was introduced to China in the later half of the Han dynasty (see p. 9). Early Chinese Buddhist beliefs and practices intermingled with those of Daoism. As a result, the aspects of the faith that were emphasized most were those that were similar to Daoist ideals. The religion caught on quickly; by the Sui dynasty, Buddhism had become the state religion.

Toward the end of the Tang, however, Emperor Wuzong undertook a large-scale **persecution** of Buddhism most likely

Zhuanzi, a Daoist philosopher, was more witty than his elder counterpart. When told that he could not possibly know how a fish feels, he replied: "You're not me, so how do you know that I don't know how a fish feels?"

Popular worship of Buddha figures is widespread in Chinese Buddhism; among the most prominent are **Amitabha** (*Amitofo* in Chinese), the Buddha of Infinite Light, and **Avalokiteshvara** (or **Guanyin**), the Goddess of Mercy.

Buddhism has a number of competing **sects.** The Tiantai and Huayan schools emphasize doctrinal distinctions. The "Pure Land" (or Jingtu) sect was named for the paradise into which enlightened worshipers would be reborn. It stressed faith as the route to salvation.

Chan Buddhism, better known as Zen Buddhism, teaches that one can only become enlightened through meditation.

Because of Buddhism's spread throughout China in the 3rd-6th centuries AD, Han emperors sent emissaries to India to translate texts into Chinese.

When Buddhism first came to China, it was widely believed that Buddha was a reincarnation of Laozi, the founder of Daoism.

A unique form of Buddhism is practiced in Tibet, where Buddhist traditions have combined with the indigenous religion, Bön (see p. 801).

Some claim that Islam was introduced to China by a companion of Muhammad's around AD 700.

In the 16th century, the Italian Jesuit priest **Mateo Ricci** entered China. He mastered Chinese and was granted permission by the Kangxi emperor to dwell and proselytize in the capital.

Chinese Jews trace their lineage patrilineally, unlike most other Jews. In the Ming dynasty, the emperor designated seven surnames specifically for the Jews.

China contains approximately 12,000 churches, 30,000 mosques, and innumerable temples.

The PRC officially recognizes four religions: Daoism, Buddhism, Islam, and Christianity. However, devotees are allowed to worship only in establish-

inspired by fear of the fiscal and political power of the Buddhist clergy. Chinese Buddhism never quite recovered from this blow. Although it continued to flourish as a religion, its power was tightly controlled, and state-sponsored liquidations of Buddhist assets were regularly undertaken.

Not surprisingly, the Cultural Revolution also took a heavy toll on Chinese Buddhism, as Red Guards destroyed temples and the government disbanded monasteries. In recent years, Buddhism has rebounded considerably and monasteries are active centers of worship once again. Although very few Chinese identify themselves as strictly Buddhist, a large number make trips to temples or pilgrimage sites.

OTHER RELIGIONS. Nearly nine million Chinese practice **Islam,** a faith founded in the 7th century AD by the prophet Muhammad. Many Chinese Muslims, or Hui, are descended from Persian and Central Asian merchants who traveled to China between the 7th and 13th centuries. See also **Minority Nationalities,** p. 23.

Today, there are almost 20 million **Christians** in China, concentrated mostly in the southeast. Christian missionaries first arrived in the 16th century, and despite the strong Catholic bent of foreign priests, today the majority of Chinese Christians are Protestant. The influence of Christianity on more recent Chinese history has not been negligible; the leader of the bloody Taiping Rebellion of the 19th century drew inspiration from the Bible, and the Boxer Rebellion was a local reaction against Christian missionaries (see p. 13).

When European missionaries began to flood into China in the 17th century, they found a small community of Chinese **Jews** in the city of Kaifeng, in present-day Henan province (see p. 271). Scholars aren't sure how they arrived in China, but most suspect that they arrived via the Silk Road. The Kaifeng Jewish community is no longer active, and only a few relics of their existence remain. During WWII, many Eastern European Jews found temporary refuge in the Hongkou International Settlement in Shanghai (see p. 332).

COMMUNISM AND RELIGION. Communist China is officially atheist, and faith in the state and the working people is theoretically supposed to eliminate the need for any deities. The Cultural Revolution marked the height of state-sponsored religious persecution in China. Red Guards destroyed temples and churches and monks and nuns of all faiths were forced to renounce their vows and were sent to labor camps or prisons. Confucianism was attacked as a remnant of feudal oppression, and Daoism and Buddhism were branded as reactionary superstitions. Christianity was condemned as a vestige of Western exploitation.

In the years following Mao's death, the intense anti-religiosity of the Cultural Revolution began to fade away. Traditional Chinese religion is now officially (and proudly) considered a national relic. In many cases, the government actively promotes the restoration of temples and holy mountains as tourist sites. But the authorities still closely monitor the activities of churches and monasteries, and problems continue to arise when the dictates of religious power structures come into direct conflict with those of the state power structure. Thus, the Catholic Church, which asserts the supremacy of the Pope over all temporal authorities, and Tibetan Buddhism, which claims the Dalai Lama as its spiritual and political leader, have clashed frequently with the government in recent years.

ments that have registered with and been approved by the state. Those who worship in house churches or possess unauthorized materials are often detained or arrested.

GOVERNMENT

The political structure of China has remained largely unchanged since 1949. China is a Communist, one-party republic controlled primarily by the **Chinese Communist Party** or **CCP,** although a few government-approved "opposition" parties do exist. Together, the CCP and the Chinese government control national politics, which isn't too difficult since most government officials are also members of the CCP, and leaders of the former tend to be leaders of the latter. The two institutions are *formally* separate, however. The government's main legislative body is the **National People's Congress** (governed by the **Politburo** and the **Secretariat**), and the chief executive body is the **State Council.** Local governments follow a similar pattern, with power formally in the hands of government bodies and effectively in the hands of local Communist Party leaders.

The foundations of the house that Mao built consist of the **Four Cardinal Principles:** the socialist road, the dictatorship of the proletariat, CCP leadership, and Marxism-Leninism-Maoism.

The CCP's main decision-making body, the Central Committee, consists of 151 members and 197 alternate members. The central committee is elected every five years, just before a National People's Congress.

HEAD HONCHOS

NAME/ STATS	TITLES	AND THEIR PERSONAL AD READS...
Jiang Zemin 江泽民 Aug. 17, 1926 Year of the Tiger	President CCP General Secretary Chairman of Central Military Committee	Enjoys Chinese folk music and classical poetry, fluent in 4 languages, plays bamboo flute; degree in electrical engineering
Hu Jintao 胡景涛 Dec. 1942 Year of the Horse	Vice President	"Compassionate reformer," good political instincts, degree in hydraulic engineering, best looking man in Chinese politics
Li Peng 李鹏 Oct. 20, 1928 Year of the Dragon	Chairman Politburo Member	Hobbies include basketball, calligraphy, and driving; advocates "suppression by force if necessary"
Zhu Rongji 朱熔基 Oct. 1, 1928 Year of the Dragon	Premier Prime Minister	Pragmatic, no-nonsense attitude; degree in electrical engineering

ECONOMY

The saying goes that if you're not a Communist before you're 30 you don't have a heart, but if you're not a capitalist after you're 30 you don't have a brain. The CCP seems to have taken this saying to heart (and brain). For nearly 30 years after the creation of the PRC, the nation had a highly centralized planned economy based on a Soviet model and in line with Marxist-Leninist principles. Under Mao's rule, the country aimed to modernize target industries through a series of **Five-Year Plans,**

Increased privatization has led to an improved standard of living for many Chinese. The number of rural poor dropped from 200 million to 80 million in under a decade, and the burgeoning middle class (100 million strong) now enjoys such luxuries as DVD players and digital cameras.

The creation of SEZs (Special Economic Zones) led to the quadrupling of China's GDP and doubling of its agricultural output.

China's GDP growth rate in 2001 was roughly 7.3%, making China's economy one of the fastest growing in the world.

Most workers are organized in work units (dānwèi). Members of a work unit live together and attend political meetings together, and the unit gives permission to its members to marry, have a child, or change residence.

In 1994, the government instituted a new State Security Law, which criminalized a number of activities, including making speeches that "endanger state security," and instigating "national disputes."

The PRC has not allowed outside organizations to keep tabs on their penal facilities. The government estimates that there are 1.2 million prisoners and detainees in China.

which, although successful at first, eventually led to low levels of production and a sluggish economy.

As the People's Republic neared its 30th birthday, Deng Xiaoping rose to power and immediately began to implement new free-market economic reforms. In 1979, the government named the southeastern coastal cities of Shenzhen, Zhuhai, Xiamen, and Shantou **Special Economic Zones (SEZs).** The national government allowed the local governments of SEZs to foster economic growth and develop governmental infrastructures without first getting the approval of the central government. The phenomenal success of the first four SEZs has prompted the government to establish others all along the eastern seaboard and down the Yangzi River.

China's economic growth has not been entirely painless, however. The hybrid system means that the country often suffers from the worst problems of both socialism (corruption, a bloated bureaucracy) and capitalism (income disparities, tacky tourist goods). In addition to a formidable unemployment problem, the Chinese government must also find a way to deal with the debt-ridden **state-owned enterprises,** industrial dinosaurs that still employ a large number of Chinese workers but operate very inefficiently.

Despite these potential pitfalls, the economy has continued to grow at a solid rate of about 8% a year (of course, many countries take the Chinese government's statistics with a grain of salt). China managed to keep the *yuán* on the straight and narrow during the **financial crisis** that sent most of Asia into a tailspin in late 1997. Pounding on the gates of economic greatness, China obtained **Permanent Normal Trade Relations** with the US in 2000 and subsequent membership in the **World Trade Organization (WTO)** in 2001. Still, these promising indications only mask underlying troubles. More than half of the country's labor force works in the agricultural sector; the average yearly income is US$830—less than 3% of what it is in the US. Regardless, the government presses forward, anxious to make its way in the global economy.

HUMAN RIGHTS

China's human rights violations have been cause for considerable international concern in the past few decades. The government maintains that stability and social order are more important than individual freedom, and individuals have been detained, arrested, and jailed for peacefully expressing political, religious, and social views that differ from those of the CCP.

Since the crackdown on the **Tiananmen Square Democracy Movement** in 1989 (see p. 20), the world has kept a close eye on China's suppression of individual rights. The release of high-profile political prisoners in 1997 and 1998 signaled a loosening of restrictions on personal and political freedoms. In September of 1998, the United Nations High Commissioner for Human Rights visited China for the first time at the behest of the government, and, one month later, the Chinese government signed—but did not ratify—the **United Nations Covenant on Civil and Political Rights.** The signing of the covenant also coincided with Beijing's first international human rights conference.

Beginning in November and December of 1998, the authorities conducted rounds of arrests, detaining dissidents who were registered with opposition political parties. The government also tightened control over the Internet and print publications, and continued its repression of unauthorized religious organizations, including the quasi-religious sect, **Falun Gong.**

A thorny recurrent issue for the Chinese government has been the human rights abuses in Tibet and Xinjiang. Tibetan dissidents, led by the Dalai Lama and backed by many Western groups like Free Tibet (including Hollywood stars like Richard Gere) have proved remarkably successful at rallying support abroad. At home, however, they have been threatened, arrested, detained, sentenced to hard labor, imprisoned, and even tortured (see **Tibet: History,** p. 797). The plight of the Uighurs of Xinjiang is less well known overseas, in no small part because they lack a prominent figure to champion their cause.

China's stance on human rights has also affected its foreign relations. Protestors opposed China's bid for the 2008 Olympics, pointing to evidence of the country's human rights violations, and the US Congress examined the issue in depth before it passed a bill granting China Permanent Normal Trade Relations in September 2000.

In spring 2001, during the country's "Strike Hard" anti-crime campaign, over 1700 people were executed in three months.

The government sets guidelines for its journalists; one such mandate requires that news is "80% positive and 20% negative." If reporters don't follow these rules, they risk censure, demotion, or imprisonment.

CULTURE

CUSTOMS & ETIQUETTE

BATHROOMS. Culture shock can't be measured in volts, but the jolt sent through most Westerners the first time they see and smell a Chinese toilet is roughly equivalent to sticking a fork in a socket. Most Chinese toilets are squat toilets: basically, a hole in the ground. There are variations, to be sure: some toilets are recessed porcelain basins with running water; some are noxious, stagnant pits. Stall partitions are at knee-height and few have doors. None have toilet paper. And, as the final insult, most toilets charge admission (Y0.2-0.5).

Public toilets are marked with signs, usually in Chinese (公用厕所). Sometimes, the facilities are separated by gender: male (男) and female (女). Many travelers avoid public toilets and head instead for upscale hotels, new department stores, and Western restaurants, which have more modern facilities.

SPITTING. Polluted cities and poor sanitation mean that respiratory flus are common for anyone living through a Chinese winter, and the Chinese tend to be fairly up front about how they take care of their phlegm. No one is shy about hawking back and letting it fly on streets, sidewalks, trains, buses, and even restaurant floors. The preponderance of public phlegm is

Today, a well-educated person is described as "having five wagons of learning," which refers to the days when books written on bamboo strips were stacked on wagons to transfer from place to place.

According to tradition, Li Bai died while drunk out of his mind; he tried to fish out the reflection of the moon from a lake.

In the early part of the Qing dynasty, the most popular heroes and heroines of fiction were surprisingly modern; brooding swordsmen, beautiful scholars, and mystery-solving officials were frequent characters.

Erotic novels were popular in the Ming and Qing dynasties and were secretly written by members of the literati. The most famous of these is *The Golden Lotus*, an impressively graphic story of sex and murder written by Xiao Shen Shen.

In 1915, professors at Beijing University founded a new journal, *New Youth*. Many of the writers for the journal criticized Chinese traditions and encouraged contact with the West.

In *Diary of a Madman*, Lu Xun wrote that Chinese culture was "a culture of serving one's masters, who are triumphant at the cost of the misery of the multitude."

After the Tiananmen square massacre (see p. 20), many writers feared they would be targeted by the government and fled the country.

The oldest surviving instrument in the musical world is a 9000-year-old bird-bone flute found at an ancient Chinese burial site.

Bamboo plays an important role in traditional Chinese music. Many instruments make use of bamboo sticks; "making the phoe-

WHEN GOOD TOILETS GO BAD

An archaeological site in Henan province seems to indicate that the Chinese invented the flush toilet almost 2000 years ago, long before Thomas Crapper arrived on the waste disposal scene. In a Han dynasty tomb, archaeologists found a toilet that closely resembles modern facilities, with running water, a stone seat, and armrests. Perhaps in an attempt to reclaim its former glory (and impress the International Olympic Committee), the Chinese government began work in January 2001 to refurbish toilets in many Beijing tourist spots. The new facilities will have 4-star ratings as an aid for the more discerning connoisseur and will include sinks, toilet paper, automatic flushing mechanisms, and lively music.

somewhat of an embarrassment for the Chinese government, and increasingly more cities are enacting anti-spitting regulations and hanging "No Spitting" signs. All of this has little actual effect, though. You will not be able to avoid spitting; you're advised to get used to it and, when you hear the characteristic hawking sound, to get out of the way.

STARING. Staring is not quite the social faux pas in China that it is in the West, to put it mildly. Be prepared for intense, prolonged scrutiny by all you encounter, especially if you're obviously a foreigner. You will almost certainly be stared at by everyone, from small children to store clerks to businessmen. There is little that you can do to ward off the spectators; take solace in the fact that you have indeed achieved a special place in the pantheon of Chinese tourist sights. Wearing unobtrusive clothing is recommended; body piercing and brightly dyed hair are certain to make you stand out even more. Yelling to stop staring (in any language) or showing obvious annoyance will most likely just make the problem worse. If you speak Chinese, talking to onlookers is often the best way to deal with unwanted attention. Travelers should remember that staring usually represents friendly curiosity, nothing more. See also **Minority Travelers,** p. 98.

BEGGARS. At some point you are likely to be approached by panhandlers, whether in Beijing or in poverty-stricken Guizhou and Tibet. Rising unemployment means more and more people throughout the country are asking for spare change. In crowded areas like train and bus stations, elderly men and women, handicapped people, mothers with babies, or young children frequently beg for money. The children, generally around four or five years old, are quite tenacious, often grabbing hold of the legs and arms of passersby and hanging on. It is ultimately up to you, but if you do give money, you run the risk of being thronged by more beggars hoping to receive the same treatment. Keep a handful of spare change in your pockets if you don't want to draw attention to a fistful of cash. Buying food for beggars is also a good alternative as it avoids the stereotyping of foreigners as money-throwing capitalists.

WE ARE TAIWANESE, IF YOU PLEASE. China and Taiwan have, how should we say, strained relations. In order to avoid an embarrassing or even hostile situation, take care how you refer to the two depending on which area you are in. When on the mainland, avoid mentioning Taiwan at all if possible. Never explicitly refer to Taiwan as a separate country, as it is likely to be offensive to Chinese citizens. However when in Taiwan, avoid calling it "The Republic of China" or "Nationalist China" as it is offensive to the Taiwanese, who consider themselves citizens of a separate country. A safe bet is "Taiwan Province," or better yet, just "Taiwan."

FOOD & DRINK

According to a Chinese proverb, to the common man, food is as sacred as the heavens. Yet may it be said that to the rich man, food is equally sacred, but often more expensive. Regardless of budget, exposure to Chinese culture begins and ends with food. This is not without reason: China has one of the most distinctive and varied cuisines in the world. Food has commanded the interest and respect of intellectual and political leaders throughout China's extensive history. When a new emperor ascended the throne, his first duty was to appoint his personal chef. A common greeting among the ruling elite in the past was "Have you eaten yet?" And in perhaps the most vivid proof of China's illustrious culinary past, the Tang poet Su Dongpo wrote the lyrical poem "In Praise of Pork."

A MODEST PROPOSAL During the last decade of the Sui dynasty, the path of the Grand Canal was set to go through the family graves of a local landlord. The landlord knew that the project overseer loved nothing more than a good meal, and so in order to persuade the overseer to divert the canal, the landlord had his housekeeper's two-year-old son killed, steamed, and served as lamb to the overseer. The overseer loved the meat so much that each day he wanted more—even after the landlord had admitted its true origins. Eventually, thousands of children disappeared, and complaints were so grievous they reached even the emperor himself. The official was executed and the bones of the children were recovered and reburied by their parents.

Chinese cuisine stresses the importance of a balance between *fàn* (rice and grains) and *cài* (vegetables and meat dishes). Ingredients for *cài* vary greatly, from the exotic (lobster, shark fin, bear paw, deer antler, and deer tail) to the rustic (grass, tree skins, bamboo leaves, and white soil).

Rice is the staple crop in most of Southern China, but in the North, wheat is the principle crop, and meals often consist of noodles and stuffed buns. In Hong Kong, **dim sum** (small appetizer dishes) is particularly popular, and the Northwest is more heavily influenced by the cuisine of Central Asia (see p. 801).

nix dance on bamboo" is considered the highest praise a musician can receive.

Since many folk songs originally used fairly explicit language, the Communist Party made an organized effort in the 1950s to "clean up" all the songs and add "revolutionary spirit" to them.

In 2001, many Westerners were introduced to the world of Cantonese pop music when the Hong Kong star Coco Lee performed at the Academy Awards.

Chinese theater was a major form of at-home entertainment in pre-modern China. Theater troupes and their low-paid actors were hired out to rich families.

Jīngjù, even though it's officially called "National Opera," is not widely popular outside of Beijing. Most Chinese prefer local forms of theater.

In *jīngjù*, the actors indicate a wide range of feelings with a few, standard gestures. For instance, if the character is worried, he will rub his hands together; if he is formulating a plan, he will fidget for several minutes until he hits his forehead with his palm.

Buddhist murals that arrived during the Tang Dynasty via the Silk Road heavily influenced Chinese dance. Many traditional poses are taken directly from these paintings.

For the Chinese literati, the study of calligraphy was thought to be essential to a good education. Some scholars, like Wang Xizhi, were more valued for their calligraphy than for their knowledge.

Gu Kaizhi, a 4th century master, is famed for portraying a scholar's wisdom with the addition of three hairs—just three quick strokes—to his chin.

Chinese brush painting saw a brief decline in popularity under Mao. During the Cultural Revolution, painters were tortured for inadvertently drawing a realistic shadow on Chairman Mao's face, which was considered to be an attempt to "blemish the face" of Chairman Mao.

Chinese sculptors take delight in displaying their artistry in a grand fashion. In every single Buddhist temple there can be found larger-than-life gold-plated statues of Siddhartha.

REGIONAL CUISINE	SPECIALTIES
Beijing and Shandong Province	Peking Duck, elaborate banquets, dumplings and noodles.
Shanghai and Jiangsu Province	Lobster, crab, fish, fish, and more fish (did we mention fish?)
Sichuan and Hunan Provinces	Searing pain from super-spicy food, including the appropriately named hotpot.
Hong Kong and Guangdong Province	Whatever's handy: monkey, snake, pigeon, frog, turtle, etc.
Xinjiang and the Northwest	Noodle soups, lamb kebabs, and roasted meat.

Chinese **tea** comes in hundreds of flavors, with two main types: **green tea** (lǜchá; 绿茶) and **black tea** (hóngchá; 红茶). Prices range from Y1 per bag to hundreds of dollars per ounce. Hot water, on the other hand, is free and available everywhere. Grain-based **baijiu** (白酒), a traditional spirit with an extremely high alcohol content, is popular among adults, especially the elderly. The fairly potent brew is so strong that it can often be smelled through a closed bottle. China also produces **beer,** one of the most popular drinks in the country. Most towns have their own local brews; the famed Tsingtao brand is the product of Qingdao (see p. 189), and is sold overseas.

THE ARTS

LITERATURE

ANCIENT AND PREMODERN

Because of its long history, **lyric poetry** is considered to be the primary genre in classical Chinese tradition. **The Classic of Poetry,** a collection of 10th- to 7th-century BC lyrics, is rumored to have been edited by Confucius himself and is an important part of a traditional Chinese education. In later years, as scholars mastered the art form, they began to create more individualistic works; the poetry eventually lost its original ritualistic role and became a sort of diary for the literati. The millions of poems that have been passed down through the ages are now invaluable historical resources with first hand accounts of rebellions and dynastic changes.

During its height in the Tang dynasty, lyrical poetry touched upon subjects from historical issues to personal concerns. Many poets from this era are still famous today: **Li Bai** wrote bold, individualistic poems; **Du Fu** dealt with the social and historical issues of his day; and **Bai Juyi** excelled at retellings of romantic legends. A new genre of lyrical poetry was created in the Song dynasty. Set to popular musical tunes, these poems were written by male scholar-officials, most often about love and desire, and were sung by courtesans. **Su Dongpo** was the most famous of these Song authors.

Personal essays that express individual philosophies complete the classical Chinese literary canon. The **Analects** of Confucius and the **Dao De Jing** of Laozi, along with the writings of Zhuanzi and Mencius, are also considered to be foundation works of a standard classical literary education.

Fiction was long regarded as a lowly art form due to its popularity with the lower classes. In the late Ming, however, the intellectual elite began to record traditional stories in vernacular narrative and, eventually, to compose original fiction for its own entertainment. Writers like **Feng Menglong** wrote volumes of fiction in short story form; many of these stories valued individual passion over Confucian ideals.

The great **novels** of the Ming and Qing dynasties are written with a combination of vernacular and classical language. Four of these novels, called the "Four Great Works," have become nearly required reading for educated Chinese. *The Romance of the Three Kingdoms* is an epic tale of the wars following the end of the Han dynasty; *The Water Margin*, the story of a band of virtuous rebels in the Song; and *The Journey to the West*, the legend of the monk Xuan Zang's journey to India to collect Buddhist scriptures. Perhaps the best known of these four novels is the *Dream of the Red Chamber*, also translated as *Dream of Red Mansions* or *The Story of the Stone*, a tragic love story involving two youths in a declining noble family.

MODERN

In the early 20th century, Chinese writers began to favor vernacular language over staid, classical writing and realism over academic form. Influenced by Western literature, a group of intellectuals urged the use of spoken vernacular, or **baihua,** to create an accessible national literature. Soon, writing in the classical language fell out of fashion.

After the May Fourth movement of 1919 (see p. 14), young intellectuals began to address contemporary social and political problems in writing, popularizing revolutionary thought and criticism. **Lu Xun,** the most famous of these writers, produced short stories ("The Story of Ah Q") that portrayed a backward China unable to survive in the modern world. **Lao She** (*Rickshaw Boy)* documented societal ills. **Ba Jin**'s trilogy of novels (*Family*, *Spring*, and *Autumn)* depicted a traditional household confronting the influx of modern and western values. **Eileen Chang**'s short stories gave a female perspective regarding the upheavals of the May Fourth era.

After the Communist victory in 1949, professional writers worked for state-run guilds. Not surprisingly, the writing from this period was strictly controlled; only works that praised the Communist cause were published. Since the end of the Cultural Revolution, from 1980 to the present, the government has eased its grip on the literary world somewhat. **Feng Jicai** and **Su Tong** have written social satire pieces; the latter's novel, *Raise the Red Lantern*, was adapted into film by Zhang Yimou (see p.

China's most valuable pottery, *táng sān cǎi,* reflects a rainbow of colors, and is evaluated according to the vibrancy of its shades.

The phrase "sitting in the North and facing the South" is still used today (in Feng Shui practices) to convey the positive energy of a building.

The famous tomb of Qin Shihuang in Xi'an (see p. 254) houses thousands of terracotta warriors in extensive underground rooms. These soldiers are more than decoration: they defend the tomb from invaders.

When the Great Hall of the People was designed, Mao decided to emphasize elegance as well as traditional Chinese aesthetics. It then logically follows that the hall was built in a pseudo-Greek style.

Feng shui is no laughing matter; in 1876, the British built the first railroad in China without consulting a *feng shui* master. The line, which ran for 9 miles, was straight, and disturbed the *qi* of everyone living nearby. The Qing dynasty promptly bought the railroad and destroyed it.

China didn't allow kissing on film until 1926, in the provocatively titled film *Two Women in the House.*

Between 1982 and 1991, the number of movie theaters in China had fallen by over 15 million. The government, desperate to stimulate interest in the Chinese film industry, temporarily eased restrictions on content and even threw a premiere party for Zhang Yimou's *The Story of Qiu Ju.*

At the height of Hong Kong's film production, many movies were shot with only the bare rudiments of a script (back then, a novelty). The director would often tell the actors to stand in front of the camera and count to twenty—the dialogue would be dubbed in later.

Chinese card games, most of which are played with a 52-card deck, include "Struggling for Points," "Looking for Friends," and "Catch the Pig."

During the Cultural Revolution, *mahjong* was banned, and those who persisted had to answer to authorities. Today, the game is still banned on college campuses, but few heed the rule.

42). A more controversial writer, **Zhang Xianliang** wrote about his days in a government labor camp in *Grass Soup*, and wrote explicit sexual scenes in *Half of Man is Woman.* **Wang Shuo**'s novels address vice and disillusionment among China's youth. Still more novels, like **Li Dawei**'s *Dream Collector*, are being written in a post-modern narrative style.

PERFORMING ARTS

MUSIC

Legend has it that Chinese music was created in 2697 BC, when the famed emperor Huangdi sent an advisor to find bamboo pipes that could sound the call of the phoenix, thus pleasing the phoenix and harmonizing the universe. Archaeological and written records confirm that Chinese music has been around for at least this long. Remains of Shang dynasty (1600-1050 BC) instruments used for ritual music have been uncovered, and textual evidence in the **Record of Rites** (2nd century BC) and the **Classic of Poetry**, which was originally set to music, indicates the importance of music to the ancient Chinese.

Traditional Chinese music uses a 12-tone system. Major **traditional instruments** include the zither, the lute, and the two-stringed viola. Most traditional Chinese music is indigenous, but traces of Muslim music, which was popular during the Tang dynasty, can still be found.

In the early years of the PRC, communal choruses adapted folk songs originally sung by two people, and lyrics were rewritten to reflect the lives of the "common people." **The East is Red** is perhaps the most famous of these tunes, due in no small part to the now popular and quite kitschy Chairman Mao lighters that play the song when lit.

Even now, in recent times, revolutionary music still holds a special place in the nostalgic hearts of the older generation. But among China's youth, the more modern sounds from Hong Kong and Taiwan have taken hold. Hong Kong has popularized its own indigenous form of music: a bubble-gum-esque sound called **Canto-pop** that puts 'N Sync to shame. The **"Four Heavenly Kings"** (sìdà tiãnwáng; 四大天王) of Canto-pop—Jacky Cheung, Andy Lau, Leon Lai, and Aaron Kwok—have been making girls swoon for over a decade. Today, these artists from Taiwan, Japan, and the mainland are increasingly popular not only in China but also in the West.

THEATER

Traditional Chinese theater is well-known for its **opera,** a combination of vocal and instrumental music. Operas from different regions boast varying singing styles and music accompaniment, but common features include bare stages, set role types, dancing, singing actors and actresses, and tons of heavy face paint.

Chinese theater began with the **zaju** ("variety plays") of the Northern Song and the **nanxi** ("southern opera") of the Southern Song, which were written with vernacular language and set to music. Opera became more artistic in the Yuan dynasty as it emphasized lyrics over plot. **Kunqu,** a form of *nánxì*, was originally performed for the lower classes but gradually gained a large following among the literati; some *kūnqù* are still read as classics today. **Jingju** (Peking opera) rose to prominence at the end of the 18th century. Like *kūnqù*, it primarily uses the flute instead of cymbals or percussion, but its plot is quicker and its acrobatics more elaborate. Although it's considered less poetic than *kūnqù*, *jīngjù* is the most popular form of traditional opera in China today (see p. 142).

China was first introduced to Western spoken drama in the early 1900s. The Chinese added folk songs and dances to create a uniquely Chinese version of the genre called **huaju,** which was easily accessible to the masses and a handy tool for nationalist propagandists looking to capitalize on the Japanese invasion.

Beginning in 1949, Mao insisted that art should first and foremost serve the masses; 1950s operas were based on real stories of the Communist revolution. In the 1960s, Madame Mao commissioned traditional-style operas that embodied revolutionary principles. These model operas, or **yanbanxi,** were the only operas allowed during the Cultural Revolution. After 1980, however, traditional opera—with a staying power rivaled only by TV's Matlock—edged back into the public sphere and is still popular among the elderly.

HUNDRED ENTERTAINMENTS

Vaudevillian entertainments migrated into China from Central Asia around 200 BC. These trick performances, called the **"hundred entertainments,"** included sword-swallowing, fire-eating, juggling, acrobatics, and tumbling. Of these, only **acrobatics and tumbling** remain popular in many parts of China today. Traditional Chinese **dance** includes Buddhist ceremonial dance, folk dance, and operatic and theatrical dance. Each minority community possesses unique dance traditions that have mostly survived to the present.

VISUAL ARTS

CALLIGRAPHY

Traditionally, a calligraphy artist uses the "Four Treasures of the Study"—ink, inkstone, brush, and paper. Calligraphy, considered a high form of visual art, reflects the calligrapher's refined taste and graceful disposition. Because the strokes cannot be altered once on paper, a masterpiece embodies the calligrapher's foresight and confidence; during the Tang dynasty, high officials were appointed after being tested on their calligraphic skills. Calligraphy adorns gates, temples, tombs, mountains, and caves all over China, and is considered to be the most elegant form of decoration.

Translation is a tricky art, especially when it comes to movie titles. Sometimes, the Chinese titles for English-language movies are slightly off. When *The Firm* was released in China, the literal translation of its Mandarin name was *"The Setup That's Attractive."* For *As Good as it Gets* the title was *"Mr. Cat Poop."* Some translations, however, were more accurate than the English originals: the Chinese title for *Nixon* was "*Nixon, the Big Liar.*"

When Chinese schoolchildren were asked to list the most important figures in 20th-century history, Zhou Enlai was at the top—right next to Michael Jordan.

The history of Chinese soccer is a heartbreaking one. In spite of rabidly supportive fans at home, the team's dream to "Kick our way out of Asia and into the World Cups," has proved to be impossible.

Deng Yaping, a ping pong player who won numerous world competitions for China, was once as popular as Michael Jordan and was revered as a national hero.

In ancient China, a popular pastime was to place two male quails in a glass bowl and watch as they clawed each other to death.

Karaoke rooms aren't just for brutally toneless warbling: some lovers also rent private rooms to escape from prying eyes. Businessmen also use the privacy to conduct illicit deals.

According to legend, in the Han dynasty a village was tormented each year by an angry demon. One day, by lucky happenstance, the people of the town discovered that the demon was afraid of the color red. The next time he appeared, the people waved bright red banners and managed to scare him away. As a result, the Chinese believe that red is a happy color, and hand out red envelopes full of money every New Year.

When you sit down at a Chinese table, serve yourself according to seniority. It is considered polite to eat equal amounts of each dish and never to choose a specific piece.

Although chopsticks are used almost everywhere,

PAINTING

Closely related to calligraphy, painting is performed with the same brushes, ink, and paper used for calligraphy and is judged in a similar way (by the gracefulness of the brush strokes). Typically, Chinese paintings are not meant to represent reality, but rather the inner life of things. Skilled painters can represent an entire mountain range with a few light splashes of ink—much is left to the imagination.

In the early 1920s, many Chinese artists visited Europe, and movements like Impressionism helped to fuse modern Western and traditional Chinese styles. **Xu Beihong,** an influential artist, used a traditional Chinese brush to mimic the realistic effect of pencil and chalk.

After the Communist takeover in 1949, idealized representations of patriotic and revolutionary men and women became the chief subject matter for most paintings. In the tumultuous decades that followed, art production ground to a halt. Paintings could easily be construed as remnants of the "decadent imperialistic past" and used to incriminate painters. After the Cultural Revolution ended, Chinese painting primarily adopted Western styles and non-political subject matter. Today, many artists have returned to traditional brush painting due to overseas demand. But more Western styles have become widely accepted, demonstrating the diversity achieved once the government allowed increased artistic freedom.

SCULPTURE

Sculpture in China is more of a craft than an art; little is made purely for aesthetic reasons. Most sculptures, like teacups in the shape of flowers or candleholders in the shape of a birds, are everyday objects with artistic embellishments. At the end of the Han dynasty, religious sculptures were common, giving rise to the numerous giant sculptures of Buddhas throughout China. By the Tang dynasty, Buddhist temples produced some of the most innovative sculpture in the world, including delicate carvings of deities in bronze and limestone.

Pottery is a practical form of sculpture. Beginning in the Shang dynasty, lacquer glazes and jade carvings decorated coffins, weapons, and furniture. By the Tang, whiteware and tricolored glazes were the norm. Ming lacquers and vases were sought after in places as far away as Europe. As a result, "china" has come to denote all fine ceramics. The blue-and-white vases of **Jingdezhen** (see p. 420) are still highly prized, as are the Yixing ceramics centered in **Suzhou** (see p. 349).

ARCHITECTURE

Five thousand years of development and countless stylistic and religious influences have resulted in an extraordinary architectural variety in China. The country contains ancient earth-covered houses and magnificient undergrounds tombs, towering pagodas and ornate imperial residences, modern skyscrapers and cookie-cutter housing projects. A few conventions, how-

FENG SHUI Westerners are familiar with *feng shui* primarily because of overpriced designers and fluffy TV-news pieces. *Feng shui* is more than a new-age fad, however. An age-old tradition, *feng shui* (literally "wind and water"; 风水) is based on geomancy, or divination according to geographic features. *Feng shui* masters learn to balance the metaphysical energies—or *qì*—of a house in order to maximize the happiness and fortune of its inhabitants. Although *feng shui* can be applied on a large scale, helping to choose building sights and to design floorplans, it is more popularly used for interior design. Each room is divided into nine pieces and then characterized according to the position of the door. For instance, the wall opposite the door symbolizes self-fulfillment and the path to enlightenment; naturally, candles are an excellent decoration for this part of the room.

ever, do exist. Traditional Chinese buildings often have elaborate and elegantly curved **roofs.** In many residences, a **courtyard** is the center of the living compound, which is surrounded by a thick wall (such architecture is most often found in the *hutongs*, or alleyways, of cities and towns). Cities were also protected by walls, and their remnants can still be found around Xi'an, Nanjing, and Pingyao. Of course, nothing can compare to the massive **Great Wall of China** that stretches over 6000km (see p. 9). Most important buildings in China face south. According to legend, the Emperor's Palace faced south, allowing him to watch over the world. Another theory holds that the ancient Chinese didn't want the barbarian invaders in the north to ruin the view.

By the 20th century, traditional Chinese architecture was subjected to European influence. In 1925, foreign-educated Chinese architects founded the Society for the Study of Chinese Architecture, adapting traditional Chinese designs to modern needs. After 1949, concrete Soviet-style gray buildings dominated Chinese architecture. Under Mao, practicality beat out aesthetics. Exceptions to the rule include political structures such as the Great Hall of the People (see p. 132) and Mao Zedong's mausoleum in Beijing (see p. 133), grand designs in the Greek tradition.

FILM

Chinese cinema began in 1896 with "Western Peep Shows," foreign films with Western subject matters. The domestic film industry emerged in the 1920s in Shanghai, producing what is now known as the "first generation" of Chinese film. By the 1950s, the Communist Party had added the film industry to its list of propaganda tools; films featured zealous, heroic peasants and emphasized class struggle. Beginning in 1966, the Cultural Revolution and the Gang of Four (see p. 19) strengthened the role of party politics in film.

many places will have forks and knives available; if you can't use chopsticks, don't be shy about asking for a fork.

In Chinese, chopsticks are called *kuàizi,* or "fast things." Some speculate that the English word came about when Chinese traders mistook the word "chop" (as in "chop, chop!") for fast.

When eating soup, to cool the broth and maximize flavor, sip from the spoon while inhaling. You may hear a loud slurp, impolite to Western ears, but the taste is worth it.

The ultimate Chinese banquet features all the culinary marvels of the Qing dynasty, including hundreds of dishes with exotic ingredients like bear paw, monkey, duck tongue, deer antler, and bird nests.

The art of tasting tea is prominent in Southern China. A good tea is distinguished by its after taste; if a sweet taste remains in the throat long after the bitter one has evaporated, the tea is considered first-rate.

After the end of the Cultural Revolution, mainstream filmmaking veered away from political themes. The **"Fifth Generation"** of filmmakers, whose members include Chen Kaige (*Farewell My Concubine*) and Zhang Yimou *(Raise the Red Lantern*), used historical settings and interpreted China's past as a rich, but tortuous one. The Chinese government, not surprisingly, does not approve of how these images portray China to the Western world. In the 1990s, a **"Sixth Generation"** of filmmakers abandoned history in order to tell bleak, urban stories. Most of these films, including *The Days* (dir. Wang Xiaoshuai), *Frozen* (dir. Wang Xiaoshuai), and *The Postman* (dir. He Jianjun), were filmed on low budgets and have had minimal (if only underground) acceptance.

"Hong Kong cinema" has a personality all its own. Although it has produced great martial arts flicks, Hong Kong filmmakers—including Stanley Kwan, Tsui Hark, Ann Hui, and Wong Kar-wai—have grappled with more thorny issues of nationalism, Westernization, cultural modernism, and technology. Movies like Wong Kar-wai's *Chungking Express* wrap vexing issues in a visually hypnotic package that is both intellectually and viscerally satisfying. But die-hard kung fu fans need not despair—the Hong Kong action flick is still alive and kicking. Jackie Chan, the Buster Keaton of kung fu, is now world-famous for his death-defying stunts; even his decade-old films are being reproduced and mass-distributed around the world. The recent success of movies like *Rush Hour*, *Crouching Tiger, Hidden Dragon*, and *Kiss of the Dragon* has helped to make Chan, Chow Yun-fat, and Jet Li into international stars.

RECOMMENDED FILMS.

Chungking Express (1994, dir. Wong Kar-wai). Two loosely connected stories about men and women in love and their favorite fast-food joint. A young Faye Wong stars.

Crouching Tiger, Hidden Dragon (2000, dir. Ang Lee). Spectacular martial-arts action melds surprisingly seamlessly with poignant acting and exquisite photography in this period drama.

Drunken Master II (1994, dir. Woo-ping Yuen). The sequel to the 1978 film that made Jackie Chan a star; the 20min. fight scene may be one of the best ever.

Farewell My Concubine (1993, dir. Chen Kaige). A bleak but powerful movie that portrays the complex relationship between two Beijing Opera stars.

Fist of Legend (1994, dir. Gordon Chan and Woo-ping Yuen). Jet Li showcases his amazing martial arts skills in this patriotic action flick.

Hard Boiled (1992, dir. John Woo). Chow Yun-fat kills lots of men. In slow motion. Sometimes in super-slow motion.

The Last Emperor (1987, dir. Bernardo Bertolucci). A beautifully shot, written, and acted film about the life of the last Qing emperor.

SPORTS & RECREATION

GAMES

Tiaoqi (Chinese checkers) is an intensely competitive game involving marbles on a star-shaped board; it is popular among pre-schoolers. Those who'd rather not get involved in the sheer brutality of children's games can opt for the more sedate **Xiangqi** (Chinese chess), which uses a set of round, wooden pieces inscribed with characters, two "cannon" pieces, and a dividing line. Xiangqi is by far the most popular board game in China, and is commonly played in parks by young and old alike. Also popular is **Weiqi,** the ancient "game of encirclement." Players use white and black pebbles on a grid board, with each side trying to secure board territory by surrounding and conquering opponent stones. **Mahjong** is a four-person game that uses ceramic blocks as pieces. Players collect pieces in order to form certain patterns (similar to the card game gin rummy). A gentle form of gambling, *mahjong* is especially popular among women. **Card games** are also popular among the elderly, and are played in parks and on street corners everywhere; these games include bridge (Deng Xiaoping's favorite) and poker.

SPORTS

Despite the worldwide popularity of Chinese kung fu, the most popular sports in China are **basketball** and **soccer.** The NBA and Michael Jordan are hot topics of conversation, even more so since the Dallas Mavericks signed 7'1" center **Wang Zhizhi.** Wang, a former officer in the PLA, is the first Chinese citizen to be drafted by an NBA team.

And as for **soccer**, the Chinese women's teams have continuously succeeded—where their male counterparts have not (a cause of deep frustration among fans). The Chinese women's soccer team is one of the best, having won numerous Asian championships. In the summer of 1999, the women's team lost to the US in the World Cup finals only after a thrilling, sudden-death penalty kick session put America ahead of China after a 4-4 tie.

In the **Olympic Games,** China performs especially well in diving, gymnastics, women's volleyball, and table tennis. The recent win for the 2008 Olympic Games bid (see p. 21) has sparked an even greater interest in athletic competition and training. China has promised a drug-free Games, but many in the international community wonder what effect this will have on the Chinese swimming and track teams (known for their all-too-sudden improvements).

With China's high population density and overcrowded cities, the space-saving games of **ping pong** and **badminton** have become the most popular urban sports in China. Even though bowling, billiards, and tennis are also popular, the expensive fees these games charge make them widely inaccessible. Due to space constraints, golf is reserved for only the extremely wealthy.

Wushu is a traditional form of self-defense and an art form that is incorporated into many dances and opera movements. The ancient Buddhist **Shaolin Monastery** (see p. 265) in Henan and the Daoist **Wudangshan** temples (see p. 455) in Hubei are the most famous centers for *wushu* study; even today, teenagers enter Shaolin to study martial arts. **Tai chi**, a slower version of *wushu*, is popular among the elderly, who can be seen practicing en masse in parks every morning.

KARAOKE

As inevitable as spitting, staring, and suffocating crowds, karaoke (kâlā OK; 卡拉OK) is simply something visitors to China cannot avoid. Invented by the Japanese, karaoke first became a hit in China in the 1980s. Today, karaoke bars can be found on nearly every street corner in major cities. Karaoke bars are often filled with large, drunken crowds; singers of all ages croon unsteadily to anything from pop songs to old revolutionary tunes. Like restaurants, they serve a wide range of guests, and a night in one room can range in cost from a mere Y20 to thousands of dollars.

HOLIDAYS & FESTIVALS

DATE	FESTIVAL	DETAILS
Feb. 1, 2003	Lunar New Year (The Year of the Ram)	The most important holiday in all of East Asia. Families gather to prepare special meals and light fireworks. Red paper decorations and New Year's calendars are hung and given as gifts.
Apr. 4-5	Qingming (Tomb-Sweeping) Festival	A traditional holiday on which the Chinese visit and beautify their ancestors' graves.
May 4	International Youth Day	A state holiday honoring the student demonstrators who catalyzed the May 4 Movement (see p. 14).
June 4, 2003	Dragon Boat Festival	Memorializes poet and patriot Qu Yuan (see p. 582).
July 1	Anniversary of the CCP's Founding	A patriotic state holiday.
Aug. 1	Anniversary of the PLA's Founding	A state holiday honoring the armed forces.
Oct. 1	National Day	A state holiday commemorating the Communist victory of October 1, 1949.
Sept. 11, 2003	Autumn Moon (Mid-Autumn) Festival	The night on which the moon is fullest and brightest, celebrated by eating mooncakes and gazing at the moon.

ADDITIONAL RESOURCES

GENERAL HISTORY

A Concise History of China, by J.A.G. Roberts (Harvard Univ. Press, US$12). Condenses four millennia of China into 300 pages. Includes ten maps.

China: A New History, by John King Fairbank and Merle Goldman (Harvard Univ. Press, US$13). A concise and comprehensive account of China, its people, and particularly their cultural history.

China: Empire and Civilization, by Edward Shaugnessy (Oxford Univ. Press, US$36). Covers the most interesting facets of Imperial China and its legacy in the 20th century.

The Cambridge Illustrated History of China, by Patricia Buckley Wheatley and Kwan-Ching Liu (Cambridge Univ. Press, US$24). Explores recurring themes in Chinese history.

FICTION AND NON-FICTION

A Dream of Red Mansions, by Cao Xueqin, Gao E, Yang Xianyi (translator) (Foreign Language Press, US$24). A celebrated 18th century Chinese classic novel about a tragic love story and a degenerating empire.

Becoming Madame Mao, by Anchee Min (Mariner Books, US$10). A historical fiction on the life of Madame Mao, known as the White Boned Demon during her reign of terror in China.

China Dawn: The Story of a Technology and Business Revolution, by David Sheff (Harperbusiness, US$17). An investigation into the high-tech revolution in China today as it faces heavy government censorship and regulation.

Coming Collapse of China, by Gordon C. Chang (Random House, US$15). A speculation into the possible financial doom of the Chinese economy within the next five years.

AN ANGLER'S DESTINATION?

Fly-fishing in the Middle Kingdom

Fly-fishing in China? Isn't that an oxymoron? Granted, much of China's coastal area is a sprawling urban mass whose contribution to the environment has been like most industrializing nations (read: mostly unpleasant). However, heading outside of these regions, one will be amazed by the rustic beauty of the river and lakes that dot the Chinese landscape. And, of course, where there are rivers there will be fish to be landed. Given the countless odes to solitaire fishing in Chinese poetry and art, there is a surprising dearth of professional guide services for those interested in fishing in China. On the positive side this means there are far fewer anglers flocking to China, leaving those who do come all the more river with which to play. With a bit of independent research and planning, fishing in china can be a fabulous experience. You will be able to false cast under a rich tent of landscapes ranging from the Himalayan mountains to the massive limestone peaks of Guilin.

There are a number of fish species in China that will be familiar to the North American angler. Brown and rainbow trout are found in the cooler regions of the north as well as the western reaches of the Himalayas. A bass-like fish that locals call the tiger bass cruises through the expansive Jingbo lake in northeast China. For the masochistic, deep sea fishing occurs off of several boats departing from Hong Kong. Most of these boats go out for big game fish like sharks (which after a long and arduous fight, leave one's arms sore and one's thoughts pondering the rationality of paying for such a fight). China also sports a number of unique species, most notably the *taimen*. Indigenous to parts of China (as well as Mongolia and Russia), the taimen is the world's largest salmanoid, growing over 75 inches and weighing up to 100 pounds! Think of these fish as the winners of the Big Fish Toughman contest. Amazingly, these fish can be taken on fly rods; the thrill of watching your fly pattern being slammed by an adult taimen is truly a memorable experience.

There are a number of suggested itineraries for those who would like to lay down some line while in the Middle Kingdom. An ideal trip is to start in Urumqi (the capital of Xinjiang) and make it out to the Ertix River in the northwest. There, you will be able to fish for pike, Siberian sturgeon and giant taimen. For fishing with a view, try the Yarlung Zangbo River in Tibet, a magnificent river that ultimately flows into India. While fishing for the trout that occupy this river, be sure to soak in the views of the Grand Yarlung Zangbo Canyon, the largest canyon in the world. For those with a burning desire for taimen, venture out into Outer Mongolia, where there are a number of good guides that look specifically for these great fish. These tours often mix Chinese and Mongolian fishing spots and are a great way to sample the angling in both countries.

Oh, and what about those two famous rivers, the Yangzi and the Yellow river? Though these two rivers served as a fertile base for the development of Chinese civilization, there is still a significant amount of industrial fishing in some parts of the rivers today. Still, be advised that fishing here would be like fishing on any river that passes through many a city. You'll get something but it probably won't be a fish.

Bernard Chang is a graduate student at Harvard University and an avid fly fisher. He serves as a regional fly-fishing guide in New York and is the author of Fly-fishing in the Middle Kingdom, *to be published in 2003.*

Peony, by Pearl S. Buck (Moyer Bell, US$5). This quiet, beautiful novel chronicles the life of Peony, a bondmaid sold to a wealthy Chinese-Jewish family.

Wild Swans: Three Daughters of China, by Jung Chang (Anchor World Views, US$8). A history of three generations of women who braved China's political scene in the 20th century.

TRAVEL WRITING

A Truthful Impression of the Country: British and American Travel Writing in China, 1880-1949, by Nicholas R. Clifford (University of Michigan Press, US$40). An accurate representation of the unfamiliar and exotic by a college professor.

Inscribed Landscapes: Travel Writing From Imperial China, by Richard E. Strassberg (University of California Press, US$15). An anthology of impressions of Chinese landscape from native citizens, covering several centuries.

The Myth of Shangri-La: Tibet, Travel Writing and the Western Creation of a Sacred Landscape, by Peter Bishop (University of California Press, US$40). Examines Western travel writings on Tibet to delineate the complex relationship between culture, physical landscape and the sacred.

PHOTOGRAPHY

A World Away, by Larry Snider (Pegasus Publishing, US$45). Photographs done over ten years in Tibet, China, Bhutan, and Ladakh.

Children in China, by Michael Karhausen (Orbis, US$19). Ninety black and white photographs of China's children and their worlds.

Marc Riboud in China: Forty Years of Photography, by Marc Riboud (Harry N. Abrams, US$25). Contrasting old and new China, Riboud specializes in the juxtaposition of images that mark the country's evolution.

Spectacular China, by Nigel Cameron (Hugh Lauter Levin Associates, US$40). China's natural beauty, culture, and architecture all in one book.

ESSENTIALS

FACTS FOR THE TRAVELER

ENTRANCE REQUIREMENTS.

Passport (see p. 50). Required for all travelers to China, Hong Kong, or Macau.

Visa (see p. 50). Required for all travelers to China. Required for some travelers to Hong Kong or Macau.

Letter of Invitation (see p. 50). Typically required to work or study in China.

Immunizations (see p. 62). No vaccinations are required to enter China, unless entering from an area infected with yellow fever.

Work Permit (see p. 50). Required of all foreigners planning to work in China.

Driving Permit (see p. 98). Required for all those planning to drive.

EMBASSIES & CONSULATES

CHINA'S CONSULAR SERVICES ABROAD

Australia: Embassy: 15 Coronation Dr., Yarralumla ACT 2600, Canberra (☎(02) 6273 4780, visa section 6273 4783; visa fax 6273 9615; www.chinaembassy.org.au). **Consulates:** 75-77 Irving Rd. 3142, **Melbourne** (☎(03) 9822 0605; fax 9822 0320; www.chinaconsulatemel.org); 15-17 William St., 3rd fl., Australia Place 6000, **Perth** (☎(08) 9321 8193, visa section 9481 3278; fax 9321 8457); 539 Elizabeth St., Surry Hills 2010, **Sydney** (☎(02) 9319 0678; fax 9699 8258).

Canada: Embassy: 515 St. Patrick St., Ottawa, ON K1N 5H3 (☎613-789-3434; fax 789-1414; www.chinaembassy-canada.org). **Consulates:** 1011 6th Ave. SW, Ste. 100, **Calgary,** AB T2P OW1 (☎403-264-3322; fax 264-6656); 240 St. George St., **Toronto,** ON M5R 2P4 (☎416-964-7260; fax 324-6468); 3380 Granville St., **Vancouver,** BC V6H 3K3 (☎604-736-3910; fax 736-4343).

Ireland: Embassy: 40 Ailesbury Rd., Dublin 4 (☎(01) 269 1707; fax 283 9938).

New Zealand: Embassy: 2-6 Glenmore St., Wellington (☎(04) 472 1382; fax 499 0419; info@chinaembassy.org.nz; www.chinaembassy.org.nz). **Consulate:** 588 Great South Rd., Greenlane, Auckland (☎(09) 525 1588 or 525 1589; fax 525 0733).

South Africa: Embassy: 972 Pretorius St., Arcadia 0083, Pretoria (☎(012) 342 4194, visa section 342 9366; fax 430 7620; www.chinese-embassy.org.za). **Consulates:** 25 Rhodes Ave., Newlands, **Cape Town** (☎(021) 674 0579, visa section 674 0592; fax 674 0589); 45 Stirling Crescent, **Durban North** 40501 (☎(031) 563 4534, visa section 563 4986; fax 563 4827); 25 Cleveland Rd., **Johannesburg** (☎(011) 784 7241; fax 883 5274).

United Kingdom: Embassy: 49-51 Portland Place, London W1B 1JL (☎(020) 7299 4049, visa section 7631 1430; fax 7466 9178; press@china-embassy.org.uk; www.chinese-embassy.org.uk;). **Consulates:** Denison House, 49 Denison Rd., Rusholme, **Manchester** M14 5RX (☎(0161) 224 8672; fax 257 2672); 43 Station Rd., **Edinburgh** EH12 7AF (☎(0131) 334 8501, visa section 316 4789; fax 334 6954).

United States: Embassy: 2300 Connecticut Ave. NW, Washington, D.C. 20008 (☎202-328-2500, visa section 338-6688; visa fax 588-9760; chinaembassy_us@fmprc.gov.cn; www.china-embassy.org). **Consulates:** 100 W. Erie St., **Chicago,** IL 60610 (☎312-803-0095, visa section 803-0098; fax 803-0122); 3417 Montrose Blvd., **Houston,** TX 77006 (☎713-524-0780, visa section 524-4311; fax 524-8466; voffice@msn.com; www.chinahouston.org); 443 Shatto Pl., **Los Angeles,** CA 90020 (☎213-807-8088, visa section 807-8018; fax 380-1961; visachina@aol.com; www.chinaconsulatela.org); 520 12th Ave., **New York,** NY 10036 (☎212-736-9301; fax 502-0245; www.nyconsulate.prchina.org); 1450 Laguna St., **San Francisco,** CA 94115 (☎415-674-2900, fax 563-0494; visa office 928 6931, fax 563 4861; www.chinaconsulatesf.org).

CONSULAR SERVICES IN CHINA

Australia: 21 Dongzhimenwai Dajie, Sanlitun, **Beijing** (☎6532 2331, embassy ext. 129; fax 6532 4605). GITIC Plaza, 339 Huanshi Dong Lu, Rm. 1509, **Guangzhou** (☎8331 0909; fax 8335 0718; www.austcon-guangzhou.org). 23/F Harbour Centre, 25 Harbour Rd., Wan Chai, **Hong Kong** (☎2827 8881; fax 2585 4457; www. australia.org.hk). Level 22, CITIC Square, 1168 Nanjing Xi Lu, **Shanghai** (☎5292 5500; fax 5292 5511; www.aus-in-shanghai.com).

Canada: 19 Dongzhimenwai Dajie, Chaoyang District, **Beijing** (☎6532 3536; fax 6532 5544). China Hotel Office Tower, Suite 801, Liu Hua Lu, **Guangzhou** (☎8666 0569; fax 8667 0267). Exchange Square, Tower One, 14th fl., 8 Connaught Place, **Hong Kong** (☎2810 4321; fax 2810 7561). American International Centre, West Tower, Suite 604, 1376 Nanjing Xi Lu, **Shanghai** (☎6279 8400; fax 6279 8401).

Ireland: 3 Ritan Dong Lu, Jianguomenwai, **Beijing** (☎6532 2691; fax 6532 6857). Chungnam Bldg., 6th fl., 1 Lockhart Rd., Wan Chai, **Hong Kong** (☎2527 4897).

New Zealand: 1 Donger Jie, Ritan Lu, **Beijing** (☎6532 2731; fax 6532 3424). 1375 Huaihai Zhong Lu, Qihua Tower, #15A, **Shanghai** (☎6471 1127; fax 6431 0226).

South Africa: 5 Dongzhimenwai Dajie, **Beijing** (☎6532 0171). Great Eagle Centre, 23 Harbour Rd., 27th fl., Rm. 2706, Wan Chai, **Hong Kong** (☎2577 3279).

United Kingdom: 11 Guanghua Lu, Jianguomenwai, **Beijing** (☎6532 1961; fax 6532 1937; consular fax 6532 1930). Guangdong Int'l Hotel, 339 Huanshi Dong Lu, 2nd fl., **Guangzhou** (☎8335 1354 or 8333 6485; fax 8333 6485). 1 Supreme Court Rd. Central, **Hong Kong** (☎2901 3000; fax 2901 3066; www.britishconsulate.org.hk). Suite 301, Shanghai Ctr., 1376 Nan Jing Xi Lu, **Shanghai** (☎6279 7650; fax 6279 7651).

United States: 3 Xiushui Dong Jie, Jianguomenwai, **Beijing** (☎6532 3431; fax 6532 6057). 4 Lingshiguan Lu, **Chengdu** (☎558 3992; fax 558 9221). 1 Shamian Nan Jie, Shamian Island, **Guangzhou** (☎8188 8911; fax 8186 4001). 26 Garden Rd., Central, **Hong Kong** (☎2523 9011; fax 2845 1598). 1469 Huaihai Zhong Lu, **Shanghai** (☎6433 6880; fax 6474 1576). 52 Shisi Wei Lu, Heping, **Shenyang** (☎2322 1198; fax 2322 2374).

OTHER CONSULATES

India: 1 Ritan Dong Lu, Jianguomenwai, Beijing (☎6532 4864; fax 6532 4486). 1008 Shanghai International Trade Centre, 2201 Yan An Xi Lu, Shanghai (☎6275 8885 or 6275 8886; fax 6275 8881).

Indonesia: Office Bldg. B, Sanlitun, **Beijing** (☎6532 5489; fax 6532 5368). 127 Leighton Rd., 2nd fl., Causeway Bay, **Hong Kong** (☎2890 4421).

Kazakhstan: 9 Dongliu Jie, Sanlitun, **Beijing** (☎6532 6182; fax 6532 6183).

GET CARD.
TRAVEL HARD.
International Student Identity Card
STUDENT
Beijing University
LEE, M.
05/07/1978
ISIC
S 000 123 456 789
SCENIC DRIVE
FOOD + GAS
LOOKOUT

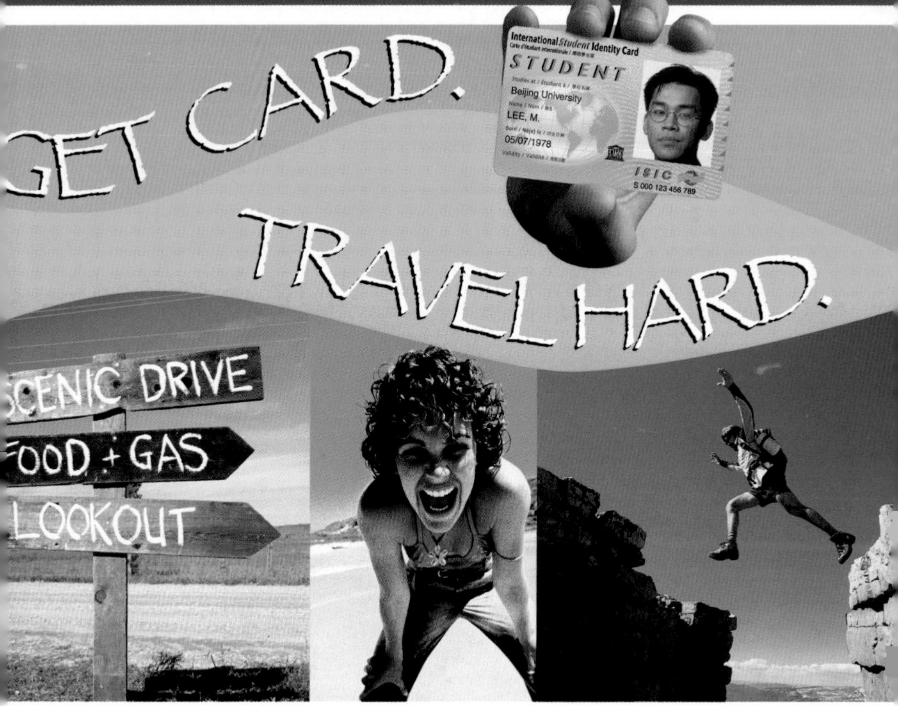

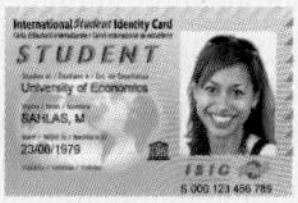

Kyrgyzstan: Tayuan Diplomatic Bldg., 14 Liangmahe Nan Lu, Sanlitun, **Beijing** (☎6532 6458; fax 6532 6459).

Laos: 11 Dongsi Jie, Sanlitun, **Beijing** (☎6532 1224; fax 6532 6748).

Malaysia: 13 Dongzhimenwai Dajie, Sanlitun, **Beijing** (☎6532 2531; fax 6532 5432). CITIC Plaza, Tianhe Bei Lu, 19th fl., **Guangzhou** (☎3877 0766; fax 3877 0769). Malaysia Bldg., 50 Gloucester Rd., 24th Fl., Wan Chai, **Hong Kong** (☎2527 0921).

Mongolia: 2 Xiushui Bei Jie, Jianguomenwai, **Beijing** (☎6532 1203; fax 6532 5045).

Myanmar: 6 Dongzhimenwai Dajie, Sanlitun, **Beijing** (☎6532 1425; visa 6532 1488; fax 6532 1344). Sung Hung Kai Ctr., 30 Harbour Rd., Rm. 2436, Wan Chai, **Hong Kong** (☎2827 7929).

Nepal: 1 Xiliu Jie, Sanlitun, **Beijing** (☎6532 1795; fax 6532 3251). 13 Luobulinka (Norbulinka) Lu, **Lhasa** (☎682 2881; fax 683 6890).

North Korea: 3 Dongsi Jie, Sanlitun, **Beijing** (☎6532 1189; fax 6532 0683). Int'l. Trade Center, 2200 Yan'an Xi Lu, 4th fl., **Shanghai** (☎6219 6420; fax 6209 2056).

Pakistan: 1 Dongzhimenwai Dajie, **Beijing** (☎6532 2504 or 6532 2581; fax 6532 2715).

Philippines: 23 Xiushui Bei Jie, Jianguomenwai, **Beijing** (☎6532 1872 or 6532 2518; fax 6532 3761). United Centre, 95 Queensway, 6th fl., Rm. 603, Admiralty, **Hong Kong**.

Russia: 4 Dongzhimennei, Beizhong Jie, **Beijing** (☎6532 2051, visa section 6532 1267; fax 6532 4853). 20 Huangpu Lu, **Shanghai** (☎6324 2682; fax 6306 9982).

Singapore: 1 Xiushui Bei Jie, Jianguomenwai, **Beijing** (☎8529 6256, visa section 8529; fax 8529 6254). Admiralty Centre, 18 Harcourt Rd., Tower I, 9th fl., Rm. 901, Admiralty, **Hong Kong** (☎2527 2212). 400 Wulumuqi Zhong Lu, **Shanghai** (☎6437 0776; fax 6474 7410).

South Korea: 14 Liangmahe Nan Lu, **Beijing** (☎6532 6775; fax 6532 6778). 8 Qinling Lu, **Qingdao** (☎897 6004; 897 6021).

Thailand: 40 Guanghua Lu, Jianguomenwai, **Beijing** (☎6532 2151; fax 6532 1748). 63 Woyihop Rd., Regent Center, Tower A, 26th fl., Kwai Chung, **Hong Kong** (☎2521 6481). 7 Zhongshan Dong Yi Lu, 3rd Fl., **Shanghai** (☎6321 9371; fax 6323 4140).

Vietnam: 32 Guanghua Lu, Jianguomenwai, **Beijing** (☎6532 5414; fax 6532 5720). 230 Wan Chai Rd., Wan Chai, **Hong Kong** (☎2591 4510).

CHINA NATIONAL TOURIST OFFICE

Australia: 19th fl., 44 Market St., Sydney, NSW 2000 (☎(02) 9299 4057; fax 9290 1958; chinainfo@cnto.org.au; www.cnto.org.au).

Canada: 480 University Ave., Ste. 806, Toronto, ON M5G1V2 (☎416-599-6636; fax 599-6382).

China: No.9A, Jianguomennei Ave., Beijing 100740 (☎(010) 6513 8866; fax (010) 6512-2096)

United Kingdom: 4 Glentworth St., London NW1 5PG (☎(020) 7935 9787; fax 7487 5842).

United States: 350 5th Ave., Ste. 6413, **New York,** NY 10118 (☎212-760 8218; fax 760 8809; cntcny@aol.com; www.cnto.org); 333 West Broadway, Ste. 201, **Glendale,** CA 91204 (☎818-545 7505; fax 545 7506).

DOCUMENTS & FORMALITIES

PASSPORTS

REQUIREMENTS. Citizens of Australia, Canada, Ireland, New Zealand, South Africa, the UK, and the US need valid passports to enter China and re-enter their home countries. China doesn't allow entrance if your passport expires in under six months; returning home with an expired passport is illegal and may result in a fine.

PHOTOCOPIES. Be sure to photocopy the page of your passport with your photo, passport number, and other identifying information, as well as any visas, travel insurance policies, plane tickets, or traveler's check serial numbers. Carry one set of copies in a safe place, apart from the originals, and leave another set at home. Consulates also recommend that you carry an expired passport or an official copy of your birth certificate in a part of your baggage separate from other documents. If you are staying in China for a significant length of time, it is a good idea to **register your passport** with your embassy. US citizens can register their passports online at the US embassy (www.usembassy-china.org.cn/english/us-citizen/regform.html).

LOST PASSPORTS. Your passport is a public document, and you may have to surrender it to a foreign government official. But it belongs to your nation's government, so they can't confiscate it; if you don't get it back in a reasonable amount of time, inform the nearest mission of your home country. If you lose your passport, immediately notify the local Public Security Bureau (PSB; gōng ān jú; 公安局) and the nearest embassy or consulate of your home government. To expedite its replacement, you will need to know all the information previously recorded in your passport and show ID and proof of citizenship. A replacement may take weeks to process and be valid only for a limited time. Any visas you've obtained will be irretrievably lost. In an emergency, ask for immediate temporary traveling papers that will permit you to re-enter your home country.

NEW PASSPORTS. Citizens of Australia, Canada, Ireland, New Zealand, the UK, and the US can apply for a passport at the nearest post office, passport office, or court of law. Citizens of South Africa can apply for a passport at the nearest office of Home Affairs. Any new passport or renewal applications must be filed well in advance of the departure date, although most passport offices offer rush services for a very steep fee. Citizens living abroad who need a passport or renewal services should contact the nearest consular service of their home country.

VISAS, INVITATIONS, & WORK PERMITS

VISAS. As of August 2001, citizens of Australia, Canada, Ireland, New Zealand, South Africa, the UK and the US need not only a valid passport to enter China, but also a visa—**a stamp, sticker, or insert in your passport specifying the purpose of your travel and the permitted duration of your stay.** Visas are issued at Chinese consulates and embassies worldwide and in Hong Kong through numerous travel agencies and even some hotels and guesthouses. Getting a Chinese tourist visa in Hong Kong is both easier and cheaper than getting one abroad (see **Hong Kong: Consulates, Visas, and Immigration,** p. 533).

VISA TYPE	aka	entry	duration of stay	passport must be valid for
TOURIST	TYPE "L"	single-, double-	up to 30 days	3 months beyond departure date
		multiple-	6-12 months	
BUSINESS	TYPE "F"	single- or double-	up to 6 months	3 months beyond
LONG-TERM WORK	TYPE "Z"	multiple-	up to 1 year	6 months beyond
STUDENT	TYPE "F"	multiple-	up to 6 months	6 months beyond
	TYPE "X"	multiple-	6-12 months	6 months beyond

Tourist visas (Type "L") are typically valid for a single entry only, but it's possible to obtain one for longer stays or for multiple entries. You might also need to obtain a visa invitation from a Chinese tour or travel agency (or a travel itinerary and airline tickets). Business ("F"), work ("Z"), and student ("F" or "X," depending on length of stay) visas generally require a **letter of invitation** from the appropriate Chinese corporation, government office, or educational institution. For multiple-entry business visas, you will also need your company's license to do business in China. For student visas, you will also need to complete a JW-202 form (further confirmation that you are indeed welcome at the school you will attend) from a school or university in China. Study abroad programs operating in China usually assist participants with getting visas and residence permits. Students enrolling directly in Chinese universities will have to contact the university to obtain necessary forms.

When applying for a visa, make sure your passport is valid six months beyond the date of your intended return (nine months for a multiple-entry visa) and has several blank pages. (For more information on finding study or work opportunities in China, see **Alternatives to Tourism,** p. 105.) If you stay in China longer than 6 months, you'll need a notarized health certificate. Students, teachers, and visiting scholars staying in China for over nine months and business persons staying for over a year must submit proof of a negative test result for HIV.

US citizens can contact the **Center for Int'l. Business and Travel** (**CIBT;** ☎800-925-2428) to secure travel visas to almost any country for a variable service charge.

Double-check entrance requirements at the nearest Chinese embassy or consulate (see **China's Consular Services Abroad,** p. 47) before departure. US citizens can also visit www.pueblo.gsa.gov/cic_text/travel/foreign/foreignentryreqs.html.

In general, you can apply in person or by mail for a visa at a Chinese embassy or consulate; you will need a completed application form, a recent passport-sized photo, a valid passport, and the appropriate visa fee.

Australia: AUS$30 for a single-entry tourist visa, AUS$45 for a double-entry tourist visa, AUS$60 for a 6-month multiple entry, and AUS$90 for a one-year multiple entry. Mail a self-addressed stamped envelope and additional AUS$10 (cash, money order, or certified check) for mail processing. Processing takes 4 working days. Rush fees are AUS$30 for 2- to 3-day service and AUS$50 for same-day service.

Canada: CDN$50 for a single-entry tourist visa, CDN$75 for a double-entry tourist visa, CDN$100 for a 6-month multiple-entry business visa, and CDN$150 for a one-year multiple-entry business visa. Mail processing costs depend on the type of visa; CDN$71.40 for a single-entry, CDN$96.40 for a double-entry; self-addressed stamped envelope required. Send mail applications to Golden Mile Travel Consultant, 203-1390 Prince of Wales Dr., Ottawa, ON K2C 3K6 (☎613-224-6863; fax 224-7863). Cash, money order, and company check are the accepted forms of payment. Processing takes 5 business days. Rush fees are CDN$35 for 2-day service and CDN$50 for next-day service (CDN$127.80 and CDN$142.80, respectively, with mail processing).

New Zealand: NZ$60 for a single-entry tourist visa, NZ$90 for a double-entry tourist visa. Accepts cash and company check. Mail processing an additional NZ$15; self-addressed stamped envelope required. Processing takes 7-10 business days. Rush fees are NZ$40 for 2- to 3-day service and NZ$60 for same-day service.

South Africa: ZAR180 for a single-entry/transit tourist visa, ZAR270 for a double-entry/transit tourist visa, and ZAR360 for a 6-month multiple-entry business visa. Cash as only accepted form of payment. Processing takes 4 business days. Rush fees are ZAR60 for 3-day service, ZAR120 for 2-day service, and ZAR180 for next-day service.

United Kingdom: UK£30 for a 3-month single entry visa, UK£45 for a 3-month double entry visa, UK£60 for a 6-month multiple entry visa, and UK£90 for a one-year multiple entry visa. Mail processing an additional UK£20. Cash only. Processing takes 3 business days. Rush fees are UK£15 for next-day service and UK£20 for same-day service.

United States: US$30 for a single-entry visa, US$45 for a double-entry visa, and US$60 for a 6-month multiple-entry business visa. Personal checks are not an accepted form of payment. Mail processing an additional US$5; self-adressed stamped envelope required; officials suggest allowing a month for mail-in applications, but processing generally takes about a week. Normal processing takes 4 business days. Rush fees: US$20 for 2- to 3-day service, US$30 for same-day service. You can obtain a visa application through a fax-back service: New York 212-868-7761; Washington 202-265-9809.

Visa extensions are the domain of the Foreign Affairs section of the Public Security Bureau (PSB) in China (listed in the **Practical Information** section of every city). Depending on where you are, it is usually not a problem to get one visa extension for an additional two weeks to a month. Getting a second extension, however, is more difficult. You might be better off heading to Hong Kong for a few days and getting a new tourist visa there. Whatever you decide, **do not overstay the duration of your visa**—you risk being heavily fined and detained when you depart China.

SPECIAL PERMITS. Only 20 years ago, much of China was off-limits to foreign travelers. These days, almost everywhere is open to tourists, but China's policy of travel restrictions still lingers. Foreigners need special **travel permits** to visit certain "sensitive" regions in China, while some areas remain entirely closed. In general, only border regions, especially those populated by ethnic minorities, require special permits to visit. The list of areas closed to foreign travelers is in a constant state of flux, and official Beijing policy can often take considerable time to reach the hinterlands of Xinjiang. So whether you'll need a travel permit to visit a particular region of the country depends on who you talk to. The areas most frequently needing special travel permits are Tibet, Northern Xinjiang, certain wilderness areas and other border regions. Travel permits are issued at the discretion of the Public Security Bureau (PSB), which decides how much they cost and how long they take to process. The local PSB reserves the right to cancel or modify your permit at any time, so it is best to get to your destination as fast as possible once you've obtained a permit for it.

WORK PERMITS. If you're planning on (legally) working in China, you must obtain a work permit, which you'll need in order to apply for a longterm multiple-entry work visa. To obtain a work permit, you must have a valid passport, be over the age of 18, and procure a number of important documents. These include but are not limited to a medical report, your credentials (diploma, resume, or transcript), a letter of intention for employment, and a report of reasons for employment. Your employer will provide documents stating your accepted employment, and they will submit your documents to Chinese authorities in order to get you a work permit. So all *you* have to do is get a check-up. You could help speed up the process by having your credentials (diploma, resume, etc.) translated into Chinese, preparing a detailed trip itinerary, and making sure you get all your shots.

IDENTIFICATION

When you travel, always carry two or more forms of identification on your person, including at least one photo ID; a passport combined with a driver's license or birth certificate is usually adequate. Many establishments, especially banks, may require several IDs in order to cash traveler's checks. Never carry all your forms of ID together; split them up in case of theft or loss.

TEACHER, STUDENT & YOUTH IDENTIFICATION. The **International Student Identity Card (ISIC)**, the most widely accepted form of student ID, provides discounts on sights, accommodations, food, and transport. However, it is not widely recognized in China. If you can get a Chinese student card, you may be able to avoid the "foreigner's surcharge" (see p. 58) that is sometimes tacked onto museum entrance fees and other travel services in China. Some places in backpacker cities like Yangshuo offer "classes" to foreigners who will then be given a Chinese student card. Anyone studying legitimately on the mainland, for no matter how short a time, can get one of these red plastic-covered wallet-sized booklets. Forged Chinese student IDs do exist in popular tourist destinations, but the government is clued in to the proliferation of fake student cards among foreign travelers; charlatans are almost always exposed. *Let's Go* does not recommend using fake IDs.

All ISIC cardholders have access to a 24hr. emergency helpline for medical, legal, and financial emergencies (in North America call 877-370-ISIC, elsewhere call US collect +1 715-345-0505), and US cardholders are also eligible for insurance benefits (see **Insurance,** p. 69). Applicants must be degree-seeking students of a secondary or post-secondary school and must be at least 12 years of age. Because of the proliferation of fake ISICs, some services (particularly airlines) require additional proof of student identity, such as a school ID or a letter attesting to your student status, signed by your registrar and stamped with your school seal.

The **International Teacher Identity Card (ITIC)** offers teachers the same insurance coverage as well as similar but limited discounts. To receive an ITIC, you must prove that you're employed at a recognized educational establishment for at least 18 hours per week. For travelers who are 25 years old or under but are not students, the **International Youth Travel Card** (**IYTC;** formerly the **GO 25** Card) also offers many of the same benefits as the ISIC.

Each of these identity cards costs US$22 or equivalent. ISIC and ITIC cards are valid for roughly one and a half academic years; IYTC cards are valid for one year from the date of issue. Many student travel agencies (see p. 83) issue the cards, including STA Travel in Australia and New Zealand; Travel CUTS in Canada; usit in the Republic of Ireland and Northern Ireland; SASTS in South Africa; Campus Travel and STA Travel in the UK; and Council Travel and STA Travel in the US. For a listing of issuing agencies, or for more information, contact the **International Student Travel Confederation (ISTC),** Herengracht 479, 1017 BS Amsterdam, The Netherlands (☎ +31 20 421 28 00; fax 421 28 10; istcinfo@istc.org; www.istc.org).

ISICONNECT SERVICE. If you have an ISIC and want to avoid buying individual calling cards or wish to consolidate all your means of communication during your trip, you can activate your ISIC's ISIConnect service, a powerful new integrated communications service (powered by eKit.com). With ISIConnect, one toll-free access number (in China ☎ 108 00 140 0208 or 108 00 180 0072) allows access to many services. To activate your ISIConnect account, visit the service's compre-

ESSENTIALS

hensive website (www.isiconnect.ekit.com) or call the customer service number of your home country (which is also your home country's access number): in Australia 800 114 478; in Canada 877-635-3575; in Ireland 800 555 180 or 800 577 980; in New Zealand 0800 114 478; in the UK 0800 376 2366 or 0800 169 8646; in the US 800-706-1333; and in South Africa 0800 992 921 or 0800 997 285.

CUSTOMS

Upon entering China, you must declare certain items from abroad and pay a duty on the value of those articles that exceeds the allowance established by China's customs service. Tourists are allowed to bring into China no more than 50g of gold or silver jewelry, perfume (a "reasonable quantity"), and *one* of the following electronic appliances: camera, portable tape-recorder, portable video camera, or computer. (During your trip, electronic goods cannot be sold if they were imported duty-free for personal use.) Tourists staying less than 6 months can bring 400 cigarettes and 2 bottles of wine or spirits. Stay over six months and you can bring 600 cigarettes and 4 bottles of your favorite pastime. All gifts and items imported on behalf of others must be declared and may be charged duty. What souvenirs are you allowed to take out of China? Y300 per person and 4 cartons of tobacco products! Exporting jewelry will require special invoices (issued by China). For cultural relics, you'll need to get an invoice permit or export license from the cultural administrative department. Antiques (real and imitation) need to be marked with a red wax seal. For both import and export, Chinese customs has a long list of prohibited items: fire arms and explosives, pornographic or political literature, narcotics, infected plants, animals, or foodstuffs, and radio transmitters, to name a few. Furthermore, the Chinese government prohibits the export of valuable cultural relics, rare animals and plants, and precious metals and gems. It is wise to make a list, including serial numbers, of any valuables that you carry with you from home; if you register this list with customs before your departure and have an official stamp it, you will avoid import duty charges and ensure an easy passage upon your return. Be especially careful to document items manufactured abroad.

Note that goods and gifts purchased at **duty-free** shops abroad are not exempt from duty or sales tax at your point of return and thus must be declared as well; "duty-free" merely means that you need not pay a tax in the country of purchase. Upon returning home, you must similarly declare all articles acquired abroad and pay a duty on the value of articles in excess of your home country's allowance. Also be sure to keep receipts for all goods acquired abroad. For more information, contact your local customs office or visit the website www.customs.ustreas.gov.

MONEY

CURRENCY & EXCHANGE

The standard unit of Chinese currency is the **renminbi** (RMB; 人民币; "people's currency"), commonly referred to as the **yuan** (元). The *yuán* is divided into 10 units of *jiâo* (角) and 100 units of *fēn* (分); 10 *fēn* equals 1 *jiâo*. Be aware that the size of coins and bills increases with value; some vendors try to trick foreign tourists by giving change in the smaller *jiâo* rather than the bigger *yuán*. Almost all prices in China, as well as those in this book, are posted in *yuán* decimal form (which is equal to RMB). When referring to prices orally, the Chinese usually substitute the colloquial *kuài* for *yuán* and *máo* for *jiâo*.

ESSENTIALS

In Hong Kong the standard currency is the Hong Kong dollar (HK$), which can also be used in parts of Guangdong province.

The currency chart below is based on September 2002 exchange rates between Chinese *renminbi* (RMB) and Australian dollars (AUS$), Canadian dollars (CDN$), New Zealand dollars (NZ$), South African Rand (ZAR), British pounds (UK£), US dollars (US$), European Union euros (EUR€), and Hong Kong dollars (HK$). Check the currency converter on the Let's Go Homepage (www.letsgo.com/Thumb/index.htm) for the latest exchange rates.

THE YUAN (Y)

AUS$1 = Y4.53	Y1 = AUS$0.22
CDN$1 = Y5.29	Y1 = CDN$0.19
NZ$1 = Y3.89	Y1 = NZ$0.26
ZAR = Y.79	Y1 = ZAR 1.27
UK£1 = Y12.88	Y1 = UK£0.08
US$1 = Y8.28	Y1 = US$0.12
EUR€1 = Y8.11	Y1 = EUR€0.12
HK$1 = Y1.06	Y1 = HK$0.94

The RMB is not traded on international markets, so you can only purchase or exchange it in China. Occasionally, American Express Travel Service Outlets have been known to exchange RMB for US dollars. In China, you can exchange currency at any one of Bank of China's 30,000 branches, not to mention the airports, upscale hotels, and tourist stores where Bank of China has set up shop. State administration controls the exchange rate, so it's the same no matter where you go in China. The fee for each exchange is also standardized, set at 7.75% of the transaction. All money exchanges are open from 8am-7pm, and hotels exchange from 7am-11pm (although service is sometimes restricted to guests, and travelers should watch out for commission rates).

Check newspapers for the standard rate of exchange. Banks generally have the best rates, but random individuals on the street also offer good rates (perhaps because they have no overhead cost). No matter where you exchange money in China, there's always the possibility that you'll end up with a few counterfeit bills, but the chances are probably slightly greater on the street than in a bank. Keep all receipts from financial transactions. You will not be allowed to exchange RMB back into foreign currency unless you have proof of how you got the RMB in the first place. Also, using an ATM card or a credit card (see p. 56) often gets you the best rates, although ATM access is sparse outside major urban centers. In **Hong Kong** and **Macau,** it should be possible to exchange most major currencies, but in China, bank tellers are more likely to exchange US dollars than other currencies.

TRAVELER'S CHECKS

Traveler's checks (**American Express** and **Visa** are the most recognized) are one of the safest and least troublesome means of carrying funds. Several agencies and banks sell them for a small commission. Each agency provides refunds if checks are lost or stolen and many provide additional services, such as toll-free refund hotlines abroad, emergency message services, and stolen credit card assistance.

While traveling, keep check receipts and a record of which checks you've cashed separate from the checks themselves. Also leave a list of check numbers with someone at home. Never countersign checks until you're ready to cash them and always bring your passport with you to cash them. If your checks are lost or

ESSENTIALS

stolen, immediately contact a refund center of the company that issued your checks to be reimbursed; they may require a police report verifying the loss or theft. Ask about toll-free refund hotlines and the location of refund centers when purchasing checks, and always carry emergency cash.

American Express: Checks available with commission at select banks and all AmEx offices. US residents can also purchase checks by phone (☎888-887-8986) or online (www.aexp.com). AAA (see p. 57) offers commission-free checks to its members. Checks available in US, Australian, British, Canadian, Japanese, and Euro currencies. *Cheques for Two* can be signed by either of 2 people traveling together. For purchase locations or more information contact AmEx's service centers: in the US and Canada 800-221-7282; in the UK 0800 521 313; in Australia 800 25 19 02; in New Zealand 0800 441 068; elsewhere US collect +1 801-964-6665.

Visa: Checks available (generally with commission) at banks worldwide. To find the nearest issuing location call Visa's service centers: in the US 800-227-6811; in the UK 0800 89 50 78; elsewhere UK collect +44 020 7937 8091. Checks available in US, British, Canadian, Japanese, and Euro currencies.

Travelex/Thomas Cook: In the US and Canada call 800-287-7362; in the UK call 0800 62 21 01; elsewhere call UK collect +44 1733 31 89 50. Call for the location of their nearest office. As with Thomas Cook MasterCard, their traveler's checks can be exchanged at most banks, including Banks of China and China Construction Banks.

Exchange rates for traveler's checks are actually more favorable than those for cash in China, making traveler's checks the preferred way to carry money on the mainland. There is only one drawback: although traveler's checks are easily exchanged at most banks and upscale hotels, they are not generally accepted at budget hotels and guesthouses, restaurants, or sights.

CREDIT CARDS

Where they are accepted, credit cards often offer superior exchange rates—up to 5% better than the retail rate used by banks and other currency exchange establishments. Credit cards may also offer services such as insurance or emergency help and are sometimes required to reserve hotel rooms or rental cars. **MasterCard** and **Visa** are the most welcomed; **American Express** cards work at some ATMs and at AmEx offices and major airports. Budget travelers will probably find that few of the establishments they frequent will accept credit cards; aside from the occasional splurge, you will probably reserve use of your credit card for financial emergencies.

Credit cards are also useful for **cash advances,** which allow you to withdraw *yuán* from associated banks and ATMs throughout China. Unfortunately, transaction fees for all credit card advances (up to US$10 per advance, plus 2-3% extra on foreign transactions after conversion) tend to make credit cards a more costly way of withdrawing cash than ATMs or traveler's checks. In an emergency, however, the transaction fee may prove worth the cost. To be eligible for an advance, you'll need to get a Personal Identification Number (PIN) from your credit card company (see **Cash Cards (ATM Cards)**, below). Be sure to check with your credit card company before you leave home; in certain circumstances companies have started to charge a foreign transaction fee.

CREDIT CARD COMPANIES. Visa (US ☎800-336-8472) and MasterCard (US ☎800-307-7309) are issued in cooperation with banks and other organizations. American Express (US ☎800-843-2273) has an annual fee of up to US$55. AmEx cardholders may cash personal checks at AmEx offices abroad, access an emergency medical and legal assistance hotline (24hr.; in North America call 800-554-2639, elsewhere call US collect +1 715-343-7977), and enjoy American Express Travel Service benefits (including plane, hotel, and car rental reservation changes; baggage loss and flight insurance; mailgram and international cable services; and held mail). The **Discover Card** (in US call 800-347-2683, elsewhere call US +1 801-902-3100) offers cash-back bonuses on most purchases, but it may not be widely accepted in China.

CASH CARDS (ATM CARDS)

While it should be no problem finding **ATMs** (Automated Teller Machines) that accept foreign ATM cards in Hong Kong and Macau, most ATMs on the mainland only take cards issued by Chinese banks. In Hong Kong (and Macau to a lesser extent), nearly every ATM is linked to an international money network, like Cirrus, PLUS, NYCE, Maestro, Global Access, and many others. Travelers who are going to be in China for an extended time period and wish to carry less local currency with them should consider opening a local account at the Bank of China or another Chinese bank and getting a domestic ATM card that can be used in many mid- to large-sized Chinese cities.

ATMs get the same wholesale exchange rate as credit cards, but there is often a limit on the amount of money you can withdraw per day (around US$500), and computer networks sometimes fail. Some ATMs may have a surcharge of US$1-5 per withdrawal. Be sure to memorize your PIN code in numeric form since machines elsewhere often don't have letters on their keys. Also, if your PIN is longer than four digits, ask your bank whether you need a new number.

The two major international money networks are **Cirrus** (to locate ATMs US 800-424-7787 or www.mastercard.com) and **Visa/PLUS** (to locate ATMs US 800-843-7587 or www.visa.com). In China, most ATMs are found in Beijing, Shanghai, Hong Kong, Macau, and Guangdong Province.

Visa TravelMoney is a system allowing you to access money from any ATM on the Visa/PLUS network. You deposit an amount before you travel (plus a small administration fee) and can then withdraw up to that sum. TravelMoney cards are available at Travelex/Interpayment locations worldwide; US residents may also obtain them through AAA offices (see p. 63) or by calling 877-394-2247. **American Express Express Cash** allows AmEx cardholders to withdraw money from American Express ATMs worldwide. To enroll, US cardholders may call 800-227-4669.

GETTING MONEY FROM HOME

If you run out of money while traveling, the easiest and cheapest solution is to have someone back home make a deposit to your credit card or cash (ATM) card. Failing that, consider one of the following options.

WIRING MONEY. It is possible to arrange a **bank money transfer**, which means asking a bank back home to wire money to a bank in China. Travelers from the US, Canada, and the UK can wire money abroad through Western Union's international money transfer services. In the US, call 800-325-6000; in Canada 800-235-0000; in the UK 0800 83 38 33; in China (010) 6318 4313. The rates for sending cash are generally US$10-11 cheaper than with a credit card, and the money is usually available at the place you're sending it to within an hour. To locate the nearest Western Union location, consult www.westernunion.com. Although the service is rather expensive, money can be transferred instantly to Beihai, Beijing, Changsha, Chengdu, Chongqing, Dalian, Dandong, Fushun, Fuqing, Fuzhou, Guangzhou, Guilin, Haikou, Hangzhou, Harbin, Hong Kong, Hu Lu Dao, Kunming, Lhasa, Liuzhou, Nanjing, Nanning, Qingdao, Shanghai, Shantou, Shenyang, Shenzhen, Suzhou, Taiyuan, Ürümqi, Wenzhou, Wuhan, Wuxi, Wuzhou,

Xiamen, Xi'an, Yichang, Yingkou, and Yulin. Except in Hong Kong where a variety of money changers and travel services receive the wire, the service is usually handled by the local post office or EMS (Express Mail Service) office. Look for foreign remittance windows in the main post offices of these cities. Some branches may only accept transfers in US currency, so be sure to call ahead if you wish to wire money in another currency. Money transfer services are also available at **American Express** and **Thomas Cook** offices.

FEDERAL EXPRESS. Some people choose to send money abroad in cash via FedEx to avoid transmission fees and taxes. Note that this method is illegal. In the US and Canada, FedEx can be reached by calling 800-463-3339; in the UK, 0800 12 38 00; in Ireland, 800 535 800; in Australia, 13 26 10; in New Zealand, 0800 733 339; and in South Africa, 011 923 8000. FedEx has two dropoff locations in Beijing and one in Shanghai; dropoff locations in Hong Kong are numerous.

DHL Worldwide Express, another shipping option, has offices in the following cities: Beijing, Chengdu, Dalian, Fuzhou, Guangzhou, Hangzhou, Harbin, Hefei, Nanjing, Ningbo, Qingdao, Shanghai, Shenyang, Shenzhen, Shijiazhuang, Suzhou, Tianjin, Wuhan, Wuxi, Xi'an, and Xiamen. For more detailed information, go to the website www.dhl.com/wrd/cn.html or call (010) 6466 5566.

US STATE DEPARTMENT (US CITIZENS ONLY). In dire emergencies only, the US State Department will forward money within hours to the nearest consular office, which will then disburse it according to instructions for a US$15 fee. If you wish to use this service, you must contact the Overseas Citizens Service division of the US State Department (☎202-647-5225; nights, Sundays, and holidays ☎202-647-4000).

COSTS

TIERED PRICING SYSTEM. China is gradually getting rid of the government-sanctioned **tiered pricing system** that charges foreigners more than overseas Chinese and overseas Chinese more than mainlanders. Many admission prices levied at many of the most popular sights in the country still charge foreigners one-and-a half or two times more than Chinese.

The cost of your trip will vary considerably, depending on where you go, how you travel, and where you stay. The single biggest cost of your trip will probably be your round-trip (return) **airfare** to China (see **Getting to China: By Plane,** p. 83). Before you go, spend some time calculating a reasonable per-day **budget** that will meet your needs.

STAYING ON A BUDGET. The average income and cost of living in China are much lower than in the West, but this doesn't always translate into cheap accommodations and transportation for travelers. A dorm bed in Yangshuo runs a mere US$2 a night, but the cheapest accommodations in Tianjin (and the other booming coastal cities) start at US$15-20. Some hotels or hostels also may not accept foreigners. To give you a general idea, a bare-bones day in China (sleeping in a dormitory, buying food on the street) would cost about US$10-15 (Y80-120) in the West (Yunnan, Guangxi, Tibet, Sichuan, Gansu, Xinjiang) and about US$30 (Y240) on the Eastern Coast; a slightly more comfortable day (sleeping in a private room, eating one meal a day at a restaurant, going out at night) would run US$45-50 (Y360-400); and for a luxurious day, the sky's the limit (especially in Hong Kong). Also, don't forget to factor in emergency reserve funds (at least US$200) when planning how much money you'll need.

THE ART OF THE DEAL Bargaining in China is a given: no price is set in stone and vendors and drivers raise prices at the mere scent of a *lâowài* (foreigner); it's up to you to get them down to a reasonable rate. Don't underestimate the importance of bargaining–for many merchants, being able to overcharge foreigners is a matter of pride. The following tips may help:

1. Overcome the language barrier. Although body language and a big, smiling face can be one of your greatest weapons, Chinese merchants will immediately drop the price if you throw out a few words of Chinese. Useful phrases include:

Duōshâo qián? (How much is it?)
Tài gùi le! (That's too expensive!)
Dùi wô kànlái, zhōnggúo shì shíjìe shàng zùi piáoliâng de gúojiā. (In my opinion, China is the most beautiful country in the world.)

Be careful, though–in minority areas, where Han Chinese aren't necessarily beloved, using Chinese might just annoy the merchant. In this case, act stupid and loveable and do your best.

2. Use your poker face. The less your face betrays your interest in the item the better. Be cool.

3. Know when to bargain. Except when in large department and grocery stores, expensive boutiques, and foreign shops and restaurants, you can expect to bargain for what you buy in China, Hong Kong, and Macau. In most cases, it's quite clear when it's appropriate to bargain. When in doubt, ask tactfully, "Can you lower the price?" *(Nî néng piányi yïdiân ma?)* or whether discounts *(zhékòu)* are given.

4. Know when to turn away. Feel free to refuse any vendor or driver who bargains rudely and don't hesitate to move on to another vendor if one will not be reasonable about the final price. However, to start bargaining without an intention to buy is a major *faux pas*, especially in minority areas. Agreeing on a price and declining it is also poor form. Turn away with a smile and *"búyào"* (I don't want it) upon hearing a ridiculous price–the price may plummet.

5. Start low. Never feel guilty offering what seems to be a ridiculously low price. Chances are, even after bargaining hard, you'll still pay twice what a local would.

TIPPING & BARGAINING

Tipping and especially bargaining in the developing world are quite different and much more commonplace practices than you may be accustomed to; there are many unspoken rules to which tourists must adhere. **Tipping** is still very uncommon in Asia. In China, don't feel obligated to tip anyone—they shouldn't expect you to. The same thing goes in Hong Kong and Macau, except in the fanciest of hotels. **Bargaining,** however, is commonplace. Travelers to China should make an attempt to learn the basics of bargaining etiquette, both in order to conduct themselves courteously in a foreign culture and to prevent unwittingly paying too much (See **The Art of the Deal,** p. 59).

As a rule of thumb, if there is no set price given, it is almost certainly negotiable, and even if there is a set price, it may well be negotiable too. This is true whether you're buying souvenirs, ordering dumplings at a food stall, checking into a guesthouse, or hiring a guide to take you sightseeing.

SAFETY & SECURITY

PERSONAL SAFETY

EXPLORING. To avoid unwanted attention, try to blend in as much as possible. Respecting local customs (in many cases, dressing more conservatively) may placate would-be hecklers. Familiarize yourself with your surroundings before setting out and carry yourself with confidence; if you must check a map on the street, duck into a shop. If you are traveling alone, be sure someone at home knows your itinerary and **never admit that you're traveling alone.**

When walking at night, stick to busy, well-lit streets and avoid dark alleyways. Do not attempt to cross through parks, parking lots, or other large, deserted areas. Look for children playing, women walking in the open, and other signs of an active community. If you feel uncomfortable, leave as quickly and directly as you can, but don't allow fear of the unknown to turn you into a hermit. Careful, persistent exploration will build confidence and make your stay even more rewarding.

EMERGENCY! **Police (PSB)** ☎ 110. **Fire** ☎ 119. **Ambulance** ☎ 120.

SELF DEFENSE. There is no sure-fire way to avoid all the threatening situations you might encounter when you travel, but a good self-defense course will give you concrete ways to react to unwanted advances. **Impact, Prepare, and Model Mugging** can refer you to local self-defense courses in the US (☎ 800-345-5425). Visit the website at www.impactsafety.org/chapters for a list of nearby chapters. Workshops (2-3hr.) start at US$50; full courses run US$350-500.

TRANSPORTATION. Although the national **train** system is safe mechanically, travelers should be wary of long-distance **buses.** Old or low-quality equipment, dangerous road conditions, and reckless drivers can make for risky journeys. Look at your bus before you buy your ticket—if a vehicle looks unsafe, it very likely is. Public city buses, which tend to be overcrowded and (sometimes) recklessly driven, also may be more dangerous than those you are accustomed to at home. Avoid **driving** altogether in China. For info on the perils of **hitchhiking,** see p. 98.

CRIME AND TERRORISM. With China swiftly changing from a planned economy to a market-driven one, the number of unemployed workers and struggling peasants is on the rise. The increase in crime has led the Communist Party to launch campaigns favoring swift justice and stiff punishments (including execution) against any "unstable factors" in society, including mafia-style gangs, currency counterfeiters, smugglers, and drug peddlers.

Lately, terrorist activity has been on the rise. Although political violence and terrorist bombings are largely the work of ethnic (mostly Uighur) separatist groups and the growing army of unemployed workers, underground pro-democracy organizations and quasi-Buddhist sects are also involved.

Despite the rise in crime and terrorist activity, China's violent crime rate is low by international standards, and it is rare for foreigners to be targets of such crimes. Travelers should be aware that property crimes most often occur in areas undergoing rapid economic development. On the whole, though, China is a relatively safe country, and local citizens will often watch out for the safety of travelers. If you are the victim of theft or assault, report immediately not only to the local PSB, but also to your embassy in China.

TRAVEL ADVISORIES. The following government offices provide travel information and advisories by telephone, by fax, or via the web:

Australian Department of Foreign Affairs and Trade: ☎1300 555135; faxback service 02 6261 1299; www.dfat.gov.au.

Canadian Department of Foreign Affairs and International Trade (DFAIT): In Canada and the US call 800-267-6788, elsewhere call +1 613-944-6788; www.dfait-maeci.gc.ca. Call for their free booklet, *Bon Voyage...But.*

New Zealand Ministry of Foreign Affairs: ☎04 494 8500; fax 494 8506; www.mft.govt.nz/trav.html.

United Kingdom Foreign and Commonwealth Office: ☎020 7008 0232; fax 7008 0155; www.fco.gov.uk.

US Department of State: ☎202-647-5225, faxback service 202-647-3000; http://travel.state.gov. For *A Safe Trip Abroad*, call 202-512-1800.

ESSENTIALS

FINANCIAL SECURITY

PROTECTING YOUR VALUABLES. There are a few steps you can take to minimize the financial risk associated with traveling. First, **bring as little with you as possible.** Leave expensive watches, jewelry, cameras, and electronic equipment (like your Discman) at home; chances are you'd break them, lose them, or get sick of lugging them around anyway. Second, buy a few combination **padlocks** to secure your belongings either in your pack—which you should **never leave unattended**—or in a hostel or train station locker. Third, **carry as little cash as possible;** instead carry traveler's checks and ATM/credit cards, keeping them in a **money belt**—not a "fanny pack"—along with your passport and ID cards. Fourth, **keep a small cash reserve separate from your primary stash.** This should entail about US$50 (US dollars are best) sewn into or stored in the depths of your pack, along with your traveler's check numbers and important photocopies.

CON ARTISTS & PICKPOCKETS. Among the more colorful aspects of large cities are **con artists.** They often work in groups, and children are among the most effective. They possess an innumerable range of ruses. Beware of certain classics: sob stories that require money, rolls of bills "found" on the street, mustard spilled (or saliva spit) onto your shoulder to distract you while they snatch your bag. Don't ever hand over your passport to someone whose authority you question (ask to accompany them to a police station if they insist), and **don't ever let your passport out of your sight.** Similarly, don't let your bag out of sight; never trust a "station-porter" who insists on carrying your bag or stowing it in the baggage compartment or a "new friend" who offers to guard your bag while you buy a train ticket or use the restroom. Beware of **pickpockets** in city crowds, especially on public transportation. Also, be alert in public telephone booths. If you must say your calling card number, do so very quietly; if you punch it in, make sure no one can look over your shoulder.

ACCOMMODATIONS & TRANSPORTATION. Never leave your belongings unattended; crime occurs in even the most demure-looking hostel or hotel. Bring your own **padlock for hostel lockers, and don't ever store valuables in any locker.**

Be particularly careful on **buses and trains;** horror stories abound about determined thieves who wait for travelers to fall asleep. Carry your backpack in front of you where you can see it. When traveling with others, sleep in alternate shifts. When alone, use good judgement in selecting a train compartment: never stay in an empty one, and use a lock to secure your pack to the luggage rack. Try to sleep on top bunks with your luggage stored above you (if not in bed with you), and keep important documents and other valuables on your person.

If traveling by **car,** don't leave valuables (such as radios or luggage) in it while you are away. If your tape deck or radio is removable, hide it in the trunk or take it with you. If it isn't, at least conceal it. Similarly, hide baggage in the trunk—although savvy thieves can tell if a car is heavily loaded by the way it sits on its tires.

DRUGS & ALCOHOL

Penalties concerning the possession, use, or trafficking of **illegal drugs** are steep—drug dealers and smugglers are regularly sentenced to death. Remember that you are subject to the laws (and the penalties) of the country in which you travel, not to those of your home country, and it is your responsibility to familiarize yourself with these laws before leaving. If you carry **prescription drugs** while you travel, it is vital to have a copy of the prescriptions themselves and a note from a doctor; keep these readily accessible whenever you cross national borders. **Avoid public drunkenness;** it can get you in trouble with the authorities very quickly and jeopardize your safety and earn the disdain of locals.

ESSENTIALS

HEALTH

Common sense is the simplest prescription for good health while you travel. Drink lots of fluids to prevent dehydration and constipation, wear sturdy, broken-in shoes and clean socks, and use talcum powder to keep your feet dry.

BEFORE YOU GO

Preparation can help minimize the likelihood of contracting a disease and maximize the chances of receiving effective health care in the event of an emergency. For tips on packing a basic **first-aid kit** and other health essentials, see p. 70.

In your **passport,** write the names of any people you wish to be contacted in case of a medical emergency, and also list any **allergies** or medical conditions of which you would want doctors to be aware. Matching a prescription to a foreign equivalent is not always easy, safe, or possible. Carry up-to-date, legible prescriptions or a statement from your doctor stating the medication's trade name, manufacturer, chemical name, and dosage. While traveling, be sure to keep all medication with you in your carry-on luggage. Allergy sufferers might want to obtain a full supply of any necessary medication before the trip.

IMMUNIZATIONS & PRECAUTIONS

Travelers over two years old should be sure that the following vaccines are up to date: MMR (for measles, mumps, and rubella), DTaP or Td (for diptheria, tetanus, and pertussis), OPV (for polio), HbCV (for haemophilus influenza B), and HBV (for hepatitis B). Adults traveling to the developing world for longer than four weeks should consider the following additional immunizations: Hepatitis A vaccine and/or immune globulin (IG), an additional dose of polio vaccine, and typhoid and cholera vaccines, particularly if traveling off the tourist path. While yellow fever is only endemic to parts of South America and sub-Saharan Africa, many countries may deny entrance to travelers arriving from these zones without a certificate of vaccination. **Hepatitis A vaccine** and/or immune globulin (IG), as well as the **Hepatitis B vaccine**, are recommended for travelers to China. An inoculation against **Japanese encephalitis** is recommended for summer travelers or visitors planning to stay

INOCULATION REQUIREMENTS AND RECOMMENDATIONS. No vaccinations are required to travel to China, except yellow fever if arriving from infected areas (parts of tropical South America and sub-Saharan Africa). Vaccines against measles, diptheria, tetanus, polio, Hepatitis A, and Hepatitis B are all recommended.

longer than two weeks in rural areas. If you will be spending more than four weeks in the country, you also should consider being vaccinated for **typhoid.** For recommendations on immunizations and prophylaxis, consult the **CDC** (see below) in the US or the equivalent in your home country and check with a doctor for guidance.

USEFUL ORGANIZATIONS & PUBLICATIONS

The US **Centers for Disease Control and Prevention (CDC;** ☎877-FYI-TRIP; tollfree fax 888-232-3299; www.cdc.gov/travel) maintains an informative website. The CDC's comprehensive booklet *Health Information for International Travel*, an annual rundown of disease, immunization, and general health advice, is free online or US$25 via the Public Health Foundation (☎877-252-1200). Consult the appropriate government agency of your home country for consular information sheets on health, entry requirements, and other issues for various countries. For quick information on health and other travel warnings, call the **Overseas Citizens Services** (☎202-647-5225; after-hours 202-647-4000), or contact a passport agency or an embassy or consulate abroad. US citizens can send a self-addressed, stamped envelope to the Overseas Citizens Services, Bureau of Consular Affairs, #4811, US Department of State, Washington, D.C. 20520. For information on medical evacuation services and travel insurance firms, see the US government's website at http://travel.state.gov/medical.html or the **British Foreign and Commonwealth Office** (www.fco.gov.uk).

For detailed information on travel health, including a country-by-country overview of diseases, try the **International Travel Health Guide,** by Stuart Rose, MD (Travel Medicine, US$19.95; www.travmed.com). For general health info, contact the **American Red Cross** (☎800-564-1234; www.redcross.org).

MEDICAL ASSISTANCE ON THE ROAD

Pharmacies, indicated by green crosses, abound in larger cities. Few are open 24 hours a day; even fewer pharmacists speak English. The selection of local and imported pharmaceuticals has increased in recent years, but you may still want to bring your own supplies. In an emergency, go to the nearest major hospital, which is almost certainly open all night with an in-house pharmacy. Outside big cities, the going is a bit rougher, but major towns should have at least one pharmacy.

The quality of China's **hospitals** and other medical services varies by region. Major metropolitan centers typically have better facilities than rural areas, but even so, hospital accommodations tend to be basic, and medical technology is not up-to-date. While most doctors and nurses are trained and competent professionals, they often do not speak English. You may have to struggle with charades and use the handy **Phrasebook** (see p. 833). **Expect to pay cash on the spot for treatment.** Foreigners are often charged more than Chinese for medical services, but the costs are still considerably cheaper than in most developed nations. For non-emergency care, you can contact your embassy and ask for a suggested list of doctors.

If you are concerned about being able to access medical support while traveling, there are special support services you may employ. The *MedPass* from **GlobalCare, Inc.,** 2001 Westside Pkwy., #120, Alpharetta, GA 30004, USA (☎800-860-1111; fax

ESSENTIALS

BIGGER IS BETTER Oh, the charm of small hospitals: spartan accommodations, ill-equipped facilities, technologically-antiquated medical instruments! What more could you want? Perhaps the sanitary conditions and sheer massiveness of a foreigner-friendly *big* hospital. Although some smaller hospitals can provide adequate medical service, you can bet your backless hospital gown on the chance that you'll get better attention and more sanitary service from a larger hospital. Once there, you will have to *guà hào* ("take a number"), which means you'll pay a small fee (Y1-5) for a card telling you which department to visit. Although the physician will see his patients in rapid succession, the care you receive is likely to be competent. If the doctor prescribes medication, keep in mind that hospital-manufactured drugs (Y2-4) are much cheaper than externally manufactured ones (Y30). For those concerned about possibly losing limbs or appendages while traveling, consider purchasing insurance, which is fairly inexpensive (less than US$100 for a 30-day visit) and offers comprehensive coverage, including medical evacuation.

770-475-0058; www.globalems.com), provides 24hr. international medical assistance, support, and medical evacuation resources. The **International Association for Medical Assistance to Travelers** (**IAMAT;** US ☎716-754-4883, Canada ☎416-652-0137, New Zealand ☎03 352 20 53; www.sentex.net/~iamat) has free membership, lists English-speaking doctors worldwide, and offers detailed info on immunization requirements and sanitation. If your regular **insurance** policy does not cover travel abroad, you may wish to purchase additional coverage (see p. 69).

Those with medical conditions (diabetes, allergies to antibiotics, epilepsy, heart conditions) may want to obtain a stainless-steel **Medic Alert** ID tag (first year US$35, annually thereafter US$20), which identifies the condition and gives a 24hr. collect-call number. Contact the Medic Alert Foundation, 2323 Colorado Ave, Turlock, CA 95382, USA (☎888-633-4298; www.medicalert.org).

ONCE IN CHINA

ENVIRONMENTAL HAZARDS

Air quality: A disproportionate number of the world's most polluted cities are in China. Most of the country burns coal for heat in the winter and industrial emissions tend to be alarmingly high. This will aggravate existing respiratory problems such as allergies and asthma, and even healthy travelers will fall victim to chest colds, respiratory infections, and bronchitis. This is particularly the case in China's biggest cities, such as Beijing, Shenyang, Chongqing, Shanghai, Xi'an, and Guangzhou. If you suffer from respiratory difficulties, be certain to take inhalers and/or any prescription medication with you and consult with your doctor for advice before departure.

Heat exhaustion and dehydration: All areas of China, particularly the deserts of the northwest and the subtropical areas of the south and southwest, can be brutally hot in the summer. Heat exhaustion, characterized by dehydration and salt deficiency, can lead to fatigue, headaches, and wooziness. Avoid it by drinking plenty of fluids, eating salty foods (e.g. crackers), and avoiding dehydrating beverages (e.g. alcohol, coffee, tea, and caffeinated soda). Continuous heat stress can eventually lead to **heatstroke,** characterized by a rising temperature, severe headache, and cessation of sweating. Victims should be cooled off with wet towels and taken to a doctor.

Sunburn: If you're prone to sunburn, bring sunscreen with you, as it's hard to find when traveling in China. If you get sunburned, drink more fluids than usual and apply

Calamine or an aloe-based lotion. The dangers of sunburn are especially acute in high elevation areas, such as parts of Sichuan and Tibet.

Hypothermia and frostbite: A rapid drop in body temperature is the clearest sign of overexposure to cold. Victims may also shiver, feel exhausted, have poor coordination or slurred speech, hallucinate, or suffer from amnesia. **Do not let hypothermia victims fall asleep** or their body temperature will continue to drop and they may die. To avoid hypothermia, keep dry, wear layers, and stay out of the wind. When the temperature is below freezing, watch out for **frostbite.** If skin turns white, waxy, and cold, do not rub the area. Drink warm beverages, get dry, and slowly warm the area with dry fabric or steady body contact until a doctor can be found. **In China, you will need to be particularly careful on long-distance bus rides;** faulty heaters and mechanical breakdowns can be deadly in cold weather or at high elevations at all times of the year.

High altitude: Travelers to high altitudes areas, particularly Tibet and parts of Sichuan, must allow their bodies a couple of days to adjust to lower oxygen levels before exerting themselves. Note that alcohol is more potent and UV rays are stronger at high elevations (see **Acute Mountain Sickness** (AMS), p. 797).

INSECT-BORNE DISEASES

Many diseases are transmitted by insects—mainly mosquitoes, fleas, ticks, and lice. Be aware of insects in wet or forested areas, especially while hiking and camping. **Mosquitoes** are most active from dusk to dawn. Wear long pants and long sleeves, tuck your pants into your socks, and buy a mosquito net. Use insect repellents, such as DEET, and soak or spray your gear with permethrin (licensed in the US for use on clothing). Consider natural repellents like vitamin B-12 or garlic pills. To stop the itch after being bitten, try Calamine lotion or topical cortisones (like Cortaid), or take a bath with a half-cup of baking soda or oatmeal. **Ticks**—responsible for Lyme and other diseases—can be particularly dangerous in rural and forested regions. Pause periodically while walking to brush off ticks using a fine-toothed comb on your neck and scalp. Do not try to remove ticks by burning them or coating them with nail polish remover or petroleum jelly.

Malaria: Transmitted by Anopheles mosquitoes that bite at night, the incubation period of the disease varies from 6-8 days to as long as several months. Early symptoms include fever, chills, aches, and fatigue, followed by high fever and sweating, sometimes with vomiting and diarrhea. See a doctor for any flu-like sickness that occurs after travel in a risk area. Left untreated, malaria can cause anemia, kidney failure, coma, and death. It is an especially serious threat to pregnant women. To reduce the risk of contracting malaria, use mosquito repellent, particularly in the evenings and when visiting forested areas, and take oral prophylactics, like mefloquine (sold under the name Lariam) or doxycycline (ask your doctor for a prescription). Be aware that these drugs can have very serious side effects, including slowed heart rate and nightmares. Risk is greatest in rural areas, so if hiking or staying overnight in certain areas, take weekly anti-malarial drugs. The type of drug you should take depends upon the strain of malaria present in the region you are traveling to; chloroquine is generally recommended for travelers to areas that do not have chloroquine-resistant malaria, while mefloquine is recommended for travelers to areas that do (most of southern China, especially Hainan Island, Guangxi, and Yunnan).

Dengue fever: An "urban viral infection" transmitted by *Aedes* mosquitoes, which bite during the day, causing flu-like symptoms and often indicated by a rash 3-4 days after the onset of fever. Symptoms for the first 2-4 days include chills, high fever, headaches, swollen lymph nodes, muscle aches, and in some instances, a pink rash on the face. If you experience these symptoms, see a doctor, drink plenty of liquids,

MALARIA RISK Malaria is a risk in most rural areas in China, with the notable exceptions of Heilongjiang, Qinghai, Tibet, and the northern provinces bordering Mongolia. For travelers visiting cities and popular tourist destinations, the risk is generally very small, and anti-malarial medication is usually not needed. In Guangdong, Guangxi, Yunnan, and Hainan Island, malaria infection is a year-round risk; most of the Yangzi River region and Sichuan is at risk from May to December; north of this area, risk of infection is only from July to November.

and take fever-reducing medication such as acetaminophen (Tylenol). *Never take aspirin to treat dengue fever.*

Tick-borne encephalitis: A viral infection of the central nervous system transmitted during the summer by tick bites or by consumption of unpasteurized dairy products, symptoms range from nothing to headaches and flu-like symptoms to swelling of the brain (encephalitis). While a vaccine is available in Europe, the immunization schedule is impractical, and the risk of contracting the disease is relatively low, especially if precautions are taken against tick bites.

Japanese encephalitis: Another mosquito-borne disease, it is most prevalent during the rainy season in rural areas near rice fields and livestock pens. Aside from delirium, most symptoms are flu-like: chills, headache, fever, vomiting, muscle fatigue. Since the disease carries a high mortality rate, it's vital to go to a hospital as soon as any symptoms appear. While the JE-VAX vaccine, usually given in 3 shots over a 30-day period, is effective for a year, it has been associated with serious side effects. According to the CDC, there is little chance of being infected if proper precautions are taken, such as using mosquito repellents containing DEET and sleeping under mosquito nets.

Lyme disease: This bacterial infection is carried by ticks and marked by a circular bull's-eye rash of 2 in. or more. Later symptoms include fever, headache, fatigue, and aches and pains. Antibiotics are effective if administered early. Left untreated, it can cause problems in joints, the heart, and the nervous system. If you find a tick attached to your skin, grasp the head with tweezers as close to your skin as possible and apply slow, steady traction. Removing a tick within 24 hours greatly reduces the risk of infection.

Yellow fever: A viral disease transmitted by mosquitoes, it derives its name from one of its most common symptoms, the jaundice caused by liver damage. While most cases are mild, the severe ones begin with fever, headache, muscle pain, nausea, and abdominal pain before progressing to jaundice, vomiting of blood, and bloody stools. While there is no specific treatment, there is an effective vaccine that offers 10 years of protection.

Other insect-borne diseases: Filariasis is a roundworm infestation transmitted by mosquitoes. Infection causes enlargement of extremities and has no vaccine. In scattered, localized areas of China, the plague and relapsing fever, which are transmitted through fleas and ticks, still occur. Treatment is available for both, and a vaccine can prevent the plague. The risk to travelers, however, is usually quite low.

FOOD- & WATER-BORNE DISEASES

Prevention is the best cure: be sure that your food is properly cooked and the water you drink is clean. Peel fruits and veggies and avoid tap water (including ice cubes and anything washed in tap water, like salad). Watch out for food from markets or street vendors that may have been cooked in unhygienic conditions. Other culprits are raw shellfish, unpasteurized milk, and sauces containing raw eggs. **In all parts of China, only drink bottled water or treated water.** All hotels, restaurants, and trains boil their water. Always wash your hands before eating or bring a quick-drying liquid hand cleaner. Your bowels will thank you. **In risk areas,** don't brush your teeth with tap water or rinse your toothbrush under the faucet, and keep your mouth closed in the shower. Ice cubes are just as dangerous as impure water in liquid form. You can treat your water with **iodine tablets**, but note that some parasites such as giardia have exteriors that resist iodine treatment, making boiling a more reliable treatment for water. Keep in mind that the water is just as bad for locals as it is for foreigners, so you should have no difficulty in finding potable water.

Traveler's diarrhea: This can result from drinking untreated water or eating uncooked foods or is a temporary (and fairly common) reaction to the bacteria in new food ingredients. Symptoms include nausea, bloating, urgency, and malaise. Try quick-energy, non-sugary foods with protein and carbohydrates to keep your strength up. Over-the-counter anti-diarrheals (e.g. Imodium) may counteract the problems, but can complicate serious infections. The most dangerous side effect is dehydration; drink 8 oz. of water with ½ tsp. of sugar or honey and a pinch of salt, try uncaffeinated soft drinks, or munch on salted crackers. If you develop a fever or your symptoms don't go away after 4-5 days, consult a doctor. Consult a doctor for treatment of diarrhea in children.

Dysentery: A serious intestinal infection caused by certain bacteria, the most common type is bacillary dysentery, also called shigellosis. Symptoms include bloody diarrhea (sometimes mixed with mucus), fever, and abdominal pain and tenderness. Bacillary dysentery generally only lasts a week, but it is highly contagious. Amoebic dysentery, which develops more slowly, is a more serious disease and may cause long-term damage if left untreated. A stool test can determine which kind you have; seek medical help immediately. Dysentery can be treated with the drugs norfloxacin or ciprofloxacin (commonly known as Cipro). If you are traveling in high-risk (especially rural) regions, consider obtaining a prescription before you leave home.

Cholera: An intestinal disease caused by a bacteria found in contaminated food. Cholera has recently reached epidemic stages in Central and South America, but the risk is low for travelers to China, especially if food and water precautions are observed. If you suffer from symptoms of diarrhea, dehydration, vomiting, or muscle cramps, see a doctor immediately. Left untreated, cholera may be deadly. Antibiotics are available, but the most important treatment is rehydration. Consider getting a (50% effective) vaccine if you have stomach problems (e.g. ulcers) or plan to stay where water is not reliable.

Hepatitis A: A viral infection of the liver acquired primarily through contaminated water, its symptoms include fatigue, fever, loss of appetite, nausea, dark urine, jaundice, vomiting, aches and pains, and light stools. Risk is high in China, especially in rural areas and the countryside; it is also present in urban areas. Ask your doctor about the vaccine (Havrix or Vaqta) or an injection of immune globulin (IG; formerly called gamma globulin).

Parasites: These include microbes, tapeworms, and other organisms that hide in unsafe water and food. **Giardiasis,** for example, is acquired by drinking untreated water from streams or lakes all over the world. Symptoms include swollen glands or lymph nodes, fever, rashes or itchiness, digestive problems, eye problems, and anemia. Boil water, wear shoes, avoid bugs, and eat only cooked food.

Schistosomiasis: Also known as bilharzia, it is a parasitic disease caused when the larvae of flatworm penetrate unbroken skin. Symptoms include an itchy localized rash, followed in 4-6 weeks by fever, fatigue, painful urination, diarrhea, loss of appetite, night sweats, and a hive-like rash on the body. If exposed to untreated water, rub the area vigorously with a towel and apply rubbing alcohol. Schistosomiasis can be treated with prescription drugs. Avoid swimming in fresh water. Risk is present in Southern China.

Typhoid fever: Caused by the salmonella bacteria, typhoid is common in rural areas in South China. While mostly transmitted through contaminated food and water, it may also be acquired by direct contact with another person. Early symptoms include fever, headaches, fatigue, loss of appetite, constipation, and sometimes a rash on the abdomen or chest. Antibiotics can treat typhoid, but a vaccination (70-90% effective) is recommended.

OTHER INFECTIOUS DISEASES

Rabies: Transmitted through the saliva of infected animals, rabies can be fatal if untreated. By the time symptoms appear (thirst and muscle spasms), the disease is in its terminal stage. If you are bitten, wash the wound thoroughly, seek immediate medical care, and try to have the animal located. A rabies vaccine, which consists of 3 shots given over a 21-day period, is available but is only semi-effective.

Hepatitis B: A viral infection of the liver transmitted via bodily fluids or needle-sharing with symptoms not surfacing until years after infection. Vaccinations are recommended for health-care workers, sexually-active travelers, and anyone planning to seek medical treatment abroad. The 3-shot vaccination series must begin 6 mo. before traveling.

Hepatitis C: This form of hepatitis is similar to Hep B, but the mode of transmission differs. IV drug users, those with occupational exposure to blood, hemodialysis patients, and recipients of blood transfusions are at the highest risk, but the disease can also be spread through sexual contact or sharing items like razors and toothbrushes that may have traces of blood on them.

AIDS, HIV, & STDS

The AIDS epidemic has hit China with such force that it will likely become one of the world's most critical areas of AIDS infection within the next decade. In Yunnan alone there are an estimated 50,000 AIDS victims. For detailed information on **Acquired Immune Deficiency Syndrome (AIDS)** in China, call the **US Centers for Disease Control's** 24hr. hotline at 800-342-2437 or contact the **Joint United Nations Programme on HIV/AIDS (UNAIDS),** 20, av. Appia, CH-1211 Geneva 27, Switzerland (☎+41 22 791 36 66; fax 22 791 41 87). The Council on International Educational Exchange's pamphlet, *Travel Safe: AIDS and International Travel*, is posted on their website (www.ciee.org/Isp/safety/travelsafe.htm), along with links to other online and phone resources. Note that China screens incoming travelers for AIDS, primarily those planning extended visits for work or study (see **Visas,** p. 50), and denies entrance to those who test HIV-positive. Contact a Chinese consulate for up-to-date information.

Sexually transmitted diseases (STDs) like gonorrhea, chlamydia, genital warts, syphilis, and herpes are easier to catch than HIV and can be just as deadly. **Hepatitis B** and **C** are also serious STDs (see **Other Infectious Diseases,** p. 68). Though condoms may protect you from some STDs, oral or even tactile contact can lead to transmission. Warning signs include swelling, sores, bumps, or blisters on sex organs, the rectum, or the mouth; burning and pain during urination and bowel movements; itching around sex organs; swelling or redness of the throat; and flu-like symptoms. If these symptoms develop, see a doctor immediately.

WOMEN'S HEALTH

Women traveling in unsanitary conditions are vulnerable to **urinary tract** and **bladder infections,** common and very uncomfortable bacterial conditions that cause a burning sensation and painful (sometimes frequent) urination. To try to avoid these infections, drink plenty of vitamin-C-rich juice and clean water and urinate frequently, especially right after intercourse. Untreated, these infections can lead to kidney infections, sterility, and even death. If symptoms persist, see a doctor.

Tampons and **pads** can be found in most, but not all, areas of China. Preferred brands are very likely not to be available, so take supplies along. **Reliable contraceptive devices** may also be difficult to find outside of large cities. Women on the pill should bring enough to allow for possible loss or extended stays. Bring a prescription, since forms of the pill vary a good deal. Women who use a diaphragm should bring enough contraceptive jelly. Though condoms are increasingly available, consider bringing your favorite brand, as availability and quality vary.

Vaginal yeast infections may flare up in hot and humid climates. Wearing loose-fitting trousers or a skirt and cotton underwear will help, as will over-the-counter remedies like Monistat or Gynelotrimin. Bring supplies from home if you are prone to infection; they're hard to find in China. In a pinch, some travelers use a natural alternative such as a plain yogurt (suānnǎi; 酸奶) and lemon juice douche.

Abortion in China is legal. Parental authorization is required for those under 18, and abortion may not be used to abort the fetus of an unwanted gender. Mifepristone, commonly known as RU-486, has been available in China since 1988. Women who need an **abortion** while abroad should contact the **International Planned Parenthood Federation,** European Regional Office, Regent's College Inner Circle, Regent's Park, London NW1 4NS, UK (☎ +44 (20) 7487 7900; fax 487 7950) for more information, or the **China Family Planning Association (CFPA),** No.1 Shenggu Beili Yinghuayuan Xijie, Beijing (☎ +86 (10) 6441 3375; cfpa@public.fhnet.cn.net).

INSURANCE

Travel insurance generally covers four basic areas: medical/health problems, property loss, trip cancellation/interruption, and emergency evacuation. Although regular insurance policies may well extend to travel-related accidents, you may consider purchasing travel insurance if the cost of potential trip cancellation, interruption, or emergency medical evacuation is greater than you can absorb. Prices for travel insurance purchased separately generally run about US$50 per week for full coverage, while trip cancellation/interruption may be purchased separately at a rate of about US$5.50 per US$100 of coverage.

Medical insurance (especially university policies) often covers costs incurred abroad; check with your provider. **US Medicare does not cover foreign travel. Canadians** are protected by their home province's health insurance plan for up to 90 days after leaving the country; check with the provincial Ministry of Health or Health Plan Headquarters for details. **Homeowners' insurance** (or your family's coverage) often covers theft during travel and loss of travel documents (passport, plane ticket, railpass, etc.) up to US$500.

ISIC and **ITIC** (see p. 53) provide basic insurance benefits, including US$100 per day of in-hospital sickness for up to 60 days, US$3000 of accident-related medical reimbursement, and US$25,000 for emergency medical transport. Cardholders have access to a toll-free 24hr. helpline (run by the insurance provider **TravelGuard**) for medical, legal, and financial emergencies overseas (US and Canada ☎ 877-370-4742, elsewhere call US collect +1 715-345-0505). **American Express** (US ☎ 800-528-4800) grants most cardholders automatic car rental insurance (collision and theft, but not liability) and ground travel accident coverage of US$100,000 on flight purchases made with the card.

INSURANCE PROVIDERS. Council and **STA** (see p. 83) offer a range of plans that can supplement your basic coverage. Other private insurance providers in the **US and Canada** include: **Access America** (☎800-284-8300); **Berkely Group/Carefree Travel Insurance** (☎800-323-3149; www.berkely.com); **Globalcare Travel Insurance** (☎800-821-2488; www.globalcare-cocco.com); and **Travel Assistance International** (☎800-821-2828; www.europ-assistance.com). Providers in the **UK** include **Columbus Direct** (☎020 7375 0011). In **Australia,** try **AFTA** (02 9375 4955).

PACKING

Pack lightly: lay out only what you absolutely need, then take half the clothes and twice the money. The less you have, the less you have to lose (or store, or carry on your back). Any extra space left will be useful for any souvenirs or items you might pick up along the way.

LUGGAGE. If you plan to cover most of your itinerary by foot, a sturdy **frame backpack** is unbeatable. (**For the basics on buying a pack,** see p. 76.) Toting a **suitcase** or **trunk** is fine if you plan to live in one or two cities and explore from there, but a very bad idea if you're going to be moving around a lot. In addition to your main piece of luggage, a **daypack** (a small backpack or courier bag) is a must.

CLOTHING. No matter when you're traveling, it's always a good idea to bring a **warm jacket** or wool sweater, a **rain jacket** (Gore-Tex® is both waterproof and breathable), sturdy shoes or **hiking boots,** and **thick socks. Flip-flops** or waterproof sandals are must-haves for grubby hostel showers. You may also want to add one outfit beyond the jeans and t-shirt uniform, and maybe a nicer pair of shoes if you have the room. If you plan to visit any religious or cultural sites, remember that you'll need something besides tank tops and shorts to be respectful.

CONVERTERS & ADAPTERS. In China, electricity is 220 volts AC, enough to fry any 110V North American appliance. Americans and Canadians should buy a **converter** (biànyāqì; 变压器; US$20); residents of Australia, Ireland, New Zealand, South Africa, and the UK won't need one. Chinese plugs are three-pronged, similar to those in Australia; generally, mid-range hotels have two-pronged outlets in bathrooms, but residents of all other countries who want to use appliances outside the bathroom will have to buy an adapter to change the shape of the plug. The electricity in China is not especially stable, especially in rural areas, so if your trip takes you out of city areas, pack light on appliances and heavy on battery power.

TOILETRIES. Toothbrushes, towels, cold-water soap, talcum powder (to keep feet dry), deodorant, razors, tampons, and condoms are often available, but may be difficult to find, so bring extras along. **Contact lenses,** on the other hand, though inexpensive, are often difficult to find, so bring enough extra pairs and solution for your entire trip. Also bring your glasses and a copy of your prescription in case you need emergency replacements.

FIRST-AID KIT. For a basic first-aid kit, pack: bandages, pain reliever, antibiotic cream, a thermometer, a Swiss Army knife (do not pack in carry-on luggage during flights), tweezers, moleskin, decongestant, motion-sickness remedy, diarrhea or upset-stomach medication (Pepto Bismol or Imodium), an antihistamine, sunscreen, insect repellent, burn ointment, and a syringe for emergencies (get an explanatory letter from your doctor).

FILM. Chinese brands of film are widely available and inexpensive. Most imported brands, including Japanese, are easy to find in cities, but they are not as cheap as Chinese brands. Slide or black-and-white film can be impossible to purchase outside of major cities. Less serious photographers may want to bring a **disposable camera or two rather than an expensive permanent one.** Despite disclaimers, airport security X-rays *can* fog film, so buy a lead-lined pouch at a camera store or ask security to hand-inspect it. Always pack film in your carry-on luggage, since higher-intensity X-rays are used on checked luggage.

OTHER USEFUL ITEMS. For safety purposes, you should bring a **money belt** and small **padlock.** Basic **outdoors equipment** (plastic water bottle, compass, waterproof matches, pocketknife, sunglasses, sunscreen, hat) may also prove useful. **Quick repairs** of torn garments can be done on the road with a needle and thread; also consider bringing electrical tape for patching tears. Doing your **laundry** by hand (where it is allowed) is both cheaper and more convenient than doing it at a laundromat—bring detergent, a small rubber ball to stop up the sink, and string for a makeshift clothes line. **Other things** you're liable to forget: an umbrella; sealable **plastic bags** (for damp clothes, soap, food, shampoo, and other spillables); an **alarm clock;** safety pins; rubber bands; a flashlight; earplugs; garbage bags; and a small **calculator.**

IMPORTANT DOCUMENTS. Don't forget your passport, traveler's checks, ATM and/or credit cards, and adequate ID (see p. 50). Also check that you have any of the following that might apply to you: a hosteling membership card (see p. 71); driver's license (see p. 98); and travel insurance forms.

ACCOMMODATIONS

The country's budget accommodations may be the low point of a trip through China. Travelers can face a host of accommodation-related annoyances, including exorbitant rates, poor sanitation, noise, insects, and bureaucratic red tape. Since quality often varies more than price, choose carefully.

RESTRICTIONS. In most cities, foreigners are barred from staying at the cheapest lodgings and may be relegated to mid-range hotels. China has a five-star (wû xíngjí; 五星级) rating system for hotels and most hotels authorized to accept foreigners (shèwài bīnguân; 涉外宾馆) are one star or higher. Those who speak Mandarin or are overseas Chinese sometimes talk the management into letting them stay in a place that officially does not accept foreign guests. In dire circumstances, hotel staff can sometimes be persuaded to call the local PSB to ask for permission to lodge you for one night, but this is by no means guaranteed. Some establishments accepting foreigners insist that they occupy standard rooms even if dorm rooms exist. Most establishments also refuse to allow Chinese and foreigners to **share a room,** especially if of the opposite sex. Less frequently, **unmarried foreign couples** are also barred from staying together; a wedding band or marriage certificate, authentic or not, goes a long way in overcoming this regulation. Remember that an English sign outside does not always indicate a foreigner-friendly establishment.

If you plan on staying in a private residence while in China, you must register with the local branch of the PSB (Public Security Bureau) upon arrival (usually within the first day or two of your stay in the area).

PRICES. A wave of renovations is converting many old budget standbys into upmarket hotels. While dorm beds in popular backpacker destinations like Yunnan, Guangxi, and Tibet continue to cost around US$2 per night, in many cities along the eastern seaboard it's now hard to find a room for under US$20 a day. The only respite in sight is the low-occupancy rate that plagues most Chinese hotels; this gives travelers bargaining power. At any type of establishment, **always ask for a discount;** discounts of at least 10-20% are common and as much as 50% is not unheard of. Many low-end hotels use their price charts only as paperweights, giving discounts or padding room rates based on a guest's appearance. Although the two-tiered (foreigner and Chinese) pricing system is disappearing in most places (see p. 58), foreigners are still easy targets for price hikes. Telling the staff that you're a student may help.

CHECKING IN. When checking in to your hotel, you will invariably be required to fill out a **registration form** (usually in English and Chinese, but sometimes only in Chinese) with vital statistics like your nationality (guójì; 国籍), passport number (hùzhào hàomâ; 护照号码), and type of visa (qiãnzhèng; 签证 ; see p. 50 for an explanation of visa types—most travelers have an "L"-type tourist visa). In the past, hotels commonly kept passports as a **deposit** on the room, but most establishments have converted to cash; nonetheless, should you be asked by hotel staff to leave your passport, refuse and offer an expired one, some other form of identification, or cash instead. For any deposit you do leave, remember to keep the receipt in order to get a refund upon check-out. Check-out is typically noon, while check-in is generally anytime. Reservations for standard rooms are often accepted, but usually not necessary.

HOTELS

UPMARKET HOTELS. These establishments generally offer several restaurants, business and travel services, IDD/DDD phones and TVs in every room, laundry, 24hr. hot water, A/C, private baths with Western-style toilets, massage parlor, salon, and just about every other amenity under the sun. The luxury doesn't come cheap, however—doubles typically go for US$40 and up.

MID-RANGE HOTELS. Even more common than upmarket deluxe mega-hotels are the somewhat cheaper mid-range hotels. A dime a dozen, these places usually come with a more limited selection of similar amenities (restaurant, TV, A/C, phones, laundry, and karaoke parlor) and a smaller price tag, usually US$15-40 for doubles. Many of these hotels are large, multi-storied buildings with worn linens and upholstery, paper-thin walls, and aging bathrooms. They often have several buildings, wings, or floors with different levels of quality, often called "economy" (jìngjì; 经济), "standard" (biãozhûn; 标准; or pûtõng; 普通), and "deluxe" (háohuà; 豪华). Receptionists will sometimes try to make you stay in the most expensive rooms, so always ask about cheaper options.

LOW-END HOTELS. Often near the train and/or long-distance bus stations, these establishments may not even have a star. Amenities may stil include TV, laundry, a restaurant, sometimes phones, and perhaps Western-style toilets. These hotels, sometimes called hostels, often rent rooms by the bed, with most thrifty Chinese happy to bed down next to strangers at a fraction of the price of a room of their own; sadly, this option is rarely open to foreigners. Nonetheless, some budget hotels do let foreigners stay in these "dorm" rooms, especially when they're not full—the best of both worlds, since you pay for only the bed but almost always get the room to yourself. In these dorm accommoda-

TYPES OF ACCOMMODATIONS. Mandarin has several words to distinguish between different types of establishments that are generally all translated as "hotel" in English. In general, the most upmarket hotels are called *dàjiŭdiàn* (大酒店), or *fàndiàn* (饭店), and mid-range hotels are called *bīnguân* (宾馆). However, many run-of-the-mill establishments masquerade as *fàndiàn* in an attempt to justify exorbitant room rates. These three types of accommodations are usually the only places in town that accept foreigners. Low-end hotels are called *læguân* (旅馆), while guesthouses are *zhāodàisuô* (招待所), but both of these rarely accept foreigners.

tions, bathrooms are usually communal, hot water only available limited hours, and cleanliness questionable at times. But the price is right, usually US$3-8 per person per night.

HOSTELS

Hostels are generally laid out dorm-style, often with large single-sex rooms and bunk beds, although some offer private rooms for families and couples. They sometimes have kitchens and utensils for your use, bike or moped rentals, storage areas, and laundry facilities. There can be drawbacks: some hostels close during certain daytime "lockout" hours, have a curfew, don't accept reservations, impose a maximum stay, or, less frequently, require that you do chores.

Joining the youth hostel association in your own country automatically grants you membership privileges in **Hostelling International (HI),** a federation of national hosteling associations. HI hostels can be found in several Chinese cities and accept reservations via the **International Booking Network** (Australia ☎02 9261 1111; Canada ☎800-663-5777; England and Wales ☎01629 58 14 18; Northern Ireland ☎01232 32 47 33; Republic of Ireland ☎01 830 1766; NZ ☎03 379 9808; Scotland ☎08701 55 32 55; US ☎800-909-4776; www.hostelbooking.com).

Most HI hostels also honor **guest memberships**—you'll get a blank card with space for six validation stamps. Each night you'll pay a nonmember supplement (one-sixth the membership fee) and earn one guest stamp; get six stamps, and you're a member. Most student travel agencies (see p. 83) sell HI cards, as do many national hosteling organizations.

Except in those cities listed above, travelers to China will see few hostels. Due to the growing number of budget travelers, though, the number of hostels is increasing. For more information, contact:

Guangdong Youth Hostel Association of China, 185 Huanshi Xi Road, Guangzhou (☎(20) 8666 6889, ext. 8719; fax 8666 5039; gdyhac@public.guangzhou.gd.cn).

Hong Kong Youth Hostels Association, Shek Kip Mei Estate, Sham Shui Po, Room 225, Block 19, Kowloon (☎(852) 2788 1638; fax 2788 3105; hkyha@datainternet.com).

OTHER TYPES OF ACCOMMODATIONS

YMCAS & YWCAS

Young Men's Christian Association (YMCA) lodgings, though far from widespread in China, can be found in China's largest cities. YMCA accommodations are often more comfortable than many mid-range hotels, but the prices usually reflect this.

ESSENTIALS

National Committee of YMCAs of China, 123 Xizang Nan Lu, Shanghai (☎(21) 6311 1765; fax 6320 3053; chinay@public4.sta.net.cn).

Y's Way International, 224 E. 47th St., New York, NY 10017, USA (☎212-308-2899; fax 308-3161). For a small fee (US$3 in North America, US$5 elsewhere), this "booking service" makes reservations for the YMCAs in Beijing, Chengdu, Shanghai, Guangzhou, Hangzhou, Nanjing, Tianjin, Wuhan, Xiamen, and Xi'an.

World Alliance of YMCAs, 12 Clos Belmont, 1208 Geneva, Switzerland (☎+41 22 849 5100; fax +41 22 849 5110; office@ymca.int; www.ymca.int).

ESSENTIALS

MONASTERIES AND TEMPLES

Especially in remote areas, monasteries and temples often provide accommodations for just a few *kuài* a night. Frequently lacking electricity and running water, these tend to be the most basic of accommodations (essentially, a bed or a piece of the floor), but those who don't mind roughing it a little are often lured by the thought of trading in the noisy concrete high-rises of the cities for a little serene rusticity. Keep in mind, though, that on popular pilgrimage routes like Emeishan, every other traveler probably has the same idea, so spaces may be scarce.

UNIVERSITY DORMS

Many **colleges and universities** open their residence halls to travelers when school is not in session; some do so even during term-time. Beijing, Changsha, Hangzhou, Hefei, Nanjing, Suzhou, and Xi'an are among the cities that offer such accommodations. These dorms are often close to student areas—good sources for information on things to do—and can be great places to find English speakers, but more often than not, campuses are far from the major sights of downtown areas. The quality of the accommodations varies widely, with some schools offering dorm beds for as little as US$7 a night and others offering upscale, even swanky rooms at rates equivalent to those of mid-range hotels. Getting a room may require advanced planning, but rates tend to be low, and many offer free local calls.

HOME EXCHANGES & HOME RENTALS

Home exchange offers the traveler various types of homes (houses, apartments, condominiums, villas, even castles in some cases), plus the opportunity to live like a native and to cut down on accommodation fees. For more information, contact **HomeExchange.Com,** US (☎805-898-9660; www.homeexchange.com), **Intervac International Home Exchange** (www.intervac.com), or **The Invented City: International Home Exchange,** 41 Sutter St., San Francisco, CA 94404, USA (US ☎800-788-CITY, elsewhere US ☎415-252-1141; www.invented-city.com). **Home rentals** are more expensive than exchanges, but they can be cheaper than comparably-serviced hotels. Both home exchanges and rentals are ideal for families with children, or travelers with special dietary needs; you often get your own kitchen, maid service, TV, and telephones.

CAMPING & THE OUTDOORS

Camping in one of China's beautiful scenic areas and nature reserves might be an attractive option, but it is unfortunately a largely unfeasible one. Nowhere are there designated camping facilities, and the PSB frowns upon setting up your own site. A few tour groups are permitted to organize camping expeditions, but these are few and far between. *Let's Go* does not recommend camping in China.

This does not mean, though, that there aren't opportunities for outdoor activity in China. Many national parks have hiking areas, and trekking is the preferred method of travel in parts of Southwest China.

USEFUL PUBLICATIONS & RESOURCES

A variety of publishing companies offer hiking guidebooks to meet the educational needs of novice or expert. An excellent general resource for travelers planning on spending time in the outdoors is the **Great Outdoor Recreation Pages** (www.gorp.com). For information about hiking and biking, write or call the publishers listed below to receive a free catalog.

Sierra Club Books, 85 Second St., 2nd fl., San Francisco, CA 94105, USA (☎415-977-5500; www.sierraclub.org/books). Publishes general resource books on hiking, camping, and women traveling in the outdoors.

The Mountaineers Books, 1001 SW Klickitat Way, #201, Seattle, WA 98134, USA (☎800-553-4453 or 206-223-6303; fax 223-6306; www.mountaineersbooks.org). Over 400 titles on hiking, biking, mountaineering, natural history, and conservation.

NATIONAL PARKS

China has some spectacular scenery, and since 1979 the government has been working to keep it that way. Under the jurisdiction of the National Parks Agency of China, over 100 national parks have been established. These areas, generally nature reserves, provide travelers with the opportunity to hike amongst lush greenery and exotic wildlife. Most parks charge admission; prices vary and sometimes depend on the mode of transportation. Some parks are more tourist-friendly than others and have wide, paved roads welcoming busloads of visitors. Others require visitors to hire a guide and/or a 4WD vehicle.

In May 2001, China established 11 new National Geological Parks. These parks, which include volcanoes in Heilongjiang and dinosaur discovery sights in Shaanxi, were established in order to encourage tourist interest and scientific discovery.

WILDERNESS SAFETY

THE GREAT OUTDOORS. Stay warm, stay dry, and stay hydrated. The vast majority of life-threatening wilderness situations can be avoided by following this simple advice. Prepare yourself for an emergency, however, by always packing **raingear, a hat** and **mittens,** a **first-aid kit,** a **reflector,** a **whistle, high energy food,** and extra **water for any hike.** Dress in wool or warm layers of **synthetic materials** designed for the outdoors; never rely on **cotton for warmth, as it is useless when wet**.

Check **weather forecasts** and pay attention to the skies when hiking, since weather patterns can change suddenly. Whenever possible, let someone know when and where you are going hiking. Do not attempt a hike beyond your ability—you may be endangering your life.

WILDLIFE. China has over 4400 species of vertebrates, so it's no wonder that a few creatures can pose a threat to soft-skinned humans. China is home to a wide variety of animals, including pandas, snow leopards, tigers, and alligators. Normally, though, these animals will avoid humans. China also contains 57 species of **poisonous snakes,** including king cobras and sea snakes. In case of snake bite, the American Red Cross suggests that you wash the afflicted area with soap and water, keep it immobile and lower than the heart, and seek immediate medical attention.

Somewhat surprisingly, another potentially threatening animal is the **monkey.** In heavily touristed areas, monkeys grow accustomed to humans and are not afraid to come close enough to bite. In short, monkeys can be vicious, evil little animals. Some travelers carry large walking sticks when in wilderness areas in order to discourage their approach. For minor bites, clean with soap and water and apply a dressing; for wounds with heavy bleeding, control the bleeding but do not clean the wound. Zoos and research facilities should have facilities and procedures to help you; in other areas seek immediate medical assistance.

Most other animal attacks in China occur in zoos, circuses, or reserves, usually when viewers taunt or hurt the animals in question. Be intelligent; **teasing a tiger is never a good idea.** For more information, consult *How to Stay Alive in the Woods*, by Bradford Angier (Macmillan Press, US$12).

CAMPING AND HIKING EQUIPMENT

WHAT TO BUY...

Good camping equipment is both sturdy and light. Camping equipment is generally more expensive in Australia, New Zealand, and the UK than in North America.

Sleeping Bag: Most sleeping bags are rated by season ("summer" means it can withstand 30-40°F at night; "four-season" or "winter" often means below 0°F). They are made either of **down** (warmer and lighter, but more expensive, and miserable when wet) or of **synthetic** material (heavier, more durable, and warmer when wet). Prices range US$80-210 for a summer synthetic to US$250-300 for a good down winter bag. **Sleeping bag pads** include foam pads (US$10-20), air mattresses (US$15-50), and Therm-A-Rest self-inflating pads (US$45-80). Bring a **stuff sack** to store your bag and keep it dry.

Tent: The best tents are free-standing (with their own frames and suspension systems), set up quickly, and only require staking in high winds. Low-profile dome tents are the best all-around. Good 2-person tents start at US$90, 4-person at US$300. Seal the seams of your tent with waterproofer, and make sure it has a rain fly. Other tent accessories include a **battery-operated lantern,** a **plastic groundcloth,** and a **nylon tarp.**

Backpack: Internal-frame packs mold better to your back, keep a lower center of gravity, and flex adequately to allow you to hike difficult trails. **External-frame packs** are more comfortable for long hikes over even terrain, as they keep weight higher and distribute it more evenly. Make sure your pack has a strong, padded hip-belt to transfer weight to your legs. Any serious backpacking requires a pack of at least 4000 cubic inches (16,000cc), plus 500 cubic in. for sleeping bags in internal-frame packs. Sturdy backpacks cost anywhere from US$125-420—this is one area in which it doesn't pay to economize. Fill up any pack with something heavy and walk around the store with it to get a sense of how it distributes weight before buying it. Either buy a **waterproof backpack cover,** or store all of your belongings in plastic bags inside your pack.

Boots: Be sure to wear hiking boots with good **ankle support.** They should fit snugly and comfortably over 1-2 pairs of wool socks and thin liner socks. Break in boots over several weeks first in order to spare yourself painful and debilitating blisters.

Other Necessities: Synthetic layers, like those made of polypropylene, and a **pile jacket** will keep you warm even when wet. A **"space blanket"** will help you to retain your body heat and doubles as a groundcloth (US$5-15). Plastic **water bottles** are virtually shatter- and leak-proof. Bring **water-purification tablets** for when you can't boil water. Also don't forget a **first-aid kit, pocketknife, insect repellent, Calamine lotion,** and **waterproof matches** or a **lighter.**

...AND WHERE TO BUY IT

The mail-order/online companies listed below offer lower prices than many retail stores, but a visit to a local camping or outdoors store will give you a good sense of the look and weight of certain items.

Campmor, 28 Parkway, P.O. Box 700, Upper Saddle River, NJ 07458, USA (US ☎888-226-7667; elsewhere US ☎+1 201-825-8300; www.campmor.com).

Discount Camping, 880 Main North Rd., Pooraka, SA 5095, Australia (☎08 8262 3399; fax 8260 6240; www.discountcamping.com.au).

Eastern Mountain Sports (EMS), 1 Vose Farm Rd., Peterborough, NH 03458, **USA** (☎888-463-6367 or 603-924-7231; www.shopems.com)

L.L. Bean, Freeport, ME 04033, USA (US and Canada ☎800-441-5713; UK ☎0800 891 297; elsewhere, call US +1 207-552-3028; www.llbean.com).

Mountain Designs, 51 Bishop St., Kelvin Grove, Queensland 4059, Australia (☎07 3856 2344; fax 3856 0366; info@mountaindesigns.com; www.mountaindesigns.com).

Recreational Equipment, Inc. (REI), Sumner, WA 98352, USA (☎800-426-4840 or 253-891-2500; www.rei.com).

YHA Adventure Shop, 14 Southampton St., Covent Garden, London, WC2E 7HA, UK (☎020 7836 8541; www.yhaadventure.com). The main branch of one of Britain's largest outdoor equipment suppliers.

ORGANIZED ADVENTURE TRIPS

Organized adventure tours offer another way of exploring the wild. Activities include hiking, biking, skiing, canoeing, kayaking, rafting, climbing, photo safaris, and archaeological digs. Tourism bureaus can often suggest parks, trails, and outfitters; other good sources for info are stores and organizations that specialize in camping and outdoor equipment like REI and EMS (see above). In China, many travel agencies can help to arrange specific tours; see the travel agency listings in each city section for more detail.

iExplore, 600 W. Fulton St., Ste. 601, Chicago, IL 60661, USA (☎800-439-7567; experts@iexplore.com; www.iexplore.com). Offers travel advice and lists regional tours and customer ratings on their website.

Specialty Travel Index, 305 San Anselmo Ave., #313, San Anselmo, CA 94960, USA (☎800-442-4922 or 415-459-4900; www.specialtytravel.com). An extensive index of tour operators in China and the rest of the world.

KEEPING IN TOUCH

BY MAIL

SENDING MAIL HOME FROM CHINA

Airmail is the best way to send mail home from China. **Aerogrammes,** printed sheets that fold into envelopes and travel via airmail, are available at post offices. Write "par avion" (hángkōng; 航空) on the front. Most post offices will charge exorbitant fees or simply refuse to send aerogrammes with enclosures. **Surface mail** is by far the cheapest and slowest way to send mail. It takes one to four months to cross the Pacific—good for items you won't need to see for a while, such as souvenirs or other articles you've acquired along the way that are weighing down your pack.

Sending a post card out of China costs Y3.2. Sending a letter out of China costs Y4.40 (1-20g) or Y8.20 (21-50g). Airmail charges an additional Y10 per gram. Sending letters within China costs Y0.8; within a particular city Y0.6. The most reliable way to ship documents and packages abroad from China is by **EMS** (Express Mail Service; tèkuài zhuāndì; 特快专递; ☎185), a service of China Post. Not all post offices offer EMS; *Let's Go: China* indicates if the service is available in the Practical Information section of each city. Sending packages via surface mail costs Y29 (less than 500g) and Y47 (less than 2kg). Be aware that mail traveling from smaller towns or outer regions may take longer than normal. These are standard EMS rates for mail from China to:

Australia & New Zealand: Allow 3-5 days for regular airmail home. Packages up to 0.5kg Y160-210, up to 1kg Y215-265.

UK & Ireland: Allow 4-6 days for regular airmail home. Packages up to 0.5kg Y220-280, up to 1kg Y295-355.

US & Canada: Allow 4-7 days for regular airmail home. Packages up to 0.5kg Y180-240, up to 1kg Y255-315.

ESSENTIALS

SENDING MAIL TO CHINA

Mark envelopes "air mail" or "par avion" (hángkōng; 航空), or your letter or postcard will never arrive. In addition to the standard postage system whose rates are listed below, **Federal Express** (Australia ☎13 26 10; US and Canada ☎800-247-4747; New Zealand ☎0800 73 33 39; UK ☎0800 12 38 00) handles express mail services from most home countries to China; for example, they can get a letter from New York to Beijing in 4 days for US$30.75 and from London to Beijing in 4 days for UK£32.10.

Australia: Allow 4-6 days for regular airmail to China. Postcards and letters up to 20g cost AUS$1; packages up to 0.5kg AUS$6, up to 2kg AUS$30.50. **EMS** can get a letter to China in 3-4 days for AUS$28. www.auspost.com.au/pac.

Canada: Allow 4-7 days for regular airmail to China. Postcards and letters up to 20g cost CDN$1.05; packages up to 0.5kg CDN$10.20, up to 2kg CDN$34. www.canadapost.ca/CPC2/common/rates/ratesgen.html#international.

Ireland: Allow 5-7 days for regular airmail to China. www.anpost.ie.

New Zealand: Allow 4-10 days for regular airmail to China. Letters up to 20g cost NZ$1.50; small parcels up to 0.5kg NZ$8.10, up to 2kg NZ$20.66. www.nzpost.co.nz/nzpost/inrates.

UK: Allow 5-7 days for airmail to China. Letters up to 20g cost UK£0.65; packages up to 0.5kg UK£4.95, up to 2kg UK£19.20. UK Swiftair delivers letters a day faster for UK£3.5 more. www.royalmail.com.

US: Allow 4-7 days for regular airmail to China. Postcards/aerogrammes cost US$0.70/0.80; letters under 1 oz. US$1. Packages under 1lb. cost US$9.25; larger packages cost a variable amount (around US$15). **US Express Mail takes** 2-3 days and costs US$15. **US Global Priority Mail** reaches select Chinese cities (Beijing, Chongqing, Dalian, Guangzhou, Nanjing, Qingdao, Shanghai, Shenyang, Shenzhen, Suzhou, Tianjin, Wuhan, Wuxi, Xiamen, and Zhuhai) and delivers small and large flat-rate envelopes to China in 3-5 days for US$5-9. http://ircalc.usps.gov.

RECEIVING MAIL IN CHINA

There are several ways to arrange pick-up of letters sent to you by friends while you are abroad. Mail can be sent via Poste Restante (General Delivery; cúnjú hòulîng; 存局候领) to almost any city or town in China with a post office, with varying reliability. When addressing letters to China, an attempt—however unskilled—to include Chinese characters will improve the letter's chances of arriving at the correct destination; Let's Go provides the characters for each province (shêng; 省) and city (shì; 市). Address mail like the example below:

Marco POLO
Poste Restante 存局候领
Shaanxi Province, Xi'an 陕西省西安市
CHINA 中国 710000

The mail will go to a special desk in the central post office, unless you specify a post office by street address or postal code. It's best to use the largest post office since mail will probably end up there regardless. It is usually safer and quicker, if more expensive, to send mail express or registered. Bring your passport (or other photo ID) for pick-up; there may be a small fee. If the clerks insist that there is nothing for you, have them check under your first name as well. Sometimes it may help to write your name on a sheet of paper and hand it to the clerk. *Let's Go* lists post offices in the **Practical Information** section for each city and most towns.

American Express's travel offices throughout the world offer a free **Client Letter Service** (mail held up to 30 days and forwarded upon request) for cardholders who contact them in advance. Address the letter to the AmEx office. Some offices will offer these services to non-cardholders (especially AmEx Traveler's Check holders), but call ahead to make sure. *Let's Go* lists AmEx office locations for Beijing, Guangzhou, Hong Kong, Shanghai, and Xiamen in their respective **Practical Information** sections.

BY TELEPHONE

CALLING HOME FROM CHINA

A **calling card** is probably your cheapest bet. Calls are billed collect or to your account. You can frequently call collect without even possessing a company's calling card just by calling their access number and following the instructions. **To obtain a calling card** from your national telecommunications service before leaving home, contact the appropriate company listed below (using the numbers in the first column). **To call home with a calling card,** contact the operator for your service provider in China by dialing the appropriate toll-free access number (listed below in the second column).

COMPANY	TO OBTAIN A CARD, DIAL:	TO CALL ABROAD FROM CHINA, DIAL:
AT&T (US)	800-222-0300	108 11
British Telecom Direct	0800 34 51 44	108 440
Canada Direct	800-668-6878	108 186
Ireland Direct	800 500 500	Not available
MCI (US)	800-444-4444	108 12

ESSENTIALS

COMPANY	TO OBTAIN A CARD, DIAL:	TO CALL ABROAD FROM CHINA, DIAL:
New Zealand Direct	0800 00 00 00	108 640
Sprint (US)	800-877-4646	108 13
Telkom South Africa	10 219	108 270
Telstra Australia	13 22 00	108 610

You can usually also make direct international calls from pay phones, but if you aren't using a calling card, you'll find that the time on your phone card disappears at an alarming rate. Where available, prepaid phone cards (see below) can be used for direct international calls, but they are still less cost-efficient. Using major credit cards is also expensive, and credit cards can't be used as extensively. Most China Telecom offices offer IDD service at expensive (but not exorbitant) rates. (See **Placing International Calls** for instructions on how to place a direct international call.)

Placing a **collect call** through an international operator is even more expensive, but may be necessary in an emergency. You can place collect calls through the service providers listed above even if you don't have one of their phone cards.

PLACING INTERNATIONAL CALLS. To call China from home or to call home from China, dial:

1. The **international dialing prefix.** To dial out of **Australia,** dial 0011; **Canada** or the **US,** 011; the **Republic of Ireland, New Zealand,** or the **UK,** 00; **South Africa,** 09; out of **China,** 00.
2. The **country code** of the country you want to call. To call **Australia,** dial 61; **Canada** or the **US,** 1; the **Republic of Ireland,** 353; **New Zealand,** 64; **South Africa,** 27; the **UK,** 44; **China,** 86; **Hong Kong** and **Macau,** 852.
3. The **city/area code.** *Let's Go* lists the city/area codes for cities and towns in China opposite the city or town name, next to a ☎. If the first digit is a zero (e.g., 010 for Beijing), omit the zero when calling from abroad (e.g., dial 10 from Canada to reach Beijing).
4. The **local number.**

CALLING WITHIN CHINA

The simplest way to call within the country is to use a coin-operated or public phone. Be aware that sometimes the public phones have extra fees for long distance calls that would not be applied otherwise. **Prepaid phone cards** (diànhuà kâ; 电话卡; available at China Telecoms and on street corners everywhere) carry a certain amount of phone time depending on the card's denomination and usually save time and money in the long run. Be aware that prepaid phone cards are sometimes only available for use within the home province; Y200 phone cards can supposedly be used anywhere in China. Be sure to ask about such restrictions before purchasing a card. Be aware also that phony phone cards are sometime sold in less official places (China Telecom offices are the best bet for official and valid cards).

Another kind of prepaid telephone card comes with a Personal Identification Number (PIN) and a toll-free access number. Instead of inserting the card into the phone, you call the access number and follow the directions on the card. These cards can be used to make international as well as domestic calls. Phone rates typically tend to be highest in the morning, lower in the evening, and lowest on Sunday and late at night. **MOBILE TELEPHONES.** China's mobile phone network, or Global Mobile Systems (GMS) network, runs at 900MHz, which means that most

OPERATOR, PLEASE. China's telephone system is far from straightforward: even the number of digits in a telephone number varies between and sometimes even within cities. Large cities and municipalities, like Beijing, have as many as eight digits, while small border towns can have as few as four. Macau has 6-, 7-, *and* 8-digit numbers. If you have trouble connecting to a number, try adding another digit to the beginning; "2" and "6" are popular new prefixes. If you still don't have any luck, consult an online directory, like www.chinabig.com. In desperate circumstances, you can try China's directory assistance: dial 114 from any phone.

European and Oceanic mobile GMS phones will work in China. Some phones will require the purchase of a new SIM (Subscriber Identity Module) or Smart card before they can be used; try electronics stores in major cities like Beijing and Guangzhou. Many North American (particularly US) phones will not work, but several mobile service providers rent out compatible phones; contact your service provider for more information. Due to the popularity of mobile phones in China, it's not possible to rent a phone once there; phones can be purchased for as little as Y800. Registering your phone numbers costs an additional Y100. The cheapest plans offer local calls at Y0.2 per minute and international calls at Y2.5 per minute. For more information, contact China Mobile (in China, ☎ 1860).

TIME DIFFERENCES

Although China is nearly 5000km from east to west, it has only one time zone. As a result, the working day in western regions like Xinjiang starts long before sunrise; these areas sometimes keep different hours to compensate (see p. 751). The country is officially 8 hours ahead of **Greenwich Mean Time (GMT).** In the summer, since China doesn't follow **daylight savings time,** the time difference may be an hour less.

MIDNIGHT	3AM	8AM	10AM	3PM	4PM	6PM	7PM
Vancouver Seattle San Francisco Los Angeles	Toronto Ottawa New York Boston	London (GMT)	Johannesburg	Hanoi Bangkok Jakarta Phnom Penh	China Hong Kong Manila Singapore	Sydney Canberra Melbourne	Auckland

BY EMAIL AND INTERNET

For the most convenient public Internet access venues, try China Telecom (zhōngguó diánxìn; 中国电信) or China Post offices, cybercafes, university campus computer rooms, libraries, and the business centers of upmarket hotels. Though nationwide coverage is still patchy, *Let's Go* lists at least one establishment where travelers can surf the net in almost every city's **Practical Information** section.

Though in some places it's possible to forge a remote link with your home server, in most cases this is a much slower (and thus more expensive) option than taking advantage of free **web-based email accounts** (e.g. www.hotmail.com and http://mail.yahoo.com). Travelers with laptops can call their home Internet service provider via a **modem.** Long-distance phone cards specifically intended for such calls can defray high phone charges; check with your long-distance phone provider to see if it offers this option. Be aware, though, that many calls go through switchboards or use antiquated phone systems, making dial-up access impossible. It is also possible to subscribe to a Chinese service provider, making long-distance dial-ups unnecessary.

ESSENTIALS

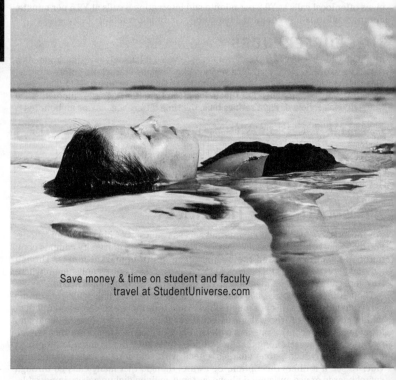

RULES AND REGULATIONS. In April 2001, the Chinese government enacted new internet regulations to block surfers from sites relating to pornography, violence, gambling, and superstition. Surfers in China will also find that many Western news sources and human rights organizations are blocked as well. Travelers should be aware that it is illegal in China to use a computer to "copy or publish material that harms government interests," spread viruses, or hack into databases. In addition, those under 18 can only enter Internet cafes during daytime hours on weekdays and holidays, and those under 14 must be accompanied by an adult. As a result of these regulations, many Internet cafes now operate with a certain amount of stealth, ushering in underage customers from behind curtains or through back-alley entrances. Most, though, simply ignore the rules, especially for foreigners.

GETTING TO CHINA

BY PLANE

When it comes to airfare, a little effort can save you a bundle. If your plans are flexible enough to deal with the restrictions, courier fares are the cheapest. Tickets bought from consolidators and standby seating are also good deals, but last-minute specials, airfare wars, and charter flights often beat these fares. The key is to hunt around, to be flexible, and to ask persistently about discounts. Students, seniors, and those under 26 should never pay full price for a ticket.

AIRFARES

Airfares to China peak between June and September; holidays are also expensive, although most foreign airlines (unlike their Chinese counterparts) don't raise their prices for Chinese New Year. Weekday round-trip flights run US$40-50 cheaper than weekend flights, but they are generally more crowded and less likely to permit frequent-flier upgrades. Traveling with an "open return" ticket can be pricier than fixing a return date when buying the ticket. Round-trip flights are by far the cheapest; "open-jaw" (arriving in and departing from different cities, e.g. London-Beijing and Hong Kong-London) tickets tend to be pricier. Patching one-way flights together is the most expensive way to travel. Flights between China's regional hubs—Beijing, Shanghai, and Hong Kong—will tend to be cheap.

If China is only one stop on a more extensive globe-hop, consider a round-the-world (RTW) ticket. Tickets usually include at least 5 stops and are valid for about a year; prices range US$1200-5000. Try **Northwest Airlines/KLM** (US ☎800-447-4747; www.nwa.com) or **Star Alliance,** a consortium of 14 airlines including United Airlines (US ☎800-241-6522; www.star-alliance.com).

In the summer, fares for round-trip flights to Beijing, Shanghai, or Hong Kong from the US or Canadian east coast start at US$800-1400; from the US or Canadian west coast US$600-1600; from the UK UK£450-800; from Australia or New Zealand AUS$1000-1500. Fares are generally US$100-300 less expensive in the off-season.

BUDGET & STUDENT TRAVEL AGENCIES

Unlike many international destinations, the cheapest tickets to China are usually not offered by conventional student or budget travel agencies (i.e. Council Travel or STA), but by smaller Chinatown agencies that cater mainly to overseas Chinese. These agencies are often able to find prices as much as 20-30% lower than other budget travel agencies. We highly recommend scouring the

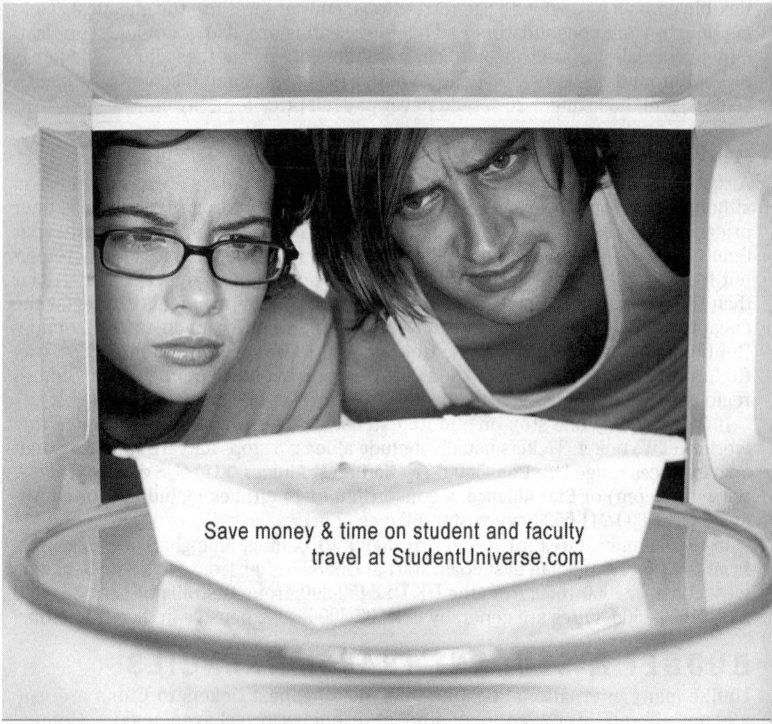

phone book for travel agencies in your local Chinatown or picking up a copy of a local Chinese newspaper and flipping to the travel advertisements page to find an agency near you.

When this option is unfeasible, budget travel agencies are your best bet. Knowledgeable agents specializing in flights to China and Asia can make your life easy and help you save, even if they may not spend the time to find you the lowest possible fare in order to maximize their commissions. Travelers holding **ISIC and IYTC cards** (see p. 53) qualify for big discounts from student travel agencies. Most flights from budget agencies are on major airlines, but in peak season some may sell seats on less reliable chartered aircraft.

usit world (www.usitworld.com). Over 50 usit campus branches in the UK, including 52 Grosvenor Gardens, **London** SW1W 0AG (☎0870 240 10 10); **Manchester** (☎0161 273 1880); and **Edinburgh** (☎0131 668 3303). Nearly 20 **usit NOW** offices in Ireland, including 19-21 Aston Quay, O'Connell Bridge, **Dublin** 2 (☎01 602 1600; www.usitnow.ie), and **Belfast** (☎02 890 327 111; www.usitnow.com). Offices also in Athens, Auckland, Brussels, Frankfurt, Johannesburg, Lisbon, Luxembourg, Madrid, Paris, Sofia, and Warsaw.

Council Travel (www.counciltravel.com). Countless US offices, including branches in Atlanta, Boston, Chicago, L.A., New York, San Francisco, Seattle, and Washington, D.C. Check the website or call 800-2-COUNCIL (226-8624) for the office nearest you. Also an office at 28A Poland St. (Oxford Circus), **London,** W1V 3DB, UK (020 7437 7767).

CTS Travel, 44 Goodge St., **London** W1T 2AD, UK (☎020 7636 0031; fax 0207 637 5328; ctsinfo@ctstravel.co.uk).

STA Travel, 7890 S. Hardy Dr., Ste. 110, Tempe AZ 85284, USA (24hr. reservations and info ☎800-781-4040; www.sta-travel.com). A student and youth travel organization with over 150 offices worldwide (check their website for a listing of all their offices), including US offices in Boston, Chicago, L.A., New York, San Francisco, Seattle, and Washington, D.C. Ticket booking, travel insurance, railpasses, and more. In the UK, walk-in office 11 Goodge St., **London** W1T 2PF or call 020 7436 7779. In New Zealand, Shop 2B, 182 Queen St., **Auckland** (☎09 309 0458). In Australia, 366 Lygon St., **Carlton,** VIC 3053, a suburb of Melbourne (03 9349 4344).

Travel CUTS (Canadian Universities Travel Services Limited), 187 College St., **Toronto,** ON M5T 1P7 (☎416-979-2406; fax 979-8167; www.travelcuts.com). 60 offices across Canada. Also in the UK, 295-A Regent St., **London** W1R 7YA (☎020 7255 1944).

FLIGHT PLANNING ON THE INTERNET. The Web is a great place to look for travel bargains–it's fast, it's convenient, and you can spend as long as you like exploring options without driving your travel agent insane. Many airline sites offer special last-minute deals on the Web. Try Air China: www.airchina.com.cn; China Eastern: www.chinaeasternair.com; Cathay Pacific: www.cathaypacific.com; Korean Air: www.koreanair.com; All Nippon Airways: www.ana.co.jp; Asiana Airlines: www.asiana.co.kr. **STA** (www.sta-travel.com) and **Council** (www.counciltravel.com) provide quotes on student tickets, while **Expedia** (http://msn.expedia.com) and **Travelocity** (www.travelocity.com) offer full travel services. **Priceline** (www.priceline.com) allows you to specify a price, and obligates you to buy any ticket that meets or beats it; expect odd hours and routes.

COMMERCIAL AIRLINES

As more and more airlines fly to China, travelers have an increasingly large number of carriers to choose from. The cheapest are often Korean Air, Air China, and China Eastern Airlines. Canadian Airlines, Cathay Pacific, All Nippon Airways, and Asiana Airlines also offer ultra-competitive fares with good service, although some flights may involve overnight stays or lengthy layovers in Tokyo or Seoul.

The commercial airlines' lowest regular offer is the **APEX** (Advance Purchase Excursion) fare, which provides confirmed reservations and allows "open-jaw" tickets. Generally, reservations must be made seven to 21 days ahead of departure, with seven- to 14-day minimum-stay and up to 90-day maximum-stay restrictions. These fares carry hefty cancellation and change penalties (fees rise in summer). Book peak-season APEX fares early; by May you will have a hard time getting your desired departure date.

AIR COURIER FLIGHTS

Those who travel light should consider courier flights. Couriers help transport cargo on international flights by using their checked luggage space for freight. Generally, couriers must travel with carry-ons only and must deal with complex flight restrictions. Most flights are round-trip only, with short fixed-length stays (usually one week) and a limit of one ticket per issue. Most of these flights also operate only out of major gateway cities, mostly in North America. Round-trip courier fares from the US to China run about US$300-500 and usually go to Hong Kong, though tickets to Beijing and Shanghai are sometimes available. Most flights leave from New York, Los Angeles, San Francisco, or Miami in the US; and from Montreal, Toronto, or Vancouver in Canada. Generally, you must be over 21 (in some cases 18). In summer, the most popular destinations usually require an advance reservation of about two weeks (you can usually book up to two months ahead). Super-discounted fares are common for "last-minute" flights (three to 14 days ahead).

Groups such as the **Air Courier Association,** USA (☎800-282-1202; www.aircourier.org) and the **International Association of Air Travel Couriers,** 220 South Dixie Hwy., P.O. Box 1349, Lake Worth, FL 33460 (☎561-582-8320; iaatc@courier.org; www.courier.org) provide members with lists of opportunities and courier brokers worldwide for an annual fee. **Micom America,** US (☎718-656-6050) has daily courier flights to Hong Kong and allows travelers to stay up to 30 days. For more information, consult *Air Courier Bargains* by Kelly Monaghan (The Intrepid Traveler, US$15) or the *Courier Air Travel Handbook* by Mark Field (Perpetual Press, US$10).

STANDBY FLIGHTS

Traveling standby requires considerable flexibility in arrival and departure dates and cities. Companies dealing in standby flights sell vouchers rather than tickets, along with the promise to get you to your destination (or near your destination) within a certain window of time (typically 1-5 days). You call in before your specific window of time to hear your flight options and the probability that you will be able to board each flight. You can then decide which flights you want to try to make, show up at the appropriate airport at the appropriate time, present your voucher, and board if space is available. Vouchers can usually be bought for both one-way and round-trip travel. You may receive a monetary refund only if every available flight within your date range is full; if you opt not to take an available (but perhaps less convenient) flight, you can only get credit toward future travel. Carefully read agreements with any company offering standby flights as tricky fine print can leave you in the lurch. To check on a company's service record in the US, call the Better

Business Bureau (☎212-533-6200). It is difficult to receive refunds and clients' vouchers will not be honored when an airline fails to receive payment in time.

TICKET CONSOLIDATORS

Ticket consolidators, or **"bucket shops,"** buy unsold tickets in bulk from commercial airlines and sell them at discounted rates. The best place to look is in the Sunday travel section of any major newspaper (such as the *New York Times*), where many bucket shops place tiny ads. Call quickly, as availability is typically extremely limited. Not all bucket shops are reliable, so insist on a receipt that gives full details of restrictions, refunds, and tickets, and pay by credit card (in spite of the 2-5% fee) so you can stop payment if you never receive your tickets. For more info, see www.travel-library.com/air-travel/consolidators.html.

TRAVELING FROM THE US & CANADA

Travel Avenue (☎800-333-3335; www.travelavenue.com) searches for the best available published fares and then uses several consolidators to attempt to beat that fare. Other consolidators worth trying are Interworld (☎305-443-4929; fax 443-0351); **Pennsylvania Travel** (☎800-331-0947); **Rebel** (☎800-227-3235; travel@rebeltours.com; www.rebeltours.com); **Cheap Tickets** (☎800-377-1000; www.cheaptickets.com); and **Travac** (☎800-872-8800; fax 212-714-9063; www.travac.com). Yet more consolidators on the web include the **Internet Travel Network** (www.itn.com); **Travel Information Services** (www.tiss.com); **TravelHUB** (www.travelhub.com); and **The Travel Site** (www.thetravelsite.com). Keep in mind that these are just suggestions to get you started; *Let's Go* does not endorse any of these agencies. As always, be cautious and research companies before you hand over your credit card number.

TRAVELING FROM THE UK, AUSTRALIA, & NEW ZEALAND

In London, the **Air Travel Advisory Bureau** (☎020 7636 5000; www.atab.co.uk) can provide names of reliable consolidators and discount flight specialists. **From Australia and New Zealand,** look for consolidator ads in the travel section of the *Sydney Morning Herald* and other papers.

CHARTER FLIGHTS

Charters are flights a tour operator contracts with an airline to fly extra loads of passengers during peak season. Charter flights fly less frequently than major airlines, make refunds particularly difficult, and are almost always fully booked. Schedules and itineraries may also change or be cancelled at the last moment (as late as 48 hours before the trip and without a full refund) and check-in, boarding, and baggage claim are often much slower. However, they can also be cheaper.

Discount clubs and **fare brokers** offer members savings on last-minute charter and tour deals. Study contracts closely; you don't want to end up with an unwanted overnight layover.

FROM RUSSIA, WITH LOVE

TRANS-SIBERIAN RAILROAD

The term Trans-Siberian Railroad is generally misused to refer to three different rail lines. The real Trans-Siberian line runs from Moscow to Vladivostok, con-

ESSENTIALS

necting the gilded domes and tinted windshields of Moscow with the rest of her proud but crumbling empire. The two lines that are of interest to the traveler in China are the Trans-Mongolian and the Trans-Manchurian. The **Trans-Mongolian** runs from Beijing through Mongolia to Moscow; the **Trans-Manchurian** runs north from Beijing, crossing the Chinese-Russian border at Manzhouli in Inner Mongolia before going straight to Moscow. The trip takes five or six days depending on the route (the Trans-Mongolian is the shorter of the two). Regardless of which route you take, the train rolls through two continents, seven time zones, and thousands of miles of flat land.

TRANS-MONGOLIAN RAILROAD

FROM	DEPARTS	TO	ARRIVES	VIA	PRICE (Y)
Beijing	W 7:40am	**Moscow**	M 2:10pm (Moscow time)	**Ulaan Batar** (arrives Th 2:10pm; Y925-950)	Y2700-3000
Moscow	T 11:42pm (Moscow time)	**Beijing**	M 3:33pm	**Ulaan Batar** (arrives Su 8:15am)	Y2700-3000

TICKETS. Tickets for the Trans-Mongolian can be obtained from **CITS** in Beijing, which allows travelers to reserve tickets in advance with a Y100 deposit. **Tianhua International Travel Service** (see p. 122) in the Jinghua Hotel in Beijing also helps arrange tickets and visas. In Hong Kong, the helpful **Moonsky Star Travel Agency** (see p. 531) offers an assortment of special packages and can help obtain Russian and Mongolian visas.

VISAS. Because the Trans-Mongolian cuts through Ulaan Bataar, both a Mongolian visa and a Russian visa are necessary to travel this route. You can obtain a Mongolian visa at the border (single entry US$40, express US$60; double US$60/US$80). Both Mongolian and Russian visas are available from the Mongolian consulate (see p. 49) in Beijing or can be obtained with the help of travel agencies mentioned above. Visitors can either get transit visas (good for 2 days) or tourist visas (90 days). The transit visa requires that the applicant hold an onward ticket and a visa for their next destination, so you will have to get a Russian visa before you can get a Mongolian visa. CITS gives travelers ticket vouchers to obtain the required visas.

TRANS-MANCHURIAN RAILROAD

TICKETS. Tickets for the Trans-Manchurian (route #19) are obtained in the same places and in the same manner as for the Trans-Mongolian (see above). Only the **CITS** head office in the Beijing International Hotel (see p. 122) books tickets.

FROM	DEPARTS	TO	ARRIVES	VIA	PRICE (Y)
Beijing	Sa 11:10pm	**Moscow**	F 7:50pm (Moscow time)	**Manzhouli** (arrives M 4:54am)	Y2700-3000
Moscow	F 8:25pm (Moscow time)	**Beijing**	F 5:30am	**Manzhouli** (arrives W 7:30pm)	Y2700-3000

VISAS. A trip on the Trans-Manchurian line only requires passengers to obtain either a Russian transit visa or tourist visa, but getting your hand on either of these documents requires quite a bit of organization. The transit visa is only valid for 10 days. Since the train ride takes about six, there is very little time to get off the train, especially since you will have to leave time to go from Moscow to your next destination. It is wise to arrange transportation out of Moscow in

ESSENTIALS

advance. To obtain a transit visa, you must already have a train ticket and a visa for your next destination in hand. The tourist visa lasts much longer but is a major hassle to obtain. You must present tourist confirmations from hotels you will be staying in during your journey, which means that you will have to have planned your itinerary in advance. Furthermore, you must stay in hotels that are registered with the Russian Ministry of Foreign Affairs, which tend to be expensive. Russian visas can be obtained with the help of the same travel agencies that book tickets, though it's cheaper to obtain visas from the Russian embassy in Beijing (see p. 49).

LIFE ABOARD THE TRAINS. Food in dining cars (as well as that sold by locals) is priced according to local currency, so bringing Russian rubles as well as Chinese *yuán* will prove useful. Bringing US dollars is more convenient, since dollars are more easily exchanged at border crossings. Many travelers also opt to bring their own snacks. Instant noodles are a good idea, since hot water is available.

Try to avoid the first or last compartment in the car because these are next to the toilets, and on trains which don't have attendants, the stench can become unbearable. And, as always, remember to bring your own toilet paper.

INTO SIBERIA. Rail routes connect cities in Heilongjiang province with Russian cities. Visas cannot be obtained at the border and since getting a Russian visa is even more difficult than getting a Chinese visa, it's best to deal with visas in Beijing. Train #607 departs Harbin Main Station and branches off to Khabarovsk and Vladivostok. The return trains (#608) meet up, heading to Harbin together.

ROUTE	FROM	DEPARTS	TO	ARRIVES	PRICE (Y)
#607	**Harbin**	W, Sa 8:10pm	**Khabarovsk**	F, M 6am	Y172-309
			Vladivostok	Th, Su 11:11pm	Y106-197
#608	**Khabarovsk**	M, Th 11:20am	**Harbin**	W, Sa 6:50am	same as above
	Vladivostok	M, Th 4:40pm			

A SLOW BOAT TO CHINA

While travel by ship may hold romantic appeal for those who like to imagine themselves pulling into ports-of-call with boatloads of silk or spices, the reality today is that international boat travel is too expensive and time-consuming to be worthwhile except between China and its near neighbors across the East China Sea.

FROM AUSTRALIA AND NEW ZEALAND. A freighter cruise is the best option; these boats generally have only a few cabins for passenger travel, so be sure to book in advance. Travel from Australia or Oceania to China generally costs US$50 a day. For more information, check www.freighter-cruises.com.

FROM SOUTH KOREA. Many coastal cities have international ferry terminals with boats arriving from Inchon, particularly Dalian (see p. 239), Tianjin's port of Tanggu (see p. 161), and Qingdao (see p. 189). Citizens of Australia, Canada, South Africa, the US, most Western European countries, and New Zealand can stay in South Korea visa-free for 30 days.

FROM JAPAN. Ferries head from Japan to several cities in China, including Tanggu (see p. 161), Qingdao (see p. 189), and Shanghai (see p. 313). High-priced cruise lines offer trips from Osaka to Hong Kong or Beijing. Citizens of North America, Western Europe, and Oceanic countries can stay visa-free for 90 days.

BORDER CROSSINGS

In general, odd-numbered international trains depart from China, and even-numbered trains arrive in China. International train tickets are usually sold at **China International Travel Service (CITS)** or other travel agencies, not at train stations.

SOUTHEAST ASIA

LAOS. The border crossing between China and Laos is located at the town of **Mohan** in the Xishuangbanna region of Yunnan province (see p. 642), which is accessible only by buses or minibuses. Laos visas are not issued at the border; they must be obtained in Beijing or at the Lao consulate in Kunming (see p. 595). For more information, see **Border Crossing into Laos: Mohan,** p. 642.

MYANMAR (BURMA). From **Ruili,** minibuses go to **Jiegao,** where the border between China and Myanmar has recently opened. You must obtain a visa from a consulate (try the Burmese Consulate in Kunming, p. 595), since border guards don't issue them. For more information, see **Border Crossing into Myanmar,** p. 631.

VIETNAM. Most travelers cross between Vietnam and China via one of two border posts: **Pingxiang** in Guangxi province or **Hekou** in Yunnan province (for more information, see **Border Crossing into Vietnam: Hekou,** p. 603). The crossing at Pingxiang can be reached via train or bus from Nanning (see p. 574). The crossing at Hekou can be reached via train from Kunming (see p. 591). Also, train T5 goes from Beijing West Station to Hanoi. Visas cannot be obtained at either crossing. The cheapest and safest plan is to take care of Vietnamese visas in Beijing or Hong Kong (see p. 47). Chinese visas can be obtained at the Chinese embassies in Hanoi and Bangkok.

FROM	DEPARTS	TO	ARRIVES	VIA
Kunming	F, Su 4pm	**Hanoi**	Sa, M 8:15pm (Hanoi time)	**Hekou** (arrives Sa, M 6:15am)
Beijing (West Station)	M, F 10:51am	**Hanoi**	W, Su 11:30am (Hanoi time)	**Nanning** (arrives T, Sa 5:22pm, departs 8:20pm)
Hanoi	T, F 2pm (Hanoi time)	**Beijing (West Station)**	Th, Su 5:18pm	**Nanning** (arrives W, Sa 8:43am, departs at 11:02)

THE 'STANS

KAZAKHSTAN. Kazakh visas can be obtained at the embassy in Beijing.

ROUTE	FROM	DEPARTS	TO	ARRIVES	PRICE (Y)
#895	**Ürümqi**	M, Sa 9:30am	**Almaty**	W, Su 10:45am (Moscow time)	Y96-192
#896	**Almaty**	M, Sa 8:30pm (Moscow time)	**Ürümqi**	W, M 7:08am	Y96-192

PAKISTAN. Buses leave from the the Kashgar International Bus Station (see p. 777) for Sost, Pakistan, via Tashkurgan and the Khunjerab Pass (16hr. plus overnight stay in Tashkurgan, daily in summer only, Y270). Visas are required and are not issued at the border; the Pakistani embassy in Beijing (see p. 49) is the nearest source of Pakistani visas (see p. 783).

KYRGYZSTAN. Buses also leave from the Kashgar International Bus Station (see p. 777) for Bishkek, Kyrgyzstan via the Torugut Pass (16hr., M, US$50). To take this bus, you'll have to obtain a transit permit (pīzhào; 批照) beforehand. However, only travel agencies can issue these permits; they often require travelers to take a tour, but if you ask you may be able to purchase a permit separately (Y300-350 for groups of 2-5). John's Information Cafe (see p. 778) in Kashgar can also arrange permits and tours to Bishkek. Travelers to Kyrgyzstan must also obtain valid entry visas, which are only available in Beijing or Hong Kong (see p. 49).

MONGOLIA

Travelers who want to visit Mongolia must have either a transit visa or a tourist visa (see p. 89). Several **trains** go from China to Mongolia each week. In addition to the Trans-Mongolian train to Russia (see p. 89), train #23 goes from Beijing to **Ulaan Bataar.** Tickets can be purchased in Beijing at CITS (see p. 122) or the Tianhua Travel Agency (see p. 122). Train #4602/4603 and #4604/4601 travel between Hohhot and Ulaan Bataar and cross the border at **Erinhot.** You can also take a **plane** to Ulaan Bataar from **Beijing** (2hr.; M,W, Sa-Su) or **Hohhot** (1½hr.; M and Th).

ROUTE	FROM	DEPARTS	TO	ARRIVES	PRICE (Y)
#23	**Beijing**	T 7:40am	**Ulaan Bataar**	W 1:10pm (Ulaan Bataar time)	Y560
#4602/ 4603	**Hohhot**	W, Su 10:50pm	**Ulaan Bataar**	F, Tu 11:05am (Ulaan Bataar time)	Y154-281
#4604/ 4601	**Ulaan Bataar**	W, Su 9:15am (Ulaan Bataar time)	**Hohhot**	Th, M 8:15pm	Y154-281

NEPAL

The **Friendship Highway** runs from from Lhasa, in Tibet, to Kathmandu, crossing the border at **Zhangmu/Kodari.** Visitors travel in both directions, but in terms of visas and logistics, it's much easier to go from Tibet to Nepal than the other way around. Nepali visas are required and can be obtained at the border crossing for US$30, although it is far more convenient to get one at the Nepali consulate in Lhasa (see p. 804 and p. 831).

NORTH KOREA

Views of North Korea from Changbaishan (see p. 228) or from across the Yalu River in Dandong (see p. 237) may be the closest you'll come to this isolated country. Generally, only organized tourist groups authorized by the North Korean government are permitted into the country. One such tourist group is **Koryo Tours** (☎/fax (010) 6418 1722; northkorea8@hotmail.com; www.koryogroup.com), which has been run by Nicholas Bonner (mobile (136) 2109 9277; nicholasbonner@cs.com) since 1993. Independent tourism is extremely limited, and US or South Korean citizens absolutely cannot obtain visas. Contact the North Korean embassy in Beijing (see p. 49) for more information.

GETTING AROUND CHINA

BY PLANE

An enormous country, China has enough geographical barriers and unbearably long bus and train rides for even the stingiest of travelers to consider domestic air

ESSENTIALS

travel. While the cost of flying is two to five times the price of a hard sleeper, air travel saves precious time and energy for you to enjoy your destination more fully. Air travel is also more convenient, thanks to the Chinese government, which has embarked on a vigorous expansion program, especially in the Northwest. The new terminal at Beijing Capital Airport, Shanghai's Pudong Airport, and Hong Kong's Chep Lap Kok all have made air travel easier as well. Nearly all domestic flights are less than three hours in duration; *Let's Go* provides frequencies and approximate prices in Practical Information or Transportation sections for available destinations. Domestic airline schedules are revised in April and October.

DOMESTIC AIRLINES. The domestic airline industry is overseen by the state-run monopoly of the **Civil Aviation Administration of China** or **CAAC** (zhōngguó rénmín hángkōng; 中国人民航空). Long infamous for its suspect safety record, unsatisfactory service, and mismanagement, the CAAC has begun a massive reform program, buying new aircrafts and safety equipment, training air traffic controllers abroad, and improving its organization. Perhaps its boldest move yet has been to decentralize the industry by forming semi-independent regional airlines that will eventually assume complete autonomy. The six largest are:

Air China (CA), US and Canada ☎800-986-1985; San Francisco ☎415-392-2162, fax 392-6214; London ☎(020) 7630 0919; Sydney ☎(02) 9232 7277; Beijing ☎(010) 6601 7755, www.airchina.com.cn. The flagship of the CAAC services mainly international routes, as well as a few domestic destinations.

China Eastern Airlines (MU), US and Canada ☎800-200-5118; Los Angeles ☎626-583-1500; San Francisco ☎415-982-5115; Sydney ☎(02) 9290 1148; Shanghai international reservations ☎(021) 6247 2255, domestic reservations ☎(021) 6247

5953, www.cea.online.sh.cn. Centered in Shanghai, with daily flights to Los Angeles from Beijing and Shanghai.

China Southern Airlines (CZ), US and Canada ☎888-338-8988; Hong Kong ☎(852) 2973 3733; Guangzhou ☎(020) 8666 1907, www.cs-air.com. Based in Guangzhou, with flights to Europe, Japan, and Southeast Asia.

China Northwest Airlines (WH), Xi'an ☎(029) 831 4452, http://china-window.com/Shaanxi_w/brief/cnwair/main.htm. Flies to over 50 cities, both in China and abroad. Based primarily in Gansu and Shaanxi provinces, it dominates Xi'an and Lanzhou.

China Southwest Airlines (SZ), Chengdu ☎(028) 666 8080, www.cswa.com. Centered in Chengdu and Chongqing. Administers most domestic flights to Tibet.

China Northern Airlines (CJ), Shenyang ☎(024) 2319 7188, www.cna.ln.cninfo.net. Hubs in Shenyang, Changchun, and Harbin.

Major regional airlines include: Great Wall (G8), Shanghai (FM), Shenzhen (4G), Sichuan (3U), Xiamen (MF), Xinjiang (XO), Yunnan (3Q), Zhejiang (F6), and Zhongyuan (Z2). **Dragon Air (KA),** a non-CAAC domestic carrier, operates out of Hong Kong.

ESSENTIALS

AIRCRAFT SAFETY. Flying in China is safer than it used to be, but crashes are still far more frequent than in more developed nations. When booking a domestic flight, be sure to inquire what type of aircraft is flying your route, as the CAAC fleet is a grab bag of some of the world's most advanced and most ancient planes. While flights in and out of more traveled regions utilize modern aircraft, flights in border regions (especially the Southwest and Northwest) often employ older, Russian-built aircraft, such as the accident-prone Tupolev 154s (Tu5) or Ilyusin 86 (YLW). The *Official Airline Guide* (www.oag.com) and many travel agencies can also tell you the type and age of aircraft on a particular route.

For more information about region-specific safety, contact the **International Airline Passengers Association** (US ☎800-821-4272, UK ☎020 8681 6555). The **Federal Aviation Administration** (www.faa.gov) reviews the airline authorities for countries whose airlines enter the US. **US State Department** travel advisories (☎202-647-5225; travel.state.gov/travel_warnings.html) sometimes involve foreign carriers, especially when terrorist bombings may be a threat.

BUYING DOMESTIC AIR TICKETS. Standard rates are fixed between cities (i.e. Beijing to Shanghai costs the same as Shanghai to Beijing). The round-trip price is always simply twice the one-way price. Prices for foreigners and Chinese are the same. Children over the age of 12 must pay the adult fare, those between the ages of 2 and 12 pay half-price, and those under the age of 2 pay 10% of the adult fare.

While it is possible to purchase a limited selection of domestic airline tickets from travel agencies abroad, most travelers find it simpler to buy them in China. Most airports have airline ticket offices that sell tickets for domestic flights on any carrier. Although availability varies depending on the route, many travelers report no problems walking in and buying a ticket for the next departure. Note that it may be more difficult to obtain tickets during Chinese New Year and for some flights in the Northwest, Southwest, and to major tourist destinations. If you purchase return or connecting tickets, be sure to reconfirm your reservation more than two days before departure; otherwise, your ticket may be cancelled.

AIRPORT PROCEDURES. CAAC instructs its passengers to arrive at the airport at least 90 minutes before departure time; check-in stops 30 minutes before departure. Be prepared for a possible headache at the baggage claim, as most older and under-equipped Chinese airports have several arriving flights sharing one baggage claim. Lost baggage is compensated at no more than Y50 per kg weighed at check-in, and the maximum compensation for checked baggage is Y8000 (US$900).

CHANGES AND REFUNDS. Travelers wishing to modify the departure time, date, or class of a ticket may do so only once, and must do so more than 24hr. before departure. If the new flight is also offered by the same carrier, than the transaction is straightforward. But if the new flight is aboard a different airline under the CAAC umbrella, then the passenger must buy a new ticket and cancel the old ticket at the airline office of the old ticket. Refunds requested less than 24hr. before departure are subjected to a 10% cancellation fee; if less than 2hr., the fee is 20%. No-shows are entitled to only 50% of the original ticket value.

BY TRAIN

Unless you are planning to stay in one city for the duration of your trip to China, you'll certainly have an opportunity to tango with China's extensive train system, which covers every part of China except Tibet. The convenience, speed, and relative comfort of train travel have made it so popular, though, that tickets can occasionally be hard to come by. Some travelers buy a ticket for their next destination as soon as they can; unfortunately, in some cities, same-day tickets are as early as they get. If you are having real trouble acquiring a ticket, most upscale hotels and travel agents can help with travel arrangements for a fee (generally Y10-50). Paper **train schedules** (shíkèbiâo; 时刻表) are available at most major stations for about Y1 and up. The **Chinese Ministry of Railways** also offers comprehensive information on schedules and regulations (www.chinamor.cn.net). Most schedules, printed or online, are only in Chinese; still, with some patience and reference to the characters for city names, anyone can decipher them. A "K" in front of the number means that train is an express (kuài; 快) and will make fewer stops, while a "Y" indicates that the train is a double-decker tourist (læyóu; 旅游) or travel class train. For a helpful guide to deciphering train tickets, see the **Appendix,** p. 832.

Once you have a ticket, you'll need to show it to access the track area; keep in mind that at the larger stations, there will be many tracks and multiple trains boarding at once and that gates are generally closed about 3 minutes before the train is due to leave. Hold onto your ticket, as attendants at many stations scrutinize your ticket again before allowing you to exit the station.

BY BUS

China's long-distance bus system has several advantages. It goes virtually everywhere, tickets are almost always easier to purchase than train tickets, and they are often cheaper. On the other hand, unpredictable road conditions, poorly maintained vehicles, and unreliable drivers can conspire to make bus trips long, uncomfortable, and even dangerous. It is not uncommon for roads, particularly in the Northwest and Southwest, to be washed out or otherwise impassable for weeks or months at a time.

Virtually every city or town has a **long-distance bus station** (chángtú qìchë zhàn; 长涂汽车站) or designated location at which buses can drop off and pick up passengers. **Tickets** are sold at the station itself and need not be booked in advance. A number of routes are traversed by both rickety, old Chinese buses and newer, relatively posh, foreign buses (for which tickets are more expensive). It is generally a good idea to look at the bus in which you will be riding before you buy your ticket;

THE LONG RIDE
China Through the Train Window

Few travelers recount their time in China without waxing poetic about the train rides. The tight quarters become the social space for a sampling of Chinese middle-class society. Laptops and Palm Pilots are rare sights; instead, the passengers are forced into close interaction. The train becomes a test tube where the commonalties and schisms of national politics and culture come to the forefront.

Riding the train from Beijing to Urumqi (the capital of the Xinjiang Uygur Autonomous Region), I traveled China's length. In 48 hours, we saw a near-total transformation. The crowded east-coast cities gave way to rice paddies and farmland on the first day. The second day, we arose to the view of a vast rocky desert. The following morning, we finally reached the oasis metropolis of Urumqi.

I say "we" because China stubbornly holds on to travel as a collective experience. Contact between passengers was sparse during the first 12 hours of the train ride, with only brief communication to resolve issues of physical space. But the Chinese have a way of overhearing, staring, and interjecting into others' conversations that Americans might find rude. In time, however, these customs created moments of community with cross-generational discussions that one finds lacking in American life. It was not long before our living area had become a forum for debating all kinds of national issues, intertwined with loud games of Chinese poker.

Conversational topics included politics, the educational system, my Chinese name, the differences between local and "foreigner" culture, and the recent (but very limited) phenomenon of open homosexuality. During a discussion, the group would often split into two camps. There were the loud types, who loved to argue and to lead discussion, and then there were the quiet types, generally the elderly, who would participate with long, friendly smiles and affirmative nods.

It so happened that on this train ride, we were a week away from the International Olympic Committee's decision on the site of the 2008 Summer Games. A level of excitement filled China unlike anything I have ever seen in the Unitesd States. Amidst millions of T-shirts and daily news flashes, the train ride was the only time I heard skeptical opinions regarding the Beijing Olympics. I was reading a book when a medical student and recent addition to our group called on me by a joke name: "Mistah Leeee! What do you think of the Olympics?" I said I thought that people were perhaps making too big a deal of it, and asked him his opinion. He then began to describe the phenomenon of *Luan shufei*. According to him, *Luan shufei*, or "forced donations," is one of the largest problems in China. Whether the government is building a school, a road, or Olympic buildings thousands of miles away, *Luan shufei* takes effect. Premier Zhu Rongji has publicly criticized the practice. However, he described it as *daode*, a moral problem, rather than a political one. Some of my conversational companions stressed the need for *falu*, law and order, to end corruption in China. However, as the medical student described, "According to the Confucian tradition, to make politicians operate by law would be to claim that they are immoral, and that would be disgraceful." Confucian philosophy maintains that the country should be governed by virtuous, paternalistic leaders. In turn, subjects should trust and obey officials. Thus, immorality can be self-perpetuating. The result has arguably been rampant corruption, which has pervaded much of Chinese history (yet we must not forget that this is also the history of the world's longest-lasting civilization).

Our train pushed on into the evening. It was soon 10 p.m.; lights out and music off. Conversation petered out, and everyone was soon asleep except for me and a businessman named Mr. Liu, who was brushing his teeth. Unbuttoning my shirt, I remarked on how much I love Beijing night culture: "Everyone hangs out on the street and relaxes together. The men, out there with their shirts off, drinking bottles of beer to stifle the summer heat.

"Ah yes, but we can't do that right now," he said jokingly. "Nowadays, what would people think!" I took my shirt off anyway and lay down. We both laughed, staring up at the ceiling, then drifted off into sleep.

Josh Levin is a Harvard graduate and Let's Go veteran. This article appeared previously in the Harvard International Review (February,2001).

IS THIS SEAT TAKEN? Chinese trains have four classes, and depending on how much you are willing to pay, you can travel in any position—from squatting to sitting to supine to spitting.

Hard seat (yìng zuò; 硬座): Hard seat is the cheapest and most popular class. Generally, a hard seat ticket entitles the bearer only to a *space* on the train—the seat part is often optional, since many trains are overbooked. Moreover, crowded cars, clouds of cigarette smoke, and blaring loudspeakers also help to make the trip a less-than-soothing experience. Some of the more popular routes have new, more comfortable trains; hard seat perks include A/C, cleaner bathrooms, seat assignments, and, ironically, well-cushioned seats.

Soft seat (ruân zuò; 软座): Soft seat cars exist only on certain routes, usually short trips between major cities. The soft seat section is similar to the passenger sections of many Western trains; that is, considerably more comfortable than the hard seat. Passengers are assigned seats, cars generally have A/C, and smoking is (allegedly) prohibited.

Hard sleeper (yìng wò; 硬卧): Hard sleeper cars consist of several doorless sleeping compartments off a main aisle. Each compartment has room for six people with three bunks on each side; sheets, blankets, and pillows are provided. The choice of bunk is a difficult one: in the summer, the claustrophia-inducing top bunk (shàng; 上) can be too hot, too cold, or too loud; the middle bunk (zhõng; 中) is only slightly removed from the hubbub below; the bottom bunk (xìa; 下) inevitably becomes the communal bench during the day. Bunk assignments are printed on the ticket and it is possible to make requests at the ticket window (ticket prices rise with bunk elevation). Once on board, the attendant exchanges your paper ticket with a metal or plastic piece. Be sure to retreive your ticket from the attendant before you disembark.

Soft sleeper (ruân wò; 软卧): Soft sleeper passengers ride as close to the lap of luxury as is possible on a Chinese train. Compartments are less cramped and more comfortable, with four well-padded bunks, a door, wall-to-wall carpeting, and curtains on the windows. For travelers faced with the unpleasant possibility of a night (or two or three) in hard seat because of sold-out hard sleeper cars, soft sleeper may provide a possible, albeit pricey, solution. Soft sleepers may cost nearly as much as airplane tickets.

a few travelers report having been charged the price for a trip on a higher-quality bus only to find themselves on a rattling, run-down vehicle. On overnight trips, more expensive **sleeper buses** with a semi-reclining bunk for each traveler now ply many routes. **Minibuses** run shorter routes, particularly between large, neighboring cities, and pick up passengers in front of train or bus stations or along major thoroughfares. Typically, you pay for your ticket once onboard the minibus, which leaves when full and stops when the driver feels like it.

Be sure to prepare yourself well for any long trip by bus; trips often take longer than anticipated. For travel in cold or high-altitude areas, even in summer, bring plenty of **warm clothing;** buses are all too frequently not equipped with working heaters, and mechanical breakdowns in remote areas can prove deadly for those not properly prepared (see **Environmental Hazards,** p. 64). It is also a good idea to bring enough **food and water** for the trip, since stops may be few and far between.

BY CAR

What are you, nuts? Most travelers to China wisely never get behind the wheel of an automobile. Foreign tourists are expressly forbidden to drive in and between most Chinese cities, more for their own safety than anything: drivers in China consider traffic laws to be no more than loose suggestions and routinely drive on both sides of the road, run traffic lights, speed, and are generally a menace to society. For local use, cars can be rented in Hong Kong, Macau, Beijing, and Shanghai, but public transportation and taxis will save you a great deal of time and worry.

If you do plan to drive a car while in China, you must be over 18 and must have either an **International Driving Permit (IDP)** or, sometimes, just a current driver's license from your home country. In mainland China, you drive on the right, while in Hong Kong and Macau you drive on the left. It may be a good idea to get an IDP anyway, in case you're in an accident (not at all uncommon in China); information on the IDP is printed in ten languages, including Chinese.

Your IDP, valid for one year, must be issued in your own country before you depart. An application for an IDP usually needs to include one or two photos, a current local license, an additional form of identification, and a fee. To apply, contact the national or local branch of your home country's Automobile Association.

BY THUMB

Let's Go strongly urges you to consider the risks before you choose to hitchhike. Bus travel in China seems to be almost as casual as hitchhiking, with travelers shouting out their destinations to passing minibuses. Some travelers don't see the difference between hitchhiking and taking buses, and some hitchhike to get around, especially in the west and on roads that are closed to foreigners. Remember that getting into a stranger's private car is always risky. You also cannot count on the experience of the driver, which can be especially perilous in areas with bad roads. We do not recommend hitchhiking as a safe means of transportation.

SPECIFIC CONCERNS

Bear in mind that traveling in the world's most populous country requires that most Westerners relax their standards for personal space and privacy. Private space is at a premium in most places, and travelers should expect to be jostled about in crowded buses, trains, and buildings. Many Chinese will not hesitate to read over your shoulder, grab notes and papers and examine them, and ask immediate, personal questions. Try to be open and adaptable, but remember not to disregard behavior that makes you feel threatened or in danger.

WOMEN TRAVELERS

China is one of the safest parts of Asia for women travelers: rape or assault of foreign women in China, although not unheard of, is uncommon. While women exploring on their own inevitably face some additional safety concerns, it's easy to be adventurous without taking undue risks. If you are concerned, consider staying in hostels which offer single rooms that lock from the inside or in religious organizations with rooms for women only. Communal showers in some hostels are safer than others; check them before settling in. Stick to centrally located accommodations and avoid solitary late-night treks or metro rides.

Always carry extra money for a phone call, bus, or taxi. **Hitchhiking** is never safe for lone women, or even for two women traveling together. Choose train compartments occupied by women or couples; ask the conductor to put together a women-only compartment if there isn't one. Look as if you know where you're going and approach older women or couples for directions if you're lost or uncomfortable.

Dress conservatively, especially in less-touristed rural areas and in the Muslim areas of China's northwestern provinces. Some Chinese men assume that foreign women traveling alone are in fact seeking out sexual gratification — the chance to practice English and become "good friends" with a foreign woman can be too much too resist. In general, anyone who asks you to come visit in a hotel and any hotel that doesn't cast a second glance as you head upstairs without proper documentation should be viewed with a certain amount of skepticism. Unwanted late night phone calls are best avoided by unplugging the phone. Also, never open your hotel door to strangers. Wearing a conspicuous **wedding band** may help prevent unwanted overtures. Even the mention of a husband or group of male friends waiting back at the hotel can be enough to deter unwanted male attention and discount your unattached appearance. Some travelers report that pictures of a "husband" or "children" are extremely useful to help document marriage status.

Your best answer to verbal harassment is no answer at all; feigning deafness, sitting motionless, and staring straight ahead at nothing in particular will do a world of good that reactions usually don't achieve. The extremely persistent can sometimes be dissuaded by a firm, loud, and very public "Go away!" or "zǒukāi!" Don't hesitate to seek out a police officer or a passerby if you are being harassed. Memorize the emergency numbers in places you visit and consider carrying a **whistle** or airhorn on your keychain. A self-defense course will not only prepare you for a potential attack, but will also raise your level of awareness of your surroundings as well as your confidence (see **Self Defense,** p. 60). Also be sure you are aware of the health concerns that women face when traveling (see p. 69).

For general information, contact the National Organization for Women (NOW), 733 15th St. NW, Fl. 2, Washington, DC 20005, USA (☎202-628-8669; www.now.org), which has branches across the US that can refer women travelers to rape crisis centers and counseling services.

TRAVELING ALONE

There are many benefits to traveling alone, including independence and greater interaction with locals. On the other hand, any solo traveler is a more vulnerable target of harassment and street theft. Lone travelers need to be well-organized and look confident at all times. Try not to stand out as a tourist, and be especially careful in deserted or very crowded areas. If questioned, never admit that you are traveling alone. Maintain regular contact with someone at home who knows your itinerary. For more tips, pick up *Traveling Solo* by Eleanor Berman (Globe Pequot Press, US$17) or subscribe to **Connecting: Solo Travel Network,** 689 Park Road, Unit 6, Gibsons, BC V0N 1V7, Canada (☎604-886-9099; www.cstn.org; membership US$35).

Alternatively, several services link solo travelers with companions who have similar travel habits and interests; for a bi-monthly newsletter for single travelers seeking a travel partner (subscription US$48), contact the **Travel Companion Exchange,** P.O. Box 833, Amityville, NY 11701, USA (☎631-454-0880 or 800-392-1256 in the US; www.whytravelalone.com; US$48).

OLDER TRAVELERS

Unfortunately, the senior citizen discounts that are so common in North America and Europe are virtually nonexistent in China, and the lack of creature comforts in much of China may make independent travel particularly taxing for senior citizens. However, agencies specializing in senior citizen group travel are growing in enrollment and popularity and can ease the stress of traveling in China. The books *No Problem! Worldwise Tips for Mature Adventurers* by Janice Kenyon (Orca Book Publishers; US$16) and *Unbelievably Good Deals and Great Adventures That You Absolutely Can't Get Unless You're Over 50* by Joan Rattner Heilman (NTC/Contemporary Publishing; US$13) are both excellent resources for those interested in individual travel. For more information on group travel, contact one of the following organizations:

ElderTreks, 597 Markham St., Toronto, ON M6G 2L7, Canada (☎800-741-7956; www.eldertreks.com). Adventure travel programs for the 50+ traveler in Tibet, Yunnan, Xinjiang, and Inner Mongolia.

Elderhostel, 11 Ave. de Lafayette, Boston, MA 02111, USA (☎877-426-8056; www.elderhostel.org). Organizes 1- to 4-week "educational adventures" on varied subjects for those 55+, including trips to Tibet and cruises down the Yangzi.

The Mature Traveler, P.O. Box 15791, Sacramento, CA 95852, USA (☎800-460-6676). Deals, discounts, and travel packages for the 50+ traveler. Subscription $30.

BISEXUAL, GAY, & LESBIAN TRAVELERS

Attitudes regarding sexual orientation vary considerably in China, Hong Kong, and Macau. Some Chinese (both male and female) hold hands with members of the same sex as an expression of friendship, at times making it difficult to distinguish between heterosexual friends and homosexual couples. While heterosexual kissing and other romantic acts are becoming more acceptable in public, similar expressions of homosexuality are not. Nevertheless, many Chinese are tolerant of homosexual behavior as long as it does not interfere with one's responsibility to produce children and raise a family.

The official view of homosexuality is slowly becoming more accepting: in April 2001, homosexuality was removed from the Chinese Psychiatric Association's list of mental disorders. However, the government still continues to regard homosexuality as somewhat of a perversion brought to China by the decadent West, despite historical and literary evidence of its ancient prevalence in Chinese culture. The legal status of homosexuality remains ambiguous, and police persecution of homosexuals and bisexuals is not uncommon. Foreigners need not worry too much, but police raids of gay clubs and meeting places are becoming more frequent, especially in Beijing, Shanghai, Guangzhou, and Hong Kong.

Resources for bisexuals, gays, and lesbians are easier to access from abroad and from select websites than from within China itself. **Utopia,** "the Obi-wan Kenobi of the Asian gay cyber community," has more complete infomation about Chinese attitudes toward homosexuality; the Chinese gay, lesbian, and transgender community; and bars, clubs, and meeting-places around the country. Listed below are contact organizations and mail-order bookstores for more specific concerns. **Out and About** (www.planetout.com) has a bi-weekly newsletter and comprehensive site that address gay travel concerns.

Gay's the Word, 66 Marchmont St., London WC1N 1AB, UK (☎+44 20 7278 7654; www.gaystheword.co.uk). The largest gay and lesbian bookshop in the UK, with both fiction and non-fiction titles. Mail-order service available.

Giovanni's Room, 1145 Pine St., Philadelphia, PA 19107, USA (☎215-923-2960; www.queerbooks.com). An international lesbian/feminist and gay bookstore with mail-order service (carries many of the publications listed below).

FURTHER READING: BISEXUAL, GAY, & LESBIAN

Spartacus International Gay Guide 2001-2002. Bruno Gmunder Verlag (US$33).

Ferrari Guides' Gay Travel A to Z, Ferrari Guides' Men's Travel in Your Pocket, and *Ferrari Guides' Inn Places.* Ferrari Publications (US$16-20). Purchase the guides online at www.ferrariguides.com.

The Gay Vacation Guide: The Best Trips and How to Plan Them, Mark Chesnut. Citadel Press (US$15).

International Lesbian and Gay Association (ILGA), 81 rue Marché-au-Charbon, B-1000 Brussels, Belgium (☎+32 2 502 2471; www.ilga.org). Provides political information, such as homosexuality laws of individual countries.

TRAVELERS WITH DISABILITIES

China, including Hong Kong, is ill-equipped to deal with disabled travelers. Despite the efforts of Deng Pufang (one of the sons of the late Chinese leader Deng Xiaoping) and the China Disabled Persons Federation, physical improvements in disabled access are still slow to be implemented. Attitudes toward disabled Chinese have gradually improved, particularly in larger cities like Beijing, Shanghai, Nanjing, Guangzhou, and Hong Kong. The May 2000 Asian Special Olympics Games in Beijing represented another means of increasing public awareness.

That said, hospitals cannot be relied upon to replace broken braces or prostheses; orthopedic materials, even in large cities, are undependable. Public transportation in mainland China is almost entirely inaccessible. Some buses in Hong Kong now have special wheelchair lifts, but there may be no room to get on and off. Train and long-distance bus stations may have escalators in the main waiting areas, but platform access is almost always via steps. All but the newest airports offer only stairway access to airplanes. While classier hotels often have elevators (which may or may not be wheelchair accessible), most budget accommodations don't. Rural areas have potholed roads and no sidewalks, and larger cities are packed with curbs and steps. Even in areas that are accessible, crowded streets and informal pushing and shoving matches present another potential challenge.

Those with disabilities should inform airlines and hotels of their disabilities when making reservations; some time may be needed to prepare special accommodations. Call ahead to restaurants, museums, and other facilities to find out about the existence of ramps, the widths of doors, the dimensions of elevators, etc. **Guide dog owners** should inquire as to the quarantine policies of each destination country. At the very least, they will need to provide a certificate of immunization against rabies.

USEFUL ORGANIZATIONS

Mobility International USA (MIUSA), P.O. Box 10767, Eugene, OR 97440, USA (☎541-343-1284, voice and TDD; www.miusa.org). Sells *A World of Options: A Guide to International Educational Exchange, Community Service, and Travel for Persons with Disabilities* (US$35).

Society for the Advancement of Travel for the Handicapped (SATH), 347 Fifth Ave., #610, New York, NY 10016, USA (☎212-447-7284; www.sath.org). An advocacy group that publishes free online travel information and the travel magazine *OPEN WORLD* (US$18, free for members). Annual membership US$45, students and seniors US$30.

TOUR AGENCIES

Directions Unlimited, 123 Green Ln., Bedford Hills, NY 10507, USA (☎800-533-5343). Books individual and group vacations for the physically disabled; not an info service.

MINORITY TRAVELERS

Every non-Asian traveler to China will find him- or herself in the minority. People will inevitably point and stare, crowds will gather around you, and you will be trailed by a constant murmur of "*lâowài!*" (foreigner) wherever you go. People will want to practice their English with you or take your picture. Your best strategy is simply to take it all in stride and to go about your business politely but firmly. The Chinese reaction to you is more likely to be curiosity than malice.

For any foreign tourist, traveling in China means dealing with often incorrect assumptions about who you are based on your skin color; this problem is exacerbated if you are not white or not overseas Chinese. Non-white and non-Chinese tourists in China face a unique set of challenges and prejudices. Unfortunately, the darker your skin, the worse your treatment in China. While incidents of racial violence or serious harassment are few and far between, discrimination on the basis of skin color is alive and well, be it from hotel owners, shopkeepers, travel agents, or government officials. Overseas Chinese may face a different set of challenges. People assume that anyone who looks Chinese can understand Mandarin like a native and are surprised and sometimes offended if the opposite is true.

TRAVELERS WITH CHILDREN

Family vacations often require that you slow your pace and always require that you plan ahead. When deciding where to stay, remember the special needs of young children; call ahead and make sure your hotel or hostel is child-friendly. Be sure that your child carries some sort of ID, with information in both English and Chinese, in case of an emergency or in case he or she gets lost.

Many museums and attractions have a children's rate. Exact age and height restrictions (often under 1.3m) vary. Children under two generally fly for 10% of the adult airfare on flights (this does not necessarily include a seat). International fares are usually discounted 25% for children from two to 11. Finding a private place for **breast feeding** can be a problem when traveling, so plan accordingly.

For more information, consult one of the following books:

Backpacking with Babies and Small Children, Goldie Silverman. Wilderness Press (US$10).

How to Take Great Trips with Your Kids, Sanford and Jane Portnoy. Harvard Common Press (US $10).

Have Kid, Will Travel: 101 Survival Strategies for Vacationing with Babies and Young Children, Claire and Lucille Tristram. Andrews McMeel Publishing (US$9).

Adventuring with Children: An Inspirational Guide to World Travel and the Outdoors, Nan Jeffrey. Avalon House Publishing (US$15).

Trouble Free Travel with Children, Vicki Lansky. Book Peddlers (US$9).

DIETARY CONCERNS

Although Chinese food often contains meat or uses meat bases, **vegetarian** dishes abound. Buddhists constitute the largest group of Chinese vegetarians and one of the best places for a good vegetarian meal is often the nearest Buddhist monastery. Very few non-Buddhist Chinese are vegetarians, but non-meat-based dishes, many of which use tofu, are popular nonetheless. Vegetarian restaurants can be found in many cities and vegetarian dishes (sùcài; 素菜) are available at virtually every Chinese restaurant (see **Phrasebook,** p. 833). However, even meatless dishes are usually prepared using animal-based cooking oils and other products; it may be hard, if not impossible, to find food cooked otherwise. Strict vegetarians and vegans may want to consider preparing their own food while traveling.

Pork is the most popular meat in China and as a result, **kosher** meals are practically nonexistent. A strong Muslim presence, however, makes **halal** (qīngzhēn; 清真) food a large part of the cuisine, especially in the north and west and in Xinjiang. Restaurants and stores certified *halal* are recognizable by their trademark green awnings and Arabic characters and are considered by some to offer more sanitary food than their non-*halal* counterparts.

Travelers who keep kosher should contact synagogues in larger cities for information on kosher restaurants. Your own synagogue or college Hillel should have access to lists of Jewish institutions across the nation. If you are strict in your observance, you may have to prepare your own food on the road. A good resource is the *Jewish Travel Guide*, by Michael Zaidner (Vallentine Mitchell; US$17).

For more information, visit your local bookstore, health food store, or library and consult *The Vegetarian Traveler: Where to Stay if You're Vegetarian*, by Jed and Susan Civic (Larson Publications; US$16).

JOURNEY TO YUNNAN PROVINCE

China's new ecotourism industry

The concept and implementation of ecotourism in China is still an entirely new endeavor despite the fact that the year 2002 was named the International Year of Ecotourism by the United Nations. Since China is currently the world's number one tourist destination (with 31.2 million visitors as quoted in 2000 *Newsweek* July 22/July 29, 2002), it is imperative to illustrate the potential outlet for ecotourism which China holds. The definition of ecotourism is travel to fragile, pristine, usually protected areas that strive to be low impact and usually small-scale. It thus follows that such travel serves to educate the traveler and in doing so, also fosters respect for different cultures as well as for human rights (Martha Honey in *Ecotourism & Sustainable Development*, 1999, Island Press).

Yunnan Province, in southwest China is a wonderful place for ecotourism. Roughly the size of France or California (at 5% of China's total land mass), it is the sixth largest of China's 27 provinces and contains both towering, icy mountains, as well as lush jungles. Of the approximately 56 recognized nationalities found in China, 24 are found only in Yunnan. Yunnan has abundant natural resources and the highest level of biodiversity in China (half of all China's animal and plant species can be found somewhere in Yunnan), and yet has China's most poorly developed infrastructure.

Geologically, Yunnan is an offshoot of Tibet, whose soaring tableland spreads eastwards creating a plateau of red earth over a mile high. In Western Yunnan, the ranges of the eastern Himalayas spread south from Tibet's border, channeling some of southern Asia's greatest rivers through deep canyons. The Salween, the Mekong,and the Yangzi Rivers race side by side far below the snow capped peaks, barely 50 miles apart. Movements in the earth's unstable crust further subject Yunnan to periodic earthquakes.

Fertile lake basins lie in the geological faults on the plateau. These form the agricultural, political, and cultural heart of the province. Among these, Kunming's Dianchi Lake is the largest. The red soil produces rice in abundance, along with year-round vegetable crops and teas that are considered among the best in China.

Botanical gardens in Kunming and in tropical Xishuangbanna display an astonishing array of plant species. Botanists come to see the camellias and rhododendrons, the province's special pride, as all species of these shrubs trace their ancestry to Yunnan. Wild animals and birds exist in great variety. Species of elephants, tigers, bears, snow leopards, takin, slow loris, golden monkeys, and gibbons can all be found in Yunnan, thus making it an unparalleled natural biological museum.

Though ecotourism is new to China, Yunnan is the most fertile ground for its beginnings; in 1994, the Chinese Minstry of Forestry allotted thousands of acres in the Gaoligongshan National Nature Reserve for tourism development. The estimated total carrying capacity for the area is 215,000 visitors per year. Since then, there have been several attempts at surveying and identifying eco- and heritage tourism sites within the area, but none have been implemented. In 2002, the Reserve revised their approach and delineated 6 areas for tourism development, including the Baihualing Area.

There are few locations in the world that possess the biodiveristy and unique character of the Gaoligongshan National Nature Reserve. Due to its climactic location (there are 7 climactic zones present) just north of the Tropic of Cancer, it gained an unusually strong repertoire of biodiversity. There is also the tremendous landform diversity, which adds to its tourism appeal. To the east, the three previously mentioned rivers cut dramatic gorges and fertile valleys. On the western slopes, the Tengchong Volcano system is regarded as one of the densest clusters of volcanoes in the world. It has over 90 pot-like volcanoes which in conjunction with hot springs or "terrestrial heat" reach 98 C.

Therefore, though the seeds for ecotourism in China are just starting to be planted, it can be expected that they will blossom fruitfully. With provinces such as Yunnan, and reserves such as Gaoligongshan, China seems well on its way to achieving the status of not only the most touristed nation, but the most ecotouristed as well.

Victoria Drake has worked for the Smithsonian Institute and The Great Lakes Conservation Fund; started IUCN-US in Washington, DC; and was the first program director for Global Alliance for Africa in Chicago.

ALTERNATIVES TO TOURISM

As fun and exciting as traveling the world (or even just part of it) can be, actually living in a country and working, volunteering, or studying for an extended period of time can often be a more rewarding and complete way to truly appreciate the local culture and environment. This chapter outlines some of the different ways to get to know a new place, whether you want to pay your way through, study, or volunteer.

Volunteering, working, or studying in a foreign country can be extremely rewarding, both financially and personally. And, in most cases, these alternatives to tourism result in a longer, more meaningful experience—something that the average budget traveler often misses out on.

Opportunities for work and study abound in China. Most foreigners go to teach English or to study Mandarin, but there are many other options for more intrepid folk. For an extensive listing of "off-the-beaten-track" and specialty travel opportunities, try the **Specialty Travel Index,** 305 San Anselmo Ave., #313, San Anselmo, CA 94960, USA (☎888-624-4030 or 415-455-1643; www.specialtytravel.com; US$6). **Transitions Abroad** (www.transabroad.com) publishes a bimonthly online newsletter for work, study, and specialized travel abroad.

STUDYING ABROAD

Studying abroad—whether for a few weeks or for a few years—is a great way to get to know both a language and a country. Programs range from basic language and culture courses to college-level classes, often for credit. When choosing a program, find out what kind of students participate in the program and what the accommodations are. In programs that have large groups of students who speak the same language, the opportunity to practice a foreign language or to befriend locals and other international students is diminished.

As for accommodations, students in some programs live with families, while in others dorm-like apartments or housing are made available to students. There are benefits and drawbacks to both—living in dorms provides better opportunities to mingle with fellow students, but there is less of a chance to experience the local scene. If you live with a family, there is a potential to build lifelong friendships with natives and to experience day-to-day life in more depth, but conditions can vary greatly from family to family.

Foreign students constitute one of the largest parts of China's expatriate population. Summer-, semester-, and year-long programs, especially for Chinese language study, are increasing in number all the time. Many are in Beijing, but Harbin, Nanjing, Shanghai, and many smaller cities also run programs. Many foreign language programs are run by foreign universities or independent international organizations, in cooperation with Chinese universities.

UNIVERSITIES

For semester- or year-long programs for college credit, most American undergraduates usually enroll in programs sponsored by US universities. If your Chinese is already proficient, applying directly to Chinese universities can be much cheaper than a US university program, though it can be hard to transfer academic credit. Most university-level study-abroad programs are meant as language and culture enrichment opportunities, and therefore are conducted in Chinese. Still, many programs do offer classes in English, beginner- and lower-level language courses; ask around. A good resource for finding programs that cater to your particular interests is www.studyabroad.com, which has links to various semester abroad programs based on a variety of criteria, including desired location and focus of study. The following is a list of organizations that can help place students in university programs abroad, or have their own branch in China.

Beijing University of Aeronautics and Astronautics (BUAA) Study Abroad Program, 241 Cliff St., Cliffside Park, NJ 07010, USA (☎201-313-7132; www.us-china.org). 8-week program offers three levels of language proficiency classes, field trips, an optional trip to Inner Mongolia and costs US$3000.

CET Academic Programs, 1000 16th St. NW, Ste. 350, Washington, D.C. 20036 (☎800-225-4262; fax 202-342-0317; cet@academic-travel.com; www.cetacademicprograms.com). Runs fall, spring, summer, and January term language programs in Beijing, Harbin, and Nanjing.

China Scholarship Council, 160 Fuxingmennei Dajie, Beijing 100031 (☎(010) 6641 3249; fax 6641 3198; webmaster@csc.edu.cn; www.csc.edu.cn), a division of the Ministry of Education. Provides financial support and resources for Chinese citizens wishing to study abroad and for foreign students wishing to study in China. Maintains a comprehensive directory of Chinese universities admitting foreign students.

Council on International Educational Exchange (CIEE), 633 3rd Ave., 20th floor, New York, NY 10017-6706 (☎800-407-8839; www.ciee.org) sponsors work, volunteer, academic, and internship programs in China.

International Association for the Exchange of Students for Technical Experience (IAESTE), 10400 Little Patuxent Pkwy. Suite 250, Columbia, MD 21044-3519, USA (☎410-997-2200; www.aipt.org). 8- to 12-week programs in China for college students who have completed 2 years of technical study. US$25 application fee.

Princeton in Beijing, 211 Jones Hall, Princeton University, Princeton, NJ 08544-1008 (☎609-258-4269; fax 258-6984; pib@princeton.edu; www.princeton.edu/~pib). Summer-long intensive Mandarin programs in conjunction with Beijing Normal University. US$3900 fee includes room, textbooks, and selected meals.

School for International Training, College Semester Abroad, Admissions, Kipling Rd., P.O. Box 676, Brattleboro, VT 05302, USA (☎800-336-1616 or 802-257-7751; www.sit.edu). Semester- and year-long programs in China run US$12000. Also runs the **Experiment in International Living** (☎800-345-2929; fax 802-258-3428; www.usexperiment.org), 3- to 5-week summer programs that offer high-school students cross-cultural homestays, community service, ecological adventure, and language training in China and cost US$5000.

LANGUAGE SCHOOLS

In general, *Let's Go* recommends traditional university study-abroad programs, both for summer study and during the regular school year. Unlike American universities, language schools are frequently independently-run international or local organizations or divisions of foreign universities that rarely offer college credit. Language schools are a good alternative to university study if you desire a deeper focus on the language or a slightly less rigorous courseload. These programs are also good for younger high school students who might not feel comfortable with older students in a university program. Some good options include:

EVERYBODY WAS KUNG FU FIGHTING Though most students go to China to study Mandarin, braver souls have another option: **martial arts academies**. The two famous centers of martial arts in China, Songshan (p. 265), home to Shaolin temple, and Wudangshan (p. 453), the setting of *Crouching Tiger, Hidden Dragon*, are covered in temples that may offer instruction, if you can speak enough Chinese to convince them. One academy that offers a more structured program is the Northern China Shaolin Martial Arts Academy, Ye He Ancient Castle, Siping City, Jilin Province 136523 (☎(434) 549 6648; fax 329 0265; www.shaolins.com). Tuition is US$300 a month; room, board, and transportation are extra. English is spoken at the academy, but the monks are willing to teach Mandarin. For more information on programs in China, contact your national martial arts association or visit a general website such as www.martialinfo.com.

FLS International: China, 101 E. Green St., Suite 14, Pasadena, CA 91105, USA (☎626 795 2912; www.fls.net). Study Chinese in Gaungzhou while assisting in the teaching of English to Chinese students.

Hong Kong Language Learning Center, 2/F Tai Shing Commercial Building, 498-500 Nathan Road, Yaumateii, Kowloon, Hong Kong (☎852 2385 5331). Leading language school specializing in Cantonese and Mandarin. For students of all ages.

WORKING ABROAD

There are two main schools of thought in terms of working abroad. Some travelers want long-term jobs that allow them to get to know another part of the world in depth, such as teaching English or working in the tourist industry. Other travelers work in short-term jobs to finance their travel. They seek employment usually in the service sector or in agriculture, working for a few weeks at a time to finance the next leg of their journey. This section discusses both short-term and long-term opportunities for working in China.

You must obtain a **"Z" Visa** to obtain employment in China. Applications and instructions for this can be found at www.china-embassy.org, the Chinese embassy in Washington, D.C., or one of the five consulates in New York, NY; Chicago, IL; Los Angeles, CA; San Francisco, CA; or Houston, TX. Requirements include: an **Employment License of the People's Republic of China for Foreigners,** which should be obtained by the employer in China from provincial or municipal labor authorities; a **Physical Examination Certificate,** issued in your country, if you plan to work for more than a year; a **Visa Application Form with one additional passport photo,** black and white; your **passport** with twelve months of validity left and one blank Visa page; and a **Foreign Specialist's License issued by the Chinese Foreign Special Bureau** if you plan to work on a scientific research project or offer technical or economic assistance. Visa applications take about two weeks to be processed, and cost US$30. They are usually valid for 90 days after date of issue.

For US college students, recent graduates, and young adults, the simplest way to get legal permission to work abroad is through **Council Exchanges Work Abroad Programs.** Fees are from US$300-425. Council Exchanges helps you obtain a three- to six-month work permit/visa and also provides assistance finding jobs and housing.

LONG-TERM WORK

If you're planning on spending a substantial amount of time (more than three months) working in China, searching for a job in advance is often the way to go.

International placement agencies are often the easiest way to find employment abroad, especially for teaching English. **Internships,** usually for college students, are a good way to segway into working abroad, although they are often unpaid or poorly paid (many say the experience, however, is well worth it). Be wary of advertisements or companies that claim the ability to get you a job abroad for a fee—often times the same listings are available online or in newspapers, or even out of date; it's best, if going through an organization, to use one that's somewhat reputable, such as:

Council Exchanges, 52 Poland St., London W1F 7AB, UK (☎44 020 7478 2000; US☎ 888-268-6245; www.councilexchanges.org) charges a US$300-475 fee for arranging authorizations for short-term work, as well as extensive information on different job opportunities in China.

TEACHING ENGLISH

There are many opportunities to teach English in China. It is possible to apply directly to a Chinese school or university, and occasionally job openings are posted on the web. Many US organizations help arrange teaching positions. Compensation is minimal by Western standards, but housing is usually provided and the salary should be enough to cover all living expenses. **CIEE** (see **Studying Abroad,** p. 105) also arranges teaching positions in China. In almost all cases, you must have at least a bachelor's degree to be a full-fledged teacher, although often times college undergraduates can get summer positions teaching or tutoring. Furthermore, many schools require teachers to have a **Teaching English as a Foreign Language (TEFL)** certificate, although not having one doesn't exclude you from finding a teaching job (but having one often times means higher salaries). Native English speakers working in private schools are most often hired for English-immersion classrooms where no Chinese is spoken. Those volunteering or teaching in public, poorer schools, are more likely to be working in both English and Chinese. To find a teaching job in China, placement agencies or university fellowship programs at home are a safe bet. The alternative is to contact schools directly or just try your luck once you get there. If you are going to try the latter, the best time of the year is several weeks before the start of the school year. The following organizations are extremely helpful in placing teachers in China:

Amity Institute, Amity Volunteer Teachers Abroad Program, 10671 Roselle St., Suite 100, San Diego, CA 92121-1525, USA (☎858-455-6364; fax 858-455-6597; www.amity.org). Offers both full-year and semester-long positions. $25-50 processing fee and $500 placement fee.

Asia/US Public Service and Educational Exchange Programs, P.O. Box 20266, Stanford, CA 94309 (☎650-723-3228; info@viaprograms.org; www.volasia.org). Places volunteers in schools. Provides round-trip airfare, accommodations, monthly stipend, travel allowance, a bicycle, and 3hr. of Chinese language training. US$950-1425 depending on length of stay. Applications due in Feb./Mar.

Colorado China Council, 4556 Apple Way, Boulder, CO 80301 (☎303-443-1108; fax 443-1107; alice@asiacouncil.org; www.asiacouncil.org). Places US college graduates and professionals in universities (Sept.-July or Feb./Mar.-July) to teach English, American history, culture, business, economics, or law. US$3250 (less for professionals and married couples) provides three-week intensive training in Shanghai, medical insurance, housing, four-week paid winter vacation, and a monthly stipend of US$300-400.

International Schools Services (ISS), 15 Roszel Rd., Box 5910, Princeton, NJ 08543-5910, USA (☎609-452-0990; fax 609-452-2690; www.iss.edu). Hires teachers for more than 200 overseas schools; candidates should have experience teaching or with international affairs, 2-year commitment expected.

WorldTeach, Inc., Center for International Development, Harvard University, 79 John F. Kennedy St., Cambridge, MA 02138, USA (☎800-4-TEACH-0 or 617-495-5527; fax 617-495-1599; www.worldteach.org). Volunteers primarily teach classes in spoken English to students of all ages in China. Fee includes airfare, health insurance, training, room, and board. Fees range from $4000-6000.

SHORT-TERM WORK

Traveling for long periods of time can get expensive; therefore, many travelers try their hand at odd jobs for a few weeks at a time to make some extra cash to carry them through another month or two of touring around. Howevery, it is illegal to accept payment for a job in China if you do not have a "Z" Visa and Employment License.

VOLUNTEERING

Volunteering can be one of the most rewarding experiences you can have—you may work with or help out locals and language skills will develop quickly. With ample time, and money, there is little that you can't do. Many volunteer services charge a surprisingly hefty fee to participate in the program and to do work, but these fees frequently cover airfare and most, if not all, living expenses. Try to do research on a program before committing—talk to people who have previously participated and find out exactly what you're getting into, as living and working conditions can vary greatly. Different programs are geared toward different ages and levels of experience, so be sure to make sure that you are taking on a level that is suitable for you. The more informed and realistic expectations you have, the more enjoyable the program will be.

Volunteer jobs in China are abundant. Most people choose to go through a parent organization, which takes care of logistical details, and frequently provides a group environment and support system. You can sometimes avoid the high application fees charged by the organizations that arrange placement by contacting the individual workcamps directly; check with the organizations. There are two main types of organizations—religious (usually Catholic), and non-sectarian—although there are rarely restrictions on participation for either. The truly adventurous travelers can search for a non-profit organization once in a country, and then only pay living expenses rather than the costly program fees for organized volunteer projects.

Cross-Cultural Solutions, 47 Potter Ave., New Rochelle, NY 10801, USA (☎800-380-4777 or 914-632-0022; fax 914-632-8494, www.crossculturalsolutions.org). Operates short- and long-term humanitarian work in health care, education, and social development. Fees range from US$2100-4200.

Earthwatch, 3 Clocktower Pl. Suite 100, Box 75, Maynard, MA 01754 (☎800-776-0188 or 978-461-0081; www.earthwatch.org). Arranges 1- to 3-week programs in China to promote conservation of natural resources. Fees vary based on program location and duration, costs average US$1700 plus airfare.

Elderhostel, Inc., 11 Avenue de Lafayette, Boston, MA 92111-1746, USA (☎877-426-8056; fax 877-426-2166; www.elderhostel.org). Sends volunteers age 55 and over around the world to work in construction, research, teaching, and many other projects. Costs average US$100 per day plus airfare.

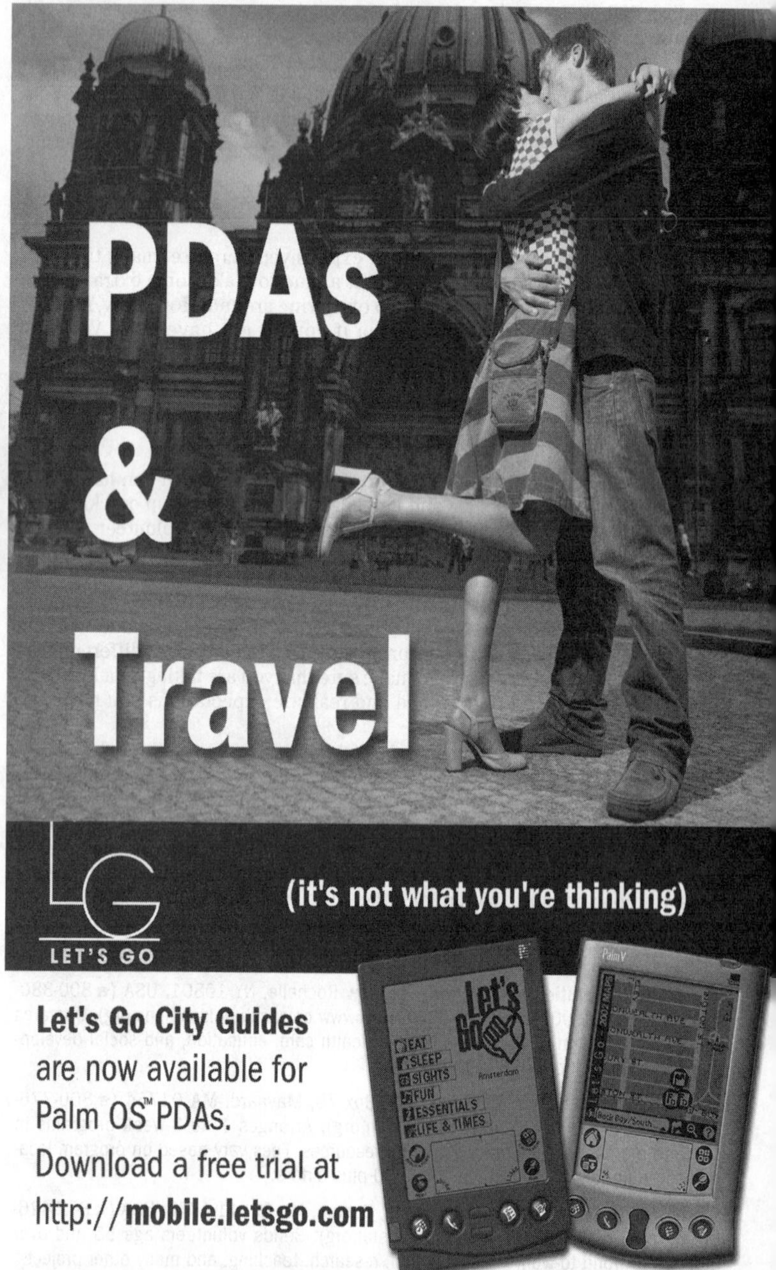
PDAs
&
Travel
LET'S GO
(it's not what you're thinking)
Let's Go City Guides
are now available for
Palm OS™ PDAs.
Download a free trial at
http://mobile.letsgo.com
EAT
SLEEP
SIGHTS
FUN
ESSENTIALS
LIFE & TIMES
Amsterdam
AMSTERDAM BARCELONA BOSTON LONDON PARIS ROME NEW YORK CITY SAN FRANCISCO WASHINGTON D
Palm OS is a registered trademark of Palm, Inc. Let's Go is a registered trademark of Let's Go Publications, Inc. Guidewalk is a registered trademark of Guidewalk LLC.

Global Volunteers, 375 E. Little Canada Rd., St. Paul, MN 55117-1628 (☎800-487-1074 or 651-407-6100; fax 482-0915; email@globalvolunteers.org; www.globalvolunteers.org). Work with a team of volunteers in a self-selected service program. US$2095/$2395 for 2-3 week program (19-day college summer program US$1595). Includes all meals, lodging, in-country ground transportation, and administrative expenses. Early applications encouraged. No teaching experience is required.

Habitat for Humanity International, 121 Habitat St., Americus, GA 31709, USA (☎229-924-6935 x2551; www.habitat.org). Volunteers build houses in over 83 countries for anywhere from 2 weeks to 3 years. Short-term program costs range from US$1200-4000.

Peace Corps, Office of Volunteer Recruitment and Selection, 1111 20th St., NW, Washington, D.C., 20526 USA (☎800-424-8580; www.peacecorps.gov). Opportunities in 70 developing nations, including China.

Volunteers for Peace, 1034 Tiffany Rd., Belmont., VT 05730, USA (☎802-259-2759; www.vfp.org). Arranges placement in work camps in China. Membership required for registration. Annual *International Workcamp Directory* US$20. Programs average US$200-500 for 2-3 weeks.

Volunteer Services Organization, 317 Putney Bridge Rd., London, SW15 2PN, UK (☎(020) 8780 7200; fax 8780 7300; www.vso.org.uk). Offers several programs (mostly long-term) for volunteers of all ages. Provides a financial package that covers all expenses (except travel) and even supports your re-adjustment to life back home.

FOR FURTHER READING ON ALTERNATIVES TO TOURISM

Alternatives to the Peace Corps: A Directory of Third World and U.S. Volunteer Opportunities, by Joan Powell. Food First Books, 2000 (US$10).

How to Get a Job in Europe, by Sanborn and Matherly. Surrey Books, 1999 (US$22).

How to Live Your Dream of Volunteering Oversees, by Collins, DeZerega, and Heckscher. Penguin Books, 2002 (US$17).

International Directory of Voluntary Work, by Whetter and Pybus. Peterson's Guides and Vacation Work, 2000 (US$16).

International Jobs, by Kocher and Segal. Perseus Books, 1999 (US$18).

Overseas Summer Jobs 2002, by Collier and Woodworth. Peterson's Guides and Vacation Work, 2002 (US$18).

Work Abroad: The Complete Guide to Finding a Job Overseas, by Hubbs, Griffith, and Nolting. Transitions Abroad Publishing, 2000 ($16).

Work Your Way Around the World, by Susan Griffith. Worldview Publishing Services, 2001 (US$18).

BEIJING AND THE NORTH COAST

Snobs. To the majority of the Chinese population, that's what most North Coasters are. After all, who can stand the way they parade with their "trends" and "fashion"? Who can stand the way they flaunt their illustrious history and traces of imperial grandeur? It's downright appropriate that self-absorbed Beijing sits right smack in the middle of this flashy region—after all, the Chinese world revolves around Beijing, an independent municipality, the nation's capital, the *crème de la crème*. Of course, being the best can also be quite taxing. So after Beijing's bigwigs finish writing the rules, they saunter over to Hebei province for a little R&R. In fact, taking advantage of this region's natural splendor is a tradition; emperors used to lounge in the shade of the Summer Villa in Chengde (p. 169) and government officials continue to cavort and sunbathe in Beidaihe (p. 173). Even today, balding big shots still enjoy some splashing at the gorgeous retreats and port cities along the North Coast.

Even though the region, from the rough-and-tumble provincial capitals of Shijiazhuang and Ji'nan to the most refined areas of Beijing, is one of China's most developed areas, it never ignores its illustrious past. Scattered throughout this prosperous region are the legacies of China's rich and famous; the Forbidden City and Summer Palace are two of China's grandest reminders of its dynastic past; the European architecture in former foreign concessions in Tianjin and Qingdao recall the age of imperialism; the grandiose monuments in Beijing's Tiananmen Square commemorate the founding and achievements of the Communist era. This area isn't just the political center of the country—it is also the cultural capital of China, and it has no intention of giving up that title. Or giving up the right to boast about it.

HIGHLIGHTS OF BEIJING AND THE NORTH COAST

BASK IN THE IMPERIAL MAJESTY of Beijing, where the magnificent Forbidden City (p. 133), Tiantan Park (p. 137), Lama Temple (p. 136), and the Summer Palace (p. 140) testify to an immensely rich cultural past unrivaled by modern highrises.

FIND YOUR INNER BARBARIAN and scale the best-preserved section of the **Great Wall** (p. 150), perched atop lush hills a few hours from Beijing.

GUZZLE GALLONS OF BEER at the beachside town of Qingdao (p. 189), where the famous international brew flows freely from factory taps.

BEIJING 北京 ☎010

Beijing is a city built for giants. From the gargantuan boulevards to the sprawling Forbidden City, everything here seems to aspire to greatness. As China's

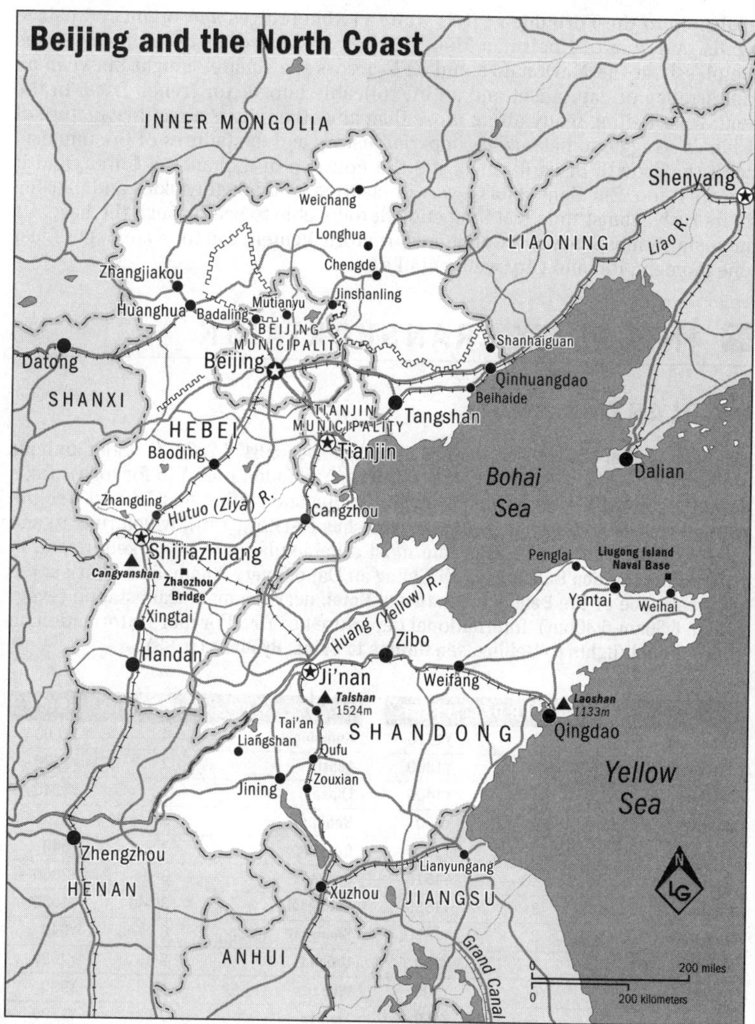

political, economic, and cultural nucleus for nearly 700 years, Beijing is the hope, future, future hope, and hopeful future of China. The pulsing heart that is Beijing never ceases to beat, as busy businessmen and frantic tourists, officious PSB officers and uniformed school children hurry down the streets always rushing, always moving forward, working toward a bright, promising future. Did we mention that Beijing has an overbearing melodramatic streak? Nonetheless, Beijing deserves its fame. Full of the palaces, temples, and parks where generations of emperors once roamed, the regal city of Beijing is a fascinating mix of history and change, a character that is most clearly illustrated by its city center. Here, Tiananmen Square, the site of the 1989 Democracy Movement, sidles up to the Forbidden City's white marble bridges and bright red palace walls. A statue of Chairman Mao, perched above a crimson archway, gazes helplessly at the McDonald's and KFC across the square, caught between an abhorrence of capitalism and an inexplicable hunger for french fries. In the end, what Beijing really offers *more* than any other city is a real live picture of China's struggle to balance its imperial history and the failures of Communism with the growth of capitalism. It's the epitome of a changing China, and it knows it too. But Beijing has a way of clearing its thick gray skies and pausing in its rush against time just long enough to be able to see through the haze. Its imposing atmosphere and Communist rhetoric lighten, and for a moment, if just one moment, it could very well feel like home.

INTERCITY TRANSPORTAION

BY PLANE

Beijing's **Capital Airport** (shǒudū jīchǎng; 首都机场; ☎6456 2580) is about an hour from the city. A taxi to the city costs at least Y80 (additional Y15 for tolls). Taxis from the airport are notorious for overcharging and getting "lost"; insist that the ride be metered. Or, take the **CAAC shuttle bus** (1-1½hr., Y16), which runs to and from various points in Beijing. The most reliable places to be picked up are: in front of the **Aviation Building,** 15 Xi Chang'an Dajie (every 30min. 5am-8pm); at the west entrance of the **Beijing International Hotel,** near the main train station (every 30min. 6:30am-6:30pm). International departure tax Y90. For more information on international flights to Beijing, see **Getting to China: By Plane** (p. 83).

TO	PER DAY	PRICE
Changsha	7-8	Y1110
Chengdu	8	Y1300
Chongqing	4	Y1400
Dalian	8	Y660
Fuzhou	5	Y1390
Guangzhou	10	Y1510
Guilin	3	Y1580
Haikou	3	Y1950
Harbin	8-10	Y880
Hefei	2	Y900
Hohhot	5	Y460
Hong Kong	5	Y2830

TO	PER DAY	PRICE
Kunming	4	Y1600
Lanzhou	2	Y1220
Lhasa	1	Y1240
Nanjing	5-6	Y920
Qingdao	3-5	Y640
Sanya	3	Y2000
Shanghai	30-40	Y1030
Shenyang	6-7	Y640
Ürümqi	2-3	Y2080
Wuhan	4	Y980
Xiamen	3-5	Y1520
Xi'an	7-8	Y960

Domestic Airlines: CAAC headquarters in the Aviation Bldg., 15 Xi Changan Jie, 1st fl. (24hr. service 6601 7755, domestic inquiry 6256 7811, international inquiry 6601 6667). Take the bus or subway to Xidan and walk 5min. east; look for the airline symbol on the building. Most tickets can be purchased at any counter in the foyer or the right wing. Open 24hr. Counters for other domestic airlines are in the left wing. Open daily 8:30am-5pm. Summer and winter holidays, 40% discounts are possible on domestic flights for exchange students with ID. **Dragon Air,** Henderson Center, 18 Jianguomennei Dajie, Tower 1, Ste. 1710 (☎6518 2533).

Asian Airlines: Air Macau, SCITECH Tower Place, 22 Jianguomenwai Dajie, Ste. 807 (☎6515 8988 or 6515 9398). **All Nippon Airways,** Fortune Bldg., 5 Dongsanhuan Bei Lu, Ste. N200 (☎6590 9191). **Asiana Airlines,** Lufthansa Center, Kempinski Hotel, 50 Liangmaqiao Lu, Ste. W102 (☎6468 4000). **Japan Airlines,** Changfugong Office Bldg., Hotel New Otari, 26 Jianguomenwai Dajie, 1st fl. (☎6513 0888). **Malaysian Airlines,** China World Trade Center, Tower 2, Ste. 1005 (☎6505 2681 or 6505 2683). **MIAT Mongolian Airlines,** China Golden Bridge Bldg., A1 Jianguomenwai Dajie, East Gate (☎6507 9297). **Pakistan International Airlines,** China World Trade Center, Ste. 617 (☎6505 1681). **Singapore Airlines,** China World Trade Center, Tower 2, 8th fl. (☎6505 2233). **Thai Airways International,** Lufthansa Center, Ste. S102B (☎6460 8899).

Other Airlines: Aeroflot, Hotel Jinglun, 3 Jianguomenwai Dajie (☎6500 2412). **Air Canada,** Lufthansa Center, Ste. C201 (☎6468 2001). **Air France,** Fenglian Plaza, Chaoyangmenwai Dajie, Ste. 515 (☎6588 1388). **Austrian Airlines,** Lufthansa Center, Ste. S103 (☎6462 2164). **British Airways,** SCITECH Tower Place, Ste. 210 (☎6512 4085). **KLM Royal Dutch Airlines,** China World Trade Center, Ste. W501 (☎6505 3505). **Lufthansa,** Lufthansa Center, Ste. S101 (☎6465 4488). **Northwest Airlines,** China World Trade Center, Ste. W501 (☎6505 3505). **Qantas,** Lufthansa Center, Ste. S120 (☎6467 3337). **Swissair,** SCITECH Tower Place, Ste. 608 (☎6512 3555). **United Airlines,** Lufthansa Center, 1st fl. (☎6463 1111).

BY TRAIN

Hotels can help book train **tickets,** but often charge a Y30-50 commission. Travelers may have to fight to get to the front of the crowds at the train station counters, but ruthless individuals shouldn't have too much difficulty obtaining a ticket. **CITS** (see p. 122) handles reservations and booking for all international train travel.

Beijing has several train stations. The **Beijing Train Station** (běijīng huǒchē zhàn; 北京火车站; ☎6512 8931 or 6512 9525) is just southeast of the city center, sandwiched between Jianguomennei Dajie and Chongwenmendong Dajie. Take the subway to Beijing Zhan; buses also make the trip. The **booking office** for international travelers is in the left back corner on the first floor, through the soft seat waiting room. International trains include the Trans-Mongolian to **Moscow** (6 days, W and Sa, Y1602-3014; see p. 89) and trains to **Ulaan Bataar, Mongolia** (30hr., Tu, Y559-949) and **Pyongyang, North Korea** (22½hr.; M, W-Th, and Sa; Y396-767).

Beijing West Train Station (běijīng xī zhàn; 北京西站; ☎6321 6253) is on Lianhuachi Dong Lu near Lianhuachi Park, at the southern end of Yangfangdian Lu, accessible by buses #5, 48, 52, 320, and 845; or, take a minibus from Beijing Train Station. Destinations include **Kowloon, Hong Kong** (28hr., every other day 9:12am, Y662-1028) and **Hanoi, Vietnam** (3 days, M and F 10:51am). The **foreigners' ticket office** is on the second floor, immediately to left of the escalators.

Beijing South Station (běijīng nán zhàn; 北京南站; ☎6303 0031), off Yonganmen Dongbinhe Lu, is accessible by buses #20 and 102. Trains to **Shidu** leave from here. **Beijing North Station** (běijīng běi zhàn; 北京北站; ☎6563 6223) is on the northwest corner of Erhuan Lu; take the subway to Xizhimen.

The following table provides the departure station, number of direct trains per day, duration of travel (in hours), and the price (in *yuán*) for all major Chinese cities serviced by trains from the Beijing Train Station **(B)** and the West Station **(W).** Prices listed are for hard seat and hard sleeper; short routes may only have hard seats available. Travel times vary; faster trains are generally more expensive. For help reading your train ticket, see the **Appendix,** p. 832.

BEIJING

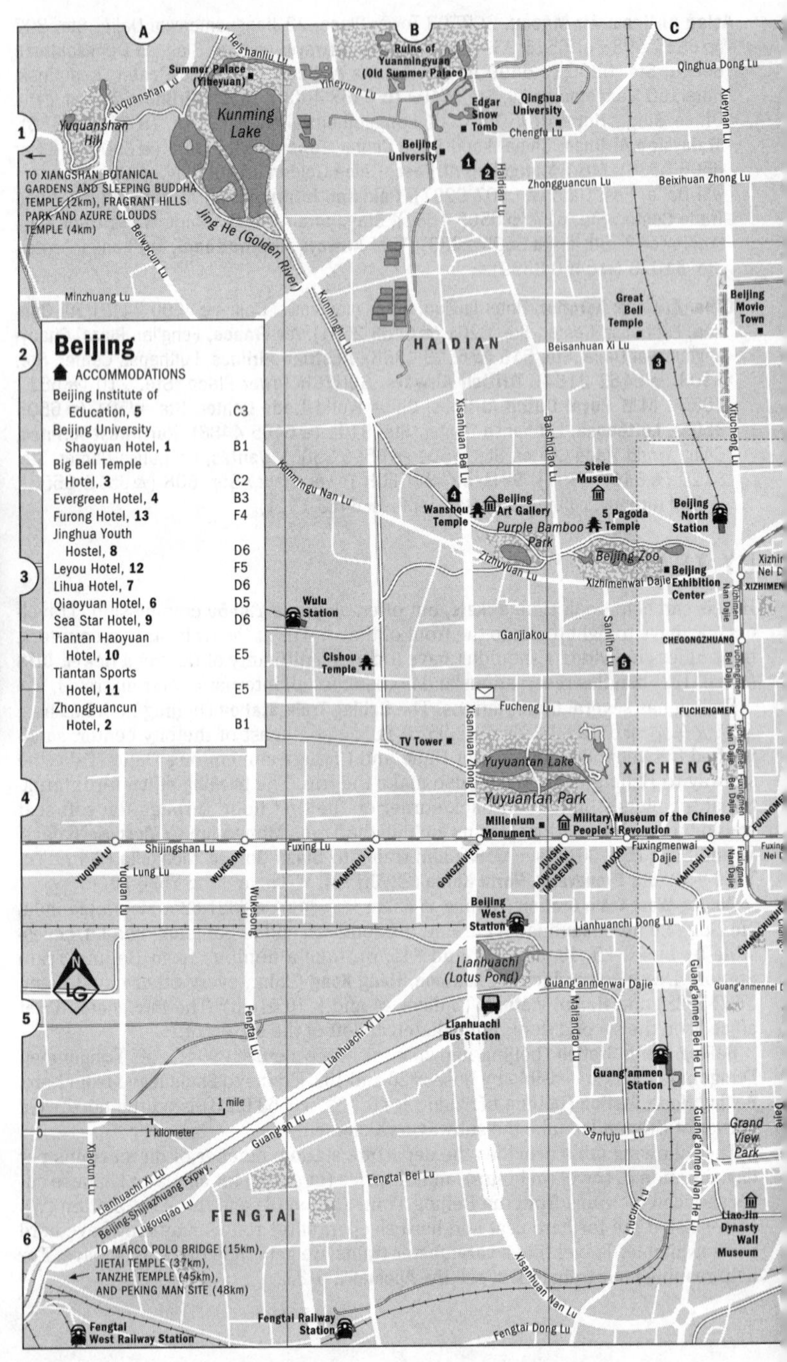
Beijing
ACCOMMODATIONS
Beijing Institute of Education, 5 C3
Beijing University Shaoyuan Hotel, 1 B1
Big Bell Temple Hotel, 3 C2
Evergreen Hotel, 4 B3
Furong Hotel, 13 F4
Jinghua Youth Hostel, 8 D6
Leyou Hotel, 12 F5
Lihua Hotel, 7 D6
Qiaoyuan Hotel, 6 D5
Sea Star Hotel, 9 D6
Tiantan Haoyuan Hotel, 10 E5
Tiantan Sports Hotel, 11 E5
Zhongguancun Hotel, 2 B1
A
B
C
1
2
3
4
5
6
Summer Palace (Yiheyuan)
Ruins of Yuanmingyuan (Old Summer Palace)
Heishanliu Lu
Yiheyuan Lu
Qinghua Dong Lu
Yuquanshan Lu
Yuquanshan Hill
Kunming Lake
Edgar Snow Tomb
Qinghua University
Chengfu Lu
Beijing University
Haidian Lu
Xueyuan Lu
TO XIANGSHAN BOTANICAL GARDENS AND SLEEPING BUDDHA TEMPLE (2km), FRAGRANT HILLS PARK AND AZURE CLOUDS TEMPLE (4km)
Zhongguancun Lu
Beixihuan Zhong Lu
Jing He (Golden River)
Beiwucun Lu
Minzhuang Lu
Kunmingyu Lu
Great Bell Temple
Beijing Movie Town
HAIDIAN
Beisanhuan Xi Lu
Xisanhuan Bei Lu
Baishiqiao Lu
Xituchang Lu
Kunmingu Nan Lu
Stele Museum
Wanshou Temple
Beijing Art Gallery
5 Pagoda Temple
Beijing North Station
Purple Bamboo Park
Beijing Zoo
Zizhuyuan Lu
Beijing Exhibition Center
Xizhimenwai Dajie
XIZHIMEN
Wulu Station
Ganjiakou
Sanlihe Lu
CHEGONGZHUANG
Cishou Temple
Fucheng Lu
FUCHENGMEN
TV Tower
Xisanhuan Zhong Lu
Yuyuantan Lake
Yuyuantan Park
XICHENG
Military Museum of the Chinese People's Revolution
Millenium Monument
Shijingshan Lu
Fuxing Lu
Fuxingmenwai Dajie
YUQUAN LU
WUKESONG
WANSHOU LU
GONGZHUFEN
JUNSHI BOWUGUAN (MUSEUM)
MUXIDI
NANLISHI LU
Yuquan Lu
Lung Lu
Wukesong
Beijing West Station
Lianhuachi Dong Lu
Lianhuachi (Lotus Pond)
Guang'anmenwai Dajie
Guang'anmen Bei He Lu
Fengtai Lu
Lianhuachi Xi Lu
Lianhuachi Bus Station
Maliandao Lu
Guang'ammen Station
0
1 mile
1 kilometer
Guang'an Lu
Sanluju Lu
Grand View Park
Xiaotun Lu
Fengtai Bei Lu
Guang'anmen Nan He Lu
Beijing-Shijiazhuang Expwy.
Lugouqiao Lu
FENGTAI
Liuculi Lu
Liao-Jin Dynasty Wall Museum
TO MARCO POLO BRIDGE (15km), JIETAI TEMPLE (37km), TANZHE TEMPLE (45km), AND PEKING MAN SITE (48km)
Xisanhuan Nan Lu
Fengtai Railway Station
Fengtai Dong Lu
Fengtai West Railway Station

TO MING TOMBS (50 km), BADALING GREAT WALL (65 km), AND HUANGHUA GREAT WALL (100 km)
TO CAPITAL AIRPORT (25km), MUTIANYU GREAT WALL (70km), AND SIMATAI GREAT WALL (120km)
Beijing College of Tourism
International Olympics Center
Chinese Ethnic Culture Park
Sino-Japanese Friendship Hospital
Hepingli Station
Liuyin Park
Ditan Park (Temple of the Earth)
SEE CENTRAL BEIJING MAP
Lama Temple
Museum of Agriculture
CHAOYANG
Chaoyang Park
Workers' Stadium
Houhai Lake
Xihai Lake
Beihai Park
Beihai Lake
Jingshan Park
FORBIDDEN CITY
Zhonghai Lake
Nanhai Lake
DONGCHENG
Ritan Park
Tuanjie Lake Park
Honglingjin Park
TIANANMEN SQUARE
Beijing Station
Beijing East Station
CHONGWEN
Majuan Bus Station
International Post Office
Tianqiao Bus Station
Tiantan Park (Temple of Heaven)
Longtan Park
Panjiayuan Flea Market
Yaowa Park
Taoranting Park
Yongdingmen Bus Station
Beijing South Station
Wanfangting Park
Muxiyuan Bus Station
Tonghui River
Ba River
Moat
BEIJING

BEIJING

A
B
C
1
2
3
4
5
6
Deshengmen Watch Tower
JISHUITAN
Xihai Lake
Deshengmen Dong Dajie
GULOU DAJIE (DRUM TOWER)
Anding Xi Dajie
Ande Lu
Qingnian
Jiugulouwai Dajie
Jiugulou Dajie
Gaoliangqiao Jie
Deshengmen Xi Dajie
Xizhimen Bei Dajie
Beijing North Railway Station
Beijing Exhibition Center
Xu Beihong Museum
Song Qingling Museum
Gulou Xi Dajie
Houhai Lake
Houhai Beiyan
Houhai Nanyan
Xinjiekou Dong Jie
Yangfang Hutong
Guanghua Temple
Bell Tower
Drum Tower
Gulou Dajie
Xizhimennei Dajie
Xizhimen Wai Dajie
XIZHIMEN
Xizhimen Nan Dajie
Guanyuan Park
Xinjiekou Nan Dajie
Xinjiekou Bei Dajie
Deshengmennei Dajie
Huguo Temple
Beijing Normal University
Liuyin Jie
Prince Gong's Residence
Dingfu Jie
Longtoujing Jie
Dianmenwai Dajie
Qianhai Lake
Chegongzhuang Dajie
Ping'anli Xi Dajie
Di'anmen Xi Dajie
Di'anmen Dong Dajie
CHEGONGZHUANG
Jingxin Zhai
Nine Dragon Screen
Five Dragon Pavilion
Beihai Park
Beihai Lake
Zhanlanguan Lu
Fuchengmen Bei Dajie
Zhaodengyu Lu
Xisi Bei Dajie
Xishiku Dajie
Dianmennei Dajie
Lu Xun Museum
Gongmenkou Santiao
Gongmenkou Ertiao
White Temple
Jingshanhou Jie
Jingshan Xi Jie
Jingshan Dong Jie
Jingshan Park
White Dagoba
Guangji Temple
Xishiku Church
Fuchengmenwai Dajie
Fuchengmennei Dajie
Bank of China
Geological Museum
Xi'anmen Dajie
Round City
Wenjin Jie
Jingshanqian Jie
FUCHENGMEN
Gate of Martial Prowess
Sanlihe Dong Lu
Fuchengmen Nan Dajie
Taipingqiao Dajie
Xisi Nan Dajie
Zhongnanhai Government Offices
Yuetan Bei Jie
XICHENG
Yuetan Park
Zhonghai Lake
Beichang Jie
Palace Moat
FORBIDDEN CITY
Yuetan Nan Jie
Fuxingmen Bei Dajie
Naoshikou Bei Jie
Xidan Bei Dajie
Xidan Emporium
Fuyou Jie
Meridian Gate
Nanchang Jie
Zhongshan Park
MUXIDI
NANLISHI LU
Parkson Store
Nationalities Cultural Palace
Xidan Food Market
XIDAN
Nanhai Lake
TIANANMEN WEST
Fuxingmenwai Dajie
FUXINGMEN
CITS
Fuxingmennei Dajie
Xichang'an Jie
Tiananmen Gate
Sanwei Bookstore-Tea House
CAAC Business Mansion
Concert Hall
Monument to the People's Heroes
Great Hall of the People
TIANANMEN SQUARE
Fuxingmen Nan Dajie
Xuanwumennei Dajie
Beixinhua Jie
Baiyun Lu
White Cloud Temple
Nantang Cathedral
Chairman Mao Mausoleum
CHANGCHUNJIE
HEPINGMEN
Zhengyangmen Gate
Lianhuachi Dong Lu
Xuanwumen Xi Dajie
Xuanwumen Dong Dajie
XUANWUMEN
Qianmen Xi Dajie
QIANMEN
Lao She Tea House
Zhengyici Theater
Arrow Tower
Tianning Temple
Xuanwu Park
Changchun Jie
Xuanwumenwai Dajie
Liulichang Culture Street
DAZHALAN
Nanxinhua Jie
Dazhalan Jie
Qianmen Dajie
Tongrentang Medicinal Hall
XUANWU
Dazhalan Xi Dajie
Guang'anmennei Dajie
Luomashi Dajie
Zhushikou Xi Dajie
Niujie Mosque
Laman Hutong
Qianmen Hotel
Yong'an Lu
Guang'anmen Nanbinhe Lu
Niu Jie
Fayuan Temple
Hufang Lu
Friendship Hospital
Beiwei Lu
Tianqiao Nan Dajie
You'anmennei Dajie
Taiping Jie
LG
N
Beizhifang Xi Jie
Baizhifan Dong Jie
Taoranting Lu
Joyous Pavilion (Taoranting) Park
Xiannongtan Temple
0
1000 yards
1000 meters

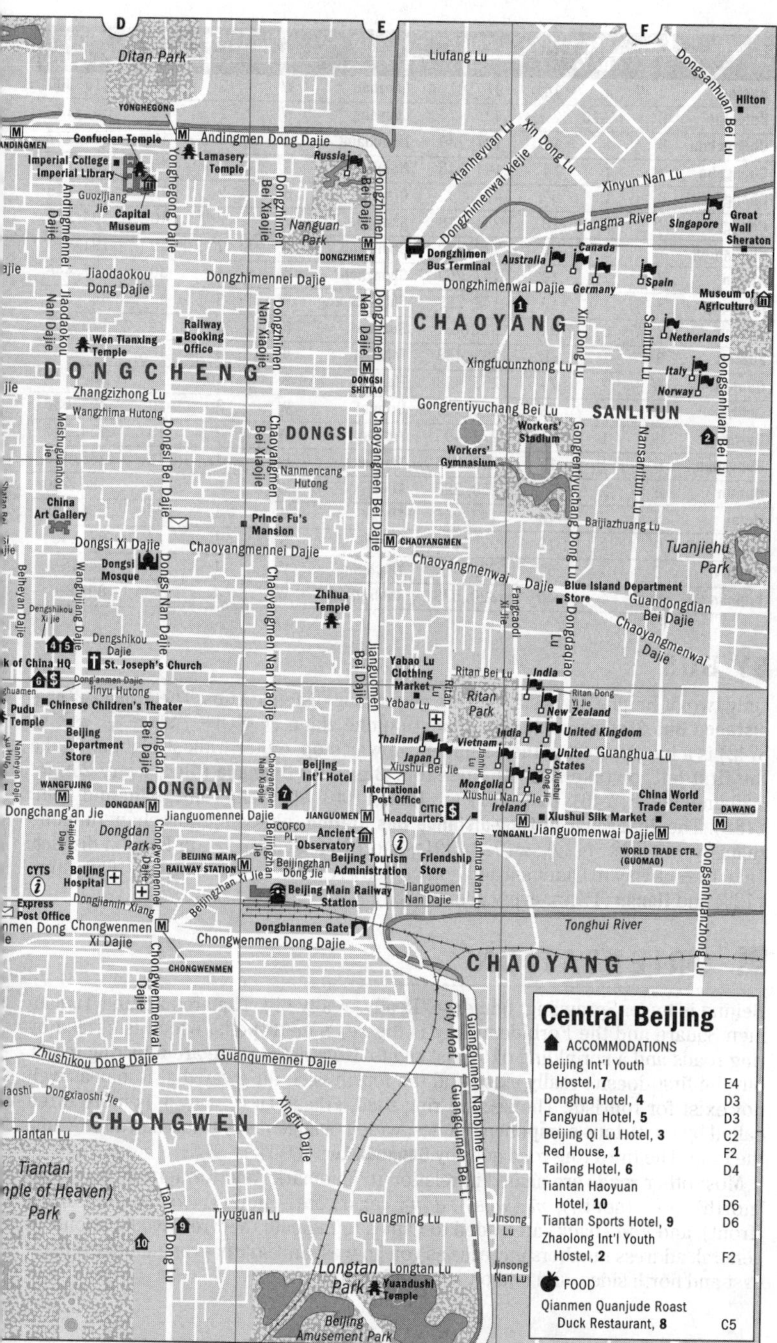
Central Beijing
ACCOMMODATIONS
Beijing Int'l Youth Hostel, 7 E4
Donghua Hotel, 4 D3
Fangyuan Hotel, 5 D3
Beijing Qi Lu Hotel, 3 C2
Red House, 1 F2
Tailong Hotel, 6 D4
Tiantan Haoyuan Hotel, 10 D6
Tiantan Sports Hotel, 9 D6
Zhaolong Int'l Youth Hostel, 2 F2
FOOD
Qianmen Quanjude Roast Duck Restaurant, 8 C5
DONGCHENG
CHAOYANG
SANLITUN
DONGSI
DONGDAN
CHONGWEN
Ditan Park
Confucian Temple
Imperial College
Imperial Library
Capital Museum
Lamasery Temple
Andingmen Dong Dajie
Nanguan Park
Dongzhimen Bus Terminal
Dongzhimennei Dajie
Dongzhimenwai Dajie
Workers' Stadium
Workers' Gymnasium
Prince Fu's Mansion
China Art Gallery
Dongsi Mosque
Chaoyangmennei Dajie
Chaoyangmenwai Dajie
Zhihua Temple
St. Joseph's Church
Chinese Children's Theater
Beijing Department Store
Ritan Park
Beijing Int'l Hotel
International Post Office
CITIC Headquarters
Ancient Observatory
Beijing Tourism Administration
Friendship Store
Beijing Main Railway Station
Dongbianmen Gate
Jianguomennei Dajie
Jianguomenwai Dajie
Xiushui Silk Market
China World Trade Center
Tonghui River
Chongwenmen Dong Dajie
Zhushikou Dong Dajie
Guangqumennei Dajie
Tiantan Lu
Longtan Park
Yuandushi Temple
Beijing Amusement Park
City Moat
Tuanjiehu Park
Blue Island Department Store
Great Wall Sheraton
Hilton
Museum of Agriculture

BEIJING

TO	站	PER DAY	HR.	PRICE (Y)	TO	站	PER DAY	HR.	PRICE (Y)
Baotou	B, W	3	14½	97, 181	**Lanzhou**	W	3	24	215, 390
Beidaihe	B	2-10	2½	42	**Luoyang**	W	2	12	53, 113
Changchun	B	1	12	137, 249	**Nanchang**	W	1	16	151, 277
Changsha	W	1	14	191, 345	**Nanjing**	B	2	10	150, 274
Chengde	B	1	5	41	**Qingdao**	B	2	10	116, 215
Chengdu	W	2	28	231, 418	**Shanghai**	B	2	10	184, 322
Chongqing	W	2	30	238, 430	**Shenyang**	B	2	10	191
Dalian	B	2	10	147, 269	**Shenzhen**	W	1	30	257, 448
Dandong	B	1	13	143, 263	**Shijiazhuang**	W	5	4	44
Datong	B, W	6	8-9	31-105,	**Suzhou**	B	1	14	170, 309
Fuzhou	B	1	35	253, 458	**Taiyuan**	B, W	3	10	79, 179
Guangzhou	W	2	24	253, 448	**Tianjin**	B	10	2	35
Guilin	W	1	28	276, 499	**Ürümqi**	W	3	60	363, 636
Guiyang	W	1	31	271, 490	**Wuhan**	W	2	13	154, 277
Hangzhou	B	1	12	200, 363	**Xiamen**	B	1	72	256, 415
Harbin	B	2	11	158, 290	**Xi'an**	W	4	29	150, 280
Hefei	B, W	2	13	143, 246	**Xining**	W	1	33	238-430
Hohhot	W	1	12	92, 170	**Yantai**	B	1	14	67, 145
Ji'nan	B	1	6	73	**Yinchuan**	W	1	21	94, 188
Kunming	W	1	40	320, 578	**Zhengzhou**	W	4	7-11	80,180

BY BUS

Only two of Beijing's bus stations are major long-distance hubs. The **Xizhimen Long-distance Bus Station** (xīzhímén chángtú qìchē zhàn; 西直门长途汽车站; ☎6217 8742) is a long way from the Xizhimen subway stop; either walk straight and take the first left, or take bus #16 one stop. Buses to: **Chengde** (4hr., every 20min. 6:20am-6:40pm, Y46); **Dalian** (17hr., 4pm, Y100); **Shenyang** (9hr., 9am and 1pm, Y188). The **Zhaogongkou Long-distance Bus Station** (zhàogōngkǒu chángtú qìchē zhàn; 赵公口长途汽车站; ☎6722 9491), is off Nansanhuan Lu, in Fengtai district. Take the subway to Qianmen and hop on bus #17. Buses go to **Qingdao** (16hr., 4pm, Y123) and **Tianjin** (1½hr., every 10min., Y31).

ORIENTATION

Beijing is huge. Sprawling. Immense. Really, really big. The area around Tiananmen Square and the Forbidden City is the city's metropolis, which is circled by ring roads and a sprinkling of tourist sights. Nominally, there are four ring roads, but the first doesn't really exist, and the fourth is so far away that it may as well not exist for tourists. The second ring road, **Erhuan Lu** (二环路), is more often called by its various component names, which change many times as you traverse the loop. The third ring road goes by **Sanhuan Lu** (三环路).

Most other roads are named in relation to landmarks and former city gates; *běi* (north), *nán* (south), *xī* (west), *dōng* (east), *nèi* (inner), *wài* (outer), *qián* (front), and *hòu* (back) are added to names to indicate their relative locations. In general, address numbers increase as you go west and south; even numbers are on east and north sides, and odd on west and south.

The most important thoroughfare is **Chang'an Jie** (长安街), which runs east-west between the Forbidden City and Tiananmen Square; it changes names continually and is also known as Jianguomenwai Dajie, Jianguomennei Dajie, Chang'an Dong Dajie, Chang'an Xi Dajie, Fuxingmennei Dajie, and Fuxingmenwai Dajie.

The **Forbidden City** and **Tiananmen Square,** on either side of Chang'an Jie, form the city center. From the south side of the square, **Qianmen Dajie** (前门大街) runs through a crowded business district to **Tiantan** before heading to budget hotels in the south. **Xidan** and **Wangfujing,** northwest and northeast of the square, respectively, are full of shopping options; cheaper goods abound at **Dazhalan** at Qianmen, directly south of the square. To the northeast is **Gongren Tiyuchang Bei Lu** (工人体育场北路), commonly known as Gongti Bei Lu, which leads to **Sanlitun,** an embassy compound. Older neighborhoods and alleyways are preserved in the northern areas around the **Drum Tower** and **Lama Temple.** The zoo, the silicon district, and Beijing and Qinghua Universities are in the far northwest; the **Summer Palace** and **Old Summer Palace** are even farther out.

LOCAL TRANSPORTATION

BY BUS

The Beijing bus system can be mystifying; but using the crowded buses, especially in combination with the subway, is a cheap way to get around Beijing. Most buses run from 5am to 11pm or midnight. Fare is generally Y1 regardless of destination; buses with air-conditioning cost Y2. The bus stops are pretty far apart, and sometimes the driver will skip entire stops if no one appears ready to get on or off. Most stops are in pinyin, but knowing the characters for your destination is helpful for finding the right bus. If all else fails, ask the ticket taker to tell you when you arrive at your destination. The scramble for seats at each stop can prevent successful disembarking, so get close to the door before you reach your stop.

There is a method to the madness of Beijing's 200-odd bus routes. As a general rule, buses #1-125 navigate the city center while #300 and above ply Beijing's periphery; #200s indicate late-night buses; #800s and #900s are air-conditioned. The **minibuses** that trail the regular buses follow the same routes and cost Y2. The table below lists some main bus routes and the areas they serve.

BUS #	ROUTE DESCRIPTION	BUS #	ROUTE DESCRIPTION
1, 4, 58	Chang'an Jie	5	North-South: Deshengmen-Qianmen Dajie
14	Jiaomen Nan Zhan-Yangqiao-Beihai	20	Beijing Main–Beijing South
21	Beijing West-Fuchengmen	44	Circle Line subway
54	Beijing Main-Yongdingmen	66	Beijing West-Yangqiao-Qianmen
103	Beijing Main-Wangfujing-Beihai-Zoo	106	Dongzhimen Bei Dajie-Yongdingmen
116	Tiantan-Dongsi Dajie-Ditan	300	Sanhuan Lu-Liangmaqiao-Sanlitun
322	Zoo-Summer Palace	808	Beijing Main-Qianmen

BY SUBWAY

Despite a relatively limited reach, the subway is a clean and reliable way to escape the Beijing traffic and construction. Trains run frequently from 5am to 11pm and cost Y3 regardless of destination. Beijing's subway system has two intersecting lines: the **Loop Line** (blue) cruises beneath the old city wall, circumnavigating the center of Beijing; and **Line #1** (red) runs directly under Fuxingmen Dajie/Chang'an Dajie/Jianguomen Dajie. To transfer between lines, follow the English signs and the rushing hordes at the **Fuxingmen** or **Jianguomen** stops. Signs are in both characters and pinyin, and stops are announced in Chinese and English.

BY TAXI

Base fare is Y10 (Y11, 11pm-5am) and each additional km is Y1.2-2. Pricier ones are slightly nicer and larger, but all taxis have air-conditioning. Always insist that drivers use the meter. Almost no cabbies speak English, few read pinyin, and Beijing is so large that many locations are first-time trips for taxi drivers. Many carry cell phones, so bring the telephone number of your destination and have them call to get good directions. Call **Beijing Taxi** (☎6837 3399) or **Beijing Tourism Taxi** (☎6832 2561) for pickup. For **taxi complaints,** call ☎6835 1150.

BY BIKE

As millions of locals have figured out, a bike is a pretty handy way to get around Beijing. Be warned, however, that there are no road rules here—motorists, cyclists, and pedestrians cross, weave, dash, cut, and crash at their own peril. Many hotels and hostels that rent bikes often lend out only the dregs; ensure that the bicycle is rideable before renting it. Also be aware that bike theft is common in Beijing. Hotels have been known to lend out a bicycle and a lock, only to send someone with another set of keys to trail the hapless biker and make off with the bike, so use a different lock if you have one. Bike parking generally costs Y0.2.

PRACTICAL INFORMATION

TOURIST AND FINANCIAL SERVICES

Tourist Offices: The vast majority of accommodations in Beijing have on-site travel agencies or arrange tours to popular sights. They can also book air and train tickets. There is a **tourist information service** in Beijing (☎6513 0828), but no tourism bureau. The **Beijing Tourism Administration,** Tourism Bldg., 28 Jianguomenwai Dajie (☎6515 8252), handles tourist complaints and large groups.

CITS: Beijing International Hotel, 9 Jianguomennei Dajie, west lobby. Airline office (☎6512 1368; fax 6528 2017). Open M-F 9am-noon and 1-5pm, Sa 9am-noon. International train office (☎6512 0507; fax 6512 0503). Y50 commission. Open M-F 8:30am-noon and 1:30-5pm. A branch in the World Trade Tower #2, 1 Jianguomenwai Dajie, Rm. 301 (☎6505 3775 or 6505 3776; fax 6505 3105) books airline tickets. Open M-F 9am-noon and 1-5:30pm, Sa 9am-noon.

Hualong International Travel Service (huálóng guójì lǚxíng shè; 华龙国际旅行社), Beijing International Hotel, 9 Jianguomennei Dajie, 4th fl. (☎6522 9444; fax 6512 4448). Open daily 8:30am-5pm.

Beijing Hotel Travel Service (běijīng fàndiàn lǚyóu bù; 北京饭店旅游部), Beijing Hotel, 33 Dong Chang'an Dajie (☎6523 2370; fax 6523 2372). Open daily 8am-10pm.

Jinghua Hotel (jīnghuá fàndiàn; 京华饭店), Xiluoyuan Nanli, Yongdingmenwai (☎6722 2211, ext. 3359; fax 6721 6383), off Nansanhuan Lu. Books domestic train (Y50 commission) and plane tickets. Open daily 8am-midnight. **Tianhua International Travel Service** (tiānhuá guójì lǚxíng shè; 天华国际旅行社; ☎8727 5387; fax 8727 5389), to the left of the business center and lobby of Jinghua. Books international and domestic train and plane tickets. Open daily 8:30am-8pm.

Embassies: Sanlitun and Jianguomenwai, near the Silk Market, are the main embassy compounds. See **Essentials: Consular Services in China** (p. 48) for complete listings.

Banks: Bank of China, 410 Fuchengmennei Dajie, 2nd fl., Counter #1 or 2 (☎6601 6688). Other branches: **Capital Airport; Asia-Pacific Bldg.,** 8 Yabao Lu, Chaoyang;

Lufthansa Center, 50 Liangmaqiao Lu, 1st fl.; **China World Trade Tower,** 1 Jianguomenwai Dajie, Ste. L204; **1 Dongchang'an Jie** at Wangfujing; **19 Dong'anmen Dajie** near Wangfujing; **CITIC Industrial Bank** (zhōngxìn shíyè yínháng; 中信实业银行), CITIC Bldg., 19 Jianguomenwai Dajie, Chaoyang; the **Friendship Store** (yǒuyí shāngdiàn; 友谊商店), 17 Jianguomenwai Jie. All exchange currency and traveler's checks. Most branches open M-F 9am-5pm.

ATM: There are over 70 ATMs in Beijing, with more sprouting up all the time. Nearly all accept **AmEx, Cirrus, MC, Plus,** and **Visa** cards. Locations include: **Bank of China,** 8 Yabao Lu, Chaoyang; 138 Wangfujing Dajie, in the Sun Dong An Plaza; 1 Dongchang'an Jie, at Wangfujing; **Palace Hotel,** 8 Jinyu Hutong, Dongdan Bei Dajie; **Landmark Towers,** 8 Dongsanhuan Bei Lu, Chaoyang; **Central Garden Hotel,** 18 Gaoliangqiao Lu, Haidian; **Capital Airport; Everbright China,** Chang'an Bldg., 7 Jianguomennei Dajie; **SCITECH Shopping Center,** 22 Jianguomenwai Dajie; **China World Hotel,** 1 Jianguomenwai Dajie, basement entrance.

American Express: China World Trade Center, 1 Jianguomenwai Dajie, Ste. 2101 (☎6505 2888), deals with lost American Express credit cards. For lost checks, first call the office in Sydney, Australia (toll free ☎1080 0610 0277).

LOCAL SERVICES

Bookstores: The following bookstores have a wide selection of English-Chinese dictionaries. **Wangfujing Xinhua Bookstore**, 218 Wangfujing Dajie, 2nd. fl. (☎6525 2592), left of the escalators. A gigantic bookstore with a fantastic selection of English-language classics, Chinese literature, and popular novels from *Harry Potter* to *The Hitchhiker's Guide to the Galaxy*. Open daily 9am-9:30pm. **Friendship Store** (yǒuyí shāngdiàn; 友谊商店), 17 Jianguomenwai Dajie, 1st fl., has a great bookstore and sells magazines.

Library: National Library (běijīng túshū guǎn; 北京图书馆), 39 Baishiqiao Lu (☎6841 5566), Haidian, near the zoo, next to the Purple Bamboo Park. Accessible by bus #332. Large foreign language section. Open daily 9am-5pm.

Movie Theater: Cherry Lane Movies (zhōngrì qīngnián jiāoliú zhōngxīn; 中日青年交流中心), Sino-Japanese Youth Exchange Center, 40 Liangmaqiao Lu (☎6461 5318), near the Lufthansa Center. Shows recent Chinese movies with English subtitles every Friday at 8pm. Y50.

Weather Conditions: ☎121 in Chinese and English.

EMERGENCY AND COMMUNICATIONS

PSB: 9 Qianmen Dong Dajie (☎6524 2063, foreigners' section 8401 5292, visa extensions 6532 3861).

Medical Services: All have English-speaking staff members. **Beijing International SOS Clinic** (formerly the **Asia Emergency Assistance International (AEA)**), BITIC Leasing Center, 1 Bei Lu, Xing Fu San Cun, Bldg. C, Sanlitun (24hr. ☎6462 9100, clinic 6462 9112). The state-of-the-art **Sino-Japanese Friendship Hospital** (zhōngrì yǒuhǎo yīyuàn; 中日友好医院; ☎6422 1122, foreigners ext. 5121), on Hepingjie Beikou, Chaoyang, just north of Sanhuan Lu, is renowned for treating foreign dignitaries. Accessible by bus #119 from Andingmen or #62 from Yonghegong. **Beijing United Family Hospital** (běijīng hémù fù'ér yīyùan; 北京和睦妇儿医院), 2 Jiangtai Lu, Chaoyang (24hr. ☎6433 3960), 5min. east of the Holiday Inn Lido, specializes in family medicine. Other hospitals: **International Medical Center (IMC),** Lufthansa Center, 50 Liangmaqiao Lu,

Ste. S106 (☎6465 1561); **Hong Kong International Center,** Swissôtel Hong Kong Macau Center, Ste. 93 (☎6501 2288, ext. 2346).

Internet Access: Qianyi Internet Cafe (qiányì wǎngluò kāfēi wū; 前艺网络咖啡屋; ☎6705 1722), Station Shopping Mall, 3rd fl., opposite the southeast corner of Tiananmen Square. Y10 per 30min. Drinks and snacks (Y15-25). Open daily 9:30am-11pm. **Spark Ice Internet Cafe,** China World Trade Center, 1 Jianguomenwai Dajie, 2nd fl. (☎6505 2288, ext. 80207), next to China World Hotel. Y15 per hr. Open 24hr. Deposit Y50. Midnight-noon Y4 per hr., noon-midnight Y8 per hr. **Feiyu Internet Cafe** (fēiyǔ wǎng bā; 飞宇网吧), 36 Haidian Lu, just east of the south gate of Beijing University. Y4-7 per hr., 7-9am free. Small discount for students. Open 24hr. Several other branches with the same rates also line Haidian Lu.

Post and Telecommunications: International Post Office (guójì yóujú; 国际邮局; ☎6512 8120), on the west side of Jianguomen Bei Dajie. Open daily 8am-6:30pm. EMS, IDD service, and Poste Restante. **Post and Telecommunications Office of the New Century** (☎6519 6630), on Jianguomennei Dajie, west of the Henderson Center, at Beijing Zhankou bus stop. Open daily 8am-6:30pm. EMS, IDD service, Internet (Y12 per hr.), Poste Restante, and Western Union.

Western Union: International Post Office, in the Postal Savings Money Order Hall; **China Post,** 7 Qianmen Dong Dajie; **Post and Telecommunications Office of the New Century** (see above).

Private Couriers: DHL Worldwide Express, China World Trade Center, 1 Jianguomenwai Dajie, Ste. 217, Sinotrans Express Center (☎6505 2173, ext. 8103). Open M-F 8am-8pm, Sa 8:30am-4:30pm, Su 9am-1pm. **UPS,** Sinotrans Pekair Parcel International Express Co., Ltd. (liánhé bāoguǒ yùnshū; 联合包裹运输), Beijing Kelun Plaza, 12 Guanghua Lu, Tower B, 1st fl., Chaoyang (☎6581 2088). **Federal Express** (liánbāng kuàidì; 联邦快递), Gaolan Plaza, 32 Liangmaqiao, 3rd fl., Chaoyang (☎6468 5566).

ACCOMMODATIONS

In Beijing, "budget" usually means "in a bad location"—most cheap accommodations cluster around the city's southern periphery. The hostels and hotels along **Nansanhuan Lu,** between the Yangqiao and Muxiyuan exits, teem with backpackers. These outposts provide dirt-cheap dorms, bike rental, ticket and tour booking, and Internet access. But the state of budget travel here is in constant flux; **Beijing International Youth Hostel** and **Zhaolong International Youth Hostel** are two shining examples of the the growing merger of budget and convenience.

During the summer, cheaper rooms are snatched up quickly, and hotels generally don't accept reservations. Your best bet is to suck it up and take a more expensive room for one night, then ask them to hold a cheaper room for you when one becomes available (and it inevitably will) in the morning. Those willing to splurge can find four- and five-star hotels almost everywhere. Most hotels have on-site restaurants and currency exchange, but do not accept foreign credit cards.

CITY CENTER (WITHIN THE SECOND RING ROAD)

Beijing International Youth Hostel (HI) (běijīng guójì qīngnián lǚshè; 北京国际青年旅舍), behind the Beijing International Hotel, 9 Jianguomennei Dajie, Bldg. 2, 10th fl. (☎6512 6688, ext. 6145 or 6146; fax 6522 9494), at the end of the road that heads north from the main train station. Accessible by bus to Beijing Zhan, the subway, and airport buses. Clean rooms, wooden bunk beds, and convenience for unbeatable prices. Packed with chatty foreigners. Bike rental (Y5 per hr., deposit Y300),

Internet (Y10 per 30min.), and laundry facilities (Y10). Reservations recommended. 6- to 8-bed dorms with A/C Y50, for non-HI members Y60. ❶

Beijing Qi Lu Hotel (běijīng qílǔ fàndiàn; 北京齐鲁饭店), 103 Dianmen Xi Dajie (☎6618 0966), near the north gate of Behai Park, accessible by buses #13, 107, 111, and 118 to Dongguanfang. Rooms have soft carpets and standard amenities. 24hr. hot water. Breakfast included. Currency exchange. Singles Y236; doubles with shower Y248, with bath Y272; triples Y258. Discounts depend on current occupancy. ❸

OFF WANGFUJING DAJIE

There are only a few comfortable hotels off the center road that are affordable. Their greatest asset is their location, a 25-minute walk from Tiananmen Square and the Forbidden City. The hotels are a 15-minute walk from the subway, and also accessible via bus (south on #10, 54, 120; north on #103, 104, 108, 111).

Tailong Hotel (tàilóng bīnguǎn; 泰龙宾馆), 51 Donganmen Dajie (☎6525 3498), right behind the Donghuamen night market. Lovely bedrooms. Clean baths have great water pressure. Deposit Y100. Doubles Y100, with bath Y200-280; triples Y240. ❷

Fangyuan Hotel (fāngyuán bīnguǎn; 芳园宾馆), 36 Dengshikou Xi Jie (☎6525 6331). Walk north on Wangfujing past the Starbucks; it's the first street on the left. Large rooms and claustrophobic halls. Breakfast included. Bike rental Y20 per day; deposit Y100. Reservations morning of arrival only. Deposit Y5. One (hard-to-get) single Y126; doubles Y177-267; triples Y342. ❷

Donghua Hotel (dōnghuá fàndiàn; 东华饭店), 32 Dengshikou Xi Jie (☎6525 7531), near the Fangyuan Hotel. Unbeatable location, but small rooms. Clean doubles and serviceable singles. 24hr. hot water. Breakfast included. Check-out 2pm. Usually-taken singles Y188. Doubles Y200-288. ❸

NORTHEAST OF CITY CENTER (SANLITUN AREA)

Zhaolong International Youth Hostel (HI) (zhàolóng qīngnián lǚshè; 兆龙青年旅舍), 2 Gongren Tiyuguan Bei Lu (☎6597 2299 ext. 6111; fax 6597 2288), at Sanhuan Lu, just behind the Zhaolong Hotel. Take bus #3, 43, or 300 to Baijiazhuang; it's a 5min. walk north. A cozier, less crowded, multi-level version of the Beijing Youth Hostel. Boasts sparkling rooms with A/C, bunk beds, tile floors, kitchen, and reading room. Common showers have fantastic water pressure. HI members: 3- to 6-bed dorms Y50, 2-bed dorms Y60. Non-members: Y60/Y70. ❶

Red House (ruìxiù bīnguǎn; 瑞秀宾馆), 10 Chunxiu Lu (☎6416 7810 or 6416 7500), off Gongti Bei Lu, a 10-15min. walk west of Sanlitun. Surprisingly comfortable dorms have A/C, bunk beds, and carpet. Each spacious 12-person suite has its own attached bath with Western-style toilet. 24hr. hot water. 12-bed dorms Y70. ❶

EAST OF CITY CENTER

Furong Hotel (fúróng bīnguǎn; 芙蓉宾馆; ☎6557 2921), on Shilipu, next to Hua Tang Shopping Center. Take bus #9 to Xiaozhuang and then #112 or 115 to Balizhuang. Sort of near the Silk Market shopping alley and far from everything else. Soft beds. 24hr. hot water. Breakfast included. Deposit Y50. Doubles with bath Y260-298. ❹

Leyou Hotel (lèyóu fàndiàn; 乐游饭店), 13 Dongsanhuan Nan Lu (☎6771 2266), in the Panjiayuan area east of Longtan Park. Take bus #28, 35, 52, 58, or 368 to Jinsong Dongkou. Flea market is a 10min. walk away. Ordinary rooms. Baths are bright and clean, and toilets offer a choice of big flush or small flush. 24hr. hot water. Breakfast included. Deposit Y50. Singles Y320; doubles Y320-430; triples Y398. ❹

SOUTHEAST OF CITY CENTER (NEAR TIANTAN)

Tiantan Haoyuan Hotel (tiāntán hǎoyuán bīnguǎn; 天坛昊园宾馆), 9A Tiantan Dong Lu (☎6701 4499; front bldg. ext. 3288; back bldg. ext. 2511 or 2512). Accessible via bus #34 or 36; or walk south from Tiantan's east gate, and it's down the first alley on the right; look for the red arch. As of July 2001, closed for renovation.

Tiantan Sports Hotel (tiāntán tǐyù bīnguǎn; 天坛体育宾馆), 10 Tiyuguan Lu (☎6711 3388), on the street opposite Tiantan's east gate. Buses (#6, 35, 39, 41, 43, 60) stop nearby. Cozy rooms. 24hr. hot water. Doubles Y260; triples Y380. ❹

SOUTH OF CITY CENTER

Jinghua Youth Hostel (jīnghuá fàndiàn; 京华饭店), Xiluoyuan Nanli, Yongdingmenwai Dajie, Fengtai (☎6722 2211, ext. 3359; fax 6721 1455), east of the smelly canal and McDonald's. Take bus #66 from Qianmen to Yangqiao. With co-ed dorms, a pool, and an unending flow of travelers, the Jinghua is a cauldron of carousal, arousal, and extra-spousal scandal. 24hr. Waley's Bar serves french toast and french fries. Cheaper dorms downstairs are basic; newer ones are a bit nicer. Tourist services galore. Bike rental Y10 per day (deposit Y100). Internet Y10 per hr. (deposit Y50). 20-bed dorm Y25; 4-bed dorms Y30-35; 3-bed dorms with bath and A/C Y50; doubles with bath Y140-230. ❶

Qiaoyuan Hotel (qiáoyuán fàndiàn; 侨园饭店), 135 Youanmen Dong Binhe Lu, Fengtai (☎6301 2244, ext. 3161; fax 6303 0119), a 500m walk west along the main street from the South Train Station (take bus #20 from Tiananmen East or Beijing Zhan, or #102). Thanks to Mr. John, budget travel coordinator extraordinaire, Qiaoyuan is chock full of foreigners looking for cheap, clean rooms. Nice common baths and fantastic doubles. Generally friendly staff, but a not-so-welcoming reception desk. Also has Internet access, discount airline tickets, bike rental (Y5 per day), and cheap tours. 4-bed dorms Y21-31. Deposit Y200. Doubles with shower Y132-192; triples Y150. ❷

Lihua Hotel (lìhuá fàndiàn; 丽华饭店), 71 Majiapu Dong Lu, Fengtai (☎6721 1144; fax 6721 1367), near Yangqiao. Accessible via bus #14, 66, or 343 from Lihua and bus #300, 324, or 368 from Yangqiao. Recently renovated. Nicely furnished, but higher priced doubles have bath and standard amenities. Deposit Y50. Doubles Y258. ❹

Sea Star Hotel (hǎixīng dàjiǔdiàn; 海兴大酒店), 166 Haihutun (☎6721 8855, ext. 3358; fax 6722 7915), Yongwai Mu Xu Yuan, Fengtai. Accessible via bus #2, 40, 54, 324, or 366. Basic dorms are downstairs. Fantastic 7-8 person dorms are in the works. The plush carpeted rooms were once luxury suites and have A/C, phone, and sparkling baths. Standard doubles boast large tubs. Internet Y10 per hr. Deposit Y100 and up. 5-bed dorms Y25; 4-bed dorms Y30; doubles with bath Y170 and up. ❶

WEST OF CITY CENTER (NEAR THE ZOO)

Beijing Institute of Education (běijīng jiàoyù xuéyuán; 北京教育学院), 2 Wenxing Jie (☎6835 2701). Take a bus to the zoo, then walk through the bus station across the street from the main gate; cross the street and walk down the alley opposite the back of the station, beside the shopping complex; take the first right, walk about 50m, and the entrance is a gate on the left. Go to either the right or left building to ask for a room (you may need to tell them about your "friend" who was a student here). Great prices for clean, spacious doubles with A/C. Usually home to picky CET foreign exchange students. Common showers and western-style toilets are scrubbed constantly. Call ahead to confirm availability. Laundry Y10 per load. Key deposit Y50. Doubles Y91. ❷

Evergreen Hotel (wànniánqīng bīnguǎn; 万年青宾馆), 25 Xisanhuan Bei Lu (☎6842 5154). Take bus #300, 323, or 374 to Wanshousi; or take bus #360 from the zoo to

Beiwa Lu, walk east to Sanhuan Lu, and head north for 10min. Ordinary standard rooms face a courtyard with the loudest cicadas known to man. The only convenient sight is the Wanshou Temple that houses the Beijing Art Gallery. Doubles Y262; triples Y282. ❸

NORTHWEST OF CITY CENTER

Beijing University Shaoyuan Hotel (běijīng dàxué sháoyuán bīnguǎn; 北京大学勺园宾馆), Bldg. 7 (☎6275 2218 or 6275 2200). Take bus #320, 332, 355, 732, 832, or 808 to Beida Ximen. Enter the west gate of the university on Yiheyuan Lu, walk between two lakes, and bear right past the basketball courts until you see Bldg. 7. If you use the pedestrian entrance, turn right first. Large rooms on one of China's prettiest campuses. Baths boast the whitest towels ever. The pleasant chatter of students buzzes from the basketball, tennis, and volleyball courts right outside. No hot water past midnight. Key deposit Y50. Singles Y200; doubles Y230-280. ❸

Zhongguancun Hotel (zhōngguāncūn jiǔdiàn; 中关村酒店), 19 Haidian Lu (☎6256 5577, ext. 2001 or 2002), about 2 blocks east of the smaller Beijing University south gate. Take bus #320, 332, or 808 to Zhongguancun, turn left, and walk down any street or alley on your right to Haidian Lu; the hotel is on your left. Ordinary standard rooms with nice wooden floors and vibrant surroundings. Internet cafes abound. Deposit Y102-132. Doubles Y268-298. Accepts credit cards and traveler's checks. ❹

Big Bell Temple Hotel (dà zhōng sì fàndiàn; 大钟寺饭店), 18 Beisanhuan Xi Lu (☎6211 3388, ext. 2138), under the expressway, about a block east from Big Bell Temple. Heralded by a fountain and a tall bowling pin. Cozy rooms with lacy curtains hide the unkempt, overgrown courtyard. Deposit Y50. Doubles with bath Y232-282. ❹

FOOD

The streets of Beijing boast dirt-cheap, delicious food options. Almost every little road-side restaurant serves up standard *jiāchángcài* (everyday family food; 家常菜). Few of these places have English menus, but they offer an unending selection of tasty, filling meals for about Y10-20 per person. Avoid being charged ridiculously inflated prices by asking to see the menu first.

Beijing is full of can't-miss culinary experiences. The two night markets off **Wangfujing Dajie** are filled with delectable delicacies and all the bubble tea you can drink. Red-and-white carts line **Donganmen,** off the north end of Wangfujing Dajie, tempting passersby with fried bananas with sugar and more exotic fare like whole sparrows on a stick (open daily dusk-10:30pm). Near the south end of Donganmen is the just-completed **Wangfujing Snack Street** (wángfǔjǐng xiǎochī jiē; 王府井小吃街). Here, excited vendors madly grill lamb, chicken, and every meat imaginable, stab a stick through it, and cover it with mouth-watering spices. Grab a seat and devour sizzling plates of rice and roodles (Y8) while opera singers perform on the outdoor balcony. To satisfy late-night cravings, take the subway to Dongzhimen to the popular 24-hour restaurants that, along with glowing red lanterns, line Dongzhimennei Daijie, also known as **Ghost Street** (guǐjiē; 鬼街). Help yourself to a mug of beer, a pile of crayfish, and platefuls of sumptuous food.

If there is one dish close to the heart (or stomach) of every Beijing local, it's the ubiquitous **jiānbǐng** (scallion pancakes; 煎饼), the mother of all snack foods. Look for carts with a black round frying skillet and feast on these delicious concoctions, made with globs of batter, an egg, tasty brown sauce, a pinch of scallions, and—if you're lucky—sesame seeds.

For fans of self-catering, supermarkets and shopping centers are scattered throughout the city. Some convenient locations include **Park N Shop,** in COFCO

BEIJING

Plaza, 8 Jianguomennei Dajie, Tower B, basement, diagonally opposite the Beijing International Hotel (open daily 8am-10pm); **Hualian Shopping Center,** across from the Vantone New World Plaza; and **Friendship Store Supermarket** (yǒuyì chāojí shāngchǎng; 友谊超级商场), at 17 Jianguomenwai Dajie.

BY REGION

CITY CENTER	PAGE	CUISINE
Fangshan Restaurant	130	Regional
No. 1 Kaifeng Sausage Dumpling Restaurant	129	Dumplings
The Sichuan	131	Sichuanese
DONGCHENG (EAST)	**PAGE**	**CUISINE**
Donglaishun Restaurant	129	Hotpot
Green Tianshi Vegetarian	131	Vegetarian
Hong Kong Food City	129	Cantonese
Shaoshan Mao	130	Special
Wonton Pavilion	129	Dumplings
E. OF CITY CENTER	**PAGE**	**CUISINE**
A Funti Hometown	130	Muslim
Almuhan Xinjiang	130	Muslim
Golden Elephant	129	Indian
Huajia Yi Yuan	131	Special

E. OF CITY (CONT.)	PAGE	CUISINE
Yuntai	131	Sichuanese
Omar Khayyam Indian	129	Indian
N. OF CITY CENTER	**PAGE**	**CUISINE**
Nine Headed Bird	131	Special
Nengren Ju	128	Hotpot
Pearl River Restaurant	129	Cantonese
Haiwan Dan	130	Special
Serve the People	130	Special
W. OF CITY CENTER	**PAGE**	**CUISINE**
Huahua Restaurant	128	Beijing Duck
S. OF CITY CENTER	**PAGE**	**CUISINE**
Dai Family Village	130	Special
Gongdelin Vegetarian	131	Vegetarian
Qianmen Quanjude	128	Duck

BY TYPE

BEIJING DUCK

A delicacy fit for a king at a price budget travelers can stomach, Beijing duck (kǎoyā; 烤鸭) is as important to Beijing history as the Forbidden City.

Qianmen Quanjude Roast Duck Restaurant (qiánmén quánjùdé kǎoyā diàn; 前门全聚德烤鸭店), 32 Qianmen Dajie (☎6511 2418 or 6701 1379). Founded in 1864, the Qianmen location is the oldest of 25 branches, and cooks 2000 quackers a day to fill the bellies of demanding patrons including Fidel Castro and Yanni. If you're going to splurge on a duck, do it with style–head through the archway to the fancier section. A duck can feed 3 people (Y168; with sauce, scallions, and pancakes Y184; carving extra). The fast-food area in front serves the same delicious duck (Y54 per person), but with less panache (read: paper plates). Meals Y75-100. "Fancier" part open daily 11am-1:30pm and 4:30-8:30pm; "less fancy" part 10am-10pm. ❹

Huahua Restaurant (huāhuā jiǔdiàn; 花花酒店; ☎8837 2129), on Wenxing Jie, a 5min. walk west of the Beijing Institute of Education. Good family-style food, oh-so-delicious Beijing duck. A duck serves 3 (with sauce, scallions, pancakes, and head Y38). Open 11am-2pm and 5-10pm. ❸

BEIJING HOTPOT

With vats of bubbling soup, vials of unnerving sauces, and heaps of raw meat, hotpot is like fondue on steroids. Vegetarians need not despair—all-veggie broths and non-meat ingredients (see **Appendix,** p. 833) are available.

Nengren Ju (néngrén jū; 能仁居), 5 Taipingqiao Dajie (☎6601 2560 or 6606 6993), near the White Pagoda Temple. Take bus #102 or 103 to Baita Si, and walk west; at the first crossing, head south. Nengren Ju is a hot spot for hotpot. Beijing style hotpot broth Y18-25; animal parts Y18-25; veggies Y4-5. Open daily 11am-2am. ❷

Donglaishun Restaurant (dōngláishùn fànzhuāng; 东来顺饭庄), Sun Dongan Plaza, 138 Wangfujing Dajie, 5th fl. (☎6528 0932), to the right of the escalators. Once the only place to go for hotpot, this busy restaurant still deserves its reputation. Hotpot broth Y15; most meat Y15-25; vegetables Y4. Open daily 11am-2pm and 5-9pm. ❷

CANTONESE

Hong Kong Food City (xiānggǎng měishí chéng; 香港美食城), 18 Dong'anmen Dajie (☎6525 7349), near Wangfujing Dajie. This huge, posh restaurant holds its own against the night market across the street. Specialities include bamboo cooked rice and shark fin soup. Skip the non-complimentary tea for a "Kiwi Kiss" (Y9), an icy blend of kiwi and pineapple. Most dishes Y25-100. 10% service charge. Open daily 11am-3am. ❸

Pearl River Restaurant (zhūjiānglóu cāntīng; 珠江楼餐厅), New Century Hotel, 6 Shoudu Tiyuguan Nan Lu, 3rd fl. (☎6849 1155). Take bus #105, 107, or 111 to Baishi Qiao and look for the white high-rise just south of Xizhimenwai Dajie. Behind its glitzy facade, Pearl River offers melt-in-your-mouth *dim sum* lunches Sa-Su. Eat to your heart's content, but skip the drinks (can of Coke Y20). Entrees and entrails Y30-80. 15% service charge. Open daily 11:30am-2:30pm and 5:30-10pm. ❸

DUMPLINGS

No.1 Kaifeng Restaurant (dìyīlóu kāifēng làcháng xiǎolóngbāo; 开封第一楼), 83 Qianmen Dajie (☎6303 0268). This *bāozi* shop is renowned for its traditional buns (Y9 per dozen) and tasty fillings. Open daily 8:30am-10:30pm. ❶

Wonton Pavilion (húndùn hóu; 馄饨侯), 11 Donganmen Dajie (☎6525 1892), at Wangfujing Dajie. Watch the chef behind a glass case creating delectable wontons (soups Y3-6) in a stuffing frenzy. Sesame cakes (Y2.5) and pickles are popular sides. Y15 per person. Open daily 7am-1am. ❶

FAST FOOD

The capital has over 60 **McDonald's** (màidāngláo; 麦当劳) restaurants, and there are few places where the insidious golden arches don't rear their ugly heads. **Kentucky Fried Chicken** (kěndéjī jiāxiāng jī; 肯德基家乡鸡) has been around since 1987; **Domino's Pizza** and **Pizza Hut** (bìshèng kè; 必胜客) have several branches around town. **Marrybrown Family Restaurant, Yongke Da Wang, Uncle Sam's,** and **Viva Curry** all do fast food with a twist. **Sammie's Cafe** delivers sandwiches. (☎6234 4487. Open daily 7am-midnight.) **Starbucks** (xīngbākè; 星巴克) continues its path toward world domination, setting up shop in the China World Trade Center, the Friendship Store, Wangfujing, and even inside the Forbidden City.

INDIAN

Omar Khayyam Indian Restaurant (wèiměijiā yìndù cānguǎn; 味美佳印度餐馆), Asia-Pacific Bldg. 8 Yabao Lu, M-01, Chaoyang (☎6513 9988, ext. 20188), behind the Bank of China. Delicious, authentic food, a charming, romantic atmosphere, and a great motto: "love all, serve all." Entrees Y38-82. Set lunch specials Y55. 15% service charge. Open daily 11:30am-2:30pm and 6-10:30pm. Credit cards accepted. ❹

Golden Elephant Spicy Restaurant (jīnxiàngyuàn dōngfāng cāntīng; 金象苑东方餐厅; ☎6417 1650 or 6417 1651), to the right of Sanlitun Lu; look for the sign. Master chefs from Thailand and India cook tempting South Asian cuisine like mandarin fish and shish kebabs. Entrees Y28-68. Weekday lunch buffet Y48. Open daily 11:30am-10:30pm. ❸

MUSLIM

Beijing is blessed with a large number of Uighur neighborhoods, though sadly, the largest one, which was near the zoo, has since been replaced by high-rises. Typical Muslim fare includes noodles (*miàn*; 面), *nang* flatbread, sumptious kebabs (*ròuchuàn*; 肉串), and Uighur tea.

A Funti Hometown Restaurant (āfántí jiāxiāng yīnyuè cāntīng; 阿凡提家乡音乐餐厅), 2A Houguaibang Hutong (☎6525 1071 or 6527 2288), in an alley just south of the Chaonei Xiaojie stop; take bus #101, 110, or 112. This Uighur funhouse serves up delectable Xinjiang fare, like melt-in-your-mouth "fried mutton with toothpick" (kebabs; Y32). A wild song-and-dance troupe performs M-Th at 8pm in what a flier describes as a "very impressive performance, which eventually includes at least one drunk *lǎowài* making a complete idiot of himself, great stuff." Entrees Y30-90. 2hr. Havana band F-Su. Open daily 10am-10:30pm. ❹

Almuhan Xinjiang Restaurant, 26 Dongzhimenwai Dajie, Chaoyang (☎6417 4888 or 6417 3568), opposite the Australian embassy, a 15min. walk east of the Dongzhimen subway stop. Crisp fried lamb breast, lamb kebabs, toasted lamb dumplings, and more lamb. An excellent music and dance troupe enlivens the crowd (daily 8:30pm); at other times, racy Arab music videos almost do the trick. Most entrees Y20-60. Open daily 11:30am-2pm and 5:30-11pm. ❸

REGIONAL/SPECIAL CUISINE

Shaoshan Mao Family Cuisine (sháoshān máojiā cài; 韶山毛家菜), 30 Yonghegong Lu (☎8404 6729), just south of the main entrance to the Yonghegong Temple. This laid-back restaurant is run by Chairman Mao's family and includes photos of Mao, paintings of Mao, and excellent Hunan cuisine. Enjoy the Great Helmsman's favorite dishes, including red-braised pork with chestnuts (hóngshāo ròu; 红烧肉). Meals (Y50) come with free Mao pins. Open daily 10am-10pm. ❸

Dai Family Village Restaurant (dǎijiā cūn; 傣家村), Guandongdian Nan Jie, Chaoyang (☎6585 8709), near Sanhuan Lu, about a block north of the Kerry Center Hotel. Also at 13 Tiyuguan Lu, Chongwen (☎6711 1616), east of Tiantan Park. Dai meals of mushroom, turtle, and snake are complemented by booze served in fat bamboo trunks and dancing performances in the aisles. Most dishes Y30-70; crispy scorpions Y80, meter-long snakes (slayed and brained before your eyes) Y150, camel paws Y320. Open daily 9:30am-2:30pm and 4:30-9:30pm; performances at 12:30, 6:30, and 7:30pm. ❸

Fangshan Restaurant (fǎngshàn fànzhuāng; 仿膳饭庄; ☎6401 1879 or 6401 1889), inside Beihai Park, halfway along the corridor that runs around Qiong Island. Those who'd rather eat than put a down payment on a new house can opt to invest in the outrageously priced 108-course banquet, a favorite of Empress Dowager Ci Xi. If that's too pricey, try the next best thing: *wowotou,* dry little corncakes that Ci Xi ate after she fled Beijing and had nothing to eat for 3 days. 14- to 16-course set banquets Y150-400 per person. A la carte option available for lunch. Open daily 11am-1:30pm and 5-7:30pm. ❺

Serve the People (☎6415 3242), Sanlitun Bar St., to the right of Sanlitun Lu, next to the Golden Elephant Restaurant. Communism was never so chic; sultry lighting accentuates simple, elegant decor. Sumptious Southeast Asian cuisine, with curries served in small fire-lit cauldrons, and flavored with coconut juice and bamboo. Entrees Y20-65. Open daily noon-10:30pm. ❸

Haiwan Dian (hǎiwǎn diàn; 海碗店), 11 Zhengguang Lu, East End, Haidian (☎8837 4993), near the zoo, just off the north end of Sanlihe Lu; look for a bright red awning and lanterns. Bus #102 to Ganjiakou Shangchang stops nearby. Dozens of young male waiters shout greetings as you enter (or break into spontaneous yelping just for the hell of it) and serve big bowls of *zhájiàng miàn* (炸酱面), a famous noodle dish with fresh veggies and savory brown sauce. The place is packed, the menu English, the service exciting, and the food fantastic. Entrees Y6-25; noodles Y8-10. Open daily 11am-11pm. ❷

Huajia Yi Yuan (huājiā yíyuán; 花家怡园), 99 Dongzhimennei Dajie, Dongcheng (☎6403 0677), on Ghost Street; take the subway to Dongzhimen. Bright red crayfish stream out of a gigantic cauldron (medium-sized platter Y20) and other delicious food is topped off by mugs of home-brewed beer (Y6). Most dishes Y20-40. Open 24hr. ❷

Nine Headed Bird Restaurant (jiǔtóuniǎo jiǔjiā; 九头鸟酒家), 141 Dianmen Xi Dajie (☎6651 9001), northwest of Behai and in front of the Behai Hotel; take bus #13, 42, 107, 111, or 823 to Changqiao. This monstrous creature was once a derogatory term for Hubei province residents, who have come to embrace their name just as Beijing has learned to embrace their food. Nearly every table has a plate of *dòupí* (rice and meat stuffed within thin layers of tofu; 豆皮) and some variation of lotus root (ǒu; 藕), a popular Hubei ingredient. English menu. Open daily 11am-9:30pm.

SICHUANESE

Sichuanese food is spicy, pickled, spicy, hot, and spicy—did we mention spicy? It packs enough punch to stun even the most dedicated spice-lovers and really isn't authentic unless it leaves your eyes teary, sinuses clear, and tongue numb.

The Sichuan (sìchuān fàndiàn; 四川饭店), A14 Liuyin Jie, Xicheng (☎6615 6924), left of Prince Gong's Former Residence, behind Beihai Park; follow the blue and white signs from Dianmen Dajie. Zhou Enlai called for the Sichuan's establishment in 1959, making the facial tissue market what it is today. A political bigwig favorite. Good service, friendly staff. Entrees Y26-98. Open daily 11am-2pm and 4-9pm. ❹

Yuntai Restaurant (yúntái cāntīng; 云台餐厅), Great Wall Sheraton Hotel, 10 Dongsanhuan Bei Lu (☎6590 5566, ext. 2295). The 3-pepper dishes here are hot enough to melt glass, while no-pepper dishes are for those who shouldn't be eating Sichuanese food in the first place. The hanging lanterns, floating candles, stellar food, and a posh 21st fl. location make the prices (mostly Y45-88) palatable. 15% service charge. Open daily 11:30am-2pm and 6-10pm. ❹

VEGETARIAN

Green Tianshi Vegetarian Restaurant (lǜtīanshǐ cāntīng; 绿天使餐厅), 57 Dengshikou Dajie, 2nd fl. (☎6524 2476), Dongcheng, east of Wangfujing Dajie. This lovely little restaurant's specialty is "the imitation of real meat, not only in appearance, but also in taste," achieved with ingredients like soybean protein, taro powder, mushrooms, and tofu. The "prawn" is interesting at the very least. Photo album menu also has helpful explanations about the magic of tea. Most dishes Y26-88. Open daily 10am-10pm. ❹

Gongdelin Vegetarian Restaurant (gōngdélín sùcài fànzhuāng; 功德林素菜饭庄), 158 Qianmen Nan Dajie (☎6702 0867); ride a bus to Zhushikou. Established in 1922, the Gongdelin is a pro at culinary deceit. Meals Y25-34. Open daily 10:30am-10pm. ❹

WESTERN

Western-style bakeries, like their fast-food counterparts, are spreading like hotcakes. **Déli France** sells authentic croissants and other pastries; some Sanlitun bakeries sell convincing French loaves. **Mrs. Shanen's Bagels** (shuānglóng wùzī gōngsī; 双龙物资公司), A3 Zhaojiu Lu, Jiuxianqiao, Chaoyang, turns out bagels by the dozen. (Delivery ☎6435 9561. Open M-Sa 8am-6pm, Su 8am-4pm.)

For an overpriced and overcommercialized Western experience, try the **Hard Rock Cafe,** at Landmark Towers, 8 Dongsanhuan Bei Lu (☎6590 6688, ext. 2571. Open Su-Th 11:30am-2am, F-Sa 11:30am-3am.) **TGI Friday's** (xīngqīwǔ cāntīng; 星期五餐厅), Huafeng Mansions, 19 Dongsanhuan Bei Lu, Chaoyang, also dishes up generic Western fare. (☎6597 5314. Open daily 11am-midnight.)

SIGHTS

CITY CENTER

TIANANMEN SQUARE

Between Chang'an Dajie and Qianmen Dajie. Take the subway to Qianmen. Buses #1, 4, 10, and 20 stop along Chang'an Jie to the north, while #5, 9, 17, 22, 47, 53, 54, 59, and 307 reach Qianmen to the south. Bus #116 runs along the side of the square.

Tiananmen Square (tiānānmén guǎngchǎng; 天安门广场), one of the largest and most notorious public meeting spaces in the world, has created enough historical and political cannon fodder to last for generations. As the political epicenter of popular protest in modern China, the square has witnessed May Fourth anti-imperialist demonstrations, anti-Japanese protests, Mao Zedong's proclamation of the People's Republic of China, Red Guard rallies of the Cultural Revolution, politically charged outpourings of grief for Zhou Enlai, and pro-democracy protests. For most Chinese, Tiananmen Square is an ideological mecca, a place to pay tribute to the heroes and victims of China's tumultuous history. Despite the bloody events of 1989 (see p. 20), the square seems rooted in an eternally celebratory atmosphere, a prime site for kite-flying and picture-taking. On certain occasions, when crowds fill this vast expanse of cement, as they did after the announcement of Beijing's victorious Olympic bid, nationalistic fervor and contagious enthusiasm will stir even the most skeptical of disbelievers.

TIANANMEN GATE (tiānānmén; 天安门). On the gate, a huge banner proclaims "Long Live the People's Republic of China, Long Live the Unity of the World's Peoples." It was on the rostrum of this gate, literally the "Gate of Heavenly Peace," that Chairman Mao declared the founding of the PRC in 1949, and his portrait (touched up yearly) still gazes serenely over the square. The climb to the top of the gate itself is not very interesting—there's only an off-limits collection of dining tables. Still, it does offer the best view of the square. Two stone lions guard each of the five bridges of **Jinshui (Gold Water) River,** which is actually a very small stream. *(At the northern end of Tiananmen Square. Open daily 8:30am-4:30pm. Y15, students Y5; bag deposit Y2.)*

ZHENGYANGMEN GATE (zhèngyángmén; 正阳门). Of the nine imperial gates *(mén)* that once guarded Beijing, only Zhengyangmen's character for *mén* (门) lacked the little hook at the lower corner. The emperor often traveled through this gate; since he was a descendent of a dragon—an aquatic creature—it was believed that the emperor could be snagged by a hook. In 1964, when the Beijing walls were torn down to make room for the subway and second ring road, only Zhengyangmen, better known as **Qianmen,** was left standing. A small exhibit has photos of Old Beijing. *(At the south end of Tiananmen Square. Open daily 8:30am-4:30pm. Y5, student Y3.)*

GREAT HALL OF THE PEOPLE (rénmín dàhuìguǎn; 人民大会馆). Home to the National People's Congress, this hall features a selection of province-themed reception rooms amid chandeliers and marble pillars. Room after room of chairs and rolled up carpet quickly loses its appeal, but the Grand Auditorium is worth a look for its 10,000 seating capacity. *(On the western edge of the square. Open daily 7:30am-3pm, except when the Congress is in session. Y20, student Y10.)*

CHINESE HISTORY AND REVOLUTION MUSEUMS (zhōngguó gémìng lìshǐ bówùguǎn; 中国革命历史博物馆). The **Museum of History** is on the right. Artifacts and pseudo-artifacts dating from 3000 BC to 1919 are arranged in a timeline defined by Marx's four stages of human development: primitive communal groups, slavery, feudalism, and capitalism/imperialism. As of August 2001, the museum was being "earthquake proofed," leaving curators to display only the most interesting 180 of 300,000 relics on the top floor. The **Museum of the Revolution,** on the left, would pick up where the Museum of History left off, beginning with the founding of the CCP (1919-21), were it not for earthquake worries. This museum is completely closed, with plans to reopen by summer 2002. No big loss. The museum experiences frequent re-fittings to accommodate the latest re-inventions of history. *(On the east side of the square. Open Tu-Su 8:30am-4:30pm; last admission 3:30pm. Museum of History Y20, students Y10, audio language tour Y20, deposit Y100 or passport; Museum of the Revolution Y5, students Y3.)*

CHAIRMAN MAO MAUSOLEUM (máozhǔxí jìniàn táng; 毛主席纪念堂). Before the Monument to the People's Heroes lies the resting place of China's famed Chairman, who has lain flag-draped in waxy splendor since 1976. Mainlanders flock to the Mausoleum for the allotted quick peek; the cult-like adoration that Mao enjoyed during his lifetime has obviously been little diminished by his demise. Epic lines of reverent visitors are shepherded with strict authority and white gloves through the dimly lit, red-carpeted tomb. Signs enjoin viewers to take off their hats and remain silent so as not to disturb the Great Embalmed One. Don't expect to see much—you're in and out of the building within five minutes thanks to the no-nonsense PLA. *(In the middle of Tiananmen Square; enter from the north door. Prepare for long lines, unless you time it right; try to go at 11-11:15am. No bags or cameras allowed; bag check across the street Y5-10. Open M-Sa 8-11:30am. Free.)*

BEIJING UNDERGROUND CITY (dìxià chéng; 地下城). Any civilization worth its salt should have a subterranean labyrinth. Beijing's chilly underground city was constructed in the 1960s when an ultra-idealist China faced nuclear threats from "hegemonic imperialist and revisionist powers" (namely the US and USSR). Hundreds of thousands of city residents could supposedly scurry down here within minutes of a raid. Following his death, Mao's body was taken down and a wax effigy constructed lest anything happen to the corpse (naturally, rumors abound). The dark, damp tunnels are not extraordinarily fascinating, but visitors emerge—of all places—into a full service silk factory, where they can watch the entire process of making silk quilts. *(62 Xidamochang Jie. Walk south on Qianmen Dajie and take the 1st alley on the left, just past the underground crosswalk stairs; continue for 15min., bearing right at the fork. Open daily 8:30am- 5:30pm. Y20, student Y15.)*

FORBIDDEN CITY

*Take any **bus** to Tiananmen Square. Go under Tiananmen Gate and continue until you reach the ticket booths for the Palace Museum. For the North Gate, take bus #101, 103, or 109. Open daily in summer 8:30am-5pm; in winter 8:30am-4:30pm; last admission 1hr. before closing. All halls have English translation; English tour guides (Y200) and highly recommended audio tours (10 different languages; Y30, Y100 deposit) offer a more in-depth understanding. Palace Museum Y40; ticket to Palace Museum, Jewelry Hall, and Clocks Hall Y60. Students half-price off palace ticket, children under 1.2m free.*

During the palace's 500-year history, only 24 emperors and their most intimate attendants could have known every part of its 800 buildings and 9000 chambers. The Forbidden City (zǐjìn chéng; 紫禁城), so named because commonfolk were barred from entering, was finally opened to the public in 1949. Now referred to as the **Imperial Palace** (gù gōng; 故宫), the complex is the largest and most impressive example of traditional architecture in China. The signs in the Forbidden City usually give at least three dates—of construction, destruction, and reconstruction. The palaces have seen so many face-lifts that it is hard to tell what is original anymore, but no amount of fresh paint can diminish the epic weight they carry.

Construction of the Forbidden City began in 1406, the 4th year of Ming Emperor Yongle's reign; the palace was significantly expanded during the Qing Dynasty. The first few halls of the Outer Court are the largest and most magnificent. It is within these ceremonial halls that the Son of Heaven conducted his stately affairs, often seated atop his imperial throne at the **Hall of Supreme Harmony.** All around are signs of the royalty, from lions at the gates (for loyalty), to the crane and tortoise incense burners (for good luck and longevity), to winding dragons (symbolizing the emperor himself). The Inner Court, where the royal couple, eunuchs, and concubines lived, was naturally a place of passion and intrigue. Take a peek at the silk flowered beds of the wedding chamber in the **Empress' Palace of Earthly Tranquility.** Finally, out back is the **Imperial Garden,** where visitors linger to appreciate the tranquil beauty and shade.

The Nationalist party took most of the palace treasures, which are now displayed at the National Palace Museum in Taipei, Taiwan; what remains still inspires gasps of awe. The **Hall of Paintings** to the west, just before Qianqinggong, is a dimly lit cavern of famous scriptures and paintings. The must-see **Hall of Clocks,** behind the Hall of Preserving Harmony, has rooms filled with unabashedly ostentatious European timepieces; some are so cluttered with gold leaf and dancing mechanical animals that it's impossible to tell the time. *(Open daily 8:30am-5pm; last ticket sold 4pm. Y10.)* Head north to the **Hall of Jewelry** and its splendid relics; visitors must shuffle about in neon orange overshoes (Y2) to preserve the brick floors. A **large theater** within this courtyard was once the stage for extravagant productions of Beijing opera. Before leaving, visitors pass a small well, where a beloved concubine of Emperor Guangxu was ordered drowned by Empress Dowager Ci Xi. *(Open daily 8:30am-5pm; last ticket sold 4pm. Y5.)*

Outside the Forbidden City, two parks offer an unexpected respite from the hordes of camera-clicking tourists. To the southwest is **Zhongshan Park** (zhōngshān gōngyuán; 中山公园), where the emperor would pay sacrifice to the gods of land and grain at the Altar of Five-colored Soil. *(Open daily 6am-10pm; last admission 9pm. Y3, students Y1.5, children under 1.2m free.)* To the southeast is the **Working People's Cultural Palace** (láodòng rénmín wénhuà gōng; 劳动人民文化宫) and **Imperial Ancestral Temple.** The inner court is like a tiny Forbidden City, surprisingly resplendent with marble terraces and stairways, but admission is an unjustifiable Y15. *(Open daily 6am-9pm. Temple 9am-4pm. Park Y2, students Y1, children under 1.2m free.)*

OTHER SIGHTS IN THE CITY CENTER

BEIHAI PARK (běihǎi gōngyuán; 北海公园). Home to the Liao dynasty palace some 800 years ago, this park is one of the world's earliest imperial gardens. Built in 1651, it sits on **Qiong Island,** home to temples (check out the esoteric deities) and cragged rocks. This central island was made from the mud collected as the lake was dug out by hand; it's connected to the surrounding land via a bridge, ferry, and Y20 per hour rental boats. The **Nine-Dragon Screen,** a 5m-long depiction of nine dragons batting pearls about in the turquoise water, the **Jade Buddha,** carved out of a single piece of white jade, and the 35.9m-tall **White Dagoba** (a Tibetan-style temple) are worth a look. The eastern and western shores boast gardens, religious buildings, and a small temple where Empress Dowager Ci Xi raised silkworms. *(Northwest of the Forbidden City. Buses #6, 101, 103, 109, 111, 202, and 802 stop outside its* *main gate in the south. Buses #13, 42, 107, 111, and 118 stop at the less crowded North Gate entrance. Open daily 6am-10pm. Park Y5; park and White Dagoba Y10; Round City Y5.)*

JINGSHAN PARK (jǐngshān gōngyuán; 景山公园). Only while standing atop Jingshan's highest pavilion can you truly appreciate the grand scale of the Forbidden City. The park presents visitors with picture-perfect views of the emperor's domain, a capsule of history against the backdrop of the modern city. Here, the Emperor Chongzhen, wracked with despair after insurgents captured the Forbidden City, hanged himself from a locust tree and ended the Ming dynasty. *(Jingshan Qianjie, directly opposite the north (rear) gate of the Forbidden City. Accessible by buses #101, 103, 109, 111, 114, 202, 211, 802, 810, and 812. ☎6404 4071. Open daily 6am-10pm. Y2.)*

AROUND THE SECOND RING ROAD

The second ring road roughly traces Beijing's old city wall. Subway stops are marked by the old locations of the city gates; although the gates are no longer standing, Beijingers still use the gate names as landmarks. Most sights around the second ring road are easily accessible by subway. Beginning with Deshengmen north of city center, the following gates are arranged clockwise.

DESHENGMEN 德胜门

PRINCE GONG'S RESIDENCE (gōngwáng fǔ; 恭王府). One of the few royal Qing residences remaining in Old Beijing, this jewel would be an idyllic paradise, were it not jam-packed with summer tour groups. The tourism bureau has taken over, and though the surrounding *hútòng* (胡同) remain unscathed (save for the bumper-to-bumper tour buses), you'll find yourself squeezing for space in the nine small courtyards of Prince Gong's hideaway. The residence is reputedly the model for the setting of the 18th-century literary classic *Dream of the Red Chamber*. Bamboo-lined paths open onto gardens of fuchsia flowers that are surrounded by a haze of white moths. *(14 Liuyin Jie, north of Beihai Park. Hard to get to except by taxi or pedicab. The closest bus stop is the Beihai Park North Gate. Open daily 8:30am-4:30pm. Guided tours with tea and performance Y60. Y5, student Y2.5.)*

DRUM TOWER (gǔ loú; 鼓楼). This vast structure has seen a few facelifts since 1272, including a major one in August 2001. Nevertheless, you can still climb steep, 600-year-old stairs for a peek—albeit an obstructed one—at the surrounding sights. With luck, the new Hutong museum will be more exciting than the downstairs "art museum" (i.e. comprehensive tourist shop). Nearby is the **Bell Tower** (zhōng loú; 钟楼) and its 63-ton bell. These two towers were once the keepers of "Beijing time," and would signal the closing of the city gates. *(At the northern tip of Gulou Dajie. Take bus #5, 58, 60, or 107; or take the subway to Gulou Dajie, then walk south on Jiugulou Dajie. Open daily in summer 9am-6pm; in winter 9am-4:30pm. Each tower Y6, both towers Y10.)*

SONG QINGLING MUSEUM (sòng qìnglíng gùjū; 宋庆龄故居). These grounds were owned by Song Qingling, wife of Sun Yat-sen and politically active in her own right. Named Honorary President of the PRC, Song was known as a proponent for democracy and civil rights. After her death in 1981, her home was turned into a museum. English translations describe photos, artifacts, and meticulously preserved rooms. *(46 Hanhai Beiyan. On the north edge of Houhai Lake, heralded by an ornate gateway. Take bus #5, 210, or 819 to Guozishi; or take the subway to Jishuitan and walk south on Gulou Xi Dajie. Open Tu-Su 9am-4:30pm. Last admission 4pm. Y8, students Y4.)*

XU BEIHONG MUSEUM (xú bēihóng jìniàn guǎn; 徐悲鸿纪念馆). Hailed as the father of modern Chinese painting and realist art, Xu Beihong enjoyed a long and distinguished career of "making ancient things serve the present" and "making foreign things serve China." This large and tastefully arranged museum features Xu's artwork as well as exhibits tracing his life history and travels. *(53 Xinjiekou Bei Dajie. South of the Jishuitan subway stop; also accessible by bus #22 from Qianmen. Open Tu-Su 9-11:30am and 1-4pm. Y5, students Y2.)*

BEIJING HUTONG TOUR. As Hong Kong tycoons turn vast swaths of Beijing's old neighborhoods into office buildings and hotels, tourism may be the last savior of the city's urban cultural heritage. For those not confident enough to navigate the narrow maze of *hútòng* (alleyways), this 2½-3hr. tour by rickshaw traverses one of Beijing's nicest gray brick neighborhoods, with stops at Prince Gong's Residence and the Drum and Bell Towers. *(☎6615 9097. Tours depart at 8:50am and 1:50pm from 26 Dianmen Xi Dajie, at Qianhai Xi Jie, 200m west of Beihai Park's North Gate. English tours available. Call ahead to reserve. Y180 per person, admission to sights included.)*

ANDINGMEN 安定门

LAMA TEMPLE (yōnghé gōng; 雍和宫). If you have time to see only one temple in the city, this colorful Tibetan Lamasery (a.k.a. **Yonghe Lamasery**) should be it. Wafting clouds of incense do little to obscure the brilliance of the blue, green, and gold detail of the red pagodas; the intricacy of the decoration both inside and out is breathtaking. Constructed in 1694 and converted into a lamasery in 1744, Yonghe successfully combines Han, Mongol, Manchu, and Tibetan architectural elements. The temple boasts three "matchless treasures": an 18m high sandalwood **Buddha statue,** with a plaque from the Guinness Book of World Records certifying that the Buddha was carved from one really big tree; the **Mountain of 500 Arhats,** made of precious stones and less-precious metals; and the **"niche of Buddha"** carved out of wood. One exhibition hall displays portraits of Dalai Lamas; the other, more interesting one chronicles (in English) the life of Emperor Qianlong, who promoted the spread of Tibetan Buddhism. *(28 Yonghegong Dajie. Take bus #13, 116, or 807 to Yonghegong or Guozijian, or walk south from the Yonghegong subway stop; enter at the tail end of the temple. Open daily 9am-4:30pm. Y15; temple and exhibition halls Y20.)*

BEIJING

CONFUCIUS TEMPLE (kǒng miào; 孔庙) **AND IMPERIAL COLLEGE** (guózǐ jiān; 国子监). Less grand than the Lama Temple and its counterpart in Qufu (p. 188), this quiet refuge is mostly overlooked by tourists. Inside, 198 stone stelae list the names of over 50,000 successful candidates for the *jìnshì* degree, the highest level of academic achievement in the imperial civil service examination system. Like most academic records, these heavy tablets are stored in an old, dim warehouse way in the back. The complex also houses the small **Capital Museum** (shǒudū bówùguǎn; 首都博物馆), which traces the history of Beijing, beginning 400,000 years ago with Sinanthropus Pekinensis (Peking Man; see p. 150) and ending with "liberation" in 1949. *(13 Guozijian Jie, diagonally opposite the main gate of the Lama Temple. Enter through a decorated archway and walk straight for 3min. Open daily 8:30am-5pm; last admission 4:30pm. Y10, elders Y6, students Y3.)*

JIANGUOMEN 建国门

BEIJING ANCIENT OBSERVATORY (běijīng gǔ guānxiàngtái; 北京古观象台). Within Beijing's busy financial district lies one of the world's oldest observatories. Built in 1442 and still in terrific condition, this sanctuary displays amazingly sophisicated navigational and astrological instruments—pieces of art in themselves. On the rooftop, eight such instruments bear exotic names like "Azimuth Theobolite," "Equatorial Armilla," and "Celestial Globe." *(West of the Friendship Store, southwest of the intersection of the Erhuan Lu and Jianguomennei Dajie. Take the subway to Jianguomen and take the southwest exit; it's around the corner. Open daily 9am-5:30pm. Y10, children Y5.)*

RITAN PARK (rìtán gōngyuán; 日坛公园). Ritan Park, shielded from the bustle of Jianguomen, is one of Beijing's oldest and most pleasant parks. Winding paths and bamboo fences lead to cragged rock formations and sleepy waterways near the south gate. Ritan ("Temple of the Sun") has a lofty heritage as a place of sacrifice. *(South, main gate at the end of Jianhua Lu, in the heart of the embassy district behind the Friendship Store. West gate at the end of Yabao Lu, opposite the Russian shopping district. Buses #1 and 4 stop nearby on Jianguomenwai Dajie. Open daily 6am-9pm. Y1.)*

CHONGWENMEN 崇文门

TIANTAN (TEMPLE OF HEAVEN) PARK

South of the city center, between Erhuan Lu and Sanhuan Lu, bordered by Tiantan Lu, Yongdingmennei Dajie, Tiantan Dong Lu, and Yongdingmen Dongbinhe Lu. Buses #2, 15, 17, 34, 35, 36, 110, 105, 610, 812, and 943 stop at 1 of the 4 gates. Open daily 6am-9pm; sights open 8am-5:30pm. High season: park Y15, students Y8, through ticket (to all three sites) Y35; low season: park Y10, through ticket Y30.

A total of four *tán* (imperial shrines) were constructed in Beijing as the sacrificial altarplace for *tiān* (heaven), *dì* (earth), *rì* (sun), and *yuè* (moon). The largest of these, Tiantan Park (tiāntán gōngyuán; 天坛公园) was designed as a venue for the annual imperial ceremony to appease the heavens, secure good harvests, atone for sins, and receive divine direction. The 273-hectare complex is rounded at its northern edge and square along the southern, reflecting the traditional Chinese belief that the earth is square and the heavens are round. Within the park compound, a long, unshaded stone boulevard once carried imperial processions from "earth to heaven." Constructed in 1420 and opened to the public in 1949, Tiantan draws crowds of *tai chi* practitioners, bird cage bearers, and opera singers at dawn.

HALL OF PRAYER FOR GOOD HARVEST (qínián diàn; 祈年殿). The highlight of Tiantan, this 38m-high, 30m-wide round hall features a triple-eaved roof covered with blue-, yellow-, and green-glazed tiles that represent the heavens, earth, and mortal world. A hallmark of Ming engineering, the hall was built entirely without the use of nails, cement, or beams, and is held together by an elaborate network of interlocking pillars. Inside, four gigantic "dragon" pillars represent the seasons and two dozen smaller ones symbolize the 12 months of the year.

ECHO WALL (jiǔlóng bǎi; 九龙柏). Thanks to its perfect curvature, a mere murmur at one side of this 65m-in-diameter wall will supposedly travel with perfect clarity all the way to the other. But with visitors hooting and howling all around, it's impossible to put that theory to the test. The **Triple Echo Stones** (sānyīn shí; 三音石), immediately in front of the hall, are similarly hindered by all the din. Stand on the first stone and clap, and the echo comes back once; on the second stone, the sound returns twice; and on the third, three times. Though you might be hard pressed to actually hear an echo, what you will hear is a continuous, "I think I heard something..." murmur thoughout the courtyard. Clamor aside, this courtyard was designed to enclose the **Imperial Vault of Heaven** (huáng qióng yǔ; 皇穹宇), which housed tablets used in sacrificial rites. A smaller version of the main hall, this vault is likewise topped by a blue-tiled, mushroom-cap roof, on which a blue-green gilded dragon plays with a pearl. *(South of the Hall of Prayers for Good Harvests.)*

ROUND ALTAR (yuán qiū; 圆丘). This sight will tickle a numerologist's fancy; its structure, surrounding stairs, and railings are all based on the lucky imperial number "9." The three tiers of the altar represent the heavens, earth, and humankind. Join the other stamping, yelling, and occasionally mooing visitors eager to test out the timeless qualities of physics from the central stone on the top tier; the sound will bounce off the stones. *(Farther south along the main park axis.)*

STAYIN' ALIVE With a 5000-year history lurking around every corner and a traditional preoccupation with brute longevity, it's not surprising that the Chinese have fine-tuned intricate workout routines to keep themselves fit and long-lasting. A good exercise regime includes several of the following:

Tree Slapping: A sort of basic man-to-nature catharsis, this activity allows the slapper (we don't know about the trees) to breathe in fresh air while expelling bad energy.

Head Standing: Meditating with your head and feet in swapped positions promotes clearer thinking by increasing blood circulation to the brain.

Walking Backward: Ancient records of an immortal who walked backwards at the speed of light have inspired many to lightfoot it butt-first through the parks. Karmic reversal is also hoped to be an associated benefit. Avoid busy highways.

Walking Barefoot: Because the body's major acupuncture channels connect to the soles of the feet, walking barefoot is a cheap and easy way of revitalizing the body's main meridians.

Primal Scream: A good, loud yell can drive out built-up bad energy in your system; usually practiced in the workplace by competing hawkers.

Finally, at the end of all the exercise, there's nothing better for keeping the spirit alive than squatting by the side of the road and smoking a pack of Chinese cigarettes while staring at the *lǎowài* (foreigner).

FASTING PALACE. Emperors would sequester themselves here, away from the wily reaches of meat, drink, and women for three days before sacrificial rites. The buildings, as one would expect of a fasting palace, are not terribly exciting, but do contain the original furniture from Qianlong's reign. *(Near the West Gate.)*

OTHER SIGHTS IN CHONGMENWEN

NATURAL HISTORY MUSEUM (zìrán bówùguǎn; 自然博物馆). The largest museum of its kind in China, this place hardly takes itself seriously; it even quotes Gorky ("Man, oh what an arrogant creation!") and has displays on Tsingtao beer. The main halls focus on flora, fauna, and human evolution. There is a graphic excess of pickled worms and deformed fetuses preserved in formaldehyde, but you can easily avoid those and spend your time with enormous dinosaur fossils. English translations are patchy if you can't decipher Latin genus names. *(126 Tianqiao Nan Dajie, an ivy-covered building 7min. north of Tiantan Park's West Gate. Take bus #2, 6, 20, 54, 120, or others to Tianqiao or Tiantan. Open daily 8:30am-5pm; last admission 4pm. Y15, students and elderly Y10.)*

XUANWUMEN 宣武门

GRAND VIEW GARDEN (dàguān yuán; 大观园). Grand View Garden was planned and built according to depictions of the garden in Cao Xueqin's *Dream of the Red Chamber;* in fact, the TV movie was filmed here. The landscape is surreally pristine, with romantic names like "Dripping Emerald Pavilion" and "Grave for Flowers." Familiarizing yourself with the story beforehand is a good idea, given the lack of English translation. Lakeside paths make for a gorgeous walk in this imagined world. *(Nancaiyuan Jie, west of Taoranting along Yongdingmen Dongbinhe Lu. Buses #59 and 351 terminate at the park, and #19, 59, 122, 395, 816, and others stop nearby. Open daily 8:30am-5:30pm; last admission 4:30pm. Carriage rides Y10. Y15, student Y8.)*

TAORANTING PARK (táorántíng gōngyuán; 陶然亭公园). Taoranting is one of the city's most serene parks. Behind the family-friendly amusement parks and waterslides are picturesque lakes where lovers snuggle and the elderly stroll. Look for the Yuan dynasty **Temple of Mercy,** which was used as a base by May 4th revolutionaries. *(19 Taiping Jie, between Taoranting Lu and Yongdingmen Dongbinhe Lu. Buses #20, 54, 102, and 106 stop at Taoran Qiao, in front of the park. Open daily 6am-10pm; in spring and autumn 6am-9pm; in winter 6:30am-8:30pm. Y2.)*

NIUJIE MOSQUE (niújiē lǐbài sì; 牛街礼拜寺). Built in AD 996 by the Arab scholar Nasuratan, the mosque combines Arab and traditional Chinese palace architecture. The intricately decorated **main hall** opens up onto panel after panel of gold Arabic script on a red background. The breathtaking hall spills into a courtyard of green plants and pink flowers. The mosque is fully operational, and visitors must respect all rules regarding personal appearance. Don't despair; the mosque lends out garish checkered pants to anyone not appropriately dressed, to the amusement of its friendly inhabitants. *(On Niu Jie, south of Guanganmennei Dajie. Accessible by bus #40, 61 from Xidan, and 88. Open daily 8am-4pm. No skirts or shorts. Y10, students Y5.)*

WHITE CLOUD TEMPLE (báiyún guān; 白云观). White Cloud, Beijing's most active Daoist temple complex, is a sleeper of a tourist attraction. The **Shrine Hall for the Jade Emperor** houses two large, very out-of-place, light-up, revolving cones that are reminiscent of Christmas trees. Beyond that, White Cloud's biggest attraction is the "wind-containing" bridge. Visitors can hurl tokens (Y0.2) at a large coin with a bell in its center underneath the bridge; a hit brings good luck, granted to you by a tiny voice that booms metallically out from under the bridge. *(6 Baiyun Lu, Xibianmenwai. Take bus #40 to Tianning Si; head north. Open May-Sept. daily 8:30am-5pm; Oct.-Apr. 8:30am-4pm. Last admission half-hour before closing. Y10.)*

FUXINGMEN 复兴门

NATIONAL MILITARY MUSEUM (jūnshì bówùguǎn; 军事博物馆). With an overwhelming number of camera flashes and enough artillery to start a revolution, this museum very quickly begins to resemble the set for *Pearl Harbor*. They've got missiles, tanks, mine-layers, and fighter planes on the ground floor, and every type of handheld weapon known to mankind on the second. Just to remind people that peace *is* better than war (it's easy to get a bit carried away downstairs), the top floor has a quiet display of friendship gifts presented to China from various countries. But few make it up this far, instead prefering to drool over the grenade and torpedo displays. *(9 Fuxing Jie. ☎6686 6244. Accessible by bus #1, 4, or 57 from Tiananmen, or take the subway to Junshi Bowuguan; it's the huge building with the unmistakable PLA star perched atop. Open daily 8:30am-5:30pm; last admission 4:30pm. Y5, students Y2.)*

FUCHENGMEN 阜成门

GUANGJI TEMPLE (guǎngjì sì; 广济寺). Built by a villager during the Jin dynasty (AD 280-316) and excavated during the Ming, this temple features images of Buddha, stone turtles, and pillar fragments that confirm the ruined temple's original location. Lovely to the eye, it is little wonder why the Chinese Buddhist Association chose this quiet refuge as its headquarters in 1953. Bright red columns enclose a library of 100,000 volumes of scriptures in over 20 languages. *(25 Fuchengmennei Dajie, at Xisi Dajie. Take bus #13 or 103 to Xisi. Open daily 6am-6pm. Free.)*

WHITE PAGODA TEMPLE (báitǎ sì; 白塔寺). The temple's huge, chalky form was designed to look like an upside-down alms bowl. There is a small collection of Qing-era Buddhist relics, and one room houses more Tibetan-style Buddha statues than you can imagine. Going around the pagoda clockwise, from west to east, is said to bring "merits and happiness and dispels evils and disease." *(171 Fuchengmennei Dajie. Take bus #13, 103, or 814 to Baitasi, or walk 8min. east from the Fuchengmen subway stop. Open daily 8:30am-5pm; last admission 4:30pm. Y10, students and elders Y5.)*

LU XUN MUSEUM (lǔxùn bówùguǎn; 鲁迅博物馆). This museum offers an in-depth perspective on the author of *The Madman's Diary* and *The Story of Ah Q*. *(19 Gongmenkou Ertiao. Take the 1st left as you walk east on Fuchengmennei Bei Dajie from the Fuchengmen subway stop; it's at the end of the road. Open Tu-Su 9am-4pm; last admission 3:30pm. Y5, students Y3.)*

XIZHIMEN 西直门

BEIJING ZOO (běijīng dòngwùyuán; 北京动物园). Weeping willow-shaded paths, placid lakes, and chirping birds make the zoo a pleasant spot for a stroll. The zoo's permanent residents, however, don't have it nearly so nice: most live in dusty, dirty enclosures and appear bored or on the verge of serious depression, except for the occasional overly excited monkey. Adorable pandas are the major tourist attraction, and live in more comfortable surroundings. *(West of the Xizhimen subway stop. Accessible by bus #7 from Hepingmen, #15 from Fuxingmen, #27 from Deshengmen, #102 and 105 from Xuanwumen, #103 from Wangfujing, #107 from Dongzhimen, and #111 from Chongwenmen: the terminus for several buses. Virtual tour at www.beijingzoo.com. Open daily 7:30am-6pm. Y10, students Y5, children under 1.2m free. Pandas an additional Y5.)*

PURPLE BAMBOO PARK (zǐzhúyuàn gōngyuán; 紫竹院公园). This is where Beijing's lovers go to grow drowsy in one another's arms. The park is a gorgeous emerald maze of waterways and footbridges, with sprawling lawns, pavilions, and lots of bamboo. *(On Zizhuyuan Lu, west of Xizhimenwai Dajie. Until construction finishes, catch bus #4, 6, or 332 to Baishi Qiao and use the west gate. Otherwise, take bus #114, 332, or 360 to Zizhuyuan. Open daily 6am-10pm; last admission 9pm. Y2, students Y1.)*

BEIJING

BEYOND THE THIRD RING ROAD

SUMMER PALACE

The quickest way to the Summer Palace is minibus #375 from Xizhimen station. Bus #332 from the zoo, 726, 826, and 832 terminate here. From Qianmen, the Palace is about 2hr. away by bike. Open daily 6:30am-6pm; in winter 7am-5pm. All halls close 1hr. beforehand. Apr. 1-Oct. 31 Y30, in summer students Y15, through ticket Y50 (includes Garden of Virtue and Harmony Y5, Tower of the Fragrance of Buddha Y10, and Suzhou Jie and the Hall of Serenity Y10); Sept. 1-March 3 Y20, students Y10, through ticket Y40. English maps Y5.

Constructed in 1750, the magnificent **Summer Palace** (yìhé yuán; 颐和园) is the largest imperial palace and garden complex in China. The emperors' enormous summertime playground houses over 3000 halls, pavilions, towers, and courtyards. From the main, east entrance and the **Hall of Benevolence**, turn right to view the **Hall of Preserving Harmony.** Old buggies and carriages are displayed in the first hall, which is in front of **Garden of Harmonious Virtue** (déhé yuán; 德和园). The grand **theater** that dominates the center of the courtyard held Beijing Opera performances. The **side rooms** display "everyday" artifacts and many rooms are furnished as they would have been a hundred years ago.

Backtrack a bit and turn left past the Hall of Benevolence for a stroll along the stunning 728m **Long Corridor** (cháng láng; 长廊) as it meanders along the **Kunming Lake.** Admire the 14,000 pastoral pictures painted on the ceiling as you head toward the **Tower of the Fragrance of Buddha** (fóxiāng gé; 佛香阁), atop Longevity Hill. Perfectly situated for emperors seeking divine guidance without leaving their vacation resort, this octagonal structure also provides a gorgeous view of the lake. Nearby is the **Buddhist Tenants' Hall** and the **Pavilion of Fragrant Rocks,** where you can duck in and out of the oddly shaped stone passageways.

Along the back lake is a must-see, albeit slightly artifical, re-creation of the southern Chinese city of Suzhou (see p. 349) where empresses could go "shopping" for fine silk. Within **Suzhou Jie** (苏州街), cool green water laps the sidewalks, stylized gondolas idle beside dumpling restaurants, and stone walkways wind between water on one side, and shops, snack stands, and street artists on the other. Follow the signs to get to the less-traveled, northern area of the park. Here you'll find the **Hall of Serenity**, which displays a collection of imperial furniture, and the **Garden of Harmonious Pleasures.** This "garden within a garden" boasts photogenic waterside pavilions and tranquil lily ponds.

Other sights include Empress Dowager Ci Xi's infamous **Marble Boat** (built in 1888 courtesy of embezzled funds), the **Seventeen Arch Bridge** topped with 544 stone lions, the **Pavilion for Listening to Orioles,** and the **Porcelain Pagoda.** *(Stations open daily 8am-around 6pm. Y30-40 per hr., deposit Y100-200. Small, imperial style ferries make one-way trips to different areas along the lake 9am-6pm. Y6.)*

OTHER SIGHTS BEYOND THE THIRD RING ROAD

OLD SUMMER PALACE (yuánmíng yuán; 圆明园). Unlike its splendid younger counterpart, the desolate Old Summer Palace remains in ruins from its plunder and pillage by French and British troops during the Second Opium War; only the winding stone **labyrinth,** an imitation European-style maze, remains unscathed. Today, only broken stone fragments—some haphazardly piled together—and the gardens' pretty names (like Eternal Spring Garden) offer a glimpse of the palace's former grandeur. *(Northeast of the Summer Palace. From the Summer Palace, take a minibus (Y5) or taxi (Y10). Bus #375 from Xizhimen, and #333 and 318 from Fragrant Hills stop outside. Open daily 9am-6pm. Tour guide Y60. Grounds Y10, student Y5; European Palaces and Labyrinth Y15, students Y5.)*

GREAT BELL TEMPLE (dàzhōng sì; 大钟寺). This endearingly enthusiastic temple believes that "every bell is a nutshell of a part of history and culture." The "bell forest" contains several hundred bells, from primitive pottery bells to utilitarian Mao-era bells. One of the world's oldest bells and China's largest, the **Great Bell** has over 230,000 characters from the Buddhist scriptures and prayers carved onto it (duck your head inside for a look). For Y2, visitors can climb a set of stairs and toss a coin in the hole of the bell for happiness. *(31A Beisanhua Xi Lu. Buses #300, 367, and 601 from the zoo stop outside. Open daily 8:30am-4:30pm. Y10, students Y5.)*

ENTERTAINMENT

ACROBATICS

Chinese acrobatics is a dizzying pinnacle of artistic achievement: plates spin on poles and grinning contortionists fold in half while trapeze artists, tumblers, and dozens of girls perch precariously on unicycles.

Chaoyang Theater (cháoyáng jùchǎng; 朝阳剧场), 36 Dongsanhuan Bei Lu, Hujialou, Chaoyang (☎6507 2421). Tickets Y100-150. Performances nightly 7:15-8:30pm.

Tiandi Theater (tiāndì jùchǎng; 天地剧场), 10 Dongzhimenwai Dajie (☎6502 3984 or 6502 2649), 3min. north of the Poly Plaza. Features the **Children's Team of the China Acrobatics Troupe.** Tickets Y120. Performances nightly 7:15-8:30pm.

Wansheng Theater (wànshèng jùchǎng; 万胜剧场), 95 Tianqiao Shichang, Xuanwu (☎6303 7449 or 6702 2324). Features the **Beijing Acrobatics Troupe.** Tickets Y100-150. Performances nightly 7:15-8:45pm.

A NIGHT AT THE JINGJU There are as many types of Chinese opera as there are Chinese dialects, but **Beijing opera** (jīng jù; 京剧) has by far the best reputation. Established in 1790 during the Qing dynasty, Jingju has entertained audiences with dramatic (though not entirely accurate) accounts of Chinese history and classical tales. In Beijing opera, there are four main role types: *shēng* (male role), *dàn* (female role), *jìng* (painted-face role), and *chǒu* (clown). Each type has unique costuming and facial makeup; the different colors of painted faces represent different personalities. Yellow or white signifies cunning; red, uprightness and loyalty; black, valor and wisdom; blue or green, vigor (often rebellious); and gold or silver, mysticism or supernatural power. Performances are accompanied by an orchestra of wind, string, and percussion instruments and often by scrolling translations on an electronic screen (a concession to the modern era). So sit back and ponder the fate of "The Drunken Concubine" or "The Unicorn-Trapping Purse."

BEIJING OPERA

The sounds of Chinese opera (jīngjù; 京剧) may be an acquired taste, but they're worth sampling (see **A Night at the Jingju,** above). Beijing has "training operas" for foreigners, which make things a little easier for the hapless musical wanderer. The all-night, top-volume acting, singing, dancing, and acrobatics performances are toned down to two-hour versions with translations flashing on electronic screens.

Liyuan Theatre (líyuán jùchǎng; 梨园剧场), 175 Yongan Lu (☎6301 6688, ext. 8860), in the Qianmen Hotel. Bite-sized segments of opera with senseless English subtitles. Tickets Y30-120; Y30 for balcony seating. Performances nightly 7:30-8:45pm.

Huguang Guild Hall (húguǎng huìguǎn; 湖广会馆), 3 Hufanqiao, Xuanwu (☎6351 8284 or 6352 9134). Scenes from famous operas presented in an old-style theater. Tickets Y100-180. Performances nightly 7:30-8:30pm.

Zhengyici Theatre (zhēngyǐcí xìlóu; 正乙祠戏楼), 220 Xiheyan Jie (☎6303 3104). Take the subway to Hepingmen; head south and turn left at the Quanjude Roast Duck Restaurant branch and follow the colorful flags. China's first opera house. Traditional setting and free snacks. Tickets Y150, students Y80. Performances nightly 7:30-9pm.

Chang'an Grand Theatre (chángān dàxìyuàn; 长安大戏院), Chang'an Bldg., 7 Jianguomennei Dajie, Dongcheng (☎6510 1309 or 6510 1308). Features 2½hr. performances with scenes from various operas in a Western-style theater. Little acrobatic work apart from swordplay. Tickets Y20-120. Performances daily 1:30 and 7:30-10pm.

GALLERIES

Red Gate Gallery (hóngmén huàláng; 红门画廊; ☎6525 1005), Dongbianmen Watchtower, Chongwenmen, on the west side of the street. From the Jianguomen subway stop, walk 15min. south on Jianguomen Nan Dajie, past the Gloria Plaza Hotel. One of the first private galleries in Beijing to challenge the boundaries of acceptable art. Exhibits change monthly. Free (tell the gatekeepers you're here for the gallery, not the watchtower). Open Tu-Su 9am-5pm.

Courtyard Gallery (sìhéyuàn huàláng; 四合院画廊), 95 Donghuamen Dajie, Basement (☎6526 8882), by a moat east of the Forbidden City. The small gallery displays art using old mediums in modern expression; overhanging eaves shelter a posh Western restaurant. Exhibits change monthly. Free. Open M-Sa 11am-7pm, Su noon-7pm.

Poly Art Museum (☎6500 1188), on Dongzhimenwai Dajie, at Poly Plaza. An extensive collection of Chinese bronzes from the Shang and Zhou dynasties to the present. Open Tu, Th, and Sa 10am-3pm. Y50.

TEA HOUSES

Typical Beijing tea houses not only serve up tea and traditional snacks like sunflower and watermelon seeds, but also feature performances of Beijing opera, acrobatics, magic tricks, traditional music, and more. Tea ceremonies take place at several venues, including **Purple Vine Tea House,** 2 Nanchang Jie (☎6606 6614; open daily noon-2am), on the corner of Xihuamen near the Forbidden City, and **Xichan Tea House** (xīchán chálín; 西禅茶林), 7 Meishuguan Dong Jie, Dongcheng (☎6404 3486; open daily 9am-midnight). Here are two others of note:

Lao She Tea House (laǒshè cháguǎn; 老舍茶馆), Dawancha Bldg., 3 Qianmen Dajie, 3rd fl. (☎6304 6334 or 6303 6830), about a block west of KFC. Lacquered wood and covered lanterns evoke an atmosphere of days long past. Quick bits of opera, instrumental music, and acrobatic swordplay deserve accolades; magic tricks do not. 2-man sound studio recreates a forest of birds and World War II for comic relief. The cheapest seats have a terrific view. Free snacks. Tickets Y40-130. Shows daily 7:40-9:20pm.

Sanwei Bookstore (sānwei shūwū; 三味书屋), 60 Fuxingmennei Dajie (☎6601 3204), at an alley corner off the main street, across from the Minzu Hotel (民族饭店); take the subway to Xidan, head west. Candles, birdcages, and expensive tickets. Chinese folk music Sa nights; a translator explains the history of each traditional instrument. *Bābăo* tea Y25. Cover Y30. Open Sa 8:30-10:30pm.

SHOPPING

Wangfujing Dajie, an upscale street with lots of stores and lots of action, runs north-south a bit east of Tiananmen Square. The street sells real designer labels and boasts the huge Oriental Sun Dong An Plazas. **Xidan,** a shopping area in the west off Chang'an Jie, is home to cheap European and American fashions. The vast **Friendship Store** (yǒuyí shāngdiàn; 友谊商店), 17 Jianguomenwai Jie, is a self-contained commercial cosmos with outlandish prices. (Open daily 9am-9pm.)

For upscale products, try **Watson's** (wòtèsēn; 沃特森) at the Holiday Inn Lido; the **Lufthansa Center** (yànshā shāngchéng; 燕沙商城), 50 Liangmaqiao Lu, also known as the **Kempinski Hotel** (kǎibīnsījī fàndiàn; 凯宾斯基饭店); or the **China World Trade Center** on Jianguomenwai. The glitzy **Hualian Shopping Center** (huāliǎn shāngshà; 花脸商厦), across from Vartone New World Plaza at Fuchengmenwai Dajie, also has designer goods as well as a sprawling basement supermarket.

PANJIAYUAN FLEA MARKET (pānjiāyuán jiǔhuò shìcháng; 潘家园旧货市场). Wake up at the crack of dawn to peek at one of Beijing's best shopping spots. Antiques and not-so-antiques stretch for what seems like miles beneath a vast overhead canopy. Nowhere else will you find such a huge selection of high quality, dirt-cheap goods (large scrolls Y30-35), including unique wares like traditional Chinese shadow puppets. *(At Panjiayuan, in the southeast part of the city. Accessible by buses #34, 51, 63, 64, and 368. Open Sa-Su from 5am-6pm to around 1pm.)*

SILK ALLEY (xiùshuǐ shìchǎng; 秀水市场). Oceans of silk spill into the street in the form of shirts, lingerie, teddy-bear pajamas, and traditional Chinese dresses. The market also peddles brand-name (sometimes authentic) merchandise, but it might fall apart before you even get home. Pirated CDs (Y7-10) abound; don't be surprised to have a shifty character lead you down an alley and pull out a duffle

BEIJING

bag full of American pop CDs. Accustomed to rich tourists, vendors scrutinize their potential prey with a practiced eye, on the prowl for easily swindled shoppers. The clientele is almost completely foreign, resulting in the ear-screeching sounds of "Lookie, lookie!" and much higher prices than what a local would ever dream of paying. Nevertheless, it's a whole lot cheaper than anything you could find at home. *(On Xiushui Dong Jie, a tiny street stretching from the north side of Jianguomenwai Dajie, between the Friendship Store and the Jianguo Hotel to the US Embassy. Take bus #1,4, 120, or 802 to Yong An Li.)*

LIULICHANG (liúlìchǎng; 琉璃厂). An amazingly modern-looking antique market, Liulichang combines the brilliant reds, blues, and golds of sleek antique restoration with the timeless art of the con. Stores overflow with vases, scrolls, calligraphy, and carpets, both genuine antiques and convincing imitations. Prices are high to exorbitant; compare first, then bargain. *(Off Nan Xinhua Jie, perpendicular to Qianmen Dajie, southwest of Qianmen. Take bus #14 or 66, or take the subway to Hepingmen and walk south on Nanxinhua Dajie. Most stores open daily 9am-5pm.)*

PEARL MARKET (hóngqiáo shìchǎng; 红侨市场). Rows of pearls in every color, style, and quality imaginable fill the third floor of this indoor market. Real pearls should have a grainy surface that you can test by biting. The lower levels of the market sell "Prada" handbags and other brand-name imitations for a fraction of the prices at the Silk Market. The basement has a seafood market, no doubt to make use of all those oysters. *(A few min. northeast of Tiantan's east gate. Take bus #39 from the train station; 60 or 106 from Dongzhimen; or 812 from the zoo to Hongqiao. Open daily 8:30am-7pm.)*

BEIJING

YABAO LU CLOTHING MARKET (yábǎolù shìchǎng; 雅宝路市场). This bizarre bazaar is a veritable Little Russia; store signs are written in Cyrillic, and Russian salutations fill the air. Russian immigrants have been running import businesses in Beijing since the early 90s, mostly on Yabao Lu. Cheap clothing, handbags, furs, and the softest blankets ever line the street. *(Off Jianguomenbei Dajie, opposite the west entrance to Ritan Park. Accessible by bus #44 from Qianmen or the subway to Jiangguomen.)*

QIANMEN DAJIE AND DAZHALAN. These two streets are lined with stalls selling virtually every article of clothing and clothing-related product known to mankind, including "leather" jackets, luggage, purses, shoes, toys, and more. Two more exotic shops in the Dazhalan Pedestrian Zone are **Zhangyiyuan Tea Hall** (zhāngyìyuán cházhuāng; 张一元茶庄) and **Tongren Medicinal Hall** (tóngrén táng; 同仁堂), the place to buy antlers, cicada shells, traditional Chinese herbal remedies, and obscenely cheap CDs (Y5). Haggling is the norm. *(Just south of Tiananmen Square. Take bus #2, 54, 59, or 66, or take the subway to the Qianmen stop.)*

NIGHTLIFE

Welcome to China, Beijing Journal offers an insider's look at fun stuff to do, from bungee-jumping to bar-hopping; *City Weekend* and *Metro* also list great night spots and restaurants. Pick up these free magazines in shopping districts, universities, and large hotels; go forth and party. Just don't expect to find the "real China."

The decadent embassy district of **Sanlitun** (sānlǐtún; 三里屯) in northeast Beijing should be called "*lǎowài* central"—every bar and street is busting at the seams with foreigners. There are two main bar streets in Sanlitun: **Sanlitun Lu,** frequented mainly by local night owls, and **Sanlitun Nan Lu,** packed with expat bars and expats. The new favorite place is a mini-Las Vegas at the south gate of **Chaoyang Park.**

BARS

Havana Cafe (hāwǎnnà kāfēi; 哈瓦那咖啡; ☎6586 6166), at the north gate of the Workers' Stadium, Chaoyang. This beautiful hovel, once the Workers' Stadium ticket booth, is Beijing's first Cuban bar. The *comida* is Latin American, the *bebidas* are international, and the *sangria* is best enjoyed on the candlelit, outdoor terrace. Drinks Y30-35. A live band blasts hot and sweaty samba beats during summer nights (around 10:15pm). Open daily 6pm-3am.

The Big Easy (kuàilè zhàn; 快乐站), 8 Chaoyang Gongyuan Lu (☎6508 6776), at the south gate of Chaoyang Park. A piece of New Orleans dropped in China. Delicious, authentic cajun and creole food (Y48-135). The Big Easy band, fronted by the fabulous Jacqui Staton (nightly 9:30pm), plays feel-good tunes. Motown, R&B, and blues. One of the best bars around. Happy Hour daily 5-8pm. Open daily 5pm-2am.

CD Cafe (CD kāfēi wū; CD咖啡屋; ☎6501 8877, ext. 3032), on Dongsanhuan Lu, Chaoyang, east of Xiaobawang overpass and 200m south of the Great Wall Sheraton. Excellent bands play nightly (typically jazz or rock) starting around 9:30pm. Special concerts regularly. Drinks Y30-40. Open daily 6pm-2am.

Durty Nellie's (dūbólín xī cāntīng; 都伯临西餐厅), 12 Sanlitun Nan Lu (☎6502 2808), on Dongdaqiao Xi Jie off Gongren Tiyuguan Bei Lu. One of 2 places in Beijing to have Guinness on tap. Everything here has the flavor of an old Irish pub, even if drinks are a bit weak. In the winter, people come to warm up (and end up staying); in the summer, they come to get liquored up (before hitting the dance clubs). Drinks Y25-30. Live band F-Sa. Open Su-Th noon-1:30am, F-Sa noon-2:30am.

The Loft (cáng kù; 藏酷), 4 Gongren Tiyuguan Bei Lu (☎6501 7501). Follow the signs next to Pacific Century Place around to the bar. Easily one of the coolest hangouts around, this sexier-than-thou bar features bamboo chairs, leafy plants, and risqué computerized images that illuminate the floor. The live DJ turns the Loft into a so-so disco (F-Sa from 10:45pm), but a more mature crowd comes for dinner (until 10pm) and drinks (Y28-120). Entrees Y42-120. Cover Y30-50. Open daily 11am-2am.

Minder Cafe (míngdà xīcānguǎn; 明大西餐馆), Xinyi Bldg., Gongren Tiyuguan Bei Lu, 1 Houpingfang, Nansanlitun (☎6500 6066). Classic American rock? Check. Faux Tiffany lamps? Check. Darts? Check. If it looks like an expat bar and sounds like an expat bar, chances are it *is* an expat bar—and a good one at that. An older crowd chats the night away while swaying to the rhythms of a Filipino band (9:30-12:30pm). Cover Y30 after midnight. Drinks Y20-35. Open M-F 11am-2am, Sa-Su 11am-4am.

Jam House (jièmò fáng; 芥茉房), 1 Sanlitun Nanlixi, Chaoyang (☎6506 3845). Foreigners begin the night here before hitting the dance clubs. Live music (Th-Sa 10pm-1am). Outdoor patio upstairs. Drinks Y25-40. Open daily from 5pm, usually until 2am.

CLUBS

Solutions (hélùshén; 和路神; ☎6255 8877), down the little lane across from the west gate of Beijing University. With Japanese rap, French hip-hop, and dirty old American booty-shakin' tunes, Solutions is the place to go if you're dying for music that won't be popular in China for another year. Weekends and nights are packed with foreign exchange students, sipping cheap mixers and jamming to the best beats in town. Most drinks Y15. Su-Th no cover, F-Sa Y10-40. Open Su-W 7pm-2am, Th-Sa 7pm-5am.

Vogue (shíshàng fēnggé; 时尚风格), 88 Gongti Bei Lu (☎6416 5316), near the City Hotel. The trendiest place to strut your stuff. No one sneaks into this techno haven—the enormous, but otherwise friendly bouncer Kay guards the door. Regular special parties. Su-Th no cover, F-Sa cover Y50. Open Su-Th 6pm-4am, F-Sa 6pm-8am.

Vics (wēikèsī; 威克斯; ☎6593 6215), at the north gate of the Workers' Stadium, next to the Outback Steakhouse. Couples get (a little too) slinky on the dance floor to R&B and reggae beats. Su-Th no cover, F-Sa Y20. Open Su-Th 8pm-2:30am, F-Sa 8pm-6am.

The Den (dūnhuáng xī cāntīng; 敦煌西餐厅), 4A Gongti Dong Lu, Chaoyang (☎6592 6290), next to the City Hotel in Sanlitun. Go before midnight, and you'll be sorely disappointed. Arrive fashionably late (past 1am) to a packed dance floor upstairs. For some breathing room, gravitate downstairs to a smoky chamber of exotic vices. Supposedly cover is Y30 (or 1 drink) F-Sa after 10pm, but it's a well known fact that scantily clad beauties get in for free. 18+. Open Su-Th 10:30am-3am, F-Sa 10:30am-7am.

Orange, 2 Xingfu Yicun (☎6415 7413), off an alley directly across from the Havana Cafe and the north gate of the Workers' Stadium; look for the tell-tale orange sign. Peculiar geometric shapes and designs create an artsy atmosphere, futher enhanced by blaring trance and techno rhythms. Th cover charge Y15, but all drinks are Y10. F has a 2-for-1 deal. Open Su-Th 8pm-2am, F-Sa 8pm-4am.

Nightman (láitè màn; 莱特曼), 2 Xibahe Nanli, Chaoyang (☎6466 2562). Features dizzying lights, strobes, smoke, TV screens, multiple levels, and unremittingly erotic dancers. Full of Chinese students hopping to English pop and techno. Drinks Y20-30. No cover for foreigners, otherwise Y25-35. Open Th and Su 8pm-3am, F-Sa 8:30pm-5am.

Nasa Disco (NASA dísīkè; NASA迪斯科), 2 Xitucheng Lu, Jimenqiao Beice, Haidian (☎6203 2906). A gangplank leads to this weird, multi-level world with an under-utilized but highly sophisticated lighting system. Young Chinese bounce or bang their heads to the strobe lights. Fake rockets and old jeeps round out the decor. Drinks Y15-30. Cover 20-30. No cover for students M, W-Th; for women Tu. Open daily 7:30pm-3am.

BEIJING

DAYTRIPS FROM BEIJING

FRAGRANT HILLS AND ENVIRONS

FRAGRANT HILLS PARK

Several buses go to Fragrant Hills Park and the adjoining Azure Clouds Temple. Bus #318 departs from Pingguoyuan; from the subway stop walk down Pingguoyuan Nan Lu and take a right at the first intersection (30min., Y1-2). Bus #333 runs from the Summer Palace on Yiheyan Lu, and #360 from the zoo. The bus terminus is at the foot of the hills, and rickshaws swarm like flies to take you to the park's north entrance (Y3-5 or a 15min. walk). Open daily 6am-6pm. Cable car runs daily 8:30am-5pm (Y30 one-way, Y50 round-trip, children under 1.2m Y10). Admission Y5, students Y2.5.

Fragrant Hills Park (xiāngshān gōngyuán; 香山公园) boasts cloudy mists resembling the exotic haze of incense, an impressive peak that resembles an incense burner, ripe cherry tree blossoms that erupt in a burst of floral aroma, a dash of history, a smattering of architecture, and a lot of retired old folks. Built in 1745 under Emperor Qianlong and ravaged by foreign imperial forces in 1860 and 1900, the park underwent some cosmetic surgery after 1949 and is now one of Beijing's most idyllic spots. The park's greenery opens up to reveal an architectural gem or two—namely the faux-Tibetan **Temple of Brilliance** and a glazed-tile pagoda—that managed to escape the razings of the last century, and its natural harmony is sullied only slightly by the vendors hawking the plastic-encased red maple leaves that lend the Fragrant Hills their fiery autumnal glow. Fall and spring, with their glorious colors, are the most popular times to visit the park, but summertime with its shady greens and well-kept gardens will still please the eye.

If the hike to the summit doesn't tickle your fancy, a **cable car** can whisk you up, up, and away in 18 exertion- and perspiration-free minutes. Otherwise, it's a long and winding path up, without much to see except trees. The best route is to enter through the North gate, visit the Azure Clouds Temple, take the cable car to the summit and then walk down. Just within the north gate of the Fragrant Hills Park lies the **Azure Clouds Temple** (bìyún sì; 碧云寺). Built in 1331, the temple complex is comprised of several halls, including the Hall of Lokapalas, with 18 *arhats* surrounded by rolling clouds and seas and a memorial hall to Sun Yat-Sen, whose remains were temporarily housed here. The red walls and tiled roofs of the other buildings give way to the cool white marble and Indian-style stupas of the Vajra **(Diamond Throne Pagoda)** in back. *(Open daily 8am-5pm. Y10.)*

OTHER SIGHTS IN FRAGRANT HILLS

FRAGRANT HILLS BOTANICAL GARDENS (xiāngshān zhíwù yuán; 香山植物园). A huge scientific and ornamental complex, these gardens are home to 30 varieties of bamboo and 2000 Chinese herbaceous peony trees. A space-age, climate-controlled conservatory houses thousands of species, from monstrous ferns to hanging orchids. Within the gardens, the **Sleeping Buddha Temple** (wòfó sì; 卧佛寺) houses a 250,000kg, 5.3m-long bronze statue of a reclining Sakyamuni, which rests beside several pairs of his enormous cloth shoes—and only 7000 people had to be enslaved to build it in 1321. *(A 15min. walk or a Y2 minibus ride from the foot of Fragrant Hills Park. Accessible by bus #318 from the terminus or from Pingguoyuan subway stop. Open daily in summer 6am-8pm; in winter 7:30am-5pm. Tropical conservatory and gardens Y50, students Y40; gardens only Y5, students Y2.5; Sleeping Buddha Temple Y5.)*

BADACHU (bādà chù; 八大处). A short ride from the Fragrant Hills are these "eight great sites." Along the path to the left, seven of the eight ancient temples are open for viewing, including the recently refurbished Lingguang Temple and a 13-story pagoda that houses the tooth relic of Buddha. To the right is the **landsled;** here, visitors can pay to ride at breakneck speeds down mountainside aluminum tubes (cable car up Y20, slide down Y40, round-trip Y55). *(From Pingguoyuan terminus, take bus #318 to Pingguoyuan Dong; then hop on #389 to Badachu. A minicab from the Botanical Gardens costs Y15-20. Open daily 5am-8pm. Y10, students Y5.)*

MING TOMBS

*About 50km northwest of Beijing proper, not far from the Badaling Great Wall. Take **bus** #5 or 44 from Qianmen to Deshengmen (or take the **subway** to Jishuitan); from the Watch Tower, walk a few minutes west, under the pedestrian overpass, to the bus terminal. Take **bus or minibus** #345 or the faster #345 (支) to Changping (昌平) or Changping Dongcheng (50-80min., Y4). **Tour buses** often visit both the tombs and Badaling (see p. 151). The three tombs that are open to the public (Changling, Dingling, and Zhaoling tombs) are far apart and hard to get to by any other means except by **taxi** (Y20 from bus stop to Changling, Y10 between tombs; it's cheapest to hire a cab to take you around to all the sites). High season Apr. 1-Oct. 31, low season Nov. 1-Mar. 31. Tombs open daily 8am-5pm. Changling Y20-30. Dingling Y30-35, museum Y10. Zhaolong Y20. Sacred Way open daily 7am-8pm, Y15-20. Students half-price; children under 1.2m free.*

At the foot of the Tianshou Mountains lie the famed Ming Tombs (míng shísān líng; 明十三陵). Zhu Di (Emperor Yongle) moved China's capital to Beijing and in 1409 commissioned his tomb to be built on the outskirts of the new capital. A who's who of entombed corpses includes 13 emperors, 23 empresses, eight concubines, and one prince. The famed **Sacred Way** (shéndào; 神道), or the **Divine Road to the Changling Tomb,** is a path lined with 36 white stone ministers, soldiers, and mythical beasts. It once stretched 4km north, crossing the **Seven-Arch Bridge** before reaching its final destination, but has since been shortened to a 20min. willow-shaded stroll beside a veritable circus of animals. **Changling** is the first and largest tomb here, built for the emperor who started it all. **Zhaoling,** the resting place of the 12th Ming emperor is just a miniature version; most tours pass it and head instead to **Dingling,** the only tomb where you can actually descend into the Underground Palace, and discover what's beneath the large mound of dirt.

The Ming Tombs ought to be an impressive reflection of Ming achievements in artistry and engineering. They're not. The **Upper Palaces** are no more extraordinary than any other temple, and the one actual tomb you can see has little more than large, damp tunnels. The descriptions only convey the rooms' dimensions, and the chambers are decorated with only a few replicas of the coffins and scattered money that visitors have tossed in as somewhat belated offerings to the emperors.

EASTERN QING TOMBS

150km east of Beijing. Near Zunhua and Hebei, but best reached from Beijing. On weekends and holidays, a tour bus (3hr., 7am, Y70 roundtrip) departs when full from Xuanwumen Church and leaves for Beijing around 7:30pm. A Y10-20 round-trip pedicab ride should cover several tombs, including the Cian and Ci Xi Tombs. Open daily 8am-5:30pm. 10-tomb admission Y80, students Y30-40, groups over 30 Y70, children under 1.3m free.

China's largest and most complete set of imperial tombs, the Eastern Qing Tombs (qīng dōng líng; 清东陵) are home to two princesses, three princes, five emperors, 15 empresses, 136 concubines, and an impressive amount of dust bunnies. The imperial superstars Empress Dowager Ci Xi, the dragon lady (her tomb is appropriately lit with a spooky green fluorescent light) who ruled China from behind two puppet emperors (see p. 14), and Emperor Qianlong, China's longest reigning emperor (see p. 14), are interred here.

Although the Qing Tombs are more of a hassle to reach than their Ming counterparts (you're basically stuck there until your tour bus returns), there is a lot more to see, even if Ci Xi and Qianlong's undergound tombs are the only ones actually opened. The sprawling 15-tomb estate has been turned into an impromptu, somewhat run-down, collection of bejeweled knicks, knacks, clocks, and corpses. At least the coffins and bodies here are the real thing. Most impressive is **Emperor Qianlong's tomb,** comprised of three magnificently carved chambers with Tibetan and Sanskrit engravings. "Imperial performances" showcase a gaggle of ruffians donning faded costumes and pretending to be royalty. These spectacles take place at **Xiaoling Tomb** (the tomb farthest to the north) Tu-Su at 10am and 2pm.

SHIDU

Southwest of Beijing. Trains run to Shidu from Beijing South Train Station (2hr.; 2 per day; "dirty" one leaves at 6:36am and returns at 6:57pm, Y7; A/C one leaves at 8:15am and returns at 3:55pm, Y12). Bus #917 (3hr., 10 per day 6am-5:08pm, returning 5:30am-5:30pm) runs from Tianqiao. A tour bus (2hr., 6:30-8am, Y40) leaves from Xuanwumen Church on weekends; it may take a while to attract enough passengers for the driver to leave. From Shidu Train Station to Solitary Hill Camp costs about Y10 one-way; taxis abound for the return trip.

You've hiked the Great Wall, gazed at the Taishan's sea of clouds, and conquered Wudangshan's peak. So you think, what's another mountain range? Nooo. Shidu (十渡) is the stuff dreams are made of. Rippling mountains with layered trees and stone swirl above a twisting river that must be crossed 10 times (hence its name, "10th Crossing") to get to the next city. At the train station, new arrivals are greeted by throngs of cabs and horse-drawn carriages. Choose a reputable-looking one for the trip to **Solitary Hill Camp** (gūshān zhài; 孤山寨). Following the winding path through the mountain valleys and bubbling creek beds, you will run into herds of snow white **goats,** nibbling on grass or resting by the flowing water. The path leads to the **Thread of Sky,** a fissure in the rocks just wide enough for a person to pass through to peek at the thin sliver of sky high above. *(Open daily 7am-7pm. Y25.)* A short cab ride away is **Immortal Peak Gorge** (xiānfēnggǔ; 仙峰谷) and the wonderful chance to scramble through a dry river bed to a small pool tucked away in a niche in the mountain. *(Open daily 7am-7pm. Y22.)* Finally, head back to **Badu** or **Jiudu** (8th and 9th crossings) to find more pure tourist traps. A **cable car** from Jiudu (Y25, roundtrip Y35) blesses you with a heartwrenching view of the surroundings, and a chance to see a moss-covered rock that bears an uncanny resemblence to a Buddha. Nearby, zip down a **glider** (Y35), sail along a **bamboo raft** (Y35), or leave all sense of sanity behind and try **bungee jumping** (Y180).

TANZHE AND JIETAI

Tour bus #7 (6-8am, Y42) leaves from the northeast corner of Qianmen on weekends; tours include the two temples and the beautiful Stone Flower limestone cave. Otherwise, take the subway to Pingguoyuan (the last stop), turn right from the station exit, walk down the street for about 5min., and hop on bus #931, which stops at both temples (about 1hr., leaves every 10min., Y2-2.5); a minicab costs about Y30.

TANZHE TEMPLE (tánzhè sì; 潭柘寺). This temple lies at the end of a scenic drive through mountains and lush valleys. Here presides the Liao dynasty emperor's gingko tree, with numerous trunks growing from the same root. The monastery dates back over 1700 years to the Jin dynasty. It takes its name from **Dragon Pool** (lóng tán; 龙潭) behind the complex, and the mulberry trees (zhè) on the surrounding hills. The central section houses the largest and most ornate of the buildings. The eastern section contains the **Floating Cup Pavilion,** whose etching on the pavilion floor supposedly resembles a dragon from one direction and a tiger from another. It is quite possible that the Qing-dynasty poets who saw these images could very well have been a bit delusional. *(Open daily in summer 8am-6pm; in winter 8:30am-4:30pm. Y30, children under 1.2m free.)*

JIETAI TEMPLE (jiètái sì; 戒台寺). Also known as **Temple of the Ordination Altar,** Jietai was built in AD 622 but didn't acquire its famed white marble altar until several hundred years later. Over 100 niches featuring the God of Ordination are carved into the altar, which was once used to celebrate graduation into full monkhood. The **Chinese Scholar Tree,** the protector of Buddhism, and many others such as the Phoenix-tailed Pine and Sleeping Dragon Pine, are over 1000 years old. Though a bit of imagination is needed for the others, the **Embracing Pagoda Pine,** true to its name, wraps its branches around a small pagoda. *(11km southeast of Tanzhe, on Ma An Hill. From the #931 bus stop in front of the large sign, its a 10min. walk up. Open daily in summer 8am-6pm; in winter 8:30am-4:30pm. Y30, children under 1.2m free.)*

MARCO POLO BRIDGE

88 Lugouqiaochengnei Xi Jie. 15km southwest of Beijing. Accessible by taxi from Tanzhe and Jietai Temples (Y30-40), or by bus #1 or 4 to Liuliqiao and bus #339 or 309 to Lugouqiao Xin Qiao. Walk straight from the bus stop and take the first right; follow the river until you reach the bridge. Open daily in summer 6:30am-7:30pm.; in winter 8am-5pm; Y10, students Y5.

Marco Polo Bridge (lúgōu qiáo; 卢沟桥), the oldest bridge in Beijing, is topped by stone lions of all different designs; legend has it that you can't count how many lions there are because they frolic about at night, but the official count is 501. Built in 1192, the bridge is noted for its part in stories Marco Polo brought back to Europe and for the Qing Emperor Qianlong's original calligraphy. It is best remembered, however, for the Marco Polo Bridge Incident of July 7, 1937, when Japan attacked Beijing, catapulting China into the fray of World War II (see p. 16). Apart from history buffs, many visitors find that the bridge is not quite worth the hike.

MUSEUM OF THE ANTI-JAPANESE WAR

101 Lugouqiaochengnei Jie, 10min. east of the Marco Polo bridge. Open daily 8:30am-5pm; last admission 4:30pm. Y15, students Y8.

The Museum of the Anti-Japanese War (zhōngguó rénmín kàngrì zhànzhēng jìniànguǎn; 中国人民抗日战争纪念馆), in the old Ming-dynasty garrison town of Wanping, is only slightly more interesting than the nearby Marco Polo Bridge. Don't let the sterilized depictions in the first hall fool you. The back room, with a dripping red introductory sign and grim background music, reveals pictures of bodiless heads, starving torture victims, and piles of dead children. A screening of the Japanese invasion shows Japanese armies swarming over some of Beijing's more renowned tourist sights. *(Chinese explanations, with the occasional Japanese translation.)*

PEKING MAN SITE AT ZHOUKOUDIAN

50km southwest of Beijing, on the boundary between Taihang Range and the North China Plain. Take bus #917 (1½-2hr., Y4.5) from the Tianqiao bus station to Fangshan; then grab a taxi (Y10). Open daily 8am-6pm. Site admission Y15, students (through high school) Y8; with museum Y20/Y10.

All the action happened here half a million years ago, when *homo erectus pekinensis* liked it so much he left his bones and artifacts here to be discovered in 1921. The Peking Man Site at Zhoukoudian (zhōukǒudiàn běijīng yuánrén yízhǐ; 周口店北京猿人遗址) is an exciting site in theory, but the original findings that set archaeological hearts all aflutter have since been "lost" at sea; all that remains are excavated, fenced-off caves, and a dismal museum housing some bone chips and stone tools. Only **Cave #1,** huge and separated from the outside world, is of any interest. Outside the site, there are plastic dinosaur exhibits and two mummies with the overwhelming stench of decayed flesh.

GREAT WALL 长城

From Shanhaiguan (see p. 171) on the Bohai Sea to Jiayuguan (see p. 739) in Gansu province, this mammoth wall winds 6400km across the northern periphery of China, a distance longer than the width of the United States. And, as all schoolchildren know, it is the only manmade structure visible from the moon.

In 221 BC, the first emperor of the Qin joined together various defensive walls to create the Great Wall to protect the newly unified nation and to permit communication between the capital Xianyang (near modern-day Xi'an) and the most far-flung outposts of the country. In an ironic twist of fate, the construction project was eventually held up as one of the emperor's crimes against the people because of its enormous cost. Although the skeleton of the Great Wall is more than 2000 years old, it owes most of its length to the Ming dynasty, when the threat of Mongol invasion spurred emperors to reconstruct the Great Wall and extend it for a 1000km to protect Shaanxi.

At the Mutianyu portion of the Great Wall, a plaque reads, "Once intended to ward off enemy attacks, today it brings together peoples of the world." To facilitate this exchange and capitalize on a huge money-making potential, the government has opened three sections in Beijing to tourists: Badaling, Mutianyu, and Simatai. Huanghua, typically refered to as the "Wild Wall," is the most remote section, so far untouched by tourism. Each section has its own personality, its own majesty. Yet, when it all comes down to it, from wherever you stand, you can gaze at this stone monument weaving atop the mountainous peaks for as far as the eye can see. And there *you* are, walking along one of the greatest achievements of civilization. Words can never describe it; but once you're there, you'll understand.

BADALING GREAT WALL 八达岭长城

*Take **bus** #5 or 44 from Qianmen to Deshengmen; hop on bus #919 (Y5) from in front of the monstrous Watchtower to Badaling (1½hr., Y5). The next best way to Badaling is a local **train** from Xizhimen Train Station to Qinglongqiao (before 10am, Y7). Official **tour buses** (Y38) #1, 2, and 4 leave for Badaling Great Wall and the Ming Tombs from the northeast corner of Qianmen (5:30-10:30am), Xuanwumen Church (6:30-9:30am), Beijing Train Station (6-10am), and the zoo (6-11am). Hotel services and **tour guides** are the most expensive means of getting there. **Open** daily in summer 6am-10pm; in winter 7am-6pm. **Admission** includes the museum and film Y45, students and elderly Y25.*

Badaling is the part of the wall to visit if you want to take pictures and have admirers back home recognize them as the Great Wall. The government has taken great pains to restore this part of the wall to its "original" condition. Every tower and turret stands just as it did when the Mongols overran the country 700 years ago, give or take a few massive souvenir shops and gaudy pastel flags. Guard rails and two **cable cars** (open daily 8am-4pm; one-way Y40, round-trip Y50) make Badaling the safe—almost easy—way to see the Great Wall. You'll get to rub elbows (literally) with tourists from all around the world. A **museum** (open 9am-4pm) displays photos of dozens of world leaders huffing and puffing up the wall, and the 360° Great Wall **Circle Vision Theatre** (open 9am-5:45pm) shows a 15-minute film on the history and legends of the wall. Despite scant English subtitles and the more-than-a-bit-artificial battle reenactment, the stomach-wrenching bird's eye views of the sweeping mountains and valleys leaves visitors satisfied.

MUTIANYU GREAT WALL 慕田峪长城

70km northeast of Beijing. Special bus #6 from the Xuanwumen Church (weekends 6:30-8am, Y43) is probably the best way to get to Mutianyu. On weekdays, take the subway to Dongzhimen (use the northeast exit) and turn left; from the long-distance bus station about 7min. down on your left, take bus #936 (Y5) or #916 (with A/C Y8) to Huairou. Minibuses (Y20-30) take passengers to Mutianyu. Open daily in summer 6am-8pm; in winter 8:30am-4:30pm. Y35, student Y17.5; plus Y1 insurance.

The Great Wall at Mutianyu was constructed during the Northern Qi Dynasty over 1400 years ago. Its splendor has held up well, with a little help from its friends in the government tourism bureau. Mutianyu was opened to take the pressure off Badaling. It's less overrun with tourists and peddlers, but plenty of both still exist. Look no further for an "I climbed the Great Wall" **panda t-shirt.** Higher up in the mountains than Badaling, Mutianyu has a much more dramatic view. A **cable car** runs to the top in 3 minutes. *(Daily 8:10am-4:30pm. One-way Y35, round-trip Y50; students half-price.)* This section of the wall also features unusual double-serrated ramparts. All in all, Mutianyu is less accessible and more expensive than Badaling, but worth it. Even the trip there on a twisting route into the mountains is gorgeous.

SIMATAI GREAT WALL 司马台长城

Special bus #12 (Y60) departs from Xuanwumen Church on weekends between 7-8am, and leaves Simatai at 4pm. Jinghua Youth Hostel (see p. 126) runs tours every other day (departs 8:30am, returns 2:30pm; Y60, excluding admission). Chartering a miàndí taxi costs around Y360. Open daily 8am-5pm. Y30, student Y15.

Reputedly the most dangerous part of the Great Wall, Simatai is also hands-down the most impressive. As the only unrestored section of the wall open to tourists, Simatai provides a glimpse of what the old wall once looked like. There are no

BEIJING

guardrails or handholds along the wall, and if you walk far enough, parts of the wall sport 70° inclines and 500m drops, bringing many hikers down on all fours. Simatai's high elevation grants an absolutely glorious view of the surrounding mountains; stairways lead to cloud-enshrouded turrets, and the unrestored wall curls away 19km into the distance. A stretch of rolling hills stands between you and the wall; save your energy to conquer Simatai itself and use the **cable car** (Y30, Y50 round-trip). The remaining hike isn't too bad, but if you're willing to shell out a bit more, a **"train"** can finish the job (Y15, Y20 round-trip). Although this section of the wall is rough and undeveloped, hawkers and restaurants are quickly starting to capitalize on tourists. Go now to Simatai, before the tourism bureau kicks in.

HUANGHUA GREAT WALL 黄花长城

About 90km north of Beijing, 22km from Mutianyu. Take the subway to Dongzhimen (use the northeast exit) and turn left; from the long-distance bus station about 7min. down on your left, take bus #961 (7:40, 9:40am, 3:30, and 5pm; Y7-8) which also returns to Beijing (5:20, 6:50am, 1, and 2:30pm). Alternatively, bus #936 (Y5) or 916 (with A/C, Y8) frequently leaves Dongzhimen for Huairou (about 2hr.), hop on connecting bus #961 (1hr., approx. every hr. 5:30am-5:40pm, Y2.5) to Huanghua. A minicab is much faster and costs Y20-30. No tourist infrastructure, no hours of operation, no admission price.

Built by General Cai Kai, Huanghua took so long to construct that the unfortunate general was deemed inefficient and beheaded. As testament to his tenacity, his headless body stood vigilant without toppling for three days and three nights before the locals had him interred. When the Mongols attacked, Cai Kai's efforts paid off; Huanghua was the only fortress that successfully warded off the enemy. Cai's body was exhumed and reburied with honor near the wall.

Even today, Huanghua is the part of the Great Wall that you conquer to become, as the Chinese say, a true man. This is un-restoration at its very best. Winding through the mountain peaks, the wall is overgrown with brush and many of the steps have dissolved into treacherous bits of crumbly pebbles that slip and slide beneath your feet. Be careful, put on your hiking boots, and don't walk the wall alone. No sissy cable cars or guardrails here, and some areas are so steep that descending them leaves climbers clinging to the side of the wall for dear life. The danger makes it exciting, the beauty makes it breathtaking, and the damage of time makes it real. This is truly the Great Wall experience of choice for hardy backpackers who scorn rampant commercialism, as there are few postcard and water vendors (locals are more interested in their sheep than in you) and no annoying tour groups. Many hikers choose to spend the night on the wall. Alternatively, there's the **Jintang Mountain Lodge** (jīntāng shān zhuāng; 金汤山庄; ☎6165 1134), across from the reservoir. Unfortunately, a face-lift has transformed dorms to relatively luxurious standards with a corresponding price hike. But after a long trek and a dip in the lake, it might be worthwhile for your tired feet. (Doubles Y258; triples Y288.)

TIANJIN 天津 ☎022

A center of trade during the Ming dynasty, Tianjin is China's fourth largest city, a major manufacturing center, and the largest port in northern China. Downtown, megastores and trendy shops abound, but the city's smaller streets and alleys are still infused with the culture and history of old China. Taxis scour the streets, and a mere wave of the hand would inspire a daring five-lane U-turn among busy traffic. Despite being a modern city, however, Tianjin still manages to maintain an unspoiled small-town mentality. For every high-priced restaurant, there are ten cheap fried dough vendors; for every fancy yellow minivan, there are hundreds of old bycicles, filling up entire streets. Unusually affluent but uniquely unspoiled by its wealth, Tianjin has retained a charm all its own.

TRANSPORTATION

Flights: Zhangguizhuang Airport (zhāngguìzhuāng fēijīchǎng; 张贵庄飞机场; ☎2490 1114). Book tickets at **Tianjin CITS Ticketing Centre,** 22 Youyi Lu (☎2835 8866; fax 2835 4653), right next to the tourism office. Open M-F 8:30am-5pm, Sa-Su 8:30am-4pm. To: **Chengdu** (Sa-Th, Y1240); **Guangzhou** (2 per day, Y1360); **Kunming** (4 per week, Y1510); **Qingdao** (daily, Y530); **Shanghai** (3 per day, Y840); **Xi'an** (daily, Y800).

Trains: The 24hr. bus #24 serves both the Main and West Stations, shuttling passengers between Heping Lu and the two stations (Baihuo Dalou stop). During the day, buses #624 and 824 service the same route. Train tickets can be bought 5 days in advance. Tickets are cheaper and easier to obtain at the Main Station. The **Main (Tianjin) Train Station** (tiānjīn zhàn; 天津站; ☎2430 6444) is on Haihe Dong Lu, just across Jiefang Qiao in downtown. To **Beijing** (1½hr., 8 per day, hard seat Y11-30) and **Shanghai** (17hr.; 4 per day; hard seat Y81, hard sleeper Y149). The **West Train Station** (xī zhàn; 西站; ☎2618 2662), on Xizhan Qian Jie. To: **Beijing** (1½hr., 17 per day, Y12); **Guangzhou** (33hr., daily, Y366); **Harbin** (18hr., daily, Y122); **Nanjing** (16hr., 2 per day, Y64); **Shanghai** (17hr.; 3 per day; hard seat Y81, hard sleeper Y149). **North Train Station** (tiānjīn běi zhàn; 天津北站; ☎2635 2214), is off Zhongshan Bei Lu.

Buses: There are three main bus stations in Tianjin. **Balitai Bus Station** (bālítái chángtú qìchē zhàn; 八里台长途汽车站; ☎2334 4749), near Shuishang Park, runs buses to **Ji'nan. West Station** (tiānjīn chángtú xī zhàn; 天津长途西站), 2 Xiqing Dao (☎2732 0688), down the road from the West Train Station, runs buses to **Shijiazhuang** and **Zhengzhou** (9hr., daily, Y140). **Northeast Station** (běidōng jiǎo chángtú qìchē zhàn; 北东角长途汽车站; ☎2635 2214), opposite Shizilin Dajie/Bei Malu entrance of Ancient Culture Street. To: **Beijing** (1½hr., 6 per day, Y30); **Chengde** (6½hr., 2 per day, Y40); **Guangzhou** (32hr., daily, Y166). **Beijing Zhao Gong Kou Bus Station** (北京赵公口站; ☎2771 9945), on Rongye Dajie in front of Food Street. To: **Beijing** (1hr., every hr. 7am-7:30pm, Y30).

Ferries: Tianjin Harbor Passenger Terminal (☎2570 6728) is open daily 8:30am-6:50pm. Take the train from the Main Train Station to the Tang Gu Passenger Terminal (tánggūxīnggǎng kèyùn mǎtóu; 塘沽新港客运码头); take bus #102 from there. Ferries go to **Kobe, Japan** (48hr., 1 per week, Y1875) and **Inchon, South Korea** (28hr., 1 every 4 days, Y988).

Local Buses: Tianjin's labyrinth-like bus system is intimidating, but worth deciphering. Fare Y1, with A/C Y2. Buses run 5am-11pm. Hours of operation are listed on bus stop signs; buses numbered 1-100 tend to run later than others. The following buses stop near the end of Heping Lu at Baihuo Dalou (百货大楼) before trundling on to other major locations: **#8:** Main Train Station, Balitai (right beside Nankai University on Weijin Lu), Waterside Park; **#24** (runs 24hr.): Tianjin Train Station, West Train Station; **#658:** Food Street, Nankai University, Tianjin University; **#693:** Anshan Dao, Hebei Lu; **#818:** North Train Station, Hubei Lu; **#860:** Food Street, Fu An Dajie; **#904:** Hubei Lu, Yingkou Dao, Northeast Bus Station.

Subway: Has 8 stops along Nanjing Lu in the direction of the West Train Station (Y1).

Taxis: Minivan taxis are cheapest. For red minivans, Y5 for the first 3km, each additional km Y1.2; for yellow ones, Y5 for the first 5km, each additional km up to 10km Y1, each additional km thereafter Y1.5.

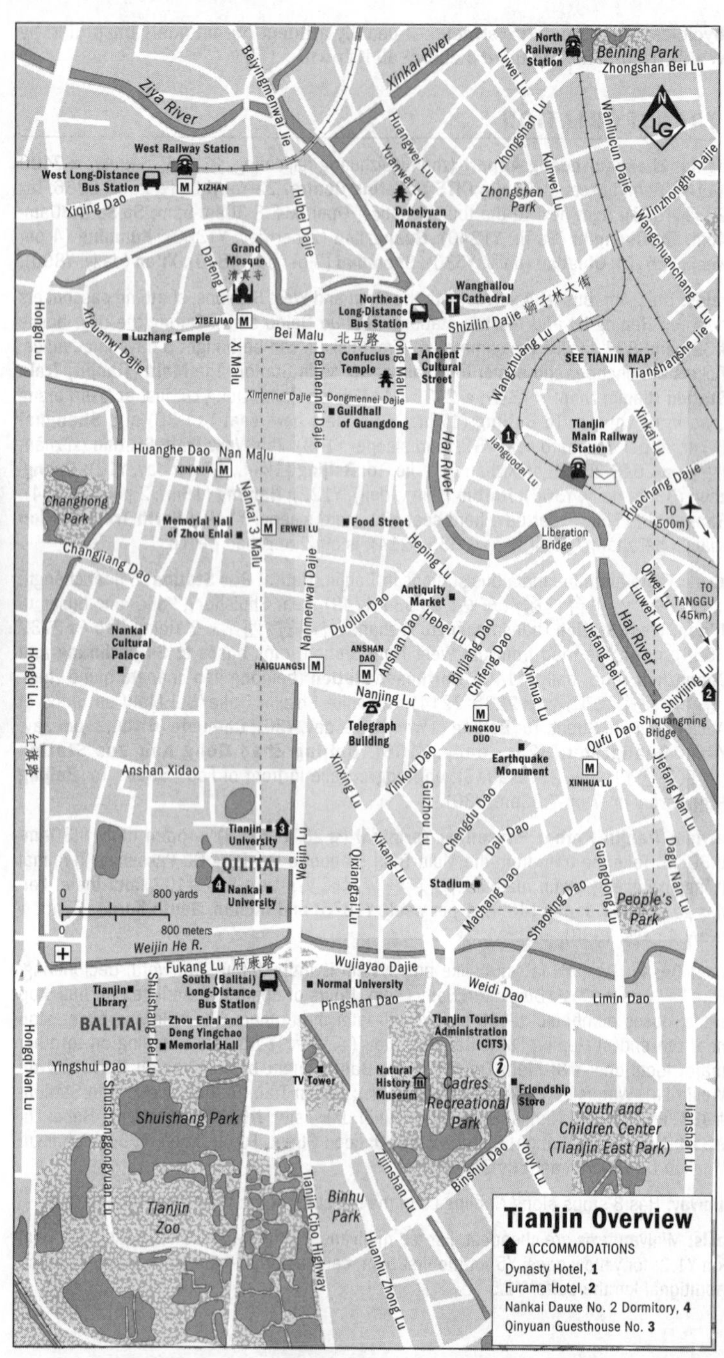
Tianjin Overview
ACCOMMODATIONS
Dynasty Hotel, 1
Furama Hotel, 2
Nankai Dauxe No. 2 Dormitory, 4
Qinyuan Guesthouse No. 3
West Railway Station
West Long-Distance Bus Station
North Railway Station
Beining Park
Zhongshan Bei Lu
Ziya River
Xinkai River
Grand Mosque
清真寺
Dabeiyuan Monastery
Zhongshan Park
Northeast Long-Distance Bus Station
Wanghailou Cathedral
Shizilin Dajie 狮子林大街
Bei Malu 北马路
Luzhang Temple
Confucius Temple
Ancient Cultural Street
Guildhall of Guangdong
SEE TIANJIN MAP
Tianjin Main Railway Station
Changhong Park
Memorial Hall of Zhou Enlai
Food Street
Liberation Bridge
Hai River
Antiquity Market
Nankai Cultural Palace
Telegraph Building
Earthquake Monument
Tianjin University
QILITAI
Nankai University
Stadium
People's Park
Weijin He R.
Fukang Lu 府康路
South (Balitai) Long-Distance Bus Station
Normal University
Tianjin Library
BALITAI
Zhou Enlai and Deng Yingchao Memorial Hall
Tianjin Tourism Administration (CITS)
TV Tower
Natural History Museum
Cadres Recreational Park
Friendship Store
Youth and Children Center (Tianjin East Park)
Shuishang Park
Tianjin Zoo
Binhu Park
TO TANGGU (45km)
TO (500m)
800 yards
800 meters
BEIJING

ORIENTATION AND PRACTICAL INFORMATION

Tianjin is just the right size—big enough to be interesting but small enough to be easily navigable. The city center is formed by a jumble of commercial streets and old-style alleys branching off **Heping Lu** (和平路) and **Binjiang Dao** (宾江道), Tianjin's main shopping arteries and pedestrian thoroughfares. The old city northwest of downtown, dubbed **"Chinatown"** by Europeans, is marked by **Bei** (北), **Nan** (南), **Dong** (东), and **Xi Malu** (西马路). Three universities converge on **Balitai,** in the oft-overlooked, tranquil southwest corner of the city.

The **Hai River** cuts through the city diagonally. Some of Tianjin's large temples are sprinkled along its northwest corner. The famed architectural legacy of the European concessions is visible throughout the city, but various national styles are concentrated together along **Jiefang Bei Lu,** which runs parallel to Machang Dao (literally, Race Horse Road) and the Hai road. The **Main Train Station** is north of the Hai, just across Jiefang Qiao (Liberation Bridge).

Travel Agency: CITS, 22 Youyi Lu (☎2835 8499 or 2835 8309), opposite the Friendship Store. Open M-F 8:30am-5pm. Shares the office with **Tianjin Overseas Tourist Corporation** (tiānjīnshì hǎiwài lǚyóu zǒnggōngsī; 天津市海外旅游总公司; ☎2313 9424). Open M-F 8:30am-5pm.

Bank of China: 80-82 Jiefang Bei Lu (☎2710 2207). Exchanges traveler's checks and currency. **ATM** (Cirrus/MC/Plus/V). The **Credit Card Department** (xìnyòngkǎ bù; 信用卡部) on 2nd fl. issues advances. Open M-F 9am-noon and 1:30-5pm.

Bookstore: Xinhua Bookstore (☎2712 9784), on the corner of Binjiang Dao and Xingan Lu, consists of five floors (with elevators) and covers everything from picture books to economic theory. Decent selection of classic English literature, with a "Learn how to speak Chinese" section for foreigners. Open M-F 9:30am-8pm, Sa-Su 9:30am-8pm.

Shopping: Tianjin Department Store (tiānjīn bǎihuò dàloú; 天津百货大楼), 172 Heping Lu (☎2730 0723, ext. 3106). Open in summer daily 9am-9pm; in winter 9am-8pm. **China Photography Store** (zhōngguó zhàoxiàng guǎn; 中国照相馆), 251 Heping Lu (☎2712 6139). Kodak film and express processing (1hr., Y28). Open daily 9am-8pm.

PSB: 26 Tangshan Dao (☎2731 9000). The **Foreigners Office** (wàiguǎn chù; 外管处), 19 Minzhu Dao, grants visa extensions.

Hospital: No. 1 Hospital (yīzhōngxīn yīyuàn; 一中心医院; ☎2336 6914), on Fukang Lu, supposedly has English-speaking staff.

Internet Access: Friends Network Coffee House, 133 Weijin Lu (☎2784 7130; http://beck.3322.net/), down the road from Tianjin University. Looks like a hole in the wall, decorated with clippings from teen/fashion magazines. 8am-noon, Y2 per hr.; noon-midnight, Y3 per hr.; midnight-8am Y10 flat. Open 24hr. **E-space** (E kóngjiān; E空间), 85 Anshan Dao (☎2722 9358). Y2 per hr. Open 24hr.

Post Office: China Post Dongzhan Post Office, gigantic building right next to the Main Train Station. EMS and Poste Restante. Open daily 8:30am-8pm. The **China Post** across from the Nankai University entrance also has EMS. Open daily 8:30am-6:30pm. **DHL** (zhōngguó wàiyùn dùnhào gúojì hángkōng kuàijiàn gōngsī; 中国外运顿号国际航空快件公司; ☎2430 3388) is a private courier service. Open daily 8am-5:30pm. **Postal Code:** 300000.

ACCOMMODATIONS

Tianjin is a great place to visit for the day, but can be quite pricey if you spend the night. Budget options for foreigners are limited. To stay in the city center, your

BEIJING

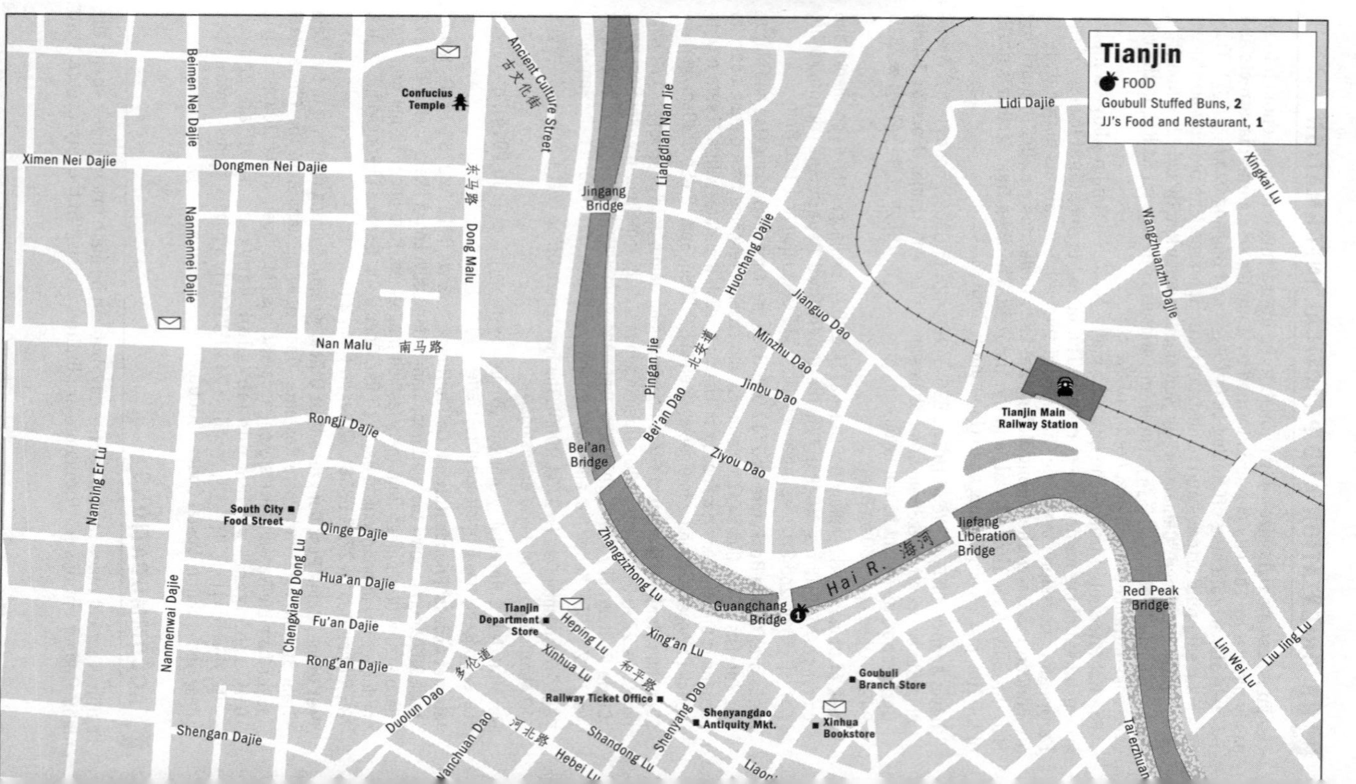
Tianjin
FOOD
Goubuli Stuffed Buns, 2
JJ's Food and Restaurant, 1
Lidi Dajie
Xingkai Lu
Wangzhuanzhi Dajie
Tianjin Main Railway Station
Beimen Nei Dajie
Confucius Temple
Ancient Culture Street
古文化街
Ximen Nei Dajie
Dongmen Nei Dajie
东马路
Dong Malu
Liangdian Nan Jie
Jingang Bridge
Huochang Dajie
Nanmennei Dajie
Jianguo Dao
Minzhu Dao
Jinbu Dao
Nan Malu
南马路
Pingan Jie
北安道
Bei'an Dao
Rongji Dajie
Bei'an Bridge
Ziyou Dao
Nanbing Er Lu
South City Food Street
Qinge Dajie
Jiefang Liberation Bridge
Hai R. 海河
Zhangzizhong Lu
Red Peak Bridge
Hua'an Dajie
Chengxiang Dong Lu
Nanmenwai Dajie
Tianjin Department Store
Guangchang Bridge
Fu'an Dajie
Heping Lu
Xing'an Lu
Rong'an Dajie
多伦道
Xinhua Lu
和平路
Lin Wei Lu
Liu Jing Lu
Goubuli Branch Store
Duolun Dao
Railway Ticket Office
Shenyang Dao
Shenyangdao Antiquity Mkt.
Xinhua Bookstore
Shengan Dajie
河北路
Shandong Lu
Hebei Lu
Tai'erzhuan

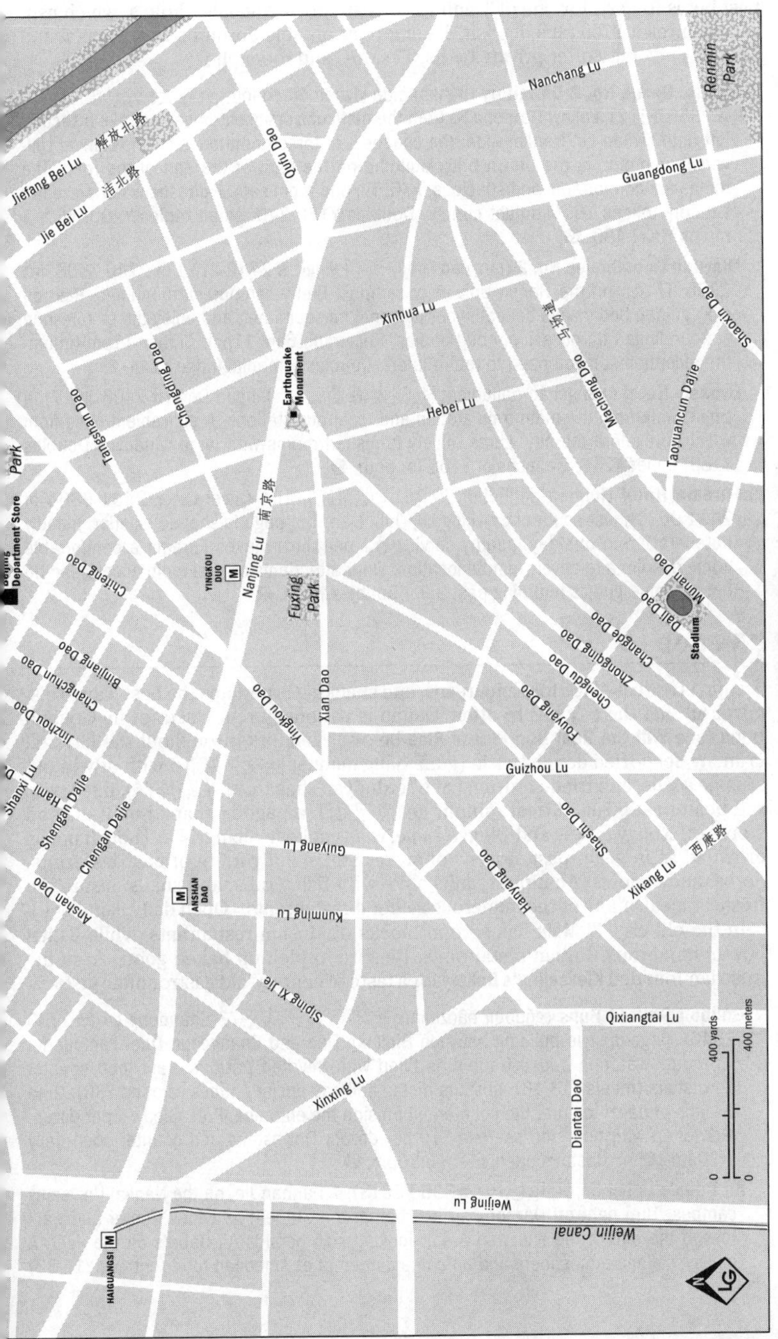
Nanchang Lu
Renmin Park
Jiefang Bei Lu 解放北路
Jie Bei Lu 洁北路
Qufu Dao
Guangdong Lu
Shaoxin Dao
Xinhua Lu
Earthquake Monument
Chengding Dao
Tangshan Dao
Park
Beijing Department Store
Hebei Lu
Machang Dao 马场道
Taoyuancun Dajie
Nanjing Lu 南京路
YINGKOU DUO
Chifeng Dao
Fuxing Park
Munan Dao
Dali Dao
Stadium
Changde Dao
Chongqing Dao
Chengdu Dao
Binjiang Dao
Changchun Dao
Jinzhou Dao
Xian Dao
Yingkou Dao
Fouyang Dao
Guizhou Lu
Shanxi Lu
Hami Dao
Shengan Dajie
Chengan Dajie
Shashi Dao
Guiyang Lu
Hanyang Dao
Xikang Lu 西康路
ANSHAN DAO
Kunming Lu
Anshan Dao
Siping Xi Jie
Qixiangtai Lu
0 400 yards
0 400 meters
Xinxing Lu
Diantai Dao
Weijing Lu
Weijin Canal
HAIGUANGSI
N

best bet is to head for one of Tianjin's consistently high-quality hotels, which usually requires a Y100 plus deposit. The more affordable dormitories at Nankai and Tianjin University offer private baths, TVs, A/C and room phones.

Nankai Daxue No. 2 Dormitory (nánkāi àidà yíyuán èrhào lóu; 南开大学谊园二号楼; ☎2350 1832). Follow Dazhong Lu from the main university entrance and take a second left onto Yiyuan Lu. Nankai Aida, the cheapest of three dormitories on the Nankai University campus, is the brown brick building on the right at the end of the road. The rooms are comfortable and spacious. A/C, TV, and room safe. Fantastic water pressure. Laundry tokens Y6. Midnight curfew. Doubles Y150-240; small triples Y200. With 2 rooms Y300-480. ❸

Qinyuan Guesthouse No. 2 (qìnyuán lìshǔ; 沁园隶属; ☎2740 7711 or 2740 7508; fax 2335 8714), on the Tianjin University campus. Pretty campus surroundings. Rest on silky golden bed covers beneath your personal mosquito net, and enjoy the picturesque surroundings with occasional bug bodies. Reception 6am-11pm. Curfew 11pm (inform the receptionist if you need to return later). Doubles with mini-fridge Y144. ❷

Dynasty Hotel (wángcháo dàjǐudiàn; 王朝大酒店), 42 Jianguo Dao (☎2403 1617), a 5min. walk from the main train station and local bus stations. A convenient base from which to explore the city. Large, nicely furnished rooms with large windows. Doubles Y188; triples Y218. Deposits of Y400 for both. ❸

Furama Hotel (fùlìhuā dàjiǔdiàn; 富利华大酒店), 104 Qiwei Lu (☎2431 9864 or 2431 0670), just south of Shiyijing Lu/Qufu Dao. The pagoda-shaped exterior, friendly hotel staff, and one-day laundry service (Y2 per shirt) makes Furama a comfortable home despite a relatively remote location. Floor attendants control room access and do not welcome guests returning past 3am. Doubles Y200. ❸

FOOD

Tianjin is a great place for Epicureans, and snacking is perhaps the best way to discover all that the city has to offer. Tianjin is nationally renowned for its Goubuli buns (see **Will the Real Bun Please Rise** below). Vendors throughout the city sell crunchy deep-fried dough twists (guīfāxiáng máhuā; 桂发祥麻花) with or without sesame seeds, and fried-eardrum cake (ěrduōyǎn zhágāo; 耳朵眼炸糕), filled with red bean paste. **Food Street** (shípǐn jīe; 食品街), a pagoda-shaped mall of food stores off Rongye Dajie and Qingge Dajie, is a snacker's Shangri-La. Though not as crowded as in years past, dozens of stores still sell a variety of pastries, fruits, herbs, and candies. Aquarium tanks alive with fish, crabs, and snails ensure the freshest meal at any of the numerous seafood restaurants. (Open daily 9am-5pm.)

In the old city, **Xi Malu** has several blocks of Muslim restaurants, while **Balitai** boasts numerous Korean restaurants. Be sure to pick up baked goods from the Austrian-founded **Kiesseling's Bakery** for a taste of century-old gastronomic history.

Goubuli Stuffed Buns (gǒubùlǐ bāozidiàn; 狗不理包子店), 77 Shandong Lu (☎2730 2540), pagoda-style building between Binjiang Dao and Changchun Dao. Famous for its mouth-watering *bāozi*, Goubuli is filled with devoted patrons. Fast food counter downstairs (meals Y13-16); upstairs dining hall has pricier entrees (around Y30). Grab 2 kinds of *bāozi* to go at the counter right inside the entrance. Pork-filled Y6 per dozen; red-dotted with pork and seafood Y10 per dozen. Downstairs and counter open daily 7:30am-10pm; upstairs open 11am-8:30pm. ❶

Ali Baba's (ālǐ bābā; 阿里巴巴; ☎2350 5613), 7 Tiannan Jie, on the Nankai University campus. Turn right off Dazhong Lu just before the Student Activities Center and walk toward the end of the alley; an Arabic-looking sign heralds Ali Baba's on the right. A messy, college atmosphere and an earnest attempt at American food (entrees Y15-30)

WILL THE REAL BUN PLEASE RISE? Of Tianjin's specialty pastry shops, the most famous by far is the Goubuli Stuffed Bun. The creator of Goubuli, Gou (literally, Dog), created it while apprenticing for a Tianjin dough-bun master in the Qing. Goubuli *baozi* was praised by the emperor and eventually became the favorite of former US President George H.W. Bush. The word Goubuli literally means "dog doesn't bother," supposedly because the master bun-maker never bothered to talk to his customers. Another version of the legend says that the unfortunate Gou was so ugly that even dogs wouldn't look at him.

Goubuli buns have become so internationally renowned (there are franchises in Singapore, Japan, Korea, and the US) that imitation Goubuli bun restaurants have sprung up throughout Tianjin. Possibly the most bizarre is Maobuwen (mǎobùwén; 猫不闻), or "cat doesn't smell" dumplings, produced since 1995. These dumplings aspire to be the fourth Tianjin pastry specialty but lack the extra flavor of a century-old legend.

draw crowds of foreign exchange students. Many stay late to down beers and watch Chinese music videos. Open daily 11am-3am. ❷

JJ's Food and Restaurant (Tianjin) Inc. (jiājiā xiāngdòujiāng zhījiā; 家家香豆浆之家; ☎2721 6289), 1 Dagu Bei Lu , immediately south of Guangchang Bridge. If China had highway pitstops, this would be it. Shiny checkered floors adorn this plastic kingdom which has an English menu, with pictures. A cool mug of soybean milk (Y3) completes spicy, fast food noodle dishes (average Y8-10). Open 24hr. ❶

CJ & Y's Gourmet Co., 125 Machang Dao (☎2325 6000 or 2325 8000). After a stroll through the lantern-lined streets of European concessions, enjoy a sumptuous meal of Shanghai cuisine surrounded by English architecture. Dinners look and taste much more expensive than they actually are, and the English menu makes ordering a breeze. Try sliced eggplant spiced with coconut crumbs and served in a wooden boat for Y18. Meals average Y22. Open daily 11am-9:30pm. ❷

BEIJING

SIGHTS

Colorful streets and museums make up Tianjin's tourist sights; most of them are close to the city center and accessible only by taxi. The city has been called a living museum of international architecture, and the energetic walker can explore either bank of the **Hai River** for the 19th-century British, French, German, Russian, and Italian buildings, remnants of old days of foreign concession.

DABEIYUAN MONASTERY (dàbēiyuàn; 大悲院). A colorful array of red charms, fruit offerings, and miniature figurines line the way to the monastery's entrance. Inside, the well-preserved prayer rooms are still sites of active worship, as evidenced by the incense-scented air and sounds of solemn chanting. Arrive around 2pm on Wednesdays and Sundays to catch a glimpse of afternoon rituals. *(40 Tianwei Lu. To the north of Jingang Bridge, Tianwei Lu is the first left off Zhongshan Lu. The monastery is on the right just past Shiwei Lu. ☎2626 1768. Open Tu-Su 9am-4pm. Y4.)*

ANCIENT CULTURE STREET (gǔwénhùa jīe; 古文化街). With its pagoda-topped buildings and delicatedly engraved eaves, this pedestrian walkway was built to mimic the look and feel of ancient China. Here an unending stream of swords, scrolls, teapots, and miniature peeing figurines awaits. *(West of the Hai River, between Jingang Bridge and Jintang Bridge, with an entrance on the corner of Dong Malu and Bei Malu. Open daily 9am-6pm.)* At the heart of Ancient Culture Street lies **Tianhou Temple** (tiānhoù gōng; 天后宫), built during the Yuan dynasty (1279-1368) and restored in 1985. This intricately ornate temple honors Empress Tianhou (born in AD 960) with incense altars and offerings of money, food, and flowers. Her death at the age of 27 came as no surprise; she had led an exhausting life "curing disease, helping the poor, and vanquishing demons and monsters." *(80 Ancient Culture Street. ☎2735 5517. Open daily 9am-5pm. Y3.)*

ZHOU ENLAI AND DENG YINGCHAO MEMORIAL HALL (zhōu ēnlái dèng yǐngchāo jìniàn guǎn; 周恩来邓颖超纪念馆). Old photographs, revolutionary scripts, wax figures, and documentary films fill this ultra-modern museum dedicated to the life and achievements of two of China's most revered revolutionary heroes, Zhou Enlai and his wife Deng Yingchao. While the latter worked for women's liberation in China, former Premier Zhou is especially respected for his lifelong work in the Chinese Communist party and for being the sole voice of reason and moderation during the turmoil of the Cultural Revolution. The downstairs hall showcases their life and achievements, while the upstairs Qing Huai Hall displays personal trinkets. Zhou's personal jet sits outside. *(Near end of Shuishang Gongyuan Lu. Southeast of Nankai University, just across from Waterside Park. ☎2352 9246. Open Tu-Su 8:30am-5pm, last ticket sold at 4pm. Y10, students Y5. Admission to jet Y10. Wheelchair accessible.)*

BEIJING

SHENYANG DAO ANTIQUE MARKET (shènyángdào gǔwù shìchǎng; 沈阳道古物市场). A complex neighborhood of winding alleyways, beginning at Shenyang Dao, where jostling vendors display their wares on roadside mats. There are ceramics and antiques galore (some real, some laughable). The same bronze dragon will cost you anywhere from Y35-200, depending on your bargaining skills. *(Shenyang Dao, south of Heping Lu. A nondescript alley directly opposite the Shijie Shangsha leads to the market. Open daily 9am-4pm. Th and F mornings are the best times to go.)*

OTHER SIGHTS. Seven minutes east of Ancient Culture Street, Tianjin's **Confucian Temple** (wénmiào; 文庙) sits on the northern side of Dongmennei Dajie and offers a quiet escape under the shadow of the huge Carrefour megastore. Umbrella-shaped trees, chirping birds, and an arched stone bridge lead to some beautifully ornate (but rather dusty) pagodas dedicated to the life of Confucius. *(☎2727 2812. Open Tu-Su 9:30am-4pm. Y4)*

The **Tianjin Radio & TV Tower** (tiānjīn guǎngbō diànshì tǎ; 天津广播电视塔) on Weijin Nan Lu is an impressive sight from afar, especially when lit up at night (until 10pm). Though the fee for an elevator ride to the top is as steep as the ascent, the view of Tianjin's flat, building-filled landscape in the city haze is quite remarkable, as you watch hundreds of bicyclers boldly dodge traffic. *(☎2335 5775 or 2334 3557. Open daily 8:30am-10pm. Tower Y50, children under 1.3m. Y25. Elevator on 2nd fl. Entrance fee to lake Y1.)* Across Weijin Nan Lu from the TV Tower sits the **Waterside Park** (shǔishàng gōngyuán; 水上公园). Relax beneath makeshift pavilions while gazing at the shady cobblestone walkways, meandering duck boats, and amusement park at the eastern corner of the park. *(☎2335 8454, ext. 8023. Open daily 5am-9pm; winter 5am-6:30pm. Y10.)*

NIGHTLIFE

Not too many years ago, Tianjin was a quiet little town; today, however, reckless carousers abound. Foreigners congregate at **Sgt. Pepper's** (see below) and **Ali Baba's** (see p. 158), where the music is loud and the beer plentiful. An exploration of Tianjin's fountains and night markets that stretch along the north side of the river affords even cheaper delights. (Open daily 6-9:30pm.)

Kanghao (kānghǎo; 康好), 47 Minzhu Dao (☎2446 2686). Kanghao awakes at 9pm, when the strobes turn on, the lights come up, and a disco full of locals starts grooving to the tunes—American remixes, Chinese pop songs, and more. The happening place for mass mobilization. Open Su-Th 8pm-2:30am, F-Sa 8pm-3:30am.

Sgt. Pepper's Music Hall Grill & Bar (shājīn yīnyuè xīcāntīng; 沙金音乐西餐厅), 62 Jiefang Bei Lu (☎2312 8138). One of the hottest places to mix and mingle, Sgt. Pepper's fun yet classy atmosphere makes it a favorite place for foreigners and locals alike to grab a beer and have a smoke. Entrees average Y40, drinks Y20 and up. Hot Stuff, "the best band in Tianjin," is just that. The Filipino group ignites the stage with both classic and modern rock (Tu-Su 9:15-12:30pm). F-Sa Y60 minimum charge. Open daily 6pm-2am.

NYC Music Kitchen (niúyuē yīnyuè chúfáng; 纽约音乐厨房), 212 Weidi Dao (☎2353 9600), near Machang Dao, on the 2nd fl. above Big Bowl Restaurant. Proclaiming the "Style of New York, Taste of China," NYC touts a classy restaurant and bar with live entertainment Tu-Su. Open daily 11am-1am.

DAYTRIP FROM TIANJIN: TANGGU 塘沽

Buses leave Tianjin for Tanggu from many locations, including the Main Train Station and the South Bus Station (1½hr., buses leave when full, Y4). Trains (Y3.5) cover the distance in 30 minutes and leave frequently. Tanggu is surprisingly vast and quite difficult to get around. Taxis are the safest bet.

The **Seaside Amusement Park** (haĭbīn yùchăng; 海滨浴场) is home of the largest waterslides and manmade beaches in China. Visitors can look out over the brown waters of the Bohai Gulf as happy music blares from speakers. (On Haifang Lu. ☎2531 9020. Accessible by a 30-minute taxi ride (Y40-50). Open daily 6am-10pm. Free.) Nearby, **Bohai Children's World** (bóhăi értóng shìjie; 渤海儿童世界), a little park with greenery, has a small castle-shaped history museum, several peacocks, and some kiddie rides. **Dagu Fort** (dàgū pàotái; 大沽炮台) boasts little more than a rusty old war plane and several decaying cannons. The fort has been around since the mid-16th century, but 450 years haven't clarified (or translated) the signs in its small museum. Climb up the lone preserved post for an unobstructed view of the barren landscape. (☎2588 8544. Open daily 8:30am-4:30pm. Y5, students Y2.) Travelers consigned to Tanggu's shores overnight should try one of the two hotels across from the passenger terminal. The **Kangda Hotel** (kāngdá zhùsè; 康达住宿; ☎2579 5941) is bright, friendly, and affordable. Doubles with A/C and bath Y100. Next door, the **International Seamen's Club** (tiānjīn xīngăng gúojì hăiyuán jùlèbù; 天津新港国际海员俱乐部), true to its name, caters mainly to sailors and fishermen, and offers clean rooms with A/C, bath, phone and TV. (☎6577 0333. Doubles and triples Y160-180)

HEBEI 河北

Take the phrase "struggles in the shadow of" and add it to each of Beijing's superlatives—now you, too, can discuss Hebei province! "Second fiddle." "Unglamorous." "Lackluster." The number of derogatory statements that have been directed at Hebei is enough to reduce a province to tears. With the powerful municipalities of Beijing and Tianjin geographically (but not administratively) within its borders, Hebei struggles to prove its own worth. But this pitiable province just isn't sexy—the mountainous tableau in the north is bleak and barren and the uninspiring plains in the south are dotted by drab industrial mining towns. Still, there is *some-*

thing about Hebei. For centuries, Hebei has been the vacation spot of choice for the ruling elite. Chengde, home to the Imperial Summer Villa (literally "Flee-the-Heat Villa"), was a favorite destination for Qing emperors in the 18th century. These days, the beach and surf of Beidaihe and Shanhaiguan lure city-weary CCP hotshots and throngs of other not-quite-as-hot-shots. In the end, despite Hebei's drab repuation, this province manages to make the most of what it has.

SHIJIAZHUANG 石家庄 ☎0311

The informal slogan of Shijiazhuang is: "Give us five years." The implied conclusion to this unrealistic declaration is: "And we'll be more like Beijing." Although this industrial town is only 250km from Beijing, Shijiazhuang still has a long way to go before it can compete with China's capital. The city, also the capital of Hebei province, does house the largest pharmaceutical plant and PLA military academy in China and sees itself as one of the forerunners of progress in the region. Indeed, the construction of the railway line has brought the region prosperity and a booming population. There are not, however, many interesting sights within the city itself; Shijiazhuang is best used as a base from which to see the surrounding sights.

TRANSPORTATION

Flights: Shijiazhuang Airport (shíjiāzhuāng jīchǎng; 石家庄机场), 45km northeast of the city. Shuttle buses leave from the CAAC office on Zhongshan Dong Lu (☎505 4084, about 6 per day, Y15). **China Eastern Airlines** (zhōngguó dōngfāng hángkōng gōngsī; 中国东方航空公司), Aviation Building, 128 Zhongshan Dong Lu (☎698 1824 or 698 1124). To: **Guangzhou** (M, Th, Sa; Y1400); **Shanghai** (daily 7:20am, Y900); **Shenzhen** (W and Su 8:30am, Y1360).

Trains: Shijiazhuang Train Station (shíjiāzhuāng huǒchē zhàn; 石家庄火车站; ☎702 2227) is accessible by almost every bus in the city. Tickets available 10 days in advance. Luggage storage Y3-5 per day. To: **Beijing** (2½hr.; many per day, 4 express trains; Y21-42); **Chengde** (8hr., 7:44pm, Y38); **Datong** (13hr., 9pm, Y45); **Harbin** (20½hr., 2:26 and 8:53pm, Y350); **Qinhuangdao** (9hr., 9:01pm, Y156); **Shanghai** (16½hr., 1:50pm, Y300); **Xi'an** (12hr., Y220-230).

Buses: The **Long-distance Bus Station** (chángtú qìchē zhàn; 长途汽车站; ☎702 5775) is south of the train station. Head as far south as you can on the pedestrian street immediately in front of the train station and go past the jungle of minibuses; look for a gold-pillared entrance. Ticket counter open daily 5am-5:30pm. To: **Beijing** (3½hr., every 20min. 6am-7:30pm, Y45-69); **Ji'nan** (5hr., every 45min. 6am-5:30am, Y130); **Qinhuangdao** (8-12hr.; 4 per day; Y104, express Y130).

Public Transportation: Local **buses** ply the streets of downtown Shijiazhuang; most of them start from, stop at, or run past the train station. Two major bus depots are on Zhanqian Lu, just south of the train station. Buses **#1, 5,** and **6** run east-west along Zhongshan Lu; **#9** runs east along Xinhua Lu.

Taxis: Base fare Y5. Y10-15 should suffice for most places around town.

ORIENTATION AND PRACTICAL INFORMATION

Most activity is centered around the plaza outside the train station, and along **Zhongshan Xi Lu** (中山西路) and **Zhongshan Dong Lu,** which run west and east,

respectively, from the station. **Zhanqian Jie** runs past the train station and nearly all of the town's hotels and 24hr. fast food restaurants. **Yucai Jie** branches off Zhongshan Dong Lu, just past the Provincial Museum.

Travel Agencies: The **CITS** (☎581 5639) and **CTS** (☎581 4076 or 581 4656) main offices are in the Tourism Building, 175 Yucai Jie, 4th and 5th fl., opposite the Hebei Grand Hotel. Both have a few English-speaking staff members, and are open M-F 8am-noon and 3-6pm. **CITS branch,** 171 Yucai Jie (☎582 7777). Open daily 9am-5pm. **CTS branch,** 140 Yucai Jie (☎667 4225). Open daily 8am-noon and 3-6pm.

Bank of China: 83 Zhongshan Xi Lu, Dongfang Plaza, 1st fl. (☎861 1257 or 861 1258), 7min. northwest of the train station, around the corner from the Dongfang Shopping Plaza entrance. Exchanges currency and traveler's checks. Credit card advances. Open M-F 8:30-11:30am and 3-6pm.

Shopping: Dongfang City Plaza Shopping Center (dōngfāng chéngshìguǎngchǎn gòuwù zhōngxīn; 东方城市广场购物中心), 83 Zhongshan Xi Lu (☎861 1061), about a block west of the train station. Open daily 9am-9pm. Farther east is the **Beiguo Commercial Building** (běiguó shāngchéng; 北国商城), 188 Zhongshan Dong Lu (☎697 4448). Open M-F 9am-7:45pm, Sa-Su 9am-8:30pm.

Internet Access: Internet Club (wǎngluò jùlèbù; 网络俱乐部), 86 Yucai Lu (☎667 0616), a block and a half south of Zhongshan Dong Lu. Y3 per hr., Y10 deposit. Open 24hr. **Sinbad's Internet Info Center** (xīnbādà wǎngluòxìnxī gǎng; 辛巴大网络信息港), 261 Yuhua Dong Lu (☎669 1414). Same prices and hours as the Internet Club.

PSB: 216 Zhongshan Dong Lu.

Post Office: China Post, 1 Gongli Jie (☎702 5736), on the corner of Gongli Jie and Zhongshan Dong Lu, just across the bridge from the train station. Main entrance on Gongli Jie; at later hours, use the entrance around the corner on Zhongshan Lu. EMS, IDD service, and Poste Restante. Open 24hr. **Postal Code:** 050000.

ACCOMMODATIONS

If you're in Shijiazhuang, you're probably a reluctant itinerant. The hotels know that you're stuck here, and as a result budget options are limited. Most of the hotels are near the train station and are fiercely competitive, so it won't hurt to check out several before making a choice.

Bailin Hotel (báilín dàshà; 白林大厦), 24 Zhanqian Jie (☎702 1398; fax 702 1887), opposite the train station. Within spitting distance of the next train out of town and unofficial award winner for best baths in town. Rooms have all standard amenities. Breakfast included. Singles (with a huge bed) Y150; doubles and triples Y220-420. ❷

Hualian Hotel (huālián héběi fàndiàn; 花联河北饭店), 10 Zhanqian Jie (☎702 5991), across from the area between the train station and the bus station, next to the Hualian Commercial Building. Comfortable bedrooms are identical; baths are noticeably better in more expensive rooms. Deposit Y100. Check-out 2pm. Doubles Y110-360. ❸

Silver Spring Hotel (yínquán jǐujiā; 银泉酒家), 12 Zhanqian Jie, across the street from the long-distance bus station. At night, the blue fluorescent lights give the lobby an eerie submerged feeling. Clean rooms with A/C, bath, phone, and TV. Currency exchange. Doubles Y128-200; triples Y198. ❷

FOOD

The biggest food fads in town are fill-me-up-quick box lunches and stuff-me-to-the-brim buffets. On **Zhongshan Dong Lu,** 50m east of Beiguo Department Store, **Changan Yuan** (长安园) alley is filled with inexpensive restaurants—the Y6-12 buffets are unbeatable. For sit-down meals, a strip of restaurants serves up aquatic delicacies along **Yucai Jie,** south of the Hebei Teachers' University.

SIGHTS

Shijiazhuang has a few interesting sights along Zhongshan Lu, but if you just want to kill some time here, wander through the massive markets south of **Xinhua Dong Lu** (新华东路) and along **Shengli Bei Jie** (胜利北街). More exciting sights lie outside the city proper, but they are more difficult and expensive to reach.

HEBEI PROVINCIAL MUSEUM (héběi shěng bówùguǎn; 河北省博物馆). This massive columned building is an impossible-to-miss local landmark. Skip the free commercial exhibition downstairs unless you collect pamphlets. The main gallery space features various exhibits and the occasional trade show. A suit of jade armor, a terracotta army, and a complete mammoth tusk can be found upstairs. *(Zhongshan Dong Lu, 3 blocks east of the Beiguo Commercial Building. Take bus #1, 5, or 35 from the train station. ☎604 5642. Open Tu-F 8-11:30am and 3-5:30pm, Sa-Su 9am-4pm. Y5.)*

MARTYRS MEMORIAL (lièshì língyuán; 烈士陵园). Never has war looked so orderly. In this perfectly geometric, expansive park, superhuman statues and busts are surrounded by refreshing greenery. Several stately buildings lovingly display all sorts of weaponry, including glass-encased machine guns and rusted shells. The photo collections and relics depict every aspect of the lives of those who dedicated themselves to the revolution. Socks and old shoes remind visitors of the men and women behind the unfeeling warfare machinery. *(343 Zhongshan Xi Lu. Take bus #1 or 25 from the train station to Lieshi Lingyuan and continue west for 3min. ☎702 2904. Open daily 7:30am-6pm. Y3.)*

DAYTRIPS FROM SHIJIAZHUANG

ZHENGDING 正定

15km northeast of Shijiazhuang. Take bus #201 from the south side of the train station to the last stop (40min., Y3). From there, jump aboard (or get shoved into) bus #1 to Dafo Si (10min., Y1). Open daily in summer 8am-6pm; in winter 8:30am-5pm. Y30, children under 1.3m Y15.

Zhengding used to be an important regional center but it has since been eclipsed by the burgeoning economic clout of Shijiazhuang. Now, Zhengding tries to sell itself as a weekend getaway with ghastly theme parks like **The Wild Kingdom** (yě chéng; 野城), a walk-through tour of plastic fairy-tale figures and the occasional Bible story (open daily 1-7pm; Y15, children Y7), and **The Hall of the Journey to the West** (xīyóujì gōng; 西游纪宫). Visit only if you are caught in a downpour and there is no other shelter. The real attraction here is **Longxing Temple** (lóngxīng sì; 隆兴寺), popularly known as the **Great Buddha Temple** (dàfó sì; 大佛寺), home to a giant, multi-armed copper Goddess of Mercy that dominates the main hall. At 21.3m, the Goddess of Mercy bronze statue with "one thousand hands and eyes" (a gross exaggeration—it's more like forty-two), was the highest statue in ancient China, and is one of the four "wonders" of Hebei Province. According to locals, a climb into the upper rafters to shake one of the Buddha's many burnished hands, to touch his nose, or to risk injury in any way, demonstrates one's piety.

CANGYANSHAN MOUNTAIN 苍岩山

90km southwest of Shijiazhuang. Two buses leave for Cangyanshan daily at 7:30am and 5:30pm (2hr., Y10) from the Dongfang Bus Station (take bus #111) on the corner of Xinhua Lu and Youyi Bei Lu. More conveniently, take a bus from the Dongfang Bus Station to the Jingling Bus Station (1hr., every 10min., Y5), and from there catch another bus heading to Cangyanshan's main entrance (1hr., about 1 per hr., Y5). Another option is to charter a taxi for Y180-200. ☎232 4104. Open 24hr. Y32.

This complex of pagodas and monasteries, set against a dramatic landscape of moutain peaks and marvelously twisted cypresses, has been carefully stitched into the mountainside—often as perilously as possible. The hike up the mountain is enjoyable and not too strenuous, passing 16 scenic spots. The climb should take about 1-2hr.; an eight-minute cable car ride can also take you directly to the summit. (Open daily in summer 7am-7pm; in winter 8am-5pm. Y26, round-trip Y42.) The **Hanging Palace** particularly merits attention; it is a spectacular, suspended temple that straddles a cleft between two cliffs. The generic temples along the way and at the summit are guarded by gatekeepers who will ask for further admission fees (Y5). You might as well skip these; there's enough to see on the free hike. Should you find yourself stranded for the night, the **Cangyanshan Hotel** ❷ (cāngyánshān bīnguǎn; 苍岩山宾馆), across from the parking lot, has decent rooms. (☎232 4114. Doubles Y120; triples Y150.)

CHENGDE 承德 ☎0314

Chengde rests roughly 200km northeast of Beijing. Once called *Rèhé* (Hot River), this small town has an appeal that increases immeasurably when Beijing's summer heat and traffic become too much for the city-dwellers to bear. Early in the 18th century, the Qing emperor Kangxi built a small mountain lodge in Chengde; later, during the reign of his son Qianlong, it grew into an immense Imperial Summer Villa. To add to the splendor, Qianlong had the surroundings dotted with temples replicating distinctive minority architecture, even going so far as to build a miniature version of Lhasa's Potala Palace inside the garden.

In the 19th century, after the emperors Jiaqing and Xiangeng both passed away in Chengde, the city's courtly bustle slipped into morbid slumber. Although this period of neglect did little to improve the condition of the city's architecture and relics, it did not lessen the appeal of the breathtaking rock formations and the cultivated gardens around them. Today, after plenty of restoration, Chengde can again boast not only of the grandeur its surrounding mountains, but also the distinctive charm of refurbished artifacts.

ORIENTATION AND PRACTICAL INFORMATION

Chengde rests in a valley bisected by the **Wulie River.** Giant rocks and stones crowd the rowdy roads, the principal of which is **Nanyingzi Dajie** (南营子大街). To the north sprawl the **Imperial Summer Villa** and its **Eight Outer Temples.**

Trains: Chengde Train Station (chéngdé huǒchē zhàn; 承德火车站; ☎208 4499), east of the river. 24hr. luggage storage (xíngbāo fáng; 行包房; Y2 day). Ticket office open daily 5-7:45am and 8:10am-11pm; advance tickets 8:40-11am and 2-4pm. To: **Beijing** (4-7hr., 5 per day, Y17-41); **Shenyang** (12hr., daily, Y45); **Shijiazhuang** (12hr., daily, Y38); **Tianjin** (9hr., daily, Y30).

Buses: Chengde Long-distance Bus Station (chéngdé chángtú qìchē zhàn; 承德长途汽车站; ☎207 3476), at the junction of Xinhua Lu and Wulie Lu. Luggage storage 5:30am-10pm (Y10 per day, depending on size). Open daily 5am-10pm. To: **Beijing** (3½hr., every 20min. 6am-6pm, Y45); **Qinhuangdao** (6hr., 4 per day, Y64.5); **Tianjin** (6hr., 3 per day, Y65.5). Private **minibuses** also depart frequently for **Beijing** (3hr., Y45) from the front of the building.

Local Transportation: Public buses (numbered #1-15) run 6am-7pm. Bus **#5** goes from the train station to the Imperial Summer Villa; **#6** from Nanyingzi Dajie to the Northern Temples via the Villa; **#7** between the train station and Nanyingzi Dajie; **#10** from Nanyingzi Dajie to the Eastern Temples. More frequent are the **private buses** (numbered in the 100s), which run later, but travel only to more central locations. Unnumbered **minibuses** run along the main streets between the train station and the city center. Fare Y1.

Taxis: Base fare officially Y5; each additional km Y1.4. To most sights in the city Y10; agree on the price in advance.

Bike Rental: Look for a stand on the right side of Tiaoli Jie, near the intersection with Xinhua Lu. Y10-20 per day. Open daily 6am-10pm. Another stand at the southwest corner of the train station square, left of the post office has a limited selection. Y5 per day, deposit Y100-200. Open daily approx. 6am-6:30pm.

Travel Agency: CITS, 11 Zhonghua Lu, 2nd fl. (☎202 6827), in the right wing of the courtyard of a gray building, 2min. up the street from the Summer Villa's Dehuimen Gate. Organizes foreign language tours (Y200 and up per day); staff members speak impeccable English. Open daily 8:30am-noon and 2-5pm.

Bank of China: 3 Dong Dajie. Exchanges traveler's checks. Credit card advances.

Hospital: Chengde City Central Hospital (chéngdéshì zhōngxīn yīyuàn; 承德市中心医院), on Xi Dajie, about 1½ blocks west of Nanyingzi Dajie. English-speaking staff. Open 24hr.

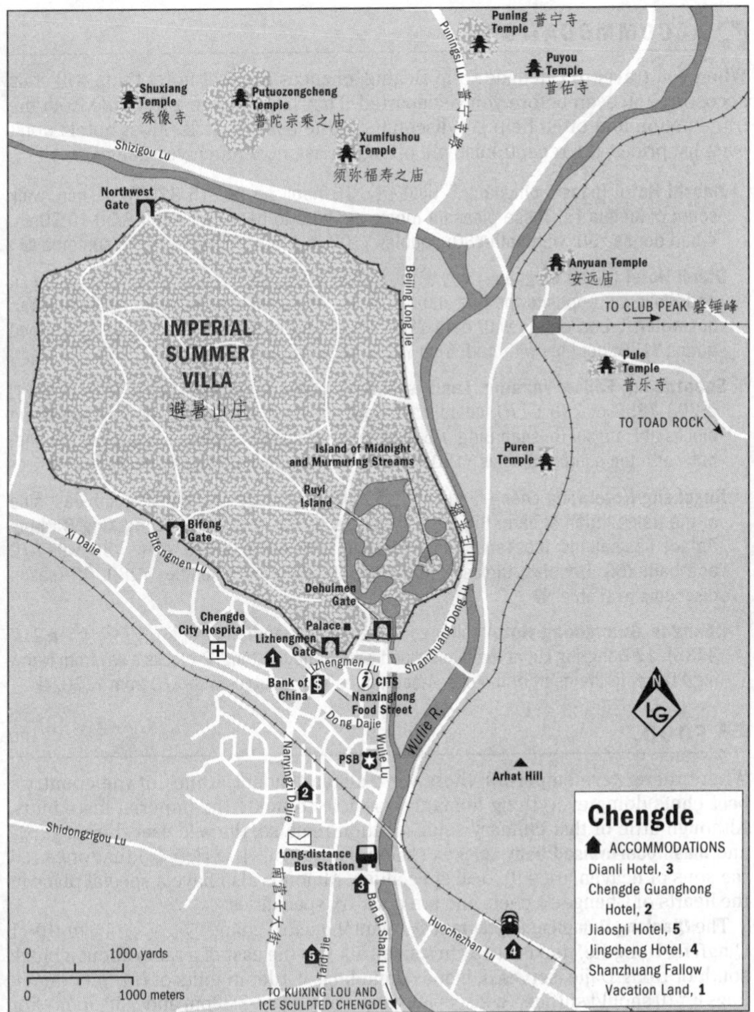

Internet Access: Chengde's Internet cafes can be difficult to spot. The 2 most centrally located Internet cafes are on Nanyingzi Dajie, opposite Chengde's only skyscraper-like building, left of the cinema. Follow the signs leading to the Mingxing Hotel (明行宾馆); the entrance is on Nanxinglong Food Street, between Lizhengman Dajie and Dong Dajie (open 10am-2am). Both Y2 per hr.

Post Office: About half a block north of the southern tip of Nanyingzi Dajie. EMS. Open daily in summer 8am-8pm; in winter 8am-6pm. **Postal Code:** 067000.

ACCOMMODATIONS

When you travel to Chengde from Beijing, chances are that hotel touts will start accosting you even before you've departed. They'll guarantee a free ride from the train station and often help get discounts at the better hotels. Most hotels don't even list prices; the receptionist will often just ask how much you can pay.

Jiaoshi Hotel (jiàoshī bīnguǎn; 教师宾馆), 16 Tiaoli Jie (☎215 3268), a 7min. walk south of Xinhua Lu. These pleasant rooms are hard to beat. Hot water 8:30-10:30pm. 4-bed dorms Y30, with bath Y80; doubles Y100, but may be pricier in the summer. ❶

Dianli Hotel (diànlì bīnguǎn; 电力宾馆; ☎217 3735), at the intersection of Xinhua Lu and Wulie Lu, opposite the bus station. Similar to the Jiaoshi, but with A/C and 24hr. hot water. 5-bed dorms with bath Y100; 4-bed dorms Y60; 3-bed dorms Y80; 2-bed dorms Y120; doubles with bath from Y200, depending on season. ❶

Shanzhuang Fallow Vacation Land (shānzhuāng xiūxián dùjiàcūn; 山庄休闲度假村; ☎203 7858 or 203 5770; cdhldjc@163.com), hidden among the growing apartment blocks at Liangshi Beishan Bldg. #6, next to the statue of emperor Kangxi. Hard to find, but worth the search. Singles Y150; doubles Y200. Haggling may be necessary. ❷

Jingcheng Hotel (jīng chéng fàndiàn; 京承饭店; ☎208 2027), on the south-east side of the train station square. Big, nice, clean, solid. The neighboring **Long Xing Bathing Palace** has saunas; foot (and other) massage Y120 per hr. 4-bed dorms Y30, with A/C and bath Y60. Doubles, triples, and quads with standard amenities Y280. Off-season discounts available. ❶

Chengde Guanghong Hotel (chéngdé guānghóng fàndiàn; 承德光宏饭店; ☎217 3735), 17 Dongxing Lu, at the intersection with Wutiao Hutong; 2 blocks away from Nanyingzi Dajie. In the heart of the city. 4-bed dorms Y30; doubles with A/C from Y120. ❶

FOOD

Where there were emperors, there were also attendant armies of the country's best chefs doing everything humanly possible to tickle the imperial taste buds. Although little of that culinary sophistication remains, the **wild deer** (lùròu; 鹿肉) and **mushroom-braised baby chicken** (xiǎojī dùn mógū; 小鸡炖蘑菇) that once fed the sons of heaven are still local specialties. Almonds also have a special place in the hearts of Chengde's chefs and are must-try specialties.

The **Qianlong Dumpling Restaurant** ❶ (qiánlóng jiǎozi guǎn; 乾隆饺子馆), on 10-11 Qingfeng Dong Jie, tucked away in a small alley to the east of a ramp about a block south of Dong Dajie, serves delicious dumplings. Order in units of *liǎng* (7 dumplings); Y10 should suffice. (☎202 8559. Open daily 11am-2:30pm and 5:30-9pm.) For true connoisseurs of local cuisine, **Nanxinglong Food Street** (nánxīnglóng xiǎochī jiē; 南兴隆小吃街) has it all. The bustling, bubbling, brewing street opposite the Lizhengmen entrance to the Imperial Villa dishes up hotpot (Y8-18) and every kind of almond snack imaginable. In the evening, open-air stalls on **Yihua Lu,** about one block west of the bus station, serve up plenty of fresh fruit and vegetables; try Chengde's specialty, **Lulu Almond Juice** (Y0.5 from street vendors; canned Y2).

SIGHTS

Temples, palaces, and curious rocks abound in Chengde. The fast and easy way to see them all is to take a minibus tour through the city (see **Travel Agency,** p. 176).

IMPERIAL SUMMER VILLA

At the end of Nanyingzi Dajie, north of the city center. The best entrance is Lizhengmen Gate on Lizhengmen Dajie. Take bus #5 from the train station or #6 from Nanyingzi Dajie. Tour buses (40min., 8am-5pm, Y40) leave from the area between the courtyards and the lake. Open daily 5:30am-9pm; last admission 6:30pm. Y50, children under 1.2m free.

At the Imperial Summer Villa (bìshǔ shānzhuāng; 避暑山庄), the grounds are impressive, the dealings important, and the former residents imperial. This massive 18th-century estate is twice the size of Beijing's Summer Palace and has seen nearly as many Qing intrigues. Since the Summer Villa fell from imperial favor over 100 years ago, the once-resplendent retreat has slipped slowly into a state of neglect. But even those who claim the park is a bit over-hyped have to admit that it is still one of Chengde's must-see sights.

There are 120 groups of ancient buildings; the main palace, including the elegant **Hall of Frugality and Sincerity,** has been converted into a museum of weaponry and furniture. In the side halls, the walls are lined with shelves that hold a gargantuan encyclopedia of books and illustrations. Behind the courtyard is the lavish **Hall of Refreshing Mists and Ripples,** where Emperor Xiangfeng signed the 1860 Treaty of Beijing and took his last breath, and the Dowager Empress Ci Xi succeeded in wresting political control from the male-dominated court.

The majority of the space has since been taken over by lakes and hills. Emperors used to test their hunting prowess on these grounds, but it would be foolhardy to explore the land alone; the hills are the perfect place to get lost. The lake is a patchwork of islands, the prettiest of which are **Ruyi Island** and the **Island of Midnight and Murmuring Streams.** You can walk to all of the islands, but renting a boat (Y10-20 per hr., deposit Y50-100) is more fun.

BEIJING

EIGHT OUTER TEMPLES

There were once 12 great temples in the area around Chengde, but four have fallen gracefully into disrepair. Of the eight Outer Temples (wàibā miào; 外八庙) remaining, only six are open to visitors. Built according to various ethnic styles, these temples were commissioned by Emperors Kangxi and Qianlong less for religious reasons than to intimidate ethnic envoys. The older and smaller **Eastern Temples** (Anyuan, Pule, and Puren), on the east bank of the river are a perfect place to escape the tumultuous tourist crowds. The bigger money-makers are the **Northern Temples** (Putuozongcheng, Xumifushou, Puning, Puyou, and Shuxiang). The smaller Puren Temple (pǔrén sì; 溥仁寺) and Shuxiang Temple (shūxiàng sì; 殊像寺) are not open to the public. While it may be tempting to strike out independently to cover all the temples, it is easy to overdose; most organized tours only take in two or three.

PUNING TEMPLE (pǔníng sì; 普宁寺). Of the Northern Temples, this is the only one where the religious chanting isn't pre-recorded. Called the "Temple of Universal Peace," this active temple commemorates Qianlong's defeat of the Mongolian rebels in 1755. The star of the temple is the 22m Thousand-Armed-and-Eyed Goddess of Mercy, the largest wooden statue in the world. It is accompanied by two smaller Buddha statues and 10,090 small "Buddhitas" that climb the walls. *(At the end of Puningsi Lu, east of the villa. Take bus #15 till the end or get off at Dafosi (大佛寺). ☎ 202 4548. Open daily 7:30am-6pm; last admission 5:30pm. Y30. Credit cards accepted, but the machine has a tendency to break.)*

PUYOU TEMPLE (pǔyòu sì; 普佑寺). This small, quiet compound was originally the center for the study of Buddhist scripture. In 1937, Japanese occupation forces moved 500 statues here from Arhat Temple; many were destroyed in a lightning fire in 1964, but 178 remain today. See such disciples as Liu Haichan, who teased toads, "The Crazy Monk," who swept up treacherous officials with his trusty broom, and "Crazy Ji," who "acted like a lunatic and gave no damn to rules." *(A 2min. walk east from Puning Temple, to the right of the gate. Open daily 8am-6pm; last admission 5:30pm. Y10.)*

XUMIFUSHOU TEMPLE (xūmífúshòu zhī miào; 须弥福寿之庙). The outstanding feature of Ximifushou Temple are the eight dragons made of sparkling gold, each weighing over 1000kg, that perch on its roof. This "Temple of Happiness and Longevity" was built in 1780 for the 6th Panchen Lama when he came to celebrate the emperor's birthday. The poor lama enjoyed neither happiness nor longevity, however; he contracted smallpox (some say he was poisoned) and was sent home in a coffin. *(On Shizigou Lu, the 1st of the Northern Temples, north of the Imperial Villa and a 10min. walk west from Puning Temple. Open daily 8:30am-5:30pm; last admission 5pm. Y20.)*

PUTUOZONGCHENG TEMPLE (pǔtuózōngchéng zhī miào; 普陀宗乘之庙). The oldest of the Chengde temples, Putuozongcheng is generally considered a happy alternative for those who can't make it to Tibet. The Putuozongcheng, also known as the Temple of Potaraka Doctrine, is a one-third scale model of the Dalai Lama's Potala Palace in Lhasa (see p. 809). Even though the great red wall surging up from the mountainous landscape is reminiscent of the Potala, so many Chinese pagodas have been added since its construction that as an impression of the original, it is limp at best. The tantric statues, however, are anything but. *(A few hundred meters west of Xumifushou. Open daily 8:30am-5:30pm; last admission 5pm. Y20.)*

EASTERN TEMPLES. Bus #10 drops you off at a big square, where a lady offers a glance at some curious stones and rocks (Y2-5) and a horse ride to the sights (Y5). Inconspicuous English signs show the way to **Pule Temple** (pǔlè sì; 普乐寺), **Anyuan Temple** (ānyuǎn miào; 安远庙), and **Club Peak.** Pule Temple is a quiet spot with a circular pavilion in the back that resembles that on Beijing's Temple of Heaven (see p. 137). The building was constructed by visiting Mongols, and the architecture is a mixture of Mongolian, Tibetan, Chinese, and Islamic styles. *(Open daily 8am-6pm; last admission 5:30pm. Y20.)* Anyuan Temple, built with Central Asian architectural styles, was once used by Mongolian troops. Today, it's the most tranquil place in town. *(A 10min. walk north of Pule Temple. Open daily 8am-5:30pm. Y10.)*

OTHER SIGHTS

CLUB PEAK (qìngchuí fēng; 磬锤峰). Looking like a large sore thumb sticking out of the eastern horizon, Club Peak is Chengde's most beloved rock formation, which, according to legend, was created by a dragon. **Toad Rock** (háma shí; 蛤蟆石) lies 2km south. Visitors scramble until they find the perfect angle and then exclaim with delight, "It's a toad, it's a toad!" The climb is especially enjoyable in the early morning, when the paths lack mounds of tourists and early risers can watch the sun rise over the Chinese countryside. *(At the end of Hedong Lu, between Anyuan and Pule Temples. Take bus #10 to its terminus. Open daily 6:30am-6pm. Y15. Cable car round-trip Y15.)*

TWIN PAGODA HILL (shuāngtǎ shān; 双塔山). Compared to Club Peak, which is visible from all over the city, Twin Pagoda Hill seems like a better deal to most travelers since it has not just one but *two* exciting protuberances. The area also boasts a treacherous metal staircase that is at the frightening mercy of the wind (Y20). In place of the toad, a smaller squat rock looks like a tortoise bowing before the two pagodas. Another formation resembles a pair of kissing lovers. *(About 15km west of Chengde. Accessible by bus #5. Open daily 6am-7pm. Park Y20; cable car one-way Y10.)*

CHENGDE ICE SNOW CITY (chéngdé bīng xuě chéng; 承德冰雪城). Lit by extraneous neon lights and boasting a mini-amusement park, this rather cheesy, but fun, mountain villa is the way to beat the summer heat. While you're here, try your hand at Chinese crossword puzzles and take a peek at the city and the surrounding mountains from **Kuixing Lou** (kuíxīng lóu; 魁星楼). The pavilions aren't extraordinary, but make for excellent viewing spots. Chinese-readers can also get an astrology lesson. *(Accessible by taxi (Y10); or take bus #9 and get off at the dirt road to the right, just outside the city. Ice-cave open daily 8:30am-8:30pm. Admission Y30, warm coats Y5. Kuixing Lou open daily 7am-10pm. Y20.)*

SHANHAIGUAN 山海关 ☎0335

Famous as the place where the Great Wall meets the sea, Shanhaiguan challenges the visitor with all sorts of contradictions. It is the site where general Wu Sangui let in the Qing armies, effectively sealing the demise of the Ming dynasty (see **Going Postal**, p. 12). Today, huge housing developments and highways surround this petite village that is confined by ancient city walls and has streets too narrow for public buses. Shanhaiguan's sights are also peculiar: the older buildings seem too well-restored, the mountains too conquered, nature too tamed—all evidence of a growing, increasingly modern China.

ORIENTATION AND PRACTICAL INFORMATION

The center of Shanhaiguan is the small village within the city walls, plus a few blocks to the south and east, where the train station and the **First Pass Under Heaven** are found. The center of town is divided into a grid pattern, anchored by **Bei Dajie** (北大街), **Nan Dajie** (南大街), **Dong Dajie** (东大街), and **Xi Dajie** (西大街); the entire village is easily navigable on foot. Around it blooms the new Shanhaiguan, an impressively uniform and unexciting flower of post-modern Chinese architecture. The whole town is encircled by mountains, the sea, and the area's other sights, many of which are beyond the reach of public transportation.

Trains: Shanhaiguan Train Station (☎504 4102), at the end of Nanguan Dajie. Luggage storage Y3 per hr. To: **Beijing** (3-7hr., 21 per day, Y24-65); **Changchun** (7-9hr., 3 per day, Y49-99); **Harbin** (10-12hr., 6 per day, Y62-125); **Shenyang** (4-7hr., 7 per day, Y31-63); **Tianjin** (4-5hr., 3 per day, Y24-75).

Local Transportation: The **bus station** at the junction of Guangcheng Dong Lu and Guangcheng Nan Lu serves **city buses** (Y1), which can also be caught on any major street outside the city walls. **Bus #25** runs from Qinhuangdao to Old Dragon Head; the seasonal **#24** goes to Yansai Lake; **#23** goes to the Mengjiannu Temple.

Taxis: Base fare Y5, each additional km Y1.4. The only way to get to Longevity Mountain and Jiaoshan Great Wall.

Travel Agency: CITS (☎505 2952), above the restaurant next to the ticket booth for the First Pass Under Heaven. English-language tours. Open daily 8:30am-5:30pm.

Bank of China: 60 Diyiguan Lu (☎505 2195). Exchanges traveler's checks. Credit card advances. Open M-F 8:30-11:45am and 3-5:30pm. In winter, times subject to change.

PSB: on 23 Guangcheng Nan Lu.

Hospital: People's Hospital (rénmín yīyuàn; 人民医院), 46 Nan Dajie (☎505 1023).

Internet: A small **cafe** at 24 Nan Dajie, half-way up the street through the South Gate. Several other establishments are open as late as 2am.

Post office: 31 Nan Dajie. EMS and Poste Restante. Open daily 8am-6pm. **Postal code:** 066200.

ACCOMMODATIONS AND FOOD

Shanhaiguan puts Beidaihe to shame when it comes to inexpensive places to stay. The **North Street Hotel** ❶ (běijiē zhāodàisuǒ; 北街招待所), 1 Mujia Hutong, to the right of Bei Dajie, has housed generations of travelers. Peeling and mossy, with stone floors and round doorways, this hotel is half-hostel, half-abandoned monastery. (☎505 1680. 6- to 8-bed dorms Y20-30; doubles with bath Y120-160.) Those not interested in spiritual renewal can try the **Rongcheng Grand Hotel** ❷, 1 Nanguan Dajie, which has 24hr. hot water, A/C, and attached baths. (☎506 4488. 2-bed dorms Y94; singles Y168; doubles Y258.) The **Shanhaiguan Hotel** ❹ (shānhǎiguān dàjiǔdiàn; 山海关大酒店), 107 Guangcheng Nan Lu, outside and east of the South Gate, is more luxurious. (☎506 4488 or 506 4988. Doubles from Y288.)

Shanhaiguan burns with a love for Middle Eastern cuisine. Many restaurants have Arabic signs or call themselves Islamic taverns. Unlike in most places in China, bread is a street vendor staple (Y2) and is served with most meals. The local specialty, *mènxiōngkǒu* (braised meat; 焖胸口), can be found at any of the family restaurants within the old city walls or on Nanguan Dajie.

BEIJING

SIGHTS

There are a fair number of sights in Shanhaiguan, most of which are wildly overpriced and not particularly interesting; at worst, they are commercialized displays of bad taste. **Beaches** are why most Beijingers flock to the coast. Don't, however, expect luxurious white sand and crystal clear water; it's not difficult to see why Shanhaiguan is so much cheaper than its neighbor, Beidaihe. From the city center to the coast, a taxi ride costs Y10.

GREAT WALL MUSEUM (chángchéng bówùguǎn; 长城博物馆). This museum is arguably the most interesting place to visit in Shanhaiguan. It features a well-curated and well-displayed history of the Great Wall, and if you can read Chinese, there's enough information here to answer any Great Wall trivia questions that backpackers can sling at you. Even if you can't read Chinese, the excellent pictures should make you itch to adjust your travel itinerary. Equally, er, fascinating is the hall of freakish-shaped rocks. *(On Diyiguan Lu, 3min. south of the First Pass Under Heaven, following the Old City Wall. Open daily 7:45am-6:30pm. Y5; bag check Y1.)*

JIAOSHAN GREAT WALL (jiǎoshān chángchéng; 角山长城). As you approach from a broad, smooth avenue, Jiaoshan looks like a promising and incredible Great Wall experience. Stately and breathtaking, it surges up along the precipitous peaks of a mountain ridge that faces the Bohai Sea, earning itself the name "Horn Mountain," as it resembles the ridges on the back of a writhing dragon. Legend holds that this section of the Great Wall spontaneously dissolved to reveal the bones of human workers that had been used to fill in its base. That might explain the extensive restoration since then; up close, Jiaoshan is disappointingly well made. Past the first two towers, however, the wall all but disappears, and determined hikers must scramble hard to make it up to **Qixian Monastery.** The view of Yansai Lake from the upper cablecar station and above is worth your sweat. *(3km north of Shanhaiguan. Accessible by taxi (Y10). Open daily from dawn until 2hr. before dusk. Y15. Cable car operates 8:30am-4:30pm; round-trip Y20.)*

FIRST PASS UNDER HEAVEN (tiānxià dìyī guān; 天下第一关). This gate was China's outermost gate to the world at one point—at least until the Manchu armies stormed in (followed soon after by souvenir vendors). The main sight of the First Pass Under Heaven is an overpowering tower of the Great Wall that now stands tall and lonesome amid squalid tourist splendor. *(At the end of Diyiguan Lu on the eastern edge of town. Open daily 6am-7pm. Y35.)*

MENGJIANGNÜ TEMPLE (mèngjiāngnǚ miào; 孟姜女庙). An entire complex dedicated to a woman who knew how to be a good wife, Mengjiangnu Temple was built in the Song dynasty and restored during the Ming. The temple bears witness to the folklore surrounding Mengjiangnu, a woman said to have traveled thousands of miles in search of her husband who died as a forced laborer at the Great Wall. So many times did she pace back and forth that she left "footprints in the stones," and so moving were her virtuous cries that the wall crumbled to reveal her husband's bones. *(6km east of Shanhaiguan, on Fenghuangshan. In July and August accessible by bus #23. Open daily 7am-dusk; Y30, children 1.1-1.4m free.)*

OLD DRAGON HEAD (lǎo lóng tóu; 老龙头). Restored in 1987 at a cost of three million *yuán*, this easternmost edge of the Great Wall juts out 124m into the Bohai Sea and is said to be a perfect juxtaposition of manmade miracle and gorgeous natural scenery. The masses of happy tourists who flock here apparently agree. *(3km from Shanhaiguan. Minibuses (Y2) leave from South Gate; bus #25 takes forever to get to the same place. Park open daily 4am-7:30pm; the wall opens at 7:30am. Y35.)*

If you ask to be taken to the Old Dragon Head, most taxis will drop you off instead at the nearby **Great Wall Cultural Center** (chángchéng wénhùa yóudōngyuán; 长城文化游东园). The exhibitions include a *papier maché* Great Wall, a model of a gruesome attack scene, and what appears to be a Buddhist temple, Elvis-style—it's covered with sparkles. *(At the head of the 500m strip leading to the Old Dragon Head. Open daily 7am-6pm. Y20.)*

LONGEVITY MOUNTAIN (chángshòu shān; 长寿山). This hiking ground is made of massive granite rocks stacked like Legos to form impressive mountains that derive their names from the frequent rock face etchings. Rare natural rock formations like the "Fish-eye stone," which looks like a giant fish with its mouth open, and the "Stone Grotto of Highly Skilled Doctors" also provide entertainment. *(9km northeast of Shanhaiguan. Accessible by taxi (30min., Y30). Open daily 8am-7pm. Y15.)*

BEIDAIHE 北戴河 ☎0335

Until Beidaihe was "discovered" in the 19th century by Europeans living in Tianjin, it was just a little fishing village. The foreigners' proclivity for sun and surf, however, quickly turned Beidaihe into China's equivalent of the Riviera. Westerners have since fled, and the coastal city has become a watering hole for Communist cadres and *yuán*-laden Chinese vacationers. If the promise of Party bigwigs shedding their comrade garb is too much to resist, join the scantily clad mainlanders and head to this sparkling oceanic oasis. But be sure to pack lots of money with your swimsuit; seaside fun has its price.

ORIENTATION AND PRACTICAL INFORMATION. Beidaihe's two main streets, **Xi Haitan Lu** and **Dongjing Lu,** run along the seashore, off of which branch a bunch of numbered alleys, named **Bao"number" Lu** (Baoyi Lu, Baoer Lu, etc.; 保"X"路). One of the fastest ways to get to **Beijing** is to take a **minibus,** which leaves daily from the square near the post office on Haining Lu (3½hr.; 6am, noon, and

4pm; Y70). Otherwise, **trains** run from the remote though modern-looking **Beidaihe Train Station** to **Beijing** (2-6hr., 13 per day, Y21-90), **Changchun** (10hr., 2 per day, Y81 and up), **Dalian** (10hr., daily, Y81), **Harbin** (13hr., 2 per day, Y160 and up) and **Tianjin** (4hr., 4 per day, Y18 and up). While trains to **Qinhuangdao** depart almost constantly, during the day a more practical option is to take one of the frequent **local buses** (Y1, 6am-7pm). Useful routes include **#5, 15, 22** (30min.) from the Beidaihe Train Station via West Beach to the Beidaihe Haibin Bus Station (a few blocks from Dongjing Lu up **Haining Lu**); and **#34** from Beidaihe to Qinhuangdao (1hr.; to get to Shanhaiguan, hop on **#25** when you reach the downtown area). **Taxi** rides (base fare Y5; each additional km Y1.2) from the train station to most hotels cost Y10; any public bus travels the same route for less. The expensive **bike rentals** are necessary only if you intend to venture to quieter beaches in the east, where taxis and buses are not allowed. Check out the array of tandems, tridems, and bigger specials at the entrance to East Beach at **Qiqiao Nan Lu,** opposite the Bank of China (up to Y10 per hour).

Bank of China, 17 Dongjing Lu, between Anwu Lu and Liuchi Lu, exchanges traveler's checks and issues credit card advances. (☎404 0397. Open daily 8-11:40am and 3-5:40pm.) The local **PSB** can be reached at ☎404 4841. **China Telecom,** 76 Dongjing Lu, has IDD service and Internet access for Y0.3 per minute. (☎404 1029. Open 24hr.; Internet access may be out at certain times, so it's best to try 6am-10pm). The **EMS post office,** on Haining Lu, about half a block north of Dongjing Lu, also books tickets and has Poste Restante. (☎404 2781 or 403 3999. Open daily 8am-6:30pm.) The **postal code** is 066100.

BEIJING

ACCOMMODATIONS AND FOOD. Those not willing to shell out Y600-700 per night have few options. The **Guesthouse for Diplomatic Missions** ❸ (wàijiāo rényuán bīnguǎn; 外交人员宾馆), 1 Baosan Lu, off Dongjing Lu, uses a different definition of "budget," and offers decadent oceanfront bungalows with access to a pool and tennis courts. (☎404 4287. Open Apr.-Oct. Doubles and triples from Y200, depending on the season.) The plush **Yuehua Hotel** ❹ (yuèhuá bīnguǎn; 悦华宾馆), 90 Dongjing Lu, is in a big white building at the intersection with Baosan Lu. (☎404 0470. 2-bed dorm rooms Y240; doubles from Y480. Credit cards accepted.) As a last resort, **Beidaihe Jiudian** ❸ (běidàihé jiǔdiàn; 北戴河酒店; ☎404 2086), on Haining Lu, 100m from the bus station, may host you for Y200 or less after some haggling.

The quality of the **seafood** in Beidaihe is nothing short of spectacular; pick out the creature of your choice from the red and green tubs on the sidewalk. The **Juan Restaurant** ❷ (jūān cāntīng; 居安餐厅; ☎403 8299), a favorite among travelers, is at the intersection of Dongjing Lu and Haining Lu, in front of the pavilion. The delicious *jìngyú* (镜鱼) and *qìpào yú* (气泡鱼) can't be missed (Y20). (Open 9am-11pm.) From Haining Lu all the way down Baoer Lu toward Tiger Rock is a row of clean, lively, and airy seafood restaurants. **Kiesslings** ❷ (qǐshìlín cāntīng; 起士林餐厅; ☎404 1043), a branch of the famous Tianjin chain, is near the Guesthouse for Diplomatic Missions, where Baosan Lu and Dongjing Lu meet. Feast on *borscht*, caviar, and the sinfully good pastries that the Austrians brought to Tianjin during the concession days. (Dishes Y5-35. Open July-Aug. daily 9am-11pm.)

SIGHTS AND BEACHES. You don't come to Beidaihe for much more than the beach, but if you start to yearn for something other than blue skies and green seas, Lianfengshan Park (liánfēngshān gōngyuán; 联峰山公园) is a pleasant refuge. Gaze at the ocean and hunt with your camera for some rare birds. *(Bus #5 will bring you to the gate; get off when the bus takes a turn at the top of a hill. Open daily 7am-6pm. Admission Y22, students Y12.)*

Of the three stretches of beach in Beidaihe, the closest and busiest is **Middle Beach.** The **West** and **East Beaches** offer more tranquility, perhaps owing to the abundance of men in uniform who cordon off choice sections for party leaders. Most of the beaches' entrances "officially" charge admission, but they seldom bother, especially in the off-season.

SHANDONG 山东

Good beer and good company has brought Shandong more than its fair share of fame in the last three millennia. The province has traditionally been one of China's poorest, due in no small part to the caprices of the Yellow River, which has spilled over its banks more times than historians can count. But this scrappy little province is also responsible for a disproportionate number of China's proudest cultural achievements, the birthplace of such colorful figures as Confucius, Mencius, and Jiang Qing, and the home of some of Daoism's most revered spirits and sprites. Even China's most highly regarded beer, Tsingtao, is brewed here. Shandong is a province full of cultural wonders that are perfectly complemented by green hills, craggy coastline, and maybe a beer or three.

JI'NAN 济南 ☎0531

For most travelers, Ji'nan is just a convenient stopping point en route to Qingdao or Taishan and Qufu. But the capital of Shandong province also offers some surprising treasures beneath its dusty big city exterior. Despite the ultra-modern offices that line the major streets and the pounding construction heard from afar, this busy city still takes life one step at a time, never pushing, never rushing. After work, Ji'nan's hard-working inhabitants find comfort on the marble benches in the city square, their eyes fixated on the final quarter of a televised football match from a huge overhead screen. The splendor of Thousand Buddha Mountain and the quiet grace of the tree-covered hills surrounding the Four Gate Pagoda add to the town's unexpected beauty. The people of Ji'nan walk with a relaxed pace, reminding visitors that life should be a stroll, not a frantic race.

TRANSPORTATION

Flights: Yaoqiang International Airport (yáoqiáng guóji jīchǎng; 遥墙国际机场; ☎694 9400). Tickets can be booked by calling the **Shandong Airlines Co. Ltd.,** 71 Jingsi Wei Yi Lu (☎603 3747 or 603 3737; fax 691 1145; www.shandongair.com), on the corner of Jingsi Lu and Wei Yi Lu. **Shuttle buses** run from the **Silver Plaza Shopping Center** (yínzuò shāngchéng; 银座商城), at the intersection of Luoyuan Dajie and Qianfoshan Lu. To: **Beijing** (2-4 per day, Y500); **Chengdu** (1-3 per day, Y1240); **Chongqing** (1-3 per day, Y1000); **Dalian** (1-2 per day, Y730); **Guangzhou** (3 per day, Y1420); **Guilin** (M, W-Th, Sa; Y1500); **Haikou** (1-2 per day, Y1770); **Harbin** (1-2 per day, Y1030); **Nanjing** (daily M, W, F; Y640); **Shanghai** (4-5 per day, Y700); **Shenyang** (1-2 per day, Y790); **Xi'an** (1-2 per day, Y800).

Trains: Ji'nan Train Station (jínán huǒchē zhàn; 济南火车站), on Jingyi Lu, in the city center. To: **Beijing** (4hr., several per day, Y74); **Fuzhou** (18hr., daily, Y208); **Harbin** (19hr., 2 per day, Y140); **Nanjing** (12½hr., 2 per day, Y45); **Qingdao** (4½hr., 3 per day, Y48); **Shanghai** (18hr., 5:30pm, Y101); **Shenyang** (15¼hr., 3 per day, Y166); **Tianjin** (3½hr., several per day, Y52).

Buses: The bus station opposite the train station (☎691 0927) is the most centrally located and most convenient. To: **Beijing** (8hr., 8 am, Y72); **Qingdao** (4½hr., every half-hour, Y54); **Qufu** (2hr., every 20min. 5:30am-5:30pm, Y21); **Shanghai** (20hr., 8:30am, Y169); **Tai'an** (1½hr., every 10min. 5:30am-7:30pm, Y8); **Yantai** (5½hr., 12 per day, Y66); **Weihai** (over 6hr., 5 per day, Y73-138).

Local Transportation: Buses #2, 48, and **51** run along Jingshi Lu to the Thousand Buddha Mountain. Many buses, including **#3, 11, 18,** and **34,** also run to and from the train and bus stations. Bus fare Y0.5-4, depending on distance.

Taxis: Base fare Y5-6. Add Y0.5-1 for A/C.

ORIENTATION AND PRACTICAL INFORMATION

Ji'nan's **train station** is in the western part of town, on **Jingyi Lu** (经一路), a major east-west street. **Daming Lake** (大明湖), surrounded by Daming Lake Park, is the major landmark in the eastern half of the city, surrounded by **Daming Hu Bei Lu** (大明湖北路) to the north and **Daming Hu Lu** to the south. **Quancheng Square,** the main business and shopping center, is to the south of the lake. The major north-south thoroughfare of **Lishan Lu** (历山路) is to the east. **Qianfoshan Lu** (千佛山路) runs through the southern half of the city, toward Thousand Buddha Park; it intersects with **Jingshi Lu** (经十路), which runs from east to west past the Shandong Provincial Museum.

In the southwestern part of the city, the east-west streets are designated as **Jing (number) Lu;** from north to south, the traveler encounters Jingyi Lu, Jinger Lu, Jingsan Lu, and so on. The north-south streets are designated **Wei (number) Lu,** and the numbers increase from east to west. A number of smaller streets between are prefixed with a **Xiao** (小).

Travel Agency: CITS, 88 Jingshi Lu, 4th fl. (☎296 5858, ext. 6401 or 6402; fax 296 5651; sdcitsaa@public.jn.sd.cn), near Lishan Lu. Open M-F 8am-6pm. **Ji'nan Tourism Bureau,** 117 Jingqi Weisi Lu, 5th fl. (☎793 0899), on the corner of the intersection.

Bank of China: 22 Luoyuan Dajie (☎699 5026 or 699 5029). Exchanges currency and traveler's checks. Credit card advances. Open M-F 8am-6pm.

PSB: 145 Jingsan Lu (☎691 5454), near Weiwu Lu.

Hospital: Shengli Hospital (shěnglì yīyuàn; 省立医院), 324 Jingwu Lu (☎793 8911), opposite the intersection with Weiqi Lu. 24hr. emergency care. Pharmacy. Within the complex, the main building is on the left, down an alley.

Internet Access: Close to the station, **The Fossick Network Bar,** 19 Jinger Weisan Lu, (☎605 0385), is through a parking lot, and down an alley to the right, beside a room with pool and ping-pong tables. Y3 per hr., 1hr. minimum. Open daily 8:30am-11pm.

Post Office: China Post, 162 Jinger Lu (☎605 7274), at Weier Lu. EMS and Poste Restante. Open daily in summer 8am-7:30pm; in winter 8am-7pm. **Postal Code:** 250001.

ACCOMMODATIONS

Accommodations in Ji'nan are, in general, pretty much identical. All come with air-conditioning, phone, TV, and a slightly stained carpet. However, baths are less common. Evaluate hotels based on location and convenience.

Shandong Longqiantan Hotel, 11-12 Jingyi Weisan Lu (☎605 7777; fax 605 5678), on Weisan Lu, less than 10min. southeast of the train and bus stations. Major buses,

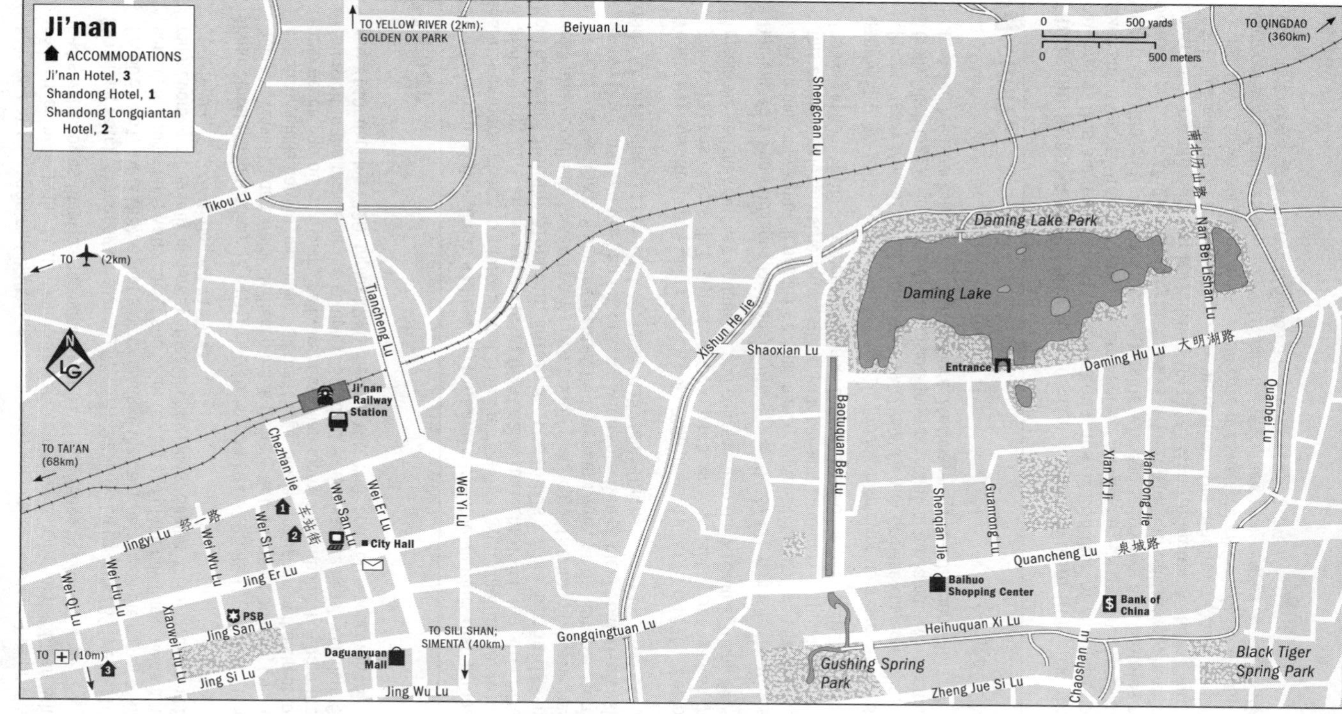
Ji'nan
ACCOMMODATIONS
Ji'nan Hotel, 3
Shandong Hotel, 1
Shandong Longqiantan Hotel, 2
TO YELLOW RIVER (2km); GOLDEN OX PARK
Beiyuan Lu
0 500 yards
0 500 meters
TO QINGDAO (360km)
Tikou Lu
TO (2km)
Shengchan Lu
南北历山路
Nan Bei Lishan Lu
Daming Lake Park
Daming Lake
Tiancheng Lu
Xishun He Jie
Shaoxian Lu
Entrance
Daming Hu Lu 大明湖路
Quanbei Lu
Ji'nan Railway Station
TO TAI'AN (68km)
Chezhan Jie 车站街
Baotuquan Bei Lu
Wei Yi Lu
Wei Er Lu
Wei San Lu
City Hall
Jingyi Lu 经一路
Wei Wu Lu
Wei Si Lu
Shenqian Jie
Guanrong Lu
Xian Xi Ji
Xian Dong Jie
Quancheng Lu 泉城路
Wei Qi Lu
Wei Liu Lu
Jing Er Lu
Baihuo Shopping Center
Bank of China
PSB
Xiaowei Liu Lu
Jing San Lu
TO SILI SHAN; SIMENTA (40km)
Gongqingtuan Lu
Heihuquan Xi Lu
TO (10m)
Daguanyuan Mall
Jing Si Lu
Jing Wu Lu
Gushing Spring Park
Zheng Jue Si Lu
Chaoshan Lu
Black Tiger Spring Park

including #51 to 1000 Buddha Mountain, all stop right outside the door. This relatively new, cheap hotel is the best place to stay for comfort and convenience. Clean, white baths with shower. Breakfast included. Doubles Y180. Deposit Y120. ❸

Shandong Hotel (shāndōng bīnguǎn; 山东宾馆), 92 Jingyi Lu (☎605 7881, ext. 3100; fax 605 7881, ext. 3188), about a block south of the train station, on the corner of Weisan Lu. All rooms have water cooler and bath. The old age of the building is evident, but renovations are currently underway. Breakfast included. Singles Y130; doubles Y150-180; triples Y210-240. Deposit Y150. ❷

Ji'nan Hotel (jǐnán fàndiàn; 济南饭店), 240 Jingsan Lu (☎793 8981; fax 793 2906), between Weiliu Lu and Weiqi Lu. Reception in Building 4, the farthest building from the entrance. A little hard to find behind all the foliage, but far enough from the street for a little peace and quiet. Gloomy hallways, but clean rooms with a bathtub, and a pretty courtyard in the middle of the complex. Standard amenities. Breakfast included. Singles Y140; doubles Y220; triples Y240. Deposit Y60, Y80, and Y60 respectively. ❷

FOOD

Luscious produce fills Ji'nan's alleys, as fruit and vegetable vendors dish up mangos, cucumbers, cherry tomatoes, and some gargantuan watermelons. A strip of up-and-coming bars and eateries is on **Qianfoshan Lu,** right down the street from the Thousand Buddha Mountain entrance. The locals gather for on-the-spot snacks and noodle dishes in the Weiwu Lu alley opposite the hospital. The basement of the **Silver Plaza Shopping Center,** 66 Luoyuan Dajie, at the intersection of Luoyuan Dajie and Qianfoshan Lu, offers a wide selection of clean, palate-pleasing foods for ultra-cheap prices (Y1-10. Open daily 9am-10pm).

Yuedu Restaurant (yuèdū jiǔlóu; 粤都酒楼), 588 Jingqi Lu (☎793 4825). Seafood galore. Patrons choose their dishes (Y8-20) from a window display, and wait as their meals are caught from their aquariums and cooked. Open daily 10am-2:30am. ❶

Tianlong Fast Food (tiānlóng kuàicān; 天龙快餐; ☎602 3742), opposite the train station, to the left. Brightly lit outside beckons hungry arrivals and bored departees alike to this tin tray, cafeteria-style eatery where your chosen, styrofoam-wrapped dishes are cooked in front of you at a supersonic pace. Dishes Y7-10. Open daily 5:30am-10pm. ❶

Millionaire, 37 Weier Lu, just before Jingsi Lu. Proudly displaying its award of "The Best Prices Clearly Marked Unit," Millionaire is McDonald's with Chinese characteristics. Literally. Their logo is an arch with an upside-down reflection of the famous M. Mix french fries and fried chicken with lo mein and rice. Meals average Y6-10. Open 24hrs. ❶

SIGHTS

THOUSAND BUDDHA MOUNTAIN (qiānfó shān; 千佛山). Within the dark chilly caverns of this magnificent mountain, thousands of Buddhas of all shapes and sizes stand carved into the stone. A dim, smoky passage leads to a massive, gold-plated Buddha and souvenir stalls. Outside, shaded stairways and temples rest beneath ancient gingkos and cypresses. A hike to the summit takes about one hour; cable cars to the temples halfway up (Y15) take 7 minutes. A slide ("Magical Function Skidway") sends visitors careening down the mountain (Y20), laughing all the way. *(18 Jingshi Lu, on the southern edge of town. Accessible via buses #2 and 48, which run along Jingshi Lu and Lishan Lu, and 51, which runs along Jingshi Lu. ☎291 2074. Ticket office open daily 6am-7pm. Y15 into park, another Y15 into cave.)*

FOUR GATE PAGODA (sìmén tǎ; 四门塔). Officially, the pagoda is 33km south of town, but locals swear that it is much farther, and your only mode of transportation—a packed, wooden plank bus,—makes you believe them. Sleeping would make the journey bearable, if only the flies would stop landing on your face. Nevertheless, the trip is well worth it. The pagoda is a small square stone hut built in AD 611, impressive for its unassuming dignity and gracious sense of history. Like the ancient scroll paintings, the surrounding tree-covered hills are adorned with pagodas and staircases—all in gentle harmony with nature. *(A 1½hr. ride on bus #22 from Ji'nan (Y4), last stop is directly at entrance. Chinese tour guides available. ☎284 3051. Open daily 6:30am-7:30pm. Y20, student Y10.)*

SHANDONG PROVINCIAL MUSEUM (shāndōngshěng bówùguǎn; 山东省博物馆). This imposing concrete block houses one of China's more intriguing provincial museums. View a Ming dynasty ship, huge dinosaur fossils, and truckloads of thousand-year-old pottery. An interesting animal exhibit upstairs includes exotic birds, huge sea turtles, and a freakish stuffed six-legged calf. *(14 Jingshi Lu. A 5min. walk from Thousand Buddha Mountain; accessible via buses #2, 31, and 48. Open M-F 8:30am-noon and 2:30-6pm with last ticket sold at 11am and 5:15pm; Sa-Su 9am-5pm, last ticket sold at 4pm. Y10, student Y5.)*

DAMING LAKE (dàmíng hú; 大明湖). Picturesque Daming Lake sits in the center of the park's amusement grounds. In the mornings, focused locals practice *tai chi* along the lake's shores. The paths that meander through the park and the breezy willow trees overlooking the lime-green waters have a soothing effect. *(271 Daminghu Nan Lu. Take bus #11 or 41. ☎608 8928. Open daily 6am-7pm. Y15.)*

TAI'AN 泰安 ☎0538

Tucked humbly at the foot of the illustrious Taishan Mountain, compact little Tai'an could easily be mistaken for nothing more than a gateway to—if not some puny wart on the foot of—its giant companion. But every emperor who conquered Taishan's summit stopped first at Tai'an's glorious and infinitely elaborate Dai Temple. When a cloudy haze obscures Taishan from view, as is often the case, Tai'an sparkles with the glow of blinking Christmas lights from makeshift karaoke stands and pool halls which appear on the street at night. The city is filled with the sound of people singing—all the time. All in all, with accommodations and food far better in quality and value than on Taishan, Tai'an is an ideal base from which to explore the towering mountain.

TRANSPORTATION

Trains: Taishan Station (tàishān zhàn; 泰山站; ☎824 6222) is in the western half of the city, just south of Dongyue Dajie. To: **Beijing** (7hr.; many per day; hard seat Y80, hard sleeper Y150); **Ji'nan** (1hr., every 30min., Y6); **Qingdao** (5½hr., 11am and 2:30pm, Y70); **Yantai** (9½hr., 10pm, Y41).

Buses: Tai'an Long-distance Bus Station (tài'ān chángtú qìchē zhàn; 泰安长途汽车站), on Dongyue Dajie, about 3 blocks east of the train station. To: **Beijing** (12hr., daily, Y60); **Ji'nan** (1½hr., every 30min. 6am-6:40pm, Y21); **Qufu** (1hr., every 20min. 6am-6pm, Y13).

Public Transportation: Several **buses** ply downtown Tai'an, but their routes are rather limited. Y1. Bus **#3** runs along Hongmen Lu from the station area to the east and west entrances to Taishan; **#4** bumps along Dongyue Dajie.

Local Transportation: Minivans Y5 for first 5km, each additional km Y1.5. **Taxis** Y8 for first 2km, each additional km Y1.8. Red cabs are relatively expensive.

ORIENTATION AND PRACTICAL INFORMATION

With barely 500,000 residents and a compact center, Tai'an is quite manageable. The mountain, positioned directly north of town, is a useful landmark when not hidden by haze. Activity is concentrated along **Hongmen Lu** (红门路), which runs directly south of the mountain before ending at the entrance to the Dai Temple and **Dongyue Dajie** (东岳大街), the major east-west street. The train station is just south of Dongyue Dajie, but everything else of interest to visitors is in the northeastern portion, just south of the base of Taishan.

Travel Agency: CITS, 22 Hongmen Lu, 2nd fl. (☎822 3259; fax 833 2240), a 2min. walk from the Taishan Guesthouse. Open M-F 8:30am-noon and 2:30-6:30pm.

Bank of China: 48 Dongyue Dajie (☎829 6701), a newly built office on the corner of Dongyue Dajie and Zhaotong Jie. Exchanges currency and traveler's checks. Credit card advances. Open M-F 8am-noon and 2:30-6:30pm.

PSB: 71 Qingnian Lu (☎822 4004). Main gate is around the corner on Dongyue Dajie.

Hospital: Central Hospital (zhōngxīn yīyuàn; 中心医院), 29 Longtan Lu (☎822 4161), near the intersection with Kangfu Lu. English-speaking doctors. Pharmacy.

Internet Access: Internet Bar (wǎng bā; 网吧), 133 Hushan Lu, 2nd fl. (☎820 8989).Y3 per hr. Open daily 8:30am-11pm.

Post Office: China Post (☎822 7824), opposite the train station. EMS and Poste Restante. Open daily 8am-7pm; in winter 8am-6pm. **Postal Code:** 271000.

ACCOMMODATIONS

The traffic of pilgrims and tourists through Tai'an keeps accommodation pricing competitive. Dongyue Dajie, in particular, is crawling with hotels. Hotels at the base are considerably cheaper and more comfortable than those at the summit, though most spend the night up there anyway, lest they miss the famous sunrise. Most hotels at the base will store your belongings while you climb (Y1 per piece of luggage). Rumors fly that Chinese-only hotels in the train station area will sometimes accept foreigners who are willing to use Mandarin, although success is entirely dependent upon luck and personal charm. Deposits are based on the difference between room price and the next hundred *yuan*.

Mian Ma Hotel (miánmá bīnguǎn; 棉麻宾馆), 129 Dongyue Dajie (☎826 5800), about a 5min. walk west of the long-distance bus station. A budget traveler's heaven, with the cheapest rooms in town. Leaky toilets make bathroom floors sopping wet. Those truly immersed in the local culture will appreciate the spitoons in every room. Midnight curfew. Hot water 8:30am-11pm. Rooms contain up to 5 beds. Each bed Y12-50, with A/C, TV, and shower Y60-120. ❶

Longtan Hotel (lóngtán bīnguǎn; 龙潭宾馆), 14 Longtan Lu (☎822 6511), at Dongyue Dajie. Clean, comfortable rooms and a convenient location. Bus #3 stops across the street to take you to Taishan's east entrance, and train and local bus stations are less than a 10min. walk away. All rooms have A/C, showers, phone, and TV. 24hr. hot water. Doubles Y200-240; triples Y240; quads Y280. ❸

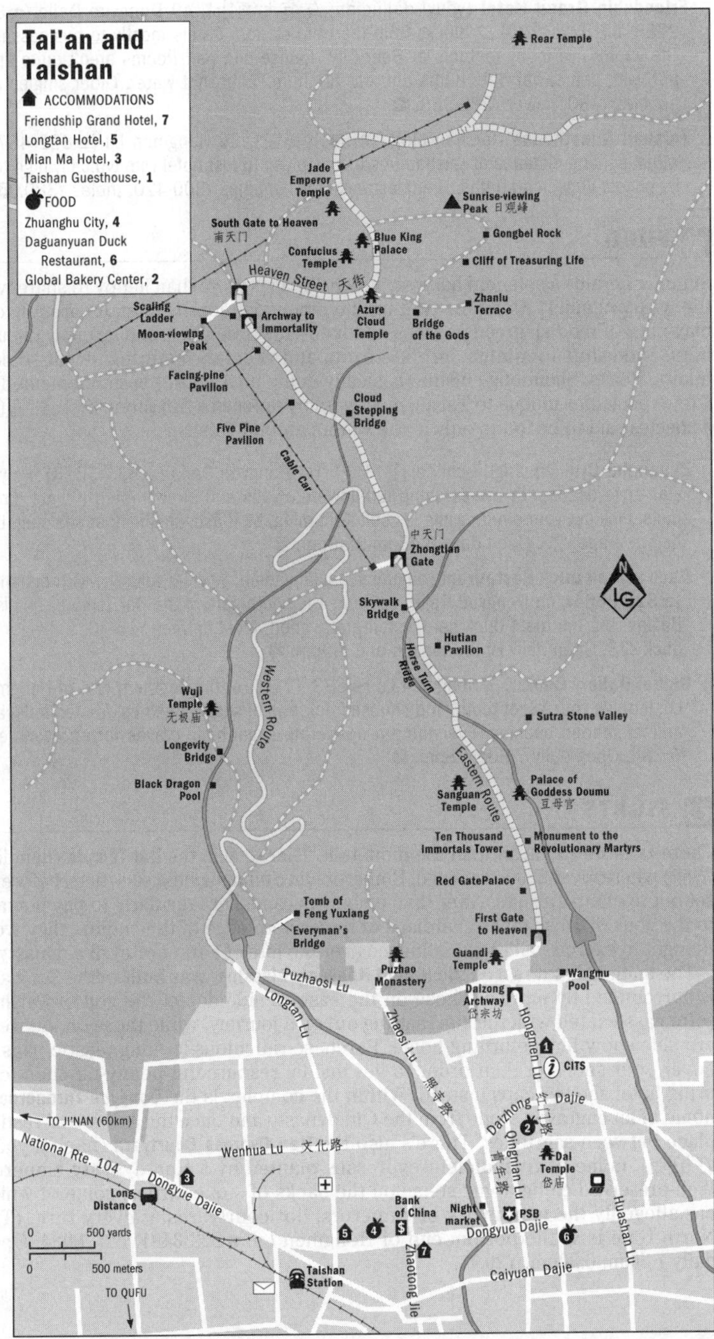

Tai'an and Taishan
ACCOMMODATIONS
Friendship Grand Hotel, 7
Longtan Hotel, 5
Mian Ma Hotel, 3
Taishan Guesthouse, 1
FOOD
Zhuanghu City, 4
Daguanyuan Duck Restaurant, 6
Global Bakery Center, 2
Rear Temple
Jade Emperor Temple
Sunrise-viewing Peak 日观峰
South Gate to Heaven 南天门
Blue King Palace
Gongbei Rock
Confucius Temple
Cliff of Treasuring Life
Heaven Street 天街
Scaling Ladder
Archway to Immortality
Azure Cloud Temple
Zhanlu Terrace
Bridge of the Gods
Moon-viewing Peak
Facing-pine Pavilion
Cloud Stepping Bridge
Five Pine Pavilion
Cable Car
中天门
Zhongtian Gate
Skywalk Bridge
Hutian Pavilion
Horse Turn Ridge
Western Route
Wuji Temple 无极庙
Sutra Stone Valley
Longevity Bridge
Eastern Route
Black Dragon Pool
Sanguan Temple
Palace of Goddess Doumu 斗母宫
Ten Thousand Immortals Tower
Monument to the Revolutionary Martyrs
Red GatePalace
Tomb of Feng Yuxiang
Everyman's Bridge
First Gate to Heaven
Puzhao Monastery
Guandi Temple
Wangmu Pool
Puzhaosi Lu
Daizong Archway 岱宗坊
Longtan Lu
Zhaosi Lu 照寺路
Hongmen Lu
CITS
Daizhong Dajie 红门路
TO JI'NAN (60km)
National Rte. 104
Wenhua Lu 文化路
Qingnian Lu 青年路
Dai Temple 岱庙
Dongyue Dajie
Long Distance
Bank of China
Night market
PSB
Huashan Lu
0 500 yards
0 500 meters
Zhaotong Jie
Taishan Station
Caiyuan Dajie
TO QUFU

BEIJING

Friendship Grand Hotel (yǒuyí dàjiǔdiàn; 友谊大酒店), 49 Dongyue Dajie (☎822 2288; fax 822 4100), 2 blocks from the train station. Caters mostly to businessmen. The impressive lobby features a "Beer City" lounge and bar. Rooms aren't quite up to par, with somewhat dirty baths and old furniture. 24hr. hot water. Older singles and doubles Y180, newer Y280-360. ❸

Taishan Guesthouse (tàishān bīnguǎn; 泰山宾馆), 26 Hongmen Lu (☎822 4678), within spitting distance of Taishan. A typically plush tourist hotel with typically high tourist prices. Very clean baths. Breakfast included. Doubles Y300-420; triples Y380. ❹

FOOD

Summer heralds a splendid harvest, which Tai'an is more than happy to share with the weary climber. Along the trail up the mountain, dozens of stalls proudly display piles of reddish-green peaches, ready-to-burst tomatoes, and crunchy cucumbers. Makeshift fountains sprinkle fruits and veggies, tempting sweat-soaked hikers. Hearty Shandong cuisine (basically dumplings galore) is supplemented by a few specialties unique to Tai'an, most notably **red-scaled fish** (hóng lǐ yú; 红鲤鱼), a species said to be found only in the waters around Taishan.

Zhuanghu City (zhuānghù chéng; 庄户城), 54 Dongyue Dajie (☎833 3373). Polynesian-style decor with eye-catching red-flowered walls and straw roofed private dining halls. Pick out your dinner while it's still swimming, be it fish, shellfish, or sea slug. Dinners average Y20. Open daily 8:45am-9:30pm. ❷

Daguanyuan Duck Restaurant (dàguānyuán kǎoyādiàn; 大观园烤鸭店), 8 Tongtian Jie (☎826 0664), on Dongyue Dajie, opposite the south gate of the Dai Temple. This isn't Beijing, but the roast duck here is still pretty good. Most entrees Y15-30, Beijing roast duck Y28. Open daily 8:30am-noon and 5-9pm. ❷

Global Bakery Center, 7 Hongmen Lu (☎833 7720), at the southern end of Hongmen Lu. Indulge your sweet tooth, and choose from rows of sugary pastries, frosted rolls, and animal-shaped cookies. Everything a desperate sugar-holic craves for an average of Y1.2-4. Open daily 7:30am-8pm. ❶

SIGHTS

There *is* more to Tai'an than the mountain. There's also the **Dai Temple** (dàimiào; 岱庙) where, over 2200 years ago, Emperor Qin Shihuang held sacrifices before he set out to climb Taishan. After that, emperors came here regularly to pay homage to the gods of Taishan; as guardians of the eastern edge of the empire, they were thought to exercise a crucial influence over the fate of a ruler or even a dynasty.

The main hall, known as the **Hall of Heavenly Blessing,** was built in the Song and is surrounded by murals. Those on the eastern side depict the god of Taishan (often associated with the sun) setting out on a journey, while those on the western side show him returning home. Purchase ridiculous-looking plastic bags to cover your shoes (Y1) in order to get inside; resourceful penny-pinchers can bring hotel shower caps instead. Within the complex is the **Dongyue Throneroom,** home of an engraved stone from the Qin dynasty and once the emperors' resting place between sacrifices. There's also the **Han Cypress Courtyard** (hànbǎi yuàn; 韩柏院), home of five ancient cypresses planted by a Han dynasty emperor. Well-preserved calligraphic stelae on the backs of stone turtles, some of which are allegedly the handiwork of emperors, dot courtyards at every turn. (The North Gate is at the bottom end of Hongmen Lu. ☎822 3491, ext. 8034. Open daily 7:30am-6:30pm. Y20.)

NEAR TAI'AN: TAISHAN MOUNTAIN 泰山

This is it. The fabled Taishan, the easternmost and holiest of China's five sacred Daoist mountains, a site of both spiritual and political importance for longer than anyone knows. Confucius climbed it. The founder of the Qin dynasty climbed it. Emperors and their retinues lined up to climb it. Even Mao lumbered up in his day. Now it's your turn. Countless Chinese travel for miles to offer prayers to the various deities associated with the mountain and to watch the first rays of morning light; watching the sunrise from the summit is considered an indispensable part of the Taishan experience. Trust us: this is one bandwagon you do want to jump on.

Stone stairs, built into the side of the mountain years ago, line the trails to the summit; wide railings provide ample sitting space for rests. A succession of temples and shrines mark visitors' upward progress. Souvenir and food vendors have staked out every trailside spot from base to summit; prices rise with the altitude.

While Taishan still remains an active place of worship, the temples and shrines that line the paths are frequented by all sorts—from businessmen to tourists to teenagers in platform shoes. Both the tradition and the spell-binding beauty at the summit urge visitors up the mountain's steep steps. Those lucky enough to come during July or August will enjoy waterfalls and streams. And despite the strenuous journey, the view from the summit is not to be missed. Above the clouds, an ocean of haunting mist floats through the forest and slowly evaporates as it drifts toward the mountaintop. It's as if you've stepped into heaven.

CLIMBING TAISHAN

The climb can take anywhere from three to eight hours. The 6600 stairs are not to be trifled with; going up and coming down in one day is recommended only for those accustomed to severe leg beatings. Spend the night at the summit to experience a breathtaking morning sunrise. Food and drink are exorbitantly priced but readily available along the trail or at the summit. Naturally, the temperature at the summit is quite a bit cooler than at the base; bring warm, waterproof clothing. Big, cozy PLA coats can be rented at the summit for Y2. Those daring a night climb should carry a flashlight, as lampposts are scarce and usually not working. The exhausted can either hire a carriage for Y100-150 or hop on a cable car to the summit from Zhongtian Gate, the halfway mark. (Open daily 7am-6pm. Y45 one-way, children Y20.) You can also take a bus (Y16 up, Y15 down) from the Western entrance up to Zhongtian Gate. The ticket gates are open 24 hours, and some frugal pilgrims often make the climb at night to arrive in time for the sunrise. Year-round admission from the Eastern entrance is Y62, student Y42, payable at the first arch along the rail; from the West Entrance Y82.

EASTERN ROUTE

This is the more traveled and more interesting of the two routes to the summit. To get to the trailhead, follow Hongmen Lu north from the Dai Temple to the **Daizong Archway** (dàizōng fáng; 岱宗坊), the first Taishan landmark. Built during the Ming dynasty, the arch is covered with calligraphic carvings that extol the traditional virtues of generosity and beneficence. Hongmen Lu ends at the **First Gate to Heaven** (yì tiān mén; 一天门), which marks the beginning of the ascent.

The next major landmark is the **Red Gate Palace** (hóng mén gōng; 红门宫), named for the two door-like scarlet stones on the southern face of the nearby peak. Temples, littered with money and offerings to their affiliated deities, surround the gate; it's also a good place to stop and gather your strength and count your blessings before the real strain begins. Next is the **Ten Thousand Immortals**

Tower (wànxiān lóu; 万仙楼), built in 1620 and dedicated to Wangmu, the popular "mother goddess." Entrance fees are paid here. One kilometer farther up is the **Palace of Goddess Doumu** (dòumǔ gōng; 豆母宫), a dusty temple that houses a statue of the child-faced goddess, sitting atop a lotus leaf.

More minor sights (the Sutra Stone Valley, Feng'an Stele, and Cypress Cave) line the path to **Zhongtian Gate** (zhōngtiān mén; 中天门), the midpoint of the ascent, perched 850m above sea level. Here, the Eastern route intersects with the Western route, and a village of trinket shops awaits visitors. The truly spent can hop on a cable car to the summit or collapse at the busy **Zhongtianmen Guesthouse ❶** (zhōngtiānmén bīnguǎn; 中天门宾馆; ☎825 3574). Other hotels are uniform in quality, or lack thereof—with dirty baths and dirty sheets; opt for the cheapest. Hope you brought mosquito repellent. (Dorm beds Y15-50; doubles Y200.)

The first major sight along the second half of the climb is the **Cloud-stepping Bridge** (yúnbù qiáo; 云步桥), about 1km past Zhongtian Gate. The bridge offers striking views of a waterfall and glistening streams full of water only in July and August. Crossing it is supposed to be an experience akin to "stepping among the clouds" (though these clouds look an awful lot like vertigo-stricken Chinese tourists snapping photos like there's no tomorrow).

A sprinkling of temples and smaller shrines like **Facing-pine Pavilion** gather along the final stretch. The very last landmark before the summit, and the bane of weary climbers, is the **Scaling Ladder to the Gate of Heaven** (tiānmén yúntī; 天门云梯), comprised of 18 bends and 1600 very steep steps that must be conquered before the weary pilgrim can reach "heaven." Don't give up. If that little grandmother with her walking stick beside you can make it, surely you can too.

WESTERN ROUTE

Temples, calligraphy, and fellow climbers are much more scarce along the western route, but it's a slightly less strenuous climb than the eastern route. The western route begins at the northern tip of Longtan Lu, runs through **Tianwai Cun** (tiānwài cūn; 天外村), then follows a winding path up to **Zhongtian Gate;** western and eastern routes converge between **Zhongtian Gate** and the summit.

After entering through Tianwai Cun, the first major sight is the **Black Dragon Pool** (hēilóng tán; 黑龙潭), home to Tai'an's famed red-scaled fish. Farther along the trail is **Longevity Bridge** (chángshòu qiáo; 长寿桥), stretching between craggy cliffs. The brook flowing beneath it feeds a tall waterfall; the bridge known by some as "the boundary between life and death." The last major sight before Zhongtian Gate is **Wuji Temple** (wújí miào; 无极庙). Built in 1925 by the warlord Zhang Zongchang in memory of his late wife (whom he hoped would become a Daoist immortal), the temple is a testament to the endurance of Taishan's mystique.

SUMMIT

Pat yourself on the back, stretch your aching muscles, and then explore the summit's maze of buildings and temples. The magnificent view of the mist-covered mountains has a poetic majesty, and the air feels redolent with mystery. The **South Gate to Heaven,** or **Nantianmen Gate** (nántiān mén; 南天门), built during the Yuan dynasty, marks the very end of the climb. From there, walk along wide-pathed **Heaven Street** (tiān jiē; 天街), which is lined with shops, restaurants, and stalls; continue onto the *raison d'etre* of modern Taishan, the **Azure Clouds Temple** (bìxiá cí; 碧霞祠). The Princess of the Azure Clouds is Taishan's premier cult figure, a Daoist deity with a fanatical following among the elderly peasant women who make the difficult climb. Myths claim that the princess was the daughter of the Taishan god, while others list her as one of seven special women sacrificed by the mythical Emperor Huangdi to the gods of Taishan. Over 40 monks, identifiable by their distinctive topknots, live and study here (Y5; fortune telling Y5). Other highlights on the summit include the **Blue King Palace** (qīngdì diàn; 青帝殿). Emperors and commoners alike have gathered here to ask for the blessings of this god, who controlled mankind according to legend. Their final destination is the **Jade Emperor Temple** (yùdì diàn; 玉帝殿), where sacrifices to heaven would be held. One of the many scenic spots is **Aishen Cliff,** or the Cliff of Treasuring Life. Filial duty in days of yore were extreme, to say the least; in order to ensure their parents' happiness, children would pray to the gods, and then fling themselves off this cliff.

In the pre-dawn stillness, crowds of tourists appear seemingly out of nowhere, tumbling out of bed and stumbling over to the **Sunrise-Viewing Peak** (rìguān fēng; 日观峰). Unfortunately, clear days are a rarity in this part of Shandong (concentrated mostly in spring and autumn); only the very lucky will see an unobscured sunrise from Taishan. Still, even shrouded in haze, that great surge levitating out of the east makes for an impressive sight.

Hotels tend to get crowded by the late afternoon, so secure rooms early. Dorm rooms are cheap, but anything close to comfortable demands an outrageous price. The **Daiding Hotel ❶** (dàidǐng bīnguǎn; 岱顶宾馆), at the end of the alley up the stairway from Nantianmen Gate is small but comfortable, with decent baths. (☎823 6519. 24hr. hot water. Laundry. Dorm beds Y10; doubles with bath Y120.) The most expensive of the contenders, the **Shenqi Hotel ❺** (shénqì bīnguǎn; 神憩宾馆), next to the Blue King Palace, about 15 minutes past the South Gate, is everything you'd expect from a three-star hotel. (☎822 3866 or 833 7025; fax 820 7619. Doubles with bath Y580; quads without bath Y160.) For privacy on Sunrise Viewing Park, head for the lofty, slightly intimidating **Meteorological Observation Hotel ❶** (rìguānfēng qìxiàngtái bīnguǎn; 日观峰气象台宾馆). A half-completed staircase is the main entrance. (☎822 6995. 8-bed dorms Y20; 4-bed dorms Y40-80; doubles Y240-300; triples with your own Chinese-style toilet Y380-460; pricier rooms have an eastern view, private rooms don't have baths.)

QUFU 曲阜 ☎0537

In the *Analects*, Qufu's famed former resident Confucius said, "Is it not a joy to have friends come from afar?" The rhetorical question seems to have proved quite prophetic for this tranquil little town, its city center swollen with tour groups eager to pay homage to Master Kong. Their overwhelming presence and loud chatter can be a bit distracting to the otherwise scholarly atmosphere. Nevertheless, present-day Qufu is a miracle of architectural preservation, a rare skyscraper-free zone full of traditional wooden buildings. The great Sage stressed that descendants are the key to immortality, and his words did not go unheeded. In a town where one of every five residents proudly shares Confucius's surname, Kong, reflections of a life lived 2500 years ago still appear very strongly.

TRANSPORTATION

Trains: The nearest train station is a 20min. cab drive away in **Yanzhou** (兖州). Travelers are probably better off making connections in Ji'nan (see p. 175).

Buses: Qufu Long-distance Bus Station (qūfù chángtú qìchēzhàn; 曲阜长途汽车站), 1 Jingxuan Lu (☎441 1241). As of June 2001, the main entrance on Jinxuan Lu is closed; the temporary entrance is on Shendao Lu. To: **Beijing** (7hr., 5 per morning, Y61); **Ji'nan** (3hr., every 30min. 6:30am-6pm, Y21); **Qingdao** (8hr., 3 per day, Y80);

Tai'an (1hr., every hr. 6:30am-6pm, Y12); **Zhoucheng** (40min., every 15min. 6:30am-6pm, Y3.5).

Local Transportation: Pedicabs run to anywhere in town for Y2-5; bargain and set the price beforehand. Tours of all of Qufu's sights average Y30-40. Red minivan **taxis** start at Y5, but many are unwilling to use the meter and charge Y10 to go anywhere.

ORIENTATION AND PRACTICAL INFORMATION

Qufu is compact and easily navigable; pedicabs or your own two feet should get you anywhere. The Confucian Temple and Confucian Mansions are right in the center of town, bordered to the east and west by **Gulou Jie** (鼓楼街) and **Banbi Jie** (半壁街), respectively. Gulou Jie becomes **Lindao Lu** (林道路) in the north, where the Confucian Forest sits. Farther south on this road is the bus station near the intersection with Jingxua Lu. **Shendao Lu** (神道路) runs between it and the south end of the Confucian Temple.

Hospital: People's Hospital (rénmín yīyuàn; 人民医院; ☎441 2440), on Tianguan Dajie.

Travel Agency: CITS, 1 Jingxuan Lu (☎441 5315 or 441 2491), off Dacheng Lu; easiest access is straight through the lobby of the Luyou Hotel. Open daily 8am-6pm.

Bank of China: 96 Dongmen Dajie (☎441 5862), east of Gulou Jie. Exchanges currency and traveler's checks. Credit card advances. Open daily 8am-noon and 2:30-6pm.

PSB: 1 Wuyuan Tan Lu (☎441 1403).

Post Office: China Post, 8 Gulou Bei Jie (☎441 2214), near the Qufu Post Hotel. EMS. Open daily 8am-6:30pm; in winter 8am-6pm. **Postal Code:** 273100.

BEIJING

ACCOMMODATIONS AND FOOD

Qufu has a decent range of accommodation options, most of which are conveniently close to sights. Since most travelers make a whirlwind daytrip to Qufu from Tai'an, hotels may lower prices by at least Y20 if you ask for a cheaper room.

Across the street from the Confucian Temple and Mansions is a bustling night market. Dozens of carts offer fresh *jiǎozi*, and barbecued pork sticks over hot-coal furnaces. Stuff yourself for under Y10.

Qufu Post Hotel (qūfúshì yóuzhèng bīnguǎn; 曲阜市邮政宾馆), 8 Gulou Bei Jie (☎448 3888), just opposite the Confucian Mansions (the real ones, not the hotel listed below). The spacious rooms feel much, much more expensive than they actually are; and you couldn't ask for a more convenient location. Doubles Y120, with bath Y260; triples Y160; deluxe singles and doubles Y280, with bath Y388-588. ❷

Luyou Hotel (lǚyóu bīnguǎn; 旅遊宾馆), 108 Datong Lu (☎441 1625; fax 441 6207), opposite and right of the bus station. Comfortable, if slightly deserted. Rooms with bath are much nicer than those without. A/C, phone, and TV. Curfew 11pm. Hot water 8am-11pm. Doubles with bath Y180; triples Y69, with bath Y150; quads with bath Y200. ❶

Confucian Mansions Hotel (kǒngfǔ fàndiàn; 孔府饭店), 9 Datong Lu (☎441 2686 or 441 1783; fax 441 3786), opposite the bus station; enter through a stone gateway on Jingwua Lu, right before its intersection with Gulou Dajie/Datong Lu. Hardly as resplendent as the real Confucian Mansions. All have baths and standard amenities. Doubles Y100; triples Y80. ❶

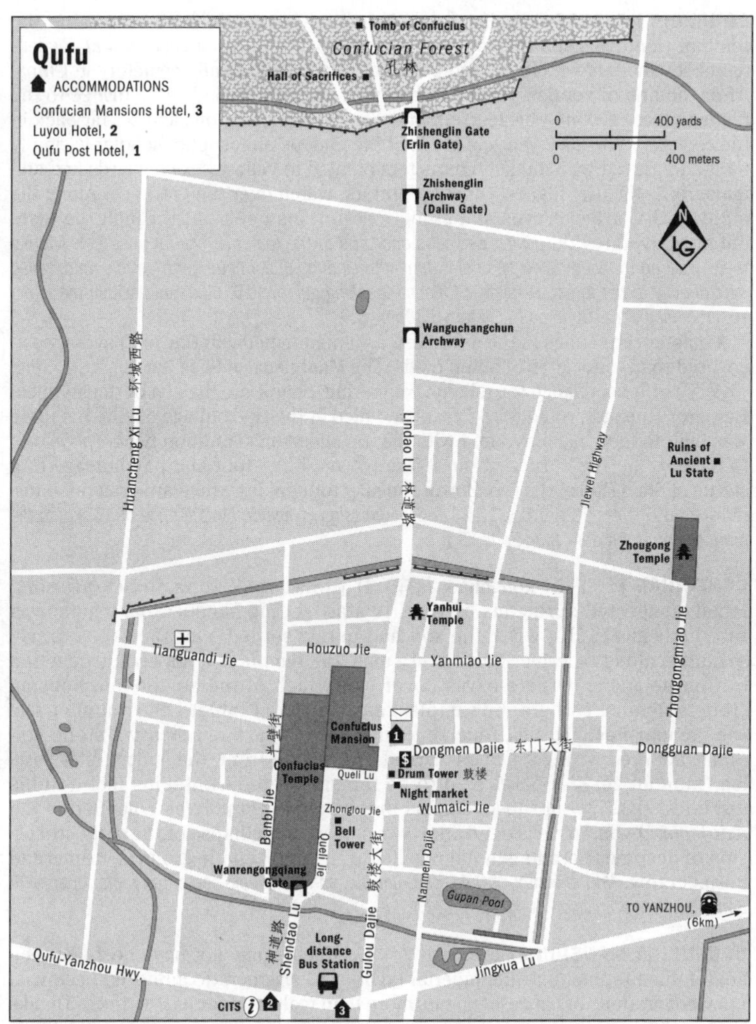

SIGHTS

Confucius is the hot topic in town, and that seems unlikely to change anytime soon. Be aware of unending streams of tourists in day-glo t-shirts reading, in Chinese, "I paid homage to Confucius." Do your best to fend off tour guides ready to pounce on the bewildered traveler. Politeness does not work; stern rejections might; running away may be best. Despite all this, these old haunts of the Great Sage pass on memories of tradition and the origins of profound wisdom.

CONFUCIAN FOREST (kǒnglín; 孔林). North of town, the forest contains the tomb of Confucius and the graves of a mere 100,000 of his ancestors and descendants; it's the largest, oldest, and best-preserved single-family cemetery in China. After the line of vendors, turn left, and pass over an arched stone bridge to the resting place of Confucius himself. Surprisingly unpretentious and set far back in the cemetery, the 2500-year-old grave of the famous philosopher/scholar is simply built and carved with ancient characters painted in yellow. Stone guards and animals, reflecting the highest funerary honors, watch over the entrance. Along the many paths, other graves and stone inscriptions peek out through the lush, untamed overgrowth. *(Hiring pedicabs and taxis to the forest is nice for your feet. Alternatively, walk north along Gulou Jie until it turns into Lindao Lu; continue north on this road, which runs directly to the forest. Persistent Chinese-speaking guides Y10. Bike rental within the forest Y5. Free minibuses. Open daily 7:30am-6:30pm. Y20.)*

A quieter retreat lies to the northeast, a 30-minute pedicab ride (Y6) over wheat-covered roads and acres of onion fields. The **Mausoleum of Shao Hao** (shǎohào líng; 少昊陵) offers a chance for relaxed wandering. Shao Hao, the son of the mythical Emperor Huangdi, ruled for 84 years and died at the ripe old age of 100. His tomb was built to look like a pyramid with the top sliced off. Tradition beckons visitors to clamber up the corner of the 8.73m pyramid barefoot and pay homage to a statue of Shao Hao at the top. Beware sneaky tour guides who may spout out information and then demand a Y5-20 fee. *(Admission is included in the price of a ticket to the mausoleum. Open daily 8am-5pm. Y5.)*

BEIJING

CONFUCIAN TEMPLE (kǒngmiào; 孔庙). It didn't take long for Confucius, largely neglected during his lifetime, to start getting his due; this temple was first built in 478 BC, when the soil had barely settled over the sage's grave. Arranged along a perfect north-south axis, the temple is a stately introduction to Confucianism. Ornate eaves cover every inch of the compound, housing stone columns, calligraphy samples, and ancestral tablets. Surrounding the spectacular **Dacheng Hall** (dáchéng táng; 达成堂) are ten massive stone columns, adorned with gorgeously carved dragons. In front, the **Apricot Altar Pavilion** (xìngtán gé; 杏坛阁) is said to be the site where Confucius lectured his disciples, spitting out those maxims that would eventually be compiled in the *Analects*. If you arrive around 3pm, you can catch a glimpse of the daily procession of devotees parading in full regalia through the temple grounds, drums and horns in tow. *(In the center of Qufu, off Gulou Jie, an unmissable sea of red roofs. Open M-Th 8am-5pm, last admission at 4:30pm. Y30.)*

CONFUCIAN MANSIONS (kǒngfǔ; 孔府). Confucius may not have been appreciated in his lifetime, but the imperial favors and aristocratic authority bestowed upon generations of his descendents more than makes up for past wrongs. Thanks to their illustrious ancestor, those of the direct male line lived a rather cushy life in the Confucian Mansions, said to have been the second most luxurious residence in all of ancient China, after that of the imperial family (see p. 188). Many members of the Kong family milked their glorious genetic heritage to the fullest, at times ruling western Shandong as their own private fiefdom. Features of the mansions include the **Front Chamber,** where patriarchs lived with their wives; the **Upper Front Chamber,** where celebrations were held; the **Third Hall,** where important family affairs were handled; and the **Great Hall,** where official decrees were received. The last of the Kongs did not leave the mansions until 1949, when they fled to Taiwan in fear of Communist persecution. *(Off Gulou Jie in the town center. Open daily 8am-5pm, last admission at 4:30pm. Y20.)*

CONFUCIUS Confucian ethics stresses two virtues: *lĭ* (礼), the rules of proper conduct and etiquette, and *rén* (仁), benevolent love or human-heartedness. Confucian morals consist of five fundamental principles in human relations: love between parents and children, justice between king and subject, difference between husband and wife, order between old and young, and trust between friends. Here are some of his quotable quotes as recorded in the *Analects*:

The obvious: "Shall I teach you about knowledge? What you know, you know, what you don't know, you don't know. This is knowledge."

The inspiring: "The virtuous won't be lonely; he will always have friends."

The mind: "To study and not think is a waste. To think and not study is dangerous."

The profound: "It is quite rare to see someone who applies himself to the study of something for three years without having a noticeable result."

The one that never made it into a fortune cookie: "I have never seen one who loves virtue as much as he loves sex."

DAYTRIP FROM QUFU: ZOUCHENG

Zoucheng (zōuchéng; 邹城), formerly Zouxian, is a tiny, struggling town less than one hour from Qufu. Its claim to fame is that it was the hometown of the philosopher Mencius, one of Confucianism's greatest proponents. The whole place is something of a poor man's Qufu, less grand and far calmer. Visitors may soon have another reason to come besides wandering the largely deserted sites—construction has begun on an enormous state-of-the-art soccer field.

The **Mencius Temple** (mèng miào; 孟庙), on Yashengfu Jie, is just a pedicab ride from the bus station (Y3). Birds of all species and sizes make their nests among the knotted trees (except in winter), evidenced by the white goop covering pathways and temple tops. Walk fast or carry an umbrella. *(Open daily 8am-6:30pm. Y20.)* Just around the corner, the **Mencius Mansions** (mèng fŭ; 孟府) are an impeccably manicured reminder of the glory once bestowed upon the descendents of the "other" semi-divine ancient philosopher. (Open daily 8am-6:30pm. Admission included in price of temple ticket.)

QINGDAO 青岛 ☎0532

Qingdao is a celebrity in the West thanks to its most famous export, Tsingtao beer. Many people enjoy the beer, and even more enjoy Qingdao, whose charms are as richly satisfying as a good brew. This coastal city boasts green hillsides, numerous beaches, and red-roofed Bavarian buildings. Before the Qing imperial court began garrisoning troops in the area in 1891, Qingdao was just a small scenic fishing village: unrefined and undistilled. In 1897, along came a German concession, which gave this modest beauty a full-scale makeover and—more importantly—some full-bodied beer.

By the time the Japanese invaded in 1937, Qingdao had blossomed into the stunning temptress that it is today, with a healthy economy, a fascinating mix of architecture, and a breezy attitude. Chinese tourists flock here on holidays, and foreign travelers pour in at increasing rates, but coy Qingdao gracefully resists their advances with a smile and a fabulous beer in hand.

TRANSPORTATION

Flights: Liuting International Airport (liútíng guójì jīchǎng; 流亭国际机场), on Kaiyang Lu (☎484 3331 or 484 2139), 32km northeast of the city. Shuttle buses (every 30min., Y10) run between the airport and 30 Xianggang Lu, where bus #25 and 316 run to the train station. For more info, contact the **CAAC ticket office,** 29 Zhongshan Lu (☎287 4275). Taxis from the airport to the city center cost at least Y90. Open daily 8am-6pm. To: **Beijing** (2-3 per day, Y650); **Dalian** (1-2 per day, Y430); **Guangzhou** (1-2 per day, Y1420); **Hong Kong** (M and F, Y2400); **Shanghai** (1-2 per day, Y590). International flights to: **Seoul, South Korea** (2hr., 2-3 per day, Y1170); **Singapore** (6hr., Th and Su, Y4980); **Tokyo, Japan** (Tu and Sa).

Trains: Qingdao Train Station (qīngdǎo huǒchē zhàn; 青岛火车站), 2 Tai'an Lu (☎286 5741 or 286 4571), north of Taiping Lu. Ticket offices also at 9 Guantao Lu (☎284 3014) and 2 Fuqing Lu (☎587 1814). To: **Beijing** (11hr., 10am and 9:25pm, Y102-213); **Chengdu** (12½hr., 1:30pm, Y160); **Dandong** (27hr., 1:55pm, Y100-212); **Guangzhou** (19½hr., 4pm, Y153-302); **Ji'nan** (4-7hr., 5 per day, Y48-53); **Shanghai** (20hr., 11am, Y150-287); **Shenyang** (21hr., 10:05am and 1:55pm, Y88-217); **Tai'an** (5½hr., 7:55am, Y60); **Weihai** (6hr., 9pm, Y28); **Wuhan** (24hr., 4:40pm, Y168-320); **Yantai** (4hr., 8:21am and 2:27pm, Y22-36).

Buses: Long-distance Travel Bus Station (chángtú lǚyóu qìchē zhàn; 长途旅游汽车站; ☎267 6842), at the terminus of bus #8. To: **Beijing** (18hr., 10am every other day); **Shanghai** (20hr.; 10:30am, 1:30, and 6pm); **Weihai** (6hr.; every 16min. 5:45am-noon, every 20min. 12:20-5:30pm); **Yantai** (3½hr., every 20min. 6am-5:30pm). **Sifang Bus Station** (sìfāng qìchē zhàn; 四方汽车站), 2 Wenzhou Lu (☎371 8061), is at the other end of route #8. To: **Beijing** (18hr., 10pm every other day, Y127); **Ji'nan** (4hr., every 30min. 6am-7pm, Y92); **Nanjing** (9hr., 4 per day 8am-4pm, Y153); **Penglai** (5hr., every 30min. 6:10am-2:40pm, Y31); **Shanghai** (20hr.; 9, 11am, and 12:30pm; Y187); **Tai'an** (5½hr., 7:30am and 1pm, Y51); **Tianjin** (10hr., 8am, Y126); **Weihai** (6hr., every 30min. 6am-5pm, Y41); **Yantai** (3½hr., every 30min. 5:50am-5:20pm, Y31-32). **West Station** (qìchē xī zhàn; 汽车西站), 36 Guantao Lu (☎267 6842), just south of the train station. To: **Beijing** (18hr., 10am, Y120); **Ji'nan** (4hr., every 20-35min. 6am-6:30pm, Y50); **Shanghai** (20hr., 4 per day 10:30am-6pm, Y160); **Yantai** (3½hr., every 20min. 6am-5:30pm, Y30).

Ferries: Qingdao Ferry Terminal (qīngdǎogǎng kèyùn zhàn; 青岛港客运站), 6 Xinjiang Lu (☎282 5001). To: **Shanghai** (26hr., every 3 days 4pm, Y98-345). International boats to **Inchon, South Korea** (20-22hr., Su-M and W-F 6pm, around Y1180) and **Shimonoseki, Japan** (36hr., Th 2pm, Y1160). **Lundu Dock** (lúndù mǎtóu; 轮渡码头; ☎287 4275), 21 Sichuan Lu, and **Small Harbor Ferry Terminal** (xiǎogǎng kèyùn zhàn; 小港客运站; ☎284 4247), 16 Xiaogang Yilu, both have boats to **Huangdao,** Qingdao's Development Zone (30min., every 30min. 6:30am-5pm, round-trip Y6-8).

Local Transportation: Fare Y1, smaller buses with A/C Y2. Useful **bus** routes include: **#1,** which runs from Hubei Lu to Sifang District via Yan'an Lu; **#2** and **5** run down Zhongshan Lu; **#8** from Lundu Dock to the Sifang Bus Station via the train station and Qingdao Ferry Terminal; **#26** from the train station to eastern Qingdao along the coastal Yang Lu, Wendeng Lu, and Xianggang Lu; **#31** from Zhongshan Park to Qingdao University; **#317** along the coast to the Stoneman scenic area, close to Laoshan.

Taxis: Base fare Y7. Each additional km Y1.2.

ORIENTATION AND PRACTICAL INFORMATION

Qingdao isn't easy to navigate; its seven urban districts and five counties are spread far and wide along the coast. The western side of the city, the tip of the peninsula on which Qingdao sits, contains the train station, the ferry terminal, No. 6 Beach, and a number of main roads. **Zhongshan Lu** (中山路) runs north-south to **Zhanqiao Pier** and is intersected by **Hubei Lu** (湖北路), which leads to the train station. **Taiping Lu** (太平路) runs east-west along the coast. **Jiangsu Lu** (江苏路), **Daxue Lu** (大学路), and **Yan'an Yi Lu** (延安一路) run north-south along the coast, eventually crossing Taiping Lu. No. 1 and 2 Beaches and the Qingdao World Trade Center lie east of here. **Nanhai Lu** (南海路) and **Shanhaiguan Lu** (山海关路) is roughly parallel to the coast from **Huiquan Bay** (汇泉角) to **Taiping Bay** (太平角).

Travel Agency: CITS, 9 Nanhai Lu (☎287 0876), in the eastern part of town, on the 4th fl. of the building behind the Huiquan Dynasty Hotel, just south of Huiquan Square. Open daily 8:30am-noon and 1:30-5pm.

Bank of China: 68 Zhongshan Lu (☎286 1106), next to Parkson Plaza. Exchanges currency and traveler's checks. Credit card advances. Open M-F 8am-noon and 2-5pm.

Bookstore: Foreign Language Bookstore (wàiwén shūdiàn; 外文书店), 165 Zhongshan Lu (☎282 8230). Open daily 9am-6pm.

PSB: 29 Hubei Lu (☎286 2787), between Tai'an Lu and Zhongshan Lu. **Foreign affairs office,** 272 Ningxia Lu (☎579 2555), in the eastern part of town. Take bus #301 from the train station to Xiaoyao Lu. Open M-F 8:30-11:30am and 1:30-5pm.

Pharmacy: No. 1 Pharmacy (huádìyī dàyàodiàn; 华第一大药店), 14 Hubei Lu (☎296 5757), has Chinese and Western medicines. 24hr. window. Open daily 8:30am-9pm.

Hospital: Qingdao Southern District People's Hospital (qīngdǎoshì shìnánqū rénmín yīyuàn; 青岛市市南区人民医院), 29 Guangzhou Lu (☎261 9783), west of the train station. English-speaking doctors. Open 24hr.

Internet Access: Xinyue Parkson Internet Cafe (xīnyuè báishèng wǎngbā; 新月百盛网吧), Parkson Plaza, 6th fl., on Zhongshan Lu at Hubei Lu. 25 computers. Y3 per hr., measured in half-hour increments. Open daily 9am-9pm.

Post Office: China Post, 51 Zhongshan Lu, across from Parkson Plaza. EMS and Poste Restante. Open daily 8am-6pm. **Postal Code:** 266001.

ACCOMMODATIONS

Cheaper establishments crowd the train station and ferry terminal areas. More upscale resort hotels line the south coast.

Jinhai Hotel (jīnhǎi dàjiǔdiàn; 金海大酒店), 2 Tai'an Lu (☎288 7788), has a very nice staff. Rooms that face the railway are noisy and dingy. 24hr. hot water. Doubles Y280. Discounts of 50% possible, especially during the off-season. ❷

Railway Hotel (tiědào dàshà; 铁道大厦), 2 Tai'an Lu (☎286 9927), just north of the train station exit. Recently renovated. A glass elevator offers great views, and bright rooms boast lots of amenities. Doubles with A/C and bath Y280 can be brought down to Y190; quads Y480. 30% discount when business lags, usually in July-Aug. ❸

Friendship Hotel (yǒuyí bīnguǎn; 友谊宾馆), 12 Xinjiang Lu (☎282 8165), next door to a popular Korean restaurant and the Friendship Store. Tacky decor, poor lighting, and a vertigo-inducing elevator—perfect for the adventurous budget traveler. Dorms available

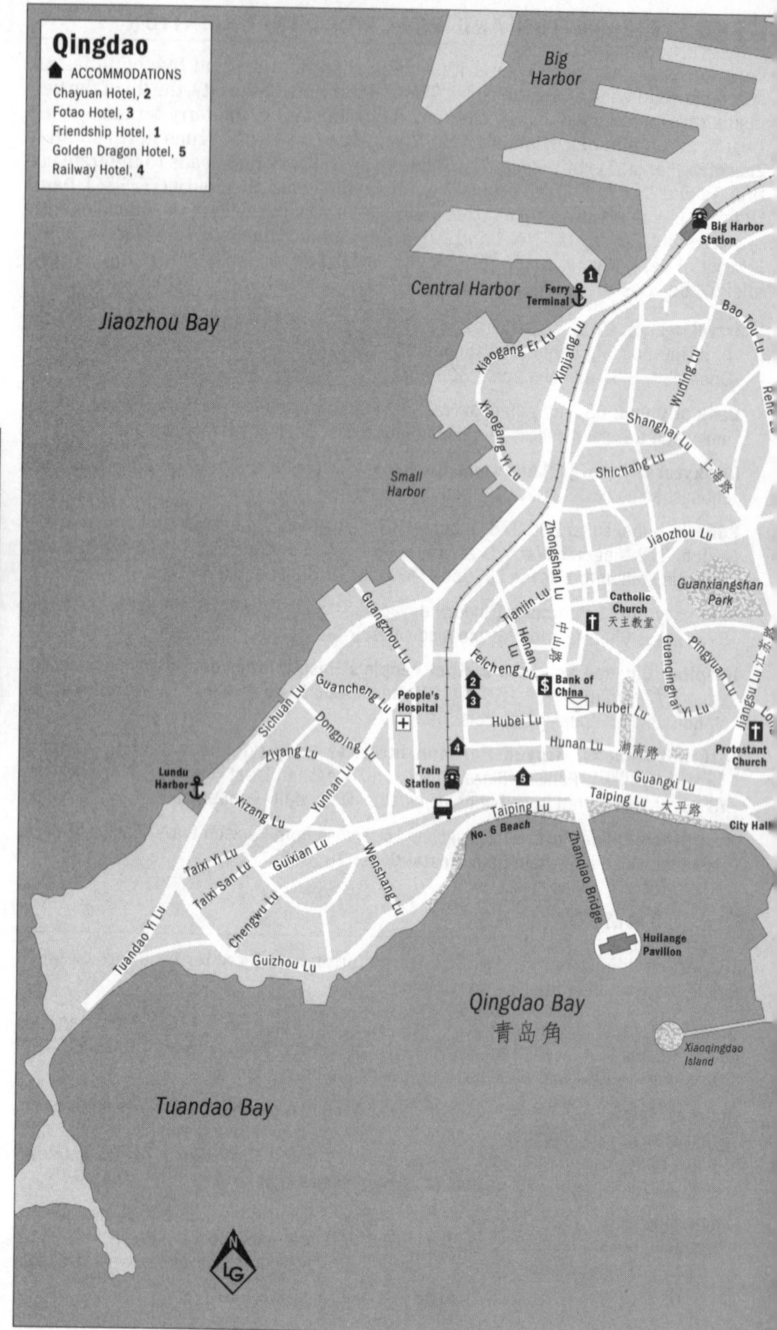
Qingdao
ACCOMMODATIONS
Chayuan Hotel, 2
Fotao Hotel, 3
Friendship Hotel, 1
Golden Dragon Hotel, 5
Railway Hotel, 4
Big Harbor
Big Harbor Station
Central Harbor
Ferry Terminal
Jiaozhou Bay
Bao Tou Lu
Xiaogang Er Lu
Xinjiang Lu
Wuding Lu
Xiaogang Yi Lu
Shanghai Lu
上海路
Shichang Lu
Small Harbor
Zhongshan Lu
Jiaozhou Lu
Guanxiangshan Park
Guangzhou Lu
Tianjin Lu
Catholic Church
天主教堂
Henan Lu
中山路
Pingyuan Lu
Feicheng Lu
Guanqinghai Yi Lu
Bank of China
Guancheng Lu
People's Hospital
Hubei Lu
Jiangsu Lu
Sichuan Lu
Dongping Lu
Hunan Lu
湖南路
Protestant Church
Ziyang Lu
Lundu Harbor
Yunnan Lu
Train Station
Guangxi Lu
Taiping Lu
太平路
Xizang Lu
City Hall
No. 6 Beach
Guixian Lu
Taixi Yi Lu
Taixi San Lu
Wenshang Lu
Zhanqiao Bridge
Chengwu Lu
Huilange Pavilion
Tuandao Yi Lu
Guizhou Lu
Qingdao Bay
青岛角
Xiaoqingdao Island
Tuandao Bay
N
LG

BEIJING

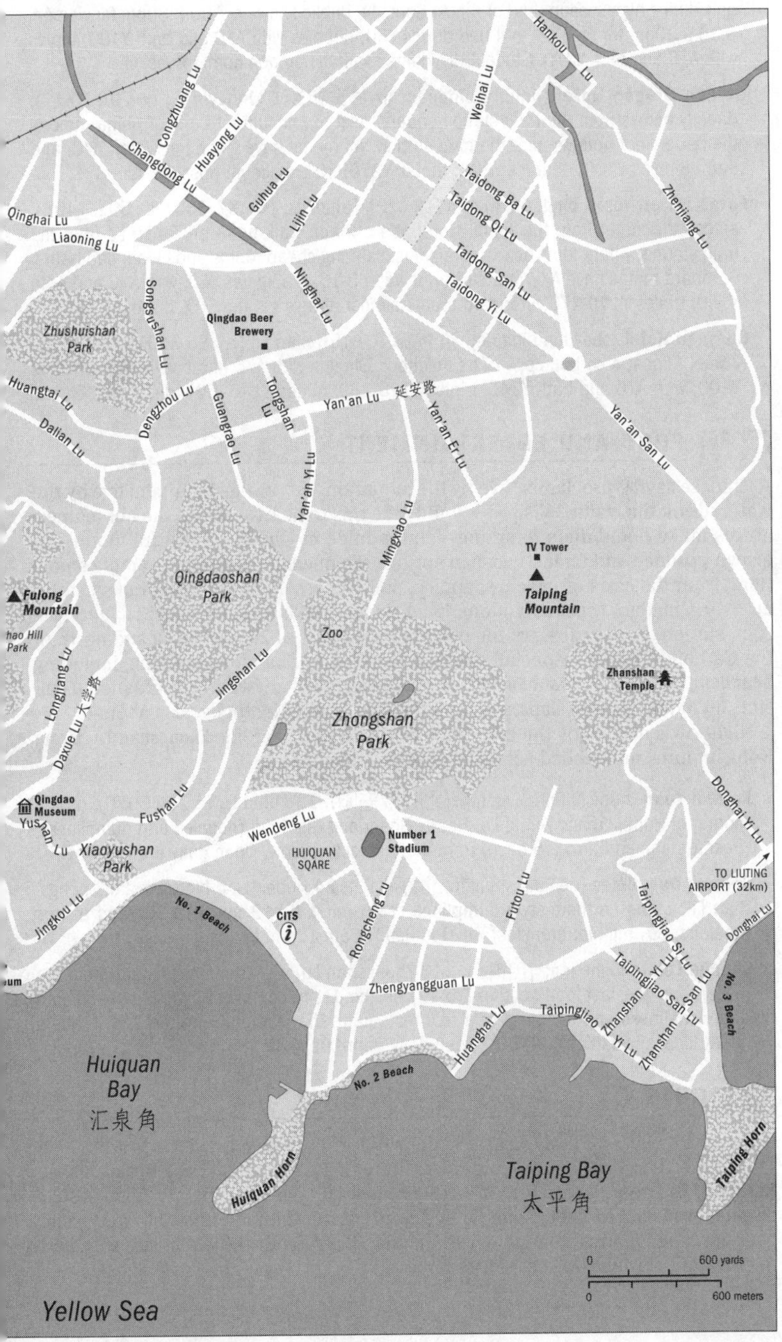
Hankou Lu
Congzhuang Lu
Weihai Lu
Huayang Lu
Changdong Lu
Guhua Lu
Lijin Lu
Taidong Ba Lu
Taidong Qi Lu
Zhenjiang Lu
Qinghai Lu
Liaoning Lu
Ninghai Lu
Taidong San Lu
Taidong Yi Lu
Songsushan Lu
Zhushuishan Park
Qingdao Beer Brewery
Huangtai Lu
Dengzhou Lu
Guangrao Lu
Tongshan Lu
Yan'an Lu 延安路
Yan'an Er Lu
Yan'an San Lu
Dalian Lu
Yan'an Yi Lu
Mingxiao Lu
TV Tower
Qingdaoshan Park
Fulong Mountain
Taiping Mountain
Zoo
Longjiang Lu
Jingshan Lu
Zhanshan Temple
Daxue Lu 大学路
Zhongshan Park
Fushan Lu
Qingdao Museum
Donghai Yi Lu
Wendeng Lu
Number 1 Stadium
Xiaoyushan Park
HUIQUAN SQARE
TO LIUTING AIRPORT (32km)
Futou Lu
Jingkou Lu
No. 1 Beach
CITS
Rongcheng Lu
Taipingjiao Si Lu
Donghai Lu
Taipingjiao Yi Lu
Zhengyangguan Lu
Taipingjiao San Lu
Huanghai Lu
Taipingjiao Zhanshan Yi Lu
Zhanshan San Lu
No. 3 Beach
Huiquan Bay
汇泉角
No. 2 Beach
Huiquan Horn
Taiping Bay
太平角
Taiping Horn
0
600 yards
600 meters
Yellow Sea

BEIJING

only during high season (end of July to Sept. 1). Public showers 7:30-8:30pm for women, 8:30-9:30pm for men. 2- to 4-bed dorms Y50; doubles with A/C and bath Y180; triples with A/C and bath Y270. Student discounts available on non-dorm rooms. ❶

Golden Dragon Hotel (jīnlóng bīnguǎn; 金龙宾馆), 1 Mengyin Lu (☎296 3741), directly across from the train station square, next to Agricultural Bank of China. Among the better-kept options near the train station. All rooms have 24hr. hot water, A/C, and bath. Singles Y180; doubles Y220; triples Y270. 30% discount possible. ❸

Fotao Hotel (fótáo bīnguǎn; 佛桃宾馆), 13 Tai'an Lu (☎287 1581 or 591 1406), across the street from the Jinhai Hotel. It's a 2min. walk north on Tai'an Lu from the train station, where touts accost foreigners claiming cheap rooms and clean tiled baths. Standard rooms have A/C and bath. Hot water 8-10pm. Singles Y60, with A/C and bath Y160; triples Y120-270. Standard rooms almost always get the 50% discount. ❶

Chayuan Hotel (cháyuàn bīnguǎn; 茶苑宾馆), 15 Tai'an Lu (☎286 3101), next to the Fotao. Almost a carbon copy of its neighbor. Singles with A/C and bath Y180; doubles Y100, with A/C and bath Y240; triples Y120-280; quads Y140. 50% discounts. ❷

FOOD AND ENTERTAINMENT

A Chinese saying proclaims "live by the mountain, eat off the mountain; live by the water, drink the water." Visitors should take this to heart—even if the hot temperatures make liquid diets tempting—and indulge in Qingdao's fruitful mountain-grown produce and famed Laoshan springs. To quench your thirst, sample something from the carts of peaches, apples, and lychees. Seafood restaurants scatter all over Qingdao, especially along **No. 1 Beach, Tai'an Lu,** and **Hubei Lu,** near the train station. For kebabs, try the neighborhood east of **Zhongshan Lu** and north of the Catholic Church (especially **Boshan Lu**). Hearty Shandong cooking, including **Shandong Corn** (Y0.8-1) and **dumplings,** can be sampled anywhere. International cuisine, including Muslim, Japanese, and the ever exotic Kentucky, also abound.

Night-owls may enjoy the numerous **movie theaters** that line **Zhongshan Lu.** Hong Kong imports and dubbed US flicks cost less than than Y10.

Jin Mai Yuan (húběilù jīnmàiyuán; 湖北路金麦园), 18 Anhui Lu (☎289 3070), on the corner of Hubei Lu and Anhui Lu. Hearty Shandong fast food (noodles and dumplings), freshly steamed *bāozi* (Y5 each) from the take-out window. Open daily 6am-9pm. ❶

Beifang Dumplings (běifāng shuǐjiǎo; 北方水饺), 24 Hubei Lu, a block west of Zhongshan Lu, offers northern-style dumplings (Y3.6 per 18, Y12 per 60). Stir-fried dishes upstairs. Soy milk for breakfast Y1. Open daily 6am-10pm. ❶

Chunhe Lou (chūnhé lóu; 春和楼), 146 Zhongshan Lu, a 5-10min. walk north from the waterfront. The fast-food section (Y5-12) on the 1st fl. combines lightning speed with the cleanliness and tastiness of a real restaurant; the restaurant on the 2nd fl. offers great local specialties (Y10-50). Open daily 6am-10pm. ❷

SIGHTS

Qingdao locals accurately describe their colorful peninsula with 8 words: "red roofs, green trees, aqua water, blue sky." Take in the scenery at **No. 2 Beach, Xinhao Hill Park,** the commercial action of **Zhongshan Lu,** and the intimate **German-style neighborhood** east of Zhongshan Lu and north of the Catholic Church. Every year, beer-guzzling fanatics stumble to the Qingdao Beer Festival (held in late summer) to do what beer-fans do best—drink.

QINGDAO BEER BREWERY (qīngdǎo píjiǔ chǎng; 青岛啤酒厂). This brewery provides a taste of history amid the odor of hops and barley. Qingdao's most famous export has been fermenting since 1903, when German expats established this, the country's best-known brewery. Mineral water from nearby Laoshan is said to be the secret behind the beer's great taste and purported medicinal properties. Drink Tsingtao—live forever. *(56 Dengzhou Lu. Take bus #1 or 25 from the train station to Shiwuzhong (十五中) on Yan'an Lu. ☎ 383 3437. Open daily 8-11am and 1:30-5pm. Call ahead. 15min. tour of the bottling workshop and unlimited tasting for Y10.)*

WUSI SQUARE (wǔsì guángchǎng; 五四广场). Twelve marble pillars (representing China's 12 dynasties) welcome visitors to Wusi (literally "May 4th") Square. The square features several fountains, including one you can walk through. Take a leisurely stroll from the #3 Beach and enjoy Qingdao's skyline or walk along the jetty and feel the crashing waves tickle your feet. *(West of #2 and #3 Beaches.)*

SIGNAL HILL PARK (xìnhàoshān gōngyuán; 信号山公园). This park derives its name from a former beacon that once sat atop the steep hill. The narrow, weed-covered paths that wind their way up to the top are not really for strolling; the 20-minute hike to the top is rewarded by majestic views of the city. Ascend the **Rotary Sight-seeing Building,** an onion-dome-like structure that offers a rotating 360° view of the city. *(☎ 279 4141. 18 Longshan Lu, just east of Jiangsu Lu. Open daily 7am-7pm. Y12, students can sometimes get in for Y6. Rotary Sight-seeing Building free with admission.)*

CATHOLIC CHURCH (tiānzhǔ jiàotáng; 天主教堂). Officially called **St. Michael's Cathedral,** this grand neo-Gothic cathedral was built in 1934 by German architects. The church was heavily damaged in the Cultural Revolution, but it was reopened in 1981. Today it is an active, but essentially empty place of worship, with few priests and nuns in residence. This quiet, cool church is nonetheless a good place to escape the heat. *(At Zhejiang Lu and Feicheng Lu, east of Zhongshan Lu. ☎ 286 5960. Open M-Sa 8am-5pm, Su 9am-5pm. Y5. Service Su 7-8:30am.)*

PROTESTANT CHURCH (jīdū jiàotáng; 基督教堂). Like its Catholic counterpart, this stone and stucco-roofed church stills serves an active community and is a prominent reminder of Qingdao's colonial past. Completed in 1908 by Germans, it houses a bell and clock tower that visitors can climb up to see. *(15 Jiangsu Lu, at Zheshui Lu. ☎ 286 5790. Open daily 8-11:30am and 1:30-4:30pm. Y3. Service Su 9-10:30am.)*

BEACHES

NO. 2 BEACH (dì'èr hǎishuǐ yùchǎng; 第二海水浴场). Finding a beach in Qingdao is only marginally harder than finding a disgruntled bureaucrat in Beijing. And of them all, No. 2 runs circles around the competition; lush hills hem it in on three sides, and clean sands and sapphire water take care of the fourth. Only algae, seaweed, and the occasional sharp rock litter the shores; only the crash and hiss of waves disturbs the quiet. *(Open 24hr. Y2; free after 5pm. Locker and shower Y10.)*

At the eastern end of the beach is **Huashi Villa** (huāshí lóu; 花石楼), or "Granite Castle." This old-world stone villa was built in 1930 for a Russian aristocrat and later owned by a succession of Chinese cadres. Apart from its lookout tower, the villa is only mildly interesting; one exhibit displays some of Chiang Kai-shek's belongings. *(18 Huanghai Lu, at Shanhaiguan Lu. Open daily 7:30am-6pm. Y5.)* Over 200 European-style villas of the concession era line the broad avenues that run through the thick greenery of **Badaguan Scenic Area** (bādàguān fēngjǐngqū; 八大关风景区), located in the surrounding hills. *(South of Zhongshan Park, in the eastern part of town. Accessible by buses #6, 26, 214, 219, and 304.)*

NO. 1 BEACH (dìyī hǎishuǐ yùchǎng; 第一海水浴场). Qingdao's longest beach is flooded with tourists, hotels, restaurants, and shark-proof nets. This kind of high-drama swimming and sunbathing can be avoided at the more deserted No. 2 Beach. *(In the eastern part of town, just south of Nanhai Lu. Accessible by buses #6, 15, 26, 312, and others. Only open July-Sept. Free; swimming Y3.)*

NO. 6 BEACH (dìliù hǎishuǐ yùchǎng; 第六海水浴场). Far too close to the downtown area, the No. 6 Beach is number 1 in terms of population density, litter, and noise level. It is, however, the gateway to **Huilan Pavilion** (huílán gé; 回澜阁) and **Zhanqiao Pier.** The pier, built in 1891, is one of the most well-known sights in Qingdao, and the octagonal pavilion at the far end echoes with the pounding rhythms of the ocean and the sound of chattering tourists. *(At the southern end of the city center, south of the train station. The pier is on Taiping Lu at Zhongshan Lu. Open 24hr. Ticketing time ends earlier in the winter. Y2 8:30am-6pm, free after 7:30pm.)*

TEENY-WEENY BIKINI When pundits talk about the hyper-politicization of every aspect of life in China, they aren't joking; even the micro-sized configuration of lycra known as the bikini was once the subject of serious national debate. The bikini debuted in China in 1986 at a Shenzhen body-building contest. At that time, the sight of the nation's precious feminine resources strutting their stuff so shamelessly was a huge (ahem) headache for government officials. The vice-manager of the Shanghai Advertising Corporation declared that bikinis were "not acceptable to oriental sensibility." One of the judges, however, exclaimed that women "taking part in such a contest clad in bikinis in front of a crowd of onlookers shows that the women of China, after thousands of years of imbibing traditional feudalistic thinking, are opening their minds." (Presumably, the sight opened the minds of more than a few male onlookers as well.) In 1992, swimsuit calendars were legalized; since then, advertisements for cars, cigarettes, and even law and democracy magazines have featured scantily clad women displaying their products—as well as whatever it is they're selling.

DAYTRIP FROM QINGDAO: LAOSHAN

*40km east of Qingdao. Laoshan is most conveniently seen with a **tour bus** (Y25 for tour guide and transportation; admission extra); megaphone-touting ticket sellers abound near the train station. All tours are in Chinese and may feature annoying stops at pearl shops, but you can ditch the group after arrival. There are several **park entrances,** including Liuqinghe (流清河), Yakou (垭口), and Yangkou (仰口). **Liuqinghe** is near Weizhu Nunnery, Liuqing River, and Jufeng Peak; **Yakou** is near Taiping Palace, Shangqing Palace, Mingxia Caves, and Longtan Waterfall; **Yangkou** is near a beach, Taiping Palace (cable car Y30 one-way, Y50 round-trip), Youlong Cave, Mitian Cave, and several small temples. Tour buses usually go only to Yakou. To explore on your own, **bus #304** runs from the train station (Y6.5) to Yakou or Liuqinghe, and **#312** runs from the train station (Y6.5) or Zhongshan Park (Y6) to Yangkou. The last bus to Qingdao departs Yangkou at 4:40pm, Yakou at 5pm. **Minibuses** (30min., every 30min. 7am-4pm, Y3) run between Yakou and Yangkou. Y50; individual sights Y10-15.*

The fabled Daoist fairyland of Laoshan (崂山) makes for a magical daytrip from Qingdao. Rising 1133m above sea level, the source of the Laoshan Mineral Spring Water is dotted with temples, monasteries, waterfalls, and limestone cliffs that hang over the Yellow Sea. Sights along the scenic paths are staggeringly numerous, and the arduous hikes are an incomparable experience. Among the most prominent are the **Shangqing Palace,** the oldest monastery in the area; the roaring

Longtan Waterfall, the sight of frequent aquatic rainbows; the bamboo-shrouded **Weizhu Nunnery; Taiqing Palace** (太清宫), a famous monastery whose active Daoist community is not allowed to eat meat, marry, or cut their hair; and the **Jufeng Peak** viewing platform. The monasteries and temples in Laoshan are active worship sites, home to Daoist monks and nuns and host to pilgrims and ordinary tourists.

YANTAI 烟台

☎0535

Despite its grime-coated Communist concrete architecture, Yantai should not be dismissed as a simple stopover on the way to the marvelous Penglai castle, Dalian, or Tianjin. A few outdoor markets, beaches, and a neighborhood of well-preserved Western-style buildings give the city a surprising dose of charm.

TRANSPORTATION

Flights: Yantai Airport (yāntái jīchǎng; 烟台机场; ☎624 1330), 17km south of Yantai. A taxi from the city costs Y40. Shuttles (Y10) leave 2hr. before flights from the **CAAC ticket office,** 6 Dahaiyang Lu (☎624 5596), just south of the train station. Open daily 8am-6pm. To: **Beijing** (5-6 per day, Y630); **Changchun** (Tu and F, Y640); **Guangzhou** (Tu-Th and Sa, Y1540); **Harbin** (daily, Y760); **Hong Kong** (W and Sa-Su, Y2610); **Ji'nan** (Tu-Su, Y470); **Shanghai** (2-3 per day, Y630); **Shenyang** (daily, Y570).

Trains: Yantai Train Station (yāntái huǒchē zhàn; 烟台火车站), 135 Bei Malu (☎624 3917). To: **Beijing** (15hr., 6am and 9pm, Y65-143); **Ji'nan** (8hr., 5 per day 6:20am-10:20pm, Y36-141); **Qingdao** (4hr., 4 per day 8:25am-6:20pm, Y21-36); **Shanghai** (24½hr., 2:40 and 5:35pm, Y86-188); **Xi'an** (16hr., 8:55am and 9:50pm, Y96-208).

Buses: Yantai Bus Station (yāntái qìchē zhàn; 烟台汽车站), 86 Xi Dajie (☎624 2716), at Qingnian Lu, 2 blocks west and 1 block south of the train station. To: **Beijing** (17hr., 10:30am, Y125.5); **Ji'nan** (6½hr., every 45min.-1hr. 6:45am-5:30pm, Y86.5-99.5); **Penglai** (1½hr., every 20min. 3:30am-5:30pm, Y8); **Qingdao** (4hr., every 30min. 6am-4pm, Y30); **Tai'an** (10hr., 6:30am, Y73.5); **Tianjin** (17hr., 1pm, Y110.5); **Weihai** (1hr., every 15min. 6am-6:30pm, Y15). The **Train Station Bus Station** (huǒchē zhàn qìchē zhàn; 火车站汽车站; ☎626 2604) is in front of the train station. To: **Beijing** (17hr., 7 and 8:30pm, Y130); **Ji'nan** (6½hr., every 40min. 5am-6:30pm, Y65); **Weihai** (1hr., every 15min. 5:30am-6:30pm, Y16).

Ferries: Yantai Passenger Ferry Terminal (yāntái kèyùn zhàn; 烟台客运站), 155 Bei Malu (☎674 1774), east of the train station. Ticket office is on Dahaiyang Lu, 50m south of Bei Malu. To: **Dalian** (express: 3hr., 4 per day 8:30am-2pm, Y192; regular: 8hr., 6 per day 8am-9:30pm, Y72-560) and **Tianjin** (16hr., July-Aug. 4pm, Y76-214).

Local Transportation: Minibuses (Y5), **public buses** (Y1), and **double-decker buses** (Y1.5-4) go almost anywhere. Buses **#2, 48,** and **52** ply Nan Dajie; **#10** and **17** from train station to the beaches to Yantai University; **#21** and **22** to the Development Zone.

Taxis: Base fare Y5. Each additional km Y1.3-1.5.

ORIENTATION AND PRACTICAL INFORMATION

Yantai spreads along the southern shore of the Yellow Sea. **Bei Dajie** (北大街) turns into **Bei Malu** (北马路) 5min. east of the train station and runs east-west, parallel to **Nan Dajie** (南大街). **Dahaiyang Lu** (大海阳路), **Xinanhe Lu** (西南路), **Shengli Lu** (胜利路), and **Jiefang Lu** (解放路) all run north-south.

BEIJING

Travel Agency: CITS, 181B Jiefang Lu, 2nd fl. (☎623 4144), at Si Malu, south of the Bank of China. Organizes English-language tours of Penglai. Some staff members speak English, Japanese, or Korean. Open M-F 8am-6pm.

Tourist Information: ☎625 3679.

Bank of China: 166 Jiefang Lu (☎623 8888), next to the Int'l Hotel, south of Nan Dajie. Exchanges traveler's checks. Credit card advances. Open M-F 8am-noon and 2-5:30pm.

PSB: 78 Shifu Jie (☎653 5621), at Chaoyang Jie. **Foreign affairs office** is on the 6th fl. Some English speakers. Contact CITS for visa consultations. Open M-Sa 8am-5:30pm.

Pharmacy: Bei Dajie Pharmacy (běidàjiē yàodiàn; 北大街药店), 30 Bei Dajie (☎622 2988), in a fancy Chinese-style building on Bei Malu. Open daily 7:30am-9pm.

Hospital: Yantaishan Hospital (yāntáishān yīyuàn; 烟台山医院), 1 Jiefang Lu (☎660 2108), at Binghai Bei Lu. Some English-speaking staff members. Open 24hr.

Internet Access: Fengye Internet Bar (fēngyè wǎngbā; 枫叶网吧), 38 Shifu Jie (☎615 1075), across from the Taipingyang Restaurant. Y4 per hr. Open 24hr. **Meigui Internet Cafe** (méiguī wǎngbā; 玫瑰网吧), 164 Bei Dajie, on Bei Malu east of the Golden Gilder Hotel. Y3 per hr. Open 24hr.

Post Office: China Post, 172 Nan Dajie, at Dahaiyang Lu. EMS, IDD service, and Poste Restante. English signs. Open daily 7:30am-6pm. **Postal Code:** 264000.

ACCOMMODATIONS

Hotels officially open to foreigners in Yantai are overpriced and drab.

Golden Gilder Hotel (jīnxiáng dàjiǔdiàn; 金翔大酒店), 172 Bei Malu (☎621 6495), a 5min. walk east of the train or ferry stations. All that gilders is not gold, as shown by this rather uninspiring place. Doubles Y128-198; triples Y228; quints Y200. Discounts of over 20% possible. ❷

Yantaishan Hotel (yāntái shān bīnguǎn; 烟台山宾馆), 38 Haian Lu (☎622 4491), at Chaoyang Jie, in the heart of the town's most interesting neighborhood, near the pier and beaches. Clean rooms have A/C and 24hr. hot water. Doubles include breakfast. Singles Y160; doubles Y228; triples Y278. 20-30% discount possible. ❷

Haiyuan Hotel (hǎiyuán bīnguǎn; 海员宾馆), 68 Bei Malu (☎624 3425), across from the train and ferry stations. The old hotel is labeled as the "International Seamen's Club"; no nautical feel, but rooms are well-kept. Singles and doubles have 24hr. hot water, dorms 7pm-midnight. 4-bed dorms Y26; singles Y100; doubles Y160-200, you can buy individual beds. ❶

FOOD AND ENTERTAINMENT

Thoroughfares like **Bei Malu** and **Nan Dajie** and Yantai's oceanfront street, **Haian Lu,** are strewn with eateries that serve local seafood. Bars, including a spin-off of the Beijing's **Keep In Touch** (open 2:30pm-late), line Chaoyang Jie north of Bei Malu. **Shengli Lu** offers great sit-down lunch and dinner options.

Yantai Beer City (yāntái píjiǔ chéng; 烟台啤酒城), 174 Xianhe Lu, south of Bei Dajie, half a block north of Jingjing Fast Food. Beer on tap may be their most popular item, but entrees (Y15-35) can add to the revelry. Try the famous Shandong *pāi huángguā* (cucumber salad; 拍黄瓜). Open daily 10am-10:30pm. ❷

Tudali (tŭdàlì; 土大力), 32 Bei Malu, near Chaoyang Jie. This Korean restaurant specializes in skewered meats and veggies. Entrees Y10-40. Open daily 10:30am-10:30pm. ❷

SIGHTS AND BEACHES

Although Yantai doesn't have much to offer tourists, one day of exploring can still prove well-spent. **Yantai Museum** (yāntáishì bówùguăn; 烟台市博物馆), 257 Nan Dajie at Shengli Jie, was built in 1884 by merchants from Fujian. The architecture and decoration, rather than the exhibits, are worth a peek. The buildings are filled with colorful carvings of dragons, phoenixes, flowers, and figurines inspired by the *Romance of the Three Kingdoms*, *Eight Immortals*, and other Chinese folk stories. (Open daily 8-11:30am and 1-4:30pm. Y5.) North of Bei Malu, the intimate streets lined with Western-style architecture lead to **Yantai Hill Park** (yāntáishān gōngyuán; 烟台山公园). The remains of a fort (Y2) and a 1905 lighthouse (Y5) are among the attractions. (Open 24hr. Y5 6am-8pm; after 8pm free.)

No. 2 Beach (dì'èr hăishuĭ yùchăng; 第二海水浴场) pales in comparison to **No. 1 Beach** (dìyī hăishuĭ yùchăng; 第一海水浴场), with its attractive, clean path winding along the waterfront. The man-in-the-moon statue, in the next cove, is a popular spot for marriages and parties. The No. 2 is a bit down the road. Tourists, trash, and fishing boats litter the horizon of this unfortunate runner-up. Locals seem to be proudest of its **Yellow Sea Beach** (huánghăi hăishuĭ yùchăng; 黄海海水浴场), farther down the coast. All three beaches are accessible by bus #17 and free.

DAYTRIP FROM YANTAI: PENGLAI

Buses to Penglai leave from the Yantai Bus Station (1½hr., every 20min. 5am-6pm, Y8) and the station on Bei Malu (buses leave whenever full 5am-6:30pm, Y8). Buses for the return trip (1½hr., every 30min. 6am-6pm, Y8) leave from the Penglai Long-distance Bus Station, 166 Zhonglou Bei Lu (☎564 2018), at Beiguan Lu. Pavilion open daily in summer 7am-6pm; in winter 8am-5pm. Y55. Cable car Y18.

The name Penglai (pénglái; 蓬莱) is familiar to those who know Chinese mythology. Qin and Han dynasty emperors, including Qin Shihuang and Han Wudi, are said to have come here to find the secrets of immortality and to appease the gods of the sea. Visitors today may not find the fountains of youth or the hoary immortals described in folktales, but at least there's the **Penglai Pavilion** (pénglái gé; 蓬莱阁), which sits atop oceanside cliffs in all its regal majesty. The garden- and temple-lined path to the pavilion winds over bridges and hills, rewarding patient trekkers with a beautiful ocean view. The pavilion's main hall has a golden statue of the **Sea Goddess,** surrounded by images of oceans, clouds, and sea dragons. The grounds are also the site of a fort, maritime history exhibition, and the fantastically unexciting line between the Bohai and Yellow Seas. Penglai is also famous for the **Penglai Mirage,** which is said to occur every few decades. Some see just a hazy mist around them, but others claim to glimpse entire cities through the clouds, complete with busy villagers, intricate temples, and mule-drawn carts.

WEIHAI 威海 ☎0631

Originally a home port from which the Chinese fleet fought off Japanese pirates, Weihai is now home to some of China's most beautiful beaches. The city became China's Pearl Harbor in 1895, when the Qing dynasty's entire North Sea Fleet, the most advanced armada in Asia, was destroyed by a smaller Japanese flotilla. Now eclipsed by the larger ports of Qingdao and Yantai, Weihai holds tenaciously onto its small niche as a hub for ferry connections to South Korea, which makes for a sizable Korean population and lots of Korean businessmen.

TRANSPORTATION

Flights: Weihai Airport (wēihǎi jīchǎng; 威海机场), 80km away in neighboring Wendeng County, is accessible by taxi (1hr., Y70-80). **CAAC ticket office,** 24-1 Qingdao Bei Lu (☎531 7915), just south of the Bank of China. Open daily 8am-8pm. To: **Beijing** (10:30am and 4:10pm, Y530); **Changchun** (W and Sa 12:25pm, Y630); **Guangzhou** (W and Sa 4:25pm, Y1460); **Shanghai** (W and Sa 10:30am, Y610).

Trains: Weihai Train Station (wēihǎi huǒchē zhàn; 威海火车站), off Qingdao Zhong Lu in the south of the city. Take bus #1 or 12 from downtown. To: **Beijing** (15hr., 9:30pm, Y69-258); **Ji'nan** (13hr., 3-4 per day, Y51-167); **Xi'an** (27hr., 8:55am, Y327).

Buses: Weihai Long-distance Bus Station (wēihǎi chángtú qìchē zhàn; 威海长途汽车站; ☎522 2867), at the intersection of Jiefang Lu and Dongcheng Lu, at the terminus of buses #3, 4, 6, 7, and 9. A kiosk next to the bus station's ticket counter also sells train and boat tickets. To: **Beijing** (15hr., 10am and 2:45pm, Y142.5); **Ji'nan** (8hr., every 30min. 8am-5pm, Y79.5-139.5); **Qingdao** (3½hr., every 15min. 6am-6pm, Y42.5); **Yantai** (1½hr., every 15min. 6am-6:30pm, Y10-17.5).

Ferries: Weihai Passenger Ferry Terminal (wēihǎi kèyùn zhàn; 威海客运站), 53 Haibin Bei Lu (☎523 3220). To: **Dalian** (7-8hr.; 8:30, 9:30am, 8, 9pm; Y69-299) and **Inchon, South Korea** (17hr.; W, F, Su 5pm; Y75-810).

Local Transportation: Buses run about 6am-7pm. Fare Y1, exact change only. Bus **#1** runs from the Ferry Terminal to the south of the city, along Qingdao Lu; **#2** runs along Huangshan Lu; **#7** runs from the International Beach, past the ferry, to the long-distance bus station; **#12** runs to the train station.

Taxis: Base fare Y5. Each additional km Y1.3-1.5.

BEIJING

ORIENTATION AND PRACTICAL INFORMATION

The city sits on a rugged outcropping that juts into the Yellow Sea, forming a natural harbor with Weihai Gulf to the east. **Haibin Lu** (海滨路) runs along the gulf shore and intersects **Kunming Lu** (昆明路) in front of the ferry terminal. **Qingdao Lu** (青岛路), **Xinwei Lu** (新威路), and **Tongyi Lu** (充一路) run roughly parallel to Haibin Lu. **Wenhua Lu** (文化路) runs east-west from the **City Government Square** (shìfǔ guǎngchǎng; 市府广场) to the International Beach.

Travel Agencies: CITS, 96 Guzhai Dong Lu (☎521 6175 or 581 8616), across from the broadcasting station. Helpful staff. Open M-F 8am-6pm. **Weihai Ticket Center,** on Xinwei Lu (☎523 1874 or 523 1577), 100m north of Weihaiwei Mansion. Arranges tickets for tours, train, bus, and flights. Open daily 8am-7pm.

Bank of China: 38 Xinwei Lu, next to the post office. Exchanges currency and traveler's checks. Credit card advances. Open in summer M-F 8am-6pm; in winter 8am-5pm.

PSB: 111 Chongqing Jie (☎521 3620).

Hospital: Central Hospital (zhōng yīyuàn; 中医院), 29 Qingdao Bei Lu (☎532 1811), south of the Bank of China and north of the train station.

Internet Access: Lingdian Internet Club (língdiǎn wǎngbā; 零点网吧), down an alley to the north of Weihaiwei Mansion, across from the post office. Y3 per hr. Open 24hr..

Anqier Internet Bar (ānqíér wǎngbā; 安琪儿网吧; ☎582 0002), in an alley across from the Bank of China. Y3 per hr. Open 24hr.

Post and Telecommunications: Weihai City Post Office, 40 Xinwei Lu. EMS and Poste Restante. Open daily in summer 8am-6pm; in winter 7:30am-5:30pm. **China Telecom,** 40 Xinwei Lu, next to the post office. IDD/DDD service. Open daily in summer 7:30am-6:30pm; in winter 7:30am-5:30pm. **Postal Code:** 264200.

ACCOMMODATIONS AND FOOD

Most of Weihai's accommodations are quite expensive, but a few bargains can be found. **Shandong University Foreign Students Dormitory** ❷ (shāndōng dàxué liúxuéshēng sùshè; 山东大学留学生宿舍), off Wenhua Xi Lu, is just west of the International Beach; take bus #7 to the Shandong stop and walk through campus. The dormitory has a cafeteria, laundry facilities, and Internet access. (☎568 1414. Doubles with bath Y120, with A/C Y160.) **Weihai Grand Hotel** ❸ (wēihǎi dàfàndiàn; 威海大饭店), 9 Dongping Lu, in an alley east of Tongyi Lu, is one of Weihai's cheapest two-star hotels. (☎523 3888. Singles Y198; doubles Y228; triples Y298.)

Restaurants are dispersed throughout the downtown area, especially on side streets off **Xinwei Lu.** Small seafood eateries are clustered near the International Beach. Among the numerous Korean food options is **Tudali** ❶ (tǔdàlì; 土大力), on 73 Guangming Lu, east of Xinwei Lu. To taste Shandong's famous northern buns and dumplings, try **Qingdao Big Buns** (qīngdǎo dàbāo; 青岛大包), 103 Tongyi Lu. *Bāozi* are only Y0.8-1 each. (☎522 4730. Open daily 6am-11pm.) A popular local spot is **Fengshengyuan Restaurant** ❷ (fēngshēngyuán càiguǎn; 丰盛园菜馆), 61 Tongyi Lu, on the 2nd floor. Don't be deceived by the exterior; the restaurant serves delicious seafood (Y10-25) and other local specialties. The first floor offers fast food service. (Open daily 2nd floor 11am-midnight, 1st floor 5am-10pm.)

SIGHTS AND BEACHES

Weihai itself has few notable sights, but a walk through its coastal streets provides a respite from the rushed pace of city life. In the city center, south of the grandiose city government building, **People's Square** is a popular meeting place, especially at night when ballroom dancers take to the streets. The **International Beach** (guójì hǎishuǐ yùchǎng; 国际海水浴场), on Beihai Lui, is perfect for strolling, swimming, or sunbathing. This beach alone makes a trip to Weihai worthwhile; the sand is fine, and the water crystal clear—or at least clearer than in Qingdao, and certainly Yantai. *(Accessible by buses #7 and 12. Open 24hr. Y2. Inflatable boats Y10-20 per hr., water bikes Y25 per hr., parasailing for Y80. Public changing room with shower and lockers Y5.)*

DAYTRIP FROM WEIHAI: LIUGONG ISLAND

Summer tourist ferries (20min., every 10min. 7am-5pm, round-trip Y25) shuttle visitors to the island from Weihai Tourist Dock (wēihǎi lǚyóu mǎtóu; 威海旅游码头; ☎523 1985), 100m south of the main ferry terminal. There is no accommodation on the island, so don't miss the last boat back to Weihai at 6pm.

Weihai's biggest attraction, Liugong Island (liúgōng dǎo; 刘公岛) lies in the Weihai Gulf 5km off the coast. During the Qing dynasty, after suffering humiliating defeats at the hands of Western powers in the Opium Wars (see p. 13), China was further embarrassed when its navy, one of the strongest in Asia, was forced by the

Emperor to surrender to the Japanese. The war ended with the infamous Maguan Treaty, in which China ceded control of Dalian, Lushun, and Taiwan to Japan.

Not surprisingly, the island is best known for the **Museum of the 1894-95 Sino-Japanese War** (jiǎwǔ zhànzhēng bówùguǎn; 甲午战争博物馆), housed in the old offices of the North Sea Fleet commanders. Exhibits include photos of warships and relics salvaged from ships sunk in Weihai Gulf. *(Open daily 7am-5:30pm. Some English translations. Y25.)* Visitors had best bypass the **Sino-Japanese Sea War Hall** (jiǎwǔ hǎizhàn guǎn; 甲午海战馆; Y25) and head instead for the six 20-ton Krupp cannons atop the forested hills and hiking trails of **Liugong Island Park** (liúgōngdǎo gōngyuán; 刘公岛公园), on the rugged north coast. *(Open 24hr. Y10. Canons Y8-10.)*

THE NORTHEAST

China's Northeast dwells on the cultural and geographic fringes of a vast and glorious empire. Known as Manchuria to Westerners and as Dongbei to the Chinese, the Northeast is, in many ways, a traveler's biggest nightmare. Accommodations tend to be expensive, the landscape can be dreary, and the established tourist sights are often dull. But, the Northeast does have some virtues that can't be found in (and don't flee to) the empire it abuts. Despite the monotonous stretches of plains and wheat fields, bitter winters, and overbearing smokestacks, this area north of the Great Wall boasts a rich historical background, gorgeous scenic wonders, and friendly residents.

Han Chinese have been trying to control these hinterlands since the 3rd century BC, but the region's plucky, stubborn, and just plain volatile inhabitants refused to give in. Over the centuries, Khitans, Manchus, Mongols, Jurchen, and a host of other peoples fought (and usually beat) the Chinese in this massive region. In the 17th century, the Manchus burst through the Great Wall and founded the Qing dynasty, uniting Manchuria and the rest of China for the first time in history (see **Going Postal,** p. 12). Foreign invasions and Civil War conflicts made the 20th century a particularly tumultuous time in the Northeast; today, the area struggles with unemployment and other economic woes. But if history is any indication, the Northeast's diverse and industrious inhabitants will no doubt find a way to fight back and prosper.

HIGHLIGHTS OF THE NORTHEAST

PEEK INTO THE COLONIAL PAST of Harbin, as you stroll past the 19th-century European-style buildings, the last remnants of Russian influence.

FIND YOUR INNER KIM IL SUNG when hiking along the lush North Korean border, where craggy rock cliffs afford glimpses into one of the most isolated nations in the world.

VENTURE INTO THE WORLD OF 1984 in the grim industrial city Jilin (p. 223), where hydroelectric plants cause the eternally leafless tree branches to drip with "ice rims," products of evaporated waste gas.

HEILONGJIANG 黑龙江

God only knows why anybody would want to visit this industrial stronghold. Perhaps it is so they can exclaim, "I have been to China's northernmost province!" or "Why, yes, I *have* suffered through very harsh climatic extremes!" Or maybe they, like the Chinese goverment in the 1950s, are attracted to rich natural resources like coal, petroleum, and thermal power—after all, thick layers of industrial grime can be quite beautiful. Despite the province's occasional sheer ugliness, Heilongjiang is a fascinating cultural crossroads, shaped by Russians, Koreans, Manchus, and sub-Arctic minorities. Harbin's European architecture, luminous Lake Jingbo, and the area's forested mountains can't quite counteract the aesthetic horror of mammoth-sized factories and gloomy commercial districts. But if you're in the country, be it in sweltering summer heat or biting winter chill, you'll discover majestic peaks and sprawling plains, Heilongjiang's true beautiful side.

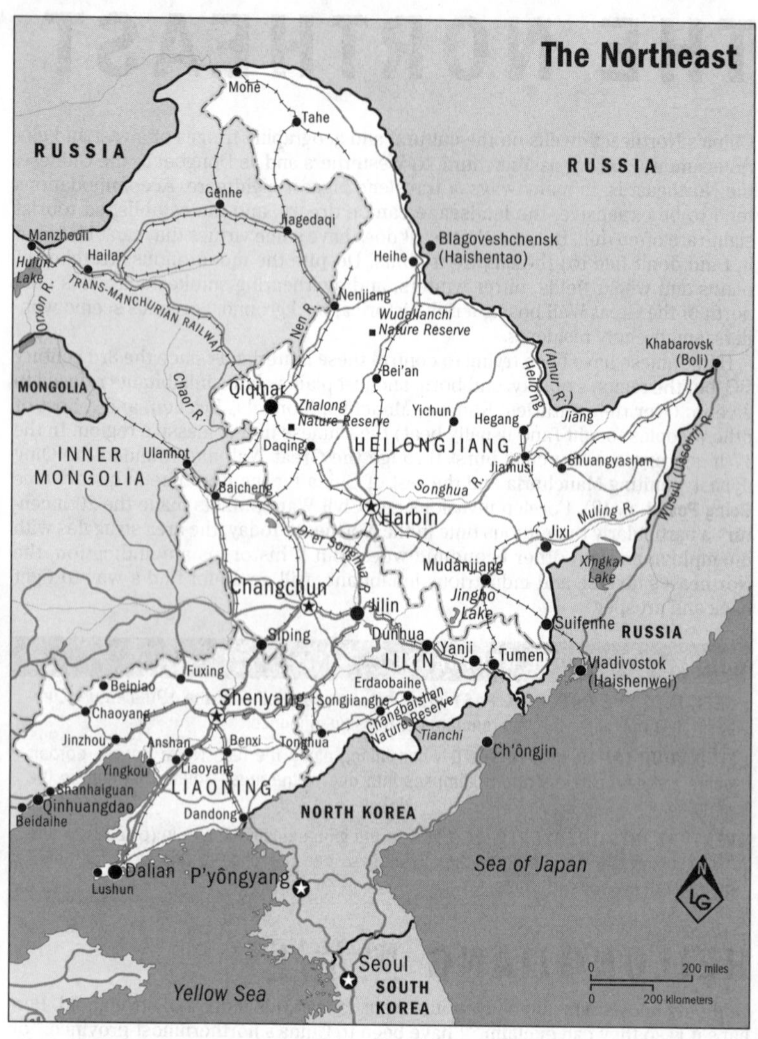

NORTHEAST

HARBIN 哈尔滨

☎0451

Were it not for the construction of the China Eastern Railway, Harbin might still be the sleepy village that it was before the turn of the 20th century. Instead, due in large part to the Russian-built railway line that once passed through here, Harbin is now the second largest city in northeastern China, with a population of nearly four million. Much of the city was built in the early 20th century by European expatriates, and as a result, the downtown area boasts an eclectic mix of Russian domes, traditional Chinese architecture, and industrial concrete eyesores. Harbin

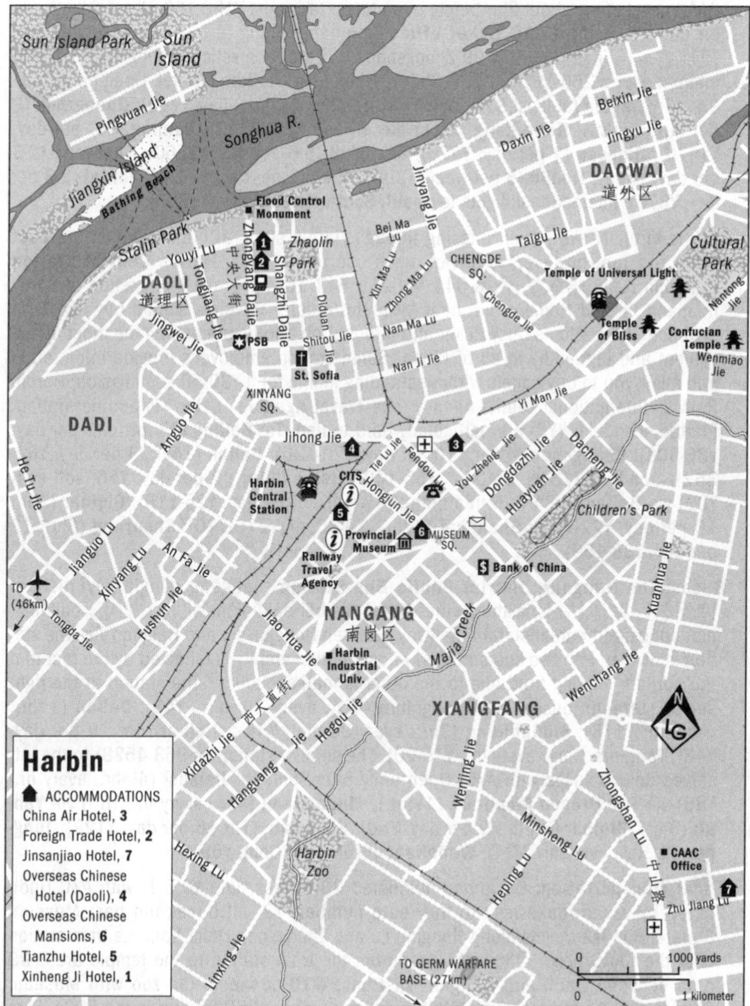

is aesthetically confusing and often startling, juxtaposing the drab and mundane with the elegant and exotic. Regardless of its visual stimuli, however, Harbin is a pleasant stop on any traveler's itinerary, be it during the harsh winter months to see the famous ice-sculpting festival or during the summer to enjoy a cool respite from the burning sun.

TRANSPORTATION

Flights: Harbin's **Taiping International Airport** (tàipíng guójì jīchǎng; 太平国际机场; ☎289 4219), 45km southwest of the city center. Airport shuttles (Y20) leave from the

CAAC ticket office about 2hr. before departures; taxis cost Y120-150. Plane tickets can be booked at the **CAAC ticket office** (mínháng shěng jú hā'ěrbīn shòupiàochù; 民航省局哈尔滨售票处), 99 Zhongshan Lu (24hr. domestic ticketing ☎265 1188, international ☎266 1924 or 289 6874); take bus #2 to Tian E Hotel. Open daily 6am-9pm. To: **Beijing** (at least 8 per day, Y880); **Dalian** (3-4 per day, Y760); **Guangzhou** (2 per day, Y2180); **Hong Kong** (2 per day Th and Sa, Y2250); **Nanjing** (2-3 per day, Y1470); **Qingdao** (2 per day, Y870); **Shanghai** (5-6 per day, Y1560); **Shenyang** (2-3 per day, Y470); **Tianjin** (5 per week, Y900); **Xi'an** (2 per day, Y1490); **Yantai** (2-3 per day, Y870). International flights to **Seoul, South Korea** (daily, Y1950).

Trains: Virtually every train passing through Harbin stops at both stations; the **East Train Station,** however, is not of much use to travelers. **Harbin Central Station** (hā'ěrbīn zhàn; 哈尔滨站; ☎643 4152 or 643 1642), at the intersection of Songhuajiang Jie and Hongjun Jie, near Museum Square. Travelers should buy tickets in advance; the station's busy ticket and information booths are among the most inconvenient and unfriendly in all of China. Some station employees provide information and allow you to buy tickets without standing in line for a Y30-50 commission; Harbin Railway International Tourist Agency (see **Travel Agencies** below) is another option. Printed schedules (Y5) are particularly hard to find. To: **Beijing** (13-24hr., 8 per day, Y86-308); **Changchun** (4½hr., 10 per day, Y20-136); **Dalian** (14hr., 3 per day, Y62-352); **Dandong** (13hr., 9:40pm, Y55-140); **Heihe** (11hr.; 2 per day; Y56, soft seat Y82) via **Bei'an** (6-8hr.); **Mudanjiang** (4½-7hr., 6 per day, Y26-116); **Qiqihar** (3hr., 10 per day, Y22-111); **Shanghai** (32hr., 10:30pm, Y276-770); **Shenyang** (8hr., 12 per day, Y38-159).

Buses: The **Nangang District Public Bus Station** (nángāng gōnglù kèyùn zhàn; 南岗公路客运站) is in the **Beibei Hotel** (běiběi dàjiǔdiàn; 北北大酒店) building, just opposite the train station, halfway between Hongjun Jie and Haiguan Jie. The station is divided into two sub-stations, whose mutual enmity is reflected by the fact that the corridor leading from one to the other is marked "toilet." The station to the right serves state-run buses. To: **Changchun** (4hr., every 30 min., Y43); **Dalian** (14hr., 4:40pm, Y178); **Mudanjiang** (5hr., every 30min., Y54); **Qiqihar** (5hr., 8 per day, Y46); **Tonghua** (2hr., every hr., Y15-20). The smaller station (☎363 4528) to the left serves deluxe buses with A/C. Open daily 5am-6pm. To: **Jiamusi** (4½hr., every hr., Y85) via **Two Dragon Mountain** (1½hr.); **Mudanjiang** (4hr., every hr., Y80) via **Yabuli** (3hr.); **Qiqihar** (3-4hr., 9 per day, Y60); **Shenyang** (7hr., 6 per day, Y129); **Tonghua** (1½hr., every hr., Y24); **Wudalianchi** (5hr., 1:30pm, Y69).

Local Transportation: On routes numbered 28 or less, fare Y0.5-1, with A/C (indicated by a snowflake next to the route number) Y2. All buses run past Museum Square: Bus **#2** travels along Hongjun Lu and Zhongshan Dajie from the train station past the CAAC ticket office; **#6** goes from the train station to the temple area; **#8** runs between Daoli and Nangang districts; **#10** connects the zoo with Museum Square and the temple area. **Minibuses** are numbered 50-99 and in the 300s. Fare Y1-2. Minibus **#64** runs between Museum Square and Daoli district; **#338** and **343** go from the hub near the train station to the Germ Warfare Base via the zoo. **Trolley buses** (Y0.5-1) are numbered in the 100s. Trolley **#101** runs between Dongli and Daoli districts via Museum Square; **#104** runs from Daowai district to the temple area; **#109** goes from Daowai district to the Children's Park via the train station. All buses run approx. 5am-10pm.

Ferries: Boats cross the Songhua River from the Flood Control Monument and travel to Sun Island from the riverbank along Stalin Park in Daowai district. Cheaper passenger boats (Y2) depart from the docks beneath the funicular railway; taxi-boats (Y10) run from farther down the river. Boats run 6am-1hr. after dusk.

Cable cars: Run from the station in Stalin Park to Sun Island. Adults one-way Y20, round-trip Y30; children Y10/20; passengers 1.1-1.4m free. Run daily 8:30am-5:30pm.

Taxis: Base fare Y6-9, each additional km Y1.6-1.9. Taxis between districts Y9-20.

ORIENTATION AND PRACTICAL INFORMATION

The railway is the city's economic and geographic center, but crossing the tracks to get from one district to another can be cumbersome. The **main train station** and **Museum Square** (bówùguǎn guǎngchǎng; 博物馆广场) comprise the center of the commercial **Nangang District** (南岗区), which is bisected by **Xi Dazhi Jie** (西大直街) and **Dong Dazhi Jie** (东大直街). The latter leads toward the distant **Taiping District** (太平区) in the east via the **temple area.** The city's architectural treasure trove, **Daoli District** (道理区), is on the west side of the railroad, bisected by **Zhongyang Dajie** (中央大街). Just east of Daoli district is its counterpart, **Daowai District** (道外区), which is full of street markets and Russian architecture. Both Dao Districts rest on the bank of the **Songhua River** (sōnghuā jiāng; 松花江), which marks the northern border of the city; beyond it lie the attractive **Sun Island** and **Siberian Tiger Parks.** In the confusing cobweb of Harbin's alleys, rivers, channels, and railways, it can be difficult to find other districts. Hop on a bus to get to the southern **Dongli District** (动力区), home to the zoo and botanical garden, and to **Pingfang District** (平房区), farther south and home to the Germ Warfare Base.

Travel Agencies: Heilongjiang CITS, Hushi Bldg., 2 Tielu Jie, 11th fl. (☎366 1159 or 366 1992; fax 366 1190 or 362 1088; cits@mail.hrb.hl.cninfo.net), next to the train station. In winter, they can arrange 1-day trips to Yabuli, Two Dragon Mountain, and other ski-resorts (Y200 includes transportation and ski-pass), along with independent ski-trips for groups of 10 or more (Y300 and up). Individual interpreters Y250 per day. English-, French-, German-, Japanese-, Korean-, and Russian-speaking staff. Open M-F 8:30am-5pm. Branch offices in most major hotels. **Harbin Railway International Tourist Agency** (hā'ěrbīn tiědào gúojì lǚxíngshè; 哈尔滨铁道国际旅行社), 8 Tielu Jie, 7th fl. (☎363 0780), behind the Hushi Building, in the Kunlun Hotel; look for the swarm of minibuses. Sells domestic as well as international tickets. To **Khabarovsk** (Y687) and **Vladivostok, Russia** (Y482). Open M-F 8am-5pm.

Bank of China: 19 Hongjun Jie (☎ 363 3518), near Museum Square in a clearly marked, tall building. Exchanges currency (1st fl.) and traveler's checks (M-F, 3rd fl.). Credit card advances. Open M-F 8:30am-noon and 1-4pm, Sa-Su 9am-3pm. A conveniently located branch at 29 Xishi Daojie (☎463 7043), between Zhongyang Dajie and Shangzhi Dajie. Open M-F 8:30am-4pm, Sa-Su 9am-3pm.

Supermarket: The Third Grocery Store (zhōngyāng shāngchéng;中央商城), 118 Zhongyang Dajie. Open daily 9am-9pm.

PSB: 9 Hongxing Jie, near the intersection of Zhongyang Dajie and Jingwei Jie. Foreign affairs, 26 Duan Jie (☎464 3497), is hidden behind the building. Processes visa extensions. Open daily 8:30-11:20am and 1:30-4:40pm.

Pharmacy: Zhongyang Dajie is dotted with pharmacies. **Baofeng Medical Co.** has a multi-story pharmacy on Zhongyang Dajie, at Xi Shisi Daojie (☎465 0129). Open 24hr.

Hospital: Heilongjiang Province Hospital (hēilóngjiāngshěng yīyuàn; 黑龙江省医院), 405 Fendou Lu.

Internet Access: In **Daoli district:** 129 Zhongyang Dajie, 2nd fl. Over 100 computers. Open daily 8:30am-10pm. In **Nangang district:** 49 Xuefu Lu (open daily 8:30am-10pm) and 399 Fendou Lu (open daily 8:30am-8pm), near McDonald's. The building facing the train station houses a fast, clean and amazingly quiet 24hr. **Internet cafe;** enter the courtyard between the entrances to Beibei Hotel and the bus station. Y3 per hr. Small, noisy hole-in-the-wall cafes are ubiquitous; usually Y2 per hr.

Post Office: Nangang Post and Telecommunications Office (nǎngáng yóudiànjú; 南岗邮电局), 104 Dongda Zhi Jie (☎363 8717), just east of Museum Square at Fendou Lu. Film processing and currency exchange. Open daily in summer 8am-7pm; in winter 8am-6:30pm. Another large post office at 12 Tiedao Lu, near the train station. Open daily 8am-10pm. In Daoli district, go to the post office on Xi Shisi Daojie. Open daily in summer 8am-6:30pm; in winter 8am-6pm. All have EMS and Poste Restante. **Postal Code:** 150001 for Poste Restante, 150000 for the city.

ACCOMMODATIONS

Many of Harbin's accommodations are expensive, but a few bargains can be found. The most conveniently located hotels cluster around the main train station and Zhongyang Dajie. During the Ice Lantern Festival, the prices may more than double and reservations are highly recommended. When you arrive at the train station, a gargantuan advertisement will entice you with what the **Beibei Hotel** calls "standard doubles" for Y100. However, livable rooms (read: with air-flow and windows that aren't bricked up) cost Y180-plus.

Foreign Trade Hotel (wàimào dàjiǔdiàn; 外贸大酒店), 9 Xi San Daojie (☎232 7101; fax 463 5824). A 2min. walk from the Ice Lantern Festival. Fantastic staff. 24hr. hot water, A/C, comfortable rooms, and large windows. 4-bed dorms Y30; doubles Y168. ❶

Tianzhu Hotel (tiānzhú bīnguǎn; 天竹宾馆), 6 Songhuajiang Jie (☎363 7261 or 363 7262; fax 364 3720), opposite and to the right of the main train station. The unassuming exterior hides comfortable rooms and a wide range of amenities. The best value in the train station area. 2-bed dorms Y50; 3-bed dorms Y35; doubles Y140, with A/C Y160; triples Y160 and up. ❶

China Air Hotel (zhōngháng zhāodàisuǒ; 中航招待所), 122 Youzheng Jie (☎364 4330, 364 2809, or 364 2122), 200m from Fendou Lu. Economical prices, exceptional in the Fendou Lu area, and comfortable rooms. 4-bed dorms Y35; 3-bed dorms Y45; 2-bed dorms Y50; doubles with A/C Y140; triples with A/C Y150; suites Y220. ❶

Overseas Chinese Mansions (huáqiáo dàshà; 华侨大厦), 18 Jihong Jie (☎469 6584), in a beautiful but dilapidated Russian building. Well-maintained, quaint rooms within walking distance of Nangang and Daoli districts. Doubles Y160; triples Y180; look at the rooms, pretend you're disappointed, and the price may mysteriously drop. ❷

Xinheng Ji Hotel (xīnhéng jī bīnguǎn; 新恒基宾馆), 38 Xitou Daojie (☎463 2384; fax 463 2494), 1 block east of Zhongyang Dajie. Four reasons for excitement: the 1913 Russian building, the central Daoli district location, free breakfast, and individual A/C remotes for each room. Doubles Y218; triples Y368; quads Y388. ❸

Overseas Chinese Hotel (huáqiáo fàndiàn; 华侨饭店), 72 Hongjun Jie (☎364 1341, fax 362 3429). From the train station, walk 5min. up Hongjun Jie; it's on the right, opposite the glass towers of the North Sinoway Hotel. Helpful staff, but aging rooms. A/C and sporadic hot water (5-9am, evening till 11pm). Doubles Y100, with A/C Y150. ❷

Jinsanjiao Hotel (jīnsānjiǎo bīnguǎn; 金三角宾馆), 16 Zhujiang Lu (☎232 7101), a few blocks from the Swan Hotel; take a bus along Zhongshan Lu to Tian E Hotel. Distinguished by the glass pyramid on its side, this hotel is vaguely reminiscent of the Louvre; rooms are surprisingly unpolished but cheap. 3-bed dorms Y40; singles Y60; doubles Y110, with A/C 160; triples Y120. ❶

NORTHEAST

FOOD AND ENTERTAINMENT

Local specialties in Harbin tend toward the rich and hearty. **Mongolian hotpot** (shuàn yángròu; 涮羊肉) is a do-it-yourself mutton dish (usually Y50 for an ample dinner for two). Local *jiǎozi* are first-rate and available everywhere. The price range of a restaurant is easily determined with a code unique to Harbin: the more **lanterns** in front of an establishment, the more expensive the meal. Most restaurants have red lanterns; blue lanterns indicate Muslim restaurants, which serve a range of mutton dishes but no pork; white lanterns with Korean flags indicate a Korean restaurant, notable for healthy *bibimbap* (bànfàn; 拌饭). The best places to trawl for Western or fast food are **Zhongyang Dajie** and the corner of **Fendou Lu** and **Dong Dazhi Jie,** near Museum Square. The latter area, especially on small streets behind the main post office, houses a peculiar Little Russia, in which *borscht* (Y3-10) and *golubtsi* (Y3-5) are standard dinner items.

A big hit with locals is the **Beibei Big World Club** (běi běi hànbīng dītǔ gāo; 北北旱冰迪土高) in an underground passageway on the corner of Hongjun Jie and Tielu Jie, across from the train station. Listen for the techno music; watch for the glow-in-the-dark murals. This combination bar/dance-club/roller-rink should not be missed. (Open daily 9am-midnight. Cover Y20; includes a pair of rental skates.)

Eastern Dumpling King (dōngfāng jiǎozi wáng; 东方饺子王), 39 Zhongyang Dajie (☎465 3920 or 465 3921). Food fit for a king. Even at off-peak hours, this branch of the well-known chain draws a crowd for truly regal fare. A sure bet (not to mention a well-rounded meal) is the cabbage and pork dumpings (báicài zhūròu shuǐjiǎo; 白菜猪肉水饺). A number of other locations throughout town. Entrees Y12-60. Open daily 10am-10pm. ❷

Portman Western Food Hall (bōtèmàn xī cāntīng; 波特曼西餐厅), 63 Xiqi Daojie (☎468 6888), overlooking an open-air seating area off Zhongyang Dajie. The menu choices (available in English) include salads, pasta, burgers, pizza, and baby-back ribs. Live music 6-11pm. Entrees Y12-30. Open daily 11am-2am. ❷

Huamei Western Restaurant (huáméi xīcāntīng; 华梅西餐厅), 112 Zhongyang Dajie (☎467 5574 or 467 5573), directly across from the Modern Hotel. Almost universally billed as the best Western restaurant in town, the Huamei offers Russian specialties and other fine continental dishes like french fries. Try the *golubtsi* (cabbage rolls; Y15) and borscht (dubbed "red soup"; Y3). Entrees Y15-30. Open daily 11am-9pm. ❷

Festivity Hotpot City (dàqìng huǒguō chéng; 大庆火锅城), 190 Majia Jie (☎364 9988), between Fendou Lu and Hongjun Jie, behind the Bank of China. Something for everyone: Chinese, Mongolian, and Russian cuisine in one place. The helpful staff is perhaps inspired by the inscription on the wall: *Not hardworking today, hard job-searching tomorrow*. Entrees Y10-30. Open daily 9am-11pm. ❷

Paris Bakery (bālí miànbāo fáng; 巴黎面包坊), 4 Xi Dazhi Jie (☎362 6838), and 174 Zhongyang Dajie (☎464 9109). Escape the bustling Chinese streets by entering this "Parisian" cafe (simulated with jazz and photos of Parisian sights). Coffee (Y5-20) and pastries with kiwi or red beans (Y5-7) are favorites. Open daily 7:30am-10pm. ❶

SIGHTS

WINTER SIGHTS. The **Ice Lantern Festival** (bīng dēng jié; 冰灯节) takes place each winter, and a remarkable number of tropic-dwellers make it all the way to Heilongjiang province for this exceptional ice performance in Zhaolin Park (zhàolín gōngyuán; 兆林公园) near the end of Zhongyang Dajie in Daoli district. Officially, the festival runs from January 5 to February 25, but the ice sculptures that glow from within (with the help of colored lights) can be viewed from the end of December until early March. *(Admission to the park during the festival Y20; in summer Y2. Tickets to special exhibits up to Y200.)*

The Ice Lantern Festival is not without competition, however. A short ferry ride away, the run-down **Sun Island Park** (tàiyángdaǒ gōngyuán; 太阳岛公园) houses the **Snow Sculpture Festival,** which occurs around the same time and tends only to attract confused tourists. *(Park Y13, students Y7.)* Many travelers come to Harbin to ski at the nearby resorts. The most prominent skiing areas are **Two Dragon Mountain** (èrlóng shān; 二龙山), on the road to Jiamusi (includes summer skiing facilities), **Jade Fountain Ski Resort** (yùquán huáxuě chǎng; 玉泉滑雪场), and **Yabuli Ski Resort** (yàbùlì huáxuě chǎng; 亚布力滑雪场), on the road to Mudanjiang (p. 215). Each area is fairly difficult to reach using public transportation. The best way to do it while in Harbin may be via CITS, which along with the usual overpriced selection, offers skiers a convenient Y200 per day deal.

ZHONGYANG DAJIE (zhōngyāng dàjiē; 中央大街). On the surface, this is just another cobblestoned, pedestrian street, laden with old Russian buildings. There is something magnetic about this esplanade, however; even locals who in any other city would escape the gloom of skyscrapers to head for a remote park take time here to sip coffee in a cafe or stroll around and enjoy street performances. For inquisitive historians, all the original buildings have English captions; for movie-buffs, the square by Xijiu Daojie has outdoor screenings (starting at 8-9pm). The street ends at **Stalin Park** (sīdàlín gōngyuán; 斯大林公园), which extends along the riverbank. Here, find the curious combination of classic Greek and social realist styles in the **Flood Control Monument** (fánghóng shènglì jìniàn tǎ; 防洪胜利纪念塔) that commemorates the victory over the deluge of 1956.

NORTHEAST

CHURCH OF SAINT SOPHIA (shèng suǒfēiyà jiàotáng; 圣索菲亚教堂). This massive Russian church sticks out like a sore but beautiful thumb in this commercial area. At present, the decaying church is home to a truly fascinating photographic exhibition on the Russian influences in Harbin. Standing on the square in front, in the center of a metropolis, it's almost hard to believe that when the church was first built in 1907, the nearest building was on today's Zhongyang Dajie and the plains to the north sprawled uninhabited all the way to Europe. The sight of the church illuminated by the evening lights is worth an extra trip. *(On Toulong Jie. Open daily 8:30am-5pm. Y10.)*

JAPANESE GERM WARFARE BASE, 731ST DIVISION (qīnhuá rìjūn qīsānyī bùduì zuìzhèng chénlièguǎn; 侵华日军731部队罪证陈列馆). This museum is located on the grounds of a former secret biological warfare research station built by the Japanese army in 1935 to test on the local population. Because the troops blew up the camp before fleeing in 1945, the exhibitions are primarily limited to illustrations of the horrors these grounds have witnessed. The passionate reactions that the exhibits evoke are further aggrevated by controversial documents, some of which insinuate that the US government traded the freedom of the perpetrators for their research results. *(Approx. 20km south of the city center. To get to the museum, take bus #337 to its terminus (45min.); the entrance is across the street. Both depart from Tiedao Lu, near the train station. Open daily 8-11:30am and 1-4:30pm. Y10, students Y5.)*

TEMPLE AREA. These temples provide a welcome alternative to the Slavic atmosphere of tourist Harbin. The **Temple of Universal Light** (pǔzhào sì; 普照寺), near the Cultural Park (wénhuà gōngyuán; 文化公园), is a gem of a temple. You have to be lucky enough to happen upon a large ceremony; sometimes, the doors may be closed (try the little dirt road passage to the left). For those who do get in, beautiful traditional constructions and a solemn atmosphere of worship await. Next door, in the **Pagoda Courtyard** (tǎ yuàn; 塔院), live chants set the rhythm for diligent monks as they work to raise a big golden Buddha. *(Construction was planned to be completed by 2002. Y5.)* The more commercialized **Temple of Bliss** (jílè sì; 极乐寺) attracts more visitors despite its rather mundane look. *(Y5, a few booths within charge an additional Y2.)* Past the noisy intersection, a 10-minute walk down Wenmiao Jie (文庙街) brings you to the **Confucian Temple** (wén miào; 文庙; Y15). The charming sanctuary, home to the only jade bridges in Harbin, is visited by few, but praised by all. *(All temples except Temple of Universal Light are open daily 8am-4pm; come early.)*

CITY PARKS. Probably because of the city's metropolitan chaos, Harbiners take a lot of pride in their parks. The promenade in **Stalin Park** (sīdàlín gōngyuán; 斯大林公园), on the Daoli District riverbank and the somewhat forsaken **Sun Island Park** (tàiyángdaǒ gōngyuán; 太阳岛公园) across the river are nice places to stroll or paddle about in boats (from Y5 per hour). *(Sun Island Park open daily 7:30am-5:30pm. Y13, students Y7.)* None of these activities can be enjoyed in **Siberian Tiger Park,** unfortunately; not even by the caged tigers, who react to the honking tour bus drivers with benign indifference. *(Take bus #12 from Flood Control Monument to the big intersection by the bridge and then #85 to the end; taxis charge Y30 one-way. Tours run 8am-6pm; Y50, children Y25. Optional livestock to feed the animals Y10-1500.)*

The **Harbin Zoo** (dòngwùyuán; 动物园) has a more diverse assortment of animals. *(95 Hexing Lu, southern Nangang District. Take bus #10 from Museum Square along Xi Dazhi Jie. Animal shows 9, 9:30am, 1:30, 3:30pm. Open daily 5am-8pm; exhibit rooms 9am-5pm. Y10, children Y5.)* Children who are less interested in zoology should take their parents to **Children's Park** (értóng gōngyuán; 儿童公园) where little trains driven by little schoolchildren take you from little Beijing to little Harbin—in a little more than 20 minutes. *(295 Fendou Lu, a few blocks from Dong Dazhi Jie. Train rides daily 8:30am-6:30pm, Y5. Park Y2, children Y1.)*

NORTHEAST

QIQIHAR 齐齐哈尔 ☎0452

Like many cities in Heilongjiang province, Qiqihar was a Russian outpost in the early years of the Trans-Siberian Railroad. Unfortunately, Qiqihar boasts none of the graceful Russian architecture that can be found in Harbin. Instead, Qiqihar's engineers seem to have preferred unpaved roads and masses of concrete. If you do go to Qiqihar, it's probably for the city's proximity to the Zhalong Nature Reserve.

TRANSPORTATION

Flights: Qiqihar Airport (qíqíhāěr fēijīchǎng; 齐齐哈尔飞机场; ☎234 6338), 15km from downtown Qiqihar. Taxis to the airport take 20min. (Y20). **CAAC ticket office,** 2 Minhang Dajie, 2nd fl. (booking ☎242 4903), in the Civil Aviation Mansion Hotel on the corner of Bukui Dajie. Open daily 8am-4:30pm. To **Beijing** (M, W, Sa 12:10pm, Y1020) and **Shanghai** (Tu and Th 2:15pm; Y1630).

Trains: Qiqihar Train Station (qíqíhāěr huǒchē zhàn; 齐齐哈尔火车站; ☎212 3111 or 292 9115), on the corner of Zhanqian Dajie and Longhua Lu. Luggage storage in the inconspicuous basement waiting room (up to Y8 per day). Ingenious English signs will entertain you while you wait. To: **Beijing** (21hr., 4 per day, Y81-191); **Changchun** (7hr., 4 per day, Y34-66); **Dalian** (19hr., 2 per day, Y73); **Harbin** (3-6hr., 8 per day, Y40); **Hohhot** (daily, Y74-129); **Manzhouli** (11hr., 2 per day, soft sleeper Y203).

Buses: Qiqihar Long-distance West Bus Station (qíqíhāěr chángtú kèyùn xīzhàn; 齐齐哈尔长途客运西站), on Longhua Lu, at the intersection with Dongxi Daojie, 2 blocks east of Bukui Dajie. Practically impossible for the average traveler to use. If you can make it through the crowd of quick-fingered touts, the ticket office is on the little dirt road to the side of Dongxi Daojie; it has no schedule or set prices. **Minibuses** run to **Zhalong** (1hr., 10am and 2:30pm, Y5); show up early, push through the crowd and keep repeating "Zhalong!" Chances are they'll put you on the right bus. **Qiqihar Long-distance East Bus Station** (qíqíhāěr chángtú kèyùn dōngzhàn; 齐齐哈尔长途客运东站; ☎213 3166) is somewhat more user-friendly. Luggage storage 5:30-11:40am (Y5). To **Wudalianchi** (approx. 6hr., 8:30am, Y37.5). Open daily 5:30am-4:30pm. Neither station has connections to any major cities.

Minivans: To get to **Zhalong,** take local **bus #14** from Bukui Dajie, Longhua Lu, or the train station to **Tie Dong** (铁东), the end of the line. At the big intersection, a number of minivans depart for Zhalong every few minutes. They're fast (20min.), but the price depends on your bargaining skills; don't go above Y20 for a one-way ticket.

Local Transportation: Most buses run 6am-7pm; major streets are covered until 10pm. Fare Y1, minibuses Y0.5. On Longhua Lu and Longsha Lu, all buses except #8 and #12 go from the train station to Longsha Park; hop on either bus to get from one side of town to the other. **Bus #14** is useful in reaching **Zhalong** (see above).

Taxis: Base fare Y6, each additional km Y1.5. Destinations within the city limits up to Y10; one-way to Zhalong approx. Y60.

ORIENTATION AND PRACTICAL INFORMATION

Every visitor in Qiqihar goes to northern **Longsha Lu** (龙沙路) for food and southern **Longhua Lu** (龙华路) for shelter. Both streets run near the train station and are the backbone of Qiqihar's tourism industry; they lead right to the city center, concentrated around **Bukui Dajie** (卜奎大街), and to **Longsha Park** (lóngshā gōngyuán; 龙沙公园). The area between Bukui Dajie and the park is filled with perpetually busy little streets, stuffed with street vendors and travel agencies.

Travel Agencies: Xinsheng Lu and the surrounding area between Longsha Park and Bukui Dajie is dense with travel agencies, all of which organize English and Russian tours to the Zhalong Nature Reserve. **Qiqihar Guangda Travel Company** (qíqíhāěr guāngdà lǚyóu gōngsī; 齐齐哈尔光大旅游公司), on 35 Gongyuan Lu, Jinggu Hotel, Rm. 201, is across from the Xinsheng Lu entrance to Longsha Park.

Bank of China: 3 Bukui Dajie (☎240 9933), near Longhua Lu. Exchanges currency (window #6) and traveler's checks (M-F; window #30). Credit card advances. Open M-F 8am-6pm, Sa-Su 8:30am-6pm.

PSB: On the corner of Bukui Dajie and Longsha Lu. The **Foreign Affairs Office** (wàishì; 外事; ☎248 6227) is on the 2nd fl. Open daily 8-11:30am and 1:30-5pm.

Hospital: No. 1 Hospital (dìyī yīyuǎn; 第一医院; ☎242 5981), on Gongyuanhou Hutong, north of Longsha Park. Staff speaks English, Japanese, and Russian.

Pharmacy: (☎292 0999), on Longhua Lu, 1 block west of the train station. Open daily 5:30am-10pm.

Internet Access: The pink building in the left corner of the train station houses a 24hr. Internet cafe (wǎngbā; 网吧). Y2 per hr. There are also a number of small Internet places on every major street.

Post and Telecommunications: The minuscule **Qiqihar Central Post** (☎242 8601), on the corner of Bukui Dajie and Xinsheng Lu, next to China Mobile. EMS and Poste Restante. To the left is the **China Telecom** building (☎240 3796). All possible telephone services. Both open daily 8am-5pm. **Postal Code:** 161000.

ACCOMMODATIONS

The most expensive hotels are near the train station and along Bukui Dajie; in between, Longhua Lu has the best budget accommodations.

White Crane Hotel (bái hè bīnguǎn; 白鹤宾馆), 25 Zhanqian Dajie (☎292 1112; fax 212 7639), across the street and south of the train station. This two-star hotel is a better-than-two-star value, with on-site sauna, bar, and revolving restaurant. A/C and 24hr. hot water. 5-bed dorms Y28; 4-bed dorms Y35; 3-bed dorms Y38; 2-bed dorms Y50; singles Y88, with bath Y160; doubles with bath Y220. ❶

Junzheng Hostel (jūnzhèng zhāodàisuǒ; 军政招待所), 11 Longhua Lu (☎212 2821), near the train station. Clean, comfortable rooms. 24hr. hot water. 4-bed dorms Y17.5; 3-bed dorms Y19.5; 2-bed dorms Y35; doubles with bath and A/C Y110; suites Y280. ❶

Military District Hostel (jūn fēnqū zhāodàisǔo; 军分区招待所), 2 Longbei Jie (☎241 1027 or 241 1037), near Longhua Lu. Run and mainly frequented by PLA members. Rooms are appropriately spartan and well-kept. 24hr. hot water. 4- and 3-bed dorms Y30; doubles with bath Y78, with A/C and bath Y88. ❶

Batehan Hotel (bātèhàn fàndiàn; 巴特旱饭店; ☎244 4384 or 242 8244), across the street from the Military District Hostel. Similar to the Military District Hostel; they might throw in an extra breakfast here, but hot water is available only 7:30-10pm. 4-bed dorms Y20; 2-bed dorms Y48; doubles with bath Y108 and up. ❶

FOOD

Qiqihar's main food street is **Longsha Lu.** The busiest and best restaurant in town is the **Modern Barbecue Place** ❸ (shídài shāokǎo guǎngchǎng; 时代烧烤广场), between Dongxi Daojie and Junjiao Jie. Each table has its own charcoal stove; don't miss the venison (lù ròu; 鹿肉; Y32) and the excitement of frying it yourself. (Open daily 10am-early morning hours.) Just next door, the **Fat Mutton Hotpot Place** ❸ (féiyáng huǒguō měishí guǎngchǎng; 肺羊火锅美食广场) serves Mongolian hotpot with an impressive array of meats, vegetables, and condiments (Y48). (Open daily 9am-midnight.) Many Chinese and Korean (marked with flags) restaurants are on Longsha Lu and in the area between the park and Bukui Dajie, around Xinsheng Lu. At night the latter area also houses outdoor crustacean extravaganzas.

SIGHTS

For lack of better attractions, visit the Qiqihar train station and its extraordinary collection of English creative writing. Locals like to while away their idle hours in the tree-lined lanes of **Longsha Park** (lóngshā gōngyuán; 龙沙公园), which offers a pleasant retreat from the bustle of the train station and the noise of the city streets. *(Open daily 6am-9pm. Y2.)* The streets east and northeast of the park are filled with markets from morning until night.

ZHALONG NATURE RESERVE (zhālóng zìrán bǎohùqū; 扎龙自然保护区) Established in 1979, this reserve is home to over 200 different bird species with several varieties of rare crane, including the endangered red-crowned and white-naped cranes. During the spring and summer, tens of thousands of birds are said to stop here en route to southern migration areas.

MR. SMITH GOES TO QIQIHAR When the enthusiastic Mr. Smith left for his trip to Qiqihar, he knew that straight-forward communication might be elusive; but compared to his zeal and excitement, the language barrier seemed to be trivial. After all, he thought, most public places have English signs and labels, and as a last resort he could always use a dictionary.

Indeed, in Qiqihar the omnipresent English signs left no room for misunderstanding. Though the Qiqihar station platform greeted him with a somewhat unfriendly *Forbid Vomiting Hlegm*, Mr. Smith's face brightened with pleasure after reading the solicitous *Keep Health*. When he discovered that the first station kiosk he'd wandered into was affably named *Love Style*, his mood improved again, reinforced by the comforting plaque stating that the establishment is a *Civilization Unit of Faith by Customers*. But Mr. Smith had no time to waste: the fortuitously placed inscription *Forbid Lying Seat* reminded him that he must look for shelter. How disappointed was he when the *Inn in Station* turned out to be full! The only place to go was the idyllically christened *Bumper Harvest Hotel* just out of town, but that could only be reached by bus. So, Mr. Smith patiently made his way to the ticket counter, maneuvering between the overflowing *Discard Thing Boxes*. Just when he was about to ask for his ticket at the *Genuine Goods at a Fair Price Satisfied Shop*, the lady at the counter, terrified by Mr. Smith's Caucasian (by inference, illiterate) face, decided this was the time for her lunch break and without a word pointed the stupefied Mr. Smith to the all-explaining piece of paper: *Wait a Jiffy!* Tired and overwhelmed by the journey, our hero left his cumbersome luggage at the *Little Piece Consignation* and indulged in a zip of a soothing liquid, whose origin was *The Factory of the Cold-Drink of the State Operated Hailar.*

Unfortunately, for all but the most seasoned bird-watchers, sightings of airborne species will likely be limited to the dozen or so caged animals, the occasional dragonfly, and maybe a mosquito. The park's two narrow paths encourage more avian than human visitors. A better place is the observation deck (Y1), which offers free binoculars; this is about the only location from which to observe the size and beauty of the reserve's wetlands and birds. Motor boats are available for rent (Y10 per person for a short ride), but engine noise tends to scare the birds away.

The best bird-watching experience is enjoyed in the morning before the first bus from Qiqihar (approx. 11am) arrives or, better yet, at sunrise. In the **hotel ❸** on the reserve grounds, you may be the only visitor. Hot water is not available. The hotel also has a restaurant. (☎245 3031. Triples Y180, with bath Y240, with bath and TV Y280; doubles, triples and quads with A/C Y360.) *(26km southeast of Qiqihar. Buses from Qiqihar to Zhalong leave the West Bus Station at 10am and 2:30pm; buses from Zhalong to Qiqihar depart from the area before the hotel at 8am and 1pm. In both cases, show up early to get a seat. Fare Y5 one-way. Taxis can be hired for Y50 one-way. Admission Y20.)*

WUDALIANCHI 五大连池 ☎0456

Wudalianchi—literally "the five great linked lakes"—was formed nearly three centuries ago after the eruption of a nearby volcano stopped up the Bai River. Today the small town that bears the lake's name is famous for its spring water, believed to have medicinal properties. As a scenic destination Wudalianchi is disappointing; the scenery falls short of childhood images of *Journey To The Center Of The Earth*—the area is flat, the volcanoes small, and the lakes depressingly ordinary.

The only sights worth visiting in Wudalianchi are **Black Dragon Mountain** (hēi lóng shān; 黑龙山; Y30) in the north and **Pulled Drawer Mountain** (gé lā shān; 格拉山; free) and its crater lake **Tianchi** (tiānchí; 天池) in the east. If you do choose to join a tour, make sure that your route includes these two places; don't let your guide take you for an exorbitantly priced meal or charge extra admission at free sites. Always buy your own tickets and don't pay for the tour until you're satisfied with the service. It is generally much easier to visit the sites independently by hiring a motorcycle taxi to each destination (Y25 after bargaining; ignore demands for Y50); this way you'll avoid the formidable task of explaining to the driver that you prefer to skip the **White Dragon Cave** (bái lóng dòng; 白龙洞; Y20) and its fluorescent ice sculptures. Some (read: tourist brochures) call the cave a "gorgeous refuge"; others (read: everyone else) call it a "tourist trap."

Don't expect to know it when you have arrived in Wudalianchi— an uninteresting traffic circle comprises the tourist village in its entirety. **Long-distance buses** depart from the traffic circle or from the adjacent parking lot. Getting to Wudalianchi is easy; getting back is much harder. Buses travel to **Harbin** (5hr., 7:30am, Y69) and **Bei'an** (1½hr.; 6:30, 7:30, 11am, and 3:30pm; Y10.5). Unless you want to endure a six-hour layover in Bei'an before catching the 10pm bus to Harbin, you have to leave Wudalianchi by 11am. Traveling by train also has a catch: the first train to Harbin (1:25am) is more expensive and arrives later than the next train (2:55am).

There is a **first aid center** and **post office** in the village. Two family-run hostels at the main intersection accept foreigners. **Rice Paddy Hotel** ❶ (shǔi hétián jiǔdiàn; 水禾田酒店), next to the general store, has dorms and common baths. (☎722 2837. 2- and 4-bed dorms Y25.) Around the corner, the **Yingbin Hotel** ❶ (yíngbīn lǚdiàn; 迎宾旅店) provides similar facilities but a little less privacy. (☎722 1502; dorm beds Y15 after bargaining.) **Yinchi Du Jia Cun** ❶ (yínchí dùjiăcūn; 银池度假村) near the gate of the monastery near the traffic circle, has particularly attentive staff members, with not-so-attractive starting prices (doubles Y150, with bath Y180); bargain for some of the best values in the village. (☎722 2913. 18-bed dorms Y20; 4-bed dorms Y35; doubles Y150, with bath Y180, with discount Y100.) For comfort-seekers, expensive hotels abound along the main street; doubles with bath (but no hot water) usually cost Y150. Be warned: the bus from Harbin may drop you off at the parking lot of one such overpriced inn.

Cheap eateries are everywhere; the restaurant at the Rice Paddy Hotel is a sure bet. The town specialty is soy sauce tofu (jiàng dòufǔ; 酱豆腐), along with, of course, the town's famous—and rather mysterious—mineral water. Locals will demonstrate to you why the mineral water may not be mixed with green tea; a chemical reaction causes an allegedly poisonous black precipitate to form.

MUDANJIANG 牡丹江 ☎0453

Mudanjiang is a moderately sized city five hours southeast of Harbin. Foreigners rarely visit here; those who do are usually en route to Jingbo Lake or Russia. Happily, the city's transportation is convenient, and there are a few reasonably priced hotels from which to choose. The lively street markets add a dash of flavor to an otherwise bland city.

TRANSPORTATION. The region is an important transportation hub; naturally, transportation options are numerous and varied. Mudanjiang's **airport** (mǔdānjiāng jīchǎng; 牡丹江机场) is 10km south of the city. CAAC airport buses (Y10) leave 1½ hours prior to departure from the **CAAC Ticket Office**, on the corner of Dong Ertiao Lu and Aimin Jie, to: Beijing (1-2 per day, Y950); Shanghai (3 per week, Y1460); Shenyang (2 per week, Y450). (24hr. ticketing ☎693 9627. Open daily 8am-5pm.) The **train station** (mǔdānjiāng huǒchē zhàn; 牡丹江火车站; ☎674 6432 or 674 3442) is at the intersection of Guanghua Lu and Taiping Lu. To: Beijing (22hr., 11:42am, Y79-550); Dalian (21hr., 9:34am, Y65-217); Harbin (4½-7hr., 11 per day, Y21-50).

Also to: Ji'nan (28hr., 10:14am, Y90-600) via Tianjin (23hr.); Shenyang (12¼hr., 4 per day; Y39 and up); Tumen (6hr., 9:26am, Y22).

The **bus station** is the parking lot outside the train station. (Open 5am-6pm.) Frequent minibuses to **Jingbo Lake** (2-4hr.; Y20 one-way, Y30 round-trip) leave from the left parking lot; all other connections depart from the right parking lot to: Harbin (5hr, every 30min., Y54-80); Suifenhe (2hr., every 20min., Y26); Tumen (8hr., 2pm, Y37); Yabuli (2hr., every hr., Y17.5); Yanji (7hr., noon, Y41). **Sleeper buses** travel to **Shenyang** (15hr., 1pm, Y130). **Public buses** run approximately 5am-7pm and span all major streets. (Fare Y1.) **Taxi** base fare is Y5; each additional kilometer is Y1.6. Destinations within the city shouldn't cost more than Y10. **Motorcycle-taxis** (Y2) are more convenient for short distances.

ORIENTATION AND PRACTICAL INFORMATION. Mudanjiang is cut roughly in half by the train tracks. The **train station** is in the center, at the intersection of **Guanghua Lu** (光华路), which runs east-west, and **Taiping Lu** (太平路), which runs north-south. The heart of the commercial district is the pedestrian street **Dong Yitiao Lu** (东一挑路), one block away from and parallel to Taiping Lu.

CITS, 34 Jingfu Lu, between Dong Yitiao Lu and Dong Ertiao Lu, arranges group tours to Jingbo Lake or Changbaishan in Jilin province. (☎695 0061; fax 695 0064. Open daily 8am-5pm.) The **Bank of China,** 9 Taiping Lu, 200m from the train station, exchanges currency and traveler's checks at window #3. (☎667 8005. Open daily 8am-4pm.) The **PSB** is at 96 Guanghua Lu. A 24-hour **pharmacy** is at 108 Dong Yitiao Lu (☎692 0094). At the intersection of Taiping Lu and Pingan Jie is **No. 2 People's Hospital** (dì èr rénmín yīyuàn; 第二人民医院). A 24-hour **Internet cafe** (wǎngbā; 网吧) with fast connections and over 100 computers, is on Pingan Jie, past the hospital. The **post office,** 33 Taiping Lu, has EMS. (Open in summer daily 8am-5:30pm; in winter 8am-5pm.) **Postal code:** 157000.

NORTHEAST

ACCOMMODATIONS AND FOOD. Most cheap, foreigner-friendly hotels are within a 10-minute walk of the train station. The accommodating staff at the **Jinyuan Hotel** ❶ (jīnyuán bīnguǎn; 金园宾馆), 139 Guanghua Jie, offers clean rooms for princes and paupers alike. (☎691 6845 or 692 3236, ext. 8071 or 8888. 2-bed dorms Y30; 3-bed dorms Y25; 4-bed dorms Y20; 5-bed dorms Y15; 6-bed dorms Y12; 8-bed dorms Y10; singles Y100, with A/C from Y140; doubles from Y80; triples Y90.) Across the street, the freshly renovated, two-star **Mudanjiang Hotel** ❷ (mǔdānjiāng fàndiàn; 牡丹江饭店), 85 Guanghua Lu, will soon reopen its doors. (☎692 5631. Doubles Y136.) **Daguan Yuan** ❷ (dàguǎn yuán; 大馆园), 98 Guanghua Jie, just behind the PSB, has comfortable rooms with A/C. (☎693 5068 or 693 5098. Doubles Y128; triples Y188.)

Many small restaurants line the side streets off Taiping Lu and Guanghua Lu; most department stores along Taiping Lu and Dong Yitiao Lu also have food halls. Night markets in this area offer the possibility of open-air meals in the summer. The **Golden Chopsticks Big Filling Dumpling Restaurant** ❷ (jīn kuaìzi dàxiàn jiǎozi cūn; 金筷子大馅饺子村), 5 Shizheng Lu (☎628 9561), cooks up tasty *xiānglà tǔdòutiáo* ("Delicious Spicy Potato"; 香辣土豆条; Y16) and delicious dumplings.

YABULI 亚布力

If you want to ski in China, you want to ski at **Yabuli.** In the summer, Yabuli is just another sleepy resort town, but in the winter it comes alive, attracting skiers from all over China. The infrastructure is somewhat less developed than it could be given that Yabuli hosted the 1996 Asian Winter Games, but it's about as good as skiing gets in China.

The skiing grounds (admission Y10) are located up the village road. Ski-lifts ascend 500m; a one-day pass costs Y200 and up. A **luge facility** is up the little road to the right. Speeding down **the longest tobogganing lane in the world** can quench anyone's thirst for adventure. (One chair-lift plus luge-ride package Y100.) Ski rentals, available in hotels, cost Y100-200, depending on the season.

Arriving in Yabuli via public transportation is far from easy. **Buses** and **trains** departing for Yabuli from Harbin and from Mudanjiang drop off flabbergasted skiers in the small town, whose location on the flattest plains ever can be puzzling to downhill skiers. From there, a taxi ride (20km, Y30) brings visitors to the real skiing area, where posh hotels line both sides of the road. The accommodations are ridiculously expensive in the winter. Budget travelers often elect to make Yabuli a daytrip from Mudanjiang. To return, take a taxi to Yabuli town and then catch a train or bus. After 4:30pm, however, transportation is more difficult to find; ask to be driven to the Harbin-Mudanjiang highway instead (15km, Y25) and hunt for passing buses (last bus passes approx. 8:30pm.)

In the summer, Yabuli is desolate and cheap; in the winter hotel prices are sky-high. Those who opt to spend the night can try the **Senfang Mountain Villa ❷** (sēnfáng shānzhuāng; 森防山庄; ☎(0139) 4512 4373), the only affordable place in town. (Dorms don't exceed Y200; in the off-season Y20.)

JINGBO LAKE 镜泊河 ☎0453

Jingbo, or "Mirror" Lake, south of Mudanjiang, was formed by volcanic explosions near the Mudan River over 5000 years ago. While the lake and the surrounding scenery has its natural splendor, a visit today is likely to be dampened by swarms of motorboats and tourists. Cold weather makes Jingbo inaccessible for much of the year. Tourists are rare and prices are low in the summer; counterintuitively, many of the lake's attractions are open only during these warm months.

ORIENTATION AND PRACTICAL INFORMATION. The historic entrance to Jingbo Lake has been recently replaced by a more modern (read: Y20-admission-charging) front gate. From there, a 4km road leads to a rotary with well-placed signs in Chinese and English directing the traffic. The main tourist access point, with parking lots, a beach, and a dock, is **Jingbo Village,** 2.6km past the roundabout, marked by signs reading **"Villa."** The village has a **first aid center** and a **post office.** (Open daily 8:30am-5:30pm.) **Postal code:** 157438. A **waterfall** is north of the village, 1.2km up a road from the traffic circle; sporadic minibuses connect the waterfall with the village (Y5-10).

The most convenient way to reach Jingbo Lake is to take one of the frequent minibuses that depart from the square in front of the **Mudanjiang train station** (round-trip Y30; one-way Y20). Otherwise, you'll need to travel by train through the town of **Dongjing,** either from Mudanjiang (2hr., 2 per day, Y4) or Dunhua (3hr., daily, Y6). A **bus** also makes the trip from Dunhua to Dongjing (3hr., many per day, Y19). Frequent **minibuses** go from Dongjing train station to Jingbo Lake village (45min., Y7; ask to go to the Villa or else you'll be dropped off at the front gate.)

ACCOMMODATIONS AND FOOD. Many hotels do not open until June 1, so if you're visiting in the off-season, call in advance. Prices are significantly lower in May and June than they are later in the summer. The best places at which to crash are the **Harbin Industrial University Dorms ❶** (hāgōng dàdìyī tǐyǎngsuǒ; 哈工大第一体养所; and hāgōng dàdièr zhǎodàisuǒ; 哈工大第二招待所), two minutes up the road from the docks. Here you can trade stories with fellow Chinese students in English and Chinese. No matter how many guests they have, they'll always find you a bed. (☎627 0015 and 627 0039, respectively. Individual beds

Y50.) A slightly more upscale (and less sociable) alternative is the **Shanzhuang Hotel** ❷ (shānzhuāng bīnguǎn; 山庄宾馆), near the lake, past the post office. (☎627 0012. Open May-Sept. Doubles Y100-120, triples Y150-200; in July and Aug. doubles Y200, triples Y300.) For food, the best options are at hotel restaurants.

SIGHTS. Although most tourist facilities and beaches are in Jingbo Village, on the northeastern shore of the lake, the tourist attractions are scattered all over the lake's shore. To see the **Solitary Mountains** (gūshān; 孤山), **White Precipice** (bái shílòuzi; 白石落子), and **Pearl Gate** (zhēnzhū mén; 珍珠门), take a two-hour boat ride (Y30; Y50 for two people; longer, more expensive tours also available). The tours are easiest to organize in the morning, when the busloads of tourists arrive from Mudanjiang.

Infrequent minibuses run from the village to the **Diaoshuilou Waterfall** (diàoshuǐlóu pùbù; 掉水楼瀑布), formed from a volcanic eruption about 10,000 years ago. In mid-summer, water from the river cascades over the lava rock and into the 60m-deep crater left by the eruption. From the top of a hill facing the waterfall, visitors can take a cable car to a **Korean minority village** (20min., Y30).

Those who don't take the minibus to Jingbo Lake directly from Mudanjiang might see some attractions on the way to the village. Y5-10 will buy you a 4km motorcycle ride from Dongjing to the ruins of the 7th- to 10th-century capital of the Bohai Kingdom, **Shangjing.** Today, little remains of the city that was once the most powerful in Asia; instead, see the archaeologists in action and the fruit of their work in the adjacent museum. Thirty kilometers farther along the road, the lake, about 15km before the village, is Heilongjiang's own **Underground Forest** (dìxià sēnlín; 地下森林), a wild garden located in a volcanic dip. The road to the forest branches right off the road from Dongjing to Jingbo, and is clearly marked—in Chinese. Transportation is difficult to arrange if you're not willing to pay the Y75 taxi fare from Dongjing or join a tumultous and overpriced CITS tour from Mudanjiang. If you're approaching Jingbo Lake from the south, stop at Dunhua and hop in a taxi (Y10) to Asia's second largest Buddhist temple, **Six-Peak Mountain Zhengjue Temple** (liù dǐng shān zhèngjuě sì; 六顶山正觉寺; Y10).

NORTHEAST

SUIFENHE 绥芬河 ☎0453

Traveling into Siberia from the Middle Kingdom can be quite a culture shock. Fifty years ago, when Mao and Stalin defined the Sino-Soviet borders, they unwittingly charged the task of cushioning the impact of cross-cultural travel to Suifenhe. The city's Russian-only nightclubs are incontestible proof that the town takes its responsibility very seriously. If you're off to Russia, or just curious about its culture, spend some time in Suifenhe to taste its culture beforehand.

TRANSPORTATION. The **train station** (huǒchē zhàn; 火车站) on Zhanqian Lu, down Wenhua Jie from Central Square, has domestic departures to Harbin (11hr., 8:06pm, Y32 and up) and Qiqihar (16hr., 3:43pm, Y64-131), both via Mudanjiang (4hr., Y13), and international departures to Vladivostok (8:50am and 12:10pm; for ticket and passport control show up at least 1½hr. before departure). Ticket booths are open 7:30am-8pm; international tickets may be easier to buy at the **Railway Travel Agency** (tiědào lǚxíngshè; 铁道旅行社; ☎392 8429 or 395 9990) across the street. The **bus station** (kèyùn zhàn; 客运站), at the intersection of Tongtian Lu and Xinxing Jie, 10 minutes from Central Square, has buses to Yanji (10hr., 4:40am, Y55) and Harbin (6hr., 9:10am, Y120). **Minibuses** go to Mudanjiang (2hr., at least every 20min. 6am-6pm, Y26); **sleeper buses** to Harbin (17hr., 8:30pm, Y70) depart from the square in front of the train station. **Local buses** (6am-7pm; Y1) all go to or from the train station. **Taxi** base fare is Y5, each additional kilometer Y1.6; many are unmetered. Destinations within town should cost about Y5.

ORIENTATION AND PRACTICAL INFORMATION. Central Square (zhōngxīn guǎngchǎng; 中心广场) is at the intersection of Tongtian Lu and Wenhua Jie, which runs to the train station. In the north, separated from the city center by the Harbin-Vladivostok highway, is the Temple of Light (guāngmíng sì; 光明寺), a conspicuous landmark that can help travelers get their bearings. (Admission Y5.) The **Bank of China,** 41 Shancheng Lu (parallel to Tongtian Lu, near Central Square), is open in summer M-F 8-11:30am and 1:30-5pm; in winter 1-4:30pm. The **PSB** is at 22 Guanghua Lu, 200m from Wenhua Jie. In the western wall of Central Square is a **pharmacy** (☎392 9867). Xinxing Jie, the big street at the end of Tongtian Lu, near the bus station, has a large and useful **supermarket.** (Open daily 8:30am-9pm.) Just opposite is a 24hr. **Internet cafe.** (Y3 per hr.) The post office is at 25 Yinxing Jie, a block away from Wenhua Jie and Central Square. (☎392 2103. Open M-F 7:30am-5:30pm.) Postal code: 157300.

ACCOMMODATIONS AND FOOD. Russian food is an integral part of the true Suifenhe bicultural experience; sadly enough, however, the majority of the local Russian establishments fall short of expectations. A brilliant exception to Suifenhe's gastronomic drabness is **Sevan ❶** (Севан), at the end of Xinrong Jie, 2-3 minutes from the intersection of Shancheng Jie and Tongtian Lu. Pleasant Russian waitresses and vibrant Russian music testify to the establishment's authenticity. The experience is further enlivened by the delicious Armenian cuisine, embellished by Russian appetizers. Don't miss the red-beet borscht (борщ, Y5) and Armenian goat cheese (армянский сыр, Y6). (☎392 1084. Open daily 8am-midnight.) For a more raucous culinary experience, go to **Restoran Wanda** (Ванда), a block down Tongtian Jie from Central Square. The establishment is the most easy to find (head for the noise) and most exclusive (filled with apoplectic caucasians) in town.

NORTHEAST

JILIN 吉林

Much like its northern neighbor Heilongjiang, Jilin province is an ambiguous blend of industrial banality and scenic beauty. Formerly known as Kirin, the area was once the home of the Hurka tribe, steppe- and forest-dwellers who sent fur and ginseng as tribute to the Ming court. The Manchus conquered the region in the late 16th century, and Han Chinese began settling here in the 18th. These days, the sooty cities of Jilin and Changchun can be haunting or dreary, depending on how good your vision is. The stunning mountain scenery of Changbaishan, however, justifiably attracts scores of tourists, and ethnic Korean villages along the North Korean border help to break up Jilin's cultural monotony.

CHANGCHUN 长春 ☎0431

Changchun literally means "eternal spring" and, although springtime here is indeed lush and green, this designation seems to ignore the reality of the region's frigid winters. The capital of Jilin province is nonetheless an unexpected mixture of greenery and urbanity. During the Japanese occupation from 1931 to 1945, Changchun was the capital of the Japanese-ruled state of Manchukuo; today the somewhat neglected palace from which the puppet emperor Pu Yi ruled the region is the city's biggest claim to tourist fame. Changchun may lack dazzling must-see sights, but its streets are great for travelers seeking a Chinese city undisturbed by

Western influences, as Changchun surges instead toward China's own unique brand of hyper-modernity.

TRANSPORTATION

Flights: Changchun Airport (chángchūn jīchǎng; 长春机场), 28 Luyuan Chuyingbin Lu (☎869 0215), west of the city. Bus #364 connects the airport with Renmin Guangchang; a taxi to the airport costs Y20-25. **CAAC ticket office,** 23-1 Changbai Lu, 2nd fl. (☎298 8888), between the train station and the Post Hotel. Open daily 8am-4:30pm. To: **Beijing** (6-9 per day, Y880); **Chengdu** (3 per week, Y1780); **Dalian** (1-3 per day, Y520); **Fuzhou** (3 per week, Y1600); **Guangzhou** (1-3 per day, Y2100); **Nanjing** (1-2 per day, Y1320); **Qingdao** (1-2 per day, Y730); **Shanghai** (2-4 per day, Y1280); **Yantai** (2 per week, Y730).

Trains: Changchun Train Station (chángchūn huǒchēzhàn; 长春火车站; ☎282 4022), at the north end of Renmin Dajie. 24hr. luggage storage (Y5). To: **Beijing** (11-14hr., 8 per day, Y83-165); **Dalian** (11hr., 5 per day, Y61-121); **Dandong** (8-10hr., 2 per day, Y71); **Harbin** (3-4hr., 11 per day, Y25-75); **Jilin** (2-4hr., 6 per day, Y9-53); **Shanghai** (29hr., 2 per day, Y158-312); **Shenyang** (4hr., 3-4 per day, Y29-75); **Tonghua** (9hr., daily, Y21-48); **Tumen** (10-11hr., 3 per day, Y32-43).

Buses: Changchun Central Bus Station (chángchūn gōnglù kèyùn zhōngxīn zhàn; 长春公路客运中心站), 6 Renmin Dajie (☎279 2544), a block from the train station, on the left. To: **Beijing** (3pm, Y180); **Dalian** (8hr., 5 per day, Y157); **Erdaobaihe** (3hr., 6am, Y52); **Harbin** (4hr., every 30min. 5:30am-5pm, Y40); **Jilin** (2hr., every 10min. 5:10am-6pm, Y14); **Shenyang** (4hr., 5 per day, Y35); **Yanji** (10hr., 7:30am, Y85).

Local Transportation: The frequent local **buses** ply every street of the city 6am-10pm; some lines only go until 6pm. Lines numbered below 100 tend to stay on the larger roads, while the 200s and 300s cover obscure neighborhoods and dirt roads. Fare Y1. Useful lines include **#6** spanning Renmin Dajie and **#25** and **62** (via Tongzhi Jie) going from the train station to South Lake Park.

Taxis: Base fare Y5; each additional km Y1.3. Most destinations Y7-16.

ORIENTATION AND PRACTICAL INFORMATION

Changchun is a sprawling city blessed with wide streets and lots of open space. The main street, **Renmin Dajie** (人民大街), bisects the city from the train station and through **People's Square** (rénmín guǎngchǎng; 人民广场). Most major streets are arranged on a grid around Renmin Dajie, with a few thoroughfares extending radially from People's Square. All in all, the center is easy to navigate; the highly visible shapes of the skyscrapers serve as helpful landmarks.

Travel Agency: CITS, Yinmao Bldg. (the biggest building around), 14 Xinmin Lu, 7th fl. For English tours, contact Zhan Xin Sheng (☎560 9039; fax 564 5069; citsjlp@public.cc.jl.cn). Open M-F 8:30-11:30am and 1:30-5pm. **Air ticket office** (☎560 9076) on the 1st fl. Open M-F 8:30-11am and 1:30-4:30pm.

Bank of China: Yinmao Bldg., 14 Xinmin Lu, 1st fl. Exchanges currency and traveler's checks (window #8). Credit card advances (windows #2 and 3). Open M-F 8:30-11:30am and 1:30-4:30pm.

Bookstore: Foreign Language Bookstore, 44 Tongzhi Jie (☎567 5854), at Huimin Lu. Open daily in summer 8:40am-8:30pm; in winter 9am-5pm. **Learner's Bookstore,** 126 Renmin Dajie (☎566 2793), near Ziyou Square, has an large collection of bilingual books. Open daily 10am-6pm.

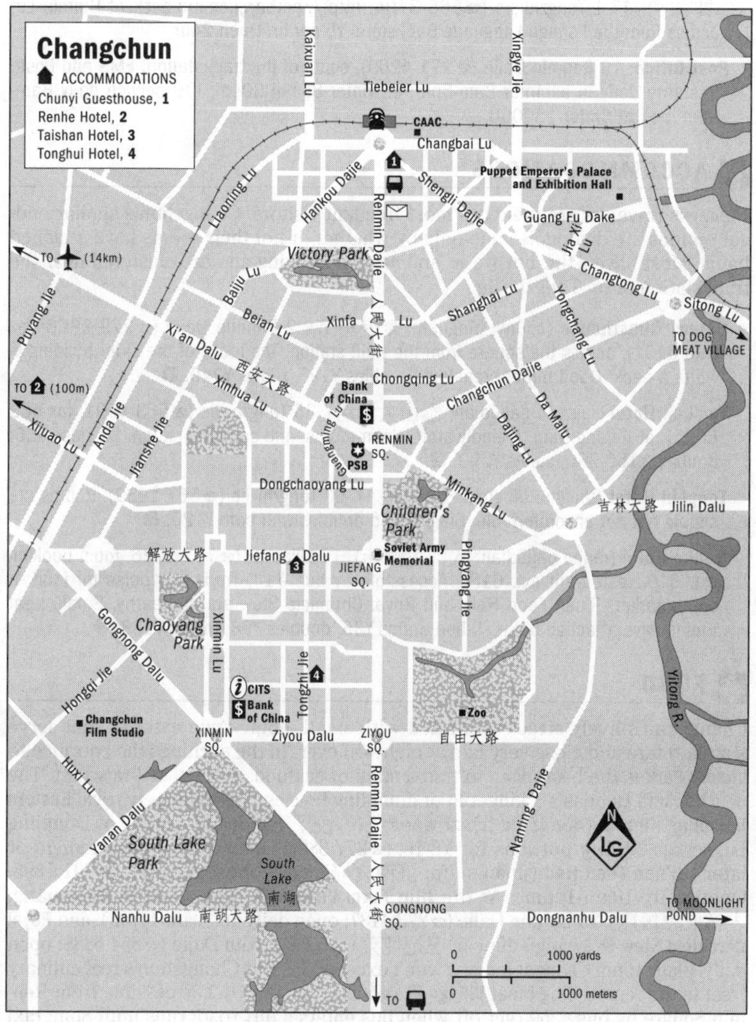

PSB: A large station occupies the area in the southwest corner of Renmin Square. An impressive exhibition in the square illustrates the PSB's success in tracing and handling public enemies. Visa extensions processed at the branch on Guangming Lu (☎898 2107). Open M-F 8:30am-5pm.

Hospital: Changchun Central Hospital (chángchūnshì zhōngxīn yīyuàn; 长春市中心医院), 64 Renmin Dajie. 24hr. pharmacy.

Internet Access: Worker's Cultural Palace Internet Cafe (wǎngbā; 网吧), 74 Renmin Dajie, 3rd fl. (☎891 3369). Over 40 computers. Y2 per hr. Open daily 8am-10pm. **Earth Village Internet and Coffee Bar** (dìqiú cūn wǎngluò kāfēi tīng; 地球村网络

咖啡厅), 47-1 Tongzhi Jie (☎565 3704; http://netbar.jl.cninfo.net), at Huimin Lu, across from the Foreign Language Bookstore. Y5 per hr. Open 24hr.

Post Office: 18 Renmin Dajie (☎271 4269), south of the train station. EMS and Poste Restante daily in summer 8am-5pm; in winter 8am-4:30pm; IDD service daily 8am-9pm. **Postal Code:** 130000.

ACCOMMODATIONS

Business travelers are the city's most frequent visitors. Changchun's similar budget options are distinguishable only by whether or not their rooms have attached baths. Most have 24hr. hot water and air-conditioning and are clustered near the train station or on Tongzhi Jie.

Chunyi Guesthouse (chūnyì bīnguǎn; 春谊宾馆), 2 Renmin Dajie (☎279 9966; fax 896 0171), across the square from the train station. The lobby of the older building is worth a peek. Good buffet breakfast. Doubles Y198; triples Y240. ❸

Taishan Hotel (tàishān dàjiǔdiàn; 泰山大酒店), 35 Tongzhi Jie (☎563 4991; fax 563 6025), at Jiefang Dalu. Friendly staff, clean rooms, and superb location. Singles Y150; doubles Y150-260; suites Y290. ❷

Tonghui Hotel (tōnghùi bīnguǎn; 通汇宾馆), 60 Tongzhi Jie (☎567 1939). Rooms are simple but not uncomfortable. Singles and doubles with bath Y120. ❷

Renhe Hotel (rénhé dàjiǔdiàn; 人河大酒店), 17 Xijiao Lu (☎792 5226, room booking ext. 619, restaurant ext. 618). Accessible by bus #14. Trade city noise for food: a supermarket, Ji'nan Food Hall, and Royal Chronicle Stew are all nearby. Small, neat rooms have attached baths. 5-bed dorms Y36; doubles Y98; triples Y138. ❶

NORTHEAST

FOOD

Changchun's lively streets are filled with small, home-style eateries that serve standard fare and close very late at night—if ever. In the evenings the entrance to **Victory Park** is the best place to find a stick of seafood, sweets, or bratwurst. The nearby **Xinfa Lu** boasts a kingdom of dumpling houses. The genuinely royal **Eastern Dumpling King** ❶ (dōngfāng jiǎozi wáng; 东方饺子王), on the corner of Dongjing Lu, serves 2-*liǎng* portions for Y8-16. (☎277 8896. Open daily 10am-midnight or later.) **Ji'nan Food Hall** (jìnǎn shífǔ; 济南食府), on 1 Chengyang Lu. (☎891 7898. Open daily 10am-10pm). At the **Jilin Farm Village** ❸ (jílín nóngjiā fànzhuāng; 吉林农家饭庄), 23 Beijing Dajie (☎273 4137; open daily 10:30am-11pm), and **Royal Chronicle Stew** ❸ (wángjì dùncài; 王记炖菜), 17 Xi Minzhu Dajie (☎854 6888; open daily 10am-10pm), a meal for two won't exceed Y50. But Changchun's real culinary treat is the remote **Dog Meat Village** ❷ (gǒuròu tún; 狗肉屯), accessible from Renmin Square by bus #259 (get off when bus enters a dirt road; runs until 8pm; taxi ride costs a fixed Y15). A savory meal including a soup with a distinctly canine look and smell should cost Y30. Mmm...puppies. **Datong River Dog Meat Restaurant** (dàtóng jiāng gǒuròu guǎn; 大同江狗肉馆; ☎464 5804) is said to be the best, but dozens of neighboring establishments are equally fido-licious.

SIGHTS

Changchun's main attraction is its streets and people, and the best places to people-watch are Changchun's parks. Full of busy metropolitan denizens seeking a place to relax, **Victory Park** (shènglì gōngyuán; 胜利公园) offers a taste of China's city-life, culinary and otherwise. *(Open daily sunrise-late night. Y3; after dusk free.)* The remote **Moonlight Pond Recreation Area** offers a more bucolic alternative. *(Take bus #102 from San Malu near Renmin Square.)*

PUPPET EMPEROR'S PALACE (wěi huánggōng; 伪皇宫). After the Japanese invaded Manchuria in 1931, they installed Henry Pu Yi, the last Qing emperor, as puppet emperor of the new state of Manchukuo. Bernardo Bertolucci's film *The Last Emperor* was filmed here; do not, however, mistake the palace for another Chinese-miniseries-set-turned-tourist attraction. The palace consists of the inner court (the private residence of the emperor and his family) and the outer court (where public affairs and ceremonies were handled). The ironically named **Mansion of Serving the Populace,** where Pu Yi signed treaties that cemented Japanese control over northern China, and **Pavilion of Joint Virtue,** where the "last concubine" Li Yuqing lived, have both been restored. Visitors expecting the opulence of the film may be disappointed, but it's enjoyable all the same. *(In the northeastern part of the city, close to the train station. Bus #268 stops at nearby Guangsha Lu; from here, go down a long dirt road. The palace is nearly impossible to find, however; take a taxi (Y5). Open daily in summer 8:30am-5pm; in winter 8:40am-4:30pm. Last admission 40min. before closing. Inner court Y20; outer court Y20.)*

CHANGCHUN FILM STUDIO (chángchūn diànyǐng zhìpiān chǎng; 长春电影制片厂). It would be unfair (and depressing) to call this studio the Hollywood of China. The crumbling remains of what is known as the cradle of the Chinese film industry are the source of much local pride, but the glamor seems to be long gone. Nevertheless, fans of *The Last Emperor* may shiver with excitement to think that it all began right here. The tour and all captions are in Chinese only. *(28 Huxi Lu, west of South Lake Park. Take bus #13 from People's Square or catch #120 on the nearby streets. ☎594 8427. Open daily 8am-4:30pm. Y20; movie show in Chinese Y10.)*

NORTHEAST

JILIN CITY 吉林市 ☎0432

Jilin's name means "lucky forest," an ironic misnomer for this industrial monster that seems to despise the color green. Even Jilin's trees are considered to be most impressive during the winter, when their branches are bedecked with dignified "ice-rims," the product of evaporation from nearby hydroelectric plants. Still, surrounding mountains liven up the horizon, and a few sights provide more intimate respites from the expansive avenues of the city.

TRANSPORTATION

Flights: Gudianzi Airport (gūdiànzi jīchǎng; 孤甸子机场; ☎306 7450), in the city's western outskirts, a Y30 taxi ride from the city center. Free shuttle buses leave 2hr. before departures from the **CAAC ticket office,** Dongmei Hotel, 199 Tianjin Jie, 2nd fl. (☎254 3638). Open M-Sa 8am-4:30pm, Su 9am-2pm. To: **Beijing** (daily, Y870); **Guangzhou** (2 per week, Y2090); **Shanghai** (2 per week, Y1320).

Trains: Jilin Train Station (jílín zhàn; 吉林站; ☎292 1222), at the end of Zhongkang Lu. To: **Beijing** (15-19hr., 2 per day, Y75-262); **Changchun** (2-4hr., 8 per day, Y9-26); **Dalian** (14½hr., 2 per day, Y56-174); **Harbin** (5½-7hr., 2 per day, Y20-170); **Shenyang** (6-9hr., 8 per day, Y31-115); **Tianjin** (18hr., 2:38pm, Y72-269); **Tumen** (8-12hr., 7 per day, Y30-115) via **Yanji.**

Buses: Main Passenger Bus Station (kèyùn zǒngzhàn; 客运总站; ☎255 5401), on Zhongkang Lu near Tianjin Jie, 5min. from the train station. To: **Dalian** (8½hr., 8:30am,

Y135); **Harbin** (5-6hr., 7 per day, Y31); **Shenyang** (4½hr., 8 per day, Y95). **Linjiang Long-distance Bus Station** (línjiáng chángtú qìchē zhàn; 临江长途汽车站; ☎484 0121), on Xi'an Lu, between Jiefang Dalu and Songjiang Lu. To: **Changchun** (1½hr., 7 per day, Y30). Sleeper buses (☎139 0444 6898) leave for **Dalian** from the square next to the train station (12hr.; 6pm; Y100, seats Y60).

Local Transportation: Most **buses** run from early morning until after 8pm, and many terminate at the Jilin Train Station. Fare Y1. Buses **#7** and **107** go to Beishan Park; **#8** and **#101** run between the train and the Linjiang bus stations; **#103** runs from the train station down Jilin Dajie; **#13** runs along Tianjin Jie between the train station and the riverfront; **#49** goes from Songjiang Lu to the terminus at Longtan Shan Park.

Taxis: Base fare Y5, each additional km Y1.2-1.8. Train station to Songjiang Lu Y5-10.

ORIENTATION AND PRACTICAL INFORMATION

Jilin's major streets run along the **Songhua River** (松花江); most of the city streets fan out from the river. **Songjiang Lu** (松江路) winds along the northwestern bank of the river bend. The main artery, **Jilin Dajie** (吉林大街), runs north-south, while **Jiefang Lu** connects the city's western and eastern neighborhoods.

Travel Agency: CITS, 3 Wenmiao Lu (☎244 3451; fax 245 3773 or 245 9204), around the corner from the Jiangcheng Hotel, next to the Confucian Temple. Organizes 3-day trips to Changbaishan's Southern Pass by train via Yanji (Y460 per person) and by bus (Y700 per person). Open M-F 8:30am-4:30pm.

Bank of China: 1 Shenchun Jie (☎467 0277), across the Linjiangmen Bridge, near the Linjiang bus station. Exchanges traveler's checks (window #5). Credit card advances (window #3). Open M-F 8:30am-4pm, Sa-Su 9am-3pm.

PSB: At the intersection of Beijing Lu and Nanjing Lu. Foreign affairs department (☎240 9323) open M-F 8:30am-5pm.

Hospitals: Jilin's largest hospital is at 4 Nanjing Jie (☎245 6181; fax 244 0643).

Internet Access: China Telecom Internet Bar (☎249 2757), at the intersection of Chongqing Jie and Jiefang Lu. Take bus #3. Y2 per hr. Open daily 8:30am-9:30pm.

Post Office: China Post (☎245 4883), on Hunchun Jie at Henan Jie. EMS and IDD service. Open daily 8:30am-5pm. **Postal Code:** 132000.

NORTHEAST

ACCOMMODATIONS

Jilin suffers from the chronic northeastern lack of budget accommodation; even the hotels near the train station are pricey.

Tourism Hotel (lǚyóu bīnguǎn; 旅游宾馆), 88 Chaoyang Jie (☎248 2087), overlooking Cultural Square. The best location in Jilin, within walking distance from Henan Jie, Jilin Dajie, and Jiefang Lu. Doubles Y140, with A/C Y160; triples with A/C Y200. ❷

Jilin Changlin Hotel (jílín chǎnglín bīnguǎn; 吉林常林宾馆), 218 Tianjin Jie (☎255 7780), near the train station. Not only do you get a clean room, but you also get to make a spectacle of yourself in the public showers. Leave your modesty at the door. 2-bed dorms Y60; 3- and 5-bed dorms Y40; doubles with bath Y160. ❶

Angel Hotel (tiānshǐ bīnguǎn; 天使宾馆), 2 Nanjing Jie (☎248 1848; fax 248 0323), just north of the Catholic Church. Sparkling carpets, comfortable beds, and an elegant atmosphere. Tea house in the lobby. Doubles Y228; triples Y248. ❸

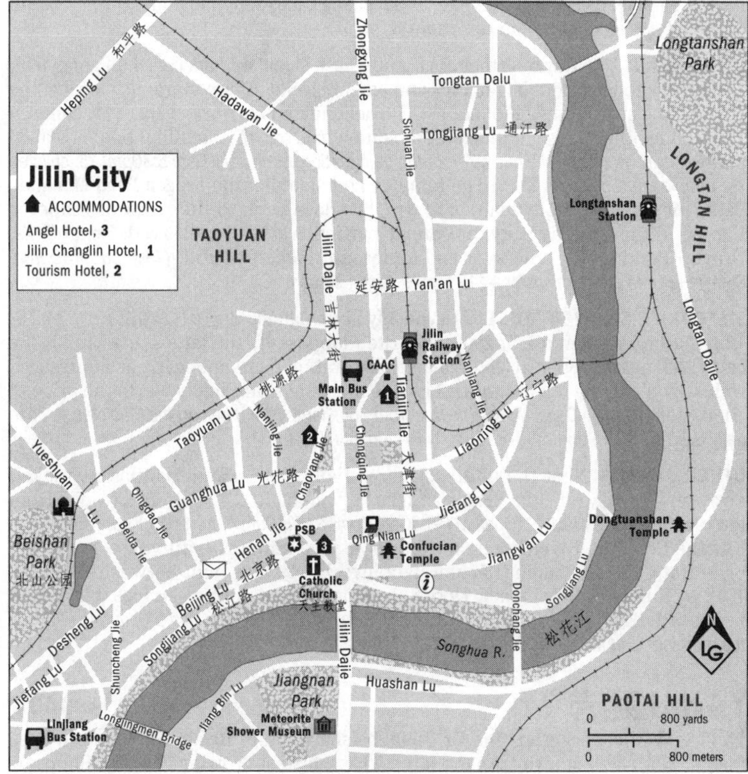

FOOD

At night, **Jiefang Lu** bathes itself in neon light and prepares for food and fun. The pedestrian street, **Henan Jie,** features everything from bakeries to dumpling houses to Sichuanese restaurants. **Chongqing Jie** is closed off to automobile traffic, and local hotpot restaurants abound north of Shanghai Lu. Tea houses cluster around **Tianjin Jie,** and fresh fruit vendors line **Qingnian Lu,** which connects Tianjin Jie and Jilin Dajie in the temple area. **Mingmen Restaurant** ❷ (míngmén fàndiàn; 名门饭店), 19 Jiefang Dajie, between Tianjin Jie and Jilin Dajie, has sophisticated entrees (Y15 and up) and an impressive view. (☎203 8888. Open daily 5:30am-10pm.)

SIGHTS

Jilin City shines most in the winter, sub-zero temperatures notwithstanding. Thanks to the manipulations of hydroelectric power companies, the Songhua River does not freeze; instead, it perspires ice-rimmed drops of sweat In the summer, there are plenty of opportunities to get out of town for a pleasant day-hike. In the winter, the **Zhuque Shan Forest Park** (zhūquèshān sēnlín gōngyuán;

朱雀山森林公园) is a treat for skiers. **Songjiang Lake** (sōngjiāng hú; 松江湖), south of the city, is also a popular destination.

CITY PARKS. The few hills that constitute **North Mountain Park** (beǐshān gōngyuán; 北山公园) house Buddhist temples and pavilions and offer panoramic views of the city and the surrounding mountains. The delapidated **Children's Park** (Y15, children Y10) sullies the spiritual atmosphere somewhat, but the paddling boats (Y20-30 per hr.) can be fun. *(Take bus #7 from the train station. Open daily 6am-5:30pm. Y5, children Y3; temples and pavilions Y1-2.)* The temples and sights of the **Dragon Pond Mountain Park** (lóngtánshān gōngyuán; 龙潭山公园) date back to the reign of Emperor Kangxi in the Qing dynasty, but aren't particularly well-preserved. Regardless, Dragon Pond is a serene spot and a pleasant place to stroll. *(Take bus #49 from Songjiang Lu to the terminus or #112 from the train station; Y2.)*

METEORITE SHOWER MUSEUM (yǔnshíyǔ bówùguǎn; 陨石雨博物馆). In 1976, Jilin got lucky when a 1.77 ton meteorite (supposedly the largest ever to hit the earth) fell nearby. Special "intergalactic decorations" are not nearly as impressive. Unless you're a big fan of large rocks, the museum is not really worth the price of admission. *(On Jilin Dajie, across the river from Songjiang Jie and behind the Mao statue. Open daily 8:30-11:30am and 1:30-4:30pm. Y40, students Y15.)*

OTHER SIGHTS. Near the intersection of Jiangwan Lu and Tianjin Jie, tucked away on Wenmiao Jie, the **Confucian Temple** (wénmiào; 文庙) offers a respite from ferro-concrete urbanity. *(Open M-F 8:30am-4pm, Sa-Su 9am-4pm. Y10.)* From here, follow the Songhua River upstream for about five minutes until you come to the beautiful **Catholic Church** (tiānzhǔ jiàotáng; 天主教堂), built between 1906 and 1912 by a French missionary. Doors are mostly open during services, but a kind nun is willing to provide a private tour. *(Services Sa-Su 8-9am and 5-6pm; also open in the mornings and for confession before each service.)*

YANJI 延吉 ☎0433

Yanji is the best access point for Changbaishan Nature Reserve's Southern Pass (see p. 228), 300km away. As the largest (and fastest growing) city in Jilin province's Korean minority region, it is an interesting cultural crossroads, teeming with bilingual residents and signs. Beyond this, Yanji offers little more than cheap, comfortable accommodations.

TRANSPORTATION

Flights: Yanji Airport (yánjí fēijīchǎng; 延吉飞机场), 10min. west of the city center. The **CAAC ticket office,** 62 Gongyuan Lu (☎271 5118), in the lobby of the Civil Aviation Mansion, is open M-F 8am-10pm. To: **Beijing** (1-2 per day, Y1040); **Changchun** (daily, Y430); **Dalian** (5 per week, Y880); **Shenyang** (5 per week, Y590).

Trains: Yanji Train Station (yánjí huǒchēzhàn; 延吉火车站; ☎221 2620), at the southern end of Zhanqian Jie, south of the rivers. Ticket booths open daily 4:30am-10:40pm. To: **Beijing** (25hr., 11:25am, Y80-588) via **Tianjin; Changchun** (9-10hr., 2 per day, Y29-220); **Dalian** (21hr., 6:05pm, Y76-275); **Harbin** (12hr., 7:40pm, Y36-170); **Jilin** (7-10hr., 5 per day, Y22-114); **Shenyang** (14hr., 3 per day, Y45-254); **Tumen** (1½hr., many per day, Y3).

Buses: Long-distance Bus Station (kěyùn zǒng zhàn; 客运总站) is the central bus station in Yanji. Buses labeled Tianchi (天池) go to **Changbaishan** (5hr.; 5:30am departure, 4pm return; round-trip Y101). Taxi drivers offer similar packages (Y105).

Minibuses to **Dunhua, Tumen** (1¼hr., 10 per day, Y8-10), and other cities; sleepers to **Changchun** (11-12hr., 5pm, Y85), **Harbin** (12-13hr., 4pm, Y96), and **Shenyang** (14-15hr., 2pm, Y120) depart from the square in front of the train station.

Local Transportation: Buses run 6am-7pm. Fare Y1. Buses **#2, 3, 4,** and **5** run between the train station and the long-distance bus station; **#3** travels along Guangming Jie; **#35** runs along Zhanqian Jie between the train station and the CAAC and CITS offices. Most **taxis** do not use meters; base fare Y5.

ORIENTATION AND PRACTICAL INFORMATION

Yanji sprawls on both sides of the **Yanji** (延吉) and **Buerhatong Rivers** (布尔哈通河). The commercial center of the city is at the intersection of **Renmin Dajie** (人民大街) and **Guangming Jie** (光明街), northeast of the rivers. The train and long-distance bus stations are across the **Yanji Bridge** (延吉桥) from the city center.

Travel Agency: CITS, 4 Yanxi Jie, 6th fl. (☎271 5018; fax 271 7906), almost directly across from CAAC. Organizes guided tours to the Southern Pass of Changbaishan; individual travelers may join 1-day tours (5am-9pm, Y270). 2-day tours to the waterfall and Underground Forest for groups of 10 or more (Y470). Open daily 8am-6pm.

Bank of China: On Renmin Dajie, 2 blocks east of Guangming Lu, next to the PSB. Exchanges traveler's checks. Credit card advances. Open daily in summer 8-11:30am and 1:30-5pm; in winter 8-11:30am and 1-4:30pm.

PSB: On Renmin Dajie, 1 block east of Juzi Jie. The approachable visa department (☎252 1372) is in the small yellow building to the right, on the 3rd fl. Open 8am-5pm.

Pharmacy: Teyao Pharmacy (tèyào dàyàofáng; 特药大药房), 40 Guangming Jie (☎252 2488), on the corner of Renmin Dajie. Open daily 7:30am-6pm.

Internet Access: On Tuanjie Lu, a block north of Renmin Lu, just east of Juzi Jie. Over 100 fast computers. Y2 per hr. Open 24hr. **Yanji Post** has Internet access on the 2nd fl. Y3 per hr. Open daily 8am-4:30pm.

Post Office: Yanji Post, on Renmin Dajie, on the corner of Juzi Jie (☎252 6989). EMS and Poste Restante. Open daily 8am-5pm. **Postal Code:** 133000.

ACCOMMODATIONS AND FOOD

The center of Yanji, particularly along Xinxing Jie, boasts mid-range hotels with exceptionally comfortable rooms. Several cheap hostels cluster near the train station square, many without hot water or showers, but some as cheap as Y10 a night.

Korean restaurants are ubiquitous in Yanji. **Jiefang Lu,** east of Juzi Jie, is lined with Korean joints specializing in dog dishes (gǒu ròu; 狗肉). **Pama's** ❷ (pāimǎsī; 啪玛嘶), on the corner of Xinxing Jie and Hailan Lu, three blocks south of Renmin Dajie, serves tasty American and European cuisine and occasionally hosts live music. (☎251 2419. Entrees Y15-36. Open daily 8:30am-2am.)

Jincheng Dasha (jīnchéng dàshà; 金城大厦), 114 Tuanjie Lu (☎251 9337), just east of Juzi Jie (☎251 9337). Huge, shining baths make the clean and comfortable rooms seem miniscule. Sumptuous breakfast included. Hot water 6-8am, 11am-2pm, and 6-11pm. Doubles Y180; bargain down to Y140. ❸

Liujin Fandian (liǔjīn fàndiàn; 流金饭店), 124 Xinxing Jie (☎291 2228; fax 256 1563), two blocks north of Renmin Dajie. These neat rooms are a study in making the most out of a little: stairs and mirrored walls make tiny rooms look like giant two-story chambers. Breakfast included. Singles and doubles Y150. ❷

NORTHEAST

Old World Hotel (lǎo shìjie fàndiàn; 老世界饭店), 122 Xinxing Jie (☎256 9900), just before the Liujin, is a 2-star hotel at its best. Bargain to: singles Y128; doubles Y158. ❷

SIGHTS

From the bridge at Renmin Dajie, bus #43 runs south to **Mao'er Mountain Park** (māo ér shān gōngyuán; 猫儿山公园), a fairly pleasant retreat with the usual paddle boats (Y5-15) and a not-so-usual ski-jump. Families may prefer to lodge here (a little house with electricity and hot water access Y100) instead of at a central hotel.

CHANGBAISHAN 长白山

No one could have said it better than Deng Xiaoping: "not climbing atop Changbaishan will be a regret harbored for life." The Changbaishan mountains feature dramatically shaped, multicolored peaks that culminate in the two-million-year-old **Tianchi Lake,** in a crater atop a dormant volcano. Tianchi, the deepest lake in China, is the source of the Songhua and Yalu Rivers, which cascade into impressive waterfalls and are replenished by steaming geysers. In Changbaishan, hardcore campers and hikers can revel in this unexplored paradise while families can easily visit the main peak via a main road.

AT A GLANCE	
AREA: 1965 km^2	**CLIMATE:** Temperate and sub-polar
GATEWAYS: Songjianghe, Erdaobaihe, Yanji (p. 226)	**FEES:** Entrance to the nature reserve Y30, students Y15
FEATURES: Tianchi Lake (p. 230), Changbaishan Gorge (p. 231), Changbai Waterfall (p. 230)	**HIGHLIGHTS:** Camping on the shores of Tianchi Lake (p. 230); Gazing across the North Korean border (p. 230)

ORIENTATION

Changbaishan is actually a gigantic volcano, surrounded by immense plains and a dozen other peaks. From China, two roads lead to the edge of the crater: one runs from **Erdaobaihe** (二道白河) to the **Southern Pass** (nán pō; 南坡); the other runs from **Songjianghe** (松江河) to the **Western Pass** (xī pō; 西坡). 350km of roads lie between these two access towns which are geographically only 7km (a 10hr., very difficult hike) apart. Hikers must take care not to tresspass into land beyond the white border stones; there are better things to do in Changbaishan than be interrogated by North Korean border guards.

TRANSPORTATION

The easiest way to travel to Changbaishan's **Southern Pass** is to go directly from **Yanji** (p. 226); buses leave from Yanji's long-distance bus station (5hr., 5:30am, Y55). If you don't come from Yanji, you'll have to travel through **Erdaobaihe,** a small city 20km south of the entrance to the nature reserve. From Erdaobaihe, **trains** go to Changchun (17hr., 11:40pm), Dandong (19hr., 4:40am), and Tonhua (8hr., 4 per day), all via Songjianghe (2hr., Y3), the access point to the Western Pass. **Buses** from Erdaobaihe travel to Dunhua (4hr., multiple departures 6am-noon, Y22), Songjianghe (3hr., 2pm, Y6), and Yanji (5hr., 7:10am, Y45). Between 4 and 6pm, buses en route to Yanji and Jilin pass through the town; although they're not listed on the bus schedule, they'll still pick up passengers.

Sonjianghe, three hours from the nature reserve, is the main access point for the reserve's **Western Pass. Trains** go to Baihe (2hr., 2 per day, Y3), Changchun (15hr., 1:48am), Dandong (17hr., 6:55am), and Tonghua (8hr., 4 per day); the train station is at the end of the main street. **Buses** depart from the Songjianghe station on the main street to **Erdao** (3hr., 8am, Y6), **Changchun** (6:35am), and **Jilin** (6am).

As of July 2001, the only way to get from Songjianghe to the Western Pass was to join a tour offered by one of Songjianghe's hotels.

PRACTICAL INFORMATION

Fees: Nature reserve Y30, students Y15.

Tours: For tours beginning at the Southern Pass, contact the **Tianchi Hotel** (tiānchí bīnguǎn; 天池宾馆; ☎(0439) 631 3077) or the **Railway Hostel** (tiědào zhāodàisuǒ; 铁道招待所; ☎(0439) 631 3742) in Songjianghe. Each arranges 1-day tours for groups of 20+ (depart approx. 5am, return 2-5pm; Y120 per person, including admission). Individual travelers may be able to join a previously established group. For tours of the Southern Pass, contact the CITS offices in Jilin (p. 224) or Yanji (p. 227).

Bank of China: In Erdaobaihe, on the main street, near the bus station; in Songjianghe, on the main street.

Post Office: In Erdaobaihe, near the bus station. Another branch near the Southern Pass gate to the nature reserve is open daily 8am-5pm. **Postal code:** 133613. In Songjianghe, near the bank. Open daily in summer 7:30am-5:30pm; in winter 7:30am-5pm. **Postal code:** 134504.

ACCOMMODATIONS

If you enter Changbaishan via the Southern Pass, stay in the nature reserve itself to cut transportation and admission costs. Accommodations may cost as little as Y30 a night; Chinese speakers may have better luck finding cheaper digs. Due to the number of affluent Japanese and Korean tourists who visit the area, the Southern Pass also boasts fairly expensive establishments; in general, the farther up the road to Tianchi you go, the more expensive the accommodations. The most unorthodox place to stay is the **tent** ❶ maintained by the local guides on the shore of Tianchi; the location can't be beat. (Open May-Oct. Y50 per night; only a few spots available.) More comfortable and arguably more exotic are the **Korean heated floors** ❶ (Y80) in a small building 500m below the waterfall ticket booth, a 20-minute walk from the last parking lot. The **Feihu Shanzhuang** ❶ (fēihú shānzhuāng; 飞狐山庄) has dorm rooms in a neat wooden structure, inconveniently located just outside the ticket gate. (☎(0422) 571 8740. 30-bed dorms Y50; standard rooms Y220.)

If you enter via the Western Pass, camping is the only option within the park. Otherwise, you'll have to spend the night in Songjianghe, in which case a few expensive (doubles Y260) and comfortable hotels can be found by the town's rotary. Or try the **Baiyuan Hotel** ❷ (báiyuán bīnguǎn; 白源宾馆) on the main street near the train station, past the bank and post office. (☎(0439) 632 4055. Clean doubles with bath Y150.) The best values can be found at the **Feng Lou Lu Hotel** ❶ (fēng lóulǚ fàndiàn; 丰楼旅饭店), home to the town's hottest disco. (☎(0439) 631 3087. Singles with TV Y20; doubles Y35.) The **bathhouse** (Y10) in the center of town and the "bath palace" of the **Railway Hostel** (Y3) have similar bathing amenities.

TREKKING IN CHANGBAISHAN

The bus depot in the parking lot 25km past the ticket gates is the hub for hitting all Southern Pass trails and destinations.

FOR NOVICES AND DAYTRIPPERS

If you want to appreciate Changbaishan's beautiful views without having to sweat or toil, you're not alone. Jeeps (30min.; Apr.-Sep. approx. 4:30am-4pm. Y80) take passengers straight to the top of **Tianwen Peak** (tiānwén fēng; 天文峰; 2670m), also known as the **Main Peak** (zhǔ fēng; 主峰).

A 4.3km road also leads to **Changbai Waterfall** (chángbái pùbù; 长白瀑布). The road begins at the parking lot, to the right of the Main Peak road, and continues along the stream. A jeep ride to the waterfall costs Y50 or less per car, but the fairly deserted road isn't steep and makes for a pleasant walk. The road also passes the **hiking path** to the Main Peak, 15 minutes from the parking lot, on the left; the road to **Small Tianchi** and the top of **White Cloud Mountain** is clearly marked and on the right. The road ends at a ticket booth (Y15) past the steamy **hot springs.** Off to the left, you can find more spectacular geysers before continuing on to the waterfall. The walk from the ticket booth to the waterfall takes 10 to 15 minutes.

FOR THE MORE ADVENTUROUS

At the waterfall, a steep path leads to the shore of **Tianchi** (2189m), where a notice informs travelers that the path is closed. During the day, guards may prevent you from hitting the path, but intrepid travelers may be able to climb up the stones on the left under the pretense of taking a photo. Once you're high enough up, step right onto the path to Tianchi. Falling stones have damaged parts of the path, but the rubble is easy to circumvent. The path continues to the top of the waterfall and along the stream to the shore of the lake, where guides maintain a permanent tent (see **Accommodations,** above). A stony trail leading to **Dragon Gate Peak** and **White Cloud Peak** branches off to the right, halfway up a paved section of the path. Just before Tianchi, a footbridge marks the beginning of a path to the left that leads to the **Main Peak.** The walk from the waterfall to the lake takes about one hour.

A 3km path branches to the right off the main access road, 5km before the parking lot, and leads to the **Underground Forest** (dìxià sēnlín; 地下森林). This path follows an extremely narrow, 50m-deep, grass-masked gorge; there are no footbridges, so hikers have to jump over the gorge a few times. The gorge eventually opens up into a gigantic abysmal dale that houses the Underground Forest. A side path leads to the **Dongtian Waterfall,** which is concealed under soil and roots.

FOR EXPERIENCED HIKERS

Two paths head for the Main Peak. The first, a long and arduous path labeled in English as a "small pedestrian road to Zhufeng," branches to the left off the road to Changbai Waterfall, a 15-minute trek past the parking lot. The trail climbs through the forest and then follows the paved road to Main Peak for about an hour. At **Black Dragon Pass** (hēilóng kǒu; 黑龙口), a pavilion with a panoramic view of the waterfall, the path swerves left and continues straight across to the peak. The route is about 6km long and takes four hours to ascend and 2½ hours to descend. The other path is a good choice for those who want to see Changbai Waterfall and the Main Peak in one day. The path to **Tianchi Lake** branches to the left (about 5min. before reaching the lake) to reveal a footbridge, this hike's starting point. The hike's first section, up a steep mountain gorge, is gritty and dangerous; after it reaches a grassy slope, the hike becomes a monotonous, albeit scenic, stair-climb. The ascent takes 2½ hours, the descent 1½ hours.

After reaching Main Peak, you can continue on to **Huagai Peak** (huágài fēng; 华盖峰; 2640m). The beautiful route spans a quarter of Tianchi's circumference and passes some of Changbaishan's most interesting geological quirks. The well-defined path soon disappears, but the easy-to-follow trail continues along the main crest. Huagai Peak is two hours into North Korea (a white post marks the border); most hikers reach the summit without any trouble. But approaching the North Korean border past the summit is dangerous. The hike takes four hours each way.

A small path off the main road from the parking lot to Changbai Waterfall, clearly marked in Chinese, leads to **Small Tianchi** (xiǎo tiānchí; 小天池). From here, a path leads to the majestic **Dragon Gate Peak** (lóngmén fēng; 龙门峰; 2595m) and **White Cloud Peak** (báiyún fēng; 白云峰; 2691m). At first, follow the trees labeled with white pieces of cloth; once you get past the tree line, the path is clearer. On a hollow alp, the path splits into two: the branch to the left leads to Dragon Gate Peak and to another path to Tianchi (1hr.); the trail to the right continues along the main crest to White Cloud Peak and, beyond it, to Western Pass. The area around White Cloud Peak is particularly difficult, and some rock-climbing experience may be necessary. The hike between Small Tianchi and the junction takes 3 hours to ascend, 1½ hours to descend; between Small Tianchi and White Cloud Peak takes 6 hours to ascend, 3 hours to descend; between Small Tianchi and Western Pass 10 hours to ascend, 8 hours to descend.

A path connects the road between Tianchi Lake and Changbai waterfall with the junction of the paths leading to Dragon Gate and White Cloud Peaks; it begins at the stone embankment and climbs all the way up to the pass, turning slightly to the left. It bisects a fragile rubble slope, is very dangerous, and should only be used to evacuate from the higher sections of Dragon Gate Peak. This path takes one hour to ascend, 30 minutes to descend.

FOR THOSE COMING FROM THE WEST

The attractions of the Western Pass are scattered along the access road from Songjianghe. There is a junction 10km before the end of the road, from which a dirt road branches to the left to the 100m-deep, precipitous **Changbaishan Gorge** (chángbáishān dàxiágǔ; 长白山大峡谷). The path overlooking the gorge passes a unique tree that is actually three different species whose trunks have merged. After 30 minutes, the path leads to a bridge over a meter-wide chasm; near here, a junction attracts jump-happy daredevils. Past the end of the road, 500m of paved stairs lead to the spectacular scenery of the pass, from which an easy path descends to Tianchi (1hr.). A difficult route to **White Cloud Peak** and **Southern Pass** begins on the left (facing Tianchi), just below the pass. Mountains to the right are easier to hike, but the North Korean border cuts them in half and wandering hikers are stopped by vigilant PSB officers.

LIAONING 辽宁

Liaoning is the golden child of China's Northeast—which isn't saying much. But Liaoning actually *is* quite splendid, with a long coastline, a booming economy, and a mild climate. And despite growing unemployment and lagging development in the countryside, Liaoning's crown jewels—the warm-water seaports of Dalian and Lushun—still shine.

Liaoning has had close ties to the rest of China ever since Qing rulers chose this area to be the site of their first capital. Liaoning suffered heavily during the Japanese occupation in the 1930s and 40s, but today the province seems blissfully unfettered by recollections of darker eras. Blessed with lush greenery and the occasional beach, Liaoning is energizing and occasionally harrowing, with its gaze focused as firmly on the pleasures of the present as on the challenges of the future.

SHENYANG 沈阳 ☎024

Shenyang is a promising metropolis, a swan amid the endless ugly-duckling wheat fields of Liaoning province. History singled out the city as the home of the Manchu court (1625-1644) at the beginning of the Qing dynasty. In 1931, Shenyang, along with the rest of Manchuria, rose to prominence when the Japanese army used the region as a base from which to launch their invasion of China. Today, with a population of 6.8 million, Shengyang is the largest and arguably the most important city in the Northeast. Modernization is more than just a buzz word here: main streets are gutted and repaved and high-rises are constructed and demolished at a frenzied pace. Luckily, the populace appears to be taking it all in stride; the historical sites that constitute the cultural heart of the city still stand undisturbed and visitors are gladly welcomed to relish in the slightly messy contrasts of old and new.

TRANSPORTATION

Flights: Taoxian International Airport (táoxiān jīchǎng; 桃仙机场; ☎8939 2000), on the southern fringe of the city, off the main highway to Dalian. **CAAC shuttle buses** (Y10) depart from the corner of Taiyuan Jie and Zhonghua Lu; a taxi costs Y60. **IATA ticket office** (guóji hángxié hángkōng shòupiào chù; 国际航协航空售票处) is at 229 Zhongshan Lu (☎2284 2925); other ticket offices abound. To: **Beijing** (5 per day, Y640); **Dalian** (1-2 per day, Y170); **Guangzhou** (1-2 per day, Y2000); **Harbin** (1-4 per day, Y470); **Hong Kong** (6 per week, Y2130); **Qingdao** (5 per week, Y620); **Shanghai** (1-3 per day, Y1190); **Xi'an** (9:25am daily, Y1350). International flights to: **Osaka** (4 per week) and other major destinations in **Japan** (1-2 per week); **Khabarovsk, Russia** (2 per week); **Seoul, South Korea** (2 per week).

Trains: Shenyang Main Train Station (shěnyáng huǒchē zhàn; 沈阳火车站; ☎2206 2222), at the end of Zhonghua Lu, on the corner of Shengli Dajie, Heping. To: **Baihe** (9hr., 4:30am, Y39-80) via **Songjianghe** (7hr.); **Beijing** (10-12hr., 8 per day, Y51-300); **Changchun** (5hr., 7 per day, Y20-75); **Dalian** (4-6hr., 8 per day, Y28-124); **Dandong** (5hr., 9 per day, Y18-54); **Harbin** (8hr., 12 per day, Y32-159); **Tumen** (16hr., 2 per day, Y47-254). **Shenyang North Station** (shěnyáng běizhàn; 沈阳北站; ☎2204 3262), on Beizhan Lu, Shenhe. To: **Dalian** (15 per day); **Dandong** (4½hr., 4 per day); **Guangzhou** (48hr., 8pm, Y286-900); **Jilin** (6-9hr., 6 per day, Y31-115); **Shanghai** (34hr., 4 per day, Y204-800); **Tianjin** (10-14hr., 4 per day, Y49-290). Most trains pass through both stations.

Buses: Shenyang South Long-distance Bus Station (shěnyáng nánzhàn chángtú qìchē kèyùn zhàn; 沈阳南站长途汽车客运站; ☎2351 3112), on Shengli Dajie, near the train station. To: **Beijing** (13hr., 2pm, Y115); **Dalian** (4½hr., 13 per day, Y72); **Harbin** (12hr., 4:30pm, Y47.5); **Tianjin** (13hr., 1pm, Y62-114). **Express Bus Station** (kuàisù kèyùn zhàn; 快速客运站; ☎2251 1222) on Huigong Jie. From Shenyang North Station, walk down Youhao Jie to a roundabout; the station is on the left. To: **Beijing** (12hr., 2 per day, Y189); **Changchun** (4hr., 8 per day, Y71); **Dalian** (4½hr., 7 per day, Y99); **Dandong** (4hr., 6 per day, Y96); **Harbin** (7hr., 2 per day, Y130); **Jilin** (4½hr., 8 per day, Y96). **Private buses** depart from the square in front of the North Train Station. Frequent departures to: **Beijing** (Y185); **Dalian** (Y98); **Harbin**

(Y80). Buses in the parking lot next door depart to: **Changchun** (3 per day, Y70); **Qingdao** (3:30pm, Y198); **Tianjin** (4pm, Y100). Local destinations are easily reached on **private cars** that depart when enough passengers arrive; many ply the area between the Main Train Station and the Long-distance Bus Station. Rides to **Dandong** (3hr.) cost Y80 after bargaining.

Local Transportation: Buses and most minibuses cost Y0.5-1, larger A/C buses and the minibuses numbered 500-plus Y2. Buses run on major streets until 10:30pm. The **first ring bus** (yī huán; 一环) loops from the Main Train Station to North Station via Xishuncheng Jie; **#202** runs between the Main Train Station and North Tomb Park via City Government Square; **#225** loops from the Main Train Station to South Lake Park and up Qingnian Dajie to City Government Square.

Taxis: Base fare Y7-8, each additional km Y1.6-2.

ORIENTATION AND PRACTICAL INFORMATION

The most important districts are the west-central **Heping** (和平), the east-central **Shenhe** (沈河), the eastern **Dadong** (大东), the northern **Huanggu** (皇姑), and the western **Tiexi** (铁西). **City Government Square** (shìfǔ guǎngchǎng; 市府广场) is the hub of the city; Heping and Shenhe districts are commercial and tourist centers. **Taiyuan Jie** (太原街), **Zhongjie Lu** (中街路), and the areas nearby will likely interest visitors the most. The **Hun River** (hún hé; 浑河) is Shenyang's southern border.

Travel Agency: CITS, 113 Huanghe Nan Dajie, Huanggu (☎8612 2445 or 8680 9834), near the North Tomb. Open M-F 8-11:30am and 1-5pm. For cheaper, private tours, minibuses depart frequently from the gates of the Imperial Palace (Y140).

Consulates: Japan, 50 Shisi Wei Lu (☎2322 7490). Open M-F 8:45am-noon and 1-5:15pm. **Russia,** 109 Huanghe Nan Dajie (☎8611 4963), on the 10th fl. of the Phoenix Hotel. Open M-Tu and Th-F 9am-4:30pm. Organize day visas here if you are planning to visit Russia from border towns in Heilongjiang Province. **US,** 52 Shisi Wei Lu (☎2322 1198, visas 2322 2147). Open M-F 8:30am-5:30pm.

Bank of China: 253 Shifu Dalu, on City Government Square (☎2285 7563 or 2285 7595). Exchanges traveler's checks (2nd fl., to the right). Credit card advances (3rd fl.). Open M-F 8:30am-noon and 1-4:30pm.

Bookstores: Foreign Language Bookstore (wài wén shūdiàn; 外文书店), 43 Taiyuan Bei Jie (☎2340 9324 or 2383 4565). Open daily 9am-6pm. **Dongyu Bookstore** (dōngyǔ shūdiàn; 东宇书店), 2 Heping Nan Dajie. Open daily 9am-8pm.

PSB: Visa extension department at 73 Zhongshan Lu, near the North Station, opposite Post Hotel (☎2253 4850). Enter the lobby of the Communications Bank, go to the 4th fl. and walk confidently to post 6; don't be intimidated by the horde of aggressive clerks busily planning the Chinese economy. Open M-F 8:30-11:30am and 1-4:30pm.

Hospital: Great No. 1 Hospital (yīdà yīyuàn; 一大医院), Nanjing Jie, at Zhongshan Square (☎2326 4677).

Internet Access: Linxi Internet Cafe (lǐnxī wǎngbā; 林夕网吧), 367 Zhongshan Lu, near Qingnian Dajie. Open 10am-midnight or later. **Wangba** (网吧) on Taiyuan Jie, between Nansan Malu and Nansi Malu (2nd fl.), is open 24hr. Both Y2 per hr. Dongyu Bookstore has access for Y3 per hr.

Post Office: China Post, 54 Zhongshan Lu, at Taiyuan Jie. EMS and IDD service. Open daily in summer 8am-5:30pm; in winter 8am-5pm. **Postal Code:** 110000.

ACCOMMODATIONS

Accommodations in Shenyang tend to be upscale, but there are some relatively cheap places in good locations. Construction is the sport of choice and hotels are often fully booked, so call ahead.

SHENHE

Meisan Hotel (méisǎn bīnguǎn; 梅糁宾馆), 48 Xiaoxi Lu (☎2273 5538; fax 2273 5548). The staff is overbearingly proud of its hardwood floors and location; City Government Square and the Imperial Palace are within walking distance. Singles Y80, with bath Y140; doubles Y160; triples Y240; quads Y280. ❶

Post Hotel (yóuzhèng dàshà; 邮政大厦), 78 Beizhan Lu (☎2252 8717), just west of the North Train Station. Dwarfed by the mighty Gloria Inn, the humble Postal Tower is still a good deal. 2-bed dorms Y40; doubles Y190 and up. ❶

Wangfu Hotel (wángfǔ bīnguǎn; 王府宾馆), 5 Youhao Jie (☎2273 5867), south of the North Train Station. A reliable option, with standard services and relatively clean rooms. Doubles Y120; triples Y180. ❷

HEPING

Peace Hotel (hépíng bīnguǎn; 和平宾馆), 104 Shengli Bei Jie (☎2383 3033), just north of the Main Train Station. Convenient location and a range of room options. 4-bed dorms Y30; singles with breakfast Y120; doubles Y100, with breakfast Y150-240; triples Y120, with breakfast Y180-260. ❶

South Pacific Mansion (nán yáng dàshà; 南洋大厦), 96 Zhonghua Lu (☎2341 0688), at Tongze Bei Jie. Fairly luxurious. Singles Y208; doubles Y248; triples Y368. ❸

Liaobao Hotel (liáobào dàjiǔdiàn; 辽报大酒店), 15 Beisanjing Jie (☎2284 4826), next door to the Liaoning newspaper building on Zhongshan Lu, a bit removed from the action of Taiyuan Jie. Clean rooms, solid place. Doubles Y150, with bath Y198. ❷

NORTHEAST

FOOD AND ENTERTAINMENT

Western restaurants and bars are clustered in the Heping district and near Dongbei University. **Zhongshan Market** (zhōngshān shìchǎng; 中山市场), on Beiliu Malu off Zhongshan Lu, is a good place for fresh fruit; the neighboring streets branching off Taiyuan Jie are packed with *bāozi* (Y0.5) stalls. The **Civic Convenience Shop** (xìnméng biànlì diàn; 信盟便利店) has 24hr. branches scattered throughout the city, including one on Xiaoxi Lu across from the Meisan Hotel. For more low-key entertainment, check out the Chinese-subtitled US and Hong Kong movies at the **Dream Cinema,** across from Star Hollywood (Y15).

Huaxia Folk Village (huáxià mínzúcūn dàjiǔlóu; 华夏民族村大酒楼), 11 Beiwu Malu, Heping (☎2340 9334 or 2383 2173), a short walk north along Nanjing Beijie from Zhongshan Square. A great big place where you can play with children's blow-up toys and hang out with the resident folk. The village food is luscious. Entrees Y18-25. ❷

Small Potato (xiǎo tǔdòu; 小土豆), 37 Xiaoxi Lu (☎2291 5040). This restaurant's potato dishes are so popular with locals that it's often hard to find empty tables. Entrees Y10-25. Open daily 10:30am-10:30pm. ❷

Star Hollywood Cafe (xīngchén hǎoláiwū diànyǐng zhǔtí cāntīng; 星辰好莱坞电影主题餐厅), 9 Tongze Bei Lu, Heping, off Zhongshan Lu. A live band

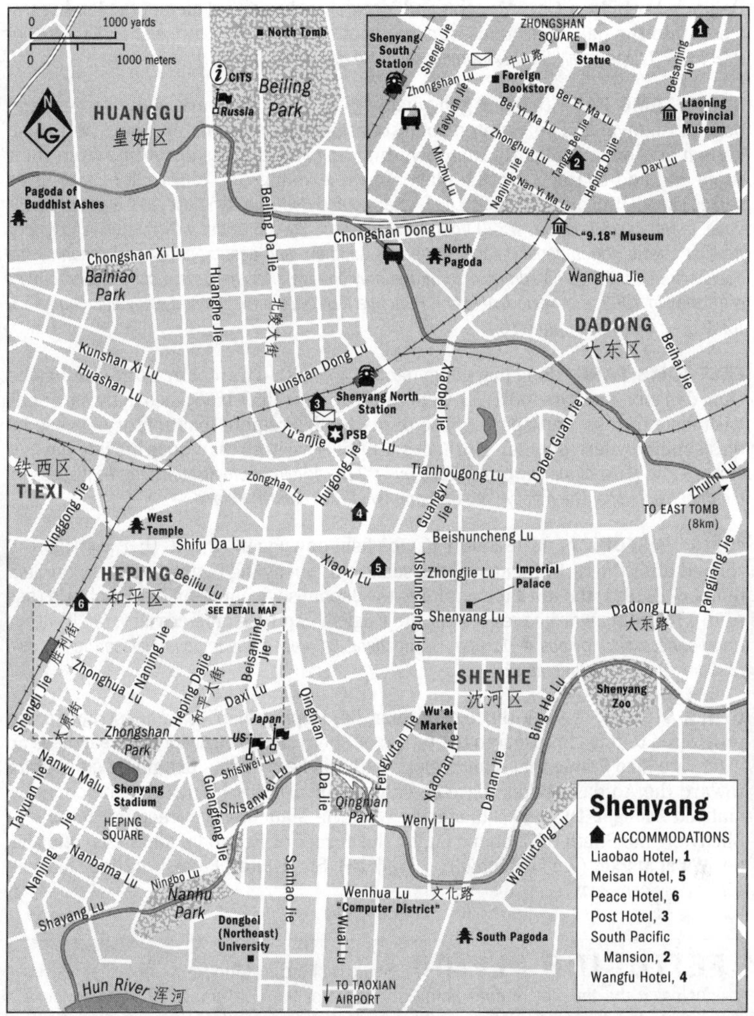

(F-Sa from 9:30pm) plays Western music. Full of foreign patrons flirting and dancing their cares away. Drinks Y28-48; entrees Y48-60. Open 11am-2am. ❹

SIGHTS

QING IMPERIAL PALACE (commonly gù gōng, 故宫; really tàiqīng gōng, 太清宫).

In the early 1600s, this splendid complex was the home of Nurhaci and Hong Taiji, the Manchu founders of the Qing dynasty. The 300 rooms are constructed largely using Han Chinese architectural principles; the palace looks like a small version of

NORTHEAST

Beijing's Forbidden City. Manchu and Mongol architectural elements blend seamlessly into the palace grounds. *(On the pedestrian Zhong Jie, Shenhe. ☎2475 4700 or 2484 6873. Open daily 8am-5:30pm; tickets sold 8am-4:30pm. Y35.)*

NORTH TOMB PARK (běi líng gōngyuán; 北陵公园). This park is the biggest and best in Shenyang. The vaunted tomb contains the remains of Hong Taiji (also known as Abahai). Slightly run-down buildings have grass sprouting from their roofs and add character to the place. In the evenings, an outbreak of kite-fever seizes the visiting folk. *(Encircled by Taishan Lu and Huanghe Nan Dajie, at the end of Beiling Dajie, in Huanggu. Take bus #220 from the North Train Station or bus #227 from Xishuncheng Jie, just west of the Imperial Palace. The park's southern and eastern gates on Taishan Lu are open 24hr. and charge no admission, but that may change after the current construction project is finished in 2002; the western gates on Huanghe Nan Dajie are open irregularly and charge Y3. Tomb open daily 7am-6pm. Y10.)*

EAST TOMB PARK (dōng líng gōngyuán; 东陵公园). The other founder of the Qing dynasty, the "Dragon Tiger General" Nurhaci (1559-1626), lies in these woods with his empress. Perhaps because of his tomb's remote location or because he was genuinely less popular, Nurhaci sees fewer visitors than does his late partner Hong Taiji. *(East of the city center. Take bus #218 (45min.) from Xishuncheng Jie just east of the Imperial Palace. Open daily 6am-6:30pm. Two ticket booths; Y2 and Y10.)*

"9.18" HISTORICAL MUSEUM (jiǔ yībā lìshǐ bówùguǎn; 九一八历史博物馆). Named after the "9.18 Incident," the seizure of Shenyang by the Japanese on September 18, 1931, the museum explores the Japanese occupation of Manchuria (see p. 16). Haunting war images render the English captions unnecessary. *(46 Wanghua Nan Jie. Accessible by bus #212 from Xishuncheng Jie, west of the Imperial Palace. Tickets sold 8:30am-4pm. Y20, students Y10.)*

OTHER SIGHTS. A walk through **Taiyuan Jie,** Heping district's pedestrian street, provides a telling glimpse into the future of Shenyang. **Zhongshan Square** houses an elaborate **Mao Statue** that stands alert, with his heavy arms extending southward toward the Adidas-trodden base of Taiyuan Jie. In Shenhe district, the commercialized **Zhongjie Lu** contrasts starkly with the Manchu-style reconstructions of Shenyang Lu. South of Zhongjie Lu, on the corner of Renao Lu and Fengyutan Jie, lies **Wu'ai Market** (wǔ'ài shìchǎng; 五爱市场), Shenyang's largest outdoor market. *(Open daily 4am-2pm.)*

FETTUCINE ALFIDO Some visitors to China may find themselves cringing at the thought of consuming dog meat or the vivid image of fluffy pooches being bred and slaughtered for a tasty meal. Han Chinese in the Northeast are actually less charmed by Fido's succulent flavors than Chinese citizens elsewhere, but the presence of ethnic Koreans in the area and the central role that dog meat plays in some regional Korean cuisines mean that restaurants offering dog meat (góuròu; 狗肉) are common. Dog hotpot also has attracted quite a following down in Guangxi province.

Dog meat is lean and recommended for those with heart problems. Known for its warming qualities, dog hotpot or broth is the rage when temperatures drop below freezing. This delicacy comes at a price, though. Restaurant owners report that a full dog goes for Y300 or more. Still unfazed? Chefs are often eager to impress tourists by showcasing the uneaten tail, paws, and head of man's best friend. Doggone it.

DANDONG 丹东 ☎415

A small, unassuming city, Dandong would make its way onto few tourist itineraries were it not for its choice location on the Sino-Korean border. Japanese, South Korean, and Chinese tourists crowd onto its shore, into boats, and along the Yalu River Bridge to catch a glimpse of the forbidden Communist kingdom beyond. The transformation of the world's most isolated nation into a tourist attraction is a spectacle every bit as bizarre as the view of North Korea itself.

TRANSPORTATION

Flights: Dandong Airport (dāndōng jīchǎng; 丹东机场; ☎617 6569), 13km from Dandong. A taxi from the city costs Y25-30. **Shuttle buses** (Y5) leave 1½hr. before departure from the **CAAC ticket office,** 50 Jingshan Dajie (☎212 3427), at 3-Wei Lu. Open daily 8am-5:30pm. To **Beijing** (Sa, Y570) and **Shanghai** (Tu, Th, Sa; Y990).

Trains: Dandong Train Station (dāndōng huǒchē zhàn; 丹东火车站; ☎202 1222), at the intersection of 10-Wei Lu and 7-Jing Jie. Ticket booths open daily 6am-6pm. To: **Beijing** (14-22hr., 2 per day, Y73-400); **Changchun** (11hr., 7am, Y41-71); **Dalian** (11hr., 6:13pm, Y53-170); **Qingdao** (24½hr., 1:53pm, Y100-330); **Shenyang** (4hr., 7 per day, Y29-54).

Buses: Dandong Long-distance Passenger Station (dāndōng chángtú kèyùn zhàn; 丹东长途客运站), 98 Shiwei Lu (☎213 4571), from the train station, a short walk to the left. To: **Beijing** (18hr., 10am, Y165); **Dalian** (6hr.; frequent minibuses 5:30am-2:30pm, a deluxe coach 4pm; Y54-64); **Harbin** (at least 20hr., 10am, Y153.5). **Huayuan Passenger Station** (huàyuán kèyùn zhàn; 化园客运站), on Huayuan Jie in north Dandong. Take local bus #11, 12 or 21. To **Shenyang** (6hr., frequent, Y54-98).

Local transportation: Local buses usually run 5am-7pm. Fare Y1. **Taxi** base fare Y6, each additional km Y1.8. **Pedicabs** within the city generally cost Y2.

ORIENTATION AND PRACTICAL INFORMATION

East of the railroad, central Dandong is a grid of numbered **Wei Lus'**, which run north-south, and **Jing Jies'**, which run east-west. Much of the city's drama takes place along the **riverbank,** past 1-Jing Jie, where cruise ships and eateries line the shore. The pedestrian **Xinan Lu,** ten minutes from the train station, is Dandong's take on a Western thoroughfare.

Travel Agency: CITS, 1 Zhanqian Dalu, 3rd fl. (☎213 7493; fax 212 5988), a large yellow building in Zhanqian Square, south of the train station. Offers tours to North Korea; package includes visas; allow a few days for processing (see **North Korea,** p. 92). Open M-F 8-11:30am and 1:30-5pm.

Bank of China: 60 Jingshan Dajie, at 2-Wei Lu. Exchanges traveler's checks. Credit card advances. Open in summer M-F 8-11:30am and 1:30-5pm; in winter 8-11:30am and 1-4:30pm.

PSB: 15 Jiangcheng Dajie, at 9-Wei Lu, across from Hualian Store (华联商店). Visas processed in room 112 (☎210 3138). Open M-F 8am-noon and 1:30-5:30pm.

Hospital: No. 1 Hospital (dìyī yīyuàn; 第一医院; ☎281 4132), on 7-Jing Jie, past the pedestrian Xinan Lu. **Pharmacy** inside.

Internet Access: Internet Cafe on 7-Jing Jie (see **Food,** below). Also on the 2nd fl. on 5-Jing Jie, at 6-Wei Lu, is open 24hr. but is slower. Both charge Y2 per hr.

NORTHEAST

Post Office: China Post, 7-Jing Jie, at 7-Wei Lu. EMS. Open M-F 8am-5:30pm. Phone booths next door in front of **China Telecom. Postal Code:** 118000.

ACCOMMODATIONS

Most of Dandong's hotels are standard and stodgy. The best locations are near the train station and the Yalu River, but the city is small enough that it doesn't matter much. Most upscale hotels are on the riverbank west of the rail tracks, near the Yalu River Bridge.

Dandong Railway Hotel (dān tiě dàshà; 丹铁大厦), 3 11-Wei Lu (☎213 1031), the tower attached to the train station. Favors convenience over class. Horn-happy taxis can make for a noisy stay. Dorms Y25-40; doubles from Y150. ❶

CITS Hotel (guólǚ bīnguǎn; 国旅宾馆), 1 Zhanqian Guangchang, 2nd fl. (☎212 2166). Standard rooms are a good value for the price. 24hr. hot water. Singles Y70; doubles Y120; triples Y180. ❶

Dandong Hotel (dāndōng fàndiàn; 丹东饭店), 31 7-Jing Jie (☎212 3529), 1 block east of the post office. Good prices and location. Almost 24hr. hot water. Dorms Y25-40; standard rooms from Y60. ❶

FOOD

Dandong's wealth of culinary options is a testament to the power of international trade. Small Korean restaurants line **10-Wei Lu** between the train station square and the river, serving cold noodles (lěng miàn; 冷面; Y3-5) and *bi bim bap* (bànfàn; 拌饭; Y5-8). For sleep-walkers (and night-eaters), **7-Jing Lu**, which runs from the train station, has food stalls open until 3am; several fancy restaurants line **6-Wei Lu.**

Andong Pavilion Restaurant (āndōng gé; 安东阁), along the riverbank, a 5min. walk past the railroad and the Yalu River Bridge; the large, elegant pavilion is easy to spot from afar. This new establishment has an original no-menu style of ordering: have the waiter walk you through a display of living creatures from which to pick and choose. The best non-bridge view of North Korea. Most entrees Y20-30. Open daily 11am-9:30pm. ❷

Deheng Fat Cow City (déhēng féiniú chéng; 德亨肥牛城), E 40 Business and Tourism Section (shāngmào lǚyóu qū; 商贸旅游区); on the little street parallel to the river-bank, between Andong Pavilion and the big square. Run by a Hui family, this restaurant serves Muslim dishes and hotpot. Dishes Y10-30. Open daily 10am-10pm. ❷

Internet Cafe (kāfēi wǎngbā; 咖啡网吧), on 7-Jing Jie, at 7-Wei Lu. Cake and tea on the left, fast connections on the right. Open daily 10am-midnight or later.

Italy Pizza (yìdàlì bǐsābǐng; 意大利比萨并), on 7-Jing Jie, at 3-Wei Lu. An Italian master chef awarded this establishment the New Kind Of Pizza Invention Certificate, which is proudly framed and displayed. A popular choice among locals. Entrees Y12-30. Open daily 8am-midnight. ❷

SIGHTS

Dandong's most interesting sights are near the Yalu River and the Democratic People's Republic of Korea. Nature-lovers can explore the hills surrounding Dandong, but even these are best-known for their bird's-eye views of The Other Bank.

YALU RIVER CRUISES. All along the Yalu River, these unconventional cruises take passengers within 10m of North Korea, one of the most isolated places on earth. Photos are allowed, but don't expect picturesque scenery; old boats, children at play, a few soldiers on patrol, and one, discreetly hidden, picture of Kim Il Sung constitute the entire visible slice of North Korean life. *(Boats run 6am-6:30pm; occasionally until later. Big boats: 20min., Y8. Speed boats get closer to the North Korean shore: 10min., Y18. If you're coming along 10-Wei Lu, don't wander right into the uninteresting park, which charges extra admission; there are lots of docks on other side of the rail tracks.)*

YALU RIVER BRIDGE (yālù jiāng qiáo; 鸭绿江桥). The bridge still bears evidence of 1950s "US aggression" against North Korea; look for shrapnel and some damage. Visitors can wear a Chinese Volunteer Anti-Imperialist Force uniform and pose with a gun in front of the North Korean border—for a fee, of course. *(West of Yalu River Park, extending halfway over the Yalu River. Open daily 6:30am-7pm. Y15.)*

DAYTRIPS FROM DANDONG

PHOENIX MOUNTAIN

50km northwest of Dandong, near the city of Fengcheng (凤城). Buses (1½hr., approx. every 30min. 5:30am-5:30pm, Y8) go from Dandong Long-distance Bus Station to Fengcheng; ask to be dropped off at Fenghuangshan Gate (凤凰山门), a few km before Fengcheng city. Buses shuttle visitors between the gate and the ticket office (Y10). Open May 1-Oct. 1. Y30.

Reputed to be China's boldest *via ferrata* (a rock-climbing route made more easily accessible with the addition of ladder-like metal tools), Phoenix Mountain (fènghuáng shān; 凤凰山) offers tourists mountaineering excitement that beats some of the world's most famous routes. Don't expect sky-high altitudes (even though scenic vistas abound); the real treat is the solid rock, which even complete beginners can scale. The path's metal protectors cut through almost vertical, polished, vertiginous rock faces and creep through dark, cramped caves, challenging agoraphobes and claustrophobes alike.

Good hiking shoes are an absolute must. The whole loop takes four hours; a cable car (Y25; one-way ascent Y15; round-trip Y40) rescues fledgling hikers halfway. Guides charge Y100 to walk less confident visitors around the loop. When you return to comfortingly horizontal landscapes, check out the Qing and Ming dynasty Daoist temples scattered between the ticket gate and the last parking lot.

TIGER MOUNTAIN GREAT WALL

15km northeast of Dandong, past the town of Jiuliancheng (九连城). Minibuses (30min., 8am-12:50pm, Y5) depart irregularly from the corner of 10-Wei Lu and Jingshan Dajie, near the bus station. Or, instead of waiting for the erratic minibus, take local bus #15 (Y1). Chinese speakers can take bus #13 (Y1) to the other side of the river; from there take a boat (Y10) to the wall; do not to stray into the North Korean grasslands on the right. Round-trip taxis cost Y80. Open daily 7:30am-5:30pm. Y15.

A small section built by the Ming dynasty in 1469, Tiger Mountain Great Wall (hǔ shān chángchéng; 虎山长城) constitutes the easternmost edge of the piecemeal Great Wall, with a half dozen towers snaking along the North Korean border. A walk atop this section of the wall, along China's modern border, is almost as thrilling as blinking at a lazy riverbank from Dandong's parks; still, the scenery is not exceptionally picturesque.

DALIAN 大连 ☎0411

In many parts of China, economic prosperity comes at the price of clean air and charm. Not so in Dalian, whose natural blessings are its biggest economic asset.

Dalian made its money through the vast shipping traffic that passes through its harbor, the third largest in China. European commercial intervention of the 19th and early 20th centuries left its architectural mark; rounding out the mix are skyscrapers, covered markets, boutiques, grassy squares, hilly terrain, and all the fresh sea air anyone could want. Today the city is vivid, rich, cosmopolitan, and, all things considered, quite fabulous.

TRANSPORTATION

Flights: The **Dalian Zhoushuizi International Airport** (dàlián zhōushuǐzi guójì jīchǎng; 大连周水子国际机场; ☎665 3388) is about 2km northwest of the city. Domestic departure tax Y50. **CAAC ticket office,** Civil Aviation Hotel, 143 Zhongshan Lu (☎363 7480), in Xiwang Square. Open daily 8am-6:30pm. To: **Beijing** (10 or more per day, Y640); **Changchun** (2 per day, Y530); **Chengdu** (1-3 per day, Y1600); **Guangzhou** (3 per day, Y1790); **Harbin** (2-5 per day, Y770); **Hong Kong** (2-3 per day, Y2870); **Qingdao** (3-5 per day, Y430); **Shanghai** (5-6 per day, Y980); **Shenyang** (1-2 per day, Y170); **Xi'an** (1-2 per day, Y1050). International flights to **Seoul, South Korea** (daily, Y1950) and **Tokyo, Japan** (2-5 per day).

Trains: Dalian Train Station (dàlián huǒchē zhàn; 大连火车站; ☎283 1002), at the head of Shengli Square. To: **Beijing** (18½hr., 2 per day, Y62-373); **Changchun** (11hr., 9:04pm, Y51-121); **Dandong** (11hr., 7:31pm, Y53-99); **Harbin** (14hr., 3 per day, Y62-352); **Jilin** (14½hr., 5:58pm, Y57-200); **Shenyang** (4-6hr., 8 per day, Y28-124).

Buses: Dalian Long-distance Bus Station (dàlián chángtú qìchē zhàn; 大连长途汽车站), 20 Anshan Lu (☎363 0119), at Xinkai Lu, west of the train station. To **Dandong** (6hr., frequent departures, Y46-58). Buses to other cities leave from the area by the train station, including the front parking lot and the hubs in front of the Bohai Pearl and Post Hotels on the sides. To: **Beijing** (14hr., several per day, Y150-210); **Changchun** (8hr., Y156); **Harbin** (13hr., Y180); **Shenyang** (4½hr., frequent departures, Y98); **Tianjin** (13½hr., Y150).

Ferries: Dalian Passenger Ferry Port (dàlián kèyùn gǎng; 大连客运港; ☎263 6061), on Gangwai Jie, at the north end of Renmin Lu. To: **Qinhuangdao** (5pm, Y120-390); **Shanghai** (36hr., 3-4 per week 4pm, Y122-662); **Tianjin** (13-15hr., 5:30pm, Y160-690); **Weihai** (7hr., frequent departures, Y80-800); **Yantai** (express 3hr., Y48-590; regular 6-7hr., Y190; both depart frequently). International ferries to **Inchon, South Korea** (18hr., Tu and F 11am, Y897-1543).

Local Transportation: Fare Y0.5-1. **Buses** run until midnight. Bus **#2** runs along Jiefang Lu; **#13** runs between the train station and the ferry port; **#19** runs from Shandong Lu to Zhongshan Square; **#23** runs along Zhongshan Lu between Zhongshan Square and Xinghai Park; **#701** shuttles from Zhongshan Square to the airport.

Taxis: Base fare Y8, at night Y10.4; each additional km Y1.2, at night Y1.56. From the city center to the beach Y15-30. **Motorcycle-taxis** shuttle arriving passengers from the train station to the central hotels for Y5.

ORIENTATION AND PRACTICAL INFORMATION

Dalian's public squares, complete with greenery and flocks of pigeons, date back to the time of Japanese rule. **Victory Square** (shènglì guǎngchǎng; 胜利广城) is opposite the train station and close to a number of hotels. To the east is **Friendship Square** (yǒuhǎo guǎngchǎng; 友好广场), home to hotels, cinemas, and bars. From here, **Zhongshan Lu** (中山路) runs farther east to the city's main square, **Zhongshan Square** (中山广场). A number of major thoroughfares radiate from here: **Yan'an Lu**

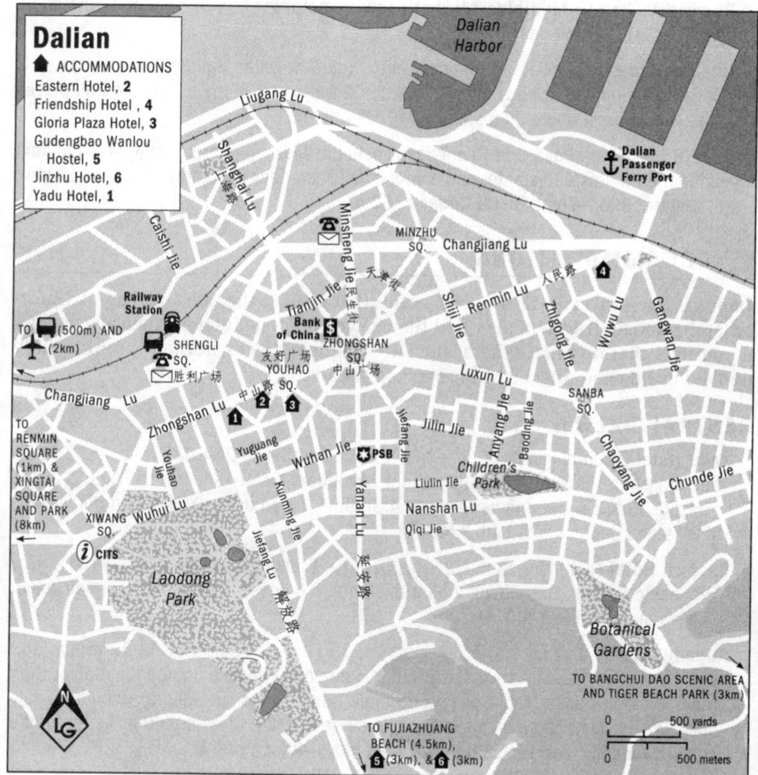

(延安路) runs south from the square; **Renmin Lu** (人民路) runs northeast to the ferry port; and **Minsheng Jie** (民生路) and **Shanghai Lu** (上海路) intersect the pedestrian **Tianjin Jie** (天津街). West of the main train station is the stately **People's Square** (rénmín guǎngchǎng; 人民广城). Dalian's beaches and scenic drives are in the south of the city along **Jiefang Lu** (解放路).

Travel Agency: CITS, 1 Changtong Jie (☎368 7843), in an architecturally unique building off Xiwang Square, opposite the Civil Aviation Hotel on Zhongshan Lu. For foreign-looking (and other) foreigners, the most official way to go to Lushun begins here. Open M-F 8am-5pm.

Bank of China: 9 Zhongshan Square (☎280 5711), in a European-style green-domed building. China's largest Bank of China exchanges traveler's checks (window #21) and issues credit card advances (window #2) M-F 8:30am-5pm. Other services M-F 8:30am-6pm, Sa-Su 9am-6pm.

PSB: 16 Yan'an Lu (☎280 2718), 2 blocks south of Zhongshan Square at Wuhan Lu. Open daily 8:30am-5:30pm.

Hospital: No. 1 Hospital of Dalian Medical University (dàlián yī xuéyuàn dì yī fùshǔ yīyuàn; 大连医学院第一附属医院), 222 Zhongshan Lu (☎363 5963), just west of People's Square.

Pharmacy: Dalian Medicine Market (dàlián yàofáng; 大连药房), 207 Tianjin Jie (☎263 0203). Open daily 8:30am-9pm.

Internet Access: Qiqi Jie a few blocks south from Zhongshan Square along Yan'an Lu is Dalian's main Internet hub, with at least ten 24hr. cafes. Many hole-in-the-wall places are scattered elsewhere throughout town. Y2-4 per hr.

Post Office: China Post, 261 Changjiang Lu, in the Youzheng Hotel, just west of the train station. EMS, Poste Restante, and a cool cafe. Open daily in summer 7:30am-7:30pm; in winter 7:30am-7pm. **Postal Code:** 116000.

ACCOMMODATIONS

Dalian is bursting at the seams with hotels that cater to the rich and playful. Unfortunately, budget travelers may find themselves outdone by the expensive accommodations that dominate the scene. Most budget places in the center are fully booked in July and August; be sure to call ahead.

CENTRAL DALIAN

Yadu Hotel (yǎdū bīnguǎn; 雅都宾馆), 11 Kunming Jie (☎264 9822; fax 265 2937), at Zhongshan Lu. New, affordable, and 1 block from Victory Square, the Yadu is a rare treasure. Public shower noon-3pm and 4:30-9pm. 3-bed dorms Y64, 2-bed dorms Y74; singles and doubles with bath Y248. ❶

Eastern Hotel (dōngfāng fàndiàn; 东方饭店), 28 Zhongshan Lu (☎263 4161), near Friendship Square. Old-school hotel with standard Chinese two-star rooms; good value. Singles and doubles Y240. ❸

Angang Dasha (āngāng dàshà; 鞍钢大厦), 33 Fengguang Jie (☎362 4265; fax 362 4264), at Zhongshan Lu, between Xiwang Square and People's Square. Central location (one bus stop from Victory Square and three from Zhongshan Square) without the city noise. Fairly clean and comfortable rooms all have A/C and bath, and make up for the aging corridors. Doubles Y252; at first staff may ask for more. ❹

Gloria Plaza Hotel (kǎilái dàjiǔdiàn; 凯莱大酒店), 5 Yide Jie (☎280 8855), off Friendship Square, a 5min. walk from Victory and Zhongshan Squares. Gloria's usual (high-priced) high-class service isn't exactly the definition of budget accommodation, but at least you won't have problems with availability. Singles and doubles Y488. Off-season discounts available. ❺

OUTSIDE THE CITY CENTER

Jinzhu Hotel (jīnzhù dàjiǔdiàn; 金铸大酒店), 87 Bayi Lu (☎268 8866), between Changchun Lu and Jiefang Lu. Take #4 from the Olympic Square, 4 stops from Zhongshan Square along Zhongshan Lu. Huge, neat, and comfortable rooms are near the beach; a solid option. Doubles Y260; triples Y320. ❹

Friendship Hotel (yǒuyí bīnguǎn; 友谊宾馆), 91 Renmin Lu (☎263 4121), a 5-10min. walk north of Zhongshan Square toward the ferry port. Fairly bland, much like most of Dalian's mid-range places. Singles Y280; doubles Y360. ❹

Gudengbao Wanlou Hostel (gǔdēngbǎo wánlóu zhāodàisuǒ; 古登堡沩楼招待所), 58 Linmao Jie (☎249 6223), perched like a little castle on a hill near Changchun Lu in the south of the city. Take #706 from Zhongshan Square and get off when the bus turns to a small road uphill. The extremely gaudy rooms will satisfy everyone's appetite for kitsch. 2- and 3-bed dorms Y25-35. ❶

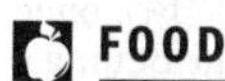

FOOD

Dalian is a port city, and it shows in the food. Seafood restaurants litter **Xiangqian Jie,** between Kunming Jie and Friendship Square, as well as the streets close to the shore. In business and tourist areas like Zhongshan Lu and Tianjin Jie, visitors will find those other unpalatable creatures that wash up on shore: **McDonald's, KFC,** and **Dairy Queen** (in the Dalian Grand Plaza Hotel, Friendship Square and the Victory Square underground mall). **Captain Nemo's ❸,** on the ground floor of the Grand Hotel (1 Jiefang Lu), just south of Zhongshan Square, serves up a Y38 Western breakfast buffet (7:30-10am). Lots of Chinese restaurants line **Renmin Lu, Zhongshan Lu,** and nearby side streets. The underground mall at Victory Square has an extensive **food court;** enter across from Tianjin Jie.

Tiantian Yugang Restaurant (tiāntiān yúgāng jiǔdiàn; 天天鱼缸酒店), 41 Yan'an Lu, 3 blocks of Zhongshan Square (☎280 1111). Sure, it's not cheap, but it's Dalian's best seafood restaurant. One *jīn* (0.5kg) of fish Y38-500 and more; frog (Y45 per *jīn*) is a treat, too. Open daily 10am-11pm. ❹

Yixin Roast Meat Restaurant (yīxīn kǎoròu diàn; 一心烤肉店), 56 Yan'an Lu, at Nanshan Lu, south of Zhongshan Square (☎265 5878). Also at 216 Youhao Lu (☎263 8202) and 246 Tangshan Jie (☎362 9203). Roast meat aficionados mob the place during peak hours, so prepare to wait. Waiters place metal "stoves" full of burning coal under a rack in the center of the table; guests cook their own pre-seasoned meats (Y15-18). The occasional third-degree burn aside, it's great fun. Open daily 11am-10:30pm. ❷

Japan Roast Meat Restaurant (rìběn kǎoròu diàn; 日本烤肉店), 9 Liulin Jie (☎280 1223), between Yan'an Lu and Jiefang Jie, south of Zhongshan Square. Don't come here expecting sushi; roast your own fish (and meat) on table stoves. The menu includes *teriyaki, tempura,* and other favorites. Join the crowds of Japanese tourists. English menu. Entrees Y10-70. Open daily 11:30am-1:30pm and 4:30-10pm. ❸

SIGHTS

Dalian is not about musty museums or ossified temples. Tourists are usually satisfied with the sea air, great shopping, glamorous atmosphere, and, oh, the beaches. After all, markets, malls, and skylines don't require admission fees. Until 1999, **People's Square**, in the west was home to one of China's best **Stalin monuments,** now relocated to neighboring Lushun. Farther east on Zhongshan Lu is **Victory Square,** a large elevated plaza with an underground shopping center, soccer field, and outdoor cafe. To the right of the Holiday Inn is **Tianjin Jie,** a jam-packed pedestrian street. A left turn on Shanghai Lu points you toward **Zhongshan Square,** lined with grandiose Western-style buildings. For a bird's-eye view of Dalian, take the **cable car** (Y25-40) over the hills of **Baiyun Yanshui Park** (báiyún yānshǔi gōngyuán; 白云妍水公园); to get to the park, take bus #407 from Changchun Lu or Go'erji Lu at People's Square to the terminus.

FUJIAZHUANG BEACH (fùjiāzhuāng hǎishuǐ yúlè chǎng; 傅家庄海水娱乐场). Barking loudspeakers, screaming children, crowded tents, and the sharp pebbled ground temper the beach fun just a bit. To avoid the crowds, walk past a string of trinket vendors and seafood restaurants to a path that leads to a clifftop. It's a good spot for a picnic and for those desperate for some ocean exposure. *(Take bus #401 from Victory Square or a taxi (Y15-20). Entry 8am-6pm Y5, 6-10pm Y3; passes for one month Y10; one summer Y15; one year Y22).*

SOUTHWESTERN DALIAN. Xinghai Square (xīnghǎi guǎngchǎng; 星海广场), once a garbage dump, is now an oceanfront square reputedly larger than Beijing's Tiananmen. A kilometer away, the rickety rides of **Xinghai Park** (xīnghǎi gōngyuán; 星海公园) are supplemented by a few record-holding attractions. **Sun Asia Ocean World** (open M-F 8am-5pm, Sa-Su 8am-5:30pm; Y70) has Asia's longest water-tank tunnel, and the **bungee jumping tower** (open 8am-5:30pm; Y180, roller-coaster Y80) is the world's highest. *(Both Xinghai Square and Xinghai Park are accessible via buses #22 from Victory Square and bus #23 from Zhongshan Square. Y10.)*

ENTERTAINMENT

Dalian's harbor brings both foreign businesspeople ansd sailors to town, and most nightlife is bound to involve one or the other. The **Holiday Inn** boasts an "English Pub" (open until midnight), and the **Swissôtel** has a gorgeous outdoor deck (performances Tu-Su 8pm-midnight). **JJ's Disco** (jiéjié dísīkē; 杰杰迪斯科), on Gangwan Jie, south of Gangwan Square near the ferry port, is a popular place for students and foreigners (no cover), although in 2001 **Ellis,** near Zhongshan Square, was the queen of Dalian's bars and discos. A half-dozen intimate cafes and bars line **Yan'an Lu** just south of the PSB, across the street from the **Night Cat** music club. A few blocks away, across from the Grand Hotel, is the extravagantly decorated **Xanadu,** where patrons listen to live performances or perform themselves in private karaoke rooms. Dalian's **soccer team,** the best in China in 2001, plays every other Saturday from September to June (the stadium is on the Olympic Square, one bus stop along Zhongshan Lu past People's Square). For more low-key spectator sports, check out the daily **soccer** matches in **Victory Square,** or head to **Zhongshan Square** at night to play **hacky-sack** and **badminton** with the student population. In the summer, the square also shows evening outdoor movies (9pm daily).

CENTRAL CHINA

Central China, the "cradle of Chinese civilization," has been a center of activity for millennia. From 3000 BC to AD 1000, it was a hotbed of cultural and political activity. Numerous ancient kingdoms and every early dynasty established capitals here; even the Qin dynasty, the first to conquer and consolidate all of China, maintained its administrative center in the city of Chang'an (present-day Xi'an). And through this incredible history, Central China has come to one profound conclusion: people don't kill people, floods kill people. The stunning Yellow River rolls through the provinces of Shaanxi, Shanxi, and Henan, providing fertile loess soil, acting as the source of irrigation to the otherwise parched land, giving life to the area and its people, and then destroying everything in its path in one fell swoop.

Aside from coping with floods from the river, also called "China's Sorrow" or "The Ungovernable," residents here have also had the pleasure of being the buffer between repeated northern invasions and the rest of China. The construction of the Great Wall made this job somewhat easier, but, of course, devastating floods can be quite distracting. Not surprisingly, Central China was one of the country's most economically poor regions until things started to pick up in the 1950s due to the industrialization of coal- and iron-rich cities.

Economic development has also made some of the world's richest historical stashes accessible to outsiders. Most visitors to China go to Xi'an, home of the Terracotta Warriors that were buried with Emperor Qin Shihuang. But this tourist hotspot is only one of Central China's many attributes, which include Wutaishan's lush valleys and mountains and Inner Mongolia's sprawling grasslands.

HIGHLIGHTS OF CENTRAL CHINA

TAKE A STEP TOWARD ENLIGHTENMENT at Buddhist **Wutaishan** (p. 286), where serene temples and mountain scenery attract devoted pilgrims from all over China.

FIND YOUR INNER STATUE among the army of Terracotta Warriors that guard Emperor Qin Shihuang's immense underground tomb near Xi'an (p. 253).

CAMP ON THE GRASSLANDS near **Hohhot** (p. 294), where you can ride on horseback, sleep in a yurt, and drink yak-butter tea.

SHAANXI 陕西

Shaanxi may once have been China's political, economical, and cultural center, but the province is really an extraordinary example of *feng shui* gone awry. Although the region has endured bad weather, floods, and the threat of attack from the north, emperors were happy to live here once they realized that Shaanxi was the geographical center of China. In fact, the Zhou, Qin, Han, Sui, and Tang dynasties all maintained their capitals here. To their credit, Shaanxi wasn't all bad. After all, it was the soft, fertile silt of the Yellow River valley in north Shaanxi that allowed farmers to settle here and cultivate crops. And during the Tang dynasty, the ancient capital city of Chang'an (modern Xi'an), located on the Silk Road, thrived as a cosmopolitan center with a population of over one million. By the end of the 9th century, however, the province's glory days came to an swift end; the capital city was sacked in 884, and Shaanxi quickly fell from grace. The next millennium left Shaanxi in a state of dreadful impoverishment, plagued by drought,

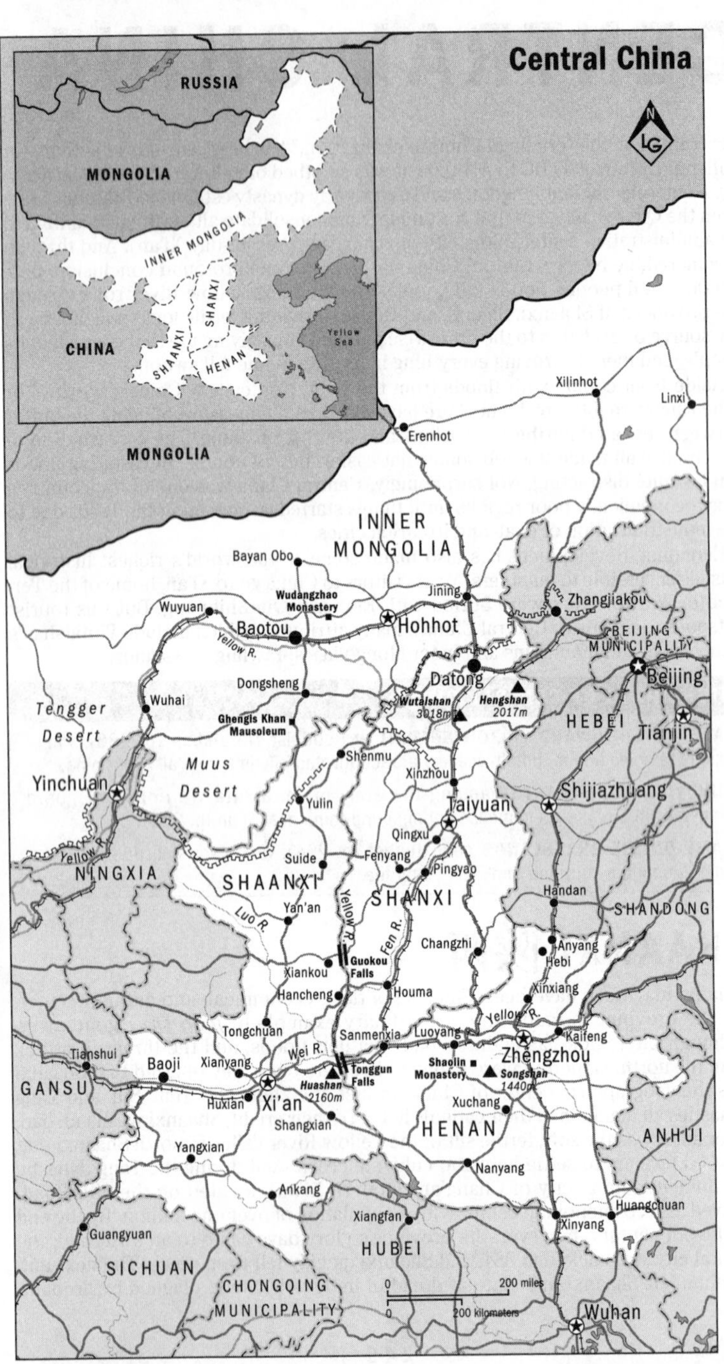
Central China
RUSSIA
MONGOLIA
INNER MONGOLIA
SHANXI
SHAANXI
HENAN
CHINA
Yellow Sea
MONGOLIA
Xilinhot
Linxi
Erenhot
INNER MONGOLIA
Bayan Obo
Jining
Zhangjiakou
Wudangzhao Monastery
Wuyuan
Baotou
Hohhot
BEIJING MUNICIPALITY
Beijing
Yellow R.
Datong
Dongsheng
Wutaishan 3018m
Hengshan 2017m
Tengger Desert
Wuhai
Ghengis Khan Mausoleum
HEBEI
Tianjin
Shenmu
Muus Desert
Yinchuan
Xinzhou
Yulin
Taiyuan
Shijiazhuang
Qingxu
Yellow
Suide
Fenyang
Pingyao
NINGXIA
SHAANXI
SHANXI
Handan
Yan'an
Luo R.
Yellow R.
Fen R.
SHANDONG
Changzhi
Anyang
Hebi
Guokou Falls
Xiankou
Houma
Xinxiang
Hancheng
Yellow R.
Tongchuan
Sanmenxia
Luoyang
Kaifeng
Zhengzhou
Tianshui
Baoji
Xianyang
Wei R.
Tonggun Falls
Shaolin Monastery
Songshan 1440m
GANSU
Huxian
Xi'an
Huashan 2160m
Xuchang
Shangxian
HENAN
ANHUI
Yangxian
Nanyang
Ankang
Xiangfan
Huangchuan
Xinyang
Guangyuan
HUBEI
SICHUAN
CHONGQING MUNICIPALITY
0 200 miles
0 200 kilometers
Wuhan
CENTRAL CHINA

rebellion, and famines. It wasn't until the Communists ended their Long March in Yan'an, where they set up a base from which to fight the Japanese and Guomindang (Nationalists), that Shaanxi regained political significance.

Today, Shaanxi seems to be pulling out of its thousand-year slump. The dry, dusty northern region of the province is still quite poor, but in the southern region, an influx of foreign and domestic investment has breathed new life into the entire province. Shaanxi has also become one of China's most popular tourist destinations, due in large part to Xi'an's Terracotta Warriors. Things are looking up for old Shaanxi; after a tough millennium, this province is poised for a comeback.

XI'AN 西安 ☎029

When tourists think of Xi'an, they immediately picture the Terracotta Warriors. But this city is no one-hit wonder; known in ancient times as Chang'an, it can back up any boast with its impressive resume. Situated on the crossroads between China and Central Asia, Chang'an grew into one of the world's wealthiest and most sophisticated cities. After the fall of the Tang dynasty, not much happened in Xi'an, although the city continued to broker trade with Central Asia.

It is this millennium of inactivity that has left Xi'an so attractive to tourists today. A latecomer on the industrialization bandwagon, Xi'an is now undergoing rapid development, and the combination of ancient architecture and development makes the city appear weathered but prosperous (not to mention modern and clean). Xi'an also contains a vibrant Muslim quarter, which adds an element of architectural and culinary diversity to the mix. This mellow giant, a favorite among both foreigners and Chinese, deserves to be on any traveler's list of greatest hits.

TRANSPORTATION

Flights: Xi'an Xianyang Airport (xīān xiányáng guójì jīchǎng; 西安咸阳国际机场; ☎870 8450), about 50km northwest of Xi'an, is accessible by shuttle bus (1hr., every hr. 5am-6pm, Y20) from the **CAAC ticket office,** 296 Laodong Lu (☎870 2299; open daily 8am-9pm); many hotels also arrange transportation. To: **Beijing** (8-9 per day, Y450); **Chengdu** (5-7 per day, Y500); **Chongqing** (Sa-Tu and Th, Y460); **Dunhuang** (daily, Y960); **Guangzhou** (3 per day, Y1190); **Harbin** (M, W, and F; Y1220); **Hong Kong** (daily, Y2440); **Jiayuguan** (seasonal, Y890); **Kunming** (up to 4 per day, Y840); **Lanzhou** (2-4 per day, Y430); **Lhasa** (Su-M, W, and F; Y1320); **Nanjing** (1-3 per day, Y860); **Shanghai** (at least 4 per day, Y1010); **Ürümqi** (3-7 per day, Y1330); **Wuhan** (3-5 per day, Y550); **Xiamen** (1-2 per day, Y1310); **Xining** (M-Tu and F-Sa, Y520). International flights to **Nagoya, Japan** (1-2 per day, Y3770).

Trains: Most commute to Xi'an by train, and tickets can sometimes be difficult to acquire, particularly in May and July. Hotels and hostels sometimes buy up tickets and jack up prices. If only hard seats are available, upgrading is often possible. **Xi'an Train Station** (xīān huǒchē zhàn; 西安火车站; ☎727 6076) is at the north end of Jiefang Lu. Foreigners can buy tickets at any window, but the foreigners' ticketing office is on the south side of the station on the 2nd floor. Lost and Found and Information booths are on the west side of station. Storage Y2 per bag. Y20-30 price difference between different level seats. Open daily 8:30-11:30am and 2:30-5:30pm. To: **Beijing** (14½-17hr., 6 per day, Y263); **Chengdu** (16-19hr., 5 per day, Y124-199); **Chongqing** (28½hr., daily Y170); **Guangzhou** (28-29hr., 2 per day, Y414); **Lanzhou** (12-14hr., 6 per day, Y104-167); **Luoyang** (9½hr., daily Y80-90); **Nanjing West** (18-22hr., 2 per day, Y163-253); **Shanghai** (20-24hr., 5 per day, Y199-301); **Taiyuan** (9½-12hr., 2 per day, Y102-163); **Ürümqi** (48hr., 1-2 per day, Y300); **Zhengzhou** (7-10hr., 4 per day, Y77-131).

Buses: Jiefang Men Bus Station (jiěfàngmén qìchē zhàn; 解放门汽车站), opposite the Xi'an Train Station. Open daily 5:30am-6:30pm. Storage Y2 per bag. To: **Huashan** (2hr., every hr. 6am-4pm, Y24); **Lanzhou** (20hr., 1 sleeper per day, Y105); **Luoyang** (14-15hr., 2 per day, Y58); **Yan'an** (8hr., 3 per day, Y54); **Yinchuan** (20hr., 6 per day, Y115); **Zhengzhou** (12hr., daily Y83). **Minibuses** to surrounding towns leave from the parking lot west of the bus station.

Local Transportation: Local buses usually cost Y1, with A/C Y2; many routes have no fare collectors and can't make change. **Minibus** prices vary with distance (Y0.5-5). Several key routes, including **#5** (train station to Yike Daxue) and **#18** (Xiaozhai to Zhangjiabao), run 6am-11pm, but most run 7am-8pm. Some have shorter winter hours. Buses **#5** and **41** serve Jiefang and Heping Lu, while **#43, 201,** and **205** run the Xi and Dong Dajie corridor. Bus **#610** is Xi'an's tourist bus; from Jiefang Men Bus Station, this minibus stops at the Bell Tower, Drum Tower, Little Goose Pagoda, Big Goose Pagoda, and the Shaanxi History Museum. Runs daily 7am-8pm.

Taxis: Base fare Y5, each additional km Y1.2-1.7. Y0.3 per km surcharge 10pm-6am. Airport to city center Y100-120; train or Jiefang Men Bus Station to city center Y8-12.

Bike Rental: The **Flats of Renmin Hotel** (p. 250) rents bikes.

ORIENTATION AND PRACTICAL INFORMATION

Although the modern metropolis has long since outgrown the confines of its ancient walls, Xi'an remains remarkably compact for a city of three million. Streets inside the walls are arranged in a grid pattern that ends abruptly in the narrow alleys of the **Muslim Quarter** in the west, and the pebble-paved streets of the **antique district** in the south. The **Bell Tower** (zhōng lóu; 钟楼) marks the city center; from this point, **Bei Dajie** (北大街), **Nan Dajie** (南大街), **Dong Dajie** (东大街), and **Xi Dajie** (西大街) extend like a cross to the city gates. **Jiefang Lu** (解放路), east of Bei Dajie, runs south from the main train and bus stations to **Heping Gate** (和平门), becoming **Heping Lu** (和平路) south of Dong Dajie. Dong Dajie, Jiefang Lu, and the surrounding quarters are lined with hotels and shops, but many of the major tourist attractions are outside the city walls.

Travel Agencies: CITS, 48 Chang'an Bei Lu (☎524 1864). Arranges tours and books tickets. Commission Y60. English-speaking staff member. Open daily 8am-5:30pm. Other branches at numerous hotels and the airport. **China Golden Bridge Travel Service** (zhōngguó jīnqiáo lǚyóu gōngsī; 中国金桥旅游公司), Bell Tower Hotel, Rm. 227 and 231 (☎725 8863 or 725 7975). Provides similar services and can arrange discounts at many hotels. Commission Y60. Open daily 8am-8pm. Also, the **Flats of Renmin Hotel** (see below), 11 Fenghe Lu (☎624 0349), arranges tours to the Terracotta Warriors and helps guests obtain train tickets in Xi'an's competitive market.

Bank of China: 306 Dong Dajie (☎726 1726). Exchanges foreign currency and travelers' checks on 2nd fl. Open M-F 8:30am-noon and 1-5:30pm.

Bookstores: Shaanxi Foreign Languages Bookstore (shǎnxīshěng wàiwén shūdiàn; 陕西省外文书店), 349 Dong Dajie (☎726 9844). Decent selection of literature classics, mysteries, Shakespeare, English newspapers, as well as the obligatory dictionaries. Open daily 9am-6pm. **Xinhua Bookstore,** 372 Dong Dajie. Selection not quite as impressive as the one at the Foreign Languages Bookstore. Open daily 9am-8pm.

Market: Parkson (bǎishēng gòuwù zhōngxīn; 百盛购物中心), 237 Dong Dajie, east of Jiefang Lu, near the Hyatt Regency. Has a supermarket with a large selection of Western brands. Open in summer daily 9:30am-10pm; in winter 9:30am-9pm.

PSB: 138 Xi Dajie (☎727 5934). Visa extensions and English-speaking staff. Open M-F 8am-noon and 2-6pm.

Hospital: No. 1 People's Hospital (dìyī rénmín yīyuàn; 第一人民医院; ☎ 721 7170), one block west of Nan Dajie. **Zhongxin Hospital,** 161 Xiwu Lu (☎ 721 8916), on the corner of Bei Dajie, is more modern but has fewer English speakers. **Xi'an #4 Hospital,** 281 Jiefang Lu (☎ 721 6916) has an STD Clinic.

Internet Access: Movie and Internet Bar, 341 Dong Dajie, 2nd fl. (☎ 721 1245). Flower garlands, mellow music, and a young crowd provide a relaxed atmosphere. Y3 per hr. Open 24hr. **Frankman,** 414 Dong Dajie (☎ 721 5552), a high-tech bar with numerous computers and fast connections. Y3 per hr. Open 24hr. The **Flats of Renmin Hotel** (see below) offers access for Y9 per hr.

Post Office: China Post, at the Bell Tower. EMS (counter #1) and Poste Restante (counter #14; Y2.3 per item). Open daily 8:30am-8pm. **Postal Code:** 710003.

ACCOMMODATIONS

Hotels that accept foreigners cater primarily to business travelers and tour groups. Backpackers and other budget travelers can find several relatively inexpensive options clustered around the train station. More upscale establishments line Dong Dajie and Xi Dajie in the center of the city. As always, bargain hard.

Flats of Renmin Hotel (rénmín dàshà gōngyù; 人民大厦公寓), 11 Fenghe Lu (☎624 0349), about 5min. from Xinghuo Lu. Bus #9 makes the 30min. trip from the parking lot on the right side of the train station; exit at Xinghuo Lu (9th stop); or take a taxi (about Y10). Despite the peeling paint, sometimes unreliable hot water, and scruffy-looking carpet, all rooms in this backpacker enclave have A/C, TV, and charming soft beds. Internet access Y9 per hr. Rents bikes. Arranges tours (see **Practical Information,** above). Helpful, English-speaking staff. 4-bed dorms in the old building Y30, new building Y40; singles and doubles with bath Y140. ❶

Jiefang Hotel (jiěfàng fàndiàn; 解放饭店), 321 Jiefang Lu (☎742 8946), to the left of the train station's main exit and across the parking lot. Spacious rooms have A/C, TV, and bath; the more expensive doubles are brighter, with newer appliances and more luxurious furnishings. Rooms facing the train station are generally noisier than those in back. Foreign currency exchange available. Reservations recommended. Doubles in back building Y198, front building Y260-280; triples Y360. ❸

YMCA Hotel (qīngniánhuì bīnguǎn; 青年会宾馆), 339 Dong Dajie (☎726 2288), a 5min. walk east along Dong Dajie from the Bell Tower; a red sign points guests down a covered alley. Central location and good deals on 5 small, windowless, spotless basement rooms with A/C, TV, phone, common bath, 24hr. hot water, and sauna. Basement: one double Y120; one triple Y150. Upstairs: doubles Y268; triples Y488. ❷

Shangde Hotel (shàngdé bīnguǎn; 尚德宾馆), 198 Shangde Lu (☎742 6164), one block west of the Jiefang Men Bus Station and a block south of the city wall. Reservations recommended. Showerless, shared triples in basement Y30 per bed; singles Y158; doubles Y158-178; triples Y188. ❶

May First Hotel (wǔyī fàndiàn; 五一饭店), 351 Dong Dajie (☎721 2212). Just minutes by foot from the Bell Tower, this establishment's fame is derived mainly from its street-level Chinese restaurant. Walk through the restaurant to the stairs indicated by the pink sign marked "Housekeeping" (客房部). Rooms have all standard amenities; the cheapest ones are windowless. Travel services available. Singles Y178-238; doubles Y198-238; triples Y288. ❸

Lijing Hotel (lìjìng jiǔdiàn; 丽晶酒店), 6 Xi Dajie (☎728 8731, ext. 100), at the southwest corner of the Bell Tower Square between Zhubashi and Nan Dajie. Well-maintained rooms with A/C, TV, IDD, and bath. Courteous staff, tropical tea house, and milk steam rooms. The central location is a plus. Room discounts available for large groups and longer stays; or you can beg. Singles Y240; doubles Y288. ❸

Xi'an Hotel (xīān fànzhuāng; 西安饭庄), 298 Dong Dajie (☎721 6120), between Juhua Lu and Nanxin Lu. Bus #201 from the train station stops on Dong Dajie, not far from the entrance. Large standard rooms with exceptional baths make this centrally located hotel appealing, if somewhat pricey. Breakfast included. The only rooms available for foreigners are singles Y230-286 and doubles Y230-260. ❹

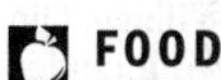

FOOD

The quality, variety, and price of Xi'an's cuisine will easily impress the budget-conscious food connoisseur. West Xi'an boasts excellent Muslim food. **Damaishi Jie** (大麦市街), **Zhubashi** (竹笆市), and the other streets near the Great Mosque in the Muslim Quarter are lined with small food stalls designated as *qīngzhēn* (Muslim; literally, "pure and true"). Lamb bread soup (yángròu pàomò; 羊肉泡馍), a mutton soup peppered with torn pieces of dry bread cake, is especially popular (usually Y4-7). Other Xi'an specialties include rice cakes with sweet filling (米糕; Y1-2), a mutton and wheat mixture (fěnzhēnròu; 粉蒸肉; Y2-3), and dark noodles (hēilāomiàn; 黑捞面; Y2-3). Although many alleys off the main roads house food-peddlers, the largest, **Tanshi Jie,** across from the bank on Dong Dajie, is open late and teems with vendors selling everything from dried spices to live fish.

Jia San Soup Parcel Restaurant (jiǎsān bāoziguǎn; 贾三包子馆), 121 Xiyangshi Jie, Muslim Quarter (☎725 7507). Customers come for the dumplings (Y5 for 10) and the uniquely flavored *zhōu* (粥; Y2), a sweet rice porridge. Open daily 7:30am to 2 or 3am. ❶

Kane's Kafe, 11 Fenghe Lu, conveniently across from the lobby of the Flats of Renmin Hotel. Friendly proprietor Kane dishes up Chinese and Western specialties as well as free travel advice in English. The extensive English menu includes Kane's special pita bread with pork, beef, or chicken filling (Y5), beer (Y4-6 per bottle), and delicious banana and honey porridge (Y5). Good company for free. English music and movies upon request. Kane always tries to make foreigners' trips to China a little brighter, and works with the Flats Hotel to arrange tours. Open daily 7:30am-2am. ❶

Dad's Home Cooking, 2 Fenghe Lu, across from the Flats of Remin Hotel. This establishment dishes up Chinese and Western food (including their famous crepe-like pancakes, Y5-7) to its backpacker clientele. Bike rental, free maps and information, next-day laundry service, tours, and help with train tickets (average commission Y50) available. English-speaking staff member sometimes present. Check out the travelers' logbooks for advice and juicy stories. Open daily 7 or 8am to 11pm or midnight. ❶

King Palace (wángfǔ dàjiǔdiàn; 王府大酒店), 333 Dong Dajie (☎725 0133), on the north side of the street. This enormous entertainment kingdom boasts 7 floors; the bottom 2 house boisterous restaurants that serve Cantonese and Sichuan cuisine. Dumplings (Y3-5); noodles (Y3-6). After eating their fill, visitors might ascend to the 5th through 7th floors, where karaoke rules the house. Open daily 10:30am-10:30pm. ❶

Laosunjia Restaurant (laǒsūnjiā fànzhuāng; 老孙家饭庄), 364 Dong Dajie (☎721 0936). Owner Ma Mingyan was schooled in Marxism, Leninism, Maoism, and yes, even Deng Xiaoping theory. The famous establishment has 5 "feature foods," including Muslim *jiǎozi* (Y0.7), salt-cured beef and mutton (Y13), beef and mutton buns, and *yángròu pàomò*. Banquet rooms serve delicacies like peacock (Y98) and fawn (Y58). Brochures explain their employee indoctrination methods. Open daily 7am-10pm. ❷

Shaanxi Food Village (xīān fànzhuāng; 西安饭庄), 298 Dong Dajie (☎725 2464), just east of Juhua Lu. Wander around this local favorite's 12 display stations of assorted plates of *jiǎozi, bāozi,* veggies, pickled seahorse, and other unidentifiable but intriguing options (Y0.5-16). Popular among locals, meals are prepared by chefs right before the eyes of hungry patrons. More expensive restaurant upstairs. Open daily 7:30am-8pm. ❶

SIGHTS

Tourist agencies and hotels arrange one-day tours that include Xi'an's famous landmarks and finish in time to catch the next train out of town. The more popular

Eastern Tour (p. 253) generally includes the Terracotta Warriors, Banpo Village, Qin Shihuang's tomb, and sometimes Huaqing Pool. The **Western Tour** (p. 255) includes the Xianyang City Museum, imperial tombs, the Qian Tomb, and Famen Temple.

XI'AN CITY SIGHTS

GREAT MOSQUE (dà qīngzhēn sì; 大清真寺). Be prepared to walk the gauntlet of hard-bargaining souvenir vendors before discovering this hidden treasure. The Great Mosque, established in AD 742, features four courtyards, each holding historically fascinating religious records including the "Moon Tablet," a stele that bears Arabic inscriptions about the Muslim calendar. Other treasures include a handwritten copy of the Qur'an (Koran) and Chinese and Arabic inscriptions from the Qur'an carved into the ceiling of the hall of worship. In the second courtyard stand tablets inscribed by famous Chinese calligraphers that are considered some of the best works of art in the country. Non-Muslims are not allowed inside the hall of worship, but the parts of the mosque accessible to the general public are popular among foreigners and well worth a visit. *(Just minutes from the Bell Tower. Buses #201, 205, and 610 from the train station stop at the Bell Tower. From Xi Dajie, take the first right onto Beiyuamen and continue north 1 block until just past the covered tunnel; red signs point the rest of the way. The entrance is down an alley called Huajue Xiang, on the left. Open daily 8am-8pm. Y12, including an English guidebook.)*

SHAANXI HISTORY MUSEUM (shǎnxī lìshǐ bówùguǎn; 陕西历史博物馆). Large Tang-style stone buildings with white tile eaves look out onto the wide courtyards of this relatively new museum. The huge space stores over 3.7 million historical relics, well-preserved by elaborate environmental control systems. The central hall features a permanent exhibit on Shaanxi's history and culture; other exhibits include displays of Bronze Age artifacts, ancient pottery, and sculpture. The exhibits all have English captions. *(91 Xiaozhai Dong Lu. Take bus #610 from the train station. ☎525 4727. Open in summer daily 8:30am-6pm; in winter 9am-5:30pm. Y25, students Y12.)*

BELL TOWER (zhōng lóu; 钟楼). First erected in 1384, this 36m pavilion was moved to its present central location at the intersection of Bei, Nan, Dong, and Xi Dajie in 1582 and then repaired and rebuilt in 1740. The second floor houses an exhibit of ancient musical instruments; the third floor displays calligraphy scroll painting. From the top, visitors get a bird's-eye view of the former capital. Elaborate musical performances (every 30min., 9-11:30am and 2:30-5:30pm) drown out the traffic below. *(Take bus #201, 205, or 610 from the train station to Zhonglou; enter through the pedestrian tunnel. Open daily 8am-7pm. Y15.)*

BIG GOOSE PAGODA (dàyàn tǎ; 大雁塔). This expansive park is comprised of temples, beautiful landscaping, visitors performing incense sacrifices and, of course, the pagoda. The pagoda, built in AD 652, houses over 600 sets of Buddhist scriptures brought to China from India by Xuan Zang, the most famous monk of the Tang dynasty. The pagoda itself, which has been restored many times in the last 1200 years, is a 64m-tall square pyramid of blue brick. On the first story, two stelae offer a Tang-era treatise on Xuan Zang's translations. The pagoda was also known in the Tang dynasty for its walls, on which imperial exam degree recipients inscribed autobiographical poems. *(Bus #610 from the train station stops outside the main entrance. ☎521 5014. Open in summer daily 8am-6:30pm; in winter 8am-6:20pm. Admission Y20 for park entrance and pagoda climbing.)*

LITTLE GOOSE PAGODA (xiǎoyàn tǎ; 小雁塔). Quiet and peaceful, this pagoda, contrary to what its name would indicate, is Big Goose Pagoda's larger neighbor. Completed in AD 709, the Little Goose Pagoda originally shot up 15 tiers, but an earthquake reduced its height to 13 or 14 perspiration-inducing flights. Earthquakes have been something of a theme in the pagoda's history: it has survived over 70 of them. A particularly violent quake in 1487 reputedly left a foot-wide fissure that ran from the top to the bottom of the temple. The crack is rumored to have been mended by an equally violent quake in 1521. *(Bus #610 stops on Youyi Xi Lu, at Xiao Yan Ta stop; coming from the train station, walk east about 1 block. Open daily 8:30am-6pm. Park Y5; park and pagoda Y10.)*

CITY WALL (chéngqiáng; 城墙). Constructed in 1370, long after Xi'an had fallen from imperial capital to mere Ming outpost, the 14km-long city wall is equipped with 5984 (now useless) battlements, 98 (now superfluous) defense towers, and a moat (just for kicks). After 1949, Beijing and other cities tore down city walls to build highways and subways, but central planners thought Xi'an was too poor to "modernize." When the city finally got funding, it chose to restore the walls and turn them into a tourist attraction, complete with Chinese and English explanatory signs. *(From the train station, bus #9 goes to the North Gate, bus #3 goes to the South Gate, and buses #5 and 41 go to Heping Gate. ☎ 725 2067. Open daily 8am-10pm. Y8, students Y4.)*

PALACE OF THE EIGHT IMMORTALS (bāxiān ān; 八仙庵). This Daoist palace offers a lovely counterpoint to China's ever-present Buddhist temples. Under Yuxian Bridge hangs the "lucky and peaceful bell." According to legend, if you hit the bell with a coin, you have a predestined relationship with Daoism and will always be lucky and peaceful. An active place of worship, the temple features two huge stelae with gorgeous, intricate etchings on their upper sections. *(East of Zhongshan Gate. Take bus #22 from the train station to the intersection with Dongxin Jie; walk east 2½ blocks. Open daily 7:30am-5pm. Y5, students Y1.)*

DRUM TOWER (gǔ lóu; 鼓楼). Since 1380, drum beats from this tower have signaled the arrival of dusk. The tower's carved beams and painted columns have held up well with a little help from the restorations bureau. The climb to the top is well worth the effort; colorful exhibits display beautifully restored frescoes from the Dunhuang Grottoes as well as furniture and vases from the Ming and the Qing. *(On Beiyuamen, across a broad square from the Bell Tower. Open daily 8am-7pm. Y12.)*

XI'AN FOREST OF STELAE (xīān bēi lín; 西安碑林). Standing among the traditional Ming and Qing Dynasty architecture and antique shops of the southern portion of the city, the Forest of Stelae contains over 1000 inscription-etched stone slabs in seven small exhibition halls. The collection includes tablets from copies of the *Analects*, works by Mencius, and the Dictionary of Terms, a veritable theme park for philosophers and etched-stone lovers. *(15 Sanxue Jie. Head east on the last street before the South Gate; turn right at the dead end and follow the curving street another 3min.; the museum is on the right side of the street. ☎ 721 3868. Open daily 8am-6pm. Y30.)*

EASTERN TOUR

The Flats of Renmin Hotel (p. 250) organizes transportation for an Eastern Tour that consists of Terracotta Warriors, Qin's Tomb, and Banpo Village (departs 8:30am, returns 3:30pm; Y35). Individual admission fees are not included, and the group must include at least four people. Almost every travel agency in Xi'an also offers the same tour with "more" included for a much higher price. Many visitors opt for the flexibility and economy of public transportation instead.

TERRACOTTA WARRIORS

Buses #306 and 307 from the train station stop outside. Alternatively, minibuses make the trip for about Y5, sometimes dropping people off at the small amusement park about a 15min. walk from the entrance. The trip from Xi'an is approximately 45min. A movie explains the history of the warriors, and displays in each vault provide English and Chinese explanations. Officially, photography is not allowed in the largest vault. ☎391 1961. Open daily 8:30am-5:30pm, no admission after 5pm. Y65, students Y35.

When current French President Jacques Chirac came to Xi'an in 1978, he declared that "with the excavation of the Qin terracotta figures and horses, the world now has its eighth wonder." Chirac's words ring true to anyone who visits the home of Xi'an's Terracotta Warriors (bīngmǎyǒng; 兵马俑). Emperor **Qin Shihuang** (see p. 9), founder of the dynasty that unified China in 221 BC, strove to construct an underground empire that would reflect the glory and dignity of his empire long after his death. So, he immortalized his soldiers by directing artisans to carve out a terracotta army for his tomb in their images. Little did he know that centuries later his efforts would restore the glory and dignity of his capital city.

In 1974, a group of peasants digging for water discovered the army, which consisted of over 7000 slightly larger-than-life clay warriors and war horses waiting in battle formation and posed according to Qin dynasty directives on the art of warfare. Each face differs from those around it, and the clay men's hands grasp for the still-sharp and still-poisoned Qin-era weapons that excited archaeologists quickly whisked away. The first vault, measuring 210m-by-60m, houses 6000 soldiers; the second contains 1000; and the third holds only 68, accompanied by a war chariot. Despite the sea of soldiers on display, some suggest that the excavated army is just one part of an even more magnificent system still buried in Qin Shihuang's tomb.

OTHER EASTERN TOUR SIGHTS

TOMB OF QIN SHIHUANG (qínshǐhuáng líng; 秦始皇陵). The Terracotta Warriors form only one section of the tomb of Emperor Qin Shihuang. The famous emperor ascended the throne of the Qin kingdom at 13 and immediately began the construction of his tomb at Mount Lishan. Seven hundred thousand conscripts built the tomb, which contained model palaces and offices, vessels, and jewels. Because of the high mercury content in the soil, the actual tomb remains unexcavated (at least until technology is invented to excavate it safely). All that visitors can see today is a large mound approximately 1.5km from the vaults of the terracotta warriors. The steps to the top lead to a spectacular view of the surrounding mountains. *(Buses #306 and 307, from both the train station and the terracotta warriors, stop a short distance away; walk in the direction of the souvenir stands. If coming from the warriors, continue in the same direction taken by the bus back to Xi'an. Walking from the warriors is not recommended; a minibus costs only Y0.5-1. Open daily 7:15am-6:30pm. Y26)*

HUAQING HOT SPRINGS (huáqīng chí; 华清池). Dating back more than 2000 years, the Huaqing hot springs have been enjoyed by a succession of emperors and other important figures. Qin Shihuang dubbed the area the "Hot Spring of Lishan Mountain," and in AD 747 Emperor Xuanzong of the Tang expanded it and named it Huaqing Palace. He made it famous by allowing his concubine, Yang Guifei, one of the four legendary beauties in Chinese history, to bathe there. In 1936, Chiang Kai-shek came here to set up his field headquarters against the CCP, and was captured in a coup known as the Xi'an Incident (see p. 16). As far as prisons go, the hot springs weren't so bad—the average temperature is 43°C. *(Bus #306 stops outside the cable car entrance. A minibus back to the train station costs Y3-4 and takes approx. 35min. Open daily 7am-7pm. Y30; hot pool and sauna Y20-120 extra.)*

BANPO NEOLITHIC VILLAGE (bànpō bówùguǎn; 半坡博物馆). Part dry archaeological exhibit and part kitschy theme park, Banpo is on most tourist itineraries. The village is the remains of a 6000-year-old matriarchal clan community in the Yellow River valley, discovered in 1953. Covering 3000m^2, the **Great Hall** is the excavated dwelling area of the Banpo people. Four houses have been reconstructed at the site, and individual graves, group graves, and children's graves have been unearthed. Near the back of the site, enter the "authentic" reproduction of the matriarchal village through an enormous statue of a reclining woman. Banpo also houses a slightly voyeuristic exhibition of photographs of "primitive man." *(Bus #105 from the train station stops at Banpo. Take a right onto Banpo Lu at the first intersection; the museum is about 5min. ahead on the left. Open daily 8am-6pm. Y20.)*

WESTERN TOUR

The Xianyang Museum is the only Western Tour sight reasonably accessible by public transportation. Minibuses (with Chinese-speaking guides) leave from the parking lot behind the train station around 8 or 9am and return around 7pm. The tours follow a tight schedule, and won't allow passengers much flexibility. Average cost is Y45 for transportation; as always, if asked to pay a flat fee in advance, be sure to clarify which sights and admission fees this covers—many tourists report being overcharged or under-tombed on this tour.

FAMEN TEMPLE (fămén sì; 法门寺). Unlike some of the other sites on the western tour, this temple and museum not only house dead bodies, but also a truly amazing collection of relics. Famen Temple is an extraordinary sight, made all the more impressive by its almost two-millennia-long history. The final resting place for four of the Buddha's finger bones (*sarira*), this 1700-year-old Eastern Han dynasty temple was one of the four ancient sacred places in the history of Buddhism. During the Tang dynasty, the temple was expanded to 24 courtyards in order to house many monks and nuns. In 1981, the *sarira* crypt was restored, yielding more than 1000 sacrificial objects preserved for over a thousand years. They are now kept in an on-site museum; the downstairs vault, in white stone and with elaborate gold decoration, is absolutely gorgeous. *(In Fufeng County, a bumpy 115km northwest of Xi'an. Open daily 8am-6pm. Temple Y15; museum Y20.)*

XIANYANG MUSEUM (xiányáng bówùguǎn; 咸阳博物馆). The city of Xianyang witnessed the founding of the Qin dynasty in 221 BC, and was home to 11 ensuing dynasties; this distinction gave rise to cutting-edge cultural and economic achievements, earning it the nickname "Oriental Pearl." The Xianyang Museum pays tribute to this long and impressive history. Originally a Confucian temple, the museum was reconstructed in 1371 during the Ming dynasty and today houses over 5000 objects, primarily relics from the Qin and Han dynasties. The first three rooms contain relics from the Qin dynasty; the fourth contains relics from excavations of Western Han mausoleums. The fifth and sixth rooms house rare colored pottery and 3000 miniature terracotta soldiers. *(Bus #3 goes from the train station to the terminal. From here bus #59 takes you to Xianyang. At the clock tower on the left, turn right; when you reach Xining Jie, turn right again. ☎ (096) 321 3015. Open daily 8am-6pm. Y25.)*

MAOLING MAUSOLEUM (màolíng bówùguǎn; 茂陵博物馆). Referred to as the crown jewel of Western Han dynasty mausoleums, the Maoling houses the tomb of Emperor Wudi (157-87 BC) and those of his relatives and assistants. Perched dramatically on a 47m high hill and overlooking the museum's lush gardens and large, ornamental fountain, Emperor Wudi's tomb once contained many ancient stone sculptures which are now lost or absent. The well-preserved artifacts, including a bronze rhinoceros-shaped vessel used for drinking wine, are now on display. *(40km northwest of Xi'an. Open daily 7:30am-6:30pm. Y21.)*

QIAN TOMB (qián líng; 乾陵). Those visitors feeling especially morbid will enjoy the largest of the surrounding tombs, the burial ground of the third Tang emperor and his wife Empress Wu Zetian the first and only female emperor in Chinese his-

CENTRAL CHINA

tory. It's a pleasant 15- to 20-minute walk from one end to the other. Sculptures of lions and other figures line the long walkway. Other nearby sites include the 17 smaller tombs of princes, princesses, and ministers. *(Open daily 8am-6pm. Y25.)*

PRINCE YI DE'S TOMB (shǎnxī gānlíng yìdé tàizimù bówùguǎn; 陕西干陵懿德太子墓博物馆). In AD 701, 19-year-old Li Zhongren, eldest son of Emperor Zhong Zong, demanded to know why certain nobles were favored in the courts. The Empress had him flogged to death for his insubordination. When Zhong Zong assumed the throne four years later, he honored his son with the title Yi De "The Virtuous" and reburied him alongside an eligible (if deceased) young lady. Excavated in 1971, the tomb was refurbished in 1996 with enough money from the Taiwanese government to restore the gorgeous Tang-style buildings, restaurants, exhibition halls, and, the burial vault itself. Corridors, tunnels, and chambers display the pride of the tomb: 450m^2 of frescoes. *(Open daily 8am-6:30pm. Y21.)*

NIGHTLIFE

Most bars, discos, and clubs are concentrated along Dong Dajie between Bei and Nan Dajie and Jiefang Lu/Heping Lu so the streets are usually filled with activity. The **Bell Tower Square** is especially lively on warm summer nights when it is filled with children, couples in love, and elderly out for a stroll. Enjoy Western film at the newly built **International Cinema** at Zhongda International Place on Nan Dajie, or cool off at **Waterworld** on the corner of Donxia Jie and Jiefange Lu (☎744 7311; open daily 10am-10pm; Y50). If bowling is your thing, try **Xi'an New Times Place,** next to the Lantai hotel, just off the Big Pagoda. (☎553 3485; Y18-24. Open daily 8am-midnight.) Weary travelers might consider forgoing the bar scene and swapping stories over a bottle of Tsingtao at Kane's Kafe (see p. 251).

Apollo Music Bar, 348 Dong Dajie (☎721 3661). Apollo is a strange mascot for this bar, which sees its action at night. The young, well-dressed patrons sit at intimate tables, and a huge stage hosts live music. Beer (Y20-30), wine (Y78-128), and cigarettes (Y10-80) get the conversation flowing. Open daily 2pm-2am.

1+1 Disco Bar (yījiāyī dīsīkē jiǔbā; 1+1迪斯科酒吧), 285 Dong Dajie (☎721 6265), on the left before Tanshi Jie as you come from the Bell tower area. Upstairs, the decor is space-age, with stars hanging from the ceiling and futuristic metal architecture. 'Romantic music' plays until 9pm, when the young crowd begins to grind to house, trance, and disco. Imported beers Y25-28. Open daily 8pm-2am.

Ferryman Bar (☎727 3560), 270 Dong Dajie. Amid a hard-partying, rock 'n roll crowd, try your luck at one of the 6 dartboards while downing a Heineken (Y35) or Budweiser (Y30). Most other drinks Y25 and up. Open daily 2pm to around 2am.

Cafe on 1st High Street, 246 Dong Dajie Lu (☎721 9911). This cafe serves up light drinks (Budweiser Y15). Enjoy traditional bar snacks (pudding Y10) with friends, or head upstairs to get a little closer. Live music starts at 9pm. Open daily 10am-1am.

HUASHAN MOUNTAIN 华山 ☎0913

Proclaimed one of the five sacred Daoist mountains by Emperor Wudi over 2000 years ago, Mount Huashan (also known as Xiyue (xīyuè; 西岳), or "Western Yue") guards the eastern gateway to Shaanxi. In the valley of the towering peak, the small village of Huashan is just another in-your-face tourist town; Mount Huashan itself, however, offers breathtaking surprises. With near-vertical cliffs and plunging ravines, the impenetrable mountain repelled countless invaders of Xi'an over the centuries. The climb to the 2158m summit—both exhilarating and terrifying—makes clear why each time would-be attackers gave up and went home.

ORIENTATION AND PRACTICAL INFORMATION

Huashan village lies at the base of the mountain, approximately 120km east of Xi'an, not far from the main Xi'an-Zhengzhou rail line. **Yuquan Lu** (玉泉路) runs perpendicular to **Jianshe Lu** (建设路), the road along which buses stop. Yuquan continues on to Yuquan Temple and the entrance to the mountain. A number of hotels, restaurants, and souvenir stands line this mainly pedestrian road. The cableway terminus is about 15 min. by minibus southeast of Huashan village. Huashan's administrative center is north of the rail line and mountain.

Trains: Huashan Train Station (huáshān huǒchē zhàn; 华山火车站; ☎438 2285), 15km away in Mengyuan, but linked with Huashan village by frequent minibuses (Y3-5). A taxi may be necessary during the evening or for return trips. To: **Luoyang** (4-5hr., 17 per day, Y26); **Taiyuan** (9hr.; 5 per day; Y48, express Y76); **Xi'an** (1¾-3hr., 19 per day, Y12). Despite its convenient location in Huashan Village, **Huashan West Train Station** (huáshān xī huǒchē zhàn; 华山西火车站) is small; departures are infrequent. To **Luoyang** (4-5hr., daily Y21) and **Xi'an** (3hr., 2 per day, Y9).

Buses: Minibuses to **Xi'an** (2-3hr., Y15-20) leave throughout the day from Yuquan Lu near the Huashan Banking Hotel. **Huashan Bus Station** (huáshān qìchē zhàn; 华山汽车站) is on Jianshe Lu, west of Yuquan Lu; due to the infrequency of departures, most travelers find it more convenient to take the minibus or the train.

Local Transportation: Minibuses #2 and **8** stop at the train station. **Taxis** are easily accessible and do not use meters; Yuquan Lu to the train station costs Y15-20.

Bank of China: On the southwest corner of Yuquan Lu and Jianshe Lu. Exchanges foreign currency but not traveler's checks. Open M-F 9am-5pm, holidays 10am-4pm.

Hospital: (☎436 3975). A 5min. walk from the intersection between Yuquan Lu and Jianshe Lu; turn right on Kangfu Lu.

Internet: Net-friend Club (☎436 6200). Walk down away from the temple and across Jianshe Lu. Turn left at the first alley; it's half-way down on the left. Y5 per hr.

Post Office: Post and Telecommunications Building, on the corner of Dongyue Lu and Dahua Bei Lu. Open daily 8am-6pm. **Postal code:** 714200.

ACCOMMODATIONS

Huashan's cheapest accommodations line Yuquan Lu near the trailhead; rates under Y50 per person are possible, but quality varies considerably. Many hotels charge much higher rates for foreigners. Discounts or the Chinese price may be possible when business is sluggish. On the mountain are more rugged accommodations.

HUASHAN VILLAGE

Huayinshi City Golden Bureau Hostel (huáyīnshì huángjīnjú zhāodàisuǒ; 华阴市黄金局招待所; ☎436 3087), a 2min. walk on Yuquan Lu past Jianshe Lu, on the right. This small family-run hotel provides rooms with A/C, TV, and bath. Storage Y4. 2-room dorms Y40; doubles Y80. ❶

Huayang Hotel (huáyáng dàjiǔdiàn; 华洋大酒店), on Yuquan Lu, 4min. beyond the intersection with Jianshe Lu, on the right. Simple, but sparkling clean rooms with equally clean baths make this small hotel stand above the rest. English-speaking manager gives discounts to foreigners. Doubles Y80-100. ❷

Huayue Hotel (huáyuè bīnguǎn;华岳宾馆; ☎436 2906, ext. 3808). Face the mountain; turn right off the intersection of Yuquan Lu and Jianshe Lu. Clean rooms with A/C. Hotel store sells cigarettes, sneakers, and more. 3-bed dorms Y30 (Y80 for the room); doubles Y128, foreigners Y198, with bath Y218/Y298; triples with bath Y258/Y328). ❶

Tielu Hostel (tiělù zhāodàisuǒ; 铁路招待所; ☎436 4723), on the left side of Yuquan Lu, just past the Huashan Banking Hotel. Rooms are functional, and water supply (especially hot water) can be unpredictable. Deposit Y100. Singles with A/C and bath Y80-100; doubles Y70. ❶

Xiyue Hotel (xīyuè fàndiàn; 西岳饭店; ☎436 4740; fax 436 4559), on the right side of Yuquan Lu, about 2min. from the Yuquan Temple entrance. Reception is down the driveway and to the right. For travelers who value material comforts. All rooms have A/C, TV, phone, and bath, and the plush 2-room singles have lounge chairs and a coffee table. Singles Y480; doubles Y198; quads Y320. MC/V. ❹

MOUNT HUASHAN

North Peak Hotel (běifēng fàndiàn; 北峰饭店; ☎436 5088), a 5min. walk from the North Peak cable car station. Clean rustic rooms, basic bathing facilities (no showers), and common toilets. Beds (during the day only) Y10 per hr.; 30-bed dorms Y30; 14-bed dorms Y40; 8-bed dorms Y50; doubles Y240; quads Y280. ❶

FOOD

Restaurants abound along Yuquan Lu in Huashan village, but proprietors are quite aware of the exploitable tourists. One traveler claims the restaurant attached to the Huangxin Binguan serves up the best dish in China: braised eggplant (Y12). Huayang Hotel, while not cheap, does offer an English menu; the manager often gives discounts. The spicy tofu and vegetables cost Y10. On the other side of Jianshe Lu, noodles and soups are dished up for Y3 per bowl. Refreshment stands are also plentiful along the trail, though the offerings at the summit are much more limited.

CLIMBING MOUNT HUASHAN

Breathtaking peaks, lush vegetation, and an inspiring summit view leave no doubt as to why many consider Huashan sacred. Though the trail is built of pebble-paved paths and stone stairs, the climb is arduous and seemingly endless. The path begins as a steep ascent, but certain stretches near the top are steep enough to transform the handrail from a simple metal chain into a lifeline. Wearing dark clothing and a pair of gloves from the village is advisable; it's hard to keep clean when you're hanging on to a rusty guardrail for dear life.

Basic accommodations at the peak are quite expensive. If you want to see the sunrise from **East Peak** but aren't a big spender, join the crowds of thrifty tourists on a night climb. At least 50 of these climbers set off around 11pm and end up on East Peak as the sun comes up. Be careful when hiking in the dark, or dawn won't be the only thing breaking. *(Flashlights for rental (Y3) or purchase are readily available on Yuquan Lu in Huashan village.)* A cable car ride to **North Peak** decreases the time commitment and thrill factor considerably. *(Minibuses between the cable car base and Huashan village Y10. ☎436 2683. Cable car runs daily 7am-7pm. Y55, round-trip Y100.)* Ticket gates are open 24 hours. Park admission is Y60 plus a mandatory registration fee for foreigners (Y5). **Yuquan Temple** (yùquán yuàn; 玉泉院), at the trailhead, is an obligatory first stop. *(Open 24hr. Y8, foreigners Y20. Try to get someone to buy you a Chinese-priced ticket.)* From there, it is a three- to five-hour climb, eased by numerous (and overpriced) refreshment stands, to **North Peak** (běi fēng; 北峰). Beer is available, as are cucumbers and hard-boiled eggs for a protein kick. It's a good idea to bring your own water, but beverages can also be bought en route. On the way up, be sure to stop and take a look at the scenery once in a while; when not shrouded by fog or mist, the sheer, white granite cliffs are quite imposing. Check out the **Thousand-Foot Cliff** (qiānchǐ chuáng; 千尺幢); it's steep, narrow, and just keeps on going. But the wind that whips off these cliffs can be chilly, so even in the summer bringing warm clothing is a good idea. Old green military jackets can be rented along the way. The climb to North Peak takes up the lion's share of the hike, and *Let's Go* does not recommend it for children. From the North Peak (which is accessible by cable car), you can turn around, or continue along the **Green Dragon Ridge** trail, which connects the North Peak to the West, South, and East Peaks. These trail hikes are shorter and more suitable for children or the less ambitious. The signs, though in English, can be misleading; ask a fellow climber rather than rely on these inaccurate markers. Most visitors continue to the **East Peak** (dōng fēng; 东峰), about one-and-a-half hours from the North Peak, and accessible by the trail above the number "6" sign. The **West Peak** (xī fēng; 西峰) is about one-and-a-half to two hours away; while the **South Peak** (nán fēng; 南峰) is about 45 minutes beyond it. Take care on the descent; while the hike up is an athletic challenge, the climb down is one of balance, patience, and poise.

YAN'AN 延安

☎0911

The final stop of the Long March in 1937, Yan'an is now the terminus for many tour groups making the same pilgrimage as Chairman Mao and the Communist Party. In the late 1930s, Yan'an's stark landscape of wind-swept sandstone cliffs provided the backdrop for the "birthplace of the revolution," and was the headquarters of the Chinese Communist Party for nine years. The city now symbolizes the heroic and idealistic phase of the revolution (see p. 16). Even though revolutionary fervor has since diminished, massive construction projects prove that this city has not been completely forgotten. With over 20 tourist sites, there is enough Mao fervor to go around.

TRANSPORTATION

Flights: Yan'an Airport (yánān jīchǎng; 延安机场) is about 5km northeast of the city center. A limited number of flights. Buses to the airport depart from the **CAAC ticket office** (☎211 3854), a 10min. walk from the bus station down Dongguan Jie away from the city center; or take a taxi (Y10). Open daily 8-11am and 2:30-5:30pm. Flights run to **Beijing** (1½hr., 4 per week, Y70) and **Xi'an** (1hr., 5 per week, Y180).

Trains: Yan'an Train Station (yánān huǒchē zhàn; 延安火车站; ☎249 6976) is at the far southern end of town on Qilipu Dajie. Buses #1, 3, and 12 stop right outside, as do numerous minibuses. The ticket office (open daily 8:30-10am, 3:30-5pm, and 8:30-10:30pm) is to the right of the waiting room when facing the station. Window #2 sells hard sleeper tickets for the evening train to Xi'an starting at 3pm; tickets sell out fast, so buy early. Same day sales only. To **Xi'an** (8-9hr., 2 per day, Y70-84).

Buses: Yan'an Bus Station (yánān qìchē zhàn; 延安汽车站; ☎211 2531 or 211 3350) is on the right side of Dongguan Jie, as you head away from the city center. Buses #4, 6, and 8 serve the station. To: **Beijing** (27hr., 11am, Y174); **Lanzhou**

CENTRAL CHINA

(25hr., 6:30am, sleeper Y127); **Xi'an** (9hr., frequent departures, Y56). Express buses also travel to **Xi'an** (6hr., 9:15am, Y80).

Local Transportation: Eleven **bus** routes run 6am-8pm. Frequent **minibuses** to and from the train station and other key areas follow the same routes as public buses. Service extends until at least 10pm. Bus fare Y0.5; minibuses Y1-3.

Taxis: Base fare Y5, each additional km Y1.

ORIENTATION AND PRACTICAL INFORMATION

Yan'an's main commercial areas and streets run parallel to the Yan and Nanchuan rivers, with the city center lying west of the confluence. **Zhongxin Jie,** which becomes **Beiguan Jie** farther north, is the main street. It intersects with **Daqiao Jie** which becomes **Dongguan Jie** on the east side of the river, next to the bus station. While the bus station, several parks, and a few sites are located near the city center, the train station and many attractions are several kilometers away.

Travel Agency: CITS, 106 Dajie (☎212 3320). Ticket commission Y10. English-speaking staff member. Open daily 8am-noon and 2:30-6pm.

Bank of China: On the right side of Beiguan Jie, a couple of minutes past the Yan'an Hotel (☎211 2423). Exchanges foreign currency and traveler's checks. English-speaking staff member at window #11. Open M-F 8:20am-noon and 2-6pm.

Hospital: Yan'an People's Hospital (yánān dìqū rénmín yīyuàn; 延安地区人民医院; ☎213 1122), on Zhongxin Jie, across from the Yan'an Hotel.

PSB: On left side of Beiguan Jie, across from Bank of China.

Telephones: China Telecom (☎211 9900), one block north of Daqiao Jie on the northwest corner of Zhongxin Jie. Open 8am-7pm.

Post Office: On Zhongxin Jie, away from Daqiao Jie toward the Yan'an Hotel; it's on the left. EMS and Poste Restante. Open daily 8am-midnight. **Postal Code:** 716000.

CENTRAL CHINA

ACCOMMODATIONS

The **Yan'an Hotel** is the only hotel officially open to foreigners. A few others that have clout with the authorities or are too obscure to be regulated may take you in.

Jiao Tong Fandian (☎213 1581). From the bus station, turn right; the hotel is a 1min. walk, on the right side of Dongguan Jie. The cheapest place in town that accepts foreigners. Rooms include TV and bath, and the staff is more than willing to fix any broken amenities. 2-room dorms Y45. ❶

Yasheng Hotel (yàshèng dàjiǔdiàn; 亚圣大酒店; ☎213 2778; fax 213 2779). From the train station, take bus #3 to the intersection between Er Daojie and Zhongxin Jie; the hotel is straight ahead on Er Daojie. Boasting a large business center, karaoke room, and revolving restaurant, the Yasheng Hotel also offers gorgeous rooms with immaculate baths, A/C, and TV. Singles Y228; doubles Y380. ❸

Yan'an Hotel (☎211 3122), on Beiguan Jie. Bus #3 from the train station stops in front; taxi costs Y7-8. Spacious doubles with A/C, sparkling baths, and TV. Doubles Y380. ❺

FOOD

Eating in Yan'an is catch as catch can. Two night markets, on either side of Daqiao Bridge, serve a number of northern Shaanxi specialties; *heluo* noodles are about Y2-3 per bowl. The chatty boardinghouse atmosphere of the **Jiao Tong Restaurant** (attached to Jiao Tong Fandian; see above) complements the cheap noodles (Y4) and delicious hotpot (Y12). Several Mongolian hotpot restaurants, mostly along Daqiao Jie and Zhongxin Jie, supplement the local cuisine.

SIGHTS

A slew of well-maintained exhibits lets visitors to get up close and personal with not only the former Chairman, but also former premier Zhou Enlai and other key members of the Communist Party. Most attractions are outside the city center, but the city's compactness makes it possible to get your Mao fix in one day.

YANGJIALING REVOLUTION HEADQUARTERS (yángjiālǐng gémìng jiùzhǐ; 杨家岭革命旧址). Set among the dry hillsides outside Yan'an are the Central Committee's meeting hall, offices, propaganda and policy research divisions, and other key administrative departments. To truly get in the revolutionary spirit, many visitors pay Y10 to don a Mao suit and have their picture taken at the podium where the former Chairman spoke. *(Take bus #1 or 3 from the train station to the last stop, then walk back toward the city for 10min. Taking a left at the first vendor-lined alley leads to the large stone gates of the entrance. Open daily 7:30am-6pm. Y11.)*

YAN'AN REVOLUTION MUSEUM (yánān gémìng jìniànguǎn; 延安革命纪念馆). After taking the obligatory picture of the massive stone carving of Mao, tourists slowly meander through the museum and its impressive collection of maps, relics, and old photographs, all without English captions. Mao's horse (stuffed, of course) holds a place of honor here; legend says that when its death was near, it turned toward Zhongnanhai, the residential complex of top CCP government officials, and gave three cries as a final farewell to its rider. *(The big orange building at the northern end of Wangjiaping Bridge. Take bus #1 or 3 from the train station and walk across the bridge. ☎211 2610. Open in summer daily 8am-6pm; in winter 8am-5pm. Y11.)*

BAO PAGODA (bǎo tǎ; 宝塔). Built in AD 766-78, the 44m high pagoda is such a fixture in the Yan'an skyline that its silhouette often appeared on Mao buttons in the 1960s. The climb up the claustrophobia-inducing staircase has its rewards: on clear days, the city and the distant desert countryside are visible. *(On the east side of Nanchuan River. Take bus #1 to Xiao Dong Men. After buying a ticket, continue along the road away from the train station, and take the first right. The walk up to the pagoda takes 15-20min.; taxis also make the trip. Open daily 7am-7pm. Park entrance Y10; pagoda climb Y5.)*

HENAN 河南

Over 90 million people call Henan home, making it the second most populous province in China. This area, the "cradle of Chinese civilization," was once home to three ancient national capitals (Luoyang, Kaifeng, and Anyang), which have left behind enough relics and ruins to satisfy even the most rapacious history buff. Recently, Henan has attracted a number of foreign investors; as a result, the province is filled with projects that are perpetually under construction. This situation is just fine with Henan, especially if projects like the Xiaolangdi Dam keep fueling the development of cities like Luoyang and Zhengzhou.

ZHENGZHOU 郑州 ☎0371

Droves of Chinese and foreign travelers pass through Zhengzhou en route to the Shaolin Monastery, Luoyang, or Kaifeng; few stick around for more than a night or two. But this capital of Henan province is far from dull; even the exterior of its train station is shiny and new, evidence of Zhengzhou's important role as a transportation hub. There are few notable tourist attractions within the city itself apart from the Henan Provincial Museum and the Erqi Pagoda shopping district.

TRANSPORTATION

Flights: Zhengzhou Airport (zhèngzhōu jīchǎng; 郑州机场), 5km east of the city center. The CAAC bus (45min., every hr., Y15) goes to the airport from the Aviation Hotel (mínháng dàjiǔdiàn; 民航大酒店), 3 Jinshui Lu (☎599 1111). To: **Beijing** (3-4 per day 8:30am-6:20pm, Y630); **Guangzhou** (3 per day 8:55am-4:35pm, Y1230); **Hong Kong** (Su-M, F 9am; Y2390); **Kunming** (2-3 per day 9:35am-3:35pm, Y1150); **Shanghai** (4 per day 8:05am-3:55pm, Y730); **Xi'an** (3:30pm, Y460).

Trains: Zhengzhou Train Station (zhèngzhōu huǒchē zhàn; 郑州火车站; ☎835 1111, ticket info ☎698 8988), in the big square at the end of Datong Lu and Zinlong Jie, southwest of the main commercial center. Tickets (especially sleepers) for trains not originating in Zhengzhou are difficult to obtain. To: **Beijing** (8hr.; many per day, 4 originating; Y95-175); **Guangzhou** (22hr.; 7 per day, 1 originating; Y25); **Luoyang** (2½hr.; many per day, 1 originating 4:48pm; Y330); **Nanjing** (9hr., 5:58 and 7:53pm, Y90-175); **Shanghai** (14hr., 5:58 and 11:45pm, Y230); **Shijiazhuang** (6hr.; many per day; hard seat Y65, hard sleepers Y150); **Taiyuan** (12hr., 5:50 and 8:44pm, Y85); **Wuhan** (5½hr.; 12 per day, 2 originating 8:10 and 10:40pm; Y60); **Xi'an** (8-9hr.; many per day, 4 originating; Y90).

Buses: Zhengzhou Bus Station (zhèngzhōu qìchē zhàn; 郑州汽车站; ☎696 3361), on Xinlong Jie, across the square from the train station. To: **Anyang** (3hr., every 30min., Y33); **Beijing** (8hr., 10 per day, Y150); **Shanghai** (20hr., 5:20pm, Y181); **Taiyuan** (8hr., 9:30am and 1:30pm, Y140).

Local Transportation: Datong Lu, opposite and to the right from the train station entrance, is a hub for local buses. Nearly every bus stops here before heading back to the Erqi Pagoda (via Fushou Jie) and then onto their individual routes. Fare Y1. Bus **#2** leaves from Datong Lu, traversing a circular route that extends as far east as Dongming Lu and north to Nongye Lu; **#32** also leaves for Datong Lu and, once past the Erqi Pagoda, travels north to the end of Jingqi Lu before turning east down Nongyue Lu; **#4** and **201** head west from the train station to the Zhengzhou University area. **Minibuses,** including **#16** to the Yellow River, ply many routes 6am-8 or 9pm. Fare Y4 and under.

Taxis: Base fare Y5-6, each additional km Y1.

ORIENTATION AND PRACTICAL INFORMATION

Zhengzhou, about 30km south of the Yellow River, is a major regional rail hub. Most activity concentrates around the train station square, which is crowded at all hours. Northeast, **Erqi Pagoda,** a notable landmark with streets that radiate from it in five directions, is a 15-minute walk from the train station. This area and, to a lesser extent, the area around the intersection of Jinshui Lu and Zijingshan Lu are home to department stores, boutiques, restaurants, and hotels. **Erqi Lu** (二七路) and **Renmin Lu** (人民路) are main thoroughfares that begin at the pagoda.

Travel Agency: CITS, Haitong Bldg., 50 Jinqi Lu, 8th fl. (☎392 7758 or 392 7768), at Weiwu Lu. Li Shengjiang, the European-US manager, speaks English well. Arranges tours to Shaolin Temple (Y80-100, not including admission). Train ticket commission Y30-50. Free airline booking. Open M-F 8:30am-noon and 2-6:30pm.

Bank of China: At the intersection of Chengdong Lu and Jinshui Lu. Exchanges currency and traveler's checks. Credit card advances. Open daily in summer 8am-6:30pm; in

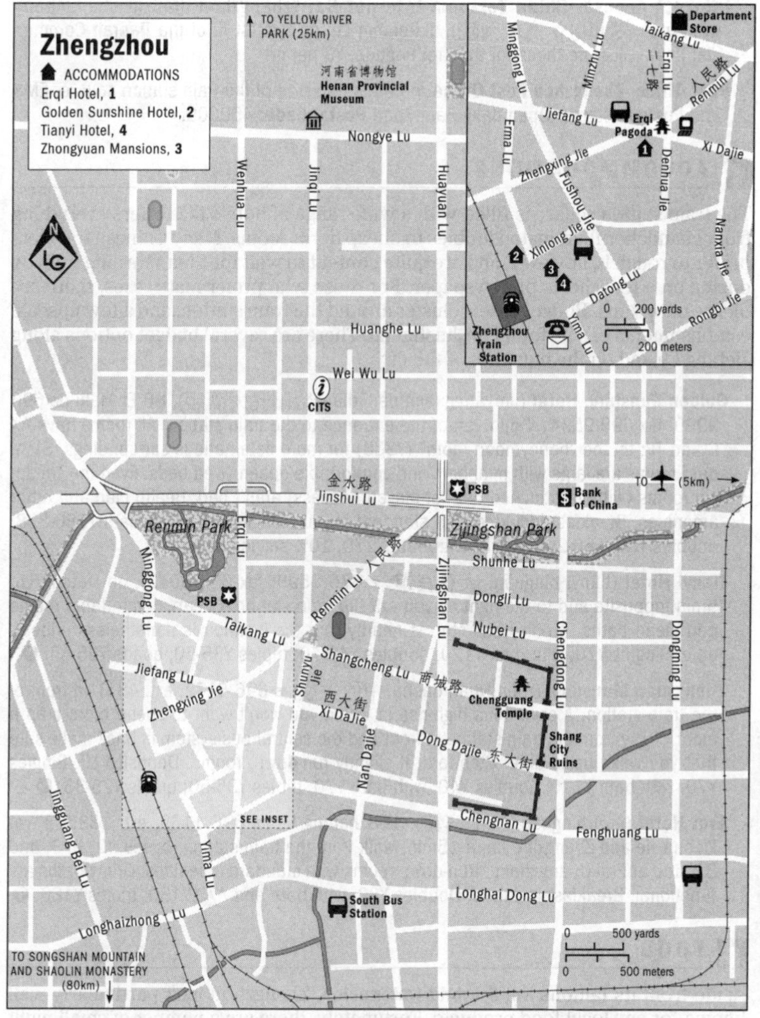

winter 8am-5:30pm. **Guangdong Development Bank** (guǎngdōng fāzhǎn yínháng; 广东发展银行), 8 Jinshui Lu, just west of the Bank of China, has an **ATM** (V).

Market: Zhengzhou Department Store (zhèngzhōu bǎihuò dàlóu; 郑州百货大楼), 49 Erqi Lu, north of Erqi Pagoda. Open daily 9am-8pm.

PSB: 110 Erqi Lu (☎622 2023), near People's Park. Open M-F 8:30am-noon and 3-6:30pm.

Hospital: First Affiliated Henan Medical University Hospital (zhèngzhōushì yīxué yīyuàn; 郑州市医学医院; ☎691 3114), where Zhengzhou Lu meets Daxue Lu.

CENTRAL CHINA

Internet Access: China Telecom Internet Bar (zhèngzhōu diànxìn shāngchéng wǎngyuàn; 郑州电信商城网院), 1 Renmin Lu, on the 1st fl. of the Tianran Commercial Center, just northeast of the Erqi Pagoda. Y3 per hr.

Post Office: Zhengzhou Post Office, on the south side of the train station square. EMS and Poste Restante. Open daily 8am-7pm. **Postal Code:** 450000.

ACCOMMODATIONS

The train station square is filled with a wide range of hotels that offers everything from chandelier-illuminated lobbies to cheap dorm rooms. Many Chinese travelers prefer to rough it, however, and are quite content to wait for their morning train by dozing on a few sheets of newspaper. For those who prefer mattresses, there are plenty of options. Budget hotels cluster around the train station, and a few upscale establishments can be found on Jinshui Lu. There are several budget options along Jiefang Lu and on the outskirts of the city.

Golden Sunshine Hotel (jīn yángguāng dàjiǔdiàn; 金阳光大酒店), 86 Er Malu (☎696 9999; fax 699 9534), 3min. left of the entrance to the train station. All rooms have A/C and TV; try the "honeymoon room" (Y388) for more ostentatious surroundings. Standard rooms are large with mini-bars and comfortable queen-sized beds. Even the cheapest rooms (without attached bath or elevator access) aren't bad. Health club and other amenities. Breakfast included with standard rooms. Singles Y40, with bath Y180-328; doubles Y60/160-298; triples with bath Y270. 10% service charge. ❶

Tianyi Hotel (tiānyì bīnguǎn; 天意宾馆; ☎676 8599; fax 696 8612), on Datong Lu, 5min. opposite and to the right as you exit the train station. Cheap, comfortable rooms and clean baths. A noisy bus stop is nearby, but the location is nonetheless unbeatable. Singles Y70, with bath Y120; doubles Y40-70; triples Y35-50; quads Y25-45. ❶

Zhongyuan Mansions (zhōngyuán dàshà; 中原大厦; ☎696 6172, ext. 481), in front of the train station. A cavernous high-rise in which you won't want to spend more than a night. Noise from the train station in front and the central bus system in back make sure that you wake up in time. Standard, if slightly run-down, rooms. Deposit Y10. Singles Y70, with bath Y120; doubles Y40, with bath Y70; triples Y35-50; quads Y25-35. ❶

Erqi Hotel (èrqī bīnguǎn; 二七宾馆), 168 Jiefang Lu (☎696 1169, ext. 183573), at Dehua Jie and Zhengxing Jie, a 15min. walk from the train station; buses #2, 6, 9, and 32 stop at Erqi Guangchang. Run-down rooms with standard amenities. Grimy baths are functional. Breakfast included. Doubles Y80, with bath and A/C Y130; triples Y180. ❶

FOOD

Aside from its famous **No. 3 hybrid watermelon,** Zhengzhou isn't particularly well known for any local food products. Fortunately, there are a number of small night market stalls around the alleys near the Erqi Pagoda. For your slurping delight, be sure to sample a bowl of *shāguō miàn* (砂锅面) or *huìmiàn* (烩面), wavy noodles flavored with seaweed and cooked in a clay pot (Y3). Stalls sell both in a small alley off Remin Lu, near the base of the pedestrian overpass; most close up around 9pm. Calm late night munchies at another market that sets up at 10pm along Dehua Jie, near the McDonald's. Many restaurants and street stands serving Muslim or Sichuanese cuisine line Ziyou Lu and Minzhu Lu off Jiefang Lu.

For Western and Chinese fusion cuisine, go to **Haoxianglai Restaurant** ❷ (háoxiǎnglái; 毫享来), 21 Minggong Lu, a 10-minute walk south of the Minggong Lu entrance to People's Park. Take bus #2 from the station to Minggong Lu and walk north for a few minutes; the restaurant is on the left. This clean, cheery place serves everything from curried chicken to *dim sum*, but the set meals (Y25), bubbling plates of egg, pasta, and meat, are the most worthwhile (☎622 6038. Open 24hr.) There is a **KFC** on the west side of Erqi Lu, just north of Erqi Pagoda, and a **McDonald's** to the south, on Denhua Jie. Summertime competition between the two results in unbeatably priced Y1 ice cream cones. (Open daily 9am-10pm.)

SIGHTS

Zhengzhou is best known as a jumping-off point for tours of Shaolin Monastery. Yet, most sights within the city provide an escape from city commotion. The cool, ultra-modern Henan Provincial Museum and the pleasant (and obviously man-made) greenery of the parks help block out the rumble of trains and honking of buses. Take bus #601 from the train station to **Zijingshan Park** (zǐjīngshān gōngyuán; 紫荆山公园), on Jinshui Lu, west of Chengdong Lu. In the evenings, vendors sell steamed corn to droves of visitors. Go fishing for Y10; if you catch anything be prepared to pay an extra Y8-16. *(Open daily sunrise-sunset. Free.)* **People's Park** (rénmín gōngyuán; 人民公园), near Erqi Lu and Xili Lu, is accessible via buses #6 and 24 from the train station, but the wide spaces in the park lanes only add to the lonely atmosphere. *(Open daily 6:30am-10pm. Y2.)*

HENAN PROVINCIAL MUSEUM (hénán shěng bówùguǎn; 河南省博物馆). The most interesting and best-preserved relics discovered in the Henan province have found their way to this gigantic pyramidal museum, whose impressive collection fills four floors of exhibition space. Oracle bone inscriptions, a full-body jade suit, fantastic replicas of classical architecture, and even the occasional vegetable (ivory cabbage and radishes from the Qing dynasty) grace the halls. Fascinating English captions enhance the experience. Tuesday through Sunday, at 10:30am and 4pm, you can enjoy a 30-minute musical performance that uses ancient instruments. *(8 Nongye Lu, at the north end of Jinqi Lu. Bus #32 stops one block to the east. ☎351 1250. Open daily in summer 8:30am-6pm; in winter 8:30am-5pm; last admission 30min. before closing. Audio tours in English Y30, deposit Y100. Y20, students Y10.)*

DAYTRIP FROM ZHENGZHOU: SONGSHAN AND SHAOLIN

Stretching 500km across central Henan is Songshan Mountain (1492m), a hotbed for Daoist worship ever since the mountain was named as one of the 5 sacred Daoist mountains in the Zhou dynasty. It's no longer quite as secluded; the area and nearby monastery attract thousands of young boys eager to master the techniques of Shaolin kung fu. Travelers don't have to face a weary climb to the top of Songshan, making the mountain an easy daytrip from either Luoyang or Zhengzhou.

SHAOLIN MONASTERY

***Minibuses** make the trip from Zhengzhou, departing from the long-distance bus station (daily 8am, returning 4pm; Y25.5, round-trip Y40.5). Most hotels arrange their own tours. The standard price for round-trip tickets is Y40, in low season Y30. A direct trip to Shaolin takes 2-2½hr., but extra stops (the Han Tombs, Zhongyue Temple, a souvenir store, the gas station, or a restaurant) can result in a 5hr. ride. Minibuses leave from the bus station next to the entrance of the train station (1½-2hr., many each morning based on demand; round-trip Y30). Stops generally include a tourist shop and the White Horse Temple. Upon arrival, you can stay with the tour bus (Y65 including admission) or visit the sights yourself. The latter option is certainly feasible; all the attractions, save only the Bodhidharma Cave, lie along the main road and are within 15min. walking distance from each other. Motorcabs can also take you around for Y3-5, but they tend to overcharge. Make sure to* *confirm the place and time to meet up with your original bus or you might have trouble finding a way back and have to pay extra.*

The cult of kung fu is going strong in Shaolin Monastery (shàolín sì; 少林寺). Although brightly colored uniforms have replaced monastic uniforms, the thousands of young trainees who fill the neighborhood still practice the kicks and jabs that made this tradition famous. Vigorous exercise certainly pays off—where else can you find dozens of 8-year-olds who could kick your butt? Almost every technique imaginable has been used to instill discipline in Shaolin martial arts (*wǔshù*; 武术) students. Training methods include ramming logs into a volunteer's stomach, meditating while suspended from a tree, using stones to crack walnuts over each other' heads, and other strength-testing and character-building exercises.

SHAOLIN TEMPLE (shàolín sì; 少林寺). Opened in AD 495, the monastery turned to Zen Buddhism after a visit by Bodhidharma in 527, when it began to adapt local martial arts to Buddhist teachings. These monks were far from secluded, showcasing their fighting prowess by helping Tang Emperor Taizong vanquish bandit rebels. The halls and shrines within the temple are in excellent condition; most were rebuilt after 1928. **Daoxong Hall,** the main hall of worship, was restored in 1985 and stands in ornate, gorgeous splendor. **Wenshu Hall,** a smaller building near Daoxong Hall, contains a stone supposedly emblazoned with the image of Bodhisattva Wenshu. **Li Xue Pavilion** (Standing-in-the-Snow Pavilion) marks the place where the master monk Huike stood deep in the snow and cut off his own left arm in order to understand the essence of Zen Buddhism. Within **Pilu Pavilion,** colored frescoes depicting the story of the 500 *arhats* adorn the walls. Forty-eight footprints cover the brick floor where monks have gathered and worshiped in this same spot for centuries. **Chuipu Hall,** an easy-to-miss courtyard to the left of the entrance to the temple, was built in 1984 and has 216 lively plaster figurines depicting Shaolin martial arts and famous temple legends. *(15min. walk on main road from the entrance, on the right. Open daily in summer 7:30am-6pm; in winter 8am-5:30pm.)*

CENTRAL CHINA

SHIFANG MONASTERY (shífāng chányuàn; 十方禅院). This small monastery features a collection of 500 colorful Buddhas with lively expressions and varied poses. As a neat fortune-telling exercise, visitors can pick the *arhat* that they find particularly appealing, count down the same number as their age (plus one year), and then read the explanatory note (in Chinese) on the Buddha statue. *(Across the street from Shaolin Temple. Open daily in summer 7am-6:30pm; in winter 8am-5:30pm.)*

OTHER SHAOLIN SIGHTS. The **Shaolin Stupas Forest** (tǎ lín; 塔林), at the end of the parking lot, a 15-minute walk from the Shaolin Temple, has many small pagodas and a nice view of the mountain range. About seven minutes farther up, the **Forest of Birds** (bǎiniáo lín; 百鸟林) has a screened-off forest of squawking birds. Near the main entrance, **Quanzhou Cinema** (quánzhōu yǐngyuàn; 全周影院) shows a laughable panoramic video, which is worth seeing for bird-training techniques and silly images of foreigners praying. **Wushu Hall** (wǔshù guǎn; 武术馆) has martial arts demonstrations daily 11am and 1:30pm. Hardly anyone makes the two-hour-plus trek up to **Bodhidharma Cave** (dámā dòng; 达摩洞), which is better seen with binoculars (Y1), and **Science Fiction Hall** (kēhuàn guǎn; 科幻馆); watching the martial arts classes and checking out the beautiful fields just inside the main entrance are far more worthwhile. *(All included in admission fee to Shaolin.)*

OTHER SONGSHAN SIGHTS. At the foot of Songshan Mountain, **Zhongyue Temple** (zhōngyuè miào; 中岳庙) is an important, although not too exciting, Daoist place of worship. Inside the compound, a bit off to the side, stand four figures known as the "Iron Men of the Song." Supposedly, rubbing the figures and then touching a sore spot on your own body will magically eliminate the pain. *(Open daily in summer 7am-7pm; in winter 7am-6pm. Y15.)*

LUOYANG 洛阳 ☎0379

As one of China's seven ancient capitals (see **The Birth of a Nation,** p. 9), Luoyang was witness to innumerable power struggles. But today, despite the city's struggles with industrial development, it boasts peaceful tree-lined boulevards and fashionable boutiques. Shaded parks are filled with people exercising in the morning, playing cards in the afternoon heat, or waltzing in the cool summer nights. The Longmen Grottoes, the White Horse Temple, and other historical sights attract many visitors, especially during the annual Peony Festival, when the Royal City Park showcases over 500 varieties of Empress Wu Zetian's favorite flower.

TRANSPORTATION

Flights: Luoyang Airport (luòyáng jīchǎng; 洛阳机场; ☎393 5301, ext. 510), over 10km north of the city. **CAAC ticket office,** 196 Chundu Lu (☎231 0121), west of the train station, at the intersection with Shachang Bei Lu. Open daily 8am-7pm. To **Beijing** (7:40pm, Y630) and **Shanghai** (10:20am, Y810).

Trains: Luoyang Train Station (luòyáng huǒchē zhàn; 洛阳火车站; ☎323 4321), on Jinguyuan Lu. To: **Beijing** (13hr., 5pm, Y113); **Guangzhou** (28hr., 15:28pm, Y211); **Shanghai** (19hr., 9:27pm, Y236); **Wuhan** (10hr., 5:28pm, Y46); **Xi'an** (7hr., several per day, Y55-87).

Buses: Luoyang Bus Station (luòyáng chángtú qìchē zhàn; 洛阳长途汽车站; ☎323 2945), on the corner of Jinguyuan Lu and Daonan Lu, diagonally opposite the train station. To: **Anyang** (5hr., every hr. 7:30am-4pm, Y48); **Guangzhou** (27hr., 6pm, Y160); **Kaifeng** (3½hr., every 30min., Y33); **Taiyuan** (11hr., 3 per day, Y81); **Xi'an** (7-8hr., several per day, Y61-65); **Zhengzhou** (2½hr., every 20min. 7am-7pm, Y26). The ticket office for deluxe buses to **Beijing** (10hr., 8am and 9pm, Y188) is to the right of the main entrance to the waiting hall.

Local Transportation: Most **buses** stop running around 8-9pm. **Minibuses** run along Zhongzhou Zhong Lu late into the night. Fare for both Y1. Buses **#5** and **48** run east along Zhongzhou Zhong Lu and up Jinguyuan Lu to the train station; **#83** goes north from the main train station to the Ancient Tombs Museum and the airport; **#102** and **103** run along Zhongzhou Xi Lu and up Jinguyuan Lu to the train station.

Taxis: Base fare Y6. Motorcycle taxis cost at least Y3.

ORIENTATION AND PRACTICAL INFORMATION

Luoyang sits on the northern bank of the Luo River, and covers an area of nearly 500km². Most of the city's hotels, shops, and restaurants are near **Zhongzhou Lu,** which runs east-west across the city, and **Jinguyuan Lu.** The main train and bus stations are on the northern edge of the city; the airport is to the northwest.

Travel Agency: CITS (☎432 3212 or 431 3701), in the Tourist Mansion on Jiudu Xi Lu. Free airline reservations; Y30 commission for train tickets. Open daily in summer 8am-6pm; in winter 8am-5:30pm.

Bank of China: 439 Zhongzhou Zhong Lu, in the Int'l Finance Building. Exchanges currency and traveler's checks. Credit card advances. Open M-F 8am-noon and 3-6:30pm.

Markets: Luoyang Department Store (luòyáng shì bǎihuò dàlóu; 洛阳市百货大楼), 287 Zhongzhou Zhong Lu (☎325 2453). Open daily 9am-7pm. **Xicheng Market** (xīchéng liàngfàn; 西城量贩), on Zhongzhou Lu 1 block west of Jinguyuan Lu. Here you can find pajamas and packaged meat in the same aisle. Open daily 8:30am-9:30pm.

PSB: 1 Kaixuan Xi Lu (☎394 8257). Open M-F 8:30am-noon and 2:30-5pm.

Hospital: The **150th Military Hospital** (150 zhōngxīn yīyuàn; 150中心医院; ☎486 1784) has a reputable Foreigner's Building. Accessible by buses #55, 101, or 103.

Internet Access: Bai Hua Lin (báihuà lín; 白桦林), 120 Zhongzhou Zhong Lu (☎349 3798). Take bus #5 or 9 to Gong Jiao Zong Gong Si; it's on the right. Y2 per hr. Open 24hr. **Kaituo Computer City** (kāituò diànnǎo chéng; 开拓电脑城), China Mobile building, 4th fl., on the corner of Zhongzhou Xi Lu and Yan'an Lu. Take bus #101 or 103 to Motuo Dalou; a block away on the left. Y3 per hr., deposit Y10. Open daily 8am-6pm.

Post Office: (☎393 8683), on the corner of Zhongzhou Zhong Lu, just east of Jinguyuan Lu. EMS and Poste Restante. Open daily 8am-7pm for packages, 8am-9pm for all other service. **Postal Code:** 471000.

ACCOMMODATIONS

Accommodations open to foreigners generally fall into one of two categories: cheap, noisy hotels near the main train station, or relatively posh establishments along Zhongzhou Lu in the city center.

Luoyang Hotel (luòyáng lǚshè; 洛阳旅社; ☎393 5181), on the corner of Daonan Lu and Jinguyuan Lu, opposite the main train station. Dorm rooms share common showers; baths are comfortable enough. 6-10 bed dorms Y10; 4-bed dorms Y12-15; 3-bed dorms Y20; singles Y50, with bath Y70; doubles Y69/Y90. ❶

Tianxiang Hotel (tiānxiāng fàndiàn; 天香饭店), 56 Jinguyuan Lu (☎391 6652), a 2min. walk from the main train station. Slightly quieter than other hotels near the station, but of similar quality. You probably don't want to spend more time than you have to in this somewhat dingy hotel. Midnight curfew. Hot water at random hours. Dorms Y20-50; doubles with bath and A/C Y100 (bargain for Y80); triples Y100. ❶

Luoyang Welcome Guesthouse (luòyáng yíng bīnguǎn; 洛阳迎宾馆), 6 Renmin Xi Lu (☎393 5156), about 3min. south of Zhongzhou Lu. Take bus #2 from the train station to Xi Gong Youyuan; the hotel entrance is on the right side of the street. Rooms have all standard amenities. Singles Y230; doubles 240-300; triples Y285. Visa. ❸

Golden Gulf Hotel (jīn shuǐwān dàjiǔdiàn; 金水湾大酒店), 319 Zhongzhou Zhong Lu (☎339 5588; fax 339 5678), in the high-rise near Remin Xi Lu. Buses #5 and 81 stop at the Luoyang Dep't Store; from there, backtrack 5min. This 3-star beauty boasts huge rooms and comfortable pillows and linens. Currency exchange. Doubles Y460 (discounted, Y303-510). Not listed but available are Y200 doubles, which are nearly identical to their more expensive counterparts. Discounts often available. ❹

FOOD

Luoyang is famous for its 24-course **Water Banquet** (see **Goodnight, Sweet Soup** below), but those who have neither the time nor the appetite have plenty of other options. Crowded street stalls and outside tables are set up at night in the city's compact alleys. There are markets off **Renmin Dong Lu,** just south of Zhongzhou Zhong Lu, **Wangcheng Lu** opposite Wangcheng Park from Zhongzhou Lu to Kaixuan Xi Lu, and at the **Xinghua Night Market** (xìnghuá yèshì; 兴华夜市) in the Old City. Don't look too closely at the fascinating food displays—they're probably still alive.

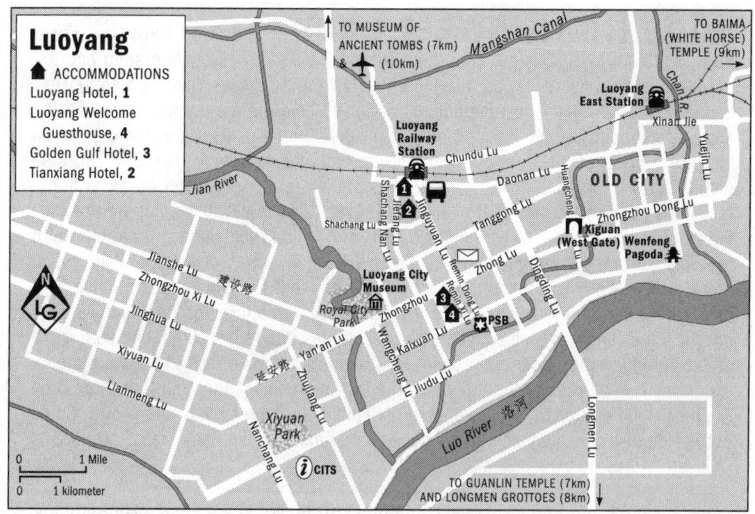

Popular snacks include lamb kebabs, *jiānbāo* (fried pastry stuffed with herbs, garlic, and other fillings; 尖包; Y0.5-2), and *jiàngmiàntiáo* (starched noodles; 浆面条), made from mung bean milk, noodles, vegetables, and various other seasonings. Another popular local dish, *tāngmiànjiǎo* (steamed dumplings in the shape of crescent moons; 汤面饺; Y0.5-1), was first prepared in Henan province, and is known for its thin wrappings and jade-like color.

One-of-a-Kind Restaurant (zhēnbùtóng fàndiàn; 真不同饭店), 359 Zhongzhou Zhong Lu (☎399 1404 or 395 5786), near the night market. Take bus #5 or 9 to Yuxi Binguan from the city center and go left about 1 block. Don't miss the 4-course mini-Water Banquet (Y20; serves 2). Open daily 9:30am-9pm or until the last guest leaves. ❷

West Gong Food Village (xīgōng fànzhuāng; 西宫饭庄), off Remin Bei Lu. Local specialties served lightning fast. Patrons slurp down bowls of hot, creamy *jiāngmiàntiáo* (Y0.8) and munch on *tāngmiànjiǎo* (10 for Y2.5). Open 24hr. ❶

Fengwei Restaurant (fēngwèi lóu; 风味楼), 46 Xigong Qu Xiaojie. From West Gong Food Village, turn right into the next alley; it's on the right, across from Big Mouth Fast Food. Orders fried fresh while you wait. *Jiānbāo* (Y1.3 per 5). Open daily 7am-10pm. ❶

SIGHTS

There is a lot here to see and do in Luoyang, but with the exception of the Royal City Park and the Luoyang Museum, most major tourist attractions are outside the city center. Luckily, none is more than a one-hour bus ride away, making independent daytrips from Luoyang a relatively simple endeavor.

LONGMEN GROTTOES

South of Luoyang. Take ***bus*** *#55 or 81 from Zhongzhou Zhong Lu to Longmen Qiao (30-40min., Y1). Get off immediately before the bridge, and walk down the steps. Visit in the morning when the crowds and the heat haven't picked up yet. Open daily in summer 6am-6:30pm; in winter 7am-5:30pm. Y45, children Y25.*

GOODNIGHT, SWEET SOUP The famed Luoyang Water Banquet (shuìxí; 水席) is so named because the main dishes contain soup and are served up almost as quickly as "flowing water." Of the 24 dishes, the first eight (evenly divided between meat and vegetables) are served cold, as are the four saved for the end of the meal. The remaining 12 dishes, divided into four sets of three, are the most important parts of the banquet. Each group includes one main dish and two side dishes, all of which are similar in taste; this method of serving is known as "a father taking his two sons to court." The famous "Luoyang Swallow Dish" is prepared by boiling shredded radishes, chicken, minced pork, and various vegetables into a thin soup; the finished product represents the spring swallow, a symbol of hope. Legend has it that Empress Wu Zetian found this dish so delicious that she consumed no other meat for three months. The highlight of the second group, "Happiness for the Whole Family," consists of a variety of braised meats and vegetables. "Eight-Treasure Rice Pudding" (a sweet porridge made from eight grains and beans), the main dish of the third group, expresses a wish for bountiful harvests. The last main dish, "Sour and Spicy Egg Drop Soup," also known as the "Farewell Soup," signifies that the meal is nearly over. Some of the side dishes served include the deceptively named "Field Snail Meat," "Turtle and Chicken," "Steamed Quails," and other delicacies.

The site of the Longmen Grottoes (lóngmén shíkū; 龙门石窟) was originally just a standard lake surrounded by hills. According to legend, one day a young shepherd heard a mysterious voice call, "*Kāi bù kāi* (shall I open?)" Perplexed, he sought out his mother, who told him to respond in the affirmative should he hear the same voice again. When the boy heard the voice again, he shouted "Open!" and the earth trembled. The hills split open and the lake flowed out into the East Sea. In its place, small streams gurgled from cracks in the cliffs; the cliffs themselves contained caves that were miraculously filled with thousands of stone statues.

History tells a slightly different story: It took over 400 years of back-breaking construction to complete the grottoes. Begun in 493 AD by Emperor Xiaowen of the Northern Wei Dynasty, the grottoes once housed over 100,000 Buddhist statues. Now, many of the 2100 niche shrines, 3600 tablets and inscriptions, and innumerable sculptured figures are missing, limbless, or in poor condition. Nevertheless, the detailed carvings and niches, ranging from tiny indentations to sizable caverns leave visitors in awe. Most of the largest caves and sculptures are found on the Western Hills, although a few temples and the possibility of a good panoramic view draw some visitors to the other side of the Yi River.

CAVES. Ten Thousand Buddhas Cave (wànfó dòng; 万佛洞) actually contains over 10,000 figurines carved into the walls, many only 4cm tall. The cave took six years to complete and was supervised by two female officials from the imperial court. Nearby, the **Lotus Flowers Cave** (liánhuā dòng; 莲花洞) houses the smallest statues (2cm) of the Longmen Grottoes, and is distinctive for the aforementioned flower high above its dome. **Fengxian Temple** (fèngxiān sì; 奉先寺) was financed by Empress Wu Zetian, who generously donated her entire annual cosmetics budget to the cause. The resulting shrine is Longmen's largest and includes the 17m-high Buddha Losana, who some say was modeled after the empress herself.

The walls of the **Medical Prescription Cave** (yàofáng dòng; 药房洞) are covered with hundreds of ancient treatments and prescriptions. The smiling statue of the Buddha Sakyamuni presides over **Guyang Cave** (gǔyáng dòng; 古阳洞), the oldest and best preserved of the Longmen Grottoes. Numerous sculptures depict the process by which Siddhartha, the founder of Buddhism, attained enlightenment.

OTHER SIGHTS

WHITE HORSE TEMPLE (báimǎ sì; 白马寺). The granddaddy of all Chinese Buddhist temples, the White Horse, built in AD 68, marks the site of the first Buddhist monastery in China. Two Indian monks who came to Luoyang to spread the Mahayana gospel carried their scriptures on a white horse—and the name stuck. Vendors sell glazed horse figurines of every color and style as two slightly droopy stone horse statues welcome you at the entrance. Many of the halls and statues are authentic works dating back hundreds of years to the Yuan or Ming dynasties; in spite of their age, they are remarkably well-preseved. In the Pilu Pavilion, 42 chapters translated from the *sutra* are inscribed on the stone walls. *(About 12km east of Luoyang, a 45min.-1hr. bus ride. Take bus #5, 9 or 101 to Xiguan; change to bus #56. Open daily in summer 7am-6:30pm; in winter 8am-5:30pm. Y25.)*

GUANLIN (guānlín; 关林). This temple commemorates Guan Yu, a warrior said to have lived from AD 160 to 219. In the *Romance of the Three Kingdoms*, Guan Yu was defeated, captured, and executed by the ruler of the Kingdom of Wu. Guan Yu was buried with full honors beneath a great mound surrounded by a stone wall. The "lin" in the name of this site refers not, as many assume, to cypress trees but instead to the burial place of a sage or saint. Only the tombs of Confucius (see **Confucianism,** p. 27) and Guan Yu have received this designation. Stone lions, each unique in their design, line the pathway to the Great Hall. Guan Yu certainly reigns supreme here—nearly every hall contains a statue of his ruddy-faced, green-robed figure or murals of his heroic adventures. *(At the end of Guanlin Nan Lu, about a 10-15min. walk from the bus #81 stop. Open daily 8am-6:30pm. Y20, children Y10.)*

ROYAL CITY PARK (wángchéng gōngyuán; 王城公园). In summer months, vendors sell over-priced ice cream and young children scamper around the sizable amusement area. But, during parts of April and May, the park really blooms; it is one of the best locations for viewing the famed Luoyang peonies. Thousands gather here during the annual Peony Festival. The **ice city** (Y15 with park admission) on the eastern edge of the park is an interesting concept, with large Buddhas and walk-through castles carved from huge blocks of ice; it's freezing cold even in the summer. *(On Zhongzhou Lu near Hedong Lu. Take bus #2, 102, or 103 from the train station to Wangcheng Gongyuan. Open daily 5:30am-9pm. Y3.)*

MUSEUM OF ANCIENT TOMBS (gǔmù bówùguǎn; 古墓博物馆). An ancient saying proclaims that while Suzhou and Hangzhou are good places to be born and live, Luoyang is a good place to die. More than 20 ancient tombs, dating from the Han to Northern Song dynasties, prove that princes, generals, and other famed figures took this advice to heart. Many of the vividly painted murals have been restored, and a number of pottery figures and other relics are on display. Duck in and out of the dimly lit tombs in the museum's long corridors; the faint of heart may want to bring along a friend. Don't miss the emperor's tomb on the left edge of the complex; this might be your only chance to see what it's like to be beneath those gigantic mounds. *(About 25min. northwest of the city. Take bus #83 from Daonan Lu in front of the main bus station to Gumu Guan. Open daily 8:30am-7pm. Y15.)*

KAIFENG 开封

☎0378

About a thousand years ago, Kaifeng was *the* place to have your dynastic capital. Seven dynasties, from 364 BC to AD 1233, set up their capitals in this city, so that the imperial court could enjoy the gentle lakes and pleasant breezes. The Northern Song settled here for 168 years, during which time Kaifeng became the most important commercial center in all of Asia. The famous scroll painting, *Up the River on Qingming Festival*, depicts the bustling life of this age in minute detail. Years later, Kaifeng welcomed a large Jewish community that has since intermarried and immersed itself in the culture of the city.

Today, Kaifeng's population of 600,000 pales in comparison to the one million people who lived there at the height of its glory. The city is not the center of trade and industry that it once was, but Kaifeng has still somehow retained that vague and elusive feeling often referred to as "cultural character." Traditional wooden-eaved buildings line the narrow back streets, and the city center keeps a light-hearted mood amidst a jumble of activity.

TRANSPORTATION

Trains: Kaifeng Train Station (kāifēng huǒchē zhàn; 开封火车站; ☎512 2222), on Zhongshan Lu, about 1km south of the old city walls. Take bus #1, 3, 4, or 9. To: **Beijing** (11hr., 7pm, Y117); **Luoyang** (3hr., several per day, Y15-30); **Taiyuan** (13½hr., 7:50 and 4:15pm, Y120); **Zhengzhou** (1½hr., several per day, Y5.5).

Buses: Kaifeng Bus Station (kāifēng qìchē zhàn; 开封汽车站; ☎595 8053), near Xinmenguan Jie and Zhongshan Lu, a 3min. walk from the train station. The terminus for bus #3 is right outside. To: **Anyang** (3hr., every hr. 6:40am-6pm, Y36); **Beijing** (9hr., 8:30am and 8:30pm, Y138); **Luoyang** (3hr., every 30min. 6am-7pm, Y3.2); **Zhengzhou** (1½hr., every 15min. 6am-7pm, Y12). **Kaifeng West Bus Station** (kāifēng kèyùn xī zhàn; 开封客运西站), 8 Yingbin Lu (☎393 3594), south of Baogong Lake. Buses #1, 4, and 9 stop outside at Xi Zhan. To: **Anyang** (5hr., 8:40am and 2:40pm, Y24); **Luoyang** (3hr., every hr. 7am-6pm, Y35); **Zhengzhou East Station** (1hr., every 15-20min. 6am-7pm, Y10-12); **Zhengzhou West Station** (2hr., 6 and 7:36am, Y10).

Local Transportation: Gulou Square is a major bus hub. Bus **#1** from the train station runs up Zhongshan Lu and past the west bus station and Song Dynasty Street before terminating 2min. from the Iron Pagoda; **#3** runs parallel to #1 along Beimen Dajie/Beitu Jie/Ximenguan Jie, terminating at the Iron Pagoda bus station; **#4** runs from Gulou Jie to the train station.

Taxis: Base fare Y5.

Bike rental: Small shops line the north side of Baogong Lake.

CENTRAL CHINA

ORIENTATION AND PRACTICAL INFORMATION

The heart of Kaifeng lies within the old city walls, which are about 3km long on each side. **Zhongshan Lu** (中山路) runs north-south from Dragon Pavilion Park, through the center of town, and past the city wall to the long-distance train and bus stations. **Shengfu Jie** (省府街) turns into **Sihou Jie** (寺后街), **Gulou Jie** (古楼街), and finally **Mujiaqiao Jie** (穆家桥街) as it moves east. The center of town is **Gulou Square** (gǔlóu guǎngchǎng; 鼓楼广场), where **Shudian Jie** (书店街) intersects with **Sihou Jie, Gulou Jie,** and **Ma Dao Jie.**

Travel Agency: CITS, 98 Yingbin Lu (☎398 0084), next to the Dongjing Hotel, near the West Bus Station. Open M-F 8:30am-noon and 3-6:30pm. **Kaifeng Guesthouse Travel Service** (kāifēng bīnguǎn lǚxíngshè; 开封宾馆旅行社), 66 Ziyou Lu (☎595 1255), left of the hotel entrance. Open daily 8am-5:30pm. Both have some English-speaking staff members. Commissions on train tickets average Y30; airline booking is free.

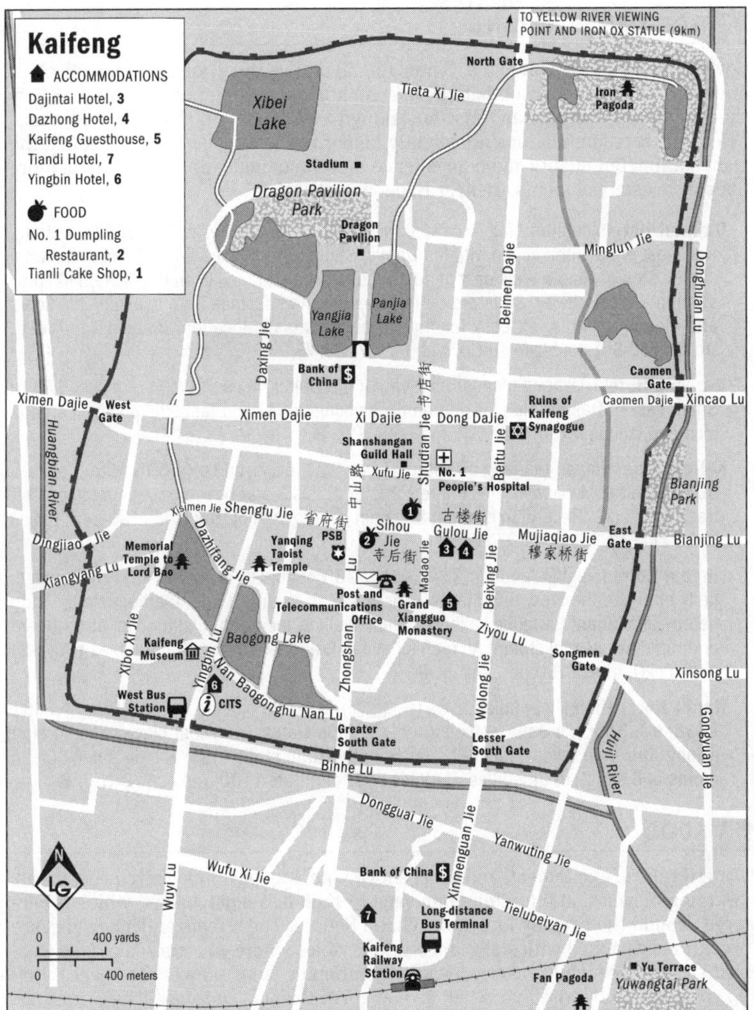

Bank of China: 31 Zhongshan Bei Lu, on the west side of the street. Open daily 8am-6pm. Another branch at 64 Gulou Jie, across from the Dazhong Hotel. Open daily 8am-6:30pm. Both exchange currency and traveler's checks.

PSB: 86 Zhongshan Lu (☎555 2014).

Pharmacy: 234 Zhongshan Lu (☎393 5818), on a curious block where all the other addresses are in the 80s. Open daily 8am-10pm.

Post Office: China Post, 33 Ziyou Lu, east of Zhongshan Lu. EMS and Poste Restante. Open daily 8am-9pm. **Postal Code:** 475000.

ACCOMMODATIONS

Several hotels along Gulou Jie, Sihou Jie, Ziyou Lu, and Zhongshan Lu are close enough to the night market that visitors can hop out of their hotel rooms to satisfy their midnight cravings and just far enough away to avoid the mess and noise. Prices for accommodations are slightly higher in the city center than around the train station, but quality and convenience more than make up for it. Several more expensive establishments are near Baogong Lake.

Dajintai Hotel (dàjīntái bīnguǎn; 大金台宾馆), 17 Gulou Jie (☎595 6677), a 3min. walk east of the intersection with Ma Daojie/Shudian Jie. Buses #4 and 7 from the train station stop at Gulou. Walk east along Gulou Jie; the entrance is on the right, marked by an ornate red archway. Standard rooms are new and spacious, with sparkling tile floors and gleaming baths. An easy landmark and a fantastic location. Breakfast included. Dorms Y20-30; doubles Y40-60, with bath Y160. ❶

Dazhong Hotel (dàzhòng bīnguǎn; 大众宾馆), 8 Gulou Jie (☎596 2796 or 598 1262), 3min. east of Dajintai Hotel. Cozy rooms, working baths, and fantastic prices in a good location. Doubles Y50, with A/C and bath Y90. ❶

Kaifeng Guesthouse (kāifēng bīnguǎn; 开封宾馆), 66 Ziyou Lu (☎595 5589; fax 595 3086), east of Ma Daojie. This entire complex of this 3-star beauty is built in the ornate, traditional style. Reception is under the main gate to the left. Doubles Y180-248; triples Y210-240. ❸

Yingbin Hotel (yíngbīn fàndiàn; 迎宾饭店), 96 Yingbin Lu (☎393 1943), 2min. diagonally opposite the West Bus Station. Buses #1, 4, 7, and 9 from the train station stop nearby at Xi Zhan; Baogong Lake is a 5min. walk to the north. Institutional atmosphere and run-down school charm. All rooms have A/C and TV. Dorms Y22; doubles Y80, with bath Y120; triples Y50 per person. ❶

Tiandi Hotel (tiāndì dàjiǔdiàn; 天地大酒店), 317 Zhongshan Lu Nan Duan (☎391 2828, ext. 3666), a 3min. walk north of the train station. A decent place to settle after a long train ride, even though it's far from the train station and a little lonely. Clean rooms and standard amenities. Doubles Y50, with bath Y100; triples Y78-150. ❶

FOOD

For adventure, excitement, and food, shove your way past indecisive pedestrians, swerving bicycles, and lurching minivans to Kaifeng's **night market,** which is centered around the brightly lit, smoky Gulou Square. The streets and sidewalks are precariously packed with stalls and outdoor tables where you can soak in the frenzied atmosphere while eagerly awaiting your spicy lamb skewers (Y1 each). Roll up your shirt and loosen your belt as you gorge through *shāguō* (砂锅), transparent noodles (chǎo liáng fěn; 炒凉粉), meat-stuffed bread, and dumplings galore. For dessert, eight-treasure rice (bābǎo fàn; 八宝饭) is an easy-to-find delicacy, but most prefer to munch on rice ice cream with flavored ice and red beans (Y3). For a small snack, follow the sweet aroma of caramelized popcorn.

No. 1 Dumpling Restaurant (dìyīlóu bāozi guǎn; 第一楼包子馆), 8 Sihou Jie (☎597 7480), just east of Zhongshan Lu. This local landmark serves up pork-filled dumplings (xiǎolóng bāo; 小笼包) for Y5 per steamer. Ever-full tables and ever-scurrying staff keep this classy place churning. Open daily 11am-2am. ❶

Tianli Cake Shop (tiānlì miànbāo xībǐngwū; 天力面包西饼屋), 43 Gulou Lu, just west of Shudian Jie. Let your nose guide the way to this small bakery under a red awning.

Fluffy sponge cake sprinkled with coconut flakes (Y2) and a large selection of breads and pastries (mostly under Y3). Open daily 6:30am-10pm. ❶

SIGHTS

A good pair of sandals and a bottle of sunscreen is all you need to sightsee in Kaifeng; many of the city's sights are either within a 30-minute walk of the city center or easily reached by local buses.

IRON PAGODA (tiě tǎ; 铁塔). The rich, iron-like forest green and burnt brown tiles with intricately carved Buddhas, ancient musicians, and celestial scenes give this pagoda its name. Built in AD 1049, this exquisitely beautiful 13-story pagoda overlooks the surrounding park and portions of the Kaifeng city wall. Since the best views can be found at the base of the pagoda (not at the top through its tiny barred openings), you can skip the pricey climb. Several of the courtyards are filled with lily-covered ponds, bonsai gardens, and green waterways. *(210 Beimen Dajie, at Tieta Xi Jie. Buses #1 and 3 terminate a block away. ☎286 2279. Open daily 7am-7pm. Y20, students Y10; pagoda additional Y10.)*

DRAGON PAVILION PARK (lóng tíng gōngyuán; 龙亭公园). Built on the ruins of the imperial palaces of the Song, Jing, and Ming dynasties, the park overlooks two scenic lakes. The Imperial Road, a 500m stone pathway, leads to the 26.7m high main hall, which features a rather disappointing life-sized, wax-figure scene of the "Founding Ceremony of Northern Song." Still, the top of the pavilion affords gorgeous views of the lakes and surrounding grounds. On hot summer days, swimmers play in the western lake; the peaceful island on the east offers a quiet respite for lakeside reading. Kitschy duck and dragon boats circle the lake (20-30min., Y10-20). **Song Dynasty Street** (sòng dū jiē; 宋都街), just south of the main entrance, is lined with restaurants and souvenir shops. *(At the north end of Zhongshan Lu. Take bus #1 from the train station, or walk from the Gulou Square area. ☎566 0142. Open daily in summer 6:30am-7pm; in winter 7am-6pm. Y25.)*

GRAND XIANGGUO MONASTERY (dàxiàngguó sì; 大相国寺). One of China's most famous Buddhist temples, this monastery was originally built in AD 555, but was later flooded and damaged by war before being rebuilt. At its proudest moments in the Northern Song dynasty, it had 64 halls and over 1000 monks in residence. The oddly-shaped Hall of Arhat houses 500 *arhats* with expressions ranging from serene to devilish; a 1000-hand Goddess of Mercy stands nearby. *(On Ziyou Lu, west of Ma Dao Jie. Open daily in summer 8am-6:30pm; in winter 8am-5:30pm. Y20.)*

TERRACE OF YU THE GREAT (yǔwángtái gōngyuán; 禹王台公园). First named the "Playing Terrace" in honor of the blind musician Shi Kuang, the terrace was renamed in 1522 to commemorate the sage king who tamed the Great Flood. The terrace itself is rather deserted and has a few unspectacular wax figures. *(Near Tielu Beiyan Jie. ☎267 8761. Open daily in summer 5am-7pm; in winter 7am-6:30pm. Y10.)*

FAN PAGODA (fán tǎ; 繁塔). It may be difficult to find, but this structure, the oldest in Kaifeng, is well worth the trouble. When it was bulit in AD 977, the pagoda stood nine stories tall; by the Ming dynasty, only three stories remained. Now, the pagoda boasts six stories built with 7000 bricks that feature 108 different designs. Be sure to grab onto the railings when making the brief but steep climb to the top. *(Hidden in a neighborhood in southeast Kaifeng; once you're in the vicinity, get a local to show you the way. From Yu Terrace, walk down Tielu Beiyan Jie and turn left onto Fanta Bei Jie; pass the railroad tracks and follow the Chinese characters painted in red on the lefthand alleyways. Open daily 8am-6pm. Y5.)*

EGG MANIA In Henan Province, there are many rituals surrounding the birth of a baby—all involving eggs. To share the good news after the birth of a baby, parents will send eggs to the baby's grandparents, dyed red to symbolize luck. If the baby is a boy, a black spot is painted on top of each egg; an even number is sent to imply that the boy will marry once he grows older. If the baby is a girl, an odd number of eggs (without black spots) are sent, implying that the girl will marry away. After receiving the eggs, the baby's grandmother bakes a cake for her son-in-law. If the man meets a dog on the way home, he throws the cake to the dog; the dog then supposedly eats all the baby's misfortunes.

Also customary is the exchanging of gifts between the new parents and their friends and relatives. When friends and relatives send gifts to welcome the baby, the baby's family must return the favor with boiled red eggs. How many eggs are given is decided according to the value of the received gifts, with, not surprisingly, an even number for a boy and an odd number for a girl.

MEMORIAL TO LIU SHAOQI (liú shàoqí chénlièguǎn; 刘少奇陈列馆). This small memorial is dedicated to Liu Shaoqi, Chairman Mao's heir apparent until he was purged at the start of the Cultural Revolution (see p. 18); he died in Kaifeng in 1969. The contrast between early photos of a robust Liu Shaoqi and those of the ailing man at an interrogation session during the Cultural Revolution is startling, even without an English translation. The architecturally and historically intriguing inner building contains the former president's deathbed and chamber pot; his last days are detailed down to his last dose of medication, body temperature readings, and the price of his cremation. *(10-12 Beitu Jie. Walk from Gulou Jie or take bus #3. ☎596 5306. Open daily 8:30am-6:30pm. Y10, students Y5.)*

MEMORIAL TEMPLE TO LORD BAO (bāo gōng cí; 包公祠). The temple documents the life history of Lord Bao, an ancient officer renowned for his noble character. Legend has it that, during the floods, he was so busy saving the city that he passed by his own house three times without stopping to see his wife and young son. The last hall features handsome frescoes that depict Lord Bao as he crushes corruption, punishes criminals, and feeds the hungry. The rock gardens and lakeside views from the pavilion are not much more impressive than what can be enjoyed by the lake for free. *(On the corner of Xiangyang Lu and Xibo Bei Jie. Buses #8 and 10 stop nearby en route to Gulou Jie or the station. ☎393 1595. Open daily 6:30am-7pm. Y20.*

KAIFENG SYNAGOGUE (kāifēng shì yóutài jiàotáng yízhǐ; 开封市犹太教堂遗址). All that remains of the oldest synagogue in China is an old well, hidden in the boiler room of the No. 4 People's Hospital, 59 Beitu Jie, south of Dong Dajie. Bus #3 stops at the Bianjing Hotel. Walk straight through the hospital courtyard, then turn left into the alleyway. After the curve, there are two sets of red doors; bang on them and someone will usually let you in.

ANYANG 安阳 ☎0372

Modern Anyang sits on the site of Yin, one of China's seven ancient capital cities, a fact confirmed by the oracle bones unearthed by local peasants over 100 years ago. Subsequent excavations revealed tombs and ruins as well as bronzes, chariots, pottery, jade, and thousands of oracle bones, the first hard evidence to support the existence of the legendary Shang dynasty (see p. 9). Although Anyang is of great interest to scholars and archaeologists, this small city has few things to see, and may hold visitors' attention for a day or two at most.

TRANSPORTATION

Trains: Anyang Train Station (ānyáng huǒchē zhàn; 安阳火车站), at the western end of Jiefang Lu. To: **Beijing** (5-6½hr.; several per day; Y63-73, hard sleeper Y103); **Taiyuan** (8½hr., 4pm, Y78); **Shijiazhuang** (2-3hr., many per day, Y32-38); **Zhengzhou** (2-3hr., many per day, Y14-25).

Buses: Anyang Bus Station (ānyáng chángtú qìchē zhàn; 安阳长途汽车站; ☎591 3951), on Heping Lu. From the train station, go south to the end of Yinbin Lu. To: **Beijing** (6hr., 6 per day 9:30am-11:50pm, Y108); **Ji'nan** (6½hr., every 30min-1hr., Y46); **Shijiazhuang** (4hr., 6 per day 8am-4pm, Y45); **Taiyuan** (6½-7hr., 3-5 per day 7:20-11:20am, Y69); **Zhengzhou** (3hr., every 20min. 6am-7pm, Y33).

Local Transportation: Fare Y1. Bus **#2** runs from the train station along Jiefang Lu, up Hongqi Lu, past Renmin Lu; **#3** runs down Jiefang Lu to People's Park; **#11** goes from the train station up Zhangde Lu, down Renmin Lu and Dongfeng Lu past People's Park.

Taxis: Base fare Y4-5.

Bike Rental: Available on the south side of Jiefang Lu, just west of Zhangde Lu. Y2 per day, deposit Y50. Alternatively, from the train station, turn right and continue about 1 block to the stand in front of Gonghang Hostel (gōngháng zhāodàisuǒ; 工行招待所). Y2 per hr.; deposit Y100.

ORIENTATION AND PRACTICAL INFORMATION

Anyang is mostly to the south of the **Huan River** (huán hé; 洹河), near the border of Henan and Hebei provinces. **Jiefang Lu** (解放路), a major east-west thoroughfare, extends from the train station to People's Park and runs parallel to **Renmin Dadao** (人民大道). **Hongqi Lu** (红旗路), running perpendicular to Jiefang Lu and Renmin Dadao, becomes **Bei Dajie** (北大街) and then **Zhongshan Jie** (中山街) as it runs south to enter the **Old City** (gǔ chéng; 古城) near the Drum Tower. The Yin Ruins and the Tomb of Yuan Shikai are in the northern part of the city.

Travel Agency: CITS, Anyang Hotel, Bldg. 3, 2nd fl. (☎592 5650). Open M-F 8am-noon and 3-6:30pm. Train ticket commission Y20.

Bank of China: On the west side of Bei Dajie, north of the Drum Tower. Open daily 8am-6pm. A new branch on Jiefang Lu, just east of Hongqi Lu (☎592 4286), exchanges currency and traveler's checks. Open daily in summer 8am-6:30pm; in winter 8am-5:30pm.

PSB: 35 Hongqi Lu (☎592 3961). Open 24hr.

Hospital: Anyang People's Hospital (ānyángshì rénmín yīyuàn; 安阳市人民医院; ☎592 3331), on Jiefang Lu, about 1 block east of Hongqi Lu near the Anyang Hotel.

Internet Access: Xiaoshi Jie Internet Bar (xiǎoshí jiē wǎng bā; 小时街网吧; ☎591 4708), on the north side of Dengta Lu, about 400m west of Hongqi Lu, past Xianzhong Jie. Y2 per hr. Open daily 8am-midnight.

Post Office: China Post (☎595 1100), 1 Yinbin Lu, just south of the train station. EMS and Poste Restante. Open daily 7:30am-9pm. Another branch on Dengta Lu, about half a block west of Hongqi Lu. Open daily 8am-9pm. EMS. **Postal Code:** 455000.

ACCOMMODATIONS

Several lodgings cluster around the train and long-distance bus stations. Unfortunately, many of the cheaper dormitory-style establishments, including those with

English signs, are either closed for renovations or do not accept foreigners. A few classier places are off Jiefang Lu.

Great Wall Hotel (cháng chéng bīnguǎn; 长城宾馆), 5 Xinxing Jie (☎591 0669), between Jiefang Lu and Heping Lu. A 3-star, often-overlooked hotel that's a 5min. walk from the train and long-distance bus stations. Spacious new rooms and a friendly staff. Cheaper doubles have scenic posters for windows, but are otherwise identical to their more expensive counterparts. Breakfast included. Check-out 2pm. Reservations recommended. Doubles Y160-280. ❸

Anyang Guesthouse (ānyáng bīnguǎn; 安阳宾馆), 1 Youyi Lu (☎592 2219; fax 592 2244), just north of Jiefang Lu, a 15min. walk from the train station. A large, blue Chinese billboard indicates where to turn. Bus #3 or 16 from the train station stop nearby at Hongqi Guangchang. Frequented by businessmen. Lovely baths and nice, carpetless rooms. All rooms have standard amenities. Reservations recommended for the Y168 doubles. Breakfast included. Doubles Y168-188. ❸

Flying Eagle Hotel (fēiyīng dàjiǔdiàn; 飞鹰大酒店), 119 Renmin Dadao (☎593 5888; fax 592 3037), west of Hongqi Lu. Take bus #2 from the train station to Er Baihuo; go north up Hongqi Lu and take a right at the first intersection. Pleasant rooms have standard amenities; the pricier the room, the cleaner the windows. Bargain. Breakfast included. Doubles Y118-268; triples Y208. ❷

FOOD

The night markets near the Drum Tower and in front of the Workers' Cultural Palace offer a wide variety of noodle and fried dishes (Y3-5), as well as lamb skewers (Y1), stuffed pitas (Y1.5), and other snacks. A scattering of outdoor tables appears in the evening near the train station along Jiefang Lu, serving cafeteria-style food. The **Kaifeng No. 1 Chain Restaurant** ❶ (kāifēng dìyīlóu tèxǔ liànsuǒ diàn; 开封第一楼特许链锁店), at the south corner of Jiefang Lu and Xianzhong Jie, serves 15 delicious dumplings for Y6. (Open daily 6:30am-11pm.) For dessert, the **Little Swan Ice Cream Stand** ❶ (xiǎo qǐ'é bīngqílín wū; 小企鹅冰淇淋屋), on the north side of Jiefang Lu between the train station and Zhangde Lu, is easily spotted by the pudgy, oh-so-cute penguin outside. It offers cold drinks and ice cream delights like the Happy Welcome Boat (yíng lè chuán; 迎乐船; Y12), a variation on the banana split. (Open daily 10am-midnight.)

SIGHTS AND ENTERTAINMENT

By day, the sights are limited to a select few. By night, not too surprisingly, full-fledged entertainment options are also rather limited. For cheap food and free people-watching, wander around the Old City (evening markets close up around 9pm, but larger crowds dance around the Wenfeng Pagoda until 10:30pm). The **Workers' Cultural Palace** (gōngrén wénhuà gōng; 工人文化宫), five minutes east of the train station at Zhangde Lu and Jiefang Lu, has a movie theater and, when the weather is warm, a huge number of pool tables out in front.

OLD CITY (gǔ chéng; 古城). When the blistering heat of the afternoon dies down, the main alley of Anyang's Old City is filled with pedestrians, bikes, and vendors selling everything from fresh bread to mosquito netting. Small lanes near the Drum Tower (gǔlóu; 鼓楼) are not clearly marked with street names but are fascinating places to wander, especially if you're looking for a fried snack. Wenfeng Pagoda (wénfēng tǎ; 文峰塔) can be reached on foot. From Jiefang Lu, walk four blocks south on Bei Dajie; turn right onto Dasi Qian Jie and continue for a couple of blocks. The 65m pagoda is open, despite the dirt and dust of construction work around its base. Be sure to duck your head and tuck your tummy; some parts of the steep climb are less than 5'3" high and 2'6" wide. A panoramic view of the city awaits at the top. *(Begins on Bei Dajie, just south of Jiefang Lu. Open daily in summer 8:30am-6:30pm; in winter 8:30am-5:30pm. Y6.)*

MUSEUM OF YIN RUINS (yīnxū bówùyuán; 殷墟博物苑). Sitting in a dusty and barren part of town, this museum is of little interest to the average visitor. The collection itself is not particularly extensive, but the unearthed horse carriages, complete with bones, make for an interesting excavation site. *(On Yinxu Lu north of Anyang Lu. From the People's Park, take bus #18 wihich terminates at the museum entrance (leaves about every 15min.). ☎393 2171. Open daily in summer 8am-6:30pm; in winter 8am-5:30pm. Y15, student Y7.5.)*

TOMB OF YUAN SHIKAI (yuán lín; 袁林). Yuan Shikai's rule as self-proclaimed emperor of China in 1916 lasted only one year, but the city seems to see the mausoleum last much longer; recent renovations have resulted in bright red buildings and shiny green-tiled roofs. A small collection of photographs and relics lie near the back of the courtyard. *(Take bus #8 from People's Square to Yuan Lin. Open daily in summer 8am-6:30pm; in winter 8am-6pm. Y20, students Y10.)*

SHANXI 山西

Shanxi boasts a unique type of ugliness that has managed to keep away most visitors to China. Its rough roads, barren mountainsides, and unremarkable coal mining cities offer little to the sight-seeker, not to mention to local residents. With such few assets, it's a wonder why anybody would want to raid such a drab province. But raid they did, and residents of this mountainous province were more than willing to pass the time by resisting incursion. Bounded to the north by the Great Wall, Shanxi played a key role in protecting China from northern nomadic tribes during the Qin and Han dynasties. During the Japanese occupation in the 1930s, Communist soldiers bided their time among the caves and crevices in Shanxi's barren mountainsides before launching guerrilla offensives. Now that all the excitement's died down, Shanxi is back to its old peaceful—and dull—self. Still, underneath the layer of smog that coats much of the province some spectacular sights do exist. Most of them are hidden well off the beaten path, like the quaint little town of Pingyao and the lush valleys, monasteries, and spectacular views of Wutaishan; the Yungang Grottoes and Hanging Monastery near Datong are also worth a look.

TAIYUAN 太原 ☎0351

The capital of Shanxi province, Taiyuan is a crucial industrial and commercial center, thriving on its rich iron and coal deposits. Foundries and furnaces provide the backdrop for the polluted city's hard-working and fast-paced atmosphere. Although gritty and in-your-face by day, Taiyuan sparkles by night. Visitors flock to Yingze Dajie for glittering, brightly lit hotels and restaurants and to May First Square for romantic encounters or quick snapshots in front of the fountains.

Although it may not be a tourist favorite, this busy city boasts a bit of historic significance. Taiyuan has long been a strategically important city. Founded in the ancient state of Zhao in 479 BC, Taiyuan was the starting point for Tang founder Li Yuan's conquest of China and served as one of the Tang's military strongholds. Today, many of the city's historical sights have been reduced to rubble, the victims of a bloody PLA siege during the struggle against the Nationalists. Taiyuan maintains a casual charm, a high-energy attitude and an impressive overabundance of karaoke bars. Most travelers either see Taiyuan as a starting point to the serene temples and fresh air of Wutaishan, or they skip it altogether.

TRANSPORTATION

Flights: Taiyuan Airport (tàiyuán jīchǎng; 太原机场; ☎701 2355) is far from the city center. Shuttle buses (30min., Y10) generally leave daily at 6, 7am, and 3pm from the **China Eastern Airlines Ticket Office,** 158 Yingze Dajie (zhōngguó dōngfāng mínháng shòupiào chù; 中国东方民航售票处; ☎404 2903), 1min. west of May First Square on the south side of the street. Open daily 8am-8pm. To: **Beijing** (daily, Y540-810); **Guangzhou** (2 per day, Y1290-1940); **Shanghai** (2 per day, Y820-1230).

Trains: Taiyuan Train Station (tàiyuán huǒchē zhàn; 太原火车站; ☎418 2913), on the corner of Yingze Dajie and Jianshe Lu. To: **Beijing** (8-10hr., 5 per day 7:30am-9pm, Y77-131); **Datong** (7-9hr., 5 per day 3-11:17pm, Y65-104); **Guangzhou** (40hr., daily Y279); **Shanghai** (22hr., daily Y304); **Xi'an** (11-12hr., 3 per day 5pm-1:29am, Y95-163).

Buses: Taiyuan Bus Station (tàiyuán qìchē zhàn; 太原汽车站; ☎404 2346), on the south side of Yingze Dajie between the train station and Bingzhou Lu. Tickets can be purchased directly from bus drivers behind the bus station. Immediately west of the Electric Power Hotel, a stand sells tickets and lists departure information for several buses per day to **Beijing, Datong,** and **Wutaishan.** Buses often stop on the way to each destination, making most surrounding cities easily accessible. To: **Datong** (5hr., every hr. 7:30am-3:30pm, Y50); **Shijiazhuang** (3hr., every 30min. 6:30am-6:30pm, Y45); **Wutaishan** (4hr., every 15-30min. 6:15am-7:15pm, Y43); **Zhengzhou** (8hr., 2 per day, Y120). Window #1 only sells tickets to **Beijing** (6hr., every 20min. 7am-4pm plus another 10 departures 4pm-midnight, Y120). Minibuses to **Datong** (Y30), **Shijiazhuang** (Y45), **Wutaishan** (Y43), and other destinations; wait in the train station parking lot.

Local Transportation: Most **buses** run approximately 5:30am to 7 or 8pm; bus **#103** to Shanxi University runs until 10pm. (Y1). **#1** shuttles incessantly along Yingze Dajie past May First Square. **Electric buses** run up and down Wuyi Lu **(#2)** and Bingzhou Lu **(#3)** and cost the same as the bus. **Minibuses** (Y1-2) also troll the city streets.

Taxis: Base fare Y7, each additional km Y1. If hired at the train station, Y1 tariff.

ORIENTATION AND PRACTICAL INFORMATION

Yingze Dajie (迎泽大街) runs west from the train station through Taiyuan's main commercial district. Transportation and accommodation options are on the eastern edge of the city, at the intersection of Yingze Dajie and **Jianshe Lu** (建设路). Ten minutes to the west, **May First Square** (wǔyī guǎngchǎng; 五一广场) marks the busy intersection with **Wuyi Lu** (五一路), which runs north, and **Bingzhou Bei Lu** (并州北路), which runs south. Most tourist attractions are near May First Square or in the southern portion of the city near the university.

Travel Agency: CITS, 38 Pingyang Lu (☎723 2188). English-speaking staff member. Commission Y20. Open M-F 8am-noon and 2:30-6pm. Another branch, next to the main Bank of China, is open M-F 8:30am-noon and 2:30-6:30pm.

Bank of China: 288 Yingze Dajie (☎404 4027), a 5min. walk west of Yingze Park. Exchanges traveler's checks. Open M-F in summer 8am-noon and 2:30-6pm; in winter 8am-noon and 2-5:30pm. The branch 2 blocks west of the train station exchanges currency only. Open M-F 8am-noon and 2:30-6pm.

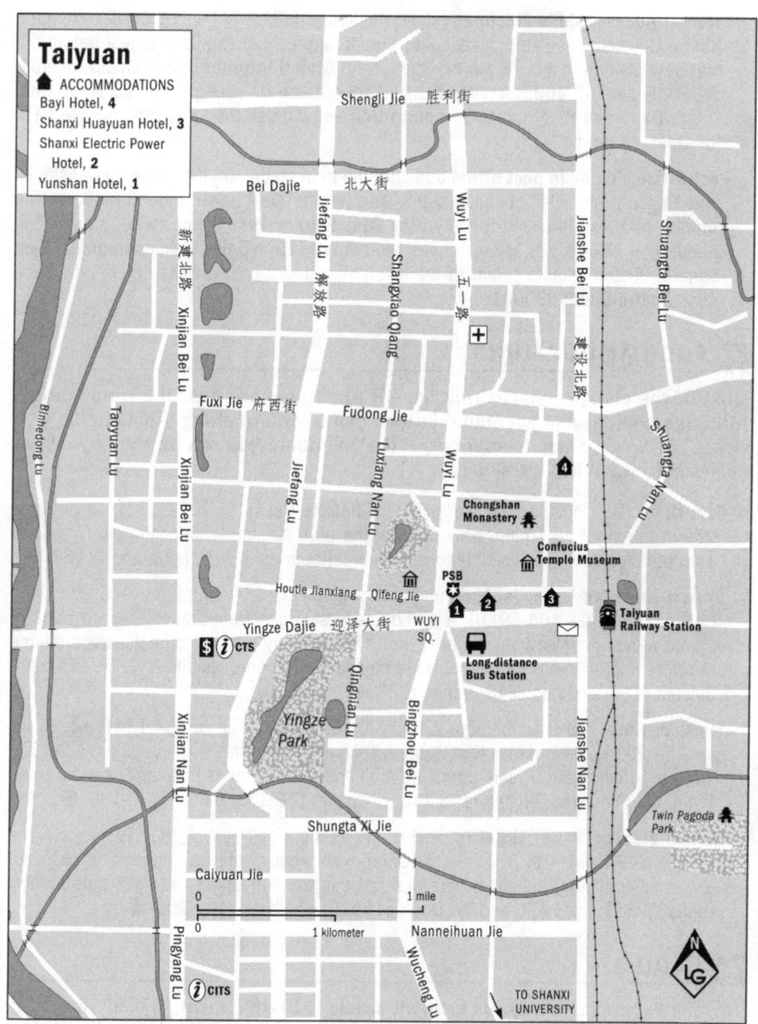

PSB: 9 Houjia Xiang (☎202 8550), 1 block northeast of May First Square. Open M-F 8am-noon and 2:30-5:30pm.

Pharmacy: On the north side of Yingze Dajie, 1min. walk east from May First Square.

Hospital: Shanxi University No. 2 Hospital (shānxī dàxué dièr yīyuàn; 山西大学第二医院; ☎307 3786), on Wuyi Lu, 1½ blocks south of Bei Dajie. Take bus #3 north from May First Square until you see the hospital on the right.

Telephones: China Telecom, 213 Yingze Dajie (☎806 9999), at Jiefang Lu. IDD service. Open 24hr.

Internet Access: Shijie Zhichuan (shìjié zhīchuān; 世界之窗; ☎783 0002). From the Shanxi University bus stop, walk south 10min. along Wucheng Lu until just before the highway; it's on the left. Y3 per hr. Open 24hr. **Global Internet Bar** (huánqiú wǎngbā; 环球网吧; ☎701 9665), on Wucheng Lu near Shanxi University. Take bus #103 from Yingze Dajie and Bingzhou Lu to Shanxi University; cross the street and double back for 1min. Y4 per hr.

Post Office: The **main post office** opposite the train station on the corner of Jianshe Lu and Yingze Dajie. EMS, English signs, and helpful staff. Open daily 8am-8pm. The smaller and less foreigner-friendly **May First Square Post Office** (wǔyì guǎngchǎng yóujú; 五一广场邮局), is on the west side of Wuyi Lu, a 3min. walk north of May First Square. Poste Restante (point to the small blackboard on the wall). Open daily 8am-7pm. **Postal Code:** 030001.

ACCOMMODATIONS

Most of the cheaper places that accept foreigners are near the train station. Although comparable accommodations can be found along Wucheng Lu (the street bordering Shanxi University), the 30-minute bus ride to the city center makes this option less attractive.

Bayi Hotel (bāyī bīnguǎn; 八一宾馆), 137 Jianshe Bei Lu (☎202 3972), on the west side of the street, a 10min. walk north of the train station; look for the red sign. Only worn but clean singles available for foreigners. Rooms with A/C, bath, and TV Y66. ❶

Shanxi Huayuan Hotel (shānxī huáyuán bīnguǎn; 山西华苑宾馆), 9 Yingze Dajie (☎404 6201; fax 404 6980), a half-block west of the train station, next to Bank of China. Although noise from the busy street below might disturb some guests, the large windows and spacious rooms are quite pleasant. All rooms include A/C, TV, and bath. Singles Y188; doubles Y218; triples Y268. ❸

Yunshan Hotel (yúnshān fàndiàn; 云山饭店), 99 Yingze Dajie (☎404 1351, ext. 6116; fax 404 2294), east of May First Square. Take any bus from the train station to the first stop (a 10min. walk). Clean rooms are a bit spartan. All rooms include TV and bath; A/C approx. Y10 extra. Singles Y108-118; doubles Y118-186; triples Y180-186. ❷

Shanxi Electric Power Hotel (shānxī diànlì dàshà; 山西电力大厦), 39 Yingze Dajie (☎404 1784; fax 404 0777), a 5-10min. walk west of the train station. Though not exactly electrifying, the rooms are nonetheless well-furnished and have notably new baths. Most include A/C and TV. Doubles Y120, with bath Y160-200. ❷

FOOD

Taiyuan is best known for its **knife-cut noodles** (dāoxiāo miàn; 刀削面), available for just a few *kuài* per bowl. If you're lucky, you'll get to see the knife-wielding chef in action. When dusk falls, the aroma of grilled meat and sizzling vegetables fills the city as street markets serve up a variety of noodles and fried dishes. Hot-pot is also quite popular. On summer nights, stands line **Bingzhou Lu** (south of Yingze Dajie) and **May First Square.** Farther south along **Wucheng Lu,** near the Shanxi University campus, fruit, steamed corn and kebab vendors fight for space with noodle stands. (Take bus #103 from May First Square to Shanxi Daxue.) A block west of May First Square, Luxiang Nan Lu runs north off Yingze Dajie; its nearby alleys also boast delicious local fare. Taiyuan's restaurants range from trendy fast-food hangouts like **Dico's** (open daily 10am-11pm) to hole-in-the-wall noodle shops and lamb kebab stands.

From fresh watermelon and fruit on sticks, to styrofoam bowls of noodles, dining in Taiyuan is casual and made to be eaten on the go. One place worthy of a special visit is **Huayuan Restaurant** ❷ (huáyuán dàjiǔlóu; 华苑大酒楼), 11 Yingze Dajie, next to the Shanxi Huayuan Hotel. Appearances can be deceiving: the prosaic restaurant offers an extensive English menu listing cheap standard dishes as well as more exotic fare. Order anything from knife-cut noodles (Y3-5) to pig's brains (Y68). Open daily 11am-10pm.

SIGHTS

Taiyuan, though not generally known as a tourist destination, has a surprising number of attractions both in the city and in nearby towns. The city streets teem with vendors and pedestrians, and on weekends the open squares host performances by schoolchildren who sing the timeless classic *B-I-N-G-O* and the all-time *Sound of Music* favorite, *Do Re Mi*. Lesser-known attractions are just as charming; at **Children's Park** (értóng gōngyuán; 儿童公园), kids find not only amusement park games and rides, but also live crabs and goldfish for sale. *(Entrance off alleyways from Wuyi Lu and Luxiang Nan Li. Open daily 7am-8pm. Y1.5.)* The gardens of **Shanxi Museum** offer a respite from city crowds and pollution. *(From May First Square walk along Wuyi Lu and take a right on the first cross street after the post office. Continue about 5min. until the dead end then turn right. Open daily 2:30-6:30pm. Y6.)*

TWIN PAGODA PARK (shuāngtǎ gōngyuán; 双塔公园). The striking twin pagodas, a.k.a. **Yongzuo Monastery** (yǒngzuò sì; 永祚寺), were constructed during the Ming dynasty and have recently been renovated. The noisy approach through commercial and industrial streets offers a stark contrast to the peaceful and beautifully maintained retreat of this garden courtyard. *(On a small street running east from Chuangta Bei Lu. Bus #19 from the train station stops at Xingyue Ge Xiecheng, the first stop after the railroad tracks; turn right on the first street and take a left before the dead end. The entrance is another 10-15min. down the road, to the right. A taxi from the train station costs about Y9. Open daily 8:30am-5:30pm, in winter 9am-5pm. Y10.)*

YINGZE PARK (yíngzé gōngyuán; 迎泽公园). Vendors at the entrance sell pineapple on a stick and blow bubbles, setting a carefree tone for the park. Notable more for its small amusement and water park than for its beautiful scenery, the area is a popular hangout for local families and cuddling couples. Boat rentals Y10-30 per hour. *(On the southern side of Yingze Dajie, between Jiefang Lu and Qingnian Lu. Buses #1 and 6 from the train station stop at Da Nan Men. Open daily 6am-9pm; in winter 6:30am-9pm. Y2.)*

JINCI TEMPLE (jìncí sì; 晋祠寺). This rambling complex (first constructed in AD 1023-1031) is filled with a diverse jumble of buildings from various dynasties and, come the summer months, plenty of tourists as well. Wandering through the maze of gardens may be more rewarding than trying to follow the twists and turns of the map; as always, visitors must run the gauntlet of souvenir stands and postcard hawkers outside the main entrance. *(25km outside the city. Take minibus #308 (1hr., Y2) from Yingze Dajie in front of the train station. Jinci Park open daily 7am-sunset. Jinci Temple open daily 8am-6pm, in winter 8:30am-5:30pm. Park Y5, temple Y16.)*

ENTERTAINMENT

It's hard to avoid the karaoke bars that line all the major streets (and many minor ones); beyond that, nightlife options are rather limited. **Wucheng Lu** is lined with several bars that are frequented by Shanxi University students. **Friday Friday** (xīngqīwǔ xīngqīwǔ; 星期五星期五), about 10 minutes south of the Shanxi Daxue

CENTRAL CHINA

bus stop is easily identifiable by its log cabin exterior. Nearby, several bars serve up Internet access instead of alcohol, as many university students in Taiyuan seem to prefer a Saturday night chatting on the Internet to an evening crooning at a karaoke bar. For those who'd rather meet people face to face, the **Chinatown "Disco Public"** (zhōngguóchéng dísīkē guǎngchǎng; 中国城迪斯科广场), 39 Bingzhou Bei Lu, features scantily clad dancers, loud music, and clientele too shy to sway with the slow songs. The club also has nightly drawings for umbrellas, travel bags, and similar prizes. (☎408 4844. Cover Y44. Open daily 8pm-midnight.)

DAYTRIP FROM TAIYUAN: PINGYAO

Easily accessible from Taiyuan. ***Trains*** *#7085 (departing Taiyuan at 7am) and 7086 (departing Pingyao for Taiyuan at 4:14pm) cost Y6-8 and take about 2½hr. Buses from Taiyuan to Pingyao are more difficult to find, but usually lurk near the train station in the mornings or park behind the bus station. Minibuses (2hr., approx. Y15) leave frequently from the Pingyao Train Station for Taiyuan when full.*

Since its construction in the 9th century BC, the 6km brick wall surrounding the ancient city of Pingyao (平遥) has warded off numerous threats, from invasion to modernization. The amazingly well-preserved city is full of outstanding examples of Ming and Qing architecture, and it's easy to envision Pingyao flourishing during these dynasties as China's premier banking center. Although the bustling city retains many of its 19th-century features (features that inspired Zhang Yimou to film *Raise the Red Lantern* here), it has managed to escape a static museum atmosphere. UNESCO recently named the city a World Heritage Site.

The layout and scale of Pingyao make it easy to travel on foot. **Bei Dajie** (北大街), **Dong Dajie** (东大街), **Nan Dajie** (南大街; actually several hundred meters east of the intersection with Bei Dajie), and **Xi Dajie** (西大街) are the main thoroughfares. Visitors first encounter the 6km **city wall** surrounding these streets. To get to the city wall from the train station, continue straight down **Shuncheng Lu** (顺城路), the road perpendicular to the train station, to the first intersection with **Xiguan Dajie** (西关大街); make a left; a 10-minute walk brings you to the west gate of the city wall. Visitors can only ascend the wall from the north and west gates. *(Open daily 7:30am-7:30pm, in winter 8am-6pm. Y16.)*

The city wall was built with rammed earth beginning in 827 BC, but the Song army set it on fire in AD 960. Savvier than the three little pigs, the residents of Pingyao learned their lesson after the first attack and rebuilt the wall with bricks in 1370. It's no wonder that this sturdier version is still standing today—its many watchtowers and imposing cannons give the wall an impenetrable feel. According to legend, the 3000 embrasures built into the wall represent the disciples of Confucius; his most venerated sages, an elite subset of that group, are represented by the 72 small watchtowers. A walk around the top from the west gate (turn right at the top of the stairs) to the small exhibition at the north gate takes about 30-45 minutes and affords a chance to glimpse into the courtyards of the city's many traditional tile-roofed houses and narrow alleyways. Bicycle rental is available for Y5 per hour at the west gate, and bicycle rides can be hired for Y25 at the top of the wall.

From the North Gate, the center of the city is a straight shot down Bei Dajie where one can find museums, restaurants, and hotels. **The Chinese Financial House Museum** (rìshēng chāng piàohào; 日升昌票号) stands next to 40 Xi Dajie. Housed in a now-defunct bank, it exhibits items dating back to its 1823 establishment. *(Walk down Bei Dajie until the dead end, then turn left. Open daily 8am-7pm, in winter 8:30am-5pm. Y10.)* Continue down Xi Dajie, which intersects Nan Dajie (its northern portion is known as Ming Qing St.) to find the ornate traditional-style buildings that line **Ming Qing Street** (明清街). These buildings house various museums, antique shops, and other enterprises. From the **Town Tower** (shì lóu; 市楼), visitors can enjoy a bird's-eye view of the town and its trademark red lanterns (Y5). Beyond this point, the streets become dustier, emptier, and less interesting.

YULIN 榆林 ☎0912

Well-preserved architecture graces Yulin, a remote, friendly town on the outskirts of the Mu Us desert in northern China. Locals are surprisingly eager to welcome visitors to this former Ming dynasty garrison and Great Wall patrol post. Their genuine enthusiasm offers a refreshing contrast to the usually jaded commerialism of the tourist industry. Whether you're visiting the beautiful surrounding countryside, a desert retreat, or a piece of the Great Wall, Yulin's hospitality will make the journey worthwhile.

TRANSPORTATION

Flights: Yulin Airport (☎328 9522), a Y10 cab ride east of the city. Small (and rather deserted), with flights serving Xi'an (daily Y500-600).

Buses: On Yuyang Zhong Lu, just west of Xinjian Lu. Buses congregate as frequently at the rotary at the east end of Yuyang Zhong Lu. There are few workers in the bus station itself; just find your bus and pay the driver. To: **Daliuta** (1½hr., every 30min., Y6); **Xi'an** (15hr., daily, Y90); **Yan'an** (5hr., 3 per day 6:30am-noon, Y43).

Local Transportation: Bus #2 follows Xinjian Lu to Renmin Lu and circles back along Great Wall Road; **#4** patrols Nanda Jie. Fare Y1. **Taxi** base fare Y4-5. **Mopeds** Y2.

ORIENTATION AND PRACTICAL INFORMATION

Although Yulin spans both sides of the **Yuxi River** (榆溪河), most of the accommodations, entertainment, and tourist attractions are on the easily navigable west side. **Yuyang Zhong Lu** (榆阳中路) runs east-west past the **bus station** and is the northern end of **Nanda Jie** (南大街), **Xinjian Lu** (新建路), and **Great Wall Rd.** (长城路). These streets run south until they terminate at **Renmin Lu** (人民路).

Travel Agency: Kang Le Travel Service (☎328 6294), in the Yuxi Hotel on Renmin Lu, just west of Great Wall Rd. Open daily 8am-noon and 2:30-6pm.

Bank of China: (☎326 7641), on Renmin Lu, just west of Great Wall Rd. The only bank in town that exchanges foreign currency and traveler's checks. English-speaking staff. Open daily 8-11:30am and 2-6pm.

PSB: (☎385 8196), on Nanda Lu, just north of the northernmost gate.

Pharmacy: Shanxi Hua Yuayi Pharmacy (☎328 1384), on Nanda Lu, just south of the northern most gate. Open daily 8am-8pm.

Hospital: Yulin #2 Hospital (☎328 3545), on Nanda Lu, north of the PSB.

Telephones: China Telecom (☎385 6135), on Nanda Lu, just south of the middle gate. Open daily 8am-noon and 2:30-6pm.

Internet Access: Next door to the China Telecom office. Y3 per hr.

Post Office: (☎326 1888), on Nanda Lu, just south of China Telecom. EMS. Open daily 8am-6pm. **Postal Code:** 719000.

ACCOMMODATIONS

Because it is still unknown to most tourists, Yulin has few accommodations. The city's south end has larger, more expensive hotels, while the north has cheaper, more hospitable family-run digs.

Yulin Hostel (☎323 5385), just north of the rotary off of Yuyang Zhong Lu. Turn left out of the bus station, walk 5min. Warm reception and friendly employees. Doubles with bath and TV Y30. ❶

Yuxi Dajiudian (☎328 0492), on Renmin Lu, half a block west of Great Wall Rd.; turn left from the bus station, then turn left at the first intersection and walk down Xinjian Lu 20min. Turn left at Renmin Lu and continue straight half a block until you see a large blue sign with the hotel's name. Clean, well-maintained baths and TV make the long trek worthwhile. Doubles Y70-130. ❷

Guangji Dasha (☎326-0557), southwest corner of Renmin Lu and Great Wall Rd. Spacious singles with double beds. Comfortable doubles. Student discounts may be available. TV and attached bath. Singles Y120; doubles Y76. ❷

FOOD

Pricey food joings line **Xinjian Lu,** but inexpensive, authentic local fare can be found east of the bus station on **Yuyang Zhong Lu. Yongchang Restaurant** ❶ (yǒngchāng jiǔdiàn; 永昌酒店), next to the Yuling Hostel, serves up delicious noodles for only Y5. Even cheaper meals can be found at the junction between Yuyang Zhong Lu and Nanda Lu or along Nanda Lu itself (large bowls of dumplings Y1).

SIGHTS

Meandering down the pebble-paved alleys of **East Yulin** is a bit like traveling through time; low brick walls encircle what were once the courtyards of Ming dynasty homes. Walk from north to south along Nanda Lu, and you will encounter three gates, each progressively more ornate and grand. Climb to the top of the last gate, Bell Tower (zhōnglóu; 钟楼), to witness a breathtaking view of the surrounding desert and the **Great Wall.** A better vantage point is from the Great Wall itself. The expansive panoramic view of desert in one direction and lush rice fields in the other explains Yulin's former strategic importance. *(Follow the winding path of the first paved alley south of the middle gate, either by foot or taxi (Y4). For the more agile, shimmy up the the southeast corner of the last rotary on Yuyang Zhong Lu.)*

It's easy to forget that a harsh desert lies just beyond the city walls, especially when strolling through the ancient streets of Yulin. Just outside the city (7.5km from downtown Yulin) sits the three-tiered fortress of **North Tower** (zhèngběi tái; 正北台). This former stronghold still projects an imposing appearance, effectively deterring many tourists. Down the road is yet another tourist-free gem: the **Red Stone Gorges.** Life as a desert-dweller seems sweet when you picnic in a river-side gazebo, duck into a refreshingly cool cave, or stroll beneath the large inscriptions chiselled into the rock face. *(Round-trip taxi to the two sites Y25. Admission to both Y10.)*

WUTAISHAN MOUNTAIN 五台山 ☎0350

A galaxy of temples and monasteries dominates the landscape of Wutaishan's five mountain peaks, which make up one of China's four sacred Buddhist mountains. The white-knuckle approach to **Taihuai Village** (tài huái; 太怀) winds through high

CENTRAL CHINA

alpine valleys before dipping into what locals call the "bowl" of Wutaishan. Bright wildflowers and grazing livestock line the path to the village and the sound of jangling bells and melodic Buddhist chants (sometimes live, othertimes from cassette players) fill the streets. It may sound idyllic, but a constant stream of photo-crazed, souvenir-hunting tourists also hope to bask in the area's monastic glow. Despite the unholy number of visitors at times, most find that Taihuai's location, beautiful surroundings, and reasonably priced accommodations make it an ideal place to appreciate the Wutaishan Mountains.

ORIENTATION AND PRACTICAL INFORMATION

All vehicles entering Taihuai must stop at the gate to the Wutaishan Scenic Area to pay the Y53 **admission fee.** Think of it less as the heavy hand of the tourist industry and more as a way to get in touch with your spiritual side (by relinquishing all worldly possessions and living a life unfettered by material things, of course).

Taihuai is a maze of narrow, hilly alleyways leading to small hotels, restaurants, souvenir shops, and temples. The only straight road in town is **Shiju Liangcheng Gonglu** (石咀凉城公路), the main highway running from north to south through town parallel to **Qingshui River** (qīngshuǐ hé; 清水河). Within Taihuai itself, most tourist attractions and services are spread along the western side of the road; Dailuo Peak is a notable exception.

The best way to get to Wutaishan is to take a bus from Taiyuan or Datong. Taking the train to Wutaishan is also an option, though trains run infrequently. **Minibuses** regularly make the 48km trip from Taihuai village (1-1½hr., Y20); they depart when full. **Trains** serve **Beijing** (6½hr., daily, Y105) and **Taiyuan** (4-5hr., 2 per day, Y17-31) and may leave at inconvenient times. **Buses** to **Datong** (5hr., 3 per day 6am-12:30pm, Y35) leave from the main road, opposite the bridge to Dailuo Peak and about two minutes south. The station is in a small courtyard with a red banner over the entrance. Buses to **Taiyuan** leave several times per day from a **long-distance bus station** at the southern end of Taihuai village, a 15-minute walk from the center of town. **Minibuses** to Taiyuan (4hr., Y43) leave when full (approx. every 30min. until 2-3pm) from the bus station at the very southern tip of town, about a 20-minute walk from the Dailuo Peak Bridge.

CITS, 18 Mingqing Jie, has no English-speaking staff but can still arrange specially (read: over-) priced tours for foreigners. (☎654 3218. Open daily 8am-noon and 2:30-6pm.) **Bank of China,** a 5-minute walk from the center of town on the west side of the main road, exchanges foreign currency only. (Open daily 8am-noon and 2:30-6:30pm; in winter 8am-noon and 3-6pm.) **China Telecom** (☎654 2666), on the road just north of CITS, has IDD service. The **post office** is on Yanling Jie, parallel to and one block west of the main road, 2 minutes south of the Dailuo Peak Bridge. (Open daily in summer 8am-8pm, in winter 8am-6pm.) **Postal code:** 035515.

CENTRAL CHINA

ACCOMMODATIONS AND FOOD

Small hostels in the north end of town compete with the larger "luxury" hotels in the south. Most solo travelers spend their nights in the former, giving in to the seductively low prices offered by relentless hostel owners. When rooms aren't full, prices may be flexible, especially at smaller establishments; mentioning the competition's rates won't hurt either. There are a number of small restaurants scattered throughout town; vegetarian as well as standard Chinese fare is served.

Wentong Hotel (wéntōng bīnguǎn; 文通宾馆; ☎654 5840), 1min. north of the bridge to the Dailuo Peak cable car parking lot, on the west side of the main road. Doubles are clean and new-looking, all with TV and bath. Doubles with outdoor entrance Y20, indoor entrance Y30. ❶

Baoyin Hotel (bǎoyín bīnguǎn; 宝银宾馆; ☎654 5648), 1min. down the alley on the west side of the main road, across from and slightly south of the bridge leading to the Dailuo Peak cable car parking lot; the hotel is marked by a red sign with white lettering. Clean, well-maintained rooms, all with TV and bath. Doubles and triples Y50. ❶

Yaojin Hostel (yàojìn zhāodàisuǒ; 跃进招待所), 32 Yingfang Jie (☎654 2586), just before the Baoyin Hotel. The inconspicuous entrance is on the right side of the street. Rooms are worn, but owners are receptive to price negotiation. 2-bed dorms Y30-60. ❶

Honglou Hostel (hónglóu zhāodàisuǒ; 红楼招待所; ☎654 2520), on the east side of the main road, 1min. south from Dailuo Peak Bridge. Doubles have fairly new baths, but dorms have cement floors and grubby showerless baths. 4-bed dorms Y20; doubles with bath Y100. ❶

Jinwei Hotel (jingwei bīnguǎn; 宾馆; ☎654 2791), a 15min. walk south from the center of town and across the bridge. A "luxury" hotel, the doubles sport new carpeting, immaculate baths, A/C, and TV. Doubles Y200. ❸

SIGHTS

TAIHUAI VILLAGE. Within Taihuai Village, there are more than enough temples to keep most visitors occupied. Wandering aimlessly among them is most enjoyable: it certainly kept the 13th Dalai Lama happy when he came here in 1908 en route to Mongolia. Landmarks such as Big White Pagoda on the western side of the village and Dailuo Peak to the east make it relatively easy to get one's bearings. Admission to most sights is Y6 or less; some are free.

The most visually striking sight is the **Tayuan Temple** (tǎyuàn sì; 塔院寺), which houses the **Big White Pagoda** (dàbái tǎ; 大白塔), a Tibetan-style, bottle-shaped pagoda topped off with a bronze cap. *(Open daily 7am-8pm. Y4.)* Northeast of the pagoda is the less conspicuous, but expansive **Xiantong Temple** (xiǎntōng sì; 显通寺), home to monks who are quick to offer a smile, a hello, or hot water. The monks can often be found praying or chanting behind the **Copper Palace** (tóng diàn; 铜殿) on the hill at the north end of the compound. *(Open daily 6:30am-7pm. Y6.)* The small **Guangning Temple** (guǎngníng sì; 广宁寺) lies at the base of Pusa Hill, northwest of the other temples. *(Open daily 6am-7pm. Free.)* Those who climb the 108 steps leading to the **Pusa Hilltop** (púsà dǐng; 菩萨顶) will be rewarded with a panoramic view of the surrounding temples and countryside.

Dailuo Peak (dàilúo dǐng; 黛螺顶), east of the main road in the northern part of the village, offers glimpses of the fog-shrouded countryside or a spectacular panoramic landscape on sunnier days. The robust route to the top is via the south face's 1080 steps, carefully planned to be a multiple of the lucky Buddhist number 108. *(Departing from the parking lot at the north end of the village are cable cars (Y16 up, Y15 down) and horses (Y20 up, Y15 down). Open daily summer 6:30am-7pm. A visit to the temple grounds at the top costs an extra Y3.)*

OUTLYING SIGHTS. Several temples are on the bus route from Wutaishan to Taiyuan; hop on a Taiyuan-bound bus or minibus and ask the driver to drop you nearby (Y10-20). Or, take a half-day minibus tour that departs each morning from the stand on the main road, north of the Bank of China. Prices vary wildly; expect to pay at least Y50-100. CITS also arranges full-day tours (Y220 per person).

The breathtaking **Nantai Temple** (nántái sì; 南台寺), 2485m high on the South Peak, provides spectacular views of the alpine vistas. Equally impressive, but more of a challenge to reach, **Thousand Buddha Cave** (qiānfó dòng; 千佛洞), also known as **Fomu Cave** (fómǔ dòng; 佛母洞), takes about 1½hr. to climb. A round-trip taxi to the two sights should cost about Y120. To get to the more remote and seldom-visited **Nanchan Monastery** (nánchán sì; 南禅寺), take a Taiyuan-bound bus and get off at **Dongyue** (东岳). From here, eager taxi drivers provide bumpy 20-minute taxi rides to Nanchan (approx Y25-30). The temple's main draw is its roof, which was constructed during the Tang Dynasty entirely without nails.

DATONG 大同 ☎0352

Although Datong had a luminous past as the capital of the Northern Wei dynasty (AD 383-534), its current condition is distinctively dingy. In far northern Shanxi province near Inner Mongolia, Datong today is a domestic leader in coal production and, unofficially, household ownership of pet dogs. Also known as the "Dragon Wall City," Datong was the site of legendary imperial exploits. Ming Emperor Zhengde, the "dragon," came to Datong on an imperial inspection tour and fell in love with Li Fengjie, the "phoenix," who was the daughter of a hotel owner. Even after his departure, the dragon left his mark, and images of this fantastical creature adorn buildings throughout the city. Sadly, as the legend ends, so too does the city's charm: outside the bustling commercial areas the streets are a dusty maze of construction projects punctuated by horse- and mule-carts and lurching minibuses, surroundings that hold little appeal for most travelers. The reason most visitors today venture out to the once-imperial, now-industrial Datong is to see the magnificent Yungang Grottoes and Hanging Monastery.

TRANSPORTATION

Flights: The nearest airport is in Taiyuan. **Datong Air Service Company** (dàtóng hángkōng fúwù zhōngxīn; 大同航空服务中心), Aviation Bldg., 1 Nanguan Xi Lu (☎204 4039), can book tickets. Open daily in summer 8am-7pm; in winter 8am-6pm.

Trains: Datong Train Station (dàtóng huǒchē zhàn; 大同火车站; ☎602 3458), at the intersection of Xinjian Bei Lu and Zhanqian Jie, in the northern part of the city. Tickets, especially those to Beijing, can be hard to come by if the train doesn't originate in Datong; some travelers have better luck at CITS. The ticket office is next to the clock tower; both same-day and advance tickets are sold. Open 24hr. in theory, but the staff might not always be there. Luggage storage near ticket office (Y2 per piece). To: **Beijing** (6½-8hr.; 9-10 per day, 3 sleepers per day; seats Y27-52, sleepers Y70-110); **Hohhot** (4-7hr., 10 per day, Y19-37); **Nanjing** (30hr., daily, Y234); **Shijiazhuang** (14hr., daily, Y91); **Taiyuan** (7½hr., 5 per day, Y65-104); **Xi'an** (18½hr., daily, Y140). The Trans-Mongolian rail (see p. 89) has a stop in **Datong** (Tu 2:15pm).

Buses: Datong Long-distance Bus Station (dàtóng chángtú qìchē zhàn; 大同长途汽车站; ☎281 4880), at Xinhua Jie and Xinjian Bei Lu, a 10min. walk from the train station. Open daily 6am-5pm; most people buy their tickets on the bus. To **Hohhot** (6-7hr., 7:20am, Y30) and **Taiyuan** (4½-5hr., every hr. 6:30am-5pm, Y40-60). Minibuses to **Wutaishan** (4hr., multiple departures 6:10am-2pm) only run May-Oct. **Datong New Long-distance Bus Station** (dàtóng chángtú xīn kèzhàn; 大同长途新客站), 20 Yantong Xi Lu (☎602 0870), west of Xinjian Bei Lu, serves similar destinations. Bus #11 stops outside. Open daily 5am-6:30pm.

Local Transportation: Most **buses** run approximately 6am-7:30pm. Some, such as #15, run 5:30am-8:40pm. Base fare Y1. Buses that leave the city (including #3) cost Y1.5. Bus **#11** follows a circular route that includes Xinkaili, the Datong Hotel, and the New Long-distance Bus Station; **#15** runs from the train station along Xinjian Lu to Yingbin Lu and several hotels; **#2, 4, 8, 14, 15, 16,** and **201** all originate at the train station.

Taxis: Base fare Y5, each additional km Y1.2. From the train station to the hotels on Yingbin Lu Y10-12.

ORIENTATION AND PRACTICAL INFORMATION

Datong's larger thoroughfares change names several times as they criss-cross the city. From the commercial center of town, **Da Xi Jie** (大西街), **Da Dong Jie** (大东街), **Da Bei Jie** (大北街), and **Da Nan Jie** (大南街) extend to the west, east, north, and south, respectively. The **Drum Tower** (gǔ lóu; 鼓楼) lies just south of the traffic circle. **Xinjian Lu** (新建路) runs from the train station to the southern reaches of the city and the terminus of several bus routes.

Travel Agency: **CITS** (☎502 2674 or 510 1836; fax 510 1326), in the train station between the 2 waiting rooms. Staffed by a friendly, knowledgeable, and mainly English-speaking staff, this is the 1st stop for most foreign travelers. Minibus guided tours of Yungang Caves and Hanging Monastery from Y100 per person (groups of 2 or more; not including admission). Sleeper ticket commission Y30. Bargain for discounts. Open daily 6:30am-6:30pm.

Bank of China: 62 Yingbin Xi Lu (☎504 4114), across the street from the Datong Hotel; bus #15 stops in front. Exchanges currency and traveler's checks. Open M-F 8am-6pm.

Market: Zhongbai Bei Jie Supermarket, 135 Da Bei Jie; bus #4 stops outside. Large selection of Chinese brands; foreign products are limited to crackers and laundry detergent. Open daily 8:30am-7:40pm.

PSB: On Xinjian Bei Lu, just north of Da Xi Jie, on the east side of the street (☎205 0778, ext. 2037). Visa extensions. Open M-F 8:30am-noon and 2:30-5pm.

Pharmacy: Tongren Pharmacy, 118 Da Xi Jie, has a few Western brands. Open daily in summer 7:30am-10:30pm; in winter 7:30am-9:30pm.

Hospital: No. 3 Hospital (dàtóngshì dìsān yīyuàn; 大同市第三医院; ☎502 1001), on the corner of Xinjian Nan Lu and Yingbin Lu. Accessible by bus #15.

Internet Access: Wangyuan Internet Bar (wǎngyuán wǎngbā; 网缘网吧; ☎280 5063), on Xinjian Bei Lu, about half a block from the train station on the left. Fast connections; blissfully uncrowded. Y3 per hr. Open 24hr. **Flying Internet Bar** (fēiyáng wǎngbā; 飞扬网吧; ☎281 8499), on Xinhua Jie. From the train station, walk down Xinjian Beilu and turn right at the first intersection; the bar is about a 15min. walk ahead, on the right. Y3 per hr. Open daily 8am-midnight.

Post and Telecommunications: ☎203 3937. On the square on the southeast side of the intersection of Xinjian Lu and Da Xi Jie. EMS and Poste Restante. Open daily 8am-8pm. **China Telecom** (☎202 2114), just east of the post office, has IDD service. Open daily 8am-6:30pm. **Postal Code:** 037004.

CENTRAL CHINA

ACCOMMODATIONS

Most of the hotels are near the train station or on Yingbin Lu; those near the train station are cheaper and more convenient. Many establishments charge foreigners more, but dorm beds (when available) are still relatively cheap.

Feitian Hotel (fēitiān bīnguǎn; 飞天宾馆), 1 Chezhan Qian Jie (☎281 3144), immediately to the left of the train station square. Popular among backpackers, the Feitian is best for those who want cheap, clean rooms near the train station; try the delicious hotpot next door. No A/C in cheaper rooms. 4-bed dorms Y35-40; doubles Y128-200. ❶

Yuwei Luguan (yǔwèi lǚguàn; 雨未旅馆; ☎281 4124), on Xinjian Bei Lu, across the street and just east of the Old Long-distance Bus Station. Dorms and doubles are clean

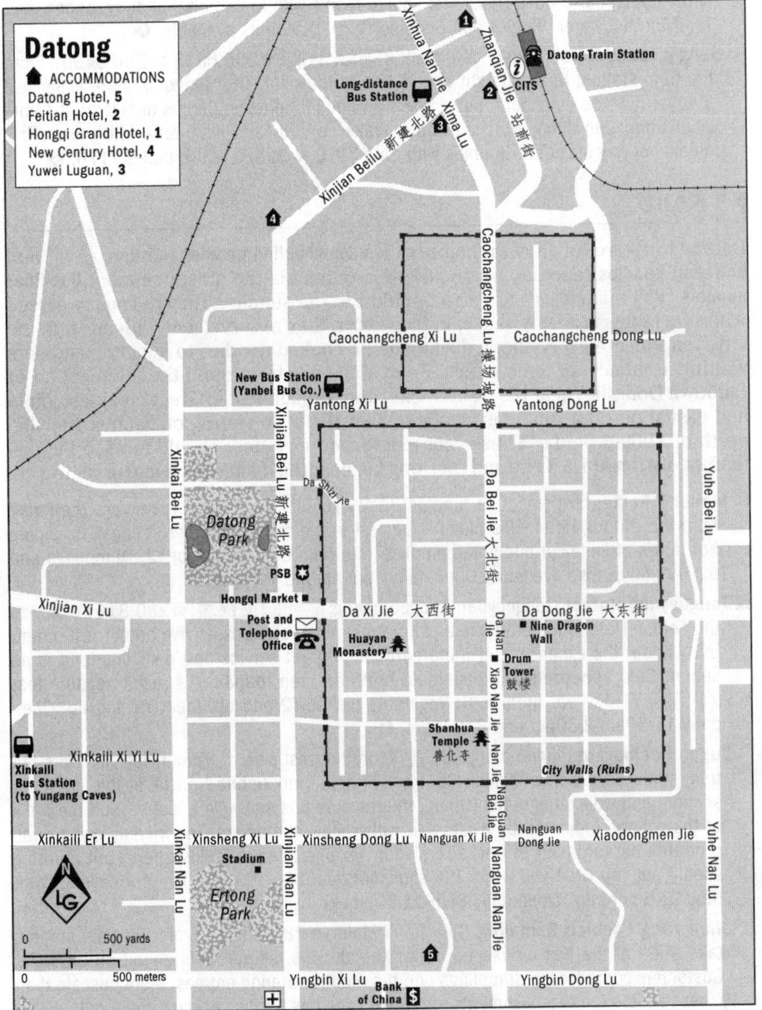

with tiled floors, and small baths are communal. 24hr. hot water. 2-bed dorms Y23 (if there are no other foreigners to share the room, you must buy both beds); doubles with attached bath Y60. ❶

New Century Hotel (xīnshìjì bīnguǎn; 新世纪宾馆; ☎706 6109 ext. 8100), on the north corner where Xinjian Bei Lu turns. From the train station, take bus #2, 15, or 16; or walk straight down Xinjian Bei Lu for 20min. With a distinctly "homey" feel, all rooms have new and brightly colored upholstery, immaculate baths, and doorbells. 24hr. hot water. Singles and doubles with baths Y88 and up. ❷

Datong Hotel (dàtóng bīnguǎn; 大同宾馆), 37 Yingbin Xi Lu (☎203 2476 ext. 2001), across from the bank, 10 stops from the train station on bus #15. This newly renovated super-hotel boasts wonderfully maintained rooms with A/C, bath, hairdryer, phone, and TV. 24hr. hot water. Singles and doubles Y228. Discounts available. ❹

Hongqi Grand Hotel (hóngqí dàjiǔdiàn; 红旗大酒店; ☎205 6813 or 206 8405). From the train station, head straight ahead and to the right. The Hongqi is more expensive than its rail-side neighbors, but it offers additional benefits. Rooms are clean, if somewhat worn, with dingy attached baths. Wake up early and jump-rope with the staff. 3 meals per day included. Doubles with bath Y170, with A/C Y190; triples Y170. ❸

FOOD

Datong folks are rough with their noodles. **Hand-pulled noodles** (lāmiàn; 拉面) and **knife-cut noodles** (dāoxiāo miàn; 刀削面) are among the most common. **Oat flour noodles** (yòu miàn; 釉面) are also popular. In the summer, they're usually served with vegetables in a tasty sauce; in the winter, they're served hot with meat. In the city, vendors are everywhere, dishing home-cooked noodles to hungry customers waiting at adjacent picnic tables. Food stalls cluster around the intersection of Baibowa Dong Jie (near the train tracks) and Xinjian Bei Lu. Great breakfast joints and casual outdoor dining is available near the train station on Xinhua Nan Jie, north of Xinjian Bei Lu. Those yearning for more choices should head to the restaurant district at Da Xi Jie and Da Dong Lu, near the main square and drum tower.

Madaha Restaurant (mǎdàhā fàndiàn; 马大哈饭店), on Yingbin Lu, across the street from the Datong Hotel. This place is busiest in the mornings, when it cooks up piping hot bowls of knife-cut noodles (complete with hard-boiled egg) for Y2. Dumplings and other noodles also available. Open daily from around 7:30am. ❶

Tongheyuan Hotpot (tónghéyuán huǒguō chéng; 同和园火锅城; ☎280 3111), next to the Feitian Hotel. All the amenities and atmosphere of an expensive hotpot restaurant, but without the expense. Get there early; their great service and delicious food is no secret. Cold appetizers and vegetable broth are free, *bābǎo chá* (eight-treasure tea; 八宝茶) Y1.5. Meat broth Y26. Vegetable dishes Y2 and up, meat Y8 and up. Open daily 11:30am-2:30pm and 6-9:30pm. ❶

Yuguo Restaurant (yùguō diàn; 御锅店), on the west side of Xinhua Nan Jie. From the train station, walk down Xinjian Bei Lu, turn right onto Xinhua Nan Jie at the first intersection, and walk straight for 10min.; the restaurant is on the left, just beyond the walls of the school, indicated by a red sign with yellow characters. The friendly owners will probably be surprised to see a foreigner; no one speaks English here, but pointing should get you what you want. The *shānshuǐ dòufǔ* (山水豆腐; Y5) is excellent. Draft beer Y2.5 per mug. Open daily 8am-11:30pm. ❶

Shen Yang Laobian Dumpling Co., 12 Xi Malu (☎281 3911). From the train station, take a left at the first intersection onto Xi Malu; the restaurant is ahead on the right. Customers come for the dumplings and the mouth-watering entrees. More upscale than most train station establishments, the Shen Yang has terrific service without outrageous costs. Entrees range Y6-18. Dumplings Y3.2. ❶

SIGHTS

Both foreign and Chinese tourists flock to Datong's most famous attraction, the Yungang Grottoes (below), although several sights within the city itself are also easily accessible and worth a visit.

HUAYAN MONASTERY (huáyán sì; 华严寺; ☎204 5185). The ancient, towering Buddhist sutras in the main **Bhagavan Stack Hall** are reason enough to visit this quiet, tourist-free monastery. Built in the Liao and Jin dynasties, only a few of the original buildings remain. During the Yuan and Ming dynasties, the complex was divided into upper and lower portions. The lower portion houses small displays of fossils, eggs, and dynastic relics, while the upper monastery's **Daxiong Treasure Hall** features colorful frescoes and a number of statues. *(South of Da Xi Jie and west of Da Nan Jie. The Upper Monastery is off Shansi Bei Xiang. To get to the Lower Monastery, walk east on Da Xi Jie, take a right on the first through street, just before the cashmere shop; the monastery entrance is ahead on the right. Open daily in summer 8am-6pm; in winter 9am-5pm. Y6. At press time, the Upper Monastery was closed for repairs.)*

NINE DRAGON WALL (jiǔlóng bì; 九龙壁). In imperial China, dragon walls served as screens to conceal palace and temple interiors from outsiders. Datong's Nine Dragon Wall was constructed in 1392 to hide the palace of Prince Zhugui, the 13th son of the founder of the Ming dynasty. The palace itself was destroyed by fire, but the sturdy wall still stands. Today, sections of the wall are scattered throughout Datong; unfortunately, the section allotted to tourists is smaller than the one dedicated to souvenir shops. The price is right for a quick look, but don't miss taking a peek at the pond below the wall—as the water moves, the dragons come alive. Most tour buses miss the wall's majesty; the colorful teal-blue sight definitely has its charm. *(About 1 block east of Da Nan Jie and Da Dong Jie, on the south side of the street. Bus #17 stops at Jiulong Bi, and bus #4 from the station stops nearby at Sipailou. Open daily 8am-6pm. Y3. Students Y1.5.)*

SHANHUA MONASTERY (shànhuà sì; 善化寺; ☎204 2898). Built in 713 during the Tang dynasty, this monastery was ravaged by war in 1122, and rebuilt a few years later. Thanks to the good monk who diligently oversaw its reconstruction, the immense, cool, incense-filled **Hall of Mahaviva** still remains. The highlight of this complex, this hall houses a magnificent collection of Buddha statues. Apart from a small section of Datong's Nine Dragon Wall, there is little more to see. *(South of Hualin Department Store and west of Nanmen Jie. From the Drum Tower, take a right on the first street south of Hualin Department Store and the first left down the alley for about 5min. Blue signs point the way. Accessible by bus #17. Open daily 8am-6pm. Y10, students Y5.)*

DAYTRIPS FROM DATONG

YUNGANG GROTTOES

About 17km west of Datong. Bus #4 from the train station goes to Xinjaili (Y1); from there, bus #3 goes to Yungang (Y1.5). Excellent Chinese and English descriptions. Open daily 8:30am-5:30pm. Y50, students Y25.

The spectacular Yungang Grottoes (yúngǎng shíkū; 云冈石窟) take cave-carving to a new, mind-blowing level with 20 caves and 51,000 Buddhist statues. Dating back more than 1500 years, these grottoes were carved out of the mountains west of Datong, the political and spiritual capital of the Northern Wei dynasty. The construction of the caves was ordered by the Northern Wei rulers to atone for their earlier persecution of Buddhism. Some 30,000 artisan families from Dunhuang (see p. 746) were forced to relocate to work on the caves. 40,000 sculptors took 50 years to complete the project, which now ranks among the finest examples of Buddhist art in China. The sculptural style was primarily borrowed from Indian Buddhist art, which itself was created from a synthesis of various foreign styles, including Persian, Byzantine, and Greek. These sculptures differ from those of the later Longmen Grottoes (see p. 269), which feature a uniquely Chinese design.

After running the gauntlet of souvenir shops, visitors enter a small gallery that describes the restoration of the caves and then come face-to-face with the pride of the Grottoes—an imposing 17m-tall Buddha. The figure is allegedly large enough for 120 people to stand on its knees, but testing this with 119 of your friends might not be appreciated by grotto staff. This is a popular tourist destination for both foreign and Chinese guests; fortunately, no number of camera-toting tourists can detract from the awe that these truly magnificent caves inspire.

HENGSHAN AND THE HANGING MONASTERY

*70km from Datong. Unscheduled **minibuses** (Y25-30) leave each morning from the train and old bus station areas in Datong, according to demand. For independent travelers, this unreliable option is the cheapest; a more secure method is to take a bus from Datong's Old Bus Station to **Hongyuan** (approx. 1½hr., Y30). Once there, you'll need to hire a taxi (20min., Y50-75 round-trip). CITS tours, which often include the monastery, may actually be cheaper. ☎(0352) 832 2142. Open daily in summer 6:30am-7pm; in winter 8am-5pm. Y35.*

One of the five sacred Daoist mountains, Shanxi's Hengshan Mountain (héngshān; 恒山) is often referred to as **beiyue** (běiyuè; 北岳) to distinguish it from *nányuè*, the Hengshan of Hunan (see p. 437). Rising 2017m into the air, Hengshan showcases its treacherous cliffs and calligraphy by Tang poet Li Bai. The most dramatic of the Eighteen Scenes of Hengshan is the Hanging Monastery (xuánkōng sì; 悬空寺), suspended precariously under an overhanging precipice. Some of the 40 halls in this temple are held up only by a single supporting pillar. Signs indicate the proper path as visitors wind their way up, down, and around to reach over 80 Buddha statues and other treasures. In the monastery, if there are a large number of tourists, this relaxed viewing can turn into a forced march. Looking down through the cracks of the flooring provides an exhilarating rush (or sheer terror for acrophobics). Hengshan Reservoir is up the stairs about 5 or 10 minutes beyond, but was closed for repairs as of July 2001.

INNER MONGOLIA 内蒙古

When most sensible individuals hear the phrase "Inner Mongolia," they think Genghis Khan, Kublai Khan, the roving Mongol armies, and brazen exploits on horseback. More often than not, that phrase will evoke a vivid image of big burly men with long, flowing hair billowing in the wind. These famous Khan leaders were dead and buried centuries ago, and things haven't been quite the same since. The unified Mongol Empire collapsed in the 14th century, and by the 20th, China and Russia were busy haggling over how to split up the nation. Inner Mongolia (not to be confused with the independent country of Mongolia) became the PRC's first autonomous region in 1947.

Those who are tempted to associate Inner Mongolia with the word "hordes" are about 700 years too late. While some inhabitants maintain their traditional nomadic lifestyle, visitors are more likely to encounter Han Chinese on horseback than Mongolians. In fact, ethnic Mongolians only make up about 10-20% of the region's population. Still, there is a non-Chinese feel that pervades the region, especially the vast areas of endless prairie near Hohhot. Organized grasslands tours may seem somewhat contrived and far from being "authentic" Mongol living (concrete-floored yurts don't fool us). Regardless, most visitors who venture north find something with which to fall in love, whether it's the endless stretches of blue sky, the potent kick of local liquor, or the dashing Mongolian tour guides.

HOHHOT 呼和浩特 ☎0471

The name Hohhot is derived from the Mongolian for "green city," but for many visitors to Inner Mongolia's capital, the grass is greener on the other side: that is, in

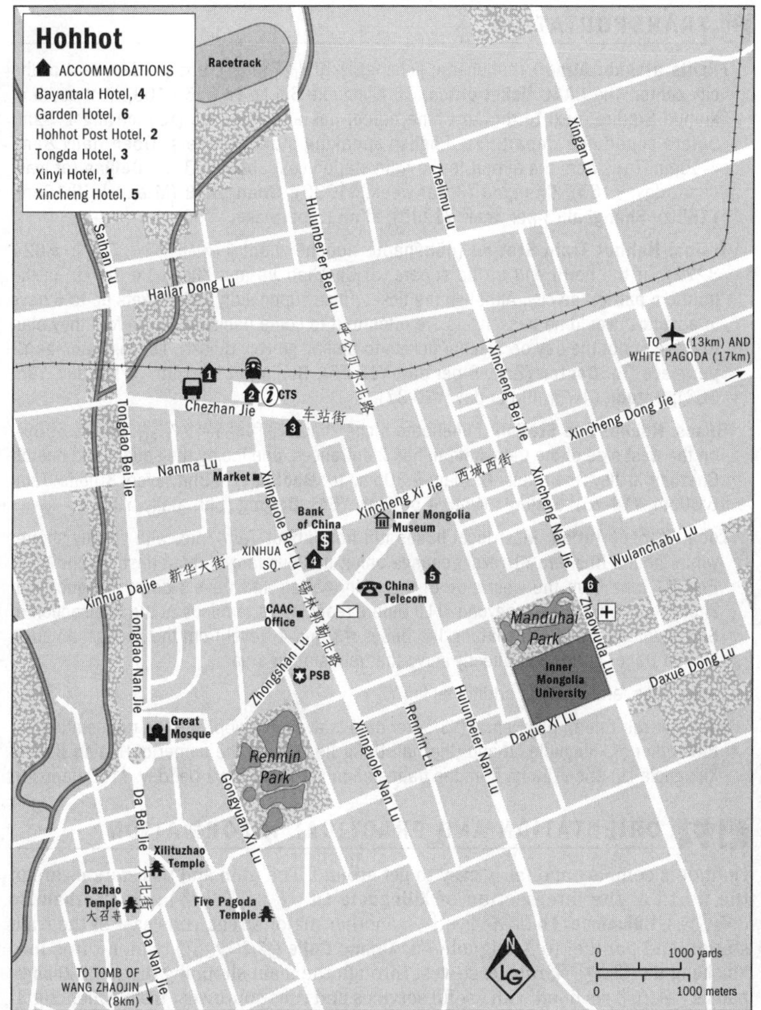

the grasslands about 100km away. Hordes of grass-loving prairie-seekers use Hohhot only as a convenient point from which to visit the surrounding plains; the city itself, originally a frontier trading post, is nonetheless a pleasant place to stay. The summer months are green and balmy, perfect for cultivating the coniferous trees that line the boulevards. Parts of the town have well-preserved architecture dating back to the early Ming dynasty, when Han Chinese first moved into the city. Today Hohhot's population, hovering around one million, is predominantly Han, but shop signs featuring Mongolian script alongside Chinese characters suggest that although the Mongol presence is outnumbered, it is not overshadowed.

TRANSPORTATION

Flights: Hohhot Airport (hūhéhàotè jīchǎng; 呼和浩特机场), about 15km east of the city center. The **CAAC ticket office,** 35 Xilinguole Bei Lu (☎696 4103), just south of Xinhua Square, next to the Air China office, has airport buses (Y5) leaving 1½-2hr. before scheduled departures. English-speaking staff members. Open daily 8am-7:30pm. Taxis from the airport to the train station cost about Y23. To: **Beijing** (at least 4 per day, Y460); **Chengdu** (3 per week, Y1230); **Guangzhou** (M and Th 8:10am, Y1650); **Shanghai** (3 per week, Y1230); **Xi'an** (5 per week, Y750).

Trains: Hohhot Train Station (hūhéhàotè huǒchē zhàn; 呼和浩特火车站; ☎624 3222), at the north end of the square, at Chezhan Jie and Xilinguole Bei Lu, in the northern part of the city. Although the ticket office supposedly sells tickets up to 6 days in advance, would-be passengers are often told to come back the day before they plan to leave, if not the day of. Sleeper tickets to Beijing go very quickly. Luggage storage Y2 per piece. To: **Baotou** (3hr., 8 per day, Y12-25); **Beijing** (11½-14hr., 5 per day, Y95-163); **Datong** (4-7hr., 9 per day, Y20-37).

Buses: Hohhot Bus Station (hūhéhàotè qìchē zhàn; 呼和浩特汽车站; ☎696 5969), on the west side of the train station, has 2 entrances, one facing the square and one off Chezhan Xi Jie. Open daily 6:30am-6:30pm. To: **Baotou** (2½-3hr., every 30min. 7am-6:30pm, Y14-25); **Beijing** (12hr., 4 per day, Y64); **Datong** (6hr., daily, Y30).

Local Transportation: Most local **buses** run from about 7am-7pm, with slightly shorter winter hours. Bus fare Y1 (exact change only); minibus fare to most destinations Y1.5. Bus **#1** runs from the west side of the train station and travels down Xilinguole Lu, Zhongshan Xi Lu, and Gongyuan Xi Lu before reaching its terminus at the intersection of Shiyangqiao Lu and Nanchafang Jie. Buses **#3** and **4** travel from the Zhongshan Lu to Xinhua Dajie, but do not directly serve the train station area.

Taxis: Base fare Y6, each additional km Y3.

Bike Rental: Cheap bike rental (Y3-5 per day) is available opposite the train station, on the corner of Xilinguole Lu and Chezhan Dong Jie, and on the corner of Hua'an Jie and Xilinguole Lu, about 5min. from the train station (Y1 for 4hr., Y2 per day, Y100 deposit).

ORIENTATION AND PRACTICAL INFORMATION

Hohhot is compact and fairly easy to get around. The train and bus stations are in the north at the intersection of **Xilinguole Lu** (锡林郭勒路) and **Chezhan Jie** (车站街). **Hulunbeier Lu** (呼仑北尔路), another major street, runs east of the train station and parallel to Xilinguole Lu. **Xinhua Dajie** (新华大街), which turns into **Xincheng Jie** (新城街), runs east-west through the main shopping districts. **Zhongshan Lu** (中山路) is lined with useful services and runs southwest from Xincheng Xi Jie, beginning near the Inner Mongolian Museum. To the west, **Tong Daojie** (通道街), which becomes **Da Bei Jie** (大北街) and **Da Nan Jie** (大南街), runs north-south through the older section of the city.

Travel Agency: CTS, Post Hotel, Rm. 208 (☎696 9211), just east of the train station. Open daily 8am-6:30pm.

Bank of China: 44 Xinhua Dajie (☎696 6738), east of Xilinguole Lu and opposite the Zhaojun Hotel. Open in summer M-F 8am-noon and 2:30-6pm; in winter 8am-noon and 2-5pm. Exchanges traveler's checks next to the VIP lounge. The **Zhaojun Hotel,** at the intersection of Xinhua Dajie and Xilinguole Lu, exchanges traveler's checks on weekends, even for non-guests (☎626 8330).

Bookstore: Foreign Bookstore, 52 Xincheng Xi Jie, just west of the bank. Good selection of English books on tape and dictionaries.

Markets: Inner Mongolian Lido Subsidiary Food Co., 195 Xilinguole Bei Lu, a 15min. walk from the train station on the west side of the street. Open daily 8am-8:30pm. **Minzu Department Store** (mínzú shāngchǎng; 民族商场) sells discount Mongolian items on the 2nd fl. Open daily in summer 9am-7:30pm; in winter 9am-7pm.

PSB: 39 Zhongshan Lu (☎696 8148), on the north side of the street. The office of the **Division of Aliens Exit-Entry Administration** is to the left, just inside the gate. Visa extensions. Open M-F 8-11:30am and 2:30-6pm.

Hospital: Inner Mongolia Hospital, 18 Zhaowuda Lu, a 10min. walk south of the intersection with Wulanchabu Lu. Bus #4 stops in front.

Telephones: China Telecom, just east of the corner of Zhongshan Dong Lu and Renmin Lu, 1 block north of the post office. Open daily in summer 8am-7pm; in winter 8am-6:30pm. 24hr. service about 50m east.

Internet Access: China Telecom Center Internet Bar (diànxìn yíngyètīng wǎngbā; 电信营业厅网吧; ☎626 5261), on the 2nd fl. of the China Telecom building on Zhongshan Dong Lu. Not usually crowded. Good connection speed. Y3 per hr. Open daily in summer 8am-6:30pm; in winter 8am-6pm.

Post Office: On Zhongshan Dong Lu, west of Renmin Lu, about a 5min. walk from Shi Zhengfu bus stop (bus #1) (☎692 4840). EMS, IDD service, and Poste Restante. Open daily in summer 8am-7pm; in winter 8am-6:30pm. **Postal Code:** 010020. The branch immediately to the left (east) as you exit the train station has the same hours but no Poste Restante. **Postal Code:** 010050.

ACCOMMODATIONS

Without a doubt, the cheapest accommodations open to foreigners are near the train station. More expensive hotels with better rooms can be found near Xinhua Square. During the summer months, hotels are often filled to capacity, so reservations are recommended, especially at more upscale establishments.

Xinyi Hotel, next to the train station (☎696 7426). The best dorm rooms in town. Large common baths are odorless, and all rooms have fan and TV. Convenient location. 24hr. hot water. 3-bed dorms Y30; 2-bed dorms Y40; doubles Y120, with living room Y200. ❶

Tongda Hotel (tōngdá fàndiàn; 通达饭店), 28 Chezhan Dong Jie (☎696 8731), across the street, half a block to the left when you exit the train station. Cheap and relatively clean, the Tongda is out of reach of the obnoxiously early train station loudspeaker, and so much quieter than other train station hotels. Only the 4th and 5th floors have guest rooms; no elevator. All rooms have fans and attached bath; doubles have phones. Hot water 7-8:30am and 9-11:30pm. Free luggage storage. Deposit Y20. Singles Y62; doubles Y100, with A/C Y138. ❶

Garden Hotel (huāyuán bīnguǎn; 花园宾馆), 83 Zhaowuda Lu (☎496 5478), at Wulanchabu Lu. From the train station, take bus #4 to the Inner Mongolia Hospital and backtrack half a block; a taxi costs about Y8. Friendly staff and clean rooms. 24hr. hot water. Breakfast included. Singles and doubles Y60, with bath Y120; triples Y60-80. Occasional discounts. MC. ❶

Hohhot Post Hotel (hūshì yóuzhèng fàndiàn; 呼市邮政饭店; ☎696 6872), to the left as you exit the train station, marked by the green China Post symbol. Cheap and convenient. More expensive carpeted rooms have bath, phone, and TV. Dorms are clean. Staff is generally unhelpful. Showers open to men M, W, F; women Tu, Th, Sa. Hot water 8-10pm. 3-bed dorms Y30; doubles Y40, with bath Y60. ❶

Xincheng Hotel (xīnchéng bīnguǎn; 新城宾馆), 40 Hulunbei'er Nan Lu (☎629 2288; fax 693 1141), north of Wulanchabu Xi Lu. Take bus #20 from the corner of Chezhan Dong Jie and Hulunbei'er Lu 2 stops to Erzhang. Or from the train station, turn left and continue straight until the traffic light; then, turn right. Once inside the sprawling complex, take a left at the first intersection to get to reception. A small golf cart motors guests to their rooms. The cheapest rooms (in building #10) are worn; but all sheets, furniture, and bathroom fixtures are new. All rooms have enormous attached baths. Doubles Y130-180, with A/C and breakfast Y300-600; triples Y120. ❷

Bayantala Hotel (bāyàntǎlā fàndiàn; 巴彦塔拉饭店), 13 Xilinguole Bei Lu (☎696 3344), across the street from Xinhua Square. Bus #1 from the train station stops across the street, at Xinhua Guangchang. Foreigners usually not allowed in dorms. A popular hotel among tourists; reservations recommended. 2-bed dorms Y60; singles Y100 and up; doubles Y130-200; triples Y180 and up. ❶

FOOD

A trip to Mongolia without hotpot is like a trip to Italy without pasta: a grievous culinary faux pas. **Mongolian hotpot with sliced mutton** (shuàn yángròu huǒguō; 涮羊肉火锅) is a specialty of the region. Although most people find the idea of boiling broth appetizing in the cold winter months, giant hotpot "palaces," hoping for more year-round business, turn their air-conditioners on full-blast in the summer to recreate a frigid feel. If the weather is warm and you're sick of sheep, there are several good areas for outdoor dining. Stands selling *bāozi* (Y2.5-3 per steamer) and other dishes set up outside the Bayantala Hotel, south of the intersection of Xilinguole Lu and Xinhua Dajie. Various *shāguō* (hotpot; 沙锅) and dumpling restaurants line Xilinguole Lu, south of the train station. The unofficial hotpot district is on **Nan Malu,** the first street on the right after crossing Chezhan Dong Jie. Those seeking beef or lamb *jiǎozi* should follow their noses to **Wulanqiate Dong Jie** and **Guoziban Xiang,** just south of the Bayantala Hotel, where restaurants dish it out for Y8 per 0.5kg (about 50 dumplings).

Wangji Dumpling House (wángjì jiǎozi lóu; 王记饺子楼; ☎629 6216), on the south side of Chezhan Dong Jie, between Xilinguole Lu and Hulunbei'er Lu, 10min. from the train station. Elbow your way through this crowded joint to get your hands on these scrumptious dumplings. Dumplings Y10-16 per 0.5kg. Hours vary. ❶

Wanglaoban Hotpot (wánglǎobán shǐguō; 王老板史锅), 178 Xilinguole Bei Lu (☎692 1291), about a 3min. walk south from the train station, on the east side of the street. Most people come here for the cheapest hotpot in town, and Wanglaoban is perpetually packed. Soup base Y10-15; vegetables Y3-6; meat Y6-16. Open daily 10:30am-2:30pm and 4:30-9:30pm. ❶

Lamb Kebab Vendor, on the east side of Xilinguole Bei Lu, a 2min. walk south of the train station. Enormous mouth-watering hunks of meat that put the sparse kebabs of other vendors to shame. Kick back with a beer, napkins, and friends at the stand's picnic table. Y1 per piping-hot kebab. ❶

Endless Love Bakery, 169 Zhongshan Xi Lu, just south of Minzu Shanchang. The aroma of freshly baked cakes, cookies, and pastries envelops visitors as they step inside this sweet haven. Goodies from Y3. Open daily 10am-noon and 4-6pm. ❶

Dairy Queen/Golden Skillet (guójì kuàicān chéng; 国际快餐城), 1 Gongyuan Dong Jie, at Zhongshan Xi Lu, across from the Minzu Shangchang. Serves both Chinese and Amer-

CENTRAL CHINA

ican fast food. Blizzards are tasty, but so small they should be called Chance of Flurries. For a change of pace, try a sesame and cashew Blizzard (Y10-16.50). Open 24hr. ❷

SIGHTS

Most visitors come to Hohhot planning to trek out to the famed grasslands outside the city. Many sights within the city are interesting enough to be included on grassland tours, but because they are easily accessible by public bus or bike, they can be visited independently as well. For sights outside the city center, including the grasslands, most of the trip can be made independently by bus.

INNER MONGOLIA MUSEUM (nèiménggǔ bówùguǎn; 内蒙古博物馆; ☎696 3766). This museum's exhibits, accompanied by both Chinese and English explanations, cover everything from dinosaurs to yurts (see **Yearning for Yurts,** p. 311). Spanning Inner Mongolia's history from the prehistoric to the Communist Revolution, an incredible number of artifacts and pictures are crammed into this 2-story museum. The exhibition on the first floor to the right of the main entrance features colorful clothing, tools, and other items representing the minority nationalities living in Inner Mongolia, particularly ethnic Mongolians. *(2 Xinhua Dajie. Take bus #20 or minibus #33 from the train station to Bowuguan. The main entrance is on Hulunbeier Lu between Xinhua Dajie and Zhongshan Dong Lu. Open in summer W-M 9am-5pm, ticket sales stop at 4pm; in winter 10am-4pm. Y8, students Y6.)*

DAZHAO TEMPLE (dàzhào; 大召). Dating back to the Ming dynasty, this large complex houses a complete set (108 volumes) of Buddhist scriptures and a rare silver statue of Sakyamuni. Sometimes, it plays host to large prayer gatherings amid the colorful decorations of the main hall. As a popular stop on grassland tours, these sprawling courtyards also play host to many camera-clicking tourists. *(On Dazhao Qianjie off Da Nan Jie, the main south street. Bus #6 from Tongda Bei Jie and Chezhan Xi Jie, west of the train station, stops nearby; from the bus stop, walk straight ahead for 3min., and then turn right onto Dazhao Qianjie. Otherwise, take bus #1 from the station to its terminus and walk north on Nanchafang Jie/Xiao Nan Jie for about 15-20min. until the large building appears on the left. Peek down the alley from Da Nan Jie to see the temple. ☎597 3154. Open daily 8am-6:30pm. Y10.)*

XILITUZHAO TEMPLE (xílìtúzhào; 席力图召). Situated off a maze of winding alleyways lined with squat adobe houses, this temple includes the largest stupa in Inner Mongolia. The main hall is filled with brightly colored dragon carpets and the overwhelming smell of incense. More secluded than the neighboring Dazhao Temple, Xilituzhao also contains many courtyards worth exploring and is the home of the Living Buddha responsible for Buddhist affairs in Hohhot. *(On a small street just east of Da Nan Jie. From Dazhao, turn left onto Dazhao Qianjie and cross the road, then continue directly across to the lane on the other side. Open daily 8am-6:30pm. Y5.)*

GREAT MOSQUE (qīngzhēn dàsì; 清真大寺). A must-see sight, if not for the gorgeous mosque itself, then for the lively atmosphere inside its walls. Surrounded by friendly, boisterous Muslim vendors, visitors munch on sweet rice and dried apricots as they stroll through the mosque's courtyards. Non-Muslims are not allowed inside the various worship halls. *(Just north of the intersection of Tong Daojie and Zhongshan Xi Lu. Bus #13 from the southeast corner of Xinhua Square terminates just beyond. Free.)*

FIVE PAGODA TEMPLE (wǔtǎ sì; 五塔寺). These five pagodas are all that remain since the Ci Deng Temple, the original anchor of the site, was destroyed. Despite their orphaned status, these five little buildings are beautifully maintained and worth a visit. The astronomical chart with Mongolian inscriptions on the back wall

FAREWELL, MY CONCUBINE Times were tough for the Han in 33 BC. The fearsome Huns were threatening Xi'an, and the Han Emperor Xuandi decided to appease the Hun Chieftain Huhanxie Chanyu by offering him the hand of a royal princess in marriage. But without a daughter of suitable age, the emperor was forced to adopt a girl from among his reserve of imperial concubines as his daughter, whom he would then marry off to the chieftan. Sixteen-year-old **Wang Zhaojun,** who had been languishing at the bottom of the concubine hierarchy, decided it was better to get out than wait forever for the emperor's attention, so she volunteered to marry the Hun chieftan. The emperor consulted his catalogue of portraits and, noting that she was somewhat frumpy, consented. But when Wang Zhaojun entered the imperial palace to be handed over to the chieftain, the emperor and his entire entourage gasped, for the young concubine was the most beautiful woman they had ever seen. It turned out that the imperial portrait painter took bribes in exchange for creating flattering paintings. Poor Wang Zhaojun was too proud to pay off the greedy painter, so he made her portrait unattractive and ruined her chances to be chosen as a favorite of the emperor. Because the Hun chieftan was present at the hand-over ceremony, the Han emperor could not take back his offer and was forced to watch glumly as the ecstatic Hun swung Wang Zhaojun (whose tomb is in Hohhot; see p. 300) up onto his horse and rode off into the sunset. She must have been a real looker; the Huns didn't try to attack again for 50 years.

is the only one of its kind in China. *(48 Wutasi Houjie, west of Gongyuang Xi Lu. Bus #1 from the train station stops at Wujing Yiyuan; from the stop, continue walking in the same direction (south) for a couple of blocks until the 5 pagodas become visible down an alley on the right. ☎597 2640. Open daily 8am-6:30pm. Y10.)*

WHITE PAGODA (bái tǎ; 白塔; ☎901 1027). Originally known as the Ten Thousand Avatamska Sutras Temple, this secluded, carefully restored pagoda towers more than 50m over the nearby fields. Although the lime on the outside gives the structure a brilliant sheen, the inside of the pagoda can be pitch black, making for a treacherous climb. Visitors may want to bring matches to the top to burn incense and pray for a safe descent. *(About 15km east of Hohhot beyond the airport. Minibus #12 to Hexi from the eastern end of Dongfeng Lu goes past the site. Some buses are unnumbered, so just catch any bus destined for Hexi (approx. Y4); Bus #33 from the train station stops at the terminus for bus #12. Open daily 8am-6pm. Y5, Y5 extra to climb the pagoda.)*

TOMB OF WANG ZHAOJUN (zhāojūn mù; 昭君墓). This rather commercial sight is the final resting place of the Han dynasty imperial concubine who was offered to a Hun chieftain (see **Farewell, My Concubine**). The top of the mound of earth affords decent views of the surrounding countryside and the well-landscaped courtyards. Many exhibits have English, Mongolian, and Chinese captions. *(About 10km south of the city. At the terminus of minibus #44 (Y1.5). Bus #1 from the train station terminates at the intersection of Shiyangqiao Xi Lu and Nanchafang Jie. Cross the intersection, and turn left. The boarding point for minibus #44 is about half a block ahead. ☎515 0061. Open in summer daily 8am-6pm; in winter 8am-5pm. Park Y10; exhibit hall Y10.)*

NEAR HOHHOT: GRASSLANDS 草原

The grasslands in the Hohhot area feel simultaneously remote and touristy. You can spend a few days in the seemingly endless prairie, but you'll probably have to share the experience with loads of other tourists. Grazing flocks of sheep still roam the famed grasslands, but the only horses you'll see are the ones that cost

Y50 per hour to ride. The dancing, singing, and wrestling, like the concrete-floored, electric-wired yurt accommodations, present varying degrees of authenticity. Despite the summer camp-meets-Club Med atmosphere, the yurt camps themselves are only small dots on an enormous landscape; a five-minute walk in any direction to watch the sunset generally gives the impression of a stark and lonely landscape. Visiting the grasslands is a must if in Hohhot; it's also a worthwhile long-weekend excursion from Beijing.

GRASSLANDS AREAS. Of the three main grassland sites around Hohhot, **Xilamuren** (希拉穆仁; 80km from the city) is the most visited, **Huitengxile** (辉腾锡勒; 120km) is the most beautiful, and the quiet, unassuming **Gegentala** (格根塔拉; 160km) just is. The best months to visit are August and September, when the grass is highest and greenest. In winter, temperatures dip below -20°C; even in summer, the weather can get chilly, so bring warm clothes. For more remote grasslands, head to the Hulunbei'er Grasslands near Manzhouli (see p. 310).

GRASSLAND TOURS. Just about everyone who visits the grasslands signs on with an official tour. Numerous tour operators—some extremely unscrupulous—solicit business throughout Hohhot. So while it's certainly no trouble to book a tour, be cautious and clarify numerous times what is included. And bargain hard—discounts of 50% and over are not uncommon. It is most prudent, if slightly more expensive, to go in person to the office of a reputable agency. A cheaper alternative is to hire a guide you meet on the street, but beware: anyone who refuses to provide printed information and official permits is a potential scam artist; in these cases, do not pay for the tour until you return and are satisfied that your conditions have been met. Likewise, keep in mind that some tourists have paid for tours to Huitengxile (easily identified by the large white windmills nearby) only to be taken to the less remote Xilamuren instead. Tour prices depend on where you want to go, how long you want to stay, the number of people going with you, and the tour agency itself. When traveling alone or in a small group, save money by finding a guide who is already leading a larger tour. *(2-day trip to Xilamuren Y200-300 per person; 2-day trip to Huitengxile Y250-350 per person.)*

Most tours last two, three, or four days and include transportation, accommodations (in a yurt), food, admission to a wrestling match or horse race, and often temple admission. While they provide the opportunity to go horseback riding across the steppes, they do not include the fee (Y50-80 per hr.). Food often includes the traditional mutton dish *shǒu bǎ ròu* (手把肉), which is eaten with a large knife and your hands. Bashful? Don't fret—all etiquette is forgotten anyway as the evening meal culminates with the *hādà* (哈达), in which local spirits are poured into goblets and passed around to the strains of Mongolian melodies. After dipping your fingers and pointing first to the sky, then to the ground, and finally touching your forehead, it's time to imbibe. Try not to gag—this stuff is potent.

VISITING INDEPENDENTLY. Good bargaining skills can result in a significantly more enriching guided tour that is only marginally more expensive than an independent grasslands visit. However, independent visits are feasible, if somewhat difficult and time consuming. Travelers can take a train from Hohhot to Jining (集宁) (one every afternoon, Y20) and hire a taxi (Y200-300) from Jining to take them to Zhongqi (中旗) near Huitengxile. Buses (daily, beginning at 7am from the bus station, Y20) also travel from Hohhot to Zhaohe, the access point for the Xilamuren grasslands. From here it is a 40min. taxi ride (Y50-80) to the grasslands. In both Zhongqi or Zhaohe, locals wait in the bus station and accost the newly arrived with offers of accommodation. Negotiate for a reasonable per-day rate (Y20-30 per bed) and you can avoid tour groups altogether.

BAOTOU 包头

☎0472

The tale of Baotou is a tale of two cities, West Baotou and East Baotou. West Baotou is the best of times, with broad boulevards lined with neatly planted trees and bright summer flowers. East Baotou is the worst of times, a maze of construction, making for a lively if somewhat noisy and bewildering atmosphere. Non-business travelers have little reason to venture to Baotou, and those who do usually use the city as a starting-off point for trips to Singing Sands Gorge, Wudangzhao Monastery, or Ghenghis Khan's Mausoleum. Counterintuitively, this coal-reliant city is extremely clean, a surprisingly pleasant layover for its few visitors.

TRANSPORTATION

Flights: Baotou Airport (bāotóu jīchǎng; 包头机场; ☎460 0160), is about 2km south of the Baotou East Train Station. **CAAC ticket office,** 26 Gangtie Dajie, Kunqu (☎513 5492), in the Aviation Building next to the Bank of China. Open daily 8:30am-noon and 2:30-6:30pm. CAAC shuttle buses Y10; call ahead to reserve a seat. To: **Beijing** (2 per day, Y540); **Lanzhou** (daily, Y1660); **Xi'an** (daily, Y730).

Trains: Baotou East Station (bāotóu dōng zhàn; 包头东站; ☎442 2962), in Donghe. Tickets sold under the large clock. **Baotou Train Station** (bāotóu zhàn; 包头站; ☎443 1011), in West Baotou, is 1.5km south of Kunqu. To: **Beijing** (15-18hr., 5 per day, Y115-199); **Hohhot** (3hr., multiple departures daily, Y12-25); **Lanzhou** (17hr., 2 per day, Y121-194); **Xi'an** (26hr., daily, Y188); **Yinchuan** (10hr., 2 per day, Y90-122).

Buses: The most convenient bus station is in Donghe, just north of the train station. Open daily 6:30am-9pm. Most travelers buy tickets once on board. To: **Dongsheng** (3hr., every 15-30min. 7am-7:30pm, Y12) and **Hohhot** (3hr., every 30-45min. 7am-5pm, Y15; express with A/C 2hr., Y25).

Local Transportation: Buses are slow and crowded; most run from 6-7am to 7-8pm. Bus **#1** runs 9am-9pm; **#5** runs 6:30am-10:30pm. Base fare Y0.5; East Baotou-West Baotou buses Y1.5, minibuses Y2.5. Be sure to hold on to the ticket until you get off the bus. Bus **#1** runs from Baotou Train Station up Aerding Dajie to Gangtie Dajie. **#5** leaves every 5min. and runs from the far eastern parking lot in Baotou East Station to Gangtie Dajie in Kunqu; the trip takes approx. 50min.

Taxis: Base fare Y5-8, each additional km Y1.2. Very accessible.

ORIENTATION AND PRACTICAL INFORMATION

Eastern Baotou, known as **Donghe** (东河), is small and compact. The Donghe train station, long-distance bus station, and airport are all in the southern part of the city. **Nanmenwai Dajie** (南门外大街) runs north from the train station, intersects **Huancheng Lu** (环城路) and forms the commercial center of the district. Western Baotou is composed of two districts, **Qingshan** (青山) and **Kundulun** (昆都仑), which is also called **Kunqu** (昆区). **Gangtie Dajie** (钢铁大街) runs east-west through Qingshan and Kunqu. **Aerding Dajie** (阿尔丁大街) intersects Gangtie Dajie near the city government building and continues south to the train station.

Travel Agencies: CITS, 9 Qingnian Lu, 4th fl. (☎515 4615; fax 515 1075), west of Shifu Xi Lu. Open M-Sa 8am-noon and 2:30-6:30pm. A more convenient branch is in the **Baotou Hotel** compound, 33 Gangtie Dajie, Kunqu (☎516 5606). Open daily 8am-noon and 2:30-6:30pm. Both offer pricey tours to Wudangzhao and Singing Sands Gorge.

Bank of China: On Huancheng Lu next to the entrance of People's Park, Donghe (☎469 0190). Currency exchange (counter #1). Open daily 8am-6:30pm; in winter 8am-6pm.

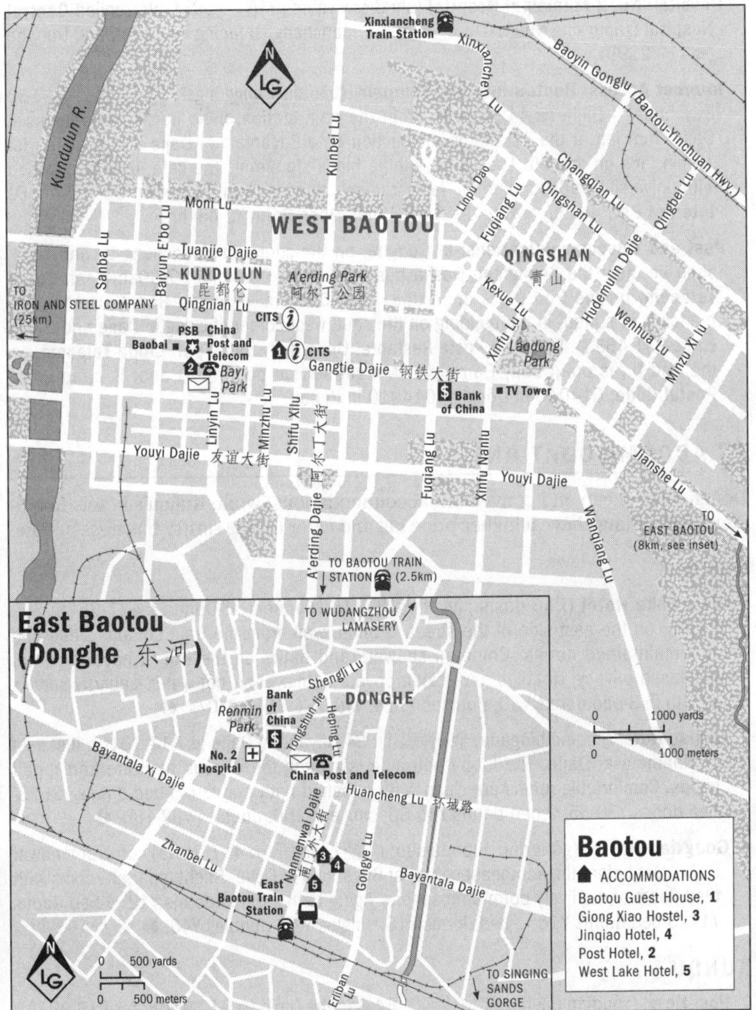

Another branch at 28 Gangtie Dajie (☎512 8888), Kunqu. Exchanges traveler's checks. Open M-F 7:30am-6:30pm; in winter 8am-6pm.

Market: The **Baotou Department Store,** known as **Baobai** (bāobǎi; 包百), 61 Gangtie Dajie, Kunqu, west of Linyin Lu. Open daily 9am-8pm; in winter 9am-7:30pm. The **Changqing Supermarket** next door has a large selection of Western candy in addition to typical Chinese goods. Open daily 8:30am-8:30pm. In Donghe, a supermarket is next to the West Lake Hotel. Open daily 8:30am-7:40pm.

PSB: 59 Gangtie Dajie (☎212 6212), just east of Baotou Department Store, Kunqu. Visa extensions. Open M-Th 8am-noon and 2:30-6:30pm, F 8am-noon.

Hospital: No. 2 Municipal Hospital (shì dièr yīyuàn; 市第二医院), also called **Central Hospital** (zhōngxīn yīyuàn; 中心医院), off Huancheng Lu facing People's Park, Donghe (☎417 2299).

Internet Access: Baotou Internet Company (bāotóu wǎnggōngsī; 包头网公司), 180 Bayantala Xi Dajie (☎442 8999). From the train station, head north on Nanmenwai Dajie. Turn left at the 1st major intersection onto Bayantala Xi Dajie and continue for 15min.; it's on the left. Look for the large black storefront. The cafe, usually crowded with university students, has the fastest connections in town. Y4 per hr. Open 24hr. **DJ Internet Bar,** Kunqu, next to the Sawa Hotel. Open 24hr. Y2 per hr.

Post and Telecommunications: In Donghe, on the corner of Huancheng Lu and Tongshun Jie, near the Shangmao Dasha bus stop. EMS. Open daily 7:30am-7pm. **China Telecom,** on the 2nd fl., is open daily 8am-6:30pm; in winter 8am-6pm. Another branch is in Kunqu, in the building on the southwest corner of Gangtie Dajie and Linyin Lu (☎251 4632). EMS and Poste Restante. Open daily 8am-7pm. **China Telecom,** on the 2nd fl., is open daily 8am-6pm. A night service booth next door is open 24hr. **Postal Code:** 014040 in Donghe, 014010 in Kunqu.

ACCOMMODATIONS

Donghe has cheap and convenient accommodations, while Kunqu's hotels in quieter surroundings have a higher price tag and cater to less-thrifty business people.

DONGHE

West Lake Hotel (xīhú dàshà; 西湖大厦), 15 Nanmenwai Dajie (☎417 2288, ext. 8108), on the east side of the street, a 5min. walk from the train station. Clean and well-maintained dorms. Common showers and baths on the 6th fl. have locks for increased privacy. Doubles have clean private baths. 24hr. hot water. Laundry service on 4th fl. 3-bed dorms Y30; doubles Y116, with A/C Y148. MC/V. ❶

Jinqiao Hotel (jīnqiáo bīnguǎn; 金桥宾馆), 84 Bayantala Dajie (☎417 1616), just east of Nanmenwai Dajie. The lobby entrance is among the various furniture and repair shops. Comfortable rooms are clean, with attached bath and fan. 5-bed dorms Y25; 3-bed dorms Y30-35; 2-bed dorms Y40-60; singles Y280; doubles Y88-180. ❶

Gongxiao Hostel (gòngxiāo zhāodàisuǒ; 供销招待所; ☎417 2869), on Nanmenwai Dajie, just before the southeast corner of Buyantala Xi Dajie. Bright, spartan rooms with tiled floors and a lively dorm atmosphere. Aging baths. 5-bed dorms Y12; 4-bed dorms Y14; 3-bed dorms Y16; 2-bed dorms Y18; singles Y25; doubles Y40. ❶

KUNQU

Post Hotel (yóudiàn dàshà; 邮电大厦), 64 Gangtie Dajie (☎212 9988; fax 213 9988), at Linyin Lu opposite Bayi Park. Bus #1 stops at Bayi Gongyuan. The best value in Kunqu. Courteous staff, attached baths, A/C, and even gold-embroidered bedspreads, but without back-breaking prices. Luxury-style rooms fill up fast; reservations recommended. Breakfast included. Doubles Y160 and up. Discounts on pricier rooms. ❷

Baotou Guesthouse (bāotóu bīnguǎn; 包头宾馆), 33 Gangtie Dajie (☎515 6655, ext. 5583), near Shifu Xi Lu. Bus #1 from Baotou Station and #5 from Donghe stop nearby. Some rooms in the west building have been recently renovated, and have soft carpets and sparkling new baths. Others have old TVs and small baths, and are still waiting for repairs. Registration in the west building. The high-rise rooms are not worth the extra money. West building doubles Y151, with A/C Y170. ❷

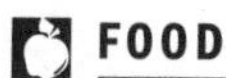

FOOD

The diverse cuisine of Baotou caters to all dining styles and tastes. In the summer, the intersection of Huancheng Lu and Nanmenwai Dajie in Donghe is filled with vendors. On **Zhanbei Lu** west of the train station, street stands sell watermelons, fresh, hot pastries, and every roastable part of a pig (hoofs Y3), and locals enjoy their meals while watching TVs dragged onto the sidewalk. Restaurants are also popular; the **West Lake Restaurant** ❶ (☎417 7505) next to the West Lake Hotel packs in customers who yearn for their extensive soup selection (Y5-10) and delicious standard Chinese dishes (stir-fried eggs and tomato Y10).

In Kunqu, both **Minzu Lu** (just south of Gangtie Dajie) and the small lane west of the Sawa Hotel are lined with restaurants offering noodles, fried dishes, and more. During the day, small stands set up on the side streets near the Baotou Department Store, selling everything from noodles to shaved ice to Mongolian souvenirs. **Old Beijing Noodle Restaurant** ❶ (lǎo běijīng zhájiàng miàn guǎn; 老北京炸酱面馆), 66 Gangtie Dajie, next to the post office in Kunqu, specializes in noodles (Y3-8 per bowl), but also has a decent selection of regional cuisine and the occasional singing waiter. For dessert, the attached bakery serves delicious pound cake (Y5). (☎212 5425. Open daily 9:30am-10pm.) **Haide Burger** ❶ (hǎidé hànbǎo; 海德汉堡) is on the south side of Gangtie Dajie, west of the Kunqu post office. Haide serves the usual fast-food fare with an unusual twist and flair—try the sauceless "pizza" for Y9-12. (☎216 0968. Open daily 9:30am-9:30pm.)

DAYTRIPS FROM BAOTOU

SINGING SANDS GORGE

Arranging a tour through CITS (Y280) may be the easiest way to visit, but independent travel is not difficult—especially if it hasn't rained recently. From the Donghe Bus Station, ***buses*** *to Dongsheng depart every 15-30min. The turn-off is recognizable by its white gate with "Singing Sands" written on it in red characters. Fare should be Y8. From there, it is an additional 8km over a dirt road.* ***Taxis*** *and* ***minibuses*** *will usually stop and pick up travelers for about Y10, but you can also walk under the railroad bridge. A more reliable strategy is to disembark at Daqi (达旗) (approx. 1hr., Y5-6), the first bus station between Baotou and Dongsheng. From there, hire a taxi (approx. 1hr., Y60 round-trip). For the* ***return,*** *it's fairly easy to flag down a Baotou-bound bus from the side of the main road.* ***Admission*** *Y25.*

One day long ago, a mean-spirited monk in the area was minding his own business when Heaven suddenly poured its sandy wrath upon him. Desperate for help, the monk belted out a tune on his trumpet. No one came to help him—some say his bad behavior had won him no sympathy. More likely, most villagers didn't realize the trumpet's wailing was a cry for help. Regardless, the monk died. Despite this lamentable tale, the dunes of Singing Sands Gorge (xiǎngshā wān; 响沙湾) offer nothing but pleasure. Filled with dazzling sand dunes, the gorge has recently been turned into a money-maker, now catering to all types of visitors. The more adventurous can climb up the rope ladder from the lower parking lot and lose themselves in the sea of dunes on the far side of the gorge, perhaps perching atop a secluded peak for a picnic lunch. Those not wishing to trudge through the sand can take the chairlift from the upper parking lot (Y35 round-trip). On the far side of the gorge, a kitschy playground atmosphere of camel rides (Y20 for 30min.), sand-skiing (Y10), and archery awaits. In the summer, colorful knee-high booties are worth the Y5 fee, as the sand gets unbearably hot.

WUDANGZHOU LAMASERY

70km northeast of Baotou. Although a tour can be arranged through CITS, it is quite feasible to go alone. ***Minibuses*** *from the parking area between the East Baotou train and long-distance bus stations make the trip, usually leaving in the morning (2hr., Y15). More reliably,* ***bus*** *#7 travels from the same point to Shiguai (every 30min. 7:45am-5:40pm), a small town 1½-2hr. north of Baotou (Y4). From there, hire a* ***taxi*** *for the remainder of the trip (Y40-50 round-trip). Starting a bidding war between feisty drivers is a great bargaining strategy.* ***Parking fee*** *Y5.* ***Open*** *daily 8am-6pm.* ***Admission*** *Y15.*

Looking for inner peace? A trip to the cool incense-filled temples of Wudangzhao Lamasery (wǔdāngzhào; 五当召) can help restore your mental balance. Built in 1749, this lamasery is the largest in Inner Mongolia and one of the three most famous in China. It houses a particularly friendly sect of lamas and consists of six halls that were once home to some 1200 lamas. In total, there are eight temples that can be visited; the white Tibetan-style buildings extend up the hillside and contain some exquisitely detailed Buddhist statues and well-maintained, colorful frescoes. During the **Mani Fair** and other festivals, pilgrims flock to the area, but at other times it is fairly deserted.

DONGSHENG 东胜 ☎0477

Dongsheng (pop. 72,000) lies in the middle of the Ordos Plateau and, like its northern neighbor Baotou, has an economy based on coal production. The bus ride in often leaves visitors covered in a thin layer of coal dust, but the city's clean streets, new buildings and friendly inhabitants can make even the grayest travelers feel fresh and shiny. Despite its best efforts, however, this quaint little city has little to offer sight-seeking tourists. The few who choose to venture out here are usually just spending the night before heading to the Mausoleum of Genghis Khan.

ORIENTATION AND PRACTICAL INFORMATION

Dongsheng is small, with an urban area of just 8.6km^2. **Hangjin Lu** (杭锦路) runs north-south through the city and intersects **E'erduosi Jie** (鄂尔多斯街), a shopping street. Navigating is easy; the bus station is at the north end of Hangjin Lu, and the intersection with E'erduosi Jie is one block south. Most of the city's cheap lodging, shops, and services are within a couple of blocks of the intersection of Hangjin Lu and E'erduosi Jie.

Buses: Dongsheng Bus Station (dōngshèng qìchē zhàn; 东胜汽车站; ☎834 1333), on the west side of Hangjin Lu, one block south of Etuoke Jie and one block north of E'erduosi Jie. Most travelers buy tickets once onboard. Open daily 5:30am-6pm. To: **Baotou** (2½-3hr., every 30min. 6:20am-6:30pm, Y12); **Beijing** (16hr., 1 sleeper per day); **Hohhot** (4½-5hr., 10 per day, Y38).

Local Transportation: Given Dongsheng's small size, walking is often the best way to get around. **Minibuses** #1, 2, and 3 all stop just south of the train station. Minibuses **#1** and **#3** serve the east and west parts of the city, respectively, while **#2** runs down Hangjin Lu to the Tianjiao Hotel at the southern tip of the city. Fare Y0.2-1.

Taxis: Base fare technically Y5, but many cars are not metered.

PSB: On the northeast corner of the intersection of Etuoke Jie and Hangjin Lu. Open M-F 8:30am-noon and 2:30-5pm.

Bank of China: On the south side of E'erduosi Jie just before the hospital (☎832 1963). Exchanges traveler's checks. Open daily 7:30-11:30am and 2:30-6:30pm; in winter 8am-noon and 2-6pm.

Hospital: Meng Hospital (méng yīyuàn; 盟医院; ☎836 7370), on the north side of E'erduosi Jie, between Wendu'er Lu and Hangjin Lu. This self-proclaimed "baby friendly" hospital is a 10min. walk west from the E'erduosi Jie/Hangjin Lu intersection.

Post and Telecommunications: East of Hangjin Lu, on the southwest corner of the intersection of E'erduosi Jie and Huaige'er Nan Lu (☎832 9957). EMS. Open daily 7:30am-4:30pm. **China Telecom** is across the street, on the southeast corner of the intersection. IDD. Open daily 7:30am-6:30pm; in winter 8am-6pm. **Postal Code:** 017000.

ACCOMMODATIONS

Most of Dongsheng's reasonably priced accommodations are on **E'erduosi Jie,** within a block of Hanjin Lu. The overpriced Tianjiao Hotel at the southern end of the city caters primarily to businessmen and wealthy tourists.

Yikejiao League Hotel (yīkè zhāoméngbīnguǎn; 伊克昭盟宾馆), 3 E'erduosi Jie (☎832 1501; fax 832 7885), at Dalate Nan Lu, one block east of Hangjin Lu; a 10min. walk from the train station. Also called the Yimeng Hotel, this is one of the few places that accepts foreigners. Rooms and small dorms are clean. 3-bed dorms Y25; 2-bed dorms Y30; singles Y40; doubles with bath Y120, with bath and A/C Y160-180. ❶

Mengjia Hotel (méngjiā bīnguǎn; 蒙佳宾馆), 1 Hangjin Lu (☎832 3699, ext. 2100), at the northwest corner of E'erduosi Jie. Small rooms come with TV, phone, clean tile floors, and fairly new attached baths. Singles and doubles Y78. ❶

Continental Grand Hotel (☎832 8117), on the southeast corner of E'erduosi Jie and Dalate Nan Lu, across the street from Yikejiao League Hotel. Big mirrors in clean bath. Rooms are bright. Doubles Y80. ❶

FOOD

There are some restaurants on Hangjin Lu and E'erduosi Jie. Fast food can be found at **Merry Holiday** (yínglè jiàrì; 迎乐假日), on the southeast corner of the intersection of E'erduosi Jie and Dalate Nan Lu. A small **night market** is in the courtyard just south of the train station. Prospective customers are also offered nylons and shoe insoles in addition to the usual fare of noodles, corn, and fruit.

DAYTRIP FROM DONGSHENG

MAUSOLEUM OF GENGHIS KHAN

50km from Dongsheng. From the Dongsheng Long-distance Bus Station, take a ***minibus*** *(2½hr., approx. every 2hr. beginning at 7am, Y14.4) to Yulin (愉林); ask to get off at the Mausoleum. For the* ***return*** *trip, flag down a Baotou-bound bus. Open 24hr.* ***Admission*** *Y25. Ticket office ☎868 1356.*

The chances that the actual remains of Genghis Khan are housed in this so-called mausoleum (chéngjísī hàn líng; 成吉思汗陵) are slim to none. But those tourists who tire of Chairman Mao's cult may be interested to see the almost god-like status to which Genghis Khan has been elevated. After his death, a tribe of Khan's followers dedicated themselves to guarding his remains and hosting memorial services in his honor. They were effective until WWII, when many relics of the great Khan were commandeered by a Japanese government intent on establishing a Mongolian puppet state. The Chinese retrieved them and in 1955 took them out of safekeeping to build this gigantic shrine, thus celebrating the creation of the Inner Mongolia Autonomous Region.

The Chinese government heralds the mausoleum as one of the "Forty Best Famous Tourism Scenic Spots," and that's just what it is—a tourist attraction. Ghenghis Khan's remains (or lack thereof) do not illicit much visual excitement. The entrance is marked by a large bronze statue of the great man himself surrounded not by galloping horses or waving grasslands, but by rows of remarkably identical souvenir shops. In the front of the main hall sits yet another massive statue of Genghis Khan (this one is marble); behind him a map shows the extent of his once-great empire. The back room contains an altar, Ghenghis Khan's "remains," and offerings of fiery Mongolian spirits. Two side halls contain remains of relatives as well as some recovered pottery and metalwork. The walls of all the halls are covered with colorful murals depicting the life and exploits of the Khan.

To the left of the mausoleum visitors can pay their respects at the recently constructed **Sacrificial Altar to Suled** (sūlèdé jìtán; 苏勒德祭坛); "Suled" is the banner of the ancient Mongolian army. **Gandeli Obo** (gāndélì áobāo; 甘德利敖包) affords a nice view of the surrounding valley. Those with more time on their hands might prefer to make the half-hour trek to the **Reviewing Stand** (diǎnjiàng tái; 点将台), on the edge of the grasslands.

The **Genghis Guesthouse** ❶ (chéngjísī bīnguǎn; 成吉思宾馆; ☎(0477) 896 1009) has accommodations for those who just can't get enough Khan. Reception is next to the parking lot, to the right of the entrance. Standard doubles have tile floors, TV, and attached bath (Y100-160); yurt accommodations are more rustic (Y20-30).

MANZHOULI 满洲里 ☎0470

Manzhouli, in the far northeast of Inner Mongolia, borders Russian Siberia to the north and Mongolian deserts to the west. The surrounding Hulun Buir grasslands, which house Han Chinese as well as Mongolian and Hun minorities, make this remote city even more attractive to travelers in search of untamed nature. For the many Russians who fill the streets of Manzhouli, piling loads of Chinese goods into their vans, Manzhouli's main appeal is not its boundless steppes, but rather its bustling commerce. As a result, the city itself lacks the wild beauty that many travelers to Manzhouli seek.

TRANSPORTATION

Flights: The airport closest to Manzhouli is **Hailar Airport** (hǎilāěr fēijīchǎng; 海尔拉飞机场; ☎827 0004). Free shuttle buses leave 1½hr. before departure from the **CAAC ticket offices** in Manzhouli, in the International Hotel, 35 Er Daojie, 2nd fl. (☎622 1436); and in Hailar, 31 Qiaodan Jie (☎833 1010). To: **Beijing** (1-2 per day, Y1650) and **Hohhot** (W-Sa, Y1200).

Trains: Manzhouli Train Station (mǎnzhōulǐ huǒchē zhàn; 满洲里火车站), on Yi Nan Daojie, south of the train tracks. To: **Beijing** (33hr., 11:48am, Y126); **Hailar** (3-4½hr.,

4 per day, Y14-18); **Harbin** (17hr., 2 per day, Y104); **Qiqihar** (11hr., 3 per day, Y46-203). There is also 1 train a week to **Moscow.**

Buses: The **Manzhouli Long-distance Bus Station** (mǎnzhōulǐ chángtú qìchē zhàn; 满洲里长途汽车站), at the west end of Yi Daojie. Frequent departures to **Hailar** (1½hr., Y26). Frequent minibuses to **Zhalainuo'er** (30min., Y3), useful If you're headed to Hulun Lake, depart from the square at the intersection of Si Daojie and Xinhua Lu.

Taxis: To any destination on the same side of the railroad tracks Y5; crossing the tracks (or going to the train station) an extra Y5.

ORIENTATION AND PRACTICAL INFORMATION

The city center is bounded by train tracks to the south and **North Lake Park** (北湖公园) to the north, traversed by **Xinhua Lu** (新华路), **Haiguan Lu** (海关路), and **Shizheng Lu** (市政路), which runs north-south, and a series of numbered (*yī*, *èr*, etc.) **Daojie** (道街) that run east-west; Yi Daojie is closest to the train tracks. Everything on the lively northern side of the rail tracks is within walking distance.

Travel Agency: CITS, 39 Er Daojie (☎622 2988; fax 622 2988), is officially limited to organizing overpriced tours (Y450 and up) for groups of 20 or more. Independent travelers are much better off directly contacting Shi Zhouyu (史轴寓), on the 3rd floor, who can arrange more flexible tours to local ethnic minority villages (taxi transport Y200; overnight stay Y100). Open M-F 8am-noon and 2:30-5:30pm.

Bank of China: On the corner of San Daojie and Xinhua Lu. Exchanges currency and traveller's checks. Credit card advances M-F 8am-5pm. Open daily 8am-6pm.

PSB: 39 San Daojie, 2nd fl. (☎622 2225, visa dept. ext. 627), next to CITS. Visa extensions; won't allow additional entries. Open daily 8am-noon and 2:30-6pm.

Hospital: No. 1 Hospital (dìyī yīyuàn; 第一医院), 14 San Daojie (☎622 2817).

Internet Access: Wangba (wǎngbā; 网吧), on Si Daojie between Xinhua Lu and Haiguan Lu, has fast connections. Y3 per hr. Open daily morning-midnight. A few other establishments line the central streets, particularly Xinhua Lu.

Post and Telecommunications: China Post (☎622 9177), on Haiguan Lu at Si Daojie. EMS, Poste Restante, and IDD service. Open in summer M-F 8am-6pm, Sa-Su 9am-4pm; in winter M-F 8am-5pm, Sa-Su 9am-4pm. **Postal Code:** 021400.

ACCOMMODATIONS

Travelers can easily find accommodations north of the railroad tracks, particularly on San Daojie. Because of the chilly climate, air-conditioning is rare; rooms with A/C begin at Y300 in the posh **International Hotel ❹,** 35 Er Daojie (☎622 2225; fax 622 2976). Russian is spoken in all hotels.

Huamei Hotel (huáměi dàshà; 华美大厦), 32 San Daojie (☎622 5225). Clean, inviting rooms near several Russian restaurants. Doubles with bath Y120. ❷

Dianli Hotel (diànlì bīnguǎn; µçÁ¦±ö¹Ý), 1 San Daojie (☎622 2549), at Shulin Lu. Small but clean doubles with comfortable baths. Doubles Y92. If the Dianli is full, go across the street to the 15-floor **Golden Wok Hotel** (jīn dǐng dàshà; 金锭大厦). Larger doubles with views Y150. ❷

Huanzhuang Central Hostel (huànzhuāng béixùn zhōngxīn zhāodaìsŭo; 换装背训中心招待所; ☎622 1747), on Daokou Lu, north of the railroad tracks. A good option if you aren't picky about baths. 4-bed dorms Y16; 3-bed dorms Y20. ❶

FOOD

Despite the city's proximity to Mongolia, Mongolian food is hard to come by; Manzhouli's best cuisine is Russian. **Russkaya Dusha** ❷ (Русская дух; literally Russian spirit), on Er Daojie opposite the International Hotel fits the bill perfectly, with gaudy, flower-adorned walls, a dance hall with incongruously synthesized, loud Russian rock-music, delicious *bosturma* (Y18), and, of course, liters and liters of vodka. (☎623 1645. Open daily 7:30-midnight and sometimes much later.) The eateries on Er Daojie, San Daojie, and Xinhua Lu are also excellent; seize the opportunity to have an exotic (in China, at least) apple dessert (Y8) at the **Jin Hongdou Jiudian** (jīn hóngdòu jiǔdiàn; 金红豆酒店; ☎622 2008), on San Daojie. In all establishments, be sure to ask for a Russian menu, or your choices will be limited to Russian-style Chinese cuisine. If you crave more genuine Chinese food, head toward any of the hole-in-the-wall restaurants in the city center.

SIGHTS

A quick walking tour of Manzhouli soon proves that the only interesting in-town activities are shopping for souvenirs of questionable Russian origin and admiring the occasional Russian-style buildings. Nearby sights prove to be more entertaining. The **Sino-Russian Trade Area** (zhōng é hùshì maòyì qū; 中俄互市贸易区) and, beyond it, endless Mother **Russia** are only a 12km taxi ride away. For many, the call of the wild and the proximitity of the **Hulun Buir Grasslands** (hūlúnbùĕr dà căoyuán; 呼伦布尔大草原) are overpowering. Punctuated by lakes, ridges, and rolling hills, the steppe is home to the Ewenki and Oroqen people in the northeast and a few Han minorities in the south; Mongolian yurt villages further enrich this ethnic and cultural kaleidoscope. Individuals may tell you about staying in "authentic" housing, but it's much better to use official companies (see **Travel Agencies,** p. 309). In the winter, most minority-inhabited areas are inaccessible.

JIN ZHANG HAN VILLAGE. Beautifully located in the middle of the grasslands, the village features a gorgeous view of the nearby, jagged mountains and meandering streams. Massive, stylized wooden constructions presumptuously imitate traditional yurts. In the beginning of July the Mongolian minority celebrates the **Naadam Festival,** a local Buddhist festival. In the winter, temperatures fall below -40°C, freezing the steppe in snow and ice. Regardless of the season, it's always a good time in Jin Zhang to sip on some Mongolian **milk tea** (naí chá; 奶茶; Y5), bricks of red tea brewed with salt and mare's milk and fat, best enjoyed with slabs of mutton (yáng ròu; 羊肉). *(Take a bus to Hailar from the Manzhouli Long-Distance Bus Station and then, for another 30min., a taxi to Jin Zhang Han Village (Y110 round-trip). Open June-Sept. Y10; overnight stay Y100 per yurt).*

HULUN LAKE (hūlún hú; 呼伦湖). Hulun Lake, known locally as **Dalai Lake** (dálài hú; 达赉湖), is the fifth largest lake in China. Rare birds inhabit the protected wetlands and grasslands that surround this salt-water lake. During the summer, sunbathers, swimmers, and avid birdwatchers line the shores; a few short months later, ice fishermen battle the bitter cold. According to legend, Genghis Khan once tied his horse to the **Horse-tethering Stake** that stands over 20m high on the western

YEARNING FOR YURTS For visitors who yearn to learn more about yurt construction, the concrete-floored yurts (ménggǔ bāo; 蒙古包) of the grasslands near Hohhot may provide little satisfaction. Even those who venture to the grasslands near Manzhouli could be left wishing that they had traveled instead to Mongolia proper. Originally derived from *gert*, a Turkish-Mongolian term for a building which is transportable and easy to set up and take down, fully collapsible yurts have been traced back to the Northern Wei dynasty (AD 386-534). It is said that experienced yurt dwellers can put up a full-size yurt in under 30 minutes. Built to withstand the fierce winds that whip through the grasslands, the yurt is a sturdy, rounded structure. The traditional Mongolian yurt, or *ger*, is built of walls made from saplings that are braided together with leather ties. These walls, known as *khana*, can either open out or fold flat and are generally divided into two sections. Wooden rafters connect the top of the *khana* to the center roof ring to provide additional support. Two belly bands wrapped outside the *khana* prevent the rafters from pushing the *khana* farther open. Felt is often used for the walls and roof. No center poles are necessary to support modest-sized yurts (up to 10m in diameter), but smoke holes provide ventilation for cooking fires and hot summer days. Innovation strikes yet again: miniature sequined yurts (Y3 and up) can be found in some department stores, and web sites touting newfangled metal "yurt" structures make it possible to set up camp just about anywhere.

bank of the lake. Seafood restaurants cluster near the parking lot of the **hotel** (☎653 1997; doubles with A/C Y170 and up; no hot water); it is also possible to arrange to stay in a yurt with access to running water for Y100. *(45km southeast of Manzhouli. Take a minibus to Zhalainuo'er and then a taxi to the lake (one-way Y30, round-trip Y50 after bargaining). Or, take a taxi directly from Manzhouli (Y150). Toll to enter the lake area with a taxi Y10; get off at the booth and walk for 5min. instead. Y10.)*

SHANGHAI AND THE YANGZI DELTA

Shanghai Municipality and Jiangsu and Zhejiang provinces huddle around the mighty Yangzi River, forming China's most densely populated and prosperous region. But to most Chinese, the defining characteristic of the area is something very different; many would inform you that the residents here are China's most shameless penny-pinchers. Perhaps the Yangzi delta's tight-fisted mentality comes from its centuries-old contact with money, tourists, traders, emperors, and luxury goods; the region had always been a busy trade center due in large part to the network of waterways that includes the Grand Canal. Parts of the Yangzi delta were inhabited as early as 5000 years ago, and cities like Suzhou, Wuxi, and Shaoxing have been lively commercial and cultural centers since the 7th and 8th centuries AD. The Song dynasty set up court in Hangzhou in the 12th century, and Nanjing served as the capital of the early Ming. In the early 20th century, Shanghai, a hub for intellectual activity, ushered in modern thought and technology.

Through all this flow and flux, it's not surprising that few remnants of the past have survived; in fact, only an occasional moat, city wall fragment, or tomb reminds the Yangzi delta's many residents of the sheer scope of their home's history—revolution, rebellion, and the passage of time have destroyed the rest. The foreign missionaries and trading companies that emerged from the East China Sea left their unmistakable mark on the region's architecture and economy. These days, outsiders still mob this well-established gateway to the Chinese mainland, but they come with different aspirations; camera-toting visitors crowd around the region's fabled scenic gems in the hopes of preserving, not altering, what remains of the ancient empire.

HIGHLIGHTS OF THE YANGZI RIVER DELTA

SCOPE OUT THE CROWDS while strolling the **Bund** (p. 328), Shanghai's glittering waterfront promenade.

FIND YOUR INNER GUANYIN (as well as fantastic sunrises) on the magical monastic island of **Putuoshan** (p. 390), in the East China Sea.

FEAST ON IMPERIAL DELICACIES while sitting on the shores of Hangzhou's radiant **West Lake** (p. 379).

SHANGHAI 上海 ☎021

Cities with long histories often view progress with a certain sort of unease. You might think that Shanghai would encounter this same problem—Shanghai's colonial past echoes strongly in the stately architecture of the Bund and the elegant streets of the French Concession; its Chinese tradition reveals itself in the pagodas of Yuyuan Gardens and the serene beauty of the Jade Buddha Temple. Yet of all cities in China, Shanghai is perhaps the most comfortable with change, still displaying the vibrance, mischief, and resilience of youth.

Until imperial powers of the 19th century set their sights on China, Shanghai was a simple fishing village, ordinary except for the fact that many fishermen chose it as the place from which "to go to sea," or *shàng hǎi*. After the Opium War (see p. 12), the village became a booming port, home to merchants and gangsters, scandal and iniquity, change and progress. Even socialist policies couldn't depress Shanghai's new-found spirit, and today it is still at the forefront of economic and cultural development. Business executives stroll along the grand colonial waterfront promenade, beepers and cell phones in hand. Skyscrapers, albeit half vacant, grace the skyline of Lujiazui in the Pudong New Area. Cozy expat enclaves boast jam-packed shops along Nanjing Lu and trendy boutiques in the French Concession that showcase the latest fashions. Shanghai is Beijing's hip little sister, well-dressed, slightly scandalous, and full of energy. The city isn't about to ignore its historical legacy, but it sure as hell won't let anything slow it down.

INTERCITY TRANSPORTATION

BY AIR

In October 1999, Shanghai opened its second major airport, **Pudong International Airport,** on the east side of the Huangpu river in the Pudong district. Although both Pudong and **Hongqiao International Airport** currently serve foreign airlines, it is expected that all foreign airlines will eventually operate out of Pudong only. Both airports feature roughly the same design: arrivals are on the lower level and departures on the upper level, with separate check-in areas for international and domestic travelers. Airline counters are generally on the upper level, while hotel, bus, and tourist information can be found on the lower level. For more information on international flights to China, see **Getting to China: By Plane,** p. 83.

For **flight** information, call **Air China** (☎6269 2999), **Air France** (☎6360 6688), **Canadian Airlines** (☎6375 8899), **China Eastern Airlines** (☎6247 5935), **DRAGONAIR** (☎6375 6375), **Japan Airlines** (☎6472 3000), **Lufthansa** (☎5830 4400), **Northwest Airlines** (☎6279 8088), **Shanghai Airlines** (☎6255 1551), **United Airlines** (☎6279 8009), or **Virgin Atlantic** (☎5353 4605).

TO	AIRPORT	PER DAY	PRICE	TO	AIRPORT	PER DAY	PRICE
Beijing	Hongqiao	18-22	Y1030	**Kunming**	Hongqiao	3-4	Y1670
Changsha	Pudong	2-3	Y810	**Lanzhou**	Hongqiao	<1	Y1550
Chengdu	Hongqiao	4-5	Y1440	**Lhasa**	Hongqiao	W, Su	Y2120
Chongqing	Hongqiao	4-5	Y1340	**Qingdao**	Pudong	6-7	Y670
Dalian	Pudong	7-10	Y970	**Sanya**	Pudong	2	Y1660
Fuzhou	Hongqiao	3-4	Y710	**Shenyang**	Pudong	3-4	Y1190
Guangzhou	Hongqiao	8-9	Y1160	**Shenzhen**	Hongqiao	7-8	Y1270
Guilin	Hongqiao	2-3	Y1190	**Tianjin**	Pudong	2	Y930
Harbin	Pudong	3-6	Y1560	**Wuhan**	Hongqiao	5-6	Y740
Hefei	Hongqiao	2	Y440	**Xiamen**	Hongqiao	2-3	Y880
Hong Kong	Hongqiao	about 15	Y2040	**Xi'an**	Hongqiao	4-5	Y1150

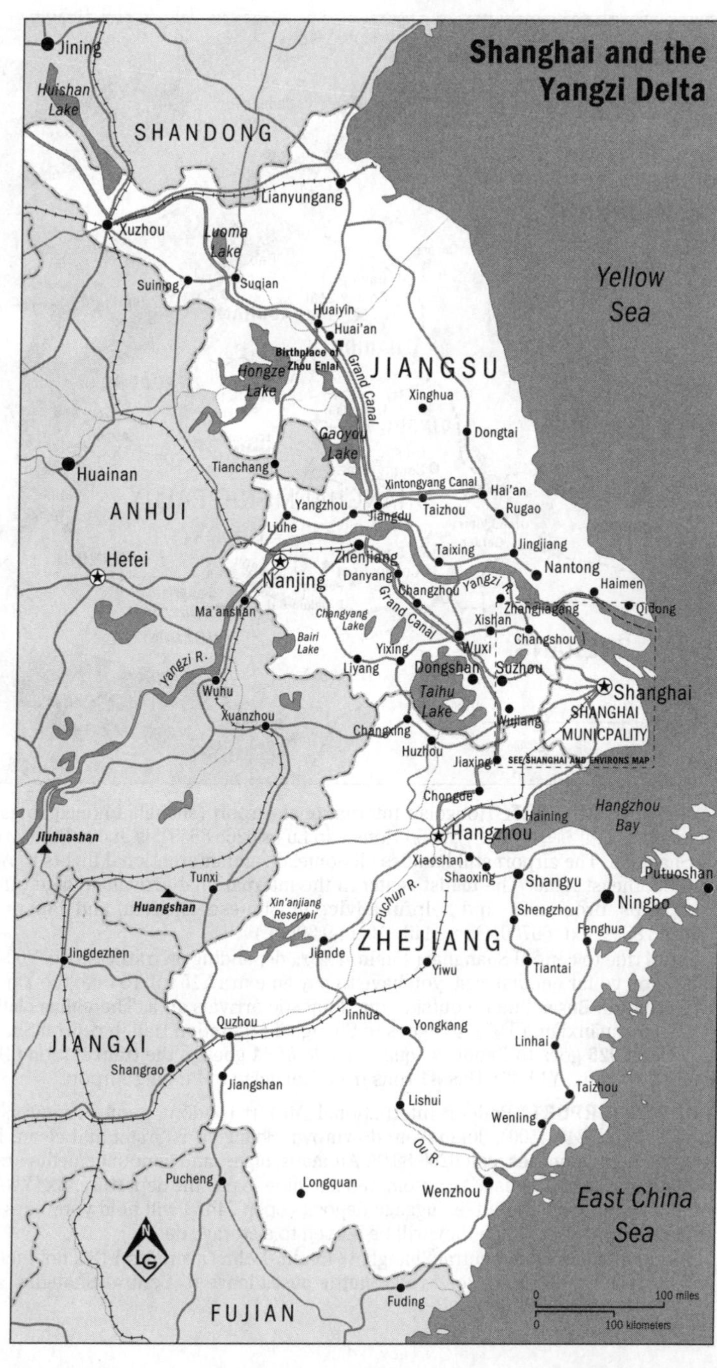
Shanghai and the Yangzi Delta
Jining
Huishan Lake
SHANDONG
Lianyungang
Xuzhou
Luoma Lake
Suining
Suqian
Yellow Sea
Huaiyin
Huai'an
Birthplace of Zhou Enlai
Grand Canal
Hongze Lake
JIANGSU
Xinghua
Dongtai
Gaoyou Lake
Tianchang
Huainan
Xintongyang Canal
Hai'an
ANHUI
Yangzhou
Jiangdu
Taizhou
Rugao
Liuhe
Taixing
Jingjiang
Zhenjiang
Hefei
Nanjing
Nantong
Danyang
Yangzi R.
Haimen
Changzhou
Qidong
Ma'anshan
Changyang Lake
Zhangjiagang
Xishan
Bairi Lake
Wuxi
Changshou
Yixing
Liyang
Dongshan
Suzhou
Wuhu
Shanghai
Taihu Lake
SHANGHAI MUNICIPALITY
Wujiang
Xuanzhou
Changxing
Huzhou
Jiaxing
SEE SHANGHAI AND ENVIRONS MAP
Chongde
Haining
Hangzhou Bay
Jiuhuashan
Hangzhou
Xiaoshan
Shaoxing
Shangyu
Putuoshan
Tunxi
Fuchun R.
Ningbo
Huangshan
Xin'anjiang Reservoir
Shengzhou
Fenghua
ZHEJIANG
Jiande
Jingdezhen
Yiwu
Tiantai
Jinhua
Yongkang
Quzhou
JIANGXI
Linhai
Shangrao
Jiangshan
Taizhou
Lishui
Wenling
Ou R.
Pucheng
Longquan
Wenzhou
East China Sea
N
LG
Fuding
FUJIAN
0
100 miles
0
100 kilometers

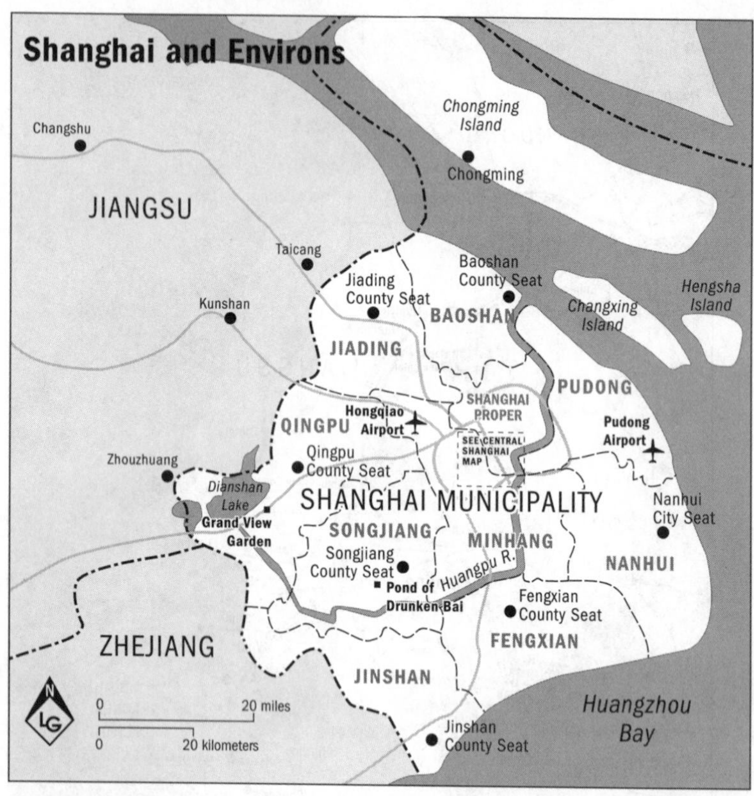

HONGQIAO AIRPORT. Hongqiao International Airport (shànghǎi hóngqiáo guójì jīchǎng; 上海虹桥国际机场), 2550 Hongqiao Lu (☎6268 3659), is about 10km west of Shanghai. The airport still handles all domestic and international flights to Asia and Southeast Asia. The **tourist center** in the international arrivals lounge offers free maps, brochures, and helpful advice in Chinese, English, and Japanese. (☎6268 8899, ext. 56750. Open daily 10am-9:30pm.)

A **taxi** ride to central Shanghai (45min.-1½hr., depending on traffic) costs Y50-70, but if you go far enough east, you have to pay an extra Y15 toll to take the Yan'an Elevated Rd. **Buses** line up outside the domestic arrivals area. The **airline shuttle** (mínbān zhuānxiàn; 民班专线) goes to Shanghai Exhibition Hall in central Shanghai. Bus **#925** goes to People's Square, while **#941** goes to the train station (1hr., every 20-30min., Y14-36). Bus **#1** runs from Hongqiao to Pudong Airport.

PUDONG AIRPORT. Pudong International Airport (pǔdōng guójì jīchǎng; 浦东国际机场; ☎3848 4500), 30km from downtown Shanghai, is bright and clean. For general flight inquiries, call 6268 8918. All maps, signs, and announcements are in both Chinese and English. An automated machine to pay the departure tax (Y90) is on the upper level. For a fee, luggage deposit (open 24hr.) will hold your bags for up to 30 days, after which they will be moved to a storage depot.

A taxi to the Bund in central Shanghai (45min.-1½hr.) averages Y120, not including the Yan'an Elevated Road toll. **Shuttle buses** leave to Central Shanghai and

Hongqiao Airport from outside the lower level (every 20-30min.). Bus **#1** goes to Hongqiao (Y30), **#2** goes to Exhibition Hall in central Shanghai (Y19), **#5** goes to Yan'an Zhong Lu and the train station (Y18 and Y20). Big signs show bus number and the next departure time. Tickets are sold on board except for #1 and 2; theirs are sold right inside the airport exit.

BY TRAIN

The main train station is **Shanghai Train Station** (shànghǎi huǒchē zhàn; 上海火车站), 330 Moling Lu (☎6354 3193, schedules 6317 9090), north of Suzhou Creek, near the intersection of Tianmu Xi Lu and Hengfeng Lu. Buses #64, 96, 104, 109, and 113 all terminate just east of the station's south square, across from the main Metro entrance. The ticket office is a large building, just east of the main square on the southern side of the station. If travelling to Suzhou, Hangzhou, or Wuxi, avoid long lines by buying same-day tickets from the little booth just to the right of the security checkpoint (look for the green and white Chinese sign). You'll need to pay with exact change. (Open daily 7-11:30am, noon-5:30pm, and 6-7pm.) Most hotels book tickets and charge commissions, including the Longmen Hotel just west of the station (commission Y5-10).

Some trains depart from the **Shanghai West Train Station** (shànghǎi xī huǒchē zhàn; 上海西火车站), 1 Taopu Lu (☎6254 9500), at the intersection of Jiaotong Lu and Caoyang Lu. Bus #106 goes here from the main train station.

The following table provides the departure station, number of trains per day, duration of travel (in hours), and the price (in *yuán*) for all major Chinese cities serviced by trains from Shanghai. Shanghai Main Train Station is indicated by "S," and Shanghai West Train Station is indicated by "W." Prices listed range from the cheapest hard seat to the most expensive sleeper. For more information on train types and train travel, see **Trains,** p. 98. For a helpful guide to reading your train ticket, see the ticket reader in the **Appendix,** p. 845.

Luggage storage is in kiosks outside the north and south exits. Prices range from Y3-8 per day depending on size. The large blue and white sign that says "luggage consigning" is a carrier service, *not* luggage storage. Lockers cost Y25-40 per day.

TO	站	PER DAY	HR.	PRICE	TO	站	PER DAY	HR.	PRICE
Beijing	S, W	3	14	Y86-321	**Huangshan**	S	1	12	Y51-177
Changsha	S	1	19½	Y86-288	**Kunming**	S	2	47-57	Y158-584
Chengdu	S	2	35-40	Y124-492	**Nanjing**	S, W	39	3-5½	Y24-111
Chongqing	S	1	45	Y155-494	**Qingdao**	S	1	18½	Y81-303
Fuzhou	S	1	21	Y83-280	**Suzhou**	S	35	1½-2	Y7-45
Guangzhou	S	2	21-23	Y116-284	**Tianjin**	S, W	7	17-18	Y79-294
Guilin	S	2	33	Y180-388	**Ürümqi**	S	1	64	Y219-721
Hangzhou	S	16	3-4	Y12-72	**Wuhan**	S	1	20	Y86-288
Hefei	S	3	10-11	Y38-165	**Xiamen**	S	1	24½	Y98-326
Hong Kong	S	1	27½	Y127-420	**Xi'an**	S	2	21-23	Y88-343

BY BUS

Buses head to destinations along the east coast and beyond. However, this may not be the best way to travel due to the region's overly congested roads, not to mention the lack of clear signs, maps, and schedules in English (and even in Chinese). There are two main long-distance bus stations, as well as several smaller ones spread throughout the city. Booths at the airport and main train station also handle departures for some destinations within the area.

Central Shanghai

ACCOMMODATIONS

Shanghai Conservatory of Music Guesthouse, **9**	B4
Education Hotel, **8**	B4
Love Inn, **1**	C1
Pujiang Hotel, **4**	F2
International Center for Cultural Exchange, **3**	E1
Shengxianju Hotel, **2**	D1
Wugong Hotel, **6**	E3
YMCA Hotel, **7**	D4
Zhongbai Hotel, **5**	D3

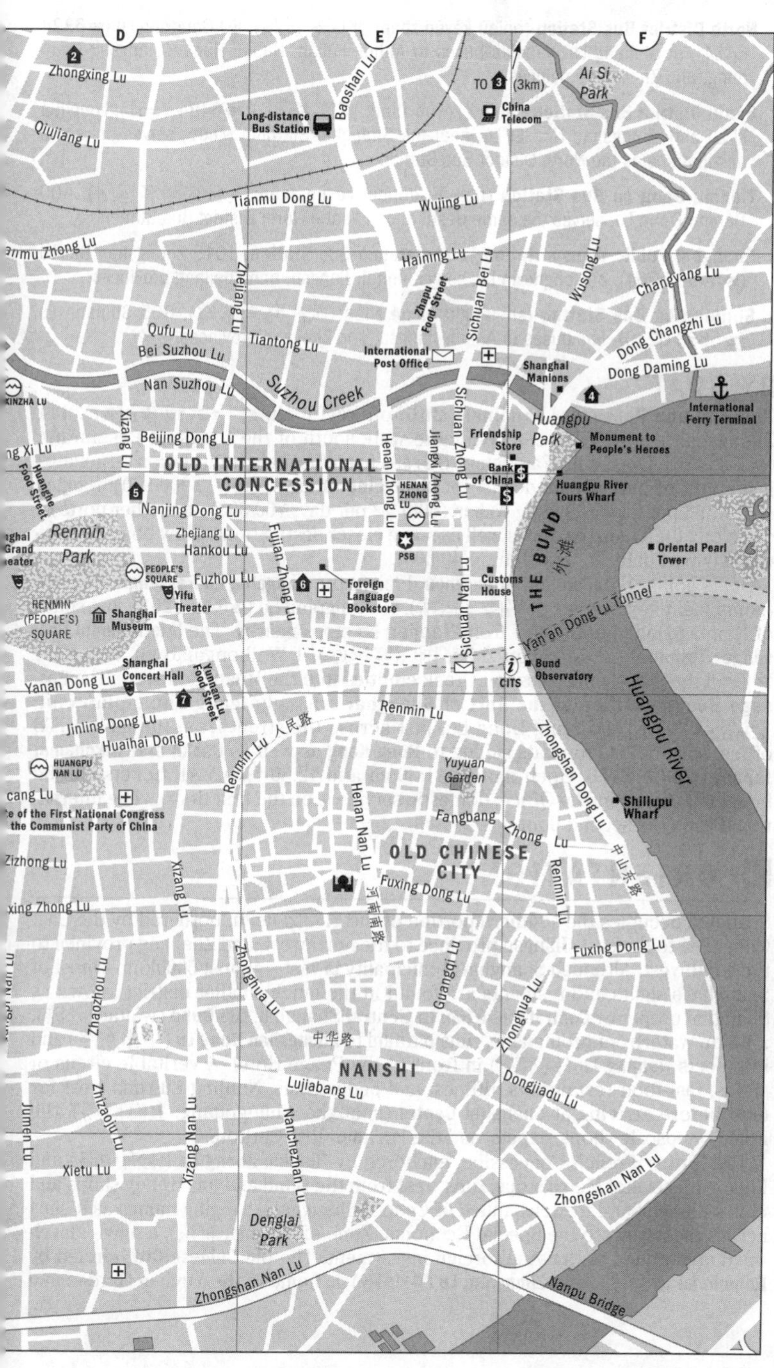
D
E
F
Zhongxing Lu
Qiujiang Lu
Long-distance Bus Station
Baoshan Lu
TO 3 (3km)
China Telecom
Ai Si Park
Tianmu Dong Lu
Wujing Lu
Haining Lu
Zhejiang Lu
Zhapu Food Street
Sichuan Bei Lu
Wusong Lu
Changyang Lu
Dong Changzhi Lu
Qufu Lu
Bei Suzhou Lu
Tiantong Lu
International Post Office
Shanghai Manions
Dong Daming Lu
Nan Suzhou Lu
Suzhou Creek
XINZHA LU
International Ferry Terminal
Huangpu Park
Monument to People's Heroes
Beijing Dong Lu
Xizang Lu
Henan Zhong Lu
Jiangxi Zhong Lu
Sichuan Zhong Lu
Friendship Store
Bank of China
Huangpu River Tours Wharf
Huanghe Food Street
OLD INTERNATIONAL CONCESSION
HENAN ZHONG LU
Nanjing Dong Lu
Renmin Park
Zhejiang Lu
Hankou Lu
Fujian Zhong Lu
PSB
THE BUND
外滩
Oriental Pearl Tower
PEOPLE'S SQUARE
Fuzhou Lu
Foreign Language Bookstore
Customs House
Yifu Theater
RENMIN (PEOPLE'S) SQUARE
Shanghai Museum
Sichuan Nan Lu
Yan'an Dong Lu Tunnel
Shanghai Concert Hall
Yunnan Lu Food Street
Yanan Dong Lu
CITS
Bund Observatory
Huangpu River
Renmin Lu
Jinling Dong Lu
Huaihai Dong Lu
Renmin Lu 人民路
HUANGPU NAN LU
Yuyuan Garden
Zhongshan Dong Lu
Shiliupu Wharf
Henan Nan Lu
Fangbang Zhong Lu
OLD CHINESE CITY
中山东路
Zizhong Lu
Xizang Lu
Fuxing Dong Lu
河南南路
Renmin Lu
Fuxing Dong Lu
Zhonghua Lu
Guangqi Lu
Zhaozhou Lu
Zhonghua Lu
中华路
NANSHI
Lujiabang Lu
Dongjiadu Lu
Jumen Lu
Zhizaoju Lu
Xizang Nan Lu
Nanchezhan Lu
Xietu Lu
Zhongshan Nan Lu
Denglai Park
Zhongshan Nan Lu
Nanpu Bridge

SHANGHAI

North District Bus Station (běiqū kèyùn zhàn; 北区客运站), 80 Gongxing Lu (☎6324 6464), at Shijiang Lu, handles buses to Anhui, Fujian, Hubei, Hunan, Jiangsu, Shandong, and Zhejiang provinces.

South District Bus Station (nánqū kèyùn zhàn; 南区客运站; ☎6484 7561), Longhua Xi Lu and Zhongshan Nan Er Lu, near the Shanghai Stadium Metro, serves the same destinations as the North District Bus Station.

Tianmu Dong Lu Bus Station (tiānmù dōnglù kèyùn zhàn; 天目东路客运站), 100 Tianmu Dong Lu, serves the same destinations as the North District Bus Station.

Shanghai Public Transportation Long-distance Bus Station, 1015 Zhongshan Bei Lu (☎5653 8064), at Gonghexin Lu, serves Anhui, Jiangsu, and Zhejiang provinces.

Shijiang Lu Bus Station (shījiānglù qìchē zhàn; 虱江路汽车站), 865 Shijiang Lu (☎5663 0230), has buses to Anhui, Jiangsu, and Zhejiang provinces.

BY BOAT

The **Shiliupu Passenger Terminal** (shíliùpù kèyùn zhàn; 十六铺客运站), 111 Zhongshan Dong Er Lu, is a 10-minute walk south of the Diamond Restaurant. (☎6326 1261. Open daily 7am-6pm.) Bus #64 from the main train station terminates just south of here. Boats depart to: **Chongqing** (4 days, daily, Y200-900); **Nanjing** (18½hr., 2 per day, Y30-200); **Wuhan** (60hr., 2 per day, Y60-300); and other ports of call along the Yangzi River, as well as some closer destinations. Slow boats to **Putuoshan** depart daily at 6pm (13hr., Y40-300).

Boats going to **Dalian** and **Guangzhou** dock at the **Gongping Lu Passenger Terminal** (gōngpínglù kèyùn zhàn; 公平路客运站), 50 Gongping Lu (☎6326 1261), just south of Daming Dong Lu. Bus #37 from Nanjing Lu stops nearby. The **International Passenger Terminal** (guójì kèyùn zhàn; 国际客运站), 1 Waihongqiao Lu, is not far beyond the point where Suzhou Creek empties into the Huangpu River. The **Passage Booking Office of the Port of Shanghai** (shànghǎigǎng chuánpiào chù; 上海港船票处), 1 Jinling Dong Lu, just across the street from the main CITS office, sells tickets to boats sailing to **Hong Kong** as well as **Osaka** and **Yokohama, Japan.** (☎6323 8750. Open daily 7-11:30am and 12:30-5pm.) All tickets can be bought at the Jinling Lu Office; domestic service is on the first floor, while international is on the second floor.

ORIENTATION

Shanghai occupies the southern portion of the Yangzi delta, bordered by the East China Sea to the east, Jiangsu province to the northwest, and Zhejiang province to the southwest. Although Shanghai Municipality is vast—almost 6000km^2—most of Shanghai's sights and residents are found in the much smaller district known as Shanghai proper or **Central Shanghai.** In Central Shanghai, the **Bund** (wàitān; 外滩), a 1.5km waterfront promenade, runs parallel to **Zhongshan Dong Lu** (中山东路) and intersects **Nanjing Lu** (南京路) in front of the Peace Hotel. A veritable circus of shops, fast-food restaurants, offices, and pedestrians, Nanjing Lu runs west for 6km before arriving at **Shanghai Centre** (shànghǎi shāngchǎng; 上海商场), the home of upscale shops, expats, and the Portman Ritz-Carlton.

The former French Concession, anchored by **Huaihai Zhong Lu** (淮海中路) and lined with several Metro stops, runs west from the Bund and has trendy shops and clubs. Zhongshan Lu circles much of Central Shanghai, changing names as it slips across the river into the Special Economic Zone of **Pudong** (浦东), a newly developed area aimed at drawing foreign investment. The **Old Chinese City,** circled by **Renmin Lu** (人民路) and **Zhonghua Lu** (中华路), is home to the Yuyuan Garden and

Bazaar. Traveling in this area is best done on foot; the narrow, winding streets can confuse even the most navigationally gifted.

Western Shanghai contains few places of touristic interest and is reputed to be somewhat unsafe; however, if the stadium complex and surrounding industrial areas inspire particular curiosity, the first Metro line has several stops in the area. North of Suzhou Creek and beyond Hongkou Park, the surroundings become more industrial, much like the area around the main train station. Fudan University at **Wujiaochang** (五角场) is a good place to find cheap food and drinks. Chinese maps (Y3-8) are widely available, and bilingual maps (Y6-15) can be bought from foreign language bookstores and street vendors.

LOCAL TRANSPORTATION

BY BUS. Using Shanghai's buses is a lot like programming a VCR: it's useful and you'll probably have to try it eventually, but damned if you actually understand what you're doing. It's impossible to find a bilingual bus map, and the buses only occasionally have English announcements, so unless you have a very good idea of where you're going and can read Chinese, riding buses can be harrowing. Buses are numbered according to their operation times. Buses **#1-200** run from about 5am-11pm, buses in the **200s** only supplement peak hours, and buses in the **300s** run between midnight-4am. Buses in the **800s** look like minibuses and go to more rural areas. Shanghai buses are crowded and sometimes lurch to sudden halts, but the system is fairly comprehensive, with service reaching all corners of the city proper. The chart below details some of the most important buses.

Fares are usually flat: Y1 if the bus is not air-conditioned and Y2 if it is (indicated by a snowflake beside the route number). Fares on double-decker buses heading to more distant corners of the city (such as #910 to Wujiaochang) depend on the destination (Y1-5). There will be one circulating fare collector who can provide change; try using anything higher than a Y10 bill, though, and you might not receive a warm reaction. Some buses also have collection boxes in front of the bus driver that require exact change.

Faster and more comfortable **minibuses** also ply many of the same routes as the buses. To catch one, wait at the regular bus stop and shout out your destination as the unmarked minibus slowly cruises past (often with a tout hanging out an open door). Prices vary, but Y2-5 is reasonable.

BUS #	ROUTE DESCRIPTION	BUS #	ROUTE DESCRIPTION
18	Lu Xun Park–People's Square	20, 37	Nanjing Lu–People's Square
64	Shiliupu Passenger Terminal–Bun–Main Train Station	917	Nanjing Lu–People's Square–Shanghai Centre
42, 126, 926	The Bund down Huaihai Lu–Library–Stadium	113	Train Station–Huaihai Lu
923	Train Station–Ji'nan Temple–Nanpu Bridge	930	Train Station—Yuyuan Area

BY METRO. The Shanghai Metro offers clean, speedy trains, with three lines serving a limited part of the city. Work on the Metro continues at an impressive pace—the third of the 11 planned Metro lines was just completed. All stations have manned ticket booths. It's also probably one of the world's few subways with velvet cordons. Announcements and most signs are in both Chinese and English. It's also possible to purchase ride cards from automatic ticket vending machines at every station.

Line #1 runs south from the main train station, underneath People's Square and along Huaihai Zhong Lu, before terminating in Xinzhuang (open 5am-11pm). **Line #2,** when completed, will run from Hongqiao Airport to Pudong Airport (open 7am-8pm). As of July 2001, it only runs from Longyang Lu, in the south of the Pudong district, to Zhongshan Park, west of the French Concession. Trains run less frequently, but since fewer people use this line, you'll probably have a luxurious green plastic bench on the train all to your lucky self. The newly completed **Pearl Line,** or elevated line, half circling central Shanghai, is done up in chrome-colored everything, and serves important stops such as the Shanghai train station, the stadium, and the west train station. **Fares** on all three lines range from Y2-Y5; route maps at ticket vending machines show fares to specific stops. While it's possible to transfer from Line #1 to #2 with the same fare card, a new ticket is required for the Pearl Line. A monthly pass for the Pearl Line is Y50.

BY FERRY. Ferries regularly make the 4-minute trip across the Huangpu River to the Pudong New Area, dodging the barges and tugboats that clog the waterways. The departure area below the Diamond Restaurant on Jinling Lu and Zhongshan Lu sells the plastic tokens needed to cross. One-way fare is Y0.5; round-trip Y1; bicycles ford across for Y1.3 extra. Boats operate from about 5am to 11:30pm.

BY TAXI. Taxis are a convenient and generally hassle-free alternative to public transportation. Base fare is Y10, and each additional kilometer costs Y2 (Y3 after 10km). From 11pm to 5am, base fare is Y13. Taxis abound after midnight when public transportation shuts down. Major cab companies operating 24 hrs. include **Dazhong Taxi** (dàzhòng chūzū qìchē; 大众出租汽车), which has just introduced new, larger taxis, and **Shanghai Qiangsheng Taxi** (shànghǎi qiángshēng chūzū qìchē; 上海强生出租汽车; ☎6258 0000).

PRACTICAL INFORMATION

TOURIST AND FINANCIAL SERVICES

Tourist Hotline: The handy **Hotline for Tourist Consultancy** (☎6252 0000) gives advice and information in Chinese, English, and Japanese. Open daily 8:30am-8:30pm, English after 9am.

Tours: Various guided tours can be booked through CITS and CTS. Options include visits to family apartments and local schools as well as main tourist attractions. For those who want more transportation flexibility, **Shanghai Tour Bus Lines** (☎6426 5555), based at Shanghai Stadium, has 10 lines that travel to sights within the city proper as well as the outer counties. Bus **#1A** goes to the Square Pagoda, **#3** to the Pearl Tower and Pudong sights, **#4** to the Shanghai Zoo, **#6A** to the Jiading District, **#9** to Wuxi and Lingshan, and **#10** to the City Center tourist route.

Travel Agencies: CITS, Guangming Bldg., 2 Jinling Dong Lu (☎6323 8741), near the Bund's southern end, a block south of Yan'an Lu. Open daily 8:30-11:30am and 1-5pm. **CTS,** 881 Yan'an Zhong Lu (☎6247 7888). Open daily 8:30-11:30am and 1:30-5pm.

Consulates: See **Essentials: Consular Services in China,** p. 48.

Bank of China: 23 Zhongshan Yi Lu (☎6329 1979), on the Bund. Exchanges currency and traveler's checks. Open M-F 9am-noon and 1:30-4:30pm, Sa 9am-noon.

ATM: Just about every ATM has connection to Cirrus and Visa/Plus networks. Citibank has two ATMs (Cirrus/DC/Plus/V) in Shanghai, one conveniently close to the Bund at 19 Zhongshan Yi Lu, and one across the river in Pudong, in the Marine Tower at 1 Pudong Dadao. Most banks and hotels now have ATMs. The Bank of China will gladly give cash advances on credit cards; be sure to bring your passport.

American Express: Shanghai Centre, 1376 Nanjing Xi Lu, Ste. 206 (☎6279 8082), card replacements and mail holding. Open M-F 9am-5:30pm.

LOCAL SERVICES

Bookstores: Shanghai Foreign Language Bookstore (shànghǎi wàiwén shūdiàn; 上海外文书店), 390 Fuzhou Lu (☎6322 3200, ext. 231), a block east of Fujian Lu. A good selection of travel books, maps, greeting cards, and other imported books. Expat magazines may include 10% discount coupons. Open daily 9:30am-6pm. **Shanghai Book City** (shànghǎi shūchéng; 上海书城) has several locations around town, including at 465 Fuzhou Lu (☎6352 2222). This 6-floor megastore has mostly Chinese books, but boasts an impressive section of imports (mostly in English). Classics Y20, bodice-rippers and sci-fi Y12. Open M-Th 9:30am-6:30pm, F-Su 9:30am-9pm.

Library: Shanghai Library (shànghǎi túshūguǎn; 上海图书馆), 1550 Huaihai Zhong Lu (☎6445 5555). Over 13 million volumes. For foreigners, a peek at just one of these books will cost Y25. Internet access available. Passport and proof of long-term residency required for foreign students to enter. Open M 1:30-8pm, Tu-Su 8:30am-8pm; some rooms later. Foreigners: Y100 deposit for a library card, card fee Y15 per month.

Ticket Agencies: Shanghai Centre Theatre Ticket Office (shànghǎi shāngchéng jùchǎng shòupiào chù; 上海商城剧场售票处), Shanghai Centre, 1376 Nanjing Xi Lu (☎6279 8663), just to the right of the main entrance. Sells tickets for performances at Shanghai Centre, the Music Hall, and other venues. Open daily 9am-7:30pm. The **Shanghai Grand Theatre** has several reservation offices around town that sell tickets for cultural events. Main office on the lower level of the theater itself, at 300 Renmin Dadao (☎6372 8701), on the edge of People's Square, next to the exit of the underpass. Open daily 9am-7:30pm. Soccer fans can buy tickets to matches at the **Shanghai Sport Stadium** (☎6438 5200), but these are usually sold out far in advance.

Markets: Lianhua Supermarket (liánhuá chāoshì; 联华超市), with a location on the corner of Fuzhou Lu and Zhejiang Lu, has a decent selection of Western food, but is a little pricey. Open daily 8am-9pm. A better choice is **Jiadeli** (jiādélì; 家得利) with locations on Wulumuqi Lu and 245 Zhapu Lu. Open daily 8:30am-10:30pm. **Kedi** (kědì; 可的), a 24hr. convenience store, has locations on many corners, including the corner of Henan Zhong Lu and Ningbo Lu. Here you'll find chips, dried noodles, and soda, as well as an assortment of toiletries and essentials like laundry detergent.

Weather Conditions: ☎121.

EMERGENCY AND COMMUNICATIONS

Crisis Lines: Al-Anon (☎6295 9551) accepts calls and holds weekly meetings. **Alcoholics Anonymous** (☎6433 6880, ext. 2244; open M, W, F) gets referrals from the US Consulate.

Pharmacies: Shanghai No. 1 Dispensary Co. (shànghǎishì dìyī yīyào shāngdiàn; 上海市第一医药商店), 616 Nanjing Dong Lu (☎6322 4567), several blocks east of Xizang Lu, near the intersection of Zhejiang Lu and Nanjing Dong Lu. Several floors of Western and Chinese medicines and 24hr. emergency service. Open daily 9am-10pm. **Watson's,** the Hong Kong pharmacy chain, sells Western over-the-counter medicine and sundries. All around town, including on the 1st fl. of Shanghai Centre and in Pudong Airport. Open daily 9am-10pm.

Hospitals: Huashan Hospital (huáshān yīyuàn; 华山医院), 12 Wulumuqi Zhong Lu, 19th fl. (☎6248 9999, ext. 1921). The foreign joint-venture section (Worldwide Medical Center) caters especially to foreigners (☎6248 3986). **No. 9 People's Hospital**

(dìjiǔ rénmín yīyuàn; 第九人民医院), 639 Zhizaoju Lu (☎6313 8341). **WorldLink Medical Centers,** Shanghai Centre, 1376 Nanjing Xi Lu, Ste. 203 (☎6279 7688), specializes in non-emergency expat medical care. English speaking doctors offer 24hr. care for members, and various hours for non-members: M and Th 8am-9pm, Tu-W and F 8am-7pm, Sa 9am-4pm, Su 10am-4pm. Call for an appointment. **New Pioneer International Medical Centre,** Geru Building, 910 Hengshan Lu, 2nd fl. (☎6407 3898), provides 24hr. medical and dental services.

Telephones: China Telecom, 30 Nanjing Dong Lu (☎6321 1130), just west of the Peace Hotel, a half-block from the Bund. Open daily 7am-10:30pm. Most hotels now have IDD/DDD phones; many offer free local calls.

Internet Access: Internet cafes come and go; check out one of Shanghai's expat journals. **Shanghai Library,** 1550 Huaihai Zhong Lu. Take the elevator to the lower level, and take the hallway to the right; also a ground-floor entrance. Passport required. Some 50 machines available; reasonable connection speed. Y6 per hr. Open daily 9am-8:30pm. **China Telecom** sells cards to access the Internet at stations in their Nanjing Dong Lu office as well as in other locations. Normally Y50 per 20hr. Occasional special offer of Y20 per 15hr. Open daily 7am-10:30pm. **Hola.net.coffee,** a newly opened Internet cafe at 333 Tangren Lu (☎6247 5559), operates daily 9am-2pm. **Raise the Red Lantern** advertises free Internet with drink purchase.

Post Office: The **main post office** is at 395 Sichuan Bei Lu, between Tiantong Lu and Bei Suzhou Lu, just north of Suzhou Creek. **Western Union** desk. International service, including EMS (☎6356 6666), open daily 9am-5pm. For Poste Restante, head to counter #17 on the Tiantong Lu side. Open daily 7:30am-7pm. For basic services such as posting letters, another post office is next door, on 2nd fl. of the Suzhou Bei Lu building. Open daily 7am-10pm.

Private Courier: DHL Worldwide Express has several locations around town, including one at Shanghai Centre, 1376 Nanjing Xi Lu, B02 (☎6536 2900). Open M-Sa 8:30am-6pm. Pick-up service available; call ahead. **Postal Code:** 200085.

ACCOMMODATIONS

Many of the city's accommodations cater to business travelers or tour groups, so rates tend to be high, especially along Nanjing Lu and in other central locations. A number of small places around the train station offer cheap rooms but almost always refuse foreigners. A new breed of hotels called "holiday hotels" (jiàrì bīnguǎn; 假日宾馆) is springing up all over the city and caters to wealthy Chinese families. Their central location, quality rooms, and low prices make them affordable alternatives to the hard-to-find dorms. Most hotels have laundry service and will book train and plane tickets.

Pujiang Hotel (pǔjiāng fàndiàn; 浦江饭店), 15 Huangpu Lu (☎6324 6388; fax 6324 3179), across Suzhou Creek from the Bund. Bus #64 from the main train station stops on the corner of Beijing Dong Lu and Jiangxi Zhong Lu. Continue along Beijing Dong Lu until you reach the Bund, then take a left and cross Waibaidu Bridge. The hotel is on the 1st righthand street. The Pujiang's high ceilings and etched glass windows whisper its past as one of the first and most luxurious Western hotels in China. Originally built in 1854, it housed the first lightbulb and telephone in China. Albert Einstein once stayed here. The Pujiang offers clean, well-kept rooms and a convenient location. A/C, lockers in some rooms (key deposit Y100). Luggage storage Y1 per bag per day. 8- to 12-bed dorms (many with baths) Y55; doubles with bath Y300-330; prices vary for larger rooms. Credit cards accepted for bills over Y1000. ❶

International Center for Cultural Exchange SISU/Shangwai Hotel (shàngwài bīnguǎn; 上外宾馆), 555 Chifeng Lu (☎6531 8882; fax 6544 8106), 1 block east of the Chifeng Lu station of the Pearl Line; or take bus #15 from the train station. A bit far from the city center, but oh-so-close to public transportation. The range of services and amenities is mind-boggling: English-speaking staff, A/C and bath in every room, free self-service laundry, IDD/DDD phones with free local calls, bowling alley, 24hr. convenience store, and eyelash perms in the salon downstairs. Reservations should be made 2-3 days in advance. Doubles range Y172-286 depending on size; extra bed Y50. Student discount 20%. Credit cards accepted. ❸

Love Inn (héjiāhuān jiàrì bīnguǎn; 合家欢假日宾馆), 1555 Zhongxing Lu (☎5672 2998; happy@bonline.sh.cn), less than 5min. from the north entrance of the main train station, or take the Xinchuan bus one stop from the main entrance of the train station and look for the hotel on the left. A lovely oasis in the northern Shanghai desert of dirt and dereliction. The rooms are clean, attractive, and lovely, as is the staff. Bath and IDD/DDD phones in every room. Breakfast included. Bonus: remote-controlled A/C. Beds may be stiff, but the prices aren't. Singles Y129; doubles Y189; triples Y159; extra bed Y40. Y50-90 discounts possible. ❷

Shanghai Conservatory of Music Guest House (shànghǎi yīnyùe xúeyuàn wàibīnlóu; 上海音乐学院外宾楼), 20 Fenyang Lu (☎/fax 6437 2577), south of Huaihai Zhong Lu. A 5-minute walk from the Changshu Lu or Shaanxi Nan Lu subway stops, or take bus #45 to Xiangyang Gongyuan. From the campus gates, take the 2nd left, walk through the basketball court-cum-parking lot, and turn left again; look for the off-white building on the right. The campus is alive with the sound of music. Really. The threat of mosquitoes is offset by the ultra-convenient location, just steps from Huaihai Zhong Lu and the lilting sounds of Chinese opera wafting through your window. 24hr. hot water. Luggage storage Y1 per bag per day. Incoming phone calls only. Self-service laundry Y5. Deposit Y100. Doubles Y80, with bath Y200 (Y200 rooms may or may not have A/C). ❶

Hailuo Hotel (hǎiluózhìxīngjiàrì jiǔdiàn; 海螺之星假日酒店), 491 Jinling Dong Lu (☎6328 2222; conchstar@citiz.net), from the People's Square, walk toward the Bund (i.e. east) on Yan'an Lu, turn right on Yongshuo Lu, walk a block and the hotel is at the intersection of Jinling Lu and Yongshuo Lu. Within walking distance of the People's Square, Yuyuan Garden, and the Bund, not to mention Yunnan Food Street. Simple, clean rooms prove that good things can come in small spaces. Rooms have bath, A/C, TV, and IDD/DDD phones. Doubles Y248-278, perennial discount of 20%. Cash only. ❹

Zhongbai Hotel (zhōngbǎi dàjiǔdiàn; 终百大酒店), 462 Xizang Zhong Lu (☎6322 3344; fax 6351 0146). Near the People's Square, at Xizang Lu and Nanjing Dong Lu. The decor may be cheesy and the lack of windows alarming, but with tourist attractions nearby, you won't be home long enough to notice. All rooms have A/C, TV, IDD/DDD phones, and bath. Singles Y200-250; doubles Y240, with windows Y280; triples Y340. ❸

Education Hotel (jiàoyù bīnguǎn; 教育宾馆), 3 Fenyang Lu (☎6466 3149; fax 6466 3149). Closer to Huaihai Zhong Lu than the Conservatory of Music, this friendly hotel offers 47 quiet but spartan rooms with hard beds. Aside from the convenient location, other perks include free local calls and a delicious Shanghainese breakfast. Dry cleaning service. Reservations accepted. Deposit Y100. 2 economy rooms without bath Y200; standard doubles Y380 (but can be bargained down to Y280); extra bed Y100. ❸

Wugong Hotel (wúgōng dàjiǔdiàn; 吴宫大酒店), 431 Fuzhou Lu (☎6326 0303), at Fujian Zhong Lu, about halfway between the Bund and People's Square. Rooms and clean and comfortable, with varied floral decorations. The hotel also offers a full range of amenities, including a sauna, Seafood World, and free breakfast. Doubles Y280-500; extra bed Y66. Credit cards accepted. ❹

Shengxianju Hotel (shèngxiánjū bīnguǎn; 圣贤居宾馆), 1032 Zhongxing Lu (☎5662 5001, ext. 100). Take bus #928 or 929 from the train station to the next stop. Continue down the street; it's less than a block away on the right. Clean, decent-sized rooms in fairly good condition. Doubles Y248-298; triples Y328. ❹

Zhongya Hotel (zhōngyà fàndiàn; 中亚饭店), 330 Meiyuan Lu (☎6354 7804), near the main train station, at Tianmu Xi Lu. The Zhongya justifies its prices by offering tidy rooms with A/C, cable, IDD, and bath, as well as access to a salon, a night club, and a billiards room. Singles Y260-480; doubles Y260-500. Credit cards accepted. ❹

YMCA Hotel (qīngnián huì bīnguǎn; 青年会宾馆), 123 Xizang Nan Lu (☎6326 1040; www.ymcahotel.com), between Jinling Lu and Yan'an Lu. Dorms are spotless, with new furnishings, attached baths, and lockers; some rooms even have a great view of central Shanghai. Bunk beds lend a nice summer-camp feel, and doubles are spacious. The bathroom floors practically glitter. Internet Y1 per min. 4-bed dorms Y125; double Y380. Credit cards accepted. ❷

FOOD

It's almost possible to forget that you're in China when eating in Shanghai. Fast-food joints and Western-style restaurants abound, especially in the French Concession, the favorite haunt of expats. A Häagen-Dazs store tempts the chocolate lover, while the new Starbucks already serves hundreds of half-crazed, twitching caffeine addicts each day.

It may be nice to have a taste of home once in a while, but the regional cuisine here is a must-try. A walk down any side street or alleyway reveals innumerable street vendors selling noodles, steamed buns (Y4-15 per dozen), wonton soup (check for clean bowls), and fried dumplings. A glance down any lane in the **Old Chinese City,** especially near Yuyuan Garden, finds open-air markets full of tasty foods and their raw—and often still moving ingredients.

Shanghai boasts several streets devoted to food. **Zhapu Lu Food Street,** north of Suzhou Creek and just east of Sichuan Bei Lu, is an explosion of neon lighting and a number of sit-down establishments. English-language menus may be scarce, but most owners will be happy to point out local favorites. Servings are large—a lone diner need not order more than two dishes to return home with a full stomach and happy heart. Zhapu Lu may be getting a little seedy these days, but living dangerously has its rewards. Street vendors sell dumplings for only Y1 per 5, and tasty *jiānbǐng* (Chinese egg crepes; 煎饼; Y1.5-2) abound.

The easiest way to sample Shanghainese specialties is to stroll along the Bund or near the Old Chinese City. Most items are on sticks: meat on a stick, melon on a stick, ice cream on a stick, squid on a stick, all for Y1-3. Conveniently located on the Bund is **Diamond Restaurant's Food Court,** where you can grab tasty Chinese and Japanese cuisine (Y10-25), corn on a stick, or some hot buns. (Open Su-Th 10:30am-9:30pm, F-Sa 10:30am-10pm. ❷) In the Old Chinese City area, the **Yuyuan Bazaar** and surrounding area, shops sell dumplings, steamed buns (try the tasty crabmeat ones; Y15 per dozen), and more for Y1-2.

Outside the boundaries of the Yuyuan Bazaar area, not too far from People's Square, is **Yunnan Lu Food Street** (yúnnánlù měishíjīe; 云南路美食街), several blocks of pure, unadulterated food. Stretching from Yan'an Dong Lu to Jinling Dong Lu, this area's restaurants stay open until nearly midnight. To the west, restaurants on **Huanghe Lu** offer local fare, and **Xizang Nan Lu,** off Yan'an Dong Lu, is another good spot for gluttons. Chinese fast food can be found on **Shashi Food Street** (shāshì shíjiē; 沙市食街), which runs south from Jiujiang Lu.

Huaihai Zhong Lu cuts through the French Concession area, where trendy restaurants and hole-in-the-wall places attract both Chinese locals and expats. Of particular note is **Yandang Lu,** running south of Huaihai Lu a block west of Chengdu Lu. Revelers can amble through the pedestrian-only zone and enjoy more *al fresco* dining than is available anywhere else in Shanghai. Hotpot is always an easy pick for the picky eater (Y10-30 for base soup, Y3-25 per ingredient).

NANJING LU AND ENVIRONS

Near People's Square, **Nanjing Lu** is crowded with fast food restaurants. **Huanghe Lu** (黄河路), between Nanjing Lu and Beijing Lu, north of People's Park, is also lined with restaurants. **Shanghai Centre,** farther along Nanjing Xi Lu, boasts well-known Western imports and smaller places serving typical Chinese fare. The residential area around **Wulumuqi Zhong Lu** offers markets and sanitary street vendors.

Gongdelin Vegetarian Restaurant (gōngdélín sùshí chù; 功得林素食处), 445 Nanjing Xi Lu (☎6327 0218). Vegetarian dishes in the grand old Buddhist tradition. Most entrees (including "saute shaped hair vegetable ball") Y15-45. Yum. Open daily 6:30-9:30am, 11am-2pm, and 5-10pm. ❷

Bi Feng Tang (bìfēng tàng; 避风塘), 1333 Nanjing Xi Lu (☎6279 0738), across the street from the Portman Ritz-Carlton. Enjoy roasted duck (Y23), taro ice cream (Y5), noodle dishes (Y13), or small frogs. Sip pearl milk tea (Y8) while watching hectic shoppers fly by in this popular *dim sum* heaven. Whether you choose to sit in the wooden boat inside or dine *al fresco,* small appetizer dishes (xiǎochī; 小吃) can be had for Y7-16 each. Beer is cheap too (Tsingtao Y8, imports Y10 and up). ❷

Sumo Sushi (yuánlù shòusī; 缘禄寿司), Lane 668, Huaihai Zhong Lu (☎5306 9136), opposite Si Nan Lu. It's a chain restaurant, but the many branches do have their purpose: to serve an Y58 all-you-can-eat sushi buffet (daily 11am-4pm and 9-11:30pm). This sashimi and nigiri paradise also has set lunches (Y28) and dinners (Y38) with sushi, tempura, and drink. Open daily 11am-11:30pm. ❸

Hard Rock Cafe, 1376 Nanjing Xi Lu, Shanghai Centre, Ste. 110 (☎6279 8133). Eating here is just like eating at the Hard Rock Cafe in London! Or Sydney! Or...Houston! Makes that soda worth the Y20, doesn't it? Burgers and other entrees Y65-85 and up. Indonesian band M-Sa beginning at 8pm. Open Su-Th 11:30am-2am, F-Sa 11:30am-3am; kitchen open until 10:30pm. ❹

OLD CHINESE CITY AREA

Kiosks inside Yuyuan Commercial City sell large bowls of wonton soup (Y8), bamboo steamers filled with buns (crabmeat Y15 per dozen, vegetable Y1), and various other delicious snacks (xiǎochī; 小吃), which are large enough to be meals.

Chang'an Dumpling Restaurant (chángān jiǎozi guǎn; 长安饺子馆), 2-8 Yunnan Nan Lu (☎6328 5156), at Yan'an Lu. 108 varieties of dumplings (Y5-50) mean that any meal here is bound to be an adventure, and if 108 doesn't cover your taste, they make personalized dumplings too, for a fee. Huge set meals on the 1st fl. for 2-10 people (Y20 and up), with more stylish (and expensive) dining on the 2nd floor. 1st fl. open daily 6am-2am; 2nd fl. 11am-2pm and 5-9pm. ❷

Old City Mid-Lake Pavilion Tea Shop (shànghǎi lǎochéng húxīntíng chálóu; 上海老城湖心亭茶楼), 257 Yuyuan Lu (☎6373 6950), just outside the entrance to Yuyuan Garden. The most famous tea shop in town plays both to world leaders (like Bill Clinton and Queen Elizabeth) and tourists. Normal tea (green, jasmine, etc.) comes by the pot on the lower level (Y15-25). Upstairs, tea fanatics savor more exceptional blends, some requiring special brewing methods and teaware (Y40 and up per cup). Nightly shows (until 9:30pm) featuring traditional music or tea ceremonies are usually scheduled by large tour groups, but if there's space, you can watch, too. Lower level open daily 5:30am-9:30pm; upper level 8:30am-6:30pm. ❷

FRENCH CONCESSION

The density of street vendors in this area is lower than in other areas, but food markets are easy to find. The **#2 Food Market,** on the corner of Huaihai Zhong Lu and Shaanxi Lu, sells dried plums, squid, beef—you name it—as well as Chinese pastries and prepared poultry, vegetables, and pig ears (open daily 8am-9pm). There are also several good places for hotpot on Huaihai Zhong Lu.

Gino Cafe (jìnuò yìdàlì xiūxián cāntīng; 季诺意大利休闲餐厅), 918 Huaihai Zhong Lu (☎6415 5245), in the Parkson Shopping Center, at Shaanxi Nan Lu. A casual atmosphere, excellent Italian food (starter salads and minestrone both Y15), and Coke floats make this place a great stop. Branches in Xujiahui and at 66 Nanjing Lu, 2nd fl. Open daily 9am-11pm. Credit cards accepted. ❷

Shenji Soup Restaurant (shěnjì tāng; 沈记汤), 41 Si Nan Lu (☎5306 5777), on the corner of Fuxing Lu. You may not find mom's chicken noodle soup here, but you're bound to find something good. Many dishes less than Y20; more exotic soups are far more expensive. Open daily 10am-2pm and 5-10pm. Credit cards accepted. ❷

Badlands (bǎilán; 百岚), 897 Julu Lu (☎6466 7788, ext. 8003), near Changshu Lu, about 10min. north of Huaihai Zhong Lu. Tex-Mex food (Y65 set meals), though quite good, appears to be only a secondary concern here. Look out back at the "Belgian Beer Garden" or check out the "Nutty Irish Man" (Y50) to discover this establishment's true passion. Y10 tacos on Tu, 2 tequila shots for Y30 on F. Open daily noon-2am. ❹

NEAR THE TRAIN STATION

Chinese fast food places across the square (on the south side) sell big bowls of fried rice (Y6), small buns (Y1 per 4), and noodle soup (Y5 and up). **Naf** ❶ (watch for the big red and white sign) and **Xinya** ❶ (xīnyà; 新亚), right across the street (with the red and yellow Chinese sign), both get the job done. (Both open 24hr.)

Big Bowl of Noodle (dàwǎntāng miànguǎn; 大碗汤面馆), 1511 Zhongxing Lu (☎5631 6653). This place may not look like much, but the staff is friendly. Gigantic bowl of noodles Y5, bottles of soda Y1.5. With value like that, you won't mind having to bring your own napkins. Delivery within a "reasonable" distance (like the Love Inn right next door). ❶

SIGHTS

Shanghai's main sights are architectural, from traces of the city's international settlements to modern wonders; plenty of religious sites, museums, and lively neighborhoods are thrown in for good measure. At present, Shanghai is "greenifying," and park fees may soon be abolished. Within various quarters of the city, walking is often preferable to using the overcrowded public buses.

THE BUND AND PUDONG NEW AREA

THE BUND (wàitān; 外滩). This stately waterfront embankment stretches 1.5km along Zhongshan Dong Lu, all the way from Waibaidu Bridge to Jinling Lu. Tracing the path of the Huangpu River, the raised walkway passes some of Shanghai's oldest reminders of foreign influence. Back in Shanghai's heyday when the Treaty of

Nanjing rendered the city a colony for international commerce, the Bund was lined with European banks and trade houses. Today, many of these relics of economic imperialism still stand in the form of colonial architecture.

At one end of the Bund, just north of Waibaidu Bridge, the towering, beige **Shanghai Mansions** (shànghǎi dàshà; 上海大厦), at various periods in history the military headquarters for both Japan and the US, have been converted into a hotel. The looming, triangular **Monument to the People's Heroes** (shànghǎi shì rénmín yīngxióng jìniàn tǎ; 上海市人民英雄纪念塔) stands on the corner of Suzhou Creek and the Huangpu River, surrounded by various depictions of the glorious masses. The 1993 inscription on the tower pays tribute to the people who have sacrificed their lives to the Socialist cause.

At the base of the tower lies the entrance to the **Bund History Museum** (wàitān lìshǐ jìniàn guǎn; 外滩历史纪念馆), a good stop for an overview of Bund history that includes an extensive collection of old photographs of the Bund. Detailed captions chronicle events such as the opening of Shanghai as a treaty port, the introduction of gas lighting, and the upheaval of the 1920s and 30s, before moving on to recent changes. *(Open daily 9am-4:15pm; last admission 4pm. Free.)* Just beyond the museum lies **Huangpu Park** (huángpǔ gōngyuán; 黄浦公园), the first park opened after the Opium War, then known as the British Public Gardens. A source of Chinese indignation and a symbol of western snobbery, the infamous sign at its gate declared: "Chinese people and dogs are not allowed." In 1928, the park was truly opened to the general public, and it has since become a popular place to practice *tai chi*, talk on cell phones, and swat away ravenous bugs. *(On the corner of Zhongshan Dong Lu and Beijing Dong Lu. Open daily May-Oct. 6am-10pm; Nov.-Apr. 6am-7pm. Free.)*

The promenade along the Huangpu River is a prime spot for people-watching. A climb to the platform of the **Bund Observatory** (wàitān tiānwéntái; 外滩天文台) yields a panoramic view. The building houses the **Bund History Exhibition** (wàitānshǐchénliè shì; 外滩史陈列室), a collection of documents and photographs from Shanghai's earlier days. *(1A Zhongshan Dong Er Lu. The only way to see it is to purchase a drink at the Museum Club 1865 bar. See **Nightlife,** p. 335. Open daily 10am-2am.)*

On the other side of Zhongshan Dong Lu, 52 buildings represent various architectural styles. Among them are the former **English Consulate** (yuán yīngguó lǐngshìguǎn; 原英国领事馆), 33 Zhongshan Dong Lu, the **City Government Building** (shìfǔ dàlóu; 市府大楼); and the **Customs House** (hǎiguān dàlóu; 海关大楼), 13 Zhongshan Dong Lu, all of which date from the 1910s and 20s. These now house Chinese government offices and are not open to tourists.

Frequent **boat tours** depart from a Bund-side dock. They provide an excellent means of escape from the Shanghai traffic, and the longer rides go all the way to the mouth of the Yangzi River. *(229 Zhongshan Dong Er Lu. Buy tickets along the Bund, north of the Diamond Restaurant. Shorter tours (6 per day 9:15am-8pm, Y25-30) last 1hr. Longer tours (2-3hr., Y45-100) leave mainly in the afternoon.)* The newest thing on the Bund is a tunnel cable car ride across the river—totally not worth the price; the view from the ferry above is better. *(One-way Y20.)*

ORIENTAL PEARL TV TOWER (dōngfāng míngzhū diànshì tái; 东方明珠电视台). Restaurants, KTV parlors, and several observation decks grace the 468m tower, the tallest in Asia. If the sky is overcast, however, be content with viewing it from the other side of the river—the admission fee is almost as high as the tower. *(On the Pudong side of the Huangpu. Buy tickets along the Bund, north of the Diamond Restaurant. Y50-100, depending on how high you go. Ferry ride across the river free when you buy a ticket. From the ferry terminal in Pudong, continue straight for about 10min. Open daily 8:30am-10pm.)*

OLD CHINESE CITY

Seven main gates mark the boundaries of the Old Chinese City, in the Southern City district. Narrow streets and labyrinthine alleyways make a trip to this area enjoyable only on foot. This part of Shanghai is still as densely populated as before, but has lost its reputation as the dirtiest, dankest part of town. The **Yuyuan Bazaar** has both upscale stores and lone street vendors—chances are that they're both selling the same overpriced souvenirs or not-so-gold jewelry. Of particular note are the stores selling only fans and chopsticks. At night, the Yuyuan Bazaar comes alive with lights and sounds, with stores and stalls open until 10pm.

YUYUAN GARDEN (yùyuán; 豫园). The Garden is an oasis of greenery and relative calm amid the carnival atmosphere of the adjoining Yuyuan Bazaar (yùyuán shāngshà; 豫园商厦). Built between 1559 and 1577 by wealthy Ming dynasty officials, the gardens suffered during the Opium War and the Taiping Rebellion, but were eventually rebuilt in the traditional style. Contemplate the Tower of Happiness or the Hall of Observing Quietness as you make your way through well-preserved traditional Chinese buildings and assorted antique and art stalls. Outside, shops sell a variety of traditional products and refreshments to ensure that the many visitors leave with their hands and stomachs full. *(218 Anren Lu, in the northeast part of the district, bounded by Fuyou Lu. Open daily 8:30am-5pm. Y25, children Y10.)*

NANJING LU AND ENVIRONS

NANJING LU (nánjīng lù; 南京路). Shanghai's answer to Hong Kong's Golden Mile (see p. 540) stretches across six upscale kilometers, from the Bund to Jingan Temple just beyond Shanghai Centre. Every day thousands of tourists and locals parade past this road, the glamorous setting of the historic Peace Hotel (hépíng fàndiàn; 和平饭店). On Saturday afternoons the street is closed to all vehicles; even then, the sidewalks sometimes seem too narrow for the crowds, and the flow of people spills onto the street.

Back in 1850, this area formed the heart of the English Concession, but it was horseracing, not shopping, that caught people's fancy. These days, **Shanghai No. 1 Department Store** (shànghǎi dì yī bǎihuò shāngdiàn; 上海第一百货商店; ☎6322 3344) anchors the corner of Xizang Lu (open daily 9:30am-10pm), and numerous other upscale establishments wait nearby. Just a few blocks south on Xizang Lu, **People's Square** (rénmín guǎngchǎng; 人民广场), the former site of the Shanghai Racecourse, invites tourists, locals, and groups of kite-wielding children to enjoy its greenery and fountains.

North of People's Square and People's Park, Nanjing Lu winds westward to the **Shanghai Centre** (shànghǎi shāngchéng; 上海商城). **Jingan Temple** (jìngān sì; 静安寺), the "Temple of Peace and Quiet," marks the official end of this raucous road and the beginning of industrial Shanghai. The temple is worth a peek, but not the Y5 admission. *(1686 Nanjing Xi Lu, at Wanhangdu Lu. Open daily 7:30am-4:45pm.)*

SHANGHAI MUSEUM (shànghǎi bówùguǎn; 上海博物馆). This modern building houses an impressive collection of ancient Chinese bronzes and ceramics, as well as exhibits on jade, the artwork of ethnic minorities, and more. The extensive exhibits can be overwhelming, but those who take their time luxuriating in the air-conditioned bliss will find the trip rewarding. Check out the beautiful collection of calligraphy, the formidable "evil spirit exorciser" from the Han dynasty pottery collection, and the cleanest bathrooms this side of the Yangzi. Helpful English signs are everywhere. Audio tours come in eight languages (Y60, deposit Y20). *(201 Renmin Dadao, in People's Square. ☎6372 3500. Open Su-F 9am-5pm, Sa 9am-8pm. Y20, students with ISIC Y5. Those with fake IDs are chastised and risk fines.)*

SHANGHAI ART MUSEUM (shànghǎi měishù guǎn; 上海美术馆). Collections of modern art are normally interesting; this museum's collection, which features works by Shanghai artists, is no exception. The artwork ranges from mildly fascinating to utterly breathtaking, and the museum's newly renovated home only adds to the enjoyment. Small but nice collection of Western oils and more contemporary Chinese art. The building itself is architectually pleasing, with A/C inside. *(325 Nanjing Xi Lu, just west of People's Square. ☎6327 2829. Open daily 9am-5pm; last admission 4pm. Y20, students Y10.)*

SHANGHAI EXHIBITION HALL OF URBAN PLANNING. Detailing the city's development, this exhibition features interesting models of Shanghai's skyline. Great for history buffs and budding architects. *(Open daily 9am-5pm. Y20, students Y16.)*

FORMER FRENCH CONCESSION

The glitzy boutiques that line Huaihai Zhong Lu may lure masses of salivating shoppers each day, but much of the area's historical significance and atmosphere is best absorbed on side streets a few blocks away from the glitter. Once the haunt of gangsters and revolutionaries, the area now conveys a more proper image, particularly in the foreign diplomatic area west of Changshou Lu.

FORMER RESIDENCE OF ZHOU ENLAI (zhōu gōngguǎn; 周公馆). This building served both as the well-loved CCP premier's living quarters and as a meeting place for early Communist revolutionaries. As a residence, it's delightful, with a lovely interior and pleasant gardens, but as a museum, it's somewhat uninteresting. Free tours in Chinese only. *(73 Si Nan Lu, south of Fuxing Lu. ☎6437 0420. Open W-Su 9-11:30am and 2:15-5pm; last admission 4:30pm. Y2.)*

FORMER RESIDENCE OF DR. SUN YAT-SEN (sǔn zhōngshān gù jū; 孙中山故居). GMD founder Sun Yat-sen (see p. 14) lived here for six years starting in 1918; after his death, his wife Song Qingling remained here until 1937. The two floors of the eerily well-preserved house contain many old portraits, a study with brushes and ink wells, and guest rooms once frequented by visiting dignitaries. *(7 Xiangshan Lu, off Si Nan Lu between Nanchang Lu and Fuxing Lu. ☎6437 2954. Open daily 9am-4:30pm. Y8.)*

FORMER RESIDENCE OF SONG QINGLING (sòng qìnglíng gù jū; 宋庆龄故居). Sun's widow spent much of her time here after 1948. A limo presented to her by Stalin and a painting by Chinese artist Xu Beihong are among the items on display. Don't miss the museum—it's one of the more interesting historical exhibits in town, with letters from Mme. Song to Stalin, Mao Zedong, and other less famous figures. *(1843 Huaihai Lu, between Yuqing Lu and Wanping Lu. Take bus #920 from Xizang Lu to Wukang. ☎6437 6268. Open daily 9-11am and 1-4:30pm. Y8, students Y6.)*

FIRST NATIONAL CONGRESS OF THE CHINESE COMMUNIST PARTY (zhōng gòng yīdà huìzhǐ jìniànguǎn; 中共一大会址纪念馆). On July 23, 1921, 11 representatives, including Mao Zedong and Chen Duxiu, initiated secret proceedings to found the CCP—secret, that is, until they were discovered by French police who forced the delegates to flee to a boat on South Lake in Zhejiang province. The building opened as a museum in 1952. *(76 Xingye Lu, at Huangpi Nan Lu. ☎6326 0664. Open daily 8:15-11am and 2-4pm, closed M and Th mornings. Y3.)*

WESTERN SHANGHAI

There are fewer obvious tourist attractions in this area of Shanghai than there are elsewhere in the city, and the distances between them are comparatively greater. **Xujiahui Cathedral** (xújiāhuì tiānzhǔtàng; 徐家汇天主堂), 158 Puxi Lu (easily accessible from Xujiahui Metro, exit #3), was built in 1906. Daily mass begins at 6:15am, with several services open to all worshipers. The large **Shanghai Stadium** (shànghǎi tǐyùguǎn; 上海体育馆; ☎6438 5200), at Tiyuguan Metro (one stop beyond Xujiahui), is part of a complex that includes a natatorium, playing fields, and other training facilities. There is also a lame water park and go-cart racing.

LONGHUA MARTYRS' MAUSOLEUM (lónghuá lièshì língyuán; 龙华烈士陵园). The gardens here are lush and verdant, a soothing counterpoint to the industrial grime of the surrounding area. The prospect of lingering and enjoying the scenery amid the tombstones, though, is slightly less appealing. An eternal flame in honor of those who died supporting the Communist cause burns in front of a giant sculpture emerging from the hillside. *(Open daily 6:30am-5pm; last admission 4:30pm. Y1.)* The Longhua Martyrs' Museum (lónghuá lièshì jìniànguǎn; 龙华烈士纪念馆) features exhibit after patriotic exhibit about the lives and achievements of those who supported the state against Imperialists and Nationalists back in the 1940s. *(2887 Longhua Lu. Open daily 9am-4pm; last admission 3:30pm. Y5.)*

The Longhua complex continues on grounds close to the main building. The halls of the illustrious **Longhua Temple** (lónghuá sì; 龙华寺) are alive with the smell of incense and the occasional clanging of the large bell near the entrance—ring it yourself (Y10) and eliminate all worries, or wait until New Year's day when it rings 108 times. *(Vegetarian restaurant open daily 11am-2pm and 5-8pm. Temple open daily 7am-4:30pm. Y5.)* Across the street stands **Longhua Pagoda** (lónghuá tǎ; 龙华塔), a seven-story octagonal tower.

AROUND SUZHOU CREEK

HONGKOU PARK (hóngkǒu gōngyuán; 虹口公园). This park, also known as Lu Xun Park (lǔxùn gōngyuán; 鲁迅公园), is a pleasant place to spend an hour or two. Bridges and covered pathways wind past a tea house. The Tomb of Lu Xun (lǔxùn mù; 鲁迅墓) is open to visitors. *(Open daily 9am-5pm; last admission 4pm. Y5.)* Though the first floor signs are entirely in Chinese, the second floor offers signs in English, and provides an overview of the life of the influential satirist and left-wing political activist (see **Modern Literature,** p. 37) who passed away here on October 19, 1936. *(2288 Sichuan Bei Lu, bordered by Dalian Lu on the north and Jiangbei Dong Lu on the west. Take bus #18 from People's Square. Open daily 6am-9pm. Y1.)*

OHEL MOISHE SYNAGOGUE (móxī huìtáng; 摩西会堂). Much of the area north of Suzhou Creek is part of Shanghai's International Settlement. Ohel Moishe Synagogue was a center for life in the "Designated Area for Stateless Refugees" during the 1930s and 40s. The museum features a few small exhibits, but its true treasure is its curator, Mr. Wang, who is happy to share his near-encyclopedic knowledge and poignant personal recollections of the area's history. *(62 Changyang Lu, 3rd fl. ☎6512 1934. Open daily 9am-4pm. Y30.)*

JADE BUDDHA TEMPLE (yùfó sì; 玉佛寺). This temple is renowned for a 2m tall white jade Buddha brought to China by a Burmese monk in 1822 and made from a single piece of jade. The statue would not be around, however, were it not for a cunning abbot and a frighteningly strict law. During the Cultural Revolution, the abbot of the Jade Buddha Temple closed the gates and plastered them with pictures of Chairman Mao. Because tearing down pictures of Mao was an offense punishable by death, the Red Guards were unable to enter and the temple was saved. Today, this big Buddha is surrounded by 688 little golden Buddhas all mounted along the ceiling. The temple is far away, but if you're only going to see one Buddhist temple in Shanghai, this is the one to see. *(170 Anyuan Lu west of Jiangning Lu. Take bus #506 one stop from the train station and follow the trail of incense sellers. Veg-*

etarian restaurant open daily 11am-2pm and 4:30-7pm. Temple open daily 7am-2pm and 4:30-9pm. Y10, additional Y5 to see the Jade Buddha himself.)

ENTERTAINMENT

That's Shanghai is the preferred entertainment magazine for young expats. The monthly publication discovers hip bars and restaurants within a week of their arrival, and lists cultural events, movies, and more importantly, where to get down. Most movies in Shanghai are dubbed, but check *That's Shanghai* or *City Weekend* for current listings on English movies (magazines Y35). In June, the Shanghai International Film Festival (SIFF) brings in many foreign films (Y25-35). Tickets for the following listings (except the Yifu Theater at times) can be purchased at the Shanghai Centre box office. Acrobatic show tickets sell out fast because of tour groups, so purchase yours in advance.

Shanghai Acrobatic Theatre (shànghǎi shāngchéng jùyuàn; 上海商城剧院), 1376 Nanjing Xi Lu (☎6279 8606), in the Shanghai Centre Theatre. The current venue is relatively small, so even the cheapest seats provide a decent view. The theater caters to tour groups, showcasing teeterboard, various comic acts, and a monkey thrown in for excitement. Performances are almost every night at 7:30pm. Box office open daily 9am-5pm if no show, 9am-7:45pm otherwise. Tickets Y30-60.

Shanghai Concert Hall (shànghǎi yīnyuè tīng; 上海音乐厅), 523 Yan'an Dong Lu (☎6386 9153), near Xizang Lu. Primarily hosts classical music performances by local groups, but sometimes sees visiting orchestras or ensembles. Tickets Y80-280, sold at the Shanghai Centre Box Office (see **Ticket Agencies,** p. 323).

Yifu Theatre (yífū wǔ tái; 逸夫舞台), 701 Fuzhou Lu (☎6351 4668), near People's Square. For those who've been craving the sweet sounds of Chinese opera, the Yifu shows traditional Beijing opera and Shanghai's own "Hu" style opera on Sunday afternoons. Tickets available at the box office outside.

Majestic Theatre (měiqí dàxìyuàn; 美琪大戏院), 66 Jiangning Lu (☎6217 4409). Shanghai's oldest theater shows a variety of programs, including ballet, tango, and opera praising the Communist Party. Tickets available at Shanghai Centre (see p. 323).

Shanghai Grand Theatre (shànghǎi dàjùyuàn; 上海大剧院), 300 Renmin Dadao (☎6386 8686), on the edge of People's Square. A sight in itself, this massive theater shows everything from Irish dancing to Russian ballet. Tickets available from the 1st fl. box office (☎6372 8701; open daily 9am-7:30pm) and other locations around town.

FESTIVALS

A number of smaller festivals take place throughout the year, and outdoor events are the norm during the summer.

FESTIVAL	TIME	LOCATION	ACTIVITIES
New Year's Festival	Dec. 31–Jan. 1	Longhua Temple in southwestern Shanghai	Ring in the New Year.
Temple Gathering	Early April	Longhua Temple	Street fair featuring guessing riddles and lots of food.
Shanghai International Tea Festival	Last Saturday in April	Zhabei Park (admission to park covers fee for festival)	Exotic and traditional blends of tea available for connoisseurs.
International Food Festival	Last weekend of June	Yandang Lu (Y100 to enter)	Taste foods from all over China and the world.

FESTIVAL	TIME	LOCATION	ACTIVITIES
Shanghai Beer Festival	Last Friday in June	A designated city park	Celebrate the second national drink of China.
Autumn Moon (Mid-Autumn) Festival	Late Sept. to early Oct.	Major streets	Stroll the streets looking at lights with riddles printed on them, and eat mooncakes.
Shanghai Seafood Festival	Late Sept.–early Oct. (week-long)	Xuhui District	Try a tantalizing array of fresh seafood.
Shanghai Tourism Festival	First week of November	Nanjing Lu	Parade down Nanjing Lu.

NIGHTLIFE

Shanghai Talk, *That's Shanghai*, *City Weekend*, and the Shanghai edition of *Metrozine* are English-language monthlies with extensive listings of activities and establishments in addition to feature articles. Free copies are available at many hotels and hangouts, like the Hard Rock Cafe (see p. 327). Although new spots are popping up all over, Shanghai's nightlife is struggling. Police are enforcing a 2am curfew and despite club efforts to go underground (complete with backdoor entrances), many just fold. Maoming Lu is no longer packed on weekends, and Julu Lu has as many women of ill repute as club-goers. But never fear: a new area filled with expats called **Xintiandi** is emerging, **Hengshan Lu** is newly-lined with bars, and the side streets off **Si Nan Lu** offer gems like **Park 97** and **Shanghai Sally's.**

Pegasus, 98 Huaihai Zhong Lu, 2nd fl. of the Golden Bell Plaza. This is the hottest disco in Shanghai (for now) and hosts international DJs on weekends. The pounding music, large dance floor, and hundreds of gyrating, sweating bodies is open to you for the nominal cover charge of Y50. Drinks Y35 and up. Open until 2am.

Park 97, 2 Gaolan Lu, Fuxing Park (☎6318 0785), on the corner of Si Nan Lu. Entry on Si Nan Lu, but when the police are blocking the front door, some people go through the back entrance. Run by the Lan Kwai Fong group of Hong Kong fame, this posh hangout features 2 restaurants and a tiny dance floor that somehow manages to pack in hundreds of screaming expats.

Rojan Disco, 283 Huaihai Zhong Lu, 4th fl. (☎6433 5086). The Chinese answer to Pegasus, this "American-style" disco draws a decidedly Chinese crowd. The music is mild, and the lighting ever so slightly brighter than in other clubs so that you can check out those new Shanghai dance moves.

Tequila Mama (bāhāmǎ cūnzhuāng; 巴哈马村庄), 24A Ruijin Er Lu (☎6433 5086), half a block from Huaihai Zhong Lu. A favorite of American students who like cheap beer (Y10), Tequila Mama is also popular for its "no cover charge for foreigners" policy. There's a game room with loud music, but most people come here to drink, not to dance. After a few of the margaritas (Y30), you too may find yourself striking a pose with this mainly international crowd. Cover Y30, foreign students (or those who look like they could be) free. Open daily until 1am.

Shanghai Sally's, 4 Xiangshan Lu (☎5382 9551), a few blocks south of Huaihai Zhong Lu, at Si Nan Lu. Don't be fooled by this lady's reserved exterior. Sure, the top floor may offer patrons the chance to sip a beer (Y35) in a pub-like setting, but there is live music in the basement with DJs on weekends. And because the dancing is downstairs, sometimes you can be let in after 2am, even after it looks dark and closed upstairs (to fool the police). Cocktails (downstairs only) Y25.

Caribe, 878 Julu Lu (☎6249 5512), one of the few places in Shanghai with salsa dancing. Two types of clientele, both of which are over 50: those who want to dance, and those who watch. Comfy chairs and Y20 drinks are the main draws.

Cotton Club, 1428 Huaihai Zhong Lu (☎6437 7110), at Fuxing Lu, is a favorite of local jazz lovers and the music is reputed to be second only to the jazz at the Portman Ritz-Carlton. The lights are dim, the tables intimate, the drinks cheap, and the music sublime. Unfortunately, the mainly expat, middle-aged, male crowd that flirts outrageously with the much younger local women tends to break the spell. Cocktails Y45, beer Y40, shots Y35; minimum tab Y25. Cover charge Y10. Live music Su-Th 9pm-midnight, F-Sa 9:30pm-1:30am. Open daily 7pm-2am.

Raise the Red Lantern (dàhóng dēnglóng; 大红灯笼), 5 Changshu Lu (☎6321 6888), north of Julu Lu. Drink here and you can enjoy not only the lovely decor and pleasantly sedate atmosphere but also the super-fast Internet access. Go ahead and email that witty remark you've been saving to the girl or guy across the bar. You know you want to. Imperial concubine chicken Y28, drinks Y30 and up (20min. free Internet access, but machines are frequently busy). Open daily 10am-5am.

Museum Club 1865, 1A Zhangshan Road (☎3313 0871). Sip your martini atop the terrace of the observatory on the Bund. Think of the Y35 you spent on drinks as the price for a spectacular view of the Pearl TV tower and the stunning architecture of the surrounding buildings.

Judy's Too, 176 Maoming Nan Lu (☎6473 1417). On a road where nightlife is dying, Judy's is not as popular as it used to be. But the owner still has a reputation for throwing slightly scandalous parties for a mainly expat crowd. Reasonably priced drinks (beer Y35), if you can find your way through the crowds to the bar. Open daily 5:30pm-2am.

A-Void Buddah Bar, 172 Maoming Nan Lu (☎6415 2688). Cool decorations, a laid-back Buddha statue, and pillowed alcoves set an atmosphere for relaxation lounging. Features 2 floors of music (top floor is more chill), but not much business on weekdays.

O'Malley's Pub, 42 Taojiang Lu (☎6474 4533), between Hengshan Lu and Wulumuqi Lu. This would be the quintessential neighborhood bar—if it were in England. The mostly expat crowd seems to be having a good time, enjoying summertime patio seating and homestyle dishes like Cottage Pie (Y120) and Fish and Chips. Guinness flows freely—or, as freely as Guinness does flow (half-pint Y40, pint Y60). Happy Hour daily 6pm-2am. Open daily 11am-2am.

DAYTRIPS FROM SHANGHAI

The counties and districts that surround Shanghai City are connected to the city proper by bus and minibus service; many leave from People's Square. Even the farthest townships are generally no more than 75km from the city center. The outlying areas themselves are a mixed bag; recently constructed amusement parks seem a bit out of place next to farmland and historical sites.

SONGJIANG COUNTY 松江县

*In southwestern Shanghai Municipality. The Huhang Gaosu Lu, an expressway linking Shanghai with Hangzhou, extends to Songjiang city. Direct buses to Songjiang leave from Songshan Lu, across from Wusheng Lu and People's Square, or from Shanghai Stadium (1hr., every 20min. 6am-8pm, Y5). Take a **sightseeing bus** from Shanghai Stadium to Sheshan or a **minibus** (30min., Y3.5) from the Songjiang county seat to Qingpu. Get off when you see the large sign that says **Sheshan Tourist District.***

The highlight of Songjiang County is Mount Sheshan, a heavily forested hill. Sheshan certainly merits a trip, and if you're out in Songjiang county, it makes sense to see the Songjiang county seat as well, though it is mainly a dull, industrial place. Songjiang's attractive cathedral, the **Holy Mother Cathedral on Sheshan** (shéshān tiānzhǔ jiàotáng; 佘山天主教堂), was built in 1863 on top of a 100m hill. The slope leading up to the cathedral bears images of the 14 Stations of the Cross, and the hillside fills with Christian pilgrims at festival times. *(Open daily until 3:30pm. Y2.)* The greenery of **Sheshan National Forest** is a soul-soothing experience, but make a whole day of it to justify the steep admission. A cable car that runs up to the cathedral and the forest offers both spectacular views and heart-stopping experiences during brisk winds. *(Open daily 7:30am-4pm. Forest admission Y28, children Y22. Cable car Y15 round-trip to the cathedral, Y10 to the forest, Y20 combination cathedral and forest.)* **Sheshan Observatory,** next to the cathedral, records earthquakes and other natural phenomena. *(Open daily 8am-4pm. Y6.)*

The Square Pagoda and Screen Wall stand inside **Square Pagoda Park** (fāngtǎ gōngyuán; 方塔公园), at 235 Zhongshan Zhong Lu, in the county seat. Take the bus that leaves from Zhongshan Zhong, by Renmin Lu across from the Industrial and Commercial Bank, to the fourth stop. The nine-story pagoda (Y5) has a history that spans over 900 years. For most people, climbing it is an enjoyable experience. For anyone over 6ft. tall, though, it may turn into a perilous adventure. The large screen wall to the north was built in 1370 during the Ming dynasty. A huge, beastly animal called Tao is carved into the center of the wall; legend has it that the greedy animal swallowed all the treasures in the world but still craved the sun. The sun shone too high for Tao, so he fell into the sea and drowned. *(Open daily 7am-9pm.)*

The **Pond of the Drunken Bai** (zuìbái chí; 醉白池) is at 64 Renmin Nan Lu, in the county seat. Walk east from the bus station until you hit Renmin Bei Lu. Turn right and walk south for about 15 minutes, past the Drunken Bai Restaurant. The pond was originally the private residence of the famous Song painter Gu Dashen, who enjoyed the work of Tang poet Bai Juyi so much that he designed a garden in his honor. Empty and a little overgrown, the gardens are still a pleasant retreat. The abandoned children's amusement park is a bit scary, though; you expect an evil clown to emerge at any moment. *(☎5774 4559. Open daily 6:30am-4:30pm.)*

The **Songjiang Mosque** (sōngjiāng qīngzhēn sì; 松江清真寺), the oldest in the Shanghai area, was built in the mid-1300s. It is surrounded by houses and is difficult to find. From Zhongshan Zhong Lu, turn south onto Renmin Lu. Take the first right into an unmarked alley and continue straight until you find the mosque on your right. The entrance is around the corner. *(☎5781 1957. Open daily 8am-4pm.)*

NANHUI COUNTY 南汇县

Southeast of the city center. A special tour bus departs from Shanghai's Shiliupu Passenger Terminal to Luchao Port. Or take the tourist bus from the stadium (2hr., every 15min. 6:30am-9pm). During the Peach Blossom Festival, buses (daily 7 and 7:30am) go from People's Square to Nanhui.

Known locally as the "Land of Peach Blossoms," Nanhui boasts over 333 hectares of orchards that dress up in bold pastels at harvest time. In the spring, the area comes alive with the scent of ripening peaches; the **Peach Blossom Festival** runs from late March to early April. At the Peachland Folk Custom Village and the Fairy Land of Peaches in Shenxi, actors play out scenes of daily life past and present. The **Peace Festival** is in mid-April. **Luchao Port** (lúcháo gǎng; 芦潮港), on the northern coast of Hangzhou Bay, features a natural harbor and several miles of beach-bedecked coastline.

JIADING DISTRICT 嘉定区

In northwestern Shanghai Municipality, linked to the city center by the Shanghai-Jiading Freeway. ***Buses*** *(M-F 6am-6pm, Sa-Su 6am-10pm) go to Jiading from Weihai Lu at Huangpi Lu, Yan'an Lu at Weihai Lu, and Hengfeng Lu near the Shanghai Train Station. Buses (daily 5am-8pm, Y6) to* ***Nanxiang*** *leave from the Shanghai North Station on Zhongshan Bei Lu.* ***Tourist Buses*** *depart from the stadium (1hr., every 20min.).*

Remnants of China's dynastic splendor are the main draw here, although the recently constructed Shanghai Global Paradise and American Dreamland Park come heavily touted as high-class vacation and entertainment spots. Jiading's **Nanxiang Town** (nánxiáng; 南翔) features a collection of pagodas and temples that should please both history buffs and casual tourists. The **Confucius Temple** (kǒngmiào; 孔庙), 183 Nan Dajie, was built in 1219 and today houses the **Jiading Museum** (jiādìng bówùguǎn; 嘉定博物馆). Those with a penchant for poetic names will enjoy a stroll through this place; even the memorial archways bear such names as "Cultivating the Talents" and "Encouraging the Virtuous." The 72 carved lions outside the temple represent the 72 highly respected disciples of Confucius. *(☎5953 0379. Open daily 8-11am and 1:30-4:30pm.)*

Just east of the temple, the **Dragon Meeting Pond** (huì lóng tán; 汇龙潭) bears the shape of "five dragons snatching at a pearl." Five small streams (the dragons) run into a pond out of which Yingkui Hill (the pearl) rises. Visitors with tired imaginations can enjoy the pleasant scenery of the **Garden of Autumn Clouds** (qīuxiá pǔ; 秋霞圃). *(3144 Dongda Lu. ☎5953 1949. Open daily 8am-5pm.)* The **Garden of Ancient Splendor** (gǔ yī yuán; 古猗园) spreads splendidly over the eastern part of town. *(2 Minghu Dong Lu. ☎5912 1335. Open daily 7:30am-5pm.)*

QINGPU COUNTY 青浦县

In western Shanghai Municipality, bordered by Songjiang County to the south and Jiading District to the north. Huqingping Lu (State Hwy. 318), a continuation of Yan'an Lu, is the main thoroughfare. The ***Qiangsheng Sightseeing Bus*** *(1½hr., 4 per day 7:30am-4pm, Y12) goes to Grand View Garden from the intersection of Jinling Lu and Yandang Lu in Shanghai.* ***Minibuses*** *(Y6) travel to the surrounding area from the Qingpu county seat.* ***Buses*** *(approx. 5am-8pm) go from Shanghai West Station on Wuzhong Lu to the Qingpu county seat.*

Activities in Qingpu County blend the old with the new, in case you haven't seen enough of that in China already. **Grand View Garden** (dà guān yuán; 大观园), on Dianshan Lake, 65km west of Shanghai, reproduces the gardens in the classic novel *Dream of the Red Chamber* (see **Ancient and Premodern Literature,** p. 36). Visitors can discuss the significance of buildings that are "Fraught with Favor, Basking in Kindness" or just take in the pleasant scenery. *(Open daily 8am-4:30pm.)*

The **Setting Free Bridge** (fáng shēng qiáo; 放生桥), in the ancient town of **Zhujiajiao** (zhūjiājiǎo; 朱家角), is the largest stone bridge in the municipality, and draws numerous visitors. Buddhists believe that setting living things free builds good karma; you can buy and set free fish caught by local fishermen and peddlers expressly for this purpose. In the northeastern part of the county, within Qingpu Town, the **Garden of Meandering Stream** sits near the Daying River. Built in 1745, the garden wins points for its lotus pond. *(Open daily 8am-4:30pm.)*

JIANGSU 江苏

Jiangsu isn't exactly the most glamorous of provinces. Some of Jiangsu's southern areas have been influenced by nearby Shanghai, but overall, this humble little region is anything but cosmopolitan. What it *is* known for is its rich soil and temperate climate, which provide the area with abundant agricultural yields and, more importantly, its vivid and exciting moniker, "Land of Fish and Rice."

But even peaceful Jiangsu cannot escape the long arm of economic development. Monstrous factories are scattered among the province's meandering rice paddies, fishing junks, and tiny cottages, belching smoke, puking waste, and pushing farmers toward already overstuffed cities. Still, the situation here is mild compared to the economic tumult of the rest of China. Jiangsu isn't an economic boom town; it's more aptly described as a historical and cultural relic. Even the Grand Canal, which runs south through the province, reflects Jiangsu's ancient character. Now outmoded in the face of modern transport, the canal starts at the less interesting northern cities of Xuzhou and Lianyungang, winds uselessly past the idyllic ancient city of Suzhou toward modern Wuxi, and crawls quietly onward to Zhejiang province.

NANJING 南京 ☎025

Legend has it that an ancient Chinese poet once wrote of Nanjing (formerly Jinling, or "golden hills") with this verse: "Oh, what a beautiful place, Jinling! Deservedly the home for many a king." And many a king did make Nanjing his home. Literally "Southern Capital," Nanjing was the Ming dynasty capital for over 50 years, the first city south of the Yangzi River to serve as the imperial seat of a united China; in the early half of the 20th century, it was the capital for a frequently fragmented China, ruled by Sun Yat-sen (1912) and then by the Guomindang (1928-49). All told, Nanjing has served as the capital of 10 governments; and even today, it is the seat of Jiangsu province. Despite the constant flux of Nanjing's history, the city's historical sights and somber monuments are testament to Nanjing's respect for the past.

With a booming economy, modern Nanjing serves as a busy gateway to the rest of China. It may not be the historical fortress of Beijing or the scenic delight that is Hangzhou, but Nanjing exemplifies the evolution of a growing city (thin coat of dust included). Luxurious five-star hotels and decadent restaurants have sprouted throughout the city, catering to pampered tourists and the business elite. But despite its growing tourism industry Nanjing remains a city for the people who live in it; its lakes, parks, and museums are more local haunts than touristed national treasures. And city life hardly implies glossy high-rises or wanton spending; instead, life in Nanjing flourishes in the small alleys off Xinjiekou, where people do laundry on traditional wooden boards and families set up tables in front of shops for a dinner of dumplings or noodles. Above all, Nanjing is promisingly, unabashedly regular—a regular city for regular folk.

TRANSPORTATION

Flights: Nanjing International Airport (nánjīng lùkǒu guójì jīchǎng; 南京禄口国际机场; ☎660 2186), has frequent flights to most destinations in China. The only frequent international flights are to Southeast Asia. Shuttle buses (1hr., every 30 min. 7am-6pm, Y25) to the airport leave from the **CAAC ticket office,** 52 Ruijin Lu (☎449 9378). Buses make the trip from Xin Han Mansion, at 180 Hanzhong Lu (starting at 6am, Y25). A taxi to the city center costs Y150. To: **Beijing** (6-7 per day, Y920); **Guangzhou** (5-6 per day, Y1070); **Hong Kong** (2 per day, Y1600); **Kunming** (2-3 per day, Y1550); **Qingdao** (daily, Y620); **Tianjin** (Tu, Th-F, and Su; Y800); **Wuhan** (2-3 per day, Y580). Another ticket office is at 1 Beijing Xi Lu (☎331 1747; fax 331 2135; xhhl1481@jlonline.com; www.hxaviation.com), 200m west of Gulou Square. Open 24hr.

Trains: Nanjing Train Station (nánjīng huǒchē zhàn; 南京火车站), 264 Longpan Lu (☎599 8202), at the terminus for buses #1, 13, 32, and 33. Buy tickets as early as possible if visiting in late June to early July to avoid the rush of students on vacation. The best place to buy tickets without commission is at the **Gulou Ticket Office,** 293 Zhongshan Lu (☎330 1692). Nanjing West Train Station tickets are also sold here. Open daily 8am-5pm. Buy tickets within 7 days before departure. To: **Beijing** (12hr., 5 per day, Y157-276); **Chengdu** (40½hr.; 2 per day; Y247, A/C Y405); **Shanghai** (3-5hr., 22 per day, Y44-82); **Xi'an** (20hr.; 2 per day; Y164, A/C Y265).

Buses: Zhongyang Gate Long-distance Bus Station (zhōngyāngmén chángtú qìchē zhàn; 中央门长途汽车站), 1 Jianning Lu (☎550 4973), a 10min. walk west of Nanjing Train Station. Accessible via buses #1, 13, 32, and 33. Open daily 5:30am-5:30pm. To: **Changsha** (24hr., 1pm, Y213); **Guangzhou** (48hr., 4:40pm, Y323); **Hefei** (2-3hr., every 20-30min. 6:30am-7:30pm, Y38-54); **Jiuhuashan** (4½hr., 9am and 2pm, Y57); **Nanchang** (10hr., 4 per day, Y126-163); **Shanghai** (3½hr., every 30min. 1am-5pm, Y82-88). **Hanfu Jie Long-distance Bus Station** (hànfǔjiē chángtú qìchē zhàn; 汉府街长途汽车站), 25 Daxing Gong (☎454 1359), east of Xinjiekou off Zhongshan Dong Lu. Take bus #5, 9, 25, or 29 to Daxing Gong. To: **Hangzhou** (5-6hr., 5 per day, Y71); **Shanghai** (3½hr., 10 per day, Y75-88); **Suzhou** (2½hr., 12 per day, Y44-64); **Wuhan** (15hr., 8 per day, Y130); **Wuxi** (2hr., 12 per day, Y37-54).

Boats: No. 4 Dock (nánjīng sìhào mǎtóu; 南京四号码头; ☎880 5501), on Xiaguan Jiangbian Lu, near the intersection of Jiangbian Lu and Da Malu. Take bus #10 to the Sihao Matou. Buy tickets a day in advance at the ticket window (open daily 8am-5pm). Offers a scenic route less taken to **Shanghai** (20hr., 8:30 and 10:30pm, Y48).

Bike Rental: Bike rental shops are few and far between, but explore the Nanjing University area for options. A stand, in a small alley 1 block south of Beijing Dong Lu, has few bikes; come either early in the day or at night. Y1 per hr. Open daily sunrise-10pm.

Local Transportation: The **public bus** system extends as far as Zijinshan and the Yangzi River Bridge. Several buses, like #9W, 11W, and 13W, run 5am-11pm; most routes run around 6:30am-8 or 9pm. Fare generally Y1, with A/C Y2; price is marked on the outside of the bus, near the door. A "W" next to the bus number means nobody is onboard selling tickets, so you should drop exact change (usually Y1) in the box next to the driver. Buses **#9, 16,** and **34** run along Zhongshan Lu; **#1, 13,** and **32** run along Fuzimiao and connect to other tourist attractions. **Minibuses** (Y1-4) follow popular bus routes. A **subway** is scheduled to be completed in 2005; it will run north-south through the city center, with 13 stops, including Xinjiekou, Gulou, and the train station.

Taxis: Base fare Y7, each additional km Y2.1-2.4. Xinjiekou to the main train and bus stations Y20-25, to the airport Y120.

ORIENTATION AND PRACTICAL INFORMATION

Nanjing's ten districts and five counties cover more than 6500km^2 on the south side of the **Yangzi River,** about 200km from Shanghai. The city is bounded by the river to the west, and **Zijinshan Mountain** to the east. Thriving commercial districts cluster in the 10km stretch between Zhongyang Gate in the north and Zhonghua Gate in the south. In the heart of the city, there are two large traffic circles, **Gulou** (鼓楼) and **Xinjiekou** (新街口). The Gulou traffic circle is the intersection of **Beijing Dong Lu** (北京东路), **Beijing Xi Lu** (北京西路), **Zhongshan Bei Lu** (中山北路), and **Zhongyang Bei Lu** (中央北路). Zhongshan Bei Lu and Zhongyang Bei Lu run south; they join to become **Zhongshan Lu** (中山路), which intersects **Hanzhong Lu** (汉中路) and Zhongshan Dong Lu to form the Xinjiekou traffic circle. Another major street is **Taiping Lu** (太平路), which runs roughly parallel to Zhongshan Lu. **Jianning Lu/Longpan Lu** runs along the city's north edge, past the Nanjing Train Station and the Zhongyang Gate Bus Station, near the West Train Station and Yangzi River docks.

TOURIST AND FINANCIAL SERVICES

Tourist Office: Nanjing Municipal Tourism Bureau (nánjīngshì lǚyóuchù shìchǎng kāifāchù; 南京市旅游处市场开发处), 4 Nan Donggua Shi, 4th fl. (☎336 2686; fax 771 1959). Take bus #13 or 65 north on Shanghai Lu 1 stop beyond the Foreign Students' Dorm. Donggua Shi alley is straight ahead; the bureau is on the left. Open M-F 8am-noon and 2-6pm. English map of Nanjing for sale (Y5) at Sheraton or Jinling Hotel.

Travel Agencies: CITS, 202-1 Zhongshan Bei Lu (☎342 8999), near Xinmo Lu, north of the Hongqiao Hotel. Take bus #13 from the train station, or #16, 26, or 34 heading northwest from Gulou for 5 stops and get off at the Nanjing Hotel stop. English-speaking staff. Average commission Y30. Open M-F 8:30am-6pm, Sa-Su 9am-4pm. **CTS,** 313 Zhongshan Bei Lu (☎343 1502). Average commission Y30. Open M-F 8am-5:30pm.

Bank of China: 29 Hongwu Lu. From the Xinjiekou traffic circle, walk 1 block east on Zhongshan Dong Lu and turn right on Hongwu Lu; the bank is on the left, 1 block down. **ATMs** (Cirrus, Visa, Plus). Open M-F 8:30am-5:30pm. Other branches scattered along Zhongshan Nan Lu all have **ATMs** accepting Visa/Plus.

LOCAL SERVICES

Bookstore: Xinhua Foreign Language Bookstore, 137 Zhongshan Lu (☎451 6465), carries English classics and best-sellers. Branch at 58 Zhongshan Dong Lu (☎664 5151), about 2 blocks east of Xinjiekou, on the right. Carries the mundane (bilingual dictionaries) and the magnificent (literary masterpieces). Open daily 8:30am-7pm.

Department Store: Xinjiekou Department Store (xīnjiēkǒu bǎihuò shāngdiàn; 新街口百货商店), 3 Zhongshan Nan Lu, is the grande dame of Nanjing department stores, with 8 imposing floors with just about every product imaginable. Open M-Th 9am-8pm, F 9am-9pm, Sa 8:45am-9pm, and Su 8:45am-8pm.

Markets: SGCS (sūguǒ chāoshì; 苏果超市), with several locations, offers snacks and ready-to-go dinners. One with a good selection is at 26 Hongwu Lu, 1 block east of Xinjiekou traffic circle, off Zhongshan Dong Lu, opposite the Bank of China building. Open daily 7am-10pm. **Zehong Supermarket** (zéhóng chāoshì; 泽红超市), 67 Zhongshan Nan Lu, 1 block south of the Xinjiekou Department Store. Good selection of Western and Chinese food, household items, basic medicines, and toiletries. Open 24hr.

EMERGENCY AND COMMUNICATIONS

PSB: 11 Hongwu Lu (☎442 0114), south of Xinjiekou traffic circle. **Foreigners' Bureau** (chūrùjìng guǎnlǐ chù; 出入境管理处; ☎442 0004) staff members speak English.

Pharmacies: They're everywhere. **Sarow Pharmacy,** on Haining Lu, a block south of Beijing Xi Lu, is open 24hr. (☎330 6810). **Baixin Pharmacy** has locations throughout the city (look for bright green and white signs), with everything from Tylenol to herbal elixirs. The Fuzimiao branch, 34 Gongyuan Xi Jie (☎662 3793), is open daily 8:30am-9pm.

Hospital: Gulou Hospital (gǔlóu yīyuàn; 鼓楼医院), 321 Zhongshan Lu (☎330 4616). From Gulou traffic circle, walk a short distance down Zhongshan Lu; the hospital is on the right. Affiliated with Nanjing University Medical School. English-speaking staff.

Telephones: China Telecom, 2 Zhongyang Bei Lu, just off the Gulou traffic circle. IDD and telegram service at the first counter to your right. Open daily 8am-6pm. Side office with separate entrance provides the same services 24hr. (toll free ☎1000).

Internet Access: Nanjing's large student population means numerous Internet options, all Y2-6 per hr. **Laiba Cafe** (láiba; 来吧), adjacent to the Nanjing University Foreign Students' Dormitory, on the corner of Jinyin Jie and Shanghai Lu. Y3 per hr. Open daily 9am-1:30am. **Internet Impression** (yīngpàishēng wǎngluò; 英派升网络), 152 Shanghai Lu, on Shanghai Lu between Beijing Xi Lu and Hankou Xi Lu, with English signs. Y4 per hr.; multiple-use cards offer great savings. **Nanjing Normal University Nanshan Hotel** has fast connections, when working, for Y0.13 per min.

Post Office: Nanjing Post Office, in the high-rise building south of Gulou traffic circle, on the corner of Beijing Dong Lu and Zhongshan Lu, with entrances on both sides (☎379 6673). EMS and Poste Restante (send to the Gulou Post Office, 鼓楼邮局). Open daily 8am-6:30pm. **Postal code:** 210005 for regular mail, 210008 for Poste Restante.

ACCOMMODATIONS

Apart from Nanjing's two university dormitories, most establishments that accept foreign guests are pricey three-star hotels. If posted room rates seem too good to be true, they very well may be; chances are the place does not accept foreigners.

Nanjing Normal University Nanshan Hotel (nánjīng shīfàn dàxué nánshān zhuānjiā lóu; 南京师范大学南山专家楼), 122 Ninghai Lu (☎371 6440), a block south of Hankou Xi Lu. Enter the campus through the main gate, when you reach a large flagpole, turn left; follow the blue sign around to the left. Renovations make this Nanjing's best budget option. Rooms have A/C, bath, phone (free local calls), Internet access (Y0.13 per min.), and TV. Gorgeous campus setting has gardens, lush foliage, a lily pond, and Qing architecture. Laundry service. Breakfast included with standard rooms. Rooms go fast (especially singles) so reserve early. Open 8am-11pm. 2-bed dorms Y30; singles with bath Y100; doubles with bath Y170. ❶

Nanjing University Foreign Students' Dormitory (nánjīng dàxué xīyuàn; 南京大学西苑), 20 Jinyin Jie (☎359 3589; fax 359 4699), 1 block to the right (if you are coming from Gulou) of the intersection of Shanghai Lu and Beijing Xi Lu. Take bus #11W or 13W to Yunnan Lu. In a lively quarter, close to eateries and bars that cater to foreign and Chinese students. Mattresses aren't plush, but rooms and halls are clean and well-kept. Laundry (self-service) Y2 per 2kg. Deposit Y10. Singles with bath Y140; doubles Y100, with bath Y140; triples Y140. ❷

Yishi Hotel (jiāngsū yìshì yuán; 江苏议事园), 81 Zhongshan Bei Lu (☎332 6826; yshotel@Public1.ptt.js.cn), behind a yellow wall bordering Zhongshan Bei Lu and Yunnan Lu, off Sanxilu Square. One stop from Gulou on buses #16, 26, 31, or 34 northbound; from the train and bus stations, take #13 to Dafang Xiang. Built in traditional Chinese style, the Yishi's smaller size and attentive staff provide a welcome respite from impersonal high-rise hotels. Breakfast included. Currency exchange. Singles Y216; doubles Y260. Student discounts possible. Credit cards accepted. ❸

Hongqiao Hotel (hóngqiáo fàndiàn; 虹桥饭店), 202 Zhongshan Bei Lu (☎340 0888), at Xinmo Lu. From the train or bus stations, take bus #13 or 32 to Hongqiao/Nanjing Binguan stop; the brightly-lit English sign can be spotted from the intersection. Bright, and clean, this hotel sees plenty of business deals struck over rounds of Tsingtao. Extra bonus: the hottest disco in town is right next door. Currency exchange. Doubles Y298. Discounts possible during mid-summer months. Credit cards accepted. ❹

Egret Hotel, 68 Dashi Ba Lu (☎662 1999; fax 662 1895), off Gongyuan Jie in Fuzimiao. Overlooking the Qinghuai River, the Egret claims the same great location as its pricier neighbors. The south building is chock-full of amenities, while cheaper rooms in the north building show wear and tear. Breakfast included. Post-discount rates: singles Y330; doubles Y510. 30% student discount possible, but bargain regardless. ❺

White Palace Hotel (bái gōng dàjiǔdiàn; 白宫大酒店), 2 Longpan Lu (☎550 9999, ext. 2200), opposite the Zhongyang Gate Long-distance Bus Station. Proximity to the train and bus stations is its biggest draw; prices are as steep as some upmarket hotels of better quality. Breakfast included with 20% discount; no breakfast for greater discounts. Singles Y385; doubles Y510. Credit cards accepted. ❺

FOOD

According to a Chinese saying, Sichuanese food is like a hot woman, Beijing food a refined young lady, and South Yangzi food a humble farm girl. Nanjing's elaborate menu of age-old delicacies and mouth-watering snacks, however, is anything but plain, and small restaurants and family-run stalls line city streets that reach their culinary apex at night; an evening stroll can quickly become a scrumptious foodfest. The night market in **Xinjiekou** (xīnjiēkǒu; 新街口), on a small lane right behind the Xinjiekou Department Store off Zhongshan Nan Lu, specializes in grilled or fried Shanghai-style chicken and beef (Y2) and smelly tofu (Y1).

The stretch of **Ninghai Lu** between Hankou Lu and Beijing Xi Lu, near Nanjing Normal University, is normally crammed with vendors serving everything from *bāozi* (Y0.50-1) to salted duck's head (Y8). Because of construction, however, these carts have temporarily relocated to **Hankou Lu** as of July 2001. Vendors offer delectable Hong Kong-style custard tarts, lychees, and yummy nectarines. After 5pm, the culinary main street turns into a **night market** where locals buy fresh veg-

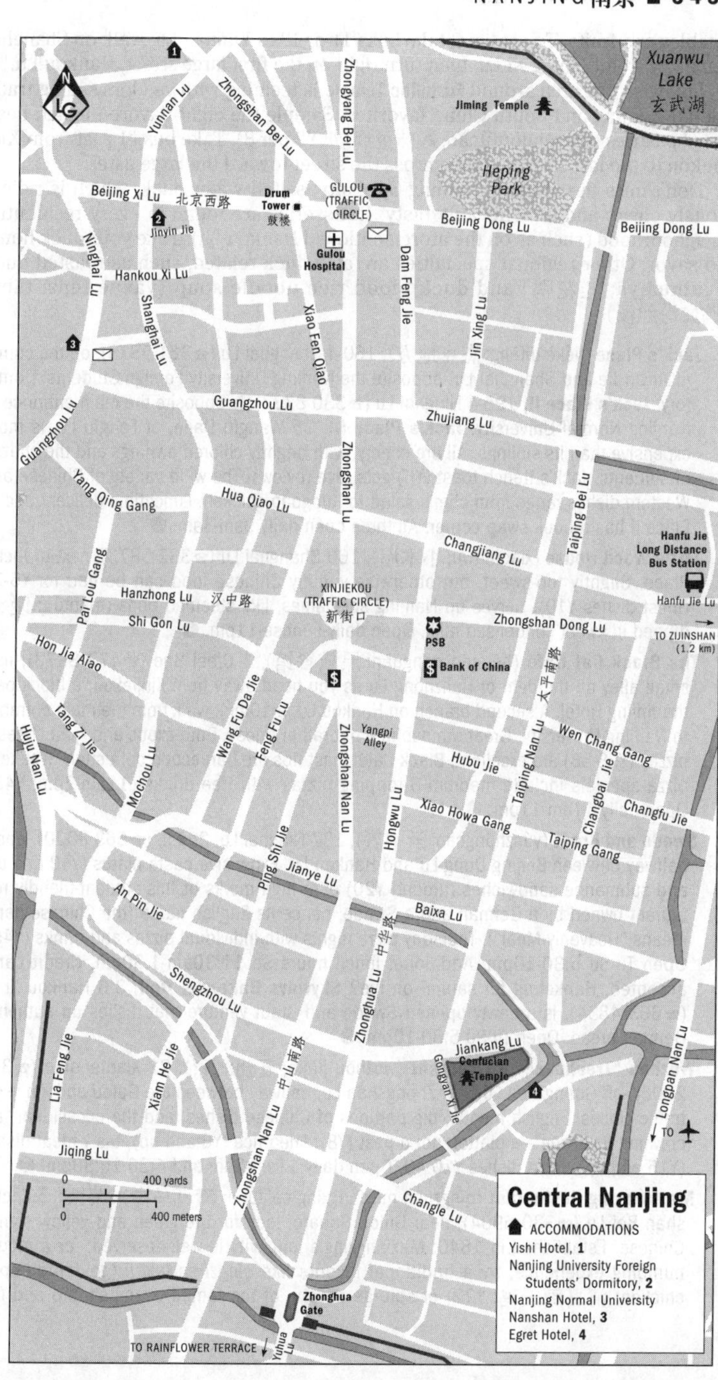
Central Nanjing
ACCOMMODATIONS
Yishi Hotel, 1
Nanjing University Foreign Students' Dormitory, 2
Nanjing Normal University Nanshan Hotel, 3
Egret Hotel, 4
Xuanwu Lake
玄武湖
Jiming Temple
Heping Park
Zhongshan Bei Lu
Zhongyang Bei Lu
Yunnan Lu
Beijing Xi Lu
北京西路
Drum Tower
鼓楼
GULOU (TRAFFIC CIRCLE)
Beijing Dong Lu
Jinyin Jie
Gulou Hospital
Ninghai Lu
Hankou Xi Lu
Shanghai Lu
Xiao Fen Qiao
Dam Feng Jie
Jin Xing Lu
Guangzhou Lu
Zhujiang Lu
Yang Qing Gang
Hua Qiao Lu
Zhongshan Lu
Taiping Bei Lu
Changjiang Lu
Hanfu Jie Long Distance Bus Station
Hanfu Jie Lu
Pai Lou Gang
Hanzhong Lu
汉中路
XINJIEKOU (TRAFFIC CIRCLE)
新街口
Shi Gon Lu
Zhongshan Dong Lu
TO ZIJINSHAN (1.2 km)
PSB
Bank of China
Hon Jia Aiao
太平南路
Tang Zi Jie
Wang Fu Da Jie
Feng Fu Lu
Yangpi Alley
Zhongshan Nan Lu
Wen Chang Gang
Huju Nan Lu
Mochou Lu
Hubu Jie
Taiping Nan Lu
Changbai Jie
Hongwu Lu
Xiao Howa Gang
Changfu Jie
Taiping Gang
Ping Shi Jie
Jianye Lu
An Pin Jie
Baixa Lu
中华路
Shengzhou Lu
Zhonghua Lu
中山南路
Jiankang Lu
Confucian Temple
Gongyan Xi Jie
Longpan Nan Lu
Lia Feng Jie
Xiam He Jie
TO
Jiqing Lu
Zhongshan Nan Lu
0
400 yards
0
400 meters
Changle Lu
Zhonghua Gate
TO RAINFLOWER TERRACE
Yuhua Lu

SHANGHAI

etables and fruits. To get here, take bus #11 or 13 to Yunnan Lu, walk on Shanghai Lu away from Beijing Xi Lu; then turn right on the first large street, Hankou Lu.

Likewise, the area around **Fuzimiao Temple** is teeming with vendors selling traditional Nanjing and South China favorites. Sample the eight-flavored jellied bean curd pastries (bāwèi dòufǔnǎo; 八味豆腐脑; Y2 per 8). Take bus #1 east from Xinjiekou to the last stop, and then cross the street toward the large gate.

Don't miss the ultimate Nanjing Specialty: salted water duck, which is ridiculously cheap and unbelievably tasty. Rotisseries are found in every residential neighborhood (such as on the aforementioned Hankou Lu). Take your duck home to savor. Other regional specialties are also duck-related, such as roasted duck (guìhuā yā; 桂花鸭) and duck blood rice noodle soup (yāxuě fěnsī tāng; 鸭血粉丝汤).

Jack's Place (jiékè dìfāng; 杰克地方), 160-4 Shanghai Lu (☎361 5873), on the corner of Jinyin Jie and Shanghai Lu, opposite the Nanjing University Foreign Students' Dormitory. **Jack's Place II,** 195-4 Ninghai Lu (☎330 8737), is opposite the main entrance of Nanjing Normal University. **Jack's Place III,** 35 Wangfu Dajie, at Fengfu Lu, is more expensive than its siblings. All are cheery, with brightly colored awnings and the chatter of students. Jack's french toast (Y6) gets rave reviews. The wide variety of Chinese and Western dishes range from chef's salad to Kungpao chicken. Lunchtime delivery. Jack's Place II has a book swap corner. All three open daily 9am-3am. ❶

Little Wood House (xiǎomùwū; 小木屋), 160 Shanghai Lu (☎332 5873), next to Jack's Place. Slightly too-sweet, but otherwise yummy Chinese food can be had for Y5-20 (most dishes Y10). Serves up Nanjing specialties, like steamed buns (mántóu; 馒头) dipped in sweet condensed milk. Open daily sunrise-11pm. ❶

The Black Cat Cafe (hēimāo cānguǎn; 黑猫餐馆), 1 Cibei She (☎472 8973), in a small alley on the right of Hanzhong Lu as you head away from Xinjiekou, a block past the Jinling Hotel. A second branch on Hankou Lu, a 10min. walk from the main entrance to Nanjing University. Great atmosphere but rather pricey. Both exotic and "just cheese" pizzas (Y28-58) are excellent; Black Cat's roast ribs are barbecued perfection. Weekend pizza specials include medium 3-topping pizzas with free drinks (11am-2pm; Y48). Open daily 11am-11pm. ❸

Swede and Kraut (yúnzhōngcān; 云中餐), 137 Ninghai Lu, 2nd fl. (☎663 8020), about halfway between Beijing Dong Lu and Hankou Lu. Expensive pasta plates (Y40 and up) and submarine sandwiches (around Y20) earn high marks at this student-friendly restaurant owned by a German and a Swede, hence its English name (the Chinese name means "Heavenly Meal"). Thursday pizza nights with individual pizzas and drinks (Y45). Open Tu-Su 5:30-10pm. Additional lunch hours Sa 11:30am-1:30pm. Credit cards accepted. Hankering for salami on rye? **Skyways Bakery & Deli,** 3-6 Hankou Xi Lu (☎663 4834), is a newly opened Swede and Kraut venture that dishes up authentic German bread. Open Tu-Su 5:30-10pm. ❸

Wuzhou "Treehouse" Restaurant (wǔzhōu jiǔjiā; 五州酒家), 22 Xiaofenqiao (☎332 2006), off Guangzhou Lu near Zhongshan Lu, halfway between the Gulou and Xinjiekou traffic circles. English menus, big portions of Chinese dishes, and the occasional "ant crawling up a tree"–a platter, not a pest (Y8). Fried rice (Y6 and up), tasty meat dishes (Y15 and up). Most dishes Y10-40. Open daily 11am-2pm and 4:30-10:30pm. ❷

Maxiangxing Restaurant (qīngzhēn mǎxiángxìng càiguǎn; 清真马祥兴菜馆), 5 Zhongshan Bei Lu (☎330 5904), near Gulou Square; look for the green and yellow sign in Chinese. Established in 1840. Maxiangxing's longevity is well-deserved; for a mouth-numbing experience, try a traditional favorite like *qīngzhēn làzi jī* (goldenrod spicy chicken; 清真辣子鸡; Y22) or splurge on one of the famed crispy shrimp and fish dishes (Y85-112). Lower level serves fast food; speedy buns and dumplings (Y1.2) available daily 6:30am-8pm. 2nd fl. open daily 10:30am-1:30pm and 5-8pm. ❷

Liu Feng Ju (liùfēngjū; 六风居), 144 Gongyuan Jie (☎662 1593), in Fuzimiao. This cafeteria-style eatery has gained acclaim among locals for dishing up the best flat rice noodles, sticky-rice meatballs, and beef kebabs this side of the Qinghuai River. Liu Feng Ju's good location and ridiculously good meatballs (shīzi tóu; 狮子头) make up for its rather pricey meals (Y20-30). Open daily 9am-10pm. ❷

SIGHTS

Most of Nanjing's main attractions are scattered around the outskirts of the city. Places of reflection and remembrance, they are reminders of Nanjing's imperial, revolutionary, and war-torn past, as well as indications of its thriving future. In July and early August, there are daily musical performances, from 7 to 10pm, at the Open Air Music Concert Hall and Bai Ma Park (báimǎ gōngyuán; 白马公园; pay at park entrance, show is free).

PURPLE GOLD MOUNTAIN

East of Nanjing. Take bus #9 from Xinjiekou to its last stop, Zhongshanling. Bicycling is a good option for those eager to avoid traffic and frequent stops; it's a 30-40min. ride from Xinjiekou. Bike storage available. The best way to shuttle between sights is the #Y2 and Y3 buses (Y2), which operate 9am-5:30pm. A Zhongshan Fengjing sightseeing bus shuttles between the sights for Y10. Open daily sunrise-sunset; in winter 7am-5:30pm. Free; separate admission to sights. Y45 for all three sights.

While neither purple nor gold, the lush, untarnished Purple Gold Mountain (zǐjīn shān; 紫金山) east of the city contains Nanjing's most renowned sights.

MAUSOLEUM OF DR. SUN YAT-SEN (zhōngshān líng; 中山陵). This grandiose mausoleum has become something of a pilgrimage site for thousands of Chinese tourists every day. A plaque at the bottom of the 392-step memorial commemorates Sun Yat-sen's devotion to the revolutionary cause, and a small picture exhibit in the garden behind the mausoleum documents the building of the memorial (see **You Say You Want a Revolution,** p. 14). Inside the mausoleum is a life-sized marble statue of Sun lying in his coffin. After the arduous climb to the top—complete with a breathtaking view of Nanjing and its surrounding hills—most visitors will be convinced that the scale of this structure indeed does justice to Sun's memory. The Tourist Info Center offers simple English help, but no tours. *(☎444 8978. Open daily 6am-6:30pm. Y25.)*

LINGGU PARK (línggǔ gōngyuán; 灵谷公园). Built in 514 and moved to its present site by the Ming Emperor Zhu Yuanzhang, **Linggu Temple** (língǔ sì; 灵谷寺) makes up for its small size with intricacy and numerous Buddhist relics. The **Beamless Hall** (wú liáng diàn; 无梁殿), the only remainder of the original structure, is constructed entirely of stone and brick, its arched ceiling supported only by paste and architectural ingenuity. The hall contains a wax figure exhibit telling the history of Chinese revolution from the reign of the Qing emperor Kangxi to Liberation in 1949. Carved on the walls are the 33,224 names of soldiers who died between 1926 and 1933. The top of **Linggu Pagoda** (línggǔ tǎ; 灵谷塔) offers a bird's-eye view of the park. *(A 30min. walk or a 10min. ride east of Sun Yat-sen's Mausoleum. Park open daily 6:30am-6:30pm, temple 7am-5pm. Park Y10, temple Y2.)*

MING FILIAL TOMB (míng xiào líng; 明孝陵). This is the burial place of the first Ming emperor Zhu Yuanzhang, Empress Ma, and 46 sacrificed concubines. The **Sacred Avenue** (mínglíng shéndào; 明陵神道) leading to the tomb entrance is lined by 12 pairs of stone animals (horses, camels, and elephants), and a nearby stone tablet features an inscription by Qing Emperor Kangxi himself. West of the tomb, reached by the last stop on the sightseeing bus, a **cable car** (Y35) goes to the top of the mountain. *(4 stops from the mausoleum on the sightseeing bus. Near the observatory (tiānwéntái; 天文台). Open daily 6:30am-7pm. Y10.)*

OTHER SIGHTS

GULOU SQUARE (gǔlóu guǎngchǎng; 鼓楼广场). Once the heart of Nanjing, before the city center shifted to the Xinjiekou traffic circle, Gulou remains the more aesthetically pleasing of the two traffic circles. The **Drum Tower,** built in 1302, sits in the middle of a traffic island, west of the traffic circle. The drums were used to signal changes in the night watch; today, you can climb to the second level to view the drums and enjoy refreshments in the tranquil **Gulou Tea House.** A tea-and-snack combo costs around Y24. *(☎ 330 1101. Open daily 8am-midnight. Y4.)* Opposite the Drum Tower, on the other side of the traffic circle, **Gulou Park** (gǔlóu gōngyuán; 鼓楼公园) fills with families on balmy summer evenings. *(On Zhongshan Lu, 2km north of Xinjiekou. Accessible via buses #1, 16, 26, and 34. Free 6am-10pm.)*

CONFUCIAN TEMPLE (fúzǐ miào; 夫子庙). This ancient temple was built in AD 103 and houses a statue of Confucius and 8 disciples. Back in the day, Confucian scholars found inspiration here on the northern shores of the Qinhua River; now this area is home to street stalls selling everything from parakeets to cheap clothing. The market is liveliest in the early evening, when lantern-lovers, dinner-goers, and die-hard shoppers stroll along the brightly-lit banks of the river. *(From Xinjiekou, take bus #1 east to the last stop, directly opposite the main Fuzimiao gate. Temple (☎ 662 8639) is open 8am-9pm. Y12. Area around temple open daily dawn-10pm. Rent a boat and view the lit-up architecture from Qinghua River. Motor boats Y20 per 30min. 4-person bike boats Y10 per 30min. Take a 15min. spin on the larger boat for a narrated tour, Y10 per person.)*

RAINFLOWER TERRACE (yǔhuā tái; 雨花台). A famous memorial to revolutionaries killed by Chiang Kai-shek in 1927, these elegant gardens contain shaded pathways, rainflower pebble stands, and a stoic monument to the Revolutionary Martyrs. Standing in front of the memorial, many groups of 30-something's come for their initiation into the Communist Party. The mountain surrounding the memorial offers great views (such as the one from the Yuhua Pavilion). There is also a peacock zoo with over 15 fowls. *(Just beyond the Zhonghua Gate at the last stop on bus #16 from Gulou and Xinjiekou. Zhonghua Lu becomes Yuhua Lu as it leads to the entrance of the Rainflower Terrace. Open daily 6am-11pm. Y15. Memorial open 8am-6pm.)*

XUANWU LAKE PARK (xuánwǔhú gōngyuán; 玄武湖公园). This park features a zoo, playgrounds, and plenty of space to roam around. Five connected islands in the middle of a gorgeous lake make this a fabulous must-see sight. *(Take bus #1, 3, 15, or 35 to the Xuanwu Lake stop. Motorboats for up to 4 people, Y25 per hour. Parasailing Y60 per 5min. Enter the gate across the street from the train station and take a ferry or motorboat across the lake for Y5. Open daily 6am-8pm. Y10.)*

MEMORIAL TO THE VICTIMS OF THE NANJING MASSACRE (qìnhuá nánjīng dàtúshā yùnàn tóngbaō jìniànguǎn; 侵华南京大屠杀遇难同胞记念馆). The memorial sits on one of the former execution sights, a somber and austere reminder of the hundreds of thousands of Nanjing residents terrorized and killed by Japanese troops in December 1937. The memorial contains outdoor exhibits, a historical museum, and a building housing the remains of some victims. English audio tapes and documentary available. *(418 Shuiximen Dajie. Take bus #37 or 41 from Xinjiekou, 3 stops past Mochou Lake. ☎ 661 2230. Open daily 8am-5:30pm. Y10, students Y8.)*

ZHONGHUA GATE (zhōnghuá mén; 中华门). One of the best preserved pieces of the old Nanjing city wall, Zhonghua Gate consists of four large archways, each with a double door and a 1000kg gate that used to shut automatically, trapping retreating enemy soldiers within the city. It was built during the Yuan and Ming dynasties, between 1366-1386, and has been restored to its original condition. The observation platform at the top provides the closest thing there is to a bird's-eye view of Nanjing, with a pretty bonsai garden that's worth a peek. *(Bus #16 south along Zhonghua Lu to Zhonghua Men Nei (2nd to last stop). Open daily 8am-6pm. Y6.)*

Mochou Lake Park (mōchóuhú gōngyuán; 莫愁湖公园), in the triangle formed by Hanzhong Xi Lu, Shuximen Dajie, and Huju Lu (take bus #13), is named after a girl who sold herself to an abusive family in order to pay for her parents' burial; she then committed suicide. Despite this poignant story, Mochou is just another park with a lake, a carousel, and locals practicing *tai chi*. *(Open daily 6:30am-9pm. Y5.)*

Far from any of Nanjing's other tourist attractions is the **Yangzi River Bridge** (nánjīng chángjiāng dàqiáo gōngyuán; 南京长江大桥公园), off Daqiao Nan Lu. An elevator at the base of the bridge takes you to the top, where zooming cars and an expansive view of Nanjing awaits *(Take bus #12, 15, or 67 from Nanjing West Train Station. Open daily 7:30am-11:30pm. Y5.)*

NIGHTLIFE

Nanjing's sizable student population frequents a constantly changing nightclub and bar scene. New watering holes seem to open every few months, replacing those that have presumably lost their mojo. Because of this dizzying turnover rate, any news heard around the major universities is likely to be as reliable as the following listings. The area near the Nanjing University Foreign Students' Dormitory offers options for casual drinks and fun: croon to karaoke favorites, jump and jive to East-West hip-hop, or just do whatever your achy-breaky heart desires. Many Nanjing universities lock their gates at 11pm, so those clubs popular among students fill up by 9:30pm and suddenly empty at the stroke of 11. (But then the foreigners rush in, along with foreign DJs.)

If the time-conscious nightclub scene doesn't float your boat, try the movie theaters in the Fuzimiao area (Chinese and Cantonese movies, Y8 and up) or the ever-popular bowling alleys.

Blowing in the Wind (dáàn jiǔbā; 答案酒吧), 13 Jinyin Jie (☎323 2486), down the street from the Nanjing University Foreign Students' Dormitory. A roomy atmosphere, pictures of past shenanigans, and reasonable drink prices (Y10 and up) make this a lively hangout for students, foreigners, and jazz-lovers. The owner and his bass guitar player often join impromptu jam sessions; monthly performances feature local bands. Open daily 6pm-2am, musical performances nightly at 9:30pm.

Orgies Club, 202 Zhongshan Bei Lu (☎341 9991), next to Hongqiao Hotel. Mostly Chinese students ensures a list of Chinese and Cantonese songs. Larger dance floor than Scarlet's. A separate karaoke area and small snack area. Open daily 9pm-3am.

Scarlet (luànshì jiārén yīnyuè xīcāntīng jiǔbā; 乱世佳人音乐西餐厅酒吧), 29 Chezhan Dong Xiang (☎335 1916), off the northwest corner of Gulou, behind Gulou Department Store, has been the disco of choice for at least 3 years among both locals and foreign students. International DJ spins hip-hop after 1am. Drinks Y30 and up. Foreigners get in free. Open daily 6:30pm-4am.

Italian Pizza Express Restaurant & Bar (yìdàlì bǐsà cāntīng; 意大利比萨餐厅), 19 Jinyin Jie (☎323 1353). Popular with students looking for late-night snacks or weekend revelry, this dimly lit restaurant and upstairs bar feature communal tables and booths perfect for conversing, wining, and dining. Big screen TV. Drinks Y10 and up. Restaurant open daily 10:30am-midnight; bar open daily 8pm-5am.

HUAI'AN 淮安 ☎0517

North of Nanjing, the landscape sheds neat rows of industrial factories to reveal sprawling flatlands, and the Grand Canal winds its way past obscure little hamlets on its way to Huai'an. The canal, along with State Hwy. 205, squeezes through this grab bag of neighborhoods. Hidden behind a barren exterior is Huai'an's lively town center, where schoolchildren play hide-and-seek in the old city fort and carts piled high with *zhāicài* (a local lake-grown vegetable). Despite the town's somewhat mundane character, it boasts 5000 years of rich history and a long list of locals who grace the pages of China's history books, including Zhou Enlai, whose framed portrait can be bought at many a town shop. Less a city of sights than one of atmosphere, Huai'an is practical, not glamorous, and those who visit quickly learn to appreciate the present.

TRANSPORTATION

Trains: Huai'an Train Station (huáiān huǒchē zhàn; 淮安火车站) will have service to Huayin and other nearby towns, but is incomplete as of July 2001.

Buses: Huai'an Long-distance Bus Station (huáiān chángtú qìchē zhàn; 淮安长途汽车站), 1 Huancheng Lu (☎591 2027). Follow Huaijiang Gonglu south past Zhenhuailou Lu; the station's on the right. Buses go to: **Hangzhou** (2 per day 6am-noon); **Nanjing** (3-5hr.; 16 per day, last bus leaves at 3:45pm; Y24-41); **Shanghai** (3 per day 6:40am-4:30pm); **Suzhou** (every other day 6:50am), with unpredictable departures.

Local Transportation: Buses #61, 62, and 63 service the Huai'an area, but are few and far between, as they are dispatched from the faraway Huayin Bus Station. Fare Y1.

Taxis: Base fare Y5. Destinations within town cost Y5-10. Hard to find.

Pedicabs: Y3 maximum to get anywhere in town. Easy to find.

Bike Rental: Available from the Xiangyu Travel Development Company.

ORIENTATION AND PRACTICAL INFORMATION

Huai'an is small enough to navigate in half a day. Walking is a good bet, particularly because of the overwhelming number of bicycles, scooters, rickshaws, and carts crisscrossing each other. Huai'an is bounded on the east by the Grand Canal and on the west by **Huaijiang Gonglu** (淮江公路), which loops around the city. Parallel to Huaijiang Gonglu, **Beimen Dajie** (北门大街) runs north-south through the town center. Between these two main streets lies the **Zhou Enlai Memorial Hall,** one of the city's main tourist draws; perpendicular to both roads are **Youyi Lu** (友谊路) and **Zhenhuailou Lu** (镇淮楼路).

Travel Agency: Xiangyu Travel Development Company (xiángyǔ lǚyóu fāzhǎn gōngsī; 翔宇旅游发展公司), 92 Xichang Jie (☎593 3501; fax 591 1412). Walk east on Zhenhuailou Lu to Xichang Jie; the office is 2 blocks south, on the left side of the street. Take bus #62 two stops beyond the hospital. Few map and brochures, but staff can arrange car and bike rental. Open daily 8am-6:30pm.

Bank of China: 82 Zhenhuailou Dong Lu (☎591 3901). Walk west on Zhenhuailou Dong Lu from the Xichang Jie intersection; the huge glass high-rise on the left. Exchanges currency and traveler's checks. Credit card advances. Open M-F 8am-5pm.

Hospital: Huai'an Renmin Hospital (huáiān rēnmín yīyuàn; 淮安人民医院; ☎591 2233), just off Zhenhuailou Dong Lu. English-speaking staff. Open 24hr.

Post Office: Huai'an Post Office, 2 Zhenhuailou Dong Lu (☎593 3209). EMS and Poste Restante. Open daily 8:30am-6:30pm. In the same building as China Telecom, which offers IDD/DDD service. **Postal Code:** 223200.

ACCOMMODATIONS AND FOOD

The only hotel in Huai'an that accepts foreigners is **Huai'an Hotel ❹** (huáiān bīnguǎn; 淮安宾馆), 2 Youyi Lu, at Beimen Dajie, a five-minute walk from the city center. This two-star establishment suffers from four-star envy, with A/C, bath, and TV in all rooms. (☎591 3700. Reserve at least 1 day in advance. Deposit Y15. Singles Y320; doubles Y160.)

There are very few restaurants and street stalls in Huai'an; locals go to Xichang Jie's **Food Street** (měishí jiē; 美食街) for good food. Three delicacies are Huai'an's claim to fame: yellow eel (shànyú; 鳝鱼), local vegetables (zhāicài; 择菜), and Pingqiao tofu soup (píngqiáo dòufǔ; 平桥豆腐). *Chasan*, fried dough string, is also popular (Y3). **Jinguchun Restaurant ❸** (jīngǔchūn cāndiàn; 金谷春餐店), 10 Xichang Jie, just south of the travel agency, serves Huai'an specialties. Garish orange chairs and minimal decor don't do much to whet the appetite, but the food (Y25-50) certainly does. (☎592 9179. Open daily 8am until whenever guests leave.)

SIGHTS

FORMER RESIDENCE OF ZHOU ENLAI (zhōu ēnlái gùjū; 周恩来故居). Know Chairman Mao's right-hand man like you've never known him before: see the room where he was born on March 5, 1898, the room where he was nursed, and the room where he studied, not to mention the well he used, the herbs he planted, and the cherry tree he didn't cut down. Pictures of Zhou and some of his letters are housed in his old sitting room. *(7 Fuma Xiang, at the intersection of Beimen Dajie and Zhenhuailou Lu. ☎591 2517. Open daily 7am-6pm; in winter 7:45am-5:30pm. Y10.)*

ZHOU ENLAI MEMORIAL HALL (zhōu ēnlái jìniànguǎn; 周恩来纪念馆). Built in 1992, this temple-like structure overlooks a lake in the center of Huai'an. The memorial hall is a gentle respite from the crowded streets of the city. The museum of Premier Zhou's life and works highlights his achievements, with a few photos of his time in Huai'an. Behind the hall is an exact replica (built in 1998) of Zhou's former Beijing residence. *(On Huancheng Lu. ☎591 2365. Open daily 8am-6pm. Y15.)*

ZHENHUAI TOWER (zhènhuái lóu; 镇淮楼). This imposing grey structure is a remnant of Huai'an's city wall. Its interior is now a mini-museum on Huai'an history, with exhibits like a calligraphy collection, a soldier's corpse, and a display on Huai'an celebrities. *(At the end of Zhenhuailou Lu. Open daily 7am-7pm. Y5.)*

FORMER RESIDENCE OF WU CHENGEN (wúchéngēn gùjū; 吴承恩故居). The home of Wu Chengen (1500-1582), author of the *Journey to the West* series, houses original manuscripts and recent translations of his work (see **Literature: Ancient & Premodern,** p. 36). Wu's kitchen, study, and living quarters are open to the public. *(12 Datong Xiang, at Beimen Dajie. ☎580 2897. Open daily 7:30am-6pm. Y10.)*

SUZHOU 苏州 ☎0512

The once poetic beauty of Suzhou's canals and gardens is now a distant memory, faintly echoed by a few preserved buildings. Today's Suzhou is filled with not just noise, but also grime, pollution, and traffic. In recent years, a surge in industrial development has smothered the surrounding farmland, dirtied the canals, and crowded the city streets. Although Suzhou's famed canals are now garbage-strewn and many of the gardens that earned the city the name "Heaven on Earth" suffer from neglect or commercialization, with effort, one can still find evidence of Suzhou's more illustrious past in this outwardly uninspiring city.

One of China's oldest cities, Suzhou dates to 514 BC,when King Helu of Wu settled here, dug numerous canals, and built the private gardens that gave Suzhou the name "Venice of the East." But Suzhou really flourished about 2000 years later, when the construction of the Grand Canal enhanced the city's position on the trading route between Nanjing and Shanghai. Traders came to Suzhou for its storied silk production; by the 12th century, Suzhou's fabrics were among China's top exports. Meanwhile, the city nourished intellectual treasures of its own, luring scholars and artists from Shanghai and Hangzhou and gaining renown as a center of high culture. Although Suzhou can no longer boast of having the 280 private gardens it had in its heyday, the town still offers enough for the horticulturally inclined to go home happy.

TRANSPORTATION

Trains: Suzhou Train Station (sūzhōu huǒchē zhàn; 苏州火车站; ☎753 2831), on the north side of town, just west of Renmin Lu after the moat. To: **Beijing** (15-22hr., 2 per day, Y68-457); **Hangzhou** (4½-5hr., 12 per day, Y16-266); **Nanjing** (3½-4hr., Y13-49) via **Wuxi** (30min., Y3-14); **Shanghai** (30min.-1hr., Y5-24).

Buses: Ping Men Long-distance Bus Station (qìchē běi zhàn; 汽车北站; ☎753 0686), on the east side of the traffic circle at the head of Renmin Lu. City bus #101 shuttles here. Open daily 5am-6:30pm. To: **Hangzhou** (many per day, Y24-41); **Nanjing** (2½hr., many per day, Y46-64); **Shanghai** (1½hr., many per day, Y22-30); **Wuxi** (1hr., 11 per day, Y15-24); **Yangzhou** (5 per day, Y51). **South Gate Long-distance Bus Station** (nán mén qìchē zhàn; 南门汽车站; ☎520 4867) is on the east side of Renmin Lu, just before the southern part of the moat. Ticket office is the first building on your right as you walk down Renmin Lu. Open daily 5:30am-5pm. To: **Hangzhou** (12 per day, Y45); **Shanghai** (4 per day, Y20); **Yangzhou** (6 per day, Y51). **Wuxian Bus Terminal** is farther south on Renmin Lu, a 5min. walk past the moat, near where buses #14 and 313 terminate. City buses #102 and 103 shuttle here. Frequent minibuses leave unpredictably for **Dongshan, Xishan,** and other **Lake Taihu** spots.

Ferries: Suzhou Shipping Terminal (sūzhōu lúnchuán gōngsī; 苏州轮船公司), 8 Renmin Lu (☎520 6681), just south of the South Gate Bus Station, on the outer moat near the Renmin Lu bridge. Open daily 5:20am-5:30pm. A boat leaves daily for **Hangzhou** (14hr., 5:30pm, Y36-280); passengers must board 30min. prior to departure. The nighttime trip may not offer much in terms of river views, but it does feature on-board entertainment (read: alcohol and karaoke) for a fee.

Public Transportation: City **buses** run to the most popular sights. Most lines run 6am-8pm and have a flat fare of Y1. Exact change only. **#1** runs along Renmin Lu from the train station to Wuxian city; **#2** covers just about every major sight between Tiger Hill and Panmen Gate; **#4** starts in the southeast, just outside the moat and zigzags northwest, passing the Master of Nets Garden, the No. 1 People's Hospital, and the Twin Pagodas before terminating on Xizhong Shi; **#9** goes east-west on Ganjian Lu through the center of town. **Tourist bus #2** goes practically everywhere (Y1, with A/C Y2).

Taxis: Base fare Y10, each additional km Y1.8. A taxi from one of the Shiquan Jie hotels to the train station should cost Y15-20. Cycle **rickshaws** (base fare Y2; each additional km Y2), affectionately labeled "tourist pedicabs," can be found almost everywhere.

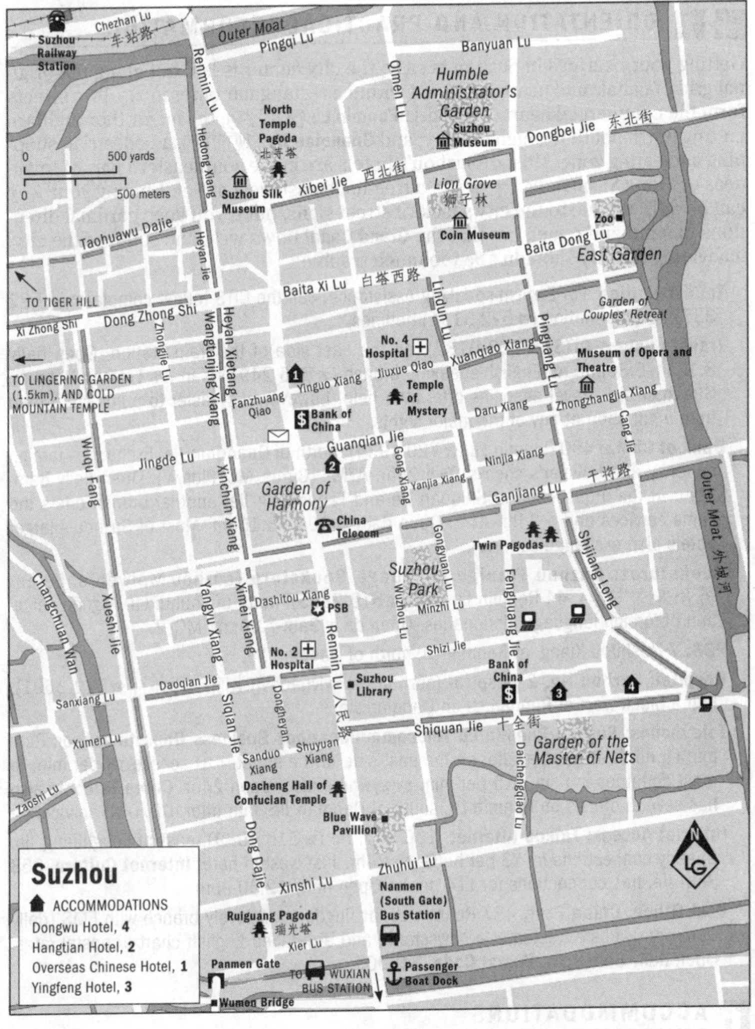

Bike Rental: Traveling by bicycle is a convenient and pleasant way to get from garden to garden to garden and can make Suzhou's polluted air and rank alleyways seem a little sweeter. Many bike rental places near the train station offer bikes of all sizes and conditions for Y2 per 3hr. or Y5 per day. Look for groups of bikes lined up on the stretch of Renmin Lu opposite the North Temple Park. **Yang Yang Bike Rental** offers the cleanest bikes in Suzhou (and friendly service, to boot). On Renmin Lu, a 5min. walk after the northern moat; or from the train station, the 1st stop on bus #102 or 103. Open daily 6am-7pm. Y5 per day with a *Let's Go* guide. Also several stands on Shiquan Jie near the Suzhou Hotel. Y15-30 per day, deposit Y200-300.

ORIENTATION AND PRACTICAL INFORMATION

Getting your bearings in Suzhou is easy; the city center is laid out along the original grid of canals and neatly confined within a rectangular outer moat. Two streets form the commercial heart of the city: **Renmin Lu** (人民路), the major thoroughfare cutting north-south through the city; and **Guanqian Jie** (观前街), a pedestrian shopping and eating zone. Most of Suzhou's hotels are in the southeastern part of town, near or along **Shiquan Jie** (十全街), a tree-lined east-west street. Finding your way can be difficult due to the city's lack of street signs, but if you keep cardinal directions in mind and remember that the **Grand Canal** flows west and south of the city, navigating the city shouldn't be too much trouble.

Tourist Hotline: For English-speaking assistance, call the CITS tourist complaint (☎522 3377) or information (☎522 3131) hotlines.

Travel Agency: CITS (☎753 0782), on the east side of the train station. Open daily 8:15am-5:30pm. An English-speaking branch (☎515 2401) is in the Lexiang Hotel on Guanqian Jie. Travel agencies offer little help, however; it's easier to purchase a map from a gift shop at any of the major sights.

Bank of China: 490 Renmin Lu (☎720 1934), north of Guanqian Jie. Exchanges foreign currency and traveler's checks. Two 24hr. **ATM**s (Cirrus/MC/Plus/V). Open daily 8am-5pm. At the intersection of Shiquan Jie and Fenghuang Jie, another branch offers the same services and a 24hr. **ATM.** Open daily 8:30am-5:10pm. Most of Suzhou's larger hotels also exchange currency.

Bookstores: Suzhou Foreign Language Bookstore (sūzhōu wàiwén shūdiàn; 苏州外文书店), 44 Renmin Lu (☎/fax 519 7355), north of Zhuhui Lu. A good selection of foreign language dictionaries. Open daily 9am-7:30pm. MC/V.

PSB: 7 Dashitou Xiang, at Renmin Lu, north of Daoqian Jie.

Hospital: Suzhou No. 2 Hospital (sūzhōu dièr yīyuàn; 苏州第二医院; ☎522 3691), half a block west of Renmin Lu on Daoqian Jie.

Telephones: Suzhou Renmin Lu Telecommunications Business Department, on Renmin Lu north of Daoqian Jie, on the east side of the street. IDD service Y8 per min. to most countries in Asia, Y15 per min. everywhere else. Open 24hr. **China Telecom** also has several offices on Renmin Lu, south of Daoqian Jie, that offer IDD/DDD service.

Internet Access: Taikoo Internet, 186 Shizi Jie (☎515 1989), east of Fenghuang Jie. Speedy connections for Y3 per hr. Open 24hr. Just west of here, **Internet Culture,** 358 Shizi Jie, has connections for Y14 per hr. Open daily 12:30-9pm.

Post Office: China Post, 487 Renmin Lu, at Jingde Lu. A lovely branch with EMS (daily 9am-5pm), Poste Restante, a newsstand, and a detailed English chart of postal rates. Open daily 8am-8pm. **Postal Code:** 215005.

ACCOMMODATIONS

Suzhou is as proud of its hotels as its gardens. Inexpensive options are scarce, but the east end of **Shiquan Jie** has something for everyone. Discounts will probably be offered even if you don't ask, but you might get larger ones if you do. The stretch of Renmin Lu between Baita Lu and Shiquan Jie offers clean and reputable, but somewhat noisy, lodgings.

Dongwu Hotel (dōngwù fàndiàn; 东吴饭店), 24 Wuheng Chang (☎519 3681), near the bridge, at the eastern end of Shiquan Jie. Rooms in this student residence are by far Suzhou's best bargain, with A/C, TVs, and clean Western-style common baths (in building #5). Beware the 11pm lockout in building #7; speak to reception if you're coming back (or going out) late. Room deposit equal to price of stay; key deposit Y50. With half the hotel's dorms set aside for long-term foreign students, travelers should reserve well in advance. Singles and doubles Y80-100, with bath Y180-280; triples Y360. ❷

Yingfeng Hotel (yíngfēng fàndiàn; 迎枫饭店), 39 Huyang Chang (☎530 0907), just off Shiquan Jie. Cross the small bridge across from the Suzhou Hotel and look for the large rooftop sign. Take the 2nd right after the canal; go through the courtyard on your left. Unremarkable rooms with A/C, bath, and TV. Doubles Y320. 50% discount available. ❹

Overseas Chinese Hotel (huáqiáo dàjiǔdiàn; 华桥大酒店), 518 Renmin Lu (☎720 2883), at Yinguo Lu, a block north of the Bank of China. It might not offer easy access to the beauty salons and souvenir shops of Shiquan Jie, but this hotel does have a friendly, helpful staff, clean rooms in good condition, and frequent discounts. Singles Y120; doubles Y180; triples Y230. ❷

Hangtian Dasha (hángtiān dàshà; 航天大厦), 1 Jiushenggang (☎522 1342; fax 521 8629). In the heart of Suzhou's pedestrian shopping zone; entrance on the little pedestrian street off Renmin Lu, south of Guanqian Jie. Standard hotel fare (A/C, bath, phone). Doubles Y180-252. Off-season discounts available. ❸

FOOD

Many visitors stick to their hotels for easy dining after long days of sightseeing. Like all Chinese cities of comparable size, Suzhou also has food streets, most notably **Tai Jian Fang** and **Jia Yu Fang,** two blocks of neon-illuminated excess north of the Garden of Harmony. The family-owned restaurants along Shiquan Jie serve heaping plates of dumplings and noodles. Across the canal on Fengmen Jie, restaurants offer long, exotic Chinese menus. The Western alphabet reasserts itself with an overabundance of KFC restaurants that seems to outnumber Suzhou's gardens. Suzhou is well known for its exquisite seafood dishes, rice pastries, tofu (both the tender silky kind and the soggy stinky kind), and a fuzzy red fruit called *yángmēi* (杨梅). Purchase this berry-like treat from basket-wielding farmers on the street. Ingesting the pit supposedly cleans your stomach of any hairballs you may have swallowed.

Yang Yang Dumpling House (yángyáng jiǎoziguǎn; 洋洋饺子馆), 144 Shiquan Jie (☎519 2728), across from the Suzhou Hotel. This hole-in-the-wall is a 2-floor haven of cheap gourmet cooking. The owners brought the secret of *jiǎozi* from northern China and serve up tender and delicious dumplings (Y5 per dozen) and southern staples like sweet and sour pork (Y18). Try the homemade hot pepper sauce. Open daily 5am-2am. ❶

Yong He Soya Bean Milk (yǒnghé dòujiāng; 永和豆浆), 191 Shiquan Jie (☎510 5918), next to the entrance to the Master of Nets Garden. A friendly and convenient pit stop with a multi-page English menu. Wonton soup (Y5), "intestines in fire pot" (Y35), jellyfish salad (Y18); the crispy fried dough sticks (yóutiáo; 油条) are perfect for dunking into some piping hot sweet soy milk (Y3). Open 24hr. ❷

Chenshifu Fried Rice (chénshīfù chǎofàn; 陈师傅炒饭; ☎522 8047; www.chinabelly.com), on the corner of Renmin Lu and a small alley a block south of Daoqian Jie Bridge, across from the Suzhou Public Library; look for the string of yellow lanterns outside. A local favorite. Savor the best egg fried rice of your life (Y4-6) inside this whimsically recreated garden restaurant. ❶

Suzhou Songhelou Restaurant (sōnghèlóu càifàn; 松鹤楼菜饭), 141 Guanqian Jie (☎727 7006), 1 block east of Renmin Lu. The preferred dining establishment for emperors and tourists alike, this is Suzhou's most famous restaurant, serving up expensive, banquet-style treats, including its 100-year-old recipe for *gulyú* (桂鱼). Open daily 5:30am-1:30pm and 2-8pm.

SIGHTS

In Suzhou, ponds become seas and rocks become mountains, living harmoniously alongside classical Chinese architecture. A garden in Suzhou is not just a pleasant expanse of ponds and greenery; often, the grounds contain subtle allusions to art or literature, and are referred to as "silent poems" or "three-dimensional paintings." To understand these verdant treasures is also to understand Daoism, Buddhism, Confucianism, and classical Chinese notions of art and beauty; they exist not only to please the eye, but also to stimulate the mind. Of course, knowledge of Chinese language and culture isn't necessary to enjoy the serenity of the gardens.

To see only one of Suzhou's gardens would be a waste; many of the 70 or so formal gardens are worth a visit. Arrive early in the morning or late in the day to beat the crowds; if possible, tag along with a tour group and pick up brochures to enjoy the entertaining anecdotes that accompany the garden's particular features.

If you're short on time, a **pedicab tour** (Y50) leaves each morning from the Nanlin Hotel. A better option is to rent a bicycle, which gives you some flexibility throughout your trip—see as many (or as few) gardens as you find interesting. Take a breather from the bewildering number of sights by stopping at one of the town's museums or use your cycling savvy to escape the crowds.

Suzhou's **antique market** features various stalls selling old jade and ceramic, as well as ubiquitous **Mao buttons.** *(On Renmin Lu, opposite the Pavilion of Surging Waves, the old temple with peach-colored walls. Open daily 9am-5pm.)*

NORTH SUZHOU

LION GROVE (shīzi lín; 狮子林). Representative of Yuan dynasty architecture, this "kingdom of rockery" was built by the monk Tianru in memory of his teacher, Zhong Feng, who lived in Lion Crag in Zhejiang province. You can easily get lost in this labyrinth of scraggly rocks pulled out of Lake Taihu; the Qing emperor Qianlong reportedly spent two hours trying to find his way out. Lion Grove is a great place to escape the tour groups, since most guides are unwilling to scale these jagged steps. Some of the rock formations are said to look like lions; others only look like lion parts. Many of the garden's buildings also contain paintings and etchings by famous calligraphers. *(About 250m south of the Suzhou Museum. Open daily 7:30am-5:30pm; last admission 5pm. Y10.)*

HUMBLE ADMINISTRATOR'S GARDEN (zhuózhèng yuán; 拙政园). Despite the name, this sprawling garden is one of Suzhou's largest and most famous. The garden was built by Wang Xianchen, a corrupt Ming dynasty official. After being cast out of his job, Wang sought solace in governing nature. "Building houses, planting trees, watering gardens, and growing vegetables," he wrote, "are a way for a humble man to manage administrative affairs." Three-fifths of the garden are covered by water, and the lush foliage overshadows the architecture. Lily-lovers will adore the overflowing lily ponds and annual lily show (June-Aug.) featuring some 70 varieties from around the world. *(On Dongbei Jie, 1km east of the North Temple. Free tours in Chinese every 30min. Open daily 7:30am-5:30pm; last admission 5pm. Y32.)*

NORTH TEMPLE PAGODA (běi sì tǎ; 北寺塔). Supposedly Suzhou's first pagoda (the original main temple was built in AD 238-251), this 76m structure is the tallest pagoda south of the Yangzi. Climb up to the seventh floor or pay an extra Y1 to go to the eighth; the kids at the top might let you use their telescopes. The top offers a fantastic 360° view of Suzhou and the green rice paddies sprawling practically all the way to Shanghai. A small garden is north of the temple, and a tea house hosts occasional amateur musical performances. *(On the corner of Renmin Lu and Xibei Jie, take buses #1, 2, 101, 103—just about anything going to the train station—and get off at Beisita. Open daily 7:30am-6pm; last admission 5:30pm. Y10; seventh floor Y5.)*

SUZHOU SILK MUSEUM (sūzhōu sīchóu bówùguǎn; 苏州丝绸博物馆). Not your average stuffy picture gallery, this museum provides an enlightening, if somewhat esoteric, introduction to the fruit of the loom. Suzhou is still one of China's primary silk producers; the museum, which claims to be the only silk-centric museum in the world, uses well-presented exhibits (with English captions) to spin the tale of Suzhou's silk trade, from the Neolithic Age through the Tang and Song dynasties (AD 618-1279), right up to today. Check out the "weaving room," where you can try out one of the looms yourself, and the "Sericulture House," where you can witness silkworms hard at work. *(661 Renmin Lu. Across the street from the North Temple Pagoda and about a half-block north. Open daily 8am-5:30pm. Y7.)*

OTHER SIGHTS. East of the Lion Grove, the now-privatized **Garden of Couple's Retreat** (ǒu yuán; 偶园) is more than just a lover's lair, with gondola rides, local story-telling, and folk music. Built by a provincial governor who wanted a place to sit with his wife, today the garden is pleasantly free of tourist mayhem. *(Open daily 8am-5pm; last admission 4:30pm. Y25 for ride and story-telling.)* The **East Garden** (dōng yuán; 东园) and **Suzhou Zoo** (sūzhōu dòngwùyuán; 苏州动物园) can be found at the end of Baita Dong Lu, near the Outer Moat. The large zoo offers visitors the chance to throw food or garbage at sad-looking animals in tiny cages—or, rather, to look on in horror as Chinese tourists do so. Grimy boats are available (Y10-15 per hr.), a sure treat for those who want to examine the dank pond in closer detail. *(Open daily 6am-5pm. Y5.)* Another interesting sight is the **Garden of Halves** (bàn yuán; 半园), in which half of everything, from the pavilion to the bridge, is missing. The owner designed the garden following in the ancient Chinese saying, "it is better to be satisfied and not seek perfection." *(60 Baita Dong Lu. Open daily 8am-5pm. Y3.)*

CENTRAL SUZHOU

GARDEN OF JOY (qià yuán; 恰园). This was once the private residence of the Qing bureaucrat Gu Wenbin and was built using stylistic elements from other gardens in the area. There are caves from Lion Grove (see above), a stone boat like the one in the Humble Administrator's Garden (see above), and so on. The plum groves make for a relaxing stop if you're in the area to send mail or change money. *(On Renmin Lu just south of Jiayu Fang. Open daily 7:30am-5:30pm; last admission 5pm. Y4.)*

TWIN PAGODAS PARK (shuāngtǎ yuàn; 双塔院). Part of the Arhat Temple complex, the Twin Pagodas are all that's left of a Buddhist temple built by three brothers in AD 1410. The site was ransacked in the early-20th century, but the pagodas were restored in 1954. The current garden is designed around the ruins of the former "Great Hall." Step back to the left from the sculpted stelae to find two large tea houses that serve tea and morning refreshments. *(Half a block east of Fenghuang Jie, just south of Ganjiang Dong Lu. Open daily 7:30am-5:30pm. Y4.)*

SOUTH SUZHOU

GARDEN OF THE MASTER OF NETS (wǎng shī yuán; 网师园). During the 12th century, Shi Zhengzhi (better known as the "Fishing Hermit") owned the **Hall of Ten Thousand Volumes.** About 200 years ago, a retired bureaucrat built the garden in its current form, declaring it his "Fisherman's Retreat." The Garden of the Master of Nets certainly knows how to net a lot—beautiful houses, a tranquil pond, a stone mountain, chambers for musical performances, Suzhou's tiniest stone bridge, even a large boulder that emits a ringing sound when struck—into a small space. Visit during the day and again at night, when the haunting melodies of Chinese folk music waft through the garden (see **Entertainment and Nightlife,** p. 357). *(On Shiquan Jie, near Fengshuang Jie. Enter through alleys off either street; follow the English signs. ☎520 3514. Open daily 8am-4:30pm. Y10. Free to "babes in arms.")*

PAN GATE SCENIC AREA (pán mén jǐng qū; 盘门景区). This area has recently been renovated. Climb to the fifth floor of **Ruiguang Pagoda** (ruìguāng tǎ; 瑞光塔) for Y6. At the far corner, the **Tower of City Gates** displays (with accurate English narration) the portcullises, cannons, stone walls, and "murder holes" used to fend off attackers. The semi-circular (and oft-photographed) **Wumen Bridge** (wǔmén qiáo; 午门桥) is on the southern edge of the park. *(At the far southwest corner of the old city. Enter from outside the moat to the south or from just east of the massive Sheraton Hotel on Zhuhui Lu. Open daily 8am-5pm; last admission 4:30pm. Y15, children under 1.2m Y8.)*

SURGING WAVE PAVILION (cāng làng tíng; 沧浪亭). This is Suzhou's oldest garden, built over 1000 years ago. The pavilion is bigger and more naturalistic and woodsy than others, but not as tidily kept; essentially, the facade is more impressive than what's inside. Notable features include the **Temple of 500 Sages,** which showcases prominent figures in Suzhou's history, and the **Green and Delicate Hall,** which is surrounded by several varieties of thick bamboo. *(East of Pan Gate, off the east side of Renmin Lu south of Shiquan Jie. Open daily 8am-5pm; last admission 4:30pm. Y8.)*

BEYOND THE OUTER MOAT

TIGER HILL (hǔqiū gōngyuán; 虎丘公园). Song poet Su Shi once declared, "To visit Suzhou without seeing Tiger Hill will be a cause for regret." While not *quite* all that, the 20-acre park still merits a visit. The area's name derives from a legend surrounding Suzhou's founder, Helu of Wu, who was buried here in 550 BC: three days after the burial, a white tiger was seen crouching by the tomb. Since then, the temple was supposedly destroyed seven times and is the setting for an unbelievable number of strange and sordid tales.

The 48m pagoda that rises—and tilts precariously—from atop the hill is surrounded by rocks, springs, and gardens. The most visible natural features are the **Sword-testing Rock,** with a huge cleft said to come from King Helu's swords, and **Sword Pond,** the alleged site of Helu's tomb. The morbid **Thousand Man Rock** is also nearby. When it rains, the rock is covered in red streaks—supposedly the blood of the 1000 workers King Helu killed in order to preserve the secrets of his tomb.

The **Giant Buddha Temple** also rests atop the hill. The truly devout are supposed to kneel and bow on each of the 53 steps leading up to the Buddha. The less devout can hire some old ladies to carry them from the entrance to the hilltop in a bright red marriage palanquin (Y20) or opt for a horse-drawn carriage (Y5). *(By bicycle, take Xizhong Shi Lu west from the city and turn right after the moat; then turn left on Shantang Jie, which follows a cobbled path directly to Tiger Hill. If you stop at the Lingering Garden, head west from the garden, and then take Huqiu Lu, the first major right off Liuyuan Lu. After about 3 blocks, bear left, and then cruise right up to Tiger Hill on the tree-lined road. Bus #2 and 5 from the train station stop outside. Open daily 7:30am-5:30pm; last admission 5pm. Y20. Chinese and English audio guides Y5 with Y50 deposit.)*

LINGERING GARDEN (liú yuán; 留园). This 400-year-old garden attracts hordes of tourists and their megaphone-wielding guides en route to Tiger Hill. Most of the garden's three hectares were destroyed during the 1949 Japanese occupation, but since then, refurbishment has restored much of its original beauty. Known for the fabulous Qing dynasty architecture at its eastern entrance, the Lingering Garden also displays peaceful water and rock arrangements, shady retreats, and a beautiful bonsai collection. *(1km west of the city's outer moat. Follow Xizhong Shi Lu west until it turns into Fengqiao Lu; turn right on Guangli Lu, and then immediately left onto Liuyuan Jie. Open daily 7:30am-5:30pm; last admission 5pm. Y16.)*

COLD MOUNTAIN TEMPLE (hánshān sì; 寒山寺). 1300 years ago, Tang poet Zhang Ji immortalized this temple in verse: "The moon is down, the raven calls, the cold frost fills the sky. Off Maple Bridge, with sleepless eyes I watch the fishing light. From far Cold Mountain near Gusu Town (Suzhou) as midnight passes by. The chiming of a temple bell comes to my boat tonight." Visitors can view the Maple Bridge (rebuilt), the bell (the Ming-era original is in Japan, but the replacement is also "Made in Japan"), and calligraphic inscriptions of the poem. Built in the 6th century, the temple is named after a Tang Buddhist monk poet known as Hanshan (Cold Mountain). Whatever hermetic asceticism is connoted in the name is drowned out by the throngs of incense-burning Chinese tourists who come to visit the famous temple from the poem they know by heart. Although the **Maple Bridge Garden** is small and quite unremarkable, it provides a welcome respite from the strangely insistent street vendors outside. *(About 8km from Suzhou. Baita Xi Lu becomes Fengqiao Lu west of the Outer Moat; Cold Mountain Temple is next to the canal. Open daily 7:30am-5pm; last admission 4:50pm. Temple Y6; tower Y5; ring the temple bell Y5; Maple Bridge Garden Y5; Maple Bridge Y2.)*

ENTERTAINMENT AND NIGHTLIFE

Suzhou may be ruled by tourists during the day, but it's dominated by party-going and merry making natives at night. Suzhou's summer evenings are its finest hour.

By far the best evening entertainment is the nightly **cultural performance** inside the **Garden of the Master of Nets** (see p. 355), on Shiquan Jie. The multi-part concert provides a great chance to see one of Suzhou's architectural masterpieces as it shimmers in the evening light. Busloads of foreign and Chinese tourists are moved through this cultural assembly line every night from opera to flute to lute. Just tag along with whichever group tickles your fancy. (May-Oct. nightly 7:30-10pm, Y60.)

The **Pulp Fiction Bar,** 169 Shiquan Jie (☎520 8067), is the only lively bar on this street, if not in all of Suzhou. Norm, the Australian owner, plies his patrons with plenty of beer (Y25 and up) and good music. The first floor of this intimate and friendly establishment plays a mix of oldies and classic rock, while the second floor features darts, a pool table, and TV lounge area. (Happy Hour 7-9pm.)

Night spots on **Shiquan Jie** charge high prices, so few are full enough to be lively. Some places get busy at night, but in an entirely different way: if you see a photo of a couple in a sumptuously decorated bedroom displayed next to the door of a "bar," be wary. You may be flattered to be chatted up by friendly, attractive women, but buy them drinks and you'll be paying for more than you expected.

DAYTRIPS FROM SUZHOU

DONGSHAN AND XISHAN

About 40km southwest of Suzhou. Getting there is simple, but finding reasonably priced transportation once there can be a hassle. Catch a ***minibus*** *from the train station (where bus #20 also leaves for the area) or from the Wuxian bus station (where buses depart to both Dongshan and Xishan). The buses should have their destinations in Chinese characters on the front ("东山" and "西山"), cost Y7, leave when full, and operate during daylight hours. Make your trip more convenient by taking a bike on board (Y5 extra). A warning: the roads on Dongshan are often steep, rocky, and not particularly well suited to* *low-quality rental bikes. Having a bike also means you'll have to travel exclusively by land; the* ***motorboats*** *that cross the lake are usually too small to carry bicycles.*

The **Dongshan** (东山) peninsula stretches out into Lake Taihu; the island of **Xishan** (西山; also known as Xidongtingshan) sits not far off the coast. Far from the fume-belching industry of the city, these areas are home to fishermen, fruit farmers, fragrant countryside, and not a whole lot else—making them a worthwhile destination for tourists who are sick of Suzhou's gardens.

Once in Dongshan, you'll be dropped near an intersection in the town proper. Head left at the intersection; the road will take you around the hill past **Purple Gold Nunnery** (zǐjīn ān; 紫金庵). The beautiful nunnery is enshrouded in bamboos, pines, and wildflowers, and contains a shrine with colored statues that are widely held to be ancient masterpieces. *(Open daily 8am-5pm; last admission 4:30pm. Y12.)* If you head right at the intersection, the road passes a small boat dock that rents **motorboats** to Xishan (30min., Y80), before coming to the Dongshan Hotel.

Whichever direction you choose, it's about 10km around the massive hill to the ferry dock to **Xishan;** taxis from Dongshan cost Y20-30. If the two daily scheduled ferries aren't running, it may be possible to hire a motorboat on the spot. Drivers will try to charge shamelessly high rates, offering to stop at various spots along the way. If you don't speak Chinese, be sure to indicate your desired destination on a map. Turn on the charm, though, and you might be able to jump onto one of the transport junks for the ride across.

Once on Xishan, make your way toward the large hill with the tower on top. The **Linwu Caves** provide relief from the summer heat, but the steps are slick and treacherous. From here, it's a short hike uphill to the **Jiatu Tower.** Climb past the souvenir and tea shops to find spectacular views of the surrounding countryside and plum trees. *(Open daily 8am-4:30pm; last admission 4pm. Y18, higher during the annual Plum Blossom Festival.)* Minibuses to the main street in Donghe, Xishan's largest town, leave from the parking lot next to the tower. Buses back to Suzhou leave from a stop across the street, from the Bank of China in Donghe.

TONGLI

About 25km southeast of Suzhou. Take a bus from Wuxian St., and ask for Tongli (frequent departures, Y5). Get off across the street from the stone gate entrance that leads to the pedestrian village. Although there's an official tourist fee for entering the scenic part of town, no one seems to collect it. The ***Tourist Service Center*** *(☎800 828 2990), near the entrance to Tuisi Garden, can book a Y50 tour that includes a guide and admission to sites. Open daily 8am-5:30pm and 7-9pm. Gondolas (Y60 per 8 people) offer 30min. tours of Tongli. Zhouzhuang, Tongli's more celebrated neighbor, is accessible by motor boat (seats 6 people; Y180 one-way for entire boat, Y250 round-trip). Overall, Tongli is better seen on land. To return, catch any bus that says Suzhou (苏州) that departs from the stone gate or take a minibus (Y6).*

If you've ever peeked at Chinese postcards of little bridges over water, most likely they're pictures of Tongli (同里) and its watery, more crowded neighbor Zhouzhuang (周庄), which, along with Suzhou, comprise the unofficial Venice of the East. Tongli is a lovely retreat, with a scenic tourist area compact enough to be seen in one hour. Although the outer edges of Tongli are not as well-kept, they offer an escape from noisy tour groups. Tongli is most famous for three bridges, **Taiping Bridge** (tàipīngqiáo; 太平桥), **Jili Bridge** (jíliqiáo; 吉利桥), and **Changqing Bridge** (chángqìngqiáo; 长庆桥), which represent peace, luck, and lasting celebration, respectively. Crossing them all in a row (guòsānqiáo; 过三桥) is good luck; elderly Tongli locals partake in this tradition on their 66th birthdays. Another worthy sight is the famous **Tuisi Garden** (tùisīyuán; 退思园), built to facilitate enlightening personal contemplation. Throughout Tongli you can snack on delicious flat flaky cakes and pastries, both salty and sweet. Roasted pigs are just as good.

WUXI 无锡 ☎0510

Many consider Wuxi to be an industrial wart on the beautifully scenic visage of Lake Taihu, one of China's largest freshwater lakes and domestic tourist draws. But just because there's little to do in Wuxi doesn't mean that there's little to love. It's true that Wuxi has never been a center of culture or innovation; early on, the city's glory lay in its tin deposits, but by the time the Han dynasty rolled around, the mines had been stripped, earning the town the name Wuxi, or "without tin." Since then, the city has functioned mainly as a trade and transportation center, and one of the town's most important purposes is to offer quick, easy access to Lake Taihu, which lies below a misty haze just a few kilometers away. Wuxi's lazy, resort town-feel is intensified by the wide, tree-lined avenues and verdant surroundings. Recently, Wuxi has begun to flourish economically, with China's film industry looking to its scenic shores as the backdrops for their newest movies about the ancient feats of warriors and kung fu masters; movie sets come and go, and are popular attractions until they leave.

TRANSPORTATION

Flights: Wuxi Airport (wúxī jīchǎng; 无锡机场), about 25km outside the city, is accessible only by taxi (approx. Y50) and serves a very limited number of destinations. Book tickets at CTS for **Beijing** (3 per week, Y680) and **Fuzhou** (4 per week, Y450), or contact **China Airlines** (☎580 5980).

Trains: Wuxi Train Station (wúxī huǒchē zhàn; 无锡火车站; ☎230 1857), at Tonghui Dong Lu and Wuhu Lu. Open daily 6am-9:45pm. **Luggage storage** to the left of the exit (Y2-4 per day, depending on size; open 6am-midnight). Foreigners can purchase tickets at window #2, but nobody here speaks English. Many trains per day to: **Nanjing** (2-3hr., Y10-39); **Shanghai** (1-2hr., Y36); **Suzhou** (30min., Y3-14); **Zhenjiang** (2hr., Y7-27).

Buses: Wuxi Main Bus Station (wúxī qìchē zhàn; 无锡汽车站; ☎230 1633), just west of the train station. The ticket office is on the east side of the station. Open daily 5am-10:30pm. The kiosk in the square in front of the train station also sells tickets. To: **Nanjing** (2hr., every 10-15min. 5:50am-6:30pm, Y37-52); **Shanghai** (1½-2hr., every 20-30min. 6:30am-6:30pm, Y37-43); **Suzhou** (1hr., every 10-20min. 6:50am-5:50pm, Y15); **Zhenjiang** (1½hr., every 30min.-1hr. 7:20am-5:30pm, Y16). Buses from the **West Bus Station** (qìchē xī zhàn; 汽车西站; ☎580 2297), on Hubin Lu across the Liangxi Bridge, only depart for destinations in Yixing county and Anhui province.

Ferries: Boats run to **Hangzhou** (13hr., several per day, Y24-294) from the dock southwest of Liangxi Bridge (☎586 5950).

Local Transportation: Buses in Wuxi are easy to use. Many lines terminate just west of the train station and most run 6am-6pm. A/C buses display "空调" (kōngtiáo) in front. Exact change only. Fare Y1, with A/C Y2. Bus **#1** runs across Baojie Bridge to Turtle Head Island; **#4** cuts through town and heads to Liangxi Bridge, near the South Bus Station; **#11** runs into the city from the train station; **#20** links the North and South Bus Stations; **#88** goes to the giant Buddha in Lingshan; **#820** shuttles around Lake Taihu tourist spots. **Motorized pedicabs** are everywhere; agree on a price in advance.

Taxis: Y8 for the first 2km, each additional km Y1.4-1.8. From the train or either bus stations to the city center Y10-15. Larger taxis Y10 base fare; prices indicated on window.

Bike Rental: A few shops are around the train station, but none have English signs.

ORIENTATION AND PRACTICAL INFORMATION

The **Grand Canal** meanders along the west side of Wuxi and several smaller canals run through the city. Across the canal, farther west, is the **Xihui Park** area, visible from much of the city. **Jiefang Lu** (解放路) circles the downtown area; **Zhongshan Lu** (中山路) crosses the city north-south and **Renmin Lu** (人民路) crosses east-west. Their intersection is the commercial (and culinary) center of the city. All the tourist sights are to the west of the city center. Trains (and most buses) arrive in the northern end of town, across the **Gongyun Bridge** (工运桥) and just a few blocks from Jiefang Bei Lu. The **Liangxi Bridge** (liángxī qiáo; 梁溪桥) connects the area near the South Bus Station to the city proper. English maps are found at major hotels like the Sheraton on Xianqian Jie and Zhongshan Lu. Act important and the concierge might be fooled into giving you one for free.

Travel Agencies: IATA, 88 Chezhan Lu, 1st and 4th fl. (☎230 0888, ext. 1725), across from the train station, next to the CTS Hotel. Look for the large "Wuxi Tourist Guide Center" sign. Booking services and an **automated information kiosk** with all sorts of practical info (and tourist propaganda) in English on the 1st fl. Open daily 7:30am-8:30pm. **CITS** (☎230 0781) is on the east side of the train station, near the soft seat waiting room. English-speaking staff. Open daily 7:40am-8pm. The main office is at 8 Zhongshan Lu (☎270 5369), at the terminus of bus #12. Open daily 7:30am-5:30pm.

Tourist Complaint: ☎16081. 24hr.

Bank of China: 258 Zhongshan Lu (☎270 5888), just south of Renmin Lu, in a sparkling new building. Exchanges currency and traveler's checks. 24hr. **ATM** to the left of the building. Open daily 7:45am-5pm.

Telephones: China Telecom, on Renmin Lu, down the street from the post office. 24hr. IDD service at window #1. Otherwise, open daily 8am-6pm.

Internet Access: The **Elite Information Technology Co.,** 196 Huaihe Lu (☎581 0417), across from the Light Industrial University Foreign Experts Hotel, is super-friendly and has super-friendly prices to match. Y2 per hr. Open 24hr.

Post Office: China Post, 226 Renmin Lu (☎272 9229), about 2 blocks east of Jiefang Lu. EMS at windows #3-8. Open daily 7:30am-6:30pm. **Postal Code:** 214001.

ACCOMMODATIONS

In the past few years, Wuxi has built several soaring hotels in the heart of the downtown area. It's hard to find good budget options; however, since supply exceeds demand, it's not too difficult to find great rooms at a good discounted price. Staff members in Wuxi hotels often speak English (those at the Sheraton are superb), a welcome relief in a city that has nearly no English speakers.

Wuxi Light Industrial University Foreign Students Hotel (wúxī qīnggōng dàxué zhuānjiā liúxuéshēng lóu; 无锡轻工大学专家留学生楼), 170 Huihe Lu (☎586 1034), across the moat and down the road from Xihui Park. Take bus #2 from the train station to Qingshan Wan (5th stop); the hotel is a half-block up the street, on the left. Far from the city, but closer to the lake. Standard rooms are small and minimal, but are the best budget options around. Super-cheap meals nearby. No A/C in 1st fl. dorms. Breakfast included. Singles Y60-100 and doubles Y110-120. ❶

China Hotel (zhōngguó fàndiàn; 中国饭店), 90 Hanchang Lu (☎230 8341), across the bridge from the train station, about 3 blocks down on the left. A/C. Singles Y58-70; doubles Y58-70, with bath Y180; triples Y90. ❶

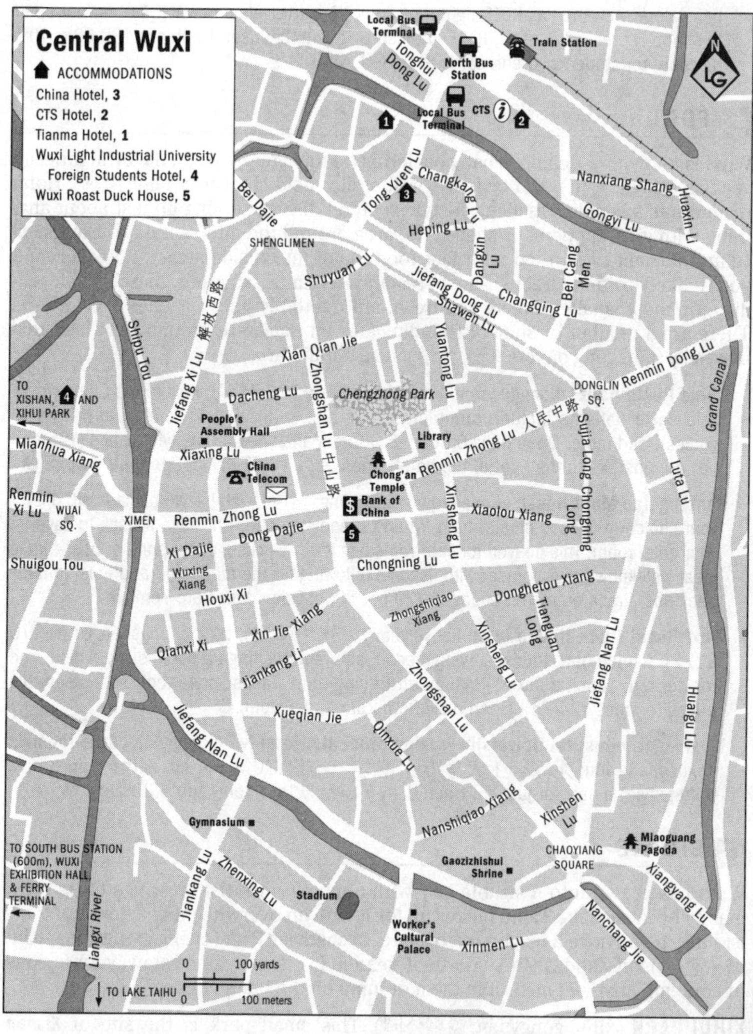

Tianma Hotel (tiānmǎ dàjiǔdiàn; 天马大酒店), 18 Liangxi Xi Lu (☎230 0788). From the train station, walk south across the bridge and turn right; the hotel is half a block down on the left. The lovely sounds of soprano sax are piped throughout this mid-range hotel. Sauna Y10. Ask for discounts. Doubles Y260; triples Y550; extra bed Y100. ❹

Wuxi Roast Duck House (wúxī kǎoyā diàn; 无锡烤鸭店), 222 Zhongshan Lu (☎270 8222), 1½ blocks south of Renmin Lu. This mega-restaurant has spacious, well-kept rooms without a quacker in sight. Doubles Y150-220, in the west building Y100. ❷

CTS Hotel (zhōnglǚ dàjiǔdiàn; 中旅大酒店), 88 Chezhan Lu (☎230 4561), across from the train station. Not your average railway fare: clean, ultra-modern rooms, and amenities galore, with the local CTS right next door. Weary travelers beware: CTS is "not open to shabbily dressed guests." Rule enforced by guard/bouncer. Doubles Y480-628. 40% discount for students. Credit cards accepted. ❺

FOOD

Wuxi is known for delicious baby back ribs (xiǎopáigǔ; 小排骨), flavorful little silver fish (yínyú; 银鱼), and tasty frogs (literally "field chicken"; tiánjī; 田鸡). Hotel restaurants specialize in Jiangsu-style seafood dishes, serving up just about anything with gills, flippers, or shells. The area around the intersection of **Zhongshan Lu** and **Renmin Lu** is filled with fast food; duck into a side street, however, and you're likely to find larger sit-down restaurants. In the summer, there's fresh produce on most smaller streets and fresh, unforgettably juicy peaches everywhere. There are a number of student-friendly cafes on **Huaihe Lu** around **Light Industrial University** (qīnggōng dàxué; 轻工大学), near Xihui Park.

China Restaurant (zhōngguó fàndiàn; 中国饭店; ☎270 7454), next to the China Hotel. A la carte delights include dumplings (Y3), eel, snails (Y3-5), *dim sum* (Y2 per 3 pieces), and more. Open daily 6:30am-8:30pm. Fancier banquet-style dishes (Y25 and up) are upstairs to the right of the hotel. Open daily 10:45am-1:30pm and 5-8pm. ❶

Sanfengqiao Meat House (sānfēngqiáo ròuzhuāng; 三风桥肉庄). No place to sit; opt for your choice of various meats—from frozen to ready-to-gnaw—and take it back to savor in your hotel room. This heaven for carnivores has it all—chicken, duck, pork, or beef—but is most well-known and popular with its local following for the marinated and roasted baby back ribs. Prepared meat starting at Y20 per 500g. Open daily 8am-7pm. ❷

Wuxi Roast Duck House (wúxì kǎoyā diàn; 无锡烤鸭店), 222 Zhongshan Lu (☎270 8222). A multi-part, tourist-serving mega-restaurant, dishing up duck, duck 'n' fish, and for dessert, "duck deluxe." High-grade Beijing- and Jiangsu-style food for reasonable prices (entrees Y24-75). Open daily 9am-2pm and 5-9pm. ❸

Wuxi Light Industrial University Foreign Students Hotel (wúxī qīnggōng dàxué zhuānjiā liúxuéshēng lóu; 无锡轻工大学专家留学生楼), 170 Huihe Lu. Large (sometimes buffet-style) meals for just Y5. Open daily 7-8am, 11am-1pm, and 5:30-7pm. ❶

SIGHTS

Wuxi has grown into a sizable city with almost no tourist offerings of its own, mainly because Lake Taihu makes up for it with an overwhelming amount of tourist junk. If you have a few hours to spare, **Chengzhong Park** (chéngzhōng gōngyuán; 城中公园), off Zhongshan Lu north of Renmin Lu, is a daytime getaway for legions of contemplative old men. Join them or jump on the bumper cars (Y3).

XIHUI PARK (xīhuì gōngyuán; 锡惠公园). This small park is the site of **Xishan** (锡山), a large hill with a distinctive pink pagoda on top. Its many forgettable attractions include gushing fountains, a zoo, an azalea garden, and a sad amusement park with a dying carousel (what the management calls "turning luxury hobbyhorses"). What Xihui is known for is its unforgettable souvenirs—namely, the small clay figurines (usually of plump senior citizens or children cuddling fish, symbols of wealth and good fortune). One of the more famous sights in Xihui is a spring that inspired the famous blind composer Ah Bing (阿丙) to write "Two Springs Reflecting Moon" (èrquán yìnyuè; 二泉映月). A plaque nearby proclaims the spring to be the "world's second best spring" (tiānxià dìèr quán; 天下第二泉), second only to the one in Zhenjiang. This one is now reduced to a stinky little pool.

Blandness aside, two attractions stand out and nearly lift the entire area to must-see status. The first is the ski-lift style **cable car** ride that connects the hill with **Huishan,** the other large hill visible from Wuxi. On clear days, the ride affords soaring views of the city and lake; beware of vertigo, though, as the trip is remarkably high and long. *(Runs daily 8:30am-5pm. Y22, children Y10.)*

Even more notable is the tunnel that cuts right through the middle of Xishan. The **Dragon Light Cave** echoes with the digital whistles and roars of a hundred scattered robotic creatures, all lurking in dark rooms off an intimidatingly long corridor. Walk from end to end, and marvel at surreal, six-foot singing carrots; fend off twitching Teenage Mutant Ninja Turtles, gasping dinosaurs, and motionless penguins; and most importantly, stay away from the huge, whistling, and highly dangerous fish-eating insects! *(Park open daily 5am-6pm. Y10-25.)*

DAYTRIP FROM WUXI: LAKE TAIHU

*Take **bus** #1 or 820 from the North Bus Station (about 45min.) and get off either at Turtle Head Island or near the Li Garden. Bus #2 stops at Plum Garden. Otherwise, travel by **bike** (if you like taking long bike rides in the rain). Follow either Liangxi Lu (toward Plum Garden) or Hubin Lu to the south, which then bends right and runs along the lake to Baojie Bridge. **Accommodations** abound, although most tourists return to Wuxi for the night.*

Covering more than 2000 sq. km, Lake Taihu (tài hú; 太湖) is one of the largest freshwater lakes in China. The lake is known for the sand ("purple sand"; zǐshā; 紫砂) found at its bottom that comes, nonetheless, in several different colors. It flavors the famous local blend of green tea and is also used to make some of the finest pottery around. Not surprisingly, the cooler air of Lake Taihu attracts droves of summer tourists; with dozens of lush islands peering through frequent (albeit polluted) haze, coastlines graced with blossoming grapes, peaches, and plums, and shallow waters teeming with fish, the lake has plenty to see. In case you need one more excuse: locals love to down their fresh seafood with cold bottles of *tàihú shǔi* (太湖水), a tasty regional beer. Spring, when fruit blossoms abound, and fall, with its mellow harvest days, are the best times to visit Lake Taihu. The

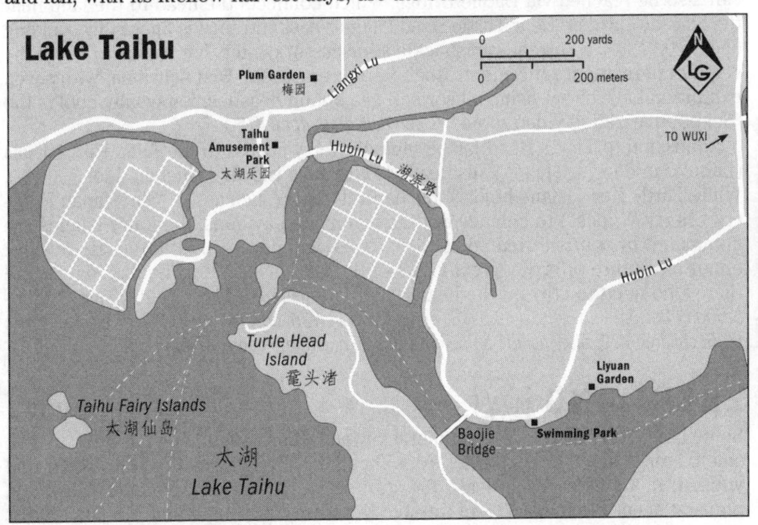

SHANGHAI

summer months can be unforgivingly hot, despite the lake breeze. At any time, though, the folks who inhabit these misty coasts will throw out the welcome mat—just take the time to sample their seed-stuffed wares.

PLUM GARDEN (méi yuán; 梅园). If you bike to Taihu from Wuxi, ride along Liangxi Lu. You will see the Taihu Amusement Park on your left, followed by a bus terminal. Across the street is the middle gate for the Plum Garden, established in 1912 by two industrialists who planted 5000 plum trees to mark their retirement. Since then, additional features have been added, including the **"In Suddenly Enlightened Hole"** (a large, dank cave); a garage-like **perfumery and greenhouse** toward the back; the **Nian Qu Tower,** which should once again afford nice views after renovation (Y2); and the **Kai Yuan Temple,** a Buddhist complex with several 20 ft. statues of snarling deities (Y2). The garden sees the occasional tourist, but it mostly provides solitude and serenity for locals—be careful not to disrupt the smooching couples. *(Open daily 6am-6pm. Y15.)*

THREE CITIES. These three recently built TV production sets have now been transformed into tourist sights. **Tang City,** the oldest of the three, was the set of a late 80s television drama series about a Tang dynasty emperor. Daily re-enactments of movie scenes and an "imperial procession," are grandiose and feature song and dance. Get in the mood; dress up in period gear. *(☎555 5019. Open daily 7:30am-5pm. Y32.)* **Three Kingdoms City** was the set of the wildly popular series "The Romance of the Three Kingdoms." Re-enactments feature famous battle scenes, ship burning, and jousts. *(☎555 5195. Open daily 7:30am-5pm. Y30.)* Last, and possibly least, is **Water Margin City,** set of the TV series "Water Margin City." Bigger and more naturalistic, but not better. *(Bus #820 goes to all three cities.)*

TURTLE HEAD ISLAND (yuántóu zhǔ; 鼋头渚). Perhaps the most renowned part of Lake Taihu is Turtle Head Island, a peninsula shaped like a turtle head, extending into the northwest part of the lake about 8km from Wuxi. This old reptilian noggin contains hidden natural gems for the daring explorer; to all others, it represents the unstoppable sprawl of pavilions and hokey tourist attractions. The island can also be reached via Baojie Bridge, which connects the head to the land near the Li Yuan Garden. Near Turtle Head Island's east entrance is **Space City** (tàikōng chéng; 太空城), a surreal, ramshackle amusement center that seems to be on the verge of permanent retirement. Much farther east is the **East Aquarium,** with seven exhibition halls showcasing all sorts of sea-bound beasties. Especially cool is the "Sci-popularization video room." *(Open daily 8am-4pm. Y15.)*

Admission to Turtle Head Island includes ferry access to the **Taihu Fairy Islands** (tàihú xiān dǎo; 太湖仙岛), also called **Three Hills Islands** (sānshān dǎo; 三山岛). While Turtle Head Island holds some natural treats (such as the "Sino-Japan Flowery Cherry Woods") to balance out the manmade pavilions, the Fairy Islands are dominated by tourist-oriented statues, caves, and pagodas. Still, the trip out is a minor adventure offerring great views of the lake (especially on misty days), and there's no need to stay on the beaten path. *(Ferries run daily every 20-40min. 8:15am-5:50pm. Be sure to pick up a map (Y3) on your way in. Y35, children Y15. More expensive tickets (Y45, children Y22) also include a ride on a shuttle bus to the center of the island.)*

ZHENJIANG 镇江 ☎0511

Some cities have distinctive landmarks or landscapes; Zhenjiang has a distinctive smell. Step a block or two away from Zhenjiang's railway station, and you'll find yourself in a pickle—or, at least, the stuff of which pickles are made. The sharp, pungent scent of vinegar drifts through the town, swirling about the jars sold at nearly every street corner and slinking about the doors of every local restaurant. The odor originates at the famed Heng Shun Sauce and Vinegar Factory, the home of a 1400-year-old recipe for China's most prized fragrant vinegar. In 1908, the recipe won the gold prize at the World Expo in Panama—a feat it repeated in Paris in 1985. The bottles of vinegar have since made their way around the world, and are as easy to find in Chinatown as in China. Today, Zhenjiang lives in relative obscurity, attracting the occasional tourist who seeks nothing more than a few bottles of top vintage for the trip home.

TRANSPORTATION

Trains: The **Zhenjiang Train Station** (zhènjiāng huǒchē zhàn; 镇江火车站) is west of the city center. Buy tickets on the far right side of the station; hours vary, but windows #8 and 9 should be open all night. Zhenjiang is another convenient city on the Nanjing-Shanghai line and has trains leaving frequently to: **Hangzhou** (5½-8hr., 6 per day, Y24-174); **Hefei** (5-5½hr., 3 per day, Y25-161); **Nanjing** (1hr., Y4-18); **Shanghai** (3-4hr., Y14-56); **Suzhou** (3-3½hr., Y9-36); **Wuxi** (2-3hr., Y7-28).

Buses: Long-distance buses leave from one of two stations across from each other on Jiefang Nan Lu, about 3 blocks south of Dashi Kou. The bus station (☎522 1606) east of the train station serves: **Hangzhou** (5 per day 6:50am-2:40pm, Y33-60); **Hefei** (4 per day 7:40am-1:30pm, Y33-56); **Nanjing** (every 10min. 6am-7pm, Y10.5-21); **Shanghai** (11 per day 7:45am-5:15pm, Y56-77); **Wuxi** (17 per day 7:15am-5:15pm, Y29-33). Privately-run **minibuses** have no posted schedule; just hop on one leaving from a station on Zhongshan Lu, a few blocks from the train station. To: **Hangzhou** (4hr., 3 per day, Y57-70); **Nanjing** (1hr., Y21); **Shanghai** (3hr., 11 per day, Y54-64); **Wuxi** (1½hr., 17 per day, Y28-32). Buses to **Yangzhou** (40min.-1hr., Y7-12) are everywhere; catch one at the ferry terminal or at either bus station. You also can hop on a minibus to Yangzhou as it waits to cross the Yangzi.

Local Transportation: City **buses** are useful for getting to major tourist sites and transport hubs in town. Most of the 23 lines run 6am-6pm, but some, like bus #2, run until 11pm. Buses with a "W" in front of their numbers don't have fare collectors and require exact change. Fare usually Y1. Bus **#2** goes up Daxi Lu in the old neighborhood, past the museum, and ends at Jinshan Temple; **#4** goes to Beigushan and then out to Jiaoshan; **#10** goes to the ferry dock; **#13** shuttles between the train station and the main bus station. **Ferries** cross the Yangzi regularly from the **dock** (dùkǒu; 渡口) in the northwest corner of town (Y8). A **taxi** from the center of town costs Y15-20.

Bike Rental: Bikes are everywhere, but the city is small enough that they're unnecessary. There are no decent bike rental shops. Those desperate for a bike can buy a cheapie (Y70-90) and resell it before leaving.

ORIENTATION AND PRACTICAL INFORMATION

Zhenjiang stretches along the south bank of the **Yangzi River**. The **Grand Canal** runs north through town, cutting through the city center before making its way to the river. The busiest part of town is in the southeast, centered around **Dashi Kou** (大市口), which is the large intersection of **Zhongshan Lu** (中山路), a major east-west thoroughfare, and **Jiefang Lu** (解放路), an avenue that runs north-south. Almost all city buses pass through Dashi Kou, the perfect reference point for navigation and home to the city's most useful tourist services. Trains and minibuses arrive in western Zhenjiang, near Zhongshan Lu, the Heng Shun factory, hotels, and restaurants. Most buses arrive at the bus station on Jiefang Nan Lu, a few blocks south of Dashi Kou.

In the west, near the river, is the oldest part of Zhenjiang, a maze of tiny shops and large-scale construction projects. Here, the streets become narrower and more closely packed. **Jinshan Temple,** farther west, marks the end of the main city.

Travel Agencies: CITS, on Jiefang Lu (☎503 7361) doesn't offer a great deal of help. Instead, try the friendly English-speaking Assistant Manager next door at the Zhenjiang Hotel. Open daily 8am-noon and 2-6pm. The **Zhenjiang China Culture Tourist Service** (zhènjiāng zhōngguó wénhuà lǚxíngshè; 镇江中国文化旅行社), 25 Jiankang Lu, Bldg. 3 (☎523 1806), has brochures in Chinese. Open daily 8am-noon and 2-6pm.

Bank of China: 235 Zhongshan Lu (☎502 6789), half a block east of Dashi Kou, on the north side of the street. Open daily 8-5:30pm.

PSB: Off a small lane next to the McDonald's near Dashi Kou.

Pharmacy: Zhongshan Pharmacy (zhōngshān yàodiàn; 中山药店), 61 Zhongshan Xi Lu. Carries Western medicine. Open daily 8am-7pm.

Internet Access: Wangshiyuan Internet Bar (wǎngshìyuán wǎngbā; 网事园网吧), 63 Zhongshan Xi Lu, 2nd fl. Fast connection. Y2 per hr. Open 24hr. **Xunda Internet Bar** (xùndá wǎngbā; 迅达网吧), on the 2nd fl. of the Telecommunications Bldg. on Zhenghuailou Xi Lu. No free machines before 3pm.

Post Office: 423 Zhongshan Dong Lu. English signs and EMS (daily 8am-6:30pm). Open daily 8am-6pm. Another branch, 65 Zhongshan Xi Lu (☎523 9236), 100m east of the train station. Open daily 8am-6:30pm. **Postal Code:** 212000.

ACCOMMODATIONS

Hotels cluster around Dashi Kou and the train station. Most post expensive rates, but in the off-season (and in Zhenjiang, there really isn't an "on" season), hotels willingly grant discounts of up to 50%. In general, rooms tend to be cheaper if you call ahead first (and speak Chinese); hotels are less willing to bargain later in the day. Avoid the **Garden Hotel** (huāyuán dàjiǔdiàn; 花园大酒店), which has dirty linen, broken beds, leaky bathroom ceilings, and not-so-secure door locks.

Jingkou Hotel (jīngkǒu fàndiàn; 京口饭店), 407 Zhongshan Dong Lu (☎522 4866), about 100m from the gate on the east bank of the Grand Canal. Cheaper rooms have A/C, bath, and TV. Newer rooms are bright and happy. Breakfast included. Doubles Y120, in new wing Y480. Rooms in the new wing can be talked down to Y280. 40% discount possible. ❷

Great Wall Hotel (cháng chéng dàjiǔdiàn; 长城大酒店), 59 Jiefang Nan Lu (☎501 8999), 2-3 blocks south of Dashi Kou, past the Yanchun Restaurant. Rooms are old, but in fair condition. Exchanges currency. Singles Y140; doubles Y200; triples Y240. Discounts start at 20%. ❷

Jinjiang (jīngjiāng fàndiàn; 京江饭店), 111 Jiefang Lu, at Dashi Kou (☎501 7788). Central location and great prices. Singles Y88; doubles Y110, with newer furniture Y160-242; triples Y132-198. Discounts start at 20% for a one-day stay. Otherwise rooms can be had for a discount of up to 50%. ❷

Zhenjiang Hotel (zhènjiāng bīnguǎn; 镇江宾馆), 92 Zhongshan Xi Lu (☎523 3888; fax 523 1055; zjhotel@public.zj.js.cn), 500m east of the train station. Views from the older rooms are dreary, but rooms themselves are big and spotless. The friendly staff likes to bargain. Breakfast included. Doubles Y300-510. Discounts start at 20%. ❹

FOOD

Zhenjiang is a veritable bonanza of food stalls and street markets. A walk down Zhongshan Lu reveals the pickled delights at the **Heng Shun Sauce and Vinegar Factory** (héng shùn jiàngcù chǎng; 恒顺酱醋厂). Since 1840, the factory has been pickling everything from turnips to cucumbers to "sacred pagoda vegetables." Not to be outdone, a few side streets off **Zhongshan Lu,** just west of the vinegar factory, have markets offering pickled eggs, pickled vegetables, pickled pecks of pickled peppers, and other local delicacies—pickled, of course. Zhenjiang is also famous for its abundance of freshwater delicacies, including the long-tailed anchovy (huíyú; 回鱼), the rare Yangzi herring (shíyú; 鲥鱼), and another trout-like creature referred to by locals as knife fish (dāoyú; 刀鱼). If seafood doesn't appeal, then **Dashi Kou,** with McDonald's, KFCs, and a range of Chinese chains, can soothe the fast-food addict's soul. There's also the delicacy, *tāngbāo* (汤包), dumplings filled with a tasty hot liquid. Poke a hole in the dumpling, suck out the filling—be careful, the juice is hot—then eat the dumpling skin dipped in vinegar.

Yanchun Restaurant (yàn chūn jiǔlóu; 宴春酒楼), 17 Renmin Jie (☎527 1615), 2 blocks east of the museum. Arguably Zhenjiang's most famous restaurant, this place has been around since 1938. The plump pork dumplings (Y15) are remarkably appetizing when dipped in that omnipresent sauce–Zhenjiang vinegar, of course. Open daily 6:15-10am, 11am-2pm, and 3-8:30pm. A newer location, on 87 Jiefang Lu (☎501 0477 or 501 0478), 2 blocks south of Dashi Kou, has cowgirl and karaoke performances. Open daily 11am-1:30pm and 5-7pm. ❶

SIGHTS

Zhenjiang's sights could easily be ingested in the course of a long day. If you have time to kill, dawdle in the **Daxi Lu** neighborhood near the museum, a part of town with labyrinthine alleys and street markets shaded by 100-year-old trees. If these sights aren't appealing, perhaps you can try your luck on the sidewalks for some entertainment; fortune tellers give face readings (kànxiàng; 看相) for Y2.

PEARL S. BUCK HOUSE (sàizhēnzhū jiùjū; 赛珍珠旧居). Pearl S. Buck (1892-1973), the Nobel-prize winning American author who astounded the world with her literary portrayals of traditional Chinese families, spent a total of 18 years in Zhenjiang. The house where she grew up has been replaced by a factory, but the home in which she spent her later years in China still stands. In 1991, by the encouragement of Zhenjiang's American sister-city, Tempe, Arizona, the house was turned into a small museum. The museum contains original furniture from Buck's residence, photos and paintings with narration, a small collection of books, and two rooms of relics from the author's houses in America and Japan, including an assortment of Santa Clauses and "I Love Tempe" mugs. *(6 Runzhoushan Lu, near the train station. From the station, head down Zhongshan Lu toward Dashi Kou. Take the 1st left onto Daxi Lu, a narrow street near the Zijin Quan Hotel. At the 2nd left, head up the road going up the hill; the house is at the top. Open daily 8:30-11:30am and 2:30-5pm. Free.)*

JINSHAN TEMPLE (jīnshān sì; 金山寺). This temple and park complex in the northwest part of town has as much water as land area. The park area contains ponds, the "Number One Spring in China," a slew of souvenir stands, and, most impressively, a 1500-year-old Buddhist temple with a towering pagoda and a still-active community of monks. In fact, Buddhists from Hong Kong and Singapore come all the way to Jinshan because they believe praying to the Buddha here is more effective than praying elsewhere. The main temple is lavishly stuffed with icons and Buddhas of all sorts. The 18 *arhats* surrounding the 3 main Buddhas are worth a peek, especially the one picking his ear wax with a stick.

Peer out from the top of the eight-sided, seven-storied, 36m tall **Ci Shou Pagoda** (císhòu tǎ; 慈寿塔) for a view of Zhenjiang's other hilltop sights, fish ponds and farmland, and the mighty Yangzi to the north. A temple was first built on this site 1400 years ago. The current pagoda was constructed in 1900 to mark the Empress Dowager's birthday. An inquiry office offers help in English. *(At the terminus for bus #2. ☎551 2992. Open daily 6am-6pm. Park Y20-24 depending on season, Ci Shou Pagoda Y4.)*

JIAOSHAN (jiāoshān; 焦山). In the far eastern portion of the town hulks a jungly island with pavilions, historical remnants, and a large tower. The mainland side of this park has a few diversions of its own, including a waterfall; but the island is the main attraction. Free ferries shuttle visitors across the river (every 20min. 7:30am-5:30pm); motorboats put visitors close enough to the river to spit in it and see it spit back (Y4 across the river, Y10 to Beigushan if you have 3 people). The most scenic route is by the **cable car** that lifts you far above the river, leaving you all alone to see the Yangzi's awesome flood potential. *(Cable car runs daily 8am-4pm. Y15 to the island, Y10 to the mainland.)*

The **Wanfo Pagoda Mountain** (literally, the "10,000 Buddhas Pagoda"; wànfó tǎ shān; 万佛) glistens after recent restorations, which seem to be as much cause for pride as the existence of the pagoda itself. You can even sponsor a Buddha (prices vary depending on yourBuddha's size and tier); but hurry before the 10,000 run out. *(Y15, but the views from the base are just as lovely.)* Near the tower on the river side is a small **calligraphy museum** (Y2), and not far away are some old **gun batteries** used during Zhenjiang's active stronghold days. On the mainland side, a cluster of buildings includes the Buddhist **Din Hui Temple** and a tree-filled pavilion. You can also wander the island's winding paths, enjoy the fragrance of ancient trees rich with centuries of river dew, and relish in those final moments of the sweet life before you get back on that big, scary cable car. Also, **Huijin Temple** is less touristy than Jinshan temple. *(Take bus #4, or head northeast on city streets until you hit Zhenjiao Lu, which winds toward the front entrance. Open daily 7:15am-5:30pm; last admission 4:45pm. Y20.)*

BEIGUSHAN MOUNTAIN (běigù shān; 北固山). The *Romance of the Three Kingdoms* tells the story of Liu Bei, the King of Shu, who was offered the hand of Sun Shangxiang, the sister of Sun Quan, King of Wu. As Liu Bei floated down the Yangzi for the wedding, Sun Quan and his treacherous advisors plotted to kill the bridegroom and annex his province of Hubei by ambushing butchers inside the **Ganlu Temple** atop Beigushan. But the girl's mother approved the marriage, and the royal hitch cemented the alliance against the Dark Side of Chancellor Cao Cao's vast Kingdom of Wei to the north. The rock in the courtyard with a gash in the middle is said to have been where the two kings swore their allegiance. Without the story, Beigushan would be just an old, overgrown garden, with silly statues and an ancient temple. Ganlu Temple, however, does house the lightning-blitzed **Iron Pagoda** and **Qinghui Pavilion,** which overlooks the river. *(Open daily 7am-5:50pm. Y10.)*

YANGZHOU 扬州 ☎0514

Scholars, artists, and foreign merchants have flocked to Yangzhou for centuries to enjoy the meandering waterways, charming bridges, and breezy avenues. The city streets seem subdued and even peaceful—and not just because of the ordinances against honking. Residents here are sublimely easy-going, relaxed, and more than willing to chat. After all, vocal braggarts have a history here too: one of Yangzhou's cultural legacies is *píng huà* (评话), a lively form of storytelling. Yangzhou also has a reputation for beautiful women; many emperors supposedly came here as much for the scenery as for the selection of imperial concubines.

Today, modern Yangzhou has even more to boast about: China's current president, Jiang Zemin, was born and raised in Yangzhou, something you'll hear mentioned often. The city has a serene atmosphere that inspires contemplation—a good thing, since there's little else to do. Stroll long enough, and you're bound to come across the city's few gardens, a monastery, and a small museum, all of which could easily provide quiet, simple distraction for a day.

TRANSPORTATION

Buses: Yangzhou Bus Station (yángzhōu qìchē zhàn; 扬州汽车站; ☎781 3658), at the intersection of Dujiang Nan Lu and Jiangyang Dong Lu, 1½km south of town. Take bus #1 or 2 from northeast Zhenjiang; or take #5, 13, or 15 from Wenhe Lu or the northwest near Shouxi Lake Park. In general, there are 3 types of long-distance buses: *kuàikè* "快客" (fastest, with A/C, priciest); *zhōngbā* "中巴" (mid-sized bus, more stops, less comfy, about 20% cheaper); and *dàbā* "大巴" (big bus, slower and another 20% cheaper). Ticket office open daily 5am-6pm. To: **Hangzhou** (6hr., 4 per day, Y78); **Hefei** (4hr., 6 per day 7:30am-3pm, Y53); **Huai'an** (practically every hr., Y20-30); **Nanjing** (1½hr., 36 per day 6:45am-5:45pm, Y22); **Shanghai** (4hr., 7 per day, Y40-69); **Wuxi** (2hr., 16 per day 6:30am-5:30pm, Y42-51). Buses to **Zhenjiang** (40min.-1hr. with ferry, multiple departures per day, Y7-12) and nearby towns leave from the **West Bus Station** (qìchē xī zhàn; 汽车西站), accessible via bus #8 (from Guoqing Lu) or 22 (from Wenhe Lu). Long-distance buses from the main station also stop here sometimes.

Local Transportation: Some of the more popular tourist destinations are best reached by **bus.** Most buses run 7am-7pm, but can be few and far between. Fare Y1-2. Bus **#15** runs from the far north of town, past Shouxi Lake and along Wenhe Lu to the main bus station; in the south, **#5** goes from the train station to Shouxi Lake; **#22** follows a similar route and continues to Daming Temple; **#4** and **12** run along Wenchang Lu. **Tourist buses** shuttle between the Imperial Dock, Shouxi Lake Park, Daming Temple, and other tourist spots (6 per day 8:30am-3:30pm, Y5).

Taxis: Base fare Y5-7, each additional km Y1.2-1.4. Taxis are hard to find on the city outskirts, but **pedicabs** are everywhere (Y3 to start). Bargain hard.

ORIENTATION AND PRACTICAL INFORMATION

Yangzhou is a relatively small city tucked next to the **Grand Canal.** Like many cities along the canal, the streets here are laid out in a grid, making navigation easy despite the fact that many streets often change names as they go along. Most hotels and services are on **Wenhe Lu** (汶河路) and **Wenchang Lu** (文昌路), which intersect at the **Wenchang Pavilion** (wénchāng gé; 文昌阁) in the center of town.

Most buses arrive at a station in the south of town, just past the Grand Canal, on a major thoroughfare that switches names three times, from **Dujiang Lu** (渡江路) in the south to **Guoqing Lu** (国庆路) and finally to **Shikefa Lu** (史可法路) in the north. In the northwest part of town is **Shouxi Lake Park,** the town's most popular attraction. **Yanfu Lu** (盐阜路) runs east from the park, along a smaller canal where imperial boats used to dock—now lined along the shores by a thriving market.

Travel Agency: CTS, 10 Fengle Shang, is very helpful. English and French speakers. Books tickets, arranges tours, and helps with visas. Open daily 8-11:30am and 2-6pm.

Tourist Complaints: ☎732 5601.

Bank of China: 28 Wenhe Bei Lu. The exchange counter will make even the most paranoid traveler feel safe, but be prepared for extensive examinations of your signature and documents. Open daily 8am-5pm. 24hr. ATM (Cirrus/MC/V/Plus).

Bookstores: Xinhua Bookstore, 65 Wenhe Lu (☎734 4427), has maps, dictionaries, and well-thumbed English classics. Open daily 8:30-11am and noon-7pm. A better option is the **Yangzhou Old Books Store,** 10 Yanfu Xi Lu (☎734 3916), with piles of dictionaries and stacks of English novels and translated Chinese classics. Open daily 8:30-11:30am and 2:30-6:30pm.

PSB: On Huaihai Lu between Siwangting Lu and Yanfa Xi Lu.

Hospital: Subei Hospital (sìběi rénmín yīyuàn; 苏北人民医院; ☎734 7693 or 797 7400), on the corner of Wenhe Nan Lu and Nantong Xi Lu.

Internet Access: Internet places come and go, but you'll find some slightly north of the Friendship Hall (next to Xiyuan Hotel). **Dingji Internet,** on the corner of Chanzheng Lu and Beimenwai Dajie, behind Xiyuan Hotel. Y2 per hr. Open 24hr.

Post Office: China Post, 37 Siwangting Lu, just west of Wenhe Lu, on the south side of the street. EMS. Another location at 162 Wenchang Zhong Lu. EMS and Poste Restante. Open daily 8am-6:30pm. **Postal Code:** 225002.

ACCOMMODATIONS

Yangzhou is high on high-end hotels, and there are few true budget options. Anywhere in the center or north of town is convenient to tourist sights, so wander around this area and try to bargain with hotel staff. May is Yangzhou's high season; bargain is much easier later in the summer.

Hongqiao Hotel (hóngqiáo bīnguǎn; 虹桥宾馆; ☎731 4701). Pass through a gate on the west side of the street between Siwangting Lu and the south entrance to Shouxi Lake; it's the white building on the right. Friendly staff. Modest rooms have dying rugs and primitive shower heads. Singles and triples Y180; doubles Y160 (can be bargained to Y120). Discounts start at 10%. ❸

Olive Hotel (aòlìwēi dàshà; 奥力威大厦), 36 Wenhe Bei Lu (☎736 1888), is a glossy newbie. Friendly staff, sparkling rooms, clean baths, and great water pressure; keycards are temperamental and rugs a bit stained. Singles Y140-288; doubles Y150-328. ❷

Xiyuan Hotel (xīyuán dàjiǔdiàn; 西园大酒店), 1 Fengle Shang Jie (☎734 4888), north of Yanfu Xi Lu and a block east of Wenhe Bei Lu, behind the museum. In a big garden with a quiet atmosphere. The exterior may resemble a riot-proof monstrosity, but the inside is fairly luxurious. Free detergent. Older buildings: doubles Y256-620; triples Y238. Luxury rooms pricier. Credit cards accepted. ❹

Yiyuan Hotel (yíyuán fàndiàn; 怡园饭店), 1 Ximen Lu (☎731 6866), on the corner of Siwangting Lu and Wenhe Lu, has great deals. Singles Y200; doubles Y240; triples Y270. Discounts start at 30%. ❷

Lantian Hotel (lántiān dàshà; 蓝天大厦), 159 Wenhe Nan Lu (☎736 0000). Dark, claustrophobic hallways lead to surprisingly large, clean rooms with refrigerators. Dreary views inside and out. Holes adorn the rugs, but beds are soft. Singles Y220-280; doubles Y280-420; triples Y360-420. 15% discounts possible. Credit cards accepted. ❸

FOOD

A Chinese city doesn't really deserve a visit unless it serves a decent dumpling. Luckily for Yangzhou, its dumplings and cakes are divine; they are best when sampled in the southeast part of town, either at the **Fu Chun Tea House** or from nearby street carts. The bazaar-like area around the Imperial Dock features several sit-down places as well as a busy market with puppies and goldfish. In the evenings, small stalls and carts line **Wenhe Lu,** between Wenchang Lu and Yanfu Lu. But this same street has also been afflicted by a festering fast-food rash of **McDonald's** and **KFC.** Yangzhou is also famous for its *dim sum* and fried rice, with reasonably-priced restaurants on **Siwanting Lu,** known as **Food Street** (měishí jiē; 美食街).

Fuchun Tea House (fùchūn cháshè; 富春茶社), 35 Desheng Qiao (☎723 3326), down an alley branching east off Guoqing Lu, between Guangling Lu and Wenchang Lu.

SHANGHAI

Indulge in a fantastic 10-piece dumpling sampler and tea (about Y25). Delicacies abound, like crab dumplings, thousand layer cake, and even the Qianlong Emperor's favorite, three-ingredient dumpling (sāndīng; 三丁). Open daily 6am-2pm and 3:30-8pm. A branch is on Yangzijiang Bei Lu outside the city center (☎787 4375). ❷

Wan Cheerful Department Store (wànjiāfú shāngchéng; 万家福商城), on Wenhe Lu just south of McDonald's, on the west side of the street near Wenchang Lu. Never before have you seen so much plastic food. The **Taiwan Noodle Shop** (táiwān dànzi miàn; 台湾担仔面) on the top floor features a smorgasbord of dishes, almost all of which cost less than Y10. Point, pay, and enjoy. The 6th fl. food court, or "dainty snacks square," offers dainty snacks. While shopping, do check out "fallow cowboy's wear" for some stylish outfits. Open M-Sa 8:30am-9:30pm, Su 8:30am-10pm. ❶

Laoma Hotpot (lǎomā huǒguō; 老妈火锅), 48 Siwanting Lu (☎734 2807), at Huaihai Lu. Look for the sign with red peppers. Pay the cashier as you enter; just point to the plastic replicas of heavenly dishes just within reach. Give the receipt to the waiter, and sit back to wait for your food to arrive, or order some cold dishes off the circulating cart. Huge Chinese families come here for cheap dumplings (Y4 for 5), bowls of noodles (Y7), taro flour *dim sum* filled with sweet red bean paste, and snails (Y5). Y15 can lead to death by over-eating. Another location is at 95 Guoping Lu. ❶

Tiantian Weilu (tiāntiān wéilú; 天天围炉; ☎736 8580), on Wenchang Lu, a block west of Guoqing Lu. All-you-can-eat hotpot or buffet. Offers lunch (11am-2:30pm, Y29), dinner (5:30pm-9pm, Y39), and night snack (yè xiāo; 夜宵; 9pm-midnight, Y29). ❷

SIGHTS

Yangzhou offers one of the more unusual sightseeing tours in the region: **Emperor Qianlong's Boat Tour** (qiánlóng shuǐshàng yóulǎn; 乾隆水上游览). A dragon boat glides along the route supposedly followed by the Qing dynasty ruler upon his visit to the city in 1757, floating past many of the sights constructed especially for him in Shouxi Lake Park. The boat can be boarded near the Imperial Dock, just south of the Xi Yuan Hotel, or at Shouxi Lake Park's south entrance (2hr., Y200 per 10 people). Open daily 6:30am-5:30pm. Most of Yangzhou's visit-worthy sights can be seen in one day; they are all clustered around Shouxi Lake Park. If visitors stay an extra day, it's usually for the *dim sum.*

SHOUXI LAKE PARK (shòuxīhú gōngyuán; 瘦西湖公园). Literally "Slender West Lake," this lake is an explicit comparison to the much more famous West Lake in Hangzhou (see p. 379). Shouxi Lake is lush, sometimes overgrown, with willows and peach trees, while pleasant paths on shore snake past a canal and a variety of interesting structures, including Dahong Bridge, Lotus Pond, Southerly Breeze, a playground, zoo, and "Long Loggie." Keep to the man-made walkways, as one poetic plaque cautions, "fragile is the grass, merciless your steps."

The vase-shaped **White Tower Pagoda** (bái tǎ; 白塔) was built by a salt merchant in 1784. Just past that, cross over **Five Pavilion Bridge** (wǔ tíng qiáo; 五亭桥), built by a local aristocrat to welcome Emperor Qianlong in 1757. This bridge has 15 "cavities," or roofed arches; as a sign declares, "When it's full moon, every cavity carries a moon, so the goldenness on the water sways and the moons contend for splendour, which is impossible to put into words." So we won't even try.

Beyond the bend at **Xi Chu Pavilion,** the path enters a less gimmicky, less crowded strip of the park, with pavilions spanning water all the way to the north entrance. Daming Temple is right outside the entrance. *(On Liuhu Lu, off Siwangting Lu near the Hongqiao Hotel; also on Pingshantang Lu, near the Daming Temple. Accessible by buses*

THE LITTLE MONK WHO COULD As you're huffing and puffing up the stairs to the top of Qiling Temple (the large pagoda at the center of Daming Temple; see p. 373), bear in mind that your efforts are piddly compared to the hardship endured by Jian Zhan (688-763), the Buddhist monk to whom the structure and the nearby Jian Zhan Memorial Hall are dedicated. Jian, an 8th-century Tang scholar, was invited to Japan to share secrets of Chinese Buddhism and reinject discipline into the Japanese branch of the religion. But as much as the monk tried to get to Japan, he was constantly forced to return by high tides and rough storms at sea. Finally, on his sixth attempt at age 66, he reached the island, where he and his followers imported all sorts of knowledge (about Buddhism as well as medicine, architecture, and other liberal disciplines) on their Japanese colleagues. The monk died and was buried in Japan, but the Japanese hardly forgot him; instead, they revere him for his wisdom and persistence even to this day. In 1974, Japanese benefactors, in joint commemoration with China, built the Qiling Temple, which was fashioned after the Toshodai Temple in Nara, Japan. The memorial hall houses a copy of a statue of the monk; the original is still a Japanese treasure.

#1, 4, 6, 16, and 18. ☎ 734 1324. Open daily 6:30am-5:45pm. Rent paddle boats for Y12 per hr., bicycle boats for Y18 per hr. (Y50 deposit), or motor boats for Y25 per hr. Admission Y30.)

DAMING TEMPLE (dàmíng sì; 大明寺). Right across from the north entrance to Shouxi Lake stands the "Great Brightness Temple," named after the enlightened dynastic era in which it was built (AD 457-465). Among the highlights are **Pingshan Hall** (píngshān táng; 平山堂), built in 1048; a nine-story pagoda; and **Jian Zhan Memorial Hall** (Y5), built in 1973 to commemorate the monk Jian Zhan (see **The Little Monk Who Could,** below). Says a sign at the front: "Monks, emperors, sages, poets, men of letters…all pious pilgrims who said their prayers [at Daming Temple], without exception, have had their prayers answered." So march up the stairs and start praying. *(Across from Shouxi Lake Park's north entrance. Take bus #21 or 22. Open daily 7:45am-5pm. Y18.)* The area northeast of the temple has a few ponds, the **Tang City Wall** (tángchéng yízhǐ; 唐城遗址), and the **Han Tomb Museum** (hànmù bówùguǎn; 汉墓博物馆), built over an archaeological site off Xiangbie Lu. **Qingling Pagoda,** first built in the Sui dynasty and rebuilt in 1993, grants gorgeous views of surrounding rice paddies, Shanxi Lake, and many old men fishing on it. The pagoda's wider steps allow for an easy climb. *(Open daily 7:30am-5pm. Y5 to climb.)*

OTHER SIGHTS. On the canal, at the north end of Guoqing Lu, is the **Imperial Dock,** where Qianlong's tour boat is said to have docked during his visit 243 years ago. Thatch-roofed buildings line Yanfu Lu all the way to the Yangzhou Museum. On summer evenings, a plaza in the front is converted into a rink for roller-skating. *(Free, but bring your own skates.)* About 500m farther east at 10 Yanfu Lu, **Ge Garden** (gè yuán; 个园) is another leftover from the days when salt merchants were the fat cats in Yangzhou. It was built in 1818 by Huang Yin-tai, a bamboo lover; the garden is bursting at the seams with 40 species of the plant. *(Open daily 7am-6pm. Y12.)*

On the south side of Yangzhou is the **Crane Mosque** (xiānhè qīngzhēnsì; 仙鹤清真寺), one of the few mosques in this part of China. The stark courtyard is highlighted by a prayer room, with a large wooden wall covered in gilded Arabic inscriptions. *(Enter the building off an alley, about 10m east of Guoqing Lu and one block north of Ganquan Lu. The gate is tended by a rather old and somewhat deaf man, so knock loudly. Open Sa-Th sunrise-sunset.)* Farther northeast on Wenchang Lu, just across the Grand

Canal, stands the **Tomb of Puhaddin** (pǔhādīng mùyuán; 普哈丁墓园), the resting place of a 16th-century descendent of Muhammad who served as a missionary in China. Look for the small, gold onion-domes; the tomb is through several gates beyond the garden and pond and atop the hill. *(Accessible via bus #12.)*

The small island **Fu Zhuang** is a gorgeous retreat teeming with chirping birds and weeping willows along the lake. And if you visit in late June (known as *yánxià*; "hot summer"; 炎夏), nary a soul will interrupt your sheltered stroll. The northern end offers several pavilions that are incredibly romantic (i.e. secluded). *(Admission includes the bonsai garden across the Hongqiao Bridge.)*

ZHEJIANG 浙江

Diehard secular infidels beware: Zhejiang's scenic wonders have the ability to infuse you with an uncontrollable sense of spirituality. From the famed beauty of Hangzhou's West Lake to the sacred Buddhist mountain on Putuoshan Island, Zhejiang's sights have been the source of legends for ages. Most of the province's most famous and interesting areas are in the northern portion of the province, not far from Shanghai. Travel inland to the south and discover densely populated towns, an occasional major city, and the fertile fields that yield some of China's richest rice harvests. In general, the farther one goes from Shanghai, the fewer travelers (and attractions for travelers) there are. Stay in northern Zhejiang to experience sites that epitomize China's cultural achievements and natural beauty.

HANGZHOU 杭州 ☎0571

A famous Chinese saying declares, "above there is heaven, below there are Suzhou and Hangzhou." Indeed, Hangzhou's famous West Lake has been fodder for artists and literati for centuries, inspiring calligraphy, paintings, poetry, and leaving behind dozens of legends in its willow-tree scented wake. Blessed with over 57 scenic spots, Hangzhou's poetic beauty and idyllic landscapes appeal to both locals and visitors who want to make the most of its visual splendor.

Hangzhou served as the capital of the Southern Song Dynasty from AD 1127 to 1279 and was one of China's most important cultural and political centers. These days, as the capital of Zhejiang province, Hangzhou struggles to maintain its scenic beauty in the face of agricultural, industrial, and commercial development. Construction cranes and large towers sprout up faster than spring blossoms. Thankfully, the energy of the city center complements (rather than intrudes upon) the serenity of the lake. There is a reason why so many of China's romances were set in Hangzhou—here, the air is sweeter, life is more languid, and the beauty of the lake casts a dreamy glow on lazy afternoons.

TRANSPORTATION

Flights: Hangzhou Airport (hángzhōu jīchǎng; 杭州机场; ☎8666 2999), northeast of central Hangzhou. A taxi to the city center costs about Y35-50 and takes about 30min. Shuttle buses (every 30min. 8am-8pm, Y20) run between the airport and the **CAAC ticket office,** 390 Tiyuchang Lu (domestic info ☎8515 4259, international ☎8515 2575), off Wulin Square. Open daily 8am-8pm. To: **Beijing** (4 per day 12:10-5:40pm, Y1060); **Fuzhou** (many per day 8:10am-5:50pm, Y590); **Guangzhou** (6 per day 1:05-6:45pm, Y960); **Hong Kong** (9:05am and 4pm, Y1570-1600).

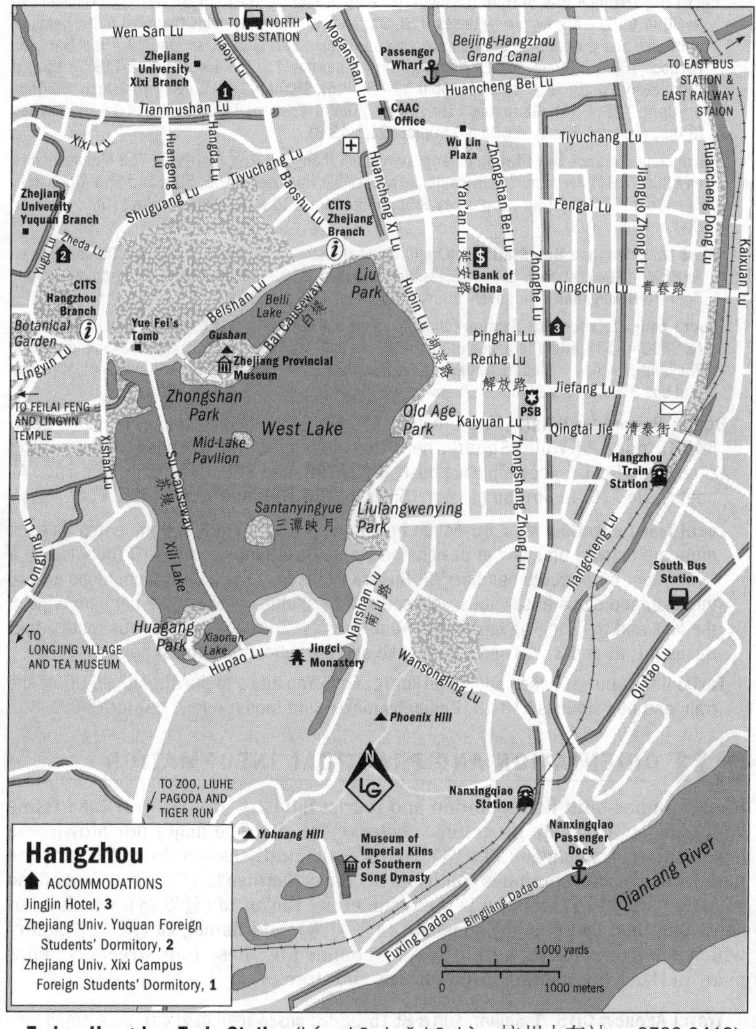

Trains: Hangzhou Train Station (hángzhōu huǒchē zhàn; 杭州火车站; ☎8782 9418), an ark-shaped building on Huancheng Dong Lu just south of Xihu Dadao. At the terminus of buses #7, 11, 39, and 151. To: **Beijing** (16hr., 9:25pm, Y200); **Fuzhou** (18hr., 4:04pm, Y125); **Guangzhou** (24hr., 11:27am, Y194); **Hefei** (11½hr., 4:46pm, Y32); **Nanchang** (10hr., 8:48pm, Y92); **Nanjing** (3hr., many per day 2:47-10:12pm, Y31-99); **Shanghai** (2-3hr., many per day 9:05am-8:31pm, Y17-33); **Suzhou** (3hr., many per day 9:05am-10:12pm, Y37-51); **Xiamen** (25hr., 2:58pm, Y73). **Hangzhou East Train Station** (hángzhōu huǒchē dōngzhàn; 杭州火车东站; ☎8782 9418), at the end of Tiancheng Lu, at the terminus of buses #5, 28, and 518, serves nearby cities.

Buses: 4 bus stations provide somewhat overlapping service.

East Long-distance Bus Station (chángtú qìchē dōng zhàn; 长途汽车东站), 215 Genshan Lu (☎8694 8251), accessible by buses #19, 31, and 56. Currently fields the most traffic because of its size and proximity to the new expressway. Tickets sold 5-11:30am and 11:40am-8pm. To: **Fuzhou** (16hr., 8:20am, Y201); **Nanjing** (5hr., 8 per day 7:20am-4:40pm, Y98-113.5); **Ningbo** (2hr., every 10-20min. 6:30am-7:30pm, Y24.8-48.5); **Shanghai** (2hr., every 10-20min. 6:20am-6:50pm, Y28.4-54); **Shaoxing** (1hr., every 20min. 6:30am-7:30pm, Y11.4-18.5); **Suzhou** (34hr., every 20-30min. 6:50am-6:50pm, Y21.5-43.8).

North Long-distance Bus Station (chángtú qìchē běi zhàn; 长途汽车北站), 758 Moganshan Lu (☎8809 7761), far from the city center, is accessible via buses #155, 503, and 555. Open daily 6am-6pm. To **Hefei** (6hr., 3 per day 8:20am-5:40pm, Y108-147) and **Nanjing** (5hr., every hr. 6:40am-6pm, Y98).

West Long-distance Bus Station (chángtú qìchē xī zhàn; 长途汽车西站), 89 Tianmushan Lu (☎8522 1304), at Yugu Lu, is accessible via buses #30, 152, and 502. Open daily 5:30am-7pm. To **Huangshan** (7hr., every 50min. 6:50am-2:40pm, Y50-70).

South Long-distance Bus Station (chángtú qìchē nán zhàn; 长途汽车南站), 417 Qiutao Lu (☎8606 4914), at the terminus of bus #501, is accessible by bus #39. To smaller cities within Zhejiang province, including **Dongyang** (express bus 2½hr., every 1½hr. 7:20am-7pm, Y45; normal bus 3½hr., every 30min. 7:20am-7pm).

Boats: Passenger Wharf (kèyùn mǎtóu; 客运码头), 138 Huancheng Bei Lu (☎8505 8458), north of Wulin Square, near the intersection of Huangshan Bei Lu and Zhongshan Bei Lu. Accessible via buses #52, 156, and 806. Open daily 6am-5pm. All boats have A/C. To **Suzhou** (13½hr., 5:30pm, Y50-100) and **Wuxi** (12hr., 6pm, Y82).

Local Transportation: Most **buses** run from around 6:30am to 8 or 9pm; hours for each route are marked on signs at designated stops. Base fare Y1, with A/C (denoted by a "K" in front of the route number) Y2. Bus **#K7** runs from the train station, loops around the lake, and stops at several scenic spots; **#27** shuttles between the northern edge of the lake and the Longjing tea village. **Minibuses** (Y1.5) follow popular bus routes; **tour buses #1, 2,** and **3** (Y2) serve West Lake and the surrounding forest area.

Taxis: Base fare Y10, each additional km Y1. From Yan'an Lu to the airport Y35-50; to the train and bus stations Y10-15. **Pedicabs** make short trips (under 1km) for Y5-8.

ORIENTATION AND PRACTICAL INFORMATION

Hangzhou has built its reputation and tourist industry around **West Lake** (xīhú; 西湖), the approximate geographic center of the city. The major downtown area lies to the east. **Hubin Lu** (湖滨路) begins at the northeastern tip of the lake and hugs its banks as it continues south and becomes **Nanshan Lu** (南山路). East of and roughly parallel to Hubin Lu is the commercial **Yan'an Lu** (延安路), which intersects **Qingchun Lu** (青春路), **Pinghai Lu** (平海路), and **Jiefang Lu** (解放路), all of which run from east to west. The area bounded by these four streets contains many of Hangzhou's more upscale hotels and stores.

Travel Agency: CITS, 1 Shihan Lu (☎8515 2888; citszj@mail.hz.zj.cn), on a small lane off the corner of Beishan Lu and Baoshu Lu. Average commission Y30-40. "English Department" offers tours, interpreters, and tickets. Open daily 8:30am-5:30pm.

Bank of China: 320 Yan'an Lu (☎8707 7996), a half-block north of Qingchun Lu. Exchanges traveler's checks. Credit card advances. **ATM** inside. Open daily 7:40am-8pm. Few other branches exchange traveler's checks.

Bookstore: Zhejiang Province Foreign Language Bookstore (zhèjiāng shěng wài wén shūdiàn; 浙江省外文书店), 56 Hubin Lu (☎8707 0243), just south of Qingchun Lu. Fair selection of bilingual tourist maps (Y4); good pickings in English classics and translated Chinese literature section on the 3rd fl. Open daily 9am-8:30pm.

PSB: 35 Huagang Lu (☎8707 6677). Visa extensions. Open daily 8am-noon and 2-5:30pm.

Hospitals: Hangzhou City Central Hospital (hángzhōu shì zhōng yīyuàn; 杭州市中医院), 453 Tiyuchang Lu (☎8515 7591). Open daily 8-11:30am and 2:30-5:30pm. **Hangzhou City No. 1 People's Hospital** (hángzhōu shì dì yī rénmín yīyuàn; 杭州市第一人民医院), 261 Wangsa Lu (☎8706 5701). Open daily 8am-noon and 2-5:30pm. English speakers at both hospitals.

Telephones: China Telecom (☎8517 4318), on the corner of Yan'an Lu and Tiyuchang Lu, in Wulin Square. 24hr. IDD service at counter #1. Open daily 8:15am-5pm.

Internet Access: Many of the newer university guesthouses and foreign student dorms offer on-site access. **China Telecom Internet Bar,** 10 Huxing Lu (☎708 0085). Y5 per hr. Open daily 8:30am-5:30pm. **Internet Cafe,** (☎8788 8011), next to the Zhejiang University Yuquan Foreign Students' Dormitory. Y3 per hr. Open 24hr.

Post Office: Hangzhou International Post Office, 1 Jiefang Lu (☎8780 0568), at Huancheng Dong Lu, 5min. north of the train station. Take bus #152 from the city center. EMS and Poste Restante. Open daily 8am-6pm. **Postal Code:** 310000.

ACCOMMODATIONS

University dormitories are the cheapest places to stay in Hangzhou if you don't mind the journey to the city center (about 15min. by bus). Travelers may be pleasantly surprised to find affordable and comfortable options surrounding the lake. Big spenders have their pick of luxury hotels, including the **Shangri-La Hotel** (xiānggélǐlā fàndiàn; 香格里拉饭店), 78 Beishan Lu (☎707 7951), where US President Richard Nixon met with Zhou Enlai in his historic 1972 visit to China. At Y900 per night, it's quite a steal.

Zhejiang University Yuquan Foreign Students' Dormitory (zhèjiāng yùquán wàiguó liúxuéshēng lóu; 浙江大学玉泉留学生楼; ☎795 1386), a 10min. bus ride from the lake. Take bus #16 from Hubin Lu or #21 west from Huancheng Xi Lu to the last stop, opposite the university's main gate. Walk on Zheda Lu away from the university entrance and turn right at the first alley; the dormitory is on the left. A nearby Internet cafe, friendly staff, and scruffy backpackers make the isolation tolerable. Rooms are bare but practical. Singles Y45; doubles with bath and A/C Y100. ❶

Zhejiang University Xixi Campus Foreign Students' Dormitory (zhèjiāng dàxué xīxī xiàoqū liúxuéshēng lóu; 浙江大学西溪校区留学生楼; ☎8827 4629), on the corner of Hangda Lu and Tianmushan Lu, Building 3. Take bus #152 from the train station or #21 from city center to Zhejiang Xixi. From the main gate, bear right along the main path, past the basketball courts on the left. An extremely loving staff and assortment of international students will take your mind off the crumbling walls and smelly common baths. 2-bed dorms Y40; doubles with A/C and bath Y120. ❶

Jingjin Hotel (jīngjìn dàshà; 京晋大厦), 50 Simadu Jiang (☎701 9663), beside Zhonghe Zhong Lu, just north of Pinghai Lu, a 5min. walk from West Lake. This comfortable hotel has bright, big rooms and free filtered water dispensers in each room. All rooms have A/C, bath, and TV. Doubles Y150 and up. ❷

Xianghai Hotel (xiānghǎi fàndiàn; 湘海饭店), 276 Yan'an Lu (☎8706 1335), 2min. from the lake. Some of the lowest prices this side of town. Rooms without A/C have mosquito nets. Doubles Y60, with A/C, bath, and TV Y100. ❶

Zhejiang University International Building (zhèjiāng zhúkějē guójìdàlóu; 浙江竺可桢国际大楼), 38 Zheda Lu (☎8795 1122), a 10min. walk through campus, at the end of the first road to the right of the main gate; take bus #152 directly to Gudang and enter through the back gate of the university on Xiqi Lu. A dormitory only in theory. Posh rooms include A/C, bath, and TV. Singles Y98; doubles Y180. ❷

FOOD AND ENTERTAINMENT

With an impressive list of dishes and enough history attached to rival West Lake itself, a routine meal in Hangzhou can easily turn into an extravaganza. Most restaurants will serve Hangzhou's fabled delicacies; pared-down versions of smelly or crispy tofu are available in any street stall (Y1-4).

The side streets off **Zhonghe Lu** (east of and parallel to Yan'an Lu), especially near the Jiefang Lu intersection, are lined with good, cheap restaurants. **Renhe Lu,** running east off Hubin Lu, is one of the most exciting culinary streets around, playing host to many small, perpetually-packed restaurants that sell a dazzling variety of local favorites, from noodles to Peking Duck to small snacks (xiǎochī; 小吃). The take-out window of the famed **Zhiweiguan** sells **almond paste cookies** (Y1) and **sticky rice-covered meatballs** (Y1) in addition to the roasted hind and front quarters of all kinds of poultry (Y12-55). Along the heavily commercial and touristed stretch of **Yan'an Lu,** vendors sell cheap pork, vegetables, and red bean paste dumplings (Y0.5-1.5). The restaurants along **Qingchun Lu,** between Hubin Lu and Zhonghe Lu, are ideal for larger groups that want to sample some of Hangzhou's finest cuisine. **Wahaha Restaurant ❹,** 169 Qingchun Lu, serves snake, yellow eel, and other delicacies. These slithery delights don't come cheap, however; a bowl of snake soup costs Y60 and up. (☎8721 9898. Open daily 11am-3am.)

Tourist kitsch and prices characterize the establishments along **Hubin Lu,** south of Qingchun Lu. Tea houses line the streets north and northeast of the lake, particularly on **Beishan Lu** and Hubin Lu. **Paradise Bird Tea House ❷** (tiāntáng pàomò hóngchá fǎng; 天堂泡沫红茶坊), 34 Hubin Lu, offers noodle soups (Y15-20) and a selection of teas and beers (Y15-25). English-language menus and photographs of Hollywood ingenues give this tea house a decidedly Western air. (☎8706 8883. Open daily noon-2am.) The **Lakeside Pavilion ❶** (wànghú lóu; 望湖楼), 12 Beishan Lu, near CITS, commands a striking view of West Lake; serving up inexpensive teas (about Y10) and sunflower and watermelon seeds. (☎8515 5843. Open daily 8:30-11:30am, 12:30-4pm, and 6pm-midnight.)

A popular gathering place at night is the night market on **Wushan Jie** (wúshān jiē; 吴山街), a tiny alley off Pinghai Lu. On hot, sticky Hangzhou nights, join locals to shop for frivolous trinkets and antiques. Lots of restaurants and street-stalls also surround the area, selling countless steamed buns (xiǎolóngbāo; 小笼包; Y5-6) and barbecued meat.

Louwailou Restaurant (lóuwàilóu càiguǎn; 楼外楼菜馆), 30 Gushan Lu (☎796 9023), near the southern end of Solitary Hill Island. Opened in 1848, this is said to be the oldest restaurant in China, and could easily be its best. This shrine to divine cuisine is a must-see sight. It is, after all, the restaurant that created Hangzhou's famous 11 dishes, and no one does them better. Don't miss succulent, melt-in-your-mouth Beggar's Chicken (Y89); light yet intensely flavorful West Lake Pure Greens Soup (Y20); and the stunning Su Dongpo Pork (Y8), so absolutely delicious it makes you want to write your own poem in praise of pork. Open daily 11:30am-2:30pm and 5:30-10:30pm. ❹

SIGHTS

Hangzhou sights are easy to find and fairly easy to reach; the challenge is to find those not overrun by large tour groups. Most of these are expansive, gorgeous parks by the West Lake; the best way to savor them is to spend lots of time in long, leisurely contemplation of their enchanting beauty.

WEST LAKE

Bordered by Beishan Lu to the north, Hubin Lu to the east, and Nanshan Lu to the south. ***Bus #K7*** *runs along Beishan Lu and the northern end of Hubin Lu; get off at any stop along that stretch. Numerous bus lines run along Hubin and Yan'an Lu, including #38 and 151; walk 1 block east from Yan'an Lu to reach the eastern shore. Some individual sights around the lake require an* ***admission*** *fee; those near the lake are all connected by public transportation.*

West Lake (xī hú; 西湖): heaven on earth, Hangzhou's *raison d'être*, fodder for countless bad pick-up lines. For centuries, men have compared the lake to women and women to the lake. Of course, some have suceeded more eloquently than others. Poets wrote that West Lake's weeping willows are as softly arched as the eyebrows of the famed beauty Xi Zi; its rippling waves sparkle like her eyes. Surrounding hills carpeted by dense forests, a wide but intimate expanse of water, and the memory of languid afternoons past combine in this earthly paradise.

Stroll along any portion of the West Lake shore or along **Bai Causeway** (bái tí; 白堤) to the north and **Su Causeway** (sū tí; 苏堤) to the west for views of the 3km long and 3km wide lake. Bai Causeway connects Solitary Hill to the north shore; Su Causeway, lined with willow trees, runs from the western end of the north shore to the south shore, connecting the Tomb of Yue Fei to Huagang Park.

ISLANDS. There's no need to linger on the banks—West Lake's waters beckon the visitor with spell-binding waves. Two islands, Mid-Lake Pavilion (hú xīn tíng; 湖心亭) and Santan Yingyue (sāntán yìngyuè; 三潭映月), are accessible only by boat, arguably the best way to see the lake. The sparkling water and the gorgeous surrounding mountains will overwhelm you. Keep an eye out for the lake's three famous Lover's Bridges, famous as the settings for some of China's most legendary love stories. The serene, forested grounds of the **Mid-Lake Pavilion,** not far from Solitary Hill Island, make for yet another peaceful stroll. *(Open daily 8am-5pm. Free.)* South of this is the delightful **Santan Yingyue** and the **Small Immortal Isle,** an island within a lake with a lake within the island. On the rest of the isle, there are many delicate pavilions, quiet bridges, and lushly shaded paths to catch your fancy, including a **Couple's Pavilion,** where lovers link their arms in a complex manner to see if their hearts are in sync. The real draw, however, are the three stone towers in the center of the lake, where the perfectly still waters reflect the **moon bridges** (sāntán yìngyuè; 三潭映月) that span the lake. *(Y13.)*

These islands may be reached, and the lake traversed, by one of several water vehicles. **Passenger ferries** leave from the eastern shore and from a dock between the Su and Bai Causeways on the northern shore, opposite the Tomb of Yue Fei. Tickets are sold at the dock. *(Every 30-40min. 7:50am-4:50pm. Roundtrip to the Mid-lake Pavilion and Santan Yingyue Y35. Boats leave all the time from the two islands.)* **Night cruises** are also available, weather permitting. *(Tickets sold F-Su 6:50-9:30pm. Y20-25.)* **Private boats** can also be arranged (Y60-80 per hr.).

HUAGANG PARK (huāgǎng guānyú; 花港观鱼). South of Solitary Hill Island along Su Causeway, Huagang Park is reputedly the best place from which to check out the fish, which is why the second half of the park's name is *guānyú* ("to view fish;" 观鱼). Built as a private garden in the early Song dynasty, the park's main draws are its peony gardens, peacock farm, and **Red Carp Pond** (hóng yú chí; 红鱼池), whose hyperactive inhabitants are constantly leaping out of the water. *(At the southwestern tip of West Lake. Enter off Nanshan Lu or the southern end of Su Causeway. Take bus #308 from Yan'an Lu to Su Ti; the entrance is 50m ahead on the right. ☎8796 7386. Open daily 6am-6pm. Y10, children under 1.4m Y5.)*

SOLITARY HILL ISLAND (gū shān dǎo; 孤山岛). Located at the north end of West Lake, this island boasts such beautiful views that nearly every tourist in Hangzhou stops by. "**Autumn Moon on a Calm Lake**" (píng hú qiū yuè; 平湖秋月), on the southeast corner, is touted as the area's best location for twilight lake-gazing (Hangzhou's sport of choice), but there are plenty of other good spots with equally breathtaking views. This island also houses the **Zhejiang Provincial Museum** (zhèjiāng shěng bówùguǎn; 浙江省博物馆) and its titillating collections of relics, gems, calligraphy, and coins. *(☎8798 0281. Open daily 8:45am-4:30pm; last admission 4:15pm. Y10, students Y5.)* **Gushan Park** (gūshān gōngyuán; 孤山公园), in the center of the island, also known as **Sun Yat-sen Park,** was established in 1752 as a private imperial resort. Although it has some of the lake's best scenery and views, this island is relatively tourist-free. *(Open daily sunrise-sunset. Y5.)*

FEILAI PEAK

At the end of Linyin Lu, 15-20min. northwest of West Lake. Take bus #K7 from Pinghai Lu to Lingyin Si, the last stop. Tourist Bus #1 circles the lake, stopping at Lingyin Temple. ☎8796 4426. Open daily 5:30am-6pm. Y20, children 1-1.3m Y10. Lingyin Temple Y15.

To the left of the entrance to Feilai Peak (fēilái fēng; 飞来峰), the **Chinese Park of Selected Grotto Carvings** (zhōnghuá shíkū jícuìyuán; 中华石窟集翠园) houses freestanding Buddhist sculptures and images culled from far-away caves and temples. Farther up the road on the left, signs point the way to the **Feilai Peak Grottoes** (fēiláifēng shíkū; 飞来峰石窟). According to legend, Feilai Peak came into existence in AD 326, when the Indian monk Hui Lai constructed Lingyin Temple and willed a well-loved peak from India to join him in his new home. The peak "flew from afar," and now houses a series of intricate statues, carvings, and etchings that bring to life the craggy limestone face and caves of the mountain. Visitors can clamber along the pathways of the mountain face and the stream that runs beside it to get a better view of the more than 470 Buddhist carvings, which date primarily from the 10th to 14th centuries. The almost pitch-black **Deep Dragon Cave** (lóng hóng dòng; 龙泓洞) is especially popular; its pinhole opening allows only a tiny shaft of light (picturesquely termed the "thread of heaven") to intrude. The **Cave of Milky Icicles** contains carvings of the characters for peace, fortune, and love; tradition has led many a hopeful tourist to rub them for good luck.

The approach to **Lingyin Temple** (língyǐn sì; 灵隐寺), known as the **Monastery of the Soul's Retreat,** is lined with two 1000-year-old *sutra* pillars and twin stone pagodas dating from AD 326, nicely interspersed with peddlers selling tea leaves, trinkets, and incense sticks. The main **Mahavira Hall** houses China's largest wooden statue (19.6m) of the sleeping Buddha, a gorgeous statue of Guanyin, and thousands of Buddhas carved into the wall.

OTHER SIGHTS

TIGER RUN DREAM SPRING (hǔ pǎo mèng quán; 虎跑梦泉). A relatively new addition, this spot is popular for a very unique reason—supposedly, no greater pleasure can be found in Hangzhou than that in Longjing tea brewed with spring water from this mountain. Chinese tourists line up for hours to collect a bucket of the precious water from the top of this small hill. According to legend, a monk came here hundreds of years ago to practice Buddhism, but the lack of available water forced him to leave. The night before he prepared to go, he dreamt that two tigers had moved a body of water to the area; the next day, a spring appeared on the summit of the mountain. Near the spring sits the **Jigong Temple,** which was named after a legendary monk, and the **Hall of the Arhats,** which contains engravings of the 500 *arhats*. *(10min. south of West Lake, accessible by bus #504 and K514 from Yan'an Lu. Open daily 8am-5pm. Y15, children below 1.4m half-price. Guides Y20.)*

TOMB OF YUE FEI (yuèfēi mù; 岳飞墓). This tomb bears the phrase "endless loyalty and devotion to one's country," the characters that, according to legend, were tattooed onto Yue Fei's back by his mother when he joined the Song army. Yue Fei (1103-42) proved to be a brilliant general, but his loyalty to a corrupt court led to his demise; he was killed as part of a Khitan conspiracy. It took another 21 years, several disastrous defeats, and strong public sentiment to convince the emperor to give Yue Fei a ceremonial reburial. **Yue Temple** (yuèwáng miào; 岳王庙), constructed in 1221, memorializes Yue and his son. Murals recount the childhood bravery and kindness to peasants that earned Yue his popularity with common folk. Try to be careful when crossing the steep **Bridge of Good and Evil,** where Qin Hui, leader of the conspiracy that killed Yue, tripped while heading toward the funeral of his victim. If you trip today, it's an indication that you have a guilty conscience. *(On Beishan Lu, near the northwest corner of West Lake. Take bus #7 to Yuewen. ☎8797 2651. Open daily 7am-6pm. Y20, children 1-1.3m Y10, children under 1m free.)*

DAYTRIP FROM HANGZHOU: LONGJING

Take bus #27 from Pinghai Lu downtown or from along the northern shore of West Lake to Longjing Cha Shi, the last stop.

Worlds away from the pandemonium and commercialism of the downtown and eastern lake shores, the Longjing tea plantations (lóngjǐng; 龙井), hidden in the hills west of the lake, are the source of China's most revered tea. The roads from Hangzhou to Longjing village follow a spectacular winding route through lush hills and sprawling terraced tea fields. An hour-long stroll or half a day spent sipping tea and admiring the bird's-eye view of the city should be enough to convert anyone into a tea enthusiast. The aromatic tea gets its name from the limestone **Longjing Spring,** which is just past the central courtyard of **Longjing Tea Room** (lóngjǐng chá shì; 龙井茶室), a few meters from the bus stop. According to popular myth, a dragon with special powers inhabits the well, which explains why it never dries up, even during a drought. The water here is cold and very clean (if unfit for drinking), and it's customary to draw up a bucketful to wash your hands and face for good luck. A short walk along the hills takes you past houses that double as business venues for residents eager to sell their fresh tea harvests. Many of these individual homes make offers that are a bit too good to be true; a good way to test if you're drinking the real deal is to see if the water that the tea leaves are put into eventually turns red—it shouldn't. Also, make sure your purchases are packed and sealed in front of you.

Two stops before Longjing village, at Shuangfeng, the beautiful **Chinese Tea Museum** (zhōngguó cháyè bówùguǎn; 中国茶叶博物馆) features replicas of tea houses and traces the history of tea from the Tang dynasty to the present. If history isn't your cup of tea, head over to the sampling room, where you can taste-test several varieties for yourself. The road down the hill also houses the famed Hangzhou pearl and silk factories. *(☎796 4221. Open daily 8:30am-4:30pm. Y10.)*

SHAOXING 绍兴 ☎0575

Although leisurely Shaoxing cannot compete economically with its frenetic, skyscraper-bedecked east coast neighbors, it can still attract travelers with its charms. This is, after all, the birthplace of many of China's greatest scholars, including the illustrious Wang Xizhi, the country's most famed calligrapher, Cai

Yuan, founder of Beijing University, and Lu Xun, modern China's greatest writer. Today, Shaoxing is a shrine to the literati and a haven for those even vaguely interested in the arts. Everywhere you turn in this aristocratic, cultured city, you find a bridge where great poems were once composed, playgrounds where great minds roamed in days past, and wineshops that celebrated pens immortalized.

TRANSPORTATION

Trains: Shaoxing Train Station (shàoxīng huǒchē zhàn; 绍兴火车站; ☎802 2584), on Chezhan Lu, at the terminus of buses #1, 2, 3, 4, 11 and 14. The ticket office is slightly to the left as you enter the main building. Open daily 6:30-10:20am, 11:20am-4:40pm, and 5-9:10pm. To: **Hangzhou** (45min.-1½hr.; 8:38am, 2:28, 9:32pm; Y13-19); **Ningbo** (1½-2hr., 12 per day 2:23am-9:19pm, Y9-28); **Guangzhou** (24hr., 10:19am, Y200-351); **Shanghai** (3-5hr.; 10:04am, 1:48, 4:37pm; Y21-64).

Buses: Shaoxing Passenger Transit Center (shàoxīngshì gōnglù kèyùn zhōngxīn; 绍兴市公路客运中心; ☎801 8852, ext. 8004), 15min. northeast of the city center. Accessible via bus #107. One of China's most luxurious bus stations; buying tickets is a breeze. To: **Fuzhou** (18hr., noon, Y179); **Hangzhou** (45min.-1hr., every 10-20min. 6:30am-7:30pm, Y18.5); **Ningbo** (1½hr., 18 per day 6:40am-8pm, Y38-43); **Shanghai** (3hr., every hr. 6:20am-6:40pm, Y56.50-70).

Local Transportation: Public **buses** run roughly 6:30am-8pm (Y1-3). Bus **#2** runs along Jiefang Lu to the Yu Mausoleum and **#3** runs the length of Shengli Lu to the Orchid Pavilion. **Huanxian Bus** (huánxiàn bāshì; 还线巴士), a private minibus line, runs along Jiefang Lu (Y1). Jiefang Lu is not very long, so a stroll between a few bus stops often takes the same amount of time as—if not less than—the bus.

Taxis: Base fare Y5, each additional km Y2.2. Most destinations under Y5-6. **Pedicabs** from Renmin Lu to the station area Y6-7, shorter distances Y3. Negotiate in advance.

ORIENTATION AND PRACTICAL INFORMATION

Jiefang Lu (解放路) is the city's main commercial street, lined with numerous shops and hotels. It runs north-south through the city, intersecting **Renmin Lu** (人民路), **Shengli Lu** (胜利路), **Dong Jie** (东街), **Luxun Jie** (鲁迅街), and **Yan'an Lu** (延安路), all of which run east-west. **Huancheng Lu** (环城路) circles the city proper. Most of Shaoxing's major sights lie outside city limits, but are easily accessible by public transportation. The train station is slightly north of the city, connected to Jiefang Bei Lu by **Chezhan Lu** (车站路); the long-distance bus station is 10 minutes northeast of the city, accessible via **Zhongxing Bei Lu** (中兴北路).

Travel Agency: CITS, 266 Fushan Xi Lu (☎516 6045; English ☎515 1565), 2½ blocks south of Shengli Xi Lu. Accessible via bus #10 from the train station. No commission for plane tickets; average train ticket commission Y20. International department on the 2nd fl. Open daily 8-11:30am and 2:30-5:30pm.

Bank of China: 201 Renmin Zhong Lu (☎522 2888), 1 block west of Jiefang Lu. Exchanges traveler's checks. **ATMs**. Credit card advances. Open daily 8am-8pm.

Bookstore: Xinhua Bookstore, on Jiefang Bei Lu, 1 block north of Shengli Xi Lu, opposite the Baida Hotel. One of the only places in Shaoxing that sells a bilingual map. English-Chinese dictionaries available. Open daily 8am-8:30pm.

Market: Gongxiao Supermarket (gōngxiāo chāoshì; 供销超市), 289 Jiefang Bei Lu (☎511 4754). Dated goods, water, and shampoo. Open daily 8am-9pm.

Hospital: Municipal People's Hospital (shì rénmín yīyuàn; 市人民医院), 61 Dong Jie (☎513 2419, emergency ext. 8539), about 200m from the post office.

Post Office: Shaoxing Main Post Office, 1 Dong Jie (☎513 5000), at Jiefang Bei Lu. EMS and Poste Restante. Open daily 7:30am-6pm. **Postal Code:** 312000.

ACCOMMODATIONS

Budget digs are easy to find, especially in the northern end of town; staff members are usually generous about allowing foreigners to stay in cheaper rooms. Many of these are really dingy, however; wads of cash (Y150) will secure creature comforts at the upper-crust establishments closer to the city center.

Shaoxing Mansions Hotel (shàoxīng dàshà bīnguǎn; 绍兴大厦宾馆), 498 Huancheng Bei Lu (☎513 6360), at Jiefang Bei Lu. Take bus #1, 2, 3, or 4 from the train station to Qiche Zhan. Pleasant standard rooms with A/C, bath, TV, and equally pleasant service. 3-bed dorms Y26; 2-bed dorms Y30; singles Y60; standard doubles Y108-148. 25% discounts available. ❶

Baida Hotel (bǎidà fàndiàn; 百大饭店), 155 Jiefang Bei Lu (☎513 4747), opposite the Shaoxing Hostel, just north of Shengli Lu. A good location in the main district, a 15min. walk from the train station. Comfortable, clean standard rooms; a considerable bargain. Breakfast included. All rooms have A/C, bath, and TV. Singles Y198; doubles from Y220; triples Y280. 40% discounts frequently available. ❸

Shaoxing Hostel (shàoxīng lǚguǎn; 绍兴旅馆), 213 Jiefang Bei Lu (☎513 2814), about 300m south of Shangda Lu. Take bus #2 from the train station. Not to be confused with the luxurious Shaoxing Hotel on Shengli Xi Lu. The dark, narrow lobby is grim and the hospital-like corridors grimmer still. Standard rooms are comfortable and well-kept. Communal baths are also well-maintained. Very helpful staff may steer you away from the non-standard rooms. Singles Y32; doubles Y50. 60% discounts often available. ❶

Jiaoyun Hotel (jiāoyùn bīnguǎn; 交运宾馆), 12 Jiefang Bei Lu (☎802 3553), south of the northern local bus station, near Huancheng Bei Lu. Walk 10min. from the train station, or take buses #1, 2, 3, or 4 to Qiche Zhan. Conveniently located just a few minutes away from the train station, the Jiaoyun is functional but otherwise unexciting. Communal baths are surprisingly clean. Dorm stays limited to one night. 4-bed dorms Y20; 2-bed dorms Y62; standard doubles with A/C, bath, and TV Y120; triples Y87. ❶

FOOD

Much of Shaoxing's local cuisine centers around wine. **Shaoxing Yellow Rice Wine** (shàoxīng huáng jiǔ; 绍兴黄酒), produced from a special kind of sticky rice, lends a potent and distinctive flavor. Drinking the brew can be a fairly heady experience—probably because it's meant to be a cooking wine. For a less intoxicating way to sample it, try the aptly-named **Drunken Chicken** (zuì jī; 醉鸡; Y15-30), a dish prepared by marinating the breast meat in the wine. Another local specialty is lima beans. These are, admittedly, more famous for their literary value—the culinary staple was immortalized by Lu Xun in his short stories. Many Chinese who grew up studying his works swear by the spiritual experience of eating this simple dish.

For cheap restaurants, look along **Luxun Lu** and on side streets off **Yan'an Lu** (the next major street after Luxun Lu as you head south of Jiefang Lu). **Renmin Lu** even has a smattering of bakeries (individual pastries Y1.5-2.5, small breads and cakes from Y5). At night, a really interesting place to look for food is **Xiada Lu**, off Jiefang Bei Lu, where **street stalls** (dàpáidàng; 大排档) sell an endless array of fresh seafood, pig's stomach, and various other goodies.

Grandma's Noodle Restaurant (āpó miànguǎn; 阿婆面馆), 100 Luxun Zhong Lu (☎513 0826), near Lu Xun Memorial Hall. Grandma's noodles never tasted so good. Noodle dishes (Y6-10), noodle soups (Y3-17), and *chǎocài* (炒菜; Y10-20) freshly made by Grandma herself are served in the downstairs dining area. Traditional restaurant fare is served in the evenings on the 2nd fl. Open daily 7am-2am; 2nd fl. 4:30pm-2am. ❶

Xianheng Restaurant (xiánhēng jiǔdiàn; 咸亨酒店), 179 Luxun Zhong Lu (☎511 6666), across from Grandma's Noodle Restaurant. An award-winning, 100-year-old establishment, the Xianheng should probably be seen more as a sight than a restaurant. The spot is, after all, a recurring character in the stories of the beloved Lu Xun, and it is said that every Shaoxing native eats here at least once in his life. The 1890s-style tea house architecture and the statue of Lu Xun make for great photo-ops. Shaoxing wine (Y2-16 a *jīn*), drunken chicken (Y15), and lima beans. Open daily 7:30am-8pm. ❶

Jubilantly Cafe (jùnlěi měishí; 俊磊美食), 558 Jiefang Bei Lu (☎513 9718), close to Dong Jie. Popular with locals, this A/C cafe serves noodle dishes (Y4-6), *jiǎozi* (Y0.4), and a la carte dishes (Y3-7). The most popular counter boasts fresh wonton soup (Y3). Open daily 6:30am-1am. ❶

SIGHTS

Shaoxing's sights pack a mighty punch. A stroll around the city center can be a thrilling experience for lovers of Chinese art and literature. Shaoxing is littered with the former residences of scholars and the spots that inspired their works.

EAST LAKE (dōng hú; 东湖). More a river than a lake, East Lake is a pleasant excursion for those up for a little exploring. One of the most enjoyable ways to see the lake is to take a ride on a **wupeng boat** (wūpéngchuán; 乌蓬船). Unique to Shaoxing, these famed boats are powered by a boatman using foot pedals. *(Y45 per boat, each boat seats 3 passengers.)* The boats can take you to areas of the lake that would otherwise be impossible to reach. The **Immortal Peach Cave** (xiāntáo dòng; 仙桃洞), **Trumpet Cave** (lǎbā dòng; 喇叭洞), and **Taogong Cave** (táogōng dòng; 陶公洞) are all spectacular cliffs with near-vertical rock faces. *(Take bus #1 to Dong Hu Fengjing Qu, which runs until 5pm; or take a 45min. boat ride from the Yu Mausoleum (Y80). ☎864 9590. Open daily 7am-5pm and 5:30-10pm. Y15, children below 1.4m Y3. MC/V.)*

ORCHID PAVILION (lán tíng; 兰亭). The pavilion, built during the Han dynasty and named in honor of the orchids planted here by the emperor, sits at the foot of Lanzhu Hill. The pavilion is sacred to devotees of Chinese calligraphy, but even those less reverent about their brush and scroll may find enlightenment here. The array of calligraphic art that graces scrolls and monuments throughout the area is merely the icing on the cake: craggy peaks and mountains form a fantastic backdrop for orchid greenhouses, densely shaded paths, and luminous pools.

The pavilion first rose to cultural and historical significance in AD 353, when renowned calligrapher Wang Xizhi and 41 of his closest friends played a drinking game along the nearby creek; those who were unable to compose a sufficiently brief and witty poem on command were required to down three shots of wine. Wang's account of the 37 poems that the amusing game produced, the **Lanting Anthology Preface** eulogizes the joyfulness of the occasion and laments the transience of happiness, and has come to be revered as the quintessential example of lucid prose and superb calligraphic style. Indeed, visitors can find numerous copies of *Wang's Preface*, including one by Emperor Kangxi, scattered around the various pavilions and within the **Ancestral Shrine to Wang Xizhi** (wáng yoù jūn cí; 王右军祠). Make like a poet—row your own bamboo raft down a lake beside the pavilion and compose a few poems. *(Y10 per raft for 30min., 4 people per raft maximum.)* The park also contains a tiny but smartly designed **Museum of Calligraphy** (shūfǎ bówùguǎn; 书法博物馆). *(On Shaoda Gonglu, 14km southeast of Shaoxing. Take bus #3 from the train station, on Shengli Xi Lu. The ride takes 35-40min., and the bus stops at Lanting, but the stop is unmarked; let the fare collector know your destination when you get on the bus. ☎460 9035 or 401 1035. Open daily 7:30am-5pm, although the gatekeeper often lets people in later. Y15, children under 1.4m Y7.5.)*

LU XUN MEMORIAL HALL (lǔ xùn jìniàn guǎn; 鲁迅纪念馆). Shaoxing was the birthplace and childhood home of Lu Xun (1881-1936), who is considered one of the best satirical fiction writers and essayists in modern China. He was especially loved for his criticism of feudal customs and oudated traditions (see p.

37). The memorial hall documents Lu Xun's life and works, from his use of literature to "wake up the Chinese people" to the original handwritten copy of his autobiography. The meticulously detailed museum has no English translations, however, so it might be worthwhile to get an interpreter. Across from the museum, **Lu Xun's Ancestral Home** (lǔxùn zǔjū; 鲁迅祖居), the site of his wealthy family's old home, is a good example of traditional Shaoxing architecture. **Lu Xun's Former Residence** (lǔ xùn gù jū; 鲁迅故居), west of the memorial hall, displays his childhood home. **Baicao Garden** (báicǎo yuán; 百草园), a small vegetable garden (described as Lu Xun's "paradise"), is also on the grounds. **Sanwei Study** ("three-flavor study"; sānwèi shūwū; 三味书屋), the school that Lu Xun attended as a child, is diagonally across the street from the other sights and still houses Lu Xun's old desk; visitors can ogle over the character for "early" (早) that Lu Xun carved when his teacher reprimanded him for being late. The saying "From Baicao Garden to Sanwei Study" (cóng báicǎoyuán dào sānwèishūwū; 从百草园到三味书屋) is still used today to describe the process of becoming educated. *(393 Luxun Zhong Lu. Take bus #2, 4, or 5 to the intersection of Jiefang Lu and Luxun Zhong Lu; the hall is a 5min. walk to the east. Bus #7 takes passengers to the front of the Memorial Hall. ☎513 2083. Open daily 8am-5:30pm; last admission 5pm. Guide Y50-100. All 4 buildings Y15, children under 1.4m half-price.)*

OTHER SIGHTS. The Zhou Enlai Memorial Hall (zhōu ēnlái jìniàguǎn; 周恩来记念馆) is dedicated to the first premier of the CCP, who is still respected for his moderate world-views during the tumultous years of the Cultural Revolution. The Memorial Hall itself is a large square; his ancestral home across the street documents his life story and houses some of his letters, furniture, and clothing. *(369 Laodong Lu, near Zhongxing Zhong Lu. ☎513 3368. Open daily 8am-5pm. Y18 to both buildings, plus entrance to Tang poet He Zhitang's museum.)* Southeast of here is the unique **Eight Character Bridge** (bā zì qiáo; 八字桥), named for its arched shape (八), which resembles the Chinese character for the number eight.

To the north of the city center, west of Zhongxing Lu, lies **Jiezhu Temple,** the site of **Wang Xizhi's Former Residence** (wángxīzhī gùzhǎi; 王羲之故宅). The famous calligrapher who turned the written word into an art form is venerated in this tiny museum that holds preserved examples of his works, including copies of the famous poems in his *Preface to the Orchid Pavilion. (72 Xi Jie. Open daily 8am-5pm. Y3.)* Slightly farther south on Caishan Jie is the **Tishan Bridge** (tíshàn qiáo; 题扇桥), where Wang Xizhi composed at least five poems. To the east of Jiefang Bei Lu, near Xiaoshan Jie, is **Cai Yuanpei's Former Residence** (càiyuánpéi gùjū; 蔡元培故居). The first president of Beijing University is an important figure in Chinese academic history; the museum documents his life story, complete with English translations. The house also showcases traditional Shaoxing architecture. *(13 Bifei Nong. Open daily 8am-5:30pm. Y8.)* Shaoxing's more famous scenic areas are all easily accessible by public transportation.

NINGBO 宁波 ☎0574

A trading port since the Tang dynasty, Ningbo has been instrumental in the exchange of goods between China and its neighbors. By the mid-19th century, Ningbo's importance as a trading harbor had declined as Shanghai, which has a more direct link to the sea, flourished. Today, sleek, modern Ningbo doesn't need to dwell on its past. Full of luxurious hotels and ever-growing skyscrapers, future-oriented Ningbo races ahead of the pack in the competition to be the brightest star on the east coast. Slick, fast-paced, and perpetually under construction, Ningbo is

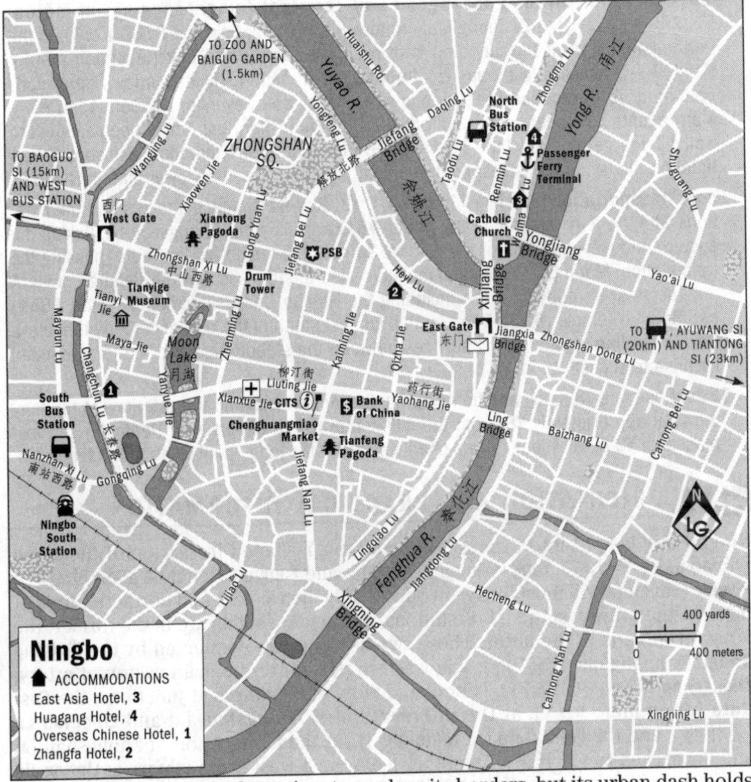

promising for those who have time to explore its borders, but its urban dash holds little appeal for those not interested in the cosmopolitan life.

TRANSPORTATION

Flights: Ningbo Lishe Airport (níngbō lìshè jīchǎng; 宁波栎社机场; ☎742 7888), a 30min. taxi ride from the city (Y40). Shuttle buses (30-45min., approx. every 30min. 6am-3pm, Y5) run to and from the **CAAC ticket office** on 91 Xingning Lu (☎8742 7700). Open daily 8am-5:30pm. To: **Beijing** (8:05am and 4:55pm, Y1080); **Fuzhou** (3 per week, Y603); **Hong Kong** (8:50am, Y1870); **Shanghai** (2:45pm, Y300).

Trains: South Station (nán zhàn; 南站; ☎8731 2084), in the southwestern corner of the city, in a plaza at the terminus of Nanzhan Xi Lu, Ma Yuan Lu, and Gong Qing Lu. Accessible by bus #1 from the ferry terminal and buses #514 and 518 from Zhongshan Xi Lu. Ticket window open daily 6am-7pm. To: **Hangzhou** (2hr., 5 per day 7:08am-7:58pm, Y29-44); **Nanjing** (10hr., 3 per day 4:36pm-5:23pm, Y71-169); **Shanghai** (4-6hr., 4 per day 8:13am-5:23pm, Y27-105).

Buses: Although Ningbo has 3 bus stations, the **South Bus Station** (qìchē nán zhàn; 汽车南站; ☎8713 1834), just west of the railway station, handles almost all long-distance traffic. Open daily 5:20am-7pm. To: **Hangzhou** (2hr., every 10-15min. 5:40am-6:30pm, Y42) and **Shanghai** (3½hr., 5:40 and 7pm, Y96).

Boats: Ningbo Harbor Passenger Ferry Terminal (níngbōgǎng kèyùn mǎtóu; 宁波港客运码头), 142 Zhong Malu (info ☎8735 6332, tickets ☎8769 1258), in the northeastern part of the city also known as the **Lunchuan Dock** (lúnchuán mǎtóu; 轮船码头). Accessible by bus #1 from the train station. Ticket windows open daily 6am-5pm. To **Putuoshan** (1hr. by bus and 1hr. by boat, every hr. 6:50am-4pm, Y57). Many agents here offer hotel room bookings for Putuoshan, but it might be cheapest to wait till you get to the island itself—at the Putuoshan ferry terminal, just about every hotel on the island has salespeople waiting, and rates are often lower than in Ningbo.

Local Transportation: Bus fare Y1, with A/C Y2. **Bus #1** connects the bus and train stations with the ferry terminal in the north; **#517** travels along Zhongshan Lu, linking the eastern and western parts of the city; **#820** runs the length of Liuting Jie, passing the train station, Moon Lake, Chenghuang Miao, and the intersection with Jiefang Bei Lu. A few routes serve outlying areas including the Ningbo University cmapus (route **#601**) and Baoguo Temple (**#332** from Renmin Lu, just south of the passenger ferry terminal). Private **minibuses** offer direct services between the station area and the ferry terminal (sunrise to sunset, Y1-2).

Taxis: Base fare Y8, each additional km Y1.5. From the bus and train stations to the ferry terminal approximately Y8; from the city center to the airport Y40. **Pedicabs** go most places for Y3-5, but many drivers charge more for the long uphill climb to the ferry area.

ORIENTATION AND PRACTICAL INFORMATION

Ningbo city is split into three sections by the Y-shaped formation of the **Yuyao** (yúyáo jiāng; 余姚江), **Yong** (yǒng jiāng; 甬江), and **Fenghua** (fènghuà jiāng; 奉化江) **Rivers.** Travelers will most likely encounter only the western and northern thirds of the city: the railway station, bus stations, and several sights are in the former; the ferry terminal is in the latter. These two sections are connected by the **Xinjiang Bridge** (xīnjiāng qiáo; 新江桥). The western portion of the main east-west artery, **Zhongshan Xi Lu** (中山西路), is bookended by two significant junctions: the **East Gate** (dōng mén; 东门), at the intersection of Zhongshan Lu and **Lingqiao Lu** (灵桥路), and the **West Gate** (xī mén; 西门), at the intersection of Zhongshan Lu and **Changchun Lu** (长春路). The other major east-west thoroughfare is **Liuting Jie** (柳汀路), which becomes Yaohang Jie (yàoháng jiē; 药行街) after the intersection with Jiefang Bei Lu, and boasts numerous shops and eateries.

Travel Agency: Ningbo CITS, 94-96 Kaiming Jie (☎8731 2890), immediately to the right past the main gate of Chenghuang Miao. Ticket commission 10% for train tickets; no commission for plane tickets. Helpful international department (open after 2pm) provides interpreters and tour guides if you join their day tours. Open M-F 8:30am-5pm.

Bank of China: 139 Yaohang Jie (☎8719 6666), between Moon Lake and the Fenghua River, 2 blocks east of the No. 1 Municipal Hospital. Accessible from the ferry terminal by southbound bus #20. Exchanges currency and traveler's checks. **ATMs** (MC/V). Credit card advances. Open daily 8-11:15am and 2:15-5:15pm.

Bookstore: Xinhua Bookstore, 91 Zhongshan Dong Lu (☎8728 1736). A 4-floor megastore selling a wide variety of English fiction and bilingual English-Chinese maps. Open daily 8:30am-9pm.

PSB: 658 Zhongshan Lu (☎8706 2000), in the municipal government's building complex (shì zhèngfǔ; 市政府), at the northeastern corner of the intersection of Zhongshan Lu and Jiefang Bei Lu. Visa extensions (☎8706 0205). Open daily 8am-5pm.

Hospital: No. 1 Municipal Hospital (shì dìyī yīyuàn; 市第一医院), 90 Xingshu Jie (☎8729 4181), off Liuting Jie between Moon Lake and Jiefang Nan Lu. English-speaking staff members. Open 24hr.

Post and Telecommunications: 258 Zhongshan Zhong Lu (☎8736 5701), at the southeast corner of the intersection of Lingqiao Lu and Zhongshan Zhong Lu. EMS and Poste Restante. International mail sent from counter #5. IDD and calling card service on 2nd fl. Open daily 7:30am-8pm. **Postal Code:** 315000.

ACCOMMODATIONS

Although most hotels in Ningbo are mid-range establishments, there are a few budget options available outside the city center. Hotels in the immediate vicinity of the ferry terminal are reasonably priced and extremely convenient, but phone in advance to double-check addresses since the pace of construction in Ningbo means short lives for buildings outside of the main commercial districts. Bargaining is possible virtually everywhere.

Huagang Hotel (huágǎng bīnguǎn; 华港宾馆), 146 Zhong Malu (☎8769 1888), left of the ferry terminal ticket office. Unbeatable location. Newly renovated rooms and helpful services. Doubles Y60, with A/C, bath, and TV from Y100. ❶

East Asia Hotel (dōng yà fàndiàn; 东亚饭店), 112 Zhong Malu (☎8735 6224), a few minutes south of the ferry terminal. Take bus #1 from the station area to Lunchuan Matou. Ningbo's oldest hotel and its very decent standard rooms come at relatively affordable prices. Buffet breakfast included. Singles Y168-180; doubles Y168-180. Year-round discounts of Y30-60. ❸

Overseas Chinese Hotel (huá qiáo fàndiàn; 华侨饭店), 130 Liuting Jie (☎8729 3175), at Changchun Lu, 2 blocks south of the Tianyige Museum. Sprawling grounds, high ceilings, and an ornate design reminiscent of 1920s Shanghai. All rooms have A/C, bath, and TV. Back building: singles Y80; doubles Y98. Main building: singles Y168-238; doubles Y168-198. ❶

Zhangfa Hotel (zhǎngfā jiǔdiàn; 长发酒店), 151 Zhongshan Dong Lu (☎8725 1828), adjacent to the Ningbo Grand Hotel, in the city center. Take bus #518 going east on Zhongshan Dong Lu to Jiefang Lu; the hotel is 2 blocks east on the left. Rooms are clean and have all standard amenities. The cheapest rooms are windowless. Chinese buffet breakfast included. Doubles Y228. ❸

FOOD

Ningbo has a wide variety of local seafood, both fresh and dried. Small restaurants that offer exotic-looking creatures from the deep (snails, eels, and squid) line **Renmin Lu** and **Zhong Malu,** south of the ferry terminal. Farther south, by the Moon Lake area, local favorite **Shipu Sea Flavor Restaurant** ❶ (shípǔ hǎiwèi fàndiàn; 石浦海味饭店), 60 Yanyue Jie, is a not-to-be-missed dining experience, with abundant seafood and vegetarian options and all the little dessert cakes, puffs, and twists you can eat. Some foods are exorbitantly priced, like yellow fish (huángyú; 黄鱼; Y120 per *jīn*) and crab (Y60 per *jīn*); but their freshness and flavor are exquisite. Shipu's excellent desserts include the tantalizing *níngbō tāngyuán* (宁波汤圆; Y8), small flour balls filled with sesame paste, and ice-cold watermelon juice (Y5). Come early. (☎8732 8777. Open daily 10am-10pm.).

For more land-dwelling options, try the **city temple** (chénghuáng miào shāngchéng; 城隍庙商城), at the southwest corner of the intersection of Yaohang Lu and Kaiming Jie. Open-air stalls and stores sell everything from grandfather clocks to novelty stationery in alleys and buildings that look like temples. Small eateries serve the usual noodles and fried foods, and large restaurants offer up regional specialties. After dark, the smells of skewered, barbecued meat and *smelly tofu* waft around the streeside stalls. In the summer, vendors also sell desserts like shaved ice with sweet toppings (bào bīng; 刨冰; Y4). In keeping with the carnival atmosphere, **Gongyuan Lu,** off Zhongshan Xi Lu, looks like the old merchant districts of Ningbo's heyday with its specialty shops, fruit juice stands, and fast food vendors selling *niángāo* (sticky rice cakes; 年糕; Y1-2).

SIGHTS

For those looking for more to do in Ningbo, the temples in the surrounding countryside may be worth a visit. The **Baoguo Temple** (baŏguó sì; 保国寺), in the Jiangbei District 15km northwest of Ningbo City, and the **Tiantong Temple** (tiāntóng sì; 天童寺), some 30km east of the city are particularly notable. Buses run from Ningbo East Bus Station to Tiantong Temple daily 6am to 5:30pm (Y4.7).

TIANYIGE MUSEUM (tiānyìgé bówùguǎn; 天一阁博物馆). Set amidst a maze of streams, gardens, and meticulously arranged rock formations, the Tianyige Museum is built around the famed **Tianyige Library** (tiānyìgé bǎoshūloú; 天一阁宝书楼), the oldest private library in China. Built between 1561-1566, the library originally held the collection of defense minister Fan Qing. Although the collection of more than 300,000 books is not open to the public, there are numerous other pavilions and exhibitions to explore, including a **Painting and Calligraphy Hall** (tiānyìgé shūhuàguǎn; 天一阁书画馆), with displays of local art and stunning scrolls for sale, the **Former Residence of Fan Qing** (fànshì gùjū; 范氏故居), with books and printing woodblocks, and the small **Ningbo History Museum** (níngbō shǐ bówùguǎn; 宁波史博物馆), which traces the 7000-year history of the city. The real highlight of the museum, however, has to be the **Mahjong Museum,** a real joy for all devotees and soon-to-be-converts. The museum details the evolution and rules of the game and exhibits gorgeous *mahjong* sets from around the world. *(On 10 Tianyi Jie. Take bus #10 or 514 from the train station to the intersection of Zhongshan Xi Lu and Changchun Lu. Walk south on Changchun Lu for about 5min.; turn left on Tianyi Jie. ☎729 3526 or 729 2442. Open daily 8am-4:30pm. Y12.)*

OTHER SIGHTS. Near the Tianyige Museum sits the oblong **Moon Lake** (yuè hú; 月湖), one of the prettiest spots in decidedly urban Ningbo. An atmospheric park on the western bank draws crowds that gather around chess players and makeshift barber shops. In mid-summer, there are Chinese opera performances in the open-air pavilions surrounding the lake. *(Open daily dawn-dusk. Free.)* Another popular pastime for some is to cross the lake on paddleboats. *(Y15-20 for 30min. Open daily 10am-11pm.)* The area north of **Xinjiang Bridge** is the site of the former Portuguese and British concessions. On Zhong Malu, the 17th-century **Catholic Church** (tiānzhǔ jiàotáng; 天主教堂) stands proudly out of place among rows of residential houses and small storefronts with its dark, Gothic influences. It still holds daily and Sunday masses, and has a congregation of 600 members. *(4 Zhong Malu. From the ferry terminal, head south on Zhong Malu for about 5min.; the church is in a gated area on the left. ☎8735 5903. Free.)*

SHANGHAI

PUTUOSHAN 普陀山 ☎0580

Saturated with the fragrance of incense and strains of Buddhist chants, the air on the tiny island of Putuoshan is worlds away from the chaotic fumes of the mainland cities. Here, ochre-tinted rocks stand unwavering against the savage waves of the East China sea. A mecca for both devout Buddhist pilgrims and wonderstruck tourists, this island boasts an abundance of temples, shrines, and monasteries. With rolling hills, rugged cliffside beaches, and views of the clear sea stretching out as far as the eye can see, Putuoshan has a timeless, tranquil beauty.

TRANSPORTATION

Boats: The only way to arrive at the island is by ferry from Shanghai, Ningbo, or one of the larger islands nearby. The **Passenger Ferry Terminal** (lúnchuán mǎtoú; 轮船码头), 1 Puji Lu (☎609 1121), also known as *kèyùn mǎtóu* (客运码头) or *kèyùn zhàn* (客运站), is at the southern tip of the island. Tickets for Ningbo may only be purchased on the day of travel, and sell out quickly, so come early to catch a particular ferry. Tickets to other destinations may be purchased 1 day in advance. Ticket window open daily 6am-5pm. To **Ningbo** (2-2½hr., 25 per day 6:40am-6pm, Y31-81) and **Shanghai** (12hr., 4:30 and 5:30pm, Y447-774).

Local Transportation: Walking is highly recommended. From the ferry terminal to Puji Temple takes 20-25min.; from Puji Temple to Fayu Temple 30-40min.; from Fayu Temple to Huiji Temple 45min.-1hr. **Minibuses** operate roughly from dawn to dusk, but service is erratic and minibuses aren't always willing to visit less-touristed attractions. They rarely stop at sign-posted bus stops, so your best bet is to go to the Puji Temple or Fayu Temple parking lots, where minibuses regularly depart for designated sights. From the ferry terminal to the Puji Temple parking lot (Y3); Puji Temple to Fayu Temple (Y3); Puji Temple to the base of Buddhist Summit Mountain, near Huiji Temple (Y6). Upscale hotels like the Putuoshan Grand Hotel also rent vans for their guests.

Taxis: The 6 **taxis** that service Putuoshan charge Y40; they're best left as a last resort.

ORIENTATION AND PRACTICAL INFORMATION

Off the coast of northern Zhejiang in the East China Sea, Putuoshan is less than 40km² and is compact enough to be traversed on foot in three or four hours. Most major roads run north-south. The ferry terminal is at the southern tip of the island. From there, the most direct route to Puji Temple and most of the island's eateries is via **Meicen Lu** (梅岑路), which runs west and then north from the terminal. **Puji Lu** (普济路) runs east and then north along the eastern coast. From the Puji Temple area, several roads run north: **Fayu Lu** (法雨路), which leads to Fayu Temple at the base of Putuoshan's principal peak, **Buddhist Summit Mountain;** and **Foding Shan Lu** (佛顶山路), which scales the western side of the mountain and ends near the entrance to Huiji Temple. There are also many small footpaths running through the hills that serve as shortcuts linking the major routes.

Tourist Office: Putuoshan Administrative Offices, Reception and Welcome Office (pǔtuóshān guǎnlǐ jú jiēdaisuǒ; 普陀山管理局接待所), 115 Meicen Lu (☎609 1224 and 609 1104), opposite and a bit south of the post office, in a large courtyard overlooking a pond. A good place to gather free maps and brochures.

Travel Agency: CITS, 112 Meicen Lu, 2nd fl. (☎609 1183), opposite the Bank of China, immediately to the left of the entrance to the courtyard. Laid-back, friendly staff arranges tours of Putuoshan (1-day tours Y300 and up) and books ferry tickets to Ningbo and Shanghai (commission Y15-20). English-, German-, Japanese-, and Korean-speaking interpreters available. Open daily 8am-5:30pm. Most hotels on the island also book plane, bus, and boat tickets with 1-day notice (commission Y10-20).

Bank of China: 106 Meicen Lu (☎609 1591), opposite CITS. Exchanges currency and traveler's checks. Credit card advances. Open daily 8-11am and 2-5:30pm.

Markets: Several small **supermarkets** cluster on Xianghua Jie (the street east of Puji Temple) and the alleys running south from it. **Fruit vendors** abound on Xianghua Jie and share space with shops selling everything from dried seafood to miniature Guanyin statuettes. A large **market** on Meicen Lu, opposite the row of banks, sells fresh seafood.

PSB: 231 Puji Lu (☎609 2000), on the right side of the road as you head south from the Puji Temple parking lot. Open daily 8-11:30am and 2:30-5:30pm.

Hospital: Puji Hospital (pŭjì yīyuàn; 普济医院), 95 Meicen Lu (☎609 2388), just past the Bank of China. Friendly staff, but no English-speakers. Open 24hr.

Telephones: Public pay phones are scarce. Calls may be made with IC phone cards bought from the post office. IDD service at China Telecom, next door to the post office.

Post and Telecommunications: 124 Puti Lu (☎609 1109), on the corner with Meicen Lu. EMS and Poste Restante. Open daily 7:30am-5:30pm. **Postal Code:** 316107.

ACCOMMODATIONS

Like everything else on this small island, hotel accommodations tend to be expensive, and the quality of the costly mid-range hotels pales in comparison to that on the mainland. Most visitors choose to grin and bear the inconvenience, but the hotels clustered on small alleys near the main temples, especially Puji and Fayu Temples, are the best options. Some local residents make some extra pocket money by opening up their homes to Chinese tourists, posting "accommodation available inside" (nèi yǒu zhùsù; 内有住宿) signs throughout the island. Foreigners, however, will have little success at these and most other cheap establishments. If all else fails, resort to these two middle- to top-end hotels: the **Xilei Little Villa Hotel** (xīlěi xiǎo zhuāng; 息耒小庄; ☎609 1505), on the corner of Puti Lu and Meicen Lu, and the **Putuoshan Grand Hotel** (pǔtuóshān dàjiǔdiàn; 普陀山大酒店; ☎609 2828), on Meicen Lu next to Puji Hospital. These luxurious options start at a whopping Y680 per night. Hotels are often filled to capacity on weekends, and prices jump Y100 on average—make an effort not to come during these times. During the summer and over the May 1 and October 1 national holidays, reservations are recommended. Rooms in the establishments below all have A/C, bath, and TV.

Sanshengtang Hotel (sānshèngtáng fàndiàn; 三圣堂饭店), 121 Miaozhuangyan Lu (☎609 1277; fax 609 1140). From Meicen Lu, turn right onto the post office road; the hotel is 10min. ahead on the left. A vast monastery-turned-hotel. Effusive service. Doubles Y214-549; triples Y300. 40-50% off-season discounts. ❸

Yinying Hotel (yíngyǐng shānzhuāng; 银影山庄), 154 Meicen Lu (609 4345). Convenient location and extremely clean rooms. Overzealous staff may burst in to clean your room in the early morning while you're still sleeping. Doubles Y160. ❷

Xilin Hotel (xīlín fàndiàn; 锡麟饭店), 9 Xianghua Jie (☎609 1303; fax 609 1199), next to the western end of Puji Temple. Newly renovated with pretty courtyards and nice, sparkling rooms. Singles Y308; doubles Y428. 20-40% off-season discounts. ❹

Silver Sea Hotel (yín hǎi fàndiàn; 银海饭店; ☎609 1556; fax 609 114), on Fayu Lu, between Jinping Mountain Villa and Fayu Temple; take the minibus from the ferry terminal to the Fayu Temple parking lot. Airy rooms with balconies that overlook Thousand-Paces Sands Beach. Doubles Y380-480; triples Y550. 50% off-season discounts. ❺

Jinping Mountain Villa (jǐnpíng shān zhuāng; 锦屏山庄), 107 Fayu Lu (☎609 1500; fax 609 1698), a few minutes south of Fayu Temple. Offers some of the nicer rooms around. Doubles Y270-490. 50% discounts possible on off-season weekdays. ❺

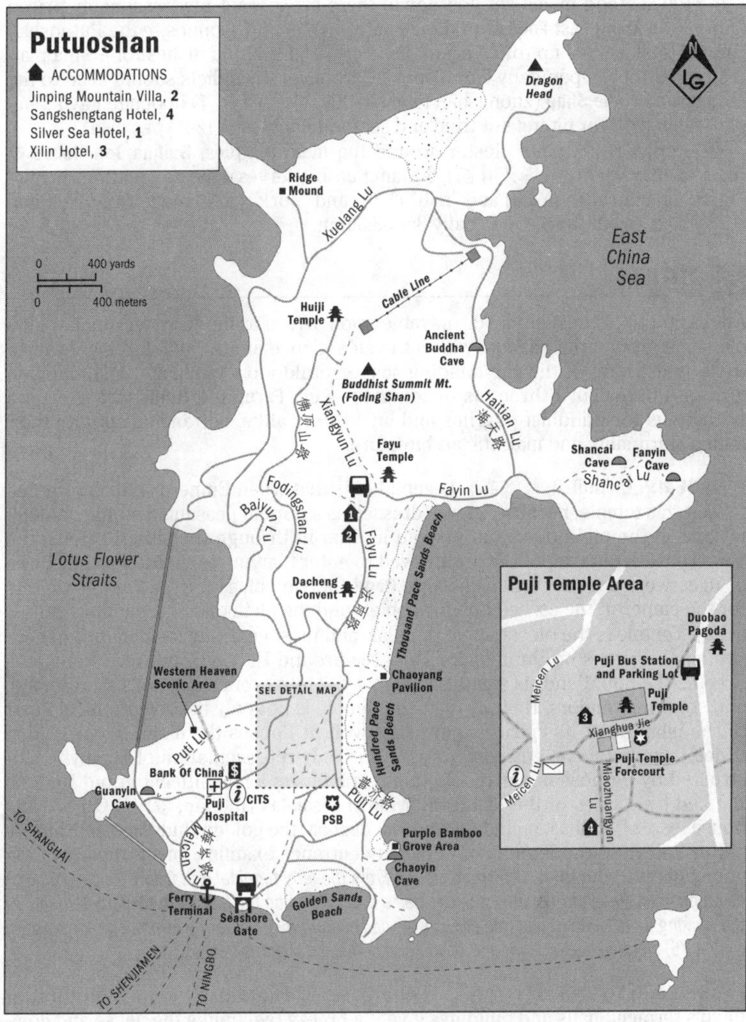

FOOD

Like neighboring Ningbo, Putuoshan is famous for its seafood. One specialty is **Zhoushan Yellow Fish** (zhōushān huáng yú; 舟山黄鱼), served steamed or sautéed with a side dish of tofu and fish-head soup (Y100 per kg). Another well-known dish is **Zhoushan Snails** (zhōushān wōniú; 舟山蜗牛), which are stirred in a special vinegar sauce (Y20). Meicen Lu and Piji Lu are littered with virtually identical expensive restaurants. Of these, the **Seafood Garden Complex** (hǎixiān yuán; 海鲜园), where Puji Lu meets Meicen Lu, is particularly good. Prices are the same everywhere on the island, but the variety here can't be beat.

SHANGHAI

If Y100 seafood meals get you down, there are a scant few reasonably priced options. **Ah Xiang Fast Food ❶** (āxiáng kuàicān; 阿祥快餐), opposite the Putuoshan Grand Hotel, serves up tofu, vegetables, pork, and seafood dishes for Y3-5 a platter. (☎609 1557. Open daily 7am-10pm.) Carbohydrate-addicts should head to the **Zhongshan Noodle Shop** (zhōngshān miànshí diàn; 中山面食店) opposite Fayu Temple's main exit, for piping hot fried and seafood noodles (Y12-20 per dish).

Vegetarian restaurants cluster around the main temples. **Baihua Tea House ❷** (báihuá cháyè guǎn; 白华茶叶馆), 6 Xianghua Jie, serves delicate creations including radish pancakes (Y4.5) and "fish" (Y20) and "pork" (Y30) made from fruit and sticky rice. (☎609 1208. Open daily 8am-8:30pm.)

SIGHTS

Admission to Putuoshan is Y60, payable upon arrival at the ferry terminal. A simple stroll around the island—without even a glance at any "official" sights—is a treat, with views of the surrounding sea, emerald mountains, and lush bamboo groves. Putuoshan's three major temples—**Puji, Fayu,** and **Huiji**—are the main attractions for Buddhist pilgrims and lay visitors alike, entrancing all with their famed spirituality and majestic architecture.

PUJI TEMPLE (pǔjì sì; 普济寺). Legend holds that when Emperor Zhuang wanted to visit this temple, because he was dressed as a normal peasant, a monk wouldn't let him in the main door and instead let him in through the side. Furious, the emperor ordered that no one be allowed to enter that entrance. Afterwards, three bridges were constructed over **Haiyin Pond** (hǎiyīn chí; 海音池)—the middle one for the emperor, the arched one for nobles, and the plain one for commoners.

Puji Temple is the oldest, most popular, and most centrally located of the three principal temples on Putuoshan. The area around Haiyin Pond (also known as Freeing-the-Soul Pond) is a gathering place for tour groups, *tai chi* practitioners, and souvenir vendors. Built in 1080, the temple is not only the geographical heart of the island, but its spiritual center as well. It houses the magnificent golden **Divine Guanyin** (shèng guānyīn; 圣观音), the only representation of Guanyin constructed by Putuoshan natives. In its main hall sits a magnificent grand Buddha flanked by statues of the **Eighteen Mythical Disciples** (luóhàn; 罗汉). Other halls house lesser Buddhas, including **Wen Shu Buddha,** the golden Buddha of learning—better known as the Buddha of university entrance examinations for many of the young people who visit. *(15 Xianghua Jie. From the ferry terminal exit, follow Meicen Lu north as it becomes Xianghua Jie; the temple is half a block down on the left. From the ferry terminal to the parking lot is a 5min. bus ride (Y3). Open daily in summer 5:30am-6:30pm; shorter hours in winter. Y5, children under 1.4m and devout-but-penniless pilgrims free.)*

FAYU TEMPLE (fǎyǔ sì; 法雨寺). At the base of Buddhist Summit Mountain, Fayu's terraced halls and buildings give it a breezy feel unlike the dense and compact Puji Temple. Built in 1580, Fayu greets visitors with its unique **Nine-Dragon Screen** (jiǔ lóng bì; 九龙壁), which is carved from 60 stones pieced together in an interlocking jigsaw fashion. Visitors will only see 8 dragons, however— the people here are reputedly the 9th dragon; after all, the Chinese somtimes call themselves the "sons of the dragon" (lóng de chuánrén; 龙的传人). A miniature golden pagoda stands between the wall and the first of the temple's several halls, where visitors can toss coins through five tiers of windows for good luck. In one hall sits the imposing statue of the **Thousand-Hand Guanyin** (qiān shǒu guānyīn; 千手观音), so called because she gave up her hands while in human form to heal her father's sickness; in return for her sacrifice, she was endowed with enlightenment. Her grateful father wanted a sculptor to commemorate his daughter by portraying her as whole and complete with her hands—the sculptor misunderstood and portrayed her with a thousand hands instead, hence setting the tradition for future portrayals of the deity. The highlight of the temple is the **Nine-Dragon Hall of Treasures** (jiǔ lóng bǎo diàn; 九龙宝殿), which was moved from Nanjing to Putuoshan during the Qing dynasty. *(1 Fayin Lu. Take a minibus from the Puji Temple parking lot, or walk 30min. north. Also accessible from Huiji Temple by descending the Buddhist Summit Mountain along a trail of 1080 steps. ☎609 1540. Open daily 5:130am-6pm. Y5.)*

HUIJI TEMPLE (huìjì sì; 慧济寺). Huiji temple, the smallest and least crowded of the three main temples, is perched at the very top of Buddhist Summit Mountain (fódǐng shān; 佛顶山). Because it's the least accessible of the three temples, reached only by cable-car or an intimidating climb, it tends to attract only the most devout pilgrims. The surrounding area features breathtaking vistas of the sea to the west and the mountainside and valley to the south and east. The long walkway leading to the temple is paved with ancient calligraphy and lotus leaves to represent Guanyin's presence and believed to purify visitors of worldly sins. The completed temple has only two main halls off an inner courtyard; the hum of praying monks emanates from side halls. *(208 Xiangyun Lu. Take a minibus to the foot of Buddhist Summit Mountain and climb for 45min.-1hr. up the 1080 steps. Alternatively, take the chairlift (6:30am-7pm, round-trip Y35, 50% off for children below 1.4m) to the top. ☎609 1126. Open daily sunrise-sunset. Y5.)*

PURPLE BAMBOO GROVE (zǐzhú lín; 紫竹林). Ironically, purple bamboo is the least exciting of this grove's many attractions. Inside a small temple, flanked by a frieze of colorful miniature murals, sits a statue of Guanyin carved entirely from a solid block of jade. Near the murals, intrepid visitors can peer into **Chaoyin Cave** (cháoyīn dòng; 朝音洞), a spine-tingling drop into which many devoted followers have plunged in their attempt to attain enlightenment. The small pavilion on the rocks looks out over **Luojia Mountain** (luòjiā shān; 洛迦山). The mountain is shaped like a sleeping Buddha; the rock depression on the beach is said to be the footprint left by Guanyin when she stepped over to Putuoshan to admire its view. The **Courtyard of the Cannot-Bear-To-Leave Guanyin** (bùkěnqù guānyīn yuàn; 不肯去观音院), a tiny shrine to the left of Chaoyin Cave, acquired its name when a Japanese monk begged to take Guanyin back to Japan. The Putuoshan monks agreed, but Guanyin apparently did not; the poor monk was shipwrecked not far offshore and returned to the island to build Guanyin a suitable temple. *(Minibuses (Y2) stop here on the way from the Puji Temple Parking Lot to the ferry. Or, walk south on Puji Lu for about 10min.; when the road forks, turn left onto Zizhu Lu. A few minutes walk down the road, a footpath leads to the entrance. ☎669 8221. Open daily 5:30am-6:30pm. Y5)*

SOUTH SEA GUANYIN (nánhǎi guānyīn; 南海观音). This 33m tall statue, set amid white limestone and marble and looming golden and impressive, has a deservedly palatial air. Around the base of the statue, exhibition halls show art and artifacts. The lower level walls are crammed with intricate wall-to-ceiling murals made with bronze, dark wood, and even colored jade. The murals illustrate scenes from the story of Putuoshan's origin and familiar pictures of present-day Putuoshan. The second level boasts hundreds of glass-encased icons of Guanyin. *(Take Puji Lu south from the Puji Temple parking lot and follow the left fork that becomes Zizhu Lu. Continue straight as Zizhu Lu becomes a footpath leading uphill for another 5-10min.; the entrance is on top of the hill, to the right. Open daily 5:30am-6pm. Y6.)*

OTHER SIGHTS. Putuoshan is sprinkled with a host of less frequent but nonetheless stunning caves, temples, and pavilions. The small **Hundred-Pace Sands Beach**

(bǎi bù shā; 百步沙), opposite and a bit north of the Puji Temple parking lot, and the more spacious **Thousand-Pace Sands Beach** (qiān bù shā; 千步沙), with its entrance along a gardened path opposite Fayu Temple, are popular summer escapes from the religiosity of the rest of the area. During the summer, you can camp in rented tents on Hundred-Pace Sands. Sunrise- and sunset-watching and tea sampling are popular hobbies for locals and tourists. Deck chairs, umbrellas, and other beach accessories can be rented for Y12-30 per hour, with a Y100 deposit. *(☎609 1418. Both beaches open for swimming 8am-7:45pm; for strolling 8pm-midnight and 3:30am-7am. Hundred-Pace Sands Y5, swimming Y15; Thousand-Pace Sands Y12. 50% off for children below 1.4m.)*

YANGZI BASIN

Like the Yellow River to the north, the Yangzi River (the third longest river in the world) and its whims dictate the fates of the countless people who dwell along its banks. Summer floods bring torrents of muddy water rushing down the river, threatening to overwhelm dikes and deluge even the most massive cities. Even in flood-free years, all that rushing water brings unbearably humid summers and damp, chilly winters to the riverside provinces of Anhui, Jiangxi, Hunan, and Hubei. All in all, the Yangzi Basin seems like a really awful place to live.

Nonetheless, the Yangzi is much gentler than the merciless Yellow River, and the lands along its banks are among China's most populous and productive and boast some of China's most dramatic scenery. The Yangzi travels 6380km from the Geladandong Glaciers of Tibet to the East China Sea, rushing through the Three Gorges in Chongqing and Hubei before giving way to sleepy hamlets and rapidly developing industrial parks. Away from the mighty river, flood plains give way to haunting, mist-enshrouded mountains that have inspired poets and painters for centuries. Today they attract tourists in search of the splendor of times past. Local history in this picturesque, enchanting area is a several thousand-year-old tale of nature at its most sensational, woven together into the rich fabric of legend.

HIGHLIGHTS OF THE YANGZI RIVER BASIN

CATCH A GLIMPSE OF MONASTIC LIFE on the sacred mountains of **Jiuhuashan** (see p. 413) and **Wudangshan** (see p. 453), where the cool religious devotees hang out.

FIND YOUR INNER CHAIRMAN at Shaoshan (see p. 434), Wuhan (see p. 443), and Jinggangshan (see p. 427), where Mao spent his formative years.

SEE THE SUN RISE OVER A SEA OF CLOUDS atop **Huangshan Mountain** (see p. 403) after climbing its craggy peaks.

ANHUI 安徽

The flat, dusty cities of northern Anhui province could never be called spectacular. But don't despair—even though Anhui is known as the "poor cousin of Jiangsu province," the province's southern areas are as jam-packed with scenic beauty as they come. Join the chattering tourists at Huangshan to catch a glimpse of the famed Beihai sunrise, or wander among the rice paddies and peasant huts that dot the idyllic countryside around Jiuhuashan, one of China's four sacred Buddhist mountains. Anhui's lush scenery and pastoral way of life is a soothing counterpoint to the frenzied coast and dusty Henan province.

HEFEI 合肥 ☎0551

The last time Hefei saw any *real* action was in AD 383, when the Battle of Feishui ripped through the city, the country; the brutal conflict ensured that north and south China would develop independently from one another well into the future. Ever since the clash, the city has been waiting for some new and exciting gem to lure tourists. But even esteemed titles like provincial capital of Anhui and home of

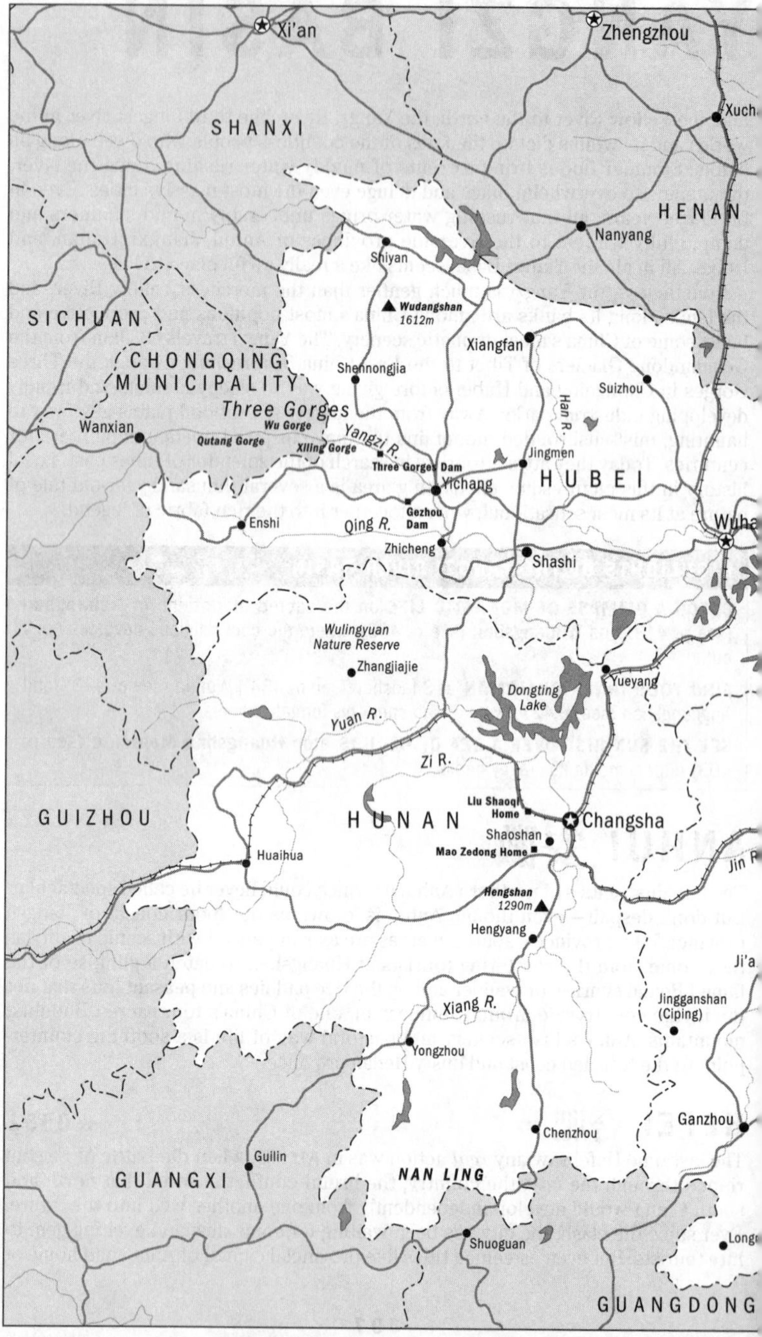

Xi'an
Zhengzhou
Xuch
SHANXI
HENAN
Nanyang
Shiyan
Wudangshan 1612m
SICHUAN
Xiangfan
CHONGQING MUNICIPALITY
Shennongjia
Suizhou
Three Gorges
Wu Gorge
Han R.
Wanxian
Qutang Gorge
Yangzi R.
Xiling Gorge
Three Gorges Dam
Jingmen
HUBEI
Yichang
Gezhou Dam
Enshi
Qing R.
Wuha
Zhicheng
Shashi
Wulingyuan Nature Reserve
Zhangjiajie
Yueyang
Dongting Lake
Yuan R.
Zi R.
Liu Shaoqi Home
Changsha
GUIZHOU
HUNAN
Shaoshan
Mao Zedong Home
Huaihua
Jin R
Hengshan 1290m
Hengyang
Ji'a
Jingganshan (Ciping)
Xiang R.
Yongzhou
Ganzhou
Chenzhou
Guilin
GUANGXI
NAN LING
Shuoguan
Longn
GUANGDONG

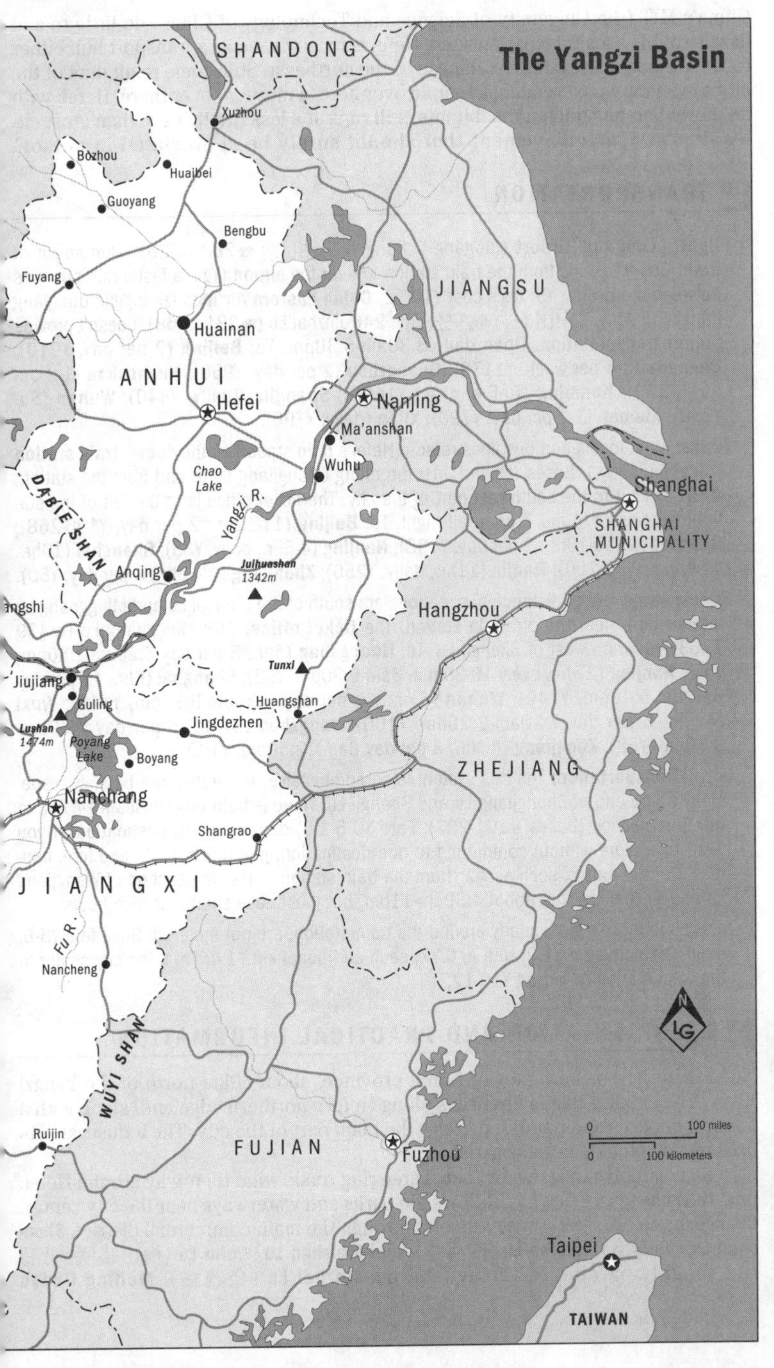
The Yangzi Basin
SHANDONG
Xuzhou
Bozhou
Huaibei
Guoyang
Bengbu
Fuyang
JIANGSU
Huainan
ANHUI
Hefei
Nanjing
Ma'anshan
Chao Lake
Wuhu
Yangzi R.
DABIE SHAN
Shanghai
SHANGHAI MUNICIPALITY
Anqing
Jiuhuashan 1342m
Hangzhou
Tunxi
Jiujiang
Guling
Huangshan
Lushan 1474m
Jingdezhen
Poyang Lake
Boyang
ZHEJIANG
Nanchang
Shangrao
JIANGXI
Fu R.
Nancheng
WUYI SHAN
Ruijin
FUJIAN
Fuzhou
0 100 miles
0 100 kilometers
Taipei
TAIWAN

China's MIT (the University of Science and Technology of China) do little to add dazzle to this squarish city. As such, Hefei is mostly used as a transport hub either to Huangshan in the south or Jiangsu to the northeast. Still, some reminders of the city's legendary past remain: a temple over here, a museum over there. Hefei, with its more than one million inhabitants, still runs at a less frantic pace than most cities its size, an achievement that should surely be appreciated in person.

TRANSPORTATION

Flights: Luogang Airport (luògǎng jīchǎng; 骆岗机场; ☎288 6626), 7km south of town. Bus #11 runs from the train station to near the airport (Y1); a faster minibus runs between the two for Y5; taxis cost Y10-12. **China Eastern Airlines** (zhōngguó dōngfāng hángkōng gōngsī; 中国东方航空公司), 246 Jinzhai Lu (☎281 2768), doesn't provide airport transportation. Open daily 8:30am-5:30pm. To: **Beijing** (2 per day, Y910); **Chengdu** (3-4 per week, Y1170); **Guangzhou** (2 per day, Y950); **Huangshan** (1-2 per day, Y330); **Kunming** (Tu-F and Su, Y1480); **Shanghai** (daily, Y440); **Wuhan** (Su, Y330); **Xiamen** (1-2 per day, Y790); **Xi'an** (daily; Y790).

Trains: Most locals and bus lines refer to Hefei's train station as the **"new" train station** (xīn zhàn; 新站). Buses #1 and 119 run along Changjiang Lu to and from the station; #101 links it to the southwest part of the city. The ticket office is to the left of the station; windows #6 and 7 open all night. To: **Beijing** (11-12hr., 2 per day, Y106-268); **Guangzhou** (15-16hr., 2 per day, Y198); **Nanjing** (4-5hr., daily, Y35); **Shanghai** (10hr., 4 per day, Y96-260); **Tianjin** (11hr., daily, Y250); **Zhenjiang** (4½-5hr., 3 per day, Y50).

Buses: About 4 long-distance bus stations are south of the Shengli Lu and Mingguang Lu intersection, near the old train station. The **ticket office,** 168 Mingguang Lu (☎429 7263), is 5min. west of Shengli Lu. To: **Huangshan** (6hr., 8 per day 6:20am-1:50pm, Y55); **Nanjing** (2½hr., every 10-20min. 6am-5:20pm, Y52); **Shanghai** (6hr., 17 per day 6:20am-5:40pm, Y149); **Wuhan** (6½hr., 6 per day 7:30am-5:30pm, Y140); **Wuxi** (4½hr., 8 per day 7:20am-2:20pm, Y100); **Yangzhou** (3½hr., 6 per day 7:30am-3:30pm, Y58); **Zhenjiang** (4½hr., 3 per day 8am-12:50pm, Y100).

Local Transportation: The bus system is comprehensive, but traffic can be slow, especially at the end of Changjiang Lu and Shengli Lu. There is both **bus** (buses #1-47) and **minibus** service (buses #101-202). Fare Y0.5-1.5, depending on destination. If you want to explore without committing to one destination, just fork over Y1 and look hapless. Certain routes, such as **#1** (from the train station to the intersection of Wangjiang Lu and Jinzhai Lu), run about 4:30am-11pm, but most have shorter service hours.

Taxis: Some taxis, particularly around the train station, are not metered. Base fare Y5-6, each additional km Y1.2; with A/C Y7, each additional km Y1.4. From the city center to the train station or airport Y10-12.

ORIENTATION AND PRACTICAL INFORMATION

Hefei is in the northern part of Anhui province, about 80km north of the Yangzi River. The smaller **Nanfei River** runs along Hefei's northern edge and, along with a handful of parks and ponds, encircles the main part of the city. The industrial suburbs recede quickly into farmland.

Hefei is largely navigable by foot. Three ring roads wind their way around Hefei; one, **Huancheng Lu** (环城路), follows the parks and waterways near the city center. **Changjiang Lu** (长江路) runs east-west through the main commercial district. **Shouchun Lu** (寿春路), **Huaihe Lu** (淮河路), and **Meishan Lu/Wuhu Lu** (梅山路/芜湖路) run roughly parallel to Changjiang Lu. **Jinzhai Lu** (金寨路), **Meiling Dadao**

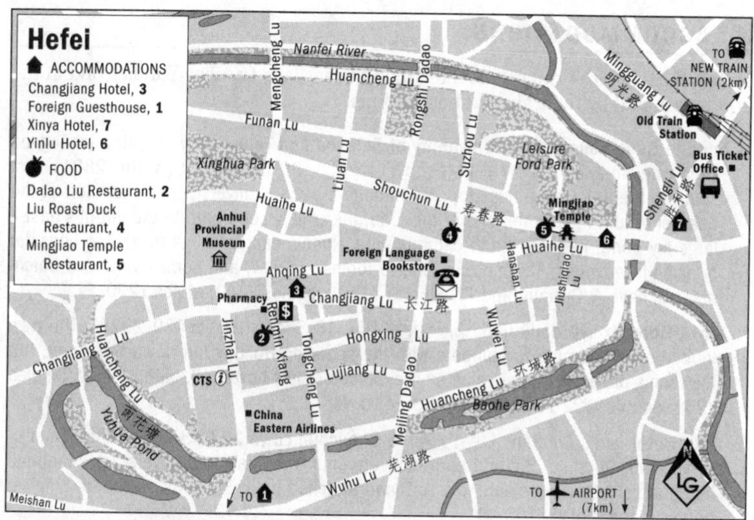

(美菱大道), and **Suzhou Lu** (苏州路) run north-south through the city. Both the train station and the main long-distance bus station are on **Shengli Lu** (胜利路), in the northeast part of the city.

Travel Agency: CTS, Jiuzhou Building, 381 Jinzhai Lu, 1st fl. (☎265 1522; fax 265 4308), near Lujiang Lu. Staff members speak English, French, German, Spanish, and Japanese. Mrs. Jane Liu in the airline booking office readily offers advice and speaks wonderful English. Open July-Sept. M-F 8am-noon and 3-6pm; Oct.-June 8am-noon and 2-5:30pm.

Bank of China: 313 Changjiang Lu (☎265 8688, ext. 2708 or 261 6719), at Renmin Xiang. Exchanges currency and traveler's checks. Credit card advances. Open M-F Mar.-Oct. 8:15am-5:30pm; Nov.-Apr. 8:15am-5pm.

Bookstores: Xinhua Bookstore (☎265 2101), on the corner of Changjiang Lu and Meiling Dadao, is large but has little more than English learners' dictionaries and creased copies of *Treasure Island.* Another location on Chiangjiang Lu near Tongcheng Lu has a similar selection. Both open daily 8:30am-7pm. **Foreign Language Bookstore** (wàiyǔ shūdiàn; 外语书店;☎265 6009), on Suzhou Lu at Huaihe Lu, has a much broader selection, including recent literature on the 2nd fl. Open daily 8:30am-7pm.

Hospital: Hefei Red Cross Hospital (héféishì hóngshízìhuì yīyuàn; 合肥市红十字会医院; ☎363 4794; 24hr. ☎365 1919), near Anhui University. From the train station, take bus #119 to Jiuhu stop and walk up a small alley.

Pharmacy: Changjiang Pharmacy (ānhuī chángjiāng dàyàofáng; 安徽长江大药房), 315 Changjiang Lu (☎264 8063), at Renmin Xiang. The 1st fl. houses Chinese versions of western drugs; upper floors sell medical devices and medicinal herbs. Open 24hr.

Telephones: China Telecom, 97 Suzhou Lu (☎267 1869). Open 24hr. IDD service.

Internet Access: On the 2nd fl. of the Suzhou Lu/Changjiang Lu post office (☎262 0782). Y5 per hr. Open daily 8am-midnight, with occasional closing at lunch time.

Post Office: Hefei Post Office, on the corner of Suzhou Lu and Changjiang Lu, near Sipai Lou bus stop. EMS and Poste Restante. Open daily 8am-8pm. **Postal code:** 230001.

ACCOMMODATIONS

Hotels in Hefei are primarily located along **Changjiang Lu,** near Yuhua Pond in the southwest, and by the train and bus stations.

Foreign Guesthouse of the University of Science and Technology of China (zhōngguó kējìdàxué zhuānjiā lóu; 中国科技大学专家楼), 96 Jianzhai Lu (☎360 2881), just south of the Keji Daxue bus stop. Go through the main university gate, turn left at the dead end; turn right at the end of the road, take the second path to the left; it's past a large lily pond, near the north campus gate. Rooms can be tough to get, so consider booking in advance. The more expensive rooms are new, and some even have balconies. All have A/C, bath, and TV. Singles Y150; doubles Y240; triples Y290. ❷

Xinya Hotel (xīnyà dàjiǔdiàn; 新亚大酒店), 18 Shengli Lu (☎429 2929). The new lobby boldly attempts to compete with the sparkling Holiday Inn down the street, but the rooms provide a better value anyway. Clean rooms have A/C, bath, and TV. Singles Y258; doubles Y228-258; triples Y336-410. ❹

Yinlu Hotel (yínlù fàndiàn; 饮路饭店), 9 Shouchun Lu (☎264 9349), on the corner of Huancheng Dong Lu. Big and unattractive rooms. The straw bed covers are unappealing, but the rooms are clean, with A/C and attached bath. Breakfast included. Singles, doubles, and triples Y100. ❷

Changjiang Hotel (chángjiāng fàndiàn; 长江饭店), 262 Changjiang Lu (☎265 6441, ext. 1117 fax 262 2295), near Tongcheng Lu. Buses #1, 3, 29, and 46 stop outside. Relatively clean rooms and a central location make up for dripping plumbing in the cheaper rooms on the 3rd fl. Refurbished rooms have newer decor but dim lighting. Singles Y90-140; doubles Y160; triples Y210-228. ❷

FOOD

Hefei's liveliest eating areas hide off the main roads. At the western edge of the city center, one block south of Changjiang Lu, small stands line the street from Jinzhai Lu almost to Gongwan Lu. A bit east of Jinzhai Lu, **Renmin Xiang** stretches south from Changjiang Lu and features several blocks of excellent eateries and an upbeat atmosphere at night; side streets that run south from Wuhu Lu, near the entrance to Baohe Park, also boast eateries. Restaurants and stalls on **Suzhou Lu** between Huaihe Lu and Shouchun Lu focus on tasty lunchtime munchies. **Street markets** are scattered throughout the city, with several right off Changjiang Lu. In all of these places, Y10 will buy a hearty meal for one. Hefei's regional speciality, **freshwater crab** from Lake Chao, is heaven at a reasonable price; look for the frisky critters at sidewalk eateries throughout the city.

The 24-hour **Haobangshou Supermarket** (hǎobāngshǒu chāoshì; 好帮手超市), two doors down from the Changjiang Pharmacy on Renmin Xiang, has a great selection. Look for the small door next to the stairs to a restaurant on the second floor, on the right side when coming from Changjiang Lu.

Dalao Liu Restaurant (dàlǎoliú xiǎochībù; 大老刘小吃部; ☎261 1461), next to 15 Renmin Xiang, proves once again the power of specialization. The friendly owners of this local favorite serve only noodle soups; the result is a bowl of basic beef noodles (Y3.5) that may well be the best you'll ever have. Soups Y2.5-14. Open daily 6am-10pm. ❶

Mingjiao Temple Vegetarian Restaurant (míngjiàosì sù cāntīng; 明教寺素餐厅), 44 Huaihe Lu (☎/fax 265 6284), inside the Mingjiao Temple entrance on the corner of

Jiushiqiao Lu. Serves imitation meat dishes (Y5-25), soups (Y10), cabbage soaked in vinegar (Y5), and fresh and well-executed fried standbys. Open daily 10:30am-9pm. ❶

Liu Roast Duck Restaurant (liú kǎoyādiàn; 刘烤鸭店; ☎265 6810), on Suzhou Lu at Huaihe Lu. This busy breakfast and lunch spot serves tasty staples to local crowds. Dumplings, noodles, pastries—all under Y4. Open daily 6:30am-9:30pm. ❶

SIGHTS

What Hefei lacks in tourist panache, it makes up for with its lush and lovely parks. In fact, the ring of parks surrounding the city center gave Hefei the honor of being named a "National Garden City" in 1992, and if you're here during the hot season, you'll quickly come to appreciate this area's shaded retreat.

ANHUI PROVINCIAL MUSEUM (ānhuīshěng bówùguǎn; 安徽省博物馆). The museum's displays include a cast of the skull of an ape-man unearthed nearby, inscriptions from Han dynasty tombs, a model of a Ming dynasty residence, and a study showcasing the "Four Scholastic Treasures" (ink, paper, brush, and stone). A walk through the museum takes around 30 minutes, but be sure to allot time to rummage through the museum's eclectic gift shop. *(268 Anqing Lu, at the northern end of Jinzhai Lu. ☎282 3299. English captions. Open daily 8:30-11am and 3-5:30pm; last admission 5pm. Y4; special exhibitions Y2.)*

BAOHE PARK (bāohé gōngyuán; 包河公园). This lakeside park is a local favorite; families enjoy paddle boats and small temples, and young lovers canoodle by the water's edge. The park contains the **Tomb of Lord Bao** (bāozhěng mù; 包拯墓), a Song dynasty judge who was posthumously honored for honest and upright service; the fact that he became the protagonist of a wildly popular Taiwanese TV show hasn't affected Hefei denizens' pride in him. *(Entrances at Ma'anshan Lu, south of Changjiang Lu; on Huancheng Lu and Wuhu Lu, off Meiling Dadao. Open 24hr. Free.)*

MINGJIAO TEMPLE (míngjiào sì; 明教寺). Cao Cao, an illustrious leader of the Kingdom of Wei, used the **Archers' Training Terrace site** to drill his troops in the early 3rd century, but this temple wasn't built until the early Tang dynasty. The halls date from the 16th century, and were recently restored after being damaged during the Cultural Revolution. *(Huaihe Lu, at Jiushiqiao Lu. Open daily 7am-6pm. Y5.)*

OTHER SIGHTS. On the northeast side of town, **Leisure Ford Park** (xiāoyáojīn gōngyuán; 逍遥津公园) was the site of a famous battle between the Kingdom of Wu and the Kingdom of Wei. A statue commemorates General Zhang Liao (of the Kingdom of Wei), whose 10,000-man fighting force defeated an army 10 times its size. The park nicely combines a carnival atmosphere with more secluded lakeside trails. *(16 Shouchun Lu. Open daily 5am-6pm. Y5.)* **Xinghua Park** (xìnghuá gōngyuán; 兴华公园) is bordered on the east by Mengcheng Lu, with an entrance between Shouchun Lu and Huaihe Lu. Other parks include **Yuhua Pond** (yǔhuā táng; 雨花塘), a popular spot for evening walks on the southwest side of the city.

HUANGSHAN MOUNTAIN 黄山

A trip to the spectacularly rugged landscape of the Yellow Mountains should be first on every traveler's itinerary. The peaks are always high on the to-do lists of many Chinese tourists, who, with all the centuries-old calligraphy scrolls and national poetry dedicated to the place, practically breathe the Huangshan air before they've even been there.

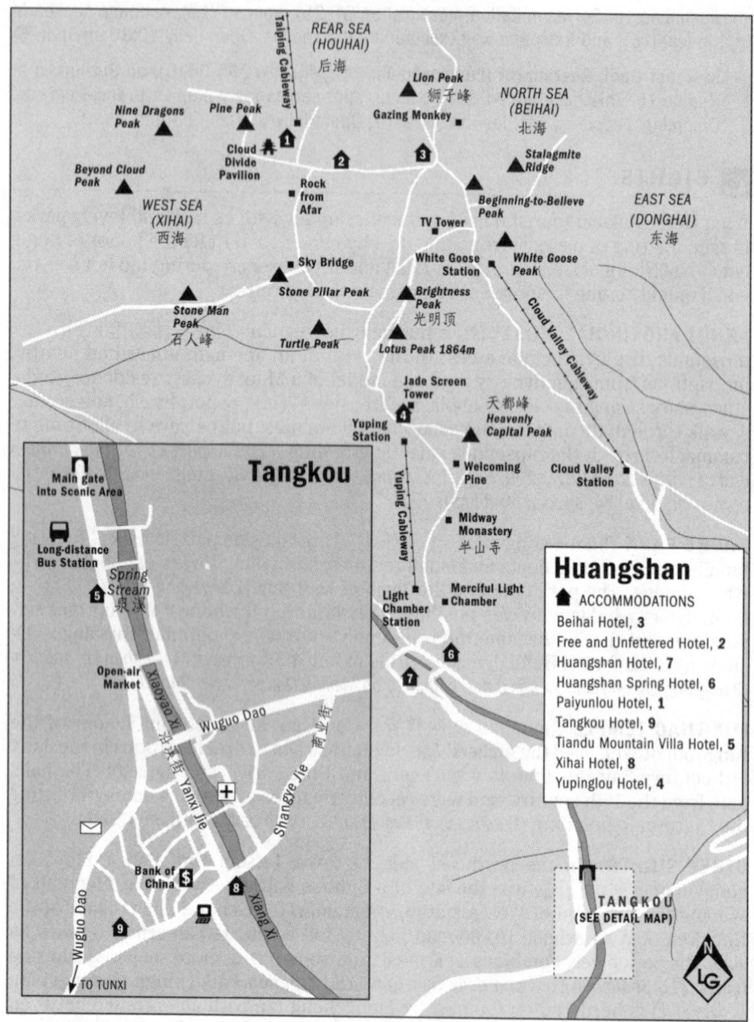

Not surprisingly, the trails along Huangshan are crowded; only the luckiest off-season climbers manage to escape the aggravating inertia of loud Chinese tour groups. And, of course, the area's rooms and food are more expensive than in other parts of China, mostly because tourism is Huangshan's greatest cash cow.

But hike for a while through the monolithic stone peaks, up through caves and clusters of crooked pines, and you'll easily understand why travelers the world over come to Huangshan. Meander through the enchanting butterfly-filled gardens on the path to Brightness Peak; clamber up Lotus Peak to see the mist-enshrouded peaks from Huangshan's highest point; or scramble with your hands and knees over the treacherous Heavenly Capital Peak, and you'll soon see why Chinese emperors wanted to live here forever. While other mountains' vistas elicit reverent sighs, Huangshan evokes breathless cries of disbelief.

As another incentive, the main outposts for Huangshan hikes are spellbinding in their own right. Nestled in the foothills of the mountains, the towns of Tangkou and Tunxi are smoky mazes of narrow streets and alleys, crowded with gritty markets and souvenir stands. The towns may be annoyingly touristy, and an amazing number of locals (i.e. everyone) seem to want to arrange your transport into the mountains, even still, the mellow and all-natural vibe of Huangshan promises more than a few gulps of fresh—albeit thin—air.

TUNXI 屯溪 ☎0559

Tunxi, also called Huangshan City, is the main transportation hub for the mighty mountain. Most travelers just pass through it on their way to Huangshan, although some buses drive directly to the base town of Tangkou. But don't just climb the mountain and hide in your hotel room—Tunxi boasts some extraordinarily well-preserved architechture from the Ming and Qing dynasties and may prove an interesting diversion from the constant Huangshan hoopla.

TRANSPORTATION

Flights: Huangshan City Airport (huángshānshì fēijīchǎng; 黄山市飞机场), about 10km west of the city center. Tickets available at the **CAAC ticket office,** 23 Huangshan Bei Lu (☎953 4111). Open daily 8am-8pm. To: **Beijing** (W-Th and Sa-M, Y990); **Guangzhou** (1-4 per day, Y880); **Shanghai** (2-3 per day, Y460); **Wuhan** (2-3 per day, Y570).

Trains: Huangshan City Train Station (huángshānshì huǒchē zhàn; 黄山市火车站; ☎251 2110), at the north end of Qianyuan Bei Lu, near the traffic circle on Guojing Lu. Ticket office (☎251 2652) in the small adjoining office on the west side of the station. Open 24hr. To: **Beijing** (21hr., 12:27am, Y182); **Fuzhou** (14hr., 5:49am, Y106); **Kunming** (57hr., 5:21pm, Y249); **Nanjing** (7-11hr., 7 per day 12:27am-11:12pm, Y27-54); **Shanghai** (12hr., 7:38am, Y44-53); **Xiamen** (24hr., 6:21am, Y64).

Buses: Huangshan City Long-distance Bus Station (huángshānshì chángtú qìchē zhàn; 黄山市长途汽车站; ☎251 5949), at the eastern end of Hehua Dong Lu. Ticket office is (☎2535 3952) in the building west of the station. Open daily 5am-6pm. To: **Hangzhou** (5hr., 6 per day 5:40am-4:20pm, Y30-48); **Hefei** (8hr., 6 per day 5:40am-12:50pm, Y42-57); **Shanghai** (12hr., 5:40 and 10am, Y47). Minibuses go to **Huangshan Scenic Area** and **Tangkou** throughout the day (1hr., Y10-25).

Local Transportation: Minibuses travel throughout the city during daylight hours. Most stop at both the train and bus stations and go along Huangshan Lu. With all the ticket sellers hanging out of buses and calling to pedestrians, chances are you'll find one that's going your way. Fare Y1.

Taxis: Taxis, pedicabs, and minibuses run throughout the region. Be careful–drivers have no qualms about ripping you off. Tunxi to Tangkou should cost about Y50-100. A pedicab from the train station to the west of the city should not be more than Y5. Always negotiate the fare in advance.

ORIENTATION AND PRACTICAL INFORMATION

The train station and **Huancheng Lu** (环城路) mark the far north of town. **Qianyuan Lu** (前园北路) runs south to the **Xinan River** (xīn'ān hé; 新安河). Several major east-west streets intersect Qianyuan Lu, including **Hehua Lu** (荷花路), which runs to the long-distance bus station in the east, and **Huangshan Lu** (黄山路), which connects **Xinan Lu** (新安路) and the commercial heart of the city in the west.

Travel Agency: CITS, 6 Xizhen Jie, 3rd. fl. (☎251 5295 or 251 2771), across from the Huaxi Hotel in the southwest part of town, just across the bridge from the Ancient Street; reach around and open the unlocked metal gate on the stairs. Exceptionally friendly and fluent English-speaking staff, with English maps and brochures to boot. Staff also speaks German and Japanese. Open in summer daily 8:30am-noon and 2:30-6pm; in winter 8-11:30am and 2-5:30pm.

Tourist Complaint Line: ☎251 7464.

Bank of China: 9 Xinan Bei Lu, at Huangshan Lu (☎251 4859). The only bank in town that exchanges currency and traveler's checks. Open daily 8am-5:30pm.

Internet Access: Yuanlai Youni Internet Bar (yuánlái yǒunǐ wǎngbā; 缘来有你网吧), on the south side of Yan'an Lu, just across the bridge from the end of Ancient Street. Y2 per hr. Open daily 8:30am-midnight.

Post Office: Huangshan City Post Office, 39 Qianyuan Bei Lu on the corner of Xinan Lu and Huangshan Lu (☎231 2110). EMS and Poste Restante. Open daily 8am-8pm. **Postal Code:** 245000.

ACCOMMODATIONS

If tourism is the lifeblood of the Huangshan region, the hotels in Tunxi would be the mitochondria. The few establishments that accept foreigners tend only to have pricey doubles. Prices listed here are for the high season (Mar. 15-Nov. 15); at other times, expect discounts (and bargaining leverage) to soar. Aim for discounts of at least 30%. All rooms listed have air-conditioning, TV, and private bath.

Huaxi Hotel (huāxī fàndiàn; 花溪饭店), 1 Xizhen Jie (☎251 4312; fax 251 4990), in the southwest part of the city, across the bridge at the western end of the Ancient Street. A 300-room monster, complete with restaurants, supermarkets, and shopping. Its cheapest rooms are Tunxi's best deal for foreigners. Singles Y580; off-season doubles in the old building Y220, in the new Y480; peak-season doubles Y280/Y680. AmEx/MC/V. ❺

Yinlian Hotel (yínlián dàjiǔdiàn; 银联大酒店), 1-8 Xianren Dong Lu (☎252 7678; fax 252 7282). Walk west of the train station and take a left on Xianren Dong Lu; the hotel is about a block down on the right. Large and impressive rooms are complemented by chandeliers in the large and impressive lobby. Bargain for at least a 20% discount. Singles Y288; doubles Y438. ❹

Huangshan Jingwei Hotel (huángshān jīngwěi jiǔdiàn; 黄山经纬酒店), 18 Qianyuan Bei Lu (☎234 5188). It's the huge, glass cylindrical building 1 block south of the train station. Costs big bucks, but ultra-convenient; large rooms have curved walls, sweeping views, and bonus fancy bath products. Doubles Y360-480; triples Y480. ❺

FOOD

Small food stands are clustered near the train and bus stations, especially along **Hehua Dong Lu,** where giant bowls of *jiǎozi* sell for as little as Y2. The street west of the bus station also has oodles of noodle and dumpling stands. **Qianyuan Bei Lu** has bigger (and more expensive) eateries. The primary nighttime activity is **karaoke,** but the tone-deaf may prefer the hopping **morning market** near the bus station. Frogs are Y3; get 'em while they're hot.

SIGHTS

Tunxi's **Ancient Street** (túnxī lǎojiē; 屯溪老街) begins near the bridge in the far western part of town and winds south toward the Xinan River. Many of the buildings lining the street date all the way back to the Song dynasty (some of the tourist maps sold here can't be much younger). Tour leaders herd their groups through this narrow lane before taking them to the mountain, so expect to see plenty of kitschy, overpriced merchandise. Some shops specialize in traditional local products, including medicine, tea, scrolls, and carved bamboo heads. Most unusual are the bottles of wine (Y30-150) with large, dead snakes inside, a delicacy that puts every tequila worm to shame. All in all, this famed street is a let-down unless you intend on some serious shopping, although the place is a lot livlier at night.

A more rewarding sight may be **Cheng's Three Residences** (chéngshì sānzhái; 程氏三宅), just off Huangshan Dong Lu, near Ancient Street. A well-preserved example of Ming architecture, this buliding was once owned by a wealthy businessman, and showcases the high walls (for the "protection" of the womenfolk) and wooden frames of ancient Anhui homes. Chinese academics have lately speculated that Chen Qiong, a former occupant of the mansion, might have been the inspiration for Lin Daiyu, the heroine of the Chinese classic, *Dream of the Red Chamber*. (Open daily 8am-6pm. Admission with guided tour in Chinese Y20, students Y10.)

TANGKOU 汤口 ☎0559

Tangkou, a small village at the base of Huangshan, is the main outpost for hikes up the mountain. The constant flow of tourists determined to photograph themselves in victorious poses atop the mountain has turned Tangkou into the archetypal tourist town: most shops sell a variety of useless hiking paraphernalia, and every corner is home to innumerable eateries and hotels. The town is otherwise unspectacular, but it is probably wise to spend a night here in order to be able to conquer Huangshan early enough to avoid the yellow-hatted, tourist-group hordes.

ORIENTATION AND PRACTICAL INFORMATION

Tangkou is a tiny cluster of hotels, shops, and restaurants spread out next to a stream that comes down from the mountain. **Yanxi Jie** (沿溪街) runs along **Spring Stream** (quán xī; 泉溪) until it dead ends at **Shangye Jie** (商业街). The two-lane highway comes in from the southwest, drawing parallel to the stream as it heads north to the main gate into the Huangshan Scenic Area. Tangkou ends here, and the highway continues up to the **Hot Springs Area** and the cable car terminal, the starting point for most mountain hikes.

Buses: Huangshan Scenic Area Long-distance Bus Station (huángshān fēngjǐngqū qìchē zhàn; 黄山风景区汽车站; ☎556 2590 or 556 5291), at the main gate. Open daily 5:30am-7:30pm. To: **Hangzhou** (7hr., 8 per day 6:20am-2:30pm, Y63-70); **Hefei** (8-10hr., 6 per day 6:05am-3:40pm, Y63-80); **Jiuhuashan** (4hr., 6:10am, Y27); **Jiujiang** (6hr., 7:40am, Y85); **Nanjing** (6-8hr., 10 per day 6:30am-4:40pm, Y57-75); **Shanghai** (12hr., 6:20am, Y101); **Wuhan** (12hr., 9am, Y153). In addition, minibuses to Tunxi ply the streets throughout the day (Y10-13).

Taxis: Taxis circle like sharks waiting for fresh tourist blood. Fares are negotiable; as always, bargain hard. From Tangkou to the base of the Eastern steps about Y10; to the Hot Springs Area about Y5.

Tour Guides: Mr. Hu, owner of the not-so-surprisingly named Mr. Hu's Restaurant (see p. 410), sells maps in English, provides quality information, and can help book bus tickets; all he asks is that you eat at his restaurant once or twice.

Bank of China: Opposite the front gate of the Free and Unfettered Hotel (☎(551) 267 5330). Open daily 8am-5pm. A branch in the **Beihai Summit Area** (☎558 5178), opposite the Beihai Hotel. Open daily 8am-4:30pm. Both branches and also many high-end hotels exchange currency.

Weather Conditions: ☎121. Weather is a crucial factor on Huangshan. Clear days can offer views of distant rock formations while cloudy weather creates seas of swirly mist. Rainy days are the worst, with slippery trails and poor visibility; but after-rain conditions are considered optimal, with fleeting cloud formation, sunshine, and the occasional rainbow. For more information, contact the **Huangshan Meteorological Observatory** (☎251 2411). Open daily 8-11am and 2-5pm.

Hospital: Beihai Emergency Center (běihǎi jiùhù zhōngxīn; 北海救护中心; ☎556 2555), in the summit area, opposite the Beihai Hotel. Open daily 8:30-11:30am and 2-5pm; a doctor is always on call for emergencies. Run by the Beihai Hotel but open to all visitors. The **Tangkou Clinic** (tāngkǒu zhěnsuǒ; 汤口诊所; ☎556 1272, emergency ☎(129) 862 8260), across the stream from Yanxi Jie just before reaching Shangye Jie, also provides medical assistance.

Internet Access: Xincheng Internet Cafe (xīnchéng wǎngbā; 新城网吧; ☎556 3001). A small store on the street next to the Free and Unfettered Hotel in Tangkou. Fast connections. Y3 per hr. Open 24hr. Upscale hotels in the Hot Springs area also have more expensive access.

Post Office: Tangkou Post and Telecommunications Office (☎556 2009), on the highway toward the south end of town, north of the Tangkou Hotel. EMS. Open daily 8am-6pm. **Postal Codes:** 242708 for Tangkou; 242709 for Huangshan Scenic Area, including Hot Springs Area.

ACCOMMODATIONS

TANGKOU

Although dorms are cheap and plentiful in theory, most foreigners will find themselves barred from all but the most expensive rooms in most establishments. Overseas Chinese, however, may be able to wheedle their way into cheaper digs. That being said, the village is still the best place to sleep if you're hiking Huangshan in a day. If you're overnighting on the mountain, ask to leave your luggage at a Tangkou hotel (Y2-5 per day), and take a daypack on your climb.

Tiandu Mountain Villa Hotel (tiāndū shānzhuāng bīnguǎn; 天都山庄宾馆; ☎556 2160), on the highway, about halfway between the bridge and the main gate to the mountains. This rare establishment offers a range of clean rooms. The cheaper rooms entail a stroll to the toilet and a trek to the shower. 4-bed dorms Y50, with bath Y60; doubles with A/C, TV, and bath Y280. ❶

Tangkou Hotel (tāngkǒu bīnguǎn; 汤口宾馆; ☎556 2400), 500m west of the Free and Unfettered Hotel on Shangye Jie, in a large white building with a blue tile roof. Friendly staff and relatively clean, though very bare dorms. More expensive rooms have A/C, TV, and bath. Communal bathrooms are damp and dimly-lit. 4-bed dorms Y35; doubles Y180-280; triples Y60-360. ❶

Free and Unfettered Hotel (xiāoyáo bīnguǎn; 逍遥宾馆; ☎556 2571). The newly renovated hotel will probably not give all travelers a free and unfettered time. The most expensive rooms are the only ones available to foreigners. Dorms Y25-60; doubles with TV, A/C, and bath Y280 and up. ❶

HOT SPRINGS AREA

Don't expect a hot tub party: the "springs" gurgle, and that's about it. There's little to distinguish the "public springs" from a big, public swimming pool. The "private springs" are even sillier: they're just bathtubs in a bathroom. Both cost Y50 and are available at the Huangshan Hotel. The area's serenity and beauty do, however, make for a welcome respite from Tangkou's unwavering obsession with tourism.

Huangshan Hotel (huángshān fàndiàn; 黄山饭店; ☎558 5808), near Peach Flower Stream. Small, standard A/C rooms with tiny bathrooms. Hot spring swimming pool on site. Singles Y380; doubles Y300-420. ❺

Huangshan Spring Hotel (huángshān wēnquán dàjiǔdiàn; 黄山温泉大酒店; ☎556 2198), down the ramp from the road at the bridge, across the stream from the Huangshan Hotel. Foreigners can stay in all of the excitingly clean rooms and admire the private stream running in front of the hotel. Be careful of what may be afoot in the bathrooms. Doubles with A/C and private bath Y380 and up. ❺

SUMMIT AREA

The same tour groups that clog the mountain trails also crowd into the dorms in the revoltingly overpriced hotels. Many travelers, however, grit their teeth and bear it. Staying in one of these hotels is the only sane way to catch the mountain at its early morning best, famed sunrises, rising cloud formations and all—and don't these hotels know it.

The following hotels are listed in the order in which they are positioned along the trail, assuming you walk from the Eastern Steps (White Goose Peak) toward the Western Steps. None of these hotels have air-conditioning, even in the most expensive rooms; most have winter heating.

Beihai Hotel (běihǎi bīnguǎn; 北海宾馆; ☎556 2555), Beihai Scenic Area, a 20min. walk from the White Goose Peak cable car. Newly renovated, this is one of the nicer hotels, with convenient access to the popular summit route. Dorm rooms are pleasant and carpeted, with wooden bunk beds and cheerful curtains. 6-bed dorms Y70; 4-bed dorms with bath Y180; doubles Y700 and up. MC/V. ❶

Xihai Hotel (xīhǎi fàndiàn; 西海饭店; ☎558 8888), Xihai Scenic Area, 20min. (2km) past the Beihai Hotel. Some of the spectacularly high-priced rooms here really do have spectacular scenic views. A pleasant cafe nearby. All rooms have attached baths, even the dorms. 4- and 6-bed dorms Y150; doubles Y960 and up. MC/V. ❷

Paiyunlou Hotel (páiyúnlóu bīnguǎn; 排云楼宾馆; ☎558 3208), Xihai Scenic Area, about 2min. beyond the Xihai Hotel, near the fork to the Taiping cable car. Rooms are relatively plain and the staff a bit distant. 10-bed dorms Y70, with shower Y170; doubles with TV and bath Y880-2000; triples Y185 per person. 10% service charge. ❶

Yupinglou Hotel (yùpínglóu bīnguǎn; 玉屏楼宾馆; ☎558 2288), in the complex at Yuping Peak, site of the Welcoming Pine. One of the few options on the Western Steps, so it fills up quickly. Dorms Y180; standard rooms Y720 and up. ❸

FOOD

Many restaurant owners here aren't afraid to take the initiative: they find you, direct you to a table, and even choose menu items. If you do venture out on your own, billboards outside the many eateries advertise roughly the same food at about the same prices, so try your luck wherever's most convenient.

An **open-air market** next to the stream sells everything from noodle and dumpling standbys to more exotic fare like eel, snake, and squirrel (each about Y3). Also here, tucked behind the first row of stalls, is **Mr. Hu's Restaurant ❶.** Look for the sign in English advertising coffee, toast, and advice. It may not be the most luxurious dining environment, but for breakfast, nothing beats a big plate of scrambled eggs and tomatoes (Y9). Save the cold beer (Y4) for later. Much of the fare is good, standard Chinese food; the English menu tells you what you're eating. For those rebelling against such standard fare, french fries (Y10) and french toast (Y5) beckon seductively. (☎(039) 5626 4286. Open daily 6am-11pm.)

Up on the mountain, snack stands and freelance cookie-and-cucumber vendors can be found at every turn; be prepared for heart-breakingly priced Y10 bottles of water. Bargaining can work; it's just not as effective when you're surrounded by tourists willing to fork over Y15 for a pack of beef jerky. Many stands sell instant noodles, but wise travelers stock up in Tangkou to avoid the exorbitant prices.

CLIMBING HUANGSHAN

Clamber past the souvenir shops to reach the area's true gem: the mountain. Admission to **Huangshan Scenic Area** (huángshān fēngjǐng qū; 黄山风景区) is Y82, for children below 1.3m and students (an ISIC card will work just fine) Y57.

There is one trail divided into three parts: the **Eastern Steps** (following the same path as the main cable car), the **Summit Area** (a variety of loop trails with relatively little up-and-down terrain), and the **Western Steps** (the Eastern Steps' brutal, crushing compatriot). Don't underestimate the physical toll of climbing several kilometers worth of non-stop steps, especially when you have to deal with maddening crowds. Try to take advantage of the frequent stone benches or buy a walking stick to help you with the ascent. Do not, however, use them to swat at other tourists, no matter how much you may be tempted to do so.

In general, of the three most famous peaks, **Brightness Peak** (guāngmíng dǐng; 光明顶) is the most accessible. **Lotus Peak** (liánhuā fēng; 莲花峰) is slightly more difficult to reach and involves a trek through caves and up irregular steps. **Heavenly Capital Peak** (tiāndū fēng; 天都峰) is frequently closed for safety reasons; the faint-hearted and safety-conscious may want to avoid it. Opt for the tried-and-true route: start at the base of the Eastern Steps and travel by foot or cable car; follow the summit across to the west; then descend the Western Steps, which, even as a downhill run, are cartilage-crushing, knee-wrecking, and exhausting. The stairs can be hypnotizing so keep your head up and remember to admire the views.

SAY CHEESE The urban legend rears its ugly head again in Huangshan. Park rangers once reported finding a tripod abandoned near a cliff at the top of the mountain. Curious as to why anyone would discard valuable camera equipment, they developed the film left inside. The prints they got back were the usual assortment of vacation photos taken by a young couple as they enjoyed the climb up Huangshan. All, that is, except for the last shot. The duo had set the camera's timer before they posed for a shot near the edge of the cliff, and the last exposure, in their final ghastly Kodak moment, had caught the surprised pair as they fell backwards off the cliff. Ghoulish and improbable? Perhaps. But the moral of the story remains: **stay on the trail.** This story may be more real than you think: accidents occur on Huangshan every year, due to overcrowded trails or less-than-conscientious travelers.

There's no shame in taking the easy way out. There are a total of three **cableways:** the **Yungu Line** (Cloud Valley line) runs up the Eastern steps; the **Taiping Line** starts from the North Gate; and the **Yuping Line** runs up the Western steps. Each makes summit runs from the scenic area gates, although from the Yuping Line you still have to conquer Brightness Peak to reach the summit proper. Unless you come early enough to beat the tour groups (a difficult feat, at best), expect long waits and exorbitant rates. If you do decide to walk, the trails are in great condition. However, some portions (particularly the route from Brightness Peak to Lotus Peak) are so steep that they're downright dangerous, especially when you add the menace of tour groups. Guides are available to lead the way for those who speak Chinese and want more detailed descriptions of the peaks and their legends. To help you find your way, signs are posted regularly along the trails. If all else fails, try pestering a Chinese tour group leader for information.

EASTERN STEPS

From the base town of Tangkou, minibuses and taxis (around Y10) make frequent trips to the **Cloud Valley Cable Car Station** (yúngǔ sì zhàn; 云谷寺站), which marks the start of the climb for most hikers. *(Cable car runs daily 6:30am-4pm. There may be as much as several hours of waiting time for the ascent. Y66 each way, children Y30.)* For those who choose to return via the Eastern Steps, the taxi fare from the Cloud Valley Temple to Tangkou is about Y10, although ridiculous fare hikes are common. Put your foot down (if your trembling muscles are in the condition to do so).

Much of the climb (ascent 1½-3hr., descent 2hr. or less) winds through forested areas; at the halfway point, hikers catch their first glimpses of the spectacular peaks, while various lookout points offer time for necessary water breaks. In general, the scenery is relatively unspectacular until you near the top, where the path reaches the upper cable car station at **White Goose Peak** (bái é fēng; 白鹅峰) and the **Beihai Scenic Area** (běi hǎi; 北海; North Sea). The walk around the summit area is a popular and not-too-tiring route. On the sharp left, an obscure path leads toward the television towers and the Western Steps. If you're doing the east-west circuit, follow the main path past the structures down to the right.

From here, there are two paths. The path upwards leads past **Beginning-to-Believe Peak** (shǐxìn fēng; 始信峰) to **Stalagmite Ridge** (shísǔn fēng; 石笋峰). The path downward leads to the Beihai Hotel and the viewing area for the Beihai sunrise. *(Daily sunrise and sunset times and weather forecast are posted in the hotel lobby and at Brightness Peak.)* From here, it's a 20- to 30-minute walk to the **Xihai Area** (xī hǎi; 西海; West Sea), a well-known stop for watching the sunset as clouds drift by in the early evening sky. The super-long **Taiping cable car** (tàipíng suǒdào; 太平索道), 3km long and with a 1km vertical drop, is supposedly the longest in Asia. *(Runs daily 7am-5pm. Peak season Y66 each way; off-season Y56.)* A short walk from the Xihai Hotel, this cableway runs from **Cloud Divide Pavilion** (páiyún tíng; 排云亭) to the distant **Songgu An** (sōnggǔ ān; 松谷庵), which leads to the North Gate.

Beyond the Xihai hotel, the path runs over **Lotus Ridge** (fūróng lǐng; 芙蓉岭), continuing past the **Rock Who Flew From Afar** (fēilái shí; 飞来石), a precipitously positioned boulder on a cliff, and Brightness Peak. From here, you can head toward the towers and loop back to the White Goose Peak cableway station or drop over the other side of the mountain for the long roller coaster hike that is the Western Steps.

WESTERN STEPS

From Brightness Peak, the path continues for five to six hours along the steep Western Steps down the mountain. From the rock formations of **Turtle Peak** (biēyú fēng; 鳌鱼峰), more steps lead to **Lotus Flower Peak** (liánhuā fēng; 莲花峰), the highest peak in the range. For a shortcut, head down and to the right at the snack stand, not up and to the left.

About halfway through the climb, the **Jade Screen Tower** (yùpíng loú; 玉屏楼) marks the terminus of the Yuping Line. *(Runs daily 6:30am-5pm. Each way Y66.)* The cable car soars by the **Moon-gazing Sky Dog** (tiāngǒu wàngyuè; 天狗望月) and the **Two Cats Capturing Mouse** (shuāngmāo bǔshǔ; 双猫捕鼠) rock formations en route to the **Merciful Light Chamber** (cíguāng gé; 慈光阁). From here, Tangkou is a short drive away. The Jade Screen Tower is near the solitary **Welcoming Pine** (yíngkè sōng; 迎客松), an eternal symbol of Huangshan. The long pine tree grows sideways out of the side of the mountain and hangs over the precipice below, awaiting photographers and painters who plaster its image in hotels and restaurants throughout the country. Just beyond the pine, at the top of an occasionally intimidating staircase, stands **Heavenly Capital Peak** (tiāndū fēng; 天都峰). The bypass for this peak branches off at the Jade Screen Tower, but meets the main trail again at the Midway Monastery. The view from the top of Heavenly Capital Peak is divine—the best on the trail.

DAYTRIP FROM HUANGSHAN: YIXIAN

47km from Tunxi. Yixian County consists of a dozen villages in the basin, with the county government in Yixian. From the Yixian Bus Station (on the main road in Yixian), ***minibuses*** *go to Tunxi (1½hr., 7:30am-5:30pm, Y7) via Yuting, and Tangkou (1½hr., 2 per day, Y13) via Xidi.* ***Hongcun*** *(10km north of Yixian) and* ***Xidi*** *(3km east of Yixian), the two main scenic spots, are accessible by* ***minibus*** *(Y2) and* ***taxi*** *(Hongcun Y20, Xidi Y5-10).* ***Admission*** *to Hongcun Y30; Xidi Y39. Foreigners require a* ***travel permit*** *to enter Yixian County (Y55), obtainable from the PSB in Tunxi. Allow a couple of days unless you go through CITS.*

Hidden in a tiny basin ringed by the Huangshan Mountains, Yixian (黟县) is one of the most isolated places in eastern China. Founded in 222 BC, the area was often a haven for refugees escaping conflicts on China's northern plains. During the Ming and Qing dynasties, residents of the county dominated commerce on the Yangzi delta and were often invited to perform opera for the emperors in Beijing, until devastating bouts of the plague in the 1800s put an end to the area's cultural and economic achievements, and doomed Yixian to obscurity. Today, over 4000 well-preserved Ming- and Qing-era homes, shops, and bridges remain (and can be seen in Zhang Yimou's film, *Judou*), a testament to Yixian's heyday and its ability to withstand the ravages of war and modernization.

While Yixian offers a quiet refuge from Huangshan's tour groups, those visitors mesmerized by the county's mist-shrouded mountains, sparkling streams, and bamboo groves should note that a PLA ballistic missile also lurks nearby. As a result, foreigners are not allowed to stay in any nearby accommodations. Local **food specialties** include "rock chicken legs," a gray-colored frog (shíjī; 石鸡), salted pork (làròu; 腊肉), and tea eggs (cháyè dàn; 茶叶蛋).

HONGCUN (hóngcūn; 宏村). Locals claim that their village is built in the shape of a kneeling ox. From above, this may indeed be the case; from the ground, though, the image is less clear. According to legend, after several fires in the 1300s, local clan elders asked a *feng shui* master for advice. (For more on *feng shui*, see **Banking on Feng Shui,** p. 547.) The master proposed giving the ox a "digestive system"—reservoirs and canals—to cleanse the village of "flammable spirits." As a result, water from a nearby stream was diverted to fill a pool in the center village. Narrow curbside aqueducts still run along every cobblestoned alleyway, carrying water from the pool throughout the village, eventually leading to South Lake. The constant flow of water past every doorstep lends a serene quality to village life and a photogenic quality as well; parts of Ang Lee's martial arts drama *Crouching Tiger, Hidden Dragon* were filmed here.

Only the **Inherit Dignity Hall** (chéngzhì táng; 承志堂) and a few smaller gardens are officially open to the public. Built by a Qing salt merchant in 1855, the Inherit Dignity Hall has over 60 rooms in seven buildings. Dubbed the "Forbidden City for Civilians," it is the largest and most elaborate example of Yixian architecture. Yixian merchants spent most of their time abroad and feared that robbers would loot their homes; thus, most of the plain, white walls have few windows. Within, the open courtyards let in natural light and are known as "sky wells." The walls are covered with ornate wood relief carvings, including two panels that depict battle scenes from the *Romance of the Three Kingdoms* and a New Year's celebration featuring over 100 boys. Wary girlfriends take note: A carving in the master's parents' hall depicts a famous opera scene in which a daughter-in-law was beaten for not kowtowing to her mother-in-law during her birthday party.

XIDI (xīdì; 西递). In AD 904, the oldest son of the last Tang emperor fled to southern Anhui after the fall of the Tang dynasty (see p. 10). Once there, he founded the Hu clan, now the biggest clan in town. Wealthy Xidi merchants, concerned about their social standing, donated generously to the imperial government. In return, the emperor awarded them various bureaucratic titles. Most of the houses display paintings of house masters dressed in mandarin attire, but few masters held any real power. Many masters had window panes carved depicting window frost (symbolizing bitterness and hard work in winter) alongside bats and grapes (symbolizing good fortune) to remind their sons that success required sacrifice. At the village entrance sit the **Governor's Arch** (cìshǐ páifǎng; 刺使牌坊), a massive stone arch with 16 lions and six crocodiles that was commissioned by the Ming emperor Shenzong to honor a loyal Xidi native. More traditional homes and mansions are open to the public in Xidi than in Hongcun.

JIUHUASHAN MOUNTAIN 九华山 ☎0566

Jiuhuashan is famous for the soaring beauty of one of China's four sacred mountains. The magnificent views from the 1350m summit have been infused with Buddhist serenity ever since a Korean prince chose these peaks as his place of meditation hundreds of years ago. Today, these hills are still alive with the sound of Buddhist *sutras* and journeying devotees emanating from over 80 temples on the mountain. Possibly more fascinating than the dazzling scenery is the frenetic capitalism of the tiny village. Villagers themselves are wont to remind you, however, that anyone who makes his refuge in this holiest of holies can't be all that bad at heart.

TRANSPORTATION

Trains: The nearest train station is the rather makeshift **Tongling station** (tónglíng zhàn; 铜陵站), 2hr. away. From there, minibuses (Y18) and taxis (up to Y200) to Jiuhuashan line up outside the station.

Buses: The **Jiuhuashan Bus Station** (jiǔhuáshān qìchē zhàn; 九华山汽车站; ☎501 1440), is 100m north of the main village gate. Open daily 5:30am-8pm. Buses run to: **Hangzhou** (7hr., 6 and 9:40am, Y55-70); **Hefei** (5hr., 7 per day 6:30am-2:10pm, Y51); **Nanjing** (5hr., 6:30am and 1pm, Y57); **Shanghai** (9hr.; 6am, 1, and 2:40pm; Y80-120); **Tangkou** (4hr.; 6:30, 7am, and 1:10pm; Y25-30). Tickets can also be bought at a kiosk (☎501 1291) inside the gates, visible from the main road. Open daily 5:30am-6:30pm. Many of the buses require you to transfer in Qingyang.

Local Transportation: Minibuses to various destinations depart throughout the day and can be found lined up along the main road, especially near the main gate. They regularly make the run to the Phoenix Tree and the cable car (Y5). Don't stress about finding one; they'll find you. Within Jiuhuashan, there isn't much need for **taxis:** the town takes about 20min. to cross on foot.

ORIENTATION AND PRACTICAL INFORMATION

Jiuhuashan is in the southern part of Anhui province, about 30km (1hr.) from **Qingyang** (青阳). The town sits cradled in a small valley, with the mountain wrapping around its south and east sides. To enter the village, buy a ticket at the main gate, in the northeast corner of town. **Admission** from March 1 to November 30 is Y60, students Y45; winter admission is Y40, students Y30, but keep in mind that snow regularly renders the roads impassable. To check road conditions in advance, call the Tourist Center (☎501 2746). From the entrance, **Jiuhua Jie** (九华街) forms a loop along the mountain, running along the east side of the mountain, turning right and curving along the front of the mountain, then hugging the main entrance. Small streets branch off from Jiuhua Jie, but none are particularly useful to tourists except the main square that branches off the eastern stretch and houses the Bank of China and the post office. Few buildings have addresses, but most hotels are either found on the main road or are directly visible from it.

Tourist Office: Jiuhuashan Tourist Center (☎501 2756), at the end of the eastern stretch of the main road, has extremely friendly staffers.

Travel Agency: CTS, 135 Jiuhua Jie, 3rd fl. (☎501 1588), provides service as ramshackle as the building. Follow the main road around to the west part of town; when you see the pond, cross over and look for the sign on the left.

Bank of China: 65 Huacheng Lu (☎501 1270), about half a block west of the main square. Exchanges traveler's checks. Credit card advances. Open daily 8am-5:30pm.

PSB: (☎501 1331), opposite the Tourist Center with officers on call 24hr. a day.

Hospital: Jiuhuashan Red Cross Clinic (jǐuhuáshān hóngshízì yīyuàn; 九华山红十字医院; ☎102) has a special examining room for tourists.

Post and Telecommunications: The **post office** (☎502 1211), on the southwest corner of the main plaza, has EMS and Poste Restante. Open daily 8am-5:30pm. **China Telecom,** in the same building, has 24hr. IDD service. **Postal code:** 242811.

ACCOMMODATIONS

It's not hard to find a small, inexpensive hotel in Jiuhuashan—the tiny town is jam-packed with hotels of all shapes, sizes, and quality, and more seem to be on the way up. It might not hurt to try some of the many family-owned businesses; though they may lack the cool detached professionalism of the larger establishments, they offer a reassuring friendliness in sync with low-key Jiuhuashan. Travelers who wish to get in touch with their spiritual sides may want to inquire at the mountain's many temples, particularly at the **Qiyuan Temple** just south of the bus station. These establishments rarely admit foreigners, though.

Yingchun Villa (yíngchūn shānzhuāng; 迎春山庄; ☎501 2749), on the main road as it curves toward the west, up a long flight of stone steps. Although slightly less posh than the larger hotels, the rooms are huge: and Mr. Liu and his extended family run the hotel with exuberant and personalized service. The cheapest rooms are bare, but clean. Most expensive rooms have A/C, bath, and TV. Mr. Liu & Co. also help book bus, train, and plane tickets for free. Doubles Y15-180. ❶

Dongya Hotel (dōngyà bīnguǎn; 东亚宾馆; ☎501 1370), a few blocks inside the main Jiuhuashan gate. Walk down the main road and turn right into a large parking lot; the hotel is at the very end. Pristine and well-kept, with strangely sweet smelling air. Bathrooms are excitingly large. Doubles and dorms include A/C, bath, and thrilling IDD phones. 4-bed dorms Y80; doubles Y240; triples Y150. MC/V. ❶

Longquan Hotel (lóngquán fàndiàn; 龙泉饭店; ☎501 1320), on the main road near its southwest corner, on the right side just before the street turns right, identifiable mostly by its bright red facade. Also a family-run enterprise. The staff is attentive and perky. Rooms are small but immaculate, with A/C, bath, and 24hr. hot water in most rooms. Foreigners may find it difficult to obtain the simpler, cheaper options. Dorms Y40; singles Y150; doubles Y200. ❶

Jiuhuashan Villa (jiǔhuá shānzhuāng; 九华山庄; ☎501 1036), turn right past Furong bridge from the main road—it's near the end of the road. Shockingly posh and sparkling. Cheerful, helpful staff. Massive gardens and gleaming rooms. All rooms have A/C, bath, and TV. Doubles Y480 and up. 20% discount possible. MC/V. ❺

Julong Hotel (jùlóng dàjiǔdiàn; 聚龙大酒店; ☎501 1368), standing by itself on the right side of the main road, not far beyond the main gate to the village. An imposing facade to match imposing prices and an imposing staff. Rooms are small, standard, and scrupulously clean. The mismatched room decor is entertainment in itself. All rooms have A/C, TV, and bath. Doubles Y280-398. ❹

Foguyuan Hotel (fógǔyuán bīnguǎn; 佛古园宾馆; ☎501 1379), on the eastern part of the road. Turn left into a small loop; the hotel is south of the CTS office, next to the sports field. Carpets are slightly worn, but rooms are faultlessly clean; all have A/C, TV, IDD, bath, and free bathroom products. Doubles Y320 and Y400; triples Y360. MC/V. ❺

FOOD AND ENTERTAINMENT

Numerous restaurants jostle for space with shops selling Buddhist paraphernalia on the main road; many are clustered on the southeast part of town. **Furong Food City** (fúróngzhuāng yǐnshíchéng; 芙蓉庄饮食城), on the corner before the road turns west, serves of plenty of food to visitors; many locals shy away, however. In just about every restaurant, you'll get to sample Jiuhuashan tea and *xiānggū* (香菇), a scrumptious dried mushroom cooked with bean curd or vegetables.

The sparkling new **Jiuhuashan Villa** (see above) comes complete with its own entertainment center. You can bowl (Y10-25 per game, depending on time; open 10am-midnight), play snooker (Y25 per hr.), or forget your spiritual surroundings and indulge in the sinful pleasure of mahjong all night long.

SIGHTS

Most tourists who journey to Jiuhuashan come to worship at (or simply admire) the area's many Buddhist temples. These holy sites may be of limited interest to a non-Buddhist, and so it may be more rewarding to soak in the sights on the two trails surrounding the village (which are centered around Buddhist sacred sites and have splendid views).

Conveniently close to the gate is **Zhiyuan Temple** (zhǐyuán sì; 祇园寺), an imposing, yellow-tiled building just inside the village. A geographically easy point of reference, the temple is off to the left after you enter and hosts the Buddhist trinity inside Mahavira Hall. It may not be particularly scintillating, but as Jiuhuashan's *raison d'être*, it is worth seeing. *(Open daily 4am-8pm. Y2.)* On the north side of this temple complex, a long staircase leads up the mountain to **Hundred Year Palace** (bǎisuì gōng; 百岁宫), the white hilltop building visible from the village. *(Open daily sunrise-sunset. Y5.)* Tread softly through the hushed palace, with its two large and separate halls. The first, an entrance hall, is occupied by monks meditating or chanting scriptures and contains the mummified body of the Ming priest Wu Xiam. Exceedingly friendly monks will happily tell the story of Wu Xiam, who was known to use gold dust and his own blood in his work on the Huayan *sutras*; his gilded body is seated in prayer. To the right is the **Five-Hundred Luohan Hall** (wǔbǎi luóhàn táng; 五百罗汉堂), where devotees gather to ask the Luohans to grant their wishes or have their fortunes read by the monks. If the steps are too much for you, you can take the overpriced cable-car, which runs from the village to the palace and enjoy the view from the upper station. *(Runs daily 6:30am-6pm. Express up Y46, down Y34; regular Y28/18.)*

Walk south along the ridge to the **Bell Tower** (zhōng lóu; 钟楼), another religious site, and the **East Peak Platform** (dōngyà yúnfáng; 东亚云舫). The latter gives a jaw-dropping view of the mountains, and the sight of the rippling trees in the distance will quickly make you forget the worldly annoyances of the village.

The eastward, uphill trail heads toward the **Phoenix Tree** (fēnghuáng sōng; 凤凰松), an ancient, jagged Huangshan pine thought to look like—surprise!—a phoenix. Minibuses regularly bring visitors up to the Phoenix Tree, where you can make your ascent to the Heavenly Platform (tiāntái; 天台). In theory, you could also hike from here to the summit. Few people do, though, and judging from the state of the trail, few people have in a long time. For the faint of heart, a **cable car** whisks travelers up to Mt. Jiuhua's 1342m summit. *(Runs daily 6am-5pm. Up Y30, down Y40, children Y10 less.)* Once at the **Golden Chicken Yelling to Heaven Gate** (jīnjī jiào tiānmén; 金鸡叫天门), take a moment to join in the heavenly chorus of poultry, and admire the view.

JIANGXI 江西

Once a relatively backwater province, Jiangxi today is a thriving and modern area. The province was a hotbed of political activity in the 1920s, and is fondly remembered by wizened Communists as the cradle of the revolution. But like Darth Vader, Jiangxi has yielded to the dark side. From the vigorous, chaotic streets of the provincial capital Nanchang to the immaculate villas in Lushan, Jiangxi is eager to make a mark on capitalist China. Despite its defection, the province's Communist legacy is still evident, and Jiangxi is dotted liberally with museums, exhibition halls, and preserved homes of the fathers of the Communist revolution—all reminders of the tumultuous days of yore.

NANCHANG 南昌 ☎0791

Lying 70km north of Lake Poyang, on the Gan River between Shanghai and Changsha, the capital of Jiangxi province is a busy trade and commerce center. Its hotels are filled with businessmen making deals by day and frequenting flashy bars and shady massage parlors by night. Vendors crowd city streets lined with billboards, plying their wares to anyone who passes.

And yet, ironically enough, this free-market capitalism-loving town is also cherished in China for its role in the development of the Communist Party. On August

1, 1927, Zhou Enlai and Zhu De, a pair of GMD officers with Communist inclinations, seized control of the city, sparking the chain of events that would eventually lead to the CCP's domination over all of China (see p. 15). Nanchang is renowned for its pivotal role in the creation of modern day China, and numerous monuments, museums, and souvenirs bear testimony to its unique status. The foundation of the People's Liberation Army is celebrated each August 1, when visitors flood the city. But visitors to Jiangxi usually pass right through Nanchang en route to Lushan or Jinggangshan; those who stick around for a while get to see a city that shows both sides of the strange, ever-changing coin that is China.

TRANSPORTATION

Flights: Nanchang Airport (nánchāng jīchăng; 南昌机场) is 30km away from the city. **China Eastern Airlines ticket offices** (zhōngguó dōngfāng hángkōng gōngsī; 中国东方航空公司), at 67 Beijing Xi Lu (☎623 1351, inquiries ☎628 2602), off Bayi Dadao; and at 87 Minde Lu (☎628 2654), just west of the Jiangxi (Binguan) Hotel. Both open daily 8am-6pm. To: **Beijing** (3-5 per day, Y750-1190); **Chengdu** (M, W, F-Sa; Y1094); **Guangzhou** (5:25 and 6:50pm, Y660); **Haikou** (daily 6:50pm, Y650); **Nanjing** (Tu and F 2:10pm, Th and Su 2:30pm; Y600); **Shanghai** (4 per day, Y650); **Xi'an** (M, W, Sa 5:30pm, Tu and Su at 9:15pm; Y920).

Trains: Nanchang is one of southern China's main rail hubs. **Nanchang Train Station** (nánchāng zhàn; 南昌站), on Zhanqian Lu, about 1km east of Fushan Traffic Circle, is beneath a huge square arch. There's also an unmarked ticket office on the eastern side of the building. Open daily 7:30am-noon, 12:20-5:15pm, 5:30pm-1:30am. To: **Guangzhou** (15½hr., 2:26 and 3:47pm, Y78-364); **Hefei** (8hr., 3:31am and 9:08am, Y27-166); **Jingdezhen** (6hr., 3 per day, Y20-155); **Nanjing** (18hr., 2:35pm, Y55-193); **Shanghai** (14hr., 4 per day until 11:30pm, Y85); **Xiamen** (22hr., 8:19 and 11:15pm, Y44-315); **Xi'an** (22½hr., 2:17 and 8:29pm, Y86-296).

Buses: Nanchang Long-distance Bus Station (nánchāng chángtú qìchē zhàn; 南昌长途汽车站; ☎670 2388 or 624 3217), in a long, shiny building on the east side of Bayi Dadao, a few blocks south of Bayi Square. The ticket office is past the luggage storage room. Open daily 5am-10pm. To: **Hefei** (6½-9hr., 3 per day 7:20am-4:20pm, Y106-125); **Jingdezhen** (5hr., every hr. 6:50am-5:50pm, Y46-70); **Jinggangshan** (7-8hr., 4 per day 6am-5:30pm, Y60-75); **Jiujiang** (2½hr., every 30min. 6am-7pm, Y35); **Lushan** (2hr., every 55min. 6:30am-4:45pm, Y37).

Ferry: Nanchang Port (nánchāng găng; 南昌港; ☎681 2515), about 1km north of Tengwang Pavilion; buy tickets just north of Bayi Bridge. Open daily 5:40am-6pm. Travel times vary greatly depending on the boat. To: **Boyang** (3-12hr., 4 per day 6:30am-6pm, Y26-61); **Duchang** (3-8hr., 3 per day 8am-7:30pm, Y24-61); **Ruihong** (2-5½hr., 4 per day 7:20-10:30am, Y18-22).

Local Transportation: Most **buses** run 7am-8pm; major buses like **#2** run 5am-10pm. Fare Y0.5-2. Bus **#2** runs along Zhongshan Lu, stops at August 1 (Bayi) Museum, turns onto Bayi Dadao, stops at the post office and long-distance bus station, and terminates at the train station; **#8** and **20** run along the river to the port and Tengwang Pavilion.

Taxis: Base fare Y6; each additional km Y1.4. Fares are negotiable; trips across town Y6.

ORIENTATION AND PRACTICAL INFORMATION

Nanchang is roughly ovular and, with the **Gan River** (gàn jiāng; 赣江) stretching along its west side. **Bayi Square** (bāyī guăngchăng; 八一广场), though not the geographic center, is the spiritual and commercial center of town. Running along the west side of the square is **Bayi Dadao** (八一大道), the major north-south thoroughfare, lined with numerous hotels, restaurants, shops and tourist-related services. Bayi Dadao runs south to the **Fushan Traffic Circle,** another service- and hotel-filled area. From here, **Zhanqian Lu** (站前路) extends east to the train station.

In the northwest part of town, Bayi Bridge crosses the Gan River just next to the ferry port on **Yanjiang Bei Lu** (沿江北路). **Minde Lu** (民德路), **Ruzi Lu,** and **Zhongshan Lu** (中山路) run east from Yanjiang Bei Lu to Bayi Dadao. **Shengli Lu** (胜利路) and **Xiangshan Lu** (象山路) both run north-south through the district.

Travel Agencies: CITS, 8 Minde Lu (☎622 4396 or 628 5014), in an unmarked office off the southeast side of the parking lot behind the Jiangxi (Binguan) Hotel; the door is by some chalkboards. Open daily 8am-11:30pm. **China Youth Travel Service** (zhōngguó qīngnián lǚxíngshè; 中国青年旅行社), 98 Fuzhou Lu (☎626 2452), about 2 blocks east of Bayi Dadao, on the south side of the street. The very friendly staff can book tickets and provide English-speaking guides. Open daily 8:30am-6:30pm.

Bank of China: 1 Zhanqian Xi Lu (☎647 1688), on the west side of Fushan Traffic Circle, across from the Nanchang Hotel. Exchanges currency (counter #23, after 2:30pm) and traveler's checks. Credit card advances. Open daily 8am-7:30pm; in winter 8am-7pm.

Bookstore: Xinhua Bookstore, 102 Bayi Dadao (☎630 1458), 3-4 blocks north of the Fushan Traffic Circle, on the west side of Bayi Dadao. Impressive collection of Agatha Christie novels, and a couple of dusty British classics. Open daily 8:30am-8pm.

PSB: Just north of the Jiujiang bus plaza in front of train station. 3 officers on call 24hr. Another branch 1½ blocks northwest of the intersection of Shengli Lu and Minde Lu.

Pharmacy: Huangqing Renzhan Pharmacy, 8 Bayi Dadao (☎626 2835), 2 blocks north of Fushan Traffic Circle. Mainly Chinese products; some Western medicine. Open 24hr.

Internet Access: China Telecom, 38 Ruzi Lu (☎810 2873), about a half-block west of the post office. Fast connections for Y2 per hr. Open daily 8am-8pm.

Post Office: China Post, 262 Bayi Dadao (☎620 0584). EMS, Poste Restante, and a "Philately" counter. Open daily in summer 8am-7:30pm; in winter 8am-6:30pm. **Postal Code:** 330003.

ACCOMMODATIONS

Nanchang hotels cater almost exclusively to business travelers; most hotels offer bellhops, karaoke bar, and mysterious phone calls from even more mysterious women. The large number of rooms means that mid-range hotels often have openings, so try bargaining. All listed hotels have rooms with A/C, bath, and TV.

Nanchang Hotel (nánchāng bīnguǎn; 南昌宾馆), 16 Bayi Dadao (☎627 1281), off Fushan Traffic Circle, between the bus and train stations. This conveniently located hotel has a friendly staff that will help you with bus and train tickets. Cheaper rooms are slightly dingier. Doubles Y165-228, triples Y278. 60% discounts possible. ❸

Jiangxi (Fandian) Hotel (jiāngxī fàndiàn; 江西饭店), 356 Bayi Dadao (☎885 8888), about 1 block south of Minde Lu, south of the other, nicer Jiangxi (Binguan) Hotel. Cheaper rooms are in a separate red building. All rooms open to foreigners. Singles Y120-240; doubles Y210-280. ❸

Ganjiang Hotel (gànjiāng bīnguǎn; 赣江宾馆), 138 Bayi Dadao (☎622 1159), opposite the bus station. Foreigners usually can't stay in rooms with a shared bath. Doubles Y80, with bath Y280-320; triples Y200. ❶

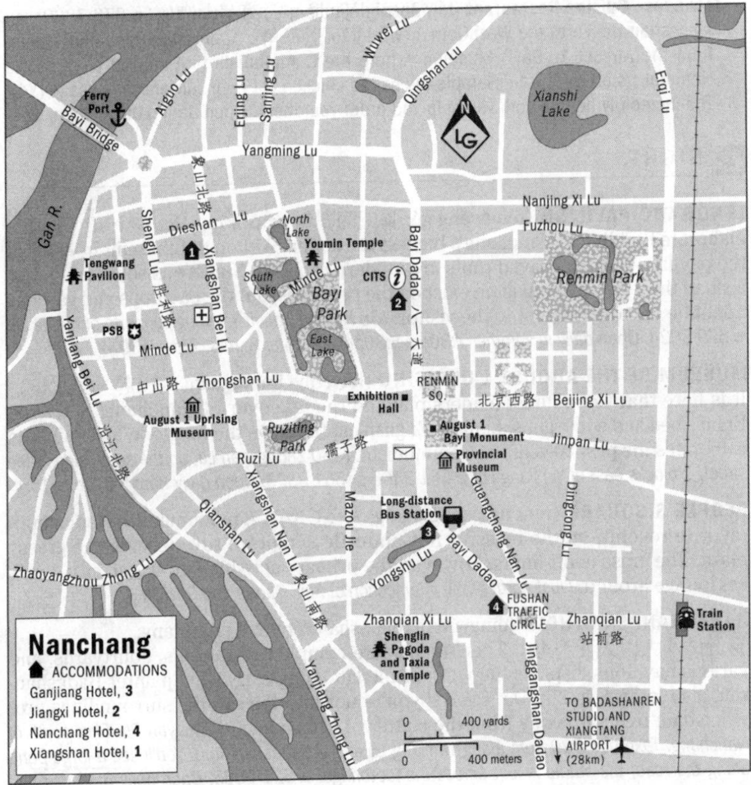

Xiangshan Hotel (xiàngshān bīnguǎn; 象山宾馆), 222 Xiangshan Bei Lu (☎678 1402), through a gate on the west side of Xiangshan Lu, 3 blocks north of Minde Lu. Rooms are large and clean. Singles Y160; doubles Y160-200; triples Y156. MC/V. ❷

FOOD AND ENTERTAINMENT

Super-cheap eats are found on the south end of the railway plaza; a number of stands and restaurants offer Chinese fastfood—pick and choose rice with one meat, two vegetable dishes, and a soup for just Y3. **Xiangshan Lu** in the north and the area around **Tengwang Pavilion** both have many stir-fry stalls. At night, hit **Culture Palace** (wénhuà gōng; 文化宫), the giant entertainment complex just north of Remin Square (人民广场). This self-contained center has a skating rink, a coffee and ice cream bar, a dance club, and a theater.

Haoxianglai Steakhouse (háoxiǎnglái niúpáiguǎn; 豪享来牛排馆), 175 Minde Lu (☎639 5678), on the north side of the street, 3 blocks west of the Jiangxi (Binguan) Hotel. A bright, cool respite from the noise of Minde Lu. Tasty steak meals come with soup, salad, rolls, and wine (Y25). Unique setting combines sizzling Western-style food with *dim sum* carts (Y5 per serving) and Japanese rice sets (Y20). Open 24hr. ❷

Taiwanese Cuisine Restaurant (táiwāncài dàjiǔdiàn; 台湾菜大酒店; ☎676 7880), on Xiangshan Bei Lu at the Wazi Corner (wǎzi jiǎo;瓦子角). Appropriately located 10min. from the August 1 (Bayi) Museum, where the Communists first started chasing the Nationalists off to Taiwan. Sample the salted chicken (Y12) or Taiwanese sausage (Y4). The incredibly helpful staff will help you order your meal. Open daily 10am-10pm. ❶

SIGHTS

TENGWANG PAVILION (téngwáng gé; 腾王阁). Overlooking the Gan River, this elaborate building is Nanchang's biggest attraction. Although first built in AD 653, the pavilion's ornate, eaved roofs are modern replicas. Numerous souvenir shops, a small theater, and a museum exist on the premises, but the pavilions and gardens might be of more interest to the visitor. *(38 Fanggu Jie, off Yanjiang Lu, north of Minde Lu. ☎670 8024. Open daily in summer 7:30am-5:30pm; in winter 8am-4:50pm. Y30.)*

MUSEUM OF THE AUGUST 1 UPRISING (bāyī qǐyì jìniànguǎn; 八一起义纪念馆). It is here that Communist leaders planned the takeover of Nanchang. See Zhou Enlai's bed and some guns. Limited English captions. On the top floor, an exhibition celebrates the past 50 years of Communism. *(380 Zhongshan Lu, on the south side of the street, 3 blocks east of Yanjiang Lu. ☎661 3806 or 661 3323. Open daily 8am-5:30pm. Y15.)*

PEOPLE'S SQUARE (rénmín guǎngchǎng; 人民广场). A monument to Nanchang's favorite revolution, the massive flag-and-rifle sculpture towers over the grassy plaza. The grass is off-limits, however; the primary activity is to watch city-dwellers lounge around. *(Just north of the intersection of Bayi Dadao and Ruzi Lu.)*

BADASHANREN STUDIO (qīngyún pǔ bādàshān rénmíng jìniàntáng; 青云谱八大山人纪念堂). This immaculate complex of gardens, courtyards, and various pavilions displays the work of the late Ming/early Qing painter Badashanren, also known as Zhu Da. Even if you're not into the art, the surroundings provide some fresh air away from the clatter of Nanchang. *(In Qingyun Pu, 5km south of Nanchang. Take bus #20 from along Yanjiang Lu to the Badashan stop. You'll see a large pond along the road; the studio is just across the footbridge. ☎521 2565. Open daily 8:30am-5pm; last admission 4:30pm. Y10.)*

JINGDEZHEN 景德镇 ☎0798

Jingdezhen put the "china" in China. In the Song dynasty (AD 960-1127), Emperor Zhengzhong first stumbled across Jingdezhen, a city capable of producing porcelain just the way he wanted: "white as jade, lustrous as mirror, thin as paper, resonant as a chime." With that, the city's destiny as the imperial porcelain factory was sealed. But unless you have a particular fetish for the history of porcelain or feel like lugging home fragile, man-sized vases, there really is no reason to go to Jingdezhen. They city is grimy, the museums monotonous, and the residents surly. An aspiring cosmopolitan city, it embraces the worst of both worlds, lacking both small-town warmth and metropolitan comforts.

TRANSPORTATION

Flights: Luojia Airport (luójiā jīchǎng; 罗家机场), 10km northwest of the city, off the road to Jiujang. The **CAAC ticket office,** 5 Lianshe Bei Lu (☎/fax 822 3458) is open daily 8am-5pm. To: **Beijing** (M and F 2:25pm, Y1140); **Guangzhou** (M and F 9:40am, Th 12:40pm; Y990); **Shanghai** (M and F 8:40pm, Th 5:30pm; Y460).

Trains: Jingdezhen Train Station (jǐngdézhèn huǒchē zhàn; 景德镇火车站; ☎822 4705), 1km southeast of the city center. The dimly lit ticket building (at the south end) has no lines; usually only 1 window is open, so either go at off-hours or book through CITS or a hotel. To: **Beijing** (24hr., 9:40pm, Y96-553); **Huangshan** (3-3½hr., 6 per day 5am-7:34pm, Y10-39); **Nanchang** (6hr., 12:19am, Y22-202); **Nanjing** (11hr., 4 per day 5am-8:04pm, Y30-214); **Xiamen** (19hr., 9:40am and 1:20pm, Y46-325).

Buses: The **bus station** (☎855 1651), across from the train station, mainly serves destinations in Jiangxi, including **Jiujiang** (6hr., frequent departures 6:30am-2:50pm, Y38) and **Nanchang** (5-6hr., frequent departures 7:40am-11pm, Y42). Ticket office open daily 6am-5:30pm. Also buy tickets here for departures from the dingy, poorly organized station across the river on **Xinfeng Lu.** To: **Guangzhou** (7:40am, Y222); **Hangzhou** (10hr., 6:40am and 3:50pm, Y80); **Hefei** (9hr., 6:15am, Y53).

Local Transportation: The bus system in Jingdezhen is fairly comprehensive, with 11 lines covering most of the city during daylight hours. **#1** runs along Zhushan Zhong Lu; **#15** runs toward the train station; **#4** plies Cidu Dadao, home of the Ceramics History Museum. Minibus taxis run across town for Y5; proper taxis charge Y10.

ORIENTATION AND PRACTICAL INFORMATION

Jingdezhen is bisected by the **Chang River** (chāng hé; 昌河); the old city in the eastern half has nearly everything a traveler needs. From the river, **Zhushan Lu** (珠山路) runs east, through the middle of town, to the city center (a rotary with a large silver sculpture). **Ma'anshan Lu** (马鞍山路) runs southeast to the train station and **Lianshe Bei Lu** (莲社北路) branches up north, a stretch of road with some nightspots and many porcelain shops.

Travel Agency: CITS, on Fengjing Lu (☎822 2939), near the Joint Venture Hotel, in a run-down building behind lonely metal gates. Arranges factory tours. Open M-F 8am-noon and 2:30-6pm.

Bank of China: On Cidu Dadao, opposite the Porcelain Museum. Open daily 7:30am-6pm.

PSB: In a tall building just north of the main Bank of China on Cidu Dadao, in the southwest part of town (☎852 1001).

Telephones: China Telecom, next to the post office on Zhushan Zhong Lu. 24hr. IDD service. Open daily in summer 8am-6pm; in winter 8am-5:30pm.

Internet Access: The **Jingdezhen Joint-Venture Guesthouse** (☎822 6416) has connections in the business center. Y12 per hr. Open daily 8am-10pm.

Post Office: Zhushan Post Office (☎822 0574) on the north side of Zhushan Lu, near the city center. Open daily 8am-7pm. EMS and *Poste Restante*. **Postal Code:** 333000.

ACCOMMODATIONS AND FOOD

Jingdezhen makes a nice daytrip, but the transportation gods have cursed the city, so chances are you're going to have to stay the night. There are few hotels in town, and even fewer that accept foreigners. As of June 2001, the **Jingdezhen Hotel** (jǐngdézhèng bīnguǎn; 景德镇宾馆) on Fengjing Lu was being renovated.

At least one thing in Jingdezhen is free of kiln grit and grime: the cooking. An unusually large number of streetside vendors, especially around the train and bus stations, whip up tasty stir-fried dishes from a variety of fresh ingredients for no more than Y5. A typical meal includes rice with 2 or 3 side dishes. For an escape from the grime and dreariness of the city, slip into **Western Food Coffee Shop** ❶ (xīcān kāfēidiàn; 西餐咖啡店), along Lianshe Beilu. French fries (Y8) and steak (Y20) served by attentive and professional staff. (☎828 3866. Open daily 9am-2am.)

Jinsheng Hotel (jīnshèng bīnguǎn; 金胜宾馆), 29 Zhushan Lu (☎823 2720), on the main commercial street near the post office. A great location, clean rooms, affordable prices, and a staff welcoming to foreigners almost make you forget the indignity of having to stay overnight in this town. All rooms have standard amenities except the cheapest double, which has A/C. Singles Y120-150; doubles Y80-180; triples Y190. ❷

Wenyuan Hotel (wényuàn dàfàndiàn; 文苑大饭店; ☎853 1227), on Qinghua Lu, half a block north of the train station. Typical hotel-near-a-train-station rooms (slighty smelly and musty). More expensive rooms are no different, so don't opt for one. Doubles Y65-95. ❶

SIGHTS

Jingdezhen has several factory tours and museums, all dedicated to the explanation and promotion of the region's tradition of churning out urn after urn's worth of shiny clay. CITS offers a **factory tour,** which features local porcelain factories, a porcelain-oriented research center, a 1000-year-old kiln site, and a museum. (Full-day tour Y160, 2 people Y240.)

If you're just in town to shop, the **Jingdezhen Arts and Crafts Corporation** (jǐngdézhèn gōngyìměishù gōngsī; 景德镇工艺美术公司), 27 Zhushan Zhong Lu (☎/fax 822 4063), about half a block east of the post office, sells porcelain pieces by renowned artists. For a bargain, hop on a bus heading toward **Jiujiang;** 3km outside the city is a mind-boggling row of shops hawking plates, vases, and more.

CERAMIC HISTORY MUSEUM (táocí lìshǐ bówùguǎn; 陶瓷历史博物馆). On Fengshushan Mountain (fēngshùshān; 枫树山), along Cidu Dadao. If you have time to see only one sight, this is the place. More of a lazy man's garden than an exhibition space, the Ming- and Qing-era restored buildings bestow ample old-school charm. Walk back past the pond and bridges toward the main display hall, with examples of porcelain and pottery through the ages. *(Accessible by bus #4. ☎852 1594. Open daily 8am-5pm. Y10.)*

ANCIENT PORCELAIN FACTORY. This factory on Fenshushan Mountain (fēngshùshān; 枫树山) was constructed in Ming and Qing styles and is currently the only place in town that still employs traditional techniques. Wander along the long assembly lines guided by skilled human hands: pieces are made from raw clay (using a manual wheel driven by a cane), baked in the cavernous, multi-story wood kiln next door (which you can walk inside), and then honed and painted. *(Next door to the Ceramic History Museum. Open daily 8am-5pm. Y10.)*

LUSHAN 庐山 ☎0792

A Chinese saying states that Huangshan is "*qí*" (strange and magnificent), but Lushan is "*xiù*" (delicate). Indeed, it is difficult not to be entranced by the impossible prettiness of this mountain resort town. Generations of Chinese political kingpins have felt the same, and the region was once famed as the "summer capital" of China's political movers and shakers (including Chiang Kai-shek, Song Meiling, and Zhou Enlai). Even the Chairman himself left his mark on the mountain, from preserved villas to collections of poetry. Today, Jiang Zemin and gang continue to make Lushan the vacation home of the old and famous. Lushan's illustrious past, however, is not as important to visitors as the area's magical present. Gurgling

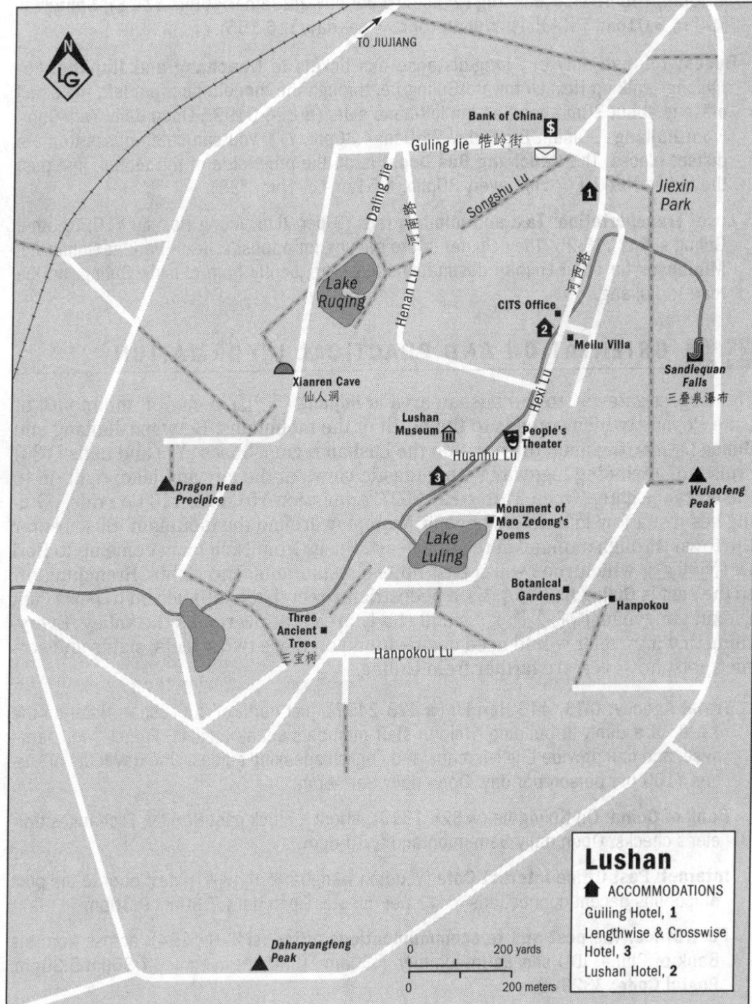

streams run past paved walkways; tranquil, misty gardens lie in the heart of commercial activity; and English explanations of monuments and plants are everywhere. Foreigners aren't common here, but the generally mellow Lushan folk will provide you with a pleasant reception.

TRANSPORTATION

Trains: Buses shuttle passengers back and forth from the **Lushan Train Station** to the mountain (Y7). Not all trains pass through Lushan, and many people transfer in Nanchang or Jiujiang stations. To: **Beijing** (21hr., 12:30pm, Y66-457); **Chongqing** (30hr.,

4:30pm, Y66-457); **Nanchang** (2½hr., 16 per day 2:23am-9:40pm, Y7-28); **Shanghai** (14hr., 8:01pm, Y50-351); **Wuhan** (5hr., 7 per day, Y16-155).

Buses: You can only buy long-distance bus tickets to **Nanchang** and **Jiujiang.** For Jiujiang, walk up Hexi Lu toward Guling Jie, through the tunnel, then turn left; the small office is about 30m ahead on the left-hand side. (☎828 0199.) Open daily 7am-9pm. From **Jiujiang** (30min., 8 per day 7:50am-4:30pm, Y7), you can catch buses to more distant places. The **Nanchang Bus Depot** is on the other side of the tunnel, just past the fork in Hexi Lu (2½hr., every 30min. 6:51am-6:21pm, Y35).

Local Transportation: Taxi and **minibus** fare Y8 per 2km. Along Hexi Lu Y10; to other Guling sights Y15-25. They cluster in the parking lot opposite Jiexin Park at Guling Jie. **Minibuses** for other Lushan destinations leave frequently from outside Guling, on the road to Jiujiang.

ORIENTATION AND PRACTICAL INFORMATION

The largest gateway to the Lushan area is **Jiujiang** (九江), a city on the mouth of Lake Poyang, which spreads to the north of the mountains. Between Jiujiang and **Guling** (牯岭), the main town within the Lushan region, buses (Y7) and taxis (Y30) cruise up a winding highway with fantastic views of the city and lake, right up to the entrance gate. (Open 24hr. ☎828 3627. Admission Y51, plus Y10 taxi ride.) Guling lies just a few kilometers beyond, wrapping around the mountain. Buses enter the town through a tunnel in the northeast. Buses from Nanchang come up to **Hexi Lu** (河西路), which runs south past hotels, restaurants, and sights. Branching off to the east is **Guling Jie** (牯岭街), a pedestrian street that continues on to **Jiexin Park** (jiēxīn gōngyuán; 街心公园), a small shady area that overlooks the valley. Everything that a traveler would need can be found on these two streets; sights and scenic spots, however, are farther from Guling.

Travel Agency: CITS, 443 Hexi Lu (☎828 2497), just north of the Lushan Hotel on the 1st fl. of a dimly-lit building. Helpful staff members speak English, French, and Japanese, and can provide English maps and English-speaking guides. One-day tours of Lushan Y100 per person per day. Open daily 8am-6pm.

Bank of China: On Guling Jie (☎828 1913), about a block past Hexi Lu. Exchanges traveler's checks. Open daily 8am-noon and 2:30-6pm.

Internet: Post Office Internet Cafe (yóudiàn wǎngbā; 邮电网吧), next door to the post office, has decent connections for Y3 per minute. Open daily 7:30am-9:30pm.

Post Office: The **post and telecommunications office** (☎828 1194), across from the Bank of China. IDD service in summer 7:30am-10:30pm, in winter 7:30am-5:30pm. **Postal Code:** 332900.

ACCOMMODATIONS AND FOOD

Few foreigners stay in Lushan, and most tour groups make the mountain a daytrip from Jiujiang. The government seems happy to keep it that way to protect Lushan's sleepy atmosphere for its higher party officials. Few hotels accept foreigners, and most are far stricter than hotels elsewhere—even overseas Chinese will not be able to scheme their way into cheaper rooms. The hotels that accept foreigners have high prices, mediocre rooms, and a habit of arbitrarily closing their doors. That said, sometimes the extra money is worth it, especially for a small villa or bungalow, which will put you right in the middle of Lushan's impressive wilderness. And what's the going rate for living like a CCP head honcho? Expect about Y680 for a villa owned by a hotel (like **Guling Hotel**) and Y800 and up for an independent one. No hotel has air conditioning during the summer since, as they will tell you, Lushan at night is cold and insect-free.

Lushan's unique atmosphere extends to eating as well: unlike most Chinese cities, the main part of Guling boasts nary a street vendor. Restaurants in town are almost all of the sit-down variety. Most meals cost Y20-30 for the standard 1-2 Chinese stir-fried dishes with rice, but don't expect anything fancy unless you head to a hotel. Luckily, there's plenty of ice cream around to beat the heat.

The following rates reflect high-season prices, so expect discounts (or bargain hard) during winter months. The following hotels all have rooms with bath and TV.

Lushan Hotel (lúshān bīnguǎn; 庐山宾馆), 446 Hexi Lu (☎828 2060), 1km south of the bus station. Rooms are in removed villas with nice views and cool summer breezes. Singles Y390; doubles Y480; triples Y260-540. 50-60% discounts possible. MC/V. ❺

Guling Hotel (gǔlíng fàndiàn; 牯岭饭店; ☎828 2200), just south of the bus station, off Hexi Lu, in a great location just opposite Guling Jie. Baths are large, but the rooms themselves are rather small and unexciting. Doubles Y380-480; villas Y680 and up. 30-40% discounts possible, especially on weekdays. ❺

Lengthwise and Crosswise Hotel (jīngwěi bīnguǎn; 径纬宾馆), 4 Jinglong Lu (☎828 2080), across the stream at the south end of the pond, next to the People's Theater. Some of the nicer rooms around, but pretty cut-off from the main commercial streets. Doubles Y480; triples Y580. ❺

SIGHTS

Countless Chinese ancients have spent long, contemplative chunks of their lives in Lushan, resulting in some legend or gushing poem associated with every cave, tree, and waterfall on the mountain. Although no single sight really stands out, wandering the trails and soaking in the oft-extolled surroundings is the best way to explore the area, whether for a day or a week.

In general, the sights closer to Guling draw larger crowds, but the Lushan area is expansive, and some of the most spectacular waterfalls and cliffs are hours away from Guling. Getting to some of these places would require the better part of the day; an easy option is to hire a minibus (found opposite Jiexin Park), which is cheaper than hotel- and CITS-organized tours. In general, the sights are organized around 2 lines, with each line containing more than 10 sights. A day-long minibus tour of one line costs Y70-80. Along the first line, there is the very pretty **Zither Lake** (rúqín hú; 如琴湖), shaped like a zither, **Xianren Cave** (xiānrén dòng; 仙人洞) where legendary folk hero Lu Dongbin became immortal, and **Dragon Head Precipice** (lóngshǒu yá; 龙首崖). The second line is a bit more entertaining and includes **Hanpokou** (hánpókǒu; 含鄱口), a vast valley that overlooks Lushan's famed Lake Poyang. At sunrise (5am in the summer, 7am in the winter), the scenic area is—as the English captions so proudly proclaim—"like a fairyland."

The area gets pretty misty at times (especialy after rain fall) but still offers amazing vistas of the numerous moutain peaks. On a clear day, the locals claim that you can see Mao's face in the mountain ridges. A can't-miss sight on the second line is Lushan's most justifiably famous spot, the **Sandiequan Falls** (sāndiéquán pùbù; 三叠泉瀑布), where sheets of water crash down three shelves of rock through a cloud of mist. Viewing the falls involves a good three-hour hike up and down some very steep steps, jostling Chinese tour groups on narrow paths, and constant taunting by human porters trying to convince you that you can't make it by yourself. But Sandiequan is definitely worth the hassle, especially after (or during) rainy weather when the falls seems to be in a world of their own; completely isolated from mild-mannered Lushan, savage rapids rush through and the falls themselves thunder out of the sky's foggy oblivion. In a word, it is magnificent. *(Admission Y28, plus another Y1 at toll gate.)*

LUSHAN MUSEUM (lúshān bówùguǎn; 庐山博物馆). Established in 1957, this is the best museum in Lushan, combining all the elements that make the mountain interesting: culture, Communism, and natural history. Highlights include Buddhist paintings, a *papier maché* model of the Lushan region, photos of some of the dignitaries who have visited Lushan, and a room full of impaled insects to help you identify that monstrous beetle in your bathroom. Limited English captions. *(1 Lulin. On Huanhu Lu, southwest of Lake Lulin. ☎828 2341. Open daily 7:45am-6pm. Y10.)*

LAKE LULIN (lúlín hú; 庐林湖). This small lake with an attached pavilion, halfway between Guling and Hanpokou, is a good starting point for short jaunts to the **Three Ancient Trees,** the **Dragon Pools,** and the **Lushan Museum.** On the lake's north end is the **Monument of Mao Zedong's Poems,** a group of huge granite slabs inscribed with Mao's own poetry and some of his personal favorites.

THREE ANCIENT TREES (sānbǎo shù; 三宝树). Standing behind fences in front of a Buddhist temple, these three old guys were supposedly planted by Tan Shen, a monk of the Eastern Jin dynasty. Don't be fooled—in reality they are only about 500 years old. Still, the trees are massive, and the on-site explanation tells you just how to feel when staring up at such towering trunks: "Sense quietness first, then darkness, and finally coldness." Down the hill from the Ancient Trees, the **Dragon Pools** (lóngchí; 龙池), a good picnic spot, sit at the confluence of two streams. *(3.5km from Guling. A 10min. walk from Lake Lulin, on the trail along the stream in Guling.)*

MEILU VILLA (měilú biéshù; 美庐别墅). An unusual range of political styles comfortably settle in this complex. Built at the turn of the 20th century by a British lord, this villa was sold during the early 30s to Song Meiling, the wife of Chiang Kai-shek. After the ruling couple's exile, the villa passed unscathed into the hands of Communists. Even Chairman Mao came to stay here several times between 1959 and 1961. Rooms display photos of Chiang Kai-shek and Mao and his entourage alongside relics of upper-class life. Limited English captions. *(180 Hedong Lu. Across the stream from Hexi Lu. ☎829 1855. Open daily 7:30am-6pm. Y15.)*

PEOPLE'S THEATER (rénmín jùyùan; 人民剧院). Also known as the **Lushan Conference Site** (lúshān huìyì huìzhǐ; 庐山会议会址), this is where the Camelot camaraderie among Long March cadres wilted. During an important conference here in 1959, Chairman Mao overruled the objections of his defense minister Peng Dehuai and steamrolled ahead with the Great Leap Forward (see p. 17). A large auditorium has a stage set up as it might have been during party meetings, with videos (in Chinese) that feature Mao, in all his fleshy glory, enjoying a swim in the Lushan lakes. In the front rooms of the hall is a small, unimpressive photo exhibit; many of the same shots are on display in the Lushan museum. *(504 Hexi Lu. At a right fork in the road, in front of a pond. ☎828 2584. Open daily 8am-6pm. Y10.)*

BOTANICAL GARDENS (zhíwù yuán; 植物园). Built in 1934, this complex houses thousands of poorly labeled plants. Those less passionate about potted specimens should probably skip the greenhouse in favor of the eastern half of the gardens, which has more nature trails. *(5.5km from Guling. From Lake Lulin, take Hanpokou Lu, following the left (north) fork. ☎828 2223. Open daily 7am-5:30pm. Y10.)*

JINGGANGSHAN MOUNTAIN 井冈山 ☎0796

Dense, wet forests blanket most of the Jinggangshan mountain range, which spread nearly 700km between Hunan and Jiangxi provinces. Seemingly anything could hide in these forest valleys, which is precisely why the battered Communist army convened here before breaking through the GMD blockades and retreating on the Long March (see **The Long and Winding Road,** p. 15).

Because of this brief but hugely significant historical congregation, Jinggangshan is known to most Chinese as "the cradle of the Chinese Revolution." Mao Zedong brought his Autumn Harvest Uprising troops here in 1927, joining forces with the remnants of Zhu De's troops from the Nanchang Uprising and Peng Dehuai's up-and-coming legions of soldiers. The leaders and their armies established residences in Jinggangshan's main village, Ciping, and other nearby towns. While most of their homes and outposts were subsequently destroyed by GMD reactionaries, the Chinese government has since resurrected the most important sites and turned Ciping into a scenic, orderly village. Despite hordes of weekend visitors, the charming village has so far managed to resist being turned into a tourist trap. Its surrounding landmarks—combined with the cool, wet air and miles of mountain hiking—persuade tourists to go out of their way to get here.

TRANSPORTATION

Trains: Jinggangshan Train Station (jǐnggāngshān huǒchē zhàn; 井冈山火车站) is actually in Taihe, a 3hr. minibus ride from the mountain. From Taihe, buses leave for Jinggangshan approx. every hr. 6:30am-2 or 3pm; flag one down on the main street. From Jinggangshan, the last express bus leaves for Taihe around 12:30pm, the last regular bus around 2pm. Fare either way is Y25. However, most visitors to Jinggangshan prefer to use the **Jian Train Station** (jí'ān huǒchē zhàn; 吉安火车站); take a bus from Ciping bus station (2½hr., every 30min. 6am-4 or 5pm) to Jian, and then hop on a Y10 taxi from the bus stop to the train station.

Buses: Jinggangshan Long-distance Bus Station (jǐnggāngshān chángtú qìchē zhàn; 井冈山长途汽车站), on the corner of Zhongxin Dadao and Nanshan Lu. To: **Changsha** (8-9hr., 12:15pm, Y69); **Hengyang** (8-9hr., 11:30am, Y50); **Nanchang** (6-7hr., 6:30am and 7pm, Y61.5).

Local Transportation: Minibuses and **tour buses** await customers at a station 1 block south of the bus station. One-day tours of Jinggangshan (8am-5pm) cover the bulk of the sights for under Y50 per person. A **taxi van** costs Y80-150; bargain as hard as you can. A taxi to any of the sights costs about Y10, but within Ciping, walking is always the best option.

ORIENTATION AND PRACTICAL INFORMATION

The town of **Ciping** (茨坪), sometimes called **Jinggangshan City,** is small enough to be traversed in 30 minutes. At the middle of the village is Yicuihu Park, which contains a large pond with an island pavilion and a pagoda on the south side. The large gold **Monument to the Martyrs of the Revolution** stands atop a hill at the north end of town, and is useful for getting your bearings, as long as the mist isn't too thick.

From the long-distance bus station in the northeast corner of town, a commercial street runs south down the hill, forking east and south along Yicuihu Park, becoming **Nanshan Lu.** On the other side of Nanshan Lu is **Nanshan Park,** with a large pagoda in its center. **Hongjun Lu** (红军路) runs north-south along the west side of the parks. **Zhongxin Dajie** (中心大街) crosses Yicuihu Park from east to west and runs parallel to **Wujing Lu** (五井路), which runs toward the bus station. **Xiao Shangpin Lu** (小商品路), the village's busiest street, runs between Wujing Lu and Zhongyang Dajie.

Travel Agencies: CTS (☎655 2504), off Hongjun Lu at the end of Shangpin Lu, next to the gate leading to the Jinggangshan Guesthouse. Staff members speak some English, offer guided tours (Y100, including transportation), and can book those hard-to-find sleeper tickets to Guangzhou (Y15 commission). The **tourist information office** next door also offers Y100 guided tours. Open daily 8am-noon and 3-6pm. **Qiu Shuigen,** 29 Ciping Xin Cun (☎655 5669), doesn't speak English, but is friendly and helpful, and also gives Y100 tours.

Tourist Hotlines: Complaints ☎655 2626. **First Aid** ☎655 2595. **Info** ☎655 6777.

Bank of China: 6 Nanshan Lu, near the southwest tip of Yicuihu Park. Exchanges traveler's checks. Open M-F 8am-6pm.

PSB: Jinggangshan Public Security Bureau (☎655 2509), on Hongjun Nan Lu.

Hospital: Jiangxi Jinggangshan Chinese Medicine Hospital (jiāngxī jǐnggāngshān zhōngyīyuàn; 江西井冈山中医院), 47 Hongjun Nan Lu (office ☎655 2268, pharmacy 655 2423).

Telephones: China Telecom, in a towering office about 100m south of Yicuihu Park. Open daily 7:30am-7:30pm.

Post Office: About 200m north of the Bank of China next to the park, across from the pagoda in the pond and near the Jinggangshan (Fandian) Hotel. EMS and *Poste Restante*. Open daily 7:30am-6pm. **Postal Code:** 343600.

ACCOMMODATIONS

This former Communist stronghold has embraced capitalism with a vengeance, leaving tourists to suffer the consequences of increasingly inflated prices. Most hotels charge Y200 and up on weekends and won't give more than a 20% discount. On weekdays, a room should not cost more than Y200—bargain hard for a 50% discount. Many hotels line Hongjun Lu; from the bus station, turn right; go up the hill and around the bend until you hit a tree-lined road.

Jinye Hotel (jīnyè dàshà; 金叶大厦), 30 Hongjun Bei Lu (☎655 8188). The best deals are in building 2, a massive Gothic cobblestone structure with large rooms. The small rooms have balconies. Rooms in the main building are newer and have A/C but don't justify the high prices. Doubles Y240-490; triples Y300; quads Y360. ❸

Jinggangshan Mansion (jǐnggāngshān dàshà; 井冈山大厦), 31 Hongjun Bei Lu (☎655 2251). This self-touted "Jinggangshan Baosteel Mountain Villa" is a cavernous stone hotel with little pretense, gorgeous high ceilings, worn rooms, and helpful service. Smelly baths have hot water from early evening to mid-morning. Dorms Y120 and up; doubles (many with balconies) Y240 and up. ❷

Jinggangshan Hotel (jǐnggāngshān fàndiàn; 井冈山饭店), 1 Xinshichang Lu (☎655 2328). From the bus station, walk south down the hill; it's about 600m down the hill, on the left. The hotel has no English sign; look for the plaque that says "Foreign Nationals." Rooms are small with Chinese-style toilets. Doubles with bath Y180. ❸

Jinggangshan Guesthouse (jǐnggāngshān bīnguǎn; 井冈山宾馆), 10 Hongjun Bei Lu (☎655 2221 or 655 2272), above a long stone wall and accessible by a ramp leading up from the road. Service can be abrupt, but ask to see Rm. 115 in the main building.

Kept just as it was when the Chairman paid a visit in 1965, the room contains the small selection of books he left behind. The rooms in the villas (including the "Nuclear Power Villa") are comparable to those in the main building, just farther away. Doubles Y320-380, in main building Y680. ❺

FOOD

Inexpensive restaurants can be found on nearly every corner. For those interested in an authentic Communist experience, you can live like the Red Army did and subsist only on puny portions of red rice and pumpkins. Otherwise, a **fresh food market** down the hill to the left of the China Telecom office sells raw meat and veggies. The road leading downhill from the bus station has a few small places to eat, and a number of quick-fry stands congregate near the **post office** and at the east end of **Zhongyang Dajie.** The street running perpendicular to Shangpin Lu is crammed with outdoor eateries that cook up Jinggangshan specialties, including just-picked Red Army lettuce (hóngjūn cài; 红军菜) with mint (Y15), roasted pheasant (shānjī; 山鸡; Y18 per *jīn*), and sautéed frog (qīngwā; 青蛙; Y18 per *jīn*).

SIGHTS

Within Ciping, all the sights are easily accessible by foot. Outside the immediate area lies much of Jinggangshan's most renowned scenery, which can all be visited in one day with a taxi and a map.

CITY SIGHTS

MONUMENT TO THE JINGGANGSHAN REVOLUTIONARY MARTYRS (jǐnggāngshān gémìng lièshì jìniàntǎ; 井冈山革命烈士纪念塔). The monument is a shimmering, angular sculpture representing a torch. The complex is also home to the **Revolutionary Martyrs' Cemetery,** a memorial hall inscribed with 15,744 names; a **Forest of Steles,** with slabs of poetry inscribed in calligraphy by national leaders and celebrities; and a **sculpture garden** featuring 19 statues of early CCP leaders, including an especially virile-looking Mao Zedong. The entrance to the monument is just up the hill to the west of the bus station; follow the loop trail to see all the sites. Not terribly interesting, but worth a visit if you're in Ciping. *(At the northern end of Ciping, towering atop a hill. Open daily 7am-7pm. Y15.)*

JINGGANGSHAN REVOLUTIONARY MUSEUM (jǐnggāngshān gémìng bówùguǎn; 井岗山革命博物馆). This museum houses an impressive collection of papers, eerie photographs, maps, scale-models, old uniforms, books, and weapons. English narrations are nowhere to be found, but the photos and relics speak for themselves. *(In the southwest part of Ciping. ☎655 2449. Open daily 8am-5:30pm. Y8.)*

COMRADE MAO ZEDONG'S RESIDENCE (máo zédōng tóngzhì gùjū; 毛泽东同志故居). This "residence" offers much insight into the stark, primitive living conditions of the early revolutionaries. Rebuilt after being burned down by the Nationalists, these former living quarters feature luxuries like threadbare uniforms and rock-hard mattresses. This place makes a budget dorm look like Shangri-La. A plaque across from Mao's quarters explains the "traditions of Mt. Jinggang," a list of the CCP principles of toil and struggle. *(About 50m north of China Telecom. Open daily 8am-6pm. Y8.)*

OUTSIDE JINGGANGSHAN

HUANGYANGJIE (huángyáng jiè; 黄洋界). Originally an army post in the Mao era, this lookout point is now a favorite spot for sunrise-seekers and landscape-lovers. Perched 1343m above sea level, it offers spectacular views of the surrounding terrain. On foggy days the entire area is like a sea of clouds. *(A 20min. drive northwest of Jinggangshan. Open 24hr. Y7.)*

FIVE DRAGON POOLS (wǔlóng tán; 五龙潭). The Five Dragon Pools are a series of drooping valleys with five gushing waterfalls and winding paths through mystical water curtains. Poetic names like "fairy waterfall" and "rainbow curtain" grace spots along this mountainous and rocky area. Those short on time or eager to see everything can use the steep cable car ride (Y50) that goes past some main waterfalls and sights. *(7km from Jinggangshan City. Open daily 5am-6pm. Y30.)*

FIVE FINGERS PEAK (wǔzhǐ fēng; 五指峰). The Five Fingers Peak, plastered on the back of the Y100 bill, can be seen life-sized here. On a clear day, the peak offers some gorgeous panoramic views. *(☎655 7667. Open daily 6am-7:30pm. Y10.)*

HUNAN 湖南

Hunan's fame as a center of fiery ideological zeal is preceded only by its reputation for fiery spicy cuisine. Beyond that, Hunan, at first glance, appears to be just another mild-mannered, lackluster Mao pilgrimage site. But somehow, the Mao buttons here seem to shine a little brighter. Perhaps it's because the province is home to Shaoshan, the much-lauded birthplace of Mao Zedong, as well as Changsha, Hunan's capital, where the CCP founder learned the ABCs of Communism as a student and a young revolutionary. In fact, following the steps of the Great Helmsman in Hunan can turn out to be quite rewarding indeed.

Apart from stops along the well-beaten Mao pilgrimage path, Hunan also lays claim to the eerie, fog-enshrouded stone outcroppings of the Wulingyuan Scenic Area in the northwest and the lakefront city of Yueyang in the northeast. Several ethnic minorities, including Miao, Tujia, Dong, and Uighur (See **Peoples, Minority Nationalities,** p. 23), inhabit the border regions of the province.

CHANGSHA 长沙 ☎0731

This provincial city embraces modernity but still wears its 3000-year-old history proudly on its sleeve. From the tomb of a 2100-year-old mummy to assorted Mao pilgrimage sights, this city offers plenty for any history buff. Changsha is not without aesthetic pleasures as well: the nearby Yuelu Mountain Scenic area boasts numerous natural sights, and in the city, massive construction has resulted in broad, tree-lined boulevards.

TRANSPORTATION

Flights: Huanghua International Airport (chángshā huánghuā guójì jīchǎng; 长沙黄花国际机场; ☎444 9500), 25km east of Changsha. Buses (every 30min. 6am-9pm, Y13) shuttle between the airport and the **CAAC ticket office,** 75 Wuyi Dong Lu (☎411 2222 or 415 5777). Open daily 7:30am-10:30pm. A taxi from the airport to town costs Y120. To: **Beijing** (2-5 per day, Y970); **Chengdu** (2-4 per day, Y730); **Chongqing** (2-5 per day, Y590); **Fuzhou** (1-2 per day, Y550); **Guangzhou** (1-3 per day,

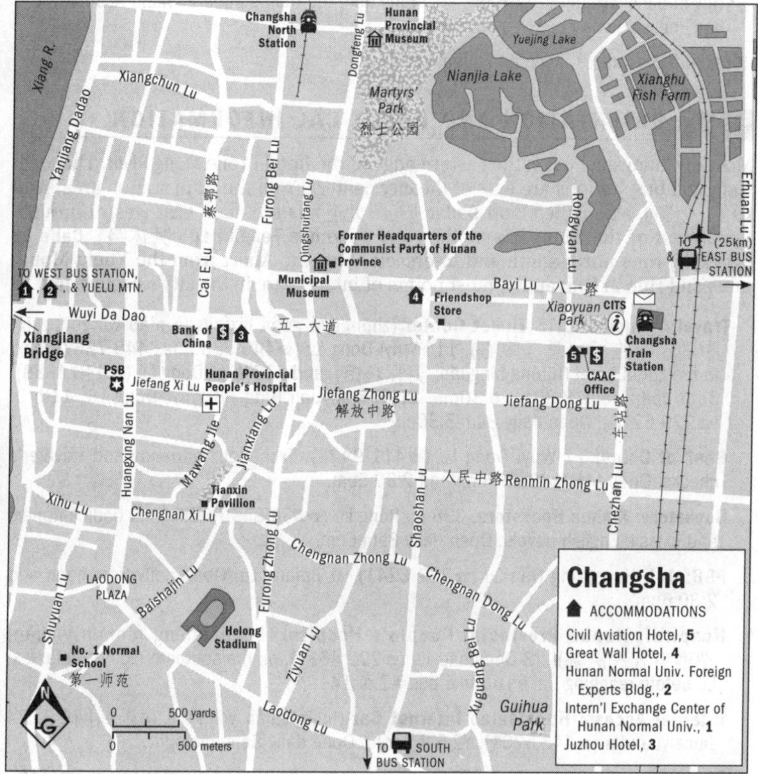

Y550); **Haikou** (2-5 per day, Y880); **Hong Kong** (daily, Y1600-2100); **Kunming** (1-3 per day, Y760); **Nanjing** (1-2 per day, Y670); **Shanghai** (1-3 per day, Y710); **Xi'an** (1-2 per day M-Th and Sa, Y710). Airport tax Y50.

Trains: Changsha Train Station (chángshā huǒchē zhàn; 长沙火车站; ☎229 6421), at Wuyi Dong Lu and Chezhan Lu, in the eastern part of town. Open 24hr. To: **Beijing** (15hr., 1daily, Y191); **Guangzhou** (9-11hr., 25 per day, Y99); **Guilin** (9-11hr., 7 per day, Y76); **Kunming** (7 hr., 3 per day, Y191); **Shanghai** (20hr., 7:50pm, Y154); **Shenzhen** (13hr., 2 per day, Y147); **Tianjin** (11hr., daily, Y201); **Wuhan** (3-5hr., 13 per day, Y50); **Xi'an** (20hr., 2 per day, Y175).

Buses: The **East Bus Station** (qìchē dōng zhàn; 汽车东站; ☎461 1731), on the east end of Bayi Lu. Accessible by bus #26. Departure times are variable. To **Wuhan** (7hr., Y75) and **Yueyang** (3hr., Y33). The **South Bus Station** (qìchē nán zhàn; 汽车南站; ☎228 2816) is considerably south of the city on Shaoshan Nan Lu; take bus #107 from the train station. To **Guangzhou** (18hr., Y73) and **Hengyang** (3hr., every 30min. 7am-6pm, Y42). Buses for **Zhangjiajie** (10hr., Y90) leave from the **West Bus Station** (qìchē xī zhàn; 汽车西站), on Fenglin Er Lu; take bus #312 from the train station.

Local Transportation: Most **buses** run 6am-8pm, but some minibuses and buses that serve the train station have extended hours. Fare Y1, with A/C Y2. **Tour Bus Line 1**

(lǚyóu bāshì yīxiàn; 旅游巴士一线) runs from the train station to Yuelu Academy and has English signs at each stop. Fare Y1.5.

Taxis: Base fare Y8, each additional km Y1.6.

ORIENTATION AND PRACTICAL INFORMATION

Most of Changsha lies on the eastern edge of the flood-prone **Xiang River.** The main train and bus stations are east of the city center. From the train station area, **Wuyi Lu** (五一路), also called **Wuyi Dadao** (五一大道), is the main east-west thoroughfare. West of the Xiang River, the road becomes **Fenglin Lu** (枫林路). **Cai'e Lu** (蔡鄂路) runs north-south and intersects Wuyi Lu. Apart from the Yuelu Mountains and Hunan University, most points of interest are in the city's eastern half.

Travel Agencies: CITS Ticket Center (zhōngguó guójì lǚxíngshè piào wù zhōngxīn; 中国国际旅行社票务中心), 114 Wuyi Dong Lu (☎446 5885; fax 446 7867), next to the Lotus Hotel (fúróng bīnguǎn; 芙蓉宾馆), and 128 Wuyi Dong Lu (☎440 1888). Both open daily 8:30am-6:30pm. **CITS,** Xiaoyuan Bldg., 8 Wuyi Dong Lu, 11th fl. (☎229 6270). Open daily 8am-5:30pm.

Bank of China: 71 Wuyi Dong Lu (☎411 9424). Exchanges currency and traveler's checks. Open M-F 8:30am-noon and 2:30-5pm.

Bookstore: Xinhua Bookstore, 338 Fu Rong Lu (☎430 8590). Bilingual bodice-rippers and classic English novels. Open daily 8am-6pm.

PSB: 445 Huangxing Nan Lu (☎222 6241), at Jiefang Lu. Open daily 8am-noon and 2:30-6pm.

Hospital: Hunan Provincial People's Hospital (húnánshěng rénmín yīyuàn; 湖南省人民医院), 28 Dongmao Jie (☎222 4611), on the southern side of Jiefang Xi Lu before reaching Cai'e Lu. Take bus #2 or 141.

Internet Access: Huanleniao Internet Bar (huānlèniǎo wǎngbā; 欢乐鸟网吧), 24 Jiucaiyuan Lu (☎443 5201). Y2.5-3 per hr. Open daily 8am-midnight.

Post Office: Changsha Post Office, on the north side of the train station square. EMS. Open daily 8am-8pm. **Postal Code:** 410001.

ACCOMMODATIONS

Restrictions on foreigners are still imposed at many of Changsha's cheapest establishments. Accommodations near the train station and around Wuyi Lu and Bayi Lu are convenient, but expensive. Cheaper hotels can be found across the river at Hunan Normal University, but these rooms often fill up quickly.

International Exchange Center of Hunan Normal University (húnánshīdàguóji xuéshì jiāolíu zhōngxīn; 湖南师大国际学士交流中心; ☎887 2188). Take bus #202 from the train station to Hunan Shida. This red building sits at the foot of the Yuelushan Mountain Scenic Area. 24hr. hot water, A/C, bath, and heat. Singles Y180; doubles Y160; triples Y180. ❸

Hunan Normal University Foreign Experts Building (húnán shīfàn dàxué wàiguó zhuānjiā lóu; 湖南师范大学外国专家楼; ☎887 2211), behind the International Exchange Building. Hot water 7-8am and 8-9:30pm. Doubles Y160; triples Y180. ❷

Juzhou Hotel (jùzhōu jiǔdiàn; 巨州酒店), 1 Wuyi Xi Lu (☎222 9148; fax 444 6685), at Jianxiang Nan Lu. The rooms aren't spectacular, but the location is conveniently close to the city's commercial center. Reservations recommended. Singles Y150-170; doubles Y150-200; triples Y150-160. 10% service charge. MC/V. ❷

Civil Aviation Hotel (mínháng dàjiǔdiàn; 民航大酒店), 7 Wuyi Dang Lu (☎417 0288; fax 414 8014). CAAC office in the same building. A relatively cheap escape from the din of the eastern end of Wuyi Dong Lu. Singles Y226; doubles Y218. ❸

Great Wall Hotel (chángchéng bīnguǎn; 长城宾馆), 28 Shaoshan Bei Lu (☎446 2888; fax 446 2321), on the corner of Bayi Lu. Luxurious rooms and facilities and a very friendly staff. Singles and doubles Y280; triples Y300. V. ❹

FOOD

Visitors to Changsha's restaurants should always be sure to have an ample supply of tissues and a gigantic jug of something cool to drink. The local cuisine is flavored with enough spice and hot pepper to make anyone's nose run; legend has it that Chairman Mao liked it that way. Spicy chicken (all parts included) is a favorite, and every year in Changsha is the Year of the Snake—at least for more adventurous diners. These Hunanese favorites can be found across the street west of the train station along **Chezhan Zhong Lu** and also one block farther west along **Chaoyang Lu.** Another hot spot for food is **Yanshan Jie,** one block south of Bayi Lu near Shaoshan Lu. The narrow lane is lined with fruit stands and restaurants serving stir-fried vegetables and noodle dishes; a meal is rarely more than Y10. Farther west along **Huangxing Lu,** south of Wuyi Dong Lu, restaurants offer everything from wonton soup (húndùn tāng; 馄饨汤) to stuffed bean curd (dòupí; 豆皮).

Songhuajiang Dumpling Restaurant (sōnghuājiāng jiǎozi guǎn; 松花江饺子馆), 106 Wuyi Dong Lu (☎446 1492). Packed every night of the week with locals gobbling up plump, piping hot dumplings into the wee hours of the morning. Vegetarian dumplings also available. Open daily 8am-3am.

Huo Gong Restaurant (huǒgōngdiàn jiǔjiā; 火宫殿酒家), 46 Pozi Jie (☎581 4896). Walk toward the river; it's to the right off Huangxing Nan Lu. A traditional red gate temple facade guards the entrance to its courtyard. The smelly tofu (chòudòu fǔ; 臭豆腐) served here garnered praise from Mao during his historic visit in 1958. Branch at 105 Wuyi Dong Lu. Tea Y2; appetizers Y4-10; meals Y12-38. Open daily 7:30am-8:30pm. ❷

Do Do Fun Cafe (dòudòufǎng kāfēi; 豆豆坊咖啡), 398 Jiefang Dong Lu (☎415 0059), right before the Huatian Hotel, at the northeast corner of Shaoshan Lu and Jiefang Dong Lu. The airy, relaxed atmosphere makes this cafe an ideal place for an afternoon breather. Mainly yuppie clientele. Specialty coffee Y18-25. Chinese and Western set meals Y20-30. Open daily 8am-1am. ❷

Mona Lisa Restaurant (méngnàlìshā zhōngxīcāntīng; 蒙娜丽莎中西餐厅), 458 Furong Zhong Lu (☎516 3222), near Renmin Zhong Lu. Part of a 5-store chain in Changsha. Set meals around Y60. Serves a wide variety of Western and Chinese cuisine (entrees Y20-40). This hotspot features an open bar (Chinese and imported beer Y20-22, cocktails Y28) and live bands starting at 8pm. Open daily 7am-2am. ❷

SIGHTS

YUELUSHAN MOUNTAIN RANGE (yuèlù shān; 岳麓山). Yuelushan is Changsha's main scenic spot. A trip to this picturesque park is part nature hike and part cultural history lesson; famous ancient philosophers lived here and modern revolutionaries are buried here. *(Take bus #202 or Tour Bus Line 1 from the train station and get off at the Hunan University stop with the Mao statue. Y2.)*

Just before the East Gate is **Yuelu Academy** (yuèlù shūyuàn; 岳麓书院), established in AD 976 as one of the four most outstanding institutions of the period. Although it's no longer a school, the traditional architecture and calligraphic inscriptions bear witness to its important position. Take Tour Bus Line 1 to the Yuelu Academy Stop. *(☎882 2316. Open daily 7:30am-5:40pm. Y14.)*

Inside the park, one of the first sites on the right hand path is the famous **Aiwan Pavilion** (àiwǎn tíng; 爱晚亭), which features a stone tablet inscribed by Mao Zedong. Those hardy enough to make it to the top can ride down the mountain to the North Gate, or careen down the mountain on a bobsled. *(Take bus #202 from the train station to the Yue Lu stop right outside the North Gate. Cable car Y15 one-way, Y25 round-trip. Bobsled Y30. Open daily 9am-5:30pm.)*

HUNAN PROVINCIAL MUSEUM (húnánshěng bówùguǎn; 湖南省博物馆). Most people come here to check out the 2100-year-old corpse of a Han dynasty woman that was unearthed in 1972. Evidence and observations regarding her final moments (she died soon after consuming a musk melon) decorate the walls. The faint-hearted might want to skip the large color photographs of the corpse as well as the glass jars carefully preserving her internal organs. The exhibition halls also hold other relics, including embroidered silk tapestries, paintings, and lacquerware; the lack of English captions may make them a bit difficult to appreciate. *(28 Dongfeng Lu. ☎451 3123. Open M-Sa 8am-noon and 3-6pm, Su 8:30am-5pm; in winter 8am-noon and 2:30-5:30pm, Su 8:30am-5pm. Y15.)*

MARTYRS' PARK (lièshì gōngyuán; 烈士公园). This park, with lakes, pagodas, and shaded walks, is the perfect place to get a breath of fresh air after visiting the macabre Hunan Provincial Museum. Inside, the Martyr's Memorial pays homage to those who died for the Communist cause. *(Take bus #112 or 113 to the park. Otherwise, the west entrance is a short walk from the Provincial Museum along Dongfeng Lu. ☎451 3029. Park open 24hr., memorial open daily 8:30am-4:30pm. Free.)*

CHANGSHA MUNICIPAL MUSEUM (chángshāshì bówùguǎn; 长沙市博物馆). Smaller than but similar to the Provincial Museum, the city museum still offers some unique exhibits, notably the Shang dynasty bronze percussion instruments and the Three Kingdoms writings inscribed on bamboo strips. The nearby **Former Headquarters of the Communist Party of Hunan Province** (zhōnggòng xiāngqū wěihuì jiùzhǐ; 中共湘区委会旧址) is also the former home of Mao and his first wife, Yang Kaihui. *(Under renovation as of June 2001. 480 Bayi Lu. Take bus #1 from the train station to Qingshuitang. ☎222 3498. Open daily 8am-noon and 2:30-5:30pm. Y10 covers both sights.)*

OTHER SIGHTS. On the southeastern bank of the Xiang River sits the **Tianxin Pavilion** (tiānxīn gé; 天心阁), one of the last remnants of the old city walls. The fortress provides a nice view of Changsha, even if the city isn't much to look at. *(On the corner of Jianxiang Nan Lu and Chengnan Xi Lu. Take bus #9 from the train station. ☎222 2404. Open daily 6am-11pm. Park Y2; pavilion Y5.)* Nearby, **No. 1 Normal School** (dìyī shīfàn; 第一师范), where Mao studied from 1913 to 1922, displays examples of his early writing and drawing. Mao studied in classroom number eight; a small placard now stands on his old desk in the second-to-last row on the right. *(From Tianxin Pavilion, follow Baishajin Lu past the intersection with Laodong Lu. ☎513 1786. Open daily 7am-7pm. Y6.)*

SHAOSHAN 韶山 ☎0732

Shaoshan looks like the China you see in the movies. Green farmlands stretch as far as the eye can see in the quiet countryside and terraced hillsides and rice paddies line the road from Changsha to this tiny town, the exalted birthplace of Mao

Zedong and probably the most important Communist pilgrimage site in the country. At the height of Mao's popularity in the 60s, more than 8000 Mao groupies paid homage to the CCP founder's hometown each day. As the fanaticism surrounding the Chairman fizzled in the aftermath of the Cultural Revolution, so too did tourism to Shaoshan. These days, however, Mao-mania is back. Mao suits, Mao badges, and Mao buttons are all collectors' items, and Shaoshan vendors hawk oodles of plastic kitsch that bears the Chairman's face.

ORIENTATION AND PRACTICAL INFORMATION. Shaoshan is divided into two parts: the **new town,** which includes the train station just south of the town center and the bus station just north of it; and **the village,** which is a few kilometers away and harbors most of Shaoshan's important Mao-related sights. The village is refered to as *gùjū* ("old house"; 故居), and all buses that go there are marked with these characters. Minibuses (Y1.5) shuttle between the two halves from the area near the Mao statue in the new town.

A daily **train** leaves Changsha at 6:40am and makes the return trip from Shaoshan at 5:25pm (3hr., Y11-17). **Buses** leave for Shaoshan from Changsha's South Bus Station (2hr., every hr. 7am-6pm, Y20; the last bus returns at 5:30pm.)

Changsha's **Huatian Hotel** (huátiān jiǔdiàn; 华天酒店), 380 Jiefang Dong Lu (☎444 2888; fax 444 2270), arranges **guided tours** of Shaoshan that include transportation and admission to sights (leave at 8am, return at 6pm; Y140). There are 14 scheduled Huatian tours per day, but the number of tours really depends on the number of tourists. At the Shaoshan train and bus stations, **minibuses** also offer tours. These informal tours include transportation to the village sights and the Dripping Water Cave and take about five hours (Y10).

ACCOMMODATIONS AND FOOD. Should you choose to stay overnight, village accommodations are generally preferable to those in town, since they're closer to Shaoshan's sights. The **Shaoshan Hotel** ❺ (sháoshān bīnguǎn; 韶山宾馆), the second most visible landmark in Shaoshan village, is more a guesthouse than a hotel. Many tour groups stay here; you won't be lonely. Private baths are available. (☎568 5080. Singles Y328; doubles Y240-280; triples Y248-280.) The **Postal Guesthouse** ❷ (yóuzhèng xiǎobīnguǎn; 邮政小宾馆), next to the Shaoshan Hotel, boasts 24hr. hot water, A/C, private bath, and TV; a restaurant is downstairs. (☎568 5488. Doubles and quads Y160; triples Y180.) **Restaurants** line the streets near the Mao Statue. A favorite local dish is braised pork (hóngshāo ròu; 红烧肉; Y20).

SIGHTS. A couple hundred meters into the village is the large Mao statue that marks the center of town. Directly opposite the statue is the **Mao Zedong Geneaology Museum** (máoshì zōngcí; 毛氏宗祠). If your Chinese is up to the task, check out Mao's family history, which dates back to an ancestral patriarch who joined the Ming revolution to kick out the Mongols. *(☎568 5364. Open daily 8:30am-5:30pm. Y6.)* Next door on the left is the **Museum of Comrade Mao** (máozédōng tóngzhì jìniànguǎn; 毛泽东同志纪念馆). Although it's all in Chinese, the museum has enough audiovisual materials to keep all travelers interested. *(Open in summer daily 7:30am-5:30pm; in winter 8am-5pm. Y7.)*

Mao's childhood home (máo zédōng tóngzhì gùjū; 毛泽东同志故居) is just outside the main village square. From the train station, take the road leading to the right after entering the village, past the souvenir market; or follow the signs in English and Chinese. Furniture, threshing tools, and pictures of the Great Helmsman clutter the house's surprisingly roomy interior. A plaque (much like the ones dotting nearly every other sight in Hunan) rests near the pond in front of the house and commemorates Mao's love of swimming. *(☎568 5125. Open in summer daily 7:30am-*

5:30pm; in winter 8am-5pm. Y6.) Next door is **Nan'an school** (nán'àn; 南岸), where Mao studied as a child. *(☎568 5121. Open daily 7:30am-5:30pm. Y6.)*

Buses run from the Shaoshan Hotel to **Dripping Water Cave** (dīshuǐ dòng; 滴水洞), approximately 3km from the village. Dripping Water Cave—actually a large park—features a steep 20-minute hike to the top of Dragon Head Hill (lóngtóushān; 龙头山), where Mao's great-grandfather is buried. The Chairman himself came here in June 1966 for a retreat; the bunker built to protect him is still visible. Near the exit, a path on the right leads to Mao's ancestral tombs. The park doesn't actually contain any caves, but it does provide a nice view of the surrounding countryside and an escape from Mao kitsch. *(Open daily 7am-6:30pm. Y18.)*

Tourists on organized tours of Shaoshan often visit **Liu Shaoqi's Childhood Home and Former Residence** (liúshàoqí jìniànguǎn; 刘少奇纪念馆), halfway between Changsha and Shaoshan. Liu Shaoqi, another Hunanese native, was the second-in-command under Mao in the 1950s and 60s but was never as popular as his superior. This large park is more architecturally impressive than any of the Mao sights in Shaoshan and is also home to several museums. *(The only way to reach the park is by taxi or tour. Open daily 7:30am-7pm. Y18.)*

HENGYANG 衡阳 ☎0734

It is no surprise that ancient Daoists made Hengshan Mountain (also known as *nányuè*) a center for spiritual enlightenment. The harmony of nature is spectacularly visible when the wind eases foggy clouds between pine trees and into the faces of mountain goats. Nearby Hengyang, a decent-sized city, transports visitors in a different way, as a major hub for rail transport to Guilin and Guangzhou.

ORIENTATION AND PRACTICAL INFORMATION

Hengyang is bisected by the **Xiang River** (湘江). The **train station** is on the eastern side, but most accommodations and points of interest are on the western side. On the western bank, **Zhongshan Lu** (中山路) and **Zhongxiang Lu** (中湘路) intersect **Jiefang Lu** (解放路), forming the commercial center of the city.

Trains: Hengyang Train Station (héngyáng huǒchē zhàn; 衡阳火车站; ☎832 3082), on Guangdong Lu. Buses #1 and 18 go to the station. To: **Beijing** (23hr., 6 per day, Y270); **Changsha** (4hr., 10 per day, Y19); **Guangzhou** (7hr., 33 per day, Y100); **Guilin** (8hr., 10 per day, Y120).

Buses: West Bus Station (qìchē xī zhàn; 汽车西站; ☎821 8742), at the junction of Jingyuan Lu and Jiefang Lu. Take a bus to Nanyue (not Hengshan) to reach the Hengshan Daoist mountains. To **Changsha** (3hr., every 30min. 7:30am-6pm, Y40) and **Nanyue** (1hr., every 30min. 7am-6pm, Y8).

Local Transportation: Bus #1 runs from the Xindu Hotel, across the river, and down Jiefang Lu to the West Bus Station, passing all major sights of interest (Y1). **Taxis** sputter about town as well; base fare Y5, each additional km Y1.4.

Bank of China: 351 Huancheng Nan Lu (☎814 4675), off Jiefang Lu. Exchanges currency and traveler's checks. Open daily 8am-noon and 3-6pm.

PSB: On the corner of Chuanshan Lu and Zhongshan Bei Lu (☎823 3171).

Hospital: People's Hospital (rénmín yīyuàn; 人民医院; ☎827 9000), on Zhongshan Bei Lu, north of Chuanshan Lu.

Internet Access: Youhao Internet Bar (yǒuhǎo wǎngbā; 友好网吧), 63 Jiefang Lu. Convenient central location. Y2 per hr. Open 24hr.

Post Office: Directly to the right of the train station exit (☎833 4742). IDD phones. Open daily 7:30am-11:30pm. **Postal Code:** 421000.

ACCOMMODATIONS

If you visit Hengshan, it's best to stay in Hengyang, since Hengshan mountain has little in terms of lodging. Hengyang's accommodations offer similar amenities at uniformly high prices. Bargain like you mean business.

Zhongjian Hotel (zhōngjiàn dàjiǔdiàn; 中建大酒店), 57 Jiefang Lu (☎826 6288), in the commercial district. The extremely friendly staff provides a warm welcome. Comfortable, well-worn rooms have A/C and 24hr. hot water. Singles Y158; doubles Y168; triples Y178. 20% discounts available. ❷

Xindu Hotel (xīndū dàjiǔdiàn; 鑫都大酒店; ☎839 7935), on Guangdong Lu. Walk out of the train station's main exit and go past the bridge; the hotel is identifiable by the bright red neon lights on your left. If you're just in town for one night, this is the most convenient place to stay. All rooms have TV, telephone, and 24hr. hot water. Singles Y168; doubles Y198; triples Y225. 20% discounts available. ❸

Huatian Hotel (huátiān dàjiǔdiàn; 华天大酒店), 20 Renmin Lu (☎828 8888; fax 828 8688). Take Jiefang Lu to Zhongshan Lu, turn right and then turn left at Renmin Lu; the hotel is on your right. Hengyang at its most decent and upscale. Billiard room and dance club downstairs. Rock on. Doubles Y228; triples Y298. ❸

FOOD

Many small shops and restaurants line the streets of Hengyang, but few stay open past 8pm. Vendors on **Yancheng Lu** serve lunchbox-type Chinese fast food during the day. The night market on **Renmin Lu** (人民路) offers cheap, tasty desserts.

Guangzhou Cake House (guǎngzhōu dàbǐngwū; 广州大饼屋), 57 Jiefang Lu (☎822 5981). Cozy wooden booths and swings and a wide variety of pastries and baked goods, pearl milk tea (Y6), and ice cream (Y5). Great for a leisurely mid-afternoon break. Open daily 7:30am-11:30pm. ❶

Zhong Hao Noodle and Fast Food Restaurant (zhōngháo miànguǎn měishí kuàicān; 中豪面馆美食快餐), 62 Jiefang Lu. Locals crowd in for fast, cheap meals and snacks. A great place to satisfy those late-night hunger pangs. Noodles Y6-8. Entrees Y5-8. Shaved ice desserts Y1-3. Open daily 8am-2am or until the last guest leaves. ❶

Meixin Ice Cream Bar (měixīn bīngbā; 美心冰吧), 4 doors from the Sanding Restaurant. Sidle up to this ice cream joint and cool down with Hengyang's popular summertime specialty: *bīng dòushā* (冰豆沙), a cold soup made with ground sweet red beans. Open daily 8am-midnight.

CLIMBING HENGSHAN

Hengyang's main sight is Hengshan Mountain, 45km outside the city. The mountain range stretches from Hengyang in the south all the way north to Yuelushan Mountain in Changsha, but Hengshan (1290m) is the tallest and most famous of the 72 peaks. Hengshan is known not only for the scenic beauty of its natural surroundings, but also for the poetry and calligraphic engravings that adorn its stelae.

Buses with A/C run from Hengyang to the mountain base (1hr., Y8). The bus stops on Highway 107 before the intersection with Zhunan Lu; the last bus back to Hengyang leaves at 6pm. From the bus stop, you can reach the mountain's main gate by walking up **Zhunan Lu,** which is dotted with vendors selling Buddhist trinkets. The ticket office is farther up the road in the foothills, past the **Nanyue Great Temple.** *(Open 24hr. Y40.)* Climbing the mountain is moderately difficult and takes about four hours. Minibuses make the trip for Y10-26. From the halfway point at **Xuandu Daoist Temple,** cable cars also ascend to the base of the highest peak; from here, it is a 30-minute hike to **Zhurong Palace.** *(Cable car Y30 up, Y25 down, Y50 round-trip.)* Those seeking an escape from the crowds should climb up the left side of the mountain to **Tianzhu Temple.** This is a more strenuous hike than the conventional route and has fewer sights along the way; however, the journey is quicker. Whichever route you choose, beware the yellow- and red-hatted Chinese tour groups.

The **Water Curtain Cave** (shuǐpù dòng; 水瀑洞), near Zhunan Lu at the eastern edge of Nanyue village, can provide a refreshing post-climb break. The new **China Construction Bank Hotel** ❹ (nányuè yínyuè bīnguǎn; 南岳银岳宾馆), on the left side of the main road into town, provides comfortable rooms. (☎566 2245. Singles Y288; doubles Y188-208; triples Y208.)

YUEYANG 岳阳 ☎0730

As a wayside stop between Chongqing and Wuhan, Yueyang has two claims to literary fame: the Yueyang Tower on Dongting Lake (the second-largest freshwater lake in the country) and Junshan Island (known for its fragrant and expensive "silver needle" tea), both of which have been the subjects of numerous well-known poems from the Tang and Song dynasties. The tea, also named *lǎo jūn méi* (the eyebrow of the old man) is a favorite drink of the elderly because its leaves resemble the white eyebrows of the Star of Longevity, thus representing good fortune and longevity in traditional Chinese folklore.

TRANSPORTATION

Trains: The **Yueyang train station** (yuèyáng huǒchē zhàn; 岳阳火车站), on Zhanqian Lu, in the northern part of the city. Trains run to **Changsha** (2hr., every hr., Y16-24) and **Guangzhou** (11½hr., 4 per day, Y230).

Buses: The long-distance bus station is south of the train station, close to the traffic circle. To **Changsha** (2½hr., Y20-30) and **Wuhan** (4hr., 3 per day, Y50).

Ferries: Yueyang Ferry Wharf, on Dongting Bei Lu, just north of the Yueyang Tower. Boats go up the Yangzi River to **Chongqing** (36 hr; 2 per day; 3rd class Y200, 2nd class Y476) and downriver to **Wuhan** (8 hr; daily; 2nd class Y98, 3rd class Y46).

Local Transportation: Bus #15 runs from the train station parking lot down Baling Lu and up Dongting Bei Lu, passing the Yueyang Pavilion and dock areas and ending at Yue Mountain Park (Y1). **Bus #22** runs an identical route as Bus #15 but ends at the Paper factory (zhǐchǎng; 纸厂). **Taxi** base fare Y5, each additional km Y2.5 (Y1 to enter the station parking lot).

ORIENTATION AND PRACTICAL INFORMATION

There are two main roads: **Baling Lu** (巴陵路) runs east-west past the bus station through the main part of the city and ends at the lakeside, where it intersects with Dongting Lu; **Dongting Lu** (洞庭路) runs north-south from the Yueyang Tower to the Old Town area. **Bus #15** stops within walking distance of many major sights.

Tourist Office: CITS, 25 Chengdong Lu (☎826 2010), next to the Yunmeng Hotel. Take bus #15 toward the lake and get off right before the Baling Bridge. Turn left down

Chengdong Lu; the Yunmeng Hotel and CITS are on your right. Offers English tours to Junshan Island and Yueyang Pavilion (Y120). Open daily 8am-noon and 2:30-5:30pm; in winter 8am-noon and 3-6pm. A CITS booking office for Yangzi River cruises and ferries is at the entrance to the Yueyang Ferry Wharf. English guides available.

Bank of China: 1 Zhanqian Lu (☎826 4560). Exchanges traveler's checks M-F. Open daily 8am-noon and 2:30-5:30pm; in winter 8am-noon and 3-6pm.

PSB: Next to the Yueyang Tower Hotel (☎861 9026).

Hospital: Yueyang Tower People's Hospital (yuèyánglóu rénmín yīyuàn; 岳阳楼人民医院), 39 Dong Maoling Lu (☎822 1211).

Internet Access: Internet Bar (☎821 3313), on Baling Xi Lu, next door to the post office. Y6 per hr. Open daily 8am-6pm. Another branch inside the train station post office. Y3 per hr.

Post Office: To the right as you exit the train station (☎826 6287). Another post office is about 100m west of the intersection of Baling Xi Lu and Dong Maoling Lu, opposite the China Telecom building. **Postal Code:** 414000.

ACCOMMODATIONS

The best places to stay in Yueyang are removed from the bustle of the train station, near Dongting Lake and the Yueyang Tower. As for food, a fresh day's catch in Dongting Lake makes a sumptuous meal in the restaurants that line **Dongting Bei Lu.** About 200m west of Baling Bridge, the alleys of the **Miaoqian Jie district** are a popular place for a late night dinner or snack, from roast duck (all parts of it) to traditional fried sweets.

Xuelian Hotel (xǔelián bīnguǎn; 雪莲宾馆; ☎832 1633), on Dongting Bei Lu, across from the Yueyang Ferry Wharf. The Xuelian is one of the best bargains in town. Very friendly staff. Clean, slightly worn rooms all have A/C and private bath. Singles Y60; doubles Y100; triples Y120. ❶

Yueyang Tower Hotel (yuèyánglóu bīnguǎn; 岳阳楼宾馆), 57 Dongting Bei Lu (☎832 1288; fax 841 4000), just opposite the Yueyang Tower. Take bus #15 from the train station to the Yueyang Tower stop, backtrack about 60m, and turn left onto a small side street; the hotel is on the right. A rather average place in the most interesting part of Yueyang. All rooms have A/C and private bath. For an additional Y20, stay in a room with a sparkling new white bathroom. Doubles Y158; triples Y198. ❷

Yunmeng Hotel (yúnmèng bīnguǎn; 云梦宾馆), 25 Chengdong Nan Lu (☎822 1115). Take bus #15 toward the lake and get off just before the Baling Bridge. Turn left down Chengdong Lu; the hotel is on the right, a 10min. walk down the road. Rooms all have standard amenities including A/C and bath. Singles Y228; doubles Y198; triples Y208. Discounts up to 33% available. ❸

FOOD

There are a couple of impressive local places worth a visit, but in general, Yueyang is not famous for its cuisine. **Zui Ming Lou Restaurant** (zuìmínglóu jiǔjiā; 醉名楼酒家), on Dongting Bei Lu across from Yueyang Tower, has an English sign above the door and sparkling kitchen and waitstaff. Be sure to try the house specialty, *hóngshāo hǎiguī* (红烧海龟; braised turtle), or one of the hotpots. (☎832 6326. Open daily 8:30am-8pm.) **Xiuyu Tea House** ❷ (xiùyù hóngchá fáng; 秀玉红茶房), down the steps underneath the Garden Hotel, is just past the Baling

Bridge. The interior combines the feel of an Italian villa, an English manor, and a Roman bathhouse. *Bǎozǎi fàn* (煲仔饭) Y16, ice cream coffee Y16. Afternoon set meals Y18. (☎831 5456. Open daily 9:30am-1am.)

SIGHTS

Yueyang Tower (yuèyáng lóu; 岳阳楼), inside Yueyang Tower Park, was originally a naval watch station built during the Three Kingdoms Period (AD 220-280). The entire structure, over 20m tall, was built without a single nail. Several famous Chinese poets have composed odes to the tower; the *Notes on the Yueyang Tower*, by Song poet Fan Zhongyan, has been drilled into the memories of generations of Chinese students. *(On Dongting Bei Lu, along the riverfront. Take Bus #15 or 22 to Yueyang Tower. ☎831 9349. Open daily 7am-6pm. Y23, additional Y5 to climb the tower.)*

A 30-min boat ride away lies **Junshan Island** (jūnshān dǎo; 君山岛), described by Tang poet Liu Yuxi as a sumptuous green conch in a silvery plate. The chance to watch tea cultivation and to sample Junshan's famous silver needle brews is worth the trip. Cobblestoned paths wind around various sights. Be sure not to miss **Monkey Mountain** (hóuzi shān; 猴子山), tucked away in the island's hilly interior, where indigenous monkeys playfully vie for your attention. *(Early morning ferries leave from Yueyang Ferry Wharf and make a late afternoon return trip (Y15 round-trip). Speedboats leave Yueyang every hr. 7:30am-5pm (Y32 round-trip). Last boat from Junshan Island to Yueyang leaves at 5pm. Admission Y32.)*

ZHANGJIAJIE 张家界 ☎0744

Part of the Wulingyuan Scenic Area and a declared UNESCO World Heritage Site, Zhangjiajie is named for the Han lord Zhang Liang who, according to local legend, lived in seclusion here and was buried under the mountain now called Zhangjiajie. The Wulingyuan landscape is dominated by sandstone pillars and underground brooks and streams that flow for long distances between enormous caves. Zhangjiajie is one of China's most beautiful nature reserves, offering lush scenery, wonderful hiking trails, and more than its fair share of enthusiastic yellow and red-hatted Chinese tour groups. Luckily for all, the reserve is still large enough for everybody to get off the beaten path and do a bit of solo exploring.

TRANSPORTATION

Flights: Zhangjiajie Airport (zhāngjiājiè jīchǎng; 张家界机场; ☎823 8294), southwest of the city center. Buses (Y5) go to and from the Daqiao Lu airport ticket office (fēijī shòupiàotīng; 飞机售票厅), across from the post office. Beware of frequent flight cancellations and massive delays. To: **Beijing** (Tu, Th, F, and Su; Y1020); **Changsha** (2 per day, Y460); **Chengdu** (daily, Y640); **Chongqing** (Tu, W, F, and Su; Y460); **Guangzhou** (2 per day, Y690); **Shanghai** (daily, Y1060).

Trains: The **Zhangjiajie Train Station** (zhāngjiājiè huǒchē zhàn; 张家界火车站) has service to: **Beijing** (27hr., daily, Y380); **Changsha** (8hr., 4 per day, Y120); **Guangzhou** (23hr., daily, Y317). Luggage storage available.

Buses: Zhangjiajie Long-distance Bus Station (zhāngjiājiè chángtú qìchē zhàn; 张家界长途汽车站), at the intersection of Renmin Lu and Huilong Lu. To: **Changsha** (11hr., 5 per day, Y49-83); **Guangzhou** (25hr., daily, Y181); **Guilin** (daily, Y160); **Wuhan** (14hr., daily, Y101).

Local Transportation: A public **minibus** shuttles between the train station and the center of Zhangjiajie city, with a stop at the entrance of the long-distance bus station. Runs daily 6am-8pm. Fare Y1. A minibus also runs from the long-distance bus station to the park entrance (1hr., every 10min., Y8). A public minibus runs from the city to the Forest Park (sēnlín gōngyuán; 森林公园) entrance (Y5), and can be flagged down anywhere. **Taxi** base fare Y5, each additional km Y1.8.

PRACTICAL INFORMATION

Tourist Office: Dragon International Hotel (xiánglóng guójì jiǔdiàn; 祥龙国际酒店), 46 Jiefang Lu (☎822 6888; fax 822 2935), arranges white-water rafting trips and tours to the cave for a hefty surcharge. English-speaking staff. Luggage storage Y5. **CITS,** 37 Jiefang Lu (☎830 0011; fax 830 0022), is across the street. In Zhangjiajie Park, **Zhangjiajie Travel Service Company** (zhāngjiājiè guójiāsēnlín gōngyuán lǚxíngshè; 张家界国家森林公园旅行社; ☎571 2162), on the 2nd fl. of the Jinbianyan Hotel, organizes tours and private drivers. The manager is quite helpful. English-speaking staff. Both offices are rather pricey.

Bank of China: 1 Xinmatou Jie (☎822 3383). Currency exchange. Open daily 8am-5:30pm.

PSB: On Ziwu Lu (☎822 5050). Open daily 8am-6pm.

Internet Access: Hong Cheng Internet Center (hóngchéng wǎnglù zhōngxīn; 洪城网路中心), 3 Bei Zheng Jie, across from the China Construction Bank. Y4 per hr. Play computer games with the owner at no extra charge. Open 24hr.

Post Office: In Zhangjiajie City, the **post office** (☎822 4757) is on Huilong Lu, just east of the long-distance bus station. Open daily 8am-8pm. Another in Zhangjiajie Park on the main street on the right of the park entrance, about 100m past Pipaxi Hotel. Open daily 8am-6pm. **Postal Code:** 427000.

ACCOMMODATIONS

Zhangjiajie's natural beauty is its chief attraction, and most tourists head straight for the scenic park. A number of hotels border the main road leading there; there are also some pricier hotels inside the park, but a reservation is needed to guarantee a room. Because of the daily influx of tourists, hotels in the area are generally pricey. If you are stuck in Zhangjiajie City overnight, try the **Doule Hotel** ❷ (dōulè bīnguǎn; 都乐宾馆), 1 Renmin Lu, opposite the long-distance bus station. (☎822 2921. Singles Y120; doubles and triples Y240.) Bargaining is a possibility in most hotels, although this becomes more difficult during the summer months when cheaper hotels are booked to their capacity. Dorms don't accept foreigners.

Jinbianyan Hotel (jīnbiānyán fàndiàn; 金鞭岩饭店; ☎571 2362), closer to the park entrance than the Zhangjiajie Hotel. Provides good Cantonese breakfast and is one of the best places to book rafting or sightseeing tours. Rooms are average, but it is the best deal near the park. Doubles Y120, with bath Y240; triples Y270. ❷

Pipaxi Hotel (pípáxī bīnguǎn; 琵琶溪宾馆; ☎571 8888; fax 571 2257), on the right side of the road as you enter the park area. Quieter and more comfortable than most other accommodations in the park. Singles and doubles Y280-548; triples Y300. ❹

Zhangjiajie Hotel (zhāngjiājiè bīnguǎn; 张家界宾馆; ☎571 2388; fax 571 2816), on the left side of the road about 100m before the last bus stop. Might be booked solid during summer tourist season; checking ahead advised. Singles and doubles Y420. ❺

FOOD AND ENTERTAINMENT

Although there are some ethnic Miaos in the area, Tujia (tǔjīa; 土家) restaurants predominate in Zhangjiajie. The restaurants near the Golden Rice Bowl Restaurant serve a variety of foods, ranging from Mao's family tofu to capitalist dumplings.

Golden Rice Bowl Restaurant (jīnfànwǎn jiǔlóu; 金饭碗酒楼; ☎571 2688), in a 2-story bamboo building overlooking the stream opposite the Zhangjiajie Hotel. Specializes in Tujia food, but the best item is another "tu": *tǔdòu bǐng* (土豆饼; potato croquettes). Excellent food and good atmosphere. Also a great place to sip a cup of tea or coffee and to snack on melon seeds. Entrees Y8-40. Open daily 8am-midnight. ❷

The Comrade Bar (tóngzhì bā; 同志吧), on Bei Zheng Jie. Despite China's turn toward market capitalism, the Comrade Bar does its best to make socialism sexy. With its chic Communist theme and a vast selection of drinks and snacks, this place is packed every night with wanna-be pop stars singing their favorite Chinese tunes. The staff is very friendly. Open daily 11am-2am.

HIKING IN ZHANGJIAJIE

Zhangjiajie National Forest Park (zhǎngjiājiè guójiāsēnlín gōngyuán; 张家界国家森林公园), the surreal realm of the Zhang family, is home to a forest of tree-covered sandstone pillars towering above mist-shrouded ravines, pristine mountain pools, and thundering rapids. Stalagtites fills palatial caverns fed by underground rivers and waterfalls. Even the crowds and the artificial lighting do not detract from the natural wonder of this place. *(☎571 2229. Y62; you can remain in the park for days without paying an additional fee.)* Travel agencies arrange half- and full-day whitewater rafting trips (generally Y120-160, plus Y35-40 for transport) and cave tours (Y35-40) in the northeastern part of the park. One popular destination is **Yellow Dragon Cave** (huánglóng dòng; 黄龙洞) about 1hr. west of the park (Y62).

Hiking trails begin just beyond the main entrance; there is also a free minibus to **Huangshizhai Mountain** (huángshízhài; 黄石寨). At 990m, Huangshizhai is the highest point in Zhangjiajie, and on a good day offers spectacular views of the forests that dot the rugged landscape. *(Admission Y110.)* Huangshizhai and **Jinbianxi** (金鞭溪) are the most popular scenic areas, with the best scenery and the most tourists. Most of the more interesting sights are on the walk down; if you don't mind large crowds, it is a good idea to ride the cable car up and walk down like most tour groups. Doing it the other way around will allow you to avoid large throngs of people, but you'll miss out on some good sights. *(Cable car runs daily 8am-6pm. Y47 up, Y37 down, Y74 round-trip.)*

Many scenic spots are surrounded by "temples" that charge an additional fee—don't bother unless you've got plenty of spare change, as most of the temples at Zhangjiajie are really just souvenir shops in disguise. Maps (Y3) point out the major hiking paths, but the more obscure trails usually make for more thrilling treks, with fewer fellow tourists and more natural scenery. Be forewarned that wild animals do roam the forests of Zhangjiajie, most notably the infamous "five-step snake." After being bitten, victims take five steps and…well, you get the idea.

If you have time to spend in Zhangjiajie City, the **Cengguang Temple** (céngguāng chánsì; 曾光禅寺), on Jiefang Lu between Bei Zheng Jie and Lingyuan Lu, is a hidden treasure. Talk to the Daoist fortune teller for a glimpse into your future (Y40) or relax to strains of traditional Tujia music. Antiques and traditional furniture are also sold here. *(☎822 2824. Open daily 8am-6pm. Y10.)*

HUBEI 湖北

Hubei province has long been at the mercy of the Yangzi River and its many tributaries. But even as the river brings yearly flooding and occasional disaster, it is also the source of livelihood for those living along its banks, bringing trade, industry, and tourists from the wealthier coastal provinces. The Yangzi meanders upstream through Wuhan, Hubei's capital and cultural center, and continues to the Three Gorges that form a magnificent backdrop for the ferries that cruise down the river. As one moves toward the northwest, the scenery turns wild and rugged, while much of the region south of the Yangzi is given over to industrial production and high tech zones. Known as the "Gateway to Nine Provinces," Hubei is central China's transportation hub, and tourists to the area are bound to spend some time here at one point or another. Summer weather can be brutal, but heaps of watermelon and a plentiful supply of local hospitality temper the stifling summer heat.

WUHAN 武汉 ☎027

Wuhan, situated in the heart of China at the confluence of the Han and Yangzi rivers, owes much of its development to its position halfway along the shipping lanes of the Yangzi. In 1842, the Treaty of Nanjing opened the district of Hankou to foreign trade, and Wuhan's European architecture is a visible reminder of its five foreign concessions. Since then, life in Wuhan has not been all peace and progress. During the 1911 Revolution, bombings and uprisings marred the city's prosperous facade, nearly leveling several parts of the city; periodic upheavals continued to wreak havoc until the end of the Cultural Revolution. Today, the hot, humid summer months bring torrential rains that threaten to flood this city of nearly five million. Thus far, Wuhan has not only survived but blossomed into a crucial regional center. Wuhan's next challenge is to satisfy the increasing number of foreign and Chinese visitors, but the city's strong collection of natural and historical sights should prove that once again, Wuhan will be up to the task at hand.

TRANSPORTATION

Flights: Tianhe International Airport (tiānhé guójì jīchǎng; 天河国际机场; ☎581 8222), 30km northwest of central Hankou. Buses (35-45min., 10 per day 6:30am-5pm, Y15-20) leave from the **China Southern Hubei Airlines office** (zhōngguó nánfāng hángkōng húběi gōngsī; 中国南方航空湖北公司), 1 Hangkong Lu (☎8361 1756 or 8361 1757; fax 8363 2264). Open daily 8am-9pm. The **CAAC Booking Service Center** (wǔhàn tiānhé jīchǎng shòupiào fúwù zhōngxīn; 武汉天河机场售票服务中心), 1089 Jiefang Dadao, Hankou (☎8360 2228). Open daily 8:30am-5pm. MC/V. To: **Beijing** (3-4 per day, Y980); **Chengdu** (daily, Y830); **Chongqing** (2 per day, Y720); **Guangzhou** (6-7 per day, Y850); **Guilin** (1-3 per day, Y710); **Hefei** (daily, Y330); **Kunming** (2-5 per day, Y1200); **Nanjing** (2-3 per day, Y580); **Shanghai** (6-9 per day, Y750); **Xi'an** (2 per day, Y630).

Trains: Most trains stop at both Hankou and Wuchang stations; in general, more trains pass through Wuchang. **Wuchang Train Station** (wǔchāng huǒchē zhàn; 武昌火车站; ☎6722 2222), on Zhongshan Lu, not far past Ziyang Lu. To: **Beijing** (12-16hr., 13 per day, Y173); **Chengdu** (27hr., daily, Y242); **Chongqing** (24hr., 3 per day, Y320); **Fuzhou** (22hr., daily, Y135); **Guangzhou** (16hr., 14 per day, Y232); **Kunming** (44hr., 2 per day, Y320); **Nanchang** (9hr., 4 per day, Y60); **Shanghai** (19hr., 2 per day, Y272); **Shiyan** (9hr., 2 per day, Y320); **Xi'an** (14-16hr., 6 per day, Y210); **Xiangfan** (5-6hr., 4 per day, Y61). **Hankou Train Station** (hànkǒu huǒchē zhàn; 汉口火车站; ☎8585

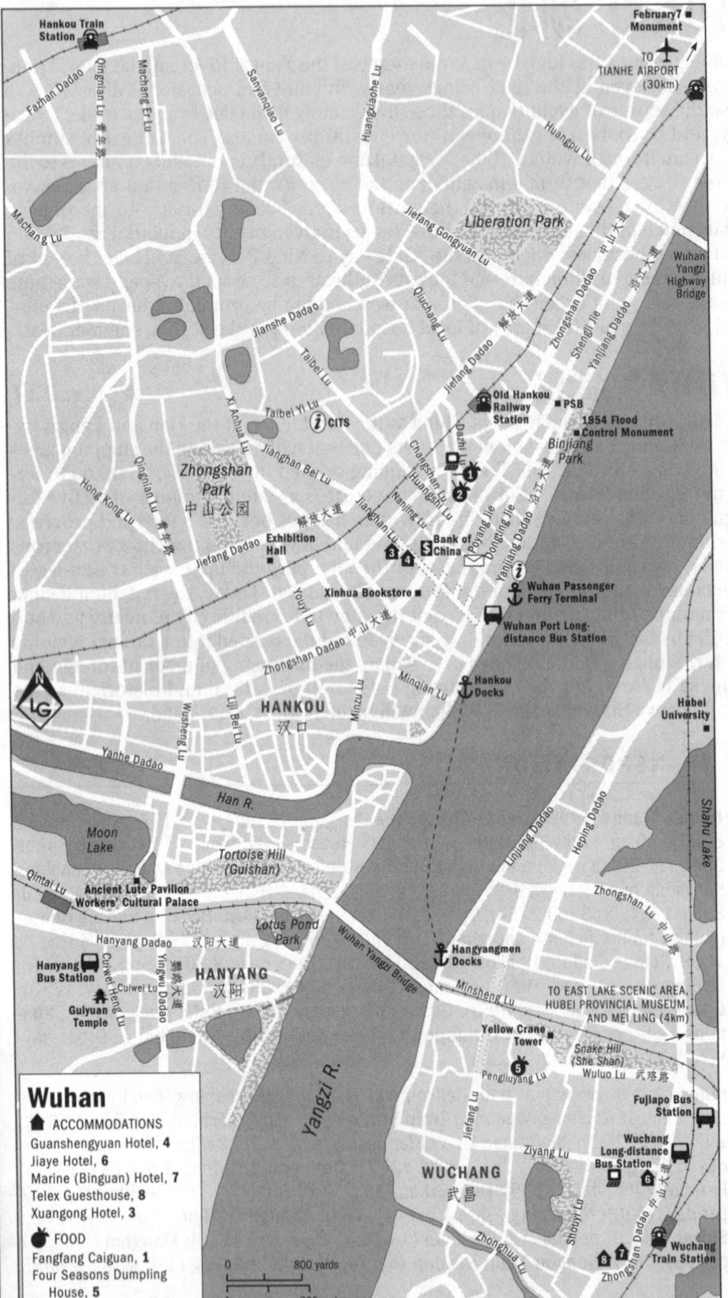

Wuhan

ACCOMMODATIONS

- Guanshengyuan Hotel, **4**
- Jiaye Hotel, **6**
- Marine (Binguan) Hotel, **7**
- Telex Guesthouse, **8**
- Xuangong Hotel, **3**

FOOD

- Fangfang Caiguan, **1**
- Four Seasons Dumpling House, **5**
- Laotongcheng Restaurant, **2**

0 800 yards
0 800 meters

Hankou Train Station
February7 Monument
TO TIANHE AIRPORT (30km)
Fazhan Dadao
Qingnian Lu 青年路
Machang Er Lu
Sanyanqiao Lu
Huangxiaohe Lu
Huangpu Lu
Machang Lu
Liberation Park
Jiefang Gongyuan Lu
Wuhan Yangzi Highway Bridge
Zhongshan Dadao 中山大道
Shengli Jie
Yanjiang Dadao 沿江大道
Jiefang Dadao 解放大道
Qiuchang Lu
Jianshe Dadao
Taibei Lu
Taibei Yi Lu
CITS
Xi Anhua Lu
Old Hankou Railway Station
PSB
1954 Flood Control Monument
Binjiang Park
Dazhi Lu
Changshan Lu
Huangshi Lu
Jianghan Bei Lu
Zhongshan Park 中山公园
Qingnian Lu 青年路
Hong Kong Lu
Nanjing Lu
Jianghan Lu
Poyang Jie
Dongting Jie
Jiefang Dadao 解放大道
Exhibition Hall
Bank of China
Wuhan Passenger Ferry Terminal
Xinhua Bookstore
Youyi Lu
Wuhan Port Long-distance Bus Station
Zhongshan Dadao 中山大道
Minqian Lu
Hankou Docks
Hubei University
Wusheng Lu
Liji Bei Lu
Minzu Lu
HANKOU 汉口
Yanhe Dadao
Han R.
Moon Lake
Tortoise Hill (Guishan)
Linjiang Dadao
Heping Dadao
Shahu Lake
Qintai Lu
Ancient Lute Pavilion
Workers' Cultural Palace
Lotus Pond Park
Zhongshan Lu 中山路
Hanyang Dadao 汉阳大道
Hanyang Bus Station
Cuiwei Heng Lu
Cuiwei Lu
Yingwu Dadao 鹦鹉大道
HANYANG 汉阳
Guiyuan Temple
Wuhan Yangzi Bridge
Hangyangmen Docks
Minsheng Lu
TO EAST LAKE SCENIC AREA, HUBEI PROVINCIAL MUSEUM, AND MEI LING (4km)
Yellow Crane Tower
Snake Hill (She Shan)
Wuluo Lu 武珞路
Pengliuyang Lu
Yangzi R.
Jiefang Lu
Fujiapo Bus Station
Wuchang Long-distance Bus Station
Ziyang Lu
WUCHANG 武昌
Shouyi Lu
Zhonghua Lu
Zhongshan Dadao 中山大道
Wuchang Train Station

YANGZI BASIN

0932), at the intersection of Fazhan Dadao and Qingnian Lu. Luggage storage in the snack kiosk out front (Y4). To: **Beijing** (12-16hr., 10 per day, Y173); **Chongqing** (24hr., 3 per day, Y154); **Fuzhou** (22hr., daily, Y135); **Guangzhou** (16hr., 10 per day, Y232); **Harbin** (2 per day); **Hefei** (10hr., daily, Y89); **Kunming** (44hr., 3 per day, Y320); **Nanchang** (9hr., 2 per day, Y60).

Buses: Wuchang Long-distance Bus Station (wǔchāng chángtú qìchē zhàn; 武昌长途汽车站), 519 Zhongshan Lu (☎8804 4703), 1 block from Ziyang Lu in the opposite direction from the train station. To: **Hefei** (9-11hr., 8 per day, Y63-140); **Nanjing** (14hr., 2 per day, Y192); **Yichang** (4-5hr., every hr. 7am-6pm, Y61-115). Wuchang's **Fujiapo Bus Station** (fùjiāpō qìchē zhàn; 付家坡汽车站; ☎8789 8687), on Wuluo Lu near Da Dong Men and Zhongshan Lu has buses to **Yichang** (every 30min. 6:30am-8pm) and less-frequent departures to **Guangzhou** (24hr., 3 per day, Y120), **Guilin** (24hr., daily, Y160), and **Shanghai** (20-22hr., daily, Y160). Hankou's **Wuhan Port Long-distance Bus Station** (wǔhàngǎng chángtú qìchē zhàn; 武汉港长途汽车站; ☎8284 0282, ext. 4557) on Yanjiang Dadao, next to the passenger ferry terminal. Open daily 7am-7pm. To: **Hefei** (10hr., daily, Y106-150); **Jiujiang** (4hr., daily, Y62); **Nanjing** (14hr., 4 per day, Y142-192); **Shanghai** (22hr., daily, Y200-306); **Yichang** (4hr., 2 per day, Y70-100).

Ferries: Wuhan Passenger Ferry Terminal (wǔhàn kèyùn gǎng; 武汉客运港; ☎8283 9546), on Yanjiang Dadao, Hankou. As you enter the ticket hall, the inquiry booth is on the right; timetables and ticket windows are against the back wall. Open daily 7am-10:30pm. Price ranges are for 3rd-2nd classes. To: **Chongqing** (62hr., 1-5 per day, Y249-588, 1st class Y1000); **Jiujiang** (9-10hr., 3-4 per day, Y56-119); **Nanjing** (33-36hr., 2-4 per day, Y131-278); **Shanghai** (43hr., 11am and 7pm, Y192-408).

Local Transportation: Most **buses** run from around 6am to 9pm. Fare Y1. **Bus #10** links the Wuchang and Hankou train stations; **#533** runs from the Hankou train station to the downtown area on Zhongshan Dadao. Other routes extend far beyond the main commercial districts. Three tourist bus lines, **#1, 401,** and **402** (Y2), connect sights and nearby scenic areas. **Ferries** link Hankou and Wuchang, with frequent departures from the **Hankou docks** along Yanjiang Lu and the **Zhonghua Lu** and **Hanyangmen docks** in Wuchang (10-15min., every 20min. 6am-11pm, Y1-4).

Taxis: Base fare Y8, each additional km Y1.4. Taxis don't get you to your destination much faster than city buses. From either train station to central Hankou around Zhongshan Dadao Y20-30.

ORIENTATION AND PRACTICAL INFORMATION

Wuhan is composed of three districts: **Hankou** (汉口) and **Hanyang** (汉阳), north of the Yangzi River, separated by the Han River, and **Wuchang** (武昌), southeast of the Yangzi. Hankou bustles with activity, while Hanyang, the smallest of the three, is a quiet center of light industry. Across the Yangzi, Wuchang has transformed from an ancient walled city into a sprawling urban settlement that recedes into green pastures out toward the East Lake Scenic Area. All three districts are linked by bridges.

Hankou is full of shops and offices, especially on **Zhongshan Dadao** (中山大道). Another important commercial thoroughfare is **Jiefang Dadao** (解放大道), which runs north of and parallel to Zhongshan Dadao. The train station is north of Hankou about 5km from the central business area. The main docks line the Yangzi along **Yanjiang Dadao** (沿江大道). Hanyang's main commercial streets are **Yingwu Dadao** (鹦鹉大道) as well as **Hanyang Dadao** (汉阳大道), which runs roughly perpendicular to the Yangzi. In Wuchang, **Zhongshan Lu** (中山路) goes past the train station to intersect **Wuluo Lu** (武珞路), another important thoroughfare. The **East Lake Scenic Area** (东湖冈景) covers much of the southeast portion of Wuchang.

Travel Agencies: Travel agencies are everywhere, especially near the ferry passenger terminal, on Jiefang Dadao in Hankou, and around the train and bus stations in Wuchang. **CITS,** 26 Taibei Yi Lu, 7th fl., Hankou (☎8578 4125), 5min. east of Xinhua Lu, opposite the Marriott Hotel. Offers English-, Japanese-, German-, French-, and Spanish-speaking staff members. Open M-F 8:30am-5:30pm. **CTS,** 142 Yanjiang Dadao (☎8284 4894; fax 8278 0820), Hankou, in front of the ferry terminal, specializes in air travel and river cruises. English-speaking staff members. Open daily 8am-7:30pm. The **Hubei CITS Ticketing Center** (húběishěng zhōngguó guójì lǚxíngshè hángkōng fúwù zhōngxīn; 湖北省中国国际旅行社航空服务中心), 26 Jianghan Lu, Hankou (☎8270 3306; fax 8270 3396), a few blocks toward the river from Yanjiang Dadao, can assist English-speaking travelers. Open M-F 8:30am-6pm, Sa-Su 8:30am-5pm.

Bank of China: 593 Zhongshan Dadao, Hankou (☎8283 4891; fax 8283 5150), at Jianghan Lu. Exchanges currency and traveler's checks at counters #11 and 12 (daily 8:30am-5:30pm). Open daily 8am-8pm. Most expensive hotels also change currency.

Bookstore: Xinhua Bookstore, 896 Zhongshan Dadao, Hankou (☎8283 2761), a few doors down from Jianghan Lu. A large selection of books, including a decent stock of English-language novels and translations of Chinese classics, plus popcultural oddities like *The X-Files* in Chinese. Open daily 9am-8pm.

PSB: 206 Shengli Jie, Hankou (☎8283 0110).

Internet Access: Three Aces Internet Bar, 48 Dazhi Lu (☎714 0255), has 100 fast computers in an air conditioned 2nd fl. hideout. Open 24hr. **Youbang Internet Bar** (yǒubāng wǎngbā; 友邦网吧), 268 Ziyang Lu, Wuchang (☎8807 6169), across from China Agricultural Bank. Y2 per hr. Open 24hr.

Post Office: International Department (guójì yíngyè tīng; 国际营业厅; ☎8283 0766) in the post office on the corner of Shanghai Lu and Dongting Jie, Hankou. EMS and Poste Restante (windows #12 or 13). Open daily 8am-6pm. In Wuchang, a branch is next to the train station. Open daily 8am-6:30pm. **Postal Code:** 430014.

ACCOMMODATIONS

Most of Wuhan's cheapest hotels are still off-limits to foreigners, but promotions during the summer and other times—and the fact that the city isn't too heavily touristed—help to bring the prices down. Accommodations are plentiful in the Zhongshan Dadao area in Hankou and near the Wuchang Train Station.

HANKOU

Wuhan City Yangzijiang Hotel (wǔhànshì yángzǐjiāng jiǔdiàn; 武汉市扬子江酒店), 104 Jianghan Lu (☎8283 1193 or 8285 4962). Walk on Zhongshan Dadao, 1 block from the river. Good price and location. Basic rooms have A/C, attached bath, and TV. Electricity Y1-3. Singles Y60; doubles Y70; triples Y80; quads Y90. ❶

Guanshengyuan Hotel (guānshēngyuán dàjiǔdiàn; 冠生园大酒店), 109 Jianghan Lu (☎8281 2658, ext. 8200, fax 8277 9067), on the left, about 1 block past Zhongshan Dadao (heading away from the Yangzi). In the heart of Hankou's main shopping district, Guanshengyuan offers nothing particularly special apart from attached baths. Singles Y138; doubles Y168; triples Y188. ❷

Xuangong Hotel (xuángōng fàndiàn; 璇宫饭店), 57 Jianghan Lu (☎8281 0365; fax 8281 6942). From Zhongshan Dadao, head up Jianghan Lu 2 blocks, away from the river; the hotel is on the left. Clean rooms with A/C and new furnishings. A classical European facade with a pleasant staff, and cheap room service. Breakfast included. 10% service charge. Singles Y268; doubles Y328; triples Y398-480. ❹

WUCHANG

Telex Guesthouse (jiànchuán zhāodàisuǒ; 舰船招待所), 450 Zhongshan Lu (☎8807 0789), across the street from and to the left of the train station, less than 5min. away. The friendly staff keep the tiled halls clean and bright. Singles Y90; doubles Y110; triples Y135. ❷

Marine Hotel (hánghǎi bīnguǎn; 航海宾馆), 460 Zhongshan Lu (☎8804 3395; fax 8807 8717). Exit the train station and cross the street; it's a short walk to the left. Pay attention to the characters; the nearby Marine (Fandian) Hotel doesn't accept foreigners. Spacious rooms and baths. Singles Y128; doubles Y138-148; triples Y168-190. ❷

Jiaye Hotel (jiāyè bīnguǎn; 嘉叶宾馆), 426 Zhongshan Lu (☎8807 2975 or 8807 2075; fax 8806 5091), at Ziyang Lu, near the train station. Bright lights outside, but little light inside. Rooms are fairly clean. Reservations recommended; proximity to the station means that rooms often fill up by 9 or 10pm, if not earlier. Singles Y128; doubles Y148; triples Y188. ❷

FOOD AND ENTERTAINMENT

Although Wuhan doesn't claim a distinctive taste as its own, catfish from East Lake are a popular treat. Floating restaurants line **Bayi Lu,** near East Lake. Also in Wuchang, several of the side streets off **Ziyang Lu** feature dense concentrations of street stands. In Hankou, **Jiefang Dadao** and especially **Zhongshan Dadao** feature a mixture of stylish establishments and local and international fast food. A mix of large restaurants and sidewalk stands make **Dazhi Lu,** which runs between Zhongshan Lu and Jiefang Lu, and **Quichang Lu,** which heads north from Jiefang Lu near the end of Dazhi Lu, lively dinnertime choices. **Jianghan Lu, Nanjing Lu,** and nearby alleyways are crowded with people day and night.

The nightlife in Wuhan isn't as happening as one might expect in such a large city. A stroll down **Zhongshan Dadao** or **Xianggang Lu** leads to a few bars and clubs, and a walk up **Jianghan Lu** uncovers a karaoke lover's pot of gold. Residents while away their evenings at the **night markets** around Jianghan Lu and Nanjing Lu. Vendors peddle clothing, footwear, food, jewelry, and more. You may see some locals heading to beauty parlors in the late hours—be aware, though, that many such establishments specialize in services other than purely beautification.

Four Seasons Dumpling House (siji jiǎozi guǎn; 四季饺子馆), 241 Pengliuyang (☎8886 7023), Wuchang, near the Pengliuyang bus stop, about 5min. from either Jiefang Lu or Wuluo Lu. This well-known spot offers almost every kind of dumpling imaginable, including mushroom-pork and tomato-garlic. Special combinations made to order. 8 dumplings, napkins, and a toothpick Y1.6-6. Open daily 10am-10pm. ❶

Fangfang Caiguan (fāngfāng càiguǎn; 芳芳菜馆), 168 Dazhi Lu, Hankou (☎8278 4083), near the intersection with Zhongshan Dadao. This popular eatery strives for the Chinese ideal in restaurant ambience: hot, noisy, and chaotic. Saxophones and traditional singers perform dueling serenades over the boisterous chatter. Vegetable dishes Y6-12; meat entrees Y20-30. Open daily 4pm-4am. ❷

Laotongcheng Restaurant (lǎotōngchéng doùpí dàwáng; 老通城豆皮大王), 1 Dazhi Lu, 2nd and 3rd fl., Hankou (☎281 0616 or 283 4559), on the corner of Zhongshan Dadao across from Tianjin Lu. Proletarian fare in one of Mao's old haunts. Stuffed bean curd (dòupí; 豆皮; Y3-6) is the house specialty. *Dim sum* Y0.5-5, Peking duck Y40. 2nd fl. open daily 6:30-8:30am; 3rd fl. open daily 10am-2pm and 5-8:30pm. ❶

SIGHTS

Wuhan first gained popular notoriety for its role in the novel *The Romance of the Three Kingdoms*, but most present-day sights here relate to 20th-century events.

HANKOU

The center of Wuhan's modern commercial life, Hankou offers more atmosphere than official sights. **Zhongshan Dadao** was the center of the foreign concessions of the early 20th century; now the swarming shopping district is the navel of consumer culture. Closer to the Yangzi River, Yanjiang Dadao is home to the old **Customs House** and several **open-air markets** (including one filled with carrier pigeons); it also leads to the hulking **Yangzi Ferry Terminal.** The mighty Yangzi River, that has shaped Wuhan's history as a trade center, has been known to take a toll for its services. In **Binjiang Park** (bīnjiāng gōngyuán; 滨江公园), next to the river at the intersection of Yiyuan Lu and Yanjiang Dadao, the towering **1954 Flood Control Monument** celebrates the complex relationship between Wuhan and its exacting natural neighbor. While summer rains are a perennial threat, 1954 remains the high water mark in Wuhan's flooding history.

HANYANG

GUIYUAN TEMPLE (guīyuán sì; 归元寺). The cavernous, incense-filled halls of this large Buddhist monastery are often crowded with visitors filing into the **Arhat Hall,** where 500 figures, sculpted between 1822 and 1831, display the many faces of enlightenment. As usual, a vegetarian restaurant vies with the temple's incense as it attempts to fill the air with the aroma of imitation meat dishes. *(On the corner of Cuiwei Lu and Cuiweiheng Lu. Take bus #61 from the Hankou train station to Zhongjiacun. From Yingwu Dadao, turn right on Cuiwei Lu and walk for several blocks. Open daily 8am-5pm. Y10.)*

ANCIENT LUTE PAVILION WORKERS' CULTURAL PALACE (gǔqíntái gōngrén wénhuà gōng; 古琴台工人文化宫). This is a nice, peaceful park, even if the intended attractions (an overgrown courtyard and a creepy waxworks display) leave you unimpressed. The part of the park that overlooks nearby **Moon Lake** is dedicated to two ancient lute enthusiasts who found friendship through their love of music. *(Near the intersection of Guishan Bei Lu, Qintai Lu, and Yingqu Dadao; near Tortoise Hill. ☎8483 4187. Open daily 7:30am-4pm. Y5.)* **Tortoise Hill** (guī shān; 龟山) marks the spot where the heroic efforts of King Yu saved the city from flooding 4000 years ago. A **cable car** (Y20) from the "extreme sports" park on top of the hill makes the 800m crossing into Hankou and offers some spectacular views along the way. *(At the intersection of Guishan Bei Lu, Qintai Lu, and Yingwu Dadao. Tourist buses #1 and 401 and buses #507 and 701 stop at Guqintai. Open daily 8am-10pm.)*

WUCHANG

YELLOW CRANE TOWER (huánghè lóu; 黄鹤楼). Just beyond the **Great Yangzi Bridge** (chángjiāng dàqiáo; 长江大桥), this park and its well-preserved, five-tiered traditional tower afford impressive views of the river and the city. Built by Huang Wu in AD 223, the tower has been the subject of over 1000 poems and numerous landscape paintings. Gardens, ponds, pagodas, and inscriptions contribute to the setting's natural beauty. On hot summer days, the sun beats down on visitors like a fly-swatter on a mosquito; come early or late in the day to avoid the worst of it.

(On Wuluo Lu. Tourist bus #1 stops outside. ☎8887 7330. Open daily in summer 7am-6pm; in winter 7:30am-5:30pm. Y30, children Y15.)

HUBEI PROVINCIAL MUSEUM (húběishěng bówùguǎn; 湖北省博物馆). This museum displays objects unearthed from a 2400-year-old tomb. With over 7000 tomb artifacts, there's little room for other exhibits. Chime bells, zithers, and other musical instruments are among the finds, but the only sounds heard here are those of the plastic booties given to each visitor. *(On Donghu Lu. The entrance is hard to miss if you backtrack from the East Lake entrance. Tourist bus #1 stops at the museum. Good English narration. Open daily 9am-5pm; tickets sold 9-11:30am and 1:30-4:30pm. Y20, students Y12.)*

EAST LAKE (dōng hú; 东湖). A watery respite from the hurried pace of downtown, East Lake and its surrounding greenery offer city-weary travelers and harried locals the chance to boat, hike, or swim—though the rather rank waters might dissuade some would-be athletes. *(In the eastern part of Wuchang. Tourist buses #1 and 401 stop here. Open 24hr. Y10, children Y5.)*

YICHANG 宜昌 ☎0717

Sleepy little Yichang marks the end of the Yangzi canyonlands and the first disembarkment point for most river cruises. Despite the nearby Gezhou Dam and the gargantuan Three Gorges Dam construction project that looms farther upstream, there's nothing electric about Yichang. Most travelers pass through quickly and catch the first available train to Chongqing, Wuhan, or Wudangshan. For longer stays, the dams make for some fascinating sightseeing, and the city's welcoming amenities make visitors feel at home. (For more on the Three Gorges, see p. 705)

TRANSPORTATION

Flights: Three Gorges Airport (sānxiá jīchǎng; 三峡机场; ☎622 8915) has flights to about 10 domestic destinations. The airport bus (Y20) picks up passengers 2hr. before departures from the Yichang International Hotel, on the corner of Shengli Si Lu and Yanjiang Dadao. To: **Beijing** (daily, Y1190); **Chengdu** (M, W, and Sa; Y720); **Chongqing** (Su-Tu and Th-F, Y590); **Guangzhou** (W-Th and Sa-Su, Y880); **Nanjing** (M-Sa, Y700); **Shanghai** (1-2 per day M-Sa, Y980).

Trains: Yichang Train Station (yíchāng huǒchē zhàn; 宜昌火车站; ☎644 5242), at the intersection of Yunji Lu and Dongshan Dadao. Tickets are sold on the left side of the station daily 5am-10pm; be prepared to find that there are no sleepers available for trains within the next 2 days; travel agents in Yichang buy up sleeper tickets, making it nearly impossible to leave Yichang in a sleeper without paying a commission or waiting 3 days. Luggage storage 8am-2am (Y2). To: **Beijing** (19hr., daily, Y298-319); **Guangzhou** (4hr., daily, Y307-330); **Xi'an** (18hr., daily, Y196-209).

Buses: Yichang Bus Station (yíchāng qìchē zhàn;宜昌汽车站; ☎644 5314), on Dongshan Dadao, 5min. from the train station. When facing the train station, turn right; the bus station is on your right. Open 24hr. Inquire about departure times and ticket prices at the "English and Dumbness Window." To: **Hefei** (3 per day 11am-9:20pm, Y235); **Shiyan** (several per day 8am-6pm, Y105); **Wuhan** (every 30min.-1hr. 7am-8pm, Y125); **Xiangfan** (several per day, Y60); **Xingshan** (every 20min. 6:30am-6pm, Y37). Unscheduled private **minibuses** leave for Wuhan from the area around the docks and from the bus depot, past the bus station on Dongshan Dadao. For early morning departures, wait on the corner of Yiling Lu and Shengli San Lu at 7:30-8am. Later in the day, take bus #1 to the bus depot. In either place, minibus operators shout "Wuhan! Wuhan!" The negotiation usually starts at Y70 and can end at Y40.

Ferries: Dagongqiao Amphibious Passenger Terminal (dàgōngqiáo shuǐlù kèyùn zhàn; 大公桥水陆客运站; ☎622 2143), on Yanjiang Dadao near Shengli Si Lu. Sells tickets to Chongqing via the Three Gorges and the Little Three Gorges (Y170). To **Chongqing** (7 per day 10:30am-2am; 1st class Y759, 2nd class Y388, 3rd class Y162, 4th class Y116, 5th class Y91) and **Jiujiang** (3 per day 10:30am-2am; 2nd class Y337, 3rd class Y159, 4th class Y117, 5th class Y78) via **Wuhan.**

Local Transportation: Buses run 6am-8pm. Fare Y1. From the dock, bus **#2** zips along Yanjiang Dadao, and **#3** and **4** run past the train station. Buses **#6** and **11** run from Gezhou Dam and the Three Gorges Hotel, respectively, to the long-distance bus station.

Taxis: Base fare Y5, each additional km Y1.2. Most trips Y5-10.

ORIENTATION AND PRACTICAL INFORMATION

Yichang's compact downtown area occupies the northeast Yangzi bank, bordered by **Yanjiang Dadao** (沿江大道). The docks are in the south, and the rail and bus stations in the north on **Dongshan Dadao** (东山大道), which runs roughly parallel to Yanjiang Dadao. **Jiefang Lu** (解放路), **Longkang Lu** (隆康路), and **Yiling Dadao** (夷陵大道) run parallel to Dongshan Dadao. Perpendicular to the river, **Yunji Lu** (云集路), the downtown street lined with stores, hotels, and entertainment options, runs for approximately 1km before intersecting with Dongshan Dadao at the train station. **Shengli Si Lu** (胜利四路) and **Shengli San Lu** (胜利三路) head away from the river farther east; **Huancheng Lu** (环城路) does so farther west. The blocks around Yunji Lu closest to the river share the main street's activity.

Travel Agencies: CITS, 18 Longkang Lu (☎624 1875; fax 622 0973; yctgcits@public.yc.ht.cn). A few members of the helpful, courteous staff speak English, French, German, Japanese, and Russian. Offers group tours to the Three Gorges Dam (daily 8 and 9am, Y45). Tickets for Little Three Gorges cruises cost Y170. Train ticket commissions: hard seat Y10, hard sleeper Y30, soft sleeper Y40. No air or cruise commissions. Open daily 8:30-11:30am and 2:30-5:30pm. **CITS Ticketing Center,** 2 Er Malu (☎623 4567), is open 24hr. Many travel agencies also line Yanjiang Dadao near the docks.

Bank of China: 10 Shengli Si Lu (☎623 6217 or 622 7483; fax 623 6217), at Longkang Lu. Exchanges currency and traveler's checks. Credit card advances. Open M-F 8-11:30am and 3-6pm. The Taohualing Hotel, on Yunji Lu, north of Longkang Lu, and the Yichang International Hotel, on the corner of Yanjiang Dadao and Shengli Si Lu, exchange currency; the Taohualing doesn't exchange Australian or Canadian dollars.

PSB: Near the intersection of Xueyuan Jie and Huancheng Dong Lu west of Yunji Lu (☎674 4861). Open M-F 8:30am-noon and 2:30-5pm.

Hospital: No. 2 People's Hospital (dì'èr rénmín yīyuàn; 第二人民医院; ☎673 2452, 24hr. service 120), on Xiling Lu near Huancheng Lu.

Telephones: The main **China Telecom** is on Yunji Lu, at Yiling Dadao, next door to the post office. IDD service and pay phones available. Open daily 8am-5:30pm.

Internet Access: There is an Internet bar (☎888 3593) off Yanjiang Dadao, across from the entrance to the Waitan Hotel Hostel. From the dock area, cross the street and walk for 1min; turn in at the red sign that says "Accommodation." The Internet bar is to the right. Open daily 8am-midnight.

Post Office: On the corner of Yunji Lu and Yiling Dadao. EMS and *Poste Restante*. Open daily 8am-7pm. **Postal Code:** 443000.

ACCOMMODATIONS AND FOOD

Wealthy Three-Gorges-cruising clientele increase Yichang's hotel rates; the best deals are along Yunji Lu, near the docks, and near the train station.

The lively riverfront restaurants and night market on **Taozhu Lu,** west of Yunji Lu, serve point-and-choose stir-fry platters for Y5-10 per person. A few hotpot restaurants also bubble up in the area. Around the train station, cheap food stands are strewn along **Dongshan Dadao** near the base of the steps. The first street that runs toward the river from Longkang Lu (when coming from Yunji Lu) is filled with fruit and vegetable stands, meat shops, and steamers of *mántóu* and buns.

Waitan Hotel Hostel (wàitān fàndiàn zhāodàisuǒ; 外滩大酒店招待所), 156 Yanjiang Dadao (☎622 4327), across from the docks. Walk toward town, and turn at the red "Accommodation" sign; it's to the left. Friendly staff, powerful fans, and laundry machine (Y5 per load) make up for the bare concrete courtyard and straw bedcovers. 24hr. hot water (cold water less consistent). Dorms Y12-25; singles Y30; doubles Y60. ❶

Yichang Railway Hotel (yíchāng tiělù dàjiǔdiàn; 宜昌铁路大酒店; ☎646 3073), in the train station square, just left of the station entrance, at the top of the steps to Dongshan Dadao. Rooms have A/C and some are quiet. 24hr. hot water. 3-bed dorms Y40; doubles Y188. MC/V. ❶

Sunshine Hotel (yángguāng dàjiǔdiàn; 阳光大酒店), 1 Yunji Lu (☎644 6075, ext. 8181; fax 644 8086), across from the steps to the train station. Rooms have A/C, bath, and unattractive but well-kept decor. 24hr. hot water. Doubles Y198-216. ❸

SIGHTS AND ENTERTAINMENT

Yichang's main points of interest are the hydroelectric wonders that rumble upstream from town. The **Gezhou Dam** (gězhōu bà; 葛洲坝) yolks the Yangzi just north of the city. Built in 1989 and soon to be dwarfed by the behemoth upriver, the 2.5km-wide, 70m-tall wall across the mouth of the Xiling Gorge is currently China's largest dam. (Take Bus #9 from Dongshan Lu. Open daily 8am-6pm. Y15, admission to ship docks are only Y8.) On hot days, locals use the nearby riverbanks as an informal swimming hole despite the questionable condition of the water. The riverside heights provide for leisurely strolls and vistas of the grand, murky Yangzi, laden with river traffic. Closer to the city center, **Binjiang Park** (bīnjiāng gōngyuán; 滨江公园) stretches along the waterfront from Shengli Lu to Xiling Lu, and has a number of places to sit and watch the powerful Yangzi current.

On **Yunji Lu** close to the waterfront and on **Er Malu,** a number of small bars with poorly spelled menus and overpriced drinks cater primarily to tourists.

XIANGFAN 襄樊 ☎0710

A place for travelers to spend the night, wash up, and make the appropriate connections, Xiangfan is devoted mainly to transport, building cars, and shuttling passengers throughout the country by way of train, plane, and bus. If you're heading to Wudangshan, you'll probably spend a few hours or even a night in this pleasant (if unexciting) town.

ORIENTATION AND PRACTICAL INFORMATION

Xiangfan is a small city, made even smaller by the fact that most travelers don't need to venture very far away from the train or bus stations. The train station is in a large square just off **Qianjin Lu** (前进路), at the head of **Zhongyuan Lu** (中原路). Eateries and hotels cluster nearby. The long-distance bus station is about two blocks down Zhongyuan Lu from the train station; the local bus station is directly across from the train station.

Flights: CAAC ticket office, 44 Qianjin Lu (☎323 9213 or 325 6492), at Zhongyuan Lu. Open daily 7am-9pm. The **Business Center of the Railway Grand Hotel** (☎322 0043, ext. 6205), on the right past the reception desk, also sells tickets. Open daily 8am-7pm for airline tickets, 7:20am-11pm for train tickets. The **airport** has limited service to: **Beijing** (Tu and Su 1:35pm, Y810); **Guangzhou** (W and Su 7:30am, Y1050); **Shanghai** (Tu and Sa, 7:10pm, Y980); **Shenzhen** (Tu and Sa 3:30pm, Y990).

Trains: Xiangfan Train Station (xiāngfán huǒchē zhàn; 襄樊火车站) is off a square at the intersection of Zhongyuan Lu and Qianjin Lu. The main ticket hall is on the right. Buy tickets early; sleeper tickets can be extremely difficult to buy even in advance. Hard seat travelers be forewarned: passengers line up at the station gates 30min. before departure, and then stampede for the trains at frightening speeds. To: **Beijing** (15-17hr., 4:14pm and 7:40pm, Y274) and **Wuhan** (3½hr-5hr., 4 per day, Y20).

Buses: Xiangfan Bus Station (xiāngfán qìchē zhàn; 襄樊汽车站; ☎322 3768) is on Zhongyuan Lu, 2 blocks from the train station, on the right. Ticket office open 24hr. Luggage storage in the ticket hall, just left of the entrance. To: **Changsha** (10hr., 5:30pm, Y108); **Shiyan** (3½hr., evey 40min. 7:30am-6pm, Y41-45); **Wuhan** (5½hr., every hr. 6am-7pm, Y65); **Yichang** (4½hr., evey 30-45min. 6am-6pm, Y60); **Wudangshan** (3hr., every hr., Y37). **Minibuses** to Yichang and Shiyan leave frequently from nearby depots.

Currency Exchange: The **Railway Grand Hotel** exchanges currency, even for non-guests. None of the Bank of China branches exchanges foreign currency.

Post and Telecommunications: The train station **post office** and **China Telecom** (☎322 3457) is down the alley next to the luggage storage office. EMS. Open daily 8am-6pm. **Postal Code:** 441003.

ACCOMMODATIONS AND FOOD

For the price of a meal, you can easily get a room for the night; but the room might be less comfortable than a damp cardboard box. If you're coming from the train or the long-distance bus station, these super-cheap deals will find you in the form of over-eager women pulling weary passengers into their nearby hostels. Foreigners may have to struggle for the cheapest rooms (Y17-20), but persistence pays off.

The streets around the train stations are filled with small stores that sell snack foods like dumplings (Y1 for 7) and a sprinkling of stalls with outside seating. Carts full of sesame seed crackers pop up everywhere. **Tiege Dumpling House** ❶ (tiěgē jiǎozi guǎn; 铁哥饺子馆), opposite and to the left of the train station, serves up delicious dumplings for cheap. (☎322 0043, ext. 6833. Open daily 9am-10pm.)

Aeolus Hotel (fēngshén bīnguǎn; 风神宾馆), 36 Qianjin Lu (☎322 3483 or 322 4035; fax 322 4968). From the train station, turn right on Qianjin Lu; look for the very tall building with the English name plastered on the side. Comfort for reasonable prices. All rooms have A/C, bath, phone, and TV. 24hr. hot water and water boiler in each room. Doubles Y168 (bargain to Y150); triples Y180. ❸

Railway Grand Hotel (tiělù dàjiǔdiàn; 铁路大酒店), 46 Qianjin Lu (☎322 0043; fax 322 1724), just across from the train station. This upscale option has French-and

English-speaking staff and sweet-smelling rooms complete with personal safe, mini bar, and VCR. Business Center in lobby books plane and train tickets. Currency exchange. Laundry service. Doubles 288-388; triples Y368. Credt cards accepted. ❹

WUDANGSHAN MOUNTAIN 武当山 ☎0719

Long before *Crouching Tiger, Hidden Dragon* exposed this majestic mountain and its devotion to the martial arts to the Western world, Wudangshan was one of China's most holy mountains. A stealthy, precise beauty pervades the mountain; the fog curls its way about craggy cliffs, slipping around trees and rocks as it moves steadily forward, creating an almost haunted atmosphere. Its temples and palaces are scattered about, built more vertically than horizontally to accommodate the mountain's steep slopes. Primarily famed as the birthplace of one of Daoism's deities, the Great Emperor Zhen Wu, the mountain is also known as the birthplace of Wudang boxing. The black-robed monks who train here use grace before strength and swiftness before power to practice the art of self-defense. With its dark forests, lofty temples, and spiritual significance, Wudangshan is a poetic gem worthy of a visit.

ORIENTATION AND PRACTICAL INFORMATION

The Wudangshan range stretches across northwestern Hubei province, between Xiangfan and Shiyan. Most travelers to Wudangshan stay in the city, which is about 25km from the main peak. One main street runs through town, going east to Xiangfan and west to Shiyan. Anything of interest is past the bridge, on this street or on one of the minor sidestreets branching off it. The main entrance to the mountain is just past the bridge to the east. From there, a sharply curving road leads up to hotels, restaurants, and the mountain's main sights.

Trains: Wudangshan Train Station (wǔdāngshān huǒchē zhàn; 武当山火车站) is south of the main road, at the end of one of the side streets. If trains arrive early and no one is there, they often do not stick around, and if they're late, they tend not to stop at all. To: **Beijing** (22hr., 1:26pm, Y114); **Shiyan** (10min., 3 per day, Y2.5-8); **Wuhan** (6hr., 11:56pm, Y63); **Xiangfan** (4 per day, Y9-23.)

Buses: A bus either to **Shiyan** (Y10) or **Xiangfan** (Y30), where it's easier to catch a train, might be the easiest way to skip town. Buses run along the main road, trolling for passengers. Frequent departures to both cities; just keep your eyes and ears open.

Bank of China: Just west of the bridge, on the main road (☎566 6154). Exchanges currency only. Open daily in summer 8am-6pm; in winter 8am-5:30pm.

Bookstore: Sanwei Bookstore (sānwèi shūdiàn; 三味书店), 3 blocks west of the bridge, opposite the Laoying Hotel. A small family-owned shop with a few classic texts and language aids. Owners Mr. and Mrs. (Victor and Juliet) Shiyi both speak English and love welcoming foreigners to their town.

Internet Access: Xiangkeji Internet Bar (xiǎngkèji wǎngbā; 想科技网吧; ☎566 8181), on the main road, about 25m east of the Xuanwu Hotel, across from the movie theater. Y2 per hr. Open daily 8am-midnight.

Post Office (☎566 0414), from the bridge, 2 blocks west along the main road, to the right; look for the pagoda-topped building on the left. EMS. Open in summer daily 7:30am-6pm; in winter 8am-5:30pm. **Postal Code:** 442714.

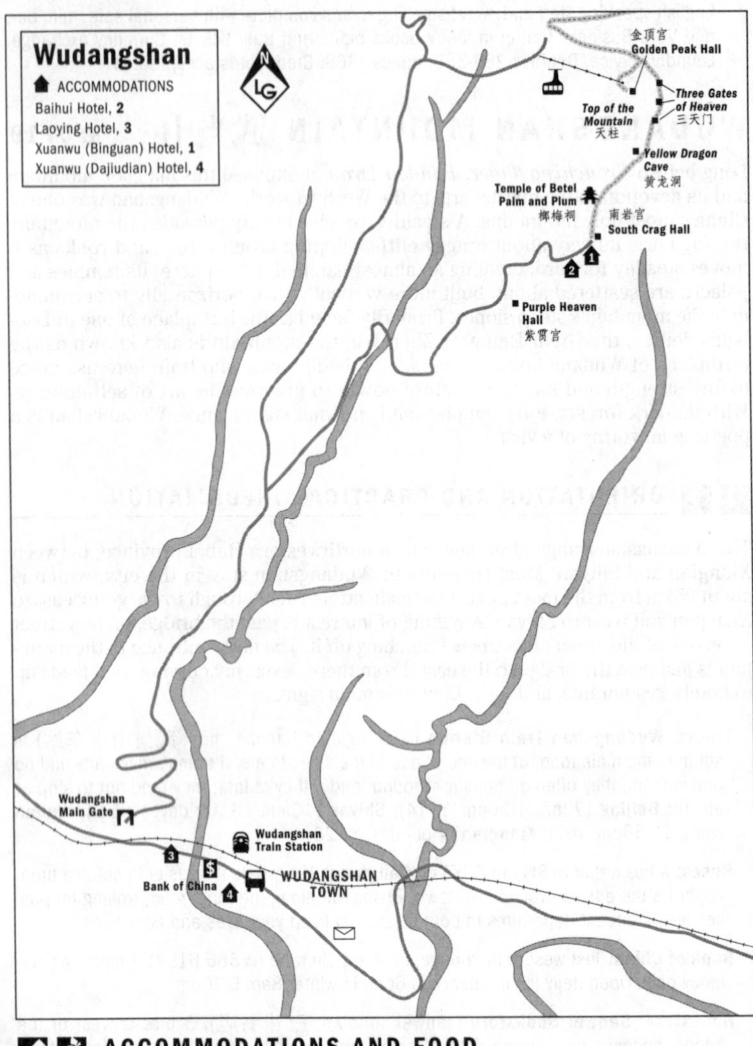

ACCOMMODATIONS AND FOOD

Staying amidst the dirt and mess of the town makes it easier to drop off your pack and make a quick daytrip to the mountain. Hotels on the mountain are slightly more expensive and not quite as nice.

Off the main road, family-owned stalls fry several varieties of scallion pancakes (Y0.5) and golden, light-as-air dough (Y1 for a bagful). A handful of sit-down places (mostly in hotels) lie along the main road.

Laoying Hotel (lǎoyíng fàndiàn; 老营饭店; ☎566 5349 or 566 5347), on the left side of the main road, across the bridge. Bargain and get a Y200 room with fluffy pillows and a queen-sized bed for Y160. Large rooms with 24hr. hot water, A/C, shower stalls, TV, but no phones. 3-bed dorms Y108; singles Y200; doubles Y200; triples Y180. ❷

Baihui Hotel (bǎihuì shānzhuāng; 百汇山庄; ☎568 9191; fax 568 9088), on the mountain, about 500m before the parking lot. If you're sweaty and tired from the hike, rent a standard double for an hour (Y20) and catch a nice nap. Rooms are clean and in good condition, with large bathtubs, phone, and TV. 4-bed dorms Y40; singles Y380; doubles Y280 per room (Y100 per person); triples Y270. ❶

Xuanwu (Binguan) Hotel (xuánwǔ bīnguǎn; 玄武宾馆; ☎568 9175), just next to the Baihui Hotel, near the end of the mountain road. Standard rooms are a world away from their cheaper counterparts: the former have 24hr. hot water and decent baths. Doubles Y120-200; triples Y120-240. ❷

Xuanwu (Dajiudian) Hotel (xuánwǔ dàjiǔdiàn; 玄武大酒店; ☎566 5347), on the main road, across from the road leading to the train station. The hotel equivalent of a hard seat. Doubles Y100 (bargain for Y80). ❷

CLIMBING WUDANGSHAN

The main gate to the **Wudangshan Scenic Area** (wǔdāngshān fēngjǐng qū; 武当山风景区) is just east of town. *(Open daily 7am-5:30pm. ☎566 5396. Y31; the extra Y1 is for insurance.)* With that in mind, speed away on a good 30-minute terror-filled ride along narrow, sharply curving roads until you reach the parking lot, the starting point for most hikers. Minivans from town to the trailhead cost Y20-30. They can also take you around to the other side of the mountain, where a cable car goes directly to the summit by way of a long, lazy ride with a few near-vertical ascents. *(Open M-F 8:30am-4pm, Sa-Su 8:30am-5pm. Up Y45, down Y35, round-trip Y70; children half-price.)* The hike itself is akin to waiting in line at an amusement park; just when you think you've arrived, you turn the corner and there's yet another steep staircase mocking your endurance. Still, the trail is in good condition and shaded from the sun by lush trees. Large numbers of souvenir stands and maddeningly temperamental weather can frustrate even the most well-intentioned climber, however. When it rains on Wudangshan, it pours, and the staircases can turn into mini-waterfalls. In good weather, a climb to the top takes about two hours.

Two trails lead from the edge of the parking lot: follow the walkway on the right to South Crag Hall, then backtrack and take the left path to the summit.

PURPLE HEAVEN HALL (zǐxiāo gōng; 紫霄宫). Purple Heaven Hall clings to the side of the mountain, about 10 min before the end of the road. Built in 1413, this temple contains shrines, a shop selling traditional Chinese herbal remedies, and Daoist monks who float down the frighteningly steep staircases with uncanny ease. *(Open daily 7am-6pm. Y10.)*

SOUTH CRAG HALL (nányán gōng; 南岩宫). South Crag Hall is about a 15-minute walk from the parking lot. From the large stone arch, go down the steps (if you head up you find only a couple of uninteresting temples). Within the South Crag Hall stands an old well that contains the sacred water that Zhen Wu drank before becoming a celestial being. Although its true powers might not extend further than thirst-quenching, the workers there still painstakingly draw water with a 17 ft. long bamboo pole. Take a left behind the main altar to **Tianyi Zhenqing Stone Palace** (tiānyǐ zhēnqìnggōng shídiàn; 天乙真庆宫石殿), where paths balance alongside rocky cliffs. Here, **Dragon Head Rock** (lóngtóu shí; 龙头石) extends beyond the mountain face. Incense still burns at the end as it has for centuries.

TEMPLE OF BETEL PALM AND PLUM (lángméi cí; 榔梅祠). The first major site on the way to the summit is a temple built during the Six Dynasties period to honor the Black Warriors, famous in Daoist legend for grafting a plum branch onto a betel palm. Much of the temple is devoted to Wudang boxing, developed by Zhang Sanfeng after he witnessed a fight between a magpie and a snake and understood their opposing natures. The diagrams and pictures inside depict techniques for overcoming strength with flexibility. *(Open daily 8am-6pm; Y2.)*

YELLOW DRAGON CAVE (huánglóng dòng; 黄龙洞). This small shrine marks the half-way point of the trail. Go up the stairs to the left to see a rather small dragon statue and a cave. Water drips from the stones above, forming a crystal clear pool. *(Open daily 8am-6pm; Y2.)*

TO THE SUMMIT. From here, it's onward and upward to the summit. At the rock, the path to the right leads to the **Three Gates of Heaven** (sāntiān mén; 三天门), a difficult trail with little to offer but the promise of sore muscles. To the left is a less strenuous and more pleasant path. At the top, pass through Harmony Palace and Lingguan Hall, dedicated to a Daoist god who punishes sinners by flinging them off the cliff. His statue, fittingly, flips you the finger. The top of the mountain (tiānzhù; 天柱) yields some spectacular views of the rugged landscape and the impressive temples that crown Wudangshan. Here, **Golden Peak Hall** (jīn dǐng gōng; 金顶宫) houses a shiny, gilded brass statue of the balding Zhen Wu, provided that your legs can manage the final walk. *(Y10.)* To head back to civilization, take the cable car back to the lower station or climb back the way you came.

SOUTH COAST

The coastal provinces of Guangdong and Fujian and the island of Hainan, have inherited their wealth and prosperity from their ambitious, driven predecessors. However, it wasn't luck or antiquated tradition that ultimately allowed these provinces to achieve greatness. No, nobody voted the South Coast to fame. In the past several decades, this region has come into its own, due in no small part to its cultural and geographic proximity to rich and indulgent Hong Kong and Taiwan. Recently, many South Coast cities have barreled ahead in the race for development. In 1979, China's first four Special Economic Zones (SEZs) were established in Shantou, Shenzhen, Xiamen, and Zhuhai.

This isn't too surprising—the South Coast has a long record of economic success. The numerous port cities along the coast and up and down the Pearl River have brought trade to the region for centuries. Exports of tea, silk, ceramics, and spices flowed out of centers of maritime trade like Guangzhou (formerly Canton). Early Arab and Muslim traders paved the way for Portuguese trade in the 16th century; Dutch, British, French, and American merchants soon followed. Migration went both ways too; the Cantonese (inhabitants of Guangdong) and Fujianese constitute the vast majority of overseas Chinese. Despite the constant onward struggle, the South Coast isn't about to forget its ancient past; between Shenzhen's theme parks and Sanya's beach resorts, hidden scenic wonders and magnificent temples remind the South Coast of the tradition of prosperity that it must uphold.

HIGHLIGHTS OF THE SOUTH COAST

DRIFT ON A BAMBOO RAFT down **Wuyishan Mountain**'s Nine-Bend River (p. 467), nestled underneath picturesque rock cliffs and mammoth green hills.

FIND YOUR INNER ELTON JOHN at Xiamen's **Gulangyu** (p. 473), the famous "Piano Isle" where the sound of classical music drifts from colonial villa balconies.

TAKE A BITE OUT OF MAN'S BEST FRIEND at Guangzhou's **Qingping Market** (p. 488), proof that the Chinese will eat *anything.*

FUJIAN 福建

Fujian province stares directly across the straits into Taiwan. While the province joins the rest of the mainland in expressing displeasure over Taiwanese independence, the flow of funds and friendship across the straits (most evident in the ostentatious riches of the provincial capital, Fuzhou) seems unlikely to slow because of mere politics. Perhaps it is because Fujian has had a centuries-long practice cavorting with outsiders. It first opened its ports to Arab and European traders hundreds of years ago, and Fujian's fabled mariners have been exploring the sea for even longer; in fact, many present-day Taiwanese are actually Fujianese. Despite the delicate situation in which Fujian finds itself, the province seems blissfully unaware of the tension created by associating with the rest of the world. Instead, it prefers to dwell upon its splendid natural attributes, from its coasts to the lush hillsides and craggy peaks of Wuyishan. Spectacular port cities like Quanzhou and Xiamen boast architecture that spells out very clearly the intriguing history of cosmopolitan Fujian.

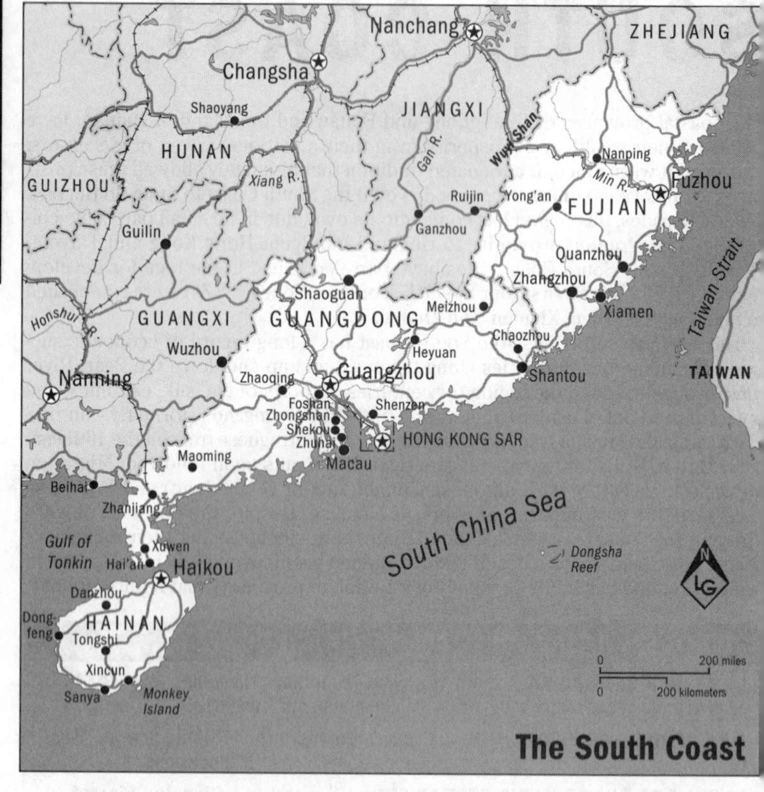

FUZHOU 福州 ☎0591

Like China, the capital city of Fujian Province is in many ways a work in progress. Full of money from Overseas Chinese, Fuzhou is constantly striving to be bigger, better, and faster—and it shows, often in aggravating ways. The unceasing construction of towering buildings makes sweltering summer days even dustier and stickier. The constant expansion and rerouting of roads makes hour-long traffic jams a very frustrating (and scary) possibility. Yet amidst the hubble and bubble of this chaos lies a truly vibrant and eclectic city. Fuzhou is a fascinating amalgam of *Mǐnnánhuà*-speaking locals of Portuguese descent, migrants from the poverty-stricken countryside eager to start anew in a wealthy provincial capital, Shanghainese expats peddling sticky rice cakes, and cell-phone-toting businessmen paying their respects at Buddhist temples. Amidst Fuzhou's frenetic pace of life lie striking contrasts, from decaying European colonial architecture and broad high-rise-lined avenues to healing hot springs and small, curving alleys. It doesn't matter, though, if the city doesn't yet know exactly where it's headed. As far as Fuzhou is concerned, it's definitely moving somewhere, and damned if it doesn't get there quickly.

TRANSPORTATION

Flights: Fuzhou Changle International Airport (fúzhōu chánglè guójì jīchǎng; 福州长乐国际机场; ☎344 0664), south of Fuzhou city. **Shuttle buses** (40min., every 15min. 8am-8pm, Y20) run to and from the **CAAC ticket office,** 185 Wuyi Zhong Lu (☎334 5988 or 331 4957), a bit north of the South Long-distance Passenger Bus Station on the opposite side of the street. Open M-F 8am-8pm. To: **Beijing** (4 per day 8:25am-2:55pm, Y1390); **Guangzhou** (several per day 8am-6pm, Y750); **Hong Kong** (3 per day 10am-2:30pm, Y1390); **Nanchang** (11am, Y410); **Shanghai** (6 per day, 9:30am-3:30pm, Y710).

Trains: Fuzhou Train Station (fúzhōu huǒchē zhàn; 福州火车站; ☎757 9350), at the terminus of Hualin Lu as it curves northward, 5min. north of the North Long-distance Bus Station. Ticket office open daily 8am-noon, 12:40-4:50pm, and 5:40-10pm. To: **Beijing** (35hr., 10:10am and 4:42pm, Y253-Y705); **Guangzhou** (27hr., 6:03pm, Y93-270); **Hangzhou** (18hr., 10:53am and 2:02pm, Y125-330); **Nanchang** (27hr., 6:03pm, Y43); **Shanghai** (21hr., 2:02pm, Y150-403).

Buses: North Long-distance Bus Station (chángtú qìchē běi zhàn; 长途汽车北站; ☎757 7849), on Hualin Lu at Beihuan Lu, 5min. south of the train station. Open daily 5:30am-10:30pm. To: **Guangzhou** (24hr., 6 per day 2:53-7:40pm, Y180-260); **Shanghai** (25hr., 10:20am, Y228); **Xiamen** (4hr., many per day 7:50am-10:30pm, Y60-80). **South Long-distance Passenger Bus Station** (chángtú qìchē nán kèyùn zhàn; 长途汽车南客运站; ☎332 2874), on Wuyi Zhong Lu at Guohuo Xi Lu, in south Fuzhou, just south of the CAAC ticket office. Bus #51 runs to the train station and the North Bus Station; #8 runs to May First Square. Open daily 5:30am-6pm. To: **Guangzhou** (24hr., several per day 10am-7:40pm, Y210-260); **Hong Kong** (24hr., 6:20 and 6:30pm, Y380-385); **Xiamen** (4hr., several per day 6:30am-7:30pm, Y49.5-80).

Local Transportation: Fuzhou's **bus** routes run 5am-10 or 11pm. Fare Y1, with A/C Y2. Bus **#1** runs down Bayiqi Lu and along the north bank of the Min River, and then crosses over to the south bank; **#5** goes from the train station down Wusi Lu to Dong Jie; **#8** heads up Wuyi Lu to the area around West Lake and Zuohai Park; **#20** and **821** continue down Bayiqi Lu from the train station; **#51** runs the length of the city from Wusi Lu to the end of Wuyi Lu, from the train station to Taijiang Lu; **#26** runs between the train station and airport; **#949** runs from the train station to Drum Mountain.

Taxis: Base fare Y7-8, each additional km Y1.8-1.4. **Pedicabs** are plentiful; fares should be settled in advance. From the train station to city center about Y7. Pedicabs can sometimes cost as much as taxis, however.

ORIENTATION AND PRACTICAL INFORMATION

Fuzhou is a vast city, spanning from the train station in the northeast to the lower bank of the **Min River** (mǐn jiāng; 闽江) to the south. **Wusi Lu** (五四路) runs north-south to the Min River and is chock-full of banks and luxurious hotels. Two other major north-south streets are **Bayiqi Lu** (八一七路) to the west and **Liuyi Lu** (六一路) to the east. **Hualin Lu** (华林路) curves northward to the train station and North Bus Station; **Dong Jie** (东街), between Bayiqi Lu and Wusi Lu, becomes **Dongda Lu** (东大路) east of Wusi Lu and is a large commercial street, home to many restaurants and department stores. **Gutian Lu** (古田路) roughly marks the heart of the city, sandwiched between **May First Square** (wǔyī guǎngchǎng; 五一广场) to the south and **Yushan Scenic Area** and a **Mao Zedong statue** to the

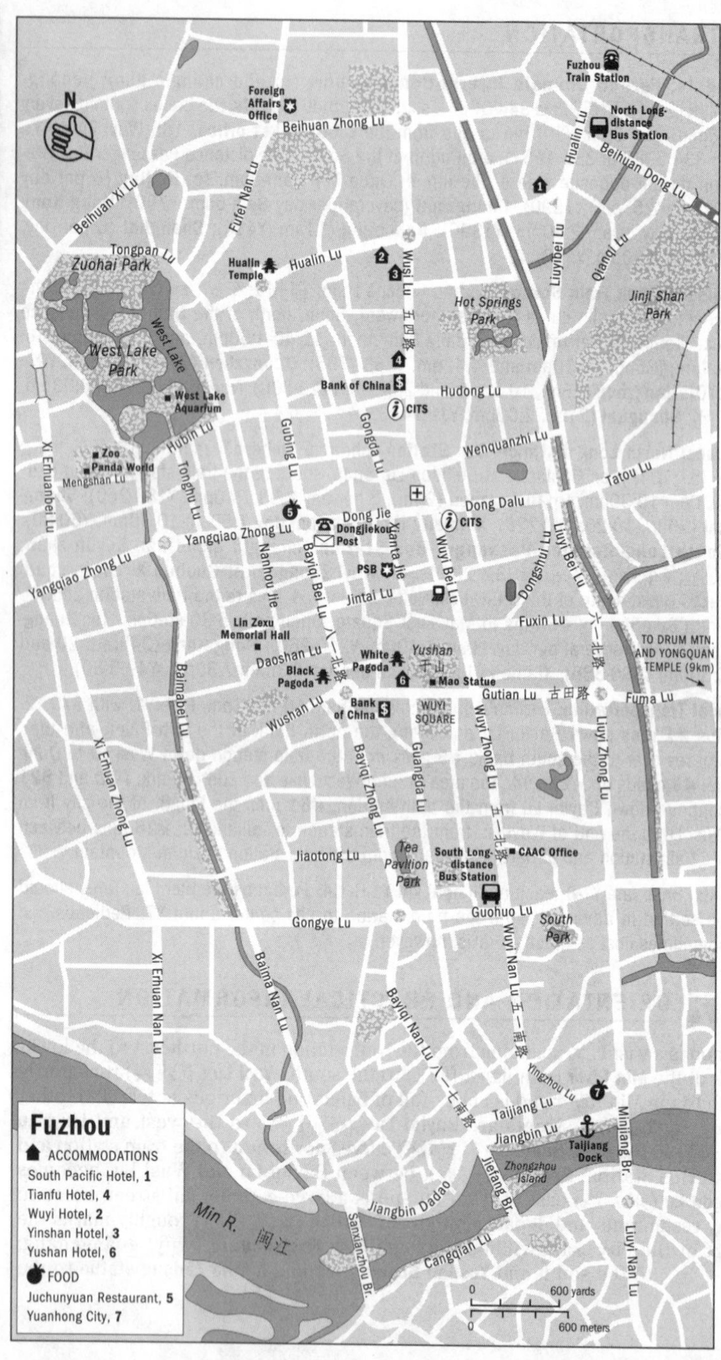
Fuzhou
ACCOMMODATIONS
South Pacific Hotel, 1
Tianfu Hotel, 4
Wuyi Hotel, 2
Yinshan Hotel, 3
Yushan Hotel, 6
FOOD
Juchunyuan Restaurant, 5
Yuanhong City, 7
N
Fuzhou Train Station
North Long-distance Bus Station
Foreign Affairs Office
Beihuan Zhong Lu
Beihuan Dong Lu
Beihuan Xi Lu
Hualin Lu
Fufei Nan Lu
Liuyibei Lu
Qianqi Lu
Tongpan Lu
Zuohai Park
Hualin Temple
Hualin Lu
Wusi Lu
五四路
Hot Springs Park
Jinji Shan Park
West Lake
West Lake Park
West Lake Aquarium
Bank of China
Hudong Lu
CITS
Hubin Lu
Gubing Lu
Gongda Lu
Wenquanzhi Lu
Zoo
Panda World
Mengshan Lu
Tonghu Lu
Xi Erhuanbei Lu
Tatou Lu
Dong Dalu
Dong Jie
Dongjiekou Post
CITS
Yangqiao Zhong Lu
Yangqiao Zhong Lu
Nanhou Jie
Bayiqi Bei Lu
八一北路
Xianta Jie
Wuyi Bei Lu
Dongshui Lu
Liuyi Bei Lu
六一北路
PSB
Jintai Lu
Fuxin Lu
Lin Zexu Memorial Hall
Daoshan Lu
White Pagoda
Yushan
于山
Black Pagoda
Mao Statue
TO DRUM MTN. AND YONGQUAN TEMPLE (9km)
Gutian Lu
古田路
Fuma Lu
Wushan Lu
Bank of China
WUYI SQUARE
Baimabei Lu
Xi Erhuan Zhong Lu
Bayiqi Zhong Lu
Guangda Lu
Wuyi Zhong Lu
五一北路
Liuyi Zhong Lu
Jiaotong Lu
Tea Pavilion Park
South Long-distance Bus Station
CAAC Office
Guohuo Lu
South Park
Gongye Lu
Xi Erhuan Nan Lu
Baima Nan Lu
Bayiqi Nan Lu
八一七南路
Wuyi Nan Lu
五一南路
Yingzhou Lu
Taijiang Lu
Jiangbin Lu
Taijiang Dock
Minjiang Br.
Jiefang Br.
Zhongzhou Island
Jiangbin Dadao
Min R.
闽江
Sanxianzhou Br.
Cangqian Lu
Liuyi Nan Lu
0
600 yards
0
600 meters

north. The South Long-distance Passenger Bus Station is at the intersection of Wuyi Zhong Lu and **Guohuo Xi Lu** (国货西路).

Travel Agencies: There are 2 **CITS** offices near the intersection of Wusi/Wuyi Lu and Dong Jie/Dongda Lu. **Tianma CITS** (☎337 0073), on the 7th fl. of the large high-rise on the corner of Wuyi Bei Lu and Dongda Lu. English and Japanese interpreters available. 1-day tours of Fuzhou (Y70) are easier to book for groups. No commission for plane tickets, but there is a commission for train tickets, depending on the price of the ticket. Open daily 9:30am-noon and 3-5:30pm. Numerous plane and train ticket booking offices line Wuyi Lu and Wusi Lu.

Bank of China: On Gutian Lu between Bayiqi Lu and Guangda Lu, west of KFC (☎332 1700). Exchanges currency and traveler's checks (counter #6). Open daily 8am-6pm. Another branch at 136 Wusi Lu (☎755 6048) exchanges currency and issues credit card advances. **ATM**. Open M-F 7:40am-5:30pm, Sa 8:30-5pm. Avoid the money changers that loiter on Wusi Lu.

PSB: 1 Jingmen Lu (☎755 7705), off Jintai Lu. Open daily 8am-noon and 3-6pm. For visa extensions, contact the **Foreign Affairs Department** (wài guǎn kē; 外管科), 109 Beihuan Zhong Lu (☎782 1000), west of Wusi Bei Lu. Open M-F 8am-noon and 3-6pm.

Hospitals: Fujian Provincial Hospital (fújiàn shěnglì yīyuàn; 福建省立医院), 34 Dong Jie (☎755 7768), on the northwest corner of the intersection of Dong Jie and Wusi Lu. The emergency entrance is off Dong Jie.

Bookstores: Antai Book City (āntài shūchéng; 安泰书城; ☎755 2619), on the 1st fl. of the Antai Building, the corner of Jintai Lu and Bayiqi Lu. A bustling book market that's home to VCD vendors and map stores as well as a **Foreign Language Bookstore** with a not-too-shabby map and English classics department. Open daily 8:30am-9pm.

Internet Access: Hongyu Internet Club, Hongyu Bldg., 96 Jingtai Lu, 2nd fl. (☎337 3117), at Wuyi Bei Lu. Y3 per hr.; passport or ID required. Open daily 8am-midnight. **Xingji Internet Bar** (xīngjì wǎngbā; 星际网吧; ☎754 1843), at intersection of Yangqiao Lu and Nanhou Lu. Fast connection speeds. Y2.5 per hr. Open 24hr.

Post Offices: Dongjiekou Post and Telecommunications (dōngjiēkǒu yóudiàn dàlóu; 东街口邮电大楼), 1 Dong Jie (☎752 2010), a high-rise on the southeast corner of Dong Jie and Bayiqi Bei Lu, opposite Juchunyuan Restaurant. EMS on the 1st fl.; *Poste Restante* at counter #4. Open daily 7:30am-7:30pm. **DHL Worldwide Express,** 197 Taton Lu (☎781 1111), off a small alley next to the Taiwan Hotel. Open M-Sa 8am-6pm. **Postal Code:** 350000 for city center, 350001 for Poste Restante.

ACCOMMODATIONS

Filthy-rich Fuzhou offers few options for dirt-poor backpackers. Establishments near the train and bus stations may prove to be the best budget option. Don't rule out high-end places altogether; they sometimes lower their prices during the summer. The following listings all have air-conditioning, bath, and TV.

Yushan Hotel (yūshān bīnguǎn; 于山宾馆), 10 Yushan Lu (☎335 1668). Take bus #8 from South Bus Station to Yushan on Gutian Lu; or #51 from the train station to Wuyi Bei Lu (keep walking, then take the first right onto Gutian Lu). Facing the Mao statue on Gutian Lu, take the stairs to the left; the entrance is across a small street, above the Shanghai Restaurant. Rooms exude an old-Orient feel, with low beds and a view of the inner garden. Breakfast included. Singles Y120-150; doubles Y180-310; triples Y250-370. 20% discounts possible. ❷

Wuyi Hotel (wǔyí dàjiǔdiàn; 武夷大酒店), 169 Hualin Lu (☎784 3038), just past Wusi Lu. Take bus #20 from the station area to Pingdong, or #51 from any station to Hualin Lu. A good location, a posh lobby, and proper service–without a shocking price tag. Cheapest rooms haven't been renovated but are nice. Singles Y300 and up; doubles Y198-338. Summer and year-round discounts make prices more likely to be Y148 and up. Y20 discount if you sacrifice the "free" breakfast. MC/V. ❹

South Pacific Hotel (nányáng fàndiàn; 南洋饭店), 346 Hualin Lu (☎757 9699), near Liuyi Bei Lu, 5-10min. south of the North Bus Station. Tiny rooms. Cheaper rooms aren't pretty, but the staff is susceptible to bargaining and sometimes charges cheaper rates for better rooms. Singles Y228; doubles Y168-248; triples Y258. 20% discounts. ❸

Yinshan Hotel (yínshān dàjiǔdiàn; 银山大酒店), 254 Wusi Lu (☎781 3688), at Hualin Lu. Accessible via bus #51 along Wusi Lu; get off at the Hualin Lu stop. One of the cheapest options available. Small, clean rooms. Includes a buffet breakfast. Doubles Y180-208, but year-round discounts make prices more likely to be Y80-110. ❸

Tianfu Hotel (tiānfú dàjiǔdiàn; 天福大酒店), 138 Wusi Lu (☎781 2328), just north of the Bank of China's main branch. Take bus #51 from the train or either bus station to Huaqiao Dasha; walk north on Wusi Lu, across Hudong Lu; it's on the left. Singles Y240-390; doubles Y325-390. 50% discounts in summer, but the staff often doesn't offer the same discounts to foreigners. ❹

FOOD

Fuzhou's absolute cannot-miss spot is the irresistible **Taijiang Lu,** known as **Fuzhou Delicious Food Street** (róngchéng měishíjiē; 榕城美食街), which is a pedestrian-only street designed to look like an endless row of traditional Chinese buildings, complete with eaved roofs and red lanterns. Shops sell everything from "real" VCDs to frivolous knick-knacks and luggage. On weekend nights, visiting opera troupes perform for free in the open-air stage at the end of the street among heaps of food, including all manner of *xiǎochī* (小吃; snacks), from steamed dumplings to noodles to skewered meat. One noteworthy stall is the award-winning **Fuzhou Fish Balls** ❶ (dàfúxīng yúwán; 大福星鱼丸). Fish-paste balls stuffed with meat are actually quite appetizing (Y6 a bowl).

If you're still standing after this eating venture, behind this Food Street is the pedestrian-only **Walking Avenue** (bùxíng jiē; 步行街). At night, locals gather along this tree-lined, fountain-scattered boulevard to enjoy the lighted terraces and balmy breeze. Dominating this street is the magnificent **Yuanhong City** ❷ (yuánhóng chéng; 元洪城), a large complex offering 1001 different kinds of foods. (Take bus #51 or 951 from Wusi lu to Laijiang Lu.) Here, savor Peking Crispy Duck (Y35 for half), steamboat feasts (both regular and Sichuan-spicy seafood), Thai food, Southeast Asian delicacies, all manner of Chinese boiled soups, Indian tandoori, Korean barbecue, and much, much—oh, so much—more.

Juchunyuan Restaurant (jùchūnyuán cāntīng; 聚春园餐厅), Juchunyuan Hotel, 2 Dongjiekou, 3rd fl. (☎750 2328 ext. 8401), across the street from the post office. This 100-year-old establishment has garnered well-earned fame from its **Buddha Jumping Over the Wall**, a pricey seafood concoction (Y200-5000 per person) served in a traditional banquet-style setting, stuffed with such goodies as abalone, scallop, and shark's fin. For the non-fabulously wealthy, its other specialties include the Eight Delicacies in a Pot (Y20), which features pig's stomach, scallops, and quail's egg among other things; the restaurant is also famed for its fried jellyfish (Y35). Ask for the English menu to avoid accidentally eating the pig tripe (猪肚). Open daily 11am-1pm and 5-9pm. ❸

TEA HOUSES

Luck Tea House (lèkè pàomò hóngchá diàn; 乐客泡沫红茶店; ☎753 0850), in the Jianxing Department Store, on Yangqiao Dong Lu, a block west from where Bayiqi Bei Lu meets Dong Jie. This tea house specializes in Taiwanese-style "foaming ice tea" (pàomò hóngchá; 泡沫红茶). The pearl milk tea (zhēnzhū nái chá; 珍珠奶茶; Y14) with tapioca pearls is also worth a try. Also serves various lunch and dinner items (ham omelette Y5; fried rice Y10). Open daily 9:30am-midnight; delivery 9:30am-8pm. ❶

Lan Fang Coffee and Tea House (kāfeī hóngchá fáng; 咖啡红茶房), 16 Shengfu Lu (☎751 9733), off the lane north from Yangqiao Lu, west of Bayiqi Bei Lu. For the young, hip, and caffeine-addicted. Espresso and tea (Y15-20). Open daily 10am-2am; food service until 11pm. ❷

SIGHTS

Except for **Drum Mountain** to the east of the city, Fuzhou's sights are pleasant but not significant. A much more worthwhile activity is to stroll through the city's various neighborhoods, particularly the ones that border the city center. West of Dongjiekou off Yangqiao Dong Lu, starting with Nanhou Jie, is the neighborhood of "**three lanes, seven alleys**" (sānfāng qīxiàng; 三坊七巷), a well-preserved cross section of old Fuzhou, with street stalls, festival lanterns, and *mahjong* groups. Among this maze of streets lie **Pagoda Alley** (tǎ jiē; 塔街) and **Literary Scholar Lane** (wénrū lù; 文儒路), both of which date back to the Ming and Qing Dynasties.

FORMER FOREIGN CONCESSION. Although very few visitors to Fuzhou have any practical reason to venture south of the South Bus Station, the banks of the Min River and the neighborhood to the south offer a tangible glimpse of Fuzhou's past. A walk across one of the three main bridges that span the Min River—from west to east, the wire-suspension **Sanxianzhou Bridge** (三县洲桥); the short, cute, and light-bedecked **Jiefang Bridge** (解放桥); and the heavily trafficked **Minjiang Bridge** (闽江大桥)—will reveal barges and larger junks traveling through the swirling waters below. Although most of the colonial architecture has recently been knocked down and replaced by skyscrapers, the remnants of the houses built into the hill, in all their medieval splendor, are still a fascinating sight. *(The terminus of bus #51 is on Taijiang Lu, just a block away from the north bank of the river; the Jiefang and Minjiang Bridges are nearby. Bus #1 from Bayiqi Lu crosses the Minjiang Bridge to the south side of the city; bus #20 does the same across the Jiefang Bridge.)*

YUSHAN SCENIC AREA (yūshān fēngjǐng qū; 于山风景区). Following the gently sloping curved path up the hill takes you past old buildings with stone archways to groups of elderly folk playing cards and *mahjong* to a rather insignificant **Fuzhou Municipal Museum** that details the city's 700-year history. *(Open daily 8am-5pm. Y3.)* The nearby **flower nursery** (lánpǔ; 兰莆) houses hundreds of varieties of orchids. *(Admission Y3.)* The **White Pagoda** (bái tǎ; 白塔) marks the western edge, and affords a bird's-eye view of the city. *(Open daily 8:30am-5:30pm. Y2.)* The crumbling remains of the old city walls still stand at the summit of Yushan. *(There are 2 entrances to the scenic area: one from a path to the left of and behind the Mao statue as you face it, the other off Wuyi Bei Lu just north of its intersection with Gutian Lu. Free.)*

WEST LAKE PARK (xīhú gōngyuán; 西湖公园). It may not be Hangzhou's West Lake, but the park makes for a pleasant outing nonetheless. It boasts a few islands in the middle of the manmade West Lake, delicate garden paths, delightful paddle boats *(Y20-30 per hr.; open daily in summer 8:30am-11pm, in winter 8:30am-10:30pm)* and children's amusement park rides (typically Y5 per ride). The only other possible point of interest is the **West Lake Aquarium** (xīhú hǎiyáng shìjiè; 西湖海洋世界) which features a small selection of tropical fish. *(Main entrance on Hubin Lu, Y6. Aquarium open daily 8:30am-10pm. Y25, children under 1.2m Y15.)*

DAYTRIPS FROM FUZHOU: DRUM MOUNTAIN 鼓山

Nine kilometers (about 20-30min.) east of Fuzhou. Several public ***buses*** *run regularly to the foot of the mountain: #7, 36, or 37 from the Chating stop on Guangda Lu, west of the South Bus Station, next to the Children's Park; #949 from the train station; and #960 from West Lake. The mountain is at the terminus for all but routes #36 and 37: in those cases, get off at the Xiayuan stop (30-40min, Y1.5).* ***Minibuses*** *go from the base up the mountain to where the Yongquan Temple is (Y5). Minibuses from downtown Fuzhou (Nan Men stop, off Gutian Lu one block east of Yushan, to your left) also offer direct services to the summit (20-30min.; one-way Y5, round-trip Y8).* ***Cable car*** *runs daily 8am-4:45pm (one-way Y25, children Y10; round-trip Y30, children Y15).*

Drum Mountain (gǔ shān; 鼓山) is Fuzhou's finest. Rising 900m above sea level, the summit offers unbeatable panoramic views of the city and the outlying maze of rivers and mountains. The 1800m ascent along sloped stone steps, with markers every 200m, takes about an hour and will get your heart pumping loud enough to make up for the silence of the drum.

At the summit, you have two options. You can wander down the path on the left of the parking lot to the mosquito-ridden 18 scenic spots; it's a steep path lined with such light pleasures as the **Eight Immortals Rock** or the **Lotus Flower Pavilion.** Alternatively, you can drop in to the impressive complex of the **Spring Gushing Temple** and its environs. *(Open daily 6am-6pm. Y6.)*

In the temple itself, there is a two-ton **Bell Tower** that faces the **Drum Tower;** these 400-year-old structures certainly warrant a visit. There is also an extremely important **Depository of Buddhist Scriptures,** in which monks have been carving scriptures since the Song dynasty; they have thus far produced a staggering 11,375 carving plates. The temple complex also houses a gigantic Goddess of Mercy statue, a vegetarian restaurant, and the **Hall of Heavenly Kings.** An interesting excursion would be to wander down the path to the right of the entrance to the **Drinking Water Rock** (hēshuǐ shí; 喝水石); formerly a place of repose frequented by the literati (as the numerous inscriptions on the surrounding rocks will attest), this has now dried up but is still a nice, eerily shady spot seemingly untouched by tourism.

WUYISHAN 武夷山

☎0599

According to legend, this idyllic mountain is the gateway between heaven and earth, where immortals cavort and all is divine. The stream water flows icy-cold and clear, every oddly shaped peak and plant has its own poetic story, and the tea is so precious and sweet that it's preserved for foreign dignitaries. Named both a natural and a cultural treasure by the government, Wuyishan boasts winding rivers, looming cliffs, and sprawling mountains, all of which can be viewed as you drift leisurely down the Nine-Bend River. Unlike many of China's other mountain towns, Wuyishan offers little of the unpleasant harrassment which are often the results of an aggressive tourist industry. In this slice of paradise, there is a gentleness to its people; after all, on Wuyishan, we're all divine, even if just for a day.

TRANSPORTATION

Flights: Wuyishan People's Airport (wǔyíshān mínháng zhàn; 武夷山民航站; ☎530 6513), on Wuyi Dadao, north of the resort town. Accessible by taxi vans (*miàndí*, 15min., Y2) from the city center. To: **Beijing** (Tu 8:45am and Su 7:45am, Y1230); **Fuzhou** (Tu and F 8:10pm, W and Sa 7:30am; Y380); **Guangzhou** (M 9:40pm, W and Sa 7:30am; Y710); **Shanghai** (M 1:15pm, Y610); **Xiamen** (M and Th 8:30am, Tu and F 2:30pm, W and Sa 7pm, Su 7:45am).

Trains: Wuyishan Train Station (wǔyíshān huǒchē zhàn; 武夷山火车站; ☎510 2745), on the outskirts of Wuyishan city. From the resort area, take bus #6 to the city center, then take bus #2 (Y1.5) or hop onto a taxi van (Y3 per person). Open daily 8am-noon and 2-6:30pm. To: **Fuzhou** (6hr., 11:55pm, Y47-147); **Quanzhou** (15hr., every other day 4:34pm, Y82-232); **Xiamen** (15hr., 3:36pm, Y82-232).

Buses: Wuyishan Bus Station (wǔyíshān qìchē zhàn; 武夷山汽车站; ☎531 1446), in Wuyishan city, accessible by bus #62 from city center. Open daily 5:30am-7pm. A more convenient option is to buy tickets from the Yulin Hotel in the resort area itself. Buses leave from in front of the hotel. To: **Fuzhou** (10hr.; 6:50pm daily, 6pm every other day; Y87); **Hangzhou** (10hr., 12:30pm, Y110); **Xiamen** (11hr., 2:30pm, Y110).

Local Transportation: Two **bus** routes service the Wuyishan area. Only bus **#6** comes into the resort area and shuttles toward the city center. From the city area, bus **#2** runs to the train and bus stations. These compact minibuses with A/C cost Y1.5 per ride.

Taxis: Yellow taxi vans (*miàndí*) are very popular. From the resort town to Wuyishan city center Y3, resort town to Wuyishan Scenic Area Y1-2. Within Wuyishan Scenic Area, **scootered pedicabs** take tourists from sight to sight (Y6-7 each trip, Y60-70 per day); some drivers may also informally serve as tour guides.

ORIENTATION AND PRACTICAL INFORMATION

Most visitors first bypass Wuyishan mountain, heading instead for the tourist services in the resort town 20km south of Wuyishan. The resort town lies to the east of a river, spanning a small stretch divided into a hotel and market area by the **Huang Hua** intersection. Crossing **Lantang Bridge** (lántāng dàqiáo; 兰汤大桥) to the west of the river leads to the scenic area, which divides into the **Nine-Bend Stream** south of the bridge, and **Water Curtain Park** and **Big Red Robe** tea plantation north of it. **Wuyishan Scenic Area** spans a whopping 60km^2. **Shanguxin Jie** (山姑新街) is the main road in the resort town, containing numerous mid-range hotels as well as tourist shops selling tea leaves, mushrooms and snake *everything*.

Travel Agencies: Wuyishan Travel Service (wǔyíshān lǚxín shè; 武夷山旅行社; ☎525 1888), on Nanwu Lu, on the foot of the sloped path leading up to the Wuyishan Mountain Villa. From the Scenic Area side of Lantang Bridge, take a left on the tree-lined path; walk straight for 5min., and turn right at the 2nd path toward the guard station. Although unaccustomed to individual travelers, WTS hands out nifty bilingual brochures and maps and arranges tours (Y100 per person). Open daily 8am-5:30pm.

Bank of China: Opposite the Yulin Hotel, next to the Popular Bowling Shop. Exchanges currency and traveler's checks. Open daily 8am-8pm.

Bookstore: Wenyou Bookstore (wényóu shūdiàn; 文友书店; ☎525 2002), in the Sanguxin Jie market area, off the 3rd alley to the left. Bilingual maps, brochures, and video CD documentaries on Wuyishan. Open daily 7:30am-11pm.

PSB: In the Wuyi Palace area of the resort town (☎525 6794).

Hospitals: No hospital exists as of yet in the resort town; the closest one is in the city center. **Wuyishan City Hospital** (wǔyíshān shìyīyuàn; 武夷山市医院), 65 Wengong Lu (☎530 2782; emergency ☎531 0463). Open 24hr.

Internet Access: Daohangzhe Internet Café (dǎohángzhě wǎngbā; 导航者网吧; ☎525 1845), along Shanguxing Jie, just next to the 3rd alley to the left. Sunny, air-conditioned, and run by friendly young people. Y3 per hr.

Post Office: Wuyishan Resort Town Post Office (☎525 2875), off Shanguxing Jie, marked by a large arched gate to the west of the Huang Hua intersection. The office is 2 blocks down this road, in an alley on the left. EMS. Open daily 5:30am-6pm. **Postal Code:** 354302.

ACCOMMODATIONS

Wuyishan's resort town is full of near identical two- and three-star hotels. The area near the Huanghua intersection is closest to the market area. Most of the budget options are directly across Lantang Bridge from the main resort town. Proprietors of these mostly family-owned inns, however, are unwilling to let foreigners stay in these hotels unapproved by the tourist bureau. Overseas Chinese might be able get the relatively basic rooms with rock-bottom prices (beginning at Y10). The following listings all offer rooms with air-conditioning, bath, and TV.

Wuyi Mountain Villa (wǔyí shānzhuāng; 武夷山庄; ☎525 1888), at the end of the sloping path off Nanwu Lu. From Lantang Bridge, turn left and walk straight along Nanwu Lu, the tree-lined path bordering the western bank of the Chongyang River; the hotel is on the 2nd path to the right, past WTS. Bus #6 stops in front of the villa. Sweeping vistas and award-winning landscaping. Ask for the underground economy doubles (with standard amenities). The staff will try to dissuade you; be firm. Economy doubles Y280, off-peak Y100; standard doubles Y480 and up. MC/V. ❹

Yulin Hotel (yùlín jiǔdiàn; 郁林酒店; ☎525 2206), west of the Huang Hua intersection on the left side of the road leading to Lantang Bridge. Central location across the street from the main market and restaurant area. Friendly staff. Doubles Y288; triples Y368. Frequent 50% discounts. ❹

Aihu Hotel (ǎihú bīnguǎn; 矮胡宾馆; ☎525 2268), directly across Lantang Bridge in the Scenic Area, at the top of a small set of stairs visible from the bridge. The oldest hotel in Wuyishan, the pleasant Aihu boasts stately wooden furniture and impeccable service. Rooms are rather old and shabby, and hot water is erratic. Singles Y180; doubles Y280. Rooms frequently go for under Y100 after discounts. ❸

FOOD

Visitors don't come to Wuyishan for the food, but lively street markets do line the resort area. Wuyishan's culinary claim to fame is its **Snake Banquet**—not yellow eel or other snake-like creatures—but the real, slithering thing from Wuyishan's mountains. This delicacy should be sampled in large hotel restaurants rather than in small street shops, since the poisonous ones, if handled improperly, can be deadly. The going rate for a bowl of snake soup is Y300. Gall bladder and blood are free (eaten separately). Most cheap options are on **Yinshe Yitiao Jie** (银蛇一条街), directly opposite the gate leading to **Shanguxin Jie.** It is liveliest from sunset to 2am and features small restaurants offering generous portions of basic dishes like tofu (Y6), noodle soups (Y10), and *bāozi* (Y3). Hotel restaurants and large air-conditioned places here tend to be more expensive (hovering over Y30 for some basic dishes), so avoid them if possible.

SIGHTS

Wuyishan is full of fascinating sights and discoveries. One of the best ways to get a feel for the breathtaking Wuyishan is to climb its peaks, from which you can admire the sea of mountains set within a spreading sea of clouds. Main trails are well-maintained and safe, even in the early morning, when falling mountain dew, glimmers of sunrise, and safety from chaotic tour groups provide ideal conditions for solitary rambles. Almost all sights have admission fees; the Y111 all-inclusive ticket (available at all scenic spots) may be your best option.

NINE-BEND RIVER

*Bamboo **rafts** (zhú fàn; 竹泛) are the most popular way to traverse this winding creek, which provides a mellow introduction to the famed sights along the riverbanks. Rafts leave from **Xingcun village,** in the southwestern corner of the Wuyishan Scenic Area. Each raft seats 6 people (5 people when the water is high); fixed **price** per raft is Y425. The ride (1½hr.), starts at the ninth bend and ends at the first. Boats run daily 7am-5pm; several go out every 30min. Ticket office ☎526 1752.*

Winding its way through 9.5km of gorges and bends in the southern portion of Wuyishan, the Nine-Bend River (jiǔqǔ xī; 九曲溪) is one of the most justifiably hyped sights in the area. It zigzags through rugged canyons and peaks, its mirror-like waters and rushing rapids pristine and unspoiled. The experience is so magical that China's most revered modern-day poet, Guo Moluo, remarked that Guilin's famed lakes could not rival even the smallest creeks in Wuyishan. Bamboo chairs are bound to bamboo rafts so that you can dip your feet into the river while the raft makes its way down the stream. For a Y40-50 tip, the boatmen will demonstrate their narrative skills.

The Nine-Bend River is an especially pleasant way to take in Wuyishan's most popular spots. From **Xingcun Village** (xīngcūn zhèn; 星村镇) and the ninth bend, the raft goes by **White Cloud Rock** (bái yún yán; 白云岩), a former gathering place for scholars and worshiping pilgrims. The eighth bend takes you past **Pinzi Rock** (pǐnzì yán; 品字岩), which is also known as **Wusha Rock** (wūshā yán; 乌纱岩), named and shaped after the squarish black gauze caps that imperial officers used to wear. Downstream at the sixth and fifth bends, the river flows by **Heavenly Tour Peak** (tiānyóu fēng; 天游峰), **Clouds' Lair,** and **Draper's Rock** (shàibù yán; 晒布岩), a cliff face whose fanlike folds give it its name. The second bend passes one of the most photographed sights in Wuyishan, **Jade Goddess Peak** (yùnǚ fēng; 玉女峰). The first bend goes by the crown-shaped **King's Peak** (dàwáng fēng; 大王峰), one of the most spectacular summits of the 36 peaks.

The raft tour wraps up at **Wuyi Palace** (wǔyí gōng; 武夷宫), a small complex of hotels, souvenir shops, and restaurants. The area also houses the **Museum of Wuyi Mountain** (wǔyí shān bówùguǎn; 武夷山博物馆), a short but lovingly designed tour that showcases images of the mountain's most famous scenic spots and its amazing array of flora and fauna in its protected reserves. (☎525 2729. Open daily 8-11:30am and 2-5:30pm. Y3.)

OTHER SIGHTS

Just across from the Bamboo Raft Pier is the **Wuyishan Tea Research Center** (wǔyí bēilín; 武夷碑林; ☎526 1997). At this flawlessly landscaped oasis of bridges and streams and stone carvings, you can learn all about the different kinds of natural tea in Wuyishan and their famously curative qualities. Try not to be so hypnotized by these serene settings that you buy a Y500 (small) tin of tea leaves. *(Open daily 8am-6pm. Admission Y6.)*

ONE LUMP OR TWO? Big Red Robe tea is one of China's most illustrious teas. Of the first generation tea, or tea from the pure, original Red Robe plants, the yearly harvest is as low as 6 liang, or 300 grams. The Big Red Robe Tea that is sold on the market is only second generation, produced from a crossover between the original plants and other kinds of tea. Chinese President Jiang Zemin gives only first generation tea his mark of his special favor. The tea was named in honor of a scholar, who was on the way to the Imperial Examinations when he fell ill in Wuyishan. A monk fed him some of the tea and the scholar miraculously recovered. After he passed the exams and became an official, the scholar used the same tea to cure the Empress when she fell ill with a strange disease. A grateful emperor gave the scholar a big red robe to wear and asked him to bring back more tea from Wuyishan. The tea was thereby named Big Red Robe for the official who made it famous throughout China.

A five-minute drive north past Lantang Bridge will take you to the **Big Red Robe Tea Mountain** (dà hóng páo; 大红袍), which houses the **Nine Dragons Nest,** a stunning group of towering rock formations that resemble nine coiled dragons. Farther up the mountain, past myriad mountain pools and waterfalls, a small tea pavilion overlooks the famed tea plantation and offers visitors a chance to sip revered tea drinks while admiring the view. *(Open daily 6am-6pm. Y12.)* Close to the summit is **Ever-happy Temple** (yǒnglè chánsì; 永乐禅寺), the largest Buddhist temple in the area. A spectacular view awaits those willing to clamber up (1½hr.) to the mist-enshrouded summit of **Heavenly Tour Peak.** *(☎525 2827. Open daily 6:30am-6pm. Y40.)*

MINYUE KINGDOM SCENIC AREA (mǐnyuèwáng chéngjǐngqū; 闽越王城景区). These ruins include a set of archaelogical discoveries confirming the existence of a lost Han civilization, the Mingyue kingdom mentioned in ancient historian Sima Qian's notes. The museum meticulously details the history of the snake-worshiping jungle warriors, who were defeated in 110 BC by a fearful Han emperor. Rare examples of Han-era weapons, ceramics, and farming implements are on display here. *(A 30km drive from the scenic area; a scootered pedicab (Y60) is probably the best way to get there. ☎511 5081. Open daily 10am-6pm. Admission Y30).*

THREAD OF SKY (yī xiàn tiān; 一线天). South of the Nine-Bend River, this mind-bending, neck-craning work of nature far surpasses the pleasant but mundane landscapes of rolling hills and brooks. The highest and narrowest of its kind, this fissured cave is formed by a split in the stone linking the Fuxi and Feng Caves. At 0.3m wide, it lets in only a beam of light and a thread of sky. There is a short climb through the seam for the slightly built and nimble. The climb is extremely dark, steep, and wet; a flashlight (Y5) can aid in maneuvering through the scarily narrow path with its man-sized steps. The admission also allows access to **Tiger Roaring Cliff,** a cliff shaped like a tiger. *(☎525 2577. Open daily 6am-6pm. Y22.)*

WATER CURTAIN CAVE (shuǐlián dòng; 水帘洞). This water curtain is a temperamental waterfall—a trickle on dry days and a gushing spout during the rainy season—over the entrance of a rocky cave. The seemingly endless staired ascent is well worth it; tourists flood the area until late afternoon. The shroud of mountain water that rains into the pond at the foot of the cave is a testament to the area's almost sacred quality. From the top of the first set of stairs leading to the cave there is a spectacular view of **Eagle's Peak** (yīngzuǐ yán; 鹰嘴岩), shaped like an eagle about to soar into flight. *(North of Lantang Bridge. Open daily 7am-6pm. Y12.)*

XIAMEN 厦门

☎0592

Xiamen, with its mild climate, interesting architecture, and fresh sea air, is undoubtedly one of China's showcase cities. Its gracious residents exude the slacker's charm, indulging in leisurely strolls, afternoon swims, and evening feasts, and imploring those seeking a fast-paced life to look elsewhere.

Over the past four centuries, this port city has seen a succession of foreign guests; Portuguese, British, French, and Japanese settlers have all exploited Xiamen's strategic trading location. But Xiamen has adapted well to the cosmopolitan influences; even today, storefronts and residences in the western waterfront district proudly don renovated colonial facades, and restaurants throughout the city serve authentic international cuisine. Enjoying the benefits of foreign investment and its status as a Special Economic Zone, Xiamen has the same looming skyscrapers and conspicuous signs of consumer affluence as any frenetic south coast city; but the city has made a point of laying the fruits of development *beside* the relics of its past, rather than bulldozing over them, and has thus maintained an air of tropical resort tranquility. If there is a method to the madness of China's development, it might just turn out to be in Xiamen.

TRANSPORTATION

Flights: Xiamen Gaoqi International Airport (xiàmén gāoqí guójì jīchǎng; 厦门高崎国际机场; ☎602 2936), about 10km northeast of downtown Xiamen, at the north end of the island, near the causeway to the mainland. Bus #37 goes from the airport to the train station. Taxis to the airport cost Y40-50 and take 30-40min. The **Xiamen Airlines Ticket Office** (xiàháng shòupiào zhōngxīn; 夏航售票中心), 931 Xiahe Lu (☎515 3601), is outside the long-distance bus station. Open daily 8am-6pm. To: **Beijing** (multiple flights per day, Y1570); **Guangzhou** (2-3 per day, Y450); **Hong Kong** (2 per day, Y1460); **Shanghai** (multiple flights per day, Y700).

Trains: As with most cities in Fujian province, trains are not the best way to travel to and from Xiamen; buses are faster and more frequent. **Xiamen Train Station** (xiàmén huǒchē zhàn; 厦门火车站), 900 Xiahe Lu (☎505 4346), on the south end of Hubin Dong Lu, east of the waterfront. Buses #3, 4, and 28 connect to the pier. A taxi from the train station to the ferry pier should cost about Y12-14. Open daily 8-11am, noon-5pm, and 6-8:45pm. To: **Beijing** (40hr., 8:34pm, Y256-715); **Hangzhou** (23hr., 9:52am, Y73-254); **Shanghai** (26hr., 5pm, Y170-472).

Buses: The **Main Long-distance Bus Station** (xiàmén chángtú qìchē zhàn; 厦门长途汽车站; ☎221 5238), on Hubin Nan Lu, sometimes called the **Hubin Long-distance Bus Station.** From here, bus #9 runs to the train station. Tickets sold daily 7:30am-10:30pm. To: **Fuzhou** (3½hr., every 20 min. 7:35am-9:35pm, Y62-85); **Guangzhou** (9hr., many per day 8:25am-10:05pm, Y110-220); **Hong Kong** (10hr., 3 per day 8:20am-9:30pm, Y250-350); **Quanzhou** (1½hr., every 30min. 6am-6pm, Y32). The **Wucun Bus Station** (wúcūn qìchē zhàn; 梧村汽车站), 931 Xiahe Lu (☎505 5525), 2min. west of the train station, serves destinations similar to those from the main station. Open daily 5:30am-10:30pm. To: **Fuzhou** (3½hr., approx. every 20min. 6:25am-10:30pm, Y50-85); **Guangzhou** (9hr., 7 per day 7:50am-10:30pm, Y110-220); **Quanzhou** (1½ hr., every 30min. 6am-6pm, Y20). More luxurious buses run the same routes. Buy tickets in the western district; buses depart from central locations like the ferry pier, in front of Xiamen University/Nanputuo Temple, and along Xinhua Lu.

Local Transportation: English transportation maps (Y5) are available at the Xinhua Bookstore. Most **buses** run 6am-10pm. Fare Y1. Buses **#1** and **21** go south toward Nanputuo Temple and Xiamen University; **#4** and **28** connect the train station to the airport; **#9** connects the main bus station to the train station; **#27** connects the airport to the ferry pier; **#37** connects the train station to the airport.

Taxis: Base fare Y7-8, each additional km Y2; all taxis should be metered. Most western district destinations (near the waterfront and Gulangyu) Y8-10; the waterfront from the bus station to Y10-12, from the train station Y12-14, and from the airport Y35-50.

ORIENTATION AND PRACTICAL INFORMATION

Xiamen city occupies the southwestern portion **Xiamen Island,** which connects to the coast of southern Fujian by the **Xiamen Causeway.** The city's most visited portion is that which faces **Gulangyu** (鼓浪屿), Xiamen's satellite islet and biggest tourist attraction. The compact and easily navigable waterfront western district is dominated by a 1km-long section of **Zhongshan Lu** (中山路), a bustling commercial street that runs east-west. Just north of Zhongshan Lu's western end is where ferries depart for Gulangyu. **Siming Lu** (思明路) runs north-south and intersects with Zhongshan Lu. In the eastern part of the city, the main long-distance bus station is on **Hubin Dong Lu** (湖滨东路), and the train station is nearby on **Xiahe Lu** (厦禾路). Xiamen's nicer night spots are also in the east, mainly along Hubin Dong Lu.

Tourist Office: Xiamen Municipal Tourism Bureau (xiàménshì lǚyoú jú; 厦门市旅遊局), Xinye Bank Bldg., 78 Hubin Bei Lu, 6th fl. (☎531 8858). Maps and travel brochures available; staff is friendly but not used to individual travelers.

Travel Agencies: Plane, train, and bus ticketing offices abound along Zhongshan Lu, Siming Lu, and near the waterfront. **CITS,** 2-3 Zhongshan Lu (☎202 0658), off a small alley around the corner from the Bank of China, across from the Hong Kong Bank. English-speaking staff. No commission for airline bookings. Open daily 8am-noon and 3-6pm. The **main CITS office** (☎504 1180) is on the 15th fl. of the Zhenxing Mansion, on Hubin Bei Lu, a block east of the tourism bureau. Take bus #31 from the pier to Te Mao. Arranges tours of Xiamen (Y100 per day), but rarely for individual travelers. English-speaking staff. Open daily 9am-6pm.

Bank of China: 6-10 Zhongshan Lu, opposite the Lujiang and East Ocean Hotels, on the same street as the McDonald's near the harbor. Exchanges currency and traveler's checks. Credit card advances. Open daily 8am-noon and 3-5:30pm.

Bookstore: Xinhua Bookstore/Foreign Language Bookstore (wàiwén shūdiàn; 外文书店), 151-153 Zhongshan Lu (☎202 4059; foreign language dept. ☎513 7768), on the north side of the road just west of Siming Bei Lu. Dictionaries, guidebooks, and a fair selection of English classics. More bookstores near Xiamen University, especially along its northwestern edge on Yanwu Lu.

PSB: 43 Xinhua Lu (☎202 5505), near Gongyuan Nan Lu, opposite the Xinhua Lu Post Office. For visa extensions, go to the **Division of Exit and Entry** (chūrùjìng guǎnlǐ kē; 出入境管理科; ☎202 2329), in a separate building in the far back corner of the compound, close to Gongyuan Nan Lu. Open daily 8-11:30am and 3-6pm.

Hospitals: Xiamen No. 1 Hospital (xiàménshì dìyī yīyuàn; 厦门市第一医院), 10 Shanggu Tie (☎213 7275, emergency ☎112), on Zhenhai Lu, parallel to and south of Zhongshan Lu, a 10-15min. walk east of the Holiday Inn. On Gulangyu: **Xiamen No. 2 Hospital** (xiàménshì dì'èr yīyuàn; 厦门市第二医院), 60 Fujian Lu (☎206 2449, emergency ☎206 3549), off Longtou Lu, a 10min. walk from the ferry pier.

Internet Access: Internet Cafe (yīntè kāfēi wū; 因特咖啡屋), 12-13 Yanwu Lu, 2nd fl. (☎209 7778), opposite and around the corner from Nanputuo Temple. Y5 per hr, deposit Y50-100; free 80s soundtrack. Open daily 9:30am-midnight. **Zizai Internet Bar** (zìzài wǎngbā; 自在网吧), 260 Zhongshan Lu (☎210 1472). Y4 per hr. Open daily

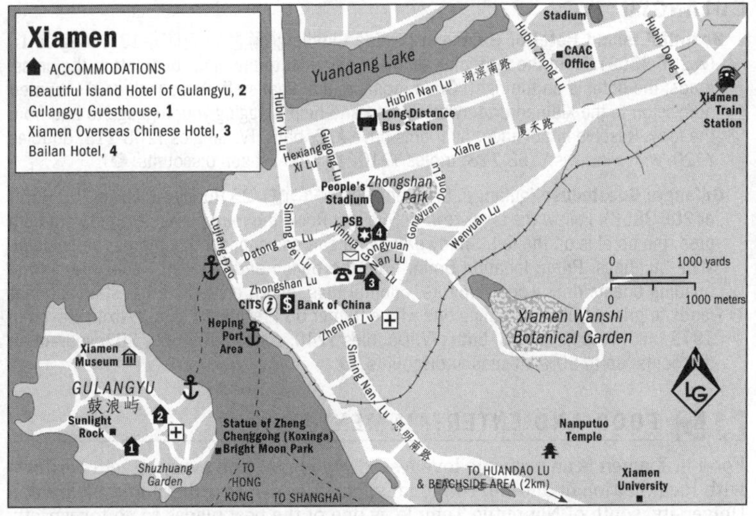

9:30am-2am. **Internet Pub** (yángyǔ wǎngbā; 洋宇网吧), 349 Zhongshan Lu (☎207 6300). High-speed connection Y4 per hr. Open daily 9am-midnight.

Post Office: 54 Xinhua Lu (☎202 2549 or 203 8277), north of Zhongshan Lu's eastern end. Open daily 7:30am-9pm. **Haihou Lu Post and Telecommunications Office** (hǎihòulù yóudiàn jú; 海后路邮电局), 58 Haihou Lu (☎202 3486), on Lujiang Dao opposite the Gulangyu ferry pier, a short walk north of Zhongshan Lu's western end. Poste Restante. Open daily 7:30am-7:30pm. EMS and IDD service at both branches. **Postal Code:** 361001 for the western district and Poste Restante, 361002 for Gulangyu.

ACCOMMODATIONS

With numerous luxury hotels and very few mid-range ones, Xiamen's accommodations may cause heart palpitations in budget travelers. On Gulangyu, however, hotels are not only affordable but breathtaking as well—especially if they overlook the beach area. A few aging colonial villas overlooking Gulangyu's shores are now inhabited by families or retirees who rent out these gorgeous, if spartan rooms for a small fee; but this option may take time, patience, and Chinese-language skills. The off-season is from September to June (excluding national holidays), when prices can fall by as much as 50%. In Xiamen city, the hotels around the train station are cheap (around Y100) but far from scenic.

XIAMEN CITY

Bailan Hotel (báilán fàndiàn; 白兰饭店), 90 Gugong Lu (☎223 1024), across the road from the large PSB, is one of the more affordable options. Central location. Comfortable standard rooms have A/C, bath, and TV. Doubles Y169-247. ❸

Xiamen Overseas Chinese Hotel (xiàmén huáqiáo dàshà; 厦门华侨大厦), 70-74 Xinhua Lu, one block from the post office. Gorgeous rooms, a posh lobby, and tender, effusive service almost make you forget the devastating price tag. The least-painful expensive option. All rooms have A/C, bath, and TV. Prices are listed in US dollars. Ask to be put in the front building, where doubles are roughly Y275. MC/V. ❹

GULANGYU

Beautiful Island Hotel of Gulangyu (lìzhīdǎo jiǔdiàn; 丽之岛酒店), 133 Longtou Lu (☎206 3309). From the ferry pier, follow Longtou Lu to the right; bear left at the crossroads; the hotel is on the right. Good rooms and a great staff. Perks include discounted admission to the Xiamen Underwater World and help dragging your luggage to and from the ferry. Reserve in advance. All rooms have A/C, bath, TV. Singles Y208-218; doubles Y120, with windows Y168-218; triples Y210. 15% off-season discounts. ❸

Gulangyu Guesthouse (gǔlàngyǔ bīnguǎn; 鼓浪屿宾馆), 25 Huangyan Lu (☎206 6050 or 206 3856). Follow the signs toward Sunlight Rock; the road passes a grassy stadium area; the hotel is on the left. Shady paths and gardens connect the impressive colonial-style buildings. Prime location 5min. from the beach and Sunlight Rock. The central building boasts dark wood furniture, oriental rugs, and a curved marble staircase that leads to pricey suites, including one where former US President Richard Nixon stayed in 1972. All rooms have A/C, bath, TV. Doubles Y240; suites Y500-800. 20% year-round discounts, up to 50% off-season discounts. ❹

FOOD AND ENTERTAINMENT

Food in Xiamen is an orgiastic love-fest; every corner and every street overflows with local, national, and international specialties. The northern end of Xiamen University, south of Nanputuo Temple, is one of the best places to go for variety. There are restaurants that specialize in **Xinjiang-style noodles** (xīběi lāmiàn; 西北拉面), **Taiwanese** restaurants around the corner from a **McDonald's,** and **Korean** restaurants farther away. Near the waterfront, the **wharf** and **western districts** teem with cosmopolitan cuisine. A few restaurants on **Siming Dong Lu** specialize in the Fujian Sha-county (shā xiàn fēngwèi; 沙县风味) style. One tiny **noodle restaurant ❶,** at 26 Zhongshan Lu, specializes in Xinjiang cuisine; its windowed kitchen reveals white-capped chefs molding perfect stringlets of noodles. Try the spicy wonton soup (húndùn tāng; 馄饨汤) with a platter of Muslim-style mixed noodles (bàn miàn; 拌面) for Y5. (☎203 1985. Open daily 8am-11pm.) Along Zhongshan Lu, streetside vendors sell skewers of Korean-style barbecue (Y2 per stick). For a more divine culinary experience, Nanputuo Temple serves Buddhist vegetarian food (Y30 per set meal).

Seafood tops the list of local specialties, especially on Gulangyu. The adventurous can seek out **turtle soup** and **grilled crayfish.** Seafood restaurants line **Longtou Lu**, the commercial market road leading inland from the pier. For Y25-40, you get soup and 3 dishes; but for Y200, you get soup and a diet-busting 8 dishes. Xiamen's specialties also include snacks like sweet fried pastries stuffed with peanut crumblies, a sweet **"soft peanut soup"** (huāshēng tāng; 花生汤), and a savory vegetable-filled pastry called *jiǔcàihé* (韭菜盒). Each costs Y1-3 and can be found along the road leading from the ferry pier on Gulangyu or Zhongshan Lu in specialty bakeries. Two other famous Xiamen dishes include paper-thin rice noodles with vegetable and seafood (miànxiàn hú; 面线糊), and gelatin (tǔsǔndòng; 土笋冻), made with wasabi, fragrant oil sauces, and a surprisingly good sea worm.

Youthful, energetic Xiamen is no newcomer to the night scene either. Clubs and pubs liberally scatter the landscape; a particularly vibrant spot is a stretch along Hubin Dong Lu, where at least four establishments line up one after another.

XIAMEN CITY

Huangzehe Peanut Soup Shop (huángzéhé huāshēngtāng diàn; 黄则和花生汤店), 22-24 Zhongshan Lu (☎212 5825), between McDonald's and the Bank of China. This wildly popular family-owned restaurant and bakery serves the famous *miànxiànhū* (Y5), and other noodle and dumpling dishes (Y3-5). Try the peanut soup (Y1), with egg (Y2), sesame-seed buns (Y2), and shaved green bean ice (Y3). Open daily 6am-9:50pm. ❶

Haoxianglai Chinese Western Restaurant (háoxiănglái zhōngxī cāntīng; 豪享来中西餐厅), 5 Haihou Lu (☎203 5212), next to the back entrance of the Lujiang Hotel and across from the East Ocean Hotel. Haihou Lu is the 1st street running north off Zhongshan Lu as you head inland from the waterfront. A popular family chain and the perfect place to satisfy cravings for Western food. Tender, juicy Western-style steak comes with a salad questionably served with ketchup sauce. Y25 set menu includes soup, vegetables, bread or rice, entree, and drink. Other good bets are the Japanese-style set dishes, complete with mackerel, soup, and steamed egg. Open 24hr. ❷

Edinburgh Pub (àidīng bǎo; 爱丁堡) 382 Hubin Dong Lu (☎507 9463), next to the Western Cowboy Pub. You're more likely to find attractive youths rocking away to jazzed-up Chinese pop and barely-clothed bartenders than kilts and bagpipes. Drinks are expensive (Y30 for a beer, Y35-40 for cocktails) but the comfy chairs and powerful sound system keep this joint packed. No cover charge. Open daily 7:30pm-2:30am. ❸

Haijiang Restaurant (hǎijiāng dàpáidàng; 海江大排档; ☎239 0460), perched on a dock opposite Gulangyu. Fishing boats from Pier No. 1 (dìyī mǎtóu; 第一码头), west of the Gulangyu ferry dock, shuttle patrons back and forth. Local patrons claim that this open-air seafood spot serves the best and cheapest seafood around. Fish your dinner from the aquarium, sit back, and admire the sunset while peeling crayfish and munching on scalloped shrimp. *Tǔsǔndòng* (bamboo shoot jello; 土笋冻) Y5 per bowl. Open daily 10am-midnight. ❶

GULANGYU

Gulong Pie House (gǔlóng bǐngjiā; 鼓龙饼家), 21 Longtou Lu (☎206 0721). From the pier, 1 block down and on the left. Paris has its croissant, New York its bagel, and Gulangyu its *xiàn bǐng* (馅饼), a pastry with sweet green bean paste filling (Y1)–made fresh only at this longtime establishment. This bakery also has fruit-flavored pastries (Y3 per box of 8), a peanut paste pastry, and yam pastries (Y1-3). Open daily 8am-8pm. ❶

Gulang Prestige Restaurant (gǔlàng xìnyù jiǔlóu; 鼓浪信誉酒楼), 4 Zhonghua Lu (☎206 3073 or 206 1996). From Sunlight Rock, walk down Huangyan Lu past the turf area; take a right and walk for half a block; it's on the left. The food doesn't come cheap, but your taste buds will thank you. Try the pearl fish (jīnzhū yú; 金珠鱼; Y90 per kg, Y120 for an average dish), steamed to tender perfection, and sip on eight-treasure tea (Y10), a concoction of chrysanthemum leaves and herbs. Open daily 10am-11pm. ❹

SIGHTS

Xiamen's largest draw is **Gulangyu,** but **Xiamen city** is also full of interesting diversions. The neighborhoods along the southwestern shore of Xiamen Island (including some renovated colonial facades along Zhongshan Lu) are worth a peek. The beach area in southern Xiamen city along the stretch of Huandao Lu (环岛路) is mile upon mile of rollicking, frolicking good fun, with uninterrupted, swimmable coastline, bike rental shops, and rows of vendors selling everything from fruit drinks to Pokémon life jackets. Perhaps more sobering is the view of Jinmen Island (金门岛), now under Taiwanese control and only 1km from shore.

GULANGYU 鼓浪屿

***Boats** to Gulangyu leave from the busy **passenger terminal** (xiàgǔ lúndù mǎtóu; 厦鼓轮渡码头), north of the western end of Zhongshan Lu (10min.; every 15min. 7:30-*

8:30am and 1:30-2:30pm, every 20min. 9:20-12:20pm, every hr. 12:20am-7:30am; round-trip ticket Y3). The ticket kiosk is just outside the docking area. Get there early to secure a spot on the upper deck for a better view. ***Speedboats*** *(seating 6 people) offer island cruises for Y100; tickets are available from the small fishing pier opposite the Underwater World or outside Shuzhuang Garden.*

Those who set foot on the multicolored cobblestoned streets of Gulangyu may come away convinced that this tiny island is the stuff of which legends are made. Long known as the "Garden on the Sea" and "Piano Isle," Gulangyu's grand assemblage of colonial-style European architecture, winding gardens, and rocky, windswept beaches have made the island a must-see for resort-seeking vacationers and culture-craving aesthetes. Even cars can't mar the island's pristine streets, which are reserved for pedestrians and the occasional electric golf cart (Y10-50). Hidden speakers and tea houses waft vague airs of Bohemian rhapsodies and Viennese waltzes, providing the slow, rolling rhythms to which Gulangyu abides.

Sensual pleasures aside, Gulangyu's sunny shores boast a great deal of historical significance. From the Xiamen waterfront, two of Gulangyu's most recognizable sights are clearly visible: at the island's southern end, the colossal **Statue of Zheng Chenggong** that honors the national military hero and native of Fujian; and near the center of the island, the stark grey protusion of **Sunlight Rock** (rìguāng yán; 日光岩), which is capped by military battlements. The island not only served as a base for Zheng Chenggong's resistance *against* foreign invaders during the 17th century, but it has also been the concession area *for* foreigners—Portuguese, British, French, and Japanese—who came to Xiamen to capitalize on its strategic commercial location. Ghosts from this checkered past survive in an eclectic jumble of **colonial architecture,** ranging from terraced patios and red brick structures to stone mansions with yellow-shuttered windows. Many of these buildings are still used as residences; a stroll along **Fujian Lu** is a showcase for these crumbling but still impressive villas, and many families are willing to open their doors and let visitors look around. Gulangyu has also produced many of China's greatest pianists, and the ratio of pianos to families here is the highest in the nation. The music school on the island strives to keep up the tradition, and the melodies of students hard at practice waft through open kitchen doors and windows. To best sample Gulangyu's many delights, take a couple days to wander through its streets, leaving China, civilization, and your cares behind.

SUNLIGHT ROCK (rìguāng yán; 日光岩). One of the most popular sights on the island is the park that contains Sunlight Rock, a 100m boulder that grants views of the entire island, the shores of mainland China, and the East China Sea in the distance. Named for being the first spot on Gulangyu to catch glimmers of the sun, the summit is a great place to watch the sunrise and join groups of *tai chi* practitioners. *(☎514 0729. Y80 admission includes a ticket to Haoyue Garden and Shuzhuang Park. Climbing after sunset and before daybreak, however, is free.)* Zheng Chenggong stationed troops on this "peak" to fight the Dutch colonialists who occupied Taiwan in 1612. Beyond a Buddhist temple near the base of the hill and near the Zheng Chenggong Memorial Hall, several paths head upward toward the peak; climb the last steep steps to the "naval command post" at the top for a bird's-eye view. The **Zheng Chenggong Memorial Hall** (zhèng chénggōng jìniànguǎn; 郑成功纪念馆), in a stately three-story colonial building, is dedicated to this national hero. *(Open daily 8am-5pm. Free.)*

From the foot of the iron-wrought stairs leading to the summit, a cable car brings you to **Hundred Bird Park** (bǎi niǎo yuán; 百鸟园), a massive net-enclosed area where rare birds roam somewhat freely, and where you can watch hourly shows that feature parrots grooving to disco tunes. *(Off Huangyan Lu, in the interior of the island beyond*

Gulangyu Guesthouse. Signs (some in English) from the ferry pier will direct you. Open daily 8am-6pm. Y40, children under 1.2m free; includes cable car and entrance to Hundred Bird Park.)

SHUZHUANG GARDEN (shūzhuāng huāyuán; 菽庄花园). Shuzhuang Garden sits on the far southeast side of the island, past rows of dried seafood, trinkets, and photo vendors, next to a pristine beach. The intensely pretty garden, done up in classical Chinese fashion, has immaculate little pavilions alongside lakes full of floating lotus flowers. Also worth a gander is the **Twelve Worlds Hole** (shí'èr dòngtiān; 十二洞天), a grotto filled with looming, oddly shaped rocks; then emerge to enjoy the evening from beachside tables. On Tianwei Lu at the end of Nine-Bend Bridge is the **Gulangyu Piano Museum** (gǔlàngyǔ gāngqín bówùguǎn; 鼓浪屿钢琴博物馆), which features over 40 different pianos from all periods and countries. *(Follow signs that lead off to the left from the main road after you disembark from the ferry. Open daily 8am-6pm. Y10, children 1-1.3m Y5, under 1m free.)*

BRIGHT MOON PARK (hào yuè yuán; 皓月园). From this point, visitors can view the **Statue of Zheng Chenggong** (zhèng chénggōng shídiāoxiàng; 郑成功石雕像) up close and personal—all 16m, 1400 tons, and 625 granite pieces of it. According to legend, Zheng threw his sword into the sea before leaving for Taiwan, and he was subsequently transformed into a huge rock to guard the motherland he loved so dearly. Designed to withstand scale 12 typhoons and 8.0 earthquakes, Zheng won't be going anywhere anytime soon. The 150 peacocks in the **Peacock Park** (kǒngquè yuán; 孔雀园) aren't shy about begging visitors for food. *(From Shuzhuang Garden, follow the coastline east until you reach the park. Open daily sunrise-sunset. Y15.)*

XIAMEN UNDERWATER SEA WORLD (xiàmén hǎidǐ shìjiè; 厦门海底世界). This compact but interesting aquarium features over 10,000 denizens of the deep. Several hundred fresh- and sea-water species are represented, including paddlefish, penguins, and piranhas. Four daily shows feature dolphins and seals doing tricks and stunts. *(2 Longtou Lu. On the main road leading off to the right from the ferry pier, after a grassy park; look for a golden octopus statue. ☎206 7668 or 206 7825. Open daily 8:30am-6:30pm. Y70, children and students Y30.)*

XIAMEN CITY SIGHTS

XIAMEN UNIVERSITY (xiàmén dàxué; 厦门大学). Xiamen University's lovely campus contains buildings that manage to be both modern and tasteful. To the left of the main Yanwu Lu entrance is the **Lu Xun Memorial Hall** (lǔxùn jìniànguǎn 鲁迅纪念馆), built in honor of the scholar and author who used to be a professor at the university. At the very center of the campus is a large and lovely lake. *(South of Nanputuo Temple. Buses #1 and 21 run south along Siming Nan Lu and terminate at a parking lot outside of the north entrance on Yanwu Lu; there is an entrance on your right.)*

NANPUTUO TEMPLE (nánpǔtuó sì; 南普陀寺). Nanputuo Temple, a huge complex with multi-colored halls, a golden Buddha statue, ponds, and pavilions, is one of the most active and best-kept monasteries in China. Built in the Tang dynasty, the temple is now the site of the **Buddhism College of South Fujian** (mǐnnán fóxué yuàn; 闽南佛学院). The temple is named after Putuoshan (see p. 390), the island off the coast of Zhejiang province that is dedicated to Guanyin, the Goddess of Mercy; Nanputuo Temple also takes Guanyin as its sacred deity. The Guanyin statues here are perhaps the most impressive aspect of the temple; three **thousand-hand gold Guanyins** sit in an elevated rotunda behind the main hall. *(On the southwestern edge of the city, north of Xiamen University. The eastern gate and entrance is next to the bus station at the terminus for buses #1 and 21, both of which run south along Siming Nan Lu. The entrance is marked by a huge pond. Open daily sunrise-sunset. Y3, children under 1m free.)*

QUANZHOU 泉州 ☎0595

There is something markedly different about Quanzhou, something that makes it seem a little less homogenously Chinese than the rest of the adamantly homogenous Chinese south coast. Perhaps it's the solid Persian walls and the ruins of the grand Qingjing Mosque, or the eerie otherworldliness of the Islamic tombs tucked away on Qingyuan Mountain. The ease with which these rather out-of-place sights fit into Quanzhou is probably the best reminder of the city's all-embracing past. During the Song and Yuan dynasties, Quanzhou was one of the largest ports in the world; its harbor shipped silk and porcelain to the Middle East in exchange for spices and ivory. Large merchant ships and a colorful mix of sailors, missionaries, and traders frequented the lively wharf area, where religions, languages, and architectural styles mixed as easily as teas and spices were traded.

Today, the port's significance lingers only in memory, and the Arab and Persian traders of yesteryear have either scattered to the winds or meshed into the local population. Although its status has diminished, its character has remained unchanged. Thousand-year-old mosques straddle the same streets as Buddhist temples and Western fast-food restaurants jostle for space with dime-a-dozen Chinese roadside stalls. Even if the times may be a-changing, Quanzhou sure ain't.

TRANSPORTATION

Buses: Quanzhou Bus Station (quánzhōu qìchē zhàn; 泉州汽车站; ☎228 4141), at the intersection of Wenling Lu and Quanxiu Jie, connects to north Quanzhou via bus #2. Like most buses that run on Fujian province's luxurious routes, Quanzhou's buses have restrooms and a stewardess who serves tea and cookies. To **Fuzhou** (2hr., approx. every 20min. 7am-7:30pm, Y60) and **Xiamen** (1½hr., 26 per day 6:40am-5:40pm, Y32).

Local Transportation: Many destinations within the city can be reached on foot, but most locals get around by **moped.** Quanzhou **buses** have comprehensive service, but some routes can get crowded—watch your belongings. Most routes run 6am-10pm. Fare Y1-2. Bus **#2** runs from the bus station up Wenling Lu, past Dong Jie, Xi Jie, and Kaiyuan Temple; **#3** runs from Guandi Temple and Qingjing Si to the Qingyuan Mountains; **#15** travels the length of Wenling Lu, continuing north to Qingyuan Mountain.

Taxis: Base fare Y8-10, each additional km Y1.4-1.8; *miàndí* taxis Y6, each additional km Y1.4 (but these pick up other passengers along the way). **Pedicabs** to most destinations within city center Y3-5, from bus station to Kaiyuan Temple Y8-10.

ORIENTATION AND PRACTICAL INFORMATION

Quanzhou is bordered by the **Jin River** (jìn jiāng; 晋江) to the west. The downtown area is bounded to the north by **Xi Jie** (西街) and **Dong Jie** (东街). Xi Jie and Dong Jie are bisected by **Zhongshan Lu** (中山路), which runs north-south. Running parallel to and east of of Zhongshan Lu is **Wenling Lu** (温陵路), which terminates in the south near the long-distance bus station, at the intersection with **Quanxiu Jie** (泉秀街). **Tumen Jie** (涂门街) and **Jiuyi Jie** (九一街) both run between Zhongshan Lu and Wenling Lu. Wenling Lu and Tumen Jie, in particular, are lively commercial streets, lined with hotels, temples, eateries, and shops, and are especially vibrant at night. Small unnamed alleys linking these two streets are full of roadside food stalls. Tumen Jie continues east of its intersection with Wenling Lu as **Fengze Jie** (丰泽街), into the newest part of town.

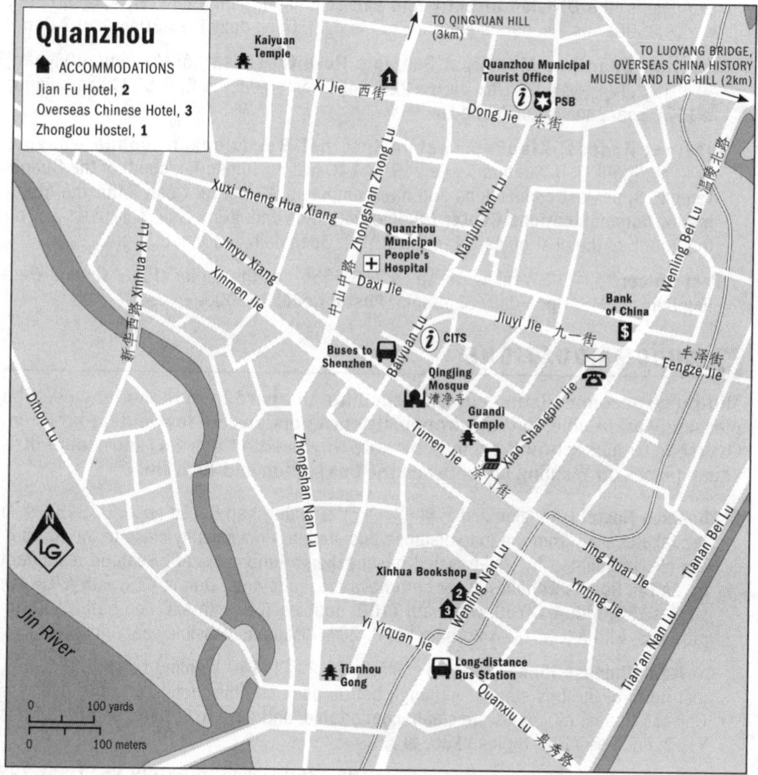

Tourist Office: Quanzhou Municipal Tourism Bureau (quánzhōu shì lǚyóu jú; 泉州市旅遊局; ☎227 4888), in the Jingweige Bldg., 3rd fl., on Dong Jie, next to the PSB. Take bus #2 to Zhonglou; backtrack a block. A small selection of English-language brochures. Welcoming, helpful staff speaks English and Japanese. Open M-F 8am-noon and 3-6pm.

Travel Agency: Quanzhou Travel Services (☎298 5940, for ticketing 228 2192), in the Huaqiao Building, on Baiyuan Lu, next to the Overseas Chinese Hotel. Private bus to Fuzhou with daily 9am departures Y55. English- and Japanese-speaking staff. Ticket commission Y10. Open daily 8:30am-6pm.

Bank of China: 1 Jiuyi Jie (☎219 1651), at Wenling Lu. Take bus #18 to Wenling Lu; look for the big sign atop the high-rise. Exchanges currency and traveler's checks. Credit card advances. Open daily 8-11:30am and 3-6pm.

Bookstore: Xinhua Bookstore/Foreign Language Bookstore (wàiwén shūdiàn; 外文书店; ☎298 4631 or 228 2496), on Wenling Lu at Yinjing Lu, a block south of the Great Wall Hotel. Sells videos of English-language movies and an impressive selection of self-help books in English. Open daily 8am-9pm.

PSB: 62 Dong Jie (☎218 0318), a few minutes east of Zhongshan Zhong Lu. From the bus station or Wenling Lu, take bus #2 to Zhonglou and backtrack a block. For visa extensions, the **Division of Entry and Exit** (chūrùjìng guǎnlǐ chù; 出入境管理处; ☎218 0308) has a separate entrance to the right. Open daily 8-11:30am and 3-6pm.

Hospital: Quanzhou Municipal People's Hospital (quánzhōushì rénmín yīyuàn; 泉州市人民医院), 54 Daxi Jie (☎228 3490, emergency ☎228 5221, ambulance ☎102), near Zhongshan Zhong Lu.

Internet Access: Xiaokan Luohua Internet Bar (xiàokàn luòhuā wǎngbā; 笑看落花网吧), 8 Wenhua Jie (☎219 4414), just off Tumen Jie, south of the Guandi Temple. Super-fast connections and new computers. Y3 per hr. Open 24hr. The **Multimedia Communications Center** (duōmeíxiūtōngxìn zhōngxīn; 多媒休通信中心), on the 2nd fl. of the post office. Y4, deposit Y50. Open daily 8:30am-6:30pm.

Post Office: 213-217 Wenling Bei Lu (☎216 6555), on the corner of Jiuyi Jie and Wenling Bei Lu. EMS. Open daily 8am-8pm. **Postal Code:** 362000.

ACCOMMODATIONS

Mid-range accommodations in Quanzhou are not hard to find and may even be pleasantly affordable, but jaw-droppingly cheap options are few and far between. Overseas Chinese, however, may be able to wheedle their way into some dirt-cheap places on Wenling Lu, between the bus station and Jiuyi Jie.

Zhonglou Hostel (zhōnglóu lǚshè; 钟楼旅社), 1 Zhongshan Bei Lu (☎237 3343), at Xi Jie; take bus #2 from the long-distance bus station. Conveniently close to the Kaiyuan Temple, frequented by well-traveled backpackers. Generous staff. Seafood restaurant on 2nd fl. Rooms without A/C or bath have mosquito nets. Dorms Y25, with A/C Y40; singles Y50, with A/C Y60, with bath Y100; doubles Y60, with A/C and bath Y100; triples Y75, with A/C Y100, with bath Y120. 20% discounts possible year-round. ❶

Overseas Chinese Home (huáqiáo zhījiā; 华侨之家), 149 Wenling Lu (☎228 3559), just north of the bus station. Although not as posh as other hotels with the Overseas Chinese trademark, rooms are clean, comfortable, and have A/C, bath, and TV. Singles Y100; doubles Y100; triples Y130. ❷

Jianfu Hotel (jiànfú dàshà; 建福大厦), 125-135 Wenling Lu (☎228 3511; fax 298 6041), on the south end of Wenling Lu, next to the Overseas Chinese Home.Reasonable prices; luxurious rooms have fridges. All rooms have A/C, bath, and TV. Singles and doubles Y320-370; triples Y360. Year-round discounts bring prices to: singles Y100; doubles Y138-158; triples Y150. MC. ❷

FOOD

Quanzhou might not have award-winning dishes of its own, but its streets are filled with restaurants and stalls selling perennial Chinese favorites. Try the **steamed sponge cakes,** snowy white rice cakes slightly fermented for a subtle sweet flavor. The **sticky rice** steamed with either chicken, pork, or red bean paste and wrapped in bamboo leaves in a pyramid shape (zòngzi; 粽子) is as fun to unravel as it is to eat. Colorful small streets in the older, northwest section of town—on and around **Dong Jie, Xi Jie,** and **Zhongshan Bei Lu** in particular—harbor a treasure of small eateries offering these snacks, as well as Sha county-style treats (shā xiàn xiǎochī; 沙县小吃). Also try the *sānhé fàn* (三合饭), a concoction of three types of grain served in a small aluminum tin. Sha county stalls can also be found in the small alleys linking Tumen Jie with Wenling Lu. After dark, food options multiply; **Xiaoshangpin Jie** (xiǎoshāngpǐng jiē; 小商品街), the street parallel to and directly west of Wenling Lu, comes alive with fruit stands, sesame cake (Y1) vendors, and neon-lit seafood restaurants. **Wenling Lu** is also transformed into a sea of all-night street stalls selling barbecued kebabs (Y0.5 a stick), smelly tofu, and much more.

SIGHTS

Quanzhou's sights reflect its colorful religious and cultural heritage; the city has a wealth of Muslim and Buddhist relics. The best way to get a feel for Quanzhou's religious and maritime history is to stroll through the old city streets, particularly along **Jubao Jie** (聚宝街) and **Xiaomen Gang** (小门巷), home to the remains of the Maritime Administration of Foreign Trade.

QINGJING MOSQUE (qīngjìng sì; 清净寺). Also known as the **Ashab Mosque,** the Qingjing Mosque has survived the forces that destroyed its counterparts. Quanzhou's only mosque is now only a shell of what it once was, and few visitors grace its halls. Still, the thousand-year-old site is fascinatingly un-Chinese. The stately Islamic building is located opposite a long, fortress-like medieval wall. From the eerily absorbing sarcophagus covers to the well-preserved stone engravings to the centuries-old well in the courtyard, there is an unnatural calm to the mosque that sets it apart from anything else you'll see in Quanzhou. To the left of the entrance a well-organized exhibition hall with English captions details the history of Islam in Quanzhou. *(On Tumen Jie, west of a minor Buddhist temple and near Baiyuan Lu. Take bus #5 from the bus station to Guandi Si. Open daily 8am-6pm. Y3.)*

QINGYUANSHAN MOUNTAIN (qīngyuán shān; 清源山). Qingyuanshan looms over Quanzhou and the surrounding area. Because it's not yet overrun with tourists, it's easy to get lost here, so prepare to bushwhack your way to the summit. Rising 615m above sea-level, this mountain is often affectionately referred to as the Wuyishan of Guangdong province. Not quite as pretty as that other Fujian mountain, Qingyuanshan is infinitely holier, with Buddhist temples, Daoist shrines, and Islamic tombs. At the base, there is the shrine to Master Hongyi, one of the most revered of Buddhist teachers, and an impressive stone statue of Laozi, the founder of Daoism. A further climb takes you to **Mituo Rock** (mítuó shí; 弥陀石) and a delicate waterfall. A backbreaking, never-ending path leads to the summit; at the very top, at the **South Platform** (nántái; 南台), you can strike a humongous bell for Y3. Another temple sits near the **Qingyuan Cave** (qīngyuán dòng; 清源洞), while the **Heavenly Cool Lake** (qīngyuán tiānhú; 清源天湖) offers a heavenly and cool respite for weary climbers. From here, **motorcycles** can take you back down (Y5 per person). The trail's few markers mke it easy for those without guides to get lost; and a simple rest stop along the paths will attract hordes of unbelievably vicious mosquitoes. *(3km north of the city. Take bus #3 from Zhongshan Lu or #15 from Wenling Lu to the last stop (30min., Y2). The Laozi and Qianshou Yan gates both lead to the scenic area. ☎279 7606. Open daily 7am-6pm. Y25, including all sights.)*

KAIYUAN TEMPLE (kāiyuán sì; 开元寺). The largest of Quanzhou's Buddhist temples, Kaiyuan is also the city's primary tourist attraction. The temple has an airy, stone-paved courtyard flanked by the impressive **East** and **West Pagodas.** Surrounded by sculptures of Buddhist icons, the pagodas are unique for their Chinese and Indian artistic styles. Although the temple dates back to AD 686, the pagodas were not constructed until more than 500 years later. The ceiling of the main hall is lined with 24 flying *apsaras*, acrobatic figurines in the early Buddhist style.

To the right of the temple, just behind the garden containing the East Pagoda, is a small but worthwhile exhibit on the history of navigation and foreign contact in Quanzhou, focusing on the Song and Yuan dynasties. The very old boats here are strangely enticing, particularly the partially reconstructed 13th-century sailing ship, discovered in Quanzhou Bay in 1973 during the dredging of an irrigation channel. *(27 Xi Jie. In the northwest part of the city. Take bus #2 from the bus station or Wenling Lu to Kaiyuan Si. Open daily 7:30am-6pm. Y4, children 1.2m and under Y2.)*

GUANGDONG 广东

A ride on the Guangshen Expressway through Guangdong is a ride through time, from the Middle Pleistocene bones of Maba Man discovered outside Shaoguan to the skyscraper skeletons under construction in Shenzhen. Somewhere in the middle, Guangzhou, the capital of the province, has nearly uprooted itself in its attempts to build a modern subway system under more than 2800 years of history. Guangdong sprawls across the fertile Pearl River basin, rich with natural resources and people. Amid the rapid economic development, trains race past farmers who live as they have for centuries, brand new highways stretch alongside rice paddies, and everywhere the marks of human labor and time are apparent.

GUANGZHOU 广州 ☎020

Beijing is famed as China's political and historical center; Shanghai is the country's new economic powerhouse; so where does that leave Guangzhou, the last city of China's "big three"? Though the hapless tourist who arrives at Guangzhou's chaotic train station may initially disagree, Guangzhou is a city where the inhabitants seem comfortable with themselves and their surroundings. Perhaps this can be attributed to Guangzhou's history of prosperity; while many Chinese cities have just recently come into their own, Guangzhou has long reaped the benefits of its proximity to SEZs like Shenzhen and Zhuhai, not to mention neighboring Hong Kong. Today, however, despite its crowded markets, glossy shops, and vibrant nightlife, Guangzhou cannot compare to the glamour of its now-mature siblings, but is still perfectly content to take a breather and move ever-so-slightly out of the spotlight it once monopolized.

ORIENTATION

Guangzhou seems to lack any apparent city planning. Fortunately, most major streets are labeled according to direction, and the new subway system helps with orientation. **Huanshi Lu** (环市路), the city's busiest road, runs west from the city center, intersecting **Tianhe Lu** (天河路) in Tianhe district. **Zhongshan Lu** (中山路) also runs east-west, bisecting the city. The subway follows most of the length of this street, before making an abrupt turn northward at Tiyu Xi Station (体育西站), continuing alongside **Tianhe Dong Lu,** and terminating at Guangzhou East Train Station. Four-lane **Dongfeng Lu** (东风路), the widest street in Guangzhou, runs parallel to Zhongshan Lu. North of the Pearl River, the newly constructed and more organized **Tianhe district** makes up the eastern part of Guangzhou. **Jiefang Lu** (解放路) and **Guangzhou Lu** (广州路) divide Tianhe district from Dongshan district. Backpacker headquarters, a.k.a. **Shamian Island**—no longer an island due to land reclamation—sits at the southwest fork in the **Pearl River** (珠江).

Each of the large thoroughfares, as well as many of the smaller streets, are divided into north (*běi*), central (*zhōng*), and south (*nán*) sections, or east (*dōng*), central, and west (*xī*) sections. Streets are numbered as well; Zhongshan Lu is divided into eight numbered sections from east to west.

TRANSPORTATION

Flights: Guangzhou's **Baiyun Airport** (báiyún jīchǎng; 白云机场; ☎8612 0000) is west of White Cloud Mountain. A taxi from central Guangzhou to the airport costs Y40-50. A **shuttle bus** leaves from the gray building next to CITS on 179 Huanshi Xi Lu (30min., every 30min. 7am-7pm, Y3-4). The following major airlines fly to Guangzhou:

Air China (zhōngguó mínháng gōngsī; 中国民航公司), 980 Jiefang Bei Lu (☎8668 1399). Open daily 8am-5pm.

China Southwest Airlines (zhōngguó xīnán hángkōng gōngsī; 中国西南航空公司), 181 Huanshi Xi Lu (☎8612 0449, ext. 477). Open daily 8am-5:30pm. To: **Chengdu** (8-9 per day, Y1300); **Chongqing** (3 per day, Y1150); **Guilin** (7-8 per day, Y530); **Harbin** (1-2 per day, Y2580); **Kunming** (3-4 per day, Y1200); **Xiamen** (2-3 per day, Y630).

Hainan Airlines (hǎinán hángkōng gōngsī; 海南航空公司), 99 Zhanqian Lu (☎8669 9999). Open M-F 8:30am-6pm, Sa-Su 8:30am-5:30pm. To **Haikou** (5 per day, Y560).

Malaysian Airlines (mǎláixīyà hángkōng gōngsī; 马来西亚航空公司), 368 Huanshi Dong Lu, 2nd fl., (☎8335 8838). In the Overseas Chinese Hotel. Open M-F 8:30am-5:30pm, Sa 8:30am-12:30pm. To **Kuala Lumpur, Malaysia** (Tu-Th; Y2500, round-trip Y3550).

Shanghai Airlines (shànghǎi hángkōng gōngsī; 上海航空公司), 194 Huanshi Xi Lu, Rm. 2832 (☎8666 8800, ext. 1248), in the Linhua Hotel. Open daily 8am-8pm. To **Shanghai** (Y1020, but ask for a Y200 discount).

Singapore Airlines, 69 Xianle Zhong Lu, 28th fl., Rm. 2807-2808 (☎8732 0600), in the Dongshan Plaza. Frequently gives discounts, especially if you buy a return fare. Open M-F 9am-1pm, Sa 9am-noon. To: **Singapore** (Tu-Th; Y3500, round-trip Y4700; prices rise during July and August).

Trains: The enormous **Guangzhou Train Station** (guǎngzhōu zhàn; 广州站; ☎8715 7222) is on the western end of Huanshi Lu. The **Guangzhou East Train Station** (guǎngzhōu dōngzhàn; 广州东站; ☎8755 0917 or 8755 8714) is considerably cleaner, safer, and less harrowing than the notorious main station. Easily accessible by subway line #1. Tourist information center open daily 6:10am-10pm (☎8714 6164 or 8714 6222). Fast and efficient service to the Kowloon KCR station in **Hong Kong** (1½-2hr., 12 per day 8:30am-8:45pm, Y200) and **Shenzhen** (1hr., every 25-45min. 7am-11:17pm, Y70). Trains to other destinations are listed in the table below; all run from the main station, although many also stop at Guangzhou East.

TO	TRAVEL TIME	PER DAY	PRICE	TO	TRAVEL TIME	PER DAY	PRICE
Beijing	24hr.	2	Y366-396	**Nanchang**	15½-18hr.	4	Y171-183
Changsha	8-10¼hr.	at least 10	Y172-276	**Nanjing**	33½hr.	1	Y341-370
Chengdu	44hr.	2	Y392-424	**Nanning**	17½hr.	5	Y171-183
Chongqing	46-47hr.	2	Y350	**Ningbo**	30hr.	1	Y305-329
Fuzhou	32hr.	1	Y276-294	**Shanghai**	24-27hr.	3	Y377
Guilin	12-13hr.	3	Y150	**Shantou**	7-10hr.	3	Y132-217
Guiyang	33hr.	5	Y254-275	**Shaoguan**	3hr.	at least 20	Y159
Hangzhou	25½hr.	1	Y194	**Shenyang**	35hr.	1	Y576
Hefei	24hr.	1	Y183	**Tianjin**	33¼hr.	1	Y383
Hengyang	4-5hr.	at least 20	Y114	**Taiyuan**	38hr.	1	Y392-424
Ji'nan	34½hr.	1	Y350-378	**Wuhan**	14-14½hr.	9	Y240-390
Kunming	44hr.	1	Y282-305	**Xi'an**	28hr.	2	Y428
Lanzhou	44hr.	3	Y491	**Yueyang**	12hr.	at least 10	Y140
Liuzhou	16¼hr.	1	Y247	**Zhangjiajie**	23hr.	1	Y317
Luoyang	28½hr.	1	Y217	**Zhengzhou**	20hr.	3	Y144

Buses: Guangzhou has an inordinate and confusing number of bus stations. The **Municipal Bus Passenger Station** (shì qìchē kèyùn zhàn; 市汽车客运站; ☎8227 9825) is down Huanshi Xi Lu from the train station, on the left at the pedestrian overpass. To **Foshan** (1hr., every 15min. 7am-10:30pm, Y12) and **Zhaoqing** (2hr., every 25min. 7am-10pm, Y30). The **Provincial Bus Station** (shěng qìchē kèyùn zhàn; 省汽车客运站; ☎8666 1297), 145 Huanshi Xi Lu, opposite the Municipal Station. Service to **Guilin** (8hr., 9:30pm, Y130) and **Haikou** (12hr., several per day 9:45am-6pm, Y250). Buses to **Hong Kong** and **Macau** board from major hotels, including the Garden Hotel (☎8333 8989), China Hotel (☎8666 6888), Hotel Landmark (☎8335 5988), and Liuhua Hotel (☎8666 8800).

Ferries: Turbo Jet (☎8222 2555) offers 4hr. boat trips from the **East River Guangzhou Ferry Terminal** (dōngjiāngsuìkèlián mǎtóu; 东江穗客连码头) to the Hong Kong China Ferry Terminal (10am and 4:30pm, HK$189-284).

Subway: The newly opened subway system (☎8755 3460, inquiries ☎8667 3366, ext. 1703) has one line that runs along Zhongshan Lu between Xilang Lu in the southwest and the Guangzhou East Train Station in the northeast. Stops are marked by a yellow sign with two red stripes. Single-ride tickets available from vending machines (accepting only Y1 coins) at every stop. Fare is Y2 per 3 stops, Y1 per additional 3 stops, with a maximum of Y6 per ride. The subway runs approximately 6am-11pm.

City Buses: The bus system is Guangzhou's most common and convenient method of travel and one of China's most comprehensive city transportation systems. Double-digit buses scour the city center (Y1, A/C Y2), while triple-digits travel to the far ends of the city (Y1-2). To board a bus, wave one down at a stop and pay exact change. Route signs are in Chinese. The most important bus routes for travelers, buses **#5** and **31,** shuttle between Shamian Island and the main train station (30min.-1hr., Y1).

Taxis: Base fare Y7, each additional km Y2.2. Taxis are not allowed to stop on Huanshi Xi Lu opposite the bus and train stations; to hail a taxi, walk onto a side street off the main road. **Motorbike** drivers provide short rides for around Y5 and usually hang around the train station, and local and long-distance bus stations.

PRACTICAL INFORMATION

TOURIST AND FINANCIAL SERVICES

Tourist Office: Guangzhou Tourism Bureau (guǎngzhōushì lǚyoújú; 广州市旅游局), 180 Huanshi Xi Lu (☎8668 7051 or 8669 8043). English-speaking staff of recent college graduates is knowledgeable and enthusiastic. Free maps, brochures, pamphlets, and advice. Open daily 8am-5:30pm.

Tourist Complaint Hotline: ☎8668 7042.

Travel Agencies: CITS, 10 Qiaoguang Lu (☎8339 9638), next to the Hotel Landmark off Yanjiang Lu. Open M-F 8:30am-6pm. **GZL International Travel Service Ltd.** (guǎngzhīlǚ guójì lǚxíngshè; 广之旅国际旅行社), 155 Huanshi Xi Lu (☎8638 4156 or 8383 5477), to the right as you exit the train station. Staff member speaks English. Open M-F 8:30am-noon and 2-5pm, Sa 8:30am-noon and 2-4pm. **White Swan Hotel Ticketing Office** (bái tiān'ér bīnguǎn piàowù zhōngxīn; 白天鹅宾馆票务中心; ☎8188 6968, ext. 14), on Shamian Nan Jie, Shamian Island. Intended for guests only, but the ground-floor office rarely asks for identification. English speakers. Open daily 7:30am-10pm.

Bank of China: Almost all city branches exchange currency and traveler's checks and issue credit card advances. Main branch ☎8190 7077. The branch on Shamian Dajie between Shamian Yi Jie and Shamian Er Jie, on Shamian Island, has English-speaking staff members. Exchanges traveler's checks M-F. Open M-F 9am-6pm, Sa-Su 9am-5pm. The branch at 91 Chandi Damalu opposite McDonald's has an indoor **ATM** that accepts international cards. Open M-F 9am-6pm, Sa-Su 9am-noon and 2-5pm. Near the bus and train stations is the branch in Guangdong International Hotel (广东国际大酒店), 339 Huanshi Dong Lu. 2 **ATMs**. Open M-F 9am-noon and 2-5pm, Sa 9am-6pm.

Western Union, 4 Zhanghai Zhannan (☎185), off Huanshi Xi Lu close to the train station. Open daily 8-11:30am and 1:30-7pm.

LOCAL SERVICES

Bookstores: The **Foreign Language Bookstore** (wàiwén shūdiàn; 外文书店), 326 Beijing Lu, near the pedestrian street; entrance is down a small alley that serves as a bike parking lot—the sign is in Chinese. The store has 2 floors, but English language books are limited to a paltry selection of classics on the top floor. Open daily 9am-8pm.

Libraries: Zhongshan Library (zhōngshān túshūguǎn; 中山图书馆; ☎8382 5710), on Wenming Lu, near Dezheng Lu has a relatively large English section on the 3rd fl. Open F-W 9:30am-4:30pm, Th 8:30am-noon. Foreigners with ID or passport can obtain library cards and borrow for free at both libraries; refundable deposit (Guangzhou Y200, Zhongshan Y20).

Supermarkets: JUSCO is a huge, recently opened supermarket that dominates the 2nd fl. of the shopping mall **China Plaza** (subway: Lei Shi Ling Yuan; follow signs for China Plaza). Sells produce, prepared foods, and sushi. Open daily 10am-10pm.

EMERGENCY AND COMMUNICATIONS

Hospital: Guangzhou No. 1 People's Hospital (shìyī rénmín yīyuàn; 市一人民医院), 602 Renmin Bei Lu (☎8108 3090). Open M-F 8am-noon and 2-5pm, Sa 8am-noon, Su emergencies only. Some English-speaking staff members.

Internet Access: Ji'nan University (jìnán dàxué; 济南大学; ☎8522 0114), Nanhai Bldg., 4th fl., Tianhe. Take bus #243 from Shamian. Y5 unlimited access for students only, but try looking like a foreign student at the university. **Internet e bar** (☎8188 6353), 18 Shamian Jie, between the Catholic Church and the Victory Hotel. Y20 per hr. Open M-F 7pm-2am. **Net Bug Club** (wǎngchóng jùlèbù; 网虫俱乐部; ☎8386 5773), on the 2nd fl. of Longchen Computer Plaza, Da Shan Tou, San Malu. Y5 per hr. **Cyber Ant** (máyǐxùn wénhuàshè; ☎8423 9220), in the Xin'an Bldg. on Jiangnan Dadao Zhong, 1st fl., Rm. 150-151. Also hosts film screenings and art exhibitions. Y5 per hr., Y20 for entire evening. Open daily 11am-2am.

Post Offices: Liuhua Post Office, on the right side of the main train station's parking lot. EMS and Poste Restante. Open daily 8am-5:30pm. **Postal Code:** 510010. On Shamian Island, **Shamian Post Office** is on Shamian San Jie. EMS. Open M-F 9am-5pm. **Xiti Post Office** (guǎngzhōushì xītí yóujú; 广州市西堤邮局), just east of Shamian Island, across the street from Cultural Park. EMS and Poste Restante. Open daily 8:30am-7pm. **Postal Code:** 510130.

ACCOMMODATIONS

Most budget establishments are in the Shamian Island area or near the train station. During the two trade fairs (the end of April and September), prices rise and rooms are scarce. Bargaining is expected in the vast majority of hotels, including five-star establishments; a standard discount is typically available on weekdays. Most hotels accept major credit cards and have a 5-10% service charge.

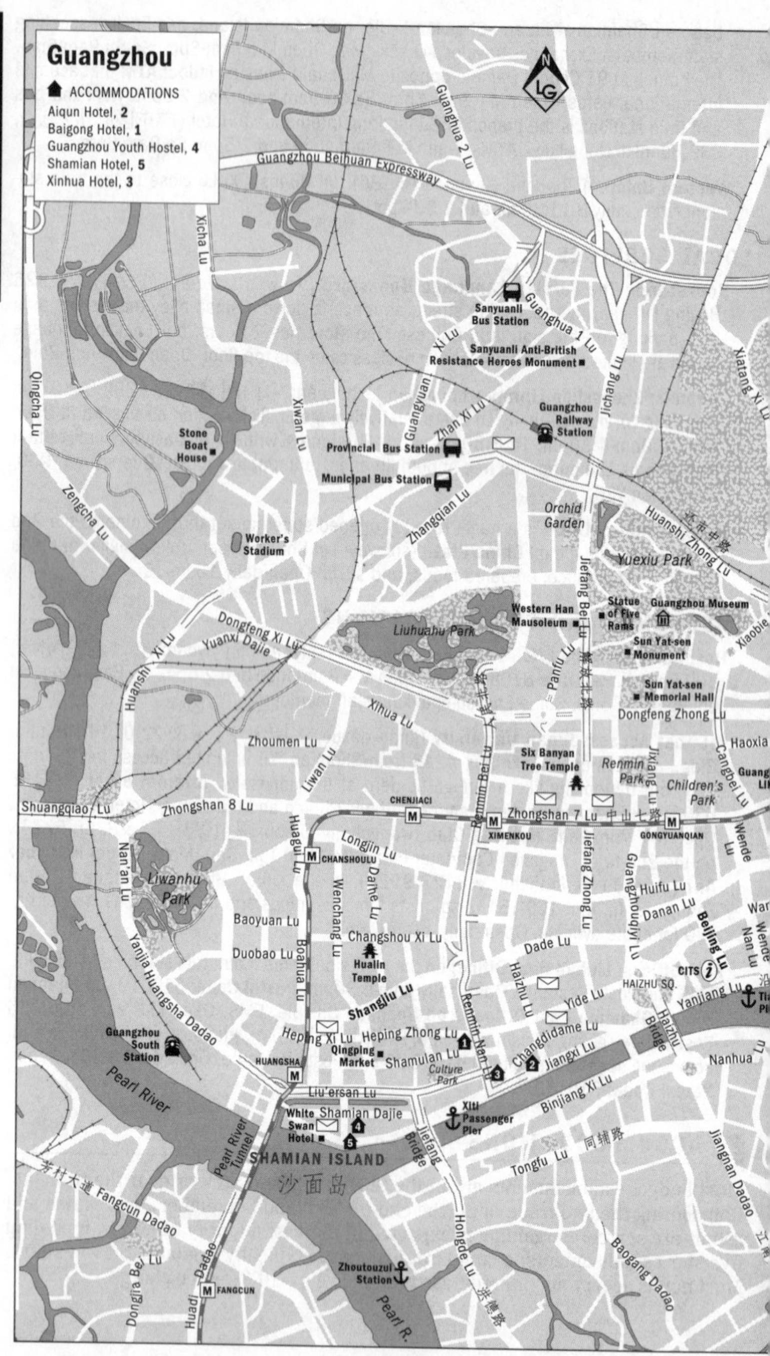
Guangzhou
ACCOMMODATIONS
Aiqun Hotel, 2
Baigong Hotel, 1
Guangzhou Youth Hostel, 4
Shamian Hotel, 5
Xinhua Hotel, 3
Guangzhou Beihuan Expressway
Guanghua 2 Lu
Xicha Lu
Sanyuanli Bus Station
Guanghua 1 Lu
Sanyuanli Anti-British Resistance Heroes Monument
Xi Lu
Jichang Lu
Xiatang Xi Lu
Qingcha Lu
Stone Boat House
Xiwan Lu
Guangyuan
Zhan Xi Lu
Guangzhou Railway Station
Provincial Bus Station
Municipal Bus Station
Zengcha Lu
Zhangqian Lu
Orchid Garden
Huanshi Zhong Lu
Worker's Stadium
Yuexiu Park
Jiefang Bei Lu
Statue of Five Rams
Guangzhou Museum
Western Han Mausoleum
Dongfeng Xi Lu
Yuanxi Dajie
Liuhuahu Park
Huanshi Xi Lu
Panfu Lu
解放北路
Sun Yat-sen Monument
Xiaobie
Sun Yat-sen Memorial Hall
Xihua Lu
Dongfeng Zhong Lu
Zhoumen Lu
Renmin Bei Lu
Six Banyan Tree Temple
Renmin Park
Jixiang Lu
Children's Park
Cangbei Lu
Haoxia
Liwan Lu
CHENJIACI
Shuangqiao Lu
Zhongshan 8 Lu
Zhongshan 7 Lu 中山七路
XIMENKOU
GONGYUANQIAN
Huagui Lu
Longjin Lu
CHANSHOULU
Daihe Lu
Wende Lu
Nan'an Lu
Liwanhu Park
Wenchang Lu
Jiefang Zhong Lu
Guangzhouqiyi Lu
Huifu Lu
Danan Lu
Baoyuan Lu
Changshou Xi Lu
Beijing Lu
Duobao Lu
Boahua Lu
Dade Lu
Hualin Temple
Haizhu Lu
CITS
Yanjia Huangsha Dadao
Shangjiu Lu
HAIZHU SQ.
Yanjiang Lu
Yide Lu
Guangzhou South Station
Heping Xi Lu
Heping Zhong Lu
Renmin Nan Lu
Changdidame Lu
Haizhu Bridge
Qingping Market
Shamulan Lu
Jiangxi Lu
Nanhua
HUANGSHA
Culture Park
Pearl River
Liu'ersan Lu
Binjiang Xi Lu
White Swan Hotel
Shamian Dajie
Xiti Passenger Pier
Jiefang Bridge
Pearl River Tunnel
SHAMIAN ISLAND
沙面岛
同辅路
Tongfu Lu
Jiangnan Dadao
芳村大道 Fangcun Dadao
Hongde Lu
Dongjia Bei Lu
Huadi Dadao
FANGCUN
Zhoutouzui Station
Pearl R.
Baogang Dadao

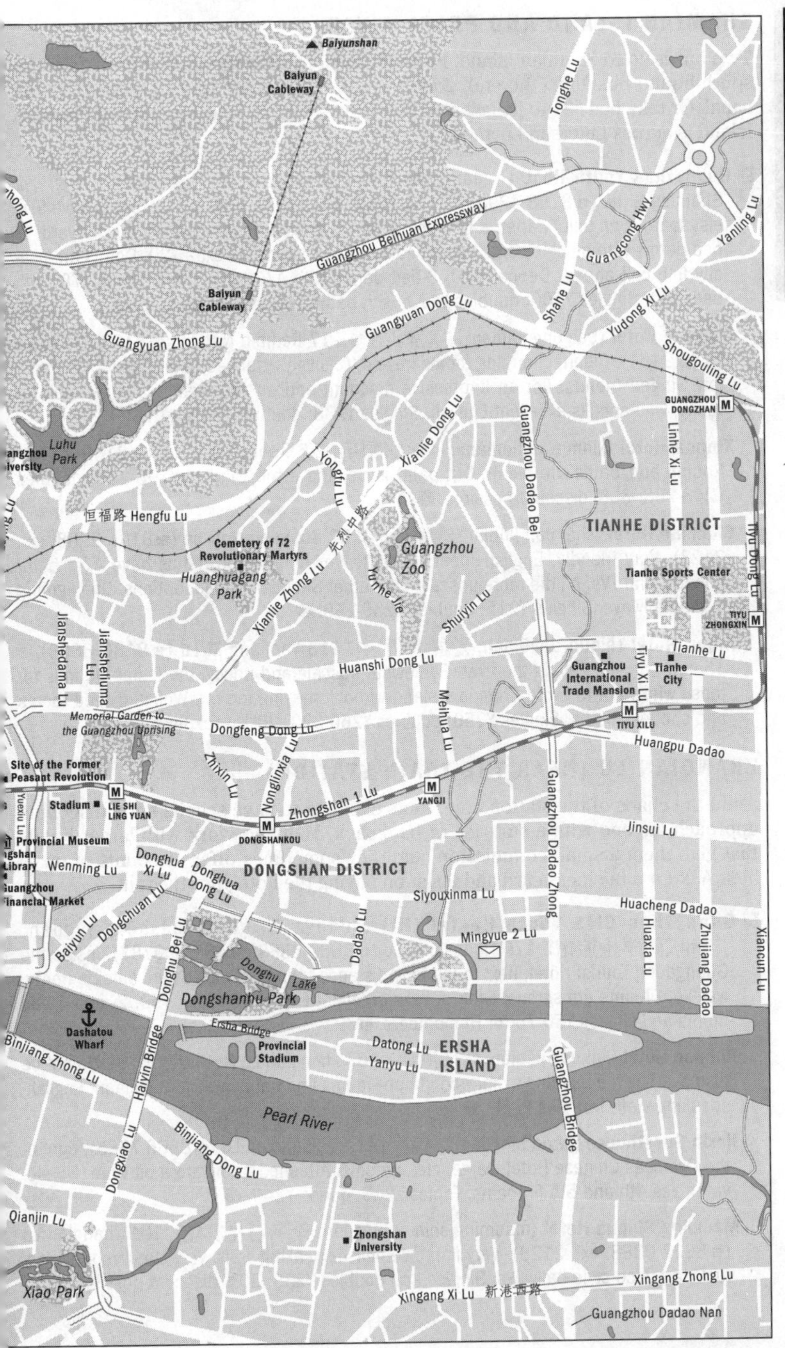

Baiyunshan
Baiyun Cableway
Guangzhou Beihuan Expressway
Baiyun Cableway
Guangyuan Zhong Lu
Guangyuan Dong Lu
Tonghe Lu
Guangcong Hwy.
Shahe Lu
Yanling Lu
Yudong Xi Lu
Shougouling Lu
GUANGZHOU DONGZHAN
Linhe Xi Lu
Luhu Park
恒福路 Hengfu Lu
Yongfu Lu
Xianlie Dong Lu
先烈中路
Guangzhou Zoo
Guangzhou Dadao Bei
TIANHE DISTRICT
Tianhe Sports Center
Tiyu Dong Lu
Cemetery of 72 Revolutionary Martyrs
Huanghuagang Park
Xianlie Zhong Lu
Yuhe Jie
Shuiyin Lu
TIYU ZHONGXIN
Tianhe Lu
Jianshedama Lu
Jiansheliuma Lu
Huanshi Dong Lu
Guangzhou International Trade Mansion
Tiyu Xi Lu
Tianhe City
Meihua Lu
Memorial Garden to the Guangzhou Uprising
Dongfeng Dong Lu
TIYU XILU
Huangpu Dadao
Site of the Former Peasant Revolution
Zhixin Lu
Nonglinxia Lu
Stadium
LIE SHI LING YUAN
Zhongshan 1 Lu
YANGJI
Guangzhou Dadao Zhong
Yuexiu Lu
DONGSHANKOU
Jinsui Lu
Provincial Museum
Library
Wenming Lu
Donghua Xi Lu
Donghua Dong Lu
DONGSHAN DISTRICT
Guangzhou Financial Market
Dongchuan Lu
Siyouxinma Lu
Huacheng Dadao
Baiyun Lu
Donghu Bei Lu
Dadao Lu
Mingyue 2 Lu
Huaxia Lu
Zhujiang Dadao
Xiancun Lu
Donghu Lake
Dongshanhu Park
Ersha Bridge
Dashatou Wharf
Haiyin Bridge
Provincial Stadium
Datong Lu
Yanyu Lu
ERSHA ISLAND
Guangzhou Bridge
Binjiang Zhong Lu
Pearl River
Binjiang Dong Lu
Dongxiao Lu
Qianjin Lu
Zhongshan University
Xiao Park
Xingang Xi Lu
新港西路
Xingang Zhong Lu
Guangzhou Dadao Nan

SHAMIAN ISLAND AND PEARL RIVER

Two buses go to Shamian Island. From Huanshi Lu near the train station, take the south-bound bus #5 to the end; go left out of the parking lot and cross over the canal. Or take bus #31 to its last stop at Culture Park; the eastern edge of Shamian Island is across Liuersan Lu and to the right.

Guangzhou Youth Hostel (guǎngzhōu qīngnián zhāodàisuǒ; 广州青年招待所), 2 Shamian Si Jie (☎8188 4298 or 8188 7912, ext. 3102). High-quality rooms have towels, soap, even toilet paper. 8-bed dorms on the ground floor face a small courtyard. 3-bed dorms with much cleaner communal baths are worth the extra Y20. Dorms are usually full; call ahead. Deposit Y50. 8-bed dorms with A/C Y50; 3-bed dorms Y70, with bath Y80. Singles Y100; doubles Y170, with bath Y190-210. Cash only. ❶

Baigong Hotel (báigōng jiǔdiàn; 白宫酒店), 13-17 Renmin Nan Lu (☎8188 2313; fax 8188 9161). Clean, charming rooms have A/C, lovely attached bath, phone, TV, and a few winged friends. For an impressive discount and an exuberant welcome, ask for Jenny, who speaks excellent English. Singles Y238; doubles Y318. ❸

Xinhua Hotel (xīnhuá dàjiǔdiàn; 新华大酒店), 2-6 Renmin Nan Lu (☎8188 2688). Rooms and baths are clean, but paint is peeling a bit. Singles Y198-228; doubles Y248-288. 30% discount possible. ❷

Shamian Hotel (shāmiàn jiǔdiàn; 沙面酒店), 52 Shamian Nan Jie (☎8191 2288, ext. 3123). Very friendly, English-speaking staff. Well-maintained rooms have A/C, bath, phones, and TVs. A little more upscale than other Shamian budget options. Dim lighting in the hallways. Singles Y215; doubles Y235-295. ❸

Aiqun Hotel (àiqún dàjiǔdiàn; 爱群大酒店), 113 Yanjiang Xi Lu (☎8186 6668), a 15min. walk east along the river. Somewhat upscale and pricey, the 3-star Aiqun is for those who want to avoid Shamian Island without straying too far. Well-furnished rooms and spotless baths. Singles Y250; doubles Y260-320. 20% weekday discount. ❹

ZHANQIAN LU (NEAR THE TRAIN STATION)

Amid the chaos of the station area, touts claiming to have special hotel discounts approach anyone with a suitcase or backpack. Many do work with larger hotels that give them a small commission, and they sometimes offer discounts of up to 50%. Ask for a business card and insist on paying the hotel, not the tout.

Guangzhou CITS Youth Hostel (HI) (guǎngzhōu guójì xuéshēng lǚguǎn; 广州国际学生旅馆), 179 Huanshi Xi Lu (☎8666 6889; fax 8667 9787), inside the Guangdong Tourist Hotel, next to the long-distance train station. Despite outside frenzy, well-kept rooms are serene. Staff speaks excellent English. Deposit Y50. 2- and 4-bed dorms and singles Y50-75 for HI members. ❶

Jinhuan Hotel (jīnhuán jiǔdiàn; 金环酒店), 103 Zhanqian Lu (☎8622 0510). Do not be dismayed by the building's dingy condition—rooms and baths are old but clean. English-speaking staff. Doubles Y160. ❷

Jiaxin Guesthouse (jiāxìn bīnguǎn; 嘉信宾馆), 92 Zhanqian Lu (☎8666 7888), right of the Overseas Chinese Hotel. Large, clean rooms. Attached baths are a bit worn. No elevator; yes 4th and 5th fl. rooms. Triples Y210; quads Y240. ❸

Maoming Shihua Hotel (màomíng shíhuà bīnguǎn; 茂名石化宾馆), 101 Zhanqian Lu (☎8622 0388, ext. 2128). Very friendly English-speaking staff. Very clean rooms. Very funky art-deco style hallways. Singles and doubles Y238. 30% discount possible. ❸

FOOD

It may be hotly disputed in China, but overseas, Guangzhou reigns as the seat of Chinese cuisine. Residents often quote the Chinese saying that a perfect life is "to be born in Suzhou, live in Hangzhou, eat in Guangzhou, and die in Liuzhou." Guangzhou's world-famous *dim sum* and snake dishes make dining an adventure, and those who enjoy unusual dishes will delight in delicious, exquisitely prepared meals for a pittance. Government-owned food stalls on every street corner boast the best deals; Y4-7 buys rice, a choice of three or four side dishes, and even soup.

SHAMIAN ISLAND

Lan Kwai Fong (lán guì fáng; 兰桂坊), 5 Shamian Nan Jie, Shamian Island (☎8191 9733 or 8192 1523). Hard to find, but not to worry—hostesses wait on Shamian Nan Jie to escort customers to this delicious Thai restaurant and bar. The food ranges from green curry (Y28) to prawns in leaves (Y38) to vegetable medleys (Y16-28). Try the *roti* with either pineapples or bananas. Even on weeknights, this place is overflowing with customers. Reservations are recommended. Open daily 11am-3pm and 5pm-4am. ❸

Shamian Coffee Shop (shāmiàn kāfēi wū; 沙面咖啡屋; ☎8190 7062), at the intersection of Shamian Nan Jie and Shamian Xi Jie, behind the White Swan Hotel; look for glass windows plastered with large red characters. Most backpackers in Shamian stop here at least once for tasty pig heart and intestines congee (Y6), steamed claws (Y8), deep-fried tentacles (Y10), or the much more exotic pan-fried Italian noodles (Y6.5). English menu available. Open daily 7:30am-1am. ❶

Kiumei Restaurant (qiáoměi shíjiā; 侨美食家), 52 Shamian Nan Jie (☎8188 4168), dishes up a culinary menagerie of Cantonese delicacies. Spiced pig's ear (Y28), fried frog (Y68), and fried sliced snake. The double-boiled crocodile with sea coconut (Y188) may not be available the day you visit, but there are certainly enough live specimens to keep things interesting. English menu. Open daily 11:30am-3pm and 5:30pm-4am. ❹

DOWNTOWN GUANGZHOU

Le Shanfang (lèshàn fáng; 乐膳坊), 8 Tongxin Lu, opposite the Bao Han Hotel (bǎohàn jiǔdiàn; 宝汉酒店; ☎8350 19191). Feast on the wonderful-smelling spicy eggplant, hot lamb, and oven-baked bread. Open daily 9am-midnight.

Black Swan Dumpling Jiaozi Restaurant (hēitiān'ér jiǎozi guǎn; 黑天鹅饺子馆; ☎8767 5687) has branches in the Gui Guan Building, 786 Jiefang Bei Lu, 2nd and 3rd floors (☎8354 8305) and at 486 Huanshi Lu, 2nd fl. (☎8757 5687). Hot, plump dumplings are dished up by the dozen to happy customers. No English menu, but "*jiǎozi*" will get you as far as you need to go. Y8-15 for a heaping plateful (vegetarian dumplings available). Open daily 9am-11pm. ❶

Monte Carlos, Yin Zheng Bldg., 338 Huanshi Dong Lu (☎8387 9146). Serves Russian borscht (Y10), African chili chicken steak (Y26), chicken curry and rice (Y16), congee, and pizza. Set meals Y26. The more daring can try a pot of frog with oyster sauce and rice (Y28). Open daily 9am-1:30am. Dance floor and performance space. Branches in the Financial Building, 199 Dongfeng Dong Lu, 1st fl. (☎8332 168, ext. 72131), and at 6 Siyou Xin Lu, 2nd fl. (☎8767 6136). ❷

SIGHTS

SHAMIAN ISLAND (shāmiàn dǎo; 沙面岛). At the beginning of the century, Shamian used to house all of Guangzhou's foreigners and their European-style customs and government buildings. These days, Shamian's wide, shaded streets are free from the incessant traffic that plagues the rest of Guangzhou. The displaced grace of Shamian architecture, its cobbled streets, and its elegant footbridge have an old-world, almost intoxicating charm. **Shamian Park** (shāmiàn gōngyuán; 沙面公园) overlooks the river. Especially popular at night, the park twinkles with electric lights along the rivers edge, where old men and women play dominoes, chess, and *mahjong*. The **Shamian Cultural Center** (shāmiàn wénhuà zhōngxīn; 沙面文化中心), 61 Shamian Bei Jie (☎8181 8558), hosts local art exhibits and has a free exercise room on the second floor.

PEARL RIVER (zhū jiāng; 珠江). Pearl River was once beautiful before industrialization and pollution set in, or so the locals claim. Regardless, Guangzhou residents still flock here to escape the grime and noise of the much more polluted city. In the morning, elderly men and women intently practice *tai chi;* in the evening, fishermen doze or wait beside their lines; and at night, neon signs and billboards flash frantically. The **Guangzhou Passenger Ship Tourism Company** (guǎngzhōushì kèlùn lǚyóu fēngōngsī; 广州市客轮旅遊分公司) at Xiti Wharf (☎8190 8190 or 8188 8932), and Tianzi Wharf (tiānzì mǎtóu; 天字码头; ☎8333 0397) on Yanjiang Lu, sells cruise tickets for river tours (6:30am-10:45pm, Y38). One-hour trips leave daily at 3pm from both wharfs; most travel agencies also sell tickets.

Shangjiu Lu (shàngjiǔ lù; 上九路), which becomes **Xiajiu Lu** (下九路), is lined with shops selling stationery, souvenirs, jewelry, shoes, and clothes. Companies hand out samples, hold contests for prizes, and put on zany shows. Pedestrians visit on weekends when the street is closed to traffic. From Shamian Island, head north past Qingping Market, away from the river for about 10 to 15 minutes.

QINGPING MARKET (qīngpíng shìchǎng; 清平市场). This market might as well be an edible zoo; a walk through it takes extreme patience and morbid curiosity. The innocuous herb and roots section closes in the late afternoon, but the poultry, fish, and meat markets farther north rage against the dying light. Everyday, 60,000 patrons visit this 2000-stall testament to the inclusive nature of Cantonese cuisine; snails, roaches, beetles, fish heads and guts, freshly killed chickens, and meat carcasses are all up for grabs. *(On the corner of Qingping Lu and Tiyun Lu, just north of Shamian Island. From Shamian, walk over the canal via the footbridge. The medicine section is at the outer fringe; the meat section lies farther in, along Shanmulan, Shibafu Nan Lu, and Tiyun Dong Lu. The wild game section is opposite the poultry street.)*

WHITE CLOUD MOUNTAIN (báiyún shān; 白云山). A popular sight for pollution-weary travelers and locals, this tidy hill draws nearly 1000 visitors a day who make the strenuous two-hour climb to the top. From the radio tower at the top, visitors can gasp their way past Qing dynasty officials' tombs, bamboo groves, and fragrant foliage. A concrete road leads to the entrance of a mountaintop park (Y5), with views of the airport, amusement park, and surrounding countryside. Side attractions include a **temple** (Y5), **Mingchun Bird Valley** (Y10), and a mountain **toboggan ride** (Y20-30) at the foot of the mountain. *(Accessible by bus #46.)*

YUEXIU PARK (yuèxiù gōngyuán; 越秀公园). The park guards the **Statue of the Five Rams** (wǔ yáng shíxiàng; 五羊石像), which Guangzhou residents have long seen as their city's emblem. A close look costs Y3. The **Guangzhou Museum** (guǎngzhōu bówùguǎn; 广州博物馆; ☎8354 5253 or 8666 2357) is housed in the beautiful **Zhenhai Tower,** which dates to 1380. *(Open daily 9am-5pm. Y10, children Y5.)* In the northwest corner of the park, the **Orchid Garden** (lán pǔ; 兰圃) is filled with over 10,000 pots and 200 varieties of orchids. The flowers bloom in fall and spring; in the dead of winter or in summer, you may end up staring at pots of dirt. *(Open daily 8am-9pm. Y8 includes tea in the central house near the ponds. On Huifu Xi Lu, near the main train* *station. Take bus #202 or 219 from the bus stop opposite the Xiti Wharf on Yanjiang Lu to the stop nearest to the huge crag or boulder on Jiefang Lu. Open daily 6am-9pm. Y3.)*

ZHONGSHAN LU 中山路

A walk along the route of the subway east on Zhongshan Lu leads to a few interesting sights in the heart of Guangzhou. **Six Banyan Tree Pagoda** (liùróng tǎ; 六榕塔) houses a multi-tiered pagoda surrounded by temples. *(Park Y1, pagoda Y6.)* The next stop, Gongyuanqian, is surrounded by a shopping bonanza that centers around **Beijing Lu** (北京路). Every night at 7pm, hundreds of stalls appear on **Xihu Lu** (西湖路) and the neighboring streets.

The **Site of the Former Peasant Movement Institute** (nóngjiǎng suǒ jiùzhǐ; 农讲所旧址; ☎8333 3936), on Zhongshan Lu next to the Guangzhou Library, preserves dormitory and study rooms and old photographs of famous students and peasant leaders on the walls. The exhibits feature limited English captions. *(Open daily 8-11:30am and 2-5pm. Y2.)* The **Memorial Garden to the Guangzhou Uprising** (guǎngzhōu qǐyì lièshì língyuán; 广州起义烈士陵园) houses a giant statue of a hand clenching a gun that casts a shadow over frightened tourists. The garden and tomb commemorate those who died during the Guangzhou Uprising of December 11, 1927. *(On Zhongshan Er Lu; subway: Lieshi Lingyuan. Open daily 6am-9pm. Y3.)*

NIGHTLIFE

Nightlife options in Guangzhou are numerous and varied: you can drink and dance, drink and sing karaoke, or just drown your sorrows in alcohol. From Shamian Island, cross Renmin Bridge and turn right; impromptu **riverside stalls** sell beer and soft drinks to customers lucky enough to grab a table. The more karaoke-oriented **Panfu Lu** scene, dominated by D&D Disco Two, keeps 'em singing all night long. The free magazine *That's Guangzhou* is in English, has extensive nightlife listings, and is available at hotels and stalls.

Windflower Music Pub, 387 Huanshi Dong Lu (☎8358 2446), next to the Holiday Inn. A choice hillside location helps make the Windflower a popular weekend hangout for Guangzhou's more sophisticated crowd. Don an all-black ensemble, and you'll be virtually indistinguishable from the other trendy patrons. Live Filipino band 4 times a week 10pm-1am. Drinks Y30-35, snacks Y20-25. Open daily 6pm-6am.

Peace Road Music Bar and Restaurant (hépíng lù jiǔbā; 和平路酒吧), 2 Heping Lu (☎8358 1720), just off Huanshi Dong Lu, next to the Holiday Inn. A friendly bar with outdoor garden seating. Live music downstairs (9:30pm-midnight) and burgers and pasta upstairs (Y15-28). Happy Hour 4-9pm and midnight-3am. Open daily 7pm-3am.

Voltage, Jinye Bldg., 422 Huanshi Dong Lu, 2nd fl. (☎8777 2888). A little tough to find; the entrance is tucked away nearly under the pedestrian overpass. Industrial-chic decor uses lots of orange and steel. Great live music. Beer Y20-30. Open daily 8pm-2am.

Face Club, 191 Dongfeng Xi Lu, in the basement of **International Bank Tower** (☎8388 0688). The dance floor gets pretty crowded, but this is still one of the best places in Guangzhou to strut your stuff, especially late at night after many other venues have closed. Music changes with the guest DJs. Open daily 8:30pm-2am.

Joe Bananas, 108 Tianhe Lu, on the 2nd fl. of the **Grand China Hotel** (jīnlái dàjiǔdiàn; 金来大酒店; ☎8559 3228, ext. 8222). The staff moves tables and chairs at night to give this small, newly-opened, laid-back bar a dance floor. Live Filipino band, Happy Hour specials provide a great excuse for midday binges. Open daily 2pm-2am.

FOSHAN 佛山 ☎0757

The quiet little town of Foshan is the birthplace of Cantonese Opera and a great place for visitors to take a breather after withstanding crowded Guangzhou.

ORIENTATION AND PRACTICAL INFORMATION. Visitors to Foshan will find almost all of their daily needs satisfied within a two-block commercial quadrangle bordered by **Qinren Lu** (亲人路) in the north, **Zumiao Lu** (祖庙路) in the east, **Chengmentou Lu** (城门头路) in the south, and **Fenjiang Lu** (汾江路) in the west. The main branch of **Bank of China** (☎224 3761) is on the corner of Renmin Xi Lu and Fenjiang Zhong Lu, and exchanges currency and traveler's checks. (Open M-F 8am-5:30pm, Sa-Su 9am-5pm.) Another branch on Zumiao Lu exchanges currency. (Open M-F 8am-5:30pm, Sa-Su 9am-5pm.) The **post office,** at 4 Qinren Lu, has EMS and Poste Restante. (Open daily 8:30am-9pm.) The **postal code** is 528000.

Most train transportation to and from Foshan is via Guangzhou. **Trains** run from the Foshan Train Station (fóshān huǒchē zhàn; 佛山火车站), in the north, to Guangzhou East Station (40min.; 8 per day; HK$180, 1st class HK$230), Hong Kong/Hung Hom Station (3hr., daily, HK$210), Shenzhen, and Zhaoqing. **Buses** from the Foshan Bus Station (fóshān qìchē zhàn; 佛山汽车站; ☎228 6700), on Fenjiang Lu, at the north end of town, run to Guangzhou (1hr., every 20min. 6:50am-6:25pm, Y11), Huizhou (3hr., 3 per day, Y55), Shenzhen (every 30min. 8am-7pm, Y75), and Zhongshan (14 per day, Y14). From the Zumiao Bus Station (zǔmiào qìchē zhàn; 祖庙汽车站; ☎222 0557 or 225 5409), on Chengmentou Lu, buses run to Guangzhou (1hr., every 15-20min. 7:30am-6:30pm, Y8-14), Shenzhen (2½-3hr., 2 per day, Y58), and Zhuhai (2 per day, Y42). **Local buses** (Y2) #1, 4, 6, 9, 11, and 12 run from the Foshan Train Station, past the Foshan Bus Station, to the Ancestral Temple. Another major local bus station is on Zumiao Lu, just opposite the Ancestral Temple. Base fare for **taxis** is Y7, and each additional km costs Y2.2-2.6. **Pedicabs** or **motorbikes** cost about Y5.

ACCOMMODATIONS AND FOOD. For those who fall in love with Foshan (or miss the last bus), the cheapest and most convenient place to stay is the **Foshan City Huasheng Hotel ❷** (fóshān shì huáshèng jiǔdiàn; 佛山市华盛酒店), 3 Fenjiang Lu, to the right of the Foshan Bus Station. It's old but decent. (☎228 7950. Singles and doubles Y55-150.) Another slightly more upscale option is the **Jiayue Hotel ❷** (jiāyuè jiǔdiàn; 嘉悦酒店), 2 Chengmentou Lu, next to Pizza Hut and amidst the action of Baihua Square. (☎222 2868. Top-floor doubles Y160.) Outside, a collection of restaurants and *dài pái dàng* (street-side cafes) presents a range of fried foods, meats, and pastry snacks. KFC, Pizza Hut, and McDonald's all cluster around **Baihua Square** (bǎihuā guǎngchǎng; 百花广场) at the intersection of Zumiao Lu and Chengmentou Lu. The **Mingren Cafeteria** (míngrén cāntīng; 名人餐厅) has Chinese fast food in a clean, brightly lit environment. (Open daily 8am-10pm.) The romantically lit **Rose Garden Coffee Shop ❷** (méiguì yuán kāfēitīng; 玫瑰园咖啡厅), 32 Zumiao Lu, serves small portions of everything from fried rice (Y15-18) to Holland cowboy steak (Y15). Ask for the daily buffet special or the four-course lunch set; English menu available. (Open daily 10am-midnight.)

SIGHTS. Foshan myth holds that a Daoist god, the Northern Emperor, rules the world's waters and holds considerable sway over the denizens of the flood-prone Pearl River region. Inside the serene, shady grounds of the **Ancestral Temple** (zǔmiào; 祖庙), a weapons collection guards the altar of this important emperor. Iron cannons from the 1840s, a life-sized carriage and boat, and an incredible collection of bonsai trees adorn the temple grounds. Inside the grounds across from the temple itself, the **Wanfu Stage,** decorated with beautiful and intricate gold inlay, is famed as the birthplace of Guangdong opera. A great little exhibit of Cantonese opera costumes and props is backstage. *(21 Zumiao Lu. Open daily 8:30am-7pm; last admission 6:30pm. Museum open daily 9:30am-4:30pm. Y20.)*

At the tiny **Renshou Temple** (rénshòu sì; 仁寿寺), on Zumiao Lu, a small but attractive tower is surrounded by a few traditional Chinese-style walkways and welcomes prayer at any of its three altars. The complex is in the process of slow renovation and is not loathe to accepting donations. *(Take bus #1, 5, or 11. ☎225 3053. Open daily 8am-5pm.)* Just north of the temple, the **Folk Art Research Institute** (mínjiān yìshù yánjiū shè; 民间艺术研究社) offers a chance to view (and buy) pricey hand-crafted items from all over China, including clothes, scarves, intricate paper cuttings, and carvings on jade, stone, and bone. The Institute was set up by the government in 1956 to promote and develop folk art. *(Open daily 9:30am-4:30pm.)*

ZHONGSHAN 中山 ☎0760

Yet another rapidly developing city, Zhongshan is unique for its strong connection to the early 20th-century reformist Sun Yat-sen. Most of the sights in this city involve the venerable leader; even the name Zhongshan is the Mandarin pronunciation of Yat-sen. About an hour east of Zhongshan, in Cuiheng, the Museum of the Former Sun Yat-Sen Residence gives everyone a chance to see the humble birthplace of the founder of the Republic of China (see p. 14). As for the city itself, Zhongshan stays bright even after the sun sets—electric and neon lights adorn every inch of available space, from pedestrian walkways to riverfront trees. An evening stroll along the newly constructed pedestrian street affords a glimpse of just how far Zhongshan has come since the glory days of its namesake.

ORIENTATION AND PRACTICAL INFORMATION

On the west side of the **Shiqi River** (shíqí hé; 石岐河), **Zhongshan Lu** (中山路) runs north-south. **Fuhua Dadao** (fùhuá dàdào; 富华大道) runs perpendicular to Zhongshan Lu, intersecting it near the Zhongshan International Hotel. On the east side of the river, Fuhua Lu becomes **Sunwen Xi Lu** (孙文西路), a beautifully paved pedestrian street that winds past pastel buildings, glossy shops, and pinewood benches. East of the pedestrian street, **Sunwen Zhong Lu** (孙文中路) continues to the commercial center of Zhongshan.

Buses: Zhongshan International Hotel Bus Station (zhōngshān guójìjiǔdiàn chēzhàn; 中山国际酒店车站; ☎863 2149), in the parking lot of Zhongshan International Hotel, on the corner of Zhongshan Yi Lu and Fuhua Lu. Buses to: **Guangzhou** (2hr., every 25min. 6am-6:30pm, Y30); **Hong Kong-Kowloon** (3hr., 4 per day, Y130); **Shenzhen** (2hr., every 30min. 7:40am-7:40pm, Y70); **Zhuhai** (50min., every 20min. 7am-7:20pm, Y15).

Local Transportation: The main bus stop (☎183 9831 or 183 9811) is on Sunwen Lu. Most **buses** run roughly 6am-10pm. Fare Y2-5. Aggressive **sampan** and **motorbike** drivers also wait impatiently to grab tourists (fares Y5 and up).

Taxis: Base fare Y7-8, each additional km Y0.5. A hotel taxi (available at Zhongshan International Hotel, on Zhongshan Yi Lu) to the Sun Yat-sen Residence costs Y30.

Travel Agencies: CTS, in the Fuhua Hotel, sells bus tickets to Guangzhou, Hong Kong, and Shenzhen. Open daily 8am-5:30pm. Credit cards accepted. **Zhongshan Traffic Travel Ltd.** (zhōngshān jiāotōng lǚxíngshè; 中山交通旅行社), directly across from the

Zhongshan International Hotel, where Zhongshan Yi Lu intersects Fuhua Lu. Friendly staff. Private car and driver to the Sun Yat-sen Residence Y70. Open daily 8am-6pm.

Bank of China: On the 1st. fl. of **Zhongshan International Hotel** (zhōngshān guójì jiŭdiàn; 中山国际酒店), on Zhongshan Yi Lu. Exchanges traveler's checks. Open daily 8:30am-5:30pm.

Post and Telecommunications: On Sunwen Lu, way past the Shiqi River. EMS and IDD service. Open daily 9am-12:30pm and 2-5:30pm. **Postal Code:** 528400.

ACCOMMODATIONS

Zhongshan's accommodations tend not to cater to budget travelers. Prices vary for weekday and weekend stays—a standard discount of at least 20% is given on weekdays. Most hotels accept major credit cards.

Tiecheng Hotel (tiěchéng jiŭdiàn; 铁城酒店), 107 Zhongshan Yi Lu (☎863 3803), at Sunwen Lu. Rooms are old but comfy, although windowless singles might leave you gasping for air. Singles Y140-185; doubles Y168. ❷

Xiangshan Hotel (xiāngshān jiŭdiàn; 香山酒店), 113 Zhongshan Yi Lu (☎863 4567). Charming rooms are clean and well-furnished, all with A/C and attached bath. Doubles Y160-260; triples Y350 and up. ❸

Zhongshan Jinyue Hotel (zhōngshān jīnyuè jiŭdiàn; 中山金悦酒店), 111 Zhongshan Yi Lu (☎862 2888), across the street from the Zhongshan International Hotel. Clean, perfumed rooms and easy access to Prince's Grill. Doubles Y460 and up. "Special offer" rooms begin at Y268. ❺

FOOD

Most hotels offer reasonably priced breakfast buffets; don't expect later meals to be such good deals. Along **Sunwen Zhong Lu,** across the river, cheap noodle shops and fast-food restaurants stay open past midnight. Noodle-weary appetites might appreciate the **McDonald's** and **Pizza Hut** on the Sunwen pedestrian street.

I Love You Cafe, 139 Fuhua Lu (☎862 6970). Large windows overlooking the street provide an abundance of light. Pine tables, tie-dyed bench covers, and a fresh atmosphere complement the 40 kinds of tea (Y15-18 per set), coffee, and floats. Open 10am-1am. ❷

Fuzhou Hotel (fùzhōu jiŭdiàn; 富洲酒店), 131 Fuhua Dao, 14th fl. A great breakfast buffet (7:30-10:30am). For Y20, it's all the *dim sum,* eggs, sausages, croissants, porridge, freshly squeezed fruit juices, and coffee you can eat. The friendly staff is eager to practice English. Lunch and dinner are also served daily. Open daily 7:30am-1am. ❷

SIGHTS

MUSEUM OF THE FORMER SUN YAT-SEN RESIDENCE (sūn zhōngshān gùjū; 孙中山故居). No trip to Zhongshan is complete without a visit here. Born in this village in 1866, Sun Yat-sen went on to head the movement that overthrew the last remnants of the Qing dynasty in 1912 (see p. 14). Visitors can gaze at the library that educated this future revolutionary, the kitchen that fed him, and the bed that cradled him. Behind the residence, another exhibit seeks to educate visitors about the living conditions of various social classes by reconstructing family homes—the wealthy family's home, the tofu-making home, and the overseas Chinese family's home are all worth a peek. The very clean, very new exhibition hall provides some truly fascinating insights into the history of Chinese nationalism and the character of Sino-Western relations, detailed in excellent English captions. *(In Cuiheng (翠亨). Bus #23 and bus #12 from the Fuzhou Hotel stop outside (approx. 1hr., Y3.5). Otherwise, take a taxi from the Zhongshan International Hotel; 30min., Y30. Y20.)*

OTHER SIGHTS. While the western bank of the Shiqi River is fairly tame, crossing the bridge and walking down the pedestrian thoroughfare of Sunwen Lu leads to a glamorous display of Zhongshan's new-found wealth. The riverbank area opposite the Fuhua Hotel becomes an impromptu **night market** from 8 to 11pm each night. A little farther east on Sunwen Lu (a 30min. walk from the Fuhua Hotel), **Sun Yat-sen Memorial Hall** (zhōngshān jìniàn guǎn; 中山纪念馆) pays homage to this city's most famous Sun. The hall hosts a number of local and international dance and music performances. *(☎882 2014. Open daily 8am-5pm. Y1.)*

ZHAOQING 肇庆 ☎0758

According to legend, the Seven Star Crags, Zhaoqing's primary attraction, formed when seven stars fell to earth and formed seven crags. For hundreds of years, these dramatic crags have inspired moving poems and essays, but the once-natural phenomena are now dressed in flashing light bulbs and are exorbitantly priced. Luckily, the crags are too big for even the Chinese tourism industry to completely destroy; the outer fringes of the crags remain free for all to walk or cycle through, and no one can charge for the stunning beauty of the crags as seen from afar.

TRANSPORTATION

Trains: Zhaoqing Train Station (zhàoqìng huǒchē zhàn; 肇庆火车站; ☎283 5114), north of town, a Y15 taxi ride from Duanzhou Lu. Bus #1 also runs from the train station to the city center. Ticket office open 24hr. To: **Guangzhou** (2-3hr., 11 per day, Y25) and **Hong Kong** (4½hr., 9:17am, Y300).

Buses: Zhaoqing City Bus Station (zhàoqìngshi qìchē zhàn; 肇庆市汽车站; ☎223 3629), on Duanzhou Lu, between Wenming Lu and Gongnong Lu. To: **Guangzhou** (2hr., at least every 30min. 6:20am-8pm, Y25); **Shenzhen** (3½hr., every 1-2hr. 8:20am-6:30pm, Y65); **Zhongshan** (2½hr., 3 per day, Y40); **Zhuhai** (3½hr., 2 per day, Y36-50).

Ferries: Zhaoqing Passenger Ferry Terminal (zhàoqìnggǎng kèyùn zhàn; 肇庆港客运站; ☎283 3231 or 226 9713), on Jiangbin Lu, a little hidden by the raised street surface. Walk or take bus #4, 5, 8, or 11 to the corner of Jiangbin Lu and Renmin Lu. Instead of taking the incline, stay on the level ground and head for the underpass. The road curves to the right as you face the river; the ferry terminal is on the right, after the bend. To **Guangzhou** (7hr., 1am) and **Wuzhou** (10hr., 9am and 11pm).

Local Transportation: Bus fare Y1-2 within the city center, Y3 on the outskirts. Aggressive **motorbike** drivers are always on hand; look for their colored helmets. Short trips approx. Y5. **Taxi** base fare is Y7, each additional km Y2.2-2.6.

ORIENTATION AND PRACTICAL INFORMATION

Zhaoqing is fairly small. Seven Star Crags and the train tracks define Zhaoqing's north border, and the **Xi River** (xī hé; 西河) marks its southern end. **Tianning Lu** (天宁路) houses tourists and their hotels, and **Gongnong Lu** (工农路) houses locals and their shops. These two streets are connected by **Jianshe Lu** (建设路) and **Duanzhou Lu** (端州路). The long-distance bus station is on Duanzhou Lu.

Travel Agencies: CITS, 46 Renmin Nan Lu (☎228 6038). On the corner of Duanzhou Lu and Tianming Lu is the **Star Lake International Travel Service** (xīnghú guójì lǚxíngshè;

星湖国际旅行社; ☎225 2033 or 223 5813), not to be confused with the Star Lake Travel Service opposite the memorial arch. Very helpful English-speaking service selling bus tickets to Guangzhou and Shenzhen (no commission). Open daily 8am-8pm.

Currency Exchange: The bank inside the **Star Lake Hotel** (xīnghú dàjiǔdiàn; 星湖大酒店), 37 Duanzhou Lu, exchanges traveler's checks. There is an international **ATM** just inside the hotel lobby, to the left. Open daily 7:30am-midnight.

Hospital: People's Hospital (rénmín yīyuàn; 人民医院; ☎283 3612).

Post and Telecommunications: On Jianshe Lu near its intersection with Wenming Lu. EMS. Open daily 7:30am-9:30pm. **Postal Code:** 526040.

ACCOMMODATIONS AND FOOD

Zhaoqing has plenty of hotels with plenty of fancy amenities; most offer discounts, but many also increase prices during the summer and on weekends and holidays.

Bakeries and tiny rice and noodle shops line **Gongnong Lu** and **Jianghe Lu.** A **night market** is on Wenming Lu, between Jianshe Lu and Qintian Yi Lu (open daily 8:30-11pm). At the northwest corner of Duanzhou Lu and Tianning Lu, **Texboy** ❶ (dézhōu niǔzǎi kuàicān; 德州牛仔快餐; ☎223 2952 or 223 3328) has swing-and-barrel seating, Western and Chinese fast food, and a ball set for kids. Staff members wear cowboy hats, plaid shirts, and bandanas—you might even catch a glimpse of the sheriff. (Noodle soups Y7; pizza Y6.50 per slice. Chinese set meals with rice, vegetable and meat dish Y13. Open daily 9am-11pm.)

Mount Dinghu International Youth Hostel (zhàoqìng dǐnghúshān guóji qīngnián lǚxíngguǎn; 肇庆鼎湖山国际青年旅行馆; ☎262 1668; fax 262 1665), at Dinghushan. Take bus #3 from Duanzhou Lu to Mt. Dinghu (the third-to-last stop); turn left at the traffic circle just ahead, and walk 10min. up the shop-lined road to the park entrance. Pay the park admission fee, hop on a park bus, and ask to be let off near the hostel (Y2); walk 10min. to the end of the road on your left; the hostel is on the right. Staff speaks exceptional English. The only downside to the hostel is that everytime you leave the park, you must buy another ticket to re-enter. Dorms have A/C, attached bath (except for the 14-person all-male dorm), lockers, toiletries, towels, and TV. Male-only 14-bed dorms and female-only 12-bed 2-bath dorms Y38; 8-, 6-, and 4-bed dorms Y38. ❶

The Seven Star Crags International Youth Hostel (HI) (☎222 6688; fax 222 4155). Take bus #19 to the Seven Star Crags Park; the hostel is outside the Middle Gate (zhōng mén; 中门). Management here also runs Mt. Dinghu Hostel and offers similar amenities in a slightly less removed setting. 4-bed dorms Y30, non-HI members Y50. ❶

Zhaoqing Friendship Guesthouse (zhàoqìngshì yǒuyì lǚguǎn; 肇庆市友谊旅馆), 45 Gongnong Lu (☎223 9298 or 223 2214). Large, clean rooms with fan, phone, and TV; and attached baths. Deposit Y50. Doubles Y60-118; triples Y90-138. ❷

SIGHTS

Zhaoqing's prime attraction, the **Seven Star Crags** (qīxīng yán; 七星岩), is said to mirror the pattern of the Big Dipper. The center of the crags has been made into a park with fishing and spelunking opportunities. Despite the unfortunate amount of kitsch, the park allows strolls along or even hikes up the crags. Romantics can hire a pedicab for a turn around the park (Y10). (Take bus #19 from the stop near the memorial arch, right below the Star Lake International Travel Service sign. ☎227 7724. Open 24hr.; tickets sold 7:30am-6pm. Y30.) Boats speed across **Star Lake** between the park and the dock (Y4-8), near **Seven Star Crags Memorial Arch.** On the corner of Duanzhou Lu and Tianning Lu, the arch frames the crag scenery from afar. Around 8pm every night, fountains near the arch shoot water into the air to the accompaniment of colored lights and music.

CLIMBING DINGHUSHAN MOUNTAIN

18km east of Zhaoqing. Take bus #3 (30min.-1hr., every 20min., Y3) from the bus stop on Duanzhou Lu, on the same side of the street as the Star Lake Hotel. Bus #3 (every 7min. 7am-10pm) to Zhaoqing leaves from the bus stop inside the park. Avoid going on weekends, when the park is crowded and bus tickets are hard to come by. Y30.

Dinghushan Mountain (dǐnghú shān; 鼎湖山) beckons as a challenge to hikers and makes for a worthwhile daytrip from Zhaoqing. Inside **Dinghushan Park** (dǐnghúshān gōngyuán; 鼎湖山公园), a concrete path winds up the mountain, revealing spectacular views of the farmland. Side routes farther up the mountain or through the woods lead to small clearings, beautiful waterfalls, and ponds. The main road passes fancifully named lakes like **Leaping Dragon Pool** and **White Goose Pond**, as well as snack stands that irregularly dot the road. Those who tire halfway can always hop on a motorbike (Y5-10). Most visit Dinghushan for its lovely **White Cloud Temple** (báiyún sì; 白云寺), a two-hour walk up the mountain from the bus stop. (Open daily 8am-5pm.)

Some travelers, enthralled by the clean air and gorgeous scenery, choose to stay a little longer at Dinghushan. The **tourist office** sells maps (Y5). The **restaurant** ❶ across the tourist office offers an English menu with dishes such as pork dumplings (Y8 for 6) and vermicelli. (Open daily 7am-2pm and 5-8pm.) Chinese fast food stands and picnic benches under the colored umbrellas are just down the road.

SHAOGUAN 韶关 ☎0751

The select few who choose to stop in Shaoguan on their way north out of Guangdong province will encounter a city that lacks the glitz and wealth of many of its South Coast neighbors—there's not a single McDonald's in sight. But Shaoguan makes up for its lack of neon lights with scenic wonders, and the surrounding area holds some of the most impressive natural and historical treasures in Guangdong, namely Danxiashan and Nanhua Temple.

TRANSPORTATION

Trains: Shaoguan Train Station (sháoguān huǒchē zhàn; 韶关火车站; ☎888290-2692), on Nanshao Lu at the Qujiang Bridge, just across from the terminus of Jiefang Lu on the peninsula. To: **Foshan** (3hr., daily, Y39); **Guangzhou** (2½-3hr., 6 per day, Y36); **Shantou** (14½hr., 2 per day, sleeper Y102-129); **Shenzhen** (5hr., daily, Y52).

Buses: Shaoguan Bus Station (sháoguān qìchē zhàn; 韶关汽车站), on Gongye Xi Lu, just east of the peninsula. To **Zhuhai** (8hr., daily, Y80) via **Guangzhou** (4hr.).

Local Transportation: Most **buses** stop at the train station square. **Taxi** base fare is Y4, but not all taxis are metered. **Motorbike** and **sampan** drivers charge about Y3.

ORIENTATION AND PRACTICAL INFORMATION

Shaoguan straddles a peninsula at the confluence of the **Wu River** (wǔ jiāng; 武江) and the **Zhen River** (zhēn jiāng; 浈江). **Fengdu Lu** (风度路) runs north-south, dividing the peninsula in half; perpendicular to Fengdu Lu are **Fengcai Lu** (风采路) and **Jiefang Lu** (解放路). Fengcai Lu is a busy shopping street full of boutiques, *dài pái* *dàng* (streetside food stalls), and restaurants. Jiefang Lu leads to the train station just off the peninsula to the east, across the bridge.

Travel Agency: Guotai Travel Agency (guótài lǚxíngshè; 国泰旅行社; ☎822 3993), in the Guotai Hotel, on the north side of the train station. Sells train tickets for a Y5 commission. Open daily 8:30am-noon, 2:30-5:30pm, and 7-10pm.

Bank of China: 158 Jiefang Lu (☎888 8338, ext. 212). Exchanges traveler's checks 3-5pm daily. The branch to the right of the train station exchanges currency only. Both open daily 8am-5:30pm.

Internet Access: Cultural Palace Internet Bar (wénhuàgōng wǎngbā; 文化宫网吧), inside the Wenhuagong building. Walk under the stone archway across the street from the Shaoguan Hotel (162 Jiefang Lu, across the bridge from the train station). The entrance to Wenhuagong is just ahead on the left, flanked by two stone lions. The bar is inside, to the right. Over 100 terminals. Y3 per hr. Free tea may be provided.

Post and Telecommunications: To the right when you exit the train station. EMS and Poste Restante. Open daily 8am-9:30pm. **China Telecom** has IDD service half-price after 9pm. Open daily 8am-10:30pm. **Postal Code:** 512023.

ACCOMMODATIONS

The cheapest accommodations are clustered around the train station square.

Gangdu Hotel (gǎngdū jiǔdiàn; 港都酒店; ☎812 2223), to the right as you exit the train station. It's the large, pink building obscured by billboards. Cheap rooms. Singles Y40-68; doubles Y60-98; triples Y120-128. ❶

Guotai Great Hotel (guótài dàjiǔdiàn; 国泰大酒店; ☎888 8999), to the left as you exit the station. Ongoing renovations have caused price increase and room selection shrinkage. Only two kinds of rooms are available: clean doubles with attached bath and A/C, and "luxury" double suites with little to merit the price. Doubles Y200-400. 20% or more discount available. 6% tax. ❸

Shaohua Hotel (shàohuá jiǔdiàn; 韶华酒店), 162 Jiefang Lu (☎888 1870, ext. 3888), across the bridge from the train station. A warm welcome to Shaoguan, with English-speaking staff. Clean, well-kept rooms have A/C, bath, refrigerator, and TV. An excellent Cantonese restaurant and gym on premises. Just 3min. away from what may be the largest Internet cafe you'll see in your life. Singles Y260; triples Y350. Major credit cards accepted. 20% discount. ❸

FOOD

Finding good, cheap food in Shaoguan is relatively easy. The ubiquitous Y5 *dà pái dàng* (streetside food stalls; 大排挡) are out in full force around the peninsula and north of the train station. **Shaoguan Restaurant Fast Food** ❶ (sháoguān jiǔjiā kuàicān; 韶关酒家快餐), 2 Xunfeng Lu, just off Jiefang Lu, serves dishes for Y5-13. (Open daily 10:30am-8:30pm.) Fast-food joints as well as smaller, pricier restaurants cluster around the mall on **Fengcai Lu.** Many hotel restaurants offer surprisingly good deals in the form of all-you-can-eat buffets (usually Y15-40).

SIGHTS

Shaoguan's sights can easily be seen in a day or two. Travel agencies organize one- or two-day tours, but it's easier and cheaper to rely on public transportation.

DANXIASHAN MOUNTAIN (dānxiá shān; 丹霞山). Danxiashan Mountain features some of the most stunning scenery in the Pearl River basin. Cliffs are mist-covered in the morning, and their red sandstone walls blaze all day. Ride a cable car to the top for Y35. *(About 1hr. north of Shaoguan. Take the pink buses (Y10) that depart from Jiefang Lu just beyond the Shaohua Hotel. The last minibus back to Shaoguan leaves around 6pm (Y15); if you miss it, take a minibus to Yunhe city and negotiate a taxi ride back to Shaoguan (Y50-100). Y43, including access to hiking trails and temples.)*

LION CRAG (shīzi yán; 狮子岩). The crag's great claim to fame is **Maba Man,** the bones of an early *Homo sapien* that dates to 600,000 BC. Admission includes a brief walking tour of the caves and a guide who describes (in Chinese) Maba Man's use of tools and division of labor. The bones and artifacts have been moved from the cave to a run-down museum to the right of the path that leads to the crag. Poorly proportioned clay statues of Maba Man and his family at work and play are just plain tacky. Still, the surrounding countryside and the crag itself are picturesque. Beware of bats on your climb into the caves. *(South of Shaoguan, outside the town of Qujiang (曲江; known as Maba). From the Shaoguan Train Station, cross the bridge to the peninsula; the bus stop is past the pedestrian overpass on the left. Blue buses (30min., every 15min., Y3) go to Maba. Open daily 8am-7:30pm, last admission 5:30pm. Y10, museum Y5.)*

NANHUA TEMPLE (nánhuá sì; 南华寺). This rather enormous temple at the base of Baolin Mountain is famous as the nexus of Zen Buddhism (see p. 29). Built in AD 502, the temple has acquired a rather impressive collection of relics, including the 2m wide "1000 Man Pot" cast in AD 191 that is still used to feed the monks on occasion. Also on display is a 1.2m drum that causes the enormous 10,000kg bronze bell in the bell tower to resonate. The temple is best known for its sixth patriarch, Huineng, an illiterate monk whose teachings later developed into Zen Buddhism; a statue of Huineng supposedly cast from his body sits in the back hall. Zhouxi Spring, where Huineng used to wash his robes, runs behind the temple; nine old cypress trees stand nearby. *(Minibuses take 30min. and cost Y10, while taxis cost around Y50 and leave from Shaoguan Train Station. Buses return to Shaoguan daily until 6pm. Open daily 8am-5pm. Y10.)*

ZHUHAI 珠海 ☎0756

For many tourists crossing the China-Macau border at Zhuhai, the city is but a brief stopover. Those who stay longer come to understand why it is a stomping ground of choice for wheelers and dealers, whether at work or at play. The privileges bestowed on Zhuhai as a Special Economic Zone have made it a hub of free enterprise of all kinds: Zhuhai's streets are filled with bargain-basement-priced electronics, food stands, and young women hoping to catch the eye of a visiting businessman. Few residents seem to notice the setting of the sun amidst the glare of flashing neon lights. Restaurants, karaoke bars, and hotels field a steady stream of customers all night long.

TRANSPORTATION

Flights: Zhuhai Airport (zhūhăi jīchăng; 珠海机场; ☎889 5494), on the peninsula southwest of Gongbei. Airport buses leave from the Zhangzhou Bldg. near Gongbei Market, or from the Xiangzhou Bus Station (40min., every 30min., Y20). A taxi to the airport costs Y100; ask for a flat rate. **Zhuhai Airlines** (zhūhăi hángkōng gōngsī; 珠海航空公司), 34 Yuehai Dong Lu (☎889 7881). Smiley Kong speaks excellent English. Open 24hr.; call first after 10pm. To: **Beijing** (1-2 per day, Y1550); **Kunming** (1-3 per day, Y900); **Shanghai** (1-3 per day, Y1150).

Buses: The best way to leave Zhuhai is by bus. **Gongbei Bus Station** (gǒngběi qìchē zhàn; 拱北汽车站), 1 Lianhua Lu or 1 Shuiwan Lu, (☎888 8554), adjacent to the Yongtong Hotel, has buses to **Zhongshan** (1hr.; every 30min. 9:10am-7pm; Y16, weekends Y18). **Xiangzhou Long-distance Bus Station** (xiāngzhōu chángtú qìchē zhàn; 香洲长途汽车站; ☎222 5345), on Shuiwan Lu, next to the Gongbei Palace Hotel, has buses to: **Guangzhou** (3hr.; every 30min. 7am-7pm; Y35, A/C minibus approx. Y50); **Guilin** (12:30pm, Y80); **Haikou** (2 per day, Y165); **Xiamen** (2pm, Y200).

Ferries: Jiuzhou Ferry Terminal (jiǔzhōu gǎng kèyùn zhàn; 九州港客运站), on Jiuzhou Lu in Jida. Take bus #4 from the border crossing to the Jiuzhou Gang stop. To: **Hong Kong** (1hr., 5 per day 8am-5pm, info ☎333 2113); **Jiuzhou Island** (1½-2hr., 1-2 per day); **Shenzhen** (1hr., approx. every 15min. 7:50am-6pm., info ☎333 3359).

Local Transportation: Buses are cream-colored with red lettering. Stops are marked by signs or a large orange pagoda roof. Most routes serve **Gongbei Bus Station** near the Macau border. Fare Y1, with A/C Y2. Bus **#2** runs along Yingbin Nan Lu and Jingshan Lu, from Xiangzhou to Lianhuashan to Gongbei; **#4** runs from the Xiangzhou Long-distance Bus Station to the Gongbei Long-distance Bus Station, passing the Gongbei Market and the Jiuzhou Ferry Terminal.

Taxis: Base fare Y10, each additional km Y2.40. **Complaints:** ☎226 2628.

ORIENTATION AND PRACTICAL INFORMATION

Zhuhai is divided into three districts: **Gongbei** (拱北), the main tourist district, borders Macau; **Jida** (吉大), the site of the ferry terminal and the famed mermaid statue; and **Xiangzhou** (香洲), to the north. **Shuiwan Lu** (水湾路) and **Yingbin Nan Lu** (迎宾南路) run through Gongbei and Jida. Two very good bilingual maps (about Y5), the *Zhuhai Tourist Map* and the *Tour and Transportation Map of Zhuhai*, are available at the border crossing and in most hotels and bookstores.

Foreign travelers to Zhuhai need **Chinese visas.** Visas can be obtained abroad before departure (see p. 50) in Hong Kong (see p. 533) or Macau (see p. 562).

Travel Agency: CTS (☎888 5777), on the corner of Yingbin Lu and Lianan Lu, next to the Overseas Chinese Hotel. More a ticket office than a travel agency; plane tickets are offered, but not tours. Open daily 8am-7pm.

Bank of China: 1148 Yuehai Dong Lu (☎888 3333), on the corner of Yingbin Lu and Yuehai Dong Lu. US or Hong Kong dollars are easiest to exchange. Also exchanges traveler's checks. Open M-F 8:30am-noon and 2-5pm, Sa-Su 9am-noon and 1:30-4pm. Hotels usually charge exorbitant exchange fees.

Bookstore: Xinhua Bookstore, on Yingbin Dadao in Gongbei, sells 3 maps of Zhuhai, and a limited selection of highly-abridged English classics. Open daily 9am-9:15pm.

Hospitals: People's Hospital (rénmín yīyuàn; 人民医院; ☎222 2571), on Kangling Lu, and **Gongbei Hospital** (gǒngběi yīyuàn; 拱北医院), 2 Lianhua Lu (☎888 5463), next to the Lianhua Hotel. Both are open 24hr. and have some English-speaking staff.

Internet Access: Fireflies (yínghuǒchóng; 萤火虫), 2091 Fenghuang Lu, 2nd fl. (☎212 5007), next to the Bank of Communications, opposite the bus #4 terminus (Xiangzhou). Y3 per hr.

Post and Telecommunications: Yuehai Post and Telecom, 1043 Yuehai Dong Lu (☎887 1821 and 336 8831, ext. 185), a few blocks east of the Guangdong Hotel. EMS and IDD service. Open daily 8am-8pm. **Postal Code:** 519020.

ACCOMMODATIONS

Most accommodations in Zhuhai cater to wealthy tourists and businesspeople. Discounts of 10-40% are often available to anyone who asks. Unless otherwise noted, major credit cards are accepted. Be forewarned that most hotels demand a deposit of at least twice the price of the room.

Zhuhai International Youth Hostel (HI) (zhūhǎi guójì xuéshēng lǚguǎn; 珠海国际学生旅馆; ☎333 3838; toll-free reservation hotline 800 830 8000; www.zhuhai-holitel.com), on the luxuriant grounds of the Zhuhai Holiday Resort Hotel on Shihua Mountain. Take bus #4 from central Zhuhai to the hotel; a free shuttle runs from the hotel to the hostel. The best deal in Zhuhai. Clean and comfortable rooms have A/C and bath. Reservations recommended. 5-bed dorms Y50, non-HI members Y60. ❶

Overseas Chinese Hotel (huá qiáo bīnguǎn; 华侨宾馆; ☎888 6288), on Yingbin Nan Lu, past Lianan Lu. Clean, comfortable rooms with dark wood paneling, plus a friendly staff, Tang-dynasty restaurant, gym, and CTS office next door. If you can squeeze out a discount, this is certainly the best value for your money. 13% service charge. Singles Y286-338; doubles Y438. 10% increase on weekends, 30% on holidays. ❹

Gongbei Hotel (gōngběi jiǔdiàn; 拱北酒店), 36 Lianhua Lu (☎888 5260). Do not be misled by the simple lobby—rooms are elegant, airy, and filled with sunlight. Deposit Y300. Singles Y300; doubles Y320. 60% discounts possible. ❹

FOOD

Most hotel restaurants serve *dim sum* and are home to Western-style cafes or coffeehouses. At night, food vendors set up makeshift tables and chairs and serve simple but tasty meals (Y10-20, beer Y7-10). *Da Pai Dang* ("street food stalls"; dà pái dàng; 大排档) are numerous, particularly along the Xiangzhou coastline and in Gongbei on **Yuehai Dong Lu** and **Yingbin Lu.** In the evening, cooks wheel carts down the streets, serving tea and snacks for Y2-3. Stall owners are friendly, but most don't speak English.

Chinese Food Street (zhōngguó dàshíjiē; 中国大食街), on the 2nd fl. of the Overseas Chinese Hotel. A not-to-be missed culinary lesson in Cantonese cuisine. Waiters in Tang-dynasty clothes pour jasmine tea and guide newcomers around the buffet (Y30) of over 80 delicious dishes. Open daily 11am-9:30pm. ❷

Haili Seafood Restaurant (hǎilì hǎixiān cāntīng; 海利海鲜餐厅; ☎888 9813), on Yuehua Lu, near McDonald's. Around 6pm, plastic tables and chairs come out and the sidewalk is transformed into a crowded outdoor restaurant. Lots of seafood. Open 24hr.

SIGHTS AND ENTERTAINMENT

If you're not shopping or belting out karaoke tunes, there's little to see or do in Zhuhai. Hop on bus #9 from the Gongbei Bus Station at the Macau border and ride it to the Jida district; here you can find Zhuhai's famed **mermaid statue,** a representation of a fishing girl handling a pearl. Near the intersection of Haijing Lu, Haibin Lu, and Lingshan Lu is **Shijingshan Tourist Centre** (shíjǐngshān lǚyóu zhōngxīn; 石景山旅游中心). Climb the stone steps up Mt. Shijing for magnificent views of Xianghu Bay. The **Lost City Water Park** (mènghuàn shuǐchéng; 梦幻水城), visible from the New Yuan Ming Palace, has a wave pool, waterfall, and river. *(Open daily noon-9pm. Y80, Y40 with purchase of palace admission.)*

Zhuhai almost never sleeps. Most of the night action is contained in the triangular region of Gongbei, between Yingbin Lu and Shuiwan Lu; a generous selection of discos and clubs thrill revelers from nearby Macau. Every night around 6pm, **Gongbei Market** (gǒngběi shìchǎng; 拱北市场) appears out of nowhere to hawk everything from watches to lingerie. *(Take bus #4 to Gongbei Shichang.)* When the market shuts down around 10pm, business picks up at the numerous karaoke clubs on the second floor of every hotel in town.

SHENZHEN 深圳 ☎0755

Other Chinese cities enjoy Special Economic Zone (SEZ) status, but none takes the title quite as seriously as Shenzhen. The well-tended city jets ahead of the rest of China in the quest to be just like Singapore, Seoul, Tokyo, and, most of all, its neighbor Hong Kong. The streets are straight and clean, the buildings tall and shiny, and the general atmosphere bustling and rich. Hong Kong natives in pursuit of entertainment flock to the region on weekends and holidays to spend time and money in the colossal theme parks nearby. This daytime host to theme park-visiting families is also a nighttime haven for weekend revelers seeking cheaper and more outrageous thrills than those of neighboring Hong Kong. Unfortunately, prosperity has left some people behind and jarringly out of place, and Shenzhen is also home to gaunt beggars and entire families of bare-bottomed children who try their hardest to tweak the heartstrings of even the city's most hardened capitalists.

TRANSPORTATION

Flights: Shenzhen International Airport (shēnzhèn guójì jīchǎng; 深圳国际机场; ☎777 6555), in the northwestern Baoan district. Take bus #330 from Hualian Mansion on Shennan Zhong Lu, west of Lizhi Park, or minibuses #501 and 507. **CAAC ticket office,** Huachang Sanyo Bldg., 1007 Huachang (☎377 9800), sells domestic tickets 20% discounts usually available. Open M-F 8am-6pm, Sa-Su 9am-4:30pm. To: **Beijing** (3 per day, Y1400) and **Tianjin** (2 per day, Y1290). **Shanghai Airlines,** 18 Shandu Lu (☎3240 1431), is open daily 8am-5pm. To: **Chengdu** (5-6 per day, Y1130) and **Shanghai** (9-10 per day, Y1120). **Eastern Airlines** (zhōnggúo dōngfāng hángkōng gōngsī; 中国东方航空公司; ☎322 7740), in the Chinese Airlines Building, 1st fl., at Huaqian Lu and Hongli Lu. Open daily 8:30am-5pm. Several flights per day to **Beijing** (Y1400) and **Shanghai** (Y1120).

Trains: (See also **Border Crossing into Hong Kong: Shenzhen,** p. 504.) **Shenzhen Train Station** (shēnzhèn huǒchē zhàn; 深圳火车站; ☎232 8647, ticket office ☎232 5043), on Jianshe Lu, a giant building connected to the customs and immigration office and the bus station by covered walkways. Electronic information kiosks in Chinese and English. Open daily 5:50am-10pm. To: **Beijing** (24hr., 2 per day, Y616); **Changsha** (10hr., 4 per day, Y291-354); **Guangzhou** (1hr., every 10-35min. 6am-9pm, Y40-70); **Guilin** (14½hr., daily, Y358); **Shaoguan** (5hr., daily, Y89); **Shanghai** (26½hr., daily, Y541); **Shantou** (9¾hr., daily, Y300).

Buses: (See also **Border Crossing into Hong Kong: Shenzhen,** p. 504.)

Luohu Bus Terminus (luóhú qìchē zhàn; 罗湖汽车站; ☎233 7378 or 232 1670), in the same complex as the train station. Most buses to **Guangzhou** depart from the basement level of the station (2hr., every 4min. 6am-10pm, Y60). Tickets sold on the 2nd fl. Open daily 7am-6pm. To: **Chaozhou** (4½hr., 3 per day, Y160); **Foshan** (2½hr., every hr. 8am-7pm, Y75); **Huizhou** (1½hr., every 15min. 7am-7pm, Y30-35); **Shantou** (4hr., every 30min. 8am-8pm, Y150); **Xiamen** (9½hr., 4 per day, Y187); **Zhaoqing** (3hr., every hr. 8am-6pm, Y90).

Shenzhen City Bus (☎540 9465 or 541 5107) services direct **Hong Kong-Shenzhen** routes. The Qiaoshe Bus Station between the Overseas Chinese Building and the Regency Overseas Chinese Hotel on Heping Lu has long-distance A/C luxury coach buses to most destinations in Guangdong Province and buses to Fuzhou, Xiamen, and Quanzhou in Fujian Province.

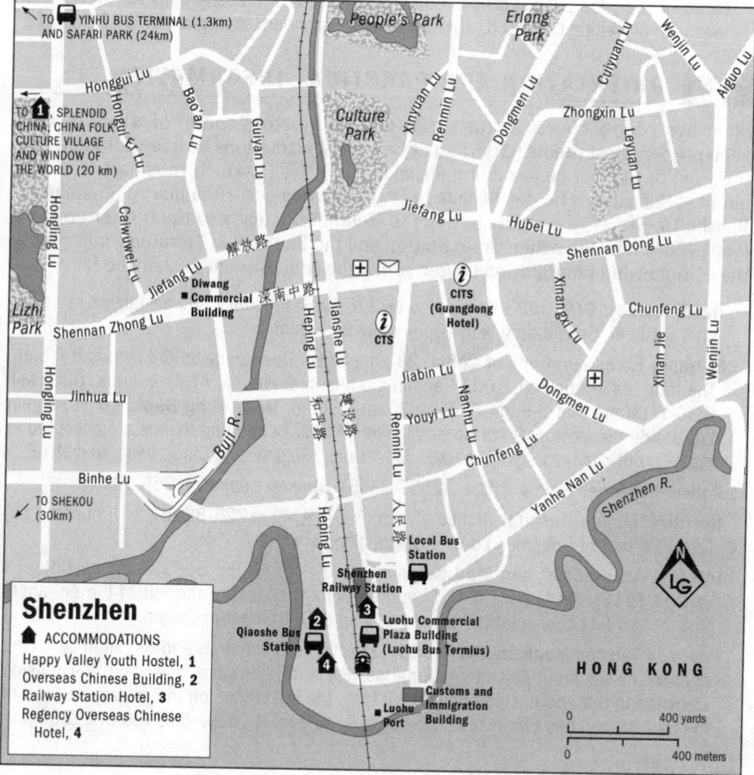

A/C double-decker bus runs from the Shenzhen Bay Hotel to **China's Hong Kong City** (3:45, 4:45, and 5:15pm). The same bus stops by the Shangri-La Hotel, near the border crossing (every 30min. 4:30-6pm). Ticket prices vary (M-F HK$65-150, children HK$45-110, depending on starting point; weekend prices rise HK$20). Credit cards accepted.

Ferries: The most convenient way to enter and exit Shenzhen is by bus or train. For those who prefer a scenic route, the nearest port to Shenzhen is **Shekou Port** (shékǒu gǎng; 蛇口港; ☎669 5600). From Shenzhen, take bus #113, heading west on Shennan Lu (Y6), or bus #204 or 217. From here, boats go to **Haikou** (16hr., Su-F 4pm, Y218-458) and **Zhuhai** (1hr., every 15-30min. 7:30am-6pm). The **ticket office** (☎669 1213), in the domestic ferry bldg., sells tickets 10 days in advance to **Hong Kong** (50min., 10 per day 7:45am-9:30pm, HK$90-125) and **Macau** (1½hr., 11am, HK$87).

Local Transportation: Many local A/C **buses** stop at the parking lot near the train station and the Luohu Commercial Plaza. Bus fares are based on the number of stops—tell the fare collector your destination. All the routes are posted in both English and Chinese. Buses within the city usually bear single- or double-digit numbers (Y1-3); buses with triple-digit numbers go far from the center (Y2-12). Bus **#3** runs down Shennan Lu, and **#101** and **113** (7am-7pm) follow Shennan Lu past the theme parks to Shekou. **Minibuses** (Y2-5) post the destination in the front window; red minibuses stay within the SEZ and green minibuses go beyond the border.

Taxis: Possibly the priciest taxis in China. Base fare Y12.5, each additional 250m or 45 seconds of waiting time Y0.6. 30% surcharge 11pm-6am. **Complaints:** ☎322 8111.

ORIENTATION AND PRACTICAL INFORMATION

Shenzhen county covers a broad area, the southeastern corner of which is Shenzhen proper. Most theme parks and other tourist attractions lie a few kilometers to the west of the city center along **Shennan Lu** (深南路), which runs east-west past many of Shenzhen's hotels. **Renmin Lu** (人民路) runs perpendicular to Shennan Lu. **Jianshe Lu** (建设路), roughly parallel to Renmin Lu, leads to the border crossing (see p. 504). The Shenzhen Train Station and the Luohu Bus Terminus, adjacent to the customs and immigration center, are at the southern end of Jianshe Lu.

Travel Agency: CTS, 3023 Renmin Lu (☎225 5888), usually has an English-speaking staff member. Sells train tickets. Open daily 9am-6pm.

Currency Exchange: Bank of China, 23 Jianshe Lu. Open daily 8:30-11am and 2-5pm. The train station branch, 1009 Renmin Lu, has international **ATM**s indoors. Open M-F 8:30-11:30am and 2-5pm, Sa-Su 9:30am-3:30pm. **Hong Kong Bank,** 1015 Renmin Lu, beside the Century Plaza Hotel, also has **ATMs.** Hong Kong dollars are accepted in the city, but change is given in RMB. Most bank ATMs service Cirrus, Plus, and NYCE.

Police: Shenzhen Police Office (☎557 6355). **Shekou** branch (☎669 1011).

Hospital: Liuhua Hospital (liúhuā yīyuàn; 流花医院; ☎223 8826), on Chunfeng Lu, just northeast of Dongmen Lu. English-speaking staff.

Internet Access: Net and Mud (wǎngluò níbā; 网络泥巴), 5033 Shennan Dong Lu (☎207 3513). On the 1st fl. of Shenzhen Book City, just to the left of the entrance. Reasonably fast connections. Y6 per hr. Open daily 8:30am-midnight.

Post and Telecommunications: At the intersection of Jianshe Lu and Shennan Lu, to the right of the hospital. For international service and telephone calls, take the outside staircase to the 2nd fl. Open daily 8am-7pm. The post office on the mezzanine level of the train station has EMS. Open daily 8am-8pm. **Postal Code:** 518000 or 518001.

ACCOMMODATIONS

With the exception of the Happy Valley Youth Hostel, just about every hotel in Shenzhen is of the luxury kind with a price to match.

Regency Overseas Chinese Hotel (huáqiáo jiǔdiàn; 华侨酒店), 1009 Heping Lu (☎559 6688; fax 558 3779). As you exit the train station, take the escalator up the pedestrian overpass to your left; the hotel is just across the street. The Overseas has slightly small, elegant rooms, and nice baths. 10% service charge. Singles Y258; doubles Y298. 30% discount may be available on weekdays. Credit cards accepted. ❹

Happy Valley Youth Hostel (HI) (☎694 9443; fax 694 9046). Across the street from the theme park, a large rainbow-colored sign indicates the entrance to the Happy Valley Plaza. Enter, bear right, and walk up the road for about 5min. Turn left into the plaza parking lot; the hostel will be on your right, opposite the bus terminal. From the train station, take minibus #473 (Y3) to the last stop or take bus #101 (40min., Y4) to Window of the World Theme Park. Dorms, all with bath and shower, are squeaky clean. Hot water 5:30pm-midnight. Lockers in every room. In the summer, reservations are recommended. 6-bed dorms Y50, non-HI members Y55; doubles Y170/180. ❶

Overseas Chinese Building (huáqiáo dàshà; 华侨大厦), 1043 Heping Lu (☎556 4762), across from the Regency Overseas Chinese Hotel on the same side of the street. People fresh off the bus constantly stream across the lobby. Standard rooms are fairly clean. 4-bed dorms with shared bath Y45; singles Y238; doubles Y138-268. 20% discount may be available, usually on weekdays. ❶

Railway Station Hotel (huǒchē zhàn dàjiǔdiàn; 火车站大酒店; ☎232 1168), in the New Railway Station Bldg. on Jianshe Lu. Just a little farther from the train station. Large, well-furnished rooms. 10% service charge. Singles HK$238; doubles HK$268. ❸

FOOD

Visitors to Shenzhen who join the crowds from the **theme parks** will be rewarded with exotic dining experiences for exorbitant prices. In the city center, most establishments are either fast-food joints or expensive restaurants. One mid-range chain restaurant, **Sandra** ❷ (xiānlè dū; 仙乐都), 1068 Heping Lu, has Asian-style Western food, from steaks (Y30-48) to "french frices" (Y18). (Open daily 8am-2am.) Along **Jianshe Lu,** McDonald's and **Cafe de Coral** join the fray. **Diwang Commercial Building,** on Shennan Zhong Lu, midway between Jianshe Lu and Hongling Lu, brings together several fast-food and Western restaurants, including the **Hard Rock Cafe.** Cheap eateries and cafeterias abound at the **train station.**

SIGHTS AND ENTERTAINMENT

Shenzhen, with no natural attractions of its own, usurps those of the rest of the world. Theme parks **Splendid China, China Folk Culture Village,** and **Window of the World** are all within walking distance of one another, but try the **Happy Line** anyway; the monorail circles the three sights and the Shenzhen Bay Hotel (Y35 between any 2 of its 7 stops). Nightlife in Shenzhen leaves the budget traveler in the dust; although discos and karaoke bars abound, they are pricey and often cater to wealthy vice-seeking businessmen rather than to common travelers.

CHINA FOLK CULTURE VILLAGE (zhōngguó mínsú wénhuà cūn; 中国民俗文化村; ☎660 0626, ext. 2020). This village was set up to teach visitors about China's many minority nationalities, and it does a surprisingly good job. It highlights the different techniques and materials used by the Bai, Dai, Dong, Mongolian, and other villages to build homes, furniture, and farming tools. Some of the other displays, such as the "Guanyin Buddha Making Her Presence," tend to be more hokey. Mini-cars with drivers run between villages (10min. drive HK$10/Y10, 1hr. drive with stops HK$150/Y150). Frequent minority drumming and dancing shows culminate in a large evening performance that most feel is well worth the extra money (7:30 and 8:30pm, Y15-20). Visitors can dress up in ethnic costumes (Y10-20) and participate in staged wedding rituals or create handicrafts. A food street (Y5-10) offers a taste of Sichuanese, Dai, Cantonese, and Northern Chinese cuisines. *(Accessible by bus #101 or 113. Free wheelchairs and baby carriages. Open M-F 10:30am-9pm, Sa-Su 10:30am-11pm. M-F Y85, Sa-Su Y80; children 1.1-1.4m tall and ages 65-69 half-price. Combination ticket with Splendid China M-F Y145, Sa-Su Y155.)*

WINDOW OF THE WORLD (shìjiè zhī hù; 世界之户). Wildly popular among Hong Kong natives and Chinese, this theme park seeks to unite the world under the global banner of kitsch. A walk through the well-landscaped park affords glimpses of the world's famous landmarks in wide variations of scale—the Eiffel Tower is impressively tall, but be careful not to trip over Notre Dame. The Taj Mahal, the Golden Gate Bridge, the Louvre, the Pyramids, and the Grand Canyon also adorn the park, and the International Street to the right of the entrance is crowded with restaurants offering everything from Viennese coffee to German sauerkraut to Turkish kebabs. *(From Shekou or Shenzhen, take bus #101 or 113 (45min., Y4) to near the*

Eiffel Tower or the Golden Gate Bridge. Open daily 9am-10:30pm; last admission 9pm. M-F Y100, Sa-Su Y110; children 1.1-1.4m tall and ages 65-69 half-price.)

SPLENDID CHINA (jǐnxiù zhōnghuá; 锦绣中华). In the words of President Jiang Zemin, Splendid China hopes "to make the world get close with China." Unfortunately, miniature versions of the Great Wall, Terracotta Warriors, Forbidden City, Seven Star Crags, and the Yangzi's Three Gorges leave a little too much to the imagination. The costumes, festivals, and houses of the Bai, Dai, Hakka, and Northern Shanxi peoples are also on display. *(Take bus #101 or 113 from the train station to Shenzhen Bay Hotel. Open daily 8:30am-6pm. M-F Y70, Sa-Su Y80; children 1.1-1.4m and ages 65-69 half-price. Combination ticket with China Folk Culture Village M-F Y130, Sa-Su Y150.)*

BORDER CROSSING INTO HONG KONG: SHENZHEN

The border is open daily 6:30am-11:30pm. To enter **Hong Kong** (see p. 525), take a train from Shenzhen (see p. 500) to Kowloon Tong (in Tsim Sha Tsui East, see p. 535), Hung Hom Station (see p. 528), or cities in the New Territories (see p. 552). The customs office abuts the Lo Wu KCR station on the Hong Kong side. To get into **Shenzhen** or any mainland destination, a valid Chinese visa is required; get one at the Hong Kong CTS office for a hefty commission or at the Chinese Visa office in Hong Kong (see p. 532). When entering Shenzhen County by **bus,** visitors must show valid travel documents. Chinese citizens may have to disembark briefly to go through inspections. Foreign passport holders usually stay on the bus. showing passports to an official, but sometimes they, too, must accompany the official to the inspection counter. In Hong Kong, **trains** depart for Shenzhen from Hung Hom Station (depart daily 5:45am-10:19pm) or the Lo Wu KCR Station (daily 6:01am-12:20am).

SHANTOU 汕头 ☎0754

Shantou today is the vision of China's dreams for the future. The country's first Special Economic Zone, this city is rich and it shows. Monstrous, gleaming skyscrapers and condominiums pop up at an alarming rate, Western fast food restaurants are a dime a dozen, and Mercedes Benzes cruise down the wide, tree-lined streets. Wander into the old city area, however, and you'll see a living reminder of the rough and tough past that Shantou is trying so hard to cast away. As a former untamed frontier and British trading port, the old city area still bears all the raggedness of its rowdy past. Decaying colonial buildings, complete with Grecian columns and elaborate carvings, fight for space with rows of stalls in the chaotic, jam-packed narrow streets. As you soak in the sea breeze, you will feel the energy, both old and new, that so marks the atmosphere of modern Shantou.

TRANSPORTATION

Flights: Shantou Airport (shàntóu guójì jīchǎng; 汕头国际机场; ☎862 6678), 15km northeast of central Shantou. From the airport, a shuttle bus takes you to the city (30min., evey hr. 6:30am-5:30pm, Y4). Taxis cost about Y50. The **CAAC ticket office,** 83 Jinsha Lu (☎825 1915), 3 blocks west of the main Bank of China. To: **Beijing** (11:50am and 5:10pm, Y1150-1250); **Guangzhou** (many per day, Y580); **Hong Kong** (8:40am and 4:55pm, Y1020); **Shanghai** (many per day, Y780).

Trains: Shantou Train Station (shàntóu huǒchē zhàn; 汕头火车站; ☎881 6487), on Taishan Lu, at the eastern edge of city. Open daily 7am-7:30pm. Accessible by buses

#2, 4, 6, 8, 11, and 12. Taxis to the station from western Shantou costs about Y35. To: **Guangzhou** (11hr., 7:06pm, Y125-224) and **Shenzhen** (9hr., 6am, Y119-328).

Buses: Shantou Passenger Transit Station (shàntóu qìchē kèyùn zhàn; 汕头汽车客运站; ☎810 2757), on Chaoshan Lu, north of Huoche Lu, 7km from the train station. Connects to Jinsha Lu by bus #4 and to Zhongshan Lu by bus #7. Open daily 6am-1am. To: **Fuzhou** (1:40, 2, and 8:30pm; Y120-140); **Guangzhou** (6hr.; every 10min. 12:25am-11:50pm; Y85-110, express Y150); **Xiamen** (4-5hr.; 9am-6:20pm; Y45-85, express Y90).

Local Transportation: Most **buses** run approx. 6am-10:30pm. Fare Y2. Buses **#2, 4, 6, 8, 11,** and **12** terminate at the train station in the far east of the city; buses **#2, 4, 6,** and **18** run along Jinsha Lu. **#11** runs from the old city dock area and along the commercial thoroughfare of Jinsha Lu. Private **minibuses** run the same routes (Y2), but are often in worse condition.

Taxis: Base fare Y8, each additional km Y2.6; with A/C base fare Y9, each additional km Y2.8. **Pedicabs** to most destinations within city center Y5-8. Motorcycle taxis are also common, but take the seat at your own risk.

ORIENTATION AND PRACTICAL INFORMATION

Shantou is vast, sprawling on the northern bank of its **harbor** (shàntóu gǎng; 汕头港) in the far north of Guangdong province. The old town center is in the southwestern end around a tiny peninsula and consists of several small streets that converge at traffic circles. The most important of these is fed by **Shengping Lu** (升平路), **Minzu Lu** (民族路), and **Anping Lu** (安平路). From the old town, the larger streets of **Wai Malu** (外马路) and **Zhongshan Lu** (中山路) run eastward into the newer parts of town. The new areas seem to have spread north and east at such a rapid pace that there is no well-defined city center. **Jinsha Lu** (金砂路) runs east-west through the city, and is a major commercial avenue, with many hotels, fast-food restaurants, and banking services.

Travel Agency: Shantou Travel Agency, 41 Shanzhang Lu (☎862 9888), in the same complex as the Overseas Chinese Hotel. 1st fl. office books local tours and tickets. Tours Y108 per day. No commission for air tickets; Y10-30 fee per train ticket.

Bookstore: Xinhua Bookstore, 26 Lian Lu (☎827 7021), just opposite the Xinhua Hotel. A limited selection of classics. Open M-F 8am-5:30pm.

Bank of China: 98 Jinsha Lu (☎826 2955), just east of the Golden Gulf Hotel. Take buses #2, 4, or 6 to Jinhaiwan Dajiudian. Exchanges currency and traveler's checks (counters #8 and 9). Credit card advances on Cirrus/MC/Plus/V. Counters open M-F 8:30-11:30am and 3-5:30pm; bank open M-F 8:30am-noon and 2:30-5pm.

PSB: 11 Yuejing Lu (☎827 2275), off Nanhai Lu, south of Wai Malu, west of the No. 2 Hospital in the old part of town.

Hospital: People's No. 2 Hospital (dì'èr rénmín yīyuàn; 第二人民医院), 28 Wai Malu (☎827 2765), east of Shengping Lu. Take bus #1 to Shengping Lu.

Post Office: Shantou Post and Telecommunications Office, 147 Wai Malu, 1st fl. (☎828 9495), in a massive building 1 block from the Xinhua Hotel. EMS. Open 24hr.

ACCOMMODATIONS

Off-season discounts are possible in Shantou, but keep in mind that prices are usually exorbitant to begin with. Budget travelers should consider spending the night in Chaozhou (see p. 507).

Xinhua Hotel (xīnhuá jiǔdiàn; 新华酒店), 121 Wai Malu (☎827 6734). In the old city area, accessible by bus #10, 11, 12. The Xinhua is slightly creaky and old, but the floors gleam and the flock of matrons running the place provide some maternal warmth. A/C, TV and bath. Doubles Y150-170; triples Y220-250. 20-30% discounts possible; students will have better luck. ❷

Swatow Peninsula Hotel (tuódǎo bīnguǎn; 鮀岛宾馆), 36 Jinsha Lu (☎831 6668; www.pihotel.com). Take bus #4 or 11 from the bus station or #2, 4, 6, or 11 from the train station to Jinsha Gongyuan. Beautiful standard rooms, with minibars, glass cabinets, and a faultlessly attentive staff. Ask for rooms with a view of Jinsha Park (they cost the same anyway). Doubles Y388 and up, suites Y788. Except during the national holidays in May and Oct., doubles are more likely to be Y240. AmEx/DC/MC/V. ❺

Qiaolian Hotel (qiáolián dàshà; 侨联大厦), 39 Shanzhang Lu (☎825 9109 or 825 0108); the non-descript building just around the corner from the Overseas Chinese Hotel. All rooms have A/C and TV; more expensive rooms have attached baths. Conveniently located communal baths are well-maintained. Singles Y65; doubles Y91-234; triples Y137-273. 30-40% discounts possible year-round. ❶

FOOD

Shantou, urban city-with-a-mission, has no official sights, and even the local CTS seems to have resigned itself to that fact. To get away from Shantou, take a 20-minute bus ride to the old town area, an interesting, aging neighborhood with small streets crammed with tatami mat vendors, vegetable stalls, and an entirely different feel from unabashedly modern Shantou. *(From the train or bus stations or from anywhere on Jinsha Lu, take bus #11 to Xiti Harbor (xītí gǎng; 西堤港).)* **Xiti Lu** (西堤路) runs north and is lined with crumbling, wooden European buildings left over from the British treaty days. Watch the harbor and picture the colonial ships that must have once rolled in here. **Anping Lu** and **Shengping Lu** run east off Xiti Lu and are brimming with local markets that sell fresh cilantro and bamboo shoots. Any of the little streets around here are good places to sniff out small restaurants that serve flat white rice noodles and delicious boiled pork and cabbage dumplings. For dessert, an absolute must-try is the **yam-paste with gingko nuts**, a thick, ultra-sweet concoction that will put a smile on your face.

CHAOZHOU 潮州 ☎0768

Chaozhou may be just 39km north of Shantou, but for all practical purposes it is a mere satellite of its more businesslike neighbor. Lacking Shantou's gleam and *nouveau riche* glamor, Chaozhou instead boasts crusty alleyways and bustling food markets lined with racks of poultry and clumps of fresh green tea leaves brought in from the countryside. Hollering vendors and early-morning revelers take full advantage of the somewhat grotty snack stands that stay open until dawn. Chaozhou is at its best in the maze of streets near the ancient city and Kaiyuan Temple. Intimate and crammed with Buddhist paraphernalia, these sleepy streets provide a welcome change of pace from the rest of breakneck Guangdong province. Don't count on staying too long in Chaozhou—it doesn't have any exciting tourist sights—but certainly indulge in its calming pleasures for a day or two.

ORIENTATION AND PRACTICAL INFORMATION

The old city walls stretch along Chaozhou's eastern border along the **Han River** (hán jiāng; 韩江), between **Huancheng Bei Lu** (环城北路) in the north and **Hua-**

ncheng Nan Lu (环城南路) in the south. **Kaiyuan Lu** (开元路) also runs west from the wall, about halfway between Huancheng Bei and Nan Lu. **Xi Malu** (西马路) runs just north of and parallel to Kaiyuan Lu. **West Lake** (xī hú; 西湖) and the sprawling **West Lake Park** (西湖公园) are not far west of the northern portion of the wall, bordered to the east by **Huancheng Xi Lu** (环城西路). From Huancheng Xi Lu, **Xihe Lu** (西河路) branches southwest and **Yonghu Lu** (永护路) branches off Xihe Lu. These two roads have many hotels and street-side stalls.

Trains: Chaozhou Train Station (cháozhōu huǒchē zhàn; 潮州火车站; ☎685 3708), off Xinfeng Lu, 7km southwest of the city. Pedicab rides from here to the old city cost about Y10. Ticket office open daily 6:30-7:50am, 8-11:30am, 2-5:20pm, 5:50-7:40pm, and 9-10:30pm. Train ticket stands throughout the city sell tickets for a Y5 commission. To: **Guangzhou** (11hr., 3 per day 8:38am-7:46pm, Y70-193); **Meizhou** (2hr., 5 per day 6:58am-1:58pm, Y19-39); **Shenzhen** (14hr., 6:28pm, Y116-208).

Buses: Chaozhou Long-distance Bus Station (cháozhōu chángtú qìchē zhàn; 潮州长途汽车站; ☎220 6052), on Chaofeng Lu, southwest of West Lake and 1km west of the city wall. Open daily 6:30am-12:30pm. To: **Guangzhou** (6½hr., 5 per day 8:20am-11:30pm, Y50-190); **Shantou** (1hr., every 20min. 6:30am-7:30pm, Y10); **Zhuhai** (3:50pm, Y110).

Local Transportation: Pedicabs are the norm here; professional drivers wear yellow helmets and vests. Most places in the old city Y5.

Travel Agency: CITS, 77 Chaofeng Lu (☎228 4177), 2 blocks west of the bus station. The staff always seems to be out to lunch or in a meeting. Try private travel agencies, which can be found in most hotels; several are located prominently along Chaofeng Lu, near the mythical CITS. Open M-F 8-11:30am and 2:30-5:30pm.

Bank of China (☎286 3020), along Yonghu Lu, about 10min. from the Chaozhou Binguan. Exchanges US and Hong Kong dollars. Open daily 8-11:30am and 2:30-5pm. The Chaozhou Hotel's business center also exchanges US currency.

Hospital: Central Hospital (zhōngxīn yīyuàn; 中心医院), 84 Huancheng Xi Lu (☎222 4092, emergency 222 4868), just north of Xi Malu. Open 24hr.

Postal Code: 521000.

ACCOMMODATIONS

Discounts and bargaining are possible at virtually all establishments year-round (except during the national holidays in May and Oct.). It may be possible to convince the hostels near the bus station to accept foreigners. All listings have rooms that feature air-conditioning, bath, and TV.

Chaozhou (Binguan) Hotel (cháozhōu bīnguǎn; 潮州宾馆; ☎226 1168), on Chaofeng Lu, opposite the front entrance of the long-distance bus station. Standard rooms are cheery and bright. A helpful staff, attention-grabbing red roofs, and generous discounts make this one of the sweeter deals in town. Doubles Y358 and up; triples Y428 and up. In Nov.-Apr., June, and Sept., prices fall to Y138 and Y288, respectively. ❺

Chunguang Hotel (chūnguāng dàjiǔdiàn; 春光大酒店; ☎226 1211), opposite the Chaozhou Hotel. Rooms have A/C, bath, TV, and a nice view. Doubles Y168; triples Y195. ❸

Chaozhou (Dajiudian) Hotel (cháozhōu dàjiǔdiàn; 潮州大酒店), 26 Xihe Lu (☎220 2128). A slew of clean, newly renovated standard rooms. Check that the price quoted to you is the price so prominently displayed. Doubles Y100-150; triples Y130-205. 15% surcharge for foreigners. ❷

SOUTH COAST

FOOD

Chaozhou, home of one of China's famed regional flavors, gets creative with its food. The flour-and-vegetable staples of the north have been traded for the tasty tripe and cow-tongue exoticisms of the coast. Chaozhou also serves up delicacies like smoked pigeon and lake-grown vegetables, local specialties gathered from the neighboring mountain area. Two items certainly worth experiencing are the **goose with plum sauce** and a post-meal tea that is served in tiny porcelain tea cups. Chaozhou is most famous, however, for its **braised meats. Yonghu Lu,** the road leading south from Chaofeng Lu past the Chaozhou Hotel, is full of street stalls that dish up liberal doses of small clams and salted vegetables, favorite pre-meal appetizers.

SIGHTS

The stretch of Kaiyuan Lu near the Kaiyuan Temple features the best shopping in town; electronics stores sit comfortably alongside merchants selling Buddhist silk brocades, banners, wooden and gilded sculptures, and precious jewelry and jade. In general, prices are the farther the store is from the temple proper.

KAIYUAN TEMPLE (kāiyuán sì; 开元寺). One of Chaozhou's quiet gems, this spacious temple is hidden along the older, narrow section of Kaiyuan Lu. Visitors can admire the ornate, intricate temple structures in one of the least-contrived environments around. A large and active temple, Kaiyuan has halls filled with golden deities that surround elegant, well-maintained courtyards, providing a pleasant respite from the merciless Chaozhou sun. Not to be missed is the **Guanyin Pavilion** (guānyīn gé; 观音阁), to the left of the main courtyard, which is dedicated to the Buddhist Goddess of Mercy. *(32 Kaiyuan Lu, about 5min. west of the city walls. From the long-distance bus station, take Huancheng Xi Lu south from the southern tip of West Lake, and take a left at Kaiyuan Lu, the first major street. Kaiyuan Lu becomes a smaller lane; the temple is on the left about 200m beyond. Open daily 8am-6pm. Y5.)*

MEIZHOU 梅州 ☎0753

The charms of Meizhou are infinite and varied. Since it's not one of China's better known cities, Meizhou has yet to suffer the indignities of a tourist boom, and residents continue to chatter in their distinct Hakka dialect, a strangely melodious tune that Mandarin speakers have difficulty understanding. Although it was originally one of Guangdong's poorest regions, today's Meizhou has a refined elegance all its own. It possesses the quiet splendor of old colonial buildings tastefully scattered throughout the old city, the mannered grace of courteous motorists on the streets, heart-breakingly well-tended tea fields, and most of all, the subtle refinement of its people. This city won't bowl you over with spectacular sights or scenery, but it does know a thing about class.

TRANSPORTATION

Flights: Meizhou Airport (méizhōu jīchǎng; 梅州机场; ☎224 2666), at Sanjiao Di Lu, 2km south of the city center. CAAC office (☎224 2716). To **Guangzhou** (M and F 1pm, W 6:20pm; Y460) and **Hong Kong** (M and F 9:45am, Y1420).

Trains: Meizhou Train Station (méizhōu huǒchē zhàn; 梅州火车站; ☎231 1742), on Binfang Dadao at the southernmost edge of the city. Accessible by bus #6 from Jiangnan Lu. Ticket window open daily 8:05am-7:50pm. To: **Chaozhou** (3hr., 5 per day,

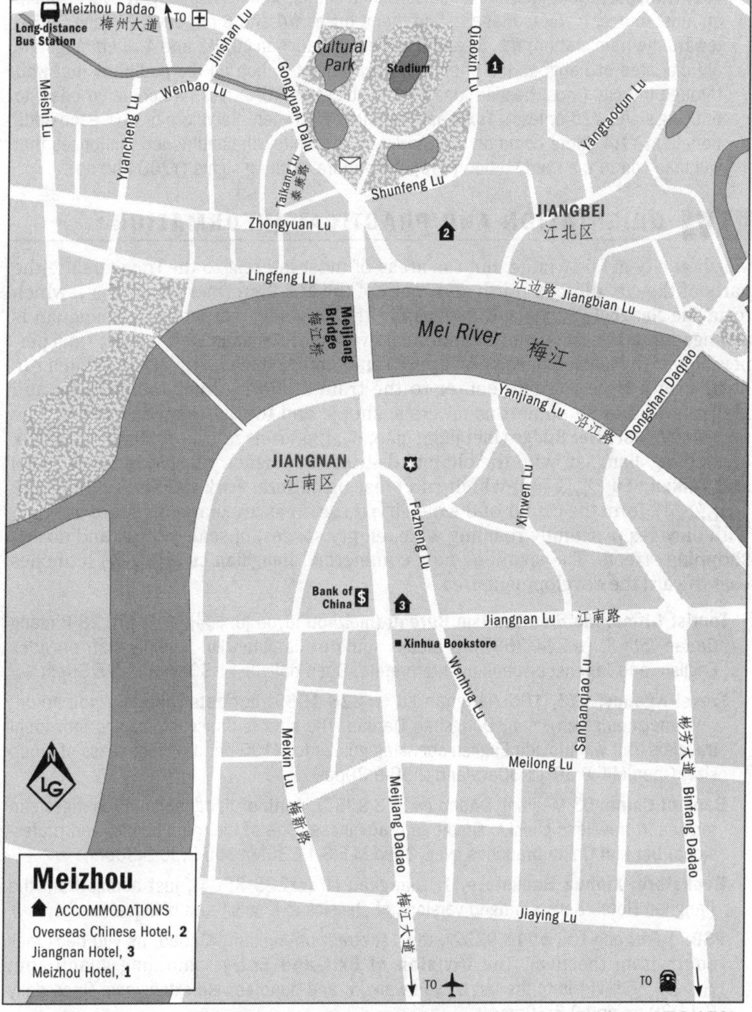

3:05am-6:27pm, Y19-39); **Guangzhon** (6-7hr., 11:15am and 5:10pm, Y56-173); **Guangzhou** (10hr., 12:56 and 10:35pm, Y60-295); **Nanchang** (5-8hr., many per day 8:45am-10:06pm, Y104-312); and **Shenzhen** (13hr.; 8:45, 10:37, 11:32am; Y63-287); **Xiamen** (10hr., 4:25am, Y64).

Buses: Meizhou Main Bus Station (méizhōu qìchē zǒngzhàn; 梅州汽车总站), 1 Meishe Lu, Jiangbei (☎222 2137). Accessible by buses #2 and 3. Tickets sold daily 8am-6:30pm. To: **Dongguan** (8:30am and 5:20pm, Y85-100); **Guangzhou** (many per day 8:20am-7:30pm, Y45-110); **Shenzhen** (many per day 9:10am-4:30pm, Y45-110). **Jiangnan Bus Station** (jiāngnán qìchē zhàn; 江南汽车站; ☎226 9568), on Binfang Dadao, accessible by bus #6, services **Dapu** (3hr., every 15min. 6am-6pm, Y20).

Local Transportation: Meizhou's bus service is erratic, with service roughly every 30min. on most routes. If you manage to find them, buses **#4** and **6** run down Binfang Dadao toward the train station; **#1, 3,** and **6** run along Jiangnan Lu; **#3** and **4** run through the old city area of Jiangbei. It's often more convenient to hop on the **pedicabs** that whiz through the city (most destinations Y1-2 for bicycles, Y5 or less for scootered ones; to outlying sights Y20 or less). **Taxis** are few and far between. Base fare of Y10, each additional km Y1.4. More common than taxis are the white, air-conditioned minibuses that will take you to the train station (Y30), or to more far-flung sights (Y200 and up).

ORIENTATION AND PRACTICAL INFORMATION

Meizhou city is fairly large, but the areas of most interest to the travelers are the parts of the city directly north and south of the **Mei River** (méi jiāng; 梅江), which form the **Jiangbei** (江北) and **Jiangnan** (江南) districts, respectively. Jiangnan is arranged in grids; the major commercial avenue of **Jiangnan Lu** (江南路) runs perpendicular to **Meijiang Dadao** (梅江大道) and **Binfang Dadao** (彬芳大道), which run north-south from the city center to the train station. Along Jiangnan Lu and Meijiang Dadao lie numerous eateries, shops, and tourist-related services. The pedestrian **Mei River Bridge** (méi jiāng qiáo; 梅江桥) runs north off Meijiang Dadao, connecting Jiangnan with the old city district of Jiangbei. **Yuancheng Lu** (元城路) and **Taikang Lu** (泰康路), which run west of **Cultural Park** (wénhuà gōngyuán; 文化公园), form the center of the old city; these areas are markedly more tranquil, with bicycles peacefully roaming wide, empty spaces, upscale hotels, and dosing shopping streets. The spanking new commercial **Jiangbian Lu** (江边路) branches east toward the development area.

Tourist Office: Meizhou Tourism Bureau (méizhōu lǚyóu jú; 梅州旅游局), 28 Binfang Dadao, 5th fl. (☎224 3687), 3 blocks south of Jiangnan Lu. Friendly staff provides English- and Japanese-speaking interpreters. Open daily 8-11:30am and 2-5:30pm.

Travel Agency: CTS, 105 Jiangnan Lu (☎226 1089; gdmzets@pub.meizhou.gd.cn; www.meizhou.gd.cn), near Dongshan Daqiao. The staff is unaccustomed to individual travelers, but will provide English-speaking guides for Y100 per day, regardless of group size. Open M-F 8:30-11:30am and 2:30-5:30pm.

Bank of China: 53 Meijiang Dadao (☎218 9287), north of Jiangnan Lu. Exchanges currency and traveler's checks. Credit card advances. One of the most helpful and professional Bank of China branches ever. Open M-F 8-11:30am and 2:30-5:30pm.

Bookstore: Xinhua Bookstore, 18 Jiangnan Lu (☎225 3504), just across from the Jiangnan Hotel. Sells abridged versions of classics in English and bilingual maps.

PSB: 1 Fazheng Lu (☎216 9332), the 1st street off Meijiang Dadao, as you backtrack south from the river. The **Division of Exit and Entry** (chūrùjìng guǎnlǐ chù; 出入境管理处) is to the left as you walk in, and handles visa extensions. Open daily 8-11:30am and 2-5:30pm.

Hospital: Meizhou No. 3 People's Hospital (méizhōu shì dì sān rénmín yīyuàn; 梅州市第三人民医院; ☎235 4244), at the terminus of Dalangkou Lu, accessible by Bus #8.

Internet Access: Taixiang Internet Cafe (tàixiáng wǎngbā; 泰祥网吧), 58 Qiaoxin Lu, (☎222 3268) near the Cultural Park. Y2 per hr. Open 24hr. **Spare Time Fast Food Restaurant** (huāshíjiān kuàicāntīng; 花时间快餐厅), 11 Meijiang Dadao (☎225 0866), opposite the Bank of China. Y2 per hr. Open daily 8:30am-11pm.

Post Office: 5 Gongyuan Lu (☎223 7586), off Jiangbian Lu, near Cultural Park. EMS and Poste Restante. Open daily 7:30am-7:30pm. **Postal Code:** 514021 for Jiangnan; 514011 for Jiangbei.

ACCOMMODATIONS

There's a surprising lack of range and quantity in Meizhou's accommodation options. For relatively low prices, you can stay at one of the city's better hotels, which suffer from a depressing lack of business and are usually willing (after some seasoned wheeling and dealing) to rent out rooms for as little as half the list price. All listings have rooms with A/C, bath, and TV.

Overseas Chinese Hotel (huá qiáo dàshà; 华侨大厦), 12 Jiangbian Lu (☎223 2388), just east of Meijiang Bridge. This former hostel turned 3-star hotel is the stuff that budget dreams are made of—lovely, clean standard rooms, a staff that will bend over backwards to make you feel welcome, and a fabulous location. Doubles Y300; suites Y380. 10% service charge. 50% discounts very possible. Am Ex/MC/V. ❹

Meizhou Hotel (méizhōu bīnguǎn; 梅州宾馆; ☎223 3530), along Qiaoxin Lu. From the main entrance of Cultural Park, go straight down Qiaoxin Lu (facing the gate across from the plaza); the hotel is along this winding road, to the right. A CTS-run hotel, rooms are clean enough, if slightly shabby. Doubles Y98; triples Y168. ❷

Jiangnan Hotel (jiāngnán dàshà; 江南大厦), 35 Jiangnan Lu (☎224 8489), at Meijiang Dadao. Located nicely along Jiangnan Lu, with decent enough rooms, but service that leaves something to be desired. Singles Y138; doubles Y158; triples Y198. ❷

FOOD AND ENTERTAINMENT

The Chinese obsession with soup is taken to new heights in Meizhou, which serves up a dizzying array of stews and broths—some boiled for a full day before serving. Scrumptious *dim sum* is available in most eateries from morning until the wee hours of the night. More compelling, however, is the local cuisine; **Ke Minority Cuisine** (kèjiācài; 客家菜) was named for present-day locals whose ancestors moved here from northern China. A must-try is *méicài kòuròu* (梅菜扣肉), a devastatingly yummy dish of roasted pork and preserved mountain vegetables. The thick layers of fat will cause heart palpitations for the health-conscious set, but will bring joy with its melt-in-your-mouth tender meat to everyone else. **Hakka wine** (kèjiā jiǔ; 客家酒), famed for its sweetness, is mixed with ginger to produce the signature Hakka sauce, especially delicious with chicken. Another Hakka chicken dish is **salt-baked whole chicken,** wrapped in butcher paper (Y25-30; enough for two).

To cleanse your palate of Hakka food, try the **Noodle King Restaurant** ❶ (miàndiàn wáng; 面店王), at the end of Wenhua Lu off Jiangnan Lu, one block east of the Jiangnan Hotel; it boasts authentic food from Heilongjiang in the Northeast. A friendly owner and obliging staff offers an extensive menu. Dumplings range from goat meat to vegetarian, and the pork-filled *xiǎolóngbāo* (Little Caged Buns; 小笼包; Y5 for 20) are especially popular. (☎226 7861. Open daily 8am-9pm.)

At night, the sixth floor of the **Riverside View Hotel Complex** features grooving Canto-pop action at the **Tianshang Renjian** (天上人间) dance club. Scantily clad platform dancers, boisterous group-croonings, and oddly infectious Chinese pop pack in the local youths. (Beer Y20. No cover charge. Open daily 7:30pm-1:30am.)

SIGHTS

The **Thousand Buddha Pagoda** (qiānfó tǎ; 千佛塔), a 15-minute drive northeast from Jiangbian Lu, is a gaudy complex worth seeing only if you've got time to spare. Overseas Chinese have donated mind-boggling amounts to this temple, resulting in a crazed frenzy of building and rebuilding that overshadows the real draw of the place: a Tang-dynasty **steel pagoda** (engraved with 1000 steel Buddhas) that has weathered wars, revolutions, and even a stint in a water-pumping factory. Now sheltered by a bigger stone pagoda, a climb to the top offers good views of Meizhou and the surrounding area. *(Open daily 8am-6pm. Y5.)*

DAYTRIP FROM MEIZHOU: YEARNING TEA PLANTATION

*About 30km from the city center. No public buses come here; **taxis** cost about Y220 round-trip. Ask at **CTS** or other travel agencies if you can hop on one of their tour buses. Visitors can spend the cost of their Y30 admission ticket at the restaurants and tea houses or put it toward defraying the cost of the villas. The villas cost more than Y30, however, requiring Y1980-7000 a night. If it's any comfort, guests can stuff their villas with as many people as they like. ☎282 8888; fax 282 6898. Open daily 8am-10pm. Y30.*

The Yearning Tea Plantation (yànnánfēi chátián; 雁南飞茶田) resort is a living testament to the ancient Chinese art of tea-growing and tea-culture. Immaculate rows of tea fields rise up on impressive mountains surrounding this resort area, and the numerous tea houses at the entrance of the resort plantation serve up constant (free) feasts of tea and sell elaborate, lovingly explained packets of China's favorite beverage (Y70-110 on average). But even the most indifferent tea-drinker will find the Yearning Tea Plantation resort irresistible. Take in the painstakingly snipped and trimmed lawns and hedges; admire the flocks of pigeons swarming around the carefully tended aviaries; strip off your clothes and plunge into the (free) swimming pools under the hot Meizhou sky. There's nothing to do here; this is simply a state of being. Spend a day drinking in the splendid greenery and explosion of roses and flowers while enjoying a truly divine cup of tea.

HAINAN 海南

Praised for its legendary beauty, Hainan is China's smallest, southernmost, and newest province, boasting lush tropical forests, hot springs, and gorgeous beaches. Part of Guangdong until it became a Special Economic Zone (SEZ) in 1988, Hainan province officially encompasses the isle of Hainan and the South China Sea archipelagos of Nansha (Spratly), Xisha (Paracel), and Zhongsha—although China's claims on all but Hainan are hotly disputed by a host of neighbors. But why bother with these reef bed islands when you have Hainan, which boasts some 1500km of glittering beaches stretching as far as the eye can see. The city of Sanya—so far south that it is known as "the End of the Earth"—attracts countless Chinese tourists with its promise of sandy bliss.

While most of Hainan's residents are Han Chinese, the island is home to three other large minority groups, the Li, Hui, and Miao. Many Li continue to live in the thatch-roofed, mud-walled cottages that dot the highlands around Tongza. With such diverse cultures and natural splendor, it's no wonder why some people call Hainan Island a paradise.

HAIKOU 海口 ☎0898

Breezy, balmy Haikou is the unofficial gateway to Hainan. The port became a center for international trade after the area was opened to foreign ships under the Treaty of Tianjin in 1876. Most people pass through Haikou on their way to and from the mainland, and few stay for very long. The happy-go-lucky tropical spirit that visitors from Hong Kong and Guangzhou find so soothing is tempered by a rash of crime. Prostitution and local gangs thrive, and tourists are often the target of pickpockets, especially along Haixiu Lu in Haikou's shopping district.

Haikou's most recent claim to fame is as the home of the Chinese air base that hosted a US spy plan for several months in 2001, after an US spy plane collided with a Chinese jet fighter near its coasts, killing the Chinese pilot, and emergency landed there. For a while, the incident made Haikou and Hainan the focus of international politics as the US government negotiated with the Chinese to release the plane and its flight crew.

TRANSPORTATION

Flights: Haikou Meilan International Airport (hǎikǒu méilán guójì jīchǎng; 海口梅兰国际机场), 20km southwest of the city. Free CAAC shuttle buses run between the CAAC office and the airport (every 30min. 6am-8pm); buses to from the airport to the city wait outside the lower level of the airport terminal (30 min.; free with a plane ticket, Y15 without). Taxis cost about Y30. **CAAC ticket office,** 9 Haixiu Lu (☎670 3306, 6676 3166 or 6672 3460), behind the International Commercial Center. Open daily 8am-8:30pm. To: **Beihai** (2 per day, Y350); **Beijing** (5-6 per day, Y1800); **Guangzhou** (10 per day, Y620); **Guilin** (1-2 per day, Y710); **Hong Kong** (2 per day, Y1350); **Shanghai** (4 per day, Y1480); **Xi'an** (2 per day, Y1530).

Buses: Buses run from **Hainan Province General Bus Station** (hǎinán hěng qìchē zǒng zhàn; 海南省汽车总站; ☎6677 2791), on Nanbao Lu, behind the Pearl Plaza. Open daily 6:30am-6:30pm. To: **Fuzhou** (72hr., 11am, Y330); **Guangzhou** (12hr., 11am, 3, 4, and 5pm; Y256); **Guilin** (15hr., 2:30pm, Y197); **Shenzhen** (12hr., noon and 2pm, Y192); **Wuhan** (2:30pm, Y252). The **East Bus Station** (qìchē dōng zhàn; ; ☎6534 0753) on Haifu Lu is accessible by bus #217 heading toward the Five Lords Temple. Hainan buses only. Open daily 6am-11pm. To: **Sanya** (luxury bus 3½hr., every 20min 7am-11pm, Y78; standard bus 5hr., runs irregularly, Y49); **Wenchang** (1hr., every 20min. 7am-8pm, Y15). The **West Bus Station** (qìchē xī zhàn; 汽车西站) on Haixiu Lu (☎6865 7306) is also on the bus #217 route but in the opposite (Xiuying) direction. Open daily 5:30am-8pm. To **Tongzha** (6hr., every hr. 6am-4pm, Y34) and **Ledong** (6hr., every hr. 7am-6:30pm, Y38).

Boats: Haikou Xiuying Port (hǎikǒu xiùyīng gǎng; 海口秀英港), on Binhai Lu, east of the city, is accessible by bus #217. The **ticket office,** 7 Haifu Dadao (☎535 1557), is across from the East Lake Hotel, at the foot of the overpass. Open daily 7:30am-5:30pm. To: **Beihai** (12hr., 6pm, Y57); **Guangzhou** (18hr.; M,W, and F 3:30pm; Y104); **Hainan** (1hr., every hr. 24hr., Y26); **Shenzhen** (18hr., Su-F 4pm, Y113); **Zhanjiang** (14hr., 9:30am, Y71). **Haikou New Port** (hǎikǒu xīn gǎng; 海口新港), north of the city center (☎6223 9744). To: **Beihai** (12hr., 6pm, Y43.5-50); **Haian** (1½hr., every 1½hr. 6:30am-6pm, Y30); **Zhanjiang** (4hr., 9:30am and 1:30pm, Y97).

Local Transportation: The ubiquitous yellow and white **bus #217,** a cross between a minibus and a full-sized bus, covers all tourist destinations, including CAAC, CITS, the main hotel strip, the International Commercial Center, the Five Lords Temple, Hai Rui's Tomb, and East and West Bus Stations (Y2).

ORIENTATION AND PRACTICAL INFORMATION

Haikou sits at the northern tip of Hainan Island, across the Qiongzhou Strait from Haian on the Leizhou peninsula in Guangdong province. **Haikou Park** (hǎikǒu gōngyuán; 海口公园) marks the central reference point in the city: from here, **Haixiu Lu** (海秀路) runs to the southwest; **Datong Lu** (大同路) runs to the northwest; **Haifu Dadao** (海府大道) runs to the southeast. One of the most important landmarks is the **Hainan International Commercial Center** (hǎinán guójì shāngyè dàshà; 海南国际商业大厦) at 38 Haixiu Lu (☎6679 2778 or 6677 4840). The shiny Pearl Plaza (míngzhū guǎngchǎng; 明珠广场) at 16 Haixiu Lu is also very visible.

Travel Agency: CITS, 17 Datong Lu (☎6670 0281, ext. 2801 or 2803 for international bookings, ext. 2804 or 2802 for domestic; fax 6670 6281 or 6677 3092; ctick@public.hk.hi.cn; www.hncts.com.cnc), next to the Haikou Overseas Chinese Hotel. Books flights (including charter flights) and organizes tour groups. English service usually available. Open daily 8am-8pm. Another branch at 8 Haifu Dadao (☎535 7999 or 537 9966), next to East Lake. Open daily 8:30am-10pm.

Bank of China: 33 Datong Lu (☎6677 7800), in the International Finance Mansion (guójì jīnróng dàshà; 国际金融大厦) behind the International Commerce Mansion. Exchanges currency and traveler's checks and provides credit card advances (windows 2 and 3). Open 8:30am-5:30pm; 9am-5pm on holidays. Two **ATM**s outside accept AmEx, Cirrus, MC, Plus, and V. Another branch at 10 Datong Lu (☎6671 8697), close to the shops on Jiefang Xi Lu, offers the same services and keeps the same hours.

Bookstore: Hainan Creation Bookstore (hǎinán chuàngxīn shūdiàn; 海南创新书店), 11 Jiefang Xi Lu 2nd and 3rd fl. (☎6621 3699; www.chuangxin.com). Novels, reference books, and Hainan travel guides in English. Internet access and a small cafe on 3rd fl. Open daily 9am-10:30pm. Credit cards accepted.

Internet Access: Ying Han Internet Garden (yīnghàn wǎngyuán; 鹰撖网园; ☎6675 4802), on the 2nd fl. of the **Huabao Building** (huábǎ dàshà; 华宝大厦) on Daying Lu. Walk down Haixiu Lu toward Haifu Lu until you see the Happy Tom Fast Food Restaurant on the right; the building is at the end of the alley adjoining it. Y3 per hr. Open daily 8:30am-3am. The **Telecommunications Mansion** (yóudiàn dàshà; 邮电大厦), 20 Nanbao Lu (☎6675 5664; www.htslong.com), is behind the Pearl Plaza; enter through the P and T Hotel lobby. 20 computers. Y3 per hr. Open 24hr.

Post and Telecommunications: 28 Haifu Dadao (☎6533 8840), in the China Telecom Building. Open daily 8am-9pm. **Postal Code:** 570203. The branch at 16 Jiefang Xi Jie (☎6622-6323) is open 24 hrs. **Postal Code:** 570206. EMS, IDD service, and Poste Restante available at both offices. No English speakers.

ACCOMMODATIONS

Budget accommodations in Haikou are scarce; bargain for cheaper rates, especially during the summer. 24hr. hot water, air-conditioning, phone, and TV are standard at all hotels officially allowed to house foreigners.

Hainan Education Hotel (hǎinán jiàoyuàn dàshà; 海南教苑大厦), 18 Haixiu Lu (☎6677 2998), on the block past and opposite the International Commerce Mansion. Rooms are small and dim but tolerable. Singles Y70. ❶

East Lake Hotel (dōnghú jiāfēng dàjiǔdiàn; 东湖嘉丰大酒店), 8 Haifu Dadao (☎6535 3333; fax 6535 8827), at Haixiu Lu, next to CITS. Comfortable and friendly. Singles and doubles Y220, off-season Y180. ❸

Trade Union Guesthouse (gōnghuì zhāodàisuǒ; 工会招待所), 2 Donghu Nan Lu (☎6533 6125), about 50m into the alley to the left of the East Lake Hotel. Fruit and food stalls line the street outside the hotel. Singles Y90, doubles Y120; prices drop to Y70 and Y80, respectively, in the summer. ❷

Hainan Civil Aviation Hotel, 9 Haixiu Lu (☎6677 2608; fax 6677 2610), right next to the CAAC ticket office. Photo developing, airline reservations, maps and phonecards, and a bite to eat at the cafe–all without leaving the bright lobby. Rooms are spacious,

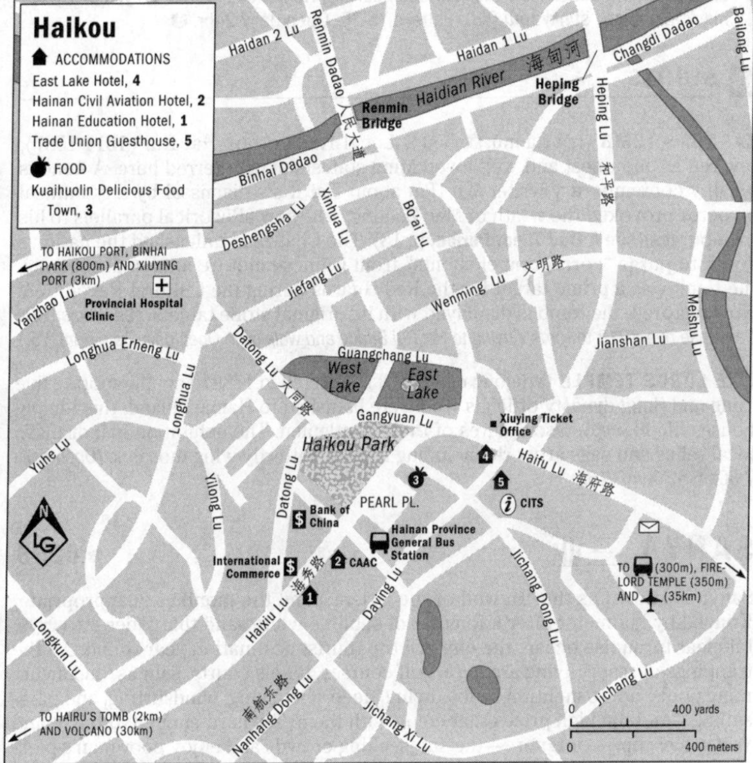

clean and modern. Singles and doubles Y488, with up to a 50% discount possible; bargain to Y220 in the summer. ❺

FOOD

Haikou's streets are lined with vendors selling mangos, coconuts, bananas, and other tropical delights. **Yilong Lu** (义龙路), parallel to Haixiu Lu, near Longkun Lu, has a market filled with rows of colorful fruit. The local cuisine is a grab-bag of styles from the mainland. One Hainan specialty is *yěcài* (野菜), a vegetable native only to the island and available at most eateries. Locals recommend **China City** (zhōngguóchéng; 中国城; ☎6588 8888) on Lungkun Bei Lu, a large food and entertainment complex serving everything from snacks to seafood.

Kuaihuolin Delicious Food Town (kuàihuólín měifàn chéng; 快活林美饭城), 2 Jichang Lu (☎678 1645), off Haixiu Lu. An unremarkable but convenient smorgasbord, with Western breakfasts, Cantonese dim sum, Taiwanese food stand favorites, and standard vegetables and meats. Huge portions. English menu. Noodle dishes Y3-8; set meals Y15. Open daily 7am-2am. ❶

Yuanmengyuang Restaurant (yuánmèngyuán jǐulóu; 圆梦园酒楼), 4 Jichang Dong Lu (☎6535 0172) before the Wuzhishan Hotel; look for the prominent "24"s painted on the storefront. Owner Mrs. Yao has been serving Hunan cuisine for 12 years. Try the black and crispy *stinky tofu* (Y8). Entrees Y5-25. Open daily 24hr. ❶

SIGHTS

HAI RUI'S TOMB (hǎi ruì mù; 海瑞墓). Local Hainan boy Hai Rui (1514-1587), revered as an honest and well-loved Ming statesman, is interred here. A famous play by contemporary writer Wu Han about Hai Rui's dismissal by a tyrannical emperor provoked the wrath of Mao Zedong, who saw allegorical parallels to his own purges (see **A Bad Time, Period,** p. 18). The Chairman unleashed the nation's youth to purge "corrupting elements" from Chinese culture and, consequently, the tomb was a prime target for the Red Guards during the Cultural Revolution. Now restored, the tomb is displayed with its original stone tablets. *(On Shugang Da Dao. Take bus #218 towards Xiuying to Hai Rui Bridge and walk over. Open daily 8am-6pm. Y5.)*

FIVE LORDS TEMPLE (wǔgōng cí; 五公祠). Erected in 1889 to commemorate five Tang and Song dynasty officials who were banished to Hainan Island, this temple houses life-like stone sculptures of these gentlemen. The exhibition hall displays local relics and sells artwork, including framed butterfly-wing mosaics. *(Open daily 7:30am-6:30pm. Y15.)*

SANYA 三亚 ☎0898

Sanya is known as the "Hawaii of the Orient," and the moniker is appropriate. Fringed by kilometer after kilometer of sublime white sand that fades into crystal-clear turquoise ocean, the city is a top tourist destination year-round. All the trappings of resort living are here: golf courses, tennis courts, saunas, and swimming pools, not to mention scuba diving, deep sea fishing, windsurfing, and parasailing—and the high prices that come with them. Try hard enough, though, and you can escape—or ignore—the sun-seeking crowds and enjoy poor man's pleasures like swimming and streetside seafood. Sanya just might be the perfect place to dig your toes into some toasty white sand, lie back, and enjoy the sun.

TRANSPORTATION

Flights: Sanya Phoenix International Airport (sānyà fènghuáng guójì jīchǎng; 三亚凤凰国际机场), is 16km northwest of town. **Sanya Phoenix International Airport Ticket Offices (SYPIA ticket offices)** at Jiefang Yi Lu (☎8827 7409, open 8am-10pm) and Jiefang Er Lu (☎8827 7820) deliver tickets for free within the city. To: **Beijing** (4hr., 2-4 per day, Y2000); **Guangzhou** (1hr., 3-5 per day, Y730); **Hong Kong** (1hr. 20min, daily, Y1680); **Shanghai** (3hr., 3 per day, Y1660).

Buses: Sanya Bus Station (sānyà qìchē zhàn; 三亚汽车站; ☎8827 2440), on Jiefang Lu. Take any bus or minibus up Jiefang Lu; the station is on the left. Open 6am-11pm. To: **Haikou** (luxury bus 3½hr., every 20min., 7am-11pm, Y79; standard bus 5hr., runs irregularly, Y50); **Lingshui** (2hr., every hr. 7am-6pm, Y13); **Tongzha** (2½hr., every 30min., 7am-3pm, Y13).

Local Transportation: Taxis, motorcabs, pedicabs, and a rickety selection of minibuses relentlessly troll the main thoroughfares and attractions and stop just about anywhere upon request. Fare Y1-5. **Minibus #2** runs up and down all of Jiefang Lu (Y1).

ORIENTATION AND PRACTICAL INFORMATION

Sanya is easy to navigate; it is divided into two main sections: **Sanya City** (三亚市) and **Dadonghai** (大东海), the beach resort area just east of the city. **Yuya Dadao** (榆亚大道) runs through Dadonghai, turns into **Gangmen Lu** (港门路) as it crosses the Sanya river, then finally veers right to the main thoroughfare of Sanya City, **Jiefang Lu** (解放路), which runs all the way out past the city limits. Jiefang Lu is divided into four sections starting from the stretch closest to Dadonghai; street numbers are functionally nonexistent.

Travel Agency: Sanya Spring-Autumn Travel Service (sānyà chūnqiū lǚshè; 三亚春秋旅行社), Room 703, Shida Department Store on Jiefang Er Lu (☎8826 5249; fax 8825 7242), has English-speaking tour guides. Open daily 9:30am-6pm.

Bank of China: 31 Yuya Lu, Dadonghai, next to Northeast King. Exchanges traveler's checks. Credit card advances. Open daily 8am-5:30pm. The branch across from the bus station on Jiefang Er Lu is open daily 9am-5pm.

Bookstores and Internet Access: Hainan Creation Bookstore (hǎinán chuàngxīn shūdiàn; 海南创新书店; ☎8826 9983), on Jiefang Er Lu and Xinfeng Jie. Open daily 9am-10:30pm). **Sea Day Bookstore** (hǎitiān shūdiàn; 海天书店), on Jiefang Er Lu across from the Sanya Hotel. Open daily 9am-1:30am. Both offer a small selection of English-language books and internet access for Y2 per hour.

Post Office: Jiefang San Lu (☎8827 2049), across from the People's Hospital. EMS and Poste Restante on the 2nd fl. Open daily 7:30am-10pm. Postal Code: 572000.

ACCOMMODATIONS

Even in China, beachfront property doesn't come cheap. Skip the budget-busting luxury resorts and hotels of Yalong Bay and Dadonghai and stay in Sanya City instead. Peak season (Oct.-May) and off season rates are indicated for the places listed below. Lodgings are almost impossible to get during national holidays.

Sanya Jingbeiqu Yingbinlou (sānyà jǐngbèiqū yíngbīnlóu; 三亚警备区迎宾楼; ☎8821 2345 ext. 0), on Yuya Lu about 500m east of Dadonghai. Newly opened in spring 2001, and it shows. Drag yourself out of your cavernous, sparkling room and catch a minibus in front of the hotel right to the beach or into Sanya city. Rooms fill up quickly, so make reservations. Doubles Y600; off-season Y140. ❺/❷

Precious Stone Hotel (huábǎoshí dàjiǔdiàn; 华宝石大酒店), 10 Jiefang Er Lu (☎8825 6588; fax 8825 7018). The convenient location near the bus station and the panoramic view of the city shoreline make up for the shabby (but spacious) rooms. The Chinese restaurant on the premises serves Sichuan, Cantonese, and northwestern cuisine. Doubles Y380; off-season Y138. ❺/❷

Oriental Cherry Guesthouse (yīnhuā bīnguǎn; 樱花宾馆) on Hedong Yi Lu (☎8826 0388; fax 8826 0347). The worn but clean and breezy rooms overlook the Sanya River. Doubles Y380; off-season 100. ❺/❷

FOOD

Sanya is justifiably famous for its seafood. **Yuya Dadao** and **Binhai Lu** along the cityshore, and **Luling Lu** and **Gangmen Lu** are lined with bustling seafood and hotpot restaurants serving up denizens of the deep, including Hainan specialties like **Hele**

crab. Seafood is typically sold by weight; the standard unit of measurement is the *jin* (斤), about half a kilogram. At night, the area around China City and Xinfeng Jie (an island in the Sanya river) is filled with seafood stalls (dishes Y5-10) and guitar-strumming troubadors earning a few yuan or a seat at the table in return for a song or a story. Another local specialty is **Yellow Oil Old Duck** (huángliú lǎoyā; 黄流老鸭), an inexplicably chewy and flavorful duck. Exercise your jaws at any of the foodstands on Shengli Lu behind the bus station.

Northeast Porridge King (dōngběi zhōuwáng; 东北粥王), 3 Hedong Lu (☎826 3684). This shop makes even porridge sexy—and you can try all 18 varieties if you please. The all-you-can-eat buffet (breakfast Y6, lunch and dinner Y12) will have you coming back for seconds. Porridge haters, don't despair: dumplings and vegetable dishes abound. Open daily 7am-9pm. ❶

Nanshan Hotpot City (nánshān huǒguō chéng; 南山火锅城; ☎825 3265), on Hexi Lu near Yuejin Lu. People come here to warm up with lamb hotpot (Y20)—a local specialty—and the lively nighttime atmosphere. Hotpots Y30-60. Open daily 9am-9pm. ❸

SIGHTS AND BEACHES

The non-sandy parts of Sanya are an afterthought for most visitors. **Luhuitou Park** (lù huítóu gōngyuán; 鹿回头公园), is on the peninsula between Sanya City and Dadonghai. The views from the nearby mountain are spectacular, especially at sunset or at night when the city lights twinkle beneath you. Try to ignore the gaudy laser lights and loud, synthesized classical music. *(Open daily 7am-11:30pm. Y23.5.)*

YALONG BAY (yàlóng wān; 亚龙湾). The beach here is 7km of glistening, picture-perfect pristine white sand, fringed with luxury resorts. The Hainan Yalong Bay Underwater World (hǎinán yàlóng wān hǎidǐ shìjiè; 海南亚龙湾海底世界) offers a variety of activities, including parasailing (Y350 per 5min.), deep-sea fishing (Y350 per hr.), boating (Y100 and up), and scuba diving (Y350 per trip). There is also an underwater excursion in a submerged viewing deck (Y170 per 30 min). *(☎8856 5588. Open daily 8am-4:30pm.)* The beach itself is extraordinary—wander off until the crowds thin and enjoy the tropical beauty. *(25km east of Sanya. Catch any minibus to Dadonghai. The green and white #102 bus runs from the East Bus Station near Dadonghai directly to the waterfront.)*

DADONGHAI (dàdōng hǎi; 大东海). Dadonghai's 2km of angel dust may not be Sanya's best beach, but it is undoubtedly its most crowded and convenient. Water sports are cheaper here than at Yalong Bay; try bargaining down to Y250 for a scuba diving trip. The beachfront plaza, currently being expanded, is a popular gathering place in the evening. Easily accessible and caters to local youths as well as tour groups. *(3km southeast of Sanya. Accessible by numerous minibuses that ply the route between the beach and the city. Minibuses Y1. Beach access free.)*

TIANYA CORNER (tiānyá hǎijiǎo; 天涯海角). Dubbed the "End of the Earth and Corner of the Sea," the southernmost point of China is a popular destination for tourists and appears on the back of the Y2 note. Its romantic name signifies a love that knows no bounds, and as a result Tianya witnesses the weddings of over 100 couples from around the world every November during the Sanya International Wedding Ceremony (sānyà guójì hūnlǐ jié; 天涯海角国际婚礼节). Festivities include a parade through Sanya City with elephants and dances, followed by a mass wedding. *(23km west of Sanya. Take any bus or minibus labeled 天涯海角 going up Jiefang Lu. Y46.5)*

MONKEY BUSINESS On this small green crag live over 300 wild macaques, personable golden-grown monkeys with red behinds. Legend has it that during the Tang dynasty, a plague left residents of this seaside port blind and near death. Local hero Yan'an set sail in search of the black pearls that provided the cure, but the young boy was shipwrecked during a fierce storm. A group of compassionate fair monkeys saved him and returned with the boy and the black pearls, saving the town and finding a new home, which the grateful villagers vowed to protect forever. Legend is strangely silent on how the monkeys' rumps turned crimson.

Folklore aside, Monkey Island offers a great chance to see these wild animals up close. Visitors can buy a pack of peanuts (Y10) and watch monkeys frolic around their feet, or undertake the 30-minute climb to the highest point on the island for an impressive view of the surrounding countryside.

DAYTRIP FROM SANYA: XINCUN AND MONKEY ISLAND

About 62km northeast of Sanya City. ***Minibuses*** *from the Sanya Bus Station to Lingshui deposit travelers to Xincun at a fork in the road 3km from town. Jump on a sidecar (Y3) for the ride along Xincun's main road, Zhongshan Lu, to the waterfront.* ***Buses*** *returning from Lingshui to Sanya (every 30min. until 6pm) stop right outside Xincun. From the Xincun waterfront,* ***motorboats*** *(5min., Y20) wind through the maze of houseboats linked by precarious boardwalks, dropping visitors at the beginning of a 2km road to the Visitors Center, accessible by foot or on a* ***motorcab*** *(Y5). A* ***cable car*** *from the Xincun waterfront (8am-5pm; one-way Y28, round-trip Y68, including admission) takes people directly to the Visitors Center on Monkey Island. Open daily 8am-5pm. Y20.*

Xincun (新村) provides access to nearby Nanwan Monkey Island (nánwān hóu dǎo; 南湾猴岛), a small peninsula that justs out into the ocean. The town itself is populated by the Hakka and Danjia minorities, many of whom earn their living from fishing; the nets and posts marking each family's fishery are clearly visible.

TONGZHA 通什 ☎0898

Tongzha (often pronounced Tongshi), a small, laid-back Li and Miao autonomous prefectural seat, is best known for its museum. Aside from this attraction, the city rarely trascends its ethnic heritage; to appreciate Tongzha's hidden treasures, one needs to visit the minority villages that dot the surrounding countryside.

ORIENTATION AND PRACTICAL INFORMATION. Tongzha is bisected by the **Nansheng River** (nánshèng hé; 南圣河), with the downtown area to the south and the museum and bus station to the north. **Haiyu Lu** (海榆路) is shaped like an "L," with one branch splayed southward across the bridge over the river and the other running northwest past the bus station and museum.

The **Tongzha Bus Station** (tōngzhā qìchē zhàn; 通什汽车站; ☎8662 2419) is on Haiyu Bei Lu. Cross the bridge and turn left; the station is 50m ahead on the right. Open daily 5:30am-5pm. To: **Haikou** (luxury buses: 4hr., 3 per day, Y64; regular buses: 5hr., every 45min.-1½hr. 6:30am-4:15pm, Y35); **Lingshui** (2½hr., 8 per day, Y16-21); **Sanya** (2½hr., every 30min. 6:30am-5:30pm, Y13). The **Bank of China,** 8 Jiefang Lu, near Xinhua Lu, exchanges traveler's checks and offers credit card advances. (☎662 3642. Open daily 8am-6:30pm.) The **Telecom Internet Bar** (tōngzhā diànxìn yīntè wǎngbā; 通什电信因特网吧; ☎8662 7773), on Hong Qi Lu at Xinhua Lu, has access for Y2 per hour. (Open M-Th 8:30am-midnight, F-Su 24 hr.) The **Main**

and Communications Post Office at Haiyu Nan Lu and Hebei Xi Lu (☎8663 2782) provides IDD service. (Open daily 7:30am-9pm.) The **postal code** is 572200.

ACCOMMODATIONS AND FOOD. Tongzha has few accommodations and restaurants. Most budget accommodations are south of the river, clustered around Jiefang Lu. The **Feicui Hotel** ❶ (fěicuì bīnguǎn; 翡翠宾馆), 1 Hongqi Lu, at Xinhua Lu south of the river, is relatively clean and well kept. All rooms but the dorms have attached bath. (☎8662 3125. Dorms Y20-30; singles Y40, with A/C Y120; doubles Y35.) Tongzha's main eateries are the food stalls near the bus station and along the river (dishes Y3-8). Li foods like **bamboo-steamed rice** and **rice wine** are served in some of the minority restaurants in the Li villages surrounding Tongzha.

SIGHTS. The main sight in Tongzha is the **Hainan Province Minority Nationalities Museum** (hǎinánshěng mínzú bówùguǎn; 海南省民族博物馆) and its collection of Li and Miao clothing, tools, and handwoven tapestries. The most beautiful part, however, is probably the view of the surrounding countryside. *(Just past the bus station, if heading north from the town center. Turn right at the sign and climb up a steep hill. ☎8662 2336. Open daily 8am-5:30pm. Y10.)* **Qiongzhou University** (qióngzhōu dàxué; 琼州大学) is a fine example of traditional Li architecture. Turn right as you exit the museum and head down toward the bus station. The **Li village of Fanmao** (fānmáo lízhài; 番茅黎寨), 2km north of Tongzha, contains numerous traditional boot-shaped houses with pyramidal huts. *(Accessible by motorcab, Y3.)* South of Tongzha, stroll the lush gardens of the faded **Culture Village of Chinese Nationalities** (zhōnghuá mínzú wénhuà cūn; 中华民族文化村), Haiyu Lu, an all-inclusive, one-stop minority experience. *(☎8662 2918. Open daily 8am-6pm.)*

HONG KONG AND MACAU

In July 1997, Hong Kong returned to Chinese rule after being under British control for nearly a century. Macau soon followed suit, when the Portuguese relinquished control in December of 1999. Although both areas interacted with mainland China over the years due to geographical proximity, socially and economically they could not have been farther apart.

After having been exposed to European influences for so many years, Hong Kong and Macau have developed a character that is best described as unique; the breadth and severity of the cultural reprecussions of re-unification remain to be seen. Hong Kong and Macau exemplify the old and the new, the East and the West, an exciting, churning mass of contradiction that defies glib comparison or introduction.

HIGHLIGHTS OF HONG KONG AND MACAU

CLAMBER OVER THE RUINS OF ST. PAUL in Macau (p. 567) and soak up some Portugese Old World charm.

FIND YOUR INNER DUMPLING at **Hong Kong**'s fabulous *dim sum* restaurants (p. 538).

PUTTER AROUND MACAU on a rented boat (p. 562) and gamble your life away on this casino-filled island.

MONEY

Legal tender in Hong Kong is the **Hong Kong dollar** (HK$), which is divided into 100 **cents.** Bronze-colored, government-issued coins come in 10¢, 20¢, and 50¢ denominations; silver-colored coins come in $1, $2, $5, $10, and $100. Three private banks issue notes in denominations of $10, $20, $50, $100, $500, and $1000. Currency can be exchanged at banks, hotels, moneychangers, or 24hr. automatic currency exchange machines called **EA$YXCHANGE,** which can be found at a few Wing Lung banks (HK$30 handling fee); banks usually have the best rates.

Anyone with a passport can open a **bank account.** Hang Seng Bank doesn't charge service fees and only requires a minimum initial deposit of HK$10. All major **credit cards** (AmEx, Diner's Club, JCB, MC, and Visa) are generally accepted in Hong Kong, although some shops charge extra for their use. **ATMs** connected to international money networks like Cirrus, Plus, Mondex, and NYCE dispense Hong Kong dollars and can be found around the city and in MTR and KCR stations. All **HongkongBank ETC** machines accept Cirrus, MasterCard, Plus, and Visa. In general, look for machines that are marked "For International Cards."

Tipping is not common, so don't feel obligated to tip waiters, bellhops, or other attendants. Most restaurants automatically levy a 10% service charge, and expect to keep the change. For taxis, round the fare up to the nearest dollar.

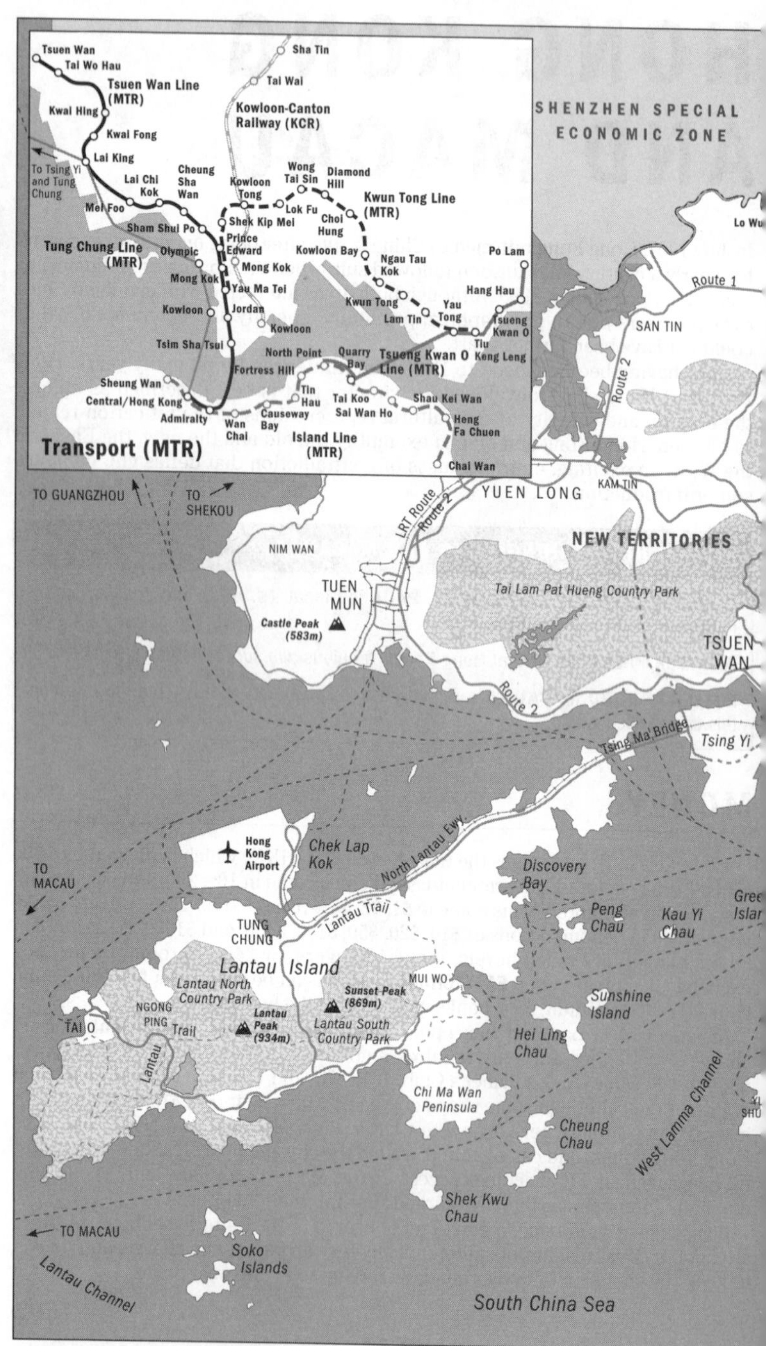

Transport (MTR)
Tsuen Wan Line (MTR)
Kowloon-Canton Railway (KCR)
Kwun Tong Line (MTR)
Tung Chung Line (MTR)
Tsueng Kwan O Line (MTR)
Island Line (MTR)
Tsuen Wan
Tai Wo Hau
Kwai Hing
Kwai Fong
Lai King
To Tsing Yi and Tung Chung
Lai Chi Kok
Cheung Sha Wan
Mei Foo
Sham Shui Po
Olympic
Mong Kok
Kowloon
Tsim Sha Tsui
Sha Tin
Tai Wai
Kowloon Tong
Wong Tai Sin
Diamond Hill
Lok Fu
Choi Hung
Shek Kip Mei
Prince Edward
Kowloon Bay
Ngau Tau Kok
Kwun Tong
Lam Tin
Yau Tong
Po Lam
Hang Hau
Tsueng Kwan O
Tiu Keng Leng
Yau Ma Tei
Jordan
North Point
Quarry Bay
Fortress Hill
Sheung Wan
Central/Hong Kong
Admiralty
Wan Chai
Causeway Bay
Tin Hau
Tai Koo
Sai Wan Ho
Shau Kei Wan
Heng Fa Chuen
Chai Wan
SHENZHEN SPECIAL ECONOMIC ZONE
Lo Wu
Route 1
SAN TIN
Route 2
KAM TIN
YUEN LONG
LRT Route
TO GUANGZHOU
TO SHEKOU
NIM WAN
NEW TERRITORIES
TUEN MUN
Castle Peak (583m)
Tai Lam Pat Hueng Country Park
TSUEN WAN
Tsing Ma Bridge
Tsing Yi
Hong Kong Airport
Chek Lap Kok
North Lantau Ewy.
Discovery Bay
TO MACAU
Peng Chau
Kau Yi Chau
TUNG CHUNG
Lantau Trail
Lantau Island
Lantau North Country Park
MUI WO
Sunset Peak (869m)
NGONG PING
Trail
TAI O
Lantau Peak (934m)
Lantau South Country Park
Sunshine Island
Hei Ling Chau
Lantau
Chi Ma Wan Peninsula
Cheung Chau
West Lamma Channel
Shek Kwu Chau
TO MACAU
Soko Islands
Lantau Channel
South China Sea

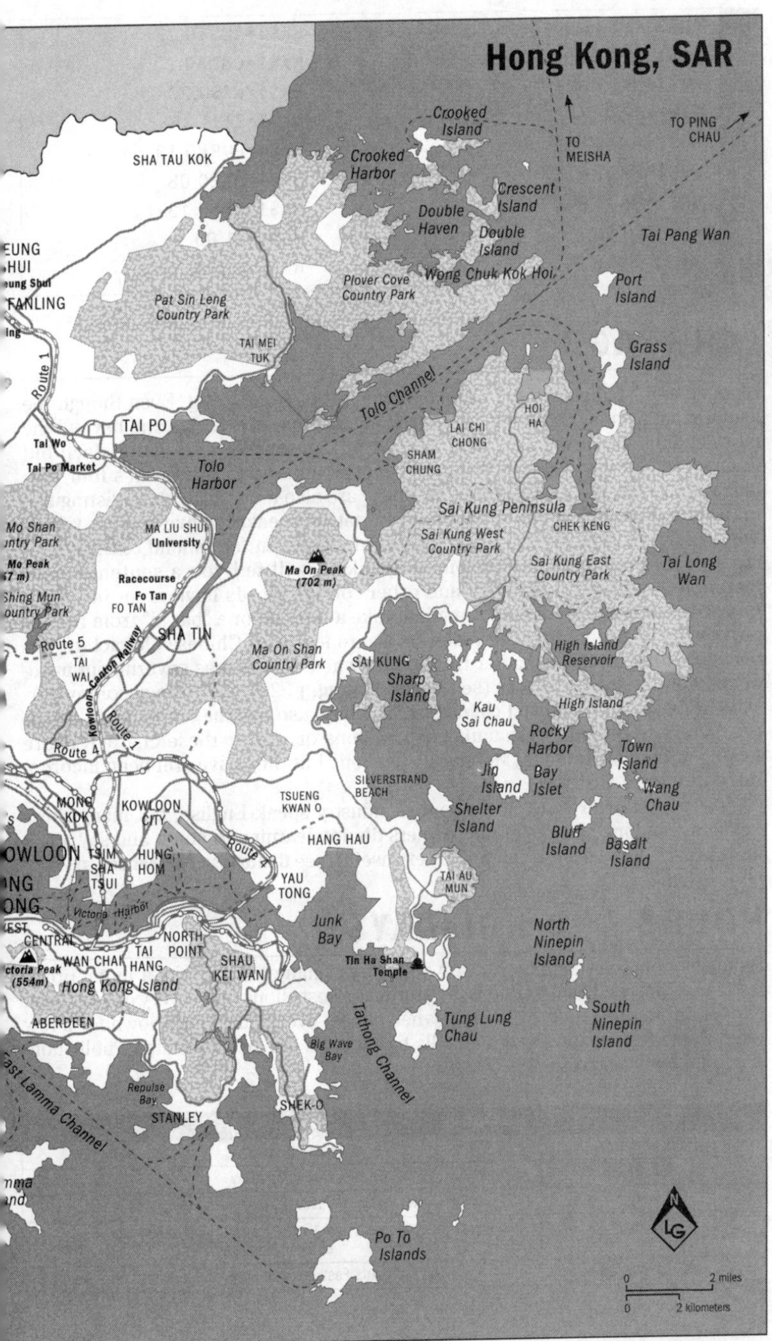
Hong Kong, SAR
Crooked Island
Crooked Harbor
TO MEISHA
TO PING CHAU
SHA TAU KOK
Crescent Island
Double Haven
Double Island
Tai Pang Wan
Plover Cove Country Park
Wong Chuk Kok Hoi
Port Island
Pat Sin Leng Country Park
FANLING
Grass Island
TAI MEI TUK
Route 1
Tolo Channel
HOI HA
TAI PO
LAI CHI CHONG
Tai Wo
Tai Po Market
SHAM CHUNG
Tolo Harbor
Sai Kung Peninsula
MA LIU SHUI
University
CHEK KENG
Sai Kung West Country Park
Ma On Peak (702 m)
Sai Kung East Country Park
Tai Long Wan
Racecourse
Fo Tan
FO TAN
SHA TIN
Route 5
High Island Reservoir
TAI WAI
Ma On Shan Country Park
SAI KUNG
Sharp Island
Kowloon-Canton Railway
High Island
Kau Sai Chau
Route 1
Rocky Harbor
Route 4
Town Island
Jin Island
Bay Islet
SILVERSTRAND BEACH
Wang Chau
MONG KOK
KOWLOON CITY
TSUENG KWAN O
Shelter Island
HANG HAU
Bluff Island
Basalt Island
TSIM SHA TSUI
HUNG HOM
Route 4
YAU TONG
TAI AU MUN
Victoria Harbor
Junk Bay
North Ninepin Island
CENTRAL
NORTH POINT
WAN CHAI
TAI HANG
SHAU KEI WAN
Tin Ha Shan Temple
(554m)
Hong Kong Island
ABERDEEN
Tathong Channel
Tung Lung Chau
South Ninepin Island
Big Wave Bay
East Lamma Channel
Repulse Bay
STANLEY
SHEK-O
Po To Islands
0
2 miles
0
2 kilometers

HONG KONG

HONG KONG DOLLAR	
AUS$1=HK$4.30	HK$1=AUS$0.23
CDN$1=HK$4.99	HK$1=CDN$0.20
NZ$1=HK$3.68	HK$1=NZ$0.27
ZAR1=HK$0.74	HK$1=ZAR1.35
EUR€1=HK$7.66	HK$1=EUR€0.13
UK£1=HK$12.16	HK$1=UK£0.08
US$1=HK$7.80	HK$1=US$0.13
Y1=HK$0.94	HK$1=Y1.06
MOP1=HK$0.97	HK$1=MOP1.03

LANGUAGE

Chinese and English are the official languages of Hong Kong. Even though the use of Mandarin is on the rise in Hong Kong, **Cantonese** is above and beyond the most widely spoken dialect. Like Mandarin, Cantonese is a tonal dialect; but Cantonese has six or seven different tones compared to Mandarin's four (see **China: Language,** p. 25). Tones in Cantonese are also more difficult to distinguish than their Mandarin counterparts—even native speakers have trouble telling them apart. Cantonese also has the habit of adding an "ah" sound to the end of most of its phrases, and Cantonese speakers will tell you a sentence feels incomplete without it. English and other foreign words have crept into Cantonese to such an extent that you might take a "teik si" or a "bas si" from the airport or buy a "fon kad" at the 7-Eleven. Cantonese uses Chinese characters, but because Hong Kong was under British rule when the Chinese government introduced simplified characters (see **China: Writing,** p. 26), the former colony persists in its use of **traditional characters.** The city also has the tendency to invent characters to express vernacular expressions or words; these characters are wholly unfamiliar to many Mandarin speakers, but they have still been incorporated into local writing.

Most people who work in the tourist industry speak English, but many shopkeepers, vendors, and restaurant owners do not; learning to count and say a few key phrases in Cantonese can prove very useful (see **Cantonese Phrasebook,** p. 843).

HOURS AND HOLIDAYS

Business hours are 9am to 5pm on weekdays (many offices take a lunch break from 1 to 2pm) and 9am to noon on Saturdays. Most shops open every day at 10am, except during the Lunar New Year, when almost everything shuts down for a few days. Some festival days vary annually based upon the local calendar. Public holidays and festivals are as follows:

DATE	HOLIDAY
Every Sunday	General Holiday
Jan. 1	New Year's Day
January	City Festival (Alternative Art Festival). More info at www.hkfringe.com.hk
mid-February	Lunar New Year, the start of a 15-day festival. Most businesses close for at least 3 days.
Feb. 10-Mar. 10	Hong Kong Arts Festival. Visit www.hk.artsfestival.org

DATE	HOLIDAY
Apr. 1	Easter Monday
May 1	Labor Day
May 20	Lord Buddha's Birthday
mid-June	Dragon Boat (Tuen Ng) Festival
July 1	SAR Establishment Day
mid-September	Autumn Moon (Mid-Autumn) Festival
Oct. 1	National Day
Oct. 14	Chung Yeung Festival
December 25	Christmas Day
December 26	Boxing Day

HONG KONG, SAR 香港 ☎852

Despite Britain's flight from Victoria Harbour and Hong Kong's status as a Special Administrative Region (SAR) of China, it's business as usual in the former colony—lightning-fast and devil-may-care. Capitalism is the name of the game, and everybody's playing; Suzie Wong has become a corporate boss, and the *taipan* of Hong Kong's mythical past are eager, Armani-clad moguls. But beneath all the ultra-modern clothes, chic haircuts, and glossy building exteriors beats the heart of old Hong Kong. CEOs head home to light joss sticks and pay homage to Buddha in front of ancestral shrines. The gliding junks and incense-clouded temples of Hong Kong's past endure, somewhat obscured by Victoria Harbour's neon lights and the all too ubiquitous golden arches. Chinese opera and Canto-pop duke it out in the streets with 'N Sync and the Beatles. Indeed, Mr. Rolex, Ms. Rolls-Royce, and little Rémy Martin lead a peaceful cheek-by-jowl coexistence with seahorse aphrodisiacs and roast-duck banquets. A city in search of free-trade nirvana, Hong Kong works hard but plays harder, leaving many visitors stunned and slightly out of breath, but invigorated nonetheless.

INTERCITY TRANSPORTATION

BY AIR

The frighteningly modern **Hong Kong International Airport** at **Chek Lap Kok** sits just off Lantau Island's northern rim, some 30km from central Hong Kong. New arrivals enjoy all the latest airport perks, including 54 moving walkways, a mall, and a high-speed rail link between the airport and Victoria Harbour. Travelers ages 12 and over must pay a departure tax of HK$50; this is sometimes included in the price of the plane ticket.

A direct **Mass Transit Railway Airport Express Line (AEL)** jets from the airport to Kowloon (20min.; single journey or same-day return HK$90, children HK$45, round-trip valid for 1 month HK$110) and to Hong Kong Island (23min.; single journey or same-day return HK$100, children HK$50, round-trip HK$180). Airport trains depart every 10 minutes. There are free check-in counters at Hong Kong and Kowloon Stations.

Airbuses run from the airport to Hong Kong Island, Kowloon, and the New Territories. **A11** goes to Causeway Bay (every 15min., HK$40); **A12** to Siu Sai Wan (every 15min., HK$45); **A21** to the Hung Hom KCR Station (every 10min., HK$33); **A22** to the Lam Tin MTR Station (every 15min., HK$39); **A31** to Tsuen Wan (every

TUEN NG FESTIVAL

Dragon Boat Racing in Hong Kong

I grew up watching dragon boat racing and eating glutinous rice dumplings wrapped in bamboo leaves during Tuen Ng Festival every year in Hong Kong. Tuen Ng (Duan Wu in Mandarin) Festival takes place on the fifth day of the fifth month in the Chinese Lunar Calendar (in 2003, Tuen Ng Festival falls on June 4).

To understand dragon boat racing on Tuen Ng Festival, one must first explore its roots in ancient China. Legend has it that over 2,000 years ago, in a time when China was divided into many warring kingdoms, a great poet named Qu Yuan was a senior court official in the kingdom of Chu. Qu Yuan was slandered by his rivals and found himself in disfavor of Chu's inept Emperor. Eventually, Qu Yuan was exiled. Qu Yuan became very distraught and, on the fifth day of the fifth lunar month, he clasped a stone to his chest and plunged into the Milo River in present day Hunan province. When villagers heard that Qu Yuan threw himself into the river, they rushed into their boats to save him but they were too late. Later, the rescue attempt became a boat race and the boats gradually turned into dragon boats.

Each year, in the months of May and June, particularly on the day of Tuen Ng Festival, many dragon boat races are held throughout Hong Kong. Teams representing various clubs, associations, and companies, race in narrow boats to the beat of rhythmic drums. The boats measure over 10 meters and feature the head and tail of a dragon. Before the start of the races, the eyes of the dragons in each boat are dotted with paint, a custom to "awaken the dragons" and dispel evil spirits that might disrupt the festivities.

In addition to dragon boat racing, celebrators eat glutinous rice dumplings wrapped in bamboo leaves on Tuen Ng Festival. When it became known that Qu Yuan drowned, villagers threw rice packets into the water to feed the fish and other sea creatures so they would not eat Qu Yuan's body. Today, Chinese people eat rice dumplings to commemorate Qu Yuan's death. In Hong Kong, rice dumplings are traditionally stuffed with ham, beans, salted egg yokes, sausages, and nuts.

Early in 2002, I signed up to race with the dragon boat team of the American Women's Association (AWA) in Hong Kong. I thought that I would have some fun and get some good exercise. I had no idea how strenuous it was to race in a dragon boat! Each stroke requires a lot of power and all the paddlers must be in sync. Unlike rowing, each stroke goes up and down instead of sideways. One must use one's arms, legs, and torso in a strong coordinated motion for each stroke.

I was totally unprepared for my first dragon boat practice session. I wore long pants and sneakers. I did not have gloves (scrapped my hands), knee pads (scrapped my knee as I anchored my knee to the side of the boat), beach shoes (my sneakers were soaked), or goggles (sea water stung my eyes even though I had sun glasses). After practice, I was exhausted. I also found out that our practice schedule would ramp up from once a week to twice a week to three times a week in the next 3 months. I briefly thought about quitting the team but was too proud. I started to hit the gym…

3 months, 2 races, and 1 badly soaked mobile phone later, Tuen Ng Festival and our big race at Stanley finally arrived. Stanley hosts one of the largest dragon boat races (www.dragonboat.org.hk) with the participation of 140 teams (20 women's and 120 men's). The race length was 300 meters and it would take our team about 180 strokes. I remember the sound of the starting gun, paddling as fast as I could, thumping noises of our paddles hitting the water, loud drums and screams from our boat and the other boats. Miraculously, our boat crossed the finished line in first place. We raced twice more and came in first each time. At the end of the day, we were crowned the Ladies Champion of the 2002 Stanley Dragon Boat Race. It was an absolute thrill to win! A fairy tale ending to my dragon boat racing season! The AWA team had never before won first place in its 20 years of dragon boat racing... and come next June, I'll be racing again.

Alice Kung is a business development consultant in Hong Kong, helping high-tech startups from Silicon Valley sell their products in Asia.

15-20min., HK$17); **A35** to Mui Wo (every 30-40min.; HK$14, Su HK$23); **A41** to Sha Tin (every 20min., HK$20); **A43** to Fanling (every hr., HK$28).

Less-expensive, conventional **bus** routes include **E11** to Causeway Bay (every 10-20min., HK$21); **E22** to Kowloon City (every 6-20min., HK$18); **E33** to Tuen Mun (every 11-20min., HK$13); **E41** to Tai Po (every 12-20min., HK$13); and **E42** to Sha Tin (every 15-20min., HK$13).

Taxis wait outside the airport terminal. A ride from the airport to Tsim Sha Tsui (TST) costs about HK$270; to Causeway Bay HK$335; to Central HK$330; and to Tsuen Wan HK$235. There is a HK$5 surcharge per piece of luggage.

Numerous carriers fly from Hong Kong to other major Chinese cities, destinations in Southeast Asia, and points beyond.

Asian Airlines: Air China (CAAC), CAAC Bldg., 10 Queen's Rd., Ground fl., Central (☎2973 3666); 54-64B Nathan Rd., Mirador Mansions, Ground fl., TST (ticketing ☎2739 0022); United Centre, 95 Queen's Way, 34th fl., Admiralty (☎2973 3733). **All Nippon,** Pacific Place Two, 88 Queensway, Rm. 2512, Admiralty (☎2810 7100, ticketing ☎2810 7100). **Cathay Pacific,** New World Shopping Centre, 20 Salisbury Rd., Basement, Shop 53, TST East. Also at Swire House, 9 Connaught Rd., 4th fl., Central (☎2747 1888, ☎ticketing 2747 1577). **China Airlines,** St. George's Bldg., Ice House St. and Connaught Rd., 3rd fl., #2, Central (☎2843 9800, ticketing ☎2843 9800). **Dragon Air,** Cosco Tower, 183 Queen's Rd., 46th fl., Sheung Wan (☎2868 6777, ticketing ☎3193-3888). **Garuda Indonesia,** Henley Bldg., 5 Queen's Rd., 7th fl., Central (☎2840 0000, ticketing ☎2216 1088). **Japan Airlines,** Gloucester Tower, 11 Pedder Landmark, 20th fl., Central (☎2523 0081). **Korean Air,** South Seas Cetre II, 75 Mody Rd., Ground fl., TST East (☎2368 6221, ticketing ☎2369 7151). **Malaysia Airlines,** Central Tower, 28 Queen's Rd., 23rd fl., Central (☎2521 8181). **Myanmar Airlines,** Shun Tak Centre, 168-200 Connaught Rd., #2206, Central (☎2526 0100). **Singapore Airlines,** United Centre, 95 Queensway, 17th fl., Admiralty (☎2520 2233, ticketing ☎2769 6387). **Thai Airways,** United Centre, 95 Queensway, 24th fl., Admiralty (☎2876 6888).

European Airlines: Air France, Alexandra House, 20 Chater Rd., 21st fl., Central (☎2769 6662, ticketing ☎2524 8145). **British Airways,** Jardine House, 1 Connaught Pl., 24th fl. (☎2882 9000, ticketing ☎2822 9090). **KLM Royal Dutch,** World Trade Centre, 280 Gloucester Rd., Rm. 2201, Causeway Bay (☎2808 2111). **Lufthansa,** Winghan Tower, 173 Des Voeux Rd., 11th fl., Rm. 1109, Sheung Wan (☎2868 2313). **Virgin Atlantic,** Kinwick Centre, 32 Hollywood Rd., 27th fl., Central (☎2532 6060).

North American Airlines: Air Canada, Wheelock House, 20 Pedder St., Rm. 1002, Central (☎2522 1001, ticketing ☎2769 6032). **American Airlines,** New World Tower, 18 Queen's Rd. Central, Tower 1, 16th fl., Central (☎2826 9269; ticketing ☎2826 9102). **Northwest Airlines,** Alexandra House, 20 Chater Rd., 29th fl., Central (☎2810 4288). **United Airlines,** Gloucester Tower, 11 Pedder St., Landmark, 29th fl., Central (☎2810 4888, ticketing ☎2801 8688).

Other Airlines: Air New Zealand, Lipo Chun Chambers, 189 Des Voeux Rd., 17th fl., Central (☎2524 9041). **Ansett Australia,** Lipo Chun Chambers, 189 Des Voeux Rd., 17th fl., Central (☎2527 7883, ticketing ☎2842 3642). **Qantas,** Jardine House, 1 Connaught Place, 37th fl., #3701, Central (☎2822 2900, ticketing ☎2842 1400).

Flights from Hong Kong to major Chinese destinations include:

DESTINATION	FREQUENCY	PRICE (HK$)	DESTINATION	FREQUENCY	PRICE (HK$)
Beijing	5 per day	2650	Ji'nan	Tu, F	2320
Changsha	M-Tu, Th-Sa	1550	Kunming	daily	1640
Chengdu	daily	2600	Nanchang	Tu, F, Su	1650

DESTINATION	FREQUENCY	PRICE (HK$)	DESTINATION	FREQUENCY	PRICE (HK$)
Chongqing	M-Tu, Th-Sa	2150	Nanjing	2 per day	1750
Dalian	daily	2600	Ningbo	daily	1630
Fuzhou	3 per day	1560	Qingdao	daily	2190
Guilin	3 per day	1620	Shanghai	6 per day	1910
Guiyang	M, F	1500	Shenyang	M, W-Th, Sa	2910
Haikou	2 per day	1370	Tianjin	daily	2450
Hangzhou	daily	1560	Wuhan	1-2 per day	1730
Harbin	W	3070	Xiamen	2 per day	1730
Hefei	M, F	1530	Xi'an	daily	2080

BY LAND

TRAINS. Hong Kong is connected to the Chinese mainland by the **Kowloon-Canton Railway (KCR)** (☎2947 7888 or 2602 7799; fax 2690 3705), which runs from **Hung Hom (Kowloon) Station** to **Lo Wu Station** (every 3-10min.; HK$33, half-price ages 3-12 and 65 and over). Passengers can cross the Chinese border at Lo Wo into **Shenzhen** (see p. 528). Trains leave from Hung Hom 5:45am to 10:19pm and return from Lo Wu 6:01am to 12:20am. Tickets to Lo Wu can be purchased at any KCR station. The KCR also has direct service to the mainland. Tickets can be purchased at any KCR station or from **CTS** (see p. 532). Trains depart from Hung Hom (Kowloon) Station to: **Beijing West** (30hr., 3pm, upper hard sleeper HK$574); **Dongguan** (1hr.; 9:25am, 1:25, and 2:30pm; 1st class HK$135-145); **Foshan** (3hr., 2:30pm, HK$210); **Guangzhou** (1½-2hr., 7 per day, premium class HK$180-230); **Shanghai** (29¼hr., 3pm, upper hard sleeper HK$508); **Zhaoqing** (4¼hr., 2:30pm, HK$235). For direct mainland service, children aged 5-9 travel for half-price. Prices rise during peak tourist season and on public holidays or festivals.

BUSES. Buses make the journey between Hong Kong and Guangdong province. **Citybus,** 33 Canton Rd., China Hong Kong City, TST (☎2736 3888) serves **Shenzhen** (1½hr., several daily 7am-2:30pm, HK$65-85) and **Guangzhou** (3½hr.; M-Sa 7:30, 9:45am, and 2:30pm; one-way HK$80, round-trip HK$150). Expect an hour's delay when crossing the border on holidays. Bus reservations are recommended on holidays. **CTS** (see p. 532) can reserve tickets in advance for no surcharge.

Even destinations as distant as London or Moscow can be reached overland from Hong Kong, via China and the **Trans-Mongolian Railroad** (see p. 88). **Moonsky Star,** 36-44 Nathan Rd., Chungking Mansions, Block E, 4th fl., Flat 6 (☎2723 1376; fax 2723 6653; MonkeyHK@compuserve.com; www.monkeyshrine.com), is the best place to book packages and tickets for the Trans-Mongolian Railway. (Open M-Sa 10am-6pm.) Moonsky Star can arrange passage from Hong Kong, Guangzhou, or Beijing to **Moscow, St. Petersburg,** and beyond. Russian and Mongolian visas are available to those who book with them. Prices vary depending on the number and length of stopovers and class of train (US$395-2790). Visit their website for up-to-date information.

BY SEA

Travel from Hong Kong to **Macau** is easiest by boat. Most boats depart from the **Macau Ferry Terminal,** Shun Tak Centre, 200 Connaught Rd., Sheung Wan (MTR: Sheung Wan), but some leave from the **China Ferry Terminal,** 33 Canton Rd., TST, behind Kowloon Park. The **Macau Government Tourist Office,** Shun Tak Centre, 200

Connaught Rd., Sheung Wan, Rm. 336 (☎2857 2287; open daily 9:30am-5:45pm) and the **Hong Kong Tourist Association** (see p. 531) provide detailed schedules and fare information. For more information about other services provided by the Macau Government Tourist Office see **Macau: Tourist Offices** (p. 562). All ferries from Hong Kong arrive at the **Macau Maritime Ferry Terminal.**

Independent ferry companies go to **Guangzhou** and **Shenzhen. CTS** (see p. 532) also arranges passage to **Shantou** (14hr.; leaves W and Sa 5pm, returns F and Tu; 1st class HK$212, 2nd class HK$202), **Xiamen** (18hr.; Tu 2pm; 1st class HK$478, 2nd class HK$428), and **Zhuhai** (1¼hr.; 10 per day; 1st class HK$186, 2nd class HK$176).

A HK$26 departure tax is included in all ferry tickets, and prices are HK$5-10 more on the return trip from Macau.

Hong Kong & Yaumati Ferry Co., Ltd. (☎2736 1387 or 2516 9581). Arranges catamaran service from China Ferry Terminal to **Macau** (1hr.; HK$113, weekends and holidays HK$134, daily after 6pm HK$154). Hoverferry service (50min., 5 per day 7:45am-6:50pm, HK$105) from the China Ferry Terminal to **Shekou** (Shenzhen port).

Far East Jetfoil Company (☎2859 3333), Shun Tak Centre, Macau Ferry Terminal. From the Macau Ferry Terminal to Macau (1hr.; every 15min. 24hr., but fewer at night; economy HK$112, weekends and holidays HK$141, after 6pm HK$161).

ORIENTATION

Sandwiched between the **Kowloon Peninsula** and **Hong Kong Island, Victoria Harbour** is the heart of Hong Kong.

KOWLOON. North of the harbor, at the tip of the **Kowloon** peninsula, is **Tsim Sha Tsui (TST),** the city's tourist center. Along the eastern banks of the harbor, **Tsim Sha Tsui East (TST East),** with upscale shopping malls and hotels, struggles to compete with Tsim Sha Tsui proper for tourism business. Quiet **Hung Hom** sits on the other side of Tsim Sha Tsui East; tourists rarely visit this area except to visit the Whampoa Gardens. **New Kowloon,** north of Tsim Sha Tsui, marks the frontier between the waterfront districts and the New Territories. (For more on Kowloon, see p. 535.)

HONG KONG ISLAND. Situated across Victoria Harbour from Kowloon, Hong Kong Island is accessible by three harbor tunnels, the MTR's island line, and the Star Ferry. To the west, **Sheung Wan** is a honeycomb of cluttered streets and alleys. Right in the thick of things, **Central** and **Admiralty** sprout vertiginous skyscrapers. **Wan Chai** is one stop east from Admiralty on the MTR; **Causeway Bay** is one stop farther. The predominantly rural southern part of Hong Kong Island boasts expat-filled **Stanley** and the beaches at **Repulse Bay.** A short skip to the west is **Aberdeen** and the Jumbo Floating Restaurant. (For more on Hong Kong Island, see p. 542.)

NEW TERRITORIES. The New Territories sprawl all the way to Shenzhen and the border with mainland China. In the New Territories, **Tsuen Wan, Sha Tin,** and **Tai Po** are fast-developing "new towns"; the **Sai Kung Peninsula** boast hiking trails and sparkling beaches. (For more on the New Territories, see p. 552.)

OUTLYING ISLANDS. The Hong Kong archipelago is not limited to Hong Kong Island. Scenic **Lamma Island** (see p. 558), off the coast of Aberdeen, has walking trails, caves, and beaches. **Lantau Island** (see p. 555), the site of the international airport, houses the giant Tian Tan Buddha and the Po Lin and Po Lam Zen Monasteries. **Cheung Chau Island** boasts flamboyant character and great scenery.

LOCAL TRANSPORTATION

MASS TRANSIT RAILWAY (MTR). The MTR (information ☎2881 8888) is Hong Kong in a nutshell: super-efficient, automated, and lightning-fast; unfortunately, it's also the most expensive of Hong Kong's public transport options. Five MTR lines connect Kowloon, Hong Kong Island, the New Territories, Chek Lap Kok Airport, and most points in between. Tickets (HK$4-13; maximum HK$26) are valid for 90 minutes of travel on the day of issue. You can also purchase a long-term, multiple-use ticket called an **Octopus** (hotline ☎2993 8880) for HK$70 (ages 3-12 and the elderly), HK$100 (for Hong Kong students), or HK$150 (for adults); the card can be used on the MTR, KCR, AEL, most KMB and Citybus cross-harbor buses, Hong Kong & Yaumati Ferry routes to the outlying islands, and even in the photo booths in subway stations. The refundable deposit is HK$50; for short-term visitors, it is probably not worth the hassle. Information centers in MTR stations sell Octopus cards, give change, and answer questions. Most tickets cost more during **rush hour** (7:30-9:30am and 5:30-7:30pm). The system runs 6am-1am, although a few stations are open 7am-midnight.

KOWLOON-CANTON RAILWAY (KCR) AND LIGHT RAIL (LR). The KCR (☎2602 7799), an older version of the MTR, runs from Kowloon Station in TST East, through the New Territories, and to the Chinese border at Lo Wu (HK$3.50-9, children and seniors half-price). Passengers can change from the MTR to the KCR at Kowloon Tong Station. Trains run every three minutes 5:30am-12:20am. The KCR also operates direct service to the mainland (see p. 528).

The LR (☎2468 7788) joins the towns of Yuen Long and Tuen Mun in the New Territories. Tickets are HK$4-5.80 and can be purchased at vending machines along the route. Trains run daily 5:40am-12:30am.

BUSES. Hong Kong's five-star bus system (HK$1.20-45) ventures into any area worth visiting. Schedules and fares are posted at bus stops and available at any tourist office. Buses with numbers followed by an "M" run to MTR stations; those with numbers followed by a "K" go to KCR stations, and those followed by "X" indicate express routes. On Hong Kong Island, **New World First Bus** (☎2136 8888) runs cream-and-blue buses; **Citybus** (☎2873 0818) operates orange buses. In Kowloon, cream-and-red caravans are run by **Kowloon Motor Bus** (☎2745 4466). Air-conditioned buses cost extra.

Red-and-cream **minibuses** stop anywhere along their routes except at busy intersections and city bus stops. Tell the driver your stop; pay as you disembark. Green-and-cream minibuses called **maxicabs** only stop at marked maxicab stops; pay once onboard. In both cases, destinations are on the front of the bus, but the English is often small and hard to read. Buses accept only exact fare (HK$1.50-20).

TAXIS. Taxis are **red** in Kowloon and Hong Kong Island, **blue** on Lantau Island, and **green** in the New Territories. Base fare for red taxis is HK$15, and each additional 200m or minute of waiting time is HK$1.40. Red taxis will take you to Hong Kong Island and vice versa, but there are surcharges for the Cross-Harbour Tunnel (HK$20), the Eastern Harbour Tunnel (HK$30), and the Western Harbour Tunnel (HK$45) to cover the cab's round-trip tunnel toll. Base fare for blue taxis is HK$12; each additional 200m or minute of waiting time costs HK$1.20. Base fare for green taxis is HK$12.50; each additional 200m or minute of waiting time costs HK$1.20. Green taxis only pick up and drop off passengers within the New Territories. Taxi drivers may also charge HK$5 per piece of luggage. Most major thoroughfares have taxi stands. Taxis are not allowed to pick up or set down passengers in areas marked with yellow lines. To file a complaint against a driver, copy down the taxi number displayed on the dashboard and call the **police hotline** (☎2527 7177).

TRAMS. Aging trams have lumbered along northern Hong Kong Island since 1904 and are an inexpensive way to see Hong Kong Island. The tram follows a route from Kennedy Town to Shau Kei Wan, past Central, Admiralty, Wan Chai, and Causeway Bay. Trams run 6am-1am. Fare is HK$2.2 (children and seniors half-price). Board at the rear and pay with exact change as you exit. The tram's last stop is written in English on the front. Contact **Hong Kong Tramways** (☎2118 6338) for more information.

TRANSPORTATION INFORMATION

For the most up-to-date information on all types of transportation into, out of, and around Hong Kong, contact one of the following companies. If all else fails, contact the **Hong Kong Tourist Association hotline** (☎2508 1234). For links to up-to-date transport information on the Internet, go to www.igsd.gov.hk.

Hong Kong International Airport (☎2181 0000).

To and From the Airport: Airbus Coach (☎2745 4466) or **Airport Express** (☎2881 8888).

Trains: MTR (☎2881 8888). **KCR:** East Rail (☎2602 7799); Light Rail (☎2468 7788); West Rail (☎2684 8833).

Buses: New World First Bus (☎2136 8888). **Kowloon Motor Bus** (☎2745 4466). **City Bus** (☎2873 0818). **Lantao Bus Co.** (☎2984 9848).

Taxis: Hong Kong Island (☎2861 1008), Kowloon/New Territories (☎2397 0922). **Taxi Union Loss Report Hotline** (☎2385 8288).

Trams: Hong Kong Tramway (☎2548 7102). **Peak Tramway** (☎2522 0922).

Ferries: Star Ferry (☎2367 7065). **Hong Kong Ferry** (☎2815 6063).

FERRIES. The **Star Ferry** (☎2367 7065) has been in operation for over 100 years. The Star Ferry Terminal in TST is at the end of Salisbury Rd. Ferries glide between TST and **Central** (every 5-10min. 6:30am-11:30pm; lower deck HK$1.70, upper deck HK$2.20) and between TST and **Wan Chai** (every 8-20min. 7:30am-11pm, HK$2.20). There is also service to **Hung Hom** from the Star Ferry pier in Central, in front of Jardine House and the post office in Exchange Square (7am-7pm, HK$5.30).

Ferries to the outlying islands leave from the **New Ferry Piers,** off the Exchange Square in Central, to **Lamma** from Pier 5 (30min.; every hr. 6:30am-12:30am; M-Sa HK$10, Su HK$14); **Cheung Chau** from Pier 6 (48min.; every hr. 6:20am-11:15pm; M-Sa HK$10, deluxe class HK$16; Su and public holidays HK$15, deluxe class HK$24); **Lantau** from Pier 7 (48min.; every 1½-2hr. 6:10am-10:30pm; M-Sa HK$10-16, Su HK$15-24); and **Peng Chau** (38min.; every 30min. 7am-11:30pm; M-Sa HK$10-16, Su HK$15-24). For schedules and fares, contact the tourist office or the **Hong Kong & Yaumati Ferry Co. Ltd.** (☎2736 1381 or 2516 9581).

PRACTICAL INFORMATION

TOURIST AND FINANCIAL SERVICES

TOURIST OFFICES

Hong Kong Tourist Association (HKTA), The Center, 99 Queen's Rd. Ground fl., Central (☎2807 6543; fax 2806 0303; info@hkta.org; www.hkta.org), Hong Kong Island. MTR: Central, D exit. Turn left on Pedder St., and then turn left onto Des Voeux Rd. Central.

Walk about 10min. until you reach a set of escalators on your left. Take the escalator one level up and walk through the maze of steel mirrors between the two water pools until you reach another set of escalators. Take the escalator down into the basement, turn left and voilà! An important stop for any visitor to the SAR. Scores of glossy new brochures and information pamphlets on events, festivals, and activities line the shelves, created in accordance with HKTA's two-year campaign for tourism since April 2001. Open daily 8am-6pm. Other HKTA offices at **Star Ferry Concourse,** TST (open daily 8am-6pm) and **Hong Kong International Airport** in Buffer Halls A and B in the transit area (open 24hr.). Weekly *Hong Kong Diary* lists current festivals and events. Visitors with foreign passports who plan to do some shopping can also ask for a free **Hong Kong VIP card** that offers special discounts at many upscale stores. Self-guided **walking tour** guides with portable CD-ROM player and headphone cost HK$50 (HK$500 refundable deposit). *Exploring Hong Kong's Countryside* by Edwards Stokes (HK$80) serves as an excellent reference for walks and hikes on Hong Kong Island, Lamma, Lantau, and New Territories. You can also request a complimentary copy of any one of the guides to Hong Kong's 18 districts, each of which lists sights and all relevant tourist information.

Multilingual HKTA Visitor Hotline (☎2508 1234). Open daily 8am-6pm.

24hr. Infofax Facsimile Information Service (☎900 6077 1128). Local calls HK$1 per min.

Online Service: Try DiscoverHongKong.com. The **Interactive Government Service Directory (IGSD)** at www.igsd.gov.hk has a directory of phone numbers and links for public services, including public transportation.

TRAVEL AGENCIES

Sincerity Travel, 835A Star House East Block (☎2730 3269), next to the Star Ferry pier. Offers discounts for ISIC holders (ISIC HK$100). Open M-F 9:30am-7:30pm, Sa 9:30am-6:30pm. Credit cards accepted (2.25% surcharge).

CTS, CTS House, 78-83 Connaught Rd., 4th fl., Central (☎2853 3888; fax 2541 9777; ctsdmd@hkstar.com). Open M-Sa 9am-5pm. Branch offices in **Alpha House** (27-33 Nathan Rd., 1st fl.; ☎2315 7188), **Central** (China Travel Bldg., 77 Queen's Rd., Mezzanine; ☎2522 0450); **Mong Kok** (62-72 Sai Yee St., 2nd fl.; ☎278 9582); **Wan Chai** (138 Hennessy Rd., Southern Centre, 1st fl.; ☎283 2388).

Shoestring Travel Ltd., Alpha House, 27-33 Nathan Rd., 4th fl., Flat A (☎2366 6222; shoetvl@hkstar.com). Enter from Peking Rd. Open M-F 8:30am-7pm, Sa 8:30am-5pm. Student discounts available. All credit cards accepted (except JCB).

Travel-Net Services, Hong Kong Pacific Centre, 28 Hankow Rd., 1st fl., G11 (☎2723 7138; trvl_net@HK.super.net). Visas to Burma, Cambodia, Nepal, Taiwan, Thailand, and Vietnam. Open M-F 9am-6pm, Sa 9am-1pm.

Sunflower Travel Service, Prestige Tower, 23-25 Nathan Rd., 6th fl. (☎2721 1682, ticketing department 2881 1788). Enter from the basement stairs below Joyce Cafe. Tours into mainland China by bus, train, car, ferry, and air. Visas for customers who book with them. Specify if you're looking for low prices. Open M-Sa 9am-8pm, Su 10am-6pm.

Traveller Services, Silvercord Tower 1, 30 Canton Rd., 10th fl., #1012 (☎2375 2222; www.traveller.com.hk). This agency was started in Chungking Mansions for backpackers; inquire about cheap air and boat fares. Open M-F 9am-6pm, Sa 9am-1pm.

Armaan Travel Service, Alpha House, 27-33 Nathan Rd., 5th fl., Flat C (☎2723 3330; atsl@armaantravel.com). Mostly deals with air travel; arranges visas to India. Open M-F 9:30am-6pm, Sa 9:30am-1pm. Credit cards accepted.

CONSULATES, VISAS, AND IMMIGRATION

The Chinese consulate is on 26 Harbour Rd., Lower Block, 5th fl., Wan Chai (☎2827 1881). For an extensive listing of other consular offices in Hong Kong, see **Essentials: Consular Services in China** (p. 48).

British citizens can stay in Hong Kong visa-free for six months; US, Canadian, Australian, New Zealand, Western European, and most Central and South American citizens can stay for three. Eastern European and African citizens usually require a visa. The Hong Kong Immigration Department handles **visa extensions.**

Most travel agencies and some guesthouse owners can arrange **Chinese visas** (see p. 50). This may take 1-5 days, and prices vary (HK$100-200 for single entry, 1 month tourist visa). Photo machines in every subway station (HK$35) and in the CTS office (HK$30) provide fast visa and passport photos.

Hong Kong Immigration Department, Immigration Tower, 7 Gloucester Rd., Wan Chai (24hr. ☎2824 6111; www.info.gov.hk/immd). For **visa extensions,** bring your passport, airplane ticket, and HK$135 and fill out form ID91. Work and study visas require an ID card, passport, a completed ID91 application form, and a letter from the appropriate company or school. Open M-F 8:45am-4:30pm, Sa 9-11:30am.

The Visa Office of the Ministry of Foreign Affairs of the People's Republic of China in Hong Kong, China Resources Bldg., 26 Harbour Rd., Lower Block, 5th fl., Wan Chai (☎2827 1881). The entrance is off Gloucester Rd., in the red-and-white building. Issues single-entry tourist visas (1 month, HK$100); dual-entry visa (1 month, HK$150); multiple-entry visa (HK$400). Visa processing takes 1 working day. Express 1hr. service (HK$150). Photos (HK$30 for 4). Open M-F 9:30am-12:20pm and 2-5:30pm.

CTS (see above). Bring HK$180, a passport, and a recent photo to fill out a visa application at the office. Processes a 3-month single-entry visitor visa in 3 days, express visas (HK$518) in 1 working day. Open daily 9am-5pm.

FINANCIAL SERVICES

Banks: Hang Seng Bank (☎2825 5111, hotline 2822 0228), at every subway station. Open M-F 9am-5pm, Sa 9am-1pm. **HongkongBank** (☎2822 1111, hotline 2749 3322). Open M-F 9am-4:30pm, Sa 9am-12:30pm. **Bank of China** (☎2826 6888). Open M-F 9am-5pm, Sa 9am-1pm.

Currency Exchange: Banks usually offer the best rates, but there are several avenues for currency exchange. In **Chungking Mansions,** 36-44 Nathan Rd., stalls on the 1st fl. (not the very first booth at the entrance) have competitive rates and are usually open daily 9:30am-6pm. AmEx cardholders can use Jetco **ATMs** for cash advances in Hong Kong currency. MC and Visa holders can use HongkongBank's "Electronic Money" ATMs as well as Citibank ATMs.

American Express: Henley Bldg., 5 Queen's Rd., 1st fl., Central (☎2277 1010, 24hr. hotline 2528 3247). MTR: Central Station, Landmark exit. Exchanges currency and AmEx traveler's checks (no fee). Handles credit card payments. Open M-F 9am-5pm, Sa 9am-12:30pm. China Plaza, 48 Cameron Rd., 1st fl., TST (☎2926 1606). Exchanges traveler's checks. Open M-F 9am-5pm, Sa 9am-12:30pm. Taikoo Place, Somerset House, 979 King's Rd., 18th fl., Quarry Branch (☎2811 6888). Offers client mail services, mail held 30 days at no fee for members and holders of AmEx traveler's checks; does not exchange traveler's checks. Open M-F 9am-5pm, Sa 9am-12:30pm.

Thomas Cook: ☎2854 4938.

Western Union: ☎2528 5631.

Lost or Stolen Credit Cards: American Express (☎2811 6122); **Citibank** (☎2823 2323; **JCB** (☎2366 7211); **Mastercard** (☎2511 6387); **Visa** (☎2810 8033).

LOCAL SERVICES

Bookstores: P.O.V. Bookstore, 137-147 Lockhart Rd., Hong Kong Mansion, Shop A, 1st fl., Wan Chai (☎2865 5116). Fiction, gay and lesbian literature, and a small selection of Chinese and foreign CDs. Open M-F 11am-10pm, Sa 11am-midnight, and Su 1-10pm. Another branch in Prosperous Garden, Shop 112, Cinema Block, 3 Public Square St., Yau Ma Tei. **Times,** Golden Crown Court, 66-70 Nathan Rd., Basement, TST (☎2367 4340 or 2367 0644). Writing supplies, maps, and fiction 20-30% off list price. Open daily 10:30am-8:45pm. Branches in Central and Causeway Bay.

Library: Hong Kong Central Library, 66 Causeway Rd. (☎2827 2833 for libraries in Hong Kong Island and Kowloon; ☎2698 0002 for libraries in New Territories; www.hkpl.gov.hk), MTR: Causeway Bay. Branch libraries in Kowloon, Sha Tin, Tuen Mun, Tsuen Wan, and Hong Kong Island. Visitors can check out a maximum of 5 books for HK$130 each (refundable). Free **Internet access** at all libraries; the Central Library has over 500 computers. Open M-Th 10am-7pm, F 10am-9pm, Sa-Su 10am-5pm.

Weather and Local Information: Time and Temperature in English (☎18501). **Weather Conditions** in English (☎187 8066). **Special Weather** such as typhoons (☎2835 1473). **English Newsline** (☎900 0038 7177).

Gay Organizations: HORIZONS, Winning Commercial Bldg., 46-48 Hillwood Rd., TST (☎2815 9268; fax 2542 3714). Information on gay nightlife and events around town as well as support and counseling. Open Tu and Th 7:30-10:30pm.

EMERGENCY AND COMMUNICATIONS

Emergency: ☎999.

Police: Crime Hotline and Taxi Complaints (☎2527 7177). To locate the nearest police station, call 2860 2000.

Medical Services: Hong Kong Island: **Queen Mary Hospital** (☎2855 3111); Kowloon: **Queen Elizabeth Hospital** (☎2958 8888); New Territories: **Prince of Wales Hospital** (☎2632 2211). **Free ambulance service:** Hong Kong Island (☎2576 6555); Kowloon and New Territories (☎2713 5555).

Internet Access: All public libraries have free Internet access (see **Hong Kong Central Library,** above), with so many computers that you usually don't have to wait too long, especially not on weekdays. Also, universities such as the Hong Kong Polytechnic University on Yuk Choi Rd., Hung Hom, often have many computers with Internet access.

Cash Online (☎2366 0060), on Nathan Rd. just before Peking Rd., TST (MTR: Tsim Sha Tsui, Hong Kong Museum of Art exit.). HK$20 per 30min.; free hot beverage, juice, or soft drink. HK$10 per additional 30min. Open daily 8:30am-10pm.

Pacific Coffee House Company, Queensway Plaza, 1st fl., Shop C34 (☎2861 2302). MTR: Admiralty exit. Free access for 15-20min. with purchase of coffee (HK$20). Open daily 7:30am-9pm. Numerous other branches around Hong Kong. The **New Territories branch** is at Festival Walk, Kowloon Tong exit (☎2265 8600). MTR: Kowloon Tong. Open M-Sa 7am-10pm, Su 9am-9pm.

Maxim's Fast Food, Newtown and Grand Central Plaza, Shop 240-244, phase 1 (☎2697 3405). KCR: Sha Tin exit. Has an impressive wall of 10 terminals. 20min. free Internet use for customers. Chinese fast-food HK$7.50-$28.50. Open daily 7am-10pm. Branch in Central MTR station also has Internet booths (☎2140 6689).

Post Offices: GPO, 2 Connaught Pl., **Central** (☎2921 2333). MTR: Central, Jardine House exit. Immediately to the right of Star Ferry and in front of the Jardine House. *Poste Restante* held for 2 weeks. Open M-Sa 8am-6pm, Su 8am-2pm. Hermes House, 10 Middle Rd., Ground fl., TST (☎2366 4111). MTR: TST, Nathan Rd. exit. Walk past

Chungking Mansions toward the harbor, and turn left onto Middle Rd.; Hermes House is at the end of the street on the left. *Poste Restante* held for 3 months. Open M-F 8am-6pm, Sa 8am-2pm, Su 8am-6pm.

Telephones: HK$70 or HK$100 IDD phonecards sold at Hong Kong Telecom Service centers, HKTA offices, or 7-Eleven and Circle K stores. Hong Kong Telecom sells cards in denominations of HK$200, HK$300, and HK$500. The office on 10 Middle Rd. is open 24hr. Local calls HK$1 per 5min. For home country operators, call the **HCD number** for your country: Telstra Australia (☎800 96 0161); British Telecom (☎800 96 0044); Canada Direct (☎800 96 1100); Telecom Eireann (☎800 96 0353); New Zealand Telecom (☎800 96 0064); Telekom South Africa (☎800 96 0027); AT&T (☎800 96 1111); MCI (☎800 96 1121); Sprint (☎800 96 1877).

Telephone Information: Directory Assistance (☎1081). **Operator assistance** (☎10010) for IDD inquiries, collect calls, or phonecard inquiries.

ENTERTAINMENT INFORMATION

Hong Kong is on the cutting edge of Chinese pop culture, dictating trends on the mainland in much the same way that Europe dominates high fashion. The opportunities for artistic and cultural enrichment can be at times overwhelming. The following are some great resources:

bc Magazine event listings (☎2976 0876; www.bcmagazine.net).
HKTA events calendar (☎2508 1234; www.hkta.org).
HK Magazine event listings (☎2850 5065; email asiacity@asia-city.com.hk).
Hong Kong Academy for Performing Arts (☎2584 8500).
Hong Kong Arts Centre (☎2734 2820; Bulletin Box ☎2824 5355; www.hkac.org.hk). Free guide to monthly program available at Centre.
URBTIX hotline (☎2734 9009).
Hong Kong City Hall (☎2921 2840; www.lcsd.gov.hk/hkch).
Hong Kong Coliseum box office (☎2895 1347). Open daily 10am-6:30pm.
Hong Kong Cultural Centre (☎2734 2009; www.lcsd.gov.hk/hkcc).
Hong Kong Stadium box office (☎2895 7895). Open daily 9am-5pm.

KOWLOON 九龙

Kowloon, the jam-packed 11 sq. km peninsula off the New Territories, is the quintessential picture of Hong Kong. Kowloon (*gau lung* in Cantonese) is named for the nine mythical dragons that are said to inhabit the peninsula—one for each of the peninsula's eight mountain peaks and one more for Ping, an ancient child-emperor. Today, the color and fury of these legendary winged beasts still lingers in the resplendent natural beauty of the area, but apartment blocks, hotels, restaurants, and plazas encroach on their traditional turf. Crowds along Nathan Rd. in TST linger in front of jewelry stores, inhale the subtle hue of saffron in restaurants, or don three-inch dancing shoes at night to paint the town red. All the while, the dragon's fiery breath still blows throughout the land—a pulsing heat that travelers to Hong Kong simply cannot avoid.

 ORIENTATION

At the southernmost tip of Victoria Harbour are the roads **Tsim Sha Tsui (TST)** and **Tsim Sha Tsui East (TST East),** separated by **Chatham Rd. South** and bounded in the south by **Salisbury Rd.** Along the waterfront are some of Kowloon's most recognizable landmarks, including the Star Ferry Pier, the Cultural Centre, the Hong Kong Space Museum, and the New World Centre. **Nathan Rd.** begins at Salisbury Rd. and runs north into the smaller districts of **Yau Ma Tei** and **Mong Kok,** both of which are famous for their crowded street markets. The red line of the **MTR** subway system runs along Nathan Rd. and under the harbor to Hong Kong Island. To the east, past the **terminus of the KCR** and the **Hong Kong Coliseum,** lies **Hung Hom.** In the north, **Boundary Rd.** separates Kowloon from the New Territories.

ACCOMMODATIONS

Tsim Sha Tsui offers numerous accommodations in the center of the chaos, dirt, noise, and decadent luxury that is Hong Kong. Budget digs in TST consist mainly of guesthouses that are tucked away inside vast "mansions"—cavernous apartment buildings where the flats have been partitioned into smaller rooms. Be wary of individuals along Nathan Rd. and outside Mirador Mansions and Chungking Mansions who aggressively tout their "very clean, very quiet, very cheap" rooms. Also, if you have decided where to stay, keep this information to yourself.

CHUNGKING MANSIONS 重庆大厦

Chungking Mansions, 36-44 Nathan Rd. (MTR: Tsim Sha Tsui, Hong Kong Museum of Art exit), is far and away the most notorious of the TST mansions. The elegant dark marble and gold lettering outside hide Chungking's chaotic interior; it is legendary for its dim labyrinth of hallways and dank staircases, crowded elevators, and disreputable inhabitants. Chungking Mansions in fact does have very quiet, very clean rooms, but it is unlikely that the touts on the ground floor are affiliated with such establishments.

Chungking Mansions is divided into five blocks, unimaginatively called A, B, C, D, and E block. From the entrance to the arcade, the A, B, and C elevators are on the left, while D and E are on the right. Each block has a pair of elevators: one services even-numbered floors, the other odd-numbered ones. Quality varies more than price, so choose guesthouses carefully; ask to look at a room before agreeing to spend the night. All guesthouses accept cash only.

Women traveling alone should take particular care: they may find themselves the object of unwanted attention from some long-term Chungking residents.

Travelers Hostel, A Block, 16th fl. (☎2368 2505 or 2368 7710; digand@hotmail.com). Spacious, fairly clean dorms popular with backpackers. Cable TV in common room. Free lockers for guests, but no padlocks provided. Luggage storage HK$5-10 per day. **Internet access** HK$10 per 15min. IDD service. 6-bed dorms with A/C HK$65; singles HK$100, with A/C HK$130 . ❶

Kyoto Guesthouse, A8, 15th fl. (☎2721 3574 or 9077 8297). Colorful rooms and cheerful staff. Singles HK$80-100, with A/C and bath HK$120; doubles with A/C and bath HK$150-160. HK$10 discount for individual travelers. ❷

Harbour Guesthouse, B8, 4th fl. (☎2721 2207 or 2367 2777). All rooms have A/C and TV. Discounts for longer stays; rates increase by about HK$10 in summer. Singles HK$100, with bath HK$110; doubles HK$160, with bath HK$200. ❷

Mandarin Guesthouse, E5, 13th fl. (☎2366 0073). A location in block E means less crowded elevators. Every room in this average guesthouse has A/C, bath, phone, sandals, towels, and toilet paper. IDD service. Singles HK$130-150; doubles HK$200. Prices very negotiable. ❷

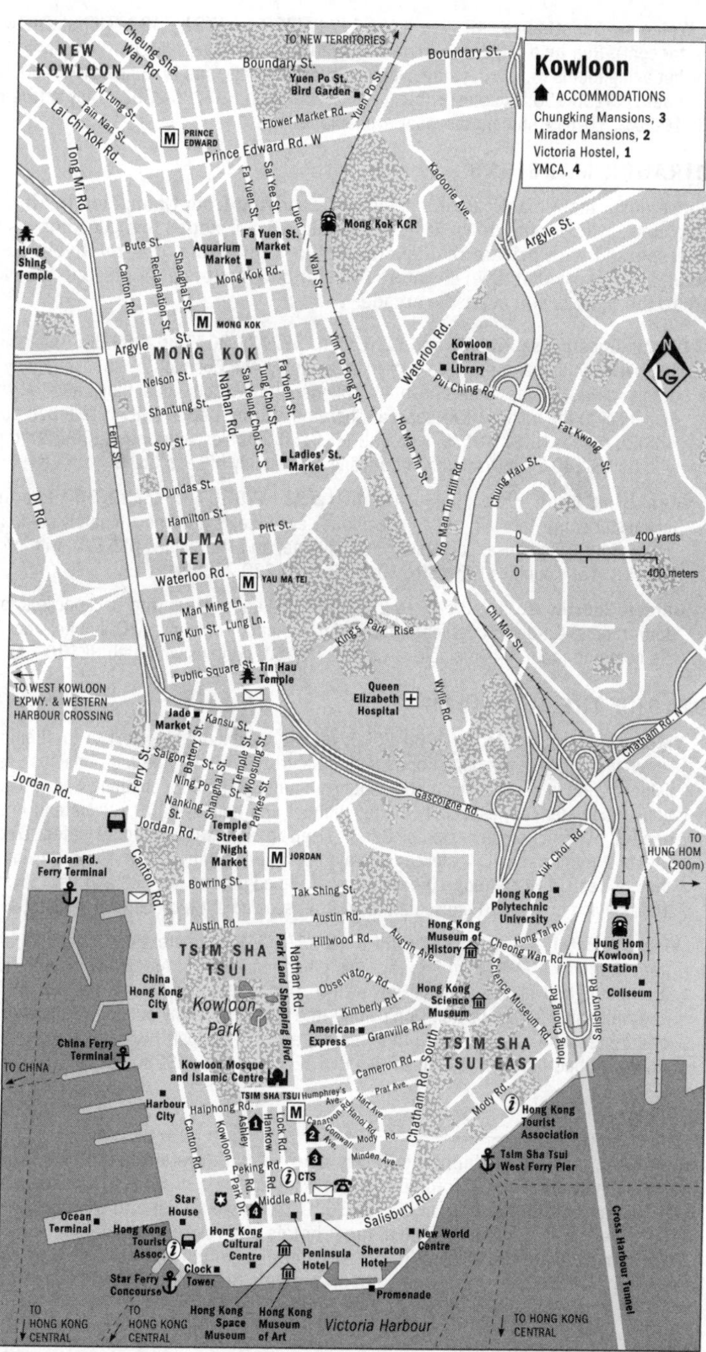
Kowloon
ACCOMMODATIONS
Chungking Mansions, 3
Mirador Mansions, 2
Victoria Hostel, 1
YMCA, 4
NEW KOWLOON
MONG KOK
YAU MA TEI
TSIM SHA TSUI
TSIM SHA TSUI EAST
TO NEW TERRITORIES
Boundary St.
Yuen Po St. Bird Garden
Flower Market Rd.
Prince Edward Rd. W
PRINCE EDWARD
Mong Kok KCR
Fa Yuen St. Market
Aquarium Market
Mong Kok Rd.
MONG KOK
Argyle St.
Kowloon Central Library
Pui Ching Rd.
Waterloo Rd.
Fat Kwong St.
Chung Hau St.
Ladies' St. Market
Hung Shing Temple
Kadoorie Ave.
Ho Man Tin St.
Ho Man Tin Hill Rd.
Pitt St.
Hamilton St.
Dundas St.
Soy St.
Shantung St.
Nelson St.
Nathan Rd.
Ferry St.
Tong Mi Rd.
Lai Chi Kok Rd.
Tai Nan St.
Ki Lung St.
Cheung Sha Wan Rd.
YAU MA TEI
Man Ming Ln.
Tung Kun St.
Lung Ln.
King's Park Rise
Public Square St.
Tin Hau Temple
Queen Elizabeth Hospital
Wylie Rd.
Chi Man St.
0
400 yards
400 meters
TO WEST KOWLOON EXPWY. & WESTERN HARBOUR CROSSING
Jade Market
Kansu St.
Saigon St.
Battery St.
Jordan Rd.
Gascoigne Rd.
Chatham Rd. N
Temple Street Night Market
JORDAN
Jordan Rd. Ferry Terminal
Canton Rd.
Bowring St.
Tak Shing St.
Austin Rd.
Hillwood Rd.
Yuk Choi Rd.
Hong Kong Polytechnic University
Hong Kong Museum of History
Cheong Wan Rd.
TO HUNG HOM (200m)
Hung Hom (Kowloon) Station
Coliseum
Kowloon Park
China Hong Kong City
Park Land Shopping Blvd.
Observatory Rd.
Kimberly Rd.
Hong Kong Science Museum
American Express
Granville Rd.
China Ferry Terminal
TO CHINA
Kowloon Mosque and Islamic Centre
Cameron Rd.
Chatham Rd. South
Harbour City
Haiphong Rd.
TSIM SHA TSUI
Mody Rd.
Hong Kong Tourist Association
Tsim Sha Tsui West Ferry Pier
Peking Rd.
CTS
Middle Rd.
Salisbury Rd.
Star House
Ocean Terminal
Hong Kong Tourist Assoc.
Hong Kong Cultural Centre
Peninsula Hotel
Sheraton Hotel
New World Centre
Clock Tower
Star Ferry Concourse
Promenade
Hong Kong Space Museum
Hong Kong Museum of Art
Victoria Harbour
TO HONG KONG CENTRAL
TO HONG KONG CENTRAL
TO HONG KONG CENTRAL
Cross Harbour Tunnel

Welcome Guesthouse, A5, 7th fl. (☎2721 7793 or 2721 7436; gloriak@netvigator.com). Run by a father-son team that readily offers travel advice, it rents out clean but aging rooms with A/C, vfridge, large windows, towels, and TV. Singles HK$100, with bath HK$130-150; doubles with twin beds and bath HK$200-220. In July prices rise 10-20%. 10-15% student discount available. ❷

MIRADOR MANSIONS

These days, many backpackers seem to be moving from Chungking to Mirador Mansions, a few doors down at 54-64 Nathan Rd.; Mirador's few guesthouses are interspersed with private residences. Unlike Chungking, it is relatively clean, quiet, and uncrowded. Two elevators (one for odd-numbered floors, one for even) are to the right as you enter the arcade.

Cosmic Guesthouse, A1, A2, and F1, 12th fl. (☎2721 3077 or 2369 6669). Open for just over 3 years, and run by a very friendly family, the Cosmic Guesthouse is truly out of this world. Spotless rooms have A/C, phone, and TV. Communal fridge and hot water dispenser in the hallway. IDD service. Check-out 11am. Deposit HK$100. 8-bed dorms HK$60; singles HK$110-130, with bath HK$150; doubles with bath $200-220; triples with bath $240-270. Discounts for anyone with a copy of *Let's Go*. ❶

Man Hing Lung Hotel, F2, 14th fl. (☎2311 8807 or 2722 0678; mhlhotel@hkstar.com). This fairly clean guesthouse even meets government safety standards, unusual for guesthouses in Mirador. A/C, phone, and TV. Singles HK$120, with private bath HK$150; doubles HK$150-220; triples HK$220-270. ❷

Garden Guesthouse, F4, 3rd fl. (☎2311 1183). Very popular with backpackers for its dorm rooms, Garden's best feature is its large outdoor balcony. A/C, phone, and TV in the common room. 6-bed single-sex dorms HK$60; doubles with bath HK$200. ❶

BEYOND THE MANSIONS

YMCA, 41 Salisbury Rd. (☎2268 7000; room@ymcahk.org.hk), next to the Peninsula Hotel and opposite the Hong Kong Cultural Centre. MTR: Tsim Sha Tsui. This posh establishment features a swimming pool, squash courts, and indoor climbing walls. Reservations recommended, especially during summer and holidays. IDD service and Internet access. Wheelchair accessible. Closet-sized lockers with personal safes. Deposit HK$150 room deposit. 7 night max stay; dorm guests must show a visa proving that they've been in Hong Kong 10 days or fewer. 4-bed dorms with A/C and bath HK$190. 10% service charge. 10% discount for YMCA associates. Credit cards accepted. ❸

Victoria Hostel, 33 Hankow Rd., 3rd fl. (☎2376 0621; vhostel@hkstar.com), 2 blocks from Nathan Rd. MTR: Tsim Sha Tsui, Hong Kong Museum of Art exit. Walk onto Middle Rd., turn right, walk ahead until Hankow Rd., turn right and walk until you see the blue-and-white sign for the hostel. Don't worry—the building's grimy outside is not indicative of its interior. A/C, common baths, phone, and TV. Deposit HK$100. 10-bed dorms HK$60; 4-bed dorms HK$140; singles HK$220; doubles HK$280. ❶

FOOD

Hong Kong is a self-acclaimed culinary heaven, with restaurants and food stalls lining every road. The *Official Dining and Entertainment Guide* (available at HKTA offices), the *HK Magazine*, and *bc Magazine* all list and rank restaurants and are free and widely available at most hotels and restaurants.

Dim sum is the soul of Hong Kong. Meaning "to touch the heart," *dim sum* is positive proof that the fastest way to someone's heart is through their stomach.

Enjoyed in the late morning or early afternoon, *dim sum* is a selection of bite-sized morsels shared by three or four people as they drink pot after pot of tea. Most Cantonese restaurants serve *dim sum* from 11am to 2pm, although some establishments devoted solely to *dim sum* continue on through the evening. The usual procedure for ordering *dim sum* involves either checking off a desired dish on a slip of paper or pointing at waiters who wander by with rolling carts.

Some of the best culinary bargains are found in **no-name shops and stalls.** Food vendors come out in the late evening (after 11pm) to refuel eager shoppers along **Nathan, Carnarvon,** and **Mody Rds.** Also, try the small streets west of Nathan Rd. While many Indian restaurants have members-only rules, the first and mezzanine floors of Chungking Mansions host a number of jam-packed but dirt-cheap stalls serving delectable South Asian dishes (often under HK$20).

Small cafes along **Haiphong** and **Canton Rds.** post menus listing Cantonese and Western food items outside their windows (HK$30-40). For those seeking Western food, **Ashley Rd.** features restaurants and pubs that serve up hearty portions of Australian, Italian, and English food at mid-range prices. **Kimberly Rd.,** which branches off Nathan Rd. farther inland, is packed to the brim with restaurants. The area bounded by **Hart Ave.** and **Prat Ave.,** on the opposite side of Nathan Rd. to Kowloon Park, has an exciting selection of both Western and Asian fare, and nightlife venues to help sated diners work away the extra calories.

Most malls in the city have **food courts,** which usually offer a great selection of cheap Asian and Western fast food. **City's Super,** inside Harbour City Mall on Canton road in TST, has a dizzying selection of international fast food cuisine that's a little more upscale than most food-court fare. Set meals run about HK$26-60. (Open Su-Th 10:30am-9:30pm, F-Sa and public holidays 10:30am-10pm. ❷)

The Sweet Dynasty, 88 Canton Rd., Ground fl., TST (☎2375 9119), opposite the Harbour City shopping plaza. Famed for its *tong shui,* sweet soups traditionally served after meals. Flour and peanut balls, pudding soups, and more curiously named dishes like *stewed snow frog fat* are also on the menu. You may want to start off with a delicious bowl of almond soup (HK$15). Open Su-Th 7:30am-midnight, F-Sa 7:30am-1am. ❶

Cheerful Ginseng Congee, Fullcorp Centre, 53-55 Chatham Rd. South, TST East (☎2368 9203), near Cameron Rd. True to its name, this restaurant serves up delicious bowls of hot congee for a palatable HK$16-30. Some meat congees are slightly more expensive (HK$38-88). Health-friendly, vegetarian-friendly, and people-friendly. English and Chinese menu. Takeout available. Open daily 7:30am-4am. ❷

Han Wo Korean Restaurant, Multifield Plaza, 3-7A Prat Ave., Ground fl., Flat 9, TST (☎2739 7798). Open atmosphere and open to all budgets, with prices ranging from HK$15 to HK$550. Open daily 11am-1am. Credit cards accepted. ❷

Wing Fat Restaurant, 448 Nathan Rd., Ground fl., Yau Ma Tei (☎2385 8167). The unpretentious fare, cheap prices, long hours, and plastic-vinyl decor are as down-to-earth as you can get. Dishes HK$30-45; french toast HK$15. Open daily 7am-4am. ❸

Jade Court Seafood Restaurant, Pacific Centre, 16-38 Hankow Rd., 2nd fl., TST (☎2723 1823). A festive atmosphere prevails in this local favorite. Light *dim sum* for 3 people (3-4 dishes) costs a reasonable HK$200. Top it off with mango pudding. Open daily 7am-midnight. Credit cards accepted. ❹

Her Thai Restaurant Shop 1, Promenade Level Tower 1, on Canton Rd. (☎2735 8898), in China Hong Kong City, TST. Outdoor tables and a stunning view of the harbor. Entrees HK$50-70, seafood dishes HK$100-120, and drinks HK$27-30. The *longan* drink is a sweet refreshment. Stick with the less expensive set menus (HK$138-298). Open daily noon-11pm, Happy Hour 3-7pm. Credit cards accepted. ❹

SIGHTS

TSIM SHA TSUI 尖沙咀

NATHAN ROAD. Nathan Road is as crazy, chaotic, and hectic as Hong Kong gets. TST's most important thoroughfare is also its greatest tourist attraction. The distinguished **Peninsula Hotel** marks one end of the boutique-packed road.; a few minutes away are the legendary **Chungking Mansions.** Covering the vast area between Nathan and Canton Rd., **Kowloon Park** (MTR: Tsim Sha Tsui, A1 exit) is a verdant oasis amid Hong Kong's endless stretches of concrete. The park features lush foliage and wildlife (flamingos and rare Asian birds share an open-air aviary) and postmodern sculptures. The footbridge to the Royal Pacific Hotel offers great views of the harbor. *(Open daily 6am-midnight.)* Near the park's Nathan Rd. entrance sits the majestic **Kowloon Mosque and Islamic Centre.** *(105 Nathan Rd. ☎2724 0095. Visitors must wear pants or long skirts. Open daily 4:30am-10pm. Free.)*

ON THE WATERFRONT. Many of TST's ultra-modern museums and landmark attractions cluster along the waterfront near the Star Ferry Pier, far from the neon lights and bargain-bonanza commotion of Nathan Rd. From the Clock Tower, a lonely remnant of the old KCR station, a concrete walkway known as the Promenade stretches along the northern banks of Victoria Harbour and into TST East. The Promenade passes by the Hong Kong Cultural Centre, the city's prime venue for Cantonese opera, Andrew Lloyd Webber musicals, and symphony concerts.

Directly adjacent to the Cultural Centre is the golf-ball-shaped **Hong Kong Space Museum,** filled with hands-on exhibits. The **planetarium** (the world's largest) and the **Omnimax Theater** each present at least three shows a day. *(10 Salisbury Rd. ☎2734 2722. Shows usually every hr. 11:30am-8:30pm. HK$32, students and seniors HK$16. Open M, W-F 1-9pm, Sa-Su 10am-9pm. Cantonese, English, Japanese, and Mandarin recorded tours. HK$10, students and seniors HK$5, free W.)* Behind the Space Museum, the **Hong Kong Museum of Art** houses well-maintained exhibits of ancient and modern Chinese art. *(☎2721 0116. Open daily 10am-6pm. HK$10, students and seniors HK$5, free W.)*

TSIM SHA TSUI EAST 尖沙咀东部

The waterfront **promenade** begins in TST and ends in TST East. Nearby, fishermen dangle makeshift lines in Victoria Harbour, but they seem to catch more oil cans, boots, and rubbish than fish as couples cuddle in corners of the second-level walkway (open daily 7am-11pm) behind the Cultural Centre. Farther down, the Promenade runs past the **New World Centre,** near an artificial waterfall and a gigantic watch embedded in a rock.

Chatham Rd. South, the boundary between the two TMTs, veers off Salisbury Rd., away from the waterfront, just after the New World Centre. Noodle, rice, and *dim sum* restaurants line one side of the street, while parks and covered rest areas proffer benches for tired sightseers on the other. At the intersection of Chatham Rd. and Austin Rd. is the brand-new **Hong Kong Museum of History.** *(☎2724 9042. Open Tu-Sa 1-6pm. HK$10; students, seniors, and handicapped HK$5.)*

NEW KOWLOON 新九龙

Squeezed between Mong Kok and the New Territories, New Kowloon has neither the glamour of Kowloon nor the seclusion of the New Territories.

CHI LIN NUNNERY. Reputedly built without a single nail over the course of 10 years, Chi Lin Nunnery is the latest architectural wonder of Hong Kong. This newly opened Tang dynasty-style Buddhist complex is visually very impressive, with 16 halls and a beautiful rock garden. Its elegant grandeur in the midst of such an urban setting is rather bizarre—as is the aura of newness for a building constructed exactly as a monastery would have been 1000 years ago. *(5 Chi Lin Dr. MTR: Diamond Hall, C exit. Follow the yellow signs. ☎2354 1604 or 2354 1882. Open Th-Tu 9am-3:30pm; Western Lotus Pond Garden open daily 6:30am-7pm.)*

WONG TAI SIN TEMPLE COMPLEX. This complex is named after a legendary healer and is dedicated to Daoist and Buddhist deities and Confucius. Old ladies sell incense sticks to temple-goers; while tourists look on, the devout come to bow and pray in this active place of worship, bringing offerings of fruit and cooked chickens. Donations go to support education and temple maintenance. *(2 Chuk Yuen Village. MTR: Wong Tai Sin, B exit. ☎2327 8141. Open daily 7am-5pm. Free.)*

SHOPPING

There is no need to go looking for good shopping in Hong Kong—it's everywhere and it's hard to resist. Serious shoppers may want to pick up *The Official Shopping Guide* from HKTA offices (see p. 531). It features shipping and insurance advice, bargaining and bargain-hunting hints, and the hours and addresses of almost every store in the city. HKTA also offers a free VIP card, which lists discounts available for tourists at upscale tours.

Bargaining is inappropriate in large boutiques and department stores, where prices are indicated. In many smaller shops and especially in street market stalls, it's expected—don't hesitate to ask for a "special price."

For short shopping sojourns near any of TST's "mansions," head to Nathan Rd.'s **Golden Mile,** the road's final stretch on the way to Victoria Harbour. **Granville Rd.,** off Nathan Rd., is also lined with shops selling clothing at incredible discounts. Street-side vendors emerge with their carts along **Salisbury Rd.** and Nathan Rd. and beside major hotels most evenings. Watches and shirts (from "Rolax" to "Tammy Hillfinger") cost about half what they do in the more crowded street markets. Buying electronics along Nathan Rd. may be tempting but is extremely risky, as vendors usually don't include the packaging, prices vary wildly, and buyers often lug their purchases home only to discover that a few key internal parts have mysteriously disappeared.

You'll find the best deals on clothing at **Fa Yuen St. Market** (MTR: Prince Edward, B2 exit). From Prince Edward Rd. West, walk against traffic (not literally, of course); Fa Yuen St. is two blocks ahead, on the right. Walk one block along Fa Yuen St. away from Prince Edward Rd. and turn right onto the street parallel to Fa Yuen St. to find the **Tung Choi St. Aquarium Market,** on Tungchoi St. Shops have walls lined with water-filled plastic bags housing goldfish, which are said to bring good luck and are always in demand. (Open daily 10am-6pm.)

Off Sai Yee St. is **Flower Market Rd.,** Hong Kong's best-smelling street. (MTR: Prince Edward, B3 exit; turn left on Prince Edward Rd. West, walk past Sai Yee St. on the left; Flower Market Rd. is on the right.) Petals give way to feathers at the end of the road and the entrance to **Yuen Po St. Bird Garden.** Recently built to replace the old Bird Street Market on Hong Lok St., the Bird Garden houses vendors selling birds, cages, and live grasshoppers. Old men also come here daily to "walk" their birds. (Open daily 10am-6pm.)

Mong Kok and **Yau Ma Tei** also bustle with street markets. **Mong Kong Market** is on Tung Choi St. (MTR: Mong Kok, D2 exit). Walk straight ahead for one block. At the traffic light, turn right and cross the street. Otherwise known as **Ladies' Street Market,** this is the place for handbags, shirts, dresses, and even underwear. (Open daily 10am-10:30pm.) To reach **Temple St. Night Market** (MTR: Jordan, Temple St.

exit), walk three blocks from the station before turning right on Temple St. Imitation designer shirts, watches, and handbags are all for sale, while palm-readers and fortune-tellers prophesize outside the temple. Shoppers can also sample snacks from stalls or enjoy performances of Chinese opera. (Open daily 7-10pm.) From Temple St., turn left on Kansu St. and walk three blocks to reach the **Jade Market,** where vendors hawk real and fake jade trinkets and souvenirs, as well as sunglasses, nail clippers, and other odds and ends. (Open daily 10am-3:30pm.)

NIGHTLIFE

Bars and pubs pack the odd quadrilateral formed by Carnarvon, Cameron, Chatham, and Mody Rd. and the area bounded by Hart Ave. and Prat Ave.

Ned Kelly's Last Stand, 11A Ashley Rd. (☎2376 0562). This Aussie saloon immortalizes a famed outlaw. For jazz lovers, this is the place to be. Live jazz band 9pm-2am. Happy Hour 11:30am-10pm. Menu items HK$48-130. Fried eggs, bacon, sausages, chips, toast, and tea/coffee/juice HK$64. Open daily 11:30am-2am.

Grammy's Lounge, Supreme House, 2A Hart Ave., Ground fl. (☎2368 3833). A favorite local hangout, Grammy's boasts multi-colored lights and Canto-pop performances. Karaoke M-Sa 5-9pm and all day Sunday. Live band M-Th 2-5pm, F-Sa 1-5pm. Happy Hour 3-10pm; most drinks HK$18. Cover HK$15, HK$10 during Happy Hour. Open M-Th 1pm-2am, F-Sa 1pm-1am, all day Su. Credit cards accepted.

Rick's Cafe, 53-59 Kimberly Rd. (☎2367 2939 or 2311 2255). When you visit this popular nightstop, dress sharp; men in shorts and anyone with sandals are not allowed inside. The DJ has a penchant for love songs. Happy Hour 5-10pm (mixed drinks and bottled beer HK$22). Open M-Th 5pm-3am, F-Sa 5pm-5am.

HONG KONG ISLAND 香港岛

ORIENTATION

When viewed from across the harbor, Hong Kong Island's impressive skyline looks like an unbroken string of high-rises. From left to right (east to west), Hong Kong Island is divided into the districts of Sheung Wan, Central, Admiralty, Wan Chai, and Causeway Bay; Stanley is farther south. The island's center is dominated by mountains like Victoria Peak, most of which are pristine and undeveloped.

SHEUNG WAN (上环). At the end of the MTR Island line, Sheung Wan is also the home of the **Macau Ferry Terminal.** Connaught Rd. Central, the area's main thoroughfare, follows the edge of the harbor. Moving south away from the coast, Des Voeux Rd. Central and Queen's Rd. Central run parallel to Connaught Rd. Central. Hollywood Rd. marks the edge of the **SoHo district,** roughly three blocks south of Queen's Rd. Central.

CENTRAL (中区) **AND ADMIRALTY.** Most of Central's major landmarks and sights are easy to find if you use the **Star Ferry Pier** as a reference point. **Connaught Rd. Central/Harcourt Rd.** runs parallel to the pier, passing **Jardine House,** a silver rectangle with glass. Queen's Rd. Central and Des Voeux Rd. Central merge to become **Queensway;** the austere black **Cheung Kong Centre,** the gleaming blue **Bank of China Tower,** and the beige pillar and dome structure of the **Legislative Council (Legco) building** can be found at this intersection. Three blocks beyond Queen's Road Central is the infamous expat playpen **Lan Kwai Fong.**

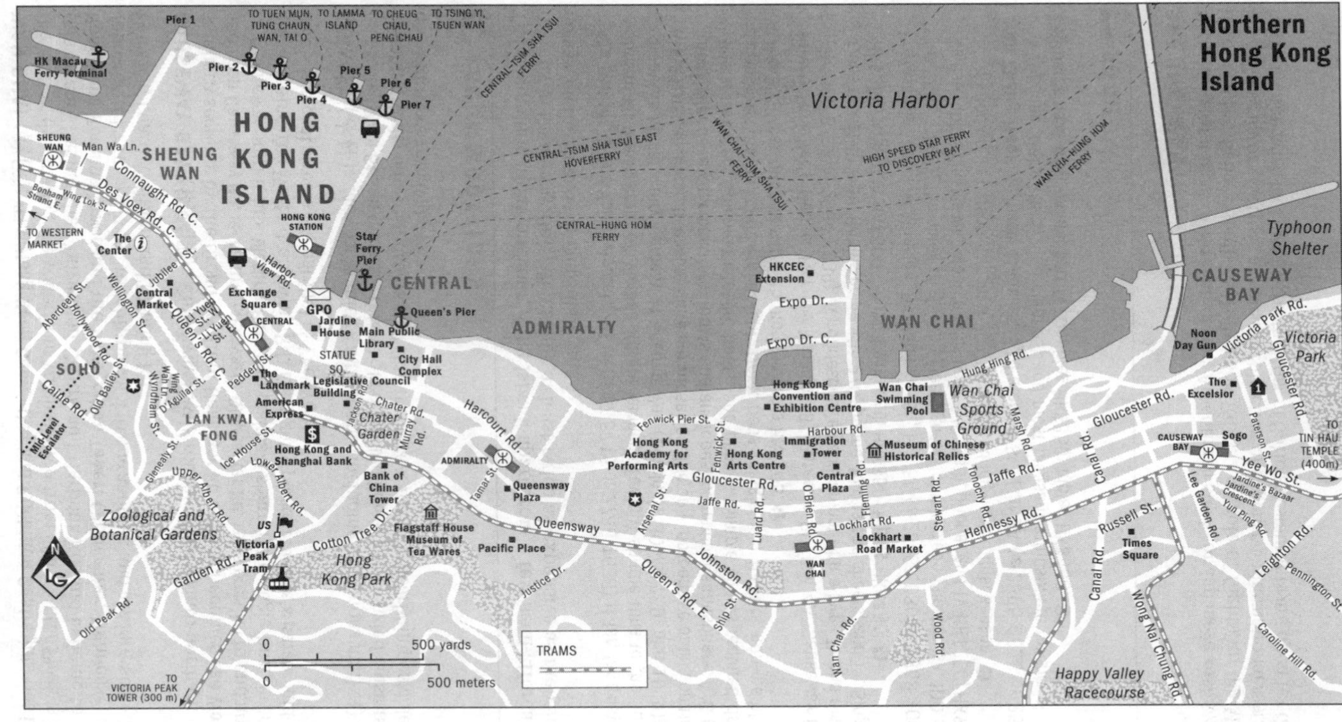
Northern Hong Kong Island
HONG KONG ISLAND
Victoria Harbor
SHEUNG WAN
CENTRAL
ADMIRALTY
WAN CHAI
CAUSEWAY BAY
SOHO
LAN KWAI FONG
HK Macau Ferry Terminal
Pier 1
Pier 2
Pier 3
Pier 4
Pier 5
Pier 6
Pier 7
TO TUEN MUN, TUNG CHAUN WAN, TAI O
TO LAMMA ISLAND
TO CHEUG CHAU, PENG CHAU
TO TSING YI, TSUEN WAN
CENTRAL–TSIM SHA TSUI FERRY
CENTRAL–TSIM SHA TSUI EAST HOVERFERRY
CENTRAL–HUNG HOM FERRY
WAN CHAI–TSIM SHA TSUI FERRY
HIGH SPEED STAR FERRY TO DISCOVERY BAY
WAN CHA–HUNG HOM FERRY
Star Ferry Pier
Queen's Pier
HONG KONG STATION
SHEUNG WAN
CENTRAL
ADMIRALTY
WAN CHAI
CAUSEWAY BAY
TO WESTERN MARKET
Mid-Level Escalator
The Center
Central Market
Exchange Square
GPO
Jardine House
Main Public Library
City Hall Complex
STATUE SQ.
Legislative Council Building
The Landmark
American Express
Hong Kong and Shanghai Bank
Bank of China Tower
Flagstaff House Museum of Tea Wares
Pacific Place
Queensway Plaza
Hong Kong Academy for Performing Arts
Hong Kong Arts Centre
Hong Kong Convention and Exhibition Centre
HKCEC Extension
Immigration Tower
Central Plaza
Wan Chai Swimming Pool
Museum of Chinese Historical Relics
Wan Chai Sports Ground
Lockhart Road Market
Times Square
Happy Valley Racecourse
Noon Day Gun
The Excelsior
Sogo
Victoria Park
Typhoon Shelter
Zoological and Botanical Gardens
Hong Kong Park
Victoria Peak Tram
US
TO VICTORIA PEAK TOWER (300 m)
TO TIN HAU TEMPLE (400m)
Man Wa Ln.
Bonham Strand E.
Wing Lok St.
Des Voeux Rd. C.
Connaught Rd. C.
Jubilee St.
Wellington St.
Aberdeen St.
Hollywood Rd.
Caine Rd.
Old Bailey St.
Wyndham St.
Wing Wah Ln.
D'Aguilar St.
Li Yuen St. W.
Li Yuen St. E.
Queen's Rd. C.
Pedder St.
Glenealy St.
Upper Albert Rd.
Ice House St.
Lower Albert Rd.
Old Peak Rd.
Garden Rd.
Cotton Tree Dr.
Harbor View Rd.
Jackson Rd.
Chater Rd.
Chater Garden
Murray Rd.
Harcourt Rd.
Tamar St.
Justice Dr.
Queensway
Queen's Rd. E.
Arsenal St.
Fenwick Pier St.
Fenwick St.
Gloucester Rd.
Jaffe Rd.
Luard Rd.
Johnston Rd.
Ship St.
O'Brien Rd.
Lockhart Rd.
Harbour Rd.
Expo Dr.
Expo Dr. C.
Fleming Rd.
Wan Chai Rd.
Stewart Rd.
Wood Rd.
Tonochy Rd.
Hung Hing Rd.
Marsh Rd.
Hennessy Rd.
Canal Rd.
Russell St.
Wong Nai Chung Rd.
Lee Garden Rd.
Yun Ping Rd.
Jardine's Crescent
Jardine's Bazaar
Paterson St.
Victoria Park Rd.
Yee Wo St.
Leighton Rd.
Caroline Hill Rd.
Pennington St.
TRAMS
0
500 yards
500 meters

WAN CHAI (湾仔). The **Hong Kong Convention and Exhibition Centre** juts out into the harbor, dominating the waterfront when viewed from afar. Center Plaza is farther inland, behind the Convention Centre and Harbour Rd. and is home to the **Hong Kong Revenue Tower** and the **Immigration Tower.** Gloucester, Hennessy, and Johnston Rd. run east-west, roughly parallel to one another, and are intersected by Fenwick, Luard, O'Brien, and Fleming Rd.

CAUSEWAY BAY (铜锣湾). Causeway Bay is roughly divided into northern and southern sections by the broad swath of **Hennessy Rd.,** which becomes **Yee Wo St.** and then **Causeway Rd.** as it runs eastward. **Gloucester Rd.** runs parallel to and north of Hennessy until it hits **Victoria Park** and makes a sharp right-angle turn, eventually crossing Yee Wo St./Causeway Rd. The tightly packed **Jardine's Bazaar** and **Jardine's Crescent** streets are parallel to Yee Wo St.

STANLEY (赤柱). Most of Stanley's attractions (including its famous market) are on **Stanley Main St.,** an intricate thread of connected lanes. The frenzied clusters of shopping stalls and restaurants that line this street make it nearly impossible to use addresses to navigate.

ACCOMMODATIONS

The accommodations on Hong Kong Island, apart from a few semi-affordable options in Causeway Bay, are usually at least twice as expensive as the guesthouses on the Kowloon peninsula.

Ma Wui Mt. Davis Youth Hostel (HI) (☎2817 5715 or 2788 1638) is far, far away on top of Mt. Davis Path, off Victoria Rd., in Kennedy Town. A shuttle runs to the hostel from the Macau Ferry Terminal in Sheung Wan (20min.; 9:30am, 7, 9, and 10:30pm; HK$10). Call ahead to ensure there are vacancies. The only inexpensive option on Hong Kong Island. Large, clean dorm rooms and an upbeat communal atmosphere. A/C and linens provided. Common kitchen, baths, and phones. Simple chores required daily. Lights out 11pm, curfew midnight. Dorm beds (single-sex) HK$65, non-members HK$95; 4-person rooms HK$75, non-members HK$105. ❶

Jetvan Traveller's House, Fairview Mansion, 51 Paterson St., Flat 4A, Causeway Bay (☎2890 8133 or 2984 8539). A nondescript establishment with a large TV and a spacious reception area. Rooms come with A/C, phone, towels and sheets, and TV. Singles HK$250, with bath HK$300; doubles with bath HK$350; triples HK$450. ❹

Payless Inn, Fairview Mansion, 51 Paterson St., Flat 5A (☎2808 1030 or 2808 1004; fax 2890 7798). The smell of ginseng greets guests of this clean guesthouse. IDD service in lobby. Singles with double beds have A/C, bath, phone, and TV HK$250; HK$50 for an additional person. Expect a 20% increase during peak tourist season. ❹

An Zhang Hang, Fairview Mansion, 51 Paterson St., Flat 2A (☎2895 0626 or 2577 5758; fax 2895 2895). The cleanest and most pleasant atmosphere on the island. Rooms have A/C, phone, and TV. Doubles HK$350; triples HK$450. ❺

FOOD

SHEUNG WAN

Hankering for a taste of Russian caviar, Argentinian steak, or Japanese *sashimi?* If so, head to **SoHo** ("South of Hollywood Rd."). A couple of flights up the Mid-Level E escalators, SoHo is an uneasy collection of expensive international restaurants on otherwise lackluster streets. Most of SoHo's restaurants are open for dinner (6-11pm); some also serve lunch (noon-3pm). Most of the culinary action happens on **Staunton St.,** parallel to Hollywood Rd., and **Elgin St.,** which begins slightly south of the intersection of Staunton St. and Peel St.

Just off the well-beaten path, **La Piazetta ●,** 5 Tsun Wing Ln., is a classy Italian restaurant that serves up pizza (HK$38-78), pasta (HK$37-60), and deer *ragout* (HK$31-48), a specialty. (☎2522 9505. Open daily noon-11:30pm.) The **Singapore Restaurant,** Alliance Building, 130-131 Connaught Rd., offers an extensive menu with low-end prices. The menu includes chicken *à la portuguese* (HK$55), shredded beef stroganoff (HK$38), and 10 kinds of ice cream sundaes. (☎2815 1566. Open daily 11am-11pm. ❷)

CENTRAL

Midnight Express, 3 Lan Kwai Fong (☎2525 5010 or 2523 4041). Serves generous portions of Greek, Indian, and Italian dishes for under HK$55; the kebabs (HK$35-55) are tasty and filling. On weeknights, the small eating booth is a refreshing escape from the glitz and sparkle of Lan Kwai Fong. On weekends, it is filled with beer-guzzling businessmen. Beer HK$20-30. Free delivery in Central and Wan Chai. Open M-Sa 10am-3am, Su 11am-3pm. ❹

Dai Pai Dong, 128 Queen's Rd. (☎2851 6389). Choose from more than 10 noodle combination meals (Y38). Those with a sweet tooth may want to try the Dai Pai Dong toast (HK$13) or a sweet Chinese pancake (HK$26). Scrambled egg on toast HK$26. 10% service charge. Open M-Sa 8am-10pm, Su 9:30am-7pm. ❷

South East Garden Vietnamese Food, 8 Queen Victoria St. (☎2525 3953). Barbecued pork HK$20; sandwiches HK$8-11. No English or Mandarin is spoken in this local hangout. Open daily 7am-5:30pm. ❷

WAN CHAI

Banana Leaf Curry House, 440 Jaffe Rd., 1st fl. (☎2573 8187). Other locations in TST, Mong Kok, Whampoa Garden, and Causeway Bay. Waitresses in traditional dress scoop rice from a wooden bucket onto a banana leaf. A comfortable setting for families. Pork satay appetizer HK$48; curry HK$24-48; vegetables HK$20. Open M-F 11:30am-3pm and 6pm-midnight, Sa-Su and public holidays 11am-11:30pm. Credit cards accepted. ❸

Healthy Vegetarian Restaurant, 51-53 Hennessy Rd., Ground fl. (☎2527 3918), uses the culinary marvels of bean curd to create uncanny meat imitations (entrees HK$38-138). The strict vegetarian can even try imitation shark's fin (HK$68). Takeout available. Open M-Sa 10:30am-11pm, Su 5-11pm. DC/MC/V. ❹

CAUSEWAY BAY

Laurel Noodle, 462 Lockhart Rd. (☎2904 7867). Eat spare ribs in pineapple sauce (HK$28) off porcelain dishes and propose a toast with mineral juice (HK$8) to the gods of cheap food. Open daily noon-11pm. ❷

Fantasy Vegetarian Restaurant, 66 Electric Rd. (☎2887 3886 or 2807 0569). MTR: Tin Hau Electric Rd. exit. One of the few vegetarian places in town features an English menu and friendly, English-speaking staff members. The lineup includes noodles (HK$17-29), congee (HK$48-60), vegetables with mock kidney (HK$52), and a dozen other dishes (HK$48-60). Open daily 11am-10pm; *dim sum* stalls open 9am-11:30pm. ❸

STANLEY

Pepperoni's, 18B Stanley Main St., Ground fl. (☎2813 8605), resembles an Italian bistro with tables that spill out onto the sidewalk. Delicious pizza is available in small (HK$50-65), medium (HK$65-85), and large (HK$80-100) sizes; ask for the special secret sauce. Open daily 10am-10pm. ❹

Al Fresco's, 30A Stanley Main St., Ground fl. (☎2813 2520), a colorful eatery with a varied menu that includes Mexican tacos (HK$65). Under the same management as Pepperoni's; both have branches throughout Hong Kong Island. Open daily 10am-10pm. ❹

SIGHTS

SHEUNG WAN

It was here that the Royal Navy raised the Union Jack in 1841. Ironically, this area is rich in local character and overflows with little shops, streetside markets, and mildewing apartments. The **Macau Ferry Terminal** sits on the northern edge of the district. Farther south, on the corner of Ladder St. and Hollywood Rd., looms **Man Mo Temple,** where the lovelorn shake fortune-telling sticks to check on the state of their star-crossed destinies. Dedicated to the ancient gods of *Man* ("Literature") and *Mo* ("Warfare"), the temple also houses shrines to the city god and the 10 divine judges. *Feng shui* advice and palm-reading is available. *(☎2540 0350. Open daily 8am-6pm. Free.)*

Hollywood Rd. curves across the center of Sheung Wan, lined by shops selling antiques and Chinese artwork (daily 10am-6pm). The **Central Mid-Level Escalators,** the longest covered escalator in the world, follow Hollywood Rd. to the eastern edge of Sheung Wan, on Cochrane and Shelley St. Over 800m of moving stairs (and a total of 20 exits) transport residents down the hill (6-10am) and up again (10am-11pm). Bars and restaurants are constantly sprouting up on the hillside along the Escalators, and toward the top is Hong Kong's own **SoHo.**

CENTRAL

VICTORIA PEAK. The quintessential Hong Kong experience is a trip to Victoria Peak. At 396m above sea level, the peak provides a spectacular view of Hong Kong; binoculars (HK$2 per 5min.) are available on levels two, four, and five of the Peak Tower. Entertainment options on the peak (shopping, a motion simulator, a theme gallery, a movie) are expensive and crowded with tourists. Sitting quietly and absorbing the panoramic view from the Level Four terrace is free, as is a walk around the trails at the top. The **peak tram** offers an exhilarating ride up a 45° incline, at a speed leisurely enough for you to take in the view. *(33 Garden Rd., behind the Murray Building. A double-decker bus (HK$3.2) departs from the Central Star Ferry pier to the tram station daily every 15min. 7am-midnight. Alternatively, walk the 600m by following Garden Rd. away from the Harbor. ☎2522 0922. Tram departs every 10-15min. 7am-midnight; HK$20, round-trip HK$30; children 3-11 HK$6/HK$9; seniors over 65 HK$7/HK$14.)*

HONG KONG PARK. For a park, this place sure boasts an impressive amount of cement, and in spite of its eight hectares, it has a cramped air. Perhaps the park's most worthwhile site is the **Flagstaff Museum of Teaware.** Constructed between 1844 and 1846, the Flagstaff House was both home and office to the Commander of the British forces in Hong Kong. The museum offers a comprehensive and innovative study of British and Chinese tea and tea customs. *(☎2869 0690. Video at 11:30am, 1:30, and 3:30pm; groups of 10 or more can inquire about additional screenings. Open Th-Tu 10am-5pm.)* The **Edward Youde Aviary, Forsgate Conservatory, K.S. Lo Gallery,** and the **Visual Arts Centre** are also on the premises, and a small but lovely bonsai and rock garden is hidden behind the aviary. *(Park ☎2521 5041; open daily 6:30am-11pm. Aviary and Conservatory open daily 9am-5pm. Gallery ☎2869 6690; open Th-Tu 10am-5pm. Visual Arts Centre ☎2521 3008; open W-M 10am-9pm. Wheelchair accessible. All free.)*

BANKING ON FENG SHUI Belief in the ancient practice of *feng shui,* or wind-water geomantic principles, still inspires modern-day engineers and architects in Hong Kong. Prime examples are the **Bank of China** and the **Hong Kong & Shanghai Banking Corporation** buildings in Central, both of which rank as internationally recognized architectural marvels. The 70-story Bank of China building earned its acclaim as the tallest building in Hong Kong until Central Plaza snatched the title a few years ago, while the Hong Kong & Shanghai Banking Corporation building, made of titanium, was the most expensive building in the world at the time of its construction.

I. M. Pei designed the Bank of China Tower to resemble a budding bamboo shoot. When it was finally completed in 1990, occupants of the surrounding structures complained of the bad *feng shui* generated by their newest neighbor. Indeed, the Hong Kong & Shanghai Banking Corporation registered a loss in profits that very year. As a defensive measure, the Hong Kong & Shanghai Banking Corporation employed a *feng shui* expert who advised the company to board up the windows of the transparent tower and to erect two arms to jut out from the side of the building closest to the rival bank. With red blinking lights and round barrels, the arms look more like guns trained on the Bank of China than manifestations of an ancient faith. In any case, business for the Hong Kong & Shanghai Banking Corporation did improve the following year. The HKTA offers a free lecture on the principles of *feng shui* every Sunday 10-11am at the HKTA office in Central (☎2564 1234).

ZOOLOGICAL AND BOTANICAL GARDENS. The Zoological and Botanical Gardens sit just off Garden Rd., a 10-minute walk from the Hong Kong Hilton past St. John's Cathedral. The main entrance is at the intersection of Garden Rd. and Upper Albert Rd. Stick to the maze of pedestrian walkways and keep your eyes alert for signs pointing to the gardens. The gardens are a pleasure for flora and fauna enthusiasts. Jaguars, reptiles, monkeys, and butterflies call this their home, but as they are for Hong Kong, space constraints are a sad reality for some of these animals. *(☎2530 0153. Open daily 6am-7pm; greenhouse open 9am-4:30pm.)*

WAN CHAI

CENTRAL PLAZA. The tallest building in Hong Kong, Central Plaza is easily spotted from most locations on the island. Its color beams serve as a clock: the color of the bottom light indicates the hour (red 6pm, white 7pm, purple 8pm, yellow 9pm, pink 10pm, and green 11pm); if the top light is a different color, it's a quarter past; if the top two and bottom two lights differ, it's half past; if the top three match, it's 45 minutes past the hour; and when all four lights match, it is on the hour.

HONG KONG CONVENTION AND EXHIBITION CENTRE (HKCEC). This grand waterfront building stands as an impressive testament to Hong Kong's ability to put on a good show. Opened in 1997 for the handover ceremonies, the Centre is a quiet, sprawling marvel of glass, sunlight, and expansive floor-to-ceiling windows. It was supposedly constructed to look like a bird on the brink of takeoff, but many claim that it slightly resembles the Sydney Opera House. Exhibits, cafes, and restaurants keep the HKCEC active at night. *(☎2582 8888. No slippers or shorts. Open 24hr.)* The outdoor garden and waterfront promenade come as a welcome surprise in this otherwise urban desert. The **Hong Kong Arts Centre,** to your right as you leave the HKCEC, sells tickets for shows in its auditoriums. Brochures and posters in front of the box office on the ground floor advertise upcoming performances. *(Program inquiries ☎2582 0202; URBTIX hotline ☎2734 9009. Box office open daily 10am-6pm.)*

CAUSEWAY BAY

VICTORIA PARK. At dawn and dusk, this haven of sprawling green lawns and leafy boulevards is peppered with *tai chi* devotees. Sports facilities include tennis courts, a roller-skating rink, a bowling green, and a swimming pool (all for a fee). Free jogging trails wind through spacious lawns, an aviary, and a topiary garden. *(Enter on Gloucester Rd., opposite the Park Lane Hotel. ☎2890 5824. Park open 24hr. Roller-skating rink open daily 9am-11pm; HK$16 per hr. Swimming pool open daily 6:30am-noon and 1-10pm; HK$19, children HK$9.)* A single footbridge in the northwest corner of the park, along the path from the Model Boat Pool, leads to **Causeway Bay Typhoon Shelter,** where floating homes bob next to sleek yachts.

HAPPY VALLEY RACECOURSE AND HONG KONG RACING MUSEUM. Built in the mid 1840s when horse racing first became popular among wealthy Hong Kong residents, Happy Valley's track was recently rewidened in 1995 to allow 14 horses to race at once. The **Hong Kong Racing Museum** on the second floor of the stand tells the story behind one of Hong Kong's greatest passions. *(MTR: Causeway Bay, exit A. From the exit , it's a 20min. walk via Leighton Rd. and Morrison Hill Rd. Racecourse ☎2966 8111. Museum ☎2966 806. Museum open Tu-Su 10am-5pm; 10am-12:30pm on race days.)*

NOON-DAY GUN. This famous gun, featured in Noel Coward's 1924 satire *Mad Dogs and Englishmen* ("In Hong Kong they strike a gong and fire a noon-day gun"), squats on the waterfront across from the Excelsior Hotel. In 19th-century Hong Kong, the famous Jardine Matheson company had their own private artillery as protection against pirates. This unlicensed show of military might finally angered a new naval officer; he demanded that the company be punished. Jardine Matheson had to fire the gun every day at noon to signal the time—a tradition that continues to this day. *(Take Jaffe Rd. toward Victoria Park; walk straight toward the alley near the Excelsior Hotel car park. Just after you pass the 7-Eleven on your left, look ahead and follow the red-letter sign to the gun. Open daily 7am-midnight.)*

STANLEY

Stanley's main attraction is **Stanley Market.** Stanley Main St. runs through clean stalls and petite shops full of every garment known to man, from snake-skin boots to the street's specialty, silk pajamas. **Stanley Main Beach,** just east of the market along Stanley Beach Rd., is often packed on weekends. **St. Stephen Beach** is a 10-minute walk south along Wong Ma Kok Rd., away from the market and toward the hills. From the bus station terminus on Stanley Village St., turn left and follow the signs in pink print all the way to the entrance. *(To get to Stanley, take bus #973 from the Star Ferry Pier in TST (HK$13) or Express Bus #260 from the Star Ferry Pier in Central. Market open daily 9am-6:30pm. Beaches open 24hr. Shower facilities available at Stanley Beach.)*

MUSEUMS

Hong Kong Museum of Coastal Defense, 175 Tung Hei Rd., Shaukei Wan (☎2569 1500). MTR: Shau Kei Wan.

Police Museum, 27 Coome Rd., Mid-level (☎2849 7019). Take bus #15 from Exchange Square in Central; get off at the intersection of Stubbs Rd. and Peak Rd. and follow the signs to the Mid-level escalators.

University of HK Museum and Art Gallery, University of Hong Kong, 94 Bonham Rd. (☎2975 5600). Take bus #23 from Pacific Place in Admiralty to Bonham Rd., opposite St. Paul's College.

SHOPPING

Unlike Kowloon, Hong Kong Island only has a few cheap street markets where budget travelers can haggle for discounts. Older, upscale tourists flex their financial might in boutiques that sell Yves St. Laurent, sparkling gold jewelry, and other 24-carat emblems of conspicuous consumption.

Li Yuen St. Market, in Central. **Li Yuen St. East** lies between Des Voeux Rd. and Queen's Rd. Excellent bargains for traditional Chinese dresses. Open daily 7am-10pm. **Li Yuen St. West** is parallel to and one block left of Li Yuen St. East, if you are standing with Jardine House behind you. More shops than its sister street and a selection of shoes that will make footware fans delirious. Open daily 7am-10pm.

Central Market, at the intersection of Queen Victoria St. and Queen's Rd., Central. Three floors packed with produce, meat, and customers. Fierce smells and questionable cleanliness, but low prices and undeniably fresh food. Open daily 6am-8pm.

Graham Street Fruit and Vegetable Market, on Graham St., off Queen's Rd., Central, between the Union Bank of Hong Kong and the V. Heun Building. This open-air market is a fruit connoisseur's fantasy, very clean and very well-stocked. Nuts, corn on the cob, and fresh tofu available. Open daily 6am-8pm.

NIGHTLIFE

Before heading out for a night on the town, stop by a restaurant, hotel, or newsstand and pick up a free copy of *HK Magazine* or *bc magazine*, two English-language weeklies with up-to-date entertainment and event listings.

CENTRAL AND ADMIRALTY

The L-shaped **Lan Kwai Fong** area overflows with trendy restaurants and bars. During the day, the area is packed with mild-mannered eateries that cater to a mellow clientele (see **Food,** p. 546). As dusk falls, Lan Kwai Fong becomes the happening hot spot for Hong Kong's expats. The city-slicker material girl regulars provide enough entertainment to justify the upwardly mobile cover charges and bar tabs at these posh, upscale places. Credit cards are accepted in most bars and clubs.

Oscar's, 2 Lan Kwai Fong (☎2804 6561). Amid high ceilings and elegant decor, Oscar's caters to a cosmopolitan crowd. Tasteful style, good music, and a great bar manager who might even buy you a drink. Happy Hour daily 4-8pm (Budweiser HK$30). Open M-F 11am-1am, Sa-Su 11am-3:30am. Check out the Australian restaurant (☎2861 1511) in Causeway Bay, run by the same management.

The Fringe Club, 2 Lower Albert Rd. (☎2521 7485). A funky art gallery and bar in one. Lunch buffet noon-2:30pm HK$75 (M-F vegetarian). Drinks HK$35-55. Happy Hour M-Sa 4-9pm. Open M-Th noon-midnight, F-Sa noon-2am.

Club 64, 12-14 Wing Wah Ln., Ground fl. (☎2523 2801), off D'Aguilar St. Popular with both expats and backpackers, this laid-back bar is normally packed on weekends. Happy Hour daily 2-9pm. Drinks normally HK$40-60; during Happy Hour a Carlsberg goes for HK$15. Open M-Th noon-2am, F-Sa 10am-3am, Su 6pm-1am.

Post 97, 9-11 Lan Kwai Fong (☎2810 9333), part of the elite 97 group that includes the members-only **Club 97** in the same building. Bottled beer HK$47. Happy Hour daily 3-7pm, dinner served until 11pm. Open M-Th 10am-12:30am, F-Sa 10am-3am, Su 10am-midnight.

LA Cafe, Lippo Centre, 89 Queensway, Ground fl., Shops 2-3 (☎2526 6863). Conjures up a stereotypical Hollywood scene with neon lights on its palm trees. Mexican dishes HK$75-125; burgers HK$90-95; pasta HK$85-105. Happy Hour daily 2-8pm with 2 for 1 drinks. Bottled beer HK$24. Open M-F 11am-midnight, Sa-Su 10am-12:30am.

Sherman's, California Entertainment Bldg., 34-36 D'Aguilar St., Ground fl. (☎2801 4946). Sophisticated patrons blow smoke rings from long, thin cigarettes in this dim bar and restaurant. Great food includes pastas HK$40, soups HK$55-60, sandwiches HK$80-110, and tiramisu HK$55. Open M-Th noon-2am, F-Sa noon-4am, Su 4pm-1am.

WAN CHAI

As the setting of Richard Mason's novel *The World of Suzie Wong*, Wan Chai will never quite shake its image of a dissolute area filled with brothels, bars, and furloughed sailors, even though the district today bears little evidence of its sordid past. Pubs and bars cluster on **Jaffe** and **Luard Rd.**, their neon signs lighting the path to drunken revelry.

Joe Bananas, 23 Luard Rd. (☎2529 1811), at Jaffe Rd. Despite the many rules—no furs, t-shirts, or shorts—this swinging spot is a Hong Kong landmark. The tropical, sunny place features palm trees and tin-foil-covered walls. Asian, European, and New World food served until midnight. Unplugged every Friday. All drinks 2 for 1 during Happy Hour 7-10pm. 21+ after 6pm. Open M-Sa noon-6am, Su 3pm-6am.

The Wanch, 54 Jaffe Rd. (☎2861 1621). MTR: Wan Chai, Lockhart Rd. exit. An ode to Hong Kong pop culture. Set lunches (HK$65-80), pub grub dinner, and Hong Kong souvenirs. Live music nightly beginning at 10pm. Happy Hour daily 11am-6pm and 7-10pm. (drinks HK$24-30); "Crazy Hour" M-Sa (drinks HK$19). Open M-Th 11am-2am, F-Sa 11am-3am, Su noon-late.

Carnegie's, 53-55 Lockhart Rd. (☎2866 6289). This popular pub has specials every night of the week. DJ every night except Th and Su, when local groups show their stuff. Cocktails HK$40-150. Happy Hour M-Sa 11am-10pm. "Crazy hour" daily 6-7pm (drinks HK$19). Open M-Sa 11am-5am, Su 5pm-2am.

Nickleby's, 57-73 Lockhart Rd. (☎2862 1023). In the basement of the Wharney Hotel, amid suspended model airplanes and clouds on the ceiling, a Filipino band plays English and Tagalog pop songs nightly (M-Th 6:15pm-12:15am, F-Sa 6:15pm-1:15am). Very mellow, relaxed atmosphere with a devoted following of regulars. Big screen broadcasts live soccer games. Cocktails HK$60. Happy Hour M-Th all day, F-Sa 4:30-9pm (all drinks 2 for 1). Open M-Th 4:30pm-1am, F-Sa 4:30pm-2am.

Cinta-J, 69 Jaffe Rd., Shop G-4, Malaysia Bldg. (☎2529 6622). A Malaysian-Filipino-Indonesian restaurant and lounge. Lunch sets M-F 11am-3pm HK$43. Happy Hour M-F 3-9pm (half-pints HK$15-16, pints HK$25-27). Live music M-Sa 5pm-1am, Su 11am-1am. Major credit cards accepted (HK$200 minimum charge). Open daily 11am-5am.

CAUSEWAY BAY

Most of the bars in Causeway Bay are joined to hotels and close early, but there are a few tucked away with relatively late hours.

Dickens, Excelsior Hotel, 281 Gloucester Rd., Lower Ground fl. (☎2837 6782). Sports buffs will appreciate the autographed pictures of tennis, soccer, and marathon champions. Very classy—don't underdress. Beer HK$50. Happy Hour 5-8pm, dinner menu 6-10pm. Open Su-Th 11am-1:30am, F-Sa 11am-2:30am.

WALKS ON HONG KONG ISLAND

Perhaps one of the most intriguing aspects of Hong Kong is that its dense urban fabric is nestled between sweeping, unspoiled hills and mountains. Over 40% of the territory has been preserved in public parks, most of which feature an intricate network of extremely well-maintained trails. The "Magic Walks" series (HK$45-85), available in major bookstores and at the HKTA, covers most hiking options. The HKTA (see p. 531) also distributes pamphlets about specific trails. Happy trekkers should bring sunscreen, proper shoes, and plenty of water.

The **Wilson Trail,** named after an ex-governor and inveterate hiker, starts in Stanley and ends in the New Territories; the **Shing Mun Jogging Trail,** the **Sai Kung Coddle Stones** path, and the southern valley of **Mount Butler** are some of the trail's highlights. The entire route takes 27 hours. The **Wan Chai Green Trail** begins at the Wan Chai Old Post Office on Queen's Rd. East and ends at Stubbs Rd. Eleven educational stations along the trail point out plants of interest. The **Hong Kong Trail** passes through five country parks on Hong Kong Island, offering scenic views of some of the island's most beautiful areas.

SOUTHERN HONG KONG ISLAND

KENNEDY TOWN 坚尼地城

Although it's a long trek to **Hong Kong University,** which is hidden on the side of a mountain in Kennedy Town on Hong Kong Island's western edge, the **University Museum and Art Gallery** is definitely worth a visit. The museum houses permanent exhibits of bronzes and ceramics that date back to the Shang (1600-1066 BC) and Zhou (1066-221 BC) dynasties. Relics from the Yuan dynasty (AD 1279-1368) also grace the display shelves. *(To get to Hong Kong University, take bus #7 from Pier 7 in Central (every 10-15min., HK$5.3) or bus #5A from along Des Voeux Rd., Queensway, or Queen's Rd. East (every 10-12min., HK$3.4). Ask a student to point out the building upon arrival at the University. ☎2241 5500. Open M-Sa 9:30am-6pm, Su 1:30-5:30pm. Free.)*

SHEK O 石澳

On the southeast coast of Hong Kong Island, not far from Stanley, lies the lovely Shek O Beach. Crowded with oiled-up sun-worshipers fanned by breezes that filter down from the mountains, this long, well-maintained stretch of shore is one of the most popular beaches on Hong Kong Island. Stake out a spot and rent an umbrella tent for the day (HK$30). Several shops rent bikes (HK$15-20 per hr., HK$35-40 per day) for exploring the surrounding hillside. Wander around the markets in Shau Kei Wan if you have time on your hands before getting on the bus. Allow at least two hours to get to the beach if you're going this way. (Bus #309 goes to Shek O from Central (50min., Su every 30min., HK$11). On weekdays, ride the tram to its last stop and board bus #9 (every 15-30min. 6am-11pm; HK$4.20, A/C HK$6.20) for Shek O at the Shau Kei Wan MTR Station, A1 or A2 exits.)

DEEPWATER BAY 深水环 AND REPULSE BAY 浅水环

Deepwater Bay beach has a long coast, a beautiful view, and powdery soft sand. Take bus #6 (every 10-30min., HK$5.30) from Central Exchange Square to the Deepwater Bay stop. Repulse Bay, ironically, is the gem of Hong Kong Island. (Take bus #6 to the Shell station stop on Repulse Bay Rd.) Sturdy nets anchored offshore keep out unwanted sea creatures and two large statues of Gwan Tum and Tin Mau, traditional protectors of local fishermen, guard the shores. Bus #73 connects Aberdeen, Repulse Bay, and Stanley (every 15-25min., HK$5.80).

ABERDEEN 香港仔

The **Aberdeen Promenade,** a smaller version of the TST walkway, passes junks, *sampan*, and teenagers fishing in waters clearly marked with pollution warnings. The **Jumbo Floating Restaurant,** the self-proclaimed "most luxurious floating restaurant in the world," offers overpriced seafood. Little old ladies waylay tourists near the bus stop for *sampan* cruises around the harbor (HK$40-50 for 30min.). Bus #70 runs between Central and Aberdeen (every 6-15min. 6am-midnight, HK$4.70).

Ocean Park features nerve-wracking, stomach-dropping roller-coasters, a goldfish pagoda, shark aquarium, dolphin university, and Hong Kong's two giant pandas, An An and Jia Jia. The pandas occupy a 2000 sq. meter habitat that is within walking distance of **Atoll Reef,** where 400 species of fish can be viewed through a glass gallery. *(A citybus shuttle runs from the Aberdeen bus terminal to Ocean Park (HK$12). Take bus #70 from Exchange Square in Central (every 6-15min., HK$4.70) or bus #72 from Causeway Bay (every 10-20min., HK$4.70); get off at the stop after the Aberdeen Tunnel and follow the blue signs to Ocean Park. ☎2552 0291. Ocean Park open daily 10am-6pm. HK$140, ages 3-11 HK$70 with purchase of adult ticket, 1 child age 3-11 free.)*

NEW TERRITORIES 新界

The quiet, rural and somewhat reserved New Territores stretch over 794 sq. km of rugged mountains and unexplored beaches. Home to almost half of Hong Kong's population, the area is rich in temples, rock carvings, hiking trails, and cultural relics. Because of its wide open spaces, the New Territories are often targeted for development. HKTA has free booklets that outline sights and hiking trails in detail for each of the New Territories' nine districts.

ORIENTATION

The best way to get around the New Territories is to use the KCR and MTR. Each stop has buses, minibuses/maxicabs, and green New Territories taxis. The KCR East Rail runs south-north, beginning at Hung Hom and zigzagging through **Mong Kok, Sha Tin, Fotan,** the **Chinese University,** and **Tai Po,** ending at **Lo Wu** on the Chinese border. From Central, the MTR red line runs north, finishing at **Tsuen Wan.** Accessible by ferry or bus, **Tuen Mun,** a residential center in the far west, is connected to **Yuen Long** in the northeast by KCR Light Rail (LR). The beaches of **Sai Kung Peninsula** and **Clearwater Bay,** in the southeast corner, are accessible by bus #299 from University KCR Station.

FOOD

Sai Kung town overflows with seafood restaurants, many of which boast live specimens in tanks. Little English is spoken in the local bars, but music proves to be a universal language—karaoke is everywhere.

Pepperoni's, 1592 Po Tung Rd. (☎2792 2083). A warm ambience and an excellent apple crumble topped with vanilla ice cream keep Pepperoni's busy; expect to wait for a table. Famed pizzas (HK$55) include small margheritas (HK$70) and small pepperoni specials. Delivery to New Territories. Open daily 9am-11pm. Credit cards accepted. ❹

Indian Curry Hut, 64 Po Tung Rd. (☎2791 2929 or 2791 2333). Serves tandoori specialties, including tandoori squid (HK$66) and chicken tikka (HK$48). Rice, bread, mutton, and vegetarian plates available. Open daily 11:30am-11:30pm. ❹

Susannah's Seafood, 76 Po Tung Rd. (☎2792 2139). The baked lobster with cheese, chili crab, and salt-fried prawns is a local favorite. Chinese dishes (HK$48-60). English menus. Open M-F noon-2:30pm and 6-10:30pm, Sa-Su noon-3:30pm and 6-10:30pm. ❹

SIGHTS

TSUEN WAN 全环

At the end of the red Tsuen Wan MTR line is a major cultural and spiritual center, the ever-expanding city of Tsuen Wan. Temples here see more prayer and incense than any others in Hong Kong. Not surprisingly, the town has capitalized on its spiritual popularity and is the most expensive place to deposit the ashes of the departed. **Tai Mo Shan,** the biggest mountain in Hong Kong, is also in Tsuen Wan.

The **Sam Tung Uk Museum,** 2 Kwu Uk Lane, is a five-minute walk from the Tsuen Wan MTR station (B3 exit). This restored, walled Hakka village dating to 1786, has rooms furnished with tools and other items. A small exhibition hall also houses a rotating exhibit. *(☎2411 2001. Open W-M 9am-5pm. Free.)*

The **Western Monastery** holds religious ceremonies on the second floor that are sometimes open to tourists. Along with its neighbor, the famous **Yuen Yuen Institute,** the temple complex is dedicated to Confucianism, Buddhism, and Daoism. A stroll around the complex reveals a bronze statue of Confucius, a bonsai garden, and a temple containing 60 statues of deities, one for each year in the Chinese 60-year cycle. Yuen Yuen also shelters three of Hong Kong's largest "Precious Buddha" statues inside its walls. *(Take green minibus #81 to Lo Wai Village. From B3 exit at Tsuen Wan MTR Station, follow the pedestrian overpass until the end. Once on the street below, with your back to the MTR station, take a left. Then, make a right turn at Chung On Street. Walk up the block, turn right at the corner, and minibus #81 will be on your right. Monastery ☎2411 5111. Institute ☎2429 2220. Both open daily 9am-5pm. Free.)*

TAI PO 大浦 AND PLOVER COVE RESERVOIR

Take the KCR to Tai Po Market, exit at Uptown Plaza, take the pedestrian underpass, and hop on bus #75K at the far back corner of the bus station (50min., HK$3.60). The reservoir is the last stop on the bus line.

Tai Po is a typical New Territories town—a mess of construction, a marvel of tall, identical apartments, and a stone's throw away from stunning panoramic views of land and sea. Plover Cove Reservoir is a favorite for both hikers and picnickers. Visitors can barbecue by the water's edge or rent boats on the weekends. A family walk begins next to the Bradbury Lodge and tours the surrounding area in under an hour; numerous side trails await exploration by the more adventurous.

Bradbury Lodge (HI), on Tai Mei Tuk Rd. (look for the sign and trail at the back of the bus terminal), puts up guests who wish to stay at the Plover Cove Reservoir for the night. The lodge has a rustic and communal atmosphere with A/C, a large, shared kitchen and dining area, a TV in the common room, and a rooftop balcony with a splendid view of Plover Cove. The drawbacks are the six shared showers, Chinese-style toilets for up to 48 guests, and cleaning duties. Reservations are recommended on weekends. (☎2662 5123. Reception daily 7-10am and 4-11pm; lockout 10am-noon. Lights-out at 11pm. 8- and 12-bed dorms HK$55; doubles HK$150.)

CHINESE UNIVERSITY 香港中文大学

A shuttle bus (☎2609 7990) runs from the University KCR station to the center of campus (every 30min. M-F 9am-5:15pm, Sa 9am-1am; HK$1). Art museum ☎2609 7416. Open M-Sa 10am-4:45pm, Su 12:30-5:30pm; closed on public holidays. Free.

The Chinese University's lovely campus, just one stop south of Tai Po Market on the KCR, is built into the side of a mountain in Ma Liu Shui. The beautiful surrounding green parks and peaceful lakes, however, are prime landslide territory during the monsoon season. A visit to the art museum (next to the university library and miniature hedge maze) is worth the risk. The museum has an extensive collection of modern and ancient Chinese art; a free audio tour is available.

SHA TIN 沙田

Sha Tin's **Shing Man River** is a popular venue for dragon boat racing during the **Dragon Boat Festival,** or **Tuen Ng.** The **Bo Fook Ancestral Worship Halls** on Tai Po Rd. also sit among Sha Tin's attractions. Situated in the mountains, these halls have a pristine tranquility that dramatically contrasts with the industrial sprawl below. Use the escalator at the base of the building for easy access. For the more athletically-inclined, the **Ten Thousand Buddhas Temple** is 450-odd strenuous steps away. The climb is steep and winds its way through heaps of rusting iron and poorer New Territories residences. Turn left at the entrance to the Worship Halls to ask for directions; watch for the little yellow signs. *(Exit through the left entrance of the Sha Tin KCR station and follow the yellow signs. Both Halls and Temple open daily 9am-5pm.)*

The **Shatin Race Course** draws thousands of spectators on race days which include Wednesday evenings, and Saturday and Sunday afternoons from late September to late June. *(Take bus #888 from the Sha Tin KCR. Overseas visitors to Hong Kong who are over 18 and have been in the area for less than 21 days can snag admission badges for entrance into the coveted Member's Enclosure at the track. Call the Hong Kong Jockey Club for details at 1817).* In the center of the track is the lush **Penfold Park** and a bird sanctuary. *(Park open Tu-Su; 9am-5pm. Closed on race days.)*

SAI KUNG 西贡

On a late Sunday afternoon, **Sai Kung** town feels like an old fishing village. It is relaxed, foreigner-friendly, and filled with hikers, campers, and beach-lovers. The area is scattered with temples over 300 years old. The **Tin Hau Temple,** built in honor of the Goddess of the Sea, is a popular place of worship for fishermen whose lives are inextricably bound to her will. *(With the waterfront behind you, walk left from the bus station. ☎2461 5725.)* You can also explore Sai Kung's **Country Park** and the famous **MacLehose Trail,** which begins in Pak Tam Chung (take bus #94 from Sai Kung station). The HKTA provides a free booklet outlining a walk in Sai Kung that includes a visit to **Sheung Yiu Village Museum,** a restored Hakka village in Pak Tam Chung. *(☎2792 6365. Open W-M 9am-4pm.)*

Sai Kung's **Clearwater Bay Beaches No. 1** and **2** are famed for their water quality. To windsurf, canoe, row a *sampan*, or kayak, contact **Chong Hing Water Sports Centre** (☎2792 6810). Clearwater Bay (清水湾), a part of Sai Kung and a popular beach, has pristine white sand and turquoise water. Beware the ominous fins that may circle offshore; the shark attack warnings plastered all over the beach are serious. Clearwater Bay (open 9am-6pm) comes fully equipped, with showers, changing rooms, a first aid station, and lifeguards who will stand between you and Jaws's jagged teeth. *(To reach the beach, take the MTR to Diamond Hill station, and take bus #91 every 12-18min. 6am-10pm; HK$4.7, with A/C HK$6.5)*

KWAI TSING 葵青

The **Kwai Tsing** district, in the southwestern corner of the New Territories, consists of Tsing Yi Island and Kwai Chung. This unpretentious urban and industrial area has some breathtaking sights, including the **Tsing Ma Bridge,** one of the world's largest suspension bridges, and the **Lantau Link View Point,** which overlooks Tsing Ma, Ting Kau Bridge, and the Ma Wan Channel. *(From Maritime Square, take minibus*

304M to the View Point. Open M-F 9:30am-6:30pm, Sa-Su and public holidays 10am-8pm.) Another way to view the surrounding area is to take a hike along the **Kwai Tsing Reunification Health Trail** which winds through Liuto Valley in Tsing Yi. *(To get to the trail, take bus 248M from Maritime Square.)*

MUSEUMS

Chinese University of HK Art Museum (☎2609 7416), Chinese University at Sha Tin. MTR: Kowloon Tong. From the MTR stop, take the KCR East Rail to University Station; then, catch a shuttle bus to the University Administration Building.

Hong Kong Heritage Museum, 1 Man Lam Rd., Sha Tin (☎2180 8107). Take KCR East Rail to Sha Tin or Tai Wai.

Hong Kong Railway Museum, Tai Po Market, 13 Shung Tak St., Tai Po (☎2653 3455). MTR: Kowloon Tong. From here, take the KCR East Rail to Tai Wo.

Sheung Yik Folk Museum (☎2792 6365), Pak Tam Chung Nature Trail, Sai Kung. MTR: Chui Hung. From here, take maxicab 1A to Sai Kung Town and then bus #94 to Pak Tan Chung.

LANTAU ISLAND 大屿山

If God lived in Hong Kong, then Lantau Island, with its breathtaking natural grandeur, would be the Garden of Eden. Lantau's craggy mountains, isolated monasteries, giant Buddha statue, and wide open skies give the island an otherworldly feel. However, even on Lantau it's hard to get away from city life entirely. The new Chek Lap Kok airport has made it easier than ever to reach the island, and Lantau greets business travelers and tourists everyday. On weekends, Hong Kong residents descend upon Lantau to dine on fresh seafood, visit temples, and picnic in the mountains. After daytrippers leave, quiet descends, leaving residents and hikers camping in the wilderness to marvel at the beautiful night sky.

TRANSPORTATION

Trains: Trains travel along the yellow Tung Chung line, beginning at Hong Kong station and ending in Tung Chung MTR Station (HK$23).

Buses: Mui Wo, Tung Chung, Pui O, Tong Fuk, Tai O, and Ngong Ping each have conspicuous bus stations with fares and schedules. Buses are run by the New Lantau Bus Co. (☎2984 9848). Blue **taxis** are available at all bus stations (☎2984 1328), but since all the major routes spiral up mountains in a leisurely fashion, taking a taxi is not recommended. Base fare HK$12 for the first 2km, HK$1.2 each additional 0.2km or 1min. of waiting time. Luggage HK$5 extra per piece.

Ferries: Ferries depart from Pier 7 at the Central Star Ferry to Mui Wo port (daily, every 30min. 1:30am-11:30pm). Free schedules are available from HKTA offices and the Star Ferry ticket office.

Local Transportation: Bus E31 leaves from Tsuen Wan and Discovery Park to Tung Chung MTR; **E32** leaves from Kwai Fong MTR on Red line via Tung Chung MTR to the Chek Lap Kok airport terminus. Both buses run every 10-20min. and cost HK$10.

Bike Rental: Friendly Bicycle Shop (☎2984 2278), behind McDonald's in Mui Wo. HK$10 per hr.; weekdays HK$30 per day, weekends HK$40 per day. HK$5 student discount on weekdays. Open daily 10am-8pm. **King of Bicycle** (☎2984 7704), two stores down from Friendly Bicycle. HK$10 per hr., HK$30 per day (overnight included). Discounts available for large groups. Open daily 10:30am-8:30pm.

ORIENTATION AND PRACTICAL INFORMATION

Lantau Island is comprised of small towns that span the island's coast. On the northeast coast, **Discovery Bay** is a tightly knit community of high-income individuals who can afford to maintain a picture-perfect neighborhood. Along the eastern coast is Lantau's ferry port, **Mui Wo,** also known as **Silvermine Bay. Pui O,** along the Southern coast, is a residential area that eventually leads to the famous beaches of **Tong Fuk Village. Tai O** is an old fishing village on the west coast. **Ngong Ping,** in the inner Western region of Lantau, is surveyed by the immense Tian Tan Buddha atop Po Lin Monastery. The quickly developing central town, **Tung Chung,** was previously the remote site of an old fort built to keep out opium traders. **Chek Lap Kok,** the site of the new airport, was once an insignificant appendage on the northwest coast, hanging onto Lantau by a thin thread of land. The newly constructed 2.2km road and rail suspension bridge, **Tsing Ma Bridge,** the longest in the world, effectively links Chek Lap Kok, Lantau Island, and Hong Kong.

Government and financial services are concentrated in **Mui Wo** and **Tung Chung.** In **Mui Wo,** banks, **ATMs**, chain grocery stores, and 7-Elevens cluster around the square surrounding the bus station. Mui Wo police station, clinic, and post office are all in the same government complex. To reach them, walk toward Silvermine Bay beach on **Ngan Kwong Wan Rd.** Just after the bridge to the beach (Mui Wo Chung Hau St.) branches off Ngan Kwong Wan Rd., you will see a gray complex on the left labeled "Government Offices." The **police** force (☎2721 2486) is in Rm. 215. The **clinic** (☎2984 2178) and **post office** are on the ground floor. (Open M-F 9am-4:30pm, Sa 9am-12:30pm.) **Tung Chung MTR Station** has a small bank with **ATM** machines; **Citygate Mall,** attached to the station, has a large grocery store.

ACCOMMODATIONS

S.G. Davis Hostel (HI), Ngong Ping (☎2985 5610). From the Mui Wo bus station at the ferry port, take bus #2 to Po Lin Monastery, Ngong Ping. Follow the sign to the left of the Buddha statue; the hostel is a 7min. walk away. Serene, and run by an exceptionally friendly couple. Reservations recommended on weekends. Simple chores required. Curfew 11pm. Dorms HK$45 for HI members, HK$75 for non-members. Doubles HK$150. ❶

Jockey Club Mong Tung Wan Hostel (HI), Pui O (☎2984 1389). From the Mui Wo bus station, take bus #7 to Pui O. Signs for the hostel are on Chi Ma Wan Rd., which loops around the bus station. Follow them; it's about a 45min. walk. Or, take the ferry from Pier 6 (Central Hong Kong Island) to Cheung Chau Island. Hire a *sampan* to the jetty at Mong Tung Wan (HK$100). The hostel is a few minutes walk away and within walking distance (45min.) of Pui O beach. Prices and curfew times same as at the S.G. Davis Hostel. ❶

Mui Wo Inn, 24 Tung Wan Tau Rd., Silvermine Bay/Mui Wo (☎2984 8597). From the Mui Wo bus station, walk toward Silvermine Bay beach; Tung Wan Tau Rd. runs along the beach. A/C, beach views, bath, refrigerator, TV, and VCR. Singles HK$280, waterfront singles HK$400; on weekends singles HK$480, waterfront singles HK$600. ❹

FOOD

MUI WO. The **Mui Wo Square** surrounding the bus station has a few small Chinese restaurants tucked between the stores. McDonald's is by the ferry terminal, and the **China Bear Bar and Restaurant** is just behind it, serving up nachos (HK$45),

HONG KONG

bangers and mash (HK$55), and an all-day breakfast platter (HK$58). The locals come here to enjoy the great waterfront view and laid-back atmosphere. (☎2984 9720. Open M-F noon-11pm, Sa-Su 11am-11pm. ❹) The **Mui Wo Cooked Food Market,** also by the ferry terminal, consists of small blocks of restaurants that share an outdoor seating area. (Open daily 6am-midnight.)

PUI O AND TAI O. Apart from Mui Wo, **Pui O** is your best bet for a selection of good restaurants in the midst of rural Lantau. From Mui Wo bus station, take bus #7 to Pui O bus terminus. A string of mostly Chinese restaurants lines the street opposite the bus station. If you want to eat as the Chinese do, take bus #1 from Mui Wo bus station and get off at **Tai O.** This small and densely populated fishing village is famous for its seafood restaurants. Unfortunately, restaurants are hard to find, and the village is hard to navigate.

OTHER OPTIONS ON LANTAU ISLAND. For vegans, **Po Lin Monastery** in **Ngong Ping** is the place to eat. On arrival at Po Lin (take bus #2 from Mui Wo station at ferry pier), walk straight from the Buddha statue through the stone gateway to the main hall. The cafeteria is on the left, in the Arhat temple. A meal ticket costs HK$60, but light snacks are available. (Noodles or tofu HK$20, desserts HK$10. ☎2985 5248. Open daily 11:30am-5pm. ❷)

The **Tung Chung** MTR station exits into the new Citygate Mall. On the other side of a Delifrance is the **Catstreet Cafe,** with outdoor seating, upscale decor, and reasonable prices. The menu includes Western and Chinese dishes, like sumptuous fried rice noodles with satay beef (HK$40) and grilled steak with black pepper sauce (HK$48). (☎2109 1131. Open daily 11am-10pm. MC/V. ❸)

SIGHTS

NGONG PING. Perhaps Lantau Island's most popular sight is the giant **Tian Tan Buddha statue,** the largest outdoor seated bronze Buddha in the world. Completed in October 1989, the statue is 33.95m tall and covers an area of 3284 sq. m. Be prepared to walk up 260 steps to view the Buddha statue up close. High atop his altar, Buddha raises his right hand as if greeting his visitors while peacefully surveying the lives of those below at the **Po Lin Monastery.** Every feature of the statue is symbolic; its broad forehead and elongated ears signify virtue, wisdom, and perfection. *(☎2985 5248. Open daily 10am-6pm. Free museum admission with food purchase.)*

The beauty of the surrounding mist-covered mountains makes for inspirational hiking. The **Lantau Trail** passes **Sunset Peak,** the second highest mountain on Lantau. Early birds who catch the sunrise from the mountain can take in this unforgettable sight. Although the path can be dangerous when wet, tourists can still manage the climb to **Po Lam Zen Monastery** (45min. from Po Lin Monastery), winding up and down through incredible scenery.

OTHER AREAS. The **Silvermine Waterfall,** a short walk from the ferry terminal in **Mui Wo,** is a hidden treasure, unknown even to many of the residents. To get to the waterfall, take a right out of the ferry terminal; continue down the road and turn right on Ngen Shek St. Follow Ngen Shek St. as it curves to the right, and then turn left onto Wong Tong Rd. Keep to the left at the two forks, and you'll soon hear the falls in the distance. The walk from the ferry to the falls takes about 35 minutes.

Pui O beach, accessible by bus #7, is popular with locals. The **Cheung Sha Upper beach,** accessible by bus #4 (specify to the driver that you are going to Cheung Sha *Upper* beach), has lovely views and high water quality. *(Beach hotline ☎2414 5555. All beaches in Lantau open daily 9am-6pm.)*

HIKING LANTAU ISLAND

Lantau is rich in country parks and hiking terrain. A large map pointing out walking trails, campsites, and country parks often greets visitors to each town. For the dedicated hiker, E. Stokes's book *Exploring Hong Kong's Countryside* is highly recommended (HK$80, available at HKTA main office and major bookstores). The HKTA (see p. 531) also publishes a free guide to five walking trails, one of which is on Lantau. **Mui Wo** is a good starting point, with a **Country Parks Information Post** in the ferry station. (Open M-F 8:30am-noon, Sa-Su 8:30am-4pm.)

LAMMA ISLAND 南丫岛

Though Hong Kong and Lamma Islands are separated only by a few miles of water, Lamma might as well be an entire planet away. On one island, life never stands still; on the other, life is in a perpetually languorous state. Lamma shuns cars, business suits, and stress, glorying instead in the beach. Needless to say, it is an escapist haven for expats in search of a more bohemian atmosphere.

ORIENTATION AND PRACTICAL INFORMATION

Lamma has a northern and southern half held together by a strip of land. The port of arrival in the north region is **Yung Shue Wan;** in the south, **Sok Kwu Wan.** A ferry shuttles from the Lamma port to Pier 5 in Central. Lamma is so small that a walk from Yung Shue Wan to Sok Kwu Wan takes under an hour.

There are no cars on the island, and most people walk or ride bikes. **Bikes** can be rented at Hoi Nam bicycle store in front of the Shai Po New Village street sign. (☎2982 2500. HK$15 per hr. Open daily 7am-11pm.) **Scorpio,** on Back St., has four terminals with net access. (☎2982 4121. Open M-Th 9am-8pm, Su noon-6pm. For HK$1 per min., 15min. minimum.) Visit **www.lamma.net** for invaluable information on Lamma Island happenings and establishments.

ACCOMMODATIONS

Man Lai Wah Hotel (☎2982 0220 or 2982 0600), right off the ferry terminal at Yung Shue Wan. A/C, bath, phone, and TV. Rooms are clean and many have balconies. Doubles HK$350-400; on weekends HK$500 and up. ❺

Lamma Vacation House, 29 Yung Shue Wan Main St., 1st fl. (☎2982 0427). A/C, bath, fridge, and TV. Doubles HK$200; on weekends HK$500. ❸

FOOD AND ENTERTAINMENT

Lamma's undisputed culinary specialty is seafood. The docks and walkways along the bay in **Sok Kwu Wan** are lined with seafood restaurants that showcase entire aquariums of edible fish. In **Yung Shue Wan,** seafood restaurants cluster around the ferry terminal; plenty of alternatives are in Yung Shue Wan.

Bookworm Cafe, 79 Yung Shue Wan Main St. (☎2982 4838). Cool your body with a pineapple smoothie or warm your heart by chatting with the friendly proprietor. Pricey but very tantalizing salads. Open Sa-M, W 10am-10pm; Tu, Th-F 10am-6pm.

Deli Lamma, 36 Main St. (☎2982 1583). Serves hefty and high-quality portions of both Western and Indian delights and occasionally hosts typhoon-watching parties. Open daily 9am-11pm.

Lamma Seaview Man Fung Restaurant, 5 Main St. (☎5982 0719). Vegetable dishes and open-air dining tables complete with fresh roses gracing each table top. Plenty of seafood, plenty of sea view. Open daily 11am-10pm. Credit cards accepted.

HIKING

The trail from **Yung Shue Wan** to **Sok Kwu Wan** passes breathtaking beaches and caves before emerging near the ferries bound for Central. From Yung Shue Wan, turn onto Yung Shue Wan Back St. and follow the concrete path through tiny villages until you hit the countryside. The trail veers past the fully equipped and staffed **Hung Shing Ye Beach** (a 25min. walk) before continuing over and around **Kamikaze Cave.** In Sok Kwu Wan, you can catch a ferry back to Central or continue on to **Mo Tat Wan** or **Lo So Shing** beaches. From Sok Kwu Wan, the trail follows the curve of the mini-bay. Walking the entire trail takes under one hour. Watch for signs for the trail in both cities.

CHEUNG CHAU 长州

Tiny in landmass but abundant in character, Cheung Chau Island is perhaps the most buoyant of the outlying islands. It boasts quite a list of flamboyant characters, from Lee Lai-Shan, Hong Kong's first Olympic gold medalist, to Cheung Po Tsai, a legendary pirate who supposedly hid in a cave that now bears his name. Ride the ferry from Pier 6 in Central and cruise through stunning visions of mountain and sea. The Cheung Chau ferry pier has **ATMs**, **grocery stores,** and the **police** station. Wander down **Pak She St.,** which runs between the waterfront and the procession of restaurants, bars, shopping stalls, and numerous ice cream stalls. The island is a colorful collection of three-tiered buildings that hosts restaurants and bars on the lower floors and sun-loving islanders on the third.

MACAU 澳门 ☎853

Portuguese traders first dropped anchor in Macau, the first European colony in Asia, in 1513, transforming this tiny peninsula into a flourishing center for trade of Oriental silks and spices. Today, every pastel colonial building or crumbling Tin Hau temple tells a story of conquest, trade, and hybridization; a scattering of elegant churches recalls the time when Jesuit missionaries came to ensure that Macau remained true to its given name, "City of the Name of God." These days, however, Macau's visitors are a very different kind of devout. Portuguese tourists and giddy Hong Kong weekenders come to gamble religiously at Macau's famed casinos or partake in the city's notoriously racy nightlife. Round-the-clock jet foils ensure a bustling tourism industry, which brings in half of Macau's yearly revenue. On December 19, 1999, Macau returned to China after an absence of more than 400 years, becoming the second of China's SARs.

MONEY

Gambler-friendly Macau takes its money seriously. The **pataca** (MOP), divided into 100 **avos,** is the official unit of currency of Macau. Coins come in 10, 20, and 50 avos and 1, 5, and 10 patacas; bills come in 20, 50, 100, 500, and 1000 patacas. All Macau businesses accept HK$, but public pay phones only take patacas. **Banks** exchange currency and traveler's checks; they can be found on every corner; **ATMs** hooked up to Cirrus, Jetco, Plus, and Visa networks are everywhere in Macau.

MACAU PATACA (MOP)	
US$1=MOP8.03	MOP1=US$0.12
CDN$1=MOP5.14	MOP1=CDN$0.19
Y1=MOP0.97	MOP1=Y1.03
HK$1=MOP1.03	MOP1=HK$0.97
EUR€1=MOP7.89	MOP1=EUR€0.13
UK£1=MOP12.53	MOP1=UK£0.08
AUS$1=MOP4.43	MOP1=AUS$0.23
NZ$1=MOP3.79	MOP1=NZ$.26
ZAR1=MOP0.77	MOP1=ZAR1.31

Most hotels and restaurants accept credit cards, but some may add a 10% service charge and 5% government tax to all bills. **Tips** are not usually expected.

INTERCITY TRANSPORTATION

VISAS AND CUSTOMS. Citizens of EU countries, Australia, Canada, New Zealand, South Africa, and the US can enter Macau with a passport or travel document and stay for 30 days. Permanent Hong Kong residents and Portuguese passport holders can stay visa-free for one year. Single-entry individual visas are available at any Portuguese consulate or at the Macau Ferry Terminal. Visas are valid for 20 days and cost HK$100, for families with children under 12 HK$200, and for members of a group of 10 or more HK$50.

Macau does not levy export duties, but Hong Kong limits the quantities of duty-free cigarettes (100) and wine (1 liter) that travelers can carry back with them.

BY AIR. Completed in 1995, the **Macau International Airport** (24hr. ☎861 111), on the eastern coast of Taipa Island, has regular flights to Beijing, Shanghai, and other cities in China, as well as to Bangkok, Brussels, Kaohsiung, Kuala Lumpur, Lisbon, Seoul, Singapore, and Taipei. More flights and carriers will be added in coming years. There is a departure tax on all flights (destinations in China MOP80, children ages 2-12 MOP50; all other destinations MOP130, children ages 2-12 MOP80). No departure tax is charged for stays under 24hr. The AP1 bus (every 15min., MOP6) runs from the airport to all major hotels. Taxis are also available.

BY SEA. Boats depart from Hong Kong's **Macau Ferry Terminal,** 200 Connaught Rd., Shun Tak Centre, Sheung Wan (MTR: Sheung Wan); some leave from the **China Ferry Terminal,** 33 Canton Rd., TST, behind Kowloon Park. A departure tax is included in the price of ferry tickets (HK$19 to Macau, MOP19 to Hong Kong).

The Hong Kong & Yaumati Ferry Co. Ltd. (☎726 301) has catamaran service (70min., 12 per day) from the ferry terminal in Macau to the China Ferry Terminal in **Kowloon, Hong Kong** (☎2516 9581). Ferries run from **Macau to Kowloon** (10:05am-11:30pm; M-F HK$119, Sa-Su and holidays before 6pm HK$140, daily after 6pm HK$160) and from **Kowloon to Macau** (8:30am-8pm; M-F HK$113, Sa-Su before 6pm HK$134, daily after 6pm HK$154).

Turbojet (Macau ☎285 9333; Hong Kong ☎790 7039) has boats from the ferry terminal to **Sheung Wan, Hong Kong** (1hr.; every 15min., less frequent in early morning; HK$112-176, HK$15 discount for adults 60 or above and children below 12). Make advance reservations for weekend tickets from Hong Kong to Macau. **Yuet Tung Shipping Company** has a daily ferry from Macau Pier 14, beside the Peninsula Hotel (2:30pm; MOP100, children MOP57), to **Shekou** and **Shenzhen.**

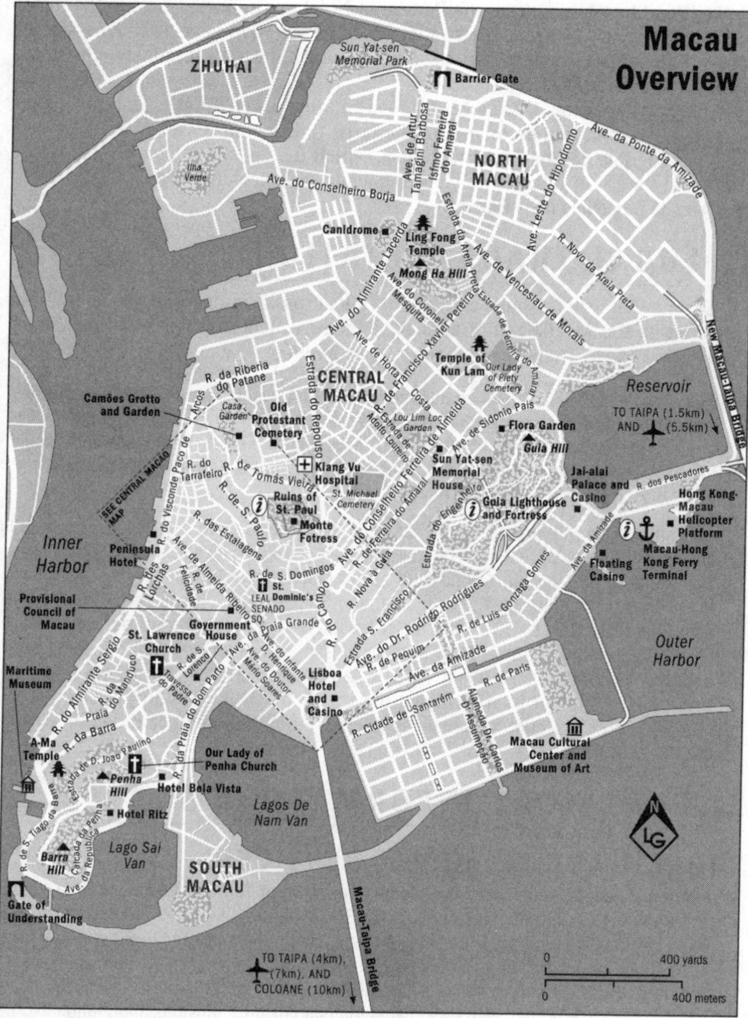

ORIENTATION

Tiny Macau Peninsula occupies the western Pearl River Delta, at the gateway to Guangdong province; **Taipa Island** and **Coloane Island** are linked to Macau by the Friendship Bridge. The Zhuhai Special Economic Zone borders **North Macau,** which has few casinos but enough bars and clubs for a lively nightlife.

Most of Macau's casinos are in **Central Macau.** Twisting, narrow streets crisscross this area, curving around Guia Hill, the Ruins of St. Paul, and St. Dominic's Church. Macau's main road, **Avenida de Almeida Riberio,** commonly known as **San**

Ma Lo (New Street), runs from the Peninsula Hotel on the West Coast to the Hotel Lisboa on the South Coast. The southern half of this road bears the name **Ave. de Infante D. Henrique.** Running from the Macau-Hong Kong ferry terminal to the Hotel Lisboa is **Ave. de Amizade.**

In hilly **South Macau,** Our Lady of Penha Church, A Ma Temple, and the Macau Maritime Museum huddle together. The large thoroughfare **Ave. de Praia Grande** becomes the **Rua de Praia do Bom Partom,** which runs past the historic Bela Vista Hotel and the Hotel Ritz before changing again (as roads in Macau are apt to do) into **Ave. de República** near Barra Hill.

LOCAL TRANSPORTATION

The Macau Peninsula is small enough to walk across in under an hour. **Transportes Colectivos de Macau (TCM)** and **Transmac** operate frequent A/C buses. Within Macau proper MOP2.5, to Taipa MOP3.3, to Coloane MOP5.

Taxis: Base fare MOP10, each additional 250m MOP1; waiting time MOP1 per min.; luggage MOP3. Surcharges for trips from the airport (MOP5), as well as to, but not from, the islands (to Coloane MOP5, from Taipa to Coloane MOP2). **Pedicabs** wait outside the ferry terminal and Hotel Lisboa; rates are negotiable (around MOP100 per hr., MOP15-20 for a ride around the bay).

Car Rental: The only reason to rent anything might be to drive a *moke*–a cute, small cousin of the jeep. Drivers must be 21+ and have a valid driver's license. **Happy Rent A Car** (☎726 868), on the ground floor of the Macau Ferry Terminal, rents *mokes*. All Hong Kong, Canadian, Japanese, Indian, and Singaporean citizens need an IDP (see **Essentials: By Car,** p. 98), valid for at least 2 years. M-F MOP480 per day, Sa-Su MOP500 (cost of gas extra). 20% discount for same-day returns. MOP4000 credit card deposit. Open daily 9am-5:30pm. **Avis** (☎726 571), also in the Macau Ferry terminal. ID for customers not from Australia, the US, or UK. M-F MOP450 per day, Sa-Su MOP500. 20% discount for same-day returns. MOP3000 credit card deposit. Open daily 9am-5:30pm.

PRACTICAL INFORMATION

TOURIST AND FINANCIAL SERVICES

Tourist Offices: In Hong Kong, the **Macau Government Tourism Office (MGTO),** Shun Tak Centre, 168-200 Connaught Rd., Ste. 336, Sheung Wan (☎2857 2287 or 2559 0147). MTR: Sheung Wan, D exit. Has maps, a comprehensive *Macau Guide Book*, and information about museums, walking tours, and accommodations. Open daily 9am-1pm and 2:30-5:30pm. In Macau, the **MGTO,** 9 Largo de Senado (☎315 566, daily 9am-6pm hotline ☎340 390; www.macautourism.gov.mo), provides information in Chinese, English, Japanese, and Portuguese. The *Official Map and Guide* is particularly useful for the islands. Provides free local calls. Open daily 9am-6pm. Other offices: at the **Macau Ferry Terminal,** near customs (open daily 9am-10pm); **Macau International Airport** (☎861 436; open daily 9am-10:30pm); **Guia Lighthouse** (☎569 808; open daily 9am-5:30pm); **Ruins of St. Paul** (☎358 444; open daily 9am-6pm).

Travel Agencies: CTS (☎700 888), on Rua de Nagasaki, Xinhua Building, 1st fl., opposite the World Trade Centre. Chinese single-entry visas MOP150; arrive before noon for pickup after noon the next day. Bring a photo or buy it there (MOP30). Open daily 9am-9pm. **Branch** at the Macau Ferry Terminal, 3rd fl., shop 1027 (☎726 756), near the MGTO. Makes hotel reservations. Open daily 9am-8:30pm.

Consulates: Portugal provides consular services in Macau; most other countries have offices in Hong Kong (see **Essentials: Consular Services in China,** p. 48).

Currency Exchange: Bank of China, on Ave. Dr. Mário Soares. Open M-F 9am-5pm, Sa 9am-1pm. **Banco Nacional Ultramarino (BNU),** 22 Ave. de Almeida Ribeiro. Open M-F 9am-5pm, Sa 9am-noon. **Hong Kong Bank,** 73-75 Rua da Praia Grande. Open M-F 9am-5pm, Sa 9am-12:30pm. The **Macau Ferry Terminal** has a currency exchange counter near the tourist office. Open daily 9am-6pm.

American Express: 23B Rua de S. Paulo R/C (☎363 262), near the Ruins of St. Paul. Traveler's checks, credit card advances, AmEx payments. Open daily 9am-5:30pm.

LOCAL SERVICES

Grocery: Yaohan Department Store, 1579 Ave. da Amizade. Follow the pedestrian walkway from the Macau Ferry Terminal. Open daily 11am-10:30pm.

Library: At Jardine de S. Francisco on Rua Do Campo, in a Chinese-style building. Open daily 9am-12pm and 7-10pm. **Provisional Municipal Council of Macau Building** on Ave. de Almeida Ribeiro, opposite the fountain, is open daily 1-7pm.

Bookstore: Plaza Cultural Macau, 32-G Ave. do Conselheiro Ferreira de Almeida. Open daily 11am-9pm.

Weather: English ☎1311.

EMERGENCY AND COMMUNICATIONS

Emergency: ☎999. **Fire:** ☎572 222. **Ambulance:** ☎577 199 or 378 311.

Police: ☎919 or 573 333.

Maritime Police: ☎559 944.

Judicial Police: ☎993.

Hospitals: Government Hospital (☎313 731), Estrada do Visconde de S. Januário. Kiang Wu Hospital (☎371 333), Rua de Coelho do Amarel. Both open 24hr.

Pharmacies: Farmacia Popular, 16 Largo de Senado (☎573 739 or 566 568). Open M-F 9am-9pm, Sa-Su 9am-8pm. **Watson's,** at the intersection of Ave. da Praia Grande, Rua do Campo, and Rua de Santa Clara.

Telephones: Companhia de Telecomunicações de Macau (CTM) offices and the snack shops on the 2nd fl. of the Macau Ferry Terminal sell MOP70 and MOP100 phone cards. For international calls, dial 00 and then the country code. For Hong Kong, dial 01. **International Directory Assistance:** ☎101. **Collect calls:** ☎191. **Local Directory:** English and Cantonese ☎181, Portuguese ☎185.

Internet Access: CTM, Long Cheon Com Bldg., 22 Rua S. Domingos, 2nd fl. (☎833 833). Look for the red ribbon logo. Free unlimited access. Open daily 10am-8pm.

Post Office: CTT de Macau, Largo do Senado, in Leal Senado Square. EMS and Poste Restante (counter #1; mail is held for 1 month). Open M-F 9am-6pm, Sa 9am-1pm.

ACCOMMODATIONS

Almost all accommdations are located in central Macau, clustered on side streets branching off **Ave. de Almeida Ribeiro,** near the harbor, or off **Ave. de Infante D. Henrique.** Many low-budget rooms were carved out of a single apartment; the vast majority let in little natural light. Consider yourself lucky to have a room with a view. On Coloane Island, two **youth hostels** *(pousada de juventude)* often have weekday discounts (see **Hostels,** below).

Anyone planning to spend more than MOP200 should first check out the travel agencies at the ferry terminal; they typically offer up to 50% discounts on larger hotels. Some packages include ferry tickets to or from Hong Kong. Advance reservations are almost universally recommended for weekend stays, when hotels are packed full of Hong Kong weekenders.

HOTELS AND PENSIONS

Vila Jing Jing, 998 Ave. da Praia Grande (☎715 037), across from the pink colonial building known as the Military Club. Friendly owner; carpeted, very pretty (albeit slightly musty) rooms with A/C, TV, rooftop balcony, and plenty of sunlight. Discounts for stays over 1 week. Singles MOP100, with bath MOP130; triples MOP230. ❷

Pensão Nam In, 3 Travessa da Praia Grande (☎710 024 or 710 008). Make sure you are on Travessa da Praia Grande, not Rua da Praia Grande. Clean, airy rooms with A/C, couch, phone, TV, and natural light. Singles with A/C and bathroom MOP150. ❷

San Va Hotel, 67 Rua da Felicidade (☎573 701; sanva@hongkong.com), off Rua dos Mercadores from Ave. de Almeida Ribeiro. Thin walls provide free evening entertainment. Many backpackers call the lovely balcony, dirty wicker chairs, and two semi-outdoor toilets and showers home. Singles MOP60; doubles MOP70. ❶

Wai Lee Guest House, 38 Ave. de Dom João IV, 1st fl. (☎710 199). Clean rooms with A/C, bath, and TV. Friendly Malaysian proprietor speaks excellent English. Check-out 1pm. Reservations recommended. Singles MOP110; doubles MOP150. ❷

Ko Wah Hotel, 71 Rua da Felicidade (☎375 599 or 375 452). Spacious rooms have A/C, bath, and TV. Reception on 4th fl. Singles MOP150; doubles and triples MOP186. Discounts for long-term stays. ❷

Vila Universal, 73 Rua da Felicidade (☎573 247 or 375 742). Clean, well-kept rooms have A/C, bath, phone, TV, and large windows. Singles MOP147; doubles MOP216. ❷

HOSTELS

Although both hostels are on Coloane Island, hostel bookings must be paid for in advance in Central Macau at the **Youth Hostel Booking Office,** on Rua de Santiago da Barra. (☎988 0712. Open M-F 9am-5:45pm.) Both hostels have a fairly comprehensive list of regulations: HI members only, midnight curfew, no cooking, and beds made by 10am. The 30-bed dorms cost MOP40-100 for foreigners, MOP20-80 for locals. In the summer, hostels are often fully booked by Hong Kong youth groups.

Hac Sa Beach Youth Hostel (☎882 701), in a gray building opposite the Water Sports Centre. Take bus #25 from the station in front of Hotel Lisboa to the 2nd to last stop; it's on the right. Has the feel of a beach resort. Spotless rooms are homey, with couches, lockers, and colorful sheets. ❶

Cheoc Van Beach Youth Hostel (☎882 024), off Estrada de Cheoc Van, on the way to the beach. From the Cheoc Van bus station, walk a few meters toward Taipa; turn left onto Rua de Antonio Francisco; the hostel is the blue and white building on the right. ❶

FOOD

Macau's eateries make up for their scarcity with impressive quality and low prices. Many restaurants serve Chinese noodles and *dim sum* with German pig knuckle, *caldo verde* soup, *tiramisu*, and Portuguese egg tarts. Vendors around **Senado Square** sell shish kebabs and fish balls, and cafes and *sopa de fitas* abound.

Rua do Almirante Sérgio, running past A Ma Temple and the Macau Maritime Museum in South Macau, is home to cheap Chinese eateries and slightly more expensive Portuguese restaurants. Upscale Portuguese and international cuisine eateries line **Alameda Dr. Carlos D'Assumçao,** which runs from the Kun Lam statue off Ave. Dr. Sun Yat Sen to the Macau Landmark on Ave. de Amizade. It eventually

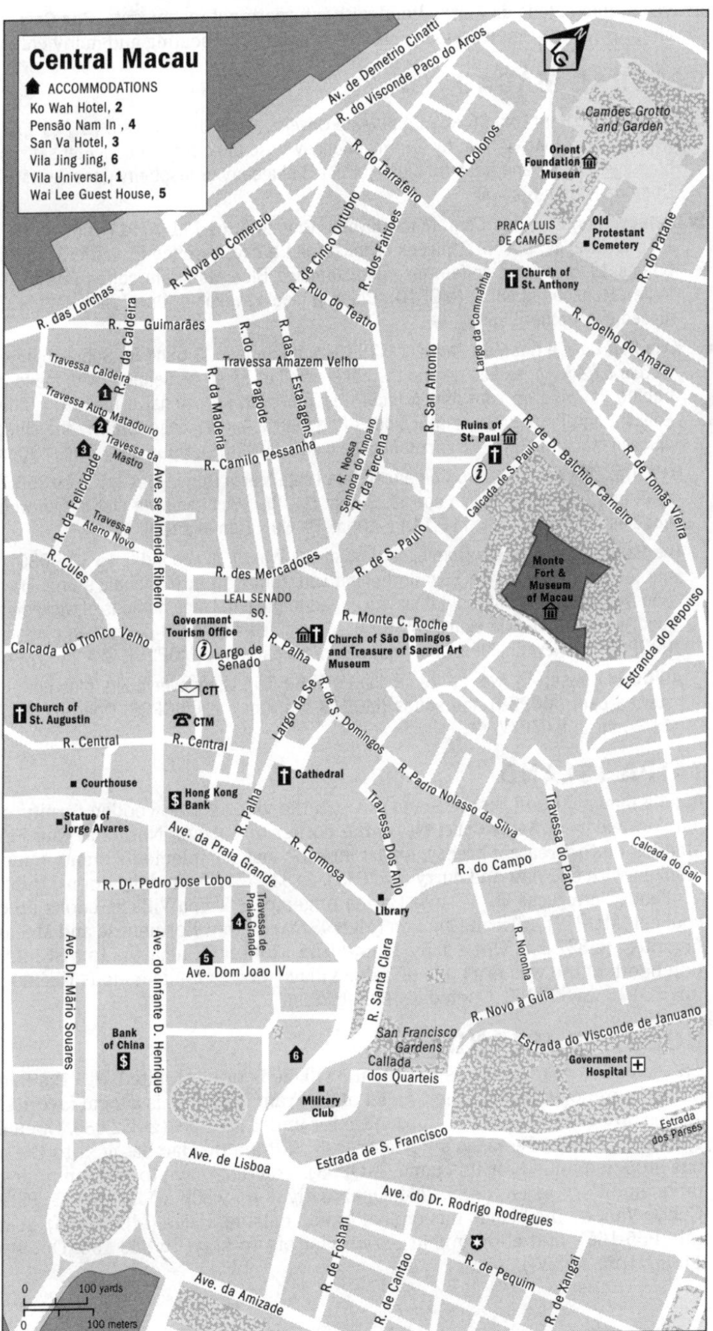
Central Macau
ACCOMMODATIONS
Ko Wah Hotel, 2
Pensão Nam In , 4
San Va Hotel, 3
Vila Jing Jing, 6
Vila Universal, 1
Wai Lee Guest House, 5
Av. de Demetrio Cinatti
R. do Visconde Paco do Arcos
R. do Tarrafeiro
R. Colonos
Camões Grotto and Garden
Orient Foundation Museum
PRACA LUIS DE CAMÕES
Old Protestant Cemetery
R. Nova do Comercio
R. de Cinco Outubro
R. dos Faitioes
Ruo do Teatro
Church of St. Anthony
R. do Patane
R. das Lorchas
R. da Caldeira
R. Guimarães
R. do Pagode
R. das Estalagens
Largo da Commanha
R. Coelho do Amaral
Travessa Caldeira
Travessa Amazem Velho
Travessa Auto Matadouro
R. da Maderia
R. San Antonio
Ruins of St. Paul
R. de D. Balchior Carneiro
Travessa da Mastro
R. Camilo Pessanha
R. Nossa Senhora do Amparo
R. da Tercena
Calcada de S. Paulo
R. de Tomãs Vieira
R. da Felicidade
Ave. se Almeida Ribeiro
Travessa Aterro Novo
R. de S. Paulo
Monte Fort & Museum of Macau
R. Cules
R. des Mercadores
LEAL SENADO SQ.
Government Tourism Office
R. Monte C. Roche
Estranda do Repouso
Calcada do Tronco Velho
Largo de Senado
R. Palha
Church of São Domingos and Treasure of Sacred Art Museum
CTT
Church of St. Augustin
CTM
Largo da Se
R. de S. Domingos
R. Central
R. Central
Cathedral
Courthouse
Hong Kong Bank
R. Padro Nolasso da Silva
Travessa Dos Anjo
Travessa do Pato
Statue of Jorge Alvares
R. Palha
Ave. da Praia Grande
R. Formosa
Calcada do Gaio
R. do Campo
R. Dr. Pedro Jose Lobo
Travessa de Praia Grande
Library
R. Noronha
Ave. Dr. Mário Souares
Ave. do Infante D. Henrique
Ave. Dom Joao IV
R. Santa Clara
R. Novo à Guia
Estrada do Visconde de Januano
Bank of China
San Francisco Gardens
Callada dos Quarteis
Government Hospital
Military Club
Estrada dos Parses
Ave. de Lisboa
Estrada de S. Francisco
Ave. do Dr. Rodrigo Rodregues
R. de Foshan
R. de Pequim
R. de Xangai
R. de Cantao
Ave. da Amizade
0 100 yards
0 100 meters

HONG KONG

arrives at **Rua Cidade da Sintra,** lined with international restaurants. **Rua Com. Mata Oliveira,** off Ave. de Dom João IV, has colorful outdoor seating and many cafes.

CENTRAL MACAU

Dili Deli, Edf. Kam Lok, 96 Rua Com. Mata Oliveira, Ground fl., Block 3 (☎713 177), off Ave. de Dom João IV. Run by an exceptionally hospitable mother-daughter set. Scrambled eggs, toast, and fresh fruit juice MOP15; blueberry or raspberry pancakes MOP10. Open daily 8am-8pm. ❶

Coffeeworks, 201 Rua Com. Mata Oliveira, Ground fl. (☎711 7771), off Ave. de Dom João IV. 2 eggs, bacon, 2 pieces of toast, and a cup of coffee for MOP13. The menu boasts 17 blends of coffee, including Jamaica Blue Mountain coffee (MOP18) and Indian Monsoon Malabar (MOP10). Chinese meals available. Open daily 8am-6:30pm; closed every other Sunday. ❶

Kam Pou Café e Casa de Pasto, 21-23 Largo de Senado, Ground fl., Sobre-Loja (☎573 986 or 572 338), tucked behind the bakery stall on Largo de Senado. With the fountain behind you, it's on your left. A local treasure, with an extensive menu (in Chinese, English, and Portuguese) that includes Portuguese and Chinese fare. Try the shredded chicken macaroni (MOP16) or mango ice cream (MOP8.5). Open daily 7am-9:30pm. ❶

B+ Cafe, Edf. Kai Fu Centro Comercial, Rua Leste Mercs Domingos, 3/5 A (☎356 778). Ham and cheese sandwich special 3-6pm (MOP5), Sichuan-style filet of fish with rice noodles (MOP10). Open M-F 11am-10pm, Sa-Su 11am-midnight. ❶

The Haven, Travessa São Domingos, Jardim Lok Wa, Bk A, Ground fl. (☎335 080). With the fountain at Largo de Senado behind you, turn right at McDonald's onto Travessa São Domingos; the outdoor tables are ahead to the left. Large portions of wickedly good food: try the Thai-style clams (MOP40), Mexican salad (MOP34), chicken cordon bleu (MOP45), or New England clam chowder in a bread bowl (MOP26). ❸

Ali Curry House, 4K Ave. da República (☎555 865). Curry everything, plus Portuguese stewed beef (MOP38) and soups (MOP13-16). Cocktails MOP28. Open daily 12:30-11:30pm. JCB/MC/V. ❸

TAIPA ISLAND

Rua da Cunha ("Food Street") cuts through the village. The wooden furniture and painted leaves at **Satay Court ❸,** on the corner of Estrada Nora and Rua Fernão Mendes Pinto, create a breezy, smart interior that complements menu items like chicken with coconut and curry (MOP48). (☎827 751. Open daily noon-11pm. MC/V.) **Panda Portuguese ❹,** 4-8 Rua Carlos Eugenio, in Taipa Village, cooks up charcoal eel (MOP78), African Chicken (MOP48), and other Portuguese and Mecanese favorites. (☎827 338. Open daily 11am-11pm.) **Tai Lei ❶,** near the tourist information booth at the western edge of Taipa village, dishes up its famous rice noodles for MOP15. (☎827 150. Open daily 6am-6:30pm.)

COLOANE ISLAND

The selection of restaurants in Coloane village is rather limited. **Nga Tim Cafe ❸,** 8 Rue Caeteno, in front of the Chapel of St. Francis Xavier, is a local favorite that serves up Portuguese and Chinese fare for under MOP50. (☎882 086. Open daily 1pm-1am. MC/V.) **Fernando's Restaurant ❹,** 9 Praia de Hac Sa, next to the main bus stop, is famous for its clams (MOP98). You may have to wait an hour for a table, but it's worth it. (☎882 264. Open daily noon-9:30pm.) **La Torre ❹,** Praia de Cheoc Van, on the beach, has typical Italian cuisine. Pasta (MOP50-60), seafood (MOP55-165), and good music entice visitors to stay. (☎880 156. Open daily 11am-11pm. MC/V.)

SIGHTS

CENTRAL MACAU

LEAL SENADO SQUARE. The fountain, pastel buildings, bakeries, and evening performances lend a fairy-tale feel to the square. The **Leal Senado** (Municipal Council) building is classic, colonial Portuguese architecture at its finest. The gray stone building, built to resemble a similar edifice in Coimbra, Portugal, houses the Senate Chamber and library. It received its name (meaning "Loyal Senate") for keeping close ties to its mother country when Spain occupied Portugal in the 17th century. Once a powerful oligarchy, the Senate now functions as a conventional political body with limited powers. *(Take bus #3 or 10a from the ferry terminal, or a 10min. walk from either the Hotel Lisboa or the Floating Casino on Ave. de Almeida Ribeiro. Open Tu-Su 9am-9pm. Library open Tu-Su 1-7pm. Free.)*

The nearby **Church of São Domingos'** white stucco moldings and green shutters belie the building's long history. Built at the turn of the 16th century by Dominican friars, the church has a graceful and airy interior that inspires hushed reverence. Some of the works in the **Treasure of Sacred Art Museum** (including gold and silver religious objects) date back to the 17th century. *(On Largo de St. Domingos in Leal Senado Square. Open daily 10am-6pm. Donations accepted.)*

RUINS OF ST. PAUL. The winding path behind the Church of São Domingos leads to Rua da Palha and the Ruins of St. Paul, once dubbed the "greatest monument to Christianity in all the Eastern lands." A devastating fire in 1835 destroyed all but the front facade (accessible by a wrought-iron staircase) and a few cornerstones. The Museum of Sacred Art, under the site of the old church, contains the bones of Japanese and Vietnamese Christian martyrs; a side hall filled with relics adds to the store of curiosities. *(Open W-M 9am-6pm. Free.)*

MONTE FORT. Monte Fort, visible from the Ruins of St. Paul, was a stronghold that once repelled a Dutch invasion in 1622. The newly opened **Museum of Macau,** built into the excavated citadel, displays old fort cannons used in its glory days. *(Museum entrances at the top and bottom of the fort; open daily 10am-6pm. Fort (☎357 911) open daily 7am-6:30pm. MOP15; children under 11 and seniors MOP8. Students 50% off.)*

CAMÕES GROTTO AND GARDEN. Away from the Ruins of St. Paul, this park sprawls behind the intersection of Rua de Terrafeiro, Rua de Tomás Vieira, and Rua de S. Paulo. Named after the Portuguese poet Luis de Camões, Camões boasts cool, shady trails and relaxing pavilions. The **Old Protestant Cemetery** to the right of the mural-covered entrance is the final resting place of 150 residents of old Macau. *(On Praça Luís de Camões. Buses #8A, 17, 18, 19, and 26 stop at the garden. Garden open daily sunrise-sunset. Free. Cemetery gates usually open during the day; if not, knock or ring the bell. Free.)* Between the Camões Garden and the Old Protestant Cemetery lies the **Cosa Garden.** Once the home of the president of the British East India Co., it now houses the Orient Foundation. *(Open daily 10am-7pm.)*

GUIA LIGHTHOUSE AND FORTRESS. Built in 1638, Guia Fort is host to a lighthouse and a small chapel, both visible from most of the Macau Peninsula. The best vantage point from which to see the two structures is Ave. de Amizade. A walk up this street from Hotel Lisboa reveals a sudden vista of the lighthouse atop a seemingly impenetrable wall of greenery. From the coffee bar on the grounds, visitors can see the mountains across the border closed to the public. *(Walk up Estrada do Engelheiro Trigo from the Guia Hotel. Open daily 9am-5:30pm. Free.)*

HONG KONG

NORTH MACAU

Watch greyhounds race and chase metal bunnies at the **Canidrome,** at the foot of Mong-Há hill (home to a fort from 1866 to 1960) on Ave. General Castelo Branco. *(☎221 199. Races M-Tu, Th-Sa 8pm.)* For something more pious, try the **Buddhist Temple of Kun Lam,** on Ave. do Coronel Mesquita, dedicated to the Goddess of Mercy. Fortune tellers and joss stick vendors surround the three altars inside. The table where the Chinese government and US Ambassador Cushing signed their 1844 friendship treaty is on display in a side room. *(Open daily 7am-6pm. Free.)*

SOUTH MACAU (PENHA PENINSULA)

AVE. DA PRAIA GRANDE. A good walking tour of Southern Macau starts on Ave. da Praia Grande at the **Statue of Jorge Alvares,** which honors the first Portuguese man to set foot on Chinese lands. Continuing along the street brings you to the pink, colonial **Government House,** a masterpiece of architect Thomaz de Aquino. Travessa do Padre Narciso, off Ave. da Praia Grande, leads to **St. Lawrence Church,** which was constructed in the 1560s. Walk through a side entrance to view the stained-glass windows and intricate artwork of the main and side altars. *(On Rua de St. Lourenço. Open M 10am-1pm and 2-6pm, Tu-Su 10am-6pm. Donations accepted.)* Ave. da Praia Grande becomes Rua da Praia do Bom Parto, and a side street off the main thoroughfare splits into two. To the left, the road leads to Bela Vista and Hotel Ritz; to the right, Calcada da Penha takes a steep climb to Penha Church. Compared to its sister church, São Domingos in Senado Square, the **Chapel of Our Lady of Penha Church** is unremarkable; but the grounds offer a lovely view of nearby bridges and Taipa Island. *(Open daily 9am-5:30pm. Free.)*

MACAU MARITIME MUSEUM. This waterfront museum is devoted to the long maritime history of Macau, and includes a special exhibit on the neighboring A Ma Temple. Electronic intercoms and telephones give audio descriptions in Cantonese, English, Mandarin, and Portuguese. A small aquarium allows close-up views of life under the sea. Visitors can also tour the harbor on a junk. *(1 Largo do Pogode da Barra, at the northern end of Rua de S. Tiago de Barro. ☎595 481. Open W-M 10am-5:30pm. MOP10, ages 10-17 MOP5, under 10 and over 65 free; Su MOP5, ages 10-17 MOP3. 30min. junk tours F-M 10:30, 11, 11:30am, noon, and 2pm. MOP10, children under 10 free.)*

A MA TEMPLE. According to legend, the goddess A Ma led a group of storm-tossed, weary sailors to what was to become Macau. The grateful survivors named the place A Ma; A Ma became A Ma Gao, which the Portuguese changed to Macau upon their arrival. Shrines to A Ma and rock paintings of the first fateful ship dot the landscape of Macau's most famous temple. On weekends, lion dances are performed in the temple's courtyard. *(Open daily sunrise-sunset. Free.)*

TAIPA ISLAND

Buses #11, 22, and 33 run through Taipa from the Hotel Lisboa (10min., MOP3.3). There is a tourist information booth on Rua Direita de Carlos Eugenio, at the western edge of Taipa village. (☎827 882. Open M-F 9am-1pm and 2:30-5:30 or 5:45pm.) Bike rental (MOP12-16 per hr.) is available from the shops at the western end of Taipa Village.

Most of the island boasts broad, new cement streets. Tiny Taipa village huddles in the shadow of its neighbors, the pink **Taipa Stadium** and the **Macau Jockey Club.** *(18+. Proper clothing required; cell phones prohibited. 1st fl. free, 2nd fl. MOP20.)* The club puts a new twist on Macau's favorite pastime. On race days, the area buzzes with excitement, and people boost their luck by lighting incense to the **Four Faces Buddha** outside.

The large, white **Taipa Monument** on the hillside greets visitors. A road follows the shoreline, passing pastel-colored houses on the way to **Our Lady of Carmel** and the lovely, if tiny, **Carmel Garden.** At night, beautifully lit steps lead up to the church; the steps below lead to the mud flat. The last blue-green house is now the **Taipa House Museum,** arranged as a middle-class Portuguese family might have had it in the early 20th century. *(Open Tu-Su 9:30am-1pm and 3-5:30pm. Free.)* Several colorful temples cluster around the main bus station in Taipa village. The 170-year-old Buddhist **Tin Hau Temple** stands on Rua Governador Tamagnini Barbosa, while the slightly larger **Pou Tai Un Temple** is close by on Rua do Legedo.

COLOANE ISLAND

From A Ma Temple on Macau proper, bus #21 runs to Coloane village (MOP4) and #21A to Hac Sa Beach (MOP4.5). From Hotel Lisboa, bus #25 runs to Hac Sa Beach (MOP4.5). Trips take 10-15min.

Coloane is generally a sleepy holiday island—most visitors head east to Hac Sa Beach for its sports complex and barbecue facilities. The thin string of the **Taipa-Coloane Bridge** becomes a road that winds along the coastline, changing from Estrada de Seac Pai Van, to Estrada de Cheoc Van, to Estrada de Hac Sa, to Estrada do Altinho de Ka-Ho. **Seac Pai Van Park,** on the island's western side, provides access to the 25km **Trilho de Coloane hiking trail,** which leads to **Alto de Coloane,** the island's highest point. At the top of this peak is the 170m white jade statue of the goddess A Ma. *(Open daily 9am-7pm. Aviary open Tu-Su 10am-4pm. Free.)*

Tiny **Coloane village,** in the southwest, is the next noteworthy stop. The **Chapel of St. Francis Xavier** is the town's claim to fame. Street stalls and cafes line the picturesque square outside; giant trees grow in the middle of the eating areas and stretch through the canopy roofs. Near the pier, right of the chapel, is the very red **Sam Seng Temple.** To the left is **Tin Hau Temple;** beyond it on Ave. de Cinco de Outubro, the larger **Tam Kung Temple** boasts a four-foot dragon boat carved from a whale bone. *(Chapel and temples open daily sunrise-sunset. Donations accepted.)*

CASINOS

In Macau, gambling is serious business; don't expect flashing neon or show girls in skimpy sequined dresses. Dealers and gamblers keep their eyes glued to the cards and numbers, rarely smile, and almost never laugh. Macau residents under 21 and visitors under 18 are prohibited. **Slot machines,** known as "hungry tigers" by the locals, devour HK$/MOP1 and HK$/MOP2 coins. Other ways to get rich quick include **baccarat, blackjack,** and **big and small,** a game in which players try to predict which numbers will show up on three dice—if the total is at least 12, it's "big"; otherwise, it's "small." Minimum bets are MOP100-500 at most casinos.

Lisboa, 2-4 Ave. de Amizade (☎375 111), part of the Lisboa Hotel. The grande dame of Macau's casinos, Lisboa boasts 5 floors filled with visitors–all day, every day–who must follow a few rules: no cameras, no caps, no guns, no shorts, no singlets for men, and no smoking on the 1st fl. Baccarat, big and small, blackjack, and *pai.* Slot machines (MOP2) on 1st and 2nd floors; VIP rooms on 5th.

Casino Macau Palace, Ave. de Amizade, Outer Harbour, by the ferry terminal. Also called **Floating Casino** since it actually does float; in fact, it recently floated over from its previous location in the Inner Harbour. Lisboa's closest competitor in terms of atmosphere, this giant palace on the water devotes an entire floor to slot machines.

Jai-Alai Palace and Casino (☎726 262), Outer Harbour, near the ferry terminal. The playing cards and dominoes on Jai-Alai's sign greet new arrivals to Macau. To avoid the thick layer of smoke coating the air, visit the health spa.

Mandarin Oriental (☎567 888), on Ave. de Amizade, next to the World Trade Centre. Plush red velvet gives a sophisticated air. Slot machines, baccarat, and blackjack.

NIGHTLIFE

After emptying your pockets at the casinos, head to one of Macau's happening **nightclubs** and **bars.** A copy of *Macau Travel Talk* (available at many restaurants, hotels, and newsstands) has weekly entertainment listings. Many locals opt instead to go to Zhuhai for a wild weekend in search of newer, racier dance clubs.

Macau proper is a round-the-clock disco-dancing center. Famous even in Hong Kong, **Oskar's Pub,** 82-86 Rua de Pequim, on the ground floor of the Holiday Inn, is popular among expats for its live music and relaxed, jovial atmosphere. A neon sign of a voluptuous woman in front of the Eiffel Tower points to the **Crazy Paris Show** at the Hotel Lisboa. (18+. MOP 300. Shows at 8 and 9:30pm.) **Taipa Island** boasts a small concentration of bars, some with pool tables, including the **Macau Jockey Club.** (Buses #22, 28A, and 33 stop across from the club.)

Irish Pub, Jardim Nam San, Taipa. Neon shamrocks and black leather couches. Drinks MOP20 and up. Happy Hour 6-8pm (buy 1, get 1 free). Open daily 5:30pm-3am.

Bar dos Namorados, across from the Jockey Club, Taipa. Decor includes lots of hearts; TV and darts accommodate the less lovey-dovey. Draft beer MOP13-28. Happy Hour 4-8pm (buy 1 glass of wine, get 1 free). Open daily 4pm-2am.

Hugo's Pub, across from the Jockey Club, Taipa. Has a graffiti wall. Drinks MOP30. Happy Hour 5-8pm (half-price drinks). Open daily 5pm-2am.

THE SOUTHWEST

The landscape in this diverse region includes the alpine highlands in northwestern Yunnan, the limestone pinnacles of Guangxi, and the steamy jungles of Xishuangbanna. The Southwest is also blanketed with a colorful patchwork of at least three dozen ethnic groups (see also **Southwestern Minorities,** p. 24), including the **Bai** (see p. 607), **Dai** (see p. 632), **Dong** (see p. 658), **Miao** (see p. 655), and **Naxi** (see p. 611), some of which have assimilated completely. Others, aware of the revenue to be had from cultural tourism, are marketed to visitors in contrived settings, uncharitably dubbed "ethnic circuses" or "human zoos." Still others live traditional lives in isolated locales and are stunned to discover travelers' interest in their lifestyles.

The government's apparent tolerance of minority peoples today hides a long history of discrimination and attempted forced assimilation. The region was long dismissed by rulers as the home of fractious "southern barbarians," but a closer peek at the history of the southwest reveals a unique cultural dynamism arising from the arrival of Miao-Yao peoples from the Yangzi region, Tibetans from the west, the Burmese, Thai, Khmer, and Vietnamese from the south, and Hui Muslim traders, lured by the promise of riches from the silk and spice trade along the ancient Southern Silk Road. Caravans no longer wind their way along the well-trodden roads of the southwest, but countless tourists do. Visitors to rowdy backpacker enclaves like Dali and Yangshuo may enjoy the rare banana pancakes, espresso, and English speakers, but ultimately, they come for the region's breathtaking natural splendor.

HIGHLIGHTS OF THE SOUTHWEST

TREK THROUGH THE TROPICS in **Xishuangbanna** (see p. 631) amidst minority villages and primeval forests.

FIND YOUR INNER KARST FORMATION while floating down the river in **Guilin** (see p. 578) and backpacker-friendly **Yangshuo** (see p. 583).

GET YOUR GROOVE ON in **Kunming** (see p. 591), the paradise city where the grass is green and the girls are pretty.

GUANGXI 广西

Mention "Guangxi" to any Chinese citizen and you're more than likely to hear something about "karst rock formations." The distinctive limestone pinnacles, arches, bridges, and caverns are Guilin and nearby Yangshuo's biggest tourist draws. Guangxi's topography also boasts terraced rice fields, misty mountains, and even a few seaside resorts. Much of the area's character derives from its diverse peoples, ranging from the Zhuang, who are almost indistinguishable from the Han, to minorities like the Yao and the Miao, who still wear traditional dress in villages far from the glare of mainstream tourism. In recognition of the Zhuang people, the largest minority group in the region, the area was renamed the Guangxi Zhuang Autonomous Region in 1958. Presently, cities like Guilin, Yangshuo, and the provincial capital of Nanning are pockets of affluence amid the continued impoverishment of the Guangxi countryside. This stark urban-rural economic divide hints that the seeming serenity of the karst rock formations and apparent complacency of Guangxi's minority peoples hides complex, underlying tensions.

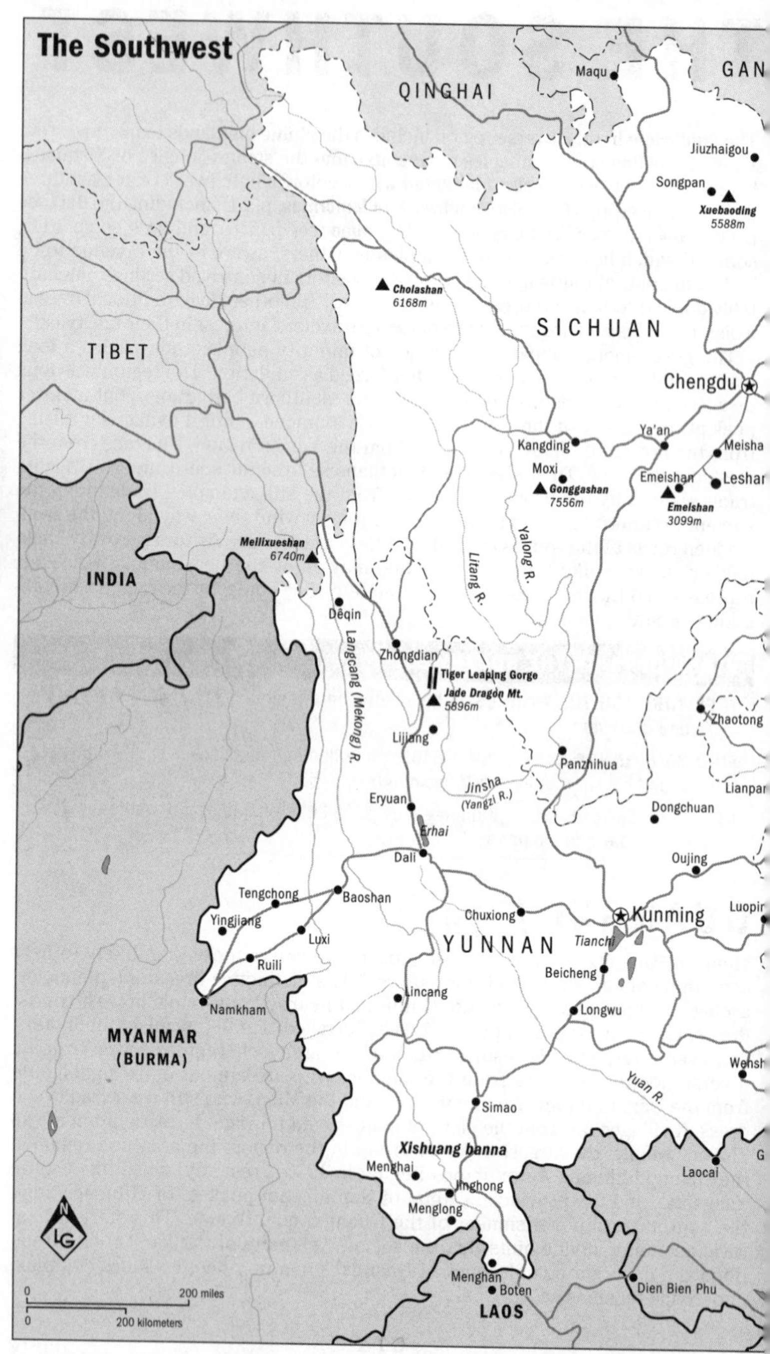
The Southwest
QINGHAI
GAN
Maqu
Jiuzhaigou
Songpan
Xuebaoding
5588m
Cholashan
6168m
SICHUAN
TIBET
Chengdu
Ya'an
Kangding
Meisha
Moxi
Gonggashan
7556m
Emeishan
Leshan
Emeishan
3099m
Yalong R.
Litang R.
Meilixueshan
6740m
INDIA
Dêqin
Langcang (Mekong) R.
Zhongdian
Tiger Leaping Gorge
Jade Dragon Mt.
5896m
Zhaotong
Lijiang
Panzhihua
Jinsha
(Yangzi R.)
Lianpar
Eryuan
Dongchuan
Erhai
Dali
Oujing
Tengchong
Baoshan
Chuxiong
Kunming
Luopir
Yingjiang
Luxi
YUNNAN
Tianchi
Ruili
Beicheng
Lincang
Namkham
Longwu
MYANMAR
(BURMA)
Wensh
Yuan R.
Simao
Xishuang banna
Laocai
Menghai
Jinghong
Menglong
Menghan
Boten
LAOS
Dien Bien Phu
0
200 miles
0
200 kilometers

Xi'an
SHAANXI
HENAN
Hanzhong
Shiyan
Xiangfan
HUBEI
Three Gorges
Fengjie
Wu Gorge
Yunyang
Xiling Gorge
Nanchong
Wanxian
Qutang Gorge
Wushan
Yichang
Wuhan
Yangzi R.
Fengdu
CHONGQING MUNICIPALITY
Fuling
Dazu
Bishan
Chongqing
Nanchuan
Wu R.
Changde
Chishui
Shunan Bamboo Sea
Changsha
Wu R.
Zunyi
HUNAN
Renhuai
Tongren
Shaoyang
Bijie
Yachi R.
Zhenyuan
Huaihua
GUIZHOU
Shibing
Chongan
Guiyang
Kaili
Jianhe
Zhijin Caves
Langde
Xijiang
Anshun
Duyun
Leishan
Longgong Caves
Danzhai
Huangguoshu Falls
Sandu
Congjiang
Longsheng
Beipan R.
Sanjiang
Rongjiang
Guilin
Li River
Dachang
Yangshuo
Yizhou
Hechi
Bose
Liuzhou
Gui R.
GUANGDONG
Hongshui R.
Wuzhou
GUANGXI
Guangzhou
You R.
Binyang
Guigang
Nanning
Cao Bang
Hengxian
Yulin
Macau
HONG KONG SAR
VIETNAM
Pingxiang
Qinzhou
Beihai
Hanoi
South China Sea
Gulf of Tonkin

SOUTHWEST

NANNING 南宁

☎0771

Tucked away on China's southern border, a few hundred kilometers from Vietnam, Nanning is an attractive, subtropical, but out-of-the-way city. An insignificant market town just a century ago, today the city is a modern transportation hub, with rail connections to Vietnam, the coast, central China, and Kunming.

Nanning has always been a quick study. When the city first opened to foreign trade in 1907, it grew so quickly that it spilled over the old city walls. During WWII, it was used as a military base by both the Japanese and the American forces. In the decades following the war, Nanning provided supplies and military support to the Vietnamese in their struggle against the French and, later, the Americans. In 1949 Nanning regained its status as provincial capital of Guangxi Zhuang autonomous region. Since then it has become an increasingly important cultural and political center. Nanning is fresh-faced, subtropical, and about as modern as cities come in southwest China.

TRANSPORTATION

Flights: CAAC ticket office, 82 Chaoyang Lu (24hr. ☎243 1459), near the bus station. Open 8am-8pm. Tickets go on sale a week in advance. Book early for discounts, and especially for the popular Hanoi flights. Buses shuttle between Nanning and the airport (40min., every hr. 8am-7pm, Y15) and meet flights at the arrivals terminal. Taxis to the airport Y70 and up. To: **Beijing** (2 per day, Y1790); **Chengdu** (daily, Y810); **Guangzhou** (3 per day, Y660); **Guilin** (M, W, F, Su; Y530); **Hong Kong** (Tu, Th-F, Su; Y1880); **Kunming** (2-3 per day, Y570); **Shanghai** (daily, Y1480). International flights to **Hanoi, Vietnam** (M and Th, Y920).

Trains: Nanning Train Station (nánníng huǒchē zhàn; 南宁火车站), on Zhonghua Lu at the north end of Chaoyang Lu. Open 24hr. To: **Beijing** (32hr., daily, Y300-490); **Changsha** (15hr., daily, Y130-230); **Guangzhou** (15hr., 1 per day, Y70-250); **Guilin** (8hr., 2 per day, Y50); **Kunming** (19hr., daily, Y180); **Shanghai** (36hr., daily, Y400); **Xi'an** (36hr., daily, Y270). International trains to **Pingxiang** on the Vietnam border (4hr., daily, Y30; 7hr., daily, Y25).

Buses: Nanning Bus Station (nánníng qìchē zhàn; 南宁汽车站), 80 Chaoyang Lu (☎242 4529). Tickets go on sale 2 days before departure. Open daily 5:30am-12:30am. To: **Beihai** (3hr., every hr. 7:30am-4:30pm, Y50); **Guangzhou** (9½hr., 3 per day, Y180); **Guilin** (4½hr., every 30min. 7am-11:30pm, Y80); **Wuzhou** (6hr., 4 per day, Y80); **Fangcheng** (2½hr., 9 per day, Y30); **Pingxiang** (4½hr., 4 per day, Y50). Buses also depart from the **Passenger Transport Center** (kèyùn zhōngxīn; 客运中心) on Youai Nan Lu to **Wuming** (every 10-15min., Y3) and other local destinations.

Local Transportation: Fare Y1-2. Buses **#6** and **10** both head down Chaoyang Lu to the train station; #6 then travels east on Minzu Dadao, while #10 heads southeast down Taoyuan Lu, passing Nanhu Lake on its way to the Blue Mountain Scenic Area. **Minibuses** from Chaoyang Square go directly to destinations such as Nanhu Park and the Blue Mountain Scenic Area. Fare Y1-3.

Taxis: Base fare Y7. **Pedicab** and **motorcab** rides average Y3-5.

ORIENTATION AND PRACTICAL INFORMATION

Nanning's railroad tracks slice the city in half, and there are definitely the right and wrong sides of these tracks. The north, especially the northwest, is the underbelly of Nanning, with roads full of potholes and gun-toting Chinese soldiers completing military maneuvers. The upscale stores and office buildings of the southern half of the city present a picture of bustling commercial affluence. Nanning's southern half

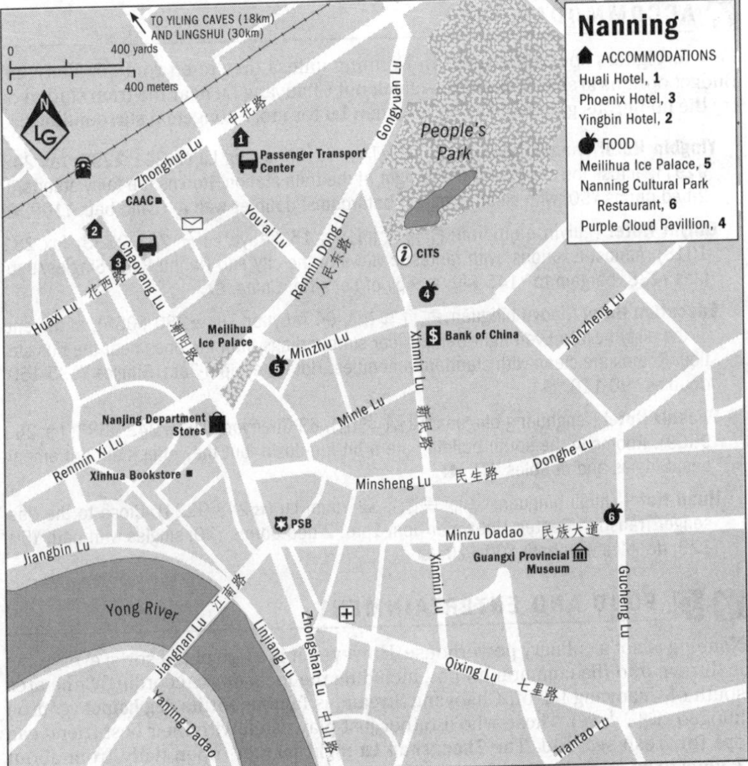

is bound by the railroad to the north and east, by department store-studded **Chaoyang Lu** (朝阳路) to the west, and by the **Pa River** (pájiāng; 邕江) to the south. The broad, highway-like **Minzu Dadao** (民族大道) runs east-west through the city center.

Travel Agency: CITS, 40 Xinmin Lu (☎262 4736). Tours and great suggestions for local tourist sites. Vietnam visas take 10 working days and cost Y750; get one in Hong Kong, Guangzhou, or Bangkok ahead of time if possible. Open daily 8am-noon and 3-6pm.

Bank of China: 45 Minzu Dadao (☎283 9224), past Xinmin Lu. Exchanges currency and traveler's checks. Credit card advances. Open M-F 8:30am-noon and 2:30-5:30pm.

PSB: 67 Donghe Lu (☎289 1264), near Minzu Dadao. **Foreign Affairs Department** (wàishì chù; 外事处), to the left of the main entrance. Open M-F 8am-noon and 3-6pm.

Hospital: Guanxi Medicine and Science University No.1 Hospital (guǎngxī yīkē dàxué dìyī fùshǔ yīyuàn; 广西医科大学第一附属医院), 6 Binhu Lu (☎535 3266). English speakers available. 24hr. pharmacy.

Bookstore: Xinhua Bookstore (xīnhuá shūchéng; 新华书城), 15 Xinhua Lu (☎281 0296), has a large English-language section on the 4th fl. Open daily 9am-9pm.

Internet Access: China Telecom (☎385 8055) Internet bar is on the 5th fl. of Nanning Department Store. Y5 per hr. Open daily 9:30am-10pm.

Post Office: On Suzhou Lu (☎243 8556 ext. 8638), near the bus station. EMS, IDD service, and Poste Restante. Open daily 8am-10:30pm. **Postal Code:** 530011.

ACCOMMODATIONS

Few foreigners spend the night in Nanning unless they're en route to Vietnam. Budget options are fairly limited—check out Chaoyang Lu near the train station or try the numerous guesthouses on Taoyuan Lu for more congenial surroundings.

Yingbin Hotel (yíngbīn fàndiàn; 迎宾饭店), 71 Chaoyang Lu (☎241 2299; fax 243 9297), across the street and to the right of the train station. Rooms are fairly standard. 2-bed dorms Y50, with clean common bathrooms; doubles with A/C and bath Y100. ❶

Guiyin Hotel (guìyín dàjǐudiàn; 桂银大酒店), 15 Jiaoyu Lu (☎283 2833; fax 281 1018). Almost luxurious, with fantastic views of the city and Nanhu Park. Singles/doubles Y238, bargain to Y145 with a copy of *Let's Go: China*. ❸

Education Hotel (jiàoyù bīnguǎn; 教育宾馆), 64 Taoyuan Lu (☎280 6056), at the end of the alley next to Everbright Bank. Nicer surroundings than the ones near the bus station. Rooms are clean with standard amenities. Hot water 6pm-3am. Singles Y135-150; doubles Y90-110. ❷

Phoenix Hotel (fēnghuáng bīnguǎn; 凤凰宾馆), 63 Chaoyang Lu (☎243 9833; fax 243 9309). Rooms in the south building are a bit run-down, but they offer standard amenities. Singles and doubles Y70. ❶

Huali Hotel (huálì bīnguǎn; 华丽宾馆), 12 Youai Lu (☎243 9224). Close to the Passenger Transport Center. Hot water 6pm-1am. 2-bed dorms Y20; singles with bath Y50-120; doubles with bath Y60-120. ❶

FOOD AND ENTERTAINMENT

Nanning is not a culinary powerhouse. However, it is a hotspot of sorts; everything is thrown into the common hotpot, including the local dog. Accordingly, the area south of Chaoyang Lu, off Chaoyang Stream, is famous for its **dog hotpot** (gǒuròu huǒguō; 狗肉火锅). Those who'd rather just play catch with their best friend can opt for fresh seafood. The **Zhongshan Lu night market** (open daily from about 7:30pm to midnight) is the place to go for fish festivities and local favorites such as snails and squid-on-a-stick. Cheap noodle and dumpling restaurants (Y3-5) also line **Zhonghua Lu** and **Chaoyang Lu** near the train station.

Meilihua Ice Palace (meǐlìhuá bīngchéng; 美丽华冰城), 51 Minzhu Lu, at Xinhua Lu, and **Meijie Ice Palace** (měijiě bīngchéng; 梅姐冰城), 12 Jiaoxu Lu (☎531 1280), both serve up tropical drinks (Y6-9), Taiwanese shaved ice (Y5-12), and rice, soup, and noodle dishes (Y5-15). Meilihua offers an English menu; Meijie is newer and brighter, but smaller. Open daily 9:30am-2:30am. ❶

Purple Cloud Pavilion (zǐyúnxuān; 紫云轩), 38 Xinmin Lu (☎280 8923), by the Mingyuan Hotel. Clean, spacious food court offers everything from fresh fries to sushi. Picture menu labeled in English. Lunch 11am-2:30pm, dinner 5pm-1am. Dishes Y4-35. ❶

Nanning Cultural Park Restaurant (nánníng wénwùyuàn jiǔlóu; 南宁文物苑酒楼; ☎281 5792), on the corner of Minzu Dadao and Gucheng Lu. Not surprisingly, this restaurant serves a variety of Guangxi's minority cuisines, including bamboo-pressed chicken and lamb kebabs. Sip Dong You tea on the pleasant upstairs terrace. Entrees Y18-35. Open daily 11:30am-2pm, and 3pm-midnight. ❷

Guangxi House (guǎngxī hǎoshí; 广西好时), 63 Taoyuan Lu (☎533 2828). The crowded dance floor, unobtrusive decor, and pounding music (2nd fl. techno, 3rd fl. disco). Come in and groove with Nanning's young trendsetters. Drinks Y20 and up. Cover Y10, ladies free except F-Sa. Open daily 8:30pm-4am. ❶

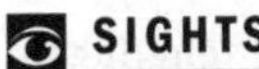

SIGHTS

Although it's not famous for any major historical or cultural sights, Nanning and the surrounding countryside can offer a day or two of relaxed sightseeing.

BLUE MOUNTAIN SCENIC AREA (qīngxiù shān fēngjǐng qū; 青秀山风景区). The rolling hills and hiking paths reward visitors with stunning views of the surrounding countryside. Take time to feed the overly eager goldfish in the pond at the base of **Dragon Pagoda** (lóngxiàng tǎ; 龙象塔) or to venture to the **Phoenix Pagoda** (fènghuáng tǎ; 凤凰塔) at the other end of the park. **Lion Forest Temple** (shī lín; 狮林), one of several on the mountainside, is not far from the cable car to the **Monument to Martyrs of the Sino-Japanese War** (kàng rì lièshìbēi; 抗日烈士碑). *(8km southeast of Nanning. Bus #10 stops at the foot of the mountain. A direct minibus (Y3) leaves irregularly 8am-5pm from Chaoyang Sq. Y8.)*

GUANGXI PROVINCIAL MUSEUM (guǎngxī shěng bówùguǎn; 广西省博物馆). This museum houses an extensive collection of bronze drums, some interesting artifacts from the Taiping Rebellion, and a wealth of information about the Miao, Dong, and Zhuang minorities. A huge second-floor exhibit displays colorful, elaborately sewn minority costumes. Exit through the back of the museum to the Cultural Park of Nanning (nánníng wénwùyuàn; 南宁文物苑) and relax in its shaded gardens amidst examples of traditional minority architecture. *(☎ 281 0907. On Minzu Dadao. Bus #6 runs from the train station and stops in front of the museum. Open W-F 8am-noon and 3-5:30pm, Sa-Su 9am-5pm. Y8, students Y3. Park open daily 8am-6pm, same admission price. Try getting in free by telling them you're eating at the restaurant; see Food, p. 576)*

PARKS. Enjoy a picnic lunch or play mahjong with Nanning's elderly residents in one of the city's large, landscaped parks. **People's Park** (rénmín gōngyuán; 人民公园) sits in the very heart of Nanning. Dense woods with boulevard-like paths wind around sculptured gardens and a lake. *(The main entrance is on Gongyan Lu, near where Renmin Lu branches off to the right; a side entrance is on Xinmin Lu. Paddle boats Y12 per hr. Open daily 6am-10pm. Y2.)* The Nanning skyline forms an impressive backdrop for **Nanhu Park.** *(Accessible by buses #3, 8, and 10. Open 24hr. Y2.)*

DAYTRIPS FROM NANNING

YILING CAVE AND WUMING

18km north of Nanning. Minibuses head to both destinations. Catch one at the Passenger Transport Center or anywhere along Youai Lu. (To the caves 40min., Y3; to Wuming 50min., Y5.) ☎ 602 0420. Open daily 8am-5pm. Gate entrance Y15, cave fee Y25. Students half price, 70+ free.

Yiling Cave (yīlǐng yán; 伊岭岩) and the village of **Wuming** (武鸣) are the biggest attractions around Nanning. Yiling is one of the largest and finest caves in Guangxi; fortunately, the wholly artificial light displays don't overwhelm the natural features. The walkways are spacious, and the tour (1hr.) is an easy stroll. Near the cave entrance, try the free Zhuang tea that is flavored with bamboo, ginger, and brown sugar. The park grounds are also home to wild monkeys, which can be spotted occasionally on roofs and in the trees. The village of **Wuming,** north of the caves, is known for its natural spring swimming pool, which is the size of a small lake. **Ling Shui** (líng shǔi; 灵水), as it is locally known, has a gate fee of Y6 for a day of swimming; inner tubes can be rented for Y5 per day. There are no lifeguards or closing hours.

ZUO RIVER SCENIC AREA

Another attraction is the Zuo River Scenic Area (zuǒjiāng fēngjǐngqū; 左江风景区). From the town of Ningming (宁明) on the Vietnamese border, a 2½hr. train ride away, take a cruise down the Zuo River (boat ride Y30) to view karst rock formations or to tour neighboring minority villages. Take a 40-minute boat ride from Ningming to see the **Huashan wall paintings,** emblazoned on the cliff rocks by Zhuang minority people (Y15).

GUILIN 桂林 ☎0773

Guilin was first founded as a military post during the Qin dynasty. Treasured for centuries as one of China's most beautiful natural settings, the city sits on the Li River surrounded by dramatic limestone hills known as karst formations. These jagged peaks and the river's green, gentle bends draw visitors from throughout China and around the world. Like any popular tourist destination, Guilin has its share of overpriced hotels and restaurants, noisy tour groups, and opportunistic touts, as well as nearly ubiquitous construction sights. None of these modern ills, however, detract from the peace of an afternoon spent by the river or the relaxing, scenic view at the top of the city's hills.

TRANSPORTATION

Flights: Lijiang International Airport (lìjiāng guójì jīchǎng; 漓江国际机场; flight info ☎284 5304). A shuttle bus (6:30am-7:30pm, Y20) runs from the airport to the train station (follow the signs to the minivan, right outside the baggage area), and also shuttles between the airport and the **CAAC ticket office** (☎384 3918, 384 7208 or 384 7209; fax 380 6463), on Shanghai Lu and Minzhu Lu, which can book domestic tickets. Open daily 7:30am-10:30pm. Taxis from downtown Guilin to the airport cost Y80-100. To: **Beijing** (3 per day, Y1580); **Changsha** (1-2 per day, Y410); **Guangzhou** (5 per day, Y610); **Hong Kong** (2-3 per day, Y1710); **Wuhan** (daily except Th, Y710).

Trains: Guilin Train Station (guìlín huǒchē zhàn; 桂林火车站; ☎383 2904), at the intersection of Zhongshan Nan Lu and Shanghai Lu. The ticket office is on the 1st fl., on the left when facing the station. Tickets go on sale 3 days in advance and frequently sell out in summer, especially hard sleeper tickets, so arrive at 8am, when the ticket office opens. Luggage storage. To: **Beijing** (30hr., 2 per day, Y420); **Guangzhou** (15hr., 2 per day, Y180); **Kunming** (31hr., 3 per day, Y200); **Nanning** (6½hr., 5 per day, Y50); **Shanghai** (27hr., 3 per day, Y330); **Xi'an** (30hr., daily, Y300). Most trains through Guilin also pass through the **Guilin North Train Station** (guìlín běi huǒchē zhàn; 桂林北火车站), on Zhongshan Bei Lu north of the city center.

Buses: Guilin Long-distance Bus Station (guìlín chángtú qìchē zhàn; 桂林长途汽车站; ☎382 0600), on the northern section of Zhongshan Nan Lu, between Yinding Lu and Nanhuan Lu, a 10min. walk north of the train station. To: **Longsheng** (4hr., every 20min. 6am-5pm, Y10.5); **Nanning** (8hr., every 1-2hr. 6:30am-8:30pm, Y75); **Sanjiang** (6hr., 8 per day, Y17); **Yangshuo** (1½hr., every 20min., Y6-10). Direct buses to Guangzhou, Longsheng, and Nanning are a bit more expensive, but twice as fast. The **Guilin South Bus Station** (guìlín nán zhàn; 桂林南站), behind the train station. Buses to **Yangshuo** usually continue on to other destinations. To **Fuli** (1hr., daily, Y8) and **Longsheng** (4hr., every 20min. 7am-5pm, Y9.5).

Local Transportation: Most **buses** leave from Zhongshan Nan Lu, outside the train station. Fare Y1-2. Maps at the bus stop indicate routes. Bus frequency within the city is every 5-10min. Bus **#1** runs from the intersection of Shanghai Lu and Zhongshan Nan Lu to the North Train Station; **#2** from Guilin Train Station, past Nanmen Bridge, Elephant Trunk Hill, Fubo Hill, Folded Brocade Hill, and west to Reed Flute Park; **#3** from

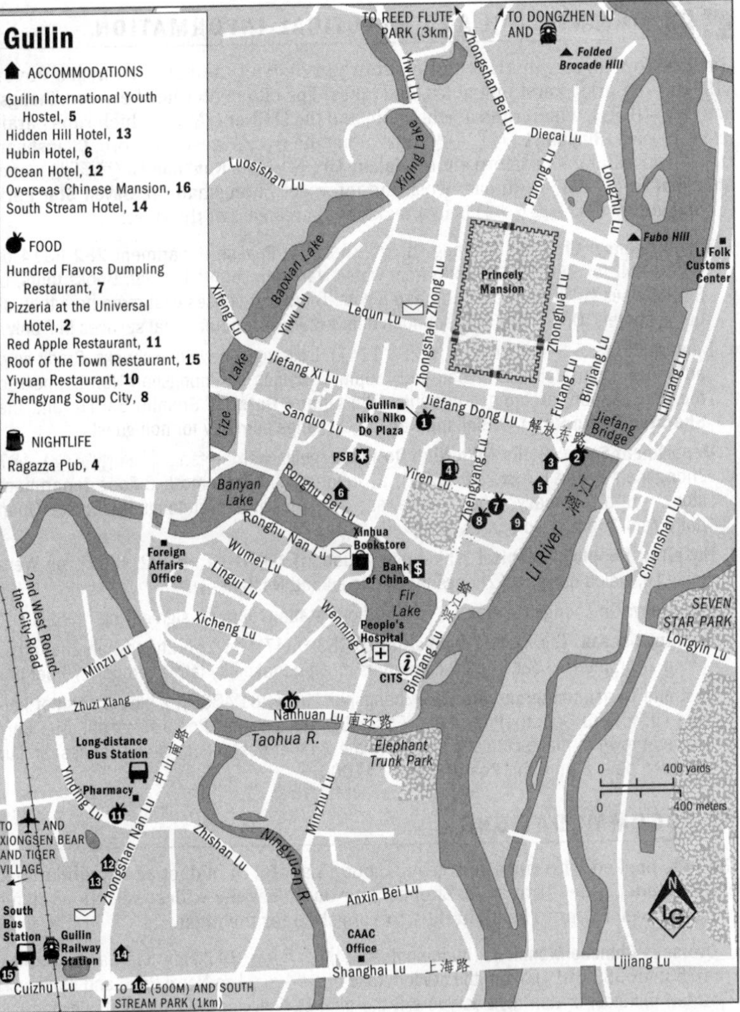

Guilin Train Station through the rice fields at the edge of town to Reed Flute Park toward Yangshuo; **#5** from Guilin Train Station, past Wayan Crossroad and Yanshan Zhen, to Yangshuo; **#11** from Seven Star Park, past Crossroad Circle, the Guilin Train Station, and South Stream Park, to Pingshan; **#13** from Seven Star Park, up Zhongshan Zhong Lu past Solitary Peak Park and Folded Brocade Hill, to Reed Flute Park; **#14** from West Hill Park, past Jiefang Bridge and Sanlidian Circle, to Wulidian.

Taxis: Taxis cluster around bus and train stations from early morning past 11pm.

Bicycle Rental: Inquire at the **Overseas Chinese Mansions,** 39 Zhongshan Nan Lu. An old man down the block rents bikes for Y15 per day. Deposit Y150 or passport; opt for the cash. Bikes due back at 7pm on the day of rental.

ORIENTATION AND PRACTICAL INFORMATION

Guilin's four urban districts, one suburban district, and two counties cover 4195km^2 of parks, karst pinnacles, and lakes. The city center lies between **Zhongshan Lu** (中山路), which runs north-south, and the **Li River** (漓江), which runs parallel in the east. **Binjiang Lu** (滨江路) runs along the river's western shore, **Chanshuan Lu** (穿山路) along its eastern shore. **Jiefang Lu** (解放路), **Nanhuan Lu** (南环路), and **Shanghai Lu** (上海路) run east-west and intersect Zhongshan Lu. **Seven Star Park** (qīxīng gōngyuán; 七星公园) is in a residential area east of the river.

Travel Agency: CITS, 41 Binjiang Lu (☎286 1801, English department 282 8314 or 282 8304; fax 280 5303), north from where Nanhuan Lu hits Li River. Books tours, Li River cruises (Y450 to Yangshuo), and flights. Tours and cruises cost more here than at budget hotels. Open daily 8:30am-noon and 3-6:30pm, international services M-F only.

Bank of China: 5 Shanhu Bei Lu (☎283 1147). Exchanges traveler's checks. Credit card advances. Open daily 8am-noon and 3-6pm. A branch on Zhongshan Nan Lu, next to the train station, exchanges currency. The **Lijiang Hotel,** 1 Shanhu Bei Lu, and the **Sheraton Guilin Hotel,** 9 Binjiang Nan Lu, exchange currency for non-guests.

Department Store: Guilin Niko Niko Do Plaza (guìlín wēixiào táng; 桂林微笑堂), 187 Zhongshan Zhong Lu (☎281 5390), at Jiefang Lu. A behemoth 6-floor department store, with a pharmacy, grocery store, and selection of English-language books. Open daily 7am-10pm. Credit cards accepted.

Hospital: People's Hospital (shìrénmín yīyuàn; 市人民医院; ☎282 3767), on Wenming Lu, which curves off Zhongshan Zhong Lu and Nanhuan Lu.

Pharmacy: On Zhongshan Nan Lu, south of bus station, under a sign saying "medicine."

Internet Access: The **Xinhua Bookstore** (☎283 0947), on 150 Zhongshan Zhong Lu, has a 24hr. Internet bar. The 20 computers might be taken by late afternoon. Y3 per hr.

Post and Telecommunications: 249 Zhongshan Lu (☎281 4339), 2 blocks north of Jiefang Lu, toward Solitary Peak Park. EMS, IDD service, and Poste Restante. The only place in town to make collect calls. There are 2 other post offices along Zhongshan Lu. All open daily 8am-8pm. **Postal Code:** 541000.

ACCOMMODATIONS

Guilin is packed with ritzy tour groups, but a handful of budget accommodations cater to independent travelers. Zhongshan Nan Lu has the widest selection; many budget travelers opt to head directly to Yangshuo for the night.

Overseas Chinese Mansions (huáqiáo dàshà; 华侨大厦), 39 Zhongshan Nan Lu (☎383 5753; fax 383 5614). From the station, take bus #4 or 11 to Nanxi Park, and backtrack a few minutes; or turn right as you exit the train station, and walk down Zhongshan Lu. Friendly staff. Clean, well-furnished rooms have 24hr. hot water, A/C, bath, phone, and TV. 10% service charge. Dorms Y44; doubles Y280-350; triples Y300. ❶

Guilin International Youth Hostel (guìlín guójì qīngnián lǚguǎn; 桂林国际青年旅馆), 90 Binjiang Lu (☎282 7115; fax 282 7118), near the intersection with Yiren Lu. Guilin's newest budget option is one of its cleanest and best-equipped. All rooms have A/C, bath, phone, and TV. Dorms are small. 24hr. hot water. Do-it-yourself laundry Y8. Internet access Y10 per hr. Bicycle rental Y20 per day. Check-in 7am-11pm. Dorms Y50; doubles Y188. Credit cards accepted. ❶

South Stream Hotel (nánxī fàndiàn; 南溪饭店), 84 Zhongshan Nan Lu (☎383 4943), opposite the train station. Convenient location for late-night arrivals. A/C, bath, phone, and TV. Hot water 7:30-11:30pm. Singles Y100; doubles Y120; triples Y150. ❷

SOUTHWEST

Ocean Hotel (hǎiyáng fàndiàn; 海洋饭店), 95 Zhongshan Nan Lu (☎383 5349), just south of the bus station. Basic rooms in this convenient location have A/C, bathtubs, phone, and TV. Hot water 7-9pm. Singles Y120; doubles Y150. ❷

Hidden Hill Hotel (yǐnshān fàndiàn; 隐山饭店), 97 Zhongshan Nan Lu (☎383 5484 or 383 3002; fax 385 8257), halfway between the bus and train stations. Predictably noisy rooms, given the proximity to the transit hubs. Rooms have A/C, bath, phone, and TV. Hot water 7am-noon and 7pm-midnight. Singles Y150; doubles Y200; triples Y260. ❷

Hubin Hotel (húbīn fàndiàn; 湖滨饭店), 2 Ronghu Bei Lu (☎282 2665), on Banyan Lake. Accessible by bus #2 from the station area to Yang Qiao (the corner of Ronghu Bei Lu and Zhongshan Lu). Rooms are scattered throughout a couple of buildings on a central courtyard. Currency exchange and IDD service. Hot water 7:30-11:30pm. Singles with A/C Y150; doubles Y150, with A/C Y200; triples 120. ❷

SOUTHWEST

FOOD

Guilin's food comes in two varieties: tourist fare in swanky settings with English menus and home cooking at sidewalk stalls. The portion of **Nanhuan Lu** between Zhongshan Lu and the river is lined with restaurants where you can observe your seafood in its prime before chowing down. The locals rave about **Linjiang Lu** (临江路), on the eastern bank of the Li River, as the best place to grab favorites like stir-fried rice noodles (mǐfěn; 米粉). From Zhongshan Nan Lu, follow the road signs to **Good Food Town** (měishí jiē; 美食街) to find Yinding Lu and another impressive collection of local noodle shops. Both areas have local specialties like turtle soup and bamboo rat. In the evening, **Binjiang Lu** hosts a lively night market.

Yiyuan Restaurant (yíyuán fàndiàn; 怡圜饭店), 106-2 Nanhuan Lu (☎282 0470), serves up tasty Sichuanese dishes in a lively setting. Huge windows, a humming evening crowd, and fresh spicy food make up for the lack of live food displays. Carp with hot bean sauce (Y35) is a house specialty. English menu available. Entrees Y6-60. Open daily 11:30am-2:30pm and 4:30-9:30pm. ❸

Red Apple Restaurant (hóngpíngguǒ měishí zhījiā; 红苹果美食之家; ☎382 4678), under the arch on Yinding Lu. This family-run establishment prepares local dishes like tortoise soup with vegetables (Y38). Beef with peppers (Y28) is spicy and delicious. Fried rice Y18. Entrees around Y48. English menu. Open daily 9:30am-11pm. ❷

Zhengyang Soup City (zhèngyáng tāng chéng; 正杨汤城), 60 Zhengyang Lu (☎285 8553), between Yiren Lu and Remin Lu. Terrific English menu has standard favorites like sweet and sour pork (Y30) and fried Guilin noodles (Y20). Open daily 11:30am-2:30pm and 5-10pm. ❷

Roof of the Town Restaurant at Hong Kong Hotel (xiāngjiāng fàndiàn; 香江饭店; ☎383 3889; fax 383 8575), on the 19th fl. of the Hong Kong Hotel. Good standard Chinese dishes play second fiddle to the outstanding views. The Cantonese breakfast buffet, served 7:30-10am, is a bargain at Y22. Entrees Y30-80. Open daily 7:30am-10:30pm. ❸

The Pizzeria at the Universal Hotel (huánqiú dàjiǔdiàn; 环球大酒店), 1 Jiefang Lu (☎282 8228; fax 282 3868), near the bridge. English menu with unbeatable sandwiches (Y20-28) and pizzas (Y30-33) made to order. A set Chinese menu offers bread, soup, an entree, fruit, and coffee for Y28. Open daily 6:30am-midnight. ❷

Hundred Flavors Dumpling Restaurant (bǎiwèi jiǎozi guǎn; 百味饺子馆), on Yiren Lu between Zhengyang Lu and Binjiang Lu. Join the locals for noodles and dumplings made with your choice of chicken brains, intestines, feet, or more pedestrian options (Y5-15). Open daily 6:30-11pm. ❶

DRAGON BOATS GALORE The Dragon Boat Festival (duān wǔ jié; 端午节) is an annual celebration in late May or early June in honor of Qu Yuan, a minister during the Warring States period who drowned himself in protest against the corrupt government. His death, which fell on the fifth day of the fifth month of the lunar calendar, was greatly mourned by patriots everywhere. After his suicide, as legend says, fishermen banged drums and threw dumplings into the water to keep the fish from eating Qu's body. Today, the festival is celebrated with feasts of *zòngzi*—a triangular-shaped dumpling made of rice wrapped in bamboo leaves—and dragon boat races to the cadence of drums. Long dragon-shaped vessels race in waters all around China, most notably in the Hong Kong harbor and around the edges of the Li River.

SIGHTS

Guilin's lush parks, misty caves, and stunning river vistas attract visitors from far and wide; and at times, especially during the summer, the city swarms with camera-toting tourists on a mission to see it all in one afternoon. Taxis offer full-day city tours for about Y100, usually bargainable to about half-price for those willing to tail tour buses. Travelers with a few days to spare will be rewarded with time to discover the relaxing, quieter parks on the north end of town.

Guilin's biggest party is the annual Dragon Boat Festival (duānwǔ jié; 端午节), which falls on the fifth day of the fifth lunar month on the Chinese calendar. During the festival, the Li River churns with Dragon Boat Races, while spectators and old Chinese drums line the shores to cheer on the rowers.

REED FLUTE PARK (lúdí gōngyuán; 芦翟公园). Reed Flute Park is home to some of Guilin's best scenery both above and below ground. The park's main attraction is **Reed Flute Cave** (lúdí yán; 芦翟岩), an enormous cavern filled with elaborate rock formations. To control the flow of people through the subterranean wonderland, Guilin has built a 500m long trail with garish neon lights. All tours are conducted in Chinese, allowing visitors who don't speak Chinese greater freedom to putz around by themselves. The rest of the park provides the rare opportunity to commune with Guilin's karst hills without paying admission. The peak across from the cave entrance offers views of the countryside. Nearby **Fragrant Lotus Pond** (fāng lián chí; 芳莲池) has bamboo rafts available for rental (Y2). *(A 25min. ride from the center of Guilin. Accessible by buses #2 and 3. Park open daily sunrise-sunset. Pond open Apr.-Nov. daily 7:30am-6pm (Y45); Dec.-Mar. 8am-5:30pm (Y40). Park free.)*

ELEPHANT TRUNK PARK (xiàng shān gōngyuán; 象山公园). This park features Guilin's most famous peak, **Elephant Trunk Hill** (xiàng bí shān; 象鼻山). The leafy limestone pachyderm stands at the meeting point of the Li River and the **Peach Blossom River** (táohuā jiāng; 桃花江). On top of the peak stands the **Puxian Pagoda** (pǔxián tǎ; 普贤塔), built during the Song dynasty as an offering to calm the flood-prone river. Visitors can also climb to the **Elephant Eye Cave** (xiàng yǎn yán; 象眼岩), watch cormorant fishing from a boat (Y10), dress up in ancient-style clothing for a souvenir photo (Y6), or simply relax on the **Three Star Island** (sānxīng dǎo; 三星岛) across the crooked bridge. *(On Nanhuan Lu, across from CITS. Open daily 6:30am-11:30pm. Y15, but some get in free around twilight when there are fewer visitors.)*

SEVEN STAR PARK (qī xīng gōngyuán; 七星公园). Guilin's largest park boasts **Seven Star Cave** (qīxīngyán; 七星岩) and the appropriately shaped **Camel Hill** (luòtuó shān; 骆驼山) among its attractions. The park's size and relative seclusion from the tour group circuit make it perfect for a quiet afternoon stroll. *(Across the Li River from the city center. Open daily 6am-11pm. Cave open 8am-5:30pm. Park Y25; cave Y30.)*

XIONGSEN BEAR AND TIGER VILLAGE (guìlín xióngsēn xiónghǔ shānzhuāng; 桂林雄森熊虎山庄). This zoo cares for some of the most endangered animals in Asia, including the South China and Siberian Tigers and the Black Bear; an assortment of crocodiles, monkeys, and ostriches is added to the mix. Skip the guided three-hour Chinese tour to roam the premises on your own. *(On Cuizhu Lu, halfway to the airport. ☎280 9257. Open daily 9am-5pm. Y80.)*

SOUTH STREAM PARK (nánxī shān gōngyuán; 南溪山公园). Two peaks shelter the park's **Buddha Cave** and **White Dragon Cave.** The first cave has a bunch of Buddha statues, and the latter is a quirky little hole containing a stalactite/stalagmite formation that slightly resembles the Three Gorges. South of the city's main tourist center, **South Stream Park** offers a park setting, a neat cavern, and no inflated admission price. *(On Zhongshan Nan Lu, a 15min. walk south of the train station. ☎280 9217. Open daily sunrise-sunset. Park Y6; Buddha Cave Y6; White Dragon Cave Y15.)*

LI RIVER FOLK CUSTOMS CENTER (guìlín líjiāng mínsú fēngqíng yuán; 桂林漓江民俗风情园). The province's largest venue created expressly for entertainment, this center showcases the culture, architecture, and art of Guangxi's minorities. Admission includes educational demonstrations and entertaining performances throughout the day. *(On Lijiang Lu, at Lijiang Kou. ☎581 5678. Open daily 8:30am-11pm. Y45, after 7pm Y60.)*

OTHER SIGHTS. In the center of Guilin, the pillar-like **Solitary Beauty Peak** (dú xiù fēng; 独秀峰) rises over 150m and offers a stunning panoramic view. *(On Zhongshan Zhong Lu, north of Jiefang Lu. ☎280 9217. Y15.)* **Fubo Hill** (fúbō shān; 伏波山), on the Li River's western bank near Solitary Beauty Peak, rises above the Li River at the point where Binjiang Lu turns into Longzhou Lu. The Tang and Song dynasties left their mark in **Thousand Buddha Cave** (qiānfó dòng; 千佛洞), where (significantly fewer than 1000) Buddhist statues and frescoes cut into the walls. *(Open daily sunrise-sunset. Y10.)* To visit **Folded Brocade Hill** (dié cǎi shān; 叠彩山), continue north on Longzhou Lu, take a left at Diecai Lu, and then a right. The hill, amid a stunning setting, resembles a stack of fabric at a Chinese silk market. Skip the creepy butterfly museum pagodas and head for the top to enjoy the view from beneath the fragrant cassia trees. *(Open daily sunrise-sunset. Y13.)*

ENTERTAINMENT AND NIGHTLIFE

The city lights up at nightfall; lasers slice the sky, neon courses over buildings, and music pulses from every storefront. The **night market** on Binjiang Lu is always crowded and worth a visit. The general nightlife ends by 11pm, leaving an assortment of large karaoke places and **bizarre discos** on Zhongshan Lu, Yiren Lu, and Binjiang Lu. The **pedestrian mall** on Zhengyang Lu boasts pricey bars and coffee shops; follow the flashing neon signs, and ask to look around before paying a cover fee (generally Y10-15). One promising lead is **Ragazza Pub,** on Yiren Lu at Zhengyang Lu. Good, canned music, a lively crowd, and no karaoke are enough to validate the sign outside proclaiming "Best Bar in Town." (Local draft beer Y20. Open daily 8pm-1am. No cover.)

YANGSHUO 阳朔 ☎0773

Yangshuo has all of Guilin's comely charms but none of its high-priced tour-group attractions. But don't assume that there's a lack of tourism in Yangshuo; it's just more focused on individual backpackers. Like Guilin, Yangshuo is set amid the craggy limestone pinnacles that are the region's hallmark; but here, prices are low and life is slower. The Li River snakes its way between the two cities, and many expensive package tours cruise to Yangshuo from Guilin, stopping only long enough to let passengers load up on cheap trinkets. When the tour boats go, the backpackers remain—often longer than they ever intended—after being charmed by the scenery here. Yangshuo's main streets are an oasis of faux familiarity to visitors who chuckle at its "Fawlty Towers Hotel," "Hard Seat Cafe," and "Planet Yangshuo." Travelers pass the days exploring the natural wonders of the nearby countryside and while away the evenings in the eateries along Xi Jie, sipping coffee and swapping stories to the sounds of Jimi Hendrix and Britney Spears.

TRANSPORTATION

Buses: The **bus station,** on Pantao Lu across from Yangshuo Park gate, services both long-distance and local traffic. Buses not going toward the Li River region usually depart from Guilin. Tickets sold daily 8am-5:30pm; but booking window is often unmanned in the middle and end of the day. To **Guangzhou** (14hr., 2 per day, Y98).

Minibuses: Minibuses make the trip to **Guilin** (1½hr., every 10-15min. or when bus fills to 110% capacity, Y6), leaving from or around the bus station. Beware of being overcharged. Minibuses go to **Xingping** (1hr., every 20min., Y5) via **Fuli** (15min., Y5).

Ferries: See the Li River description in **Sights,** p. 586.

Bike Rental: Many hotels and vendors along Xi Jie rent nearly new mountain bikes for Y10-15 per day. Bikes are due back between 6 and 7pm the same day.

ORIENTATION AND PRACTICAL INFORMATION

Yangshuo is 65km by road or 83km by river southeast of Guilin. Central Yangshuo lies between **Yangshuo Park** to the west and the **Li River** and **Green Lotus Peak** to the east. Across the street from the park gate, the bus station sits on the town's main road, **Pantao Lu** (叛逃路). From the bus station, Pantao Lu runs east toward the city center and the river. The post office is at the intersection of Pantao Lu and **Xi Jie** (西街), where you'll find Yangshuo's guesthouses, cafes, and restaurants. Visitors who arrive by boat at the **Yangshuo Quay** (yángshuò mǎtóu; 阳朔码头) on **Binjiang Lu** (滨江路) should walk along the river toward Green Lotus Peak; Xi Jie runs away from the river, on the right.

Travel Agencies: Travel agencies, backpacker cafes, and self-proclaimed tour guides crowd Xi Jie and Pantao Lu. Perhaps the most congenial CITS independent agent is **Uncle Bob** (www.unclebobtravel.com), who speaks excellent English and has attained the status of a local celebrity. Look for his sign along Xi Jie.

Bank of China: 11 Binjiang Lu (☎882 2329), near the river. Walk to the end of Xi Jie, and turn left at the river; it's 100m down on the left. Exchanges currency and traveler's checks. Another branch is on Xi Jie, near Pantao Lu. Credit card advance. Open daily in summer 8am-5:30pm; in winter 8am-5pm.

PSB: 39 Chengbei Lu (☎882 0778), on the right side of the building. Officer **Bin Yao** handles crimes against foreigners. Visa extension. Open daily 8:30am-5:30pm.

Medical Services: People's Hospital (rénmín yīyuàn; 人民医院), on Shenshan Lu, at the intersection with Chengbei Lu. **Dr. Lee** (☎882 0505, pager 127 159 8929) is **SOS International**'s Yangshuo doctor.

Internet Access: Internet cafes that line Xi Jie charge Y8 per hr. **Global Village Cultural Internet Bar,** 109 Xi Jie, across from West Street International Youth Hostel. 6 computers, fast connection, and A/C. Y10 per hr. Open daily noon-midnight.

Post and Telecommunications: Yangshuo Post Office, 28 Pantao Lu (☎882 2416), at Xi Jie. IDD and Poste Restante. Fax service 2 doors down, in the **China Telecom Office.**

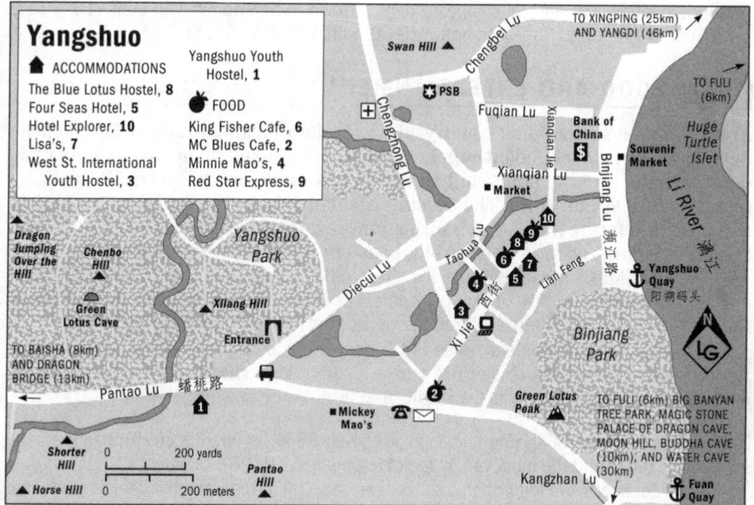

Uncle Bob and some hostel owners will let you make international calling card calls for Y2-5. Open daily 8am-10pm. **Postal Code:** 541900.

ACCOMMODATIONS

Finding a cheap room, even one outfitted with toilet seats, is usually no trouble in Yangshuo. Many of the best bargains boast not only a place to lay your head, but travel agencies, cafes, laundry services (Y1-3 per piece), and more. Bargaining hard may yield savings of up to 50% during colder months. Room prices may double or triple at certain times of the year, especially during Chinese New Year. Guests who stay for extended periods of time may also be eligible for discounts.

Lisa's (lǐshā jiǔdiàn; 李莎酒店), 71 Xi Jie (☎/fax 882 0217). The grande dame of this establishment is Lisa (lisa@public.glptt.gx.cn), who offers travel advice and tips, and is almost as famous as Uncle Bob. 24hr. hot water. Dorms with bath Y30; singles and doubles with A/C Y80; triples Y60. ❶

Four Seas Hotel (sìhǎi fàndiàn; 四海饭店), 73 Xi Jie (☎882 2013; sihai@hotmail.com). Spacious and well-lit halls. Tidy dorms. 24hr. hot water. Dorms Y15-20; singles Y20-30; doubles Y30-50, with bath Y30-60, with A/C and bath Y70-200. ❶

The Blue Lotus Hostel and Cafe (dīngdīng fàndiàn; 丁丁饭店), 62 Xi Jie (☎882 7873). Cozy rooms extend a homey feel, and the friendly owners earn praise from travelers. 24hr. hot water in shared baths. Dorms Y15; singles Y20; doubles Y30; triples Y45. ❶

Hotel Explorer (wénhuà fàndiàn; 文化饭店), 40 Xianqian Jie (☎882 8116; fax 883 7816). This sparklingly clean establishment escapes the hubbub of Xi Jie. Hot water 6am-midnight. 5-bed dorms Y20; singles, doubles, and triples Y120-140. ❶

West Street International Youth Hostel (HI) (xījiē guójì qīng nián lǚguǎn; 西街国际青年旅馆), 102 Xi Jie (☎882 0933; fax 882 0988). Brand-new, clean rooms with wooden bunk beds. Self-catering kitchen and laundry facilities (Y10 per load). 24hr. hot water. 8-bed dorms with bath and A/C Y25; doubles Y80-90. ❶

Yangshuo Youth Hostel (qīngnián zhāodàisuǒ; 青年招待所), 85 Pantao Lu (☎882 2347), a staggering step from the square outside the bus station. Cheap beds, convenient location, but not the cleanest rooms in town. 5-bed dorms with bath Y15; 3-bed dorms Y10; doubles Y30, with bath Y40-60, with A/C Y80-120. ❶

FOOD AND ENTERTAINMENT

Apart from the surrounding countryside, Yangshuo's main attraction for independent travelers is its abundant supply of Western food and company. Visitors typically pass the evening hours and an occasional rainy day in the small cafes and restaurants that line **Xi Jie.** These establishments comprise Yangshuo's nightlife and provide a forum for trading information. Several cafes have nightly double feature showings of recent American blockbusters, and the crowd sticks around until 1am or later. Make arrangements for the week's excursions, get free advice, sip coffee, knock back a few beers, play some pool, or boogie to disco. For regional fare, try the food stalls along Chengzhong Lu, between Xi Jie and Diecui Lu.

One of Yangshuo's busiest times is Chinese New Year, when Western travelers flock to this tiny mecca to see fireworks, firecrackers (illegal in some cities, but encouraged in Yangshuo), and a traditional lion dance (wǔ shī; 舞狮).

Red Star Express (hóng xīng tèkuài; 红星特快), 66 Xi Jie (☎882 2699), has the best pizza in town, and the most variety too (16 toppings, Y15-20). Cleanest kitchen around. The owner keeps the joint open into the wee hours. A mixed crowd of backpackers and locals makes for great socializing and story swapping. Apple pie Y12; beer and cocktails Y12-16. Open daily 8am-midnight (or whenever the last straggler wanders home). ❶

Minnie Mao's, 83 Xi Jie. The oldest restaurant on Xi Jie is still one of the most popular, with excellent Western and local cuisine and nightly movies. Try the stuffed tomatoes (Y6) or the steamed dumplings (Y6-8). Entrees Y8-15. Open daily 6:30am-late. ❶

MC Blues Cafe (líshì jiǔdiàn; 黎士酒店), 101 Xi Jie (☎882 0095; fax 882 7816), on the corner of Pantou Lu. Whistle while you work, listen while you eat; MC Blues has the best selection of music around. The small book swap collection (give 1, get 2) and copies of many English publications attract Anglophones from far and wide. Mushrooms witih bamboo shoots Y6; entrees Y12-35. Open daily 7am-midnight. ❷

King Fisher Cafe (xīnyúniǎo kāfēidiàn; 鑫鱼鸟咖啡店), 64 Xi Jie (☎882 2211). Israeli salad Y8; bananas with brandy Y8; beers Y10-15. Open daily 7:30am-midnight. ❶

SIGHTS

Yangshuo's striking scenery is easily explored on foot, by bike, or by boat. The countryside is overflowing with routes for lazy bike rides, and more gung ho cyclists can take to the hills with mountain bikes, determination, and big muscular legs. Even visiting couch potatoes can hop on a bus to experience Yangshuo's fantastic slice of the great outdoors.

LI RIVER (lìjiāng; 漓江). Marking the eastern border of town, the Li River is both Yangshuo's and Guangxi's main attraction. It winds for miles around fantastically shaped limestone peaks bearing names like **Camel Crossing the River** (luòtuó guòjiāng; 骆驼过江) and **Waiting for Husband Rock** (wàngfū shí; 望夫石). Most travelers explore the river by boat or by bike. The most popular method is to take a one-way boat ride to the river, and return by bike to Yangshuo. Tickets for the boats are on sale at most cafes, restaurants, and hotels along Pantao Lu and Xi Jie.

The most popular nearby destinations along the Li River are **Xingping** (3hr. by boat, 2hr. back by bike) and **Yangdi** (by boat; 5hr. to get there, 1½hr. to return), and between these two cities is the area's most impressive scenery. For most of 2001, tour operators in Yangshuo were not allowed to run boats to these destinations. A good alternative is to take a minibus to **Xingping** (30min., departs daily at 8am for an 8:30am boat, Y5), where you can take a round-trip cruise to **Yangdi** (3hr., Y50). To return to Yangshuo, bikes can be held in Xingping, or buses make the trip every 15 minutes. Those wishing to make a day-long trip to Xingping should visit on market days, the 3rd, 6th, 9th, 13th, 16th, 19th, 23rd, 26th, and 29th of each month, just like in Yangshuo. From Yangshuo, you can also rent a sidecar to Xingping (round-trip Y90-100) or Fuli (round-trip Y30).

Fuli (fúlì; 福利) is the only destination of Yangshuo boats. Most people find that the scenery on this stretch of river does not justify the inflated price. However, the shorter trip to Fuli (1hr. by boat, 40min. back by bike) makes it a good choice for travelers with only a few days in Yangshuo. Boat tickets can be purchased at the Yangshuo Dock on Binjiang Lu for Y150. You can bike to Fuli from Xingping by taking a right on the main road. Fuli has markets like those in Xingping, with an assortment of goods, including frogs, snakes, firecrackers, fishing baskets, and woven hats. Fuli also specializes in fans and calligraphy; the street perpendicular to the river is lined with calligraphy shops. Markets are on the 2nd, 5th, 8th, 12th, 15th, 18th, 22nd, 25th, and 28th of each month.

If boat rides seem too structured for your exploration of the Li River, stop in at **Mickey Mao's,** 31 Pantao Lu (☎/fax 886 0082), for an inner tube (Y20 per day) or a kayak (Y100 per day). Groups get discounted rates. (Open daily 7am-11pm.) Li River fishermen have long trained **cormorants** to dive into the river and catch fish by the light of a flaming torch, but some enterprising locals now allow tourist boats to tag along and watch them practice their trade. The whole experience feels contrived, but it's interesting nonetheless. (1-1½hr., daily around 8pm, Y25.)

MOON HILL (yuèliàng shān; 月亮山). Named for the crescent-shaped hole through its center, Moon Hill is a 50-minute bike ride or a 10-minute bus ride from Yangshuo proper. The 800 steep steps to the top are no leisurely stroll, but the pain is worth it; the view of the countryside is truly outstanding. Make your way past the aggressive hawkers on the stairs and take the short path to the top of the arch for the highest lookout. Tours of the hill and parts of the surrounding villages cost about Y50—touts will look for you along Xi Jie and at other major tourist sights. *(Ride along Pantao Lu past Green Lotus Peak, and then take Kangzhan Lu to your right when the road forks; look for the English sign. Minibuses or small trucks from around the Yangshuo Bus Station to Gaotian can drop you off at the entrance (Y2). Open daily sunrise-sunset. Y9.)*

CAVES. Tickets to the caves near Yangshuo can be found along Xi Jie. **Buddha Cave** (fó dòng; 佛洞) was used as a refuge by local villagers from the invading Japanese army during WWII. It draws its name from a tiny stalagmite inside the cave that resembles the Maitreya, or Future Buddha. It's full of narrow, maze-like, and sometimes dangerous passages, which explains why locals once thought the cave was secure from the Japanese and why portions are still off-limits to visitors; even in the areas open to the public there have been injuries during the cave's 11 years as a tourist attraction. A guide and a flashlight are necessary. Bring a bathing suit and towel for the underground waterfall pool, and be prepared to sacrifice your crummiest rags to the grubby climb. *(Down the road from Moon Hill, in the direction of Yangshuo. There are 3 tours: a 1hr. tour (Y40), a 1½hr. tour (Y50), and a 3hr. tour that visits all the caves that are open to the public (Y120). Groups of 8 or more can bargain.)* **Water Cave** (shuǐdòng; 水洞), one of the newer tours available in Yangshuo, aims to challenge Buddha Cave's reputation as the most extensive, unaltered subterranean microcosm in the area. Tours enter the cave by boat. *(From Yangshuo, a 20min. drive past Moon Hill. 2hr. tour Y78.; 4-6hr. tour Y108.)*

OTHER SIGHTS. Dragon Bridge (yùlóng qiáo; 玉龙桥) lies 13km from Yangshuo, 3 minutes beyond the town of Baisha. The bridge, built in 1412, offers stunning

SOUTHWEST

CALL ME FISHMAEL Each evening at dusk, fishermen along the Li River set out in bamboo rafts to make their living, armed with only a team of four to eight trained birds. Fishermen have been using trained cormorants to fish for over 1400 years. The green-eyed birds, originally brought to Guangxi from Qinghai province in northwest China, can dive for more than a minute at a time. As the fisherman cruises along, his team swims alongside his boat, scooping up the fish attracted to the surface by the fisherman's lantern. A good night's yield can be as much as 10 lbs. per bird, but only the cormorant knows how much he really caught. Each bird wears a thin piece of twine around its throat to keep it from swallowing the biggest fish; everything small enough to get down the bird's throat is his to keep.

views of the Li River's winding path through Yangshuo's rice fields and karst hills. *(Side car to Baisha Y5. Sidecar from Baisha to Dragon Bridge Y2.)*

To get up close and personal with a karst hill without parting with a single yuan, try **Green Lotus Peak.** The steep and often slippery 20-minute trek rewards hearty hikers with a panoramic view. *(Follow Pantao Lu south to the end of the buildings, and take the stairway from the end of the sidewalk to the beginning of the trail.)* **Big Banyan Tree Park** lies halfway on the road to **Moon Hill** (30min. bike ride, or take a Y2 minibus to Gaotian), home to an ancient tree with an over-1400-year history and a Zhuang minority cultural showcase. Those who balk at the Y18 admission just to see a tree may content themselves with a good glimpse by the roadside as they pass by on a bicycle. A little farther across the street stands the **Magic Stone Palace of Dragon Cave** (qíshígōng; 奇石宫), a museum collection of over 1000 odd geological formations found in nearby **Dragon Cave.** *(Open daily 9:30am-6pm. Y23.)*

SHOPPING

Yangshuo is the best place in China to fill your pack with priceless treasures for the folks back home. An endless variety of silk scarves, batiks, jade chopsticks, and Mao memorabilia fill the stalls along **Binjiang Lu.** Many visitors come for the custom-made silk clothing, but tailors along **Xi Jie** can accommodate unusual requests (like brocade overalls) and are quick with custom orders (same-day to one-day service). Prices run around Y50 for a skirt, Y35-40 for a shirt, and Y80 for pants. Bargain when shopping in Yangshou; the first price you hear should never be the last.

BEIHAI 北海

☎0779

Beihai is an ocean town, living and breathing at the whim of the sea. On the northern shore, freight vessels dock next to weather-beaten canoes; on the southern shore, visitors to Silver Beach swear by another kind of boat—speed cruisers that scream carefree fun and fancy. This "Pearl City" is, like its namesake, gracious and understated, with a balmy climate that makes for a pleasant and serene stop on the way to neighboring Hainan.

TRANSPORTATION

Flights: Beihai International Airport (běihǎi guójì jīchǎng; 北海国际机场; ☎207 2511), 25km northeast of the city. **Buses** (Y10) depart for the airport (1½-2hr. before flights) from the **CAAC ticket office,** 7 Beibuwan Lu (☎303 3757). Open daily 8:30am-10pm. To: **Beijing** (daily, Y1800); **Changsha** (2 per day, Y810); **Chengdu** (M, W, Su; Y1080); **Guangzhou** (2 per day, Y630); **Guilin** (1-2 per day, Y480); **Haikou** (M, T, Th-F; Y350); **Kunming** (Tu, Th, Sa; Y710); **Shanghai** (Sa-Th, Y1420).

Trains: Beihai Train Station (běihǎi huǒchē zhàn; 北海火车站; ☎305 8136), at the southern end of Beijing Lu. All destinations connect through **Nanning:** express (3hr., 7am and 4pm, Y40), regular (4¼hr., 1:48pm, Y22).

Buses: Beihai Main Bus Station (běihǎi qìchē zǒngzhàn; 北海汽车总站; ☎202 2094), on Beibuwan Lu. Open daily 6am-9pm. **Express buses** to: **Fangcheng** (2hr., 2:30pm, Y30); **Guangzhou** (10hr., 8:45am and 8:50pm, Y180); **Guilin** (7hr.; 8, 9am, 9:10pm; Y150); **Liuzhou** (5½hr., 4 per day, Y100); **Nanning** (3hr., every 30min.-1hr. 6:50am-8:30pm, Y50).

Ferries: Beihai International Passenger Dock (běihǎi guójì kèyùn mǎtóu; 北海国际客运码头), 4 Yintan Lu (☎388 1963). Open daily 7:30am-6pm. **Ticket office** (☎306 6829), on Sichuan Bei Lu, 200m north of Beibuwan Plaza, on the opposite side of the street. Open daily 7am-10pm. To **Haikou** (10hr., 6pm, Y83-211).

Local Transportation: Bus stops are clearly labeled with route numbers, direction, and route information. Bus **#2** runs along Haijiao Lu, Sichuan Lu, Beibuwan Lu, and Beijing Lu toward the train station; **#3** runs from Haibin Park past Beibuwan Plaza to Silver Beach; **#8** starts from Beibuwan Plaza and circles the entire downtown area. Y1-2.

Taxis: Base fare Y5. Pedicabs also available.

SOUTHWEST

PRACTICAL INFORMATION

Beihai is located on a peninsula that juts into the Beibuwan (literally "North Bay"; běibùwān; 北部湾). **Beibuwan Lu,** the main thoroughfare, runs from the southwest to the northeast of town. The major streets that intersect Beibuwan Lu are, from west to east, **Yunnan Lu, Guizhou Lu, Sichuan Lu, Beijing Lu,** and **Guangdong Lu.** Get directions at **Beibuwan Plaza** in the city center.

Travel Agency: CITS, 33 Chating Lu (☎206 2999), on the 3rd fl. of the Shangri-La Hotel, past Haibin Park. Service in English available. The **ticket center** (☎207 8030 or 207 9030; fax 207 8029) on the 1st fl. books plane, train, and bus tickets. Open daily 9am-6pm.

Bank of China: (☎306 1133), on the corner of Beihai Dadao and Guizhou Lu. Exchanges currency and traveler's checks. Credit card advances. Open daily 8am-noon and 3-6pm.

Hospital: People's Municipal Hospital (rénmín yīyuàn; 人民医院), 84 Woping Lu (☎202 2245). 24hr. pharmacy.

PSB: 213 Zhongshan Dong Lu (☎209 1114 or 209 1811). Visa extensions. Open daily 8:30am-noon and 3-5:30pm.

Internet Access: China Unicom Internet Bar (liántōng xīwàng wǎngxiào; 联通希望网校; ☎306 6383), on the 2nd fl. of the Qidong Shopping Center (qǐdōng shāngchéng; 启东商城), across from Beibuwan Plaza. Y5 deposit. Y2.5 per hr. Open daily 9am-9pm.

Post and Telecommunications: On Sichuan Lu, about 300m south of Beibuwan Sq., on the opposite side of the street. EMS and Poste Restante. Open daily 8am-8pm. The **Business Services Center** next door offers 24hr. fax and IDD service. **Postal code:** 536000.

ACCOMMODATIONS

No-name hostels on Silver Beach provide cheap accommodations, but are uncomfortably close to nearby karaoke restaurants. The hotels within Beihai city are your best bet for a good night's sleep.

Taoyuan Hotel (táoyuán dàjiǔdiàn; 桃源大酒店; ☎202 0919; fax 202 0520) is slightly removed from the main thoroughfare, in an alley opposite the bus station. The best amenities and cleanliness in its price range. Delicious *congee* breakfast special (7:30-10am, Y3). Singles Y78; doubles Y158; triples Y188. ❶

Hualian Hotel (huálián jiǔdiàn; 华联酒店), 1 Beibuwan Xi Lu (☎303 1998; fax 303 5636). Conveniently located near shops, local transportation, and Beibuwan Sq. All standard amenities. Singles Y150; doubles Y128; triples Y200. ❷

Ocean Hostel (hǎiyáng zhāodàisuǒ; 海洋招待所), 224 Haijiao Lu (☎390 2014). Off the beaten path, but one of the best deals in Beihai. 4-person dorms Y18. With private bath: doubles Y70; triples Y90; quads Y100. With A/C and bath: singles Y60; doubles Y100; triples Y120. ❶

FOOD

Not surprisingly, Beihai is a fish-loving town, serving up such seafood delights as fish jerky, fish soup, fresh fish, and tube worm (shāchóng; 沙虫). The northern end of Sichuan Lu connects to the small islet **Waisha,** which has a row of restaurants as well as a **fish market** selling exotic dried goods.

Waisha Danjia Restaurant (wàishā dànjiā péng; 外沙蛋家堋; ☎202 6889), on the far right side of the row of restaurants on Waisha Islet. The live seafood display puts the Beihai Aquarium to shame. Pick and choose your own dinner, then relax in an open-air cabana with a view of the ocean. Live performances nightly. Seafood Y20 and up, most regular dishes Y5-15. Open daily 9am-2am. **Danjia Food Plaza** (dànjiā měishícūn; 蛋家美食村), 4 Beibuwan Lu (☎205 4734), is another branch of the same chain, and has the same menu with more non-seafood options. Open daily 7:30am-2am. ❶

Guangdong Restaurant (guǎngdōng shíjiē; 广东食街), on Guizhou Lu about 50m north of Beibuwan Lu. A local favorite for succulent seafood, tasty corn pancakes, and tube worm. Entrees Y10-30. Open daily 7am-midnight. ❶

Dexing Restaurant (déxīng shíjiē; 得兴食街), 1 Sichuan Lu, behind Beibuwan Sq. (☎303 6178). Choose between Cantonese-style dim sum (Y2-8 per dish) or the regular entrees-and-rice menu (Y8-25 per entree). Lunch specials Y10-28. English menu available. Open daily 7am-2am. ❷

SIGHTS

MARINE MARKET (shuǐchǎn shìchǎng; 水产市场). All the ocean's magnificent creatures: dried, bagged, and on sale. **Pearl City,** on the market's second floor, sells pearls, shells, and derivative products. *(On Yunnan Bei Lu at Haijiao Lu. Take bus #8 to the Fisheries Market stop. ☎390 8333. Pearl City open daily 9am-5:30pm; downstairs market open for indefinite hours. Free.)*

SILVER BEACH (yíntān; 银滩). At Beihai's main attraction, Chinese tourists are as ubiquitious as sandcrabs, basking in droves beneath multicolored umbrellas. The best way to enjoy Silver Beach is to cruise away from the crowds by motorboat (Y8 per 10min.), or to plop down in a relatively secluded spot. *(Take minibus #3 (Y2) from Beibuwan Plaza for the 15min. ride from the city center or bargain for a taxicab ride (Y20-25). Open 24hr. Y25.)*

BEIHAI UNDERWATER WORLD (běihǎi hǎidǐ shìjiè; 北海海底世界). The complex's vibrant tropical fish and diving and feeding shows don't merit the steep admission price. Not even Fei-fei (literally, Fat-fat), the biggest turtle in China, makes this sight worthwhile. *(On Chating Lu, in the Seaside Park (hǎibīn gōngyuán; 海滨公园). ☎205 3275. Open daily 8am-5:30pm. Adults Y60, children Y30.)*

YUNNAN 云南

It would take very little to convince the blissful backpackers in Yunnan that they've actually died and gone to heaven. Tucked away in the far southwest, China's fourth largest province has, quite honestly, no unpleasant destination. From the chilly mountain passes and snow-capped peaks of the north to the upbeat urbanity of Kunming and the dormant volcanoes and luxuriant tropical rainforests of the south, Yunnan has something for everyone. The province's diversity does not begin and end with its scenic splendor, however—it is also one of China's most ethnically diverse provinces. A trip through the province leads travelers past Tibetan herders, the Bai, the Mosuo, and the matriarchal Naxi, to the Lahu, Dai, Yi, and Bulang minorities of Xishuangbanna and the Myanmese of Ruili, offering insight into distinctive ways of life that are fast disappearing elsewhere.

Yunnan has had plenty of time to adjust to its role as a cultural crossroads. The lesser-known Southern Silk Road, which connected Southeast Asia to the better-known Eurasian Route, passed right through the region; Myanmese, Thai, Khmer, and Tibetan people and goods flowed into the area, often settling here permanently. The ethnic groups that originally inhabited Yunnan acknowledged Han Chinese rule as early as the Qin and Han dynasties, but never completely fell under the mantle of Chinese culture. During the Tang, the independent Nanzhao kingdom, led by the ancestors of the present-day Bai people, ruled the region from the city of Dali. Then, in 1523, the Mongols incorporated Nanzhao into the Yuan empire and gave it its dreamy name, Yunnan—"south of the clouds."

When Ming leaders promoted Han Chinese migration to Yunnan, hoping to assimilate the local population, they failed miserably. To stop the influx of foreign influences and weaken the hold of indigenous cultures over local populations would have been as difficult as trying to drain the Yangzi with a thimble. The provincial government long ago realized that ethnic diversity holds plenty of appeal for curious visitors, and has therefore vigorously pumped money into a tasteless and insensitive marketing of minority cultures to visiting urbanites with a hankering for the "quaint" and "primitive." To its credit, the government is making a concerted effort to preserve minority cultures by creating autonomous countries and by increasing bilingual schooling; it still takes a bit of effort, however, on the part of the traveler to penetrate the Han haze that hangs about this area.

KUNMING 昆明 ☎0871

Kunming, "city of eternal spring," plays its role in style, with year-round blooms and mild weather. As a leader in China's determined march through the 21st century, Kunming maintains a precarious balance between development and natural beauty with surprising grace. The Han, Dai, and Muslim influences in local architecture and cuisine, however, only hint at the cultural clash that has shaped the surrounding area for centuries.

The 1999 International Horticultural Exposition, coupled with domestic and international investment, has transformed the city's infrastructure, including many of Kunming's historic neighborhoods and narrow *hútòngs*. Fortunately, Kunming's push for modernization seems bedecked more with flowers than with the dreary pollution that plagues other cities. The city is lively, clean, and bursting at the seams with character—a fleeting visit makes you wish for a longer one, and a longer one makes you wonder what it would be like to call this place home.

SOUTHWEST

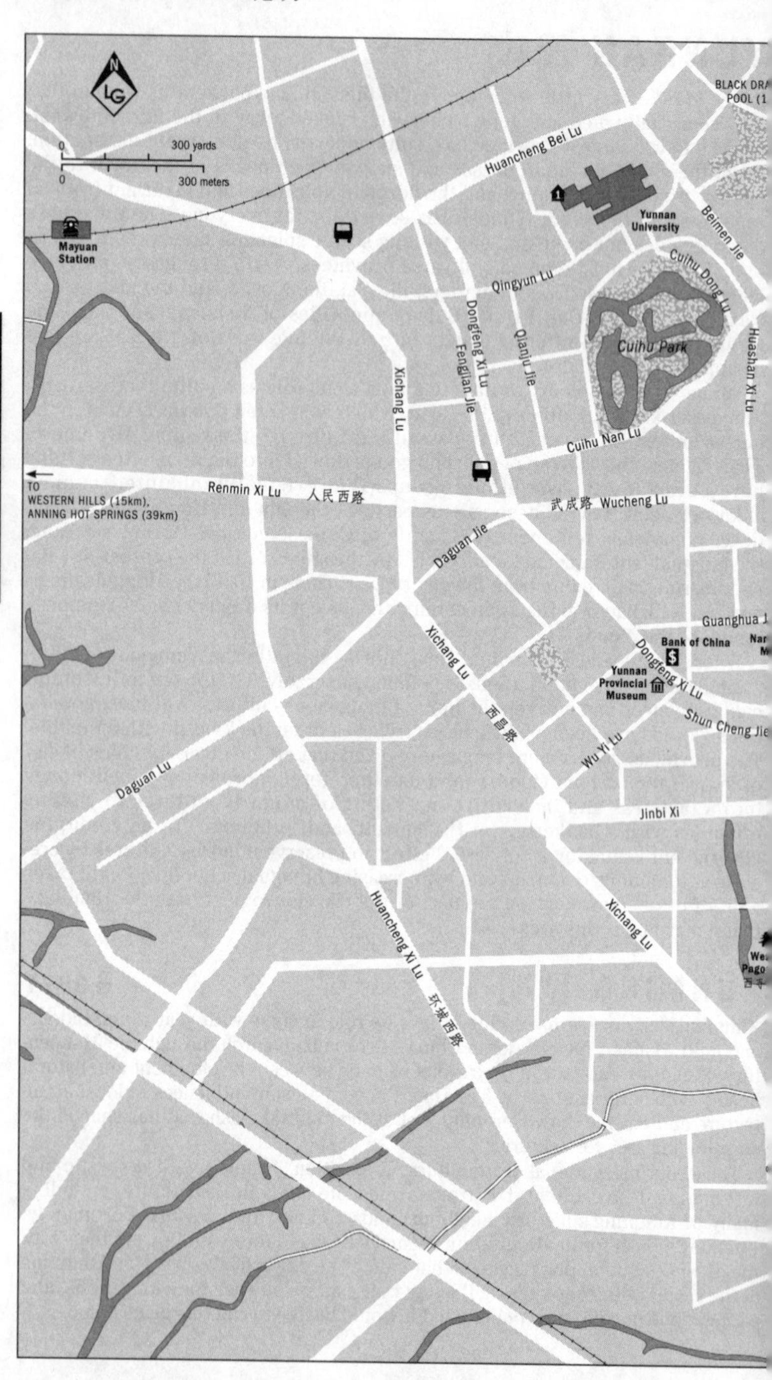

0 300 yards
0 300 meters
Mayuan Station
Huancheng Bei Lu
Yunnan University
Beimen Jie
Cuihu Dong Lu
Qingyun Lu
Dongfeng Xi Lu
Fengjian Jie
Qianju Jie
Cuihu Park
Huashan Xi Lu
Xichang Lu
Cuihu Nan Lu
TO WESTERN HILLS (15km), ANNING HOT SPRINGS (39km)
Renmin Xi Lu 人民西路
武成路 Wucheng Lu
Daguan Jie
Guanghua
Bank of China
Yunnan Provincial Museum
Dongfeng Xi Lu
Xichang Lu
西昌路
Shun Cheng Jie
Wu Yi Lu
Daguan Lu
Jinbi Xi
Huancheng Xi Lu 环城西路
Xichang Lu

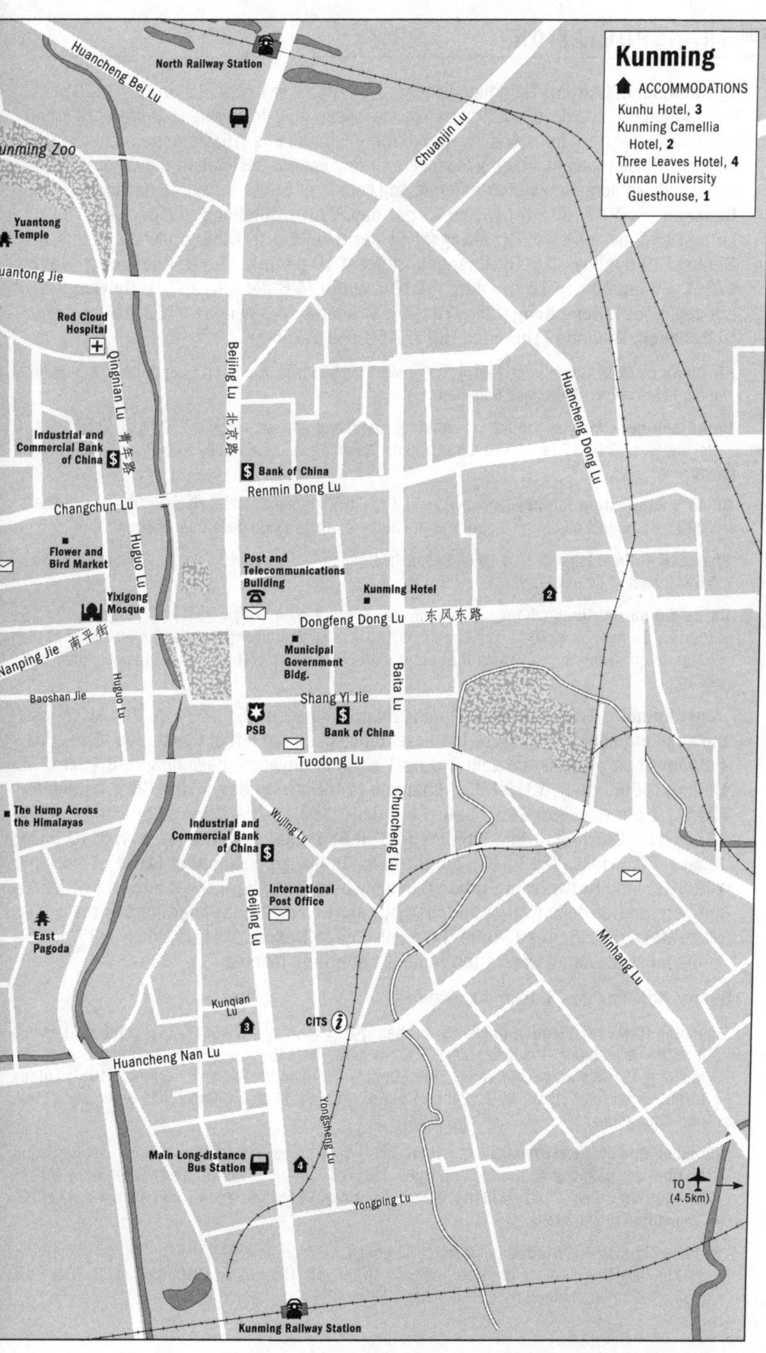
Kunming
ACCOMMODATIONS
Kunhu Hotel, 3
Kunming Camellia Hotel, 2
Three Leaves Hotel, 4
Yunnan University Guesthouse, 1
North Railway Station
Huancheng Bei Lu
Kunming Zoo
Chuanjin Lu
Yuantong Temple
Yuantong Jie
Red Cloud Hospital
Qingnian Lu 青年路
Beijing Lu 北京路
Huancheng Dong Lu
Industrial and Commercial Bank of China
Bank of China
Renmin Dong Lu
Changchun Lu
Huguo Lu
Flower and Bird Market
Post and Telecommunications Building
Kunming Hotel
Yixigong Mosque
Dongfeng Dong Lu 东风东路
Nanping Jie 南平街
Municipal Government Bldg.
Baita Lu
Baoshan Jie
Shang Yi Jie
PSB
Bank of China
Tuodong Lu
The Hump Across the Himalayas
Wujing Lu
Industrial and Commercial Bank of China
Chuncheng Lu
International Post Office
East Pagoda
Minhang Lu
Kunqian Lu
CITS
Huancheng Nan Lu
Yongsheng Lu
Main Long-distance Bus Station
TO (4.5km)
Yongping Lu
Kunming Railway Station

TRANSPORTATION

Flights: Kunming Airport (kūnmíng jīchǎng; 昆明机场; ☎717 9113 or 711 3229) is a few kilometers outside town. Accessible via buses #52 from Huguo Bridge, 78 from Qingnian Lu, and 67 from North Train Station. A shuttle bus (Y5) from the airport to the Worker's Palace usually takes passengers to any central destination they request. Different airlines sometimes offer different "discount" prices to the same destination. To: **Baoshan** (Su-M, W, F; Y440); **Dali** (3 per day, Y360); **Jinghong** (17 per day, Y520); **Lijiang** (6-7 per day, Y420); **Mangshi** (3 per day, Y530). Other domestic flights to: **Beijing** (10 per day, Y1450); **Chengdu** (at least 10 per day, Y560); **Chongqing** (daily, Y720); **Guangzhou** (6-10 per day, Y1010); **Guilin** (4-6 per day, Y670); **Guiyang** (2-5 per day, Y350); **Hong Kong** (daily, Y2400); **Shanghai** (4-6 per day, Y1520). Also flights to **Bangkok, Thailand** (1hr., daily 3:20, 3:50 and 7:15pm).

Air China (zhōngguó mínháng; 中国民航; ☎351 1591), by the main train station, left of the main ticket office. Open daily 8am-8pm.

China Southern Airlines (zhōngguó nánfāng hángkōng gōngsī; 中国南方航空公司), 433 Beijing Lu (☎310 1831 or 310 1832), near Dongfeng Lu. Open daily 8am-8pm. Credit cards accepted.

China Southwestern Airlines (zhōngguó xīnán hángkōng gōngsī; 中国西南航空公司; ☎353 1222), on Huancheng Nan Lu opposite the Bank of China. Open daily 8am-6:30pm.

Shanghai Airlines (shànghǎi hángkōng gōngsī; 上海航空公司), 46 Dongfeng Dong Lu (☎ 351 1534), east of Beijing Lu.

China Yunnan Airlines (zhōngguó yúnnán hángkōng gōngsī; 中国云南航空公司), 24-28 Tuodong Lu (☎316 4270, reconfirmation ☎316 4415). The manager in the far left corner of the office often seems to find seats that other staff can't. Open 24hr. Credit cards accepted (4% charge).

Trains: Kunming Train Station (kūnmíng zhàn; 昆明站; ☎351 1534 or 302 2122) is at the southern end of Beijing Lu. The ticket office is on the left of the station. Open daily 6:30am-11pm. Tickets are sold 3 days-1 week in advance, beginning at 8:15am. To: **Beijing** (46hr., daily, Y319-889); **Chengdu** (24hr., 2 per day, Y105-322); **Chongqing** (24hr., 2 per day, Y95-345); **Dali** (8hr., daily, Y30 or 70); **Guangzhou** (34hr., daily, Y170-515); **Guiyang** (13hr., daily, Y75-233); **Shanghai** (57hr., 2 per day, Y179-553); **Xi'an** (42hr., daily, Y218-612). For travel to **Guilin,** go to **Nanning** (16hr., 2 per day, Y98-301) first. **North Train Station** (kūnmíng běizhàn; 昆明北站; ☎515 3506), at the northern end of Beijing Lu, is to the right after walking up the road next to the underpass. Open daily 6am-10:40pm. Trains also go to **Hekou** (16-17hr., daily, Y37 or 77); in the rainy season, however, this route is not always reliable.

Buses: Kunming has 3 main bus stations.

Kunming Passenger Station (qìchē kèyùn zhàn; 汽车客运站; ☎354 3325), to the right as you face the train station. The ticket office is to the right, down the row of shops before the fence surrounding the bus area. Open daily 7am-10pm. To: **Jinghong** (24hr., 6 per day, Y165); **Lijiang** (10hr., 3 per day, Y130); **Ruili** (24hr., 4 per day, Y150); **Xiaguan/Dali** (5hr., 6 per day, Y100); and **Zhongdian** (16hr., 1-2 per day, Y200).

Kunming Bus Station (kūnmíng qìchē zhàn; 昆明汽车站; ☎351 0617), a 5min. walk up Beijing Lu from the train station, on the left. Open daily 6:40am-9pm. To: **Guiyang** (15hr., daily, Y130); **Hekou** (9hr., daily, Y101); **Lijiang** (10hr., 4 per day, Y156); **Xiaguan** (5hr., 10 per day, Y110); **Zhongdian** (12hr., daily, Y197).

Yunnan Express Bus Station (yúnnán gāosù gōnglù kèyùn zhàn; 云南高速公路客运站), next to Kunming Bus Station. The ticket office is to the left. Open daily 6:30am-9pm. To **Dali** (5hr., daily, Y103) and **Lijiang** (8hr., 2 per day, Y130).

Local Transportation: The extensive **bus** system has announcements in both English and Chinese. Fare Y1. Buses **#50, 64, 67,** and **68** run along Beijing Lu from the Kunming to North Train Stations; **#5** travels along Dongfeng Dong Lu; **#52, 67,** and **78** go to the airport; **#101** goes around Cuihu Park.

Taxis: Base fare Y7-8, each additional km Y1.6-1.8.

Bike Rental: Camellia Hotel. Y2 per hr., Y15 per day; deposit Y200-300. **Kunhu Hotel,** 3rd fl. The best shop for foreign bike parts is at 33 Tieju Jie, just off Cuihu Nan Lu. There are a number of bike shops on Renmin Dong Lu.

As in any city in China, passengers should guard valuables with particular vigilance on **long-distance buses,** especially on **sleeper buses.** Travelers have also reported incidents of robbery and fraud involving tickets sold at Kunming bus stations. Readers are advised to purchase tickets only from official sources; if someone offers you a ticket at a cheaper-than-advertised price, be suspicious.

ORIENTATION AND PRACTICAL INFORMATION

Kunming's downtown area is surrounded by **Huancheng Lu** (环城路), the first ring road. **Beijing Lu** (北京路) links the North Train Station in the north and the Kunming Train Station and the main long-distance bus station in the south. **Dongfeng Lu** (东风路) runs east-west, bisecting Beijing Lu at the Worker's Cultural Palace near the **Panlong River** (盘龙江). Most of the parks, eateries, and coffee shops are found around **Cuihu Park,** near **Yunnan University,** and to the north of the city.

Travel Agencies: CITS, 287 Huancheng Nan Lu, after the overpass. The very helpful Ma Tongchung (☎353 3276) and Wang Ping (☎355 5890) both speak English. Or try the North America and Europe bureau (☎353 5448). Open M-F 8:30am-noon and 2-5:30pm. **Camellia Travel Agency** (cháhuā lǚxíng shè; 茶花旅行社), 96 Dongfeng Dong Lu (☎316 6514). Open daily 8am-8pm. **Kunhu Travel Agency** (kūnhú lǚxíng shè; 昆湖旅行社), 202 Beijing Lu (☎313 3737). Supposedly open 24hr.

Consulates: Kunming is a good place to stock up on visas for Southeast Asian countries. There is no **Vietnamese consulate.** Travelers have reported varied success when attempting to obtain one through CITS; contact Ma Tongchung for details.

Laos, Camellia Hotel, 96 Dongfeng Dong Lu, Bldg. 3, 1st fl. (☎317 6623; fax 317 8556). Issues 15-day transit visas (US$35 for German, Japanese, and US citizens; US$30 for Australian, New Zealand, and most Western European citizens); processing takes 3 working days. Visas are not issued at the Lao border. Open M-F 8:30-11:30am and 1:30-4:30pm.

Myanmar, Camellia Hotel, Bldg. 3, 3rd fl. (☎317 6609; fax 317 6309). Issues 28-day tourist visas (Y165; no extensions). Processing takes 3 working days (rush fee: 3hr. Y100, 12hr. Y50). Tourists must change US$200 into Foreign Exchange Certificates (FEC) upon arrival in Myanmar. Open M-F 8:30am-noon and 1-4:30pm.

Thailand, Kunming Hotel, 145 Dongfeng Dong Lu, South Bldg., 1st fl. (☎316 8916 or 314 9296; fax 316 6891). Issues max. 30-day transit visas (Y70; must have proof of plane reservations from China to Thailand and from Thailand to a 3rd country), 60-day tourist visas (Y110; up to 1-month extension permitted), and 90-day "non-immigrant" business visas (Y180 with invitation letter). Processing takes 2 working days. Open M-F 9-11am.

Currency Exchange: Bank of China, 515 Beijing Lu (☎318 8974), at Renmin Dong Lu. Open daily 9-11:45am and 1:30-4:45pm. **Industrial and Commercial Bank of China** (zhōngguó gōngshāng yínháng; 中国工商银行), 275 Beijing Lu (☎317 0614). Exchanges traveler's checks. MC/V **ATM.** Open daily 9am-5pm. Major hotels may also exchange currency and traveler's checks.

SOUTHWEST

Bookstores: Xinhua Bookstore (xīnhuá shūdiàn; 新华书店), 90 Yuantong Jie. Limited selection of English books. Open M-Tu 10am-8pm, W-Su 9am-9pm. The **Journey to the East Cafe** (see p. 598) and **Wei's Pizzeria** (see p. 598) have better selections.

Markets: Sakura Shopping Center (yīnghuā gòuwù zhōngxīn; 樱花购物中心), 27 Dongfeng Dong Lu (☎314 0429), next to the Holiday Inn. An expensive **grocery section** is on the 1st fl. Open daily 9:30am-10pm. Credit cards accepted. **Paul's Shop** (bǎolì shāngdiàn; 保利商店), 40 Wenlin Jie (☎535 4210), stocks imported foods and drinks. Open daily 8:30am-9pm.

PSB: 94 Beijing Lu (☎316 1021 or 316 3585), in the big municipal building between Dongfeng Lu and Xiangxi Jie. The **visa office** is in a small side building (☎301 7585). Open daily 8-11:30am and 1-4:30pm.

Internet Access: China Telecom, 12 Dongfeng Dong Lu (☎317 7875), at Beijing Lu, has 24 computers. Y8 per hr., deposit Y20. Open M-F 8am-5pm, Sa-Su 9am-5pm. **Holiday Inn,** 25 Dongfeng Dong Lu (☎316 5888), at Baita Lu. Y20 per 2hr. Open daily 8am-10pm. **Dove Email** (xìn'gē diànnǎowū; 信鸽电脑屋), 47 Wenlin Jie (☎536 9789), toward Dongfeng Xi Lu. Y6 per hr. Open M-Sa 10am-8pm, Su noon-6pm. **Technology Service Center** (jìshù fúwù bù; 技术服务部), 221 Baita Lu, near Mama Fu's. Y10 per hr. Open daily 9am-10pm. Backpacker restaurants and hotels have access too.

Post Office: 231 Beijing Lu (☎318 4132), just above Heping Lu. EMS and Poste Restante. Open daily 8am-8pm. **Postal Code:** 650011.

SOUTHWEST

ACCOMMODATIONS

The cost of accommodations in Kunming has been rising over the last few years. All hotels provide 24-hour hot water unless otherwise specified.

Kunming Camellia Hotel (kūnmíng cháhuā bīnguǎn; 昆明茶花宾馆), 96 Dongfeng Dong Lu (☎316 3000 or 316 2918). Take bus #23 or 67 from either train station to Dongfeng Dong Lu; then, switch to bus #5, heading toward Huancheng Dong Lu. The undisputed favorite of Kunming backpackers, with cheap beds, good service, and a lovely garden. On-site travel agency, 2 consulates, Internet access (Y10 per hr.), currency exchange, and free airport shuttles. 3-, 4-, and 7-bed dorms (foreigners only) Y30; doubles with bath Y140. Credit cards accepted. ❶

The Hump Across the Himalayas (tuófēng kèzhàn; 驼峰客栈; ☎364 4197), on Shu Lin Jie, across the Panlong River from the Kunhu Hotel. The Hump is the place to stay for those who never want their party to end. Dorm beds Y15-40. ❶

Kunhu Hotel (kūnhú fàndiàn; 昆湖饭店), 202 Beijing Lu (☎313 3737), by Huancheng Lu. The lobby is dank and the corridors dim, but the rooms are much nicer. Next to 3 cafes, with travel agencies and 100 telephone stalls on the premises. 3- to 4-bed dorms Y25-26; singles Y60; doubles Y68, with bath Y128. ❶

Yunnan University Guesthouse (yúnnán dàxué zhāodàisuǒ; 云南大学招待所; ☎503 3557; ccfs@ynu.edu.cn), on Tian Jun Dian, off Yieryi Dajie, on the western edge of campus. From the North Train Station, take bus #22 down Huancheng Bei Lu to Yunnan University, near Dongfeng Xi Lu. From Kunming station, a taxi (Y14) is more convenient. From Wenlin Jie, turn onto Wenhua Xiang about halfway along the street, turn right at the end of the road, and left at Journey to the East Cafe; the university is on the left. Bright lighting, private bath, and TVs make this guesthouse's popularity well deserved. Hot water nominally 24hr. Dorm beds Y30; singles Y70; doubles Y100; triples Y150. ❶

Three Leaves Hotel (kūnmíng sānyè fàndiàn; 昆明三叶饭店), 83 Beijing Lu (☎351 2543), across from the long-distance bus station and about 200m from Kunming train station. You'll need more than just three leaves over your ears to sleep at night. Ask to see the small standard room (Y60). Singles and doubles with bath Y150. ❷

FOOD

Despite the lack of variety in Kunming cuisine, there's plenty here to make your taste buds tingle. Cheap snacks and more expensive tea houses and coffee shops surround Cuihu Park. Just north of the park, near Yunnan University, restaurants offer heartier fare and ask only Y2-5 for everything from dumplings to Muslim entrees. Another prime place for cheap food is Beijing Lu, near the long-distance bus station and Kunming Train Station. Look for the fruit market in the alley just past the entrance to the train station, to the left.

KUNMING SPECIALTIES

Kunming is most famous for its **Across-the-Bridge Noodles** (see **Bridge Over Troubled Waters**). **Across Bridge Garden** (guòqiáo yuán; 过桥园) is in an alley off Dongfeng Dong Lu, across the street from the Camellia Hotel. The third floor decor, with dark artificial trees and awkward waitstaff in Manchu costumes, is a triumph of tackiness; the noodles (Y20-180), however, are nothing but pure, unadulterated pleasure. (☎316 9135. Open daily 8am-9pm. ❹) The restaurant at 161 Qingnian Lu, halfway between Renmin Dong Lu and the zoo, on the right as you come from Renmin Dong Lu, dishes up gigantic bowls of Across-the-Bridge Noodles for just Y5. (Open daily 8am-8pm. ❶)

Another local Kunming dish is **Steampot Chicken** (qìguō jī; 汽锅鸡), chunks of tender chicken and broth that are cooked and presented in brown earthenware pots. **Chuncheng Hotel** (chūnchéng jiǔlóu; 春城酒楼), 11 Dongfang Xi Lu, diagonally opposite a Bank of China, serves this dish for Y30-35 per pot. (☎363 3271. Open daily 7:30-11am, 11:30am-2pm, and 5-8pm. ❸)

MUSLIM CUISINE

Kunming's Hui residents have long inhabited the neighborhood bounded by **Wuyi Lu, Dongfeng Xi Lu,** and **Jinbi Lu.** Parallel to Dongfeng Xi Lu, **Shuncheng Jie** (顺城街) is a vibrant alley filled with Hui restaurants that sport green store fronts with Arabic inscriptions. From Dongfeng Xi Lu, turn at Wuyi Lu, which intersects the road at the Yunnan Provincial Museum, and take the first left. Many stalls serve up

BRIDGE OVER TROUBLED WATERS Kunming's most famous local dish is Across-the-Bridge noodles (guò qiáo mǐ xiàn; 过桥米线), named for a medieval myth from Southern Yunnan. A diligent scholar preparing for the imperial examinations did his cramming on an isolated island, accessible only by a lone wooden bridge. His devoted wife brought him food everyday, but everyday he grumbled that it was cold by the time it reached him. Intent on pleasing her beloved, the woman tried various experiments. One day she discovered that she could keep the soup hot by adding a layer of oil on the top. After crossing the bridge, she would quickly mix all the other ingredients together in the soup, making the perfect meal. This same basic method of preparation continues today. Across-the-Bridge restaurants start patrons off with a selection of finger foods; they are then given bowls of boiling soup, with raw meat and vegetables placed in bowls on the side. It is up to the diners to oversee the cooking of the meat and vegetables in the soup. Prices for Across-the-Bridge Noodles range from reasonably cheap to exorbitant, according to the amount and variety of ingredients spicing up the soup. The delicious taste warrants a taste... or two or three.

spicy noodle soups (Y2-3) and pastries filled with nuts and cream (Y10-20 per kg). The **Kunming Muslim Special Flavor Restaurant** (kūnmíng qīngzhēn fēngwèi'er chéng; 昆明清真风味儿城), 76 Shuncheng Jie, near Wuyi Lu, is the only restaurant in the area with an English menu, however minimal it may be. Skinned white duck (Y18), spiced lamb kebabs (Y20), and flaky, round, sesame-covered sweet pastries (Y4) are favorites. (☎316 8806 or 313 0898. Open daily 11:30am-2pm and 5-9pm. ❷)

DAI CUISINE

One of the few Dai restaurants in town, the **White Pagoda Dai Flavor Restaurant** (bái tǎ dài wèi tīng; 白塔傣味厅), 127 Shangyi Jie, showcases heavily spiced food, often wrapped in banana leaves, grass, or bamboo. Try the house favorite, sticky black rice cooked in pineapple (Y8). Go south on Baita Lu from the intersection with Dongfeng Dong Lu and take the first right; the restaurant is a three-minute walk on the left. (☎317 2932. Open daily 5am-9pm. ❶)

WESTERN FOOD AND BACKPACKER HANGOUTS

Pizza da Rocco (☎362 7951); at the entrance to the Flower and Bird Market, turn left; continue into the market until you see a sign for Rocco's Pizza on the right. Rocco dishes out Italian food so good you'll forget you're in China. Homemade pasta, cheese, and imported wine. Try the tiramisu (Y10). Open daily 6:30am-11pm. ❶

Wei's Pizzeria (hāhā fàndiàn; 哈哈饭店), 400 Tuodong Lu (☎316 6189), a 10min. walk from Beijing Lu. From the Camellia Hotel, turn right. Then, take a left at the Holiday Inn, walk down Baita Lu, and turn right at the Green Lands Hotel; it's up the road, on the right. Good pizza (Y20-30), with a great atmosphere. The clientele is a refreshing mix of locals and foreigners. Open daily 7:30am-midnight. ❷

Golden Bay Western Restaurant (jīnhǎiàn xīcāntīng; 金海岸西餐厅), 60 Cuihu Bei Lu (☎537 9584), behind Cuihu Park's North Gate, has a friendly staff and a wonderfully relaxed air. Impressive selection of Western food (Y8-30) and drinks. Great pizza (Y15-36). Added perks: M 8-10pm buy 2 beers get 1 free; W-Th free fruit platter with orders over Y80; and Su free cup of beer with pizzas Y20 and up. Open daily 10am-midnight. ❷

Louise Bar (lòuyì cānbā; 露易餐吧), 90 Dongfeng Dong Lu (☎313 5018), before the Camellia Hotel but past Baita Lu. The most popular bar in town, now with an English book collection (Y2 per day per book) and a travelers' notebook. Most dishes Y4-15; pizzas Y20-35; beer Y10-30. Open 24hr. ❶

Journey to the East (dōngfāng zhīlǚ; 东方之旅), 15 Tian Jun Dian (☎531 7451), near the Yunda Hotel. Turn right out of Yunnan University Guesthouse and walk up the slope. More like a journey to Kunming's expat community than "to the East." Entrees Y5-15, Internet access Y12 per hr. Kunming's largest international book collection (book rentals Y1 per day). Open daily 8am-late. ❶

SIGHTS

Too many misguided travelers assume that Kunming is just another dull provincial capital, choosing to stop only for a night or two. However, Kunming has plenty of spirit and enough attractions, and its charms stem as much from the general atmosphere as from specific sights. In preparation for the Horticultural Exposition, much of the city was razed; many of the older *hútòng* and large portions of the Vietnamese and Cantonese commercial centers no longer exist. However, enough traditional architecture remains to provide an intriguing contrast to the dizzying scale and speed of Kunming's latest additions.

MUSLIM NEIGHBORHOOD. Approximately 40,000 Hui Muslims live in Kunming. The best remaining examples of Islamic architecture line **Shuncheng Jie,** which runs parallel to and one road south of Dongfeng Xi Lu, just opposite the Provincial Museum. Most older mosques are no longer standing; among the new places of worship is **Nancheng Mosque** (nánchéng qīngzhēn gǔsì; 南城清真古寺), on the corner of Zhengyi Lu and Chongyun Jie. Go north at the large intersection with Zhengyi Lu; the mosque is in an alley just past the Giordano shop. The green minarets and gold Arabic rooftop blaze bright and clear from afar. The first floor is occupied by a canteen; the prayer hall is upstairs. Devotees arrive each day around 1:30pm, particularly on Fridays. The **Yixigong Mosque** (yǐxīgōng qīngzhēn sì; 迤西公清真寺), near the corner of Qingnian Lu and Nanping Jie, just opposite the Bank of Communications, is grandiose and impressive, very different from a typical, delicate Hui mosque.

FLOWER AND BIRD MARKET (huāniǎo shìchǎng; 花鸟市场). Stalls in this sprawling market offer much more than flowers and birds; you can buy practically anything, from carved wooden animals to gerbils, maggots, and plastic cockroaches. The edges of the market, particularly toward the back, are lined with some fine examples of traditional Kunming architecture. Surrounding side streets, such as Jingxing Jie and Wenming Jie, are also dotted with old wooden structures. The shopping mall opposite the market entrance, on Jingxing Jie, has some stunning photographs of Yunnan on the third floor. *(Between Jingxing Jie and Guanghua Jie. Walk north up Zhengyi Lu from the large intersection with Dongfeng Xi Lu, and turn left where a large sign advertises "Jingxing antique and jewelry center." This market blends into the flower and bird market on the right. Plan to spend at least 1-2hr. if you want to cover the entire market.)*

EAST AND WEST PAGODAS (dōngsì tǎ; 东寺塔; and xīsì tǎ; 西寺塔). These twin relics from the Tang dynasty are the oldest standing structures in Kunming. Preserved in small parks, the timeworn gray towers provide a nice backdrop for the timeless art of relaxation. The West Pagoda is easily visible on a street flanked by old red walls; its courtyard is frequented by *mahjong* players and other gamblers. *(The East Pagoda is on Shulin Jie, halfway between Jinbi Lu and Huancheng Nan Lu. The West Pagoda is directly opposite the East Pagoda on Dongsi Jie, which runs parallel to Shulin Jie. Both open daily 7am-8pm. Y0.5 each.)*

YUANTONG TEMPLE (yuántōng sì; 圆通寺). Built over 1000 years ago, this Buddhist temple represents the Mahayana, Theravada, and Tibetan sects. The best time to go is in the early morning or late afternoon, when the ratio of serious worshipers to idle visitors is greatest. *(30 Yuantong Jie, about a 10min. walk from Qingnian Lu away from the stream. ☎517 2881. Open daily 8am-5:20pm. Y5.)*

CUIHU PARK (cuìhú yuán; 翠湖园). Cuihu is a complex of four lakes, the remnants of a swampland that was drained in the 17th century. Today, sculpted gardens, restaurants, and an amusement park all fight for space between the lakes. Even on weekdays, the tree-shaded stone benches overflow with elderly *mahjong* players and kids clamoring for rides on the lake's car-shaped boats (Y20-30 per hr., deposit Y150). More tranquil grounds can be found near the east entrance or directly to the north, across Wenling Jie, on the cool, shady campus of **Yunnan University.** *(Take bus #5 up Dongfeng Lu and get off at Xiaoxi Gate. Continue walking in the same direction; turn right on Cuihu Nan Lu and walk for 10min. to the south entrance. There are also entrances on the east, north, and west sides. ☎363 2081. Open daily 7am-10pm. Y3.)*

YUNNAN PROVINCIAL MUSEUM (yúnnán shěng bówùguǎn; 云南省博物馆). This grand building is an extravagant testament to provincial pride and ethnic diversity. The museum's main draw is on the third floor, an exhibit on textiles, costumes, handicrafts, and artifacts, with life-size mannequins of minority people in costume. The second floor has Neolithic Yunnan bronzeware and Buddhist art. *(At the intersection of Dongfeng Xi Lu and Wuyi Lu. Take bus #5 along Dongfeng Lu to Jinre Gongyuan (近日公园). Continue walking in the same direction; the museum is on the left. ☎361 1551. Open Tu and Th-Su 9am-4:30pm. Y5, students Y2.5.)*

SOUTHWEST

WORLD HORTICULTURAL EXPOSITION GARDEN (shìjiè yuányì bólǎnyuán; 世界园艺博览园). Kunming's 1999 International Horticultural Exposition closed over three years ago, but the grounds remain a prime tourist attraction. Small gardens represent Chinese provinces, Taiwan, and 34 foreign countries (the US garden is a "Texas ranch," complete with cacti and spicy chicken). Unless you really enjoy specimens of unusually large garlic, squash, and plums, the steep entrance fee is probably not worth it. *(In the northeast part of Kunming. Take bus #47, 68, 69, or 72 (Y1). From Beijing Lu, you can also walk up to the intersection with Renmin Lu, turn right onto Renmin Lu, left on Baita Lu, and follow Baita Lu around to the right as it becomes Bailong Lu. Go to the end of Bailong Lu; the entrance is on the right where the road forks. ☎501 2367. Open daily 8am-9pm. Y100, after 2pm Y50; students and teachers Y50.)*

BAMBOO TEMPLE (qióngzhú sì; 筇竹寺). This Zen Buddhist temple, dating from the late 13th century, is famous for its art and architecture. Legend has it that two princes were led by a magical rhinoceros to a group of strange monks on the site of the future temple. The monks left behind walking sticks that managed to arrange themselves into a bamboo grove. The temple's 500 quirky, life-size depictions of *lohans* are to the right of the main courtyard. *(12km northwest of Kunming. Take the bus (30min., leaves when full, Y5) from outside the Yunnan Hotel. Y7.)*

GOLDEN TEMPLE PARK (jīndiàn míngshèng qū; 金殿名胜区). The main attractions here are the **Bell Tower,** which contains China's largest ancient bell, and the **Golden Temple** itself—the largest bronze temple in China. Over 300 years old, the temple was commissioned by Wu San Gui, a military genius who was later named the King of Yunnan. There is also a Daoist and Buddhist temple on the park grounds. *(Take bus #10 or 71. Alternatively, walk toward the Expo Garden and turn left when Bailong Lu forks; turn right at Cuanjin Lu. The park is 15min. away, on the right. You can also enter via cable car from the Expo Garden (Y10 one-way, Y25 round-trip). Open daily 8am-8pm. Y15.)*

OTHER SIGHTS. About 16km from Kunming, accessible by bus #9 or 79 from North Train Station, is **Black Dragon Pool** (hēi lóng tán; 黑龙滩). This restored Ming-dynasty Daoist temple is named for a legendary black dragon whose life was spared by a Daoist immortal in return for its promise to aid mankind. The grounds contain cypresses and flowering trees that bloom in April and May; the botanical garden has even more plant life. *(Open daily sunrise-sunset. Y5.)*

With waters streaming forth at temperatures of around 38°C, **Anning Hot Springs** (ānníng wēnquán; 安宁温泉) has been a favored bathing spot for the Chinese since it was discovered in the Han dynasty. Foreigners have given it lukewarm reviews, however. Across the river and 2km south of the hot springs is **Caoxi Temple** (cáoxī sì; 曹溪寺), a Song-era monastery. A bus leaves from the bus station by the main train station for Anning.

ENTERTAINMENT

Looking for nightime entertainment in Kunming can, at times, be a lost cause. In order to make the city more "presentable" for the 1999 International Horticultural Exposition, local police shut down many of the city's nightspots. Currently, the most popular places are discos in a few major hotels; most party-goers are in their late teens or early 20s.

Camel Bar (luòtuó jiǔbā; 骆驼酒吧), 274 Baita Lu (☎317 6255). A long trek down Baita Lu, but there's live music and plenty of revelers. Drink up (Y12-15) before moving onto the hot dance floor—they don't call this the camel bar for nothing. Open 24hr.

Top One Disco, 329 Baita Lu, in the Bolan Hotel (bólán jiǔdiàn; 博兰酒店; ☎316 2118), and 98 Beijing Lu, in the King World Hotel (jǐnhuá dàjiǔdiàn; 锦华大酒店).

Cute clientele, loud techno. The branch in the Bolan Hotel is currently the more popular spot. Beer Y35 and up. Dress is smart-casual. Open daily 10:30pm-6am.

DAYTRIPS FROM KUNMING

STONE FOREST

*In Lunan Yi Autonomous County, 126km outside Kunming. Express **trains** from Kunming Main Station (90min.; 8:28 and 8:47am, returning at 3:18 and 3:54pm; Y30 round-trip) are the best bet. **Minibuses** (Y2) run to the forest from the station. Minibuses from the Camellia Hotel (30min., Y40 round-trip) depart at 8:30am, stop several times along the way, and return at 3pm; you won't actually arrive at the forest until 1-1:30pm. Minibuses also depart from outside the King World Hotel, on the corner of Beijing Lu and Yongan Lu, but the stopping problem also haunts this option. From the forest, minibuses (Y15) return to Kunming frequently. **Open** 24hr. **Admission** Y55, students Y30.*

A self-designated "wonder of the world," the Stone Forest (shí lín; 石林) covers 11.92km^2. Only one portion—home to the Big and Little Stone Forests—is open to visitors. The forest is a gigantic labyrinth of jagged karst (limestone) pillars, some over 30m high, lashed and split by ice and rain, and eroded to their present form. Formed more than 200 million years ago, some rocks were miraculously distorted into shapes that resemble "a 1000-year-old tortoise, "a baby elephant," or "a stone buffalo," thrilling the not insubstantial community of connoisseurs of rocks-that-look-like-something-else.

The Stone Forest's status as a tourist attraction means that it usually harbors dangerous packs of tour groups. Paths are narrow, making exploration slow and exhausting, and it is difficult to find any place in the main forest that is not crawling with people. For the less harrowing company of stones and some relief from the human circus, take the path to the right at the main fork, which leads to a small and quiet pavilion. Although the forest can be visited as a daytrip, perhaps the most pleasant way is to arrive in late afternoon, stay overnight, and wander around in the morning before the tour bus invasion. The surrounding area is populated by the **Sanyi** minority group, a subgroup of the Yi; many locals sell their wares or are employed as tour guides.

To stay overnight, there are two main options, neither of which are particularly cheap or in any way remarkable. The **Yunlin Hotel** (yúnlín bīnguǎn; 云林宾馆), inside the forest, is a good choice. From the main path, turn right, left, and left again; signs point the way. (☎771 1410 or 771 1058. 6-bed dorms Y30; doubles with bath Y250; triples with bath Y200-250.) The **Shilin Hotel** (shílín bīnguǎn; 石林宾馆) is just past the entrance to the forest, on the left. (☎771 1401. Singles Y200, with A/C Y300; triples Y210, with A/C Y350.)

LAKE DIAN AND THE WESTERN HILLS

*A **minibus** (8am, Y10) runs from the Yunnan Hotel, 128 Dongfeng Xi Lu; to get to the Hotel, take bus #5 along Dongfeng Lu to the stop after the Yunnan Provincial Museum. Or, take **bus** #5 all the way to the end of the line, where you can squeeze onto a crowded #6 to the base of the hills; from here, minibuses run to the Tomb of Nie Er (Y4). Buses also run back down the hill (Y6); many of these will go all the way to the beginning of bus #5. To **bike** to the Western Hills (1½-2hr), take Renmin Xi Lu; bear left when the road forks. The road leads directly to the Western Hills. Take the cable car up, and the ride down should be a breeze. Western Hills Dragon Gate area **open** daily 7am-8pm. **Admission** Y15.*

Lined with small fishing hamlets, **Lake Dian** (diān chí; 滇池) is the largest lake in Yunnan and the sixth largest in China. Many of the sights around Kunming are in fact spots that afford the finest views of the lake. By far the most spectacular view of Lake Dian is from the **Western Hills** (xī shān; 西山), nicknamed **Sleeping Beauty**

Mountain because its resembles a woman reclining. Carved into the craggy cliff faces are Yuan, Ming, and Qing dynasty temples, with a series of grottoes thrown in for good measure. Near the summit, even the most perilous passageways and stone paths have chest-high walls with guard rails.

The area between the Tomb of Nie Er and the top of the mountain is officially known as **Dragon Gate** (lóng mén; 龙门). A chairlift runs from the tomb to the top. *(Runs daily 8:30am-3:30pm. Y20.)* In 1781, the Daoist monk Wu Laiqing, aided only by a hammer, a chisel, and a dream, determinedly chipped a long corridor up the face of the mountain. Legend has it that the tip of his chisel broke as he neared the end of his work (a good 14 years later), throwing him into a fit of despair; in turn, he threw himself into the waters below. Over 50 years later, the monk's followers finally reached a natural cliff-top platform, now called Dragon Gate. Over 2400m high, it commands a breathtaking vista of Lake Dian. A 15-minute climb from Dragon Gate leads to the top of one of the hills, covered with rocks known as the Small Stone Forest, and home to a large pagoda. A 10-minute descent leads to **Sanqing Pavilion** (sānqīng gé; 三清阁). Built in the 14th century as a country retreat for a Yuan dynasty prince, the pavilion was later reincarnated as a Daoist shrine.

SOUTHWEST

The **Tomb of Nie Er** (niè ěr mù; 聂耳墓) is 20 minutes from Sanqing Pavilion, down a path lined with souvenir vendors. A native of Yunnan, Nie Er (1912-1936) composed China's national anthem before drowning en route to the Soviet Union. From the Tomb of Nie Er, buses run to the base of the hills or back to Kunming. However, walking down the hills leads to two more temples. **Taihua Temple** (tàihuá sì; 太华寺) is the next temple down the mountain, about 30 minutes from Nie Er's tomb. Known for its camellia blossoms, Taihua is a Yuan dynasty temple rebuilt during Qing Emperor Kangxi's reign. *(Open daily sunrise-sunset. Y5.)* **Huating Temple** (huátíng sì; 华亭寺) is another 30-minute walk down the main road. Beyond the ornamental lake and garden, the main temple boasts lavishly painted Buddha statues. *(Open daily sunrise-sunset. Y5.)* The mountain base is yet another 30-minute walk.

The **Taihua Mountain Hotel** (tàihuá shān zhuāng; 太华山庄) is about 150m from the entrance. (☎841 1893. Singles Y96; triples Y110. Special group rates available.)

JIUXIANG SCENIC AREA

Transportation options are limited. The East Bus Station, accessible by buses #11, 50, and 63, might have minibuses to Jiuxiang soon. Renting a minibus costs about Y220. Otherwise, try to catch a ride from Transfer International Travel Service (yúnnán shěng jiāotōng zǒng gōngsī; 云南省交通旅行游总公司), 60 Beijing Lu (☎351 4274). Y68.

Not nearly as well known as the Stone Forest but definitely just as amazing a natural wonder, Jiuxiang Scenic Area (jiǔxiāng fēngjǐng qū; 九乡风景区) contains 66 caves, of which only a few are open to the public. Human and other mammalian remains from the Paleolithic Age were discovered in the 1980s, and the caves became a scenic spot in 1989. Despite a heavy human presence (eerie neon lights, camera toting vendors, and exhibits), the Jiuxiang caves maintain a primeval feel. Main attractions include a series of rock terraces that have been dubbed the **Magic Fields** (神田) and a spectacular underground river and waterfall. We recommend that you discover this place before tour groups do.

DALI 大理 ☎0872

Lying between Erhai Lake and the Cangshan mountain range, the charming town of Dali sits on the Yunnan-Myanmar and Yunnan-Tibet trade routes. It served as the capital of the Nanzhao Kingdom from AD 739 to 937, but today, much of the prefecture's economic and political hustle and bustle is centered around the city of Xiaguan. Fortunately, Dali has none of the chaos and pollution of many other Chinese cities. The relaxing atmosphere and laid-back pace of life here have

BORDER CROSSING INTO VIETNAM: HEKOU

Hekou (hékǒu; 河口) is the small town at the Chinese border with Vietnam; on the other side of the border is **Sapa,** an old French hill station populated by Hmong people. The border crossing is actually a small bridge across a river, and border formalities take place on either side. Border officials rarely speak much English, but tend to be friendly on the Chinese side, though many travelers have to pay a small "handling fee" on the Vietnamese side. **Vietnamese visas cannot be obtained at the border crossing.** Some travelers have been able to get them from CITS in Kunming (see p. 595), but it is best not to count on that possibility. **Buses** to Kunming run from the bus station on the main road, Renmin Lu (16-18hr., 10 per day, Y100-120). Chinese time is one hour ahead of Vietnamese—be careful to not the miss the bus. **Trains** to Kunming's North Station leave in the early afternoon (16hr., Y33-77). The first thing most people need to do once in China is change money. The **Bank of China** is at the end of the main road, on the left side on the corner. The bank will not exchange Vietnamese currency for Chinese, but many locals will do so.

Hekou has plenty of **hotels.** One cluster is up the main road, and another cluster is left out of the border office and left again. Dorms go for Y10-40, but many places only have standard rooms (Y100 and up). Key deposits tend to be high. Both the **Tourism Administration of Hekou County** (☎/fax 0873 342 1259) and the **CITS** (☎0873 342 2256; fax 342 1252) are at 9 Renmin Lu.

SOUTHWEST

turned Dali into a backpacker mecca of sorts, where days mysteriously turn into weeks and weeks into months. Despite the nearly constant influx of both Chinese and foreign tourists, Dali rarely feels crowded, and winding backroads and scenic landscapes are only a few minutes away by bike or foot. Dali, home to the Bai people, a branch of the Yi minority, is a mixture of authentic history and contrived "tradition." Travelers eager for the "real" China, a mythical place free of the "damages" of tourism, may be disappointed by Dali's easy expatriate air and keen lookout for colorful pieces of *yuán*.

ORIENTATION AND PRACTICAL INFORMATION

Dali is located between **Lake Erhai** and the **Cangshan Mountains,** 1940m above sea level. The town's historical role as a defense-worthy administrative center is evident from the remnants of stone walls that mark the outer boundaries of the old, square-shaped town. **Fuxing Lu** (复兴路) runs between the **North City Gate** (běi mén; 北门) and the **South City Gate** (nán mén; 南门). **Huguo Lu** (护国路), the coffee- and pizza-laden "foreigner street," branches off from Fuxing Lu.

Buses: Dali Long-distance Bus Station (dàlǐ chángtú qìchē zhàn; 大理长途汽车站), on Dianzang Lu, about 30m from Huguo Lu, just past the No. 4 Guesthouse. Most travel agencies, hotels, and restaurants along Huguo Lu sell tickets and take people to the station. To **Kunming** (4½-5hr.; 11 per day; Y50-105, express Y100-110) and **Lijiang** (5hr.; 34 per day; Y30-35, express Y55). More buses to these and other destinations leave from **Xiaguan**.

Local Transportation: While Old Town Dali itself can be navigated entirely on foot, local buses cover the distance between Dali and nearby Xiaguan. **Buses** (Y1.2) and **minibus #4** (Y1.5) to **Xiaguan** stop frequently along Boai Lu (20min., every 10min.); visitors can easily flag down a minibus (Y2) on Dianzang Lu. For either of these options, turn left off Huguo Lu with Dali behind you, and you will be heading in the correct direction.

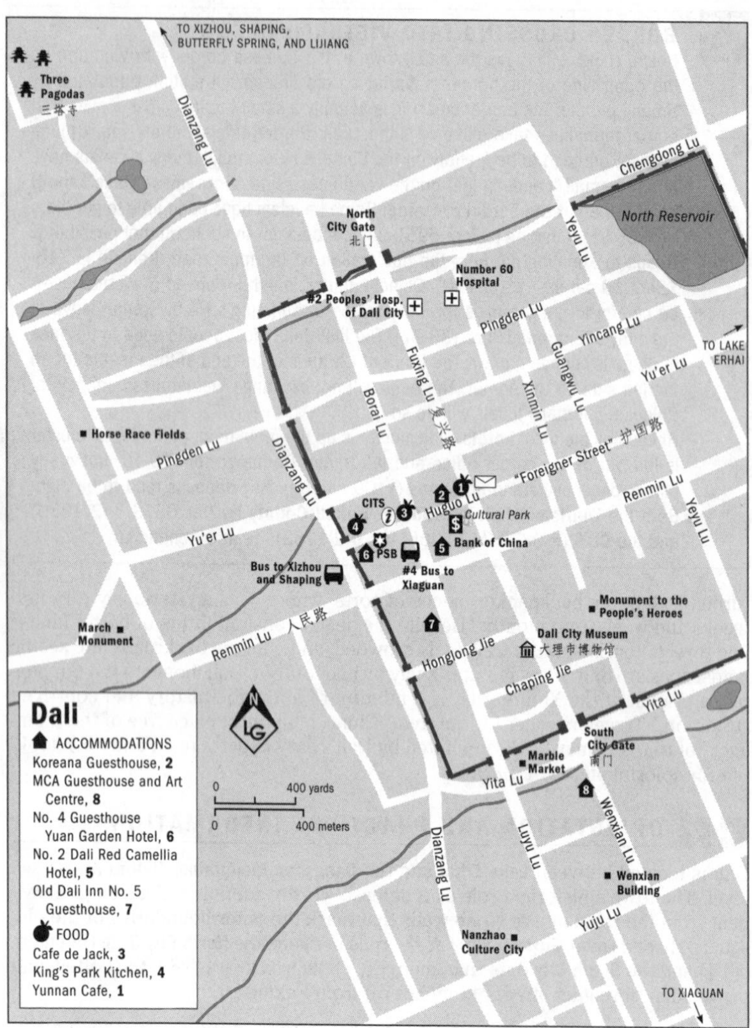

Bike Rental: The high number of rental services keeps prices relatively low and the quality of rentals relatively high. **Michael's,** 44 Boai Lu, next to Michael's Miao Art. Turn left off Huguo Lu with Fuxing Lu behind you. Y3 per hr., Y10 per day. Open daily 8am-8pm. The **No. 4 Guesthouse** on Huguo Lu and the **No. 5 Guesthouse** on Boai Lu have a small selection of bikes. Y10-15 per day.

Travel Agencies: It's not hard to find travel advice or information in Dali. **Dali Travel Information Service Bureau** (dàlǐ lǚyóu xìnxīzìxún fúwù bù; 大理旅游信息咨询服务部; ☎267 1890; mobile 13508 724 012), on Huguo Lu before the Tibetan Cafe. Open daily 7am-9pm. **Dali Travel Center** (dàlǐ gǔchéng kèchē zhōngxīn; 大理古城客车中心; ☎267 1890; mobile 13508 724 197), on the corner of Fuxing Lu and Huguo Lu. Open daily 7am-10pm. Most agencies can arrange travel to local destinations or to Kunming, Lijiang, and Zhongdian; many also provide maps.

Currency Exchange: Bank of China, 304 Fuxing Lu (☎267 0171). Exchanges traveler's checks. Credit card advances. Open daily 8am-7:30pm. The **Industrial and Commercial Bank of China** (zhōngguó gōngshāng yínháng; 中国工商银行; ☎267 0231), also on Fuxing Lu, across from the post office. Exchanges US currency and traveler's checks. Open daily 8am-8:30pm.

PSB: 4 Huguo Lu (☎267 0016), next to the No. 4 Guesthouse. Open M-F 2-5:30pm. Visa extensions available from **Dali PSB Foreign Affairs Office,** on Cangshan Lu in Xiaguan. Prices vary depending on the nationality of the applicant.

Internet Access: Tim's Internet Shop, 82 Boai Lu (☎207 1572), next to Cafe de Jack. Y3 per 10min., Y16 per hr. Open daily 8am-1am. Several shops along Huguo Lu also offer Internet access. The **No. 5 Guesthouse** offers a free email service for guests.

Post and Telecommunications: On the corner of Fuxing Lu and Huguo Lu (☎267 0111). With the mountains behind you, the post office is on the left; China Telecom is on the right. EMS and IDD service. Open daily 8am-9pm. **Postal Code:** 671003.

ACCOMMODATIONS

Most of the cheapest places in backpacker-friendly Dali cluster around Huguo Lu and Boai Lu, near the tourist cafes. All have dormitories (often co-ed), individual rooms, laundry service, and luggage storage.

Old Dali Inn No. 5 Guesthouse (dàlǐ sìjì kèzhàn; 大理四季客栈), 51 Boai Lu (☎267 0382). Attractive rooms and a garden courtyard create an inviting atmosphere. Newly renovated restroom facilities feature blissful Western-style toilets. Bike rental Y15 per day. Free Internet for guests. 24hr. hot water. 4-bed dorms Y10-15; 3-bed dorms Y20; singles Y30; doubles Y50, with TV and bath Y110-115; triples Y20. ❶

No. 4 Guesthouse Yuan Garden Hotel (yú'ān yuán huāyuán lǚshè; 榆安园花园旅社), 4 Huguo Lu (☎267 2093), above Boai Lu and several steps below the intersection with Dianzang Lu, a common stop for minibuses. The guesthouse contains a pretty courtyard where backpackers often lounge about. 24hr. hot water. Free washing machines. Bike rental Y10 per day. 5- to 6-bed dorms Y10; 3- to 4-bed dorms Y15; singles Y30, with bath Y100; doubles Y50, with bath Y100. ❶

MCA Guesthouse and Art Centre, 7000 Wenxian Lu (☎267 3666 or 267 1999), a 5min. walk out of Dali from the South Gate, about 7-8min. from the center of town. No Chinese name; ask for "MC" if you need directions. Run by artists affiliated with the Yunnan School of Art; the 10-bed dorms have been converted into a studio and gallery. Although the remote location can be inconvenient, the MCA seems to have it all, including an outdoor pool (sometimes functional), cafe, book rental (Y2 per day), pool tables, Internet access (Y18 per hr.), and bike rental (Y10 with deposit). 4- to 5-bed dorms Y10; singles Y50; doubles Y50, with bath Y150; triples Y100. ❶

Koreana Garden Cafe and Guesthouse (dàlǐ gāolì tíngcānyǐn; 大理高丽亭餐饮), 115 Huguo Lu (☎266 5083). The Koreana has a prime location, a great Korean restaurant, and a relaxed atmosphere. Friendly staff offers regional travel advice. Dorms Y15-20. ❶

No. 2 Dali Red Camellia Hotel (dàlǐ hóng shān chá bīnguǎn; 大理红山茶宾馆), 32 Huguo Lu (☎267 0423). Dark hallways and a noisy karaoke place next door. Hot water 6-10pm. 5-bed dorms Y10; singles and doubles Y30, with bath Y80; triples Y36. ❶

FOOD

The majority of Chinese restaurants are on **Renmin** and **Yuer Lu.** Most locals grab a *bāozi* (meat or red bean paste filled bun; 包子) for breakfast, but many also head to stands selling fried dough and various—usually spicy hot—sauces wrapped in a grilled rice pancake or rice noodles. Marvelous Muslim food can be found along Fuxing Lu and Renmin Lu; look for Arabic writing or the Chinese characters 清真. Many foreign visitors pounce on the opportunity to enjoy good Western food and head to the cafes and restaurants clustered around **Huguo Lu.** Bearing colorful English signs and menus, these places are hard to miss. Dali has become an increasingly popular destination for Chinese tourists; for these visitors, the Western cafes are the attraction, a place to observe the *lǎowài* in their native habitat.

Yunnan Cafe (yúnnán kāfēiguǎn; 云南咖啡馆), 151 Huguo Lu (☎267 0083), on the left side of Huguo Lu, near Fuxing Lu. Small and peaceful, with a relaxing sun deck, this is a reprieve from the noisy upper end of Huguo Lu. The best Western food around (Y8-18), including the best pizza in town (Y10-20) and a wide range of alcoholic drinks. Try the burger (Y9) or the vegetarian pizza (Y13). The cafe also offers imported books, board games, and magazines. Open daily 8am-10:30pm. ❶

King's Park Kitchen (☎ (136) 1872 0623). Coming from Huguo Lu, turn right at the alley just before the No. 4 Guesthouse. Set back off the street and with a lovely outdoor beer garden, King's Park is the perfect place to enjoy delicious Cantonese cuisine. Be sure to check out the black mushrooms with seasonal spring vegetables (Y12), the stewed beef in *chu-hau* paste (Y15), and the homemade wines (Y5 per glass). ❶

Sunshine Cafe (yángguāng kāfēi; 阳光咖啡), 16 Huguo Lu (☎267 0712). Comfy chairs, a great location, and a friendly staff. The Chinese food tends to be better than the Western. Some customers rave about the homemade bread (Y4-5) and the chocolate brownies (Y6). Dishes Y5-15. Open daily 7:30am-12:30am. ❶

Cafe de Jack (jiékè kāfēiwū; 杰克咖啡屋), 46 Boai Lu (☎267 1572), just left off Huguo Lu, run in conjunction with Tim's Internet Shop next door. The atmosphere de Jack is warm and welcoming; customers are encouraged not to order "complicated dishes" when the place is busy. Dishes Y8-15. Don't miss the clean restrooms. Open daily 8am-1am (or whenever the last customer leaves). ❶

Mr. China's Son (☎267 8234), on Bo'ai Lu. Contrary to premature reports of the owner's death, he is still alive and well. He speaks excellent English and is eager to talk to travelers about Chinese history and the Cultural Revolution. The cafe also has an excellent guidebook for travelers and an interesting collection of Bai "relics" on the side wall. 5- or 6-course Bai meals Y12-14. Open daily 8am-midnight. ❶

SIGHTS

Dali's relaxed atmosphere, unique architecture, and people-watching opportunities are far more impressive than its actual sights. For some non-law-abiding tourists, a certain locally grown herb (dàmá; 大麻) is one of the greatest attractions of Dali. Possession of marijuana is illegal in China; *Let's Go* does not recommend getting wacky with the terbacky. The **North** or **South City Gate** along the Old Town Wall affords good views of the town and Lake Erhai. *(Open daily 9am-7pm. Y2.)* From here, a visitor can get a sense of what it was like back when Dali's strategic importance was not so dependant on Internet cafes and pizza joints. The **Dali Museum** (dàlǐshì bówùguǎn; 大理市博物馆), 111 Fuxing Lu, is, sadly, not at all dedicated to Surrealism. This exceedingly bland collection of historical relics is housed in a far more interesting Bai-style building. *(☎267 0196. Open daily 8:30am-6:30pm. Y8.)* The **Dali Cultural Park** (dàlǐ wénhuà yúan; 大理文化园) is really just a regular old park.

With your back to the mountains, turn right off Huguo Lu; the park is on the right. *(Open 24hr. Free.)*

THREE PAGODAS (sān tǎ sì; 三塔寺). The oldest standing structures in Yunnan, these pagodas have come to symbolize Dali. With Cangshan in the background, the majestic towers stand on a hill an hour beyond the North Gate and are visible from almost any vantage point within Dali and the surrounding area. Erected over 42 years during the Nanzhao era, the original pagodas were destroyed in a fire in the 19th century, and built in 1997. The central **Qianxun Pagoda** stands at 69m, flanked by twin 42m pagodas on either side. From the nearby **Reflection Park** (dàoyìng gōngyuán; 倒映公园) you can see the pagodas reflected in the lake. *(Turn right off Huguo Lu onto Dianzang Lu; follow Dianzang Lu for approx. 1hr. ☎ 267 0179 or 267 1847. Horse tours Y90. Open daily 8am-8pm. Y20; Jianyi Bell Tower Y5. Reflection Park Y5.)*

OTHER SIGHTS. The ride to the avant-garde construction of **Butterfly Spring** (húdié quán; 蝴蝶泉) is beautiful. Legend tells the tale of the star-crossed lovers who threw themselves into the waters in despair; their spirits turned into butterflies and the transformed lovers return each spring to frolic (as lovers are wont to do) at the site of their last union. Despite the romantic legend surrounding the sight, the spring itself is not terribly interesting. *(Buses make the 35min. trip every 20min. starting at 7:30am for Y6. By bicycle, follow Dianzang Lu all the way to the spring; the trip will take about 2½hr. each way. Y20.)* For those who want to go shopping in **Shaping** (shāpíng; 沙坪), the market takes place every Monday morning. By bike, the trip takes about two and a half hours each way; turn right off Huguo Lu onto Dianzang Lu. *(Public buses leave Dali Bus Station on Dianzang Lu to Shaping (20min., every 20min., Y6). Travelers can also book tickets on a tour bus; tours leave at 9am, return at 1:30pm, and cost Y15.)*

THE BAI PEOPLE Numbering between 1.4 and 1.7 million people, the Bai minority live in northwestern Yunnan, clustered around Dali prefecture. Their language is part of the Yi group of the Tibeto-Burmese family and, until recently, had no written form. Although many Bai words are borrowed from Mandarin Chinese, Bai itself is a non-Chinese tonal language with a very different grammatical structure.

The religion of the Bai is similar to that of the southern Chinese, emphasizing local deities and ancestral spirits. Although the Bai maintain their distinct language and dress, their daily practices bear the influence of a long history of contact with the Han Chinese. In the Yuan dynasty, Kublai Khan conquered the Dali kingdom, and the Bai were encouraged to model themselves after Chinese literati. Today, many Bai—even those who are extensively assimilated into Chinese society—make a point of stressing their Bai ancestry to celebrate their distinct cultural heritage as well as to obtain exemptions from the one-child policy, which does not apply to non-Han ethnic groups.

SHOPPING

Shopping is the major Dali pastime. **Huguo Lu** is lined with tailors selling all manner of striped or tie-dyed clothing; if you don't like what they have, many will fill a custom order. Batik shops are also abundant; most batiks (blue tie-dyed or colorfully painted clothes), are made in Guizhou, but Dali is one of the best places in Yunnan to buy them. Peddlers at street stalls push jewelry and small potteries, while Bai women selling silver and embroidery often follow people from restaurant to restaurant; it's a bonanza for knick-knacks of varying charm and uselessness. Just outside the South City Gate is the sprawling **Marble Market,** which has tons of small stalls selling cups, animal figurines, and jewelry made of Dali's famous marble. In fact, the Chinese word for marble, *dàlǐshí* (大理石), literally means "stone of Dali."

DAYTRIPS FROM DALI

Half the joy of the sights around Dali is in getting to them. Whether cycling, taking the bus, walking, or horseback riding, visitors cannot help but be mesmerized by the region's stunning scenery.

CANGSHAN MOUNTAINS

Cangshan Temple can be reached by cable car for Y35, or on horseback for about Y70. A cheaper alternative to the cable car is to take bus #4 (Y5) on Boai Lu going toward Xiaguan to Gantong Temple. From there, take one of the many horse carriages or small vans (30min., Y5) to the foot of the mountain. Hiking from Gantong Temple to Zhonghe Temple takes 6-8hr., and the path is not clearly marked. Ask at a travel agency in Dali for a more detailed map. Admission to the temples is free; other sights Y6-10.

The Cangshan Mountains (cāng shān; 苍山) surrounding Dali offer more than just pleasant scenery. For the many monks and nuns who reside on these spectacular hills, they are also a place for religious worship and retreat. The most touristy sight is **Cangshan Temple,** which offers a stunning view of Lake Erhai and the surrounding area. From Cangshan, visitors can walk along a flat road north (the left, facing away from the mountains) to **Zhonghe Temple** (zhōnghé sì; 中和寺), or head off in the opposite direction to **Gantong Temple** (gǎntōng sì; 感通寺). If you arrive around noon, you can join the residents for a vegetarian meal. From the Gantong Temple it is a 10-minute trek to **Jizhao Monastery** (jìzhào ān; 寂照庵), where eight nuns and monks reside.

WASE

A tourist boat (leaves 9:30am, returns 4pm; Y20) shuttles between Dali and Wase. If you want to leave later in the day, many local Dali street merchants will offer to take you; it will cost more (Y30-50), but there will be fewer foreigners at the market at that time. For tourist boats exploring other parts of Lake Erhai, inquire at the Yuxing Tourist Office. Most trips take 6hr. and cost Y20-50.

The **market** in Wase (wāsè; 挖色), held every five days from the 5th to the 25th of each month, is your "typical" Bai market—teeming with life and confusion. The area near Lake Erhai's shore is the market square, where Bai merchants in traditional dress ply their peaches, rice noodles, household goods (including rat poison), and live fowl. A walk into the town offers a great opportunity to explore the small streets and local architecture. The public ferry no longer runs, but tourist boats ply the route across Lake Erhai, usually taking in sights such as **Minor Putuo Island** (xiǎo pǔtuó; 小普陀), **Tianjing Pavilion** (tiānjìng gé; 天境阁), and **Sea Island** (hǎi dǎo; 海岛). Or bike to Wase in just over four hours and meander through lakeside Bai villages. If you get stuck in Wase, stay in the **Wase Hostel** (wāsè zhāodàisuǒ; 挖色招待所). Turn left out of the market square with your back to the lake and go as far along the road as you can, following it as it turns right; the hostel is the last building on the right, before the PSB. (Dorms Y10.) If you miss the Wase market, you can still take a trip on **Lake Erhai** that visits some of the major sites around the lake; inquire at local travel agencies.

XIZHOU VILLAGE

***Buses** (30min., every 30min., Y3) leave from the Dali Bus Station. Many buses go along this route; ask to be dropped at Xizhou when you get on the bus or when buying your ticket. There are 2 attractive routes for **biking** to Xizhou (2hr. one-way). To take the low road, follow Fuxing Lu out through North Gate. If it's hot, take the high road along Dianzang Lu; the road is a little* *uneven, but the trees offer some shade. Both taking the bus and cycling along Dianzang Lu will land you at a large sign (in English) pointing to Xizhou. After a bumpy 5min. cycle ride or a 15min. walk along this cobbled path, cross the road and continue in the same direction. Arrows direct you to the main square.*

Xizhou (xǐzhōu zhèn; 喜洲镇), a military stronghold during the Nanzhao Kingdom, retained enough wealth to build huge houses whose crumbling remains remind visitors of the town's glorious past. The road to Xizhou, revealing fresh green rice paddies and the majestic Cangshan Mountains in the background, can be more of an attraction than the town's rather contrived display of Bai culture. The special sight here is **Yan's Big Courtyard** (yánjiā dàyuàn; 严家大院), in the main square. The Yans were rich industrialists who left China during the Cultural Revolution. Their massive house now offers a Bai cultural experience of traditionally clad dancers and singers performing while the "trilogy tea of the Bai clan" (named for its three flavors: bitter, sweet, and spicy) and Bai bread are served. Performances start once enough people show up. *(Open daily 8am-6pm. Y4; Y20 for meal and performance.)*

From Xizhou main square, a 20-minute walk through the rice fields, following the sign to Shiping Jie (市坪街), leads to the **Haixin Pavilion** (hǎixīn tíng; 海心亭). *(Open daily 8am-midnight. Free.)* While the pavilion itself is unspectacular, the path leading to it is picturesque. The **Xizhou Tianzhuang Hotel** (dàxǐzhōu tiánzhuāng bīnguǎn; 大喜州田庄宾馆), on Shiping Lu, is housed in a grand Bai building, and has rooms arranged around a lush courtyard. (☎245 1515. 24hr. hot water in good weather, 8-11pm otherwise. 5-bed dorms Y30; doubles Y60.)

SOUTHWEST

XIAGUAN 下关 ☎0872

At the mouth of Lake Erhai and at the foot of the Cangshan mountains, Xiaguan should have been named China's "windy city." The combination of mountains and lake makes the wind literally howl in this capital of Dali Bai Autonomous County, especially at night. Most use Xiaguan as a base for exploring nearby Jizushan, a sacred Buddhist site, or as a regional transportation hub. It's no wonder Xiaguan's name can mean "inferior pass"; it is a town for drifters, with no character, no local sites of interest, and a somewhat resentful populace.

ORIENTATION AND TRANSPORTATION

Xiaguan is sometimes referred to as **Dali City** (dàlǐ shì; 大理市) and should not be confused with Dali, the intended destination of many travelers who pass through Xiaguan. Virtually all major establishments in Xiaguan are on **Jianshe Lu** (建设路).

Flights: The new **Dali Airport** (dàlǐ jīchǎng; 大理机场; ☎216 6771 or 216 8288) is 16km outside Xiaguan and accessible only by taxi (Y20-30). To **Jinghong** (daily, Y520) and **Kunming** (3 per day, Y340). Purchase tickets in one of Dali's many travel agencies, or at the **Dali Travel Ticket Center** (dàlǐ lǚyóu piàowù zhōngxīn; 大理旅游票务中心), Dali Hotel, 1 Jianshe Xi Lu, 1st fl. (☎216 6588; fax 216 6578), at Renmin Lu, in Dali.

Trains: Dali Train Station (dàlǐ zhàn; 大理站; ☎219 1660), is 2km away from the intersection of Jianshe Xi Lu and Renmin Lu. Take bus #1 from Jianshe Lu, going away from the Cangshan mountains. To **Kunming** (9hr., daily, Y60-70).

Buses: Xiaguan has three bus terminals, all on Jianshe Lu within 10min. of each other. For information on buses to Jizushan, see below.

Dali Long-distance Bus Station (dàlǐ qìchē kèyùn zhàn; 大理汽车客运站; ☎218 9330), a modern building near the intersection of Jianshe and Renmin Lu. To: **Baoshan** (5½hr., 5 per day, Y19-26); **Kunming** (express: 4½hr., every 30min. 7:30-9:30am and every hr. 10:30am-8pm, Y90-110; regular: 7hr., every hr. 7:30am-5:40pm, Y50-70); **Lijiang** (4hr., 4 per day, Y25-50); **Ruili** (sleeper bus 12hr., daily, Y93); **Zhongdian** (8hr., 2 per day, Y82).

Bus Station of Dali Prefecture (dàlĭzhōu kèyùn zhàn; 大理州客运站; ☎217 4621), the only station with an English sign, diagonally across from the Dali Long-distance Bus Station. To: **Baoshan** (5hr., 2 per day, Y25); **Jinghong** (24hr., daily, Y140); **Kunming** (4hr., 12 per day, Y70); **Lijiang** (3hr., 6 per day 7-11:30am, Y25-50); **Ruili** (12hr., 2 per day, Y69-90).

Xiaguan Long-distance Bus Station (xiàguān qìchē kèyùn fúwù zhàn; 下关汽车客运服务站), 50 Jianshe Lu (☎212 5631, ext. 202), opposite the 35108 Military Service Station, the former Nanzhao Hotel. To: **Baoshan** (5hr., 5 per day, Y26); **Kunming** (4½hr., 27 per day, Y50-83); **Ruili** (12hr., 3 per day, Y65-90); **Zhongdian** (7hr., 2 per day, Y42-55).

Local Transportation: To get to Dali, take **bus #4** from the main station at Renmin and Jianshe Lu (20min., every 10min., Y1.2). Bus stops along Jianshe Lu are marked with yellow signs. Slower **minibuses,** also marked #4, ply the same route (Y1.5).

SOUTHWEST

ACCOMMODATIONS AND FOOD

It is usually better to take the bus to Old Dali than to put up with Xiaguan's relatively expensive accommodations and painful lack of character. However, if circumstances necessitate a night in Xiaguan, there are two fairly cheap hotels near the bus stations. **Xiaguan Hotel ❶** (xiàguān fàndiàn; 下关饭店), 1 Renmin Lu, on the corner of Jianshe and Renmin Lu, has basic rooms with nominally 24hr. hot water. (☎217 4933; fax 216 8889. Doubles Y80; triples Y60.) **Keyun Hotel ❶** (kèyùn fàndiàn; 客运饭店), 24 Jianshe Lu, next to Dali Long-distance Bus Station, has hot water available from noon to midnight. (☎212 5286. 4-bed dorms Y6; singles Y14-26; doubles Y25; triples Y24.) The sidestreets winding around Xiaguan feature tiny cubicled restaurants serving up savory local specialties.

HIKING NEAR XIAGUAN: JIZUSHAN MOUNTAIN

Towering 3240m over northwestern Binchuan County in the Dali Prefecture, Jizushan Mountain (jīzúshān; 鸡足山) has been a sacred Buddhist site ever since Jiaye, a famed disciple of the Sakyamuni Buddha, took up residence there. By the Qing dynasty, 36 temples and 72 nunneries flourished on the mountain. Now recovering from the devastation of the Cultural Revolution, the mountain and its ancient structures offer breathtaking views. While simply trekking around the mountain is rewarding in itself, there are also several sights, including **Zhusheng Temple** (zhùshèng sì; 祝圣寺), historically the most prominent of the temples, and **Jinding Temple** (jīndĭng sì; 金顶寺), at the very peak of Jizushan. The trip to the top is costly; admission is Y40, and most shell out Y25 for horses to get to the **cable lift** (Y22) at **Huideng Nunnery** (huìdēng ān; 慧灯庵), and more still if the cable car isn't working. In the rainy summer months, the ascent takes about two hours by horse and cable car; on foot it takes 30 minutes more.

Basic dorm accommodations are available at **Jinding Temple Zonghe Hostel** (jīndĭng sì zōnghé lōudài; 金顶寺宗合楼待), next to Jinding Temple. (☎935 0060. 4-bed dorms Y15.) If you don't make it to the top before nightfall or before the frequent rainstorms, there are cheap rooms (Y10 per bed) above many restaurants near the Jizu Shan Hotel, next to four gold cranes preening in a pool.

Buses go from Xiaguan's Dali Bus Station (dàlĭ kèyùn zhōngxīn; 大理客运中心) on Huangcheng Dong Lu to **Binchuan** (2½hr., last bus 7pm, Y20) and from Binchuan to the foot of Jizushan (1hr., last bus 6:30pm, Y10). The last bus to Xiaguan from Jizushan leaves at 7pm. The **Guesthouse of Binchuan No. 12 ❶** (bīnchuān bīnguăn; 宾川宾馆) is the main hostel for foreigners in Binchuan. Turn left out of the bus station and left again at the intersection; the hotel is up the road on the left. (☎714 1323. 3-bed dorms with TV Y12.)

LIJIANG 丽江

☎0888

The topography of Lijiang Naxi Autonomous Prefecture ranges from gently rolling plains to the highest mountain ranges south of the Yangzi, and the area's inhabitants are just as varied, with 22 ethnic minority groups. Activity centers around the prefectural seat, also called Lijiang, a city distinguished by an intricate system of narrow waterways and canals, all set at an elevation of 2400m. In 1996, an earthquake measuring 7.0 on the Richter scale devastated Lijiang, leveling the old part of town. Since then, for better or for worse, a replica of the original old town has been built, and Lijiang has become a UNESCO World Heritage Site. Some decry the faux antique, tourist-trap atmosphere of the old town, but off the main drags, the tourist shops dwindle, the well-worn cobblestone back alleys take on the musty air of centuries past, and traditional Naxi-style architecture remains authentic. It is here that the mysterious force of the Naxi's Dongba religion, with its synthesis of sorcery, medicine, and philosophy, is still palpable.

TRANSPORTATION

Flights: Lijiang Airport (lìjiāng jīchǎng; 丽江机场; ☎517 0987 or 512 8088), 26km from the city. Buses leave from the **Yunnan Airlines ticket office** (zhōnggúo yúnnán lìjiāng shòupiào chù; 中国云南丽江售票处; ☎516 1291), at the intersection of Yunshan Zhong Lu (known as Xueshan Zhong Lu by the locals) and Fuhui Lu. **CAAC ticket office** (☎512 0280), on the corner of Xin Dajie. Open daily 8:30am-noon and 2:30-5:30pm. All interprovincial flights go through Kunming. To **Jinghong/Xishuangbanna** (1-2 per day, Y610) and **Kunming** (3-4 per day, Y420).

Buses: Neither of the 2 main bus stations has service to Baoshan or Chengdu. To get to **Baoshan,** take the bus to Xiaguan and then catch another bus there. To get to **Chengdu,** take the bus to the railhead of Jinjiang/Panzhihua and then take a train.

Main Long-distance Bus Station (lìjiāng kèyùn zhàn; 丽江客运站; ☎512 2187 or 512 1106), at the far end of Minzhu Lu. Turn left out of the old town, and left after the post office on Minzhu Lu. To: **Jinjiang/Panzhihua** (8hr., 7 per day, Y43.5); **Kunming** (9hr., 9 per day, Y105.5-115.5); **Xiaguan** (5hr., 20-30 per day, Y31.5 or Y50.9); **Zhongdian** (6hr., 7 per day, Y27).

North Bus Station (běi qìchē zhàn; 北汽车站; ☎518 9141), on Xin Dajie, just past Mao Square, on the same side as the Lijiang International Ethnic Cultural Exchange Center. Buses leaving from this station are marked "Guluwan" (古路湾), the more common name of the bus station. Bus tickets can be bought opposite the train station. Ticket office open daily 6am-7pm. To: **Daju** (3hr., 3-5 per day, Y23); **Jinjiang/Panzhihua** (8hr., 5 per day, Y43-62); **Kunming** (9hr., 6 per day, Y115-155); **Xiaguan** (5hr., 12 per day, Y29.5-50); **Zhongdian** (6hr., 5 per day, Y21-29) via **Qiaotou** (2½hr., Y15).

Local Transportation: Several local **buses** crisscross the new city. From Xin Dajie, near Mao Square, bus **#7** (every hr. 8am-6pm) heads to Baisha (Y6) and Jade Dragon Mountain (Y8). Bus **#1** (every 15min. 7am-9 or 10pm, Y0.8-1) stops at the South Bus Station and on Fuhui Lu and Xin Dajie, near the entrance to the Old City.

Bike Rental: Hordes of small shops in Mao Square rent bikes for Y7-10 per day. The **Prague Cafe** also has a modest selection. Y15 per day.

Taxis: A flat fare of Y6 can usually get you anywhere in the city.

ORIENTATION AND PRACTICAL INFORMATION

Lijiang is divided into two very distinct entities: the New and Old Towns. The **New Town** (xīn chéng; 新城) is still under construction. Most visitors encounter the stretch of **Xin Dajie** (新大街) from the entrance of the Old Town to Black Dragon Fountain Park, via **Mao Square** and the bus station. **Minzhu Lu** (民主路) runs from the Old Town to the South Bus Station. The **Old Town** (gǔ chéng; 古城) tries just as hard to preserve (and, in some cases, commercialize) history as the New Town tries to disregard it.

Travel Agencies: There is certainly no dearth of travel agencies or travel advice in Lijiang. **Lijiang CITS Reception Center** (☎512 3508), on Xin Dajie, just past Mao Square on the right. Very friendly staff can help arrange travel to just about anywhere in the area. Open daily 7:30am-10pm. **Yak Travel** (lìjiāng máoniúpíng lǚyóu suǒdào yǒuxiàn gōngsī; 丽江牦牛坪旅游索道有限公司; ☎512 4099; fax 516 1649), on Sifang Jie in the Old Town. Attendants may not speak much English, but they can arrange for guides and bus tickets and have the best maps in town.

Currency Exchange: Bank of China, opposite and to the left of the South Bus Station. Exchanges traveler's checks. Open daily 8am-5:30pm. A more convenient branch on Xin Dajie at Fuhui Lu, just opposite the Chinese Construction Bank. Exchanges traveler's checks. **ATM**s. Open daily 8:30am-7pm. **Industrial and Commercial Bank,** on Dong Dajie, near the entrance to Market Square, exchanges traveler's checks and US, Hong Kong, and Japanese currencies. **ATM.** Open in summer daily 8am-5pm; in winter 8:30am-5pm.

Bookstore: Xinhua Bookstore, on Xin Dajie, at the turn into the Old Town. Small supply of English books plus some maps of Lijiang and Yunnan. Open daily 8:30am-9:30pm. Travelers' cafes in the Old Town often do book exchanges as well.

PSB: Near the South Bus Station, up the 1st right alley on Nanguojing Lu (☎512 1567). This office, despite its room for foreign visitors, is next to useless. Visit the more helpful prefectural office on Fuhui Lu (☎512 5318). Grants up to 2 one-month visa extensions. Open daily 8am-noon and 2:30-6pm.

Hospitals: Lijiang District Hospital (lìjiāng dìqū yīyuàn; 丽江地区医院; ☎512 1545, emergency 512 2393 or 512 2335), on Fuhui Lu. Minimal English spoken. **Lijiang County People's Hospital** (lìjiāng xiàn rénmín yīyuàn; 丽江县人民医院; ☎512 2871), on Changshui Lu, near the South Bus Station.

Internet Access: Most hostels and cafes in the Old Town offer access; the average rate is Y15 per hr. The **Prague Cafe** charges Y5 per hr., and the **Blue Page Vegetarian Restaurant** offers 30 free min. with a purchase of Y15 or more. Otherwise, Y8 per hr.

Post and Telecommunications: The main **post office** is on Minzhu Lu. Turn left out of the Old Town, and then left again; the post office is on the right. EMS. IDD service. Open daily 8am-8pm. The branch on Dong Dajie also offers IDD service. Facing the Old Town, follow the street on the right; the post office is on the left, opposite the Industrial and Commercial Bank. Open daily 8am-10pm. **Postal Code:** 674100.

ACCOMMODATIONS

Prices are roughly the same in the Old and New Towns; most travelers prefer to stay in the Naxi-style Old Town, five minutes from the North Bus Station. Most guesthouses have 24hr. hot water and prices usually begin around Y20 per bed.

Prague Cafe Guesthouse, 80 Xinyi Jie, Mishi Xiang (☎512 3757), diagonally across from Mama Fu's. The closest thing to a "home away from home," the Prague has everything: Internet access, a good restaurant, luggage storage, bike rental, laundry (Y10 per load), over 100 DVDs from which to choose, travel information, and a friendly English-speaking staff. 4-bed dorms Y10; singles Y60; doubles Y40; triples Y20. ❶

Sakura Cafe Guesthouse (☎512 5179 or 518 7619). Go to the Sakura Cafe on Xinhua Jie and ask to be taken to the guesthouse. An excellent deal. Rooms overlook a quiet courtyard. Clean 4-bed dorms Y10; doubles Y40; triples Y45. ❶

SOUTHWEST

First Bend Inn (dìyīwān jiǔdiàn; 第一湾酒店), 43 Mishi Xiang (☎518 1688 or 518 1073), off Xinyi Jie. As you go into the Old Town, veer left onto Xinyi Jie and keep going past Lamu's House of Tibet and the MCA Guesthouse. A peaceful courtyard and comfortable beds, along with excellent maps and information for Tiger Leaping Gorge trekkers. 4 days free luggage storage. Hot water 8-10am and 6-10pm. 4-bed dorms Y20; 3-bed dorms Y30; singles Y80; doubles Y40. ❶

Yizhou Inn (yízhōu kèzhàn; 怡舟客栈), 3 Wuyi Jie (☎512 7439). Follow Xinyi Jie past Mama Fu's until the bridge on the right. Turn left; the inn is 3min. ahead on the left, marked by a blue and white banner on the right. This quiet guesthouse is about as close as you can get to living with a Naxi family, but the owners only speak minimal English. Spartan rooms are immaculate and comfortable. 4-bed dorms Y15; singles Y25-30. ❶

Huang Family Flower Inn (huáng jiā huāyuán kèzhàn; 黄家花园客栈), 29 Xinyi Jie, Jishan Xiang (☎512 8679; mobile 1390 888 3030). Take the left lane when you enter the Old Town; when you reach the courtyard in front of the MCA, follow the road around the grilled piglet restaurant until you see the red and white banner about 1min. ahead. A lovely and clean Naxi home, away from the tourist rush. Non-English speaking owners. 4-bed dorms Y20-30; doubles Y50-70; triples Y25-35. ❶

FOOD

Vendors in the Old Town steam, fry, and grill an inviting selection of local delicacies, including **baba** (fried Naxi flatbreads), noodle soups, hotpot pork, and rice dishes. Anyone craving travel advice, the company of foreigners, or just some steak and chocolate cake can head to the gaily marked cafes that line **Jishan Xiang, Mishi Xiang,** and **Market Square.**

Sakura Cafe (yīnghuā kāfēi; 樱花咖啡; ☎518 7619), on Minzhu Lu. Upon entering Market Square, take the first right, and the first right again; walk parallel to the way you came. Run by an amiable Lijiang resident and his Korean wife, this comfy spot has great Korean food (Y5-18), apple pie (Y5), and Naxi food (Y6-15). Internet access Y15 per hr. Free movies. Open daily 7am until the last customer leaves. ❶

Lamu's House of Tibet (xīzàng wū; 西藏屋; ☎518 9000), on Xinyi Jie, not far past the entrance to the Old Town. A favorite with many travelers. Fabulous Tibetan food (Y6-15), especially the *momos* (Y8), served in a lovely bamboo structure with a garden. Open in summer daily 7am-midnight; in winter 8:30am-midnight. ❶

Mama Fu's Restaurant (māmāfù cāntīng; 妈妈傅餐厅), 76 Xinyi Jie, Mishi Xiang (☎512 2285), with outdoor tables overlooking the canal. The Chinese food tends to taste better than the Western food. Try the Kungpao Chicken (gōngbào jīdīng; 宫保鸡丁; Y10) and the chrysenthemum tea (Y4). Open daily 9am-12:30am. ❶

Blue Page Vegetarian Restaurant, 69 Mishi Xiang (☎518 5206), down the street from First Bend Inn, toward Market Square. A vegetarian restaurant with friendly, English-speaking staff and Internet access. Try the Chinese vegetable burger (Y12) or the cheese burrito (Y8). Open daily 8am-midnight. ❶

Big Stone Bridge Restaurant (dàshíqiáo huǒtuǐchǎofàn fàndiàn; 大石桥火腿炒饭饭店; ☎512 9866), on Xin Dajie, next to Xinhua Bookstore. Locals flock here for the hotpot (Y6) and *mǐxiàn* (rice noodle soup; 米线; Y3). The central location is great for people-watching. Open daily 7am-10pm. ❶

SIGHTS AND ENTERTAINMENT

The old town's winding cobbled streets, traditional Naxi houses with intricate wooden facades, and women in Naxi dress make wandering through Lijiang an activity in its own right. Head away from the main streets to get away from the gift shops; getting lost can be quite rewarding. Be forewarned, however, that due to the recent tourism boom, the price of admission to tourist sights has also boomed.

DAYAN NAXI MUSIC ASSOCIATION (dàyánnàxī gǔyuèhuì; 大研纳西古乐会). Word has it that this Naxi music is actually very similar to ancient Han music, as the Naxi minority has historically appropriated Han styles as part of attempts at assimilation. The music is haunting, and the charismatic director of this association, Xuan Ke, spices up his introduction of the orchestra, the music, and himself with provocative social commentary (although these witticisms are rarely translated into English). The performance also features wonderful displays of folk songs. For a more folk-flavored show, many tourists choose to go to the **Dongba Music House** (Y35), directly across the street. *(On Dongda Jie. Don't worry about missing the place—there's a large sign right outside the door, and every night you'll see countless people waiting there. ☎512 7971 or 4559. Performances nightly 8pm. Y40-50.)*

BLACK DRAGON POOL PARK (hēi lóng tán gōngyúan; 黑龙潭公园). Here you will find numerous Dongba art galleries, temples, and gardens along with the small lake that is the park's namesake. Most pictures of Jade Dragon Snow Mountain are taken from here. Visitors can spend a worthwhile, relaxing day here, despite the high entrance fee. For a little adventure, you can make the one-hour climb up **Elephant Hill** (xiàng shān; 象山), where a spectacular view awaits. Women may want to exercise particular caution in this area. *(Take a left out of the Old Town, and then a right onto Xin Dajie; follow Xin Dajie 15min. to its end. For a more scenic route, follow the stream out of the Old Town. Cross the bridge on your left just before the small waterfall; bear left when the road forks, and follow it to the end. The museum entrance is 20m to the right. Open daily 7am-9pm. Y20; some travelers report being able to get in free before 7am.)*

LION HILL (shīzi shān; 狮子山). Both the hill and the wooden structure called **Wangulou** (wàngǔ lóu; 万古楼) provide good views of the Old Town and the surrounding countryside, although few travelers find the trip worthwhile. *(Walk up the street to the right of CC's Bar and look for signs to take a left to Wangulou. The round-trip walk takes under 1hr. Open daily 8am-6pm. Climbing Lion Hill is free; Wangulou admission Y15.)*

WOULD THE REAL SHANGRI-LA PLEASE STAND UP? "Shangri-La," in a Zhongdian dialect of Tibetan, means "the slope leading to the land of the sun and moon in my heart." British author James Hilton based his novel *The Lost Horizon* (1933) on this mysterious, hidden Eden in Southwest China. The fanciful have long sought this surreal town, supposedly tucked away in the mountains between Tibet and Yunnan. Part of Shangri-La's magic is that it is a place of eternal youth; natives who left quickly aged and died.

In 1997, a team of investigators sent by the Chinese government officially declared Deqin Prefecture (the area around Zhongdian, see p. 619) to be the lost Eden described by Hilton. More recently, Lijiang (p. 611) and Daocheng (in Sichuan) have both been contending with Zhongdian for the title of the "true Shangri-La." However, every town in the area attempts to rake in tourist dollars with claims of being the Shangri-La on which Hilton's book was based. A debate has ensued between cynics and romantics; the former search for physical evidence of such a place, while the latter insist that Shangri-La is not a specific place but rather a paradise in the heart that could exist anywhere.

SOUTHWEST

DAYTRIPS FROM LIJIANG

JADE DRAGON SNOW MOUNTAIN

35km north of Lijiang. Take bus #7 (30min., every hr., Y8) from Baixin Department Store on Xinda Jie. Open daily 8:30am-4:30pm. Admission to National Park Y40.

Jade Dragon Snow Mountain (yùlóng xǔeshān; 玉龙雪山) is the dramatic 5596m peak that appears in virtually every postcard of the area. After staring at the peak every day you spend in Lijiang, it would certainly be a shame to miss the chance to go up it. Two cable cars ascend the mountain: the shorter lift (Y40) ends at **Donkey Meadow,** where you may get to see pretty shrubbery and Naxi dancing; the longer, more worthwhile lift (Y110) is one of China's longest cable car rides. At the top is a short but exhausting walk to a viewing platform; those who suck up the financial and physical abuse of the trip are rewarded with spectacular views. The fact that hawkers at the peak sell oxygen pillows (Y20-30) instead of the usual tacky trinkets is perhaps a bit alarming, but some climbers have no difficulty with the altitude and even manage to get some mileage out of the karaoke machine in the tea house, where at least they have an excuse for sounding like strangled monkeys. (For information on trekking in Tiger Leaping Gorge, across the Yangzi from Jade Dragon Snow Mountain, see below.)

SOUTHWEST

BAISHA

About 8km north of Lijiang. From Fuhui Lu or from the market right outside the Old Town, take a farm truck (Y2) marked 龙泉 (lóngquán) or 白沙 (báishā). There are two biking routes; for both, cycle along Xin Dajie and take a left where the road forks. Follow this flat road until you come to the sign that says "Shabai"; it points you down a dirt path leading right to the village. Or, turn left down any of the dirt paths off the main road and right onto another dirt path, which will lead to Baisha.

The small village of Baisha (báishā; 白沙) is best known for its frescoes. **Fuguo Monastery** (fùguó sì; 福国寺) holds scores of large frescoes of Tibetan-Buddhist, Daoist, and Han origins. The damage to the frescoes is more often due to violence during the Cultural Revolution than to natural decay. Naxi girls sometimes dance and sing in the courtyards. (Open daily 7am-8pm. Y8.) The old house around the corner, with Mao quotation wall graffiti from the 60s and 70s still visible, is one of the few unrenovated buildings that visitors are allowed to enter. Perhaps more famous than the frescoes, Dr. Ho, the "Daoist physician" made famous by travel writer Bruce Chatwin, also calls Baisha home. You may encounter him near his office, in a slightly dirtied white coat, strolling along the main street. For a small sum, he'll show you newspaper cuttings documenting his international fame as you sip his special blend of herbal tea.

To reach the **Dragon Springs** (lóng quán; 龙泉) and explore a typical Naxi village, follow the main road (identifiable by the newspaper clippings proclaiming Dr. Ho's fame) for 25 minutes by bike or 45 on foot. Go through a village and across some fields, cross the river, and look for a small building at the end of the road.

TIGER LEAPING GORGE 虎跳峡

Tiger Leaping Gorge (hǔ tiào xiá), named for the legend of a hunted tiger that leapt across the stone abyss to escape its pursuer, has become a sort of backpacker's rite of passage—a ready source of conversation and the topic of innumerable entries in travelers' notebooks. Indeed, Tiger Leaping Gorge deserves all the attention it gets. The gorge lies at the point where **Haba Snow Peak** (hābā xǔeshān; 哈巴雪山) shoots up to face the Jade Dragon Snow Mountain over the swift

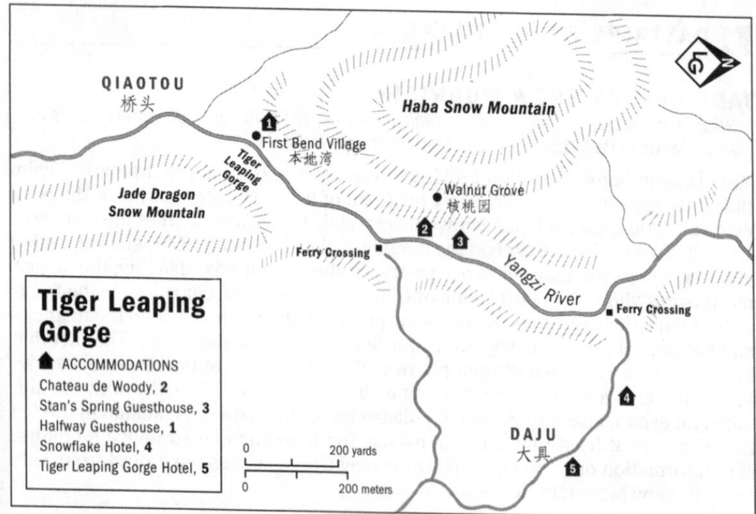

waters of the fledgling Yangzi River. Still known as the Jinsha (Gold Sand) River, it has chiseled out one of the deepest and most breathtaking gorges in the country. The 35km-long and 12km-wide gorge, the southernmost glacial mountain in China, marks the northern boundary of Lijiang Prefecture. Shanzidou, the summit of the surrounding peaks, stands a lofty 5600m above sea level. At its narrowest point, the gorge spans barely 30m.

TREKKING AROUND TIGER LEAPING GORGE

The hike is challenging and not for the faint-of-heart or out-of-shape. Leave large packs in Lijiang, and bring water and snacks. During the rainy season, the trek can be particularly treacherous; flooding and mudslides are not uncommon, and sometimes particularly nasty rains force travelers to spend more time in the gorge than they had originally anticipated. Plan wisely, but remain flexible; the situation for gorge trekkers is in constant flux. Ask other travelers what they have done and talk to locals in cafes before setting off. Many local guesthouses and restaurants may underestimate the length of time it will take to get to the next stopping point. The best places to get information include the **Prague Cafe** and **First Bend Inn** (see **Lijiang,** p. 612). The best **trekking map** of the gorge, by the Scottish engineering mapper Neil McLean, is available at First Bend Inn (Y1). Tiger Leaping Gorge is bounded on one side by the town of **Qiaotou** (qiáotóu; 桥头) and on the other by **Daju** (dàjù; 大具). **First Bend Village** (běndìwān; 本地湾) and **Walnut Grove** (hétáo yuán; 核桃园) villages lie in between. (Admission to the gorge is Y30. Some travelers have reported that security is lax near dawn.)

DAJU TO WALNUT GROVE. Buses (3hr., 3 per day, Y20-24) to Daju (大具) leave from Lijiang's North Station (see p. 611). Buses from the First Bend Inn make the trip almost every day (6am, Y13). Dorms (Y10) are available at the **Snowflake Hotel,** next to the Daju Bus Station.

From Daju, it is an hour's walk or a short taxi ride (Y5) to a lake. If you don't see a ferry man, call out for him. In the rainy season, it may be safer to take the old ferry (ask in Daju for information), but the new ferry is quick and drops you in a different location, cutting out a couple of hours of relatively uninteresting walking. Taking the old ferry often means an overnight stay in Walnut Grove; the new ferry often means an overnight in First Bend Village. The walk from the ferry crossing to **Walnut Grove** takes about four hours. If you are short on time, you can get a ride along the road between Daju and Walnut Grove and start your trek at Walnut Grove. At Walnut Grove there are two places to stay, five minutes apart: **Chateau de Woody** ❶ (báiliǎn lǚguǎn; 白脸旅馆) and **Stan's Spring Guesthouse** ❶ (shānquán kèzhàn; 山泉客栈). Both have dorm beds (Y10-20), restaurants, and hot showers. Woody can also arrange tours to Zhongdian and Baishui Terrace. Another 30- to 45-minute walk along the road leads to **Tina's House,** at the point where the low path leaves the road to join the high path (dorms Y10-20).

WALNUT GROVE TO FIRST BEND VILLAGE. The walk from Walnut Grove to First Bend Village takes three to four hours, encompassing the gorge's most gorgeous scenery. Sporadic yellow or red arrows mark most of the trails; if in doubt, head for the power lines to keep on track. At **First Bend Village,** you will see a guesthouse; from there, head straight up the steep slope. A waterfall at the top makes the climb worthwhile. The **Halfway Guesthouse** nearby has dorms with showers (Y15-20). Mr. Feng, the owner, is a specialist in natural medicine who offers tours to other local spots.

FIRST BEND VILLAGE TO QIAOTOU. Halfway Guesthouse is most people's last place of rest before the six- to eight-hour hike to Qiaotou. You'll know you're in the last village before Qiaotou because you'll come across a guesthouse that advertises "bowel and lodging." **Qiaotou** is a nondescript town, teeming with concrete structures, so try to avoid having to stay overnight. If you must stay in Qiaotou, try the **Tiger Leaping Gorge Hotel** ❶, next to the bus station and opposite the Backpacker's Cafe (dorms Y15-20). From Qiaotou, the last bus (Y15) leaves for **Lijiang** or **Zhongdian** at 6pm. Inquire at the Backpacker's Cafe.

QIAOTOU TO DAJU. **Buses** (Y13) to Qiaotou leave Lijiang's First Bend Inn starting at 6am. From Qiaotou, take a left out of the Backpacker's Cafe and follow the sign to the gorge, which will point you to a tall gate; walk 100m past the gate and take a left. When you come to the basketball court, walk across, turn right, then walk along the base of the hill until you pick up the trail on your left. Always bear left when the trail looks like it's forking; trails to the right usually lead to private houses. If you want to do the trek in two days, plan carefully. The **last ferry** across the lake to Daju leaves around 6pm.

LUGU LAKE 泸沽湖 ☎0888

The lengthy bus ride from Lijiang unwittingly discourages many potential visitors to Lugu Lake, a majestic oasis on the Yunnan-Sichuan border. Once there, however, the warmth and hospitality of the people in the surrounding Tibetan, Yi, Pumi, and Mosuo villages and the laid-back atmosphere on the lake make it difficult for travelers to leave. The Lugu Lake area is best known as home of the unique Mosuo culture. The Mosuo, a subgroup of the Naxi, is a matrilineal society whose members engage in traditional "walking marriages," in which husband and wife remain in their respective maternal homes and often have more than one partner.

According to locals, the lake is gorgeous in all seasons, but most visitors prefer to visit in late spring or fall when the sky is usually a clear blue and the weather is more mild. In winter, Lugu Lake is very cold and often snowy, with wild geese and seagulls congregating on its icy shores; in late summer, rains are frequent.

TRANSPORTATION

The easiest way to get to Lugu Lake is from Lijiang. A 9am bus (Y56) goes all the way to the lake via Ninglang. A new road to **Ninglang** (宁蒗), the Lugu County seat and stopover point for the lake, is still under construction; once completed, it will likely shorten the seven-hour trip on the old road from Lijiang to about three hours. **Buses** (7am and 2pm, Y34) leave from Lijiang South Station for Ninglang (see p. 611). It is fairly easy to get a bus from Ninglang Bus Station or the main street to Lugu Lake (3hr., Y15-20). The last buses usually leave around 6 or 7pm.

Buses from Lugu Lake to Ninglang leave from the **Mosuo Hotel** (7:30 and 8am, Y20). From Ninglang, buses go to **Kunming** (1 pm, Y105), **Lijiang** (every hr. 7am-1pm, Y36), and **Xiaguan** (7am, Y48).

ACCOMMODATIONS AND FOOD

Ninglang is noisy, dirty, and not a terribly pleasant place to stay. If you miss the last bus from Ninglang to Lugu Lake, however, the **Bus Station Guesthouse** (kèyùn zhāodàisuǒ; 客运招待所) in the bus station has rooms for Y10-15. The nearby **Ninglang Jiamei Hotel ❶** (nínglāng jiāměi bīnguǎn; 宁蒗佳美宾馆) has hot water from 6 to 10pm. Turn right out of the bus station and walk about 100m; look for the words "Jia me hote" on black marble to your right. (☎552 4489. Doubles and triples Y15.)

The bus to Lugu Lake drops off passengers at the **Mosuo Hotel,** in the village of **Luoshui.** Turn right out of the Mosuo Hotel; on your right you'll see some guesthouses that are pretty much all the same, with dorm beds (Y15) but no showers. There is a **village bathhouse** (cūnzhuāng línyù; 村庄淋浴; Y3); ask a villager and you'll be pointed the way. Accommodational uniformity aside, the owners of the **Cloud Pagoda Inn** (cǎitǎ jiā; 彩塔家; ☎588 1123) and the **Husi Tea House** (☎588 1170) are extremely friendly and are also good sources of information about the area. The Husi Tea House also has a restaurant and **Internet access** (Y15 per hr.).

Most visitors choose to eat where they stay; expect to pay Y15-20 per day for food. The food is simple but delicious, consisting of fish, bread, and potatoes. The Husi Tea House's hot cola and ginger drink (Y6) has soothed many a traveler's queasy stomach. They also have Western dishes (Y8-20) and English menus.

SIGHTS AND HIKING

The key to visiting Lugu Lake is to get away from the inn-cluttered and tourist-laden Luoshui village. **Boats** (Y35 per person) go from the Luoshui Dock to **Tusi** and **Liwubi,** two small islands with lamaseries. There's not much to see on either of them, but the boat ride is worthwhile. The rowers at times may be inclined to sing; more often, however, they're inclined to wail. Hiring a guide at the dock area costs about Y100 per day; it's best to arrive around 7 or 8am to arrange this. **Horserides** (Y60) leaving from the dock stop at a nearby meadow for tourists to wrestle with local champions. Beware: a "local tradition" is to split the opponent's pants in these wrestling matches.

Mosuo culture is at its most fascinating in the smaller, more tranquil Mosuo villages of **Lige** (里格), **Xiao Luoshui** (小落水), and **Dazui** (大咀), which have remained relatively untouched by the ever-expanding mass-marketing of the region. Some Mosuo families offer **accommodations** and **food** for Y10-20 per night. It takes over 12 hours to walk around the lake, and about seven hours to get to the three villages.

The majority of the Mosuo live in **Yongning** (永宁), an area about a one-hour bus ride from Lugu Lake. Yongning is worth a visit for further insight into Mosuo culture. **Accommodations** are available in Mosuo homes. The **bus** from Ninglang to

IF THIS PROVINCE IS A-ROCKIN' At 21:10 GMT on Wednesday, May 31, 2001, an earthquake measuring 5.8 on the Richter scale rocked the area surrounding Lugu Lake, leaving 5000 people homeless and injuring over 50. The government estimated the damage at 180 million *yuán* (approximately US$22 million). Relief efforts were hindered by the mountainous terrain and the scattered villages of Yi and Mosuo minorities hidden within the peaks and valleys. This earthquake was by no means an anomaly, however. In fact, earthquakes are so common in the region that the Yunnan Earthquake Reconstruction Program was established in order to provide an effective means of channeling aid to areas in need of relief. In 1996, when an earthquake measuring 7.0 on the Richter scale struck Lijiang, the World Bank was able to send aid quickly via this program. As one of China's poorest provinces, and with many inaccessible areas, Yunnan needs all the help it can get.

Yongning (Y5) passes by Luoshui daily at 10am; ask the manager of the Husi Tea House to take you to the bus or to arrange for transportation to Yongning.

The **trek** from Yongning to Lijiang is said to be gorgeous, and a few backpackers have done it, camping or staying at villagers' homes along the way, but it is difficult to get information about this hike once in Lugu Lake. Instead, while in Lijiang, ask other backpackers, check out travelers' notebooks, or talk to travel agencies. The folks at the Prague Cafe in Lijiang (see p. 612) are particularly helpful.

ZHONGDIAN 中甸 ☎0887

Zhongdian, the name of both the county and its capital, is part of Diqing Tibetan Autonomous Prefecture (known as Gyelthang in Tibetan) in the far north of Yunnan province. Because travel into Tibet from Zhongdian is now possible, droves of backpackers flock to the town that many believe to have been the famed Shangri-La. And even if you don't continue on to Tibet, a stay in the area can give you a fascinating glimpse of Tibetan life. Tibetan villages dot the valleys, and saffron-robed monks meander through the streets. Ranging in elevation from 1480m to 6740m, the prefecture encompasses some breathtaking scenery; prolonged travel entails bus rides along precarious but exhilirating mountain roads. Like many Chinese towns of regional import, Zhongdian seems to endure a constant frenzy of construction and a continual haze of dust; even the old section of town has been invaded by impersonal masses of concrete and faux-traditional buildings. Despite its dwindling structural character, Zhongdian's cultural diversity—a mix of Han Chinese, Tibetan, Bai, and Naxi minorities—and its resplendant natural scenery bring Zhongdian to life.

TRANSPORTATION

Flights: Diqing Airport (díqìng jīchǎng; 迪庆机场; ☎822 9916) is 3km out of town. No airport shuttles; a taxi from town costs Y15-20. The **CAAC ticket office** (☎822 9901) is on Changzheng Lu, a couple of doors down from 2 stone lions. Open daily 8:30am-noon and 2-5:30pm. To: **Chengdu** (1 per week, Y890); **Kunming** (2 per day, Y560); and **Lhasa** (1 per week, Y1250).

Bus: Zhongdian Central Bus Station (zhōngdiàn kèyùn fúwù zhōngxīn zhàn; 中甸客运服务中心站; ☎822 2972), on Changzheng Lu. The ticket office is inside the waiting room. Ignore the large timetable on the wall; the small one by the ticket booth has more up-to-date information. Luggage storage Y2 per bag per day. Open daily 6am-8pm. To: **Deqin** (7hr., 2 per day, Y31.5); **Kunming** (15hr., 5 per day, Y146); **Lijiang** (5hr., 5 per day, Y29.5); **Sanba** (3.5hr., daily, Y20.5) via **Baishuitai;** and

Xiaguan (8hr., 11 per day, Y45). Travel from Yunnan to Sichuan is easiest between Zhongdian and Xiangzheng. There are no travel restrictions and the route features some wonderful scenery to brighten the long, bumpy busrides.

Local Transportation: Bus **#3** runs every 5min. from the Long Life Tibetan Hotel down Changzheng Lu, past the bus station and bank, going toward Songzanlin Lamasery. Fare Y1. Bus **#2** travels the length of Changzheng Lu. For shorter distances, you can also take a **pedicab** (Y2-3) or a **taxi** (Y5 within the city proper).

ORIENTATION AND PRACTICAL INFORMATION

There are two distinct areas within Zhongdian. The rough-hewn, construction-crazed area around **Changzheng Lu** (长征路), the main shopping street, constitutes the modern part of Zhongdian. The old town, on the other hand, is a muddled series of dusty lanes and dilapidated houses, complete with barking dogs and wandering pigs.

Travel Agencies: CITS (☎823 1935 or 822 2238), on Sifang Jie in the old town. At the end of Changzheng Lu, walk to the end of the 1st street to the old town and turn right; the office is on the right. They can help arrange tours for 3-4 people to Baishui Terraces or Bita Lake. English-speaking staff member on the 2nd fl. The **Zhongdian Holiday Travel Agency** (zhōngdiàn jiàrì lǚxíngshè; 中甸假日旅行社; ☎822 8555; fax 822 8666), on Tuanjie Jie, just before the Long Life Tibetan Hotel. Organizes tours, gets plane tickets, and arranges permits for Tibet. The most popular Tibet travel service at the moment is run through the travel agency at the **Kangba Hotel** (☎822 9028) on Changzheng Lu. Their Y2500 package includes one-way airfare, Tibet travel permit, airport transportation, English-speaking guide, and travel insurance. Also arranges for overland travel from Zhongdian to Lhasa (2+ people) for Y5100.

Tourist Complaints: ☎822 5390.

Currency Exchange: People's Bank (zhōnggúo rénmín yínháng; 中国人民银行), on Changzheng Lu, opposite the Bita Hotel. Exchanges traveler's checks. Credit card advances. Open M-F 8:30-11:30am and 2-5pm.

PSB: On Changzheng Lu (☎822 6834), just right of the CAAC ticket office, 2 buildings past the Kodak shop. Go through the metal gates on the 3rd fl. Visa extensions. Open M-F 8:30-11:30am and 2:30-5:30pm.

Medical Services: Foreigner's First Aid Center (☎822 9979).

Internet Access: China Telecom has access. Y8 per hr. The **Long Life Tibetan Hotel** has 1 computer (Y10 per hr.), as does the **Tibet Cafe** (Y8 per hr.). Another Internet cafe marked "email" is on Changzheng Lu, one street away from the old town (Y9 per hr.).

Post and Telecommunications: China Telecom, on Changzheng Lu, to the left of the bus station. IDD service and Internet access (Y8 per hr.). Open daily 8:30am-10pm; in winter 9am-8pm. IDD service available in the Long Life Tibetan Hotel. **China Post** is to the right of the bus station. Poste Restante. **Postal Code:** 674400.

ACCOMMODATIONS

As Zhongdian grows as a backpacker hangout, more and more budget options are becoming available.

Long Life Tibetan Hotel (yǒng shēng fàndiàn; 永生饭店), 106 Tuanjie Jie (☎822 2448; fax 822 3863). Turn right out of the bus station, then turn left at the end of the road; continue 5-10min. If there are any foreigners in Zhongdian, you'll likely find them here. The hotel staff is very friendly and can offer a lot of good travel advice. Bike rental (Y3 per hr., Y25 per day), cafe with English menu, Internet access (Y10 per hr.), and IDD service. Rooms are very clean and usually very quiet. Hot water 7-11pm. Y100 deposit. 6-bed dorms Y20; 4-bed dorms Y20; 3-bed dorms Y25; doubles Y50. ❶

Old Town Guesthouse (gǔ chéng lǚshè; 古城旅社; ☎822 3629), in the old town. Walk onto the 1st street of the old town (at the end of Changzheng Lu); the guesthouse is on the left, marked by a bright yellow sign and an iron fence. Provides clean, quiet, but fairly small rooms in a building centered around an attractive courtyard. Run by a Tibetan family. Public showers nearby (Y5). Singles Y10. ❶

Jian Hotel (jiān jiǔdiàn; 季安酒店), 6 Changzheng Lu (☎823 1108), to the right of the bus station. Convenient location, but nothing special. There is, however, a Tibetan-style restaurant on the 1st fl. and a lounge on the 2nd. Rooms are clean but noisy. No hot water. 2- to 3-bed dorms Y30. ❶

FOOD

Food in Zhongdian consists mostly of Chinese standards flavored with heavy Sichuanese spices. Local favorites include hotpot and cured beef. Restaurant stalls line **Changzheng Lu** and **Heping Lu** (dishes Y5-8), and there are some dumpling stalls along **Hongqi Lu.** Try fish-scented eggplant (yúxiāng qiézi; 鱼香茄子) or dry-cooked beef (gānbiān niúròu sī; 干煸牛肉丝). A **produce and meat market** is just left of the bus station.

Restaurants with English menus are few and far between. Of these, the best is the **Long Life Tibetan Hotel Cafe** ❶ (entrees Y6-12). **Tibet Cafe** ❶, on the right side of Changzheng Lu toward the old town, serves up pizza (Y13-17), pancakes (Y8), ice cream fruit shakes (Y10), and Tibetan flower tea (Y4). (☎267 3666. Open daily 8am-11pm.)

SOUTHWEST

SIGHTS

Although Zhongdian itself may not be much to look at, it is useful as a base from which to explore the more scenic surrounding areas. The old part of town can make for interesting walks; exploration of the countryside in the direction of Lijiang can also be rewarding. **Big Turtle Park** (dàguīshān gōngyuán; 大龟山公园) provides a good view of the old town. From Changzheng Lu, go straight then turn left, and then right; from here you should be able to see the base of the small hill and a monastery. Toward the end of April or beginning of May, Tibetan families trek up to the monastery to burn incense and pray for a good harvest. *(Open daily 8am-6pm. Y3.)* There are also two small **monasteries** near the upper end of the old town. *(Open daily sunrise-sunset. Y3 and Y5.)*

SONGZANLIN LAMASERY (sōngzànlín sì; 松赞林寺). This lamasery alone justifies a trip to Zhongdian. Affiliated with the Yellow Hat sect and built by the fifth Dalai Lama, Songzanlin is the largest Tibetan Buddhist lamasery in Yunnan. The temple was first established in 1679, but was almost completely demolished during the Cultural Revolution. It has since been reconstructed and is active again (though some construction is still underway), and has many lamas in residence. The main hall (entrance ticket required) contains some stunning Tibetan art. Musical entertainment awaits the early morning visitor. *(5km northwest of Zhongdian. Take bus #3 (15min., every 5-10min., Y1) from outside the Long Life Tibetan Hotel. Open daily sunrise-sunset. Free, except the main hall, which is Y10.)*

NAPA LAKE (nāpā hǎi; 纳耙海). This "lake" only exists from July to September; at other times of the year, it is a large, idyllic meadow. The surrounding hills are blanketed with patches of wild blossoms in May and June, creating a relaxing place for a picnic and a nap. During the winter, rare black-neck cranes visit. There is a small

RIDE 'EM COWBOY The annual three-day Horse Racing Festival in Zhongdian injects a bit of life, both human and equine, into an otherwise soporific town. The festival falls around early or mid-June, the same time as the Dragon Boat Festival. Preparations begin early; tents are repaired, special foods cooked, and traditional costumes brought out.

The gathering, a tradition that dates back centuries, takes place in a flat meadow. All the horses are specially decorated for the occasion; a jockey's dress depends on the race in which he competes, and includes short tunics trimmed with silver and gold, overcoats, fox fur hats, Tibetan boots, and broad swords. The races and their accompanying festivities are taken very seriously by participants who compete for large monetary prizes, sometimes as much as Y1000 (US$120).

In addition to more conventional races, other competitions test a wide range of equestrian skills, from picking up *hada* (white prayer scarves) off the ground to archery on horseback. This is a wonderful time of year to visit Zhongdian, but be sure to book your hotel room early, before the mounted hordes invade all the accommodations.

temple nearby. *(5km from Songzanlin Lamasery. Take bus #2 (Y5) from Changzheng Lu; ask before you board, as not all of them go to Napa Lake. Lake Y10. Horse rides Y50.)*

BITA LAKE (bìtǎ hǎi; 碧塔海). Bita Lake is 3540m above sea level, 3km from the west entrance to the scenic area. For those interested in a more equine experience, it is also possible to rent a horse (about Y30). From the south entrance, it's a 2km hike down a log-covered path. Most of the hike around the lake is not grueling, and the surrounding woods are lovely, with long strands of moss hanging from the trees and wildflowers sprouting up in the most surprising places. Accommodation is available in white-shingled wood cabins (Y15-30 per person) or in campgrounds on the premises. Bring plenty of water. A visit to **Shudu Lake** (shǔdū hǎi; 属都海), also west of Zhongdian, costs as much as one to Bita Lake. *(About 1hr. west of Zhongdian. No regular public transportation. Hire a taxi and driver (Y150 for 3-4 people) from Zhongdian. Bita Lake Y30. Canoe rental Y20; speedboat Y25 per person. Shudu Lake Y10.)*

BAISHUI TERRACE (báishuǐ tái; 白水台). The limestone terraces of Baishui form the second largest natural terrace of its kind in the world. The valley, thought to be fed by a holy spring, is covered with red and pink wildflowers in the fall and is a pilgrimage site in March. Crowds can be intimidating at certain times of the year, especially in March. *(Take the bus to Sanba from Zhongdian, which leaves at 8:30am (summer) and 6:30am (winter) for the 3½hr. trip (Y20.5). Buses don't return to Zhongdian until the next morning. Unless you hire a vehicle, a trip to Baishui Terrace necessitates an overnight stay. Beds are available in guesthouses by the road for Y15-30. It is also possible to hire horses in Baishuitai and trek to the Tiger Leaping Gorge (Y400-500 per day); ask at the Long Life Tibetan Hotel for details.)*

DEQIN 德钦

Deqin Tibetan Autonomous County is Yunnan's northernmost region, nestled in the Hongduanshan Mountains on the southern edge of the Tibetan plateau. The population of the entire county is just over 55,000, 80% of which is Tibetan. The county seat, also called Deqin, is a ramshackle little mountain town, tantalizingly close to the Tibetan border. The trip between Zhongdian and Deqin passes a tributary of the Yangzi, clusters of Tibetan herders, fields of wildflowers with cattle and yaks grazing, and striking snow-capped mountains. The setting lends Deqin a certain mystique and aura of excitement, but for those who aren't mountain lovers, the town doesn't merit a visit of more than a couple days. It is mostly a spring and summer destination; roads are often impassable during winter months.

ORIENTATION AND PRACTICAL INFORMATION

Deqin is a one-street town: **Nanping Jie** (南平街) has good hotels, the bus station, the bank, the post and telecommunications offices, and many small eateries. The town is laid out on a hillside; wandering around can be interesting and even tiring, given the altitude. The **Deqin Bus Station** (déqīn kèyùn fúwù zhàn; 德钦客远服务站; ☎841 2115) is on Nanping Jie. Buses run to Zhongdian (8hr., 2 per day, Y34). It is difficult to cross into Sichuan from Deqin without going through Tibet and getting a permit. Another option is to go to Benzilan, halfway between Zhongdian and Deqin, and take a ferry across the river to Sichuan. From here, you can travel to Derong and on to Xiancheng, via a frequently traveled backpacker route.

The **bank** is on Nanping Jie about five minutes down from the Dexin Hotel, but they don't change money. The owners of the Dexin Hotel are very helpful when it comes to sightseeing; if they can't arrange the trip for you, they know someone who can. The **China Telecom** office is just next to the bus station, and the **post office** is another 100m up the hill on Nanping Jie. **Postal code:** 674500.

ACCOMMODATIONS AND FOOD

Although there are several "tourist designated restaurants" on the main street, none of these—and in fact no restaurant in town—has an English menu. Go into the kitchen of your chosen restaurant and pick the ingredients of your meal yourself (usually around Y8-12 per dish). Food is standard Chinese cuisine. A **produce** and **meat market** is at the end of Nanping Jie.

Dexin Hotel (déxīn lóu; 德薪楼), 86 Nanping Jie (☎841 2031). Walk downhill from the bus station; the hotel is on the right. With graceful Tibetan-style floral patterns on the walls, a glassed-in patio, and friendly staff, the Dexin is a relaxing place to rest after a jarring bus ride. A friendly Tibetan family runs the place; the son is an excellent tour guide. While the thin mattresses on the dorm beds in the basement don't provide much comfort, the second-floor rooms have comfy mattresses and TVs. Warm showers available on request. Dorms Y15-23; singles Y50; doubles Y80. ❶

People's Government Guesthouse (qírénmín zhèngfǔ zhāodàisuǒ; 其人民政府招待所), 25 Nanping Lu (☎841 2118), next to the bus station. Fairly noisy. Hot water 6-10pm. 3- to 4-bed dorms Y15, with TV Y25; singles Y40; doubles with bath Y65. ❶

Adunzi Hotel (ādūnzǐ jiǔdiàn; 阿墩子酒店; ☎841 3378), on Nanping Jie. Turn right out of the bus station. Rooms are clean but somewhat noisy. Travel agency. Hot water 5:30pm-10am. 4- to 7-bed dorms Y20; standard rooms also available. ❶

SIGHTS

MEILIXUESHAN MOUNTAINS (méilǐxuěshān; 梅里雪山). The Meilixueshan Mountains lie just beyond the banks of the Mekong River on the Yunnan-Tibet border. The mountain range contains Yunnan's highest peak, the 6740m **Mt. Kagebo.** The mountain is a spectacular sight, with its piercingly white peaks ascending defiantly toward the sky. The closest most travelers come to Kagebo is the fantastic hike up to **Mingyong Glacier** (míngyǒng bīngchuān; 明永冰川), which at 2700m is the world's lowest-altitude glacier. *(West of Deqin. A bus (daily 3pm, returns next day 7 or 8am; Y10) to Mingyong Glacier leaves from Nanping Jie near the bus station. A taxi to Mingyong*

SOUTHWEST

costs Y350-400 round-trip. Accommodations are available in the hotel near the glacier (Y15 per person). It takes about 2hr. to hike up the glacier. Horses are also available (one-way Y60, round-trip Y80). Y60.)

FEILAI MONASTERY (fēilái sì; 飞来寺). Feilai Monastery is the name given to both the small monastery and a viewing area 1km away; ask to have the prayer hall opened for you. The viewing terrace is a sight in itself, with a line of bright white *stupas* (small pagodas) and piles of Tibetan prayer flags raised at the Tibetan New Year and left up throughout the year. On clear days, the terrace affords stunning views of the surrounding mountain landscape. *(11km from Deqin. A bus (Y6) leaves daily from Nanping Jie (near the bus station) around 7am. You can also walk or take a taxi (Y30-50); roads are almost deserted, making other means of transportation almost impossible. Terrace open daily sunrise-sunset. Y10. Monastery free; donations accepted.)*

SOUTHWEST

BAOSHAN 保山 AND DEHONG 德宏

Baoshan Prefecture and Dehong Dai Jinpo Autonomous County, in far southwestern Yunnan, comprise one of the least visited and wildest areas of the province. A large number of Dai, Jingpo, Achang, and other ethnic minorities live in the area, and Dehong County's long border with Myanmar adds a strong international flavor to the already potent ethnic mix of the region. The area has been the site of cultural and economic transition for centuries; since the middle of the first millennium, it has been a crucial stretch of the Southern Silk Road, linking China, Southeast Asia, and India. Trade, both legal and illegal, continues today; prostitutes, drugs, and disease flow across the border alongside machinery and clothing, injecting a note of danger into the region's heavy subtropical air. China-Myanmar relations are contentious, and the authorities periodically close the border.

BAOSHAN 保山

☎0875

Perhaps more prosaic than the lively towns of Tengchong and Ruili, Baoshan city is still the seat of Baoshan Prefecture. In the 4th and 5th centuries, silk, gold, precious stones, and elephants would pass through on their way to India and Southeast Asia. Remnants of this glorious past are hardly apparent, but Baoshan is still a convenient stopping point on the way to the southwestern frontier.

ORIENTATION AND PRACTICAL INFORMATION

Most hotels and many high-end shops are on **Baoxiu Lu** (保岫路), **Shangxiang Jie** (上巷街), and **Xiaxiang Lu** (下巷街); the latter two run parallel to one another, a block apart. These three thoroughfares are bounded by the long-distance bus station on one side and **Taibao Park** on the other.

Flights: Baoshan Airport (bǎoshān jīchǎng; 保山机场; ☎212 1666) is not far out of town. Shuttle buses (20min., Y2) leave 2hr. before departure from in front of the **CAAC ticket office** (☎216 1737), on the corner of Longquan Lu and Taibao Nan Lu. Open daily 8:30-11:30am and 2:30-5:30pm. A more convenient branch (☎212 1888, ext. 660) is in the Landu Hotel, the largest hotel on Baoxiu Xi Lu. Open M-F 8am-noon and 2:30-6pm, Sa-Su 8:30am-noon and 2:30-5:30pm. To **Kunming** (daily, Y440).

Buses: Baoshan Long-distance Bus Station (bǎoshān kèyùn zhàn; 保山客运站; ☎212 2311), at the intersection of Baoxiu Dong Lu and Huancheng Dong Lu. The best place to buy maps. Open daily 6am-9pm. To: **Ruili** (7hr., approx. every hr., Y35); **Tengchong** (5hr., approx. every hr., Y25); **Xiaguan** (7hr., 10 per day, Y24); **Yingjiang** (8hr., 3 per day, Y35). Sleeper buses to **Kunming** (22hr., 7 per day, Y80-110).

Bank of China: 1 Baoxiu Dong Lu, next to the Yindu Hotel. Exchanges traveler's checks. Credit card advances. Open daily M-F 8-11:30am and 12:30-6pm.

PSB: On Lujia Jie. From Baoxiu Xi Lu, take the 2nd left after passing the Landu Hotel on your right. The staff is not particularly helpful; for visa extensions, your best bet is to visit the **regional PSB** (☎212 2445), on Zhuxi Jie, the 2nd street on the left after Zhengyang Bei Lu. Prices depend on the nationality of the applicant.

Internet Access: Landu Hotel, on Baoxiu Xi Lu. Y15 per hr. Open M-F 8am-1pm, Sa-Su 9am-5pm. Tiny computer shops around town charge Y4-6 per hr. Try **Lancheng Computer,** 34 Mali Jie (☎212 6910). Take the first road on your left after passing Landu Hotel on the right. Open daily 8:30am-9pm.

Post Office: China Post, 21 Xiaxiang Jie, at Xiaoci Jie. EMS and Poste Restante. **Postal Code:** 678000.

SOUTHWEST

ACCOMMODATIONS AND FOOD

Accommodations here are fairly basic; only an ever-friendly staff puts some establishments above others. No hotel is more than 10 minutes by foot from the bus station, and all have 24-hour hot water unless otherwise specified.

Food is cheap (Y3 for a large bowl of rice with three dishes) and delicious. Stalls set out their edible bonanza for inspection, clustering around the long-distance bus station and the market on **Xiashuihe.** For Muslim food, go to the corner known as **Qingzhen Jie** (清真街), at the intersection of Shangxiang Jie and Huancheng Xi Lu. Along Shangxiang Jie, the coffee and tea shops in bamboo stalls adorned with plastic hanging plants are a pleasant surprise. The **Cold Rice Cafe** (lěngfàn kāfēi; 冷饭咖啡), 189 Baoxin Xi Lu, opposite the Yongchang Hotel, serves more than just cold rice. Try the coffee (Y8). (Open daily 10am-11:30pm. ❶)

Yongchang Hotel (yǒngchāng bīnguǎn; 永昌宾馆), 7 Baoxiu Xi Lu (☎212 2802 or 212 2595). From the bus station, turn right and right again at the traffic circle; the hotel is 10min. up the road on the left. Clean rooms and friendly, informative staff. 4-bed dorms Y12; singles Y30; doubles and triples with bath Y120-150. ❶

Shengyang Hotel (shēngyáng fàndiàn; 昇阳饭店; ☎216 0660). Turn right out of the bus station and left at the traffic circle; the hotel is on the right. Rooms are basic by most standards, clean, and serviceable. Hot water 7-11:30pm. Singles Y30; doubles Y35, with bath Y40; triples Y36/45. ❶

Huacheng Hotel (huāchéng bīnguǎn; 花城宾馆), 16 Huancheng Dong Lu (☎212 2037), across the street from the bus station. Clean rooms with TV. Singles Y22, with bath Y40; doubles Y24/50; triples Y30. ❶

Lanhua Hotel (lánhuā bīnguǎn; 兰花宾馆), 23 Baoxin Xi Lu (☎212 2803 or 212 0835), next to the Yongchang Hotel. The lobby's attempt at chandeliered grandeur sets a chintzy tone for the rest of the hotel. Clean but unimpressive rooms. Singles Y30, with bath Y50; doubles with bath Y80; triples with bath Y75; quads with bath Y125. ❶

SIGHTS

The countryside around Baoshan is beautiful and tempting; unfortunately, there is no bike rental place in town. Within the city, all sights are concentrated on the western edge. The sights aren't terribly special, but if you're relaxing in Baoshan for a day or two, they can be an interesting diversion. Walk along Baoxiu Lu away from the bus station, past the Bank of China and the Landu Hotel, until the road forks: to the right, **Yuhuang Pavilion** (yùhuáng gé; 玉皇阁) offers a good view of the city, especially at night; to the left is the entrance to **Taibao Park** (tàibǎo gōngyuán; 太保公园), a wooded area interspersed with pagodas. (Open daily 7am-9pm. Y5.)

As with all Chinese parks, go early (around 6am) or late (after 6:30pm) to avoid the entrance fee and to mingle with locals at rest and play. From the paths that run through the park, the 13-tiered **Wenbi Pagoda** (wénbǐ tǎ; 文笔塔) is visible just to the south; unfortunately, the pagoda looks best from a distance. **Yiluo Pond** (yìluó chí; 易罗池) is just below the hill on which the Wenbi Pagoda rests; the pagoda at the center of the pond is a good place to relax and breathe some fresh Baoshan air.

TENGCHONG 腾冲 ☎0875

With its lushly covered mountains, extinct volcanoes, and still-bubbling hot springs, Tengchong boasts wilder and rougher surroundings than Baoshan. The main streets, unlike those of Baoshan, are dismal thoroughfares filled with scurrying vehicles and lined with dirty mechanics' shops, but the sidestreets are delightfully labyrinthine, lined with interesting traditional architecture that invites and rewards independent exploration.

ORIENTATION AND PRACTICAL INFORMATION

Although there is no distinction between an old town and a new town, Tengchong certainly seems divided between the maze of narrow side streets and the wide main roads that encircle them. Running vaguely northeast-southwest, **Huancheng Dong Lu** (环城东路) passes Tengchong's two bus stations; **Fengshan Lu** (风山路) runs parallel to it. Intersecting those two streets are **Yingjiang Lu** (盈江路), the larger street of **Guanghua Lu** (光华路), and **Huancheng Nan Lu** (环城南路), also known as **Feicui Lu** (翡翠路).

Buses: Tengchong's 2 **bus stations** are opposite each other on Huancheng Dong Lu; they offer comparable prices and destinations and differ only in departure times. The bus station (qìchē zhàn; 汽车站; ☎518 1450) on the same side of the street as the Tonglida Hotel has a ticket office open daily 6am-9pm. Sleeper buses to **Kunming** (16hr., 4 per day, Y100). Non-sleeper buses to: **Baoshan** (5hr., 7 per day, Y25); **Ruili** (6hr., 3 per day, Y30); **Xiaguan** (10hr., 2 per day, Y72); **Yingjiang** (3hr., 9 per day, Y24). **Tengchong Passenger Station** (téngchōng kèyùn zhàn; 腾冲客运站; ☎518 1363) is across the street. Ticket office open daily 6am-8:30pm. To: **Baoshan** (9 per day, Y25-30); **Kunming** (3 per day; Y130-140); **Ruili** (4 per day, Y30); **Xiaguan** (daily, Y72); **Yingjiang** (10 per day, Y24).

Bank of China: At the intersection of Fengshan Lu and Yingjiang Lu. Exchanges traveler's checks. Credit card advances. Open daily in summer 8am-noon and 2:30-6pm; in winter 8-11:30am and 2-6pm.

PSB: ☎513 6605. Head toward Guanghua Lu on Yingjiang Xi Lu; it's in the yellow-tiled complex on an alley. **Foreign bureau** for visa extensions open daily 8-11:30am and 2:30-5:30pm. Most travelers prefer to take care of visa problems in Xiaguan, however, where the PSB officials are more accustomed to handling such requests.

Post and Telecommunications: China Post, a 3min. walk down Fengshan Lu, just past the intersection with Yingjiang Xi Lu in the opposite direction from Guanghua Lu (☎512 3192). EMS and Poste Restante. Open daily 8am-6pm. Next door, **China Telecom** offers IDD service. Open daily 8am-9:30pm. **Postal Code:** 679100.

ACCOMMODATIONS AND FOOD

Hotels in Tengchong are rather spread out, and the budget accommodations are none too inspiring. Most hotels have standard amenities, including the ever-present 24-hour hot water, phone, and TV.

In addition to the usual Chinese fare, Tengchong has a significant number of Muslim restaurants and the occasional Myanmar-influenced menu. Most eateries are street stalls where customers can choose from ingredients to create their own culinary masterpiece. One of Tengchong's specialities is steamed buns (*bāozi*; 包子; Y1-2); the round bamboo steamers in front of restaurants are a dead giveaway that buns are near.

Tonglida Hotel (tōnglìdá bīnguǎn; 通利达宾馆), 50 Huancheng Dong Lu (☎518 7787), in a prominent white building. Tonglida's proximity to the bus station makes it a good, if somewhat noisy stop. 2- to 3-bed dorms Y25; singles with bath Y110; doubles with bath Y80; triples with bath Y100. ❶

Tengchong Guesthouse (téngchōng bīnguǎn; 腾冲宾馆; ☎518 1044), 12 Guangting Xiang, a Y5 pedicab ride or a 20min. walk from the bus station. Take Huancheng Dong Lu toward the Tonglida Hotel; at the crossroads turn right on Huancheng Nan Lu; the hotel is on the left with an English sign. The staff is friendly and professional, but rooms are basic and baths far away. Singles have hot water during the day only. Singles Y30; doubles Y130-150; triples Y80. ❶

Postal Service Training Center (yóudiàn fúwù péixùn zhōngxīn; 邮电服务培训中心), 2 Fengshan Jie (☎513 1418), next to the post office. Clean but basic 3-bed dorms Y20; singles Y180; doubles Y60. ❶

Taian Hotel (tàiān bīnguǎn; 泰安宾馆; ☎518 3382), on the corner of Huancheng Dong Lu and Huancheng Nan Lu. From the bus station, walk past the Tonglida Hotel toward the crossroads for about 15min.; a large sign marks the hotel. Clean rooms have all standard amenities. Singles, doubles, and triples with bath Y100-120. ❷

SIGHTS

Tengchong itself packs all the satisfaction of a sight. A stroll around the old wooden shops and houses of **Yingjiang Dong Lu** (盈江东路) can prove highly rewarding. Town markets tend to be vivid affairs. On **Guanghua Xi Lu** (光华西路), there is a daily market for produce and meat. Around the corner on **Huancheng Xi Lu** (环城西路), heftier items like horses and beds are traded. Another food-oriented market is just off **Fengshan Lu,** as you walk toward Yinjiang Xi Lu.

About 2km west of town, **Laifeng Temple** (láifēng sì; 来风寺) is set inside **Laifeng Mountain National Park** (láifēng shān guójiā gōngyuán; 来风山国家公园). The attraction here is more the journey than the destination. (From Tengchong, walk along Fengshan Lu (toward Guanghua Lu) to Yinjiang Lu; when the road forks, bear right. Open daily sunrise-sunset. Y10.)

DAYTRIPS FROM TENGCHONG

HESHUN VILLAGE

A few km southwest of Tengchong. Take bus #3 (15min., every 20min., Y1.5) from the intersection of Huancheng Nan Lu and Fengshan Lu, heading away from the Tongchang Hotel. Admission to the village Y20. Some travelers have reported being able to backtrack and then cross the fields in order to enter the village from the side. Yuanlong Pavilion open daily 8am-8pm. Y3. House of Ai Siqi open daily 8am-7pm. Y10.

Heshun village (héshùn xiāng; 和顺乡) is a well-preserved Qing-dynasty village. The narrow cobblestone streets, set amid undulating hills and rice fields, beckon to visitors with the prospect of real, untempered relaxation. Anyone who spends a half-day or more here is bound to be a saner person in the long run. Heshun boasts a few visit-worthy sights: the **ancient library** (túshūguǎn; 图书馆), opposite the arch that serves as the village entrance; **Yuanlong Pavilion** (yuánlóng gé; 元龙阁), a small lakeside temple; and the **House of Ai Siqi** (ài sīqí gùjū; 艾思奇故居), a museum idolizing one of Communism's great educational reformers. The latter two are on the path that runs from the village entrance around the left edge of the village, a 15-minute walk past a manmade lake on the left.

SEA OF HEAT HOT SPRINGS

12km south of Tengchong. Minibuses (25min.; 8am-6pm; Y5 per person for groups, Y10 for individuals) with the characters for Rehai (热海) leave from the traffic circle along the road between the Taian and Tengchong Hotels. You can also wait at the minibus "station" on the road opposite the orange PICC sign near the traffic circle. Taxis cost Y20-30. Open daily 8am-midnight. Admission Y20; includes bonus commemorative tourist coin.

Tengchong lies in the middle of a once-active tectonic region; its surrounding landscape features 80 geysers and some 60 volcanoes. Most geysers cluster in an area known as the "Sea of Heat" (rè hǎi; 热海). Geyser names conjure up images of nightmarish amusement park rides ("Toad Eruption Spring," "Pregnant Spring," "Big Boiler"), the fragrance of sulfur fills the air, and a naturally heated pool gets Buddha-bellied local men into bathing suits to test the waters. Despite all the human absurdity, the springs still manage to impress. The waters are rumored to have healing qualities; it's not hard to believe that dips in the steaming pool might cure a stress-induced ailment or two.

SOUTHWEST

TENGCHONG VOLCANOES

Minibuses run to Mazhan (马站) from Tengchong. Follow Guanghua Lu around the corner to the right and up Huancheng Xi Lu to the West Gate. When the road forks, bear right. Take the bus labeled Diantan (滇滩), which goes through Mazhan (40min., 7:30am-7:30pm, Y5). In Mazhan, continue down the main road and turn right onto a flat road. After 20min., turn left onto another flat road. Steps lead to the summit, a 20min. walk. Admission free.

Along with the hot springs, another remnant of Tengchong's explosive past lies in the more than 60 extinct volcanoes (huǒshān; 火山) nearby. The most accessible are north of the town of **Mazhan** (mǎzhàn; 马站). These fire-mountains-no-more are most definitely extinct; the craters are skeletal and grown over with grass. But the hike up the slopes is pleasant and not too grueling, and there is a good view of the surrounding countryside from the top.

YINGJIANG 盈江

Most often used as a connecting point for travel between Tengchong and Ruili, the bustling town of Yingjiang reflects the tropical culture found farther south. Palm trees grace the roadsides and sarong-wrapped locals take part in the rollicking nightlife. Although some buses from Tengchong to Ruili now bypass Yingjiang altogether, this town still makes for a quick, pleasant stop.

The **Yingjiang Bus Station** (yíngjiāng qìchē zhàn; 盈江汽车站) is on **Yongsheng Lu** (永胜路), the main road. (☎818 0766. Open daily 5:30am-9pm.) Sleeper buses go to **Kunming** (21hr., 4 per day, Y140), and non-sleeper buses head to: **Baoshan** (8hr., 5 per day, Y44); **Ruili** (4hr., 10 per day, Y21); **Tengchong** (3hr., 10 per day, Y24). The **post office** is on Zhengxing Lu, the road farthest to the right from the traffic circle, next to the area **hospital. Bank of China** is near the bus station, across the street and a few minutes' walk to the left.

Budget accommodations in Yingjiang are sparse; the cheapest and most convenient place to spend a night is in the **Bus Station Hostel** ❶ (qìchēzhàn zhāodàisuǒ; 汽车站招待所). This all-but-completely-drab place at least has 24hr. water. (3-bed dorms Y5; 2-bed dorms Y7; singles with bath Y35; doubles with bath Y20.) Most other hotel rates in the area start at Y120. Two **food markets** are on streets off Yongsheng Lu; one is just after the Agricultural Bank of China, diagonally across the street from the bus station, and the other one is farther up the road just before another Agricultural Bank. Most places serve up traditional Chinese fare.

RUILI 瑞丽 ☎0692

Ruili is the last major town in Yunnan before the border with Myanmar. This famous stronghold of free trade and dubious morals is dedicated to its megalithic markets and a slightly naughty nightlife. In recent years, Ruili's "openness" has unfortunately ushered in the attendant problems of heroin addiction, HIV/AIDS infection, and prostitution. In response to these escalating problems, the government has recently closed (and in some cases levelled) particularly shady areas of town. Irrepressible Ruili, however, seems to be recovering and in fine form. While the city has few conventional sights, visitors with an eye for human drama are likely to find plenty here: Ruili has all the life and grit of a border town.

TRANSPORTATION

Flights: Flights leave from **Mangshi Airport** (mǎngshì jīchǎng; 芒市机场). A shuttle leaves 3hr. before the 1st flight of the day from the **Yunnan Airlines Booking Office** (yúnnán hángkōng lǚyóubāo gōngsī; 云南航空旅游包公司; ☎414 8275), on Renmin Lu, next to the Yongchang Hotel. Or, take the minibus to Mangshi; ask the driver to drop you at the airport. Open daily 8:30am-5:30pm. To **Kunming** (2 per day, Y530).

Buses: Ruili Bus Station (ruìlì kèyùn zhàn; 瑞丽客运站), 9 Nanmao Lu (☎414 1423). Open daily 5:40am-9pm. To: **Baoshan** (8hr., 8 per day, Y35); **Kunming** (20hr., 8 per day, Y147); **Nongdao** (45min., Y8); **Tengchong** (6hr., 4 per day, Y30); **Xiaguan** (13hr., 3 per day, Y90); **Yinjiang** (4hr., 8 per day, Y20). The local **minibus** depot is opposite the bus station. Minivans leave when full for: **Jiegao** (15min., Y4); **Mangshi** (2hr., Y22); **Wanding** (40min., Y10).

Bike Rental: The **Limin Hotel** rents bikes for Y8 per day.

ORIENTATION AND PRACTICAL INFORMATION

Ruili's major street, **Nanmao Jie** (南卯街), runs east-west through town. The street's eastern portion, **Ruihong Lu** (瑞宏路), forks into two highways; the left road leads to Wangding and the right to Nongdao. **Bianmao Market** (biānmào shìchǎng; 边贸市场) runs parallel to and a block from Nanmao Jie.

Bank of China: On Nanmao Jie, down the street and opposite from the bus station. Exchanges traveler's checks. Credit card advances. Open M-F 8am-6pm.

PSB: 10 Jinshe Lu (☎414 1690). Pass the Ruili Guesthouse and take the 1st right up the hill; bear left when the road forks. Issues **visa extensions.** Not surprisingly (given the flourishing local heroin and smuggling trade), they are a suspicious crowd at this branch; non-emergency affairs are probably best handled in another town. Visas to Myanmar must be obtained in Kunming (see p. 595).

Telephones: China Telecom, on Mengmao Lu, past the post office and around the corner to the left. IDD service. Open daily 8am-9pm.

Internet Access: China Telecom, on Mengmao Lu, a few doors down from the telecommunications office. Y5 per hr. Open daily 8am-6pm.

Post Office: China Post, on Renmin Lu, across the street and up from the Yongchang Hotel. EMS and Poste Restante. Open daily 8am-8pm. **Postal Code:** 678600.

ACCOMMODATIONS

The hotel situation in Ruili is a fast-evolving one; many of the good hotels that used to accept foreigners no longer do. Most hotels have 24hr. hot water.

Taihe Hotel (tàihé bīnguǎn; 泰和宾馆; ☎414 4333), off Nanmao Jie, across from the bus station and up the 1st alley to the right. The main building features luxurious, spacious rooms; the side building has less comfortable but cheaper rooms. 3-bed dorms Y15; singles Y35, with bath Y45-80; doubles and triples with A/C and bath Y100. ❶

Limin Hotel (lìmín bīnguǎn; 利民宾馆), 2 Nanmao Jie (☎414 2249). From the bus station, turn left; the hotel is 500m away, on the left. Clean, albeit unexciting rooms. Bike rental Y3 per day. Hot water 6am-midnight. 3-bed dorms Y20; 2-bed dorms Y25; doubles with A/C and bath Y120; triples with bath Y150. ❶

Tiandu Hotel (tiāndū jiǔdiàn; 天都酒店; ☎414 4835), on Mengmao Lu, next to Ruili No. 1 Nationality Middle School. Beautifully clean beds. Hot water when there is sunlight. 4-bed dorms Y15; doubles Y45; triples Y60. ❶

Post and Telecommunications Hotel (yóudiàn gōngyù; 邮电公寓), 5 Renmin Lu (☎411 8889), opposite the Yongchang Hotel. Rooms have A/C, bath, and phone. Clean 2-bed dorms Y40; 3-bed dorms Y30; singles and doubles Y120; triples Y150. ❶

SOUTHWEST

FOOD

Small food stalls serving Chinese, Burmese, and Dai cuisine are a dime a dozen in Ruili. The Burmese signs in front of restaurants usually exist simply for the benefit of Burmese speakers and do not necessarily indicate that the restaurant serves Burmese cuisine. There's plenty to sink your teeth into during the day, but an even greater variety is available at night. Beware *sápī* (撒丕), a Dai noodle dish made with fried cow intestine, boiled cow ears, and cow tail—few report liking this concoction of unfamiliar cow parts.

Fruit stalls offering fruit and freshly squeezed citrus juices abound; look for the glasses with limes on top. Many stalls offer **lotus seeds** (liánzi; 莲子), an exquisite local specialty that looks vaguely like a nut and has a slightly bitter flavor. The **Little Bee Bar** (xiǎomìfēng jiǔbā; 小蜜蜂酒吧; ☎414 8233) serves up excellent coffee (Y6) and a wide selection of alcoholic drinks.

SIGHTS AND ENTERTAINMENT

Ruili has few sights of note; this town is more about doing (or buying, selling, or partying) than looking. More conventional sights (i.e. Buddhist temples) cluster along the palm-lined road that runs past Ruili on the way from Nongdao to Wanding. If nothing else, these sights give travelers an excuse to get out of town and explore the local countryside.

RUILI MARKET. The real heart of Ruili is its colossal market. Buyers beware: not all products are what they seem. Mango jam is probably genuine; "real" jade bracelets (Y80 to Y4000 per pair) often are not. Brightly colored Burmese sarongs (Y20-35) are good purchases. At night, drinks (Y20-35) are stiff and the stage is set for virtual orgies of karaoke. *(Between the minibus station and Jianshe Lu.)*

TEMPLES. Perhaps the most rewarding sights in Ruili are those found while biking through the countryside; if you prefer to have a specific destination, however, the surrounding area has several worthwhile temples. **Leixian Zhuang Temple** (léixiānzhuàng sì; 雷仙奘寺) is Ruili's oldest *stupa*, out-of-the-way and rarely frequented by tourists despite reports 10 years ago that a gold Buddha had fallen from the sky and landed nearby. To get to Leixian, take the minibus to Nongdao; ask to be dropped off at *léixiān zhàn*. From the road, walk toward the fields to the Dai village; any villager can lead you to the temple. On the left side of the road to Nongdao, heading away from Ruili, a mud trail veers left toward **Denghannongzhuang Temple** (děnghǎn nòngzhuāng sì; 等喊弄奘寺), a wood edifice painted red with yellow markings to distinguish it from local residences. After you get off at the stop for the temple, walk a few minutes toward a small bridge, after which you'll see the temple; a sign points the way.

The **Nong'an Golden Duck Temple** (nòng ān jīn yā tǎ; 弄安金鸭塔) complex is just southwest of town. One of the temples has elaborate white decorations and golden duck carvings on its red roof; the other has two blue dragons carved onto its walls. Past Ruili, on the way to Wanding and just past the village of Jiele, lies the popular **Jiele Golden Pagoda** (jiělè jīn tǎ; 姐勒金塔), whose name comes from the gold paint on its central *stupa*. Seven smaller *stupas* represent the seven days of the week. *(Take a pedicab (15min., Y3) from the minibus station. Y3.)*

BORDER CROSSING INTO MYANMAR

Ruili is close to two checkpoints along the Myanmar border: **Jiegao** (15min., Y4) and **Wanding** (40min., Y10), both accessible by minibus from Ruili. In Jiegao (jiěgaò; 姐告), a huge jade market sets up next to the bus stop. The border crossing into Myanmar is now open to foreigners; visas must be obtained beforehand, however (see Kunming: Consulates, p. 595). Wanding (wǎndīng; 畹町) is China's smallest open border town, distinguished by the bridge that connects it to Myanmar. Foreigners cannot cross into Myanmar from here, but it still offers a great view of the hills just across the border. For current information on border crossings, contact the PSB at the border bridge. (☎515 1541 or 515 3043. Open daily 7:30am-5pm.)

XISHUANGBANNA 西双版纳

Xishuangbanna Dai Autonomous Prefecture ("Banna" for short), an area filled with old-growth tropical rainforest that borders Laos and Myanmar, is one of China's most engaging regions. The prefecture is composed of three counties: Jinghong, Menghai, and Mengla. Jinghong, the capital and largest city, is the base from which most travelers explore this diverse region. Members of the Dai minority group make up one-third of the area's population, which also includes members of the Lahu, Hani, Bulong, Yao, and Jinuo minorities. Most of the local people are Buddhists of the Southeast Asian Theravada school; local Buddhist art and architecture closely resemble that of Thailand and Laos.

It is strongly recommended that you do not join a Chinese tour group of any kind when in Banna; else, you'll find yourself shuttled from one money-making scheme to another. Since the mid-90s, travelers wary of the area's many tourist traps have ventured into Banna less and less. As a result, the residents in the area whose livelihood depends on tourism seem increasingly desperate. As long as you wander off the beaten path, you should be able to avoid the aggressive tourist industry and enjoy the region's natural and cultural beauty.

TREKKING IN XISHUANGBANNA

Trekking is arguably the single best way to experience Xishuangbanna. Many travelers to Xishuangbanna arrange for **guides** (usually in Jinghong); this option may be more expensive than traveling alone, but guides can be invaluable on twisting

OUT, OUT, DAMNED SPOT! Each April, tourists flood into Xishuangbanna to celebrate the Dai New Year. One of the most popular events is the Water Splashing Down Dance, in which the Dai splash huge amounts of water on each other, symbolically washing away dirt and sin. Legend has it that an evil demon set his sights on the beautiful Princess Nanzongbu. He viciously captured her, forced her to be his seventh wife, and then invited her to celebrate New Year's Day with him. The princess drank, danced, and flattered him shamelessly, until he revealed to her the one way he could die: if someone were to pull a single hair out of his head and tie it around his neck, the demon's head would detach from his body. The stealthy princess decapitated the unsuspecting demon. She then returned to the human world, the first item on her to-do list being to wash that nasty demon blood from her hands—hence the Water Splashing Down Dance. Although traditionally the dance is only performed at the Dai New Year, it is now performed daily in Tinghong for the benefit of visiting Chinese tour groups, who eagerly listen to this bloody tale of unrequited love.

country roads hemmed in by dense jungle. Guides often speak both Mandarin and Dai, an important skill in a region where English speakers are almost nonexistent and a striking number of adults do not speak standard Mandarin. Guides can also scout out less-traversed routes and are almost always more effective diplomats in isolated villages than the average foreigner. If you decide to venture out without a guide, try to pick up a few Dai phrases beforehand, and remember that younger people are more likely to know Mandarin than older ones. Those who forgo a guide are also advised to find a traveling companion for the trek.

Many people spend the night in villagers' homes along the way, but don't assume that you and your party are welcome in a home unless you have what is indisputably an invitation. If possible, try to arrange a price before you have eaten or spent the night, and aim to pay slightly more than the market price. Most guides advise paying Y10-15 per person for an overnight stay; food usually should cost less than Y20. A few people report having been shouted at the next morning for not paying enough, but these cases are rare; usually, friendly locals only complain about the hangovers they suffer after an evening of drinking and talking. One other etiquette point of note: always ask (or pantomime) before taking anyone's picture, especially with monks and in temples.

When packing, bring **food** and **bottled water** or **iodine tablets,** as well as a sizable stash of **toilet paper.** Take care to dispose of your plastic and paper waste as responsibly as possible. You may need to ford a few small rivers; use **matches** to rid yourself of leeches. Before setting off, scour **travelers' notebooks** for advice and anecdotes; those at Mei Mei's and Forest Cafe in Jinghong are the most useful.

JINGHONG 景洪

☎0691

Given its beautiful surroundings, Jinghong itself is a bit of a disappointment. Dilapidated buildings and scaffolding on the city's outskirts and high-rise hotels in the city center obscure views of the luxuriant scenery. Despite the big-city pace of its construction, the residents of Jinghong still move at small-town speed. Jinghong's importance as a base for travel to more remote parts of Xishuangbanna, however, more than compensates for its lack of atmosphere.

TRANSPORTATION

Flights: A bus (Y2) goes from the **airport** to the Xishuangbanna Hotel (the expensive one); ask to be dropped off near your destination. To get to the airport, take bus #1

(Y3) from outside the Yunnan Airlines Office. Taxis cost Y25-30. **Yunnan Airlines Office** (yúnnán hángkōng gōngsī; 云南航空公司; ☎212 4774), on the corner of Jingde Xi Lu and Minhang Lu. Follow Jingde Lu toward the Nationalities Park. To **Xiaguan** (daily, Y520) and **Kunming** (5-30 per day depending on the season, Y520).

Buses: Long trips, like those to Dali and Kunming, can take up to 14hr. longer than usual, especially if roads are washed out during the rainy season. The prices below all apply to the trip out of Jinghong; return trips along the same routes vary in price.

Jinghong Banna Main Bus Station (jǐnghóng bǎnnà kèyùn zhàn; 景洪版纳客运站), 5 Minzu Bei Lu (☎212 4427 or 212 3348), at Jinghong Bei Lu. Also known as **Fantai Chang** (fāntāi chǎng; 翻胎厂). Open daily 6am-8pm. To: **Hekou** (26hr., daily, Y145); **Kunming** (18hr., 9 per day 8am-6:30pm, Y119.5); **Xiaguan/Dali** (24hr., 2 per day, Y150). Minibuses run to: **Menghai** (2hr., every 20min. 7am-6pm, Y8); **Menghan/Galanba** (45min., every 20min. 7am-7pm, Y7); **Mengla** (5hr., every 30min. 7am-5pm, Y25-29); **Menglong** (2hr., every 10min. 6:30am-7pm, Y11); **Menglun** (2hr., every 30min., Y12); **Mengyang** (1½hr., every hr. 8am-6:30pm, Y6); **Puer** (3hr., 3 per day, Y42); **Simao** (5hr., every 30min. 7am-5pm, Y24).

Jinghong Bus Station (jǐnghóng qìchē kèyùn zhàn; 景洪汽车客运站), 23 Jinghong Bei Lu (☎212 3570). Stay on Jinghong Lu as it turns from Jinghong Nan Lu into Jinghong Bei Lu; the station is on the right. Open daily 6am-9pm. Sleeper buses to **Kunming** (18hr., about 5 per day (whenever there are 15 passengers), Y146) and **Xiaguan/Dali** (16hr., daily, Y152). Minibuses to: **Menghai** (Y9); **Menghan** (Y7); **Mengla** (Y26.5); **Menglun** (Y12.5); **Mengyang** (Y6.5).

Local Transportation: Bus #3 (Y1) runs along Manting Lu. **Pedicabs** will go anywhere; arrange the price before embarking. **Taxis** to destinations within the city Y5-7.

Bike Rental: Banna Guesthouse rents standard bikes (Y8 per day) and mountain bikes (Y18 per day). The **Mekong Cafe** rents standard bikes for Y10 per day.

ORIENTATION AND PRACTICAL INFORMATION

Jinghong lies southwest of the **Lancang River** (láncāng jiāng; 澜沧江), which flows into Laos and Vietnam; the new **Lancang Bridge** (láncāng qiáo; 澜沧桥) is just east of town. The city is centered on **Peacock Lake** (kǒngquè hú; 孔雀湖), from which **Jinghong Lu** (景洪路) stretches in the four cardinal directions. **Jingde Lu** (景德路) runs south of the lake, parallel to **Jinghong Xi Lu** and **Jinghong Dong Lu.** Most restaurants and some backpacker accommodations are on **Manting Lu** (曼听路), at one end of Jingde Dong Lu. The town is easily navigable on foot, but the sweltering, muggy summers can leave travelers in a sweat in no time flat.

Travel Agencies: CITS, 6 Galan Zhong Lu (☎212 6783), opposite the Banna Guesthouse. Offers 1-day all-inclusive bus tours for about Y160; some have English-speaking tour guides. **Mengyuan Travel Service** (mèngyuán lǚxíngshè; 勐苑旅行社), Mengyuan Hotel, 3 Jinghong Nan Lu, Rm. 224 (☎212 5214; myluke@bn.yn.cninfo.net). Standard treks are about Y200 per day. 3 English-speaking guides, including the highly recommended **Luke Liu** (刘诗军). Open daily 8:30-11:30am and 3-5:30pm. James **(Jame's Cafe),** Sarah **(Forest Cafe),** and Vicky **(Mekong Cafe)** arrange and guide custom treks.

Bank of China: On 1 Jinghong Nan Lu, on the corner opposite Peacock Lake. Exchanges traveler's checks. Credit card advances. **ATM.** Open M-F 8am-5:30pm, Sa-Su 8-11am and 3-5pm. **Agricultural Bank of China** (zhōngguó nóngyè yínháng; 中国农业银行), 15 Jinghong Dong Lu, opposite the Jingyong Hotel. Exchanges traveler's checks. Open daily 8am-8pm.

Bookstore: Mei Mei's, the **Mekong Cafe,** and the **Forest Cafe** have book exchanges.

PSB: 5 Jinghong Dong Lu (☎212 2676), with an English sign. Visa extensions possible. Open daily 8-11:30am and 3-5:30pm. For more extensive visa services, go to the **main PSB** (☎212 2778, ext. 2259) on Jinde Lu, next to Mei Mei's. Open daily 7am-1am.

Post and Telecommunications: 2 Jinghong Xi Lu, opposite Peacock Lake. EMS and Poste Restante. Next door, **China Telecom** has IDD service and Internet access (Y5 per hr.). Both open daily 8am-8pm. **Postal Code:** 666100.

ACCOMMODATIONS

Lodgings here are a reprieve from rough village nights; most have 24hr. hot water.

Banna Guesthouse (bǎnnà bīnguǎn; 版纳宾馆), 11 Galan Zhong Lu (☎212 3679; fax 212 6501). From Peacock Lake, follow Jinghong Dong Lu and turn left at the end; the Banna is 5min. away, on the right. Lovely landscaped grounds and a shaded courtyard. Rooms and dorms have bath, mosquito nets, and TV. Bike rental, medical clinic, and travel agency on-site. 3-bed dorms (foreigners only) Y30; doubles Y80-390. ❶

Dai Building Hotel (dàijiā huāyuán xiǎolóu; 傣家花苑小楼), 57 Manting Lu (☎213 2592). From Peacock Lake, go down Jinghong Nan Lu, turn left onto Jingde Dong Lu, and turn right at the end of the road; the hotel is 5min. ahead, on the right, just past the White Elephant Dai Restaurant. Small, fairly clean Dai-style bamboo huts on stilts, each with a narrow balcony and charm to spare. Fans and mosquito nets provided. Solar-heated water approx. 10am-midnight depending on the weather. Deposit Y5. 2- to 4-bed dorms Y25; doubles Y50. ❶

Jingyong Hotel (jǐngyǒng fàndiàn; 景永饭店), 12 Jinghong Dong Lu (☎/fax 212 3727), right of Peacock Lake. Clean, comfortable rooms with attached bath. 2- to 3-bed dorms Y20; doubles Y168-248; triples Y198. ❶

Mengyuan Hotel (měngyuán bīnguǎn; 勐苑宾馆), 3 Jinghong Nan Lu (☎212 3028 or 212 4573). Walk 2min. away from Peacock Lake; the hotel is on the right, on a nicely shaded street. Clean rooms have bath and TV. Staff is typically receptive to bargaining. Singles Y120; doubles Y150-200; triples Y230. ❷

FOOD AND ENTERTAINMENT

Dai cuisine is a strong presence in Jinghong; restaurants serve up dishes like the rather lurid "pungent vegetables with egg," which tastes far better than it sounds. Dai food is distinguished by its emphasis on vegetables and the use of unusual ingredients like oil-fried river moss. Pineapple is often combined with salty foods or rice, which is eaten with your hands. Mint leaves make a refreshing addition. The Dai version of *shāo kǎo* (Chinese barbecue; 烧烤) consists of fish and chicken drenched in a delicious spicy sour sauce.

The Dai restaurants along **Manting Lu** are instantly recognizable by the brightly clad women who stand in front. These restaurants are a main source of Jinghong's evening entertainment; from approximately 6-9pm, Dai dancers perform as guests enjoy their food. **Mekong Cafe** and **Jame's Cafe** have English menus, but their dishes (Y10-20) are less of a bargain than at other Dai places.

Many small restaurants serve Myanmar- and Thai-style noodles (Y5-8) which taste almost exactly the same. Stalls by the bus stations and along **Galanba Lu** and **Jingde Lu** dish up standard Chinese fare, while **pastry shops** cluster on northern Jinghong Bei Lu. For imported goods and trekking supplies, try the **supermarkets** on Jinghong Nan Lu, just before Peacock Lake. Mouth-watering fruits like mango, melon, and jackfruit are sold everywhere; don't miss the sweet, abundant, and obscenely cheap pineapple (Y0.5-1). The listings below are for those with a hankering for Western flavors.

Mei Mei's (měiměi kāfēidiàn; 美美咖啡店; ☎212 7324), on Jinde Xi Lu, near the top left corner of the traffic triangle as you walk away from Manting Lu. Good Western and Chinese food (Y8-16) and a great BLT (Y7). English book collection (deposit Y100). Open daily 8:30am-10:30pm. ❶

Mekong Cafe, 111 Manting Lu (☎212 8895), just before the White Elephant Dai Restaurant. The Mekong is the youngest and prettiest of Jinghong's backpacker cafes; it's also quickly becoming the most popular. Trekking info, bike rental, limited book collection, and Internet access (Y10 per hr.). Open daily 8:30am-late.

The Forest Cafe (sēnlín kāfēi; 森林咖啡; ☎213 6957), on Galanba Nan Lu diagonally opposite Mei Mei's. Loaves of homemade bread (Y13-17; order a day in advance), Western and Chinese dishes (Y5-18), and a surprisingly large English book collection (deposit Y200). Open daily 9am-11pm. ❶

Jame's Cafe (jiémǔsī kāfēi; 杰姆斯咖啡), 153 Manting Lu (☎212 2937). Also known as the **Wanli Restaurant and Guesthouse,** even though the guesthouse is long gone. One of the few places in town that attracts both Chinese and foreigners. Good Dai, Chinese, and Western food (Y10-20). Try the *peroda* (Y6), a sweet drink made of jello, bread, ice, milk, and *peroda* (a type of fruit) juice. Open daily 8am-10:30pm. ❶

SIGHTS

Many visitors bust out of Jinghong on their way to the surrounding villages, but the city itself is not altogether lacking in sights.

XISHUANGBANNA TROPICAL FLOWERS AND PLANTS GARDEN (xīshuāngbǎnnà rèdài huā huì yuàn; 西双版纳热带花卉苑). This garden, organized around a chain of lakes and ponds, provides ample opportunity to explore outside a predetermined route. One thousand species of flowers live here, enough to make any botanist green with envy. Two monuments commemorate Premier Zhou Enlai's 1961 visit; he came to the garden, proudly stroked a rubber tree, and ponderously declared, "This is our own rubber tree." *(28 Jinghong Xi Lu. The main entrance is just past the Yilan Resort; walk under the arch and toward the end of the road. Open daily 7:30am-6:30pm. Y15.)*

MANTING PARK (mántīng gōngyuán; 曼听公园). Originally known as Chunhuang Park ("Garden of the Soul"), this park is the oldest in Xishuangbanna. When the beloved companion of one of Banna's ancient rulers fell ill and died after spending a day here, the court physician concluded that the lady must have left her soul in the garden and her body could no longer survive. The vast area includes a monument to Zhou Enlai, a Bodhi tree, 400 peacocks, and a garishly painted temple. Every day locals perform death-defying tightrope maneuvers across the Lancang River. The **Dai Water Splashing Dance** (see **Out, Out, Damned Spot!**, p. 632), a traditional dance at the Dai New Year in April, is performed daily at 2:30pm. *(1 Manting Lu, a 10min. walk from town; Manting Park is on the right, marked by English signs. Open daily 7am-7pm. Y10, students with ISIC Y5.)*

SOUTHWEST

NATIONALITIES PARK (mínzú fēngguāng yuán; 民族风光园). Informative despite its contrived nature, this is Jinghong's somewhat dubious tribute to the minority peoples of Xishuangbanna. Six small houses are dedicated to the Dai, Jinuo, Hani, Lahu, Yao, and Buan peoples. Cock-fights, dancing, music, and elephant performances are staged throughout the day. Of particular interest is the "Dance of the Lights"—look for the women in gold body suits and extended gold fingers. *(4 Minhang Lu. Follow Jingde Lu to Minhang Lu and turn left; the park is on the right. Open Su-Tu, Th-F 8:30am-7:30pm, W and Sa 8am-10pm. Y30.)*

XISHUANGBANNA PRIMEVAL FOREST PARK (xīshuāngbǎnnà yuánshǐ sēnlín gōngyuán; 西双版纳原始森林公园). The closest tropical forest to Jinghong, this park offers a glimpse of what the region was like before the invasion of construction and tourism. Parts of the forest are extremely slippery; be especially careful on the bamboo paths and bridges. The park also hosts contrived ethnic dances and staged minority "marriage ceremonies" between audience members and blushing—or at least heavily rouged—minority brides. Be prepared for officious hordes of Chinese tourists. *(8km north of Jinghong. Bike along the highway from Jinghong to Mengyang and then turn left into the park's very visible entrance after about 1hr.; or, take the bus to Mengyang and ask to be dropped off at the park. Open daily 8am-10pm. Y25.)*

MONASTERIES. Jinghong's two largest active Buddhist monasteries, both on Manting Lu, are cool, dark, and wonderfully ornate. Young boys come here to study Buddhism and to learn the Dai language and script. Respectful observers are welcome; shoes should be removed before entering the prayer hall, and photography is not permitted. Even outside the prayer hall, ask for permission before taking any pictures, as many monks dislike having their photos taken. **Manjing Temple** (mànjǐng fósì; 曼景佛寺), known in Dai as *Wat Chienglarn*, is just past the Dai Building Guesthouse on Manting Lu, guarded by golden dragons and lions. *(Open daily sunrise-sunset. Free.)* A 10-minute walk down the road toward Manting Park is the similarly dragon-guarded **Manting Temple** (màntīng fósì; 曼听佛寺), also known as *Manting Wat. (Y1.)*

MARKETS. Jinghong's main **produce market** (jímào shìchǎng; 集贸市场), between Jingde Xi Lu and Nonglin Lu, sells food, household items, and other local products. There is a **vegetable market** directly opposite the Jinghong Bus Station. The **Minority**

Crafts Market (mínzú gōngyìpǐn shāngchǎng; 民族工艺品商场), on Zhuanghong Lu across from the Banna Guesthouse, is a tacky tourist outfit that sells jade, "authentic minority dress," carved wooden animals, peacock-feather fans, and other overpriced objects for indiscriminate buyers. You can also buy minority cloth and clothing in the market on Jingde Dong Lu.

DAYTRIP FROM JINGHONG: MANTING

A 10min. walk down Manting Lu from Jinghong. It takes 15min. to traverse Manting on foot. To cross the river, head down the dirt path away from Jinghong; look for the small hut by the river and the long, simple boat (Y1) big enough to accommodate bicycles. The boat stops running at 7pm; a shout should be sufficient to call it over from the other side.

The quiet and splendid scenery of Manting (mǎntīng; 曼听) belies its proximity to dusty Jinghong. A path leads from the ferry hut, eventually turning gently to the right; a smaller trail leads to the left toward an almost-empty **animal reserve** (dòngwù yuán; 动物园) that contains a few peacocks and monkeys. Walk along the main path and turn right at the fork to reach **Manyangguang Monastery** (mànyǎngguǎng sì; 曼养广寺), an intimate temple with a few monks, a wooden prayer hall, and a white *stupa*. *(Open daily sunrise-sunset. Free.)* If you follow the main path and take the left fork, you'll come across several Dai villages. When the road forks again, the upper road leads to the hamlet of **Manhena** (mànhènà; 曼贺纳). From Manhena, paths lead deeper into the countryside.

SOUTHWEST

MENGHAN 勐罕

Menghan, also known by its Dai name, **Galanba** (gǎnlǎnbà; 橄榄坝), is 27km southeast of Jinghong, set amidst fields overflowing with rice, palms, and flowers. The town itself is very small and has few sights, but the flat roads that radiate from it make for easy biking through the countryside.

Buses stop just off the main road, near a small office. Tickets to Jinghong (45min., every 20min. 7am-6pm, Y7) can be bought inside. To go to Mengla (5hr., every 20min., Y25) or Menglun (1½hr., every 20min., Y10), stand on the road and hail down any bus traveling from Jinghong. To **bike** to Menghan from Jinghong, turn right out of Jinghong's Banna Guesthouse. When the road forks, bear right toward the river; at the bottom of the hill, follow the traffic right, past the ponds, and onto a large new road. Go left, and follow this road all the way to Menghan. The ride should take about four hours. **Rent a bicycle** opposite the Dai Bamboo House; bikes are kept in the courtyard at the end of the path. (Standard bikes Y10 per day, mountain bikes Y20. Deposit Y300.) You can't exchange currency anywhere in town, so be sure to bring sufficient cash.

The **Dai Bamboo House** ❶ (dǎijiā zhúlóu lǚshè; 傣家竹楼旅社), on the main road, is the first building past the furniture shop; look for a small yellow sign. There are thin mattresses on a bamboo floor and cold showers. (6- to 7-bed dorms Y10.) The **Galanba Guesthouse** ❶ (gǎnlǎnbà bīnguǎn; 橄榄坝宾馆) is on a small street parallel to the main street. Turn right down any of the side streets that run off the main street away from Jinghong; then left onto the next street. The guesthouse is on the right. Amenities include attached baths, bed frames, mosquito nets, and TV. (☎241 1216. Singles Y80; doubles Y100; triples and quads Y120.) Fruit sellers line the road. A **market,** off and halfway down the main road, joins the two largest streets in town.

DAYTRIPS FROM MENGHAN

The enticing Menghan countryside—flat, cultivated, gentle, and inviting—begs for casual exploration. It is hard to give particular recommendations; there are few unappealing places and the emerald backdrop of rubber plantations and rice fields can justify any trip. Those who stray from the routes outlined below are all but guaranteed to stumble upon something quite marvelous.

The Mengyuan Travel Service in Jinghong offers a two-day casual **trekking** tour of area villages and monasteries suitable even for elderly or less fit travelers. For the more ambitious, a popular route runs from Menghan to **Menglun** (see below). The Mengyuan Travel Service arranges a four-day trek between the two towns that passes through Dai, Hani, and Ahe minority villages.

MENGBALA KINGDOM PARK (mèngbālā wángguó yuánlín; 勐巴拉王国园林). This park contains some of the most distinctive monastery grounds in all of Xishuangbanna, with painted statues of peacocks and lions, white *stupas*, and a Buddha statue submerged in lotus leaves. At the back of the complex are more statues and a small bridge ringed by forest. *(After entering the park, head right when the road splits; the monastery grounds are on the right. Open daily 8am-8pm. Y7.)*

MANCHUNMAN SCENIC PARK (mànchūnmǎn fēngjǐng yuán; 曼春满风景园). An enjoyable half-day jaunt through the Manchunman Scenic Park reveals a cluster of centuries-old temples and monasteries. The first temples were built here in AD 538 and have been restored countless times. *(From Menghan, walk away from Jinghong down the main street, past the Dai Bamboo House. When the road forks, turn right down a slight slope, cross the river, and turn left at the end, toward a yellow arch announcing the park. The park is apparently always open. Y20, but ticket sellers are sometimes sleeping.)*

MENGHAN CHUNMAN TEMPLE (mènghàn chūnmǎn sì; 勐罕春满寺). The path from Mengbala Kingdom Park leads to Menghan Chunman Temple, also known as *Wat Ban Suan Men*. The resplendent gold *stupa* sits in the center of the courtyard, surrounded by smaller *stupas* and the dazzlingly colored temple. On July 21, the temple celebrates its birthday with dancing, pop music, and snacks (Y1).

MANZHA VILLAGE (mànzhà; 曼乍). From Menghan Chunman Temple, the road veers to the right, heading to the small village of Manzha. Just opposite, a small monastery marks the village. This humble wooden structure is a pleasant contrast to the garish spectacles at other area monasteries. There is no sign, but the monks hanging out in the gardens should clue you in. From the monastery, the road goes straight and then veers to the left; 10 minutes beyond is the last monastery in the complex, **Manting Buddhist Temple** (màntīng fósì; 曼听佛寺). A giant white *stupa* dominates the temple area; inside the monastery sits an enormous gold Buddha statue. A 30-minute walk from the temple leads back to Menghan. This return trip passes some gorgeous landscapes and Dai villages; many people wander off the path to explore individually.

MENGLUN 勐仑

Menglun, southeast of Jinghong, is another lazy village whose biggest draw are its luscious nearby attractions. The enormous Chinese Academy of Science tropical arboretum sets this town apart from the rest.

Buses go to Menglun from Jinghong (1½hr., every 30min., Y12), Menghan (1hr., every 20min., Y12), and Mengla (5hr., when full). From Menghan, take the bus labeled "Mengla" and ask to be dropped off at Menglun; vice versa coming from Mengla. In Menglun, buses converge around the traffic circle on the main street. Those who don't speak Chinese can ask English-speaking cafe owners in Jinghong to write their intended destination on a piece of paper; show this to the driver to avoid confusion. The **PSB** is a small, laid-back office on an alley off the main road. Walk about seven minutes past the Sinodec gas station and Wantong Inn and turn left into the alley; the office is a few minutes ahead, on the left. (☎871 5094. Open daily 8am-5pm.) **China Post** is on the left, just past the alley to the PSB, opposite the Luosuojiang Restaurant. (luósuōjiāng fàndiàn; 逻梭江饭店. Open daily 8am-5pm.)

The **Cuixinyuan Hotel** ❷ (cuìxīnyuán jiǔdiàn; 翠馨园酒店), on the main road, has rooms with 24hr. hot water, A/C, and bath. (☎871 5737 or 871 5711. Doubles and triples Y100.) Rooms in the **Scientists' Activity Center** ❸ (kēxuéjiā huódòng zhōngxīn; 科学家活动中心) have attached bath and hot water after 6pm. When entering the garden, turn left after the bridge; follow the signs. (☎871 5043. Singles Y180; doubles Y150; triples Y200.) **Wantong Inn** ❶ (wàntōng lǚshè; 蔓通旅社), on the main street next to the Sinodec gas station, about 4km from the botanical gardens, has clean rooms and hot water during the day. (☎871 6318. 3-bed dorms with bath Y50; 2-bed dorms Y20.) Small, bland **restaurants** line the main street. There are also snack stalls within the garden. In the morning **market,** *bāozi* (Y0.5) abound.

DAYTRIPS FROM MENGLUN

CHINESE ACADEMY OF SCIENCE TROPICAL BOTANICAL GARDENS (zhōngguó kēxuéyuàn xīshuāngbǎnnà rèdài zhíwùyuán; 中国科学院西双版纳热带植物园). These are sure to fulfill any botany buff's floral fantasies. Even the less horticulturally savvy should be humbled by the presence of over 120 species of bamboo and palm trees, many native to Xishuangbanna. Especially famous are the "stranglers," parasites that cling on to other trees and grow over their trunks before squeezing the life out of them, and the friendlier "dancing plant," which moves its tender leaves when you sing to it. It's advisable to get to the gardens before the midday influx of Chinese tour groups. *(Continue walking in the direction the bus travels and turn right at the market; the gardens are at the end of the road. To return to Menglun, either backtrack through the park, or take the much longer route (5-6hr. on foot) out of the East Gate and through the countryside back to town. ☎871 5071. Open daily 8am-11pm. Y35.)*

DAI GARDEN (dǎizú yuán; 傣族园). Sometimes, in the happy world of travel, a sight sticks out so much that it needs to be listed if only to steer visitors clear of it. Unless you have a special desire to see men decked out in gold crowns and glittery pink robes, this grotesque exploitation of Dai culture will probably send you hurling toward the nearest vomitorium. After half an hour of melodramatic "ethnic" dancing, seven Dai "princesses" fall in love with seven audience members, egged on by a raucous, drum-beating parade. In return, all they ask from these audience members is a Y100-300 token of affection. *(43km from the Botanical Gardens, on the left side of the main road. Open daily 8am-10pm. Y10.)*

MENGHAI 勐海

Menghai, the largest town in western Xishuangbanna, is often only visited en route to more interesting nearby areas. The Menghai region is prime tea-growing country and an important source of **pu-erh tea,** a black, earthy brew favored by dieters but few others. The town also has a sizable Muslim population, rare in Xishuangbanna; the **mosque** (qīngzhēn sì; 清真寺) is on the main street back to Jinghong. Menghai's Sunday market is particularly popular, drawing crowds from throughout Xishuangbanna. About 10 minutes down the main road to Jinghong are some small **Dai villages** and a gold **pagoda.** A path to the left leads to another small hilltop **pagoda** and attached **temple,** with commanding views of vast tea fields.

Just about everything a visitor could need is on the main street, **Xiangshan Xinjie** (香山新街). **Menghai Bus Station** (měnghǎi qíchē zhàn; 勐海汽车站) is just past the Muslim section of the main street, on the right as you head toward Jinghong; look for a large yellowish arch. The other **bus station** (kèyùn zhàn; 客运站) is across the street. Both stations run buses to Jinghong (2hr., Y8), Kunming (24hr., 4 per day, Y142), and Ruili (28hr., daily, Y120).

The **Banna Hotel** ❶ (bǎnnà lǚshè; 版纳旅社) is past the bus stations on the way to Jinghong, opposite the Industrial and Commercial Bank of China and the market; look for the English sign. Dorm beds (Y10) have mosquito nets; try not to get a room facing the noisy street. Opposite the Menghai Bus Station, the **Customs Hostel** ❷ (hǎiguān zhāodàisuǒ; 海关招待所) has clean rooms with attached bath and mosquito nets. (Singles and doubles Y80.) For dumplings and steamed buns (Y4), try the small row of open-fronted **restaurants** just up from the Banna Hotel, down the small alley to your left. For Muslim food, backtrack for five minutes in the direction of Jinghong; look for the Arabic script.

There is a bustling **Sunday market** in nearby **Menghun** (勐混), a tiny town southwest of Menghai. The surrounding area is populated by a lively mix of Dai, Bulang, and Ahe people. It is best to stay in Menghun or nearby Menghai the night before, since the market is most active in the morning; tour groups sometimes bus in around 11am. **Buses** overflowing with people, animals, and goods run from Jinghong (3½hr., Y15) and Menghai (1½hr., Y10) to Menghun. To reach a non-descript guesthouse (dorm beds Y10), turn right from where the bus stops and walk up the hill through the tiled arch. After passing two basketball courts, turn left onto a gravel path in front of a brownish-gray building. Follow the path as it curves past a brick building; the entrance is right behind a gate.

SOUTHWEST

DAMENGLONG 大勐龙

Damenglong, usually listed on bus timetables as **Menglong** (勐龙), is basically just a single street but serves as a fine base for trekking. Two marvelous temples stand at either end of town. The **Manfeilong Bamboo Temple** (mànfēilóng sǔntā; 曼飞龙笋塔) lies at the base of a hill, several kilometers back toward Jinghong. A 15-minute walk up the hill leads to the *stupa;* when the road forks, go up the stairs to the *stupa* instead of following the path onward. The white pagoda, built in AD 1204, was named for its resemblance to bamboo shoots. The whole complex is awash with carvings of plants, animals, and Buddhas. (Temple Y5.) At the other end of town, just before the road bends to the left, a path branching off to the right leads to the **Black Pagoda** (hēi tǎ; 黑塔). This monastery, fronted by a silver *stupa,* sits 50m up the hill. Another 10 minutes of scrambling gets you to the main shining gold *stupa.* There is a **small market** just before the path up to the Black Pagoda.

Buses to Damenglong depart from Jinghong Main Bus Station (3hr., every 10min. 6:30am-7pm, Y11). There's little room for luxury on Damenglong's one street. The **Bus Station Hostel** ❶ (qìchēzhàn zhāodàisuǒ; 汽车站招待所), next door to the bus station, has run-down dorms (Y10). The noisier **Damenglong Hostel** (dàménglóng zhāodàisuǒ; 大门龙招待所) is up the road and to the right, at the end of the street, in the top left corner of the government building courtyard. The Damenglong Hostel has **bike rentals** (Y3 per hr., Y10 per day).

TREKKING AROUND DAMENGLONG

The 50km stretch between Damenglong and **Bulangshan** (布朗山) usually takes two to four days. This route is fairly populated; if you have walked more than two hours without seeing anyone, chances are you're lost. This route covers some steep terrain and is definitely more rigorous than the Menghan to Menglun circuit. Water and snacks can be bought in most villages between Manpo and Bulangshan, but carry a good deal with you anyway. Beware of dogs; some travelers have reported vicious canines roaming around the villages. In the rainy season, the geography can look different; be extra observant.

BITTEN BY THE LOVEBUG In Xishuangbanna's more remote stretches, the traditional courtship rituals of the Dai and the Hani (Xishuangbanna's two largest minority groups) still continue to this day. **Dai** maidens sometimes carry **perfumed pouches** that they throw at the lucky man who catches their eye. If the man accepts the pouch, it means he likes her. If he flings it back, it's a flat-out rejection. Another Dai courtship ritual involves **barbecue chicken.** The man heads toward the poultry-seller who has stolen his heart (or stomach); if she doesn't like him, she'll charge an exorbitant price. Unfortunately, bargaining isn't an option here.

Hani men have a much quicker (though perhaps more acutely painful) way of catching a bride. When a Hani maiden goes to fetch water or firewood, her Romeo "kidnaps" her, throwing the girl on his back and running as fast as he can to his house. She usually has already expressed that she likes him, but she still has to scream and cry for her parents, who come scurrying out to hurl various objects, such as tools and vegetables, at the bandit. To prove to her lover that she really does like him, the girl must **bite** him several times on the neck and shoulder. The harder she clamps down, the more she loves him—Hani men wear these scars with pride.

DAMENGLONG TO BULANGSHAN. The following is a rough description of the trek. Check travelers' notebooks in Jinghong and ask around before you head out. The first village after Damenglong is **Manguanghan.** Follow the road south toward Myanmar, and turn right when the border guards are visible. It is also possible to grab rides in motorbike sidecars. After Manguanghan, follow the tractor trail for 20 minutes to **Guanmin,** a small Hani village. From there, it's a 5km walk to **Manpo,** a Bulang minority village.

Leave Manpo for the walk to **Nula** (1½-2hr.) from the trail starting at the back of the town. After you've climbed a steep hill and within five minutes of beginning the trail, there will be a plateau where the trail splits. The branch that forks left is quickest. The scary bamboo bridge just past Nula is an awesome test of courage and agility that is amusing only in retrospect. After braving the bridge, take the trail to the left that runs along the edge of some rice paddies. You'll soon cross a fence made of branches; within 20-25 minutes you'll see a somewhat trodden path that descends to the river. The winding path may make it seem like you're backtracking, but you're on your way to **Songer,** a Lahu village (1hr.).

From Songer, take the path that heads down for about 30 minutes until you reach a clearing near some cornfields. Follow the path toward the stream; with the cornfields on your right, bear left. The more obvious path to your right is the more difficult one, and leads to muddy rice paddies with several paths up a hill. It takes about two hours to reach **Weidong,** a Hani village. It is best to look for housing with local families here, since some travelers have reported problems finding accommodation in Bulangshan. From Weidong, follow the broad tractor trail to **Bulangshan** (3½hr.). Buses run from Bulangshan back to Menghun.

MENGLA 勐腊

Mengla's main draw is its proximity to **Mohan,** site of the border crossing into Laos. Due to the increasing flow of people and goods across the border, Mengla is growing fast, but most tourists pass through quickly. **Buses** run to Jinghong (5hr., Y27) and Menghan (5hr., Y26) from the bus station (qìchē zhàn; 汽车站; ☎812 2773). **Bank of China,** outside the bus station, on the left corner of the next intersection, exchanges currency and traveler's checks. The **postal code** is 666300. **Mengla Xumushou Veterinary Technology Training Center ❶** (měnglà xùmùshòu yīkējì péixùn zhōngxīn; 勐腊畜牧兽医科技培训中心) is a hotel that accepts foreigners. From the bus station, turn right and keep on going. It's on the left; if you can see the river, you've gone too far. (☎812 2240. Doubles Y75; bargain to Y50.)

BORDER CROSSING INTO LAOS: MOHAN

Buses (2hr., Y10) go from Mengla to **Mohan** (磨憨), the small town where China ends and Laos begins. Minibuses (Y60) also ply the route. There is no Bank of China in Mohan; other banks will change US dollars, but usually only in amounts over US$100. Small notes can be changed on the black market. Laos **visas** are not issued at the border. All visas must be obtained at the embassy in Beijing (see p. 91) or the consulate in Kunming (see p. 595). The Lao entry checkpoint is a 20-minute walk from the border.

GUIZHOU 贵州

"In Guizhou, the sky is never three days clear, the land does not have three feet that are flat, and the people haven't three cents worth of money." So, Guizhou is drizzly, hilly, and poor. More accurately, Guizhou defies easy characterization. The landscape, strewn with jagged and soft-peaked karst hills, is undeniably evocative, but Guizhou's defiant beauty is also its sorrow; the mountainous topography and low-grade soils have always hindered agriculture yields. In many ways, the province is something of a Chinese Appalachia: the site of wretched material poverty, gentle mountain beauty, and great cultural wealth.

Guizhou is, and always has been, the home of many minority nationalities; today, Han Chinese comprise 70% of the population, but the remainder includes 30 separate minority groups that cluster mainly in the south. The history of this ethnic mix has been tumultuous. The province was not brought under full Chinese control until the Ming dynasty, and later, in the Qing dynasty, major ethnic conflict broke out, mainly between the Miao, the predominant minority group, and Han Chinese. In the infamous Battle of Mount Leikong in 1726, more than 10,000 Miao were beheaded, and another 40,000 starved to death. In 1856, Guizhou Miao joined the Taiping Rebellion (see p. 56) but were defeated in 1871. Even in the 20th century, relations between minorities and Han were tense; only recently has the government begun to make efforts to protect minority cultures.

Chinese tourists visit Guizhou with two things in mind: the famed scenic sights near the town of Anshun (see p. 647) and the province's most acclaimed export, *maotai* liquor. Guizhou has much more to offer, however; restful, welcoming hamlets of Miao, Dong, and other minorities snuggle in valleys and by riversides, offering a glimpse into a life both difficult and enchanting, just like the province itself.

GUIYANG 贵阳 ☎0851

Guiyang, the capital of Guizhou, is a curious beast; it is a wealthy urban center in a province that is overwhelmingly rural and poor. Like most of the province, the city was originally populated entirely by non-Chinese peoples. Han Chinese settlement of Guiyang didn't begin in earnest until the Mongols invaded southwest China in 1279, after which the city became the diverse and contradictory area it is today. As a result of recent economic development, buoyant commercial districts often sit alongside the crumbling buildings typical of much of Guizhou. But despite its inequities, Guiyang is a vibrant city with more hope than sorrow. The city revels in its great parks, superb food, and endless shops, while Guizhou University lends this mix its own youthful air.

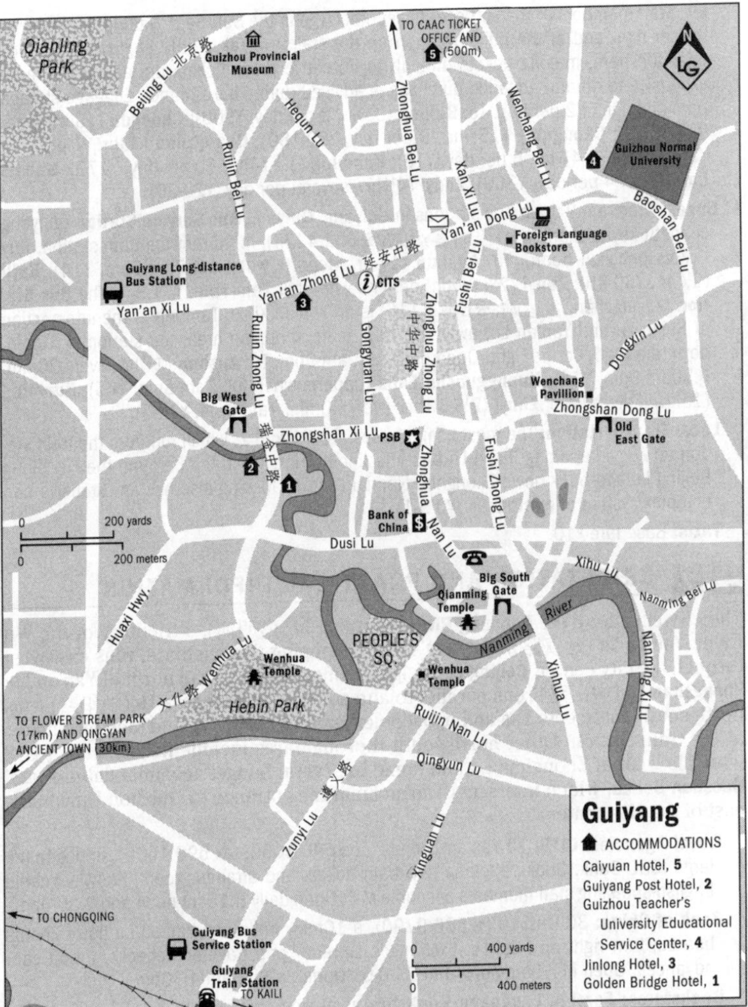

TRANSPORTATION

Flights: An airport bus (Y10) runs to and from the city center, stopping several times along the way. Board the bus at the **CAAC Ticket Office,** 304 Zhonghua Bei Lu, north of Beijing Lu. **China Southern Airlines** (zhōngguó nánfāng hángkōng gōngsī; 中国南方航空公司), 70 Zhunyi Lu (☎582 8429). Open daily 8am-8pm. To: **Beijing** (2 per day, Y530); **Chengdu** (8 per day, Y570); **Chongqing** (daily, Y420); **Guangzhou** (5 per day, Y790); **Guilin** (daily, Y500); **Kunming** (8 per day, Y400); **Shanghai** (2 per day, Y1430).

Trains: Guiyang Train Station (guìyáng huǒchē zhàn; 贵阳火车站; ☎698 1222), at the south end of Zunyi Lu. The ticket booth is slightly to the right of the train station center. Staff members at the soft seat ticket office (go in the Soft Seat Waiting Area door at the far right end of the building, then up the stairs) speak a little English. Few trains originate here, making tickets difficult to obtain; express tickets are easier but more expensive to obtain. Advance purchase is advised during the summer. Luggage storage 6am-midnight; Y2 per bag. To: **Beijing** (33hr., 2 per day, Y500); **Chengdu** (18hr., 4 per day, Y150); **Chongqing** (15½hr., 9 per day, Y80-180); **Guangzhou** (33hr., 7 per day, Y250); **Kaili** (3-4½hr., 5 per day, Y16); **Kunming** (12-14hr., 10 per day, Y170); **Shanghai** (32hr., 4 per day, Y360); **Zunyi** (4½hr., several per day, Y20-30).

Buses: There are 2 main bus stations in Guiyang. **Guiyang Bus Service Station** (guìyáng chángtú kèyùn zhàn; 贵阳长途客运站; ☎682 4224), in front of the train station. Buy tickets once on board. To: **Anshun** (1½hr., departs when full 7am-7pm, Y14); **Kaili** (2½hr., Y30-35); **Zunyi** (2½-3½hr., departs when full 7am-7pm, Y21-34). The **Bus Station** (kèyùn zhàn; 客运站; ☎687 1116) is on Yan'an Xi Lu. Turn left at the intersection of Ruijin Lu and Yan'an Lu, away from the main shopping area; the station is 10min. down the road, on the right. Open daily 5:30am-9pm. To: **Anshun** (1½hr., every 20min. 6:30am-8pm, Y14); **Huangguoshu Falls** (departs when full 7am-8pm, Y65); **Kunming** (15hr., daily, Y120); **Zunyi** (2½-3½hr., every 20min. 7am-9pm, Y25.5).

Local Transportation: The most useful **buses** are **#1** and **2,** which run from the train station up Zunyi Lu, along Ruijin Lu past the Jinqiao Hotel, and then around the city along Beijing Lu and back down Zhonghua Nan Lu (Y0.5). Guiyang also has an extensive and complex system of **minibuses** (Y0.5-1).

Taxis: Base fare Y10.

SOUTHWEST

ORIENTATION AND PRACTICAL INFORMATION

The city sits along the **Nanming River** (nánmíng hé; 南明河), a tributary of the Wu River. **Yan'an Lu** (延安路), Guiyang's main shopping thoroughfare, runs east-west through the city center. **Beijing Lu** (北京路) runs parallel to and north of Yan'an Lu; **Zhongshan Lu** (中山路) runs parallel to and south of it. **Zhonghua Lu** (中华路) runs north-south, intersects Yan'an Lu, becomes **Zunyi Lu** (遵义路), and then terminates at the train station. Other north-south thoroughfares include **Ruijin Lu** (瑞金路), which is west of Zhonghua Lu and home to several budget accommodations, and **Baoshan Bei Lu,** which intersects Yan'an Lu at the entrance to Guizhou University, east of the city center.

Travel Agencies: CITS, 20 Yan'an Zhong Lu (☎690 1660; fax 690 1600), opposite the large ICBC Bank. Books airplane and train tickets and arranges tours. Knowledgeable English-speaking staff members available M-F. Open daily 8:15am-noon and 2:30-6pm.

Bank of China: 30 Dusi Lu (☎586 9790), a 10min. walk from Yan'an Lu down Zhonghua Lu; turn right on Dusi Lu. Exchanges currency and traveler's checks. Credit card advances. Open M-F 8am-noon and 2:30-6:30pm, Sa-Su 9am-4:30pm.

Bookstores: Foreign Language Bookstore (wài wén shūdiàn; 外文书店), 62 Yan'an Dong Lu (☎581 4328), has English-language classics. Open daily 8:30am-6pm.

PSB: On the corner of Zhonghua Lu and Zhongshan Xi Lu (☎676 5230), a 10min. walk down Zhongshan Lu from Yan'an Lu. A foreign affairs officer handles visa extension requests daily 8:30am-5:30pm.

Telephones: China Telecom, 68 Zhonghua Nan Lu (☎585 0330), across from the intersection of Zunyi Lu and off Zhonghua Nan Lu. IDD in central hall. Open daily 8am-7pm.

Internet Access: Internet Bar (tiānchéng wǎngbā; 天城网吧), 13 Yun'an Dong Lu, on the 2nd fl. of a bakery. Enter through the clothing store next to the bakery. Eighteen computers with average connection speeds. Y15 per hr. Open 24hr.

Post Office: China Post, 1 Zhonghua Bei Lu (☎686 0891), at Yan'an Lu. EMS and Poste Restante. Open daily 8:30am-7pm. **Postal Code:** 550001.

ACCOMMODATIONS

Guiyang's hotels cater mainly to upscale tour groups, so budget choices are few. Call ahead to find affordable beds in July and August. During non-summer months, most hotels offer up to 20% discounts; expect price hikes during the first week of May and October. All hotels listed have 24hr. hot water unless otherwise noted.

Guizhou Teacher's University Educational Service Center (guìzhōu shīfàn dàxué jiàoyù fúwù zhōngxīn; 贵州师范大学教育服务中心), 180 Baoshan Bei Lu (☎670 2582). From the end of Yan'an Dong Lu, follow the path next to the neon-lit tea house. Guiyang's cheapest rooms are in this noisy but well-kept guest dorm next to Guizhou University. College dorm decor and atmosphere. Check your wit and sobriety at the door. Hot water until 10pm. Dorm beds Y18-38; singles Y120, doubles Y95-115. ❶

Jinlong Hotel (jīnlóng bīnguǎn; 金龙大酒店), 62 Yan'an Zhong Lu (☎528 2321; fax 528 1507), set back from the road one block toward Ruijin Lu from CITS. Clean, newly-furnished rooms. Rooms have A/C, bath, and TV. Downstairs business center allows international calling card calls at no charge. Singles Y128; doubles Y168; triples Y188. ❷

Guiyang Post Hotel (guìyáng yóuzhèng bīnguǎn; 贵阳邮政宾馆), 31 Ruijin Bei Lu (☎595 8127), near Zhongshan Xi Lu. Fine rooms with bright, clean baths and TV. Singles Y186; doubles Y168; triples Y216-368. ❸

Caiyuan Binguan (cáiyuán bīnguǎn; 财源宾馆), 346 Zhonghua Bei Lu (☎/fax 689 4100), just past where Zhonghua Bei Lu turns left. Conferences make rooms scarce at times, but newer rooms are worth the inconvenient location. Doubles Y125-168. ❷

Golden Bridge Hotel (jīnqiáo bīnguǎn; 金桥宾馆), 34 Ruijin Zhong Lu (☎582 9951 or 581 4872; fax 581 3867). Take bus #1 or 2 from the train or main bus stations. Come here to see how the other half lives—in luxury and sparkling cleanliness. Currency exchange. Singles Y238-280; doubles Y248-288; triples Y276. ❹

FOOD

The cooks in Guiyang outdo themselves making masterpieces out of the sparest ingredients. Most of the food is very spicy; the less daring might want to order less throat-burning versions of the local fare. But throw caution to the winds in order to experience this culinary capital to the fullest.

Guiyang overflows with snacks of all varieties, and meals are best taken as a series of small courses spread out over several blocks. Its culinary variety stems from its position at the crossroads of a multi-cultural province. Look for men selling delectable **kebabs** (shāokǎo; 烧烤) of spiced lamb (Y1). Of Guiyang's many grilled-on-a-stick options, these smoked delights take the prize for tastiness. Guizhou is also known for its very sour dishes, and pickled vegetables turn up by the bushel. One that sticks out in this category is the **sour radish** (suān lóbō; 酸萝卜), which looks like a tongue on a stick. Miao minority vendors contribute to the mix with grilled tofu (Y2) and a delicious sweet steamed bread speckled with candied fruits (Y5). All these treats (and many more) can be found on Ruijin Lu, between Yan'an Lu and the Jinqiao Hotel, or on the food-infested Feishan Jie, which branches off Ruijin Lu nearby. The stalls that line the road leading to Qianling Park provide another good grazing area during the day. Here patrons create do-it-yourself spring rolls by filling small crepes with noodles and vegetables.

After dark, try the **night market** on Ruijin Nan Lu in front of Hebin Park. Other night markets, offering the same delicious edibles, line Yan'an Lu and Hequn Lu. For dessert, look for a mother-daughter team about 300m from Yan'an Zhong Lu on the stir-fry side of the street. Their simple lychee sundaes (shaved ice topped with lychees, sweetened condensed milk, and peanuts, Y8) are the perfect finish to a Guiyang tasting tour. Those hungering for a real meal can try the hotpot sold at stalls opposite the night market on Ruijin Nan Lu or on Feishan Jie. The base price for hotpot tends to be Y2-3, with each additional ingredient Y3-8. **Dog hotpot** (gǒuròu huǒguō; 狗肉火锅) is quite common in Guiyang but is more expensive than other meats. Other restaurants and bars cluster around Baoshan Bei Lu, near the Guizhou University campus.

SIGHTS

Guiyang deserves a second look—and a third, and a fourth. The city's new wealth contrasts with the timeworn poverty of nearby towns, creating a layered experience that gets richer with time. In town, the city's street life and active parks provide ample entertainment; visits to towns like Qingyan reveal mazes of old houses and narrow paths that are prime for exploration.

QIANLING PARK (qiánlíng gōngyuán; 黔灵公园). This park—Guiyang's biggest—offers a fantastic mixture of forested seclusion, religious solemnity, and amusement park madness. The 383 steps to the top of Mt. Qianling, known as the "nine-winding path" for its steep switchbacks, lead to fabulous views of the city and surrounding Guizhou scenery. Wild Rhesus monkeys line this path and others in the park; they won't try to sell you souvenirs, but some can be vicious (particularly those with newborns).

The park's main attraction, however, is **Hongfu Temple** (hóngfú sì; 弘福寺), which was founded in 1672 by Master Chi Song (1634-1706) and sits at the top of Mt. Qianling. After 32 years of construction, 100 monks took up residence here and turned the temple into a regional center for Buddhist teachings. During the Cultural Revolution, Red Guards evicted the monks and did some damage to the temple; today, many monks have returned, including a few from Henan province's Shaolin monastery (see p. 265), recognizable by the nine dots on their upper foreheads. The tea house just outside the temple gate is a good place to rejuvenate after the climb. *(Park and tea house open daily 10:30am-10pm. Park Y1.)*

Family-oriented diversions pepper the rest of the park and draw a steady stream of locals and tourists. Near the entrance, the new **aquarium**'s displays of tropical fish beckon to visitors. *(Open daily 9am-6:30pm. Y30.)* Some people choose to swim in **Qianling Lake** (qiánlíng hú; 黔灵湖) even though it's not the cleanest place to take a dip. Beyond Hongfu Temple, on the far side of Mt. Qianling, a **zoo** features some of China's endangered species as well as more common specimens. *(Take bus #1 or 2 to the corner of Beijing Lu and Zaoshan Lu, or walk all the way up Ruijin Lu, past Yan'an Lu, and turn left onto Beijing Lu. The park is up a shaded path leading away from the city. Park open daily 6:30am-10pm; zoo daily 9am-6:30pm. Park Y5, zoo Y20.)*

FLOWER STREAM PARK (huāxī gōngyuán; 花溪公园). The park, 17km southwest of Guiyang, is a popular afternoon outing from the city. In the summer, visitors swim in the river or the nearby water reservoir. The distinctive **villages** surrounding the park make for a great half-day of exploration all year round. One town has houses made of stone slabs; another one rests beside a mountain that looks as though it was sliced straight down the middle. *(Take the bus from the Guiyang Long-distance Bus Station (30min., Y3). Open daily 8am-6pm. Y5; outside park hours free.)*

GUIZHOU PROVINCIAL MUSEUM (guìzhōu shěng bówùguǎn; 贵州省博物馆). The museum focuses most of its exhibitions on Guizhou's 48 minority peoples, featuring visual displays of festivals, traditional dress, and minority art. Permanent exhibits are on the second floor. *(On Beijing Lu; take bus #1 or 2 and ask to stop at the* *museum; or walk up Zhonghua Bei Lu from Yan'an Lu, turn left onto Beijing Lu, and the museum is 10min. down on the right. Open Tu-Su 9am-5pm. Y10, students Y5; ISIC may work.)*

QINGYAN ANCIENT TOWN (qíngyán gǔ zhèn; 青岩古镇). Known to locals simply as Qingyan, this bustling village contains a number of well-preserved Ming dynasty buildings. On market days (ask at Guiyang CITS for the schedule), traditional architecture is overrun by throngs of buyers and sellers. For a more relaxing visit, wander away from the main streets. Residents will happily point you in the direction of the local temple, a Christian church, and other interesting buildings. *(Take the bus (1hr., Y6) from Guiyang Long-distance Bus Station.)*

PAPER GORGE (xiāngzhǐ gōu; 香纸沟). Paper Gorge offers unspoiled woodlands of bamboo and birch, small ponds, waterfalls, and the chance to see ancient methods of paper-making. The products of this unmechanized process are thin, yellowish pieces of paper that most people buy to burn as spirit money in memory of their ancestors. *(Take the bus (1½hr., Y5) from Guiyang Long-distance Bus Station to Wudang (wūdāng; 乌当), and ask for directions from the bus stop. Open daily 8am-6pm. Y10.)*

OTHER SIGHTS. Locals head for the swimming pool at **Hebin Park** (hébīn gōngyuán; 河滨公园), on Ruijin Nan Lu near Zhunyi Lu, to escape the sweltering summer heat. Several restaurants and a tea garden lie hidden in the foliage around the park. *(Open daily 6:30am-10:30pm. Y3.)* Across the river from Hebin Park, at the intersection of Zunyi Lu and Ruijin Nan Lu, **People's Square** (rénmín guǎngchǎng; 人民广场) provides a more manicured park experience. Elderly Chinese linger to play *mahjong* or just sit and talk while the Chairman, in his stone splendor, watches over them from across the street. To Mao's right, across a twist in the river, a side street off Zunyi Lu runs along the river bank and is home to a small **flower and bird market.** Listen for talking mynah birds that speak a few Chinese phrases, like "have you eaten yet?," "buy some eggs," or "please buy me."

ANSHUN 安顺 ☎0853

On the rail line between Guiyang and Kunming, Anshun is a rough-and-tumble western town—western Guizhou, that is; the frontier here runs between China's current economic "boom" and the poverty that has long plagued the province. Despite pitted streets and ramshackle buildings, Anshun sees a steady stream of tourists thanks to its proximity to **Huangguoshu Falls** and **Longgong Caves,** Guizhou's best-known tourist attractions, and **Zhijin Caves,** Asia's largest karst caves. These attractions take at least a couple of days to see and can easily justify the bumpy bus rides and pricey admission fees required to see them.

TRANSPORTATION

Trains: Anshun Train Station (ānshùn huǒchē zhàn; 安顺火车站; ☎332-5300), at the south end of Nanhua Lu. Sleeper tickets from Anshun require a reservation slip from an office on the 2nd fl. to the left of the stairs (open daily 9am-6pm), which should then be exchanged for a receipt at window #5 downstairs (open daily 8:10-8:40am); the actual purchase is completed at window #2 (open daily 8:30-11:30am). If you need a ticket for the same day, get to the upstairs office early; if you're lucky, the window will open early enough to match the short window of activity at window #5. Luggage storage Y2; accessible 24hr. To: **Chongqing** (12hr., 2 per day, Y126); **Guiyang** (1½hr.; 3 per day, last train at 7:50pm; Y14); **Kunming** (11hr., 8 per day, Y100-130); **Shanghai** (39hr., 2 per day, Y300).

Buses: Prices and destinations are similar at the two bus stations. **Anshun Passenger Bus Station** (ānshùn kèchē zhàn; 安顺客车站; ☎322 3111), at the intersection of

Nanhua Lu and Guihuang Lu. For shorter trips, buy tickets onboard. Open daily 6am-6pm. To: **Guiyang** (1½hr., every 20-30min. 6:30am-7pm, Y13.5); **Huangguoshu Falls** (1½hr.; when full, 8am-6pm; Y6); **Kunming** (12hr., 2 per day, Y134). A small van goes to **Longgong Caves** (1hr., when 5-7 people show up, Y10). **Anshun West Bus Station** (ānshùn xī zhàn; 安顺西站; ☎322 3839), on Tashan Xi Lu. From the train or passenger bus station, head toward the large buildings on Nanhua Lu and turn left at the Bank of China; the station is a few minutes down on the left. Buy tickets on board. Open daily 6:30am-5:40pm. To: **Guiyang** (1½hr., every 20min. 7am-7pm, Y12); **Huangguoshu Falls** (1½hr., every 20min. 8am-5:40pm, Y8); **Longgong Caves** (1hr., 2 per day, Y6).

Local Transportation: Fare Y0.7. **Buses #3** and **4** go up Nanhua Lu and turn right on Tashan Dong Lu; **#7** and **8** run from the train station up Nanhua Lu and turn left on Tashan Xi Lu; **#12** runs the length of Tashan Lu.

Taxi: Y5 gets you to most destinations in town.

SOUTHWEST

ORIENTATION AND PRACTICAL INFORMATION

Nanhua Lu (南华路) runs from the train station in the southeast up through two traffic circles at **Guihuang Lu** (贵黄路) and **Tashan Lu** (塔山路). Anshun's only large modern buildings, including the Bank of China, the post office, and China Telecom, all sit at the intersection of Tashan Lu and Nanhua Lu. With only 2km separating the train station and the town center at Tashan Lu, Anshun is small enough to easily navigate on foot.

Travel Agencies: CITS (☎322 4379 or 322 4537), on Tashan Dong Lu. Turn right off Nanhua Lu; CITS is a 15min. walk, on the left, near the end of the road. Open daily 8am-6:30pm. **CPTS,** 48 Nanhua Lu (☎322 5525; fax 322 4377), at the Ruofei Hotel, is a friendly place to buy tickets for the day tour to Huangguoshu Falls and Longgong Caves (Y200). Open daily 9am-6pm.

Bank of China: 1 Tashan Xi Lu (☎/fax 322 9684), at Nanhua Lu. Exchanges currency and traveler's checks. Credit card advances. Open May-Oct. M-F 8:30-11:40am and 2:40-6:20pm; Nov.-Apr. M-F 8:30-11:40am and 2-6pm.

PSB: On Tashan Xi Lu (☎322 2391). From the train station, turn left off Nanhua Lu at the Bank of China, and walk ahead for 10min; the PSB is on the left. For visa extensions, go to the **Foreigners' Bureau** on the 5th fl. Open M-F 8am-noon and 2:30-6pm.

Internet Access: China Telecom has an Internet office (☎334 4642) next to the telecom office with 5 sluggish terminals. Y2 per hr. Open daily 8:30am-9:30pm.

Post and Telecommunications: China Post and Telecom, 2 Nanhua Lu (☎322 3336), at Tashan Lu, opposite the Bank of China. Poste Restante. Open daily 8am-7pm. **Postal Code:** 561000.

ACCOMMODATIONS

Anshun's few cheap accommodations tend to be a little rough around the edges. Hotels listed have 24-hour hot water.

Shiyou Gongsi Hostel (shíyóu fēngōngsī zhāodàisuǒ; 石油分公司招待所), 22 Guihuang Lu (☎322 5316). It isn't the Ritz, but the beds are decent. Friendly staff keeps up with the good shared baths. 3-bed dorms Y20-25; singles Y68; doubles Y56. ❶

Ruofei Hotel (ruòfēi bīnguǎn; 若飞宾馆), 48 Nanhua Lu (☎/fax 322 5374), halfway between Tashan Lu and Guihuang Lu, next to the "Wholesale Market of Small Goods in Anshun." Renovations haven't yet extended to the rooms, but quarters are clean and bright, with fans and attached baths. 3-bed dorms Y40; singles and doubles Y100-180. ❶

Xixiu Shan Hotel (xīxiù shān bīnguǎn; 西秀山宾馆), 63 Nanhua Lu (☎322 3900), opposite the Ruofei Hotel and toward Guihuang Lu. Very friendly staff and nice rooms with attached bath. Singles and doubles Y178-258. 20% off-season discount. ❸

Nationalities Hotel (mínzú fàndiàn; 民族饭店), 67 Tashan Dong Lu (☎/fax 322 2621). Coming from the train station, turn left off Nanhua Lu at the post office; the hotel is a 10min. walk on the left–a large bowling pin marks the spot. An inconvenient location with relatively high prices. Doubles Y180; triples Y220. ❸

FOOD

Those looking for gourmet thrills among the survival food of Anshun will be barking up the wrong tree. **Dog,** known as a hearty, warming staple, is immensely popular here. There is a small selection of restaurants near the Guihuang Lu traffic circle. Street stalls line the roads, and the main **market areas** are near the intersection of Nanhua Lu and Tashan Lu. **Fruit sellers** are all over the city, clustered in the markets just up from the post office and between the train and bus stations, both on Nanhua Lu.

If you find yourself looking for culinary variety in Anshun, head out to **Farm Family Love** (nóngjiā qíng; 农家情), on Guihuang Xi Lu (☎341 3183), a 30-minute walk or 10-minute taxi ride into the karst-and-paddy countryside. The easiest way to get there is to start walking on Guihuang Xi Lu and flag down cabs. Be careful if you walk back after dark—there are no street lights on Guihuang Lu and the road is strewn with ditches. This bamboo oasis serves lovingly prepared Miao and Chinese food (Y6-15 for most dishes). Try the scrumptious *hema* and egg pancake (Y12). *Hema*, a local poison ivy that induces an extreme allergic reaction if met in the uncooked wild, makes a tasty and nutritious dish once stir-fried. The broiled fish stuffed with herbs (Y25) is also delicious. After a visit here, the world will seem a brighter, friendlier place.

SIGHTS

Most people visit Anshun for the thunderous beauty of neaby Huangguoshu Falls and the inky depths of Longgong Caves. These and other nearby attractions provide excellent sightseeing, while Anshun can provide enough diversions for a pleasant afternoon in town. Tours to sights like Huangguoshu Falls, Longgong Caves, and Heavenly Star Bridge Scenic Area cost about Y200, including admission to all three sights. **CPTS** (see **Travel Agencies** p. 648) sells tickets for a tour bus that leaves from the Ruofei Hotel (departs 7am, returns 5-6pm).

HUANGGUOSHU FALLS (huángguǒshù pùbù; 黄果树瀑布). At 81m wide and 74m high, Huangguoshu Falls are Guizhou's biggest tourist attraction and one imposing wall of water. The falls, at their best after the summer's heavy rains, cascade in all directions, throwing off spray that gives rise to rainbows and wet tourists; bring a slicker if you plan to get close. The only drawback is, as usual, other tourists and the trade they inspire; batik shops, drink stands, and silver-ponchoed tour groups threaten to overwhelm the area's majestic beauty. Signs point the way to several viewing platforms around the crashing waters. Follow the signs to **Water Veil Cave** (Y10) for the opportunity to go behind the falls, an irreplaceable chance to hear and feel the force of the water's descent. The cave is also one of the best vantage points for seeing the rainbows that frequently arch over **Rhinoceros Pool** at the foot of the falls.

Huangguoshu Falls are not the only spectacular falls inside the park, and a 15-minute walk in either direction will bring you to a more secluded waterfall suitable for both quiet contemplation and a little dip. **Luositan Falls** (luósītān pùbù; 螺丝滩瀑布) lies 1km downstream along the path by the river. Continue past the small, overpriced **railway** (Y5) on the far right side of the main falls area. *(Take the bus from either Anshun (2hr., Y6-10) or Guiyang (3hr., Y65). Open daily 6:30am-7pm. Y30.)*

The only hotel near the falls that officially houses foreigners is the **Huangguoshu Hotel** ❺ (huángguǒshù bīnguǎn; 黄果树宾馆), on Huangguoshu Lu, just beyond the second park entrance to the left. *(☎359 2154; fax 359 2111. Doubles Y380-480; triples Y480.)* The cheap places downhill from the Huangguoshu Hotel may be willing to bend the rules. Try the **Chuanji Hostel** ❷(chuānjì zhāodàisuǒ; 川记招待所), on your right as you head into town from the falls. The clean, spacious rooms surround a central courtyard for a communal feel. *(☎359 2663. Singles Y60; doubles Y80; July-Aug. singles Y100, doubles Y120.)*

SOUTHWEST

LONGGONG CAVES (lónggōng dòng; 龙宫洞). Along with Huangguoshu Falls, the Longgong Caves form the backbone of any tourist jaunt through the area. They are among the most extensive karst caves yet discovered, and they house the longest underground river in China. All visitors must set sail on small yellow boats that glide into the caves (traffic jams permitting) accompanied by a Chinese-speaking guide. The 30-minute trip is something like wandering through the haunted house of a third-rate carnival, passing bits of cave lit up by red, green, and purple lights to highlight the prominent karst features. Creepiness aside, the caves are magnificent, with stalactites and stalagmites sharp enough to put out an eye. The viewing platform in the large park near the entrance allows visitors to look down onto the thundering water of **Guanputai Waterfall** (guānpùtái pùbù; 观瀑台瀑布) and grin in the face of watery death. *(Buses from Anshun West Bus Station (2 per day, Y6) and minibuses from Anshun Passenger Bus Station (depart when full, Y10) make the 1hr. trip. Y30.)*

HEAVENLY STAR BRIDGE SCENIC AREA (tiānxīngqiáo fēngjǐng qū; 天星桥风景区). A long and winding stone path strings together the four "sights" that comprise the Heavenly Star Bridge Scenic Area. Plan for at least an hour of walking to see the park, more if you want to savor the sights. It begins with a series of ponds traversed by stepping stones and a pavilion lovely enough to be a prime target for assembly-line picture-taking. This is where most tour guides end their Y10 tour, leading less-daring travelers out of the area and leaving the rest of the area truly celestial for those who strike out on their own. From here, the path twists and turns past clusters of tree roots and reveals a lovely series of waterfalls. Farther on awaits the Heavenly Star Bridge, which was formed when a boulder just happened to drop between two stone outcroppings to span a 10m ravine. The rock has since been hollowed in order to allow visitors to walk through the holy boulder. On the far side of the bridge, a cavern offers some impressive stalagmites and stalactites without the "enhancements" (i.e. colored lights and anthropomorphic name signs) usually installed by Chinese tourist authorities. A cable car (Y10) goes to the exit from this area; the car operator will also point you in the right direction from the short walk out.

The park path, clear and well-marked in Chinese signs, includes enough offshoots and alternative routes to be entertaining. It is possible to find pleasant and peaceful spots by leaving the main pathways. If in doubt about where to go, one of the strategically placed souvenir sellers will point you in the right direction. *(6km downstream from Huangguoshu Falls. Motorcycle taxis or pedicabs ply the route from the falls; don't pay more than Y8 one way. Minibuses go from the scenic area to Anshun (Y10); to return to Guiyang, you must first return to the Huangguoshu Falls area. Open daily 6am-7:30pm. Y30.)*

OTHER SIGHTS. The same **Xixiu Mountain Pagoda** (xīxiù shā tǎ; 西秀山塔) that lends its name to so many local institutions sits on a small hill overlooking Tashan Lu. *(Turn left at the intersection of Nanhua Lu and Tashan Lu, if coming from the train or bus station area; the entrance is opposite the Anshun West Bus Station.)* The secondary streets in this part of town are lined with peddlers trying to eke out a living, and sellers seem to outnumber buyers during the week; this neighborhood becomes the liveliest trade center during Anshun's **Sunday Market.**

Wen Temple (wénmiào; 文庙), off Qian Jin Lu, in the northeast corner of town, was built in the early Ming years and still contains some original structure pieces. The staff, several of whom speak a little English, love the temple and revel in showing visitors its nooks and crannies. *(The easiest way to get there is by taxi from the center of town (Y5-10). Open daily 8am-midnight. Y3.)* Anshun is famous for its **batik.** While batik sellers clog the tourist sights outside town, the best prices are usually in town. Shops line Nanhua Lu between the traffic circle and the Bank of China. Bargain hard; start at slightly less than half of the first price you hear.

SOUTHWEST

DAYTRIP FROM ANSHUN: ZHIJIN CAVES

About 150km (3hr.) from Anshun. Buses leave from Anshun's bus stations (Y30-40) and from Guiyang Long-distance Bus Station (Y60 to Zhijin), but frequently leave at unscheduled times. Inquire the day before you visit the caves. Minibuses (Y5) go from Zhijin to the caves. CPTS in Anshun can arrange daytrips (Y300-4500 per vehicle). Open daily 8am-6pm. Y60.

The spectacular Zhijin Caves (zhījīn dòng; 织金洞), the largest series of karst caves in Asia, are touted with increasing fervor as the "number one cave in the world." There are currently 12 "rooms" open to the public, with more—one reportedly the size of a soccer field—still under preparation. The immense scope of the caves and the awe-inspiring formations of stalactites and stalagmites is mind-boggling. Floor lights and guides with flashlights prevent some stumbles in the caves' inky darkness. **Zhijin Caves Hotel** (zhījīn dòng bīnguǎn; 织金洞宾馆) is next to the cave entrance. (☎(0857) 781 2046 or 762 7181. 4-bed dorms Y20; singles with bath Y120.)

KAILI 凯里 ☎0855

Although its residents are mostly Han Chinese, the little town of Kaili in eastern Guizhou is nestled among numerous minority villages and serves as a great jumping-off point for exploration. The city itself is somewhat drab and dusty, but even a short trip outside of town yields excellent views of spiky karst hills and steeply terraced rice paddies. Visitors usually alternate daytrips and overnight rambles in the surrounding towns with peaceful evenings in Kaili, where convenient accommodations and good restaurants provide all the comfort you need in a base town.

Eastern Guizhou is one of the most ethnically diverse regions in China. The Miao and Dong are the predominant groups, but the area is also home to Yao, Shui, Buyi, Mulao, and Gelao peoples. Kaili sits surrounded by Miao villages, and an hour's trip in any direction will bring you to at least one cluster of low wooden houses built in the traditional Miao fashion. Dong villages cluster in the most southeastern corner of the province, six hours by bus from Kaili. In both areas, some villages have only recently opened to non-Chinese visitors, and Westerners may be met with as much curiosity as they bring.

TRANSPORTATION

Trains: Kaili Train Station (kǎilǐ huǒchē zhàn; 凯里火车站; ☎855 2222), on Qingjiang Lu, at the far northern end of town. Take bus #2 or a taxi (Y10-15). The ticket office is on the left; although officially open 24hr., the office is more consistently staffed 8am-8pm. Because few trains originate in Kaili, sleeper tickets are easier to buy in Guiyang. To: **Guiyang** (4hr., 15 per day, Y15); **Shibing** (1hr., 2 per day, Y5-8); **Zhenyuan** (2hr., 9 per day, Y12).

Buses: Kaili Long-distance Bus Station (kǎilǐ qìchē kèyùn zhàn; 凯里汽车客运站; ☎822 3794), on Wenhua Bei Lu. From Dashizi, go east on Beijing Dong Lu and take the 2nd left up Wenhua Lu. The station is on the left, past Yingpan Dong Lu. Ticket office open daily 6am-10:30pm. Most tickets, however, are bought on board. To: **Duyun** (every 40min. 6:30am-4:20pm, Y15); **Guiyang** (2.5hr., every 30min. 6:30am-10:30pm, Y30-35); **Huangping** (3hr., every hr. 6am-6pm, Y15); **Leishan** (1½hr., 2½hr.; every 30min. 7am-6pm; Y10); **Rongjiang** (5-6hr., every hr. 6am-4pm, Y30); **Sanhui** (3-4hr., every 40min. 6am-6pm, Y20-25). **Kaili Society Bus Station** (kǎilǐ shèhuì kèyùn zhàn; 凯里社会客运站), next to the Kaili Hotel, in the south of town, mainly offers southbound buses. Sleeper buses to **Guangzhou** (24hr., 1-2 per day, Y200) and comparably priced buses to **Guiyang.**

Local Transportation: Bus #2 (Y0.5) runs from the train station to Dashizi.

Taxi: Base fare Y5.

ORIENTATION AND PRACTICAL INFORMATION

Kaili is easy to navigate. With the exception of the train station, most important places and attractions lie within a small area around the city center, easily accessible on foot. **Beijing Lu** (北京路) runs east-west and intersects **Shaoshan Lu** (韶山路), which runs north-south at **Dashizi** ("Big Cross;" 大十字). North of and parallel to Beijing Lu is **Yingpan Lu** (营盘路), which is lined with restaurants and budget accommodations. **Wenhua Lu** runs east of and parallel to Shaoshan Lu.

Travel Agencies: CITS, 53 Yingpan Dong Lu (☎/fax 822 2506 or 822 9441), on the grounds of the Yingpan Hotel, next to the tennis court. Friendly and helpful staff members speak excellent English, Japanese, and French, and can provide information on local events. Internet access Y4 per hr. One-day trips to **Langde** (see **Daytrip,** p. 654) start at Y400 per person; prices drop significantly for larger groups. Open M-F 8:30am-6pm; staff is sometimes there on weekends.

Bank of China: 6 Shaoshan Nan Lu (☎/fax 822 6304). Exchanges traveler's checks. Credit card advances. Open daily 8am-noon and 2:30-5:30pm.

PSB: On Beijing Dong Lu. From the intersection with Shaoshan Lu, it's 5min. down on the left. Handles visa extension requests. Open M-F 9:30am-noon and 2:30-4:30pm.

Internet Access: Internet Cafe, 13 Wenhua Lu (☎822 4471), between Yingpan Lu and Beijing Lu. 21 computers; mediocre connections. Open 24hr. Y10 per hr.

Post and Telecommunications: 1 Beijing Lu (☎/fax 822 3542), at Shaoshan Lu. EMS and Poste Restante. **China Telecom** is on the 2nd fl. Open daily 8am-8pm. **Postal Code:** 556000.

ACCOMMODATIONS

The days of dirt-cheap accommodations in Kaili are gone. Several hotels, however, still offer reasonable rates; the best deals are on **Beijing Lu** and **Yingpan Dong Lu.** For travelers who choose to visit the surrounding villages, all listed hotels store luggage; most have 24-hour hot water.

Longfen Hotel (lóngfēng jiǔdiàn; 隆丰酒店), on Wenhua Lu (☎822 1650). Turn left as you exit the bus station; it's on the left before the next corner. A bright, new entry on

SOUTHWEST

Kaili's budget-lodging roster. Some rooms have A/C and bath; others share well-maintained baths. TV in all rooms. Singles Y68; doubles Y80; triples Y90. ❶

Petroleum Guesthouse (shíyóu bīnguǎn; 石油宾馆), 44 Yingpan Dong Lu (☎823 4331), near Wenhua Lu. From the bus station, walk toward town on Wenhua Lu, turn right on Yingpan Lu; the hotel is on the left. Kaili's cheapest rooms fill a dilapidated old building littered with hints of former fanciness. Spartan rooms have baths, Chinese-style toilets, fans, and TVs. 5-bed dorms Y23; 2-bed dorms with bath Y34; singles Y56. ❶

Yingpanpo National Hotel (yíngpánpō mínzú bīnguǎn; 营盘坡民族宾馆), 53 Yingpan Lu (☎827 5518; fax 827 5566), between Shaoshan Lu and Wenhua Lu; look for the English sign. The hotel is up a slope and to the right. Friendly staff. Rooms are dim and baths are in poor condition. Renovated building has 24hr. hot water. Singles Y60, in renovated building Y280; doubles Y80, in renovated building Y150; triples Y75. ❶

FOOD

Cuisine in Kaili is standard Chinese fare, but with a mouth-puckering twist: sour is the flavor *du jour* every day. Kaili's pride and joy is its **sour soup** (suān tāng; 酸汤), a hotpot concoction made with a choice of meat and flavored with lemon grass that is known throughout China as a regional treat. The restaurant at the **Yingpanpo National Hotel,** on Yingpan Dong Lu outside the entrance to the hotel grounds, serves sour soup (Y10-15 per person) and fresh, delicious stir-fry dishes (Y6-10). The friendly staff keeps enough cold beer (Y3-5) on hand for a long and relaxed evening. (Open daily 10am-midnight. ❶)

Those craving puppy chow can head to the row of **dog hotpot** restaurants on Beijing Dong Lu, on the left, just past Wenhua Lu. The pick of the litter is the **Zhangjia Dog Restaurant** (zhāngjiā gǒuròu diàn; 张家狗肉店), which serves hotpot for Y30 per person. (Open daily until 10pm.)

There is a small **night market** on Beijing Lu near Dashizi, and restaurants and food stalls line the alleys off both sides of Beijing Dong Lu. One excellent option is **Dong Yi Ma Ta Gue** (zhāngmā cānguǎn; 张妈餐馆), which serves vegetable dishes and delicious fried fish. (Entrees Y10. Open daily 5-10pm. ❶) The **Xiaoqiao Restaurant** (xiǎoqiáo jiǔjiā; 小乔酒家) has tempting dinners and keeps the same hours just next door. For something sweet, head to Bejing Lu for some *bīngfēn* (冰芬), a type of jello with ice, pickled fruits, and nuts (Y1-3 per bowl).

SIGHTS

Most visitors to Kaili head elsewhere to sightsee. In town, the **Grand Pavilion** (dà gé; 大阁) is a small temple perched atop a hill, an active site of worship and an attractive spot from which to observe local life. On special occasions, the temple is open at night. *(Open daily 8am-6:30pm. Y1. To get there, walk to the end of Shaoshan Bei Lu, turn right, and then take the first left up Dage Xiang, which leads to the base of the hill.)*

For a view of daily life in Kaili, turn onto a sidestreet near the base of the Grand Pavilion Hill. This area, between Dongmen Lu and Yingpan Lu to the east of Shaoshan Bei Lu, is known as **Old Town** because it includes Kaili's first street. Many traditional wooden homes from Kaili's days as a Miao village still remain.

At the opposite end of town, Shaoshan Nan Lu leads to the **Minorities Museum,** which is set back from the road behind the Kaili Society Bus Station. The museum occupies the second and third floors of an imposing building but falls short of its potential with only four display halls that look like they were designed as part of a 5th-grade social studies project. There are a few interesting examples of Dong and Miao handiwork, but not enough to justify the admission price. *(Buy tickets at the souvenir shop on the stairway to the entrance. Open daily 8:30-11:30am and 2:30-6pm. Y10.)*

SHOPPING

Every Sunday, the **Kaili Market** sets up along Dongmen Lu, north of and parallel to Beijing Lu. Some serious mercantile action happens here, but it pales in comparison to the spectacular Sunday markets in the minority villages throughout the region (see **Markets,** p. 655). Shopping, especially for crafts made by Guizhou minorities like the Miao and Dong, is one of the best things to do in Kaili. The night market on Beijing Lu features a good selection of Miao embroidered bags and accessories, including a traditional favorite, the cell phone holder. On the weekend, across the street and to the right of the Yingpanpo Hotel, minority goods (mainly embroidered clothes and bags) are sold along a small alley.

DAYTRIP FROM KAILI: LANGDE

South of Kaili, on the road into the Leigong Hills. Take the Leishan-bound bus (45min., every 30min., Y5) from the Long-distance Bus Station in Kaili and ask to be let off at Langde. There is a small guesthouse (zhāodàisuǒ; 招待所) in Langde and one in Upper Langde (both Y6 per person). Every villager will know the way and will happily show you; you're unlikely to find it on your own in the twists and turns of identical-looking streets.

Langde (lǎngdé; 朗德), one of Guizhou's most accessible Miao villages, is a picturesque labyrinth of wooden houses and narrow cobblestone streets. For the most part, daily village life goes on as usual here; pigs and chickens rummage for lunch, children play, and adults carry out their domestic chores in the streets. A slow-moving river urges the town's waterwheels forward and cools the water buffalo that linger in its deeper spots. Unfortunately, it's becoming more difficult to visit Langde and simply observe; visitors often arrive to a flurry of activity as local residents rush from their houses to offer handicrafts for sale. Despite the mercantilist twist on traditional Miao hospitality, it still makes for an extremely warm reception. Accommodations are available with Miao families; wooden beds with thin mattresses are standard, and guest bath is in the male- and female-designated parts of the river.

Upper Langde (lǎngdé shàng; 朗德上) lies 3km up the path from Langde, across the river but on the same side of the road from Kaili. The villages look and feel quite similar, but the walk between them, especially across the double-tiered wooden bridge next to Upper Langde, justifies the effort. The views from Upper Langde will take your breath away (as will the uphill trek to get there). Tour groups from Kaili frequently visit Upper Langde, and it's easy for independent explorers to join in the scheduled festivities, in which men bring out their reed flutes (lúshēng; 芦笙) to greet guests and women stop visitors to toast them with small bowls of homemade liquor. Traditional dancing and festivities follow. Because the tour group usually will have paid for all performances, individual visitors standing with the villagers (instead of sitting at the wooden tables with the guests) do not have to pay. However, if a villager approaches you for payment, Y50 is appropriate.

KAILI MINORITY VILLAGES

The area around Kaili may well contain the single most diverse concentration of minority peoples in all of China. The two dominant groups are the Miao (to the north, south, and west of Kaili) and the Dong (to the southeast), but a scattering of Gelao, Mulao, Gejia, Yao, and Shui peoples provides cultural contrast at every turn. Thanks to the slow growth of tourist traffic through the region, villages are

KAILI MINORITIES: THE MIAO Most villages in this part of Guizhou are Miao strongholds. With over seven million members dispersed throughout Hunan, Sichuan, Guangxi, Yunnan, and (predominantly) Guizhou, the Miao people influence the culture of the entire region. The Miao ethnicity, a branch of the better-known Hmong tribes of Southeast Asia, is actually a Miao mix, comprised of seventy or more sub-groups, distinguished by fine variations in dialect, dress, and custom. In fact, the Miao language has nearly as many dialects as Chinese.

Miao culture is an eclectic blend of tradition and outside influences. The Miao tend to settle in mountainous regions and build simple, single-story houses out of wood or thatch. Agriculture and forestry are Miao mainstays, and the group has historically been known as prime producers of opium. In recent years, with the illegalization of opiates, new crops have taken precedence. Some Miao were converted to Christianity by 19th-century missionaries, but their traditional religion is profoundly polytheistic, involving numerous gods and demons and a strong emphasis on ancestor worship.

Miao traditional dress varies according to age and occasion; after marriage, women adopt a whole new wardrobe. Across the board, though, the look is elaborate. The Miao are known for their intricate embroidery and handicrafts and, in particular, for elaborate baby carriers. At festivals and weddings, women don mounds of silver jewelry, including unwieldy headdresses and neckware.

The reed flute (lúshēng; 芦笙) is the foundation of Miao music, the necessary accompaniment of Miao dances, and the symbol of Miao culture. Visitors who cannot attend the annual Reed Flute Festival (see **Festivals**) should ask around to see if they can persuade a local reed flute virtuoso to stage an impromptu performance.

SOUTHWEST

still just villages in this part of the world, and the sights and smells of everyday life have not yet been sterilized or forced to conform to the expectations of tourists.

Between the towns, roads wind around spiky green karst peaks, and the area's natural beauty compensates for the long, bone-rattling bus rides along its ill-kept roads. Don't expect to whip through three villages in a day; trips require planning and patience. Most buses back to Kaili stop running by mid-afternoon and bus trips often take longer than expected. Kaili is the point from which most roads in the area radiate, so it's easiest to approach your exploration as a series of 1- or 2-night trips from Kaili. **Langde** (see **Daytrips from Kaili,** above), **Leishan,** and **Xijiang** form a small cluster to the southeast of Kaili. **Chong'an, Shibing,** and **Zhenyuan** work as a circuit to the north of Kaili. And the **Dong villages** in far southeast Guizhou provide ample material for a third itinerary.

In each of these areas, additional villages tempt visitors to linger longer. If you venture far, remember that some towns have only recently been opened to foreign tourists and, as a result, do not yet have approved accommodations for non-Chinese guests. If you announce your presence by walking around town, the PSB may just announce its presence with a midnight visit to your hotel room. Travelers report a fine of Y200-300 for staying in unapproved lodging.

MARKETS

Part grocery, part mall, and part livestock fair, eastern Guizhou's markets bring together buyers and sellers from around the region. Souvenir hunters should expect to find intricately embroidered goods from the minority villages (without the mark-up taken by minority craft stores throughout the southwest). The Miao are known for their work with silver, and good bargainers can get small pieces for under Y20. The presence of both Miao and Gejia craftsmen makes the Chong'an market the area's best. Most markets open very early in the day and wind down by noon. On Sunday, markets are held in **Kaili** (see p. 651), **Shibing** (see p. 657), and **Zhenyuan** (see p. 658). Markets are held every five days in **Chong'an** (see p. 657) and every six days in the villages of **Leishan** (see p. 656), **Xijiang** (see p. 657), and **Zhouxi.** For more comprehensive listings and date information, check with the Kaili CITS.

FESTIVALS

Eastern Guizhou's ethnic diversity results in a nearly non-stop calendar of festivals, with at least 135 festivals per year. Local festivals are occasions for mass gathering, singing, and dancing; for many young people, they are also a prime opportunity to meet and consider potential spouses. Locals welcome the participation of outsiders; respectful behavior on your part will help to ensure that they remain open to newcomers.

Festivals follow the lunar calendar, so the dates in the Roman calendar vary from year to year. Most festivals are annual events, but some are far rarer; the **Miao Guzang** festival, for example, is held only once every 12 years (next in 2012). Kaili CITS has a full schedule of festivals throughout the region. Here is a small selection of the festivals in 2003: the **Dong Ancestor Worship** (tóngzú jìsàsuì; 侗族际萨岁), in Longtu and Conjiang; **Miao Reed Flute Festival** (miáozú lúshēnghuì; 苗族芦笙会), in different towns every two to three days; the **Miao Hill-Leaping Festival** (miáozú tiào huāpō; 苗族跳花坡), in Kaili; the **Miao Dragon Boat Festival** (miáozú lóngchuán jié; 苗族龙船节), in Shidong; and the **Shui Dragon Boat Festival** (shuǐzú duān jié; 水族端节).

LEISHAN 雷山 ☎0855

Leishan (south of Kaili) is little more than a useful mini-hub for travel farther south or northwest of Xijiang. Leishan has three roads. The bus stops at one end of town; from here, the main road runs through town and across the river. Two-thirds of the way to the river, the main road intersects the second street. At the far end of town, the third street branches right off the main road and runs parallel to it on the opposite riverbank.

Buses go to Leishan from **Kaili** (1½hr.,; every 30min. 7am-6pm; Y7), returning to Kaili whenever full; the last bus leaves for Kaili at 4pm. Buses from Leishan depart from the front of the Leishan Hotel. Buses to **Xijiang** (1½hr., 8:30am-2:30pm, Y6) leave earlier and sometimes more frequently on market days (see **Markets,** above). From the bus drop-off point, walk into town on the main road and make a right at the intersection; the road dead-ends at the hotel almost immediately.

The **Post Office Hostel** ❶ (yóudiàn zhāodàisuǒ; 邮电招待所) is on the main road just before the road turns right to cross the river. Enter beneath the China Post sign on the left side of the street; the hotel is above the post office on the second floor. Rooms have good lighting and TV; try to get one that also has air-conditioning and bath. (☎323 1436. Singles Y60; doubles Y60; triples Y75.) The **Electric Energy Guesthouse** ❶ (diànlì zhāodàisuǒ; 电力招待所) is on the left side of the main road, 200m beyond the bridge over the river. The rooms are in good condition. (☎333 1519; fax 333 1910. Singles Y50; doubles Y80; triples Y90.) Leishan's elite guests stay at the **Leishan Hotel** ❷ (léishān bīnguǎn; 雷山宾馆). From the bus drop-off point, walk into town and take a right at the intersection. The hotel is to the right of the big pink building at the end of the road. The improvement in the rooms doesn't justify the difference in price, but it's a clean third option. (☎333 4329. Singles and doubles Y86 per person; triples Y180.) Streetside food stalls, small restaurants, and fruit vendors cluster around the post office.

SOUTHWEST

XIJIANG 西江

☎0855

Xijiang, southwest of Kaili, is said to be the largest Miao village in the region. Set in the Longgong Hills, Xijiang receives accolades for its scenic beauty; many consider it the loveliest village in the area. It is also the ideal place to pass the Miao New Year (mid-Oct.), when locals pile their finest silver and enjoy a good bullfight or two. To get to Xijiang, take the **bus** from Kaili to Leishan, where you hop on another bus to Xijiang (1½hr., every 30min. 7am-6pm, Y6). To return, the last bus leaves for Leishan at 4pm, so staying the night is usually necessary. Fortunately, in endearing Xijiang, this should be no hardship. The **Government Guesthouse** ❶ (zhèngfǔ zhāodàisuǒ; 政府招待所) is just off the main road. Turn right from where the bus stops and then right again at the first road; the guesthouse is on the right. (☎334 8030. Dorms Y20. Bargaining may be possible.)

CHONG'AN 重安

☎0855

Tiny Chong'an is the place to be when the local **market** comes to life by the river. The market, which draws mostly Miao and a few Dong traders, spreads into local alleyways and produces human traffic jams. Snorting pigs and screaming chickens add to the pandemonium of buying, selling, auctioning, and haggling.

If you're unlucky enough to miss the area's wildest market, the area around Chong'an also offers some wonderful hiking options. A short walk along the river offers some good views of the lazy waterway. To venture out of Chong'an, walk up the main road in the direction away from Kaili and turn right at the end; the path leads to a **Gejia minority village** several hours away. Guides (Y20) can be arranged at area hotels. The **Xiaojiangnan Guesthouse** (☎245 1208) has a list of suggested routes, including a 10-hour trip through **Mulao minority villages,** with a stop for lunch. The guesthouse can also arrange **bus tours** of the area (6-10 people, Y100 per day), 10km trips by **horse cart** (3-4 people, Y30), 10km outings in a **fishtail boat** (10-15 people, Y80), and, for the proud and the brave, 5km trips in an "**armored wooden boat**" (Y30).

To get to Chong'an, take the direct **bus** (2hr., Y8) from Kaili or get off on the way to Huangping (黄平) or Shibing (施秉). **Chong'an Jiang Holiday Resort** (chóng'ān jiāng lǚyóu tíngcūn; 重安江旅游停村) is on the road back to Kaili, a 10-minute walk from the bus stop, on the left with an English sign. The staff here will bend over backwards for you. The **Xiaojiangnan Guesthouse** (xiǎojiāngnán zhāodàisuǒ; 小江南招待所) is in a two-story brick building just before the Chong'an Jiang Holiday Resort. The **Tourist Vacation Village** (lǚyóu dùjiàcūn; 旅游渡假村) next door to the Xiaojiangnan has similar accommodations.

SHIBING 施秉

☎0855

Shibing, a small city northeast of Chong'an, is more of a crossroads than a destination. Most travelers use the town as a base from which to explore the **Wuyang** (wǔyáng hé; 舞阳河) and **Shamu** (shāmù hé; 杉木河) **Rivers. CITS** (☎422 1177), in the Minfu Hotel on Dong Jie, can arrange cruises, rafting, and tubing trips.

Smaller than the Wuyang, the Shamu river offers calmer waters and relatively less spectacular scenery. The Shamu's slow-paced meandering does, however, allow visitors to stop and swim in deeper pools. As you drift, be sure to pull your raft to shore occasionally to savor the enticing barbecued fish, chicken, corn, frog, or crab that locals serve up. (Try to join a CITS group already heading out to the Yantai Mountains. Buses from town (round-trip Y15) and from the train station (Y100) go to the Shamu River. River admission Y100. Raft rental Y100.)

The most scenic way to travel between Shibing and Zhenyuan is by boat along the Wuyang River. Catch the bus running to Zhenyuan and ask to be let off in the

KAILI MINORITIES: THE DONG Over half of China's two and a half million Dong people live in southeast Guizhou. Historians trace the evolution of Dong culture back to the Qin and Han era, even though the people do not make an appearance in Chinese records until the Song dynasty, when the entire Dong population picked up and moved south to avoid the invading Mongols.

The Dong culture remains distinct from mainstream Han culture in many important aspects. The spoken language of the Dong is loosely related to the other languages in the Sino-Tibetan family, but it more closely resembles the languages of the Zhuang and Shui peoples. Although they use the Chinese script, the Dong spoken language utilizes over 15 tones. Their religion is based around a complex pantheon of spirits and demons, but Buddhist imagery has heavily influenced Dong architectural styles.

The Dong are widely respected throughout China for their architectural achievements. Their distinctive villages usually sit in foothills, where houses are raised up on pilings. Most Dong villages of any significant size include at least one pagoda-like wooden drum tower; in larger towns, these towers are often as high as 30m. The Dong are also known as master bridge-builders, and examples of their "wind and rain bridges" span rivers throughout Guizhou.

village of **Caizawan,** 3km from Shibing. Once in Caizawan, walk down through the village and turn left toward the hydroelectric power station, so that the village is to the right and there is a gorge in front of you. Scramble over the rocks to find available boats at the dock. With bargaining, the trip should cost about Y50 per person. All boats follow a fairly similar route through river gorges, waterfalls, and mineral formations along the lines of Peacock Rock. The one-hour trip ends about 17km from Zhenyuan, near the **Buddhist Green Dragon Temple** (Y10). To get to Zhenyuan, walk up the hill and wait for the bus. Buses to Zhenyuan (Y6) will be going in the direction that leads uphill.

DONG VILLAGES 侗村 ☎0855

This region, on the formidable road between Guizhou and Guangxi provinces, is said to be one of the single most stunning areas in China. Roads are bad, transport links spotty, and tourists rare indeed. The outlay of time and patience will be rewarded many times over by the chance to experience, amid blindingly beautiful scenery, a culture virtually unknown to most Westerners.

Buses (6hr., every hr. 6am-5:30pm, Y20-30) rumble from Kaili to **Rongjiang** (榕江). From Rongjiang, more buses huff and puff on to **Xiajiang** (下江) via **Tingdong** (停洞). Some buses go directly from Rongjiang to **Congjiang** (从江), at the Guangxi border; others terminate at Xiajiang, making it necessary to take another bus to reach Congjiang. Westbound travelers should keep in mind that the last bus from Congjiang to Xiajiang leaves in the early afternoon. If you miss it, taking a taxi to Xiajiang may be worthwhile, since no one who puts forth the effort to get to Dong county should even think of missing this remarkable town.

In general, Xiajiang is a better place to spend the night than the more expensive, less charming Congjiang. However, **Gaozhen** and **Xiaohuang,** two tiny villages near Congjiang, and **Basha,** 7km from Congjiang, are all excellent places to explore and easily justify the trip to Congjiang. Due to difficult road conditions and scarce transportation, the Kaili CITS recommends hiring a taxi (half-day Y100) in this area. Betwen Rongjiang and Congjiang lies **Zengchong,** a village famous for its 311-year-old drum tower.

ZUNYI 遵义

☎0852

In 1935, this backwater-to-end-all-backwaters made its way onto the map when the desperate, bedraggled Red Army staggered into town during the Long March (see p. 15). It was here that the central committee of the CCP met and decided to hand the chairmanship to a Hunanese peasant partisan by the name of Mao Zedong. The site where this famous agreement was made is Zunyi's only worthwhile attraction; the city itself is over-industrialized and run-down. As with other semi-major towns in Guizhou, Zunyi can also be used as a base from which to explore the marvelous countryside.

ORIENTATION AND PRACTICAL INFORMATION

The train and bus stations cluster off **Waihuan Lu** (外环路), which leads to the main shopping street, **Zhonghua Lu** (中华路). **Zijun Lu** (子君路), the fabled conference sight, and the entrances to the city park are on the other side of **Phoenix Hill** (fènghuáng shān; 凤凰山), which marks the center of town.

Trains: Zunyi Train Station (zūnyì huǒchē zhàn; 遵义火车站; ☎883 2074), just off Waihuan Lu. The ticket office is in the middle facing the station; an information window is on the left. To: **Chengdu** (14½hr., 2 per day, Y61); **Chongqing** (10hr., 12 per day, Y28); **Guiyang** (2½-4hr., 13 per day, Y14); **Kunming** (17hr., 2 per day, Y66).

Buses: Zunyi Bus Station (zūnyì qìchē zhàn; 遵义汽车站; ☎885 8084), just off Waihuan Lu, in front and to the left of the train station. Purchase tickets once on board the bus. To: **Chishui** (10-12hr., daily, Y50); **Guangzhou** (34hr., daily, Y120); **Guiyang** (1½hr., every 30min. 5am-7pm, Y20).

Local Transportation: Bus **#3** leaves from Waihuan Lu, runs along the edge of town, and then heads down Zhonghua Lu (Y0.5).

Taxi: Base fare Y5.

Bank of China: On Xinhua Lu. From the large traffic circle, turn right off Zhonghua Lu and walk for 5min.; the bank is in a huge building on the right. Exchanges traveler's checks. Credit card advances. Open daily 8am-5pm.

Internet Access: Louzhuang Computer City (lóuzhuāng diànnǎo chéng; 楼装电脑城), a computer store on Louxiang Gonglu. Y4 per hr. Open daily 8am-7pm.

Post and Telecommunications: On the corner of Xinhua Lu and Zhonghua Lu. EMS and Poste Restante. Open daily 8am-10pm. **China Telecom** is next door. Open daily 8am-6pm. **Postal Code:** 563000.

ACCOMMODATIONS AND FOOD

Cheap rooms are sadly lacking in Zunyi, but the few budget options are very budget indeed. The best places to look for accommodations are on Beijing and Shilong Lu or off Waihuan Lu.

Restaurants, snack stalls, and fruit vendors are concentrated around the train and bus stations and in small alleys off **Zhongshan Lu.** Hotpot is available in restaurants just up the road from the train station.

SIGHTS

ZUNYI CONFERENCE SITE (zūnyì huìyìzhǐ; 遵义会议址). After the GMD drove the Red Army out of their guerrilla stronghold in Jinggangshan (see p. 427) in

Jiangxi province, the rapidly dwindling forces played a deadly game of hide-and-seek with the GMD as they fled through the Guizhou countryside. When the Army stopped off in Zunyi midway through their Long March, the top CCP leaders spent three days and nights (January 15-17, 1935) engaged in acrimonious arguments over their future strategy. At the end of the meeting, a popular vote handed the chairmanship of the party to Mao Zedong.

The conference site is a mansion that originally belonged to a GMD-affiliated warlord. The house itself is nothing much, but just picturing Zhou Enlai, Zhu De, and other soon-to-be CCP big shots settling down in the various rooms is exciting enough. If you've come to Zunyi and decide to not visit this conference site, why, may we ask, have you come to Zunyi? *(On Zijun Lu. Open daily 8:30am-5pm. Y5.)*

MONUMENT TO THE MARTYRS OF THE RED ARMY (hóng jūn lièshì língyuán; 红军烈士陵园). This masterpiece of Soviet-style revolutionary art dates back to the days when Sino-Soviet relations were more friendly, and is markedly different from many other martyrs' monuments. It is also particularly poignant—three-quarters of the 80,000 Long March participants did not survive. (*Just off Fenghuang Lu. From Zunyi Park, proceed up the road and turn left at the end; the entrance is on the right. Free.)*

MILITARY FORTRESS (jūnshì chéngbǎo; 军事城堡). This fort was built in the Ming dynasty by a rebellious general who liked to stage Roman-style gladiatorial contests. The hike to the top is grueling and takes two to three hours, but it offers spectacular views. *(Free.)*

OTHER SIGHTS. The small but dense **Xiangshan Temple Complex** (xiāngshān sì; 湘山寺), off Zhonghua Nan Lu, sits on a hill that affords an impressive view of the city, factories, and TV towers. *(Continue from the traffic circle at the base of the street and turn left up a small winding alley; the temple is a few minutes up ahead. Open daily 7am-7pm. Y0.5.)* The smaller **Baiyun Temple** (báiyún sì; 白云寺), also off Zhonghua Nan Lu, is near a slightly more interesting covered market. *(Free.)*

CHISHUI 赤水 ☎0852

The little-visited but beautiful town of Chishui lies on the Guizhou-Sichuan border, about 300km northwest of Zunyi, in the middle of an isolated and untrampled subtropical forest. Chishui's landscape, cityscape, and cuisine have a distinct Sichuanese flavor, and the surrounding scenery is utterly stunning and virtually tourist-free. For those traveling from Guizhou to Chongqing and the Three Gorges, Chishui can provide a quiet and enchanting rest.

The two main attractions in the area are the **Shizhangdong Falls** (shízhàngdòng pùbù; 十丈洞瀑布), 40km south of Chishui, and the **Four Caves and Gorges** (sìdòng gōu; 四洞沟), just a few kilometers southwest of the town center. The falls may not be as high as the **Huangguoshu Falls** near Anshun, but they are far less touristed and an equally pleasant get-away. The cave and gorges, with four smaller waterfalls and a famous "sea of bamboo and ferns," are also worth a visit. Public buses and *miàndī* taxis run from the main **bus station** (chíshǔi kèyùn zhàn; 赤水客运站) in the southwest corner of town to both of these areas (to Shizhangdong Falls Y8-10; to the Four Caves and Gorges Y3-5); return transportation is available until dusk.

The best option for budget accommodation in Chishui is the **Postal Hotel** ❶ (yóuzhèng bīnguǎn; 邮政宾馆). From the main Chishui bus station, walk west to the first intersection and turn right; an English sign marks the front of the hotel. The hotel offers bright, clean dorm rooms and somewhat run-down standard rooms. (Dorms with common showers Y30; standard doubles, triples, and quads Y45-55. All prices can be bargained down 20-30%.)

Buses travel from the main bus station to **Zunyi** (14hr.; 6:30am Y70, 5pm Y80). Just across the bridge that separates Sichuan from Chishui, the **Jiuzhi Bus Station** (jiǔzhī chēzhàn; 九支车站) has buses to **Luzhou** (3hr., every 30min. 5am-5pm). At Luzhou, you can take a Y5 taxi to the **Xiaoshi Bus Station** to transfer to **Yibin** (2.5hr., Y15) or **Chongqing** (6hr., 2 per day, Y45). **Taxis** to sites within Chishui cost Y2-3. Tricyles cost Y1.

SICHUAN AND CHONGQING

Blessed with vigorous rivers, a mild climate, and endless rows of terraced greenery, Sichuan province and Chongqing municipality are justifiably known as China's "Heaven on Earth." The major breadbasket of the southwest, the area is home to a whopping 110 million people. Most live in the fertile and flat Sichuan basin centered around the provincial capital of Chengdu. The bustling city was the capital of Sichuan's own Kingdom of Shu in the 3rd century AD, spawning the hell-fire spicy food and the local dialect that are both unique to the region. Once the area's largest city, Chengdu's rival Chongqing (originally the eastern quarter of Sichuan) was penciled in as a municipality in 1997, instantly becoming the largest "city" in the world, with a population of over 30 million. In contrast, the western hinterlands of Sichuan are sparsely populated with Tibetans, Qiang, and Yi minorities, as well as wildlife such as the giant panda. The area's thundering rapids, snowy peaks, and furry yaks signal the geographic, border with Tibet. Sichuan and Chongqing boast some of China's most stunning natural features and cosmopolitan centers, truly making them must-see destinations.

HIGHLIGHTS OF SICHUAN AND CHONGQING

FIND YOUR INNER BUDDHA in the incense-filled temples of **Emeishan** (see p. 680) and at the Big Buddha of **Leshan** (see p. 676).

CUDDLE UP TO PANDA CUBS at **Chengdu's Giant Panda Research Center** (see p. 671) or the **Wolong Nature Reserve** (see p. 674).

MARVEL WHILE YOU CAN at the famed **Three Gorges** (see p. 705).

SICHUAN 四川

Sichuan has historically thrived in isolation from the rest of China. However, even isolation cannot last forever. The region's magnificent scenery has made Sichuan a popular destination for Chinese tourists. As the major state-sanctioned springboard to Tibet, Sichuan attracts its share of adventure-seeking Western tourists, as well. Indeed, Sichuan's remarkable mix of culture, nature, and adventure means that it is quickly losing its status as one of China's best-kept secrets.

CHENGDU 成都 ☎028

Beautiful tree-lined streets, soaring skyscrapers, and glitzy department stores conceal Chengdu's 2300-year history; where there were once only lush green fields there is now a major metropolis of 9.8 million residents, many of whom are riding high after the economic reforms implemented by Sichuan native Deng Xiaoping. Mobile phones, DVD stores, and multi-story McDonald's branches propel the city into the new millennium of free market economics and global communication. Despite the crowds and activity on every street corner and back alley, time passes at a remarkably slower pace within Chengdu's parks, gardens and temples, as locals finish their days with a pot of tea and a few rounds of *mahjong*.

The Qin dynasty (221-206 BC) established the city's remarkably successful Dujiangyan irrigation system, which diverts the Min River and supports one of the densest agricultural populations in the world. During the Eastern Han dynasty (AD 25-220), Chengdu garnered fame for its silk brocade, which was traded as far west as Rome. After the fall of the Han, loyalist Liu Bei and his brilliant advisor Zhuge Liang sought to revitalize the dynasty by establishing the short-lived Shu Han Kingdom (AD 221-263) and making Chengdu its capital—an endeavor immortalized by the novel *Romance of the Three Kingdoms*. During the Tang dynasty, the great poet Du Fu (AD 712-770) lived in a thatched cottage in the western part of Chengdu, where he penned over 240 poems. Numerous Daoist and Buddhist monasteries also dot the city's landscape. The ancient city wall and many other monuments were destroyed in the Cultural Revolution and replaced by tributes to Communism that include a gigantic statue of Mao that gazes over the city center to this day.

Mellow but overcrowded, Chengdu offers enough life, history, and culture to pique the interest of every traveler: spicy Sichuanese restaurants, tranquil tea houses, and famous historical sites. Chengdu's proximity to some gorgeous, mountain-in-the-clouds nature parks—notably Emeishan, Leshan, and Jiuzhaigou—makes it an ideal point for starting or ending one's journey through Sichuan.

TRANSPORTATION

Flights: Shuangliu Airport (shuāngliú jīchǎng; 双流机场; ☎570 0114), 16km southwest of the central districts. Mainly served by China Southwest Airlines, Dragon Air, and Sichuan Airlines. Public buses to the city leave from 20m outside the arrival gate (approx. every 30min. 4:30am-9pm, Y8). Taxis (40min., Y70-80) also make the trip. Airport tax Y50. To: **Beijing** (several per day, Y1300); **Guangzhou** (several per day, Y1190); **Guiyang** (several per day; Y570); **Kunming** (many per day, Y640); **Lanzhou** (many per day, Y860); **Lhasa** (3-5 per day, Y1270); **Shanghai** (several per day, Y1440); **Xi'an** (many per day, Y570); **Xining** (Tu and F, Y790).

Trains: Chengdu North Train Station (chéngdū běi huǒchēzhàn; 成都北火车站; ☎337 7523; inquiries 333 2633; schedule and reservations 666 4758), at the northernmost end of Renmin Bei Lu, at the intersection with Erhuan Lu. To: **Beijing** (33-56hr., 3-4 per day, Y390); **Chongqing** (11hr., 5 per day, Y63-179); **Emeishan** (2-3hr., 6 per day, Y12); **Guangzhou** (48-56hr., 2-4 per day, Y271-754); **Guiyang** (19hr., daily, Y72-226); **Kunming** (20-24hr., 3 per day, Y120-338); **Lanzhou** (27hr., daily, Y115-347); **Nanjing** (37hr., 3-4 per week, Y253-705); **Shanghai** (40-44hr., 2 per day, Y126-437); **Taiyuan** (30hr., daily, Y88-304); **Ürümqi** (49hr., daily, Y233-710); and **Xi'an** (19-40½hr., 2 per day, Y55-193).

Buses: Chengdu has bus stations in every direction, including **Ximen, Jiuyanqiao, Beimen,** and **Wuguiqiao** stations. Nearly all service nearby attractions like Dujiangyan.

Chengdu North Bus Station (chéngdū běimén zhōngxīn kèyùn zhàn; 成都北门中心客运站; ☎317 5758, info 317 5992, booking 317 3612), Chengdu's main bus terminal, is next to the train station. Exit North Train Station and stay on the right side of the square. Make a right on the first street from the square and go straight, following signs until the street ends and you enter a large gate. Buses #2, 16, 25, 28, 44, 64, and 65 stop nearby. Open daily 6:30am-6pm. To: **Chongqing** (4hr., every 30min., Y85); **Dujiangyan** (1hr., every 20min., Y10); **Kangding** (at least 12hr., 4:30am and 2pm, Y104).

New South Gate Bus Station (xīnnánmén qìchē zhan; 新南门汽车站; ☎543 3609), on Binjiang Lu, next to the Traffic Hotel on the south bank of the river. Open daily 8am-6pm. Buses to: **Emeishan** and **Jiuzhaigou** (10hr., 8am, Y93); **Kangding** (every hr. 7-11am, Y98); **Leshan** (every 30min. 7:30am-9:30pm, Y37); **Moxi** (6-8hr., 8:30am, Y121 plus an additional Y20 insurance fee). Buses to Moxi are also marked **Hailuogou** (海螺沟).

Shiyangchang Bus Station (shíyángchǎng qìchēzhàn; 石羊场汽车站), offers the quickest, most direct service to **Leshan** (every 20min., Y30) and often doesn't charge insurance fees like the other stations. Take bus #78 from Sam's Guesthouse.

West Gate Bus Station (xīmén qìchē zhàn; 西门汽车站), in the northwest, just beyond Yihuan Lu, on Menkou Lu by the Aba Hotel. Open daily 8am-6pm. To: **Dujiangyan** (1hr., every 15min., Y8-14); **Jiuzhaigou** (10hr., 3 per day, Y78-92); **Songpan** (1-2 per day, Y49); **Xiaojin** (10-11hr., 6:40 and 11am, Y72) via **Wolong** (Y43).

Local Transportation: The **Chengdu North Bus Station** also has a local station (☎317 6210). Exit the North Train Station and stay on the right side of the square; take the first right and the local bus station is 100m away, on the left. **Buses #55** and **64** go to the city center; **#16** runs from the North Train Station through the city center to the South Train Station. Fare Y1, with A/C Y2.

Taxis: Most taxis charge a base fee of Y5 during the day and Y6 at night, with Y1 for each additional 1.3km. **Tricycles** are a cheaper alternative; negotiate prices in advance.

ORIENTATION AND PRACTICAL INFORMATION

Chengdu's urban layout is quite confusing, with streets often changing names every few blocks and no clear axial orientation. Almost everything you will need, including banks, post office, most hotels and transportation hubs, are on or near the city's main axis: **Renmin Lu** (人民路), which extends north-south from **Tianfu Plaza** (天府广场) in the center of town to cross through the two ring roads that encircle the city. The North Bus Station and the train station sit at the far north end of Renmin Lu, where it intersects the second ring road **Erhuan Lu** (二环路). The Traffic Hotel and the New South Gate Bus Station are within a block of where Renmin Lu intersects the South River, a 20-minute walk south of Tianfu Plaza. Below the South River on Renmin Lu, inside **Yihuan Lu** (一环路), the first ring road, and near Sichuan University, you can find many Chinese and Western bars, cafes, and restaurants. Inside Yihuan Lu, several branches of the Bank of China and China Post line Renmin Lu, on either side of Tianfu Plaza. Just west of the central plaza on **Renmin Xi Lu (人民西路)** is **People's Park.** Farther west, just off the first ring road, are the city's main historical sites, including Du Fu's cottage and the Qing Yang Temple.

Tourist Office: China Chengdu Tourism Bureau (chéngdūshì lǚyóu jú; 成都市旅游局), 80 Zhengfu Jie, 7th fl. (24hr. ☎662 9858; complaints ☎662 2062; fax ☎662 0420), in the far north of the city. The office's main purpose is quality control; it settles disputes between tourists and hotels or travel agencies. Maps in Chinese, English, French, German, Japanese, and Korean. Open in summer M-F 8am-noon and 2:30-6pm; in winter 8am-noon and 2-5:30pm.

Travel Agencies: CITS, 65 Renmin Nan Lu, Er Duan (☎665 8731). Open M-F 8:30am-8:30pm, Sa-Su 9am-6pm. **CYTS** (chéngdū zhōngguó qīngnián lǚxíngshè; 成都中国青年旅行社), 6 Renmin Nan Lu, San Duan (☎558 3854), on the 7th fl. of the Baiyun Hotel. Open M-F 9am-6pm. Four travel agencies in the **Traffic Hotel** specialize in tours to Emeishan, Jiuzhaigou, Leshan, and Tibet. Open daily 8am-10pm. **Sam's Guesthouse** also arranges similarly priced tours and is a great source of unbiased information about travel in Tibet.

Camping/Backpacking Gear: China Golden Bridge Travel Service (zhōngguó jīnqiáo lǚyóu sìchuān gōngsī; 中国金桥旅游四川公司), a few doors down from Sam's Guesthouse. Sells mostly obscure but quality brands of backpacks (Y400-600), tents (Y400-500), and a small selection of hiking boots, fleece, and stoves. English spoken. Also arranges local tours.

Consulates: US (měiguó lǐngshìguǎn; 美国领事馆), 4 Lingshiguan Lu (☎558 3992, emergency ☎137 800 1422), off Renmin Nan Lu, between the 1st and 2nd ring roads. Accessible via bus #16. Open M-F 8:30am-6pm.

Bank of China: Main branch on Renmin Lu, near Qinglong Jie. Exchanges currency and traveler's checks. **ATM.** Open daily 8:30am-6pm. There are other branches throughout the city; a convenient one is on Renmin Nan Lu, a 5min. walk from Sam's Guesthouse.

Bookstore: Foreign Language Bookstore (wàiwén shūdiàn; 外文书店), 5 Zhongfu Lu (☎662 7582). A very limited range of foreign language books (mostly in English) books on Chinese culture, and a few English classics. Open daily 9am-7:30pm.

PSB: 144 Wenwu Lu (☎640 7114), 5min. north of the Mao statue. Visa extensions take 2 days at the office around the corner.

Hospitals: Sichuan People's Hospital (sìchuānshěng rénmín yīyuàn; 四川省人民医院), 32 Yiyuan Xi Lu, Er Duan (☎776 9982). **No. 1 Hospital of Huaxi Medical College** (huáxī yīkēdàxué fùshǔ dìyī yīyuàn; 华西医科大学附属第一医院), 37 Guoxue Xiang (☎555 1255). **Hospital of Chengdu Chinese Medical College,** 17 Shierqiao Lu (☎776 9902).

Pharmacy: Tongrentang Pharmacy (tóngréntáng yàodiàn; 同仁堂药店), 1 Zhongfu Lu (☎674 2926), 3min. from the Holiday Inn Crowne Plaza. Mostly Chinese medicine,

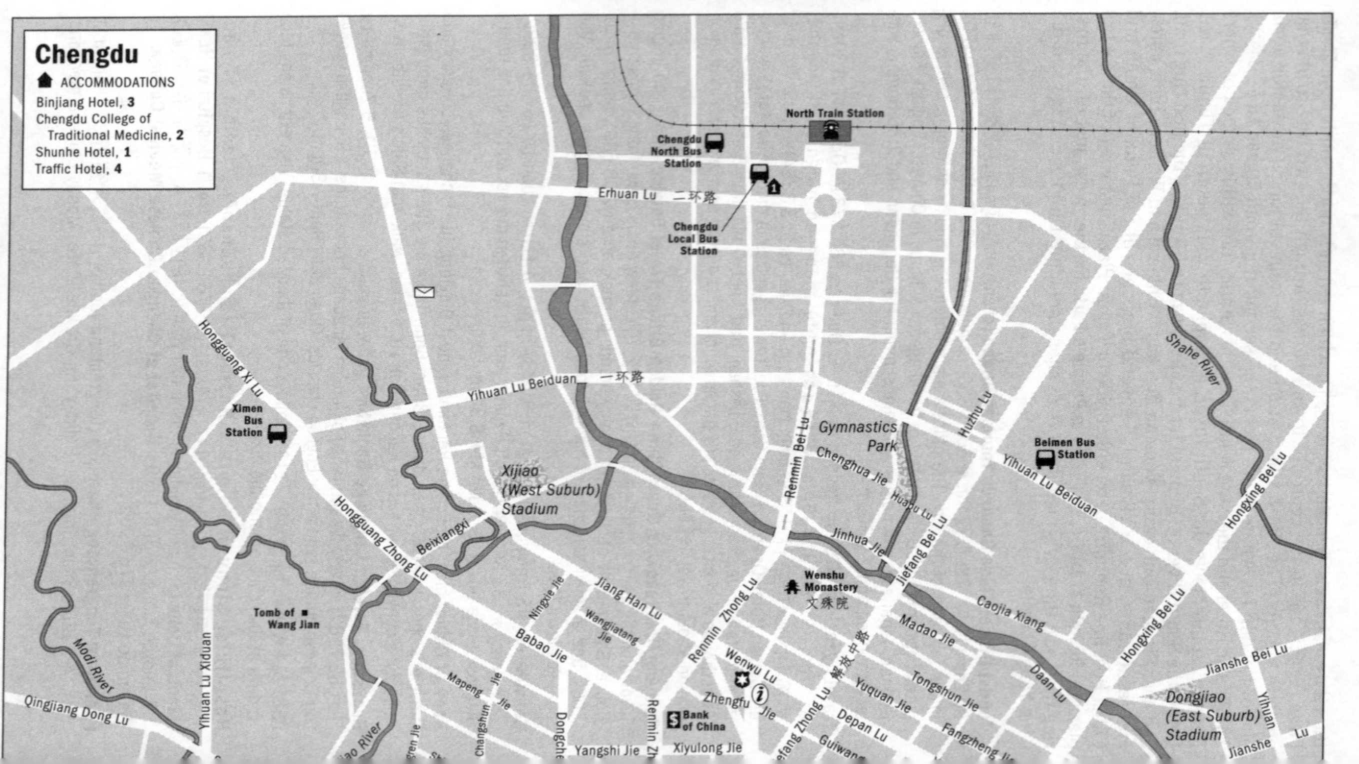
Chengdu
ACCOMMODATIONS
Binjiang Hotel, 3
Chengdu College of Traditional Medicine, 2
Shunhe Hotel, 1
Traffic Hotel, 4
North Train Station
Chengdu North Bus Station
Erhuan Lu 二环路
Chengdu Local Bus Station
Hongguang Xi Lu
Ximen Bus Station
Yihuan Lu Beiduan 一环路
Xijiao (West Suburb) Stadium
Hongguang Zhong Lu
Beixiangxi
Gymnastics Park
Renmin Bei Lu
Chenghua Jie
Huzhu Lu
Huahu Lu
Beimen Bus Station
Yihuan Lu Beiduan
Shahe River
Hongxing Bei Lu
Jinhua Jie
Jiefang Bei Lu
Wenshu Monastery 文殊院
Caojia Xiang
Madao Jie
Renmin Zhong Lu
Jiang Han Lu
Wangjiatang Jie
Ningxie Jie
Babao Jie
Tomb of Wang Jian
Modi River
Yihuan Lu Xiduan
Qingjiang Dong Lu
Mapeng Jie
Changshun Jie
Dongche
Renmin Zh
Yangshi Jie
Xiyulong Jie
Bank of China
Zhengfu Jie
Wenwu Lu
解放中路
Yuquan Jie
Depan Lu
Tongshun Jie
Fangzheng Jie
Daan Lu
Jianshe Bei Lu
Dongjiao (East Suburb) Stadium
Yihuan Lu
Jianshe

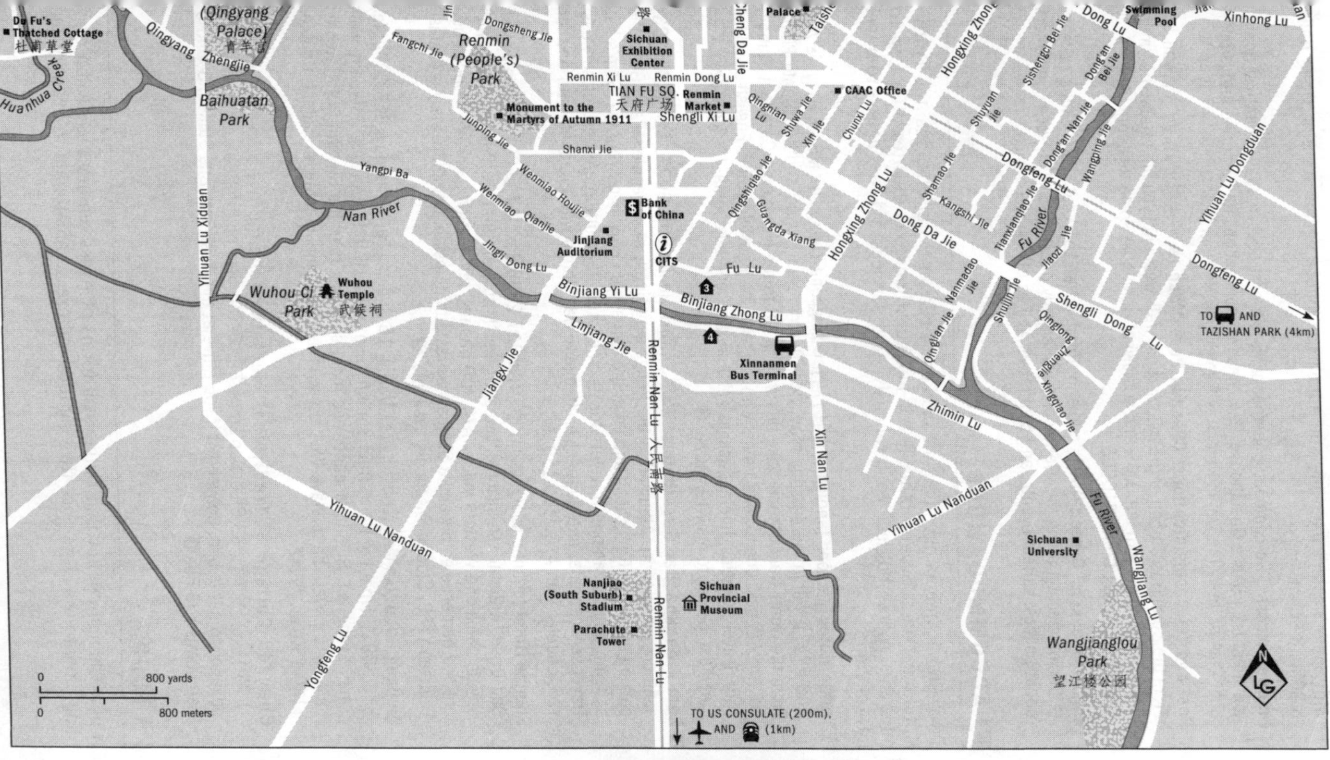

Du Fu's Thatched Cottage 杜甫草堂
(Qingyang Palace) 青羊宫
Qingyang Zhengjie
Huanhua Creek
Baihuatan Park
Dongsheng Jie
Fangchi Jie
Renmin (People's) Park
Sichuan Exhibition Center
Cheng Da Jie
Palace
Renmin Xi Lu
Renmin Dong Lu
TIAN FU SQ. 天府广场
Renmin Market
Shengli Xi Lu
Monument to the Martyrs of Autumn 1911
Junping Jie
Shanxi Jie
CAAC Office
Qingnian Lu
Shuwa Jie
Xin Jie
Chunxi Lu
Shuyuan Jie
Hongxing Zhong Lu
Sishengci Bei Jie
Dong'an Bei Jie
Dong'an Nan Jie
Wangping Jie
Dong Lu
Swimming Pool
Xinhong Lu
Yihuan Lu Dongduan
Dongfeng Lu
Yangpi Ba
Wenmiao Houjie
Wenmiao Qianjie
Nan River
Yihuan Lu Xiduan
Bank of China
Jinjiang Auditorium
CITS
Jingli Dong Lu
Qingshiqiao Jie
Guangda Xiang
Shamao Jie
Kangshi Jie
Dong Da Jie
Tianxianqiao Jie
Fu River
Jiaozi Jie
Fu Lu
Binjiang Yi Lu
Binjiang Zhong Lu
Nanmadao Jie
Qinglian Jie
Shuijin Jie
Qinglong Zhengjie
Xingqiao Jie
Shengli Dong Lu
TO AND TAZISHAN PARK (4km)
Wuhou Ci Park
Wuhou Temple 武侯祠
Linjiang Jie
Jiangxi Jie
Renmin Nan Lu 人民南路
Xinnanmen Bus Terminal
Xin Nan Lu
Zhimin Lu
Yihuan Lu Nanduan
Sichuan University
Wangjiang Lu
Nanjiao (South Suburb) Stadium
Parachute Tower
Renmin Nan Lu
Sichuan Provincial Museum
Yongfeng Lu
Wangjianglou Park 望江楼公园
0
800 yards
0
800 meters
TO US CONSULATE (200m), AND (1km)

with some Western medicine and supplies. Chinese doctor upstairs. Open daily 8:30am-8:30pm.

Internet Access: Two competing Internet cafes are next door to each other, just across the street from Sam's Guesthouse. Each has fast connections for Y3 per hr. and is open until 2am or later. The Traffic Hotel has 5 terminals. Y10 per hr.

Post and Telecommunications: Chengdu Post Office (☎674 1580), on Shawan Lu. From the North Bus Station or the train station, walk west until you hit a statue of a muscleman on a rock; turn left. EMS and somewhat unreliable Poste Restante. Open daily 8am-6pm. **Postal Code:** 610000.

English Speakers' Corner: On the corner of Renmin Nan Lu and Binjiang Zhong Lu, east of the intersection along the river. Locals will eagerly question English-speaking visitors about politics, current events, and culture—as well as offer travel advice.

ACCOMMODATIONS

Two establishments have become backpacker favorites in Chengdu: the Traffic Hotel and Sam's. Several other hotels and guesthouses in the area offer low- to mid-range rooms, but lack comprehensive tour services and easy access to travel information.

Traffic Hotel (jiāotōng fàndiàn; 交通饭店), 6 Lingjiang Zhong Lu (☎545 1017; ☎/fax 548 2777), within the first ring road, near Renmin Nan Lu, just south of Tianfu Plaza. From the North Train Station, take bus #55 or 28 to the New South Gate Bus Station; the hotel is next door. Clean rooms with A/C and TV. Knowledgeable English-speaking staff. Travel agencies, Internet access (Y10 per hr.), and bike rental (Y15 per day). Free breakfast. 3-bed dorms Y40. MC/V. ❶

Sam's Backpacker Guesthouse, 130 Shanxi Jie (☎609 9022; fax 447 6823; santour@yahoo.com). Attached to the Rongcheng Hotel, near People's Park. Go in the parking lot for the Rongcheng and enter the unmarked doorway on your left. Sam's has become popular among travelers for its price and its comprehensive tour services. Travel service, cafe, and currency exchange. 6-bed dorms with attached bath and fan Y25; doubles with A/C Y100-150. ❶

Shunhe Hotel (shùnhé jiǔdiàn; 顺和酒店; ☎317 2886; fax 317 5509), Erhuan Lu, Bei San Duan. A 2-star establishment west of the North Train Station. Pristine rooms with private baths and Western toilets. A/C, IDD phones, refrigerators, and TVs. Popular hotpot and barbecue eatery and a Sichuanese restaurant inside. Complimentary breakfast. Doubles Y180. Student discounts available. ❸

Binjiang Hotel (bīnjiāng fàndiàn; 滨江饭店), 16 Binjiang Lu, Yi Duan (☎665 6009; fax 666 8092). From the North Train Station, take bus #16 to the Jinjiang Hotel and walk 3min. to the left. Slightly cheaper and more spacious than the Shuhan Hotel. Rooms have A/C; private baths have Western-style toilets. Complimentary breakfast. Doubles Y140-180. MC/V. ❷

Chengdu College of Traditional Medicine (chéngdū zhōngyīyào dàxué; 成都中医药大学), 33 Shierqiao Lu (☎773 9909), just north of Cultural Park. Call in advance to nab a bed. Convenient if you arrive at the West Gate Bus Station. 3- and 6-bed dorms Y20-60. ❶

FOOD

A new Chengdu policy that outlaws all forms of street vending has dealt a crippling blow to the city's once-thriving food culture. In an attempt to beautify and "civilize" the city's appearance, police with pick-up trucks now make random sweeps of small alleys, confiscating any objects that lie outside the bounds of the building facades. Even buckets, brooms, and free-standing signs are hauled away by the beautifying brigades. As a result, street markets on Chunxi Lu and near the People's Park have been quieted and dining options are limited to excellent but less exciting restaurants. Various kinds of sweet dumplings and porridge are available in many shops along the downtown shopping strips.

Sichuan is famous for **hotpot** (huǒguō; 火锅), a basin of boiling, seasoned soup built right into the center of your table. Although Chongqing's hotpot is better known, there are plenty of great eateries in Chengdu as well. Streetside restaurants will generally cook meals for Y20 per person, or sell individual sticks of food for Y2-4. There is also a strip of more upscale establishments in the Sichuan Opera district along **Qintai Lu,** on the eastern edge of **Cultural Park.**

Other famous eateries include **Dan Dan Noodles** (dāndān miàn; 担担面; ☎674 4134), on the first section of Renmin Zhong Lu. **Lai Tang Yuan** (lài tāngyuán; 赖汤圆; ☎351 6011), on Zongfu Jie, right next to the Holiday Inn Crowne Plaza Hotel and Parkson Shopping Center, specializes in sticky balls (usually sweet, with ground black sesame, Y2 for 6). **Laohao Zhangyazi Duck Restaurant** (lǎohào zhāngyāzi; 老号张鸭子), down the street from Lai Tang Yuan, is also a wonderful place, where a plate of the famous duck costs Y18.

SICHUAN

Paul's Oasis, 1-28 Bingjiang Zhong Lu (☎667 3074), across from the Traffic Hotel. With graffiti-covered walls, plush couches, and Western music from breakbeat to flamenco, the Oasis is a watering hole in a desert of spices. The owner is an affable former professor of Chinese philosophy who cooks up a mean pizza (Y20-30) as well as other delicious Chinese and Western dishes. Imported beer available. A great place to meet other travelers (Paul is keen on introducing them to each other). Email access Y10 per hr. Open daily 9am until the last customer leaves. ❷

Shu Feng Garden Restaurant (shǔfēngyuán cāntīng; 蜀风园餐厅), 79 Huangmen Jie (☎558 7653), in the southwest section of the city, near Renmin Lu. The dining rooms feature Chinese paintings, ceiling lanterns, and beautiful wood carvings. A doting staff in red silk dresses serves up scrumptious food, including roast duck (zhāngchá yāpià; 樟茶鸭片; Y30), bear paw tofu (xióngzhǎng dòufǔ; 熊掌豆腐; Y15), and sizzling pork (tiěbǎn huìguōròu; 铁板烩锅肉; Y25). Open daily 11am-2am. ❷

Sucai Restaurant (sùcài cānguān; 素菜餐馆), in the Wenshu Monastery, inside the gate and to the left. This delicious vegetarian restaurant is in Chengdu's largest Buddhist monastery. Sucai provides plenty of excellent, cheap vegetarian food skillfully disguised as Sichuanese meat dishes (Y3-10 per dish). English menu. Open daily 11:30am-2:30pm and 5:30-6:30pm. ❶

High Fly Cafe (gāofēi kāfēi; 高飞咖啡), Renmin Nan Lu, San Duan (☎550 1572), a 5min. walk from the Nan River away from the city center, on the right side of the street. Western and Chinese food. After dinner, stuff down a brownie à la mode (Y10). High Fly throws Saturday night parties with dancing and live music that run until morning. Otherwise, open daily 8:30-1am. A new branch has opened at 18 Binjiang Lu, just east of Renmin Lu along the river, across from the Traffic Hotel. It specializes in pizza (Y15-32) and Italian food, and offers coupons for 30min. of free Internet access with every purchase. Pizza delivery available. English spoken. ❷

Weixiangju Hotpot Restaurant (wèixiāngjū hǔogūo; 味香居火锅), 4 Xinguanghua Jie (☎665 6180), just east of Renmin Nan Lu, 1 block south of Shanxi Jie; look for the brown sign in front. All-you-can-eat hotpot, in a clean, nice decor. A wide selection of meats, fish, and vegetables. Y13 per person, plus Y5 for the pot. ❷

Chen Mapo Doufu (chénmápó dòufǔ diàn; 陈麻婆豆腐店), 197 Xiyulong Jie (☎675 4512), right smack in the city center, north of the Chengdu Stadium; take bus #16. Refreshing A/C and delicious spicy tofu (*mápó dòufǔ*, Y6). Open daily 10:30am-9pm. ❶

Huangcheng Laoma Restaurant (huángchéng lǎomá; 皇城老马), 20 Qintailou Lu (☎613 1752), a large stone relief marks the door. Be forewarned: when purchasing *huǒguō*, take care what you order–the Chinese fill their pots with unfamiliar eats like cow brains and duck intestines. Hotpot Y25-65. If organs aren't your thing, there are many other options available. Open daily 10am-11:30pm. ❸

TEA GARDENS

Tea-drinking, accompanied by playing cards, *mahjong*, and gossiping, ranks among the favorite pastimes of Chengdu's residents. The tea gardens found in virtually every park offer an escape from the city's endless cacophony of bicycle bells and car horns; Y3-8 can buy a little peace of mind.

One of Chengdu's most attractive tea gardens is in secluded **Wangjianglou Park** (wàngjiānglóu yuán; 望江楼园; entrance fee Y2, tea Y4), near Sichuan Union University. A more buzzing and energetic tea garden is in **People's Park** (rénmín gōngyuán; 人民公园), along Jinhe Lu. Here, a tea pavilion sits beside a lake shaded by willow trees where crowds gather in the early afternoon and evening (entrance fee Y2, tea Y5). For a more secluded and introspective tea experience, check out the park surrounding the **Tomb of Wang Jian** (wángjiànmù; 王建墓; entrance fee Y3, tea Y4), in the northwest of the city. Enjoy your beverage in a pavilion over a lily pond.

SIGHTS

DU FU'S THATCHED COTTAGE (dùfǔ cǎotáng; 杜甫草堂). Chengdu's most famous cultural relic is only a few blocks west of Qingyang Temple. During the chaotic An Lushan Rebellion that divided the Tang and Late Tang dynasties, Du Fu (AD 712-770), also known as the "Poet Saint," escaped to Chengdu, stayed for four years, and wrote about his harsh life in exile. Most of the majestic present-day buildings were built after Du Fu's time here, however. The legendary Tang poet produced roughly 240 poems, including the famous "verse for the destruction of my thatched-roof cabin by the autumn windstorm." Although the cottage today is a replica, the sheer beauty and mystique of the grounds makes this site a very worthwhile visit. *(On Qinghua Lu. ☎731 9258. Open daily 7am-5pm. Y30, young children and disabled travelers free.)*

QINGYANG TEMPLE (qīngyáng gōng; 青羊宫). Qingyang Temple, also known as the Green Ram Monastery, is one of China's most famous Daoist temples, serving as an active center of worship for Chengdu and the surrounding region. The giant "Hall of Hunyuan Originator" houses a deified Laozi that holds a large golden ring representing the state of chaos before creation. In the central courtyard sits the remarkable "Eight Diagrams Pavilion," a wooden structure built entirely without nails. Dragon-lovers will appreciate the 81 carvings of the mythical creature. The main building, the "Hall of Three Purities," contains statues of the supreme Daoist deities and the 12 golden immortals. *(On Qingyang Lu, just inside Yihuan Lu, near the West Gate. ☎776 6584. Open daily 8am-8pm. Y1.)*

GIANT PANDA BREEDING RESEARCH CENTER (dàxióngmáo fánzhí zhōngxīn; 大熊猫繁殖中心). The recently opened breeding center contains 12 to 13 adorable giant and red pandas housed in a pseudo-natural environment where, besides lounging, sleeping, and napping, the favorite activities include climbing trees and eating. Come between 8:30 and 10:30am to see them while they are being fed and are most active. Otherwise, it is difficult to catch a glimpse of them in their large forested arenas. For a much more intimate encounter with the pandas, head for the **Wolong Research Center** (see p. 674) where smaller pens bring you closer to the animals. The **Giant Panda Museum** also features life-size dioramas and detailed information on the evolution, feeding, and mating behavior of pandas, not to mention an exhibit displaying one lucky panda's carefully preserved reproductive organs. Sam's Guesthouse runs tours for Y50, which includes admission and transportation. *(About 16km northeast of the city center. No buses to the breeding center; taxis cost Y80-90. It is possible to bike to the center (3-4hr.). ☎350 9613. Open daily 7am-6pm. Y10.)*

WUHOU TEMPLE (wǔhòu cí; 武候祠). Wuhou Temple is over 1500 years old and holy ground to thousands of fans of the *Romance of the Three Kingdoms*, but is less interesting to those unfamiliar with the book or television movie. It is the most famous sight honoring Zhuge Liang (AD 181-234), the outstanding Shu prime minister of the Three Kingdoms period. Surrounded by manicured gardens, green lawns, and a large red wall, the Wuhou Temple houses over 40 stone tablets, the most valuable of which is **The Tablet of Three Wonders,** carved during the Tang dynasty (AD 618-907). The 41 clay statues, each 1.7 to 3m high, are the temple's most captivating aspects. Apart from gold-coated statues and traditional paintings, the temple also houses Zhuge Liang's chapel and Liu Bei's tomb, which is surrounded by a 180m-long brick wall. Be sure to check out the **Display Hall of Three Kingdoms Culture,** which houses sculptures, ink rubbings, and maps. *(231 Wuhou Ci Jie, in the southwest, across the Nanhe River from the downtown area. Accessible by buses #1, 10, 26, 53, 59, and 306. ☎555 2397. Open daily 8am-6pm. Y30, young children and seniors 70+ free.)*

PEOPLE'S PARK (rénmín gōngyuán; 人民公园). Near the city center, People's Park is—as its name suggests—heavily populated by Chengdu urbanites. A brief respite from the frenzy of city life, the diverse park boasts sectioned-off gardens containing plums, flowers, crabapples, bonsai, and of course, a tea house. A "Children's Paradise" houses rides and a swimming pool (Y7, children Y5). At the center of the complex is a large circular lake with small rentable boats (Y15 per hr.). A 31m-tall monument honors those who perished during the Xinhai Revolution (1911), when Chengdu residents fought imperial powers to build the Chengdu-Chongqing railway. *(From Tianfu Plaza, walk 5min. east along Renmin Dong Lu. Open daily 7am-midnight. Y2.)*

TOMB OF WANG JIAN (wángjiàn mù; 王建墓). Revered for his bravery, wisdom, and kindness, Wang Jian (AD 847-918) climbed the military ranks to become emperor of the Shu Kingdom. His mausoleum is reputed to be the largest of the royal tombs from the Five Dynasties and Ten Kingdoms Period (AD 907-979). Originally built into a small hill, only the stone platform upon which Wang Jian's coffin once rested still remains. The platform is decorated by exquisite stone reliefs that include depictions of 23 different types of ancient Chinese musical instruments. The mausoleum isn't much of an attraction, but the well-kept gardens arranged around the tomb are worth a look; narrow, bamboo-lined pathways lead to collections of bonsai trees and pavilions where you can enjoy a cup of tea. *(7 Fuqing Dong Jie, inside the 1st ring road and northwest of downtown. Accessible by bus #48. ☎774 4480. Open daily 8am-5pm. Park Y1, tomb Y20.)*

WENSHU MONASTERY (wénshū yuàn; 文殊院). Founded in the Sui dynasty (AD 589-618), Wenshu is a maze of gardens, shrines, and some 400 Buddhist statues gazing upon incense-filled courtyards; some, like the fine iron figures of the 10

SICHUAN

bodhisattvas, are recognized as great works of art. Wenshu also houses the **1000 Buddha Pagoda, The Hall of 500 Arhats,** and various paintings and calligraphy. The monastery is an ideal place to have a cup of tea (Y2-3) if you enjoy observing card-playing locals. Catch the monks chanting everyday at 5pm, or come earlier to dine at the fantastically cheap vegetarian restaurant (see p. 669). *(On Wenshu Yuan Jie, close to Renmin Zhong Lu, north of the city center. Accessible by buses #16, 55, and 64. ☎693 2375. Main gate open daily 8am-6pm, back gate 6am-9pm. Y1.)*

WANGJIANGLOU PARK (wàngjiānglóu; 望江楼). Wangjianglou Park (also called River-Viewing Park) is dedicated to the famous Tang poet Xue Tao. The park is a peaceful, less-crowded alternative to People's Park (see above). The top of the its elegant 28m-tall pagoda provides a wonderful view of the Fuhe River and the surrounding area, and the park boasts a serene tea garden, relics of the poet, Qing dynasty architecture, and rare species of bamboo. The over 150 types of bamboo have earned the park the name "Kingdom of Bamboo of Endless Charms." *(On Wangjiang Lu, near Sichuan Union University. Accessible by bus #35. Open daily 6am-9pm. Y3.)*

ENTERTAINMENT AND NIGHTLIFE

SICHUAN

Chengdu has numerous entertainment options, from soccer matches to bass-thumping discos to laid-back folk and rock venues. The cafes at Sam's Guesthouse and Paul's Cafe are also tried-and-true standbys, if you feel like kicking back with other travelers over cheap beer and VCDs.

Chengdu Soccer (zúqiú bǐsài; 足球比赛). The Chengdu or Sichuan soccer teams play other cities or provinces every Saturday and Sunday morning. The provincial-level games have better attendance and play quality than the city games, but any match is still a blast. Held in the main Chengdu Stadium, just northeast of Tianfu Plaza, and usually start at 7pm. Tickets Y10.

Focus (jiāodiǎn; 焦点), 100 Yandai Jie, Transport Bldg., 6th fl. (☎666 0326). Known as Chengdu's best club, it is also the most upscale and expensive. The city's hot spot for the young, rich, and beautiful, Focus sports a pulsating dance floor, a bandstand, an enormous circular bar, 6 bowling lanes (Y60-80 per hr.), darts, two pool tables (Y40 per hr.), and private karaoke rooms. Nightly live performances feature local pop stars, dancers, and bizarre touring acts. Shows that feature well-known performers require a ticket (Y150). Beer Y25 and up. Open daily 7pm until everyone leaves.

Top One (kǎkădū; 卡卡嘟), 16 Yihuan Lu, South Section (☎555 8999), near Sichuan Province Swimming Pool. A large bar encircles an elevated stage where musical and dance acts perform until 11pm. Red lights and plush seating fill the room, which is bordered by private karaoke rooms. After the performances, much of the youthful crowd heads downstairs to a hypnotic dance room, with spinning strobes. Beer Y25 and up. Open daily 7pm-3am.

Kinglane Club (xīnlěi; 鑫磊), 8 Dongcheng Gen Lu (☎677 0408), just off Renmin Nan Lu, south of the city center. A local nightlife scene in full bloom, replete with teeny boppers and middle-aged men. Two floors of bars and table seating gaze upon a dance floor filled with smoke and strobelights, where local singing and dancing acts perform. At about 12:30am, Kinglane starts spinning good House music. Beer Y25 and up. Open daily 7:30pm-1:30am.

12 Oaks Bar (shí'èr xiàngyuán; 十二橡园), 12 Renmin Nan Lu, #7, on a strip with 5 or 6 other bars. For a more laid-back night, head to the 12 Oaks, which has the feel of an intimate jazz bar. Musicians set a mellow mood while patrons sip cold beers (Y20) and mixed drinks. Head upstairs for couches and more intimate conversation. Live folk and rock music M, F-Sa. Open daily 2pm-3am.

Garden Cinema (huāyuán yǐngchéng; 花园影城), 18 Renmin Nan Lu (☎554 4206), next to the Province Swimming Pool. Year-old undubbed English movies run all day. Surprisingly comfortable fake leather sofas. Tickets Y5-10. Open daily 1:30-11pm.

DAYTRIPS FROM CHENGDU

DUJIANGYAN IRRIGATION SYSTEM 都江堰

56km west of the city. Take the bus from the West Gate Long-distance Bus Station, northwest of downtown Chengdu (1hr.; every 10min. 7am-5pm; Y8, express bus with A/C Y14). From Dujiangyan Transportation, cross the street and take bus #1 or 4 (every 10min., Y1). Returning to Chengdu, buses run until 7 or 8am. Open daily 8am-5pm. Y60.

The Dujiangyan Irrigation System is on the Min River in the northwest of Dujiangyan City. The river, a tributary of the Yangzi, flooded frequently thousands of years ago. In 256 BC, Li Bing, the governor of the Shu prefecture, diverted the river into a manmade channel through Mount Yulei and constructed an ingenious irrigation system. This system divides the Min into an inner and outer river, with two spillways to control flooding and collect silt. Since Dujiangyan's construction, the region has become a "Land of Abundance," with a yearly bumper crop.

Dujiangyan is divided into three parts: the **Fishmouth Pier** (yúzuǐ; 鱼嘴) splits the river in two; the **Feishayan Weir** (fēishàyàn; 飞沙堰) drains flood water and flushes out sediment deposits; and the **Mouth of the Precious Jar** (bǎopíng kǒu; 宝瓶口), or the trunk canal, cuts through Mount Yulei and diverts water to irrigate nearby farmlands. A typical tour starts at the left main gate and winds through the exhibition center and main dyke structures before crossing the beautiful **Anlan Bridge** (ānlán qiáo; 安澜桥), which is suspended (at least outwardly) by woven bamboo cables. From here the trail heads into the hills and returns along the far bank. Anlan was once called Fuqi (Husband and Wife) Bridge because it was built by a devoted couple; its chain railing is held together by locks that symbolize the pair's never-ending devotion. Up the hill and overlooking the irrigation project are temples and pavilions separated by forest and gardens, the most important of which is **Erwang Temple** ("Two Kings Temple"; èrwáng sì; 二王寺), built as a tribute to Li Bing and his son. The **Chenghuang Temple** is easily the most impressive structure on the hillside, with 10 levels of flying-eaved temples. You may also run into the **oldest tree in China,** measuring 3.6m across and dating back to the Yin Shang dynasty (1700-1100 BC). Get a bird's-eye view of the whole system by continuing up to the five-story-high **Qin Yen Lou**. Cable cars (Y25 per stop) run from Yulei Hill Park to Erwang Temple and Lidui Park.

Several cheap **eateries** (Y5-15 a meal) serving basic Sichuanese food line the street close to the entrance and riverfront. Although pure scenery-seekers may find Dujiangyan disappointing, the sheer ingenuity and history surrounding the ancient complex compensate for its rather drab appearance. The Y60 entrance ticket, however, isn't worth it.

QINGCHENGSHAN MOUNTAIN 青城山

About 70km from Chengdu. Daily buses depart from the West Gate Bus Station northwest of the city (1½hr., daily 7-10am, Y10-12). You can also take a bus from Dujiangyan (1hr., every 20-30min., Y3). Buses return only to Dujiangyan (1hr.; 4, 6, and 7pm; Y3). Train ride round-trip Y12. Cable car one-way Y25. Ferry ride one-way Y3. Or hike up the mountain (3½hr). Y41, children less than 1.3m tall half-price.

SICHUAN

Immersed in a sea of green trees and veiled in layers of chiffon mist, Qingcheng (Green City) Mountain is so named for good reason. A less rigorous climb than the one at Emeishan, Qingcheng offers much of the same captivating beauty. Apart from providing spectacular views of an ocean of greenish mist, the south face of the mountain, known as **Qingcheng Front Mountain,** is also home to numerous Daoist temples. The best preserved of these, **Jianfu Temple** (jiànfú gōng; 建福宫), lies at the foot of the mountain and dates back to the Tang dynasty, when it was known as Zhangren Temple. According to myth, a fairy once lived on Zhangren Mountain, practicing Daoism in seclusion; for good luck, a king visited the fairy before heading into battle. When the king later won the battle, he built Zhangren Temple in the fairy's honor. Today, the temple houses ancient relics in the Rugian and Weixin Pavilions.

Halfway up Qingcheng lies **Tianshi Cave** (tiānshī dòng; 天师洞), a mazelike temple dedicated to the Daoist master Zhang Ling. Built up on the mountainside, it eventually dips into the cave where Zhang once lived. Tianshi houses a giant gingko tree planted by Zhang Ling in the Han dynasty and a colossal boulder that supposedly split when a sky demon hurled a lightning bolt.

The **Shangqing Temple** (shàngqīng gōng; 上清宫), a multi-layered pavilion, dominates the mountain's first peak. A wood carving of the Daoist Scriptures is here, and three Daoist deities are consecrated: the High Lord Lilaojun and Daoism's founders Chui Yang and Sin Feng. From the rear of the temple, visitors can walk farther up the mountain to enter the six-story **Laojunge Pavilion** (lǎojūn gé; 老君阁; Y3). This massive structure is the highest point on Qingcheng and offers a stunning 360° bird's-eye-view of the greenery and mist below.

Jianfu Temple, Tianfu Temple, and Shangqing Temple, near the exit of the second cable car, all offer **food** and **accommodation** (Y20-30). Qingcheng Front Mountain can be done as a long daytrip out of Chengdu, or can be shortened by taking the cable car one way. Another option is to stay one night on the mountain, perhaps at Shangqing Temple, to catch the sunrise.

About 30km from Qingcheng Front Mountain is **Qingcheng Rear Mountain** (qīngchéng hoùshān; 青城后山), the north face of Qingcheng. Minibuses run frequently from Qingcheng Front Mountain to the Rear Mountain (30min., Y5). While the south face of Qingcheng is the more famous Daoist haven, the north face is better known for its picturesque natural scenery, caverns, waterfalls, gardens, and ancient graves. Tranquil and unspoiled, Qingcheng Rear Mountain offers a more secluded and less touristed alternative to the Front Mountain. At the main back mountain gate, a trail winds up through the **Qinan Temple** before reaching a cable car, which goes about halfway up the mountain to a small village; from here the trail continues up to the **Baiyun Temple** (báiyú sì;白云寺) near the summit. Another way up the mountain is to hike up the **Feiquan Gorge** (fēiquán gōu; 飞泉沟) from the bottom of the cable car, passing a small lake before reaching the **Heavenly Bridge** (tiān qiáo; 天桥), which goes over a small waterfall and up to the **Cloud-watching Pavilion** (wàngyún tíng; 望云亭). Continue up the trail past another pavilion and up to the Baiyun temple, passing a series of caves.

WOLONG NATURE RESERVE 卧龙自然保护区

100km northwest of Chengdu, the Wolong Nature Reserve is accessible from West Gate Bus Station by a Xiaojin-bound bus (3hr., 6:40 and 11am, Y43). Another option is to take a noon bus to Dujiangyan (every 15min., Y8-14) and transfer to a bus to Wolong (2-3hr., 2pm, Y13). Hail returning buses anywhere along the road through Wolong. Three direct buses to Chengdu run in the morning, the last at 10:30am (Y20). Or, you can take an 8am or 11am bus back to Dujiangyuan (Y13). Taking the bus to Xiaojin is the better option if you plan on hiking, since you can ask them to let you off at the trailhead for the

SICHUAN

PANDA-MONIUM The charismatic giant panda—currently an endangered species—once ranged over huge tracts of land in China and Myanmar in dense, high-altitude bamboo or coniferous forests. Today, fewer than 1000 wild pandas remain in small, isolated patches of Sichuan, Gansu, and Shaanxi provinces. The Wolong Nature Reserve in Sichuan is one of 11 natural areas protected by the Chinese government to preserve pristine, bamboo-bejungled panda habitat. As of late, panda conservation has captured the attention of the entire world. The adorable creatures are the emblem of the World Wildlife Fund, and over 100 pandas have been taken from the wild and placed in Chinese and foreign zoos.

Illegal poaching continues despite stiff laws, but China's pandas are most threatened by habitat destruction due to the burgeoning Sichuanese population. Because they eat tremendous amounts of only one species of bamboo, pandas need an exceptionally large habitat to survive. When the arrow-shoot bamboo in one area goes through its normal cycle of self-destruction every dozen years or so, pandas have to be able to migrate to other areas. So in isolated patches, pandas end up starving.

Because pandas are clownish, theatrical, and adorable animals that easily win over audiences, they are highly sought-after by zoos. The Chinese government has given or lent pandas to foreign zoos in the past as a gesture of friendship and goodwill. In 1936, fashion designer Ruth Harkness brought the first giant panda to be exhibited overseas to the United States. The panda, Su-Lin, arrived as an infant at the Brookfield Zoo near Chicago, IL, and was one of the zoo's biggest attractions until his death in 1938. Mao Zedong gave President Nixon a pair in 1972; Xing-Xing (Hsing-Hsing) and Ling-Ling were installed in the National Zoo in Washington, D.C. Ling-Ling died at the ripe old age of 23 in December 1992, and Xing Xing died seven years later. In December 2000, two giant pandas were again donated to the zoo. Tian Tian and Mei Xiang will be on a 10-year loan to the zoo, which is currently doing research on panda breeding and habitat conservation.

SICHUAN

Valley of Heroes, about 10km from the Dujiangyan bus stop. Otherwise, a ride from Wolong town can cost Y20. From Jiuzhaigou, take a return bus heading toward Chengdu, and get off at the town of ***Yinxin.*** *Then take a taxi van (Y20 per person) to the town of Wolong.* ☎ *(0837) 624 6615. Admission to the Giant Panda Research Center Y30.*

The Wolong Nature Reserve was established by the Chinese government in the late 1970s to protect the highly endangered—and highly adorable—giant panda. The panda lives in some of the most stunning and dramatic wilderness in Sichuan, and you may find your face pressed against the glass during the entire last hour of the bus ride to the reserve.

The pandas are best seen in the **Giant Panda Research Center** (dàxíongmāo guǎn; 大熊猫馆), halfway up the mountain, where they can be observed from behind bars (your chances of catching a glimpse of a panda in the wild are extremely limited). These furry and innocent-looking creatures, however cute, are far from harmless; bars protect onlookers from their powerful claws and 200kg bodies. Many a lucky visitor is able to pet and even shake hands with the young panda cubs housed in similar pens, since they are very curious and will rear up to stick their muzzles and paws out through the bars. The best time to visit the center is from 8am to 3pm, when the pandas are active and more likely to take an interest in visitors. Visitors can also pose for photos with the reserve's baby pandas (Y100). 25m farther up the mountain, the **Red Panda Center** (xiǎoxíongmāo guǎn; 小熊猫馆) is home to the less rare and more raccoon-like red pandas.

Up in the mountains, pandas, golden monkeys, takins, and pheasants can be observed in their natural habitat; even if no animals are seen, visitors can still find solace in nature's wondrous beauty. Wolong lacks major tourist facilities but offers the only real pristine hiking around Chengdu. Two of the best hikes in the area start from a bridge about 10km past the town of Wolong, which is itself about 7km past the Panda Center. Cross the bridge and hike up the **Valley of the Heroes** (yíngxíong gōu; 英雄沟; 3hr.), through a beautiful gorge. From the roadside trail-head, head in the other direction up to the Yinchang Valley (4-5hr.).

Wolong is a long haul from Chengdu, and transportation is limited, so if you plan on hiking, also plan on spending the night. There is a small **hotel** outside the Giant Panda Research Center on the way to the red panda center. Doubles run for Y200, but bargain. There is also lodging available in the town of Wolong (Y30 per bed). If your only intention is to see a panda, you may opt to stay in Chengdu and visit the Giant Panda Breeding Research Base instead (see p. 670). Maps of the area are available from the Panda Center ticket booth or at the Wolong Hotel in town (Y5).

FOUR MAIDENS MOUNTAINS 四姑娘山

*From Chengdu, take a bus (5hr., 6:40 and 11am, Y43) to **Xiaojin** (小金) and disembark at **Rilong** (日隆). Or, take a taxi (roundtrip Y200-300). The China Golden Bridge Travel Service (see p. 665) also arranges transportation and guides.*

About 100km past the town of Wolong, this area offers pristine, virtually untouristed hiking and camping opportunities. Higher in elevation than Wolong, the Four Maidens area consists of 3 main hiking trails, beginning in Rilong, where there are hostels with Y20-30 dorm beds. Ascending through wildflower-filled meadows and alpine forests, spacious views are dominated by the four snow-capped peaks that give the area its name. The highest peak towers at 6240m, while the lowest of the peaks has a more gentle slope and can be climbed in several days. Though food and accommodations are available here, expect to camp while you are climbing any significant distances, or stay on the lower trails and make day hikes.

LESHAN MOUNTAIN 乐山 ☎0833

The bustling city of Leshan, with a population of six million, becomes even more crowded each summer when hordes of tourists descend upon the city to visit the celebrated Big Buddha, the tallest stone statue in the world. Leshan was once an educational center that produced several members of the Chinese literati; today it has caught the nasty building bug: massive construction efforts have turned parts of the town into busy commercial centers, complete with neon signs, skyscrapers, and glittering advertisements. In spite of these modern disturbances, however, Leshan is still quite a beautiful city. It sits at the confluence of three major rivers and overlooks the Big Buddha, carved into a cliff face on the far shore. In the early morning the parks and plazas that line the river banks are filled with *tai chi* and *wushu* practitioners from the local martial arts schools; in the late afternoon, the young and old come to sip tea and relax with the setting sun.

TRANSPORTATION

Buses: Leshan Long-distance Bus Station (lèshān zhōngxīn chángtú qìchē zhàn; 乐山中心长途汽车站), 165 Jiading Zhong Lu (☎213 1080). Buses run roughly 7am-5pm. Luggage storage in the main lobby (6am-6pm, Y2 per day). To: **Chengdu** (2-4hr., every 30min., Y31); **Chongqing** (7hr., every hr., Y86); **Emeishan** (1hr., every

30min., Y15); **Kangding** (15hr., one each morning, Y65); **Yibin** (6hr., every hr. until 2pm, Y50). Coming from Yibin or Zigong, you may be dropped off at **Changjiang Bus Station** (chángjiāng kèyùn zhàn; 长江客运站), just off the old Leshan bridge farther west on Jiading Lu.

Ferries: Near Yutang Jie and Binjiang Lu. Ticket booth open daily 8:30-11:30am and 3-6pm. A boat heads for **Yibin** (daily, Y80), where passengers can catch boats to **Chongqing.** However, the boat only runs when the seasonal river waters are favorable; check with a local travel agent.

Local Transportation: Buses run between Leshan's 2 ferry piers along Binjiang Lu, near the Taoyuan Hotel. Local bus **#1** runs between the bus station and the dock area, stopping one block from the Education Hotel. **#3** runs from the back gate of the Wuyou temple to downtown Leshan, passing the Education Hotel. **Speedboats** give 30min. tours of the Buddha and the island for Y30 (☎211 7217; open daily 7am-7pm). The cheapest and most common way to get to the Buddha is to take the **ferry** (Y1) directly across the river to the left side of Lingyun Hill. Another ferry goes to the front of Wuyou Hill (Y2). After heavy rains, the ferries cease operation. Minimum 10 passengers, so you may have to wait as much as 30min.

Taxis: Base fare Y3, each additional km Y1.

Motorcycles and Tricycles: Y1-2 for any destination in the city.

ORIENTATION AND PRACTICAL INFORMATION

About 166km southwest of Chengdu, Leshan occupies the flat northwestern shores of the T-shaped intersection formed by the **Min** and **Dadu Rivers.** All of Leshan's attractions are carved on or built atop the rocky embankment on the far shore facing the city. The **Leshan Bridge** (乐山大桥) farther upstream and the **Minjiang Bridge** (岷江大桥) closer to the docks connect the island banks with the city bank of the river. On the city side, **Binjiang Jie** (宾江街) runs along the waterfront while **Jiading Lu** (嘉定路), also parallel to the Min River, flows farther inland, connecting the bus station in the north with the waterfront in the east. Farther inland still, **Renmin Lu** (人民路) crosses **Daqiao Xi Jie** (大桥西街), the road across the Minjiang Bridge.

Tourist Office: Leshan Tourism Bureau (lèshānshì lǚyóu jú; 乐山市旅游局; ☎213 6926), on Binhe Lu, in the city government's office. Open M-F 8am-noon and 3-6:30pm. The **Foreign Affairs Office** (wàiguórén bànshì chù; 外国人办事处), 17 Shanxi Lu (☎213 0971), has some English speakers and is better for complaints or questions. Open M-F 8-11:30am and 3-6:30pm.

Bank of China: 36 Renmin Nan Lu, Huangjia Shan (☎212 5121). The only bank in Leshan that exchanges currency and traveler's checks. Credit card advances. International **ATM** outside. Open daily 8am-6pm.

PSB: 5 Chunhua Lu (☎249 9048), in the far west. Open daily 8-11:30am and 3-6pm.

Pharmacy: Leshan City Medical Company (lèshānshì yīyào gōngsī; 乐山市医药公司), 3 Tuqiao Jie (☎213 2064). Open daily 8:30am-8:30pm.

Hospitals: Leshan City People's Hospital (lèshānshì rénmín yīyuàn; 乐山市人民医院), 76 Baita Jie (☎211 9328), up the street from the Jiazhou Hotel. **Leshan City Red Cross Hospital** (lèshānshì hóngshízì yīyuàn; 乐山市红十字医院), 45 Xincun Jie (☎213 9082), appears slightly cleaner and newer than the People's Hospital. Both open 24hr.

Post and Telecommunications: Post and Telecommunications Office (yóudiàn shāngchǎng; 邮电商场; ☎211 8384), on Yutang Jie. EMS, IDD service, and **Internet** access (Y3 per hr.). Post office open daily 8am-8pm. Telecommunications office (2nd fl.) open daily 8am-10pm. **Postal Code:** 614000.

ACCOMMODATIONS

With most tourists arriving in high-rolling tour groups, individual travelers are often left stranded, and accommodations in Leshan do not cater to the average budget traveler.

Taoyuan Hotel (táoyuán bīnguǎn; 桃源宾馆), 12 Binjiang Jie, near the ferry pier and across the river from the Big Buddha. With clean, bright, carpeted rooms and an unbeatable location, this is the best value in the city. Lone travelers must pay for the whole room. Doubles with attached bath Y80. ❶

Jifenglou Hotel (jífēnglóu bīnguǎn; 集风楼宾馆; ☎230 2807), next to Lingyun Temple. Though you miss out on the lively atmosphere and good food on the city side of the river, the Jinfenglou offers a quiet stay, a gorgeous setting, and easy access to the Big Buddha park. Clean bathrooms, A/C, IDD, and TV. 24hr. hot water. Doubles Y120-180. ❷

Postal Hotel (yóudiàn bīnguǎn; 邮电宾馆), next to the Post and Telecommunications office on Yutang Jie. A 5min. walk from the waterfront, the Postal Hotel is the most reliable option for single travelers not willing to pay high prices for double rooms. Standard doubles Y260; clean triples with bath Y50. ❹

Education Hotel (jiàoyú bīnguǎn; 教育宾馆; ☎219 3951), off Jiading Lu midway between the bus station and the dock. Not too close to the waterfront, but a very pleasant place to stay for those on a tight budget. The cheapest rooms are few, so don't count on one being available. Tiny singles with fan and TV Y30; doubles Y100. ❶

B.B. House, 2 Daqiao Xi Jie, just south of the Minjiang Bridge before Renmin Lu. Sam Zhang, a private English teacher in Leshan, offers information services and Y20-40 dorm rooms with 24hr. hot water in associate school dorms. For about 2hr. of language exchange with his students, you can stay for free. The hostel and language exchange program were just starting up in July 2001, so you may want to check in advance on its status before arrival. ❶

FOOD

Leshan is renowned for its *xībà dòufǔ* (西坝豆腐), said to be an especially delicious tofu because of the waters used to prepare it. Near the Taoyuan Hotel, tofu restaurants line the streets and serve many variations of *xībà dòufǔ*. If you're looking for an upscale environment, try **Xiba Doufu Restaurant** (xībà doùfǔ dàjiǔdiàn; 西坝豆腐大酒店), 121 Binjiang Lu (☎210 0848), in the same area.

Roast meat and vegetables (Y0.2 per skewer) and dumplings (Y1-2 per bowl) can be found on the strip along the river from the pier to the Jiazhou Hotel (if coming out of Taoyuan, turn right). Visitors dine outside at the small restaurants and tea houses that pack the strip (dishes Y5-10 each). Small and dusty, **The Yang's Restaurant,** 49 Baita Jie, just across from the Leshan City People's Hospital, is a foreigner hangout with an English menu. The food is relatively inexpensive, and the English-speaking Mr. Yang arranges popular tours to the countryside. For a real (albeit expensive) escape, check out the zany and well-furnished **Newcastle Pub** (jīngdiǎn shíguāng; 经典时光), 5 Baita Jie, attached to the Jiazhou Hotel and a little closer to the river than Mr. Yang's. The pub offers imported coffee (Y20-50), milkshakes, some foods and snacks (Y5-12), and a few imported beers.

SIGHTS

BIG BUDDHA 大佛

Across the river from the city. The best way to get there is to take the ferry (Y1); make a right off the dock and walk 200m to the entrance of Lingyun Temple. Tour boats (Y30) from the Leshan pier (see ***Practical Information,*** *p. 677) drift by the Big Buddha for a quick view. Lingyun Temple and Big Buddha Y40, children under 1.2m free.*

The construction of the Big Buddha began in AD 713 and lasted 90 years. Today, the statue is the world's largest (and least imaginatively named) Buddha. The Big Buddha (dà fó; 大佛) was designed by the monk Haitong in order to control the menacing waters of the Min, Dadu, and Qingyi rivers that once wreaked havoc on the people of Leshan. Despite the Big Buddha's serene look, untouched by wear and tear, time has taken its toll on other parts of the Enlightened One, and curious patches of body hair have sprouted up in the form of green vegetation. At the top, visitors can stick a finger into the Buddha's ear or pat his nose for good luck. Doing both at the same time is not recommended. On the way down the flight of steps from his head to his manicured toes, a white scar can be detected on the Buddha's chest, where a thief dug a book of Buddhist scriptures and a jade statue of Avalokiteshvara out of the Buddha's chest. The descent down takes about 10 minutes.

OTHER SIGHTS

LINGYUN TEMPLE (língyún sì; 凌云寺). Also known as Big Buddha Temple, Lingyun Temple was built in the 7th Century and has magnificent gold-plated statues of Sakyamuni, the 5 *bodhisattvas*, and 18 *arhats*. The main courtyard is lined with corridors depicting the history of the Big Buddha and other large Buddha statues. Behind the main chapel is **Zangyanfazheng Hall,** which pays tribute to the monk Haitong and two others who contributed to the taming of rivers: Li Bing and Zhao Yu. Haitong is the statue with the missing eyes; legend has it that Haitong dug out his eyes to convey his sincerity and good faith, as well as to blind himself to the corruption of the age. Li Bing built Dujiangyan resevoir, and Zhao Yu is the hero who is said to have slain a ferocious flood-causing river dragon. The small chapel next door, dedicated to a statue of Sakyamuni, is carved out of just one piece of wood. *(On Lingyun Hill. Enter from the Big Buddha entrance.)*

WUYOU TEMPLE (wūyóu sì; 乌尤寺). Wuyou Hill and Lingyun Hill were attached until Li Bing, the engineer for Dujiangyan, sliced a waterway between them 2000 years ago to rid the island of its flooding problems. Wuyou Hill is said to resemble the head of a sleeping Buddha; a temple perches atop, granting magnificent views of the surrounding rivers and hills. The steep climb and isolated location deter most tourists, creating a quiet and mystical atmosphere. At the entrance to Wuyou Temple, four giant gods boldly stand guard. Inside the main chapel stand gold-plated statues of the Buddha of Boundless Life, Sakyamuni, Puxian, Bodhisattva of Wisdom, and Wenshu, Bodhisattva of Behavior; a statue of the Goddess of Mercy stands in a small side chapel. The rear of the main chapel holds the temple's best-regarded statues, Song dynasty iron casts of the three **Saints of the West.** While in the Wuyou Temple complex, you may want to check out **Arhat Hall,** with contemporary, life-like sculptures of each of the 500 *arhats*. *(Accessible by bridge from Lingyun Hill, or by ferry from the main pier Y5. Open daily 8am-6pm.)*

MAHAO CAVE TOMBS (máhào yámù; 麻浩崖墓). Cave tombs were popular in Sichuan during the Han dynasty, when people believed in ghosts, superstitions, and the afterlife. While the tombs themselves have little to see, the museums that are interspersed throughout the compound display a number of beautiful stone carvings and various funerary objects. *(At the foot of Lingyun Hill, left of the Haoshang Bridge. Open daily 8am-6pm. Y2, children under 1.3m free if accompanied by an adult.)*

DONGFANG FODU MUSEUM (dōngfāng fódū; 东方佛都). The museum is constructed in an Indian architectural style, complete with red earth and stylized domes. Dongfang Fodu boasts one of the largest collections of replicated Buddha statues around, ranging from the huge, 173m-long reclining Buddha on the hill (constructed in just two years) to the modern copies of statues taken from China by foreign powers. With authentic Buddha statues all over the island, you may find that this site is not worth the price or time. *(To the right of Haoshang Bridge. Take the passenger scooters Y5. If walking, go past the minibuses and down the dirt path; veer left when it becomes a paved road, and continue walking for about 1km. Open daily 8am-7pm. Y25.)*

EMEISHAN MOUNTAIN 峨眉山 ☎0833

One of the four famous Buddhist mountains in China, Emeishan lies 20km west of Leshan. In the past, worshipers impatient to become Buddhist deities believed one could compensate for not leading a life of self-sacrifice and abstinence by leaping off Sheshen Cliff near the Golden Summit onto a rocky platform resembling Buddha's outstretched palm. Today, devout Buddhists prove their faith by fending off ferocious monkeys and chattering tourist groups on their way to the various temples that are scattered throughout the peaks.

The number of temples that dot Emeishan's peaks may be impressive, but the views steal the show. Narrow, stone-paved trails thread through valleys crisscrossed by waterfalls and mineral pools, ascend towering cliff faces, and reveal views of layered peaks receding into the mist. Looking down on a sea of clouds or a sparkling sunrise, very lucky visitors may witness the phenomenon known as **Buddha's Light** (fóguāng; 佛光), said to occur only 14 times a year on unpredictable days. On these rare occasions, your shadow is cast from the peak into the mist before you, and a colorfully glowing halo encircles the shadow of your head as if you have attained Enlightenment. You will more likely be enveloped in Emeishan's frequent thick fog and drizzle, however, but the trailside scenery of jungle forest and ancient, gnarled trees will still make you feel like a mystical wanderer.

TRANSPORTATION

Trains: Emeishan Train Station (éméishān huǒchē zhàn; 峨眉山火车站; ☎547 0699), on Mingshan Dong Lu, Shengli Town, about 4km east of Emeishan. To: **Chengdu** (2½hr., 4-5 per day, Y12-22); **Chongqing** (6hr., daily, Y52); **Kunming** (19hr., 3 per day, Y109); **Panzhihua** (14hr., 4-5 per day, Y41-71); and **Xi'an** (21hr., 2 per day, Y113).

Buses: The **Long-distance Bus Station** (éméishān kèyùn zhàn; 峨眉山客运站; ☎553 3084) is on Mingshan Dong Lu. To: **Chengdu** (2hr.; every 30min. 5am-6pm; Y25, with A/C Y32); **Chongqing** (5-6hr., 8:20am, Y91); **Dujiangyan** (3hr., 4pm, Y37); **Leshan** (30-40min., every 15min. 6am-6:15pm, Y5.5); **Yibin** (5hr., 7:10am and 12:50pm, Y44); **Zigong** (3hr.; 8:20, 8:50, 11am, 1:50, 2:30pm; Y18, with A/C Y32). The **Baoguo Monastery Lianyun Bus Co.** (bàoguó sì liányún qìchē gōngsī; 报国寺联云汽车公司; ☎552 2299), next to the Teddy Bear Cafe, has buses to **Chengdu** (2hr., approx. every 45min. 6:30am-6pm, Y35) and **Chongqing** (7:30am and 4:30pm, Y95). Check the main lobby's timetable (in Chinese and English). The travel agencies in **Emeishan**

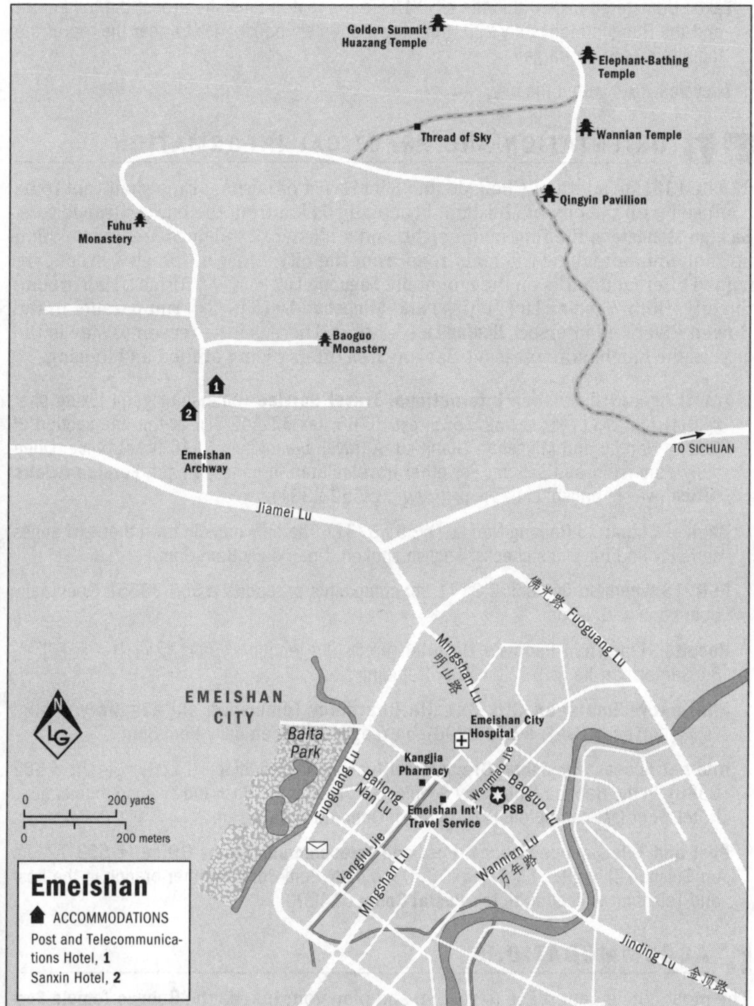

Grand Hotel (éméishān dàjiǔdiàn; 峨眉山大酒店) and **Hongzhushan Hotel** (hóngzhūshān bīnguǎn; 红珠山宾馆), near Baoguo Monastery, arranges buses to Dazu, Dujiangyan, Jiuzhaigou, Leshan, Qingcheng Mountain, and Yunnan's Xishuangbanna.

Local Transportation: Buses run throughout the city 7am-6pm. Fare Y0.5. In the Baoguo Monastery Scenic District, buses run 7am-6pm from the Lianyun Bus Station, next to the Teddy Bear Cafe, with direct service to **Quingyin Pavilion** (Y10), **Wannian Temple** (Y15), and the **Leidongping parking lot** just below the cable car station at the summit (Y30). Return buses from each of these locations are available until 6pm. Ask at the Teddy Bear Cafe about a slower local bus from the Emeishan archway (Y2). 5-seater vans (Y1) run from the fountain on Mingshan Lu, Zhong Duan, to Baoguo Monastery 6:30am-7:30pm.

Taxis: Unmetered taxis within the city Y10. To the foot of Emeishan (past the toll booth) and the Baoguo Monastery Y20, from the monastery parking lot to near the top of the mountain Y45-50. Bargain.

Tricycles: Y3-4 within the city.

ORIENTATION AND PRACTICAL INFORMATION

Situated 131km south of Chengdu and 30km west of Leshan, Emeishan (not to be confused with the city of Meishan) is actually 6.6km from the park entrance gate. **Baoguo Monastery,** the first major sight, and a cluster of lodgings are about 1.5km up the mountain along the main road from the city. Most of the city streets are named after landmarks on the mountain. **Foguang Lu** (佛光路) forms a ring around the city. Both **Wannian Lu** (万年路) and **Mingshan Lu** (明山路) run parallel to the Bowen River and intersect **Jinding Lu** (金顶路). There is little reason to stay in the city, as the much more pleasant Baoguo area offers plenty of food and lodging.

Travel Agency: Emeishan International Travel Service (éméishān guójì lǚxíng shè; 峨眉山国际旅行社; ☎552 7555, ext. 5766; fax 522 4244), at the intersection of Jinding Nan Lu and Mingshan Zhong Lu. A travel agency and CAAC ticket office. Open daily 7am-noon and 1-6pm. For other travel-related inquiries, try the **Foreign Affairs Office** (wàishì bànshì chù; 外事办事处; ☎552 2831).

Bank of China: 73 Bailong Nan Lu (☎552 3737). The only bank in town that exchanges currency and traveler's checks. English spoken. Open daily 8am-6pm.

PSB: 73 Wenmiao Jie (☎552 2741, for complaints or reports ☎553 3355). Open daily 8am-noon and 3-6pm.

Hospital: Emeishan People's Hospital (éméishān rénmín yīyuàn; 峨眉山人民医院), 81 Santaishan Jie (☎552 2408), off Jinding Nan Lu.

Pharmacy: Emeishan City Kangjia Pharmacy (éméishān shì kāngjiá yàofáng; 峨眉山市康佳药房; ☎552 0290), on Yangliu Jie. Open daily 8am-8pm.

Internet Access: Emeishan Grand Hotel (éméishān dàjiǔdiàn; 峨眉山大酒店; ☎562 6888), in the Baoguo Monastery Scenic Area, next to the Post and Telecommunications Hotel. Four fast computers (Y10 per hr.). Open daily 8am-1am.

Post and Telecommunications: Post and Telecommunications Office (☎553 7217), on Suishan Zhong Lu. EMS and IDD. Open daily 8am-8pm. Another branch in the Post and Telecommunication Hotel. **Postal Code:** 614200.

ACCOMMODATIONS

The most convenient place to rest up and plan your hike is the **Baoguo Temple Scenic Area** (bàoguó fēngjǐng qū; 报国风景区), a strip of restaurants and hotels along the main road leading up to the temple. Budget dorm rooms are plentiful among the smallest establishments on the left side of the road, and the going rate is about Y20 per bed. Since price and quality are pretty consistent, it is easiest to let the staff at the Teddy Bear Cafe set you up at their associate guesthouse. Angela or Patricia, both good English speakers, wait daily at the Emeishan bus station and will arrange everything for free. More upscale establishments are also available along the Baoguo Temple strip. On the mountain, monasteries and temples provide the cheapest and most convenient places to stay, with basic dorm beds, hot showers, and vegetarian cafeterias. With the exception of **Xi'an Feng Temple,** which charges Y30 because of its location at the top of an exhausting stretch of mountain trail, most places charge Y15-20 per night. If the Golden Summit Monastery is full or won't give you a Y15 bed, try the **Xiang Hostel** just next to the TV tower. More luxurious accommodations are clustered next to an open lot just below the peak with rooms Y80 and up. All listings below are in the **Baoguo Monastery Scenic Area.** Due to the dramatic fluctuations in the number of tourists, off-days are prime bargaining opportunities.

Teddy Bear Guesthouse (shǔxiāng jiǔdiàn; 蜀乡酒店), in an alley around the corner from the Teddy Bear cafe. Basic dorm rooms, clean public showers, luggage storage, and 24hr. hot water. 3- and 4-bed dorms Y20. ❶

Sanxin Hotel (sānxīn dàjiǔdiàn; 三鑫大酒店; ☎559 1766), just across from the well-marked Emeishan Hotel. Dorms are bright and squeaky-clean, with tiled floors, TV, and common baths. 2- and 3-bed dorms Y45; doubles with bath Y180-240. ❶

Baoguo Temple Guesthouse (bàogúosì sùshè; 报国寺宿舍), one of the more beautiful and peaceful places to begin your journey up the mountain; don't be surprised to be awakened by monks drumming and chanting at 4am. Ask at the main temple gate about getting a room. 24hr. public showers and luggage storage. Vegetarian restaurant on the temple grounds. Dorm beds Y20-40. ❶

Post and Telecommunications Hotel (yóudiàn bīnguǎn; 邮电宾馆; ☎559 0777; fax 559 0019), clearly visible on the right along the main road leading to Baoguo Monastery. Sunny rooms. IDD service. Standard doubles with attached bath Y150. ❷

FOOD

A number of restaurants line the main road to Baoguo Monastery, near the Post and Telecommunications Hotel. The **Teddy Bear Cafe** ❶ (wánjùxióng cānguǎn; 玩具熊餐馆), in the Baoguo Monastery Scenic Area, is noticeable for its teddy bear sign on the second floor. Popular among foreigners, this inviting cafe serves delicious Sichuanese and Western dishes, with menus available in various languages. Don't miss the eggplant with garlic and ginger (Y10) and the pancakes with chocolate and banana (Y10). The Teddy Bear Cafe is also a great source of information on mountain conditions and hiking routes, and can arrange train, bus, and air tickets. English-speaking management and staff. (☎559 0135. Open daily 7am until the last customer leaves.) Farther up the road from the Teddy Bear Cafe, **Dengyue Restaurant** ❶ (dēngyuè jiǔlóu; 登月酒楼) has an English menu and serves the standard Sichuanese food. The fried egg noodles (Y8) and crispy fish (Y25) are a good bet. (☎559 0085. Open daily 6:30am-midnight.) There is also an outdoor food market just up the hill from the Teddy Bear Cafe, with stalls selling cold noodles (Y4), dumplings (Y3), and cold beer (Y3-5).

CLIMBING EMEISHAN

***Buses** leave from the Baoguo Monastery Lianyun Bus Station 6am-5pm (off-season 6am-4pm), and have 3 stops: the parking lot below Qingyin Pavilion (Y10); the cable car station leading to Wannian Temple (Y15); and Leidong Terrace (Y30), 7.5km from the peak. One option is to take the bus and **cable car** (Y40) to Wannian Temple, hike 2 days to the peak, and then hike down the other path (1-2 days) to the parking lot below Qingyin Pavilion. If you have time (3-4hr.) and energy, hike all the way back to Baoguo Temple via the oft-neglected lowland path that passes the Shenshui Pavilion and Fuitu Temple. A second hiking option is to start from either the main parking lot below Qingyin, or from Baoguo Temple, and hike up the more strenuous path to the top, stopping at either Xianfeng or Xixiang temple for the night before continuing to the Golden Summit, then hiking down the* *quicker route to the Wannian temple lot. A time- and knee-saving alternative is to take the bus all the way up, catch a cable car from Jieyin Hall (a 20min. walk from the bus drop-off) to the Golden Summit (Y40), spend the night there, and hike down the next day.*

The Emeishan mountains, 7km southeast of Emeishan city, cover some 300km². In addition to the three dozen historical sites connected by 100km of trails, the 60km² park area is also a nature reserve home to red pandas, bearded frogs, and hundreds of kinds of butterflies, not to mention the bands of semi-domesticated monkey-devils that roam the trails. There are also over 3000 species of plants, including 60 varieties of Indian azaleas.

The traditional pilgrimage up the mountain begins at Baoguo Temple and winds along the Emeishan foothills through terraced farmland and bamboo forest, passing Fuitu Leiyin and Shenshui temples before reaching the **Qingyin Pavilion,** the most frequently used starting point. From here, the main trail up the mountain diverges. The left branch leads up a scenic gorge. Although this is a difficult route, including the **"99 switchbacks"** and greedy-monkey roadblocks, it is by far the more beautiful and awe-inspiring of the two routes, following a coursing waterfall through towering cliffs and misty jungle valleys. The right path, enclosed by forest on all sides and lacking the expansive views of the left path, passes through several important historical sites, including Wannian Temple. The trails eventually converge and lead to the Golden Summit.

SICHUAN

Due to the 2500m elevation difference, mountain weather can be unpredictable and much cooler (7-10°C lower) than city temperatures. Locals say that the best weather for visiting the peak is right after a rainstorm, when fast-fleeing clouds are accompanied by rainbows and, sometimes, the rare Buddha's Light (see p. 680). Climbs on clear days offer less dramatic views of verdant valleys, and visits in cloudy weather are the least rewarding, as the mountain is cloaked with dense mist. Emeishan is also popular as a winter resort, with camping, hiking, and skiing all possible in the heavy snows that last until April.

BAOGUO MONASTERY (bàoguó sì; 报国寺). Built in 1615, Baoguo is the largest monastery on Emeishan, sitting 550m above sea level at the foot of the mountain. It was originally known as the **Assembled Religions Hall,** because it united the three popular beliefs in China at the time: Buddhism (represented by Guangchengzi), Daoism (by Chukuang), and Confucianism (by Puxian, later known as Samantabhadra Bodhisattva). During the early part of the Qing dynasty, the hall was renovated and became known as Baoguo Monastery. *Bàoguó* ("dedication to one's country") is considered one of the four acts of benevolence. The temple's interior, filled with plant life, is home to many small gardens and bonsai.

Baoguo's main historic relic is the **Shengji bell.** Reputedly the second-largest bell in China (after Beijing's Great Bell), the 25-ton bronze bell was cast in 1564 and has some 61,600 words from Buddhist scripture inscribed upon it. At the start of the 20th century, the bell was taken from the monastery to make ammunition, and although safely returned later, was marred by a small crack. During the Great Leap Forward (1957-58), the bell was damaged again, and can no longer be used. Behind Daxiong Hall sits a 2m Ming dynasty porcelain Buddha that is particularly remarkable for the thousand-petal lotus that it rests upon, representing attainment of *nirvana*. *(Accommodations available in Baoguo Monastery. Open daily 6:30am-9pm. Y8.)*

FUHU MONASTERY (fúhǔ sì; 伏虎寺). Named for a tiger that used to harass the monastery's inhabitants, Fuhu (Conquering Tiger) Monastery is farther up the mountain than Baoguo. Although the monastery is ancient, it remained uninhabited until the 1980s, when a small group of nuns took up residence in it. There are few statues of note, but the temple's architecture and landscape design sets it apart from others on the mountain. With terraced layers of small gardens, **penjing** (potted landscapes), and flying-eaved halls set into the lush slopes of lowland forest, it is easy to while away a couple of hours here after a long trek, sipping tea or eating noodles (Y1.5-2). The luxuriant surrounding forests and mountains are home to the rare Withered Leaf Butterfly. This rare and ancient plant fulfilled the appetites of herbivorous dinosaurs 200 million years ago and still grows today. *(Accommodations consist of basic 4-bed dorms (Y14). Open daily 6:30am-8pm. Y6.)*

QINGYIN PAVILION (qīngyīn gé; 清音阁). Farther up the mountain, weary hikers can catch their breath at the Qingyin Pavilion, situated between the Black and White Dragon streams, flanked by symmetrical bridges and surrounded by deep green growth. The crisp sound of water cascading down sleek ebony stone gives Qingyin (literally, Clear Sound Pavilion) its name.

WANNIAN TEMPLE (wànnián sì; 万年寺). Higher up the mountain at 1020m sits Wannian Temple, which dates back to the Jin dynasty (AD 280-316). A fire in 1945 consumed the temple, leaving only one brick chapel unscathed; the ancient structure is now the mountain's oldest building. Wannian Temple was once known as Baishui Puxian Monastery, named after the famous *bodhisattva* Puxian (Samantabhadra), who is the main deity worshiped at Emeishan. In AD 980, Tang Emperor Taizong commissioned the most important statue in the temple—a bronze, 7.4m, 62-ton statue of Puxian Bodhisattva riding atop his white elephant. During the Ming dynasty, Emperor Wanli had the temple renovated and renamed it Wannian (Ten Thousand Year) Temple. The statue of Puxian is housed in **Wuliang Hall,** where it is surrounded by 1000 small copper statues of Buddha.

Wannian Temple is also famous for its melodious **musical frogs;** but since their vocal cords are usually only active in the early mornings it is unlikely that late-comers will catch the creatures in concert. *(Temple accommodations Y15 per bed. Vegetarian restaurant open during temple hours (Y5-10). Temple open daily 11am-7pm. Y10.)*

ELEPHANT-BATHING TEMPLE (xǐxiàng sì; 洗象寺). At 2100m, seated upon a small precipice with tremendous drops on both sides, Xixiang Temple used to be known as Lotus Flower Temple because a large piece of yellow rock resembling a lotus flower was once found there. Some years later, a medicine man on the mountain is said to have seen Puxian Bodhisattva bathing his white elephant in the small hexagonal pond in front of the temple. It seems doubtful that this miniscule pool could accommodate the girth of Puxian's pachyderm, but we won't argue. *(This is one of the most pleasant monasteries to spend the night in, with airy 5-bed dorms opening onto a long balcony that looks over the cliffs below. Y15 per bed. Open daily 7am-8pm. Y1.)*

EXPLORING TOUR (tànxiǎn yóu; 探险游). About 30 minutes from the Leidong Terrace, a signpost in English and Chinese directs you off the main trail up a flight of stairs to the right. This path leads to one of the wildest and most stunning areas of the whole mountain. Instead of the ubiquitous stone paving that covers most of Emeishan's trails, this section of the mountain uses hewn-log ladders and bridges to descend a precipitous cliff 450m down from the main ridge trail. Reaching the base of this towering cliff, visitors can follow a rocky trail that continues to descend into a lush valley of wildflowers and gushing waterfalls, supported by chains and ropes attached to the steep slope. The trail runs for about 4km, passing a campsite with several 2-man cabins ready for use, before abruptly ending at a 100m waterfall. From the campsite, a trail (3km) also leads up to the left to **Guigu Cave** (gǔigǔ dòng; 鬼谷洞). To the left, a trail (2.5km) leads to **Sanxiao Cave** (sānxiāo dòng; 三霄洞). Branching uphill to the right off this trail is a short hike (1km) to the **Dragon Pool** (lóngtán; 龙潭). Not including the longer treks to the two caves, the descent to the waterfall and back to the main trail takes about six hours, so plan accordingly. Bring a sleeping bag or blanket and stay overnight either in the caves or in one of the cabins where the trail splits. Locals say that the crystal-clear stream that flows down through the valley is safe to drink; you might want to use iodine tablets anyway. Bring as much food as you will need for the entire trek, as there are no vendors in the area. This "exploring tour" is technically only for guided treks, so don't expect any rescue teams. It's probably best not to hike it alone. *(Free.)*

GOLDEN SUMMIT HUAZANG TEMPLE (jīndǐng huázàng sì; 金顶华藏寺). First constructed during the Eastern Han, the Golden Summit Huazang Temple stands 3077m above sea level. The temple itself is a simple structure and not terribly interesting, but it provides a platform from which to admire the opaque and mystical scenery, from the distant cloud-clad mountains to the deep gullies below. All it takes to witness a dazzling sunrise over a sea of clouds, and perhaps even Buddha's Light, is a little luck, the determination to wake up at 5:30am, and the patience to wait around in the cold wind until daybreak. If you aren't completely exhausted from the hike up, the starry skies to the east above the summit occasionally yield a kind of electrical phenomenon that the locals call the **Buddha's Lamp** (fódēng; 佛灯), similar to the *aurora borealis*. *(Temple accommodations Y20-30 per bed. Small restaurant on site. Cable cars from Jeyin Hill to Golden Summit Y40, Y30 down. Open daily 6am-7pm. Y10.)*

SICHUAN

MOXI 磨西

☎0836

Nestled in the mountains of Luding County, about 50km away from Luding itself, the town of Moxi holds it breath, waiting to emerge as a tourist hotspot. Moxi and Hailuogou Glacier Park, the town's claim to fame, are oft-compared to northern Sichuan's Jiuzhaigou National Park, which attracts nearly half a million tourists each year. Although plans for the future are well underway, however, the spirit of the town remains firmly entrenched in the past. Away from the frenzy and tangle of construction, old men smoke pipes, women knit furiously, and children scramble around dirt roads after the chickens and ducks that wander at will. This juxtaposition of immutability and manic change makes Moxi an interesting and relaxing place to stay for a day or so; most travelers don't stick around for much longer, instead using Moxi as a base for trips into nearby Hailuogou Glacier Park.

TRANSPORTATION. Moxi is accessible only by bus; however, there is no official bus station. The bus to **Chengdu** is the only direct transportation out of Moxi; it leaves from in front of the Haiyun Hotel (6-8hr., 8am, Y100). For all other destinations besides Chengdu, it is necessary to change buses in **Luding.** Taxis and minibuses wait at the top of the hill to depart for Luding (1-2hr., daily starting at 7:30am, about Y20).

ORIENTATION AND PRACTICAL INFORMATION. The town of Moxi consists of three unnamed main streets, all of which run from the bottom to the top of the hill. If you are coming from **Chengdu,** chances are the bus will drop you off in front of the Haiyun Hotel, which is up the hill on the farthest street away from the river. If you are coming from **Luding,** you may either be dropped off at the Haiyun Hotel or near the Catholic Church, which is up the hill on the middle street. All three roads are connected by crossroads at the top and bottom of the hill.

Given Moxi's imminent rise to the ranks of tourist hotspots, it is somewhat surprising that there are no travel agencies. For travelers who are interested in 2- to 6-

day treks in Hailuogou Glacier Park, the staff at the Haiyun Hotel or at one of the shops at the entrance to the park can help hire guides. The **PSB** is on the middle road, set slightly off the street about one-third of the way up the hill. (☎326 6280. Open M-Sa 9am-5pm.) **Post and Telecommunications** are across the street from the PSB. EMS; no collect calls. (☎326 6295. Open M-Sa 9am-5pm.)

ACCOMMODATIONS AND FOOD. Haiyun Hotel ❷ (hǎiyùn fàndiàn; 海运饭店), is on the road farthest from the river, just before the massive red and orange building on the right. Rooms are spotless with 20-inch color TVs and attached Chinese-style bathrooms for your hygienic pleasure. Ask for a room overlooking the mountains. (☎326 6503. Doubles Y100.) To reach the **Glacier Restaurant and Hotel ❷** (bīngchuān fàndiàn; 冰川饭店), go up the middle road after the fork with the right road; the hotel is 100m ahead on the left. Clean, attractive rooms and a quiet location make the Glacier Hotel a relaxing place to spend a day or two. (☎326 6206. Doubles with TV Y100.) Moxi boasts a number of small, cheap restaurants that serve up the best and spiciest of Sichuanese cuisine. The middle street is lined with hotpot eateries; in the rest of town, noodles abound. The restaurant attached to the Haiyun Hotel also serves up excellent Sichuanese food for Y8-15.

HAILUOGOU GLACIER PARK. The lowest glacier in Asia, Hailuogou Glacier Park (hǎiluógōu bīngchuān gōngyuán; 海螺沟冰川公园) lies at the foot of the legendary, 7556m-tall Gonggashan Mountain (gònggāshān; 贡嘎山). A relatively new road winds its way up from Moxi to **Camp No. 3** inside the park, but pony paths and stone-paved hiking trails are more direct. Because of frequent, heavy rainfall in the summer, pesky clouds and fog often obscure the peaks of Mount Gonga. On a clear day, however, the view from the top is breathtaking. It is also possible to continue down into the glacier itself if the weather is good. Expect about a 1- to 1½-hour hike from Camp No. 3 to the **Glacier Viewing Point.** At Camp No. 3, there are also ponies for hire (about Y30 an hour). *(At the top of the hill in Moxi, turn left and walk straight for about 300m until you reach the park entrance. Buses (Y55) to the glacier depart from the park entrance at 7:30am. Ground commission ☎326 6203 or 326 6205. Trekkers should inquire at the shops around the entrance to the park about hiring a guide. Entrance ticket Y70. Maps Y2.)*

E-COMMERCE

Inspired and empowered by images of hip Western youngsters getting their groove on at discos, the Chinese have taken to the clubs en masse, and nighttime venues have become the place to see and be seen. In China, unlike in the West, relatively costly cover charges and drinks keep out the *lǎobǎixìng* (common people) and make discos a haven for the elite upper crust, gangsters, and those involved in the prostitution industry. As with most transnational institutions, however, Western-style discos have not been fully adopted in China. Instead, many of those who are accustomed to the frenetic grinding style of dancing at Western discos will come away from a Chinese night on the town shaking their heads at the somewhat different style of dancing. The drug commonly known in the West as ecstasy, which made its way from the rave scene onto the list of most commonly used clubbing drugs, has also made its way to China. In Chinese, its name is *yáotoúwán* (literally: the shaking-the-head pill). As with many other social trends in China, the habit has trickled down from the top to the masses, and now, shaking one's head—not always in time with the music—has become the preferred style of dancing in China and is an established way to show that you are having a good time on your night out.

KANGDING 康定

☎0836

Kangding (or *Dardo* in Tibetan) usually serves as a stopover point for travelers on their way to sights farther west. However, the town is more deserving of attention than the typical transportation hub. Although the town is now predominantly Han Chinese, the small side streets still smell of yak butter tea and Tibetan herbs. The people are friendly, the food and accommodation cheap, and the atmosphere both stimulating and low-key. Kangding is definitely worthy of a few days of exploration or rest before barrelling off along the Sichuan-Tibet highway.

ORIENTATION AND PRACTICAL INFORMATION

The town straddles the **Zheduo River** and has four main bridges starting at the bottom of the hill. **Yanhe Dong Lu** and **Yanhe Xi Lu** run alongside the river; most of Kangding's daily grind occurs along these main thoroughfares. Looping behind Yanhe Xi Lu from the third to the fourth bridges is **Guangming Lu** (光明路) and the greatest number of hotels. **Dong Dajie** (东大街) runs parallel to Yanhe Dong Lu and boasts many small restaurants. The bus station is about a ten-minute walk from the first bridge.

Buses: The only way to get to Kangding is by bus. The **Kangding Bus Station** (kāngdìng qìchē zhàn; 康定汽车站; ☎283 7914), 10min. from the first bridge, is teeming with activity. To: **Chengdu** (8hr., 16 per day, Y98); **Ganzi** (12hr., 2 per day, Y103); **Litang** (8hr., daily, Y78); **Leshan** (7hr., daily, Y63); **Ya'an** (6hr., 4 per day, Y60); **Xiangcheng** (16hr. excluding overnight stop in Litang, daily, Y136). **Taxis** (2hr.) to Luding costs Y15.

Travel Agency: The best travel agency in town is the **Kangding Travel Agency Tourism Co. Ltd** (kāngdìng lǚxíngshè; 康定旅行社), 41 Xi Dajie (☎283 4000 or 283 1946). From the Black Tent Hotel, turn left; turn left again at the second bridge. The agency does it all: provides information on trekking on Gonggashan Mountain, arranges transportation to out-of-the-way sites, buys bus tickets, and arranges for interpreters. Open M-Sa 9am-5pm.

Bank of China: On Yanhe Xi Lu between the first and second bridges. Neither this branch nor any other bank in Kangding exchanges currency. Open daily 8:30am-5:30pm.

PSB: On Dong Dajie, past the fourth bridge, on the left side of the street (☎281 1415, ext. 5035). Open M-F 8:30am-noon and 2:30-5:30pm.

Internet Access: A few places on Guangming Lu near the Paomashan Hotel offer Internet access for around Y5 per hr. A shop with "Internet" in green letters, located halfway between the bus station and the first bridge, has many computers and fast connections for Y5 per hr. Open daily 9am-6pm.

Post and Telecommunications: On the 2nd fl. of a building a few doors up from the Bank of China (☎283 2037). Open daily 8:45am-5:30pm. **Postal code:** 626000.

ACCOMMODATIONS AND FOOD

Given the Tibetan influences at work in Kangding, you would expect to find a lot of Tibetan food around town. In fact, only one Tibetan restaurant, next to the Kangding Travel Agency, can be found. Small restaurants serve spicy Sichuanese food along Yanhe Dong Lu and Dong Dajie, and at sunset, stalls spring up out of nowhere to sell kebabs smeared with tasty Sichuanese spices.

The Black Tent Hotel (hēi zhàngpéng zhùsù; 黑帐篷住宿; ☎283 2511), on Yanhe Xi Lu. From the bus station, turn right; at the fork in the road, veer right. At the river, turn left and cross the fourth bridge; it's the building on the corner with the porch. A small family-run operation, the Black Tent offers cozy and clean rooms, all of which come with electric blankets (necessary to withstand Kangding's chilly nights—even in the summer). Downstairs, a tea house serves up fortifying Tibetan teas. The only drawback to the Black Tent is the unenticingly smelly common bathrooms. Showers are in a nearby public bathhouse. 4-bed dorms Y17, with TV Y27; doubles with TV and carpet Y42. ❶

Paomashan Hotel (pǎomǎshān bīnguǎn; 跑马山宾馆; ☎283 3110), on Guangming Lu. Turn right out of the bus station; at the fork in the road, veer right. At the river, turn left and cross over at the third bridge. Turn left onto Yanhe Xi Lu, and make your first right onto Guangming Lu; Paomashan Hotel is about 150m ahead on the right. The rooms are spotless, and if it's Western amenities you're after, Paomashan is the place to go. All rooms have TV and attached Western bath. One disadvantage, however: no elevator—and most of the cheaper rooms are on the top floors. 3-bed dorms Y150; standard room Y240. ❷

Kangding Hotel (kāngdìng bīnguǎn; 康定宾馆) 25 Guangming Lu (☎283 3081; fax 283 3442). Turn right out of the bus station; at the fork in the road, veer right. At the river, turn left and cross over at the fourth bridge; the Kangding Hotel is at the top of the small hill in front of you. Built for Chinese tour groups, the building is rather grandiose. 3-bed dorms with common bath Y108, singles Y252, doubles Y240-288. ❷

SIGHTS

Although most of the more interesting sights are outside town, there are also a few low-key places of interest that don't require a substantial time commitment. Sandwiched between the Black Tent Hotel and the Kangding Hotel, the **Anjue temple** (in Tibetan, *ngachu gompa*) is a quiet spot. It belongs to the Yellow Hat sect of Tibetan Buddhism and, in its heyday, had more than 300 monks in residence. **Paomashan Hill** (pǎomǎ shān; 跑马山) offers a respite from the crowds and some stunning views of the area; the hike takes about 30 minutes. From town, turn right just before the bus station and continue until you reach a temple and the stairs up the hill.

For transportation to **Tagong Grasslands** (tǎgōng cǎoyuán; 塔公草园), a beautiful meadow surrounded by impressive, snowy mountains, **minibuses** leave from Yanhe Dong Lu each morning, near the second bridge. For more information on transportation to **Gongga Temple** (gònggā sì; 贡嘎寺) and trekking around Gonggashan Mountain, visit the Kangding Travel Agency (see above).

JIUZHAIGOU 九寨沟 ☎0837

Here, set against a backdrop of thundering waterfalls, snow-capped mountains, and virgin forest, 108 iridescent turquoise lakes fan out across panoramic valleys like a strutting peacock unfurling its plumage. Named after the nine Tibetan villages in the gully, Jiuzhaigou has dazzling scenery that reinvigorates jaded travelers. This northern Sichuanese national park doubles as a giant panda reserve and has been recognized as a UNESCO World Heritage Site. But fame has its price: the park is already filled with Chinese tourists hopping from sight to sight.

Although the swarming crowd of up to 10,000 visitors per day might easily sour one's impression of the place, it's easy to break free from tour routes and explore this amazing area independently. Shuttle buses cart tourists along well-paved roads while a network of small horse trails link most of the major sights via beautiful and isolated stretches of forest and meadow; and beyond the southernmost bus stop, untrammeled forest and grassy mountain peaks provide opportunities for day hikes and isolated views of the radiant pools below.

ORIENTATION AND PRACTICAL INFORMATION

Over 450km north of Chengdu, Jiuzhaigou is tucked into the Minshan Mountain Range in Nanping County, part of the Aba and Qiang Autonomous Prefecture near the Gansu border. It spreads across 60,000 hectares and has a gorgeous 80km long scenic area, largely concentrated in a Y-shaped valley that splits near the mighty Nuorilang Falls. The road leading up to the falls passes the quiet village of **Heye** (héyè zhài; 荷叶寨), about 4km, before reaching the more touristed **Shuzheng village** (shùzhèng zhài; 树正寨), about 8km up the road. Two kilometers farther is the Nuorilang area and a fork in the road. The left branch passes through **Zhechawa Village** (zéchāwā zhài; 则查洼寨) before heading to the long lake and the nearby Five Color Pool. The right branch passes through the Pearl Shoal Falls, near Panda Lake, and up to the currently closed section through the Rize Gorge and Swan Lake. Great hiking is easy to find past the last open bus stop at the Arrow Bamboo Lake. In winter, snow renders Jiuzhaigou inaccessible to travelers; even in summer, heavy rainfall can make the roads to the reserve treacherous.

Buses and Tours: Long-distance Bus Station (jiǔzhàigōu qìchē zhàn; 九寨沟汽车站; ☎773 2030), in the parking lot of the Jiutong Hotel (jiǔtōng bīnguǎn; 九通宾馆) about 200m along the road toward Jiuzhaigou city; keep right as you exit the park gates across from the gas station. To: **Chengdu** (10hr.; 7:30, 8am, 3:30pm; Y80-95); **Chongqing** (morning); **Huanglong; Songpan** (2-3hr., 7am, Y20). Also, a noontime bus to Songpan picks up passengers on the road in front of the park entrance. To Huanglong, you can fill a taxi van for about Y250; you must first pass within 10km of Songpan, so it's more practical to go there first. Inside Jiuzhaigou, buses run up and down the main road. A bus pass (Y80) gives you unlimited rides; the last bus from Long Lake leaves at 5pm; from the Arrow Bamboo Lake at 4pm. Buses (6-9pm) descend every hr. from the Nuorilang Falls.

PSB: Inside the main visitors center facing the park entrance, on the 1st fl. Some English spoken. Open daily 8:30am-5:30pm; someone is on duty 24hr.

Hospitals: Jiuzhaigou County Hospital (jiǔzhàigōuxiàn yīyuàn; 九寨沟县医院; ☎773 2156 or 2146), 43km past the turnoff to the Jiuzhaigou entrance, down the road to Nanping County, on the right. Ambulance service. Open 24hr. 5km up the road in the other direction is the **Jiuzhaigou County Clinic** (jiǔzhàigōu xiàn yīyuàn zhàngzhá fēnyuàn; 九寨沟县医院障扎分院; ☎773 4007). Open 24hr.

Post and Telecommunications: On the right (coming from Chengdu) in a 3-story building, 5-6km from the entrance to Jiuzhaigou. The visitors center offers international mail service for postcards and small packages. IDD service. Open daily 10am-5pm.

ACCOMMODATIONS

In an effort to preserve a degree of tranquility and environmental sensitivity, the Jiuzhaigou Tourism Bureau regularly informs tour groups that no accommodation is available inside the park; as a result, the strip of road near the park gates has become a breeding ground for mid- to high-end hotels, the cheapest of which charges Y30 per bed in the low season and Y40-50 in high season. Fortunately, lodging within the park is cheap (Y20-30 per bed) and quite peaceful after the crowds leave. All three villages offer similar accommodations, although Zechawa and Heye are less touristed and somewhat cheaper.

SICHUAN

INSIDE JIUZHAIGOU

Baojing Hotel (bǎojīn lóu; 保金楼), in Zechawa village, the second complex with prayer flagpoles on the roadside. This pleasantly scented wood guesthouse is run by a very friendly Tibetan family. Triples with neglected outhouse and no shower Y20 per bed; 2nd fl. rooms are most pleasant. Just next door, sparkling new rooms with 24hr. hot water, bath, and TV Y30-40 per bed. Student discounts available. ❶

Guibin Hotel (guìbīn lóu; 贵宾楼), in Shuzheng Village. The rooms in this traditional Tibetan-style guesthouse are quite beautiful, and an excellent value. Check in at the "Front Office" sign; the rooms are up the hill. Y40 per bed doubles are clean with shower; hot water available in the evenings. The Y50 per bed doubles are more spacious. ❶

Silver Fall Hotel (yíngpù bīnguǎn; 银瀑宾馆; ☎773 8038), in Shuzheng Village, facing the parking lot. Carpeted rooms are bright and clean, with private bath and TV. Doubles Y20, in high season (July-Oct.) Y30-40. ❶

Zechawa Village Hotel (zècháwā zhài bīnguǎn; 则查洼寨宾馆), in Zechawa Village, the first hotel up the hill from Nuorilang bus stop. Far inferior to its neighbor up the road, this is nonetheless a good standby if the Baojing Hotel is full. Doubles Y22; with unreliable bath, carpeted floors, and TV Y30. ❶

OUTSIDE JIUZHAIGOU

Unless you're arriving at 4am on the sleeper bus from Chengdu, there is no reason to stay outside the park; even then, head into the park and wait for the 7am bus up the gorge, since you won't have to pay the entrance fee at 4am.

Yangdong Hotel (yángdōng fàndiàn; 羊峒饭店; ☎773 9770), 50m to your left as you face the park entrance, marked by a yellow sign in English. May not be the greatest value, but Y40 gets you a bed in a bright, albeit musty, double with clean tile bathrooms and 24hr. hot water. In peak season, it may be difficult to get a single bed. ❶

Jiuzhaigou Cabins (jiǔzhàigōu mùwū; 九寨沟木屋; ☎773 4127), 25m from the entrance to the nature reserve. When facing the gate, the cabins are up a small path on the left. Newly opened, sparkling, all-wooden hotel. Some rooms overlook the river, and all have bright lighting, baths, heaters, and TVs. Singles Y100; doubles Y300. ❷

Jiuzhaigou Grand Hotel (guìbīnlóu fàndiàn; 贵宾楼饭店; ☎773 4163; fax 773 4163), just to the right of the visitors center. Luxury doubles start at Y220 per room. With a night's stay, you can get Y22 off your entrance ticket. ❸

FOOD

Jiuzhaigou's best culinary options are wild vegetable dishes, like the **sliced pork with edible tree fungus** (mùěr ròupiàn; 木耳肉片; Y30) and the **walnut flower dish** (hétáohuā; 核桃花; Y30). **Yak** (máo níu; 牦牛; Y60) is also worth trying if you have money to spare. Be forewarned: the food prices are greatly inflated within Jiuzhaigou; vendors ask Y5-8 for dried noodles and Y5 for bottles of water; budget travelers should carry their own snacks and drinks into the park. Most guesthouses in Zechawa and Heye village will happily cook you a bowl of vegetable noodles (Y3-5), a good alternative to instant noodles. There are several good and inexpensive restaurants inside the nature reserve, most serving up standard meals of rice, soup, and vegetables for Y15-20. Extra dishes cost Y10-60. In Heye Village, there is the **Lotus Leaf Restaurant** (héyè cāntīng; 荷叶餐厅). In Zechawa Village, there is the **Nuorilang Restaurant** (nuòrìlǎng cāntīng; 诺日郎餐厅), just up the hill from the

Baojin Guesthouse, offering huge breakfasts for only Y5. In Shuzheng Village, there is **Shuzheng Restaurant** (shūzhèng cāntīng; 树正餐厅).

SIGHTS

JIUZHAIGOU NATURE RESERVE. Jiuzhaigou's beauty is as legendary as its origins. According to a local tale, the warrior-god Dage presented a magic mirror, painstakingly crafted from clouds and wind, to his beloved goddess Wunosemo. One day, a meddling devil, envious of the couple's love and happiness, made Wunosemo drop her treasured mirror. It fell to Earth, where it shattered over Jiuzhaigou and formed glittering lakes. From the main gate, **Suzheng, Sleeping Dragon,** and **Sparkling Lakes** reveal branching calcium formations that create a series of multicolored terraces that step up the mountainside. Midway up the gorge, **Nuorilang Falls** (the world's widest waterfall) cascade down, over 30m tall and 320m wide. Just above Nuorilang, the main road forks; the right path passes the **Pearl Shoals** (zhēnzhū tān; 珍珠滩), where a long series of waterfalls rush between trees and flowering bushes, bifurcating the broad **Peacock River** (kǒngquè hédào; 孔雀河道) into thousands of tiny streams before cascading over the amazing Pearl Shoal Falls. Continuing up this path, the intense blues of **Five Flower Lake** (wǔ huā hǎi; 五花海) and **Panda Lake** (xióngmāo hǎi; 熊猫海) extend to mythical depths. The final bus stop is along the right fork, near **Arrow Bamboo Lake** (jiànzhú hǎi; 箭竹海). From here, the road continues up through quiet meadows, following the mountain stream past forested peaks dwarfed by the majestic snowcaps in the far distance. *(Gates open daily 7am-9pm. Y115, students and seniors 60+ Y57.)*

LONG LAKE (cháng hǎi; 长海). One of the most beautiful sights in the reserve is Long Lake, situated at the end of a 30-minute, 18km bus climb along the left branch of the road from the Nuorilang bus stop. At an elevation of 3150m, this tranquil lake is one of the least crowded areas of the park. Crystal clear and strikingly deep (130m, 40m visible depth), the azure blue waters attract migratory wild swans. Although jagged cliffs make hiking around the lake virtually impossible, to escape the clamor of Chinese tourists, simply walk left down from the parking lot along a small path that leads to a boat dock. Here, a boulder-strewn beach is sheltered from both the visual and auditory intrusions of the fray above. From the Long Lake parking lot, walk 1.5km down a small, paved footpath to the **Five Color Pool** (wǔcǎi chí; 五彩池), a radiant gem enclosed by steep, forested hills on all sides. It fades from reddish yellow through the color spectrum to the purest of deep blue violets at the center point. Most tourists arrive at Long Lake and descend to the Five Color Pool between 2 and 5pm, so head up the left branch route in the morning to avoid the crowds. **Zaru Temple** (zárú sì; 扎如寺), at the end of a small road branching left about 1km up from the main trail, is near the entrance. A small Tibetan monastery, Zaru Temple is equally happy to accept visitors and their donations. At the center of the main assembly hall is a prominent statue of Sakyamuni, and over 1000 smaller Sakyamunis line its side walls. An elderly monk (one of five who reside in Zaru) will sound the gong and chant while the devout pray to the main statue. He then presents visitors with *hadas* (Tibetan ceremonial scarves) as good luck charms. *(Open daily 8am-7pm.)*

CULTURAL EVENTS. Each of the three villages hosts an evening cultural event, usually nightly, depending on tour groups' demand. In Heye Village, from 8 to 10pm, there is a kitschy, Tibetan-style **Bonfire Party** (Y60), complete with Tibetan dancing, a Tibetan-style tug-of-war, a mock Tibetan wedding ceremony (in which a fortunate winner from the audience plays the part of bridegroom), and a whole lamb crackling delectably over the flames. In Shuzheng, from 8:30 to 10:30pm during high tourist season, there is a show that focuses specifically on different forms of **Tibetan dancing** (foreigners Y100, Chinese Y80, students Y60). But if you really want to get down and dirty, you can witness a **Yak-Slaughtering Ceremony** (Y30-50) in Zechawa Village from 8 to 10pm, and then feast on the freshly flayed flesh.

HIKING IN JIUZHAIGOU

Most tourists who visit Jiuzhaigou jump from bus stop to bus stop and congregate around demarcated scenic vistas that provide easy access photo-ops. Since Jiuzhaigou is immense, however, it's easy to avoid the swarming masses. Many horse and foot trails weave through the park, offering long intervals of quiet and solitude between major tourist sights. One of the best ways to go from the Pearl Shoal Falls back to the Nuorilang area is to hike along the opposite side of Mirror Lake from the major road. Instead of crossing the last bridge back to the road at the bottom of the Pearl Shoal Falls walkway, go through an opening in the shrubbery and walk along a well-trod horse trail that leads through several wildflower meadows, past vast expanses of brilliant green marshland and through pine forests, eventually hitting the main road just below the Nuorilang Falls. If you're hiking up to the Pearl Shoals, walk down the road from Nuorilang and head upstream on a small path just after the first bridge. In Shuzheng, reach another nice unmarked trail by crossing the small footbridge on Tiger Lake and then either heading right toward Nuorilang Falls or left toward Sleeping Dragon Lake. Another longer, more strenuous hike starts above the last bus stop at Arrow Bamboo Lake; walk up the road from the parking lot for about 20 minutes, and at the first cluster of buildings, the **Rize Protection Center** (rìzé bǎohù zhàn; 日则保护站), walk through the compound and up the grassy pastures behind it. Follow well-defined horse and yak trails up the grassy slopes of the mountain on your right, reaching the summit after about 3-4 hours. From this vantage point, the turquoise lakes fan out to the north and to the south, and several towering snowcaps rise in the distance.

A SIMPLE GAME OF ONE, TWO, THREE? A social phenomenon pervasive throughout Han Chinese culture in northwest and central China is a game called *huáquán*. This amazingly simple hand game dominates the Han social scene, and its signature sounds penetrate every street corner, restaurant, and home throughout the region, especially after dusk. Many foreigners initially mistake the matches for violent arguments, but should not be alarmed by the bursts of manic shrieking. The game is played one-on-one, with the two opponents facing one another. Each player throws one hand into the center, holding out anywhere from zero to five fingers. Simultaneously, both participants must yell out a number from zero to 10. If the total number of fingers equals the number either player called out, that player wins the round. If there is no victor, the players go right into the next round. Let the manic shrieking begin.

SONGPAN 松潘 ☎0837

Surrounded by terraced grasslands and bright fields of yellow mountain flowers, Songpan's ancient city gates guard the entry into this vibrant and diverse community of Tibetan, Hui Muslim, and Han Chinese who live and work together in a way rarely seen in other Chinese cities. A dense network of cobblestone paths and canals weaves through neighborhoods of traditional wooden houses, courtyard gardens and local mosques and temples nestled into the surrounding hills. The town center is a wide road that runs between the north and south gate towers and is filled with restaurants, Tibetan souvenir shops, and cafes. Fueled by a rapidly growing tourist industry, Songpan also sports several modern hotels, internet cafes, and backpacker hangouts catering to the handful of foreigners who arrive here for horse treks into the surrounding mountains.

Situated at the intersection of the northwest road to Gansu, the southern road to Chengdu, the eastern road to Huanlong, and the northeast road to Jiuzhaigou, Songpan is also now a popular layover point for travelers in northern Sichuan.

Songpan is centered on the intersection of four roads; each leads to a large gate tower, with the exception of the west road, which quickly branches into alleyways and market streets as you move away from the center intersection. Horse trek companies and the Traffic Hotel are just outside the north gate, and the main bus station is half a kilometer down the north road. Several other good hotels, the Pancake House, and a few Internet cafes lie between the north gate and town center; many good restaurants are clustered near the central intersection. A large fruit and vegetable market lies west of the center, as alleyways branch north to several mosques and temples in the hills and south along the river, passing garden tea houses amidst residential neighborhoods.

TRANSPORTATION. Songpan's **bus station** is just outside the north gate. Buses to: **Chengdu** (7hr., 6am, Y50); **Huanglong** (2hr., 7am, Y21); **Jiuzhaigou** (3hr., 7am, 1:30am-2pm, Y21); **Zoige** (6-7hr., 7am, Y31). Most buses leave from the second bus station about half a kilometer up the road to the northeast. Plans are in the works to consolidate Songpan's bus stations into a new central station; check with Happy Trails or backpacker guesthouses for info on where to catch your bus.

ORIENTATION AND PRACTICAL INFORMATION. There is nowhere in Songpan to exchange currency or traveler's checks. If you're in dire straits, you can **exchange US dollars** on the black market relatively easily; ask at any backpacker information center. The **PSB** is across from the Pancake House between the north gate and the city center, but does not process visa extensions. (Open daily 8:30am-noon and 3-6pm.) The cheapest place in town for **Internet access** is the **Zhiju Internet Bar** (zhīzhū wǎngbā; 蜘蛛网吧), just east of the center crossroads, on the right; a black sign with green bubbles marks the second-floor bar (Y4 per hr.). Several Internet cafes also line the northern road near the north gate and charge Y5-6 per hour. A **post and telecommunications** office, south of the Pancake House, has IDD service. International calls cost Y8 per minute. (Open in summer 9am-11pm; in winter 9am-5pm.)

FOOD AND ACCOMMODATIONS. Prices may jump Y10-20 during the busy peak season (July-October). **Songpan Hotel** ❶ (sōngpān fàndiàn; 松潘饭店), near the south gate, has clean, bright dorms (Y15 per bed) with communal showers. **Traffic Hotel** (jiāotōng bīnguǎn; 交通宾馆) is across the street from Happy Trails; its public showers (Y3) are around the corner. (Dorm beds Y15; singles with bath Y20-30.) **Jingyuan Hotel** ❶ (jǐngyuán fàndiàn; 景缘饭店), just inside the north gate, is an excellent value. Sparkling doubles with bath and lots of complimentary toiletries are Y30 per bed. (Hot water 3-10:30pm.) **Songzhou Hotel** ❶ (sōngzhōu bīnguǎn; 松州宾馆; ☎723 2371), just south of the north gate, has decent dorm rooms. (Y15 per bed. Adjacent public showers Y2.)

The **Pancake House** ❶ (yùlán fàndiàn; 玉兰饭店), halfway between the north gate and the center crossroads, is a mainstay for foreigners not wanting stir-fry. Standard fare includes bananas and chocolate pancakes (Y8), french fries, and hamburgers. **The Backpacker's Home** (bǎikèlì; 百客利), next to Shun Jiang Horse Treks, serves up Chinese and Western fare at prices similar to those at the Pancake House. They also offer helpful travel advice and a loud stereo (bring your own music). **Star Moon Restaurant** ❷ (xīngyuèlóu cāntīng; 星月楼餐厅), just south of the main crossroads on the west side, has green moons in the windows and a green sign overhead. Although these Muslim dishes are on the expensive side (Y15-20), they are well worth the price. Friendly cooks let you come into the kitchen to see how it's done.

HORSE TREKS. Many claim that the horse treks out of Songpan are the highlights of their Sichuan travels. The price (Y80 per day, including meals, tents, bedding, cold water gear, and lovable guides) has gone up Y20 since last year, supposedly the result of increasing government tax pressure. Even though you might feel somewhat less than satisfied with a short trek to **Munigou Hot Springs,** you definitely get your money's worth trekking to **Ice Mountain.** Treks to the isolated **Falling Stone Mountain** also come highly recommended. The two competing companies, **Happy Trails Horse Treks** (kuàilè de xiǎolù qímǎ lǚyóu; 快乐的小路奇马旅游; ☎723 1064) and **Shun Jiang Horse Treks** (shùnjiān lǚyóu mǎduì; 顺江旅游马队; ☎723 1201) are right next to each other and offer the same tours with the same high quality. Treks to Munigou and the Hot Springs at Er Dao Hai take two days; a detour to the Zhaya waterfall takes an extra day. The Hot Springs are actually rather cold (21°C), and the mineral pools that form the area's main attraction don't compare in the least to Huanglong's or Jiuzhaigou's, even if the 100m Zhaya Waterfall is quite beautiful. *(Entrance fees to both parks Y33. Riding time to Muigou about 4hr.)*

Treks to **Ice Mountain** (bīng shān; 冰山) take four days of hard riding (7-8hr. per day), but are said to be the most awesome of the available treks. You can also trek to **Huanglong** (2 long 7-8hr. days of riding, 1 day hiking in the park), passing close to the snowline, but since bus service is convenient and several hours of riding must be done on the public highway, this trek is not very popular.

DAYTRIP FROM SONGPAN: HUANGLONG

About 17km north of Songpan, the main road branches north toward Jiuzhaigou and east to Huanglong (56km). ***Buses*** *leave the Songpan Northeast Bus Station for the park gates daily at 7am (2hr., Y21) and cross a breathtaking pass just below the snowline.* ***Horse treks*** *from Songpan* *(see p. 695)* *involve a 1-day ride to Huanglong, crossing the same pass, 1-day hike in the park, and 1-day return. From Jiuzhaigou, you can also get to Huanglong by taking a* ***minibus*** *(Y200-300 for a 4-5 seater) from the parking lot in front of the park gates. The round-trip* ***hike*** *to Huanglong Temple and the Five Colored Pool is 7.5km and takes 3-4hr. From the park gates, buses return to Songpan at approximately noon, 2:30, and 5pm. Although there are many small restaurants along the main road in front of the park, there are no vendors inside, so bring food and drink. Park opens daily 8am-7pm. Admission Y80, with student ID Y40.*

Guarded by 10 majestic peaks, the Huanglong Scenic Reserve is famous for its radiant turquoise pools and breathtaking alpine scenery, even if the scenery is in fact quite distant. Unlike Jiuzhaigou's wide, crashing waterfalls and lakes and rivers, Huanglong consists of a long, narrow cascade of white calcium terraces, filled with luminous turquoise water unlike anything at Jiuzhaigou. This UNESCO World Heritage Site was named Huanglong ("Yellow Dragon"; huánglóng; 黄龙) by locals because it reminded them of a dragon leaping down from the mountains. Walking up the boardwalk through the narrow gorge, a line of snow is just a few hundred meters up the mountain, and the air is thin and pure. The **Five Colored Pool** at the top of the park is simply stunning and makes the long trip to Songpan worthwhile. From the veranda of the Huanglong Temple, the glowing terraces of yellow, red, and blue spread out under a massive snow-capped mountain. Looming high above, just below the temple, is a beautiful cave worth exploring if you have a flashlight. Behind the pool, a footpath leads to the hills and boulder field, offering the more energetic hiker a heart-stopping view of the entire Huanglong gorge.

While Huanglong is indeed beautiful, it is designed for easy access and convenient photo-ops, and is traversed by paved and wood-plank paths often filled with swarms of Chinese tourists. Because of the fragility of the calcium formations that cover the narrow gorge, it is nearly impossible to strike off on your own unless you head for the high ridges overlooking the valley. Ordinarily, visitors ascend to the Five Colored Pool along the main boardwalk path and descend along an uninteresting stone path through the woods to avoid congestion on the narrow boardwalk path. You may want to return along the same path to brave the mass of tourists for better views of the pool.

Accommodation in Huanglong is generally very expensive, hovering around Y200 per night, so it's probably best to make only a daytrip out of the excursion.

ZÖIGÊ 若尔盖

Pronounced *ruòěrgài* in Mandarin, Zöigê serves mainly as a night's stopover point for north or southbound bus riders. Because there are no direct buses between Songpan and Longmusi, you will have to spend the night here and catch a connection bus early the next morning. This dusty little town is somewhat inhospitable: the uniform, cement buildings block the views of the beautiful surrounding hills and grasslands, and few food options are available.

Buses leave from Zöigê every morning for **Hezuo** (4-5hr., 6am, Y37), where you can transfer to Xiahe and Lanzhou, **Langmusi** (2-3hr., 6am, Y13), and **Songpan** (5-7hr., 6am, Y29). The best place to stay is the **Panzhou Hotel ❶** (pānzhōu bīnguǎn; 潘州宾馆), with its clean, bright dorm rooms for Y15 per bed. Slightly better quality doubles (Y25 per bed) and triples (Y20 per bed) share the same communal baths and showers. Walk left out of the bus station and wind around to the right on the main road; the hotel is 200m ahead on your left. An **Internet cafe** right next to the Ruoliang Hotel (ruòliáng bīnguǎn; 若粮宾馆) has access for Y5 per hour. From the bus station, walk right and make your second left; the hotel is at the end of the street. If you are headed north to Langmusi, you can try hitching a ride on a track from the *kèyùnqiáo* (passenger transportation bridge; 客运桥), 3km out of town where the road from the south merges with the road from the west to become one small northbound road. *Let's Go* does not recommend hitchhiking. From the Zöigê town center, take a taxi (Y5-10) to this juncture point.

Most trucks and buses that you will encounter heading north will not take you directly to Langmusi, which is about 4km off the main road to Hezuo. Ask them to drop you at the entrance to the small road into town and walk or hire a taxi or motorbike. You can also try to pay the truck driver to take you into town.

LANGMUSI 郎木寺

☎0941

Langmusi is a hidden treasure on a traveler's itinerary between Chengdu and Xiahe. If it weren't for the giant mountains and rock structures that surround this tiny town, you'd think you were on the Tibetan Plateau: the streets are filled with robed Tibetan monks and women clad in the ornate costumes of Tibetan herders. It's also one of the last places in which a tourist can witness a traditional **sky-burial,** which occurs nearly every morning.

TRANSPORTATION. Buses leave daily for **Hezuo** (5hr., 7 and 8am, Y20), where you can change for **Xiahe** (2-3hr., Y9). To go south to **Zöigê** and onto **Songpan**, take a motorcycle or truck to the main road junction 4km out of town, where southbound buses (Y15) pass, and get a ride from the frequent trucks going either north to Xiahe or south to Zoige.

ACCOMMODATIONS AND FOOD. Two pleasant, friendly guesthouses sit right next to each other in south Langmusi, both offering Y15 beds in 4-bed dorms with communal baths and showers. The **Langmusi Hotel** (lámùsì fàndiàn; 郎木寺饭店; ☎667 1086) is slightly more popular due to its English-speaking manager and second-floor balcony overlooking the street. The **White Dragon Hotel** (báilóng fàndiàn; 白龙饭店) is of similar quality but is often less crowded.

Langmusi offers some tasty food and some restaurants with English menus. In **Lesha's Cafe ❶** (dīxuéwén fànguǎn; 丁学文饭馆; ☎667 1179), attempt to beat the 13-minute record for finishing a frisbee-sized yak burger (Y12). If you still have room for dessert, order a slice of the delicious apple, peach, or apricot pie (Y8). The **Hotel Restaurant ❶** (bīnguǎn cāntīng; 宾馆餐厅; ☎667 1164) just under the Langmusi Hotel offers a nice break from potatoes and yak at Lesha's, with tasty noodle soups (Y3-5) and fried vegetable dishes (Y6-10).

SIGHTS. The town's main attraction is the giant **Langmusi Temple** (làngmùsì; 郎木寺), a monastery divided into two complexes: the one upstream nestles into the valley, and the other, smaller complex on the high hill flanks the town to the east. Recently, the larger, more intricate valley temple complex has begun charging Y10 admission tickets just to walk through the small dirt roads connecting the various dormitories and shrines. If you enter from anywhere but the main road on the left of the river, however, chances are no one will hassle you for a ticket. To get to the **sky burial site,** walk to the highest temple structure on the eastern hill and follow a small dirt trail to the open grasslands. Then look for the burial grounds (surrounded by prayer flags) to the northeast. Several local nuns will quite forcefully try to make you buy a ticket, the price of which fluctuates according to what they think they can get from you. Don't pay more than Y5 per person. A great hike starts from the sky burial site, winding up through the grasslands to a row of orange cliffs that tower above the town below (3-4hr. to the highest prayer flags and back to the valley town). On the opposite side of the valley, follow a horse trail along the river north and up into the rockier and more barren mountain crags to the west (5-6hr. to the first main rock group and back to the town).

SICHUAN

YIBIN 宜宾

Situated at the confluence of the Min and Jinsha tributaries of the Yangzi River in southeastern Sichuan, the rather uninteresting industrial town of Yibin is little more than a convenient base for exploring the incredible Bamboo Sea forest preserve 60km to the southeast.

Yibin is laid out along a rough grid with a crossroads at the center. **Renmin Lu** (人民路) runs east-west and becomes **Zhongshan Jie** (中山街) east of the crossroads, dead-ending on the banks of the Min River. South of the crossroads, **Minzhu Lu** (民主路) passes the post office and becomes **Nan Jie** before crossing the Jinsha river in the south. Across the Jinsha is the **Nanchang Bus Station. Cuiping Lu** (翠屏路) winds from the train station and **West Gate Bus Station** in the southwest to the **North Gate Bus Station** in the north, intersecting Renmin Lu at the entrance to the **Cuiping City Park** at the western end of the city.

Budget accommodations open to foreigners in Yibin are incredibly scarce, and since there is little to see in the city itself, it might be better to arrive in Yibin as early in the day as possible, go directly to the **Nan'an Bus Station** (nán'àn kèyún zhàn; 南岸客运站), and catch an afternoon bus to the Bamboo Sea. If this is not possible, be prepared to shell out Y100-200 for a double room. As of July 2001, only the **Education Hostel** ❶ (jiaòyú zhāodàisǔo; 教育招待所), conveniently located across the river from the Nan'an Bus Station, allows foreigners in dorm rooms. To get there, head south on Nan Jie; about 30m from the Jinsha bridge and near an alley filled with vendors, a vertical sign with red chinese characters indicates the hostel entrance. You will probably have to fill a double room (Y40) or a single if available (Y30), but this is undoubtedly the cheapest accommodation in Yibin. Rooms come with nice TVs and ceiling fans. The owner speaks a little English and may be of some help to travelers. Students congregate in the lobby. The **Nezha Hotel** ❶ (nézhā bīnguǎn; 哪吒宾馆), just south of the intersection of Renmin Lu and Cuiping Lu, is a five-minute walk from the West Bus Station or train station, or a 10-minute walk from the North Bus Station. (3-bed dorms Y120; singles with double bed, communal bath, and TV Y70; doubles and triples with bath and A/C Y200.) The next best option is the **Xufu Hotel** ❷ (xùfǔ bīnguǎn; 叙府宾馆). It's also somewhat difficult to find and is on Renmin Lu, off an alley just before the central crossroads. (Clean doubles with A/C and bath Y142.)

If staying at the Education Hostel, cross Nan Jie and walk up the small street on the opposite side to find hotpot restaurants and roasted meat vendors. In the downtown and western areas, small alleys off Renmin Lu offer an assortment of noodle dishes (Y1-2) and grilled foods (xiǎokaǒ; 小烤). Try the lamb kebabs (Y0.5 a stick), grilled eggplant, or cucumber (Y2 for 15 or so skewers) offered with spicy Sichuan sauce and ground peanuts. In the mornings, look for meat-filled sticky buns to start the day as it should be started: with sweet goo and nourishing meat.

BAMBOO SEA

About 60km southeast of Yibin lies one of China's largest expanses of bamboo forest, stretching over 120km^2 of mountain peaks, towering cliffs, and deep, secluded valleys. A network of stone-paved trails weaves through the park, ascending steep rock faces and passing behind several waterfalls; loggging trails pass by traditional houses. One downside to the area, apart from the steep entrance fee, is the swarms of Chinese tourists that often inundate the main lower-elevation trails, especially on weekends and holidays. However, bypassing the crowds and heading high up into the hills and back country allows you to experience this amazing forest in solitude.

At the base town of Wanling, the main road splits. The left fork runs through the Flower Bamboo Valley (huāzhúxī; 花竹溪); the right fork runs past the cheap but somewhat inconvenient **Traffic Hotel** ❶ (jiāotóng bīnguǎn; 交通宾馆; 4-bed dorms Y25; double with bath Y40-50) and up into the **Forgetting Worries Valley** (wàngyōu gǔ; 忘忧谷). From here, the road continues about 8km through towering bamboo, reaching the **lake-viewing pavilion** (guānhú lóu; 观湖楼) and the entrance to a small tourist village near **Fairy Lake** (xiānnǚ hú; 仙女湖). Motorbikes ply this stretch of road for Y10. At the main fork at Wanling, just past the **Bamboo Sea Museum** (zhúhǎi bōwùguǎn; 竹海博物馆), is the **Black Brook Valley** (mòxī; 墨溪), one of the more secluded areas of the park, with several towering waterfalls in the high cliffs above. About 1km up along the Black Brook Valley road, a sporadically functioning **cable car** takes you to a village at a higher elevation.

The best bet for accommodation in the park is one of the mountain-top hotels, which range from Y50 to Y300 per night. In addition, a night on the mountain is the best way for travelers to see the sunrise and early-morning sea of clouds descending over the valleys. The **Xianyu Mountain Villa** ❶ (xiānyù shānzhuàng; 仙寓山庄), just off the mountain-top parking lot near Fairy Lake, offers summer season doubles for Y80 and low season doubles for Y40. If arriving with a heavy pack, take a motorbike or taxi (Y10-15) directly to this hotel or to one of the dozen or so others lining the mountain roads.

From Yibin, take the #2 or 4 local bus or a Y5 taxi south across the Jinshu river bridge to the **Nan'an Bus Station.** Daily buses go directly to **Zhuhai** (zhúhǎi; 竹海) every 30min. 8-10:30am; in the afternoon, buses leave at 1:25, 2, 3, 4, and 4:30pm. In the morning, there is usually a choice between a minibus (Y15) and a tour bus with A/C (Y20). The bus stops at the west gate of the park to purchase entrance tickets (Y57, half-price for students with ID), then continues up to the base town of **Wanling** (wànlǐng; 万岭). From here you can pay Y10 to continue up to higher elevations as part of a tour, walk up individually, or take a taxi or motorbike. Direct buses back to Yibin are often unavailable, requiring you to take a bus first to the nearby town of **Changning** (chángníng; 长宁; Y4), before transferring to a Yibin bus (Y7.5). The last bus from Wanling leaves around 5:30pm.

CHONGQING 重庆 ☎023

Over the years, some have come to see Chongqing (meaning "Doubly Blessed") as a lackluster interior city, but nothing could be further from the truth. The landscape of this attractive Yangzi-side city is uniquely serene, especially when juxtaposed with the city's sweltering sub-tropical climate and spicy food. Here, even the streets are mellow, with a city ordinance against honking car horns. At the same time air raid tunnels and Guomindang prison camps hint at a turbulent past.

Chongqing became an integral part of China during the Ming dynasty. This thriving Yangzi port was first opened to British trade in 1890 and then to Japanese trade in 1895. The Japanese left at the onset of the Sino-Japanese War in 1937 (see p. 13), and Chongqing became the capital of the Republic of China after the Guomindang evacuated Nanjing. This distinction made Chongqing the site of intense fighting in the final days of the civil war between the CCP and the GMD.

Part of Sichuan province until 1997, Chongqing now enjoys the special status of independent municipality, a title shared with Beijing, Tianjin, and Shanghai. About the size of Austria and home to 30 million people, Sichuan is far too large for most people to explore. Th-ese days, this booming industrial city, seething with the heat, humidity, and dust of the sultry Yangzi Valley, is best known as a starting-off point for Three Gorges cruises down the Yangzi. But Chongqing's burgeoning nightlife, historical sights, and unmistakable atmosphere make it worthwhile on its own.

TRANSPORTATION

Flights: Jiangbei Airport (jiāngběi jīchǎng; 江北机场; ☎6715 2337), 35km north of the city center. **Shuttle buses** (40-50min., every 30min. 6am-6pm, Y15) leave from the **CAAC office,** 161 Zhongshan San Lu (☎6360 0444), toward the west end of the Yuzhong district. Open daily 7:30am-6:30pm. Chongqing is mainly served by **China Southwest Airlines** (xīnán hángkōng gōngsī; 西南航空公司), which has a convenient branch (☎6382 5926) between the Liberation Monument and Huixianlou Hotel, in the basement of the Industrial and Commercial Bank of China building. Open daily 8:30am-6pm. **Sichuan Airlines** (sìchuān hángkōng gōngsī; 四川航空公司), 17 Minquan Lu (☎6370 7070 or 6383 9999; fax 6370 0818), just beyond the post office when coming from the Liberation Monument. Open daily 8:30am-10pm. To: **Beijing** (3 per day,

Y1400); **Guangzhou** (3 per day, Y1070); **Kunming** (4 per day, Y650); **Lhasa** (2 per week); **Shanghai** (3 per day, Y1340); **Xi'an** (3 per day, Y520).

Trains: Caiyuanba Train Station (càiyuánbà huǒchē zhàn; 菜园坝火车站), 4 Caiyuan Lu (☎6386 2607), in Yuzhong district's southwest corner. Ticket office open daily 8:30-11:30am, 2:30-5:30pm, and 6:30-11:30pm. Taxis opposite the exit may not use meters. The official taxi stand is on the right as you walk out of the station. To: **Beijing** (32-35hr., 2 per day, Y348-658); **Chengdu** (10hr.; 3 per day; Y88-130); **Guangzhou** (54-65hr., 4 per day, Y105-339) via **Nanning; Guiyang** (10hr., daily, Y34-120); **Kunming** (24hr., 2 per day, Y81-304); **Shanghai** (45hr., 5:14pm, Y271-756).

Buses: Chongqing Long-distance Bus Station (chóngqìng chángtú qìchē zhàn; 重庆长途汽车站), 6 Caiyuan Lu (☎6360 7768), next to the train station. English-speakers man the clearly marked info desk. Open daily 5:30am-midnight. To: **Chengdu** (4hr., every 20min. 6:30am-10pm, Y107-199); **Dazu** (2hr., every 40min. 6:30am-7pm, Y29); **Emeishan** (7hr., 8:45am, Y94); **Lhasa** (4 days, every other day, Y650).

Ferries: See the **Three Gorges,** p. 705.

Local Transportation: Buses are cheap and efficient, but the number of routes can make the system overwhelming. If you don't see the bus you're looking for, listen for your destination (each bus has someone yelling out its route at major stops) or ask the driver where he's going. Fare Y1-1.5. Bus **#102** runs along Jiefang Lu between Chaotianmen Dock and the Caiyuanba Train Station; **#103** runs near the Liberation Monument and past the Great Hall of the People; **#401** links Chaotianmen Dock with the Liberation Monument. Stops are far apart; ask drivers to let you off close to your destination. **Minibuses** (Y3) run the same routes and are more willing to stop anywhere.

Taxis: Base fare Y5, each additional km Y1.2.

ORIENTATION AND PRACTICAL INFORMATION

Situated at the confluence of the **Yangzi** and **Jialing** rivers, Chongqing municipality is divided into five central districts; of these, **Yuzhong** (渝中) contains the most conveniently located accommodations, shops, and transport facilities. **Jiangbei** (江北) to the north and **Shapingba** (沙坪坝) to the west are important gateways to sights in the outer reaches of the city. Steep and narrow winding streets make Chongqing difficult to navigate, and Yuzhong alone is too big to cover on foot. The district, bounded to the southwest by the train and bus stations on Caiyuan Lu and to the northeast by the **Chaotianmen Docks,** is best navigated by bus or taxi. However, near the **Liberation Monument,** a 15-minute walk from the docks at the intersection of Minzhu Lu and Minyuan Lu with Zourong Lu, hotels, restaurants, nightlife, and most services cluster in a compact, convenient space.

Travel Agencies: CITS, at 120 Zhaozhi Lanyan Lu (☎6385 0693, 24hr. information line 6385 2490; fax 6385 0196; citzcq@public.cta.cq.cn). Excellent English-speaking department headed by Mr. Li, a one-man army in the service of independent travelers. Inquire about travel permits for Tibet. French, Japanese, and German spoken. Open daily 8:30am-5:30pm. Another branch on the 5th fl. of the Huixianlou Hotel (☎6370 9934 or 6372 3415; fax 6372 3415) is more conveniently located, but less prepared to help non-Chinese travelers. Open daily 9am-5:30pm. **China Youth Travel Service** (zhōngguó qīngnián lǚxíngshè; 中国青年旅行社), 125 Renmin Lu (☎6386 0814), near the intersection with Zhongshan Lu. Open M-F 9am-5:30pm. The **Huixianlou Hotel** (☎6382 5148) also books tickets at no extra cost.

Consulates: Canada: Metropolitan Tower, Ste. 1705, Wuyi Lu (☎6373 8007). **UK:** Metropolitan Tower, Ste. 2801, Wuyi Lu (☎6381 0321). Both open M-F 9am-5pm.

SICHUAN

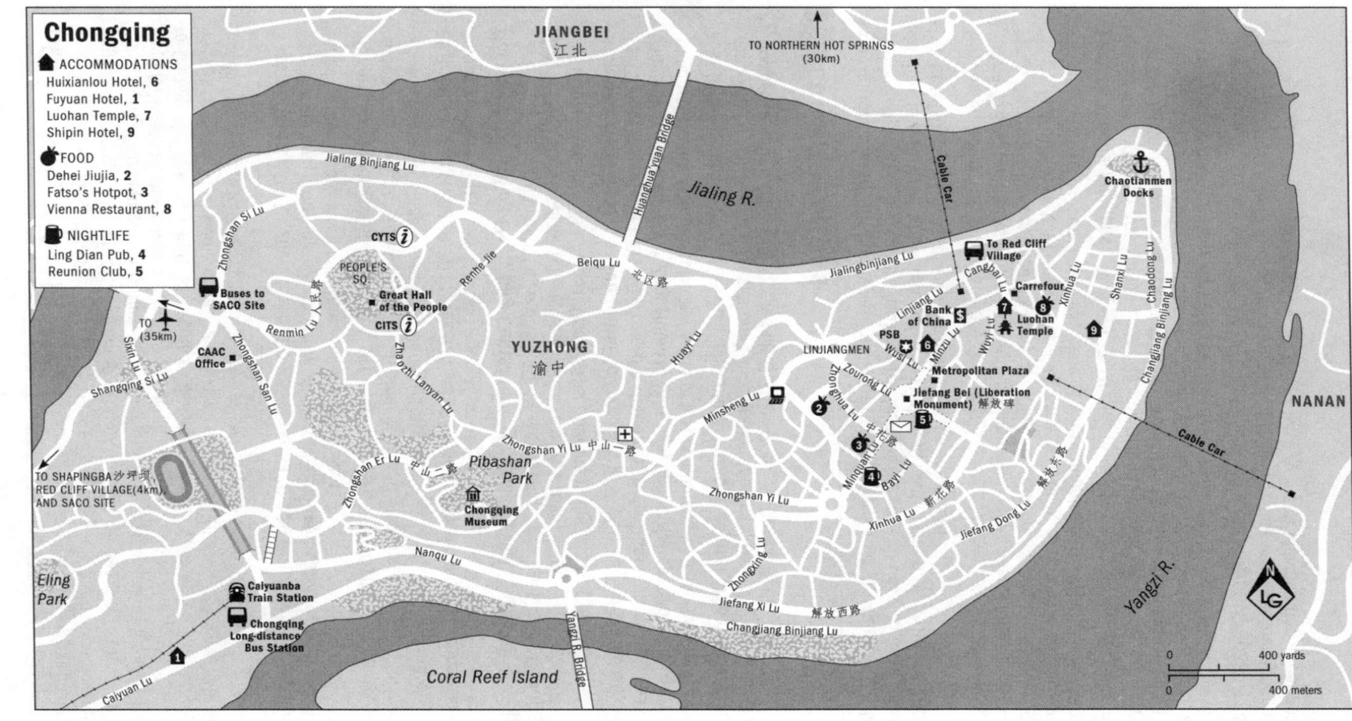
Chongqing
ACCOMMODATIONS
Huixianlou Hotel, 6
Fuyuan Hotel, 1
Luohan Temple, 7
Shipin Hotel, 9
FOOD
Dehei Jiujia, 2
Fatso's Hotpot, 3
Vienna Restaurant, 8
NIGHTLIFE
Ling Dian Pub, 4
Reunion Club, 5
JIANGBEI
江北
TO NORTHERN HOT SPRINGS (30km)
Jialing Binjiang Lu
Huanghua'yuan Bridge
Jialing R.
Cable Car
Chaotianmen Docks
Zhongshan Si Lu
CYTS
PEOPLE'S SQ.
Great Hall of the People
CITS
Renhe Jie
Beiqu Lu
北区路
Jialingbinjiang Lu
To Red Cliff Village
Cangbai Lu
Carrefour
Buses to SACO Site
TO (35km)
Renmin Lu 人民路
Sixin Lu
CAAC Office
Zhongshan San Lu
Shangqing Si Lu
Zhaozhi Lanyan Lu
YUZHONG
渝中
Huayi Lu
Linjiang Lu
Bank of China
Minzu Lu
Wuyi Lu
Luohan Temple
Xinhua Lu
Shanxi Lu
Chaodong Lu
Changjiang Binjiang Lu
PSB
LINJIANGMEN
Wusi Lu
Metropolitan Plaza
Zourong Lu
Zhonghua Lu
Jiefang Bei (Liberation Monument) 解放碑
Minsheng Lu
NANAN
中华路
Minquan Lu
Bayi Lu
Cable Car
Zhongshan Yi Lu 中山一路
Zhongshan Er Lu 中山二路
Pibashan Park
Chongqing Museum
Zhongshan Yi Lu
新华路
解放东路
TO SHAPINGBA 沙坪坝 RED CLIFF VILLAGE(4km), AND SACO SITE
Xinhua Lu
Jiefang Dong Lu
Nanqu Lu
Zhongxing Lu
Yangzi R.
Eling Park
Caiyuanba Train Station
Chongqing Long-distance Bus Station
Jiefang Xi Lu
解放西路
Changjiang Binjiang Lu
Yangzi R. Bridge
Coral Reef Island
Caiyuan Lu
0
400 yards
0
400 meters

LOOK MA, NO HANDS! Long years of battle between the Ming and the invading Manchurians of the Qing left Chongqing's population severely depleted. During the reign of Qing Emperor Kangxi, large numbers of people were brought into Chongqing from Hunan and Hubei provinces to repopulate the city. The emperor's soldiers handcuffed these forced migrants to one another for the long walk to Chongqing. The only time they could have their hands released was when they needed to use the toilet. And so the phrase "free my hands" (jiěshǒu; 解手) was born; it is still used today in Chongqing to excuse oneself to go to the bathroom.

Bank of China: 104 Minzhu Lu (☎6380 0654; fax 6370 1294), beyond the Haixianlou Hotel if coming from the Liberation Monument. Exchanges currency and traveler's checks. Credit card advances. Open daily 8:30am-9pm.

Market: Carrefour (jiālèfú; 家乐福), 2 Cangbei Lu (☎6378 9010), with an entrance around the corner at 14 Minzhu Lu. Carrefour seems to offer more dairy products than anywhere else in China. Open daily 9am-10pm.

PSB: 48 Wusi Lu (☎6386 7017; fax 6375 8106). Serves foreigners and processes visa requests. Open 24hr.

Hospitals: Chongqing Emergency Center (chóngqìngshì jíjìu yīliáo zhōngxīn; 重庆市急救医疗中心), 1 Jiankang Lu (☎6387 4000). Emergency room open 24hr. **Chongqing No. 1 People's Hospital** (chóngqìngshì dìyī rénmín yīyuàn; 重庆市第一人民医院), 40 Damen Kou (☎6384 4283). Open 24hr. Both are in the Yuzhong district.

Internet Access: Reader's Club (dúzhě jùlèbù; 读者俱乐部), 181 Minsheng Lu, 3rd fl. (☎6371 6367 or 6371 6347). From the Huixianlou Hotel, turn right at the Liberation Monument and then left on Zhonghua Lu. Stay right until the street ends; turn right and enter next to the Xinhua Bookstore. A sea of fast computers. Y3-5 per hr. Open 24hr.

Post Offices: Each district has a main post office. **Yuzhong central office**, 3 Mingnan Lu (☎6389 9110), is half a block from the Liberation Monument, on the left. IDD service downstairs until 8pm. EMS. Open daily 8:30am-9:30pm. **Postal Code:** 630011.

SICHUAN

ACCOMMODATIONS

Accommodations in Chongqing are all about skyscrapers and sky-scraping prices (US$150 per night). Foreigners looking for budget hotels will have to look far and wide. Fortunately, the cheapest district, Yuzhong, is also the most convenient. All listed hotels have 24-hour hot water unless otherwise noted.

Huixianlou Hotel (huìxiānlóu fàndiàn; 会仙楼饭店), 186 Minzhu Lu (☎6383 7495; fax 6384 4234), two blocks from the Liberation Monument, in the heart of the Yuzhong district. Dorms are the best deal in town, but they may not be around much longer. This place is plush; even the dorms have A/C, carpets, and TV. Books river cruises, plane tickets, and tours. 6-bed dorms Y50; singles Y269; doubles Y200-280; triples Y280. ❶

Luohan Temple (luóhànsì; 罗汉寺), 7 Minzhu Lu (☎6373 7169; fax 6373 7162), between Cangbei Lu and Xinhua Lu in Yuzhong district. Rooms are on the 3rd fl. of the temple complex, above the vegetarian restaurant. The monk at the door will let you in without a ticket if you're staying at the hotel. Rooms feature A/C, attached baths, and TV. 3-bed dorms Y30; doubles Y100. ❶

Shipin Hotel (shípǐn bīnguǎn; 食品宾馆), 72 Shanxi Lu (☎6384 7300; fax 6384 5844), Yuzhong district. Clean and convenient. The English-speaking assistant manager sometimes gives discounts to foreigners. All rooms have A/C and attached baths, but not all have latches on doors; ask to move if you feel that the room isn't secure. Books Yangzi cruises. Laundry Y5 per piece. Singles Y100; doubles Y80-120; triples Y90-140. ❷

Fuyuan Hotel (fùyuán bīnguǎn; 富苑宾馆), 38 Caiyuan Lu (☎6363 6564; fax 6387 3321), around the corner from the bus and train stations toward the river. Fine, clean rooms with central A/C and TV. Close to transportation hubs but not much else. Hot water 7pm-10am. Singles and doubles Y160-220; triples Y180; quads Y140. ❸

FOOD

Superhuman chili-eaters will be right at home in Chongqing. The local specialty **Sichuanese hotpot** (sìchuān huǒguō; 四川火锅) is said to have originated in the city. Unlike the clear Mongolian variety, Chongqing hotpot broth is an ultra-spicy psychedelic-red concoction that used to be laced with opium for added "flavor." The ubiquitous hotpot joints are easily recognized by the rows of tables with holes in their middles.

The hotpot craze began in the area of **Xiaomishi** (xiǎomíshì; 小米市), but the family-run joints there have been replaced by sidewalk eateries and flashy, high-end restaurants. Only a few of the original places remain; try **Fatso's Hotpot** ❶ (pàngzǐmā huǒguō; 胖子妈火锅; ☎6381 3425), where beef, mushrooms, kidney slices, and liver slices are hot add-ins (Y10-20 per plate). From the Liberation Monument, walk two blocks on Minquan Lu and take a right into the alley just before the intersection. The stir-fry (Y2-18) is also tasty. (Open daily 8am-11pm.) **Vienna Restaurant** ❸ (wéiyěnà dàjiǔdiān; 维也纳大酒店), 28 Minzhu Lu (☎6382 0652), between Xinhua Lu and Shanxi Lu, serves heavenly hotpots buffet-style. The one-price lunch and dinner hotpots (Y40) allow diners to sample dozens of meats and vegetables in either Sichuan or Mongolian broth. (Open daily 9:30am-2pm and 5-10pm.) There are more stalls near the Huxianlou Hotel; from the hotel, walk toward the Liberation Monument, take the first right, and then turn into an alley to the left. A small night market on Cangbai Lu also features hotpot; walk up Minzhu Lu away from the monument, and turn right at the Carrefour.

When you're ready to give your blistered taste buds a rest, try **Dehei Jiujia** ❶ (déhēi jiǔjiā; 德黑酒家; ☎6383 5223), on the corner of Datong Lu and Minsheng Lu. From the Liberation Monument, walk one block on Minquan Lu, take a right on Zhonghua Lu and a left on Datong Lu. This cozy corner restaurant serves sizzling stir-fries (Y6-20), with or without the chili. (Open daily 8am-2am.)

SIGHTS

It's easy to lose a day walking among Chongqing's attractive architecture and steep winding streets. The city does not have much in the way of natural scenery or ancient relics. Instead, the city's official sites focus largely on the grim and not-so-ancient past of the 1947-49 Civil War. These openly political sights offer a glimpse at some of the founding facts (and perceptions) behind the worldview of many modern Chinese citizens.

LIBERATION MONUMENT (jiěfàng bēi; 解放碑). This short tower, built to commemorate the Communist liberation of Chongqing from GMD control, is now the most prominent meeting point in Yuzhong district. Surrounded by flashing neon lights, fast food joints, and billboards, the monument today looks like it's celebrating Chongqing's "liberation" from socialist austerity. The monument area is a great place to watch fashion-conscious children strutting by with new clothes from the huge **Metropolitan Plaza** (dàdūhuì guǎngchǎng; 大都会广场), the city's largest mall.

PEOPLE'S SQUARE (rénmín guǎngchǎng; 人民广场). The massive People's Square is dominated by the **Great Hall of the People** (rénmín dàlǐtáng; 人民大礼堂), designed by the famous Chinese architect Zhang Jiade and completed in 1954. The building was modeled after the Temple of Heaven in Beijing (see p. 137), but the interior is fairly uninteresting. In 1981, "the people" sacrificed their access to the south and north wings and turned them into the palatial Chongqing People's Hotel. *(Open daily 8am-6pm. Y3.)* Visit People's Square at night, when the plaza in front of the Great Hall of the People becomes a massive dance hall; hundreds of people coordinate dance steps to music blasted over giant loudspeakers. The mixed crowd includes a good number of young people intent on learning steps from the elegant older women who rule this dance floor. The 10pm finale is an over-the-top feel-good musical bonanza. *(Dancing daily 7:30am-10pm. Accessible by bus #103 from the Liberation Monument area.)*

SITE OF SINO-AMERICAN SPECIAL TECHNICAL COOPERATION ORGANIZATION (SACO) (zhōngměi hézùosuǒ jízhōngyíng jiùzhǐ; 中美合作所集中营旧址). The SACO site is named for the alliance that lent US support to the Guomindang against the Communists. The larger camp, known as **Refuse Pit Prison** (zhāzí dòng; 渣滓洞), once held some 300 Communist Party members for questioning and, later, execution. The interrogation room, with its faintly blood-stained rope and torture apparatus, has been kept just the way it was, as have some of the prison cells. On November 27, 1949, after the Communist Party proclaimed the People's Republic of China, the Guomindang commander in charge of Chongqing ordered the massacre of the prisoners. Only 15 people managed to escape.

SICHUAN

Three kilometers down the hill, the **Bai Mansion** (báigōngguǎn; 白公馆) relates some of the same sordid past, albeit on a smaller scale. Exhibits tell the stories of prisoners, including Little Radish, who was so named because malnutrition caused his head to appear considerably larger than his body. The child entered the prison with his parents, both active Communists, when he was eight months old and died at the age of nine, in the 1949 purge. The interrogation room is in a small cave at the back of the mansion. Cool, damp air and red lights enhance the eeriness of the chamber, which still contains various 50-year-old tools.

Another 3-4km away, down the hill back toward the road, is the **Martyrs' Tomb** (lièshì mù; 烈士墓), where a large stone carving commemorates the members of the Communist Party who died at Gele Mountain. A museum displays photographs, clothes (most bearing marks of suffering), and writings of the deceased, as well as a larger collection of tools used during interrogation sessions. For visitors who can't read Chinese, the Martyrs' Tomb is the least-moving piece in the trio of sights. *(On Gele Mountain, 50min. from the city center. Take bus #215 from the Liberation Monument area, the intersection of Renmin Lu and Zhongshan Lu, or People's Square, to Shapingba and change to #210, which runs past the entrance to the Martyrs' Tomb and up the hill to Bai Mansion. Taxis run uphill to Refuse Pit Prison (Y5). ☎6531 3028 or 6351 0908. Interrogation reenactments (Y40) are held nightly at 7pm at Refuse Pit Prison; the more gruesome techniques are left out. Refuse Pit Prison and Bai Mansion open daily 8am-7pm; Martyr's Tomb open daily 8am-6pm. Combined admission to all sights and museum Y15; individual sights Y2-5.)*

RED CLIFF VILLAGE (hóngyán cūn; 红岩村). This modest complex was built by members of the Communist Party to serve as their headquarters during the shaky Communist-Nationalist alliance. A small museum near the entrance displays revolutionary photographs and essays. Slightly farther away are the southern headquarters and living quarters of the Communist Party and the 8th Route Army, where Zhou Enlai lived for several years during the war with Japan. Despite Chongqing's scorching summers, Mao's room is the only one with an electric fan.

(Take bus #104 from Cangbei Lu (35-45min.); Red Cliff village is at the terminus, on the opposite side of the road. ☎6330 1887. No English captions. Open daily 9am-5pm. Y6.)

NORTH HOT SPRINGS (běi wēnquán; 北温泉). Kiss those unsightly rashes goodbye; a dip in these three pools can reputedly cure skin ailments. Private baths and showers are also available for those who fear that the water's healing powers may be diluted by the itchy crowds. The grounds of North Hot Springs Park invite aimless wanderings or a trip to a deep mountain cave, where stalactites, stalagmites, and bats prove amiable company. *(A bus (2hr., Y6) runs daily from the Chungking Hotel, on Xinhua Lu one block from Minzhu Lu in the direction of the docks, to Bei Pei; from there, bus #516 (Y1) takes you to the springs. ☎6822 2324. Open daily 7am-8pm. Y8.)*

OTHER SIGHTS. Luohan Temple (luóhàn sì; 罗汉寺) is an unusual temple complex worth a visit; even for those who've seen their share of sacred carvings. Built over 1000 years ago, the temple has been renovated a great deal since. To the left is a large red- and yellow-painted temple, under construction as of August 2001; to the right are 500 carved and painted terracotta figures guarded by a large gold Buddha. *(7 Minzhu Lu. Open daily 9am-6pm. Y2.)* **Pibashan Park** (píbáshān gōngyuán; 批杷山公园) stretches between Zhongshan Er Lu and Pibashan Zhenjie. The central pavilion provides arid views of Chongqing that are particularly stunning at night. *(Open daily 7am-10pm. Y5.)* On the path from the road on the south side of the park is the lackluster **Chongqing Museum** (chóngqìng bówùguǎn; 重庆博物馆), which houses relics from Chongqing's past. The photo exhibition of modern Chongqing on the first floor is worth the entrance fee, especially for those interested in photojournalistic depictions of urban progress. All captions are in Chinese. *(Open daily 8:30am-5pm. Y5.)*

NIGHTLIFE

In the world of Chongqing nightlife, any pub or club that's been around for a year must be on the downswing. Word of mouth (not hard to find among the city's hip young English speakers) should always be your first guide to this booming scene. If nobody's talking, follow the packs of glittering night owls who prowl the blocks around the Liberation Monument, Yuzhong's most happening area.

Ling Dian Pub (língdiǎn jiǔbā; 零点酒吧). From the Liberation Monument, walk two blocks down Minquan Lu and cross the large modern complex on the far left corner. To the left of the large KTV sign, an elevator leads up to this 4th fl. dance party. Features DJ-mixed house music for a laid-back crowd. After midnight, tables are hard to come by. Heineken Y25. Open daily 4pm-5am.

Reunion Club (huíguī jiǔláng; 回归酒廊; ☎6376 2882), in the Yutian Bldg., 8th fl. From the Huixianlou Hotel, turn left at the Liberation Monument; the building is a block ahead on the right—the one with the McDonald's inside. Chongqing's best-dressed come here to see and be seen. The Reunion's throbbing techno and exuberant crowd keep the place moving until closing time. Corona Y25. Open daily 8pm-2am.

Ziyi Coffee House (☎6379 8007). Below and next to the Lingdian Pub. A low-key alternative for mellow insomniacs. The dusty KTV setup plays mainly English pop. Chinese and English menu. Coffee drinks Y15-25. Open daily 10am-2am.

THREE GORGES 三峡

From the White Emperor City (446km downstream from Chongqing) to Nanjingguan (6km west of Yichang), the mighty Yangzi rolls through the 196km of death-defying rapids and imposing peaks known as the Three Gorges (sānxiá). Immortalized in poetry and literature, these gorges have captivated the imagination of everyone from Li Bai to Bill Gates. However, in 2003, this ancient landmark and its nearby historical sights will begin to disappear as a result of contemporary China's obsession with development and traditional China's infatuation with undertaking outlandishly ambitious projects. The Three Gorges Dam, one of the largest civil engineering projects in history, is due to be completed in 2009. When completed, it will be one of two manmade structures visible from space (the other, of course, is the Great Wall) and will raise the water level 175m above its current level. As an intermediate step in creating the Three Gorge Reservoir the water is set to rise 135m during 2003.

The Three Gorges are a must-see for many Chinese tourists, so the cruise is steeped in Chinese tourist culture. Tourists who expect a peaceful ride down the graceful Yangzi may come away feeling disappointed by how the experience is packaged. Segments of the trip are impressive and well-narrated by an army of tour guides, but large portions feel like an ordinary (albeit long) boat ride. Overpriced, manmade attractions and the souvenir feeding frenzy that waits at each stop help to temper the sense of wonder that the trip is meant to inspire. Caveats aside, with the right expectations, the cruise through the most striking section of the Yangzi is a great way to spend a few days.

Most tourists make the downstream journey from Chongqing and disembark at either Yichang (see p. 449) or Wuhan (see p. 443) in Hubei province; some cruises go as far as Jiujiang in Jiangxi province or all the way to Shanghai. Increased numbers of ships have made it easy to find a ticket; still, advance purchase is a wise precaution. The **Official Port Ticket Office** (chóngqìng gǎng shòupiào chù; 重庆港售票处; ☎6384 2861), under the Chaotianmen Hotel at the Chaotianmen Docks (cháotiānmén; 朝天门) is perhaps the most trustworthy place to get a ticket. (Open daily 6am-11pm.) Most reputable companies have a booth here and all offer the same, fixed prices. CQG ("Chongqing Port") officials, who can be distinguished by blue shirts, black pants/skirts, and small red pins, monitor the goings-on. Questions or concerns can be addressed at the CQG desks in the back and far side of the terminal.

As always, be on the lookout for con artists. If it seems too good to be true, it probably is. The cruise tickets are computer-issued and about the same size as computer-issued train tickets. Be sure the price and class printed on your ticket corresponds to the full list price. Some tourists fall victim to English-speaking con artists who promise all-inclusive private or small-group tours led by English-speaking guides only to be herded on to the big boats once the money is handed over. There is no pre-paid board option on the regular tourist boats. While higher-end cruises with small tours do exist, they cost considerably more (Y1600-3000) and often fall below expectations. One way to avoid unpleasant scams is to travel individually; bypassing tour groups saves you commission fees and allows you to pick and choose which sights to visit. It is always possible to purchase admission tickets upon arrival at each attraction.

There are different classes of **berths:** 1st class (2 beds, A/C, TV, and bath), 2nd class (2-4 beds, A/C, TV, and sometimes bath), 3rd class (6-8 beds, A/C, TV, and sometimes a washbasin), 4th class (8-12 beds, sometimes TV), and 5th class (any space you can find on the deck). Boats go to **Yichang** (3 days; 1st class Y929, 2nd class Y482, 3rd class Y225, 4th class Y160, 5th class Y112) and **Wuhan** (4 days; 1st class Y1369, 2nd class Y704, 3rd class Y330, 4th class Y237, 5th class Y162). Children pay 5th class fare. Most departures are 5-8pm, so a three-day cruise is really one evening, two days, and two nights. The dock number and boat name are

IN THE NAME OF PROGRESS At **Sandouping,** just a little before the Nanjin Gate and some 40km from Yichang is the **Three Gorges Project** (sānxiá gōngchéng; 三峡工程), the world's largest dam construction site, an overwhelming (and depressing) sight. The sheer scale of the project dwarfs bulldozers, drills, and other mechanical monstrosities, making them look like mere sandbox Tonka toys manned by some 60,000 action figures. When completed in 2009, this 200m high, 2000m wide Great Wall across the Yangzi and its 28 superturbines will harness more energy than 18 nuclear power plants. The price tag? According to official figures, a mere US$17 billion.

When this super-project reaches its final stage in less than a decade, the Three Gorges as we know them will vanish forever, along with the homes of nearly 2 million people and the unexcavated treasures of some 8000 archaeological sites. Proponents envision railway links, rapid regional development, better living standards for residents around the Three Gorges Reservoir, and flood control downriver. Naysayers warn of silt, water pollution, inadequate compensation for dislocated residents, mountains of debt, endangered species facing extinction, rock slides, and earthquakes.

After decades of debates and countless rounds of expert testimony, the Three Gorges Dam, often described as the pet project of former Premier and Department of Hydropower Secretary Li Peng, is forging ahead. Although the pragmatic wing of the Politburo led by Zhu Rongji remains cool to the dam, most analysts believe that too much money has already been spent for the project to stop.

To visit the dam, take the #2 bus from Yanjiang Dadao in Yichang. Tell the driver where you are going, and he'll let you off at a stop where you can catch the #8 bus to the dam. From the stop, walk up the hill to enter the official viewing area (Y20).

Yichang CITS arranges tours of the site that include transportation, a guide, and visits to a couple of lookout points providing views of the cranes, boats, workers, and the river itself; admission to the dam area (Y20) is not included. Markings on cliffs indicate flood levels: by 2003, the water level is predicted to be 135m above the current river; when the dam is completed it is expected to be 175m above current levels. Tours leave from Gezhou Dam Hotel (gézhōu bà bīnguǎn) off Dongshan Lu, a 15-minute walk west of the train station, daily at 9am and 2pm, or from the CITS office, daily at 8 or 9am. Tours departing from the Gezhou Dam Hotel take 3hr.; tours from the CITS take 4hr. (Y45).

printed on the ticket. Some companies also run non-tour boats to **Shanghai** (6 days; 1st class Y2059, 2nd class Y1109, 3rd class Y519, 4th class Y372, 5th class Y256).

The cruise experience varies significantly from boat to boat. Most ships have one or two restaurants on board that sell overpriced food. Most passengers bring groceries aboard and supplement their stash with cheap snacks from the stalls at the stops. Often, the best views on the boat are from the exposed top deck, so sunscreen and a good hat normally come in handy. Some boats charge a fee of as much as Y30 for access to the top deck, but the expense is only worth it if you spend a lot of time outside, not hiding in your air-conditioned cabin. As you might expect, film is more expensive than usual along the way, so stock up in Chongqing.

FENGDU 丰都

The surrounding riverbank of this "City of Ghosts" (guǐ chéng; 鬼城) is fabled to be home to demonic spirits, and this tourist town feeds off the legend with a kitschy, carnival atmosphere. Once they open the floodgates at the Three Gorges Dam, however, the entire city of Fengdu really will be an underwater ghost town, leaving only (a much shorter) Mingshan Mountain above the water line. Most cruises allow passengers three hours in this town, usually beginning between 6 and 8am on the first full day. The visit is designed to funnel tourists directly to Mingshan Mountain, but Fengdu is a pleasant enough town in which to walk around for an hour or two.

MINGSHAN MOUNTAIN (míng shān; 名山). Said to be the hilltop capital of a ghost kingdom, Mingshan Mountain now sees just enough activity to wake the dead—and empty your wallet. From the docks, follow the crowd of visor-wearing tourists straight ahead; if arriving at Dock #4, head left along **Dongmen Lu** (东门路) and **Beimen Lu** (北门路) before turning right on **Zhongshan Lu** (中山路). The massive stone head on the hill indicates the route. The mountain has been collecting ghost-ornamented temples since the Tang Dynasty. Today, the garish **God Palace** (guǐguó shéngōng;鬼国神公) is overrun with palm readers (Y60), picture takers (Y10), tea houses (Y20), and trinket sellers (Y10-100). The suspension bridge that leads to the mountain is where a soul's destination in the afterlife, be it nirvana or hell, is said to be determined. On festival days, the demons go marching in and the temple complex overflows with goblins, ogres, and horse-headed monsters. *(☎7062 3235. Open daily 6am-6pm. Y60. Chairlift Y15. Haunted house Y5.)*

SHIBAOZHAI (shíbǎozhài; 石宝寨). Three hours and 106km downstream from Fengdu, the "Stone Treasure Stronghold" of Shibaozhai (which proclaims itself the "Pearl on the Yangzi"), is an impressive 12-storied, red-walled, green-eaved pagoda built against a sheer cliff. While some boats just cruise by Shibaozhai for a passing view, others stop for an entire hour. The short visit is just enough time to scramble up the ramp, through the vendor-crammed streets, and up the "Stairs to the Clouds" of the 56m Ming-era tower dedicated to the Jade Emperor, the omnipotent heavenly ruler of folk religion. Legend has it that Shibaozhai is the elaborately colored jade chop left behind by the goddess Nü Wa when she mended the broken sky. *(Open daily 8:30am-4pm. Y15.)*

ZHANG FEI TEMPLE (zhāngfēi miào; 张飞庙). The temple, three and a half hours from Shibaozhai, marks the spot where Zhang Fei, a famous general from the Three Kingdoms period, met his end. Two of Zhang Fei's men, who had been on the receiving end of their commander's wrath, decapitated the general and are said to have thrown his head into the Yangzi at the spot where the temple now stands. The current temple, built in 1870 after a flood destroyed an earlier version, contains statues of Zhang Fei and several noteworthy tablets and woodcuts. Boats that stop here typically arrive between 6 and 8pm and stay for just 45 minutes. Despite the temple's excellent view of the sunset over the Yangzi, the short visit is perhaps best spent getting dinner from one of the vendors that crowd the path from the boat; there is little inside the temple to warrant its steep admission charge. Visits to Zhang Fei Temple may be suspended in the near future—the temple's current spot is slated to be flooded with the creation of the Three Gorges Reservoir. In order to preserve the temple and its historical relics, the Chinese government will relocate the structure to higher ground on the opposite shore. *(Open daily 9am-9pm. Y20.)*

FENGJIE 丰节

The small, history-laden town of Fengjie guards the entrance to Qutang Gorge, at the confluence of Yangzi and Plum Creek. Two 1000-year-old coffins, discovered in the exposed valley wall, confirm that Fengjie was the capital of the Kui Kingdom of the Ba people, ancestors of today's Tujia minority. Kuizhou, the Tang-era name of Fengjie, was a hot spot for itinerant Tang poets like Li Bai, Du Fu, and Lu You, all of whom braved the gorges. But Fengjie's greatest claim to fame is White Emperor City, the site of some *Romance of the Three Kingdoms* episodes.

Many boats drop anchor for the night outside Fengjie, entering the Three Gorges early the next morning. If you have the opportunity to go ashore at Fengjie, explore the environs, which are loaded with unusual geological formations. The 500m wide, 600m deep crater-like funnel called the **Heavenly Pit** (xiǎotiān zhài; 小天寨) leads to myriad caverns fed by underground rivers.

White Emperor City (báidì chéng; 白帝城), just outside Fengjie, is a cluster of temples built during the Han dynasty by Gongsun Shu, the ruler of Sichuan. One day some white gas escaping from a well appeared to Gong as a white imperial dragon, which he took as a propitious sign for him to assume the title of White Emperor. Oddly enough, none of the statues in the temple is dedicated to him and it is not for Gong that the city is renowned. About 450 years ago, *Romance of the Three Kingdoms* buffs tossed out Gong's altar and replaced it with one for their hero, Liu Bei. According to the novel, in AD 221 Liu, the King of Shu, launched a 750,000-man invasion against a former ally to avenge the decapitation of his blood brother. Against the better judgment of his advisor, Zhuge Liang, Liu stationed his enormous army in the forests of Yichang, which were promptly burned by enemy troops. Liu Bei escaped thanks to Zhuge's brilliant **Eight Diagram Formation** (bāguà zhèn; 八卦阵), an ingenious defense that relied on a labyrinth of mist-enshrouded boulders around Fengjie that trapped pursuing troops. Many visitors feel that the sights in White Emperor City don't necessarily justify the steep admission fee. Some boats arrive as late as 11pm for the two-hour visit, and many travelers choose to stay aboard for this stop in order to rest up for their visit to the Three Gorges the next morning. Travelers who choose to go ashore but not to visit the temples are required to pay Y10 for the boat-to-shore trip (round-trip, so keep the stub) and meet with little entertainment on the lonely path to White Emperor City. *(Open daily with no set admission hours. Y40, chairlift Y15.)*

SICHUAN

QUTANG GORGE

Boats begin entering the first of the Three Gorges as early as 6am on the second full day of the cruise. Qutang Gorge (qūtáng xiá; 瞿塘峡), just east of Fengjie, is the shortest and narrowest of the Three Gorges, just 8km long and only 50m wide at its narrowest point. This spectacular stretch of river features the Gorges's fastest currents and is flanked by knife-cut sheer cliffs on both sides and vividly named rock formations like Phoenix Drinking Spring, Upside-down Monk, and Rhinoceros Gazing at the Moon. The north bank, called the **Red Armor Cliff,** was named after a battalion that was outfitted with red armor in the Spring and Autumn Period (722-481 BC). The south bank, called the **White Salt Cliffs,** still boasts the remains of a treacherous ancient plankway built by placing wooden planks into grooves in the cliff.

LITTLE THREE GORGES

Qutang Gorge ends at the town of Wushan, located at the confluence of the Daning and Yangzi Rivers. From here, the Little Three Gorges (xiǎo sānxiá; 小三峡) stretch north along the Daning and its Mandu River tributary for 50km. These narrower passes may not boast the austere majesty and historic gravity of their counterparts, but the six-hour tour to see them is widely considered to be the most rewarding portion of a trip on the Yangzi. Smaller boats provide a more intimate experience, and more time allows for visits to river caves and the archaeological site where a two-million-year-old ape-man was unearthed. As it winds through the Longmen, Bawu, and Dicui gorges, the Daning river turns into a splendid stream spindling through lush, uninhabited limestone ravines. Monkeys call and egrets karr in the dense forests high above as boatsmen propel wooden *sampan* by thrusting bamboo poles into the clear creek bed full of smooth, iridescent pebbles. Unfortunately, it too will be lost to the flood of 2009. *(Tickets bought directly from the boat steward can be fully refunded without difficulty if conditions preclude the tour; tour group members may be stuck with a partial refund or substitutes of other sights. Y100.)*

WU GORGE

Once passengers have returned from the Little Three Gorges, cruises continue from Wushan into Wu Gorge (wū xiá; 巫峡), the "gorge of witches," generally considered to be the most enchanting of the Three Gorges. The 2000m-high canyon walls block out the sun's rays, and the dappled sunlight and misty showers give the area a surreal feel. The western section of the 40km-long gorge is called **Gold-Helmet Silver-Armor Gorge,** and the eastern section is called the **Iron Coffin Gorge.** At the western end of the gorge, Wushan mountain, for which the town is named, towers over the river with 12 peaks, six on either side, that are thought to be the ossified offspring of the Empress of the Heavens.

XILING GORGE

The longest and last of the Three Gorges, the 80km-long Xiling Gorge (xīlíng xiá; 西陵峡) is no lazy homestretch. Most of this canyon's hidden shoals have been blasted clear, and the gorge is no longer known as a ship graveyard. But landslides continue to smash villages, and navigating down the treacherous 42km section that includes the Art-of-War, Cow-Liver-Horse-Lung (supposedly named after the cliffside imagery), and Yellow Cow and Yellow Cat Gorges still results in a lot of water on deck. The dam that will become the Gorges's nemesis lies an hour beyond the end of Xiling Gorge (see **Frankly My Dear, I Do Give a Dam,** p. 707). Another hour away, past the **Nanjin Gate,** boats line up in the placid Gezhou Dam Lake to await their turn at the Gezhou Dam lock. The opening of the lock's massive doors marks the end of the trip for Yichang-bound passengers.

THE NORTHWEST

Vast, sparsely populated, and blanketed by dune-swept deserts, plateaus, mountains, and inland salt seas, China's Northwest is often dismissed as an inhospitable backwater frontier. The area has historically lagged behind its coastal counterpart in terms of economic development, but a long history of contact with "outsiders" along the famed Silk Road has left a lasting legacy; imperial tombs, Buddhist grottoes, city ruins, and desert mummies offer a glimpse of past wonders. Today, the region—Xinjiang in particular—serves as a gateway to Central Asia and Pakistan. A trip in the Northwest often appears hauntingly surreal: against the flat monotone brown of the Taklimakan Desert, the eerie fluorescent orange of the masked highway sweepers, the piles of sparkling green glass raked to the side of the road, even the mottled reds and blues of passing vehicles seem brighter and more vivid than usual. The area is also home to amazing geographic diversity: within an hour or two the landscape can change from desert to rock mountains to alpine forest to snow-capped mountain peaks. A colorful collage of faces, hats, and costumes surfaces in the area's Uighur bazaars, Tibetan monasteries, Mongol yurts, and Hui mosques, showcasing the region's cultural diversity. The Northwest is also a fantastic place to delve into the great outdoors, by sheepskin-rafting down the Yellow River, traveling by camel through the vast desert, or hiking through unexplored alpine valleys.

HIGHLIGHTS OF THE NORTHWEST

CAVE IN to the charms of Dunhuang's **Mogao** (see p. 749), Guyuan's **Xumishan** (see p. 723), and Tianshui's **Maijishan** (see p. 737) grottoes.

FIND YOUR INNER PEDDLER along the fabled **Silk Road,** with stops in **Zhongwei** (see **p. 719**), **Jiayuguan** (see **p. 739**), **Turpan** (see **p. 767**), and **Kuqa** (see **p. 774**).

SHOP UNTIL YOUR DONKEY DROPS at Kashgar's **Sunday Bazaar** (see p. 780).

NINGXIA 宁夏

Roughly the size of the Republic of Ireland, Ningxia Hui Autonomous Region is quietly wedged between Shaanxi and Gansu provinces. Ningxia relies on an extensive irrigation system to sustain agriculture on its arid hills and desert dunes. Local peasants scratch out fields of corn, wheat, millet, and sorghum that are visible for miles from the winding, country roads, while herdsmen boast their very own stock of high-cashmere-wool-yielding and fast-growing Zhongwei sheep.

The majority of the region's five million inhabitants are Han Chinese, but a full third are Hui; Tibetan, Mongolian, and Manchu peoples are also scattered throughout the province. The Hui in particular have had a strong influence on Ningxia's architectural and religious landscape. For travelers to northwestern China, Ningxia is a transitional region where Han influence melts into the Islamic culture farther west. Ningxia's multicultural history and its natural beauty is reason enough to visit this slow-paced, increasingly wealthy region.

The Northwest
RUSSIA
KAZAKHSTAN
Friendship Peak
4374m
ALTAI MTS.
Hanas Lake
Hemu Kanas
Altai City
Burqin
Ertix R.
Lake Balkhash
Ulungur Lake
Karamay
Junggar Basin
Alashan Pass
GURBANTÜNGGÜT DESERT
Sayram Lake
Huocheng
Horgas Port
Shihezi
Tianchi
Yining
Almaty
Qapqal
Ürümqi
Bishkek
No. 1 Glacier
Dahey
TIAN SHAN
Turpan
Turpan Depression
-154m
KYRGYZSTAN
Luntai
Yanqi
Bosten Lake
Aksu
Kuqa
Korla
Aksu R.
Loulan Ruins
Tarim R.
Torugut Pass
3752m
Kashgar (Kashi)
TAKLIMAKAN DESERT
PAMIR
Hotan R.
XINJIANG
Yensigar
Lake Karakul
Mt. Muztagata
7546m
Miran Ruins
TAJIKISTAN
Shache (Yarkand)
Ruoqiang
Tashkurgan
Tarim Basin
Yecheng (Kargilik)
Qiemo
Khunjerab Pass
4900m
Hotan
Minfeng
ALTUN MTS.
Sost
K2 8611m
KARAKORUM MTS.
KUNLUN MTS.
PAKISTAN
INDIA
Ali
TIBET
(XIZANG)
AUTONOMOUS REGION
N
LG
0
200 miles
0
200 kilometers
NEPAL

NORTHWEST

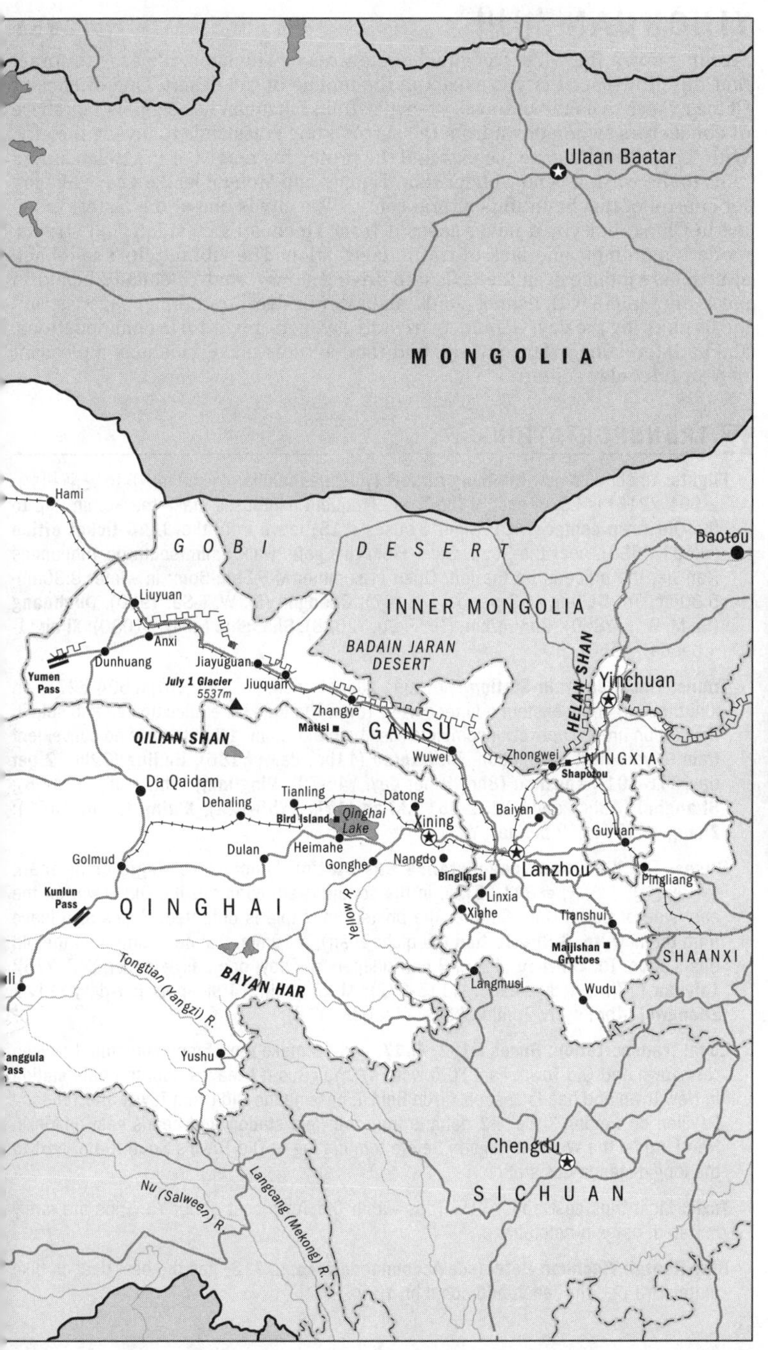

Ulaan Baatar
MONGOLIA
Hami
GOBI DESERT
Baotou
INNER MONGOLIA
Liuyuan
Anxi
Dunhuang
Yumen Pass
BADAIN JARAN DESERT
HELAN SHAN
Jiayuguan
Jiuquan
July 1 Glacier 5537m
Yinchuan
Zhangye
Matisi
GANSU
QILIAN SHAN
Wuwei
Zhongwei
NINGXIA
Shapotou
Da Qaidam
Dehaling
Tianling
Datong
Bird Island
Qinghai Lake
Xining
Baiyan
Guyuan
Dulan
Heimahe
Gonghe
Nangdo
Lanzhou
Golmud
Binglingsi
Pingliang
Kunlun Pass
QINGHAI
Yellow R.
Linxia
Xiahe
Tianshui
Maijishan Grottoes
SHAANXI
Tongtian (Yangzi) R.
BAYAN HAR
Langmusi
Wudu
Yushu
Chengdu
SICHUAN
Nu (Salween) R.
Langcang (Mekong) R.

NORTHWEST

YINCHUAN 银川 ☎0951

Strolling down the wide, tree-lined boulevards of Yinchuan, it's easy to forget that this slow-paced city is smack in the middle of the desert. One of ancient China's more dynamic outposts of civilization, Yinchuan has seen its fair share of conquerors swoop down from the surrounding grasslands to invade the city. With the Yellow River to the east and the protective ranges of the Helan Mountains to the west, it is no wonder Han, Tangut, and Mongol leaders have all vied for control of this bountiful cultural center. The city is one of the fastest growing in China, but you'd never guess it from Yinchuan's clean air and streets, modern buildings, and lack of traffic congestion. The vibrant city's laid-back atmosphere induce even the taxis into driving slowly. And Yinchuan's beautiful parks are replete with fishing ponds, alabaster bridges, traditional pagodas, and locals enjoying the day. Genuinely friendly hawkers, plentiful accommodations, and an interesting balance of Hui and Han cultures make Yinchuan a pleasant two- or three-day sojourn.

TRANSPORTATION

Flights: Yinchuan's new **Minhang Airport** (yínchuān mínháng jīchâng; 银川民航机场; ☎691 2218) is 25km east of Old Town. Frequent minibuses make the 30min. trip to the Old Town center (Y40). Shuttle buses (Y15) leave from the **CAAC ticket office** (☎691 3688), near the South Gate. From this gate, walk 5min. south on Yuhuangge Nan Jie; the office is on the left. Open in summer M-F 8am-6pm; in winter 8:30am-5:30pm. To: **Beijing** (1-3 per day, Y1107); **Chengdu** (M, W, F-Sa; Y980); **Dunhuang** (Su-M, W, F; Y860); **Guangzhou** (Tu, F, Su, Y2088); **Shanghai** (daily, Y1080); **Xi'an** (1-4 per day, Y560).

Trains: Yinchuan Train Station (yínchuān huôchē zhàn; 银川火车站; ☎504 6271) on Xingzhou Lu, in the eastern quarter of New Town. The train schedules posted and sold in the station are deceptively incomplete—ask before assuming that there is no convenient train to your next destination. To: **Baotou** (11hr., daily, Y186); **Beijing** (22hr., 2 per day, Y76-301); **Lanzhou** (8hr., 2 per day, Y46-70); **Pingliang** (9hr., daily, Y34-68); **Shanghai** (48hr., daily, Y132-261); **Xi'an** (17hr., Y55-122); **Xining** (14hr., Y160); **Zhongwei** (3½hr., 2 per day, Y13).

Buses: The **Yinchuan Long-distance Bus Station** (yínchuān chángtú qìchē zhàn; 银川长途汽车站; ☎603 1571), in the southeastern corner of the Old Town, on the east side of South Gate Square. The posted timetable is outdated. Buses also leave from the new **No. 6 Bus Station** (liù qìchē zhàn), a 10min. taxi ride north from the old bus station. To: **Lanzhou** (11hr.; 2 non-sleepers per day, one daily sleeper; Y43, Y75); **Taiyuan** (17hr., daily sleeper, Y115-122); **Xi'an** (16hr., 4 sleepers per day, Y112); **Zhongwei** (4hr., every 25min. 7:55am-5:30pm, Y13).

Local Transportation: Buses #1, 2, 4, 17, and **18** make the 15min. commute between New Town and Old Town. Fare Y0.5, with A/C Y1. Bus **#1** leaves from the train station in New Town and heads east on Yinxin Bei Lu, passing the Old Drum Tower and Yuhuang Pavilion on Jiefang Xi Jie; **#2** departs from the train station and heads east on Yinxin Nan Lu past the Western Pagoda before terminating at Old Town's South Gate, next to the long-distance bus station.

Taxis: Most trips cost about Y15. Trips within Old Town cost about Y5. Trips are rarely metered; bargain beforehand.

Bike Rental: Yinchuan Hotel (see **Accommodations,** p. 716) has the best deal on bike rentals. Y3 per 4hr., each additional hr. Y0.5.

ORIENTATION AND PRACTICAL INFORMATION

Yinchuan is divided into two distinct communities that lie 11km apart: **Old Town** (lâo chéng; 老城) in the east and **New Town** (xīn chéng; 新城) in the west. The two towns are connected by three main roads. **Yinxin Nan Lu** (银新南路) is sandwiched between **Yinxin Bei Lu** (银新北路) to the north and **Changcheng Lu** (长城路) to the south. The vast majority of accommodations in New Town are centered around the traffic circle. Hotels and sights are more liberally dispersed throughout the paradoxically more modern Old Town. Old Town's bustling main road, **Jiefang Xi Jie** (解放西街), becomes Yinxin Nan Lu in New Town. Jiefang Xi Jie and **Jiefang Dong Jie** (解放东街) intersect with **Minzu Jie** (民族街) to form the backbone of Old Town. The **Drum Tower** (gû lóu; 鼓楼), just east of Minzu Jie, is at the intersection of **Gulou Jie** (鼓楼街) and Jiefang Jie.

Travel Agency: CTS, 116 Jiefang Xi Jie, Ste. 301 (☎504 8006, 504 5555, or 504 3720; nxcits@126.com), on the southwest corner of the intersection of Fenghuang Jie and Jiefang Xi Jie, marked by a small red sign. English-speaking staff member. Organizes tours of Sand Lake (shā hú; 沙湖), the Xia tombs, and other famous destinations within Ningxia. Also a good resource for planning group excursions along the Silk Road and into Qinghai. Open M-F 8:30am-noon and 2:30-6pm.

Bookstore: Foreign Bookstore, 22 Jiefang Xijie. Open daily 9am-6:30pm.

Bank of China: On Jiefang Jie, a 10min. walk west of the Yinchuan Hotel, on the left side of the street. The only branch in town that exchanges traveler's checks (counter #13). Open M-F in summer 9am-noon and 2:30-6pm; in winter 9am-noon and 2-5:30pm.

PSB: (☎691 5080), on the northern end of Yuhuangge Bei Jie. Take bus #3 north from the South Gate stop. **Visa extensions** available M-F 2:30-6pm. Open M-F 8am-6pm.

Hospitals: Yinchuan's best hospital is **Medical University Hospital** (yīxuéyuàn fùshû yīyuàn; 医学院附属医院; ☎409 1488), 2km south of Old Town. **Shizhong Hospital** (☎602 5831), on Jiefang Xi Jie just east of the West Gate.

Internet Access: Internet Bar, 16 Minzu Bei Jie (☎601 6800), across from the Exhibition Center. Y2 per hr.

Post Office: 12 Jiefang Xi Jie (☎603 1740), across the street and just west of the Yinchuan Hotel. EMS. China Telecom upstairs. Open M-F in summer 8am-7pm; in winter 8am-6:30pm. **Postal Code:** 750001.

ACCOMMODATIONS

In New Town, most hotels are near Tiedong Lu and Xinchang Xi Jie. Take bus #1 from the train station and get off at the Tiedong Lu traffic circle, or pay Y5 for a 10-minute taxi ride. Most accommodations in Old Town are on or around Jiefang Xi Jie, with a few near the bus station in the southeast part of town.

NEW TOWN

Taoyuan Hotel (táoyuán bīnguân; 桃园宾馆), 2 Tiedong Bei Jie (☎306 6485). From the train station, take a left onto Tiedong Bei Jie; the hotel, sporting big red lanterns, is on the right. The Taoyuan has carpeting, newly painted walls, and large, bright baths with shower curtains. Deposit Y100. 3-bed dorms Y28; 2-bed dorms Y45; singles Y25, with TV, bath, and breakfast Y50. ❶

Kaiyue Hotel, 51 Xincheng Xi Jie (☎951 7875), on the southwest corner of the traffic circle, Tiedong Bei Jie. This newly renovated hotel boasts bright, sparkling clean rooms. All rooms have A/C, beautiful attached baths, and TV. Singles Y168; doubles Y100. ❸

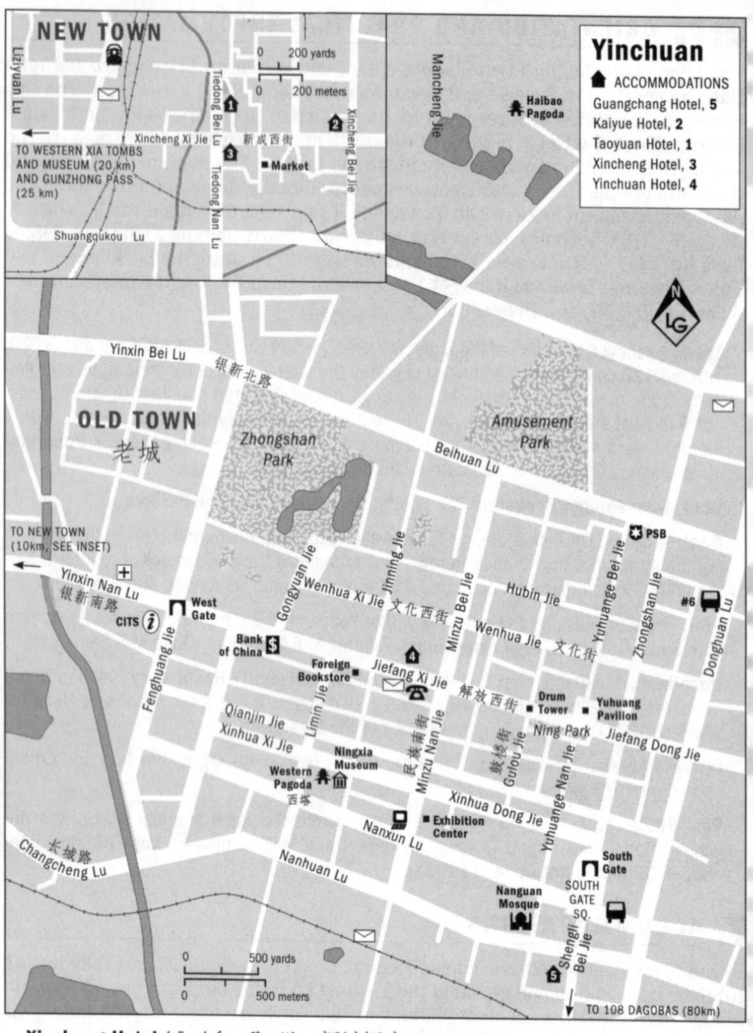

Xincheng Hotel (xīnchéng fàndiàn; 新城饭店; ☎306 6691), on the corner of Tiedong Lu and Xincheng Xi Jie, opposite the Kaiyue Hotel; a 10min. taxi ride from the station. Aging rooms have peeling paint and a musty odor, but tough-to-beat prices. Hot water 7am-11pm. Deposit is twice the room rate. 3-bed dorms with bath Y25; doubles Y25-43, with bath Y76 (ask for the double with living room); triples Y66. ❶

OLD TOWN

Yinchuan Hotel (yínchuān fàndiàn; 银川饭店), 17 Jiefang Xi Jie (☎602 3053), near Jinning Jie. Rooms are clean and spacious. On-site travel service (Y20 ticket commission). Hot water after 7pm. Lockout 1-5am; knock to be let in. Deposit Y10. Singles Y39; doubles Y45-70, with A/C Y108; triples Y75-120. ❶

Guangchang Hotel (guângchâng fàndiàn; 广场饭店; ☎410 8472), on Shengli Bei Jie, a 3min. walk south from the South Gate. Sheets are clean and baths massive. Singles Y58; doubles Y88, with living room Y98. ❶

FOOD

While not renowned for its culinary specialties, Yinchuan's proximity to the sheep herds of Ürümqi and the hotpots of Inner Mongolia makes for some delicious lamb hotpot. Establishments along **Jiefang Xi Jie, Yuhuangge Bei Jie,** and **Xinhua Dong Jie** serve up tasty lamb kebabs (yángròu chuàn; 羊肉串); Yuhuangge Bei Jie in particular has a large selection of restaurants and side-street fruit markets. One restaurant sets up a piping-hot fresh bread stand on Minzu Lu, just south of Jiefang Xi Jie—perfect for a quick breakfast. Fried rice with egg and tomatoes is a popular standby. Plentiful ice cream stands are a wonderful relief from the summer heat. Be sure to try the *mêiguó dà jiâobân* ("American Big Foot"; 美国大脚板), a delicious jab at tourists' oversized clod-hoppers.

Lao Bing Hotpot (lâo bīng huôguõ; 老兵火锅), on Jiefang Xi Jie, 1 block past the West Gate fountain, on the corner of Xi Qiao Xiang. Walk west on Jiefang Xi Jie; the restaurant is on the right. Friendly servers help you choose from over 20 kinds of noodles and vegetables to dunk in a yin-yang shaped hotpot with 2 different brews (all-you-can-eat Y10). Open daily 11am-9:30pm. ❶

Xinglongshui Restaurant (xìnglóngshuî fànguân; 兴隆水饭馆), 112 Limin Jie, just south of Jiefang Xi Jie. This small, 5-table family restaurant is a great option for breakfast or lunch. A big bowl of steaming *jiâozi* with local vegetables costs Y6. All dishes under Y12. Open daily 10am-8pm. ❶

Beijing Roast Duck Restaurant (bëijīng kâoyã fàndiàn; 北京烤鸭饭店), 158 Limin Jie (☎608 2144), half a block south of Jiefang Xi Jie on the right. Get a roast duck to go, or sit outside on the small umbrella-shaded stools and enjoy the overwhelming aroma that wafts through the streets. 1 duck Y11.8. Open daily from 9:30am and in the afternoon from 3:30pm. ❶

SIGHTS

OLD TOWN

YUHUANG PAVILION (yùhuáng gé; 玉皇阁). Built some 450 years ago, the Yuhuang Pavilion is a great starting point from which to explore the city. Breezy, cool, and devoid of tourists, the second floor contains a painting and calligraphy gallery highlighting talented local artists. Climb to the third floor to see various metal and earthenware artifacts documenting Ningxia's history, as well as a beautiful scroll with both Arabic and Chinese *kâishü* (楷书) style script. A historical survey of the area, beginning with the mysterious Xia dynasty, is displayed in Mandarin, but non-Chinese speakers can still enjoy this exceptional museum and ancient building. *(1 block east of the Drum Tower. Open daily 8:30-11am and 2-5pm. Y5.)*

HAIBAO PAGODA TEMPLE (hǎi bǎotǎ sì; 海宝塔寺). Built in the early 5th century and reinforced in the late 18th century, this nine-story pagoda is part of an active—both for prayer and construction—temple complex just beyond the northern edge of Old Town. After chatting with the friendly monk at the first shrine, climb up the pagoda for a bird's-eye view of the surrounding farmland through the windows on top. *(By bicycle, a 20min. ride north on Jinning Bei Jie; after Beihuan Xi Lu the street becomes a dirt road, from which the pagoda is clearly visible. Or, take bus #20 north from the intersection* *between Jinning Jie and Jiefang Xi Jie and get off as it turns east. Walk up the dirt road, take a left at the dead end. Open daily sunrise-sunset. Y5.)*

NANGUAN MOSQUE (nánguān qīngzhēn sì; 南关清真寺). Easily visited on the way to or from the 108 Dagobas (see p. 719), this magnificent mosque is a welcome architectural respite from typical Chinese temples. Erected in the late Ming dynasty, the mosque was rebuilt in 1981 after its destruction during the Cultural Revolution. Nanguan has lost some of its splendor over the years, but it's still worth a visit. The main dome is over 25m tall, surrounded by four turquoise domes that represent the four sects of Islam. The sound of running and splashing water greets visitors in the main courtyard. Pheasants, peacocks, and parakeets chatter in the aviary that wraps around the garden. Visitors are asked to remove their shoes before entering the back of the mosque. *(A 15min. walk south of the Yuhuang Pavilion on Yuhuangge Nan Jie, at Nanhuan Dong Lu. ☎410 6714. Open daily 8:30am-8pm. Y8.)*

NINGXIA MUSEUM (níngxià bówùguǎn; 宁夏博物馆). This regional museum has an extensive collection of Northern Zhou and Western Xia objects. Although dusty and poorly maintained, the museum is still worth a quick look. In the center of the courtyard, the **Western Pagoda** offers a commanding view of the city after an exhausting 12-story climb. Morning visitors still standing after the climb are often invited to join the groups of locals in the courtyard for some popular workout routines. *(Entrance to the courtyard on Jinning Nan Jie. Walk west along Xinhua Xi Jie and take a left onto Jinning Nan Jie; the entrance is on the right. 32 Jinning Jie. ☎818 9282. Open in summer Tu-Su 9am-5pm; in winter 9am-noon and 2-5pm. Museum Y2; pagoda Y5.)*

NEAR YINCHUAN

The Western Xia Tombs and Museum and Gunzhong Pass can be visited together in a day of sightseeing; take a taxi van from the Old Town (Y150-200 round-trip) or take the infrequent bus #2 west from the depot on Xinhua Jie to the last stop. From here the taxi fare to the Xia tombs and Gunzhong Pass should be no more than Y100 round-trip. The CAAC hotel also organizes pricey tours.

WESTERN XIA TOMBS (xī xià wánglíng; 西夏王陵). Undoubtedly the best sight in Yinchuan, the Western Xia Tombs pay silent tribute to an empire rumored to have killed Genghis Khan with poison-tipped arrows before being obliterated in 1227 by vengeful Mongol hordes. Described by proud Yinchuan residents as the Egypt of China, these large mounds of earth require visitors to have an active imagination, since only a museum accompanies the desolate tombs of the Western Xia kings. Scattered across rocky plains are the nine windswept heaps of soil said to house the remains of the nine emperors, while the 200 smaller structures that span the horizon may have been erected for various nobles. When visiting the tombs, wander out into the desert scenery, and discover the lonelier tombs on the horizon—they are well worth the walk. *(30min. from and 20km west of New Town. Open daily sunrise-sunset. Y30.)*

WESTERN XIA MUSEUM (xī xià bówùguǎn; 西夏博物馆). The first floor displays well-preserved relics of the Western Xia, ranging from 800-year-old leather shoes to imperial seals. On the second floor, massive horse, ox, and dog figures in bronze, gold, and stone maintain their ancient vigilance encased in modern glass displays. There is also a beautiful collection of Buddhist icon paintings, as well as *sutra* scrolls written in Chinese and Arabic. The museum is a good warm-up to the tombs themselves and the barren Helan Mountains rising in the distance. *(Next to the parking lot and a short distance from the largest tombs. Open daily sunrise-sunset. Admission included in tombs ticket.)*

GUNZHONG PASS (gǔnzhōng kǒu; 滚钟口). Consisting of several paved trails that wind along the red foothills of the Helanshan mountain range, this secluded hiking reserve offers spectacular views of the Yellow River valley. The greener rock faces near the pass recede into stark clay and sand farther south toward the Western Xia Tombs. There are also possibilities for longer day- or multiple-day hikes into the craggy peaks looming above, some rising over 5000 ft. The none-too-taxing trails are suitable for all ages and abilities. *(Lodging is available year-round at the small hostel just above the front gate to the left for Y10 per bed or Y30 for a double room. Ask at the front gate for information. Open daily sunrise-sunset. Y5.)*

108 DAGOBAS (qīngtóngxiá yībǎilíngbā tǎ; 青铜峡一百零八塔). These structures are a testament to good intentions gone awry. Despite the impressive scenery and attractive garden, the *dagobas* themselves are unfortunate victims of modern repair. Whereas the pictures of the old dagobas are truly impressive, the current renditions are replete with gaudy coloring and now-rusting tin roofs. *(Take a taxi Y60-100 to the dam, 3.5km from the site. Then, walk left along the east bank of the river until you reach the ferry. The ferry, or a smaller boat difficult to find, should cost around Y10. Open daily sunrise-sunset. Y5.)*

ENTERTAINMENT

Night markets abound in Yinchuan (open daily approx. 7pm-midnight). There is a large market at the very end of Gulou Nan Jie; from the Drum Tower, walk south and enter under the rainbow-colored arches. In **Ning Park** (níng yuán; 宁园), just south of the Yuhuang Pavilion, locals fish, play cards, or sip tea under the low-hanging trees and gazebos. Just south of Zhongshan Park is the lively and festive **Guangming Square** (guāngmíng guǎngchǎng; 光明广场), centered around a lit fountain. Everyone enjoys the cool, breezy Yinchuan evenings near the stadium and opposite the People's Congress Building. Unfortunately, at 10:30pm, the fountain is shut off and everyone heads home. Those not willing to call it a night can head for the bars that line Yuhuange Nan Jie, just north of Xinhua Dong Jie. Down a beer at the **Kabin Club,** dance at the **Millennium Disco Night Club,** or turn the corner to 35 Xinhua Dong Jie and rock the stainless steel boat of **9+9 Disco Club.**

ZHONGWEI 中卫

☎0953

A mere 160km southwest of Yinchuan, Zhongwei has the low-key atmosphere of a beach town—without the beach. Instead, visitors can surf sand dunes, float down the Yellow River on sheepskin rafts, explore the Tengger Desert atop occasionally cranky camels, and learn about the science of desert reclamation. These activities—all less than 40 minutes from town—are a welcome relief from the monotony of small rural villages in central Ningxia. Life in Zhongwei is enjoyed at a markedly slower pace than in most Chinese cities, evidenced by the multitude of card games littering the sidewalks, the women who gossip beneath the tree-lined avenues, and the idle markets that fill the town every Thursday. Sleepy Zhongwei wakes up at night, when families, couples, and groups of old women stroll through the streets in search of the perfect lamb kebabs, fresh ears of corn, or ice cream cones.

ORIENTATION AND PRACTICAL INFORMATION

Zhongwei's simple grid-like layout makes for easy navigation. From the **Drum Tower** (gǔ lóu; 鼓楼) in the city center, **Bei Dajie** (北大街), **Nan Dajie** (南大街), **Dong Dajie** (东大街), and **Xi Dajie** (西大街) mark the town's northern, southern, eastern, and western neighborhoods, respectively. The train station is at the northern end of

Bei Dajie, and the bus station is at the eastern end of Dong Dajie. China Telecom, the PSB, a good hotel, Internet access, and the hospital are all on Xi Dajie. Taxis and bike rentals are unnecessary; because of Zhongwei's small size, most points of interest are around the Drum Tower.

Trains: Zhongwei Train Station (zhōngwèi huǒchē zhàn; 中卫火车站; ☎709 5222), on Bei Dajie, a 15min. walk north of the Drum Tower. Taking the train from Zhongwei is often more convenient than the bus. Open daily 8am-12:30pm, 1:30-6:30pm, 7:10pm-7:30am. To: **Beijing** (28hr., 8:50am, Y179); **Guyuan** (4½hr., 5 per day 12:10am-5:58pm, Y14-17); **Lanzhou** (6hr., 2 per day, Y18-47); **Ürümqi** (20hr., 9 and 11am, Y105-122); **Yinchuan** (2½-3hr., 4 per day, Y11-25).

Buses: Zhongwei Long-distance Bus Station (zhōngwèi chángtú qìchē zhàn; 中卫长途汽车站; ☎701 2775), on Dong Dajie, a 15min. walk east of the Drum Tower. Schedules and routing often depend on demand; many trips involve stops and changes. To **Yinchuan** (4hr., approx. every 30min., Y14). Buses also run to **Lanzhou.**

Travel Agency: Ningxia Shapotou Travel Service (níngxià shāpōtóu lǚxíngshè; 宁夏沙坡头旅行社, ☎701 2961), 2 Bei Dajie, in the Yixing Hotel. There is also a branch outside the Zhongwei Hotel, at 33 Xi Dajie. Arranges group tours to Shapotou, Yellow River rafting tours (Y120 for 1hr.), and day- to week-long Tengger Desert camping expeditions (Y250-380). English-speaking guides and staff at both branches.

Bank of China: 1 Dong Dajie, next to the Drum Tower. Exchanges traveler's checks. Open in summer M-F 8am-6:30pm, Sa-Su 9:30am-5pm; in winter M-F 8am-6pm, Sa-Su 9:30am-4:30pm.

PSB: (☎701 2914, ext. 8000 or 8030), on the north side of Xi Dajie just past the intersection with Shangye Jie. Open daily 8am-noon and 2:30-6:30pm.

Pharmacy: North Street Chemist's Shop (bêi jiē yào diàn; 北街药店), on Bei Dajie, just south of the train station. Western medicines available. Open daily 8am-9:30pm.

Hospital: Kang Fu Hospital (☎701 1632) is on Xi Dajie, just west of the intersection with Shangye Jie, on the south side of the street.

Telephones: China Telecom, on Zhongshan Nan Jie, at the intersection with Xi Dajie. IDD service. Open daily 8am-7pm.

Internet Access: Computer World (diànnâo dàshìjiè; 电脑大世界; ☎703 0086), on the left side of Xi Dajie, around the corner from China Telecom. Y8 per hr. Cheaper access can be found on Shangye Bei Jie. The 2nd fl. has many small bars with fast connection speed for Y2 per hr.

Post Office: 30 Xi Dajie (☎855 6850). The new **post office** is a large glass-faced building on Xi Dajie, a 15min. walk west of the Drum Tower, on the left side of the road. EMS. Open daily 8am-7pm. **Postal Code:** 751700.

ACCOMMODATIONS AND FOOD

Zhongwei boasts tasty dining options, from the excellent noodle shops and kebab stands that line Bei Dajie to the night market stalls on Shangye Nan Jie to the sparkling restaurant in the Yixing Hotel. **Hongmei Restaurant** on Bei Dajie just north of the Gao Temple serves up mouth-watering vegetarian stir-fry from their English menu (most dishes Y10). Try the *háoyóu niúròu* (beef with onions, mushrooms, and brown sauce; 耗油牛肉; Y10), *rìshì wūdōngmiàn* (a pasta-like Japanese dish; 日式乌冬面; Y5), and *gāozi miàn* (spicy noodle soup; 蒿子面; Y3). Lamb dishes are also popular. In the summer, apricots and other fresh fruit abound.

Long Hui Hotel (☎709 5405; fax 701 9032). The new, modern building to the right as you exit the train station. Although this glitzy hotel provides high-priced luxury rooms for businessmen and tourists, the dorm rooms maintain the high quality at a much lower

NORTHWEST

cost. Closets, clean carpets, immaculate baths, a weight room, and a bowling alley. 3-bed dorms Y50; 2-bed dorms Y68; standard doubles Y268-488. ❶

Tie Lu Hotel (☎701 1441). Take a left out of the train station; the hotel is across the street on the right. The wallpaper is new, the rooms are quiet, and the prices unbeatable. Hot water after 8pm. 3-bed dorms Y25; 2-bed dorms Y33. Singles Y66. ❶

Zhongwei Hotel (zhōngwèi bīnguǎn; 中卫宾馆), 33 Xi Dajie (☎701 2609). Part of the Zhongwei government complex, this hotel makes up for its lackluster service by providing clean, bright, quiet rooms that overlook a small flower garden. Breakfast and dance tickets included. Double rooms with bath, fan, and phone Y84-128; triples Y75-90. ❷

Yixing Hotel (yìxīng dàjiǔdiàn; 逸兴大酒店; ☎701 7666; fax 701 9993), in a large, modern building next to the Drum Tower. An excellent restaurant on the 2nd fl., a travel service, and a business center. Rooms (most with bath and fan) are spacious and clean, with 24hr. hot water. Deposit Y500. Singles Y100; doubles Y120-160, with A/C Y280 and up; triples Y75-150; quads Y80. Discounts sometimes available. ❷

SIGHTS

SHAPOTOU (shāpōtóu; 沙坡头). Sandwiched between the stark and arid Tengger Desert and the loess-filled Yellow River, Shapotou is Zhongwei's prime tourist destination. Worth the visit for its natural beauty alone, Shapotou offers unique experiences in a truly fantastic setting. For outdoor enthusiasts, a day at Shapotou begins at the top of the chairlift with a heart-stopping toboggan ride (Y15) down the 100m face of the dune. Then, fly across the Yellow River on China's first zipline (Y50). Once down at the river, strap on a life jacket and raft down the Yellow River in inflated sheepskin rafts (Y30), or take a six-hour motorboat cruise to a giant waterwheel (Y180). Farther east along the river bank, land-lovers can ride lounging camels that stubbornly mosey up the dunes (Y10) or saunter into the heart of the desert (Y30 per hr.) to the Inner Mongolian border (Y150-200 includes 5hr. non-stop camel journeys and yurt accommodations).

To escape the tourist groups that normally overrun the small resort's riverbanks, ride the chairlift to the top of the sand cliff and walk along a small hiking path that meanders through flowering shrubs and patterned dunes as it skirts the high bank of the Yellow River below. The **Desert Research Center,** across the train tracks from the Shapotou resort entrance, is a treasure trove of information, and also the sight where shrubs and trees are made ready for transplanting to sensitive areas along the desert's edge. *(The cheapest mode of transportation from Zhongwei is by minibus (Y5); they leave the bus station about every hr. starting at 9am. Alternatively, take a taxi (35min., round-trip Y100) from Zhongwei; bargain hard. Upon arrival, go to the resort ticket booth and plan activities with director Dong Jianzhong (☎769 8053); the Shapotou staff is flexible and accommodating. No tours are necessary. Except for the dune ride, all activities are down at the riverbank. Tickets for individual activities can be bought from the kiosks at each site. Y20.)*

GAO TEMPLE (gāo miào; 高庙; ☎701 2620). Built between AD 1403 and 1424, the Gao Temple is an intriguing architectural and spiritual conglomeration, housing Confucian, Buddhist, and even Christian religious figures. The temple complex covers an impressive 4100m^2 of tall, spiraling towers, elegant open-air walkways, and multiple pavilions. Each feature is painstakingly unique; intricate latticework, carved faces on the end of each roofing tile, flowers engraved upon boughs, and magnificent paintings and calligraphy on every partition. Although many visitors come for the serenity and beauty of the prayer halls, an equal number come for the bizarrely fascinating haunted-house-like portion of the temple. For an extra Y5, go underground and receive an eye-opening lesson on the numerous forms of punishment waiting for you in the netherworld. Black lights, neon paint, styrofoam, and

NORTHWEST

eerie 80s music are the backdrop to "Zhongwei's High Temple of Hell." The 18 jails display unlucky souls in various stages of decapitation, disembowelment, and some acts that words simply fail to adequately convey. *(On Bei Dajie, across from the Zhongwei Hotel. Open daily sunrise-sunset. Y5.)*

GUYUAN 固原 ☎0954

Drab, dusty, and small, this southern Ningxia town serves only as a convenient staging post for a trip to the impressive Xumishan Grottoes, 55km to the northwest. Inexpensive accommodations and a lively street scene—often including fireworks on summer nights—can make a short stay in Guyuan pleasant.

ORIENTATION AND PRACTICAL INFORMATION

Guyuan's **train station** is 3km east of the town center, an eight-minute ride (Y3) on a *bèngbèng chē* (motorized three-wheeled cab; 蹦蹦车). Trains go to **Lanzhou** (10hr., 10:20pm, Y31); **Xi'an** (9hr.; 1, 3:30am, 2:05, 9:40pm; Y28); and **Yinchuan** (6hr., 4 per day, Y27). Buying tickets in advance is challenging; an attendant is only available 1½ hours before each train departure. The **bus station** is five-minutes west of the town's major north-south axis, **Zhongshan Jie** (中山街). Buses go to **Lanzhou** (8hr., daily, Y27); **Xi'an** (10hr.; 7am and 7pm; Y35-66); and **Yinchuan** (4½-7hr., 2 per day, Y27-40). All attractions are within walking distance of the bus station.

The **Bank of China,** on Zhongshan Jie, 10min. north of the intersection with Wenhua Jie, does not exchange traveler's checks. (Open in summer M-F 8:30am-5pm; in winter 8am-6pm; all year Sa-Su 9:30am-4pm.) The **hospital** is directly across the street from the Dianli Hotel. **China Telecom** is across from the post office. (Open daily 7:30am-10pm.) **Internet access** is available in the post office branch across from the main building, just west of the Guyuan Hotel, on Zhengfu Jie (Y5 per hr.). Guyuan's newly renovated **post office** is on Zhongshan Nan Jie, a block south of Wenhua Jie, and has EMS. (Open daily 8am-6pm.) The **postal code** is 756000.

ACCOMMODATIONS AND FOOD

Guyuan has only a few options for food and accommodations; most are cheap and tend to cluster around the bus station and Zhongshan Jie. Muslim restaurants are scattered along Wenhua Jie; hotel restaurants also serve inexpensive fare.

Dianli Hotel (diànlì bīnguǎn; 电力宾馆), 219 Renmin Jie (☎204 0495). From the bus station, turn right onto Wenhua Jie, walk through the intersection, and take the first right; it's on the right. The glass doors, massive reception area, and army of doormen may scare budget backpackers away, but the Dianli dorm rooms are the best value in town, with new TVs and carpets. 24hr. hot water. Scrubbed communal baths. Breakfast included. Curfew 2am, but knock and the night guard will let you in. 3-bed dorms Y25; 2-bed dorms Y35; singles with bath Y380; doubles Y70, with bath Y120. ❶

Plum Garden Hotel (méiyuán fàndiàn; 梅园饭店; ☎203 9788), near the bus station. From the bus station, turn right and walk 15m; the hotel is on the left. The Plum Garden boasts a convenient location, bright rooms with clean sheets, fans, and TV. Hot water 6:30-8am and 8:30-11:30pm. 4-bed dorms Y4; 3-bed dorms Y12; doubles with bath Y28, with living room Y60. ❶

Guyuan Hotel (gùyuán bīnguǎn; 固原宾馆, ☎203 2479), 94 Zhengfu Jie. Walk left out of the bus station, make the first left; turn right on Zhengfu Jie, the first main cross street; it's on the left. Clean common baths. Singles with bath Y150; doubles Y60, with bath Y130-180; triples Y75/120. Additional 6% Guyuan "education" fee. ❶

SIGHTS

Guyuan's main claim to fame is its majestic Xumishan Grottoes—and it deserves every bit of its reputation. For those with extra time, the surprisingly extensive Guyuan Museum is also worth a visit.

XUMISHAN GROTTOES (xūmíshān shíkū; 须弥山石窟). Beautiful, blood-red mountains and a slow march of dark green pines up crumbling ridges herald the approach to the grottoes. This expansive array of sculptures and temples is tucked into the folds of the massive rock face amid the gorgeous desert landscape. Xumishan is a surreal collection of eight cliff art sites, 70 Buddhist statues, 130 Buddhist relief carvings, and 350 caverns, originally built by the rulers of the Northern Wei (AD 386-534) and Northern Zhou (AD 557-584) dynasties. The most commanding of the statues, a 22m-high Tang-era **Maitreya Buddha,** maintains silent watch over both the river bed below and the delinquent tourists snapping pictures in this camera-forbidden zone. Caves #21, 25, 30, and 31, all containing Buddhas of various forms, are of particular interest; caves 24 and 32 are notable for their prayer columns. *(Direct buses from the Guyuan bus station to Xumishan leave irregularly. From around 7:30-11am, frequent minibuses, Y4-8, from Guyuan travel in the direction of Xumishan, stopping at a dirt road about 16km away. From here, local taxis go the rest of the way; Y20 round-trip, Y5 per hr. waiting time. Minibuses return to Guyuan until late evening. Walking around Xumishan can take a good 4-5hr., and the sun is relentless, so bring sunscreen and a wide-brimmed hat. Open daily sunrise-sunset. Y20.)*

GUYUAN MUSEUM (gùyuán bówùguǎn; 固原博物馆). The museum contains artifacts that range from the Stone Age to the Qin dynasty, a spectacular set of regional history exhibits, and an electronic map that shows routes along the Silk Road. Bronze, clay, and jade works mingle with ancient fishing weapons, musical instruments, and stone axes. The tour guide may speak only a little English, but the tour is still recommended. All posted signs and explanations are in Chinese. *(On the east end of Zhengfu Jie. Open Tu-Sa 8am-noon and 2:30-6pm. Y20, students Y10.)*

GANSU 甘肃

Reaching westward like a greedy finger of land, Gansu is bounded by the Qilian and Zoulan mountain ranges to the south and the Gobi desert to the north. Gansu province has long been a crossroads of Han, Mongolian, Tibetan, and Turkic cultures. The lush foothills in the southwest corner of the province are home to a sizable Tibetan population, centered around the enchanting town of Xiahe. West of the fertile Yellow River valley surrounding Lanzhou, the flat and featureless Hexi corridor is laced with a string of Silk Road outposts protected by the Great Wall. Oases like Dunhuang and Jiayuguan are a practice in paradox; their leafy avenues, poplar-lined parks, and fresh springs are all hemmed in by relentless desert. Corridor highlights include the spectacular Buddhist art of the Mogao Grottoes and the awe-inspiring Ming Great Wall fort. Farther west, pebble flats give way to dunes, and the Han and Hui presence fades into Uighur and Yughur culture.

LANZHOU 兰州 ☎0931

Although it's the geographical center of the country, Lanzhou (pop. 1.3 million) has long been considered a peripheral outpost of China. Initially a pit stop along the Silk Road, the city was elevated to the status of provincial capital in 1666, but didn't really shed its backwater reputation until 1949 when it became a center for petrochemical refining and bauxite smelting. Though the city bears the title of the world's most heavily polluted city, it still has some pleasant surprises. Massive skyscrapers, wide boulevards, shopping centers, and fantastic restaurants now complement the stark natural scenery of the surrounding mountains and the Yellow River. Its most popular attraction, the cave art at Bingling Temple, is a few hours away; the bustling outdoor cafes, locally brewed beer, impressive provincial museum, and rapidly developing western district also merit exploration. A mere outpost no longer, Lanzhou is one of the last bastions of modern conveniences en route to China's otherwise underdeveloped western frontier.

TRANSPORTATION

Travel insurance, compulsory for travel within Gansu, costs Y30, is valid for 14 days, and can be purchased at any hotel, travel agency, or bus station. Buying it before you leave is generally cheaper than purchasing it en route.

Flights: Zhongchuan Airport (lánzhōu zhōngchuān jīchǎng; 兰州中川机场), 73km north of the city, is a major regional hub. Buses (Y25) shuttle between the airport and the **China Northwest Airlines ticket office** (xīběi hángkōng gōngsi shòupiào chù; 西北航空公司售票处), 512 Donggang Xi Lu (24hr. ☎882 1964; free ticket delivery ☎883 9064). Turn left at the Legend Hotel and walk 5min.; the office is on the right. Open daily 8am-9pm. To: **Beijing** (2-3 per day, Y1220); **Chengdu** (1-2 per day, Y860); **Dunhuang** (4 per week, Y940); **Shanghai** (daily, Y1560); **Ürümqi** (Th and Su, Y1040); and **Xi'an** (1-3 per day, Y550).

Trains: Lanzhou Train Station (lánzhōu huǒchē zhàn; 兰州火车站; ☎882 2142), at the southern end of Tianshui Lu, and the intersection with Pingliang Lu, in Lanzhou's eastern district. Tickets sold 2-5 days in advance. Buying tickets (especially hard sleepers) for trains not originating in Lanzhou is extremely difficult, particularly in the summer. While the station undergoes renovations, the **ticket office** is to the right of the building. To: **Beijing** (25-35hr., 3 per day, Y235-390); **Golmud** (20hr., daily, Y156); **Guangzhou** (35hr., daily, Y493); **Shanghai** (31hr., 2 per day, Y438); **Ürümqi** (32hr., 6 per day, Y225); **Xi'an** (13hr., 10 per day, Y175); **Xining** (4hr., 5 per day, Y33).

Buses: East Station (lánzhōu dōng zhàn; 兰州东站; ☎841 8411), on Pingliang Lu, a 20min. walk north of the train station. To: **Dunhuang** (24hr., 2:30 and 6pm, Y140); **Jiayuguan** (17hr., 2:30 and 6pm, Y95); **Pingliang** (4½-8hr., every 30min. 6:30am-7:30pm, Y46-62); **Ürümqi** (38hr., 6pm, Y246); **Xi'an** (16hr., 6:30pm, Y86-130); and **Yinchuan** (12hr., 7am and 7pm, Y63). **West Station** (lánzhōu xī zhàn; 兰州西站; ☎233 3285), on Xijin Dong Lu, has buses to: **Linxia** (3hr., every 30min. 7am-4:30pm, Y20); **Xiahe** (6hr., 7:30 and 8:30am, Y32-43); and **Xining** (5hr., every 30min. 9am-5pm, Y31). There is also a much smaller bus station on Pingliang Lu across from the train station, but departures there are sporadic and prices erratic.

Local Transportation: The extensive and convenient public **bus** system makes the cross-town commute almost enjoyable. Fare Y0.4-1.1. Buses **#1, 7, 10,** and **31** travel north from the train station, while bus **#6** heads northwest. Bus #1 goes from the train sta-

Travelers who use the West Bus Station should beware of touts who accost foreigners outside the station, claiming to shuttle passengers to Xiahe. Only two buses travel directly to Xiahe each morning; the rest stop earlier, in Linxia. Purchase your ticket at the station to avoid buying the wrong tickets or paying full price for less than a full trip. If you do end up stranded in Linxia, don't panic: catching a connection to Xiahe should not be difficult.

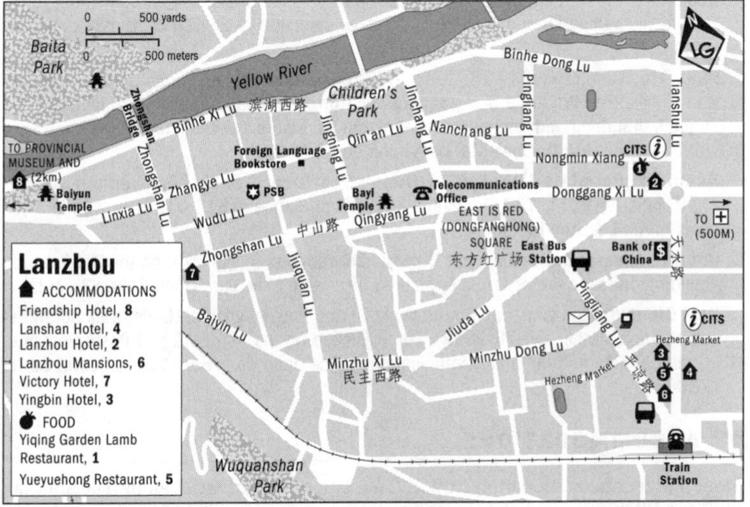

tion to the Lanzhou Hotel and the intersection of Donggang Xi Lu and Tianshui Lu before proceeding westward along Zhongshan Lu. Bus #6 heads toward the east of the town to the intersection of Pingliang Lu and Minzhu Dong Lu, where you must change to bus **#33.** From the same junction, change to bus **#34** to get to Zhongshan Bridge.

ORIENTATION AND PRACTICAL INFORMATION

Lanzhou sits on the southern shores of the Yellow River and is divided into two distinct districts. Visitors usually enter Lanzhou from the **eastern district.** The part of the city that radiates out from the train station in the south contains dozens of street markets, cheap accommodations, and bustling restaurants. In contrast, the glitzy Shanghai-like **western district** boasts fashion stores and upscale dim sum joints. The riverfront **Binhe Lu** (滨河路) and the main thoroughfare of **Xijin Lu** (西津路) link the two ends of town. **Xijin Xi Lu** forks into three main roads, each changing names several times as it crosses the eastern end of town. In the heart of the eastern district, **Tianshui Lu** (天水路) bisects Donggang Lu at the **Xiguan Traffic Circle** and terminates at the train station. **Pingliang Lu** (平凉路) cuts diagonally across the eastern end of town, from **East is Red Square** (dōngfānghóng guângchâng; 东方红广场) to the train station. The main Yellow River crossing is the **Zhongshan Bridge** (zhōngshān qiáo; 中山桥).

Travel Agencies: CITS, 10 Nongmin Xiang (☎841 6164 or 886 1333), directly behind the Lanzhou Hotel. Another location at 290 Tianshui Lu (☎862 5678), a 20min. walk north from the train station. No tours for individual travelers. Both branches open daily 9am-6pm. **Yingbin Travel Agency** (yíngbīn læxíngshè; 迎宾旅行社; ☎888 1272), next to the Yingbin Hotel. Full-day tours to Bingling Temple Y150-180. Some English spoken. **Gansu Western Tour Service** (gānsù xībù læxíngshè; 甘肃西部旅行社; ☎885 2929, 24hr. ☎908 9110), in the Lanzhou Hotel. Open daily 8am-noon and 2:30-6pm.

Bank of China: 589 Tianshui Lu (☎888 9942), a 20min. walk from the train station. Exchanges traveler's checks at counter #42. Credit card advances (4% commission) at counter #47. Open M-F 8:30am-5:30pm.

Bookstore: Foreign Language Bookstore (wàiwén shūdiàn; 外文书店), on Zhangye Lu, between Jingning Lu and Jiuhuan Lu. A large selection of English classics. Open daily 8am-6:30pm.

PSB: 310 Wudu Lu (☎846 2851, ext. 8550). From Zhongshan Lu, go north on Jiuquan Lu; turn left on Wudu Lu. A sign points you down a small street to the right, but the branch that deals with foreigners faces Wudu Lu. **Visa extensions** for UK citizens Y320, for US citizens Y250. Open M-F 8am-noon and 2:30-6pm.

Hospital: People's Hospital of Gansu Province (gānsùshēng rénmín yīyuàn; 甘肃省人民医院), 160 Donggang Xi Lu (ambulance ☎812 0120). A 10min. walk east of the Lanzhou Hotel.

Internet Access: Qidian Internet Bar (qǐdiǎn wǎngbā; 起点网吧), on the 3rd fl. of the building opposite the post office, marked by a large blue sign. Open 24hr. Y3 per hr.

Post Office: On the corner of Minzhu Dong Lu and Pingliang Lu, a 15min. walk northwest of the train station (☎878 9692). Parcel pickup on the left. EMS and Poste Restante. Open daily 8am-7pm; telecommunications office open daily 8am-11pm. **Postal Code:** 730000.

ACCOMMODATIONS

Most budget accommodations are in the city's eastern district along Tianshui Lu, within a 20-minute walk of the train station. A few cheap lodgings can also be found amid the pricey real estate in the western district.

EASTERN DISTRICT

Lanzhou Mansions (lánzhōu dàshà; 兰州大厦), 9 Tianshui Lu (☎841 7210), opposite the train station. Clean sheets, bathtubs, bed lamps, and TVs. The undisputed favorite among backpackers—due in part, no doubt, to its close proximity to the train station. Haircuts in the lobby Y10. Deposit Y100. 3-bed dorms Y26; singles with breakfast Y110; doubles Y82 and up. ❶

Lanzhou Hotel (lánzhōu fàndiàn; 兰州饭店), 434 Donggang Xi Lu (☎841 6321, ext. 8777 or 8260), on the Xiguan Traffic Circle. Take bus #1 from the train station. If you are willing to pay a little extra, this hotel offers pristine rooms with new bathrooms and a quiet back garden. Conveniently located next to the Nongmin Xiang food street. Traveler's check exchange (for guests only) and travel agency. Deposit varies. Singles Y230; doubles Y180-480; triples Y120. Credit cards accepted. ❸

Yingbin Hotel (yíngbīn fàndiàn; 迎宾饭店), 37 Tianshui Lu (☎888 6552), a 5min. walk from the train station, on the left. The Yingbin has renovated the majority of its rooms; those in the middle building were redone most recently. Pleasant, if basic, rooms; many face an unusually quiet parking lot. Hot water 8-11pm in front building, 24hr. everywhere else. Deposit Y100. Singles Y50, with bath Y158; doubles Y44-50, with bath Y178; triples Y93. ❶

Lanshan Hotel (lánshān bīnguǎn; 兰山宾馆), 6 Tianshui Lu (☎861 7211), a 5min. walk from the train station, on the right. Rooms are clean and well-lit, if a bit worn. Concrete floors and green paint in rooms with common baths. Breakfast included with singles and doubles. Deposit Y20. Singles Y40, with bath Y78; doubles Y42, with bath Y84; triples Y66. ❶

WESTERN DISTRICT

Friendship Hotel (lánzhōu yǒuyí bīnguǎn; 兰州友谊宾馆), 16 Xijing Xi Lu (☎233 3051), opposite the Provincial Museum in the western district. Take bus #1 from the train station. An excellent option for anyone planning to explore the west end, this huge hotel has a wide variety of rooms. Cheaper rooms may be available in the somewhat

NORTHWEST

WHAT'S IN A NAME? Always Coca-Cola? Not so much. Although the swirly red-and-white trademark of the Coca-Cola Corporation is recognized throughout the world, the folks at Coke wanted to give the world's most popular drink a name with more Middle Kingdom flavor. At first, the closest phonetic match they could find was "Kedou Kela" *(kēdǒu kēlà;* 蝌蚪磕蜡); but for the beverage elite from Hong Kong to Harbin, the name meant "bite the wax tadpole" or "female horse stuffed with wax" (depending on the dialect). Coke nixed the wildlife theme and, after an exhaustive search through 40,000 characters, hit upon the infinitely more successful "Kekou Kele" (kěkǒu kělè; 可口可乐), which translates roughly as "brings happiness in the mouth." Not to be outdone, Pepsi Co. made the choice of a new generation "Baishi Kele" (bǎishì kělè; 百事可乐) or "everything enjoyable." In an attempt to elbow in on the competition, the local yokel Wahaha Corporation came out with "Feichang Kele" (非常可乐) or "Future Cola," whose suspiciously curlicued, red-and-white packaging cannot mask its decidedly non-cola taste. But the phonetic fun goes beyond cola wars! American automotive giant Chrysler first thought of bombarding Chinese car buyers with advertisements for their reliable "Kuaisele" brand (kuàisǐle; 快死了), but abandoned the idea when they realized the name meant "swiftly careening toward death."

delapidated East Building (dōnglóu; 东楼). Deposit double the room rate, Y100 minimum. Doubles Y108-380; triples Y171. Credit cards accepted. ❷

Victory Hotel (shènglì bīnguǎn; 胜利宾馆), 43 Zhongshan Lu (☎846 5221, ext. 2500). Take bus #1 from the train station. Well-kept common showers and bathrooms and a few English-speaking staff members make this an economy-class winner. The best rooms are on the 5th through 8th floors. Deposit double the room rate. 3-bed dorms Y30; doubles with bath Y160-260; triples Y90, with bath Y150. ❶

FOOD

A trip to Lanzhou is not complete without a taste of its **honeydew melon** (báilánguā; 白兰瓜). Another local delight is the famed **eight treasure tea** (bābǎo chá; 八宝茶; Y1), a tasty mix of herbs and dried fruit that will leave you thirsting for more. Numerous restaurants line **Tianshui Lu** between the train station and Xiguan Traffic Circle. **Nongmin Xiang** (农民巷), a small street near the Xiguan Traffic Circle, is an old backpacker favorite; it boasts delicious Muslim noodle shops and kebab stands. Just south of Minzhu Dong Lu, running between Pingliang Lu and Tianshui Lu, is **Hezheng Market** (hézhèng shìchǎng; 和政市场). Vendors sell lamb kebabs (yángròu chuàn; 羊肉串; Y0.5), egg pancakes (jīdàn bǐng; 鸡蛋饼; Y0.8), and delicious sweet porridge blends (hēimí zhōu or xiǎomǐ zhōu; 黑米粥 or 小米粥; Y0.5 per bowl). Dozens of hotpot restaurants cluster around the Pingliang Lu gate. **Zhongshan Jie,** near the Victory Hotel, has many excellent cafes and dim sum spots unmatched in quality and atmosphere; some stay open well past midnight. Outdoor cafes abound on **Donggang Xi Lu.**

Yiqing Garden Lamb Restaurant (yīqīng yuán yánggāoròu diàn; 伊清园羊羔肉店; ☎872 0357), on Nongmin Xiang. This tiny Muslim restaurant serves up delicious lamb dishes, from the special (baby lamb; yánggāoròu; 羊羔肉) to the suspicious (baby lamb head; yánggāotóu; 羊羔头). Most dishes Y5-15. Open daily variable hours. ❶

Caigenxiang Restaurant (caìgēnxiāng dàjiǔdiàn; 菜根香大酒店), 22 Xijin Xi Lu, next to the Friendship Hotel. A large, busy restaurant with big windows and never-ending Christmas music. Try the *júejúe* lamb, served in a sizzling iron bowl (júejúe yángròu; 嚼嚼羊肉; Y20). Extensive tea menu. Open daily 11am-9:30pm. ❷

Yueyuehong Restaurant (yuèyuèhóng cānyín; 悦月红餐饮), 19 Tianshui Lu, 2min. from the Lanzhou Mansions, on the same side of the street. The food is nothing spectacular, but the English menu and stir-fry options (Y6-10) make ordering cheap and easy. ❶

SIGHTS

The provincial museum and a smattering of city parks aside, the **Bingling Temple Grottoes** outside the city are Lanzhou's most famous tourist attractions. Those with a bit of extra time may want to visit the **White Cloud Temple** (báiyún guān; 白云观), a 10-minute walk west of Zhongshan Bridge along the river. The most important Daoist temple in Lanzhou remains serene despite the street noise that manages to penetrate the darkest recesses inside. *(Open daily sunrise-sunset. Free.)*

GANSU PROVINCIAL MUSEUM (gānsùshěng bówùguǎn; 甘肃省博物馆). This splendid museum is a fountain of information on the 3000-year history of Gansu civilization. One of the most interesting sights in Lanzhou, it is a must-see for all travelers, history junkies or not. Be warned, however, that the museum is undergoing a multi-year renovation, making some galleries inaccessible. The second-floor gallery displays art and tools dating back to the Neolithic period, including bronze and jade ritual objects, Han wooden horses, and beautiful pottery artifacts from before 2000 BC. The world-renowned **Han Horse of Wuwei,** a marvelous bronze sculpture of a divine prancing horse takes center stage in the second room. Also, a massive electronic map shows the various branches of the Silk Road. Perhaps the most interesting exhibit is a Tang dynasty camel driver's woolen expense log, displayed in the final room of the front hall. *(On Xijin Xi Lu, directly across from the Friendship Hotel, in the western district. Open Tu-Sa 9am-noon and 2:30-5:30pm. Y25, students Y15.)*

NORTHWEST

WUQUANSHAN PARK (wǔquánshān gōngyuán; 五泉山公园). Far less touristed than the White Pagoda Park across town, this park boasts a series of small temples, pavilions, and tea houses terraced into the steep, rocky hills south of the city. Sheltered by towering cypress trees, the park's courtyards offer an expansive view of Lanzhou's skyline and the perfect spot to lounge and enjoy a cup of Eight Treasure Tea. *(South of town, at the terminus of bus #8. Taxi from the main train station Y7. Also accessible via bus #141 from Lanzhou West Train Station. Open daily sunrise-sunset. Y5.)*

WHITE PAGODA PARK (báitǎ gōngyuán; 白塔公园). After climbing the stairs to the right of the park entrance, visitors are likely to be overwhelmed by a barrage of circus games, neon lights, food hawkers, and animated afternoon karaoke sessions. The pagoda at the top rewards persistent visitors with a more pleasant view of Lanzhou. The covered terrace that surrounds the site is a convenient place to take a breather, and during the summer months, locals gather around tables, playing card games and nibbling on sunflower seeds. *(At the end of Zhongshan Lu, on the north bank of the Yellow River, near Zhongshan Bridge. Open daily 7:30am-7:30pm. Y5.)*

DAYTRIP FROM LANZHOU: BINGLING TEMPLE GROTTOES

*Take a **bus** (7:30 or 8:30am, Y10.5) to Liujiaxia Dam (liújiāxiá; 刘家峡), making sure that the driver knows you want to get off at Bingling Temple. The bus drops you at a ticket office along the main road; here you must pay an exorbitant "admission fee" to the dock area (Y15, students Y10). If the water level is too low, you may be forced to take a speedboat (Y50-75 per person, depending on the size of your group) rather than the ferry. Regular **admission** Y18; admission to locked caves additional Y60-300 per cave (caves #140, 144, 169, and 182 are the most expensive). Take a **bus** back to Lanzhou from the first ticket booth along the main road (last bus leaves around 5:30-6pm); or share a taxi to the far west end of town (Y10-20 per person) and then take bus #41 (1hr., Y1.1) into the center of town. Depending on whether you take the speedboat or the ferry, the whole trip includes 4-5hr. on a bus, 2-6hr. on a boat, and a mere 1-1½hr. of cave viewing. Public buses*

TWIST AND SHOUT Among other things, Lanzhou is known for being the home of Li Yang (李阳), creator of "Crazy English." As a beginning English student, Li found that he was unable to concentrate and had difficulty making any progress. He then stumbled upon a new technique: shouting. He stood outside and yelled all the English words he could think of, over and over again. Eventually, Li began telling others about his technique, and this rather peculiar method swept across China. The three main instructions are: as fast as possible, as clearly as possible, as loud as possible. Possibly because of Mr. Li's efforts, Lanzhou is home to a large population of well-educated English students. They even host an **English Corner** at the Northwest Nationalities Institute (xīběi mínzú xuéyuàn; 西北民族学院) on Wuquanshan. Take a taxi van (*miàndí*) from the train station (Y7); the English Corner is held every Sunday (3-6pm) in a pavilion to the right of the main gate. Shouting is optional.

from Lanzhou often stop many times along the way to the reservoir, leaving even less time at the caves; consider taking an all-inclusive ***tour*** *(Y180 and up) through a travel agency to save transit time and maximize cave-viewing time.*

Although hailed as one of the best-preserved collections of Buddhist cave art in China, the **Bingling Temple Grottoes** (bǐnglíng sì shíkū; 炳灵寺石窟) are becoming famous in traveling circles for not quite living up to expectations. Despite the complaints, however, the grotto art still merits a visit. The ride from Lanzhou is pleasant (if rough) and offers glimpses of vast corn fields and the distinctive red-clay banks. The upriver cruise from the dam rewards passengers with streaming landscapes of open skies, multicolored peaks, and contoured banks. As the river narrows upstream and the boats snake through a rocky gorge, spectacular finger-like stone spires, rising 30 to 50m above the rushing waters, signal your arrival at the small dirt path leading to the caves.

Reality, in the form of a pastel billboard and exorbitant prices, rudely awakens travelers upon their arrival at the caves. The extra money to visit locked caves buys the chance to climb bamboo ladders to trapdoors that lead four stories up into the cliffs, an experience hardly worth the steep price; these caves are rather dull compared to the caves included in the basic admission.

Construction on the first of the 183 caves, 694 stone statues, and 82 clay figures began in AD 366 and continued for 1000 years. Caves #69, 82, 134, 136, and the curiously black-and-white 28 (all visible when you pass to the left of the Maitreya) are well-preserved with murals and calligraphic *sutras* adorning the inner caverns. At the far end of the access bridge sits a 27m tall Tang-era Maitreya sitting Buddha. Legend has it that the upper body, carved out of the rock cliff, symbolizes the internal realm, and the lower body, molded out of excavated stone and clay, symbolizes the external. The Buddha is said to sit equally mindful of both.

LINXIA 临夏 ☎0930

Populated largely by the Hui minority, Linxia was once an important outpost on the Silk Road. Today it is still an important regional trade center. Mosques abound in this very religious town; most men wear white skullcaps and minarets issue calls to prayer five times a day. Although little can keep travelers here for too long, Linxia makes for an interesting stop on the way to Xiahe.

TRANSPORTATION AND PRACTICAL INFORMATION. Almost all travelers arrive in Linxia at the **South Bus Station** (qìchē nánzhàn; 汽车南站), which lies on Jiefang Nan Lu (解放南路), the town's main drag. Outbound buses go to: **Lanzhou** (3hr., every 20min. 6am-6pm, Y19.5-26); **Xiahe** (3hr., every 30min. 7am-5pm, Y13.5); and **Xining** (9hr., 6am, Y38). Note that competition among private operators, particularly on the Lanzhou route, is fierce; it is not uncommon for people to be manhandled into buses. Foreigners are rarely subjected to such physical treatment, but it never hurts to be careful. The much smaller **West Station** is accessible by taxi.

The **Bank of China,** 157 Jiefang Nan Lu, just after the first intersection on the left, exchanges traveler's checks. (Open M-F 8am-noon and 2:30-6pm.) The **PSB** office (☎621 7525) is located in the city government building (gōngzhèngchù; 公证处), on Jiefang Nan Lu, before the traffic circle on the left. The **post office** is also on Jiefang Nan Lu, just next to the city government building. **Postal Code:** 731100.

ACCOMMODATIONS AND FOOD. Budget accommodations can easily be found near the bus station and on or near Jiefang Nan Lu. **Shuiquan Hotel ❶** (shûiquán bïnguân; 水泉宾馆), is on Jiefang Nan Lu, near the bus station, on the right. Bathrooms are a bit rustic, but reasonably clean. Rooms are large and airy and feature comfortable easy chairs. (3-bed dorms Y10; doubles Y30, with bath Y50.) **Nationalities Hotel ❶** (mínzú bïnguân; 民族宾馆), is on the far side of the first intersection, on the right. Slightly fancier and newer than the Shuiquan, with many rooms that feature newly-renovated baths. (☎621 5472. Doubles Y80; triples Y120.)

SOME LIKE IT HOT POT A Northwestern China specialty, hotpot is literally that: a hot, steaming pot of spicy broth kept boiling by a special burner either built-in or under the table. The broth is seasoned with fish heads, Chinese dates, star of anise, and more spices than you care to count. Into this, people dunk thinly sliced meats, often beef or lamb, as well as any imaginable local vegetable or noodle. Cooked within seconds, these morsels are fished out and dunked again into a spicy peanut sauce before being devoured. Both a festive occasion and a culinary delight, hotpot brings together a sweaty, teary-eyed group of friends who linger for hours over the steaming pot, often while playing drinking games and laughing uproariously. Hotpot generally costs Y20-30 per person.

The most enjoyable food option is undoubtedly the **night market** at the end of Jiefang Nan Lu, on the traffic circle. While all manner of breads, dumplings, noodles, and chicken parts are available, nothing quite compares to China's favorite meat-on-a-stick: the lamb kebab (yángròuchuàn; 羊肉串; Y0.3-0.5). Most food stands have small seating areas and serve free tea. Muslim restaurants (denoted by 清真) abound on Jiefang Nan Lu.

SIGHTS. The **outdoor stalls,** particularly along Jiefang Nan Lu and Bei Dajie, display everything from beautiful daggers and leopard pelts to the hand-made eyeglasses for which Linxia is famous. On Jiefang Nan Lu, just before the traffic circle, stands **Nanguan Mosque** (nángüan qïngzhën dàsì; 南关清真大寺), the largest mosque in Linxia (the main building and surrounding complex can hold up to 10,000 worshipers). Mosques have stood on the site for more than 800 years; the current building, however, is just a decade old. Visitors are forbidden to enter the prayer hall, but may peek in through the open doors. The very pleasant **Red Park** (hóngyúan; 红园) can be found on Hongyuan Lu. Take the second left from Tuanjie Lu; bypass the first, smaller park and continue on the road to the right. The park is a fine place to spend an afternoon in the shade of a pondside gazebo. It offers amusement rides, including bumper cars...on water. There's also a small zoo with monkeys, camels, and some dejected-looking pheasants. (Admission Y2.)

XIAHE 夏河

☎0941

Home to the Labrang Lamasery, the largest and most important center of Tibetan Buddhism outside of Tibet, Xiahe is rapidly becoming a mecca for budget travelers. Still, the heavy influx of tourist buses has done little to diminish the charm of this quiet, spiritual town in the middle of nowhere. After a short walk into the surrounding mountains or grasslands, you are likely to encounter no one other than grizzled nomads tending their flocks; the town remains a fascinating mix of monks, devout pilgrims, and traders.

ORIENTATION AND PRACTICAL INFORMATION

Xiahe lies along a single road that runs from the bus station in the east 4-5km west to a Tibetan community complete with mud-brick houses, prayer flags, and colorful door fronts. The post office and administrative buildings are in the east, while Labrang Lamasery is out west.

Buses: Xiahe is accessible only by bus. **Xiahe Bus Station** (xiàhé chángtú qìchē zhàn; 夏河长途汽车站; ☎712 1462) is on the eastern edge of town. To: **Langmusi** via **Hezuo** (2hr., every 30min. 6:10am-5:30pm, Y9); **Lanzhou** (5-7hr., 4 per day 6:30am-2:30pm, Y32-44); and **Linxia** (3hr., every 30min. 6am-6pm, Y13.5).

PSB: Take a right up the road out of the bus station; a 3min. walk takes you to the office, which will be on your right. (☎712 1526). Open M-F 8am-noon and 2:30-6pm.

Bank: No banks in Xiahe exchange traveler's checks. Some hotels may be able to convert US dollars. The nearest **Bank of China** is in Linxia.

Internet Access: In the **Overseas Tibetan Hotel**. Open daily approximately 8am-10pm. Y16 per hr .

Post Office: From the PSB, turn left and walk 5min. (☎712 1944). IDD service next door at the telecommunications office. Both open daily 8am-6pm. **Postal Code:** 747100.

ACCOMMODATIONS

Xiahe has several pleasant and inexpensive accommodations; most are run by friendly managers and accept foreigners.

Overseas Tibetan Hotel (huáqiáo fàndiàn; 华侨饭店; ☎712 2642; othotel@public.lz.gs.cn), just before the lamasery. The friendly owner speaks perfect English and is happy to help travelers. Clean dorms with lockers and TVs. Beautiful new doubles are decorated in traditional Tibetan style. Hotel taxi, bike rental (Y10 per day), IDD service, and a book exchange. 24hr. hot water. 4-bed dorms Y15; doubles Y60, with bath Y160. ❶

Tara Guesthouse (zhúomâ læshè; 卓玛旅社; ☎712 1274), around the corner from the Overseas Tibetan Hotel near the lamasery. The upkeep and room quality varies (avoid the small, dark dorms on the bottom floor). The staff is quite friendly, however, and there are several large, sun-filled common areas where travelers congregate. All rooms have common baths. Bike rental Y10 per day. Hot water 7am-noon and 6-10pm. Somewhat small 3- to 6-bed dorms Y15-20; doubles Y25. ❶

White Conch Hotel (bái hâiluó bïnguân; 白海螺宾馆; ☎712 2486). Guests can fall asleep to the soothing sounds of the Daxia River; rooms to the right of the staircase are closest to the water. English-speaking staff member. Fairly new rooms have white sheets, heavy blankets, clean carpets, and well-kept baths. Hot water 7-11:30pm. 3-bed dorms Y31; doubles with bath Y180; suites Y250. ❶

NORTHWEST

Daxia Hotel (dàxià bīnguân; 大夏宾馆; ☎712 1546), a short walk up the road from the bus station, on the right. Big rooms have comfortable beds. Hot water 8-11:30pm. 3-bed dorms Y16-21; singles Y70-90; doubles Y52-82. ❶

FOOD

Han, Hui, and Tibetan cuisines are all widely available in their respective sections of town; a dozen or so restaurants display outdoor English menus. For genuine Tibetan food, steer clear of the "Yak Restaurant"or similar imitation restaurants in the east of town that serve indifferent faux-Tibetan food. Instead, cross the little bridge into the west of town. On the right side of the road, just before the lamasery, the **Labrang Lamasery Restaurant** ❶ (lābûlèng sì fànguân; 拉卜楞寺饭馆) is a backpacker's dream, with an English menu and particularly delicious breakfast foods, including a loaf of piping hot Tibetan bread (Y2). Just across the street, the **Snowlands Restaurant** ❶ (xuêchéng cãntïng; 雪城餐厅) is another haven for Tibetan, Han, and creative Western cuisine. The restaurant is particularly clean and tidy, with outdoor seating and a great chicken sandwich (Y5). The Nepali chef at the **Everest Cafe** ❷ (☎712 2642), attached to the Overseas Tibetan Hotel, cooks up some of the best chicken curry outside India (Y16).

SIGHTS

Within the city limits, there are few sights of interest other than the lamasery. The surrounding grasslands, however, are definitely worth a visit. Take a right onto the dirt track just before the lamasery and follow it up into the mountains for about 20 minutes, and you might just witness a sky burial (see p. 815), which is still occasionally performed in Xiahe.

LABRANG LAMASERY (lābùlèn sì; 拉卜楞寺). This lamasery, which belongs to the Yellow Hat (Gelug) sect, is spectacular inside and out. The magnificent site is surrounded by over 2500 prayer wheels, including several massive wheels housed in separate towers. It's possible to sit for hours and watch pious pilgrims performing clockwise circuits about the grounds.

The lamasery was founded in 1709 by Eang Zongahe, a monk who was named the first *Jiamuyang*, or "living Buddha." Since then, Labrang has been the site of numerous acts of violence, and any monk will forcefully attest that the lamasery you see is only a shell of its former self. Large-scale bloody disputes between Tibetan and local Hui rulers in the 1920s and the ravages of the Cultural Revolution reduced the lamasery's population by 75%. One thousand temples were destroyed; today, only 27 remain.

The main prayer hall at the entrance gate was rebuilt in 1990 after an electrical fire in 1985. Able to hold the lamasery's entire population, the hall is illuminated by yak-butter lamps, draped with hangings called "umbrellas," and filled with statues of Buddhas of the past, present, and future.

To appreciate all that the lamasery has to offer, be sure to take a tour, after which you may wander about the entire complex on your own. From the exit, take the first left and follow the right wall to a small garden. At certain times of the day, you may be able to view lamas at play, either exercising or practicing meditative gymnastics. Travel up the road from the northern complex and follow the covered prayer circuits counterclockwise until you reach the **Gongtang Pagoda** (gòngtáng bâotâ; 贡唐宝塔), which is surrounded by an impressive array of prayer wheels. *(Tours of the lamasery leave from the ticket office to the right of the entrance daily at 10am and 3pm. Office open daily 8:15am-noon and 2-6pm; lamasery open daily 9am-5pm. Entrance Y5, tours Y23.)*

SANGKE GRASSLANDS (sāngkē cǎoyuán; 桑科草原). Easily reached by taxi or bike. Heading west, a large touristy yurt village swamped with Chinese tourists from Lanzhou can be found on the right side of the road. To the left, the grasslands stretch indefinitely. *(Round-trip taxi Y25. Horses Y20 per hr. Entry to grasslands Y3.)*

GANJIA GRASSLANDS (gānjiā cǎoyuán; 甘加草原). Ganjia is vaster, more starkly beautiful, and far more isolated than Sangke. Although it's only about 35km from Xiahe, it takes nearly an hour to drive here on a primitive, winding, mountain road. In addition to the stunning vistas, there are a number of other interesting sights in the area. At **White Rock Cliff** (*takker* in Tibetan; báishíyá in Chinese; 白石崖), there is a fascinating holy cave complete with allegorical rock formations, underground pools, and a handprint made by the 10th Panchen Lama. Much of the fun is in the descent, as the cave extends deep into the mountain. Even normally brash travelers might find some parts downright terrifying, however, as they grasp a slippery rope in one hand and a sure-footed monk with the other while peeping into seemingly bottomless chasms on either side. Be very careful and be sure to bring a flashlight: the candles at the entrance are unreliable, and you may very well set yourself on fire as you crawl about on all fours. A small monastery near the cave is of no special interest. The **Eight Corners Wall Village** (bājiâo chéng; 八角城) nearby has a cross-shaped wall that dates back over 2000 years to the Qin dynasty. Much of the wall has survived, and within it lies a small, friendly Tibetan village which seems to be entirely populated by adorable 8-year-old children. *(Ganjia is accessible by private vehicle only. The Overseas Tibetan Hotel has the best deal: Y200 for a miàndí that seats 5-6, driven by Pu Zhipeng (浦致鹏), a charismatic local who is familiar with the area. Otherwise, Tara Guesthouse charges Y70 per person for tours; Tsering Gompo at the White Conch also arranges trips. Entrance to White Rock Cliff Y8. Holy cave Y7. Monastery Y5. Eight Corners Wall Village Y5.)*

PINGLIANG 平凉 ☎0933

NORTHWEST

A growing industrial town in Gansu just across the Ningxia border, Pingliang is most famous—and with good reason—for nearby Kongtongshan, a spectacular Daoist mountain. Like many other cities in central China, Pingliang is on the fast-track to modernization and boasts as many newly built hospitals as watermelon vendors. But this young city is handling its growing pains relatively well, and visitors are often pleasantly surprised by the city's festive markets and lively town square. The beautiful surrounding countryside of green, rocky cliffs and high ridges of terraced farmlands make Pingliang a pleasant stop.

TRANSPORTATION

Trains: Pingliang Train Station (píngliàng huǒchē zhàn; 平凉火车站; ☎862 8878), on Jiefang Bei Lu north of the city center. Accessible via bus #1. Open daily 9am-noon, 1:30-5:30pm, 7:10-9pm, and 10:30pm-8am. To: **Chengdu** (20½hr., daily, Y63); **Lanzhou** (11hr., daily, Y32); **Ürümqi** (12hr., 2 per day, Y118-137); **Xi'an** (8hr., daily, Y28); **Yinchuan** (9 hr., 2 per day, Y34).

Buses: The newly built **Pingliang Long-distance Bus Station** (píngliàng chángtú qìchē zhàn; 平凉长途汽车站; ☎863 1271) is on Jiefang Bei Lu, 10min. north of the city center. Open daily 5:30am-10pm. To: **Lanzhou** (5-8hr.; every hr. 6am-5pm; Y52, express Y63); **Xi'an** (8 hr., every hr. 6am-1:30pm, Y50); and **Yinchuan** (8hr., 7am and 6pm, Y45). Buses, especially those going to nearby destinations like Guyuan, also leave from the old bus station on National Highway 312, about 2.5km west of the town center.

Local Transportation: Bus #1 stops at the train station and new bus station, and **#2** runs along Zhongshan Jie to the Panxuan Lu traffic circle. Fare Y1. **Bengbengche** (motorized three-wheeled cabs; 蹦蹦车) to most destinations cost Y2.

ORIENTATION AND PRACTICAL INFORMATION

Pingliang is built on a grid, with the **Panxuan Lu** (盘旋路) **traffic circle** in the center. **National Highway 312** (sānyāoèr guódào; 312国道) runs west of the circle. **Jiefang Bei Lu** (解放北路) runs north from the city past the new bus station until it dead-ends at the train station. The other major road is **Zhongshan Jie,** parallel to and one block south of National Highway 312.

Bank of China: On Zhongshan Jie, about 5min. west of the post office. Exchanges currency and traveler's checks. Open M-F 8am-noon and 2:30-6pm.

Market: Xing Sheng Market, 8 Jiefang Nan Lu (☎861 1598), just past the Blue Star Hotel. 2 floors of grocery goodness and a large selection of western toothpaste.

Hospitals: District Hospital (dìqū yīyuàn; 地区医院), on Kongtong Dong Lu, 10min. east of Panxuan Lu traffic circle and north at the first intersection. A large blue sign indicates when to turn north. Other modern hospitals are scattered throughout the city.

Internet Access: Jianxian Internet Bar, Jiefang Nan Lu, on the northeast corner of the intersection with Zhongshan Jie, on the 2nd fl. 10 computers. Y2 per hr.

Post Office: Pingliang Post Office, on Zhongshan Jie, a 10min. walk from Xinmin Jie. From the Panxuan Lu traffic circle, walk south on Jiefang Nan Lu. Turn right onto Zhongshan Jie and walk about 20min.; the building is on the left. EMS. Open daily 8am-7pm. **Postal Code:** 744000.

NORTHWEST

ACCOMMODATIONS AND FOOD

Cheap and relatively clean accommodations are available for about Y10 per bed in the many hostels near the train and bus stations. Much nicer rooms in the town center are slightly more expensive.

The downtown area offers a lively atmosphere to walk off an evening meal, and standard, inexpensive Chinese cuisine can be found at any of the street vendors that cluster in the area.

Blue Star Hostel (☎822 1390), east of the traffic circle, just past the hospital sign. Offers guests fly swatters and friendly service. Large rooms with linoleum floors, TV, and common baths. Showers are found in another building. Singles Y30; doubles Y50. ❶

Blue Star Hotel (lánxīng fàndiàn; 蓝星饭店; ☎862 4419), on the left side of Jiefang Nan Lu, 5min. from Panxuan Lu traffic circle. Carpeted rooms with bright white walls, clean sheets, and sanitary common baths don't make up for the lack of showers. Deposit Y100-200. Singles and doubles Y25-50. ❶

Yuanheng Hotel (yuánhēng bīnguǎn; 元亨宾馆; ☎822 6831, ext. 8999), on the southeast side of the Panxuan Lu traffic circle. Spotless rooms have TV. Decent common bathrooms. The courteous staff and sparkling glass-lined lobby are icing on the cake. Deposit Y150 and up. Doubles Y90, with bath Y100-170; triples with bath Y156. ❷

SIGHTS

KONGTONGSHAN MOUNTAIN (kōngtóng shān; 崆峒山). China's most famous Daoist mountain is undoubtedly the best reason to visit Pingliang. If the number of art students at a place of beauty is an indication of its aesthetic appeal, Kongtongshan Mountain is off the charts, with hordes of easel-wielding beauty seekers making the pilgrimage. Kongtongshan, formerly the realm of the Eight Famous Immortals (bāxiān; 八仙) and the hermitage of ascetic priests, has 42 Qin- and Han-dynasty temples and pavilions built on high, forested cliffs. Once accessible only by chiseled steps and dangling chains, the area is now invaded by a newly opened road and parking lot. The spectacular view of the surrounding terraced farmland and the bright smiles of the mountain priests are more than enough to restore the sense of calm spirituality that was once so central to the place. Visitors seeking to follow the traditional pilgrimage route can start at **Qianshan** (qiánshān; 前山) and ascend the roughly 3km of steps, stopping at smaller temples along the way to burn incense. For less athletic visitors, a cable car traverses the emerald lake. *(15km west of Pingliang. A taxi from Pingliang to Qianshan costs about Y20; taxis also stop at Houshan (hòushān; 后山). From there, it is a long wait for an all-terrain vehicle (Y20) to the top. Y50.)*

OTHER SIGHTS. A post-dinner stroll through the night markets of Pingliang brings visitors to the **Bao Pagoda** (bâo tâ; 宝塔). Southeast of the Panxuan Lu traffic circle, this seven-story Ming structure houses bronze Buddha statues on each level. Walk south on Jiefang Nan Lu and turn left on Zhongshan Lu (which becomes Baota Lu after several blocks). Bao Pagoda is on the left. **Liu Lake Park** (liû hú gōngyuán; 柳湖公园) has meandering garden paths, a small zoo, paddle boat rentals (Y10), and frequent music performances. The park is near the old bus station on National Highway 312, about 10 minutes from Panxuan Lu traffic circle. Open daily until around midnight (Y2).

TIANSHUI 天水 ☎0938

When tourists gossip about their latest expedition to Tianshui, talk about this industrial city usually takes a backseat to discussions of the nearby Maijishan Grottoes. The vibrant, growing, and wonderfully clean city is somewhat of a modern city oasis. Young people come from small surrounding towns to seek employment, and they play welcoming hosts to the cave-loving tourists.

The Maijishan Grottoes themselves house amazingly well-preserved Buddhist sculptures in over 200 cliff caves that date back more than 1500 years. Tianshui also offers convenient access to several other sights of interest, most notably the Immortals' Cliff Area and the Stone Gate Mountains, both great hiking spots made more enjoyable by the breezy and dry climate. Tianshui is an ideal two- or three-day stop for those traveling along the southern route of the Silk Road.

TRANSPORTATION

Trains: Tianshui Train Station (tiānshuî huǒchē zhàn; 天水火车站; ☎261 1460), in Beidao, facing a large square, is the departure point for Qincheng- and Maijishan-bound minibuses. Ticket office open 24hr. Tickets can also be bought at the **Industrial and Commercial Bank of China** on Dazhong Lu, a 5min. walk south of the Qincheng central square. Open daily 9am-6pm. To: **Lanzhou** (7hr., 7 per day, Y26-52); **Ürümqi** (6hr., 3 per day, Y131-245); and **Xi'an** (7hr., 10 per day, Y25-51). Also trains to **Xining.**

Buses: Tianshui Long-distance Bus Station (tiānshuî chángtú qìchē zhàn; 天水长途汽车站; ☎821 4028), in the northern part of Qincheng. From the central square, walk 3 blocks east on Minzhu Lu, and turn left on Hezuo Bei Lu. Walk for 5min. until you reach the first major intersection, then turn left again; the station is on the right. Buses to local and long-distance destinations are rarely crowded; 30min. is enough time to buy a ticket and find the bus. Departure times vary by day and season. To: **Lanzhou** (8hr.; 4 per day, evening bus offers sleepers only; Y38-54); **Linxia** (13hr., daily, Y43); and **Pingliang** (8hr., 2 per day, Y32.5). The **local bus station,** servicing closer towns, is just past the Industrial and Commercial Bank on Dazhong Lu in Qincheng, and has frequent morning buses to **Gangu** and **Wushan.**

Local Transportation: Buses #1, 6, and **9** shuttle between Qincheng central square and the train station in Beidao, leaving every 10-15min. Y2. Bus #6 is an express bus (approx. 30min.); the others take about 45min. **Private minibuses** also travel between these 2 points, but take much longer. These minibuses often look very similar to city buses; city buses clearly display their numbers in the front windshield. **Taxi:** Base fare Y4, each additional km Y1. Taxis to Jade Springs Park Y3-10.

ORIENTATION AND PRACTICAL INFORMATION

Tianshui is comprised of two main sections, separated by 18km of industrial development and several small, rural communities. In the eastern section of **Beidao** (北道), several large avenues radiate out from the train station. **Longchang Lu** runs east-west and passes directly in front of the train station. Public buses and minibuses make the 45-minute trip to the modern and lively **Qincheng** district (秦城), leaving every 10 minutes and dropping passengers off at bus stops on **Dazhong Lu** (大众路), just southwest of the **central square** (zhōngxīn guǎngchǎng; 中心广场). **Minzhu Lu** (民主路) runs along the north side of the square, and **Jiefang Lu** (解放路) borders the south side and extends to the western end of the city. In most cases, walking is a good way to get around within each district. Taxis travel between districts for Y25-30.

NORTHWEST

Travel Agency: CITS (☎821 3621), on the northwest corner of Minzhu Lu and Hezuo Lu, in Qincheng. Walk east from the central square for 7-8min.; the office is on the left. Although the office staff is friendly to individual travelers, the office specializes in group package tours–including high-priced tours of Maijishan (English-speaking guides available). English-speaking staff member. Open daily 9am-6pm.

Bank of China: On Minzhu Lu, in Qincheng. From the city square, walk east for 15min.; the bank is on the left, in a clearly visible glass high-rise. Exchanges currency and traveler's checks. Open daily 8am-6pm. Another location on Long Chang Lu, in **Beidao,** across the street and slightly east of the train station.

Hospital: #1 Hospital, 105 Jianshe Lu (☎821 3722).

Internet Access: Internet Bar (wângbã; 网吧), on Qingnian Bei Lu, Qincheng. From the central square, walk east on Minzhu Lu, and take the first left onto Qingnian Bei Lu; the bar is 2min. ahead on the left, just before the first alley. Look for a small blue sign with the Chinese name. The bar is on the 2nd fl. Y2 per hr. Open 24hr.

Post and Telecommunications: (☎821 0547). On the corner of Dazhong Lu and Minzhu Lu, Qincheng, just north of the central square. EMS. Open daily 8am-8:30pm. **Postal Code:** 741000. **China Telecom** is next door. No IDD service. A **post office** is on Long Chang Lu, a 2min. walk west of the train station, Beidao. **Postal Code:** 741020.

ACCOMMODATIONS AND FOOD

Most of Beidao's accommodations are within minutes of the noisy train station. In the area, dining options are limited to a few restaurants across from the train station. Most travelers stay in Beidao if they need to catch an early morning train or if they arrive on a sleeper. Qincheng, on the other hand, offers centrally located and inexpensive lodging with easy access to major city sights and the bustling night markets near the central square.

Streetside stalls and restaurants abound; at **Wenmiao Market** (wénmiào shãngchâng; 文庙商场) in the southeast corner of the central square, over 100 vendors sell local specialties. For breakfast, try the small, round yellow breads eaten with a spiced hash and a bowl of porridge.

BEIDAO

Yindu Hostel (yíndū zhāodàisuǒ; 银都招待所; ☎261 6246), on Longchang Lu, across from and slightly east of the train station. Courteous staff. Clean, carpeted, and spacious rooms with common baths. Singles and doubles Y25-50, with bath Y100. ❶

Tianliang Hotel (tiānliàng bīnguǎn; 天凉宾馆; ☎821 3792), a small hostel across the street from the train station and slightly west of Long Chang Lu. All rooms have TV, decent bath, and comfortable beds. Singles Y35-55; doubles Y60-80. ❶

Railway Hostel (tiělù zhāodàisuǒ; 铁路招待所; ☎273 5154), near the train station. From the station, turn right; it's a few doors down Longchang Lu. The 24hr. service desk attracts late-night travelers, but don't expect service with a smile. Bright, clean rooms with cement floors and mosquito netting. 24hr. hot water. Common baths. Singles Y32, with living room and TV Y45. Foreigners should expect to pay as much as 40% more. ❶

Maiji Hotel (màijī dàjiǔdiàn; 麦积大酒店; ☎261 2207), on the right side of the train station square as you exit the station. Large rooms have electric fans, TVs, and clean showers. 24hr. hot water. Doubles Y130; triples Y180. 10% student discount. ❷

QINCHENG

Huaxi Hotel (huáxī bīnguǎn; 华西宾馆; ☎821 5356). From the Qincheng bus stop, walk straight ahead with the central square on your left and cross Minzhu Lu at the first intersection; the hotel entrance is around the corner to the left. Hospitable staff, enormous rooms, and balconies. Showers aren't on every floor. Hot water 8-11pm. Solo travelers report having luck procuring a single bed in a double room. 2-bed dorms Y29; 3-bed dorms Y24; doubles Y54, with bath Y86-106. ❶

Tianyao Hostel (tiānyào zhāodàisuǒ; 天药招待所; ☎828 7503), on Minzhu Lu one block east of the post office, down the first alley on the south side of the street. Bright rooms, with carpeting and TV. Quiet and away from the central square. Singles Y48; doubles 48-118; triples Y60-125. ❶

SIGHTS

There are several worthwhile spots to visit in and around the Qincheng district, all of which can be seen in one day. The Nanguo Temple opens at night and makes for a relaxing after-dinner excursion. The **Maijishan Grottoes,** the **Immortals' Cliffs,** and **Stone Gate Mountain Hiking Reserve** lie south of Beidao. These attractions are a must-see for outdoors enthusiasts and grotto-lovers alike.

MAIJISHAN GROTTOES

***Minibuses** leave from Tianshui's Beidao Train Station in the morning (1hr.; Y10, round-trip Y20-25). **Tours** in Mandarin Y20, in English Y70. For an additional Y100-600, visitors can see some of the caves that are closed to the general public. For information on tours, check with the tourist office to the left of the museum. Gate **admission** Y11; admission to caves Y30, groups of 2 or more students with ID Y15 per person.*

Named after their resemblance to stacks of harvested wheat, the sheer rock cliffs of Maijishan (màijīshān shíkū; 麦积山石窟) rise dramatically from the lush forest below. From a distance, a latticework of caves and exterior sculptures seems to be the natural texture of the rock. Up close, however, as you scurry up the scaffolding to the caves on the rock face, the intricacy of the carving and painting is revealed.

Each cave is dominated by a central figure—some over 16m tall—whose expression and gestures depict a particular realm of the Buddhist cosmos, reflected in the surrounding sculpture and murals. Fortunately for tourists with short attention spans, the sculpture styles and spatial arrangements continually change, progressing from late Qin styles to those of the Qing dynasty 1600 years later. Although Maijishan's caves are closed off, visitors can peer inside through the metal screens; guided tours allow guests to step inside some of these locked areas.

The **Maijishan Museum** (màijīshān bówùguân; 麦积山博物馆), near the parking lot of the main entrance, displays some of the most delicate and well-preserved objects from the site.

IMMORTALS' CLIFFS (xiānrén yá; 仙人崖). Surrounded by forested ridges and cultivated fields, this area is best known for the Buddhist and Daoist temples built under the shelter of an enormous overhanging cliff. A short but strenuous 10-minute hike is necessary to reach the cliffs and reveals breathtaking peaks and an emerald lake, the beauty of which makes the trip worthwhile. Tucked into this cave-like niche are over 50 prayer halls, each housing evocative sculptures and murals that date back over 1600 years. To get a good look at the recessed figures, approach an altar at the front of the prayer hall; as you do so, it is appropriate to burn a stick of incense and donate some small change as a sign of respect. There are also small pavilions and shrines dotting the surrounding hills; hiking to these can be the best part of the trip, as you wind through a network of small dirt trails, crisscrossing the lush, fragrant farmland. A small floating gazebo in the lake next to the main parking lot is perfect for picnicking; paddle boats can also be rented. *(Although this area merits a full day of exploration, it's cheaper to arrange with a minibus driver at Beidao Train Station to go to Maijishan and then spend a few hours at each spot; this should cost about Y40 round-trip for a group. A taxi for a full day costs Y130-150. Admission Y15.)*

FUXI TEMPLE (fúxī miào; 伏羲庙). This beautiful and expansive Ming-dynasty temple is devoted to Fuxi, the chief of a southeastern Gansu Neolithic clan society who is said to be the original ancestor of the Chinese people. In the courtyard, 1000-year-old cypress trees and a pair of enormous phoenix and dragon reliefs—reputed to be carved from a single piece of wood—frame the intricate temple facade. The **Tianshui Museum** (tiānshuî bówùguân; 天水博物馆), on the left as you enter, houses an impressive collection of Neolithic pottery, ritual vessels, and even some prized sculptures taken from Maijishan. As you walk around the temple complex, take a peek into the rooms bordering the courtyard: many are studios for local painters and calligraphers. *(On Jiefang Lu. From the Qincheng central square, walk west for 20min.; the temple is on the right. Open daily sunrise-sunset. Y5.)*

ANTIQUE MARKET (gǔwán chéng; 古玩城). Well-spoken collectors and the artists themselves run this market, a collection of fascinating art studios and antique shops that offer everything from Ming-dynasty furniture and model architecture to contemporary sculptures (gēndiāo; 根雕) that use gnarled roots and branches. *(On Jiefang Lu, underneath the Qincheng central square. The entrance is across the street from a small mosque. Open daily 8:30am-5:30pm. Free.)*

JADE SPRINGS DAOIST TEMPLE (yùquánguān gōngyuán; 玉泉观公园). First built during the Yuan dynasty, this temple in the dusty hills northwest of the Qincheng city center has only its 700-year-old cypress trees and a sweeping view of the city to distinguish it from the peaceful retreat of other temple complexes. It is, however, a pleasant place to relax and sip tea on a long, hot afternoon, and it provides a beautiful vantage point from which to watch dusk fall over the city. *(From Fuxi Temple, turn left on Jiefang Lu, take the first left on Shuangqiao Bei Lu, and turn right onto Renmin Xi Lu. Walk for 5min.; the temple will be visible up a small street to the left. Open daily sunrise-sunset. Y5.)*

NANGUO TEMPLE. This large park sits in a mountain valley and wraps around a pond that is lit by colored lights at night. Two 2000-year-old cypress trees, each 3m in diameter, guard the temple's main gate, admitting strolling couples and small families. In 759, the Tang dynasty poet Du Fu, who was at the time exiled, visited the temple and wrote a poem singing its praises. In the courtyard, another old cypress, verified to be over 1600 years old, is reputed to be the very tree that caught Du Fu's fancy. *(2km south of Qincheng. Taxi from the central square Y10. Open daily 6am-midnight. Y6.)*

NEAR TIANSHUI: GANGU 甘谷

2hr. west of Tianshui. Buses to Gangu (2hr., every hr., Y6) run from the Qincheng local bus station in Tianshui, on Dazhong Lu. Return buses to Tianshui depart every hour until 6pm. A taxi costs approx. Y100.

Gangu's wheat fields and rolling countryside stretch out beneath **Great Statue Mountain** (dàxiàng shān; 大像山), a temple complex that hugs a high ridge above the small, tourist-free town. *(Open daily sunrise-sunset. Y10. Don't let them sell you the extra temple admission ticket; it's not needed for entrance.)* It takes no more than a few hours to explore the temple, but accommodations are cheap and transportation options plentiful, making Gangu a relaxing overnight stop on the way to Lanzhou.

Virtually the only place to stay is the **Gangu Hotel ❶** (gāngû fàndiàn; 甘谷饭店), which is accessible by taxi (Y5 from the bus station, Y2 from the train station). Located on the edge of the town center, a 40-minute walk from Great Statue Mountain, the Gangu boasts a helpful staff. Dorm beds have newly painted walls, concrete floors, and one-inch thick mattresses; there are no common showers, but the bathrooms are sanitary and well kept. Other rooms have proper mattresses, TV, phone, and bath. (Singles Y24; doubles Y15, with bath Y43 and up; triples Y13.)

The best place to eat is the **Gangu Restaurant** (gāngû dàjiûdiàn; 甘谷大酒店), a multi-floor restaurant. Walk due south from the Gangu Hotel with the mountains at your back; after about 50m, you'll see a blue glass high-rise on the left. Those who miss home can enjoy the Chinese version of french fries (tûdòu kuài; 土豆块; Y4-5). For breakfast, vendors along the main street in town sell delicious sticky rice and dates (Y2).

JIAYUGUAN 嘉峪关 ☎0937

Despite the town's grim historical reputation as the Ming dynasty's final frontier, modern-day Jiayuguan is a pleasant enough place to spend a slow-paced day or two. Jiayuguan Fort, which marks the end of the Great Wall, is an impressive reminder of the splendor and limits of Imperial China. Other sights, including the Wei and Jin Tombs and the July 1st Glacier, also draw visitors. Jiayuguan, although not quite a must-see city, still makes for a worthwhile and interesting stop.

NORTHWEST

TRANSPORTATION

Flights: Jiayuguan Airport (jiāyùguān jīchǎng; 嘉峪关机场), 11km northeast of town. CAAC shuttle buses depart 1½hr. before flights (20min., Y10; don't let them overcharge). From the **CAAC ticket office,** 1 Xinhua Nan Lu (☎622 6237), about 50m before the central traffic circle, opposite the post office. Open M-Sa 8:30am-noon and 2:30-5:30pm. To **Xi'an** (M, W, F, and Su 5pm; Y1010) via **Lanzhou** (Y730). Flights are less frequent in winter.

Trains: Jiayuguan Train Station (jiāyùguān huǒchē zhàn; 嘉峪关火车站; ☎631 5074), on Yingbin Xi Lu, several km southwest of town, accessible by pedicab or minibus #1. Purchase tickets 3-5 days in advance if possible. Open 24hr. To: **Beijing** (45hr., 1-2 per day, Y466); **Chengdu** (38hr., daily, Y324); **Shanghai** (52hr., daily, Y545); **Xi'an** (13hr.,

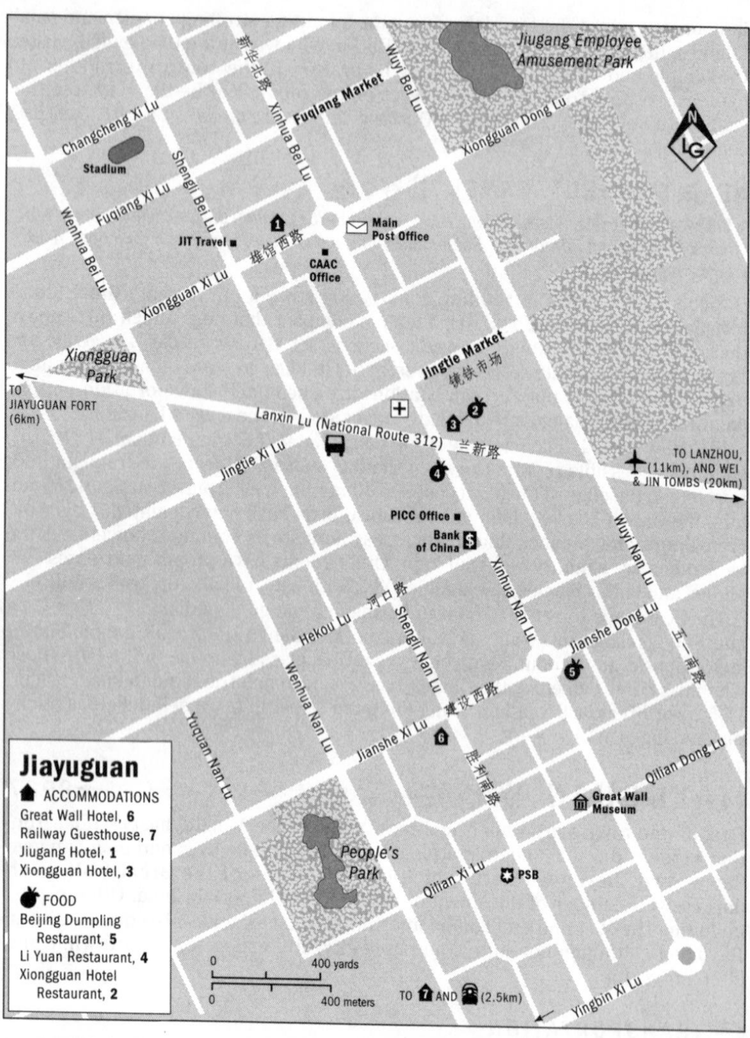

6 per day, Y185). All west-bound trains (10 per day) stop at: **Liuyuan** (6hr., Y22); **Turpan** (14hr., Y125); and **Ürümqi** (19hr., Y153).

Buses: A **Gansu PICC insurance ticket** (Y30) is required to purchase bus tickets in Gansu. The **PICC office** (zhōngguó rénmín bâoxiân; 中国人民保险, ☎622 6362), 36 Xinhua Nan Lu, is about 100m to the right of the Bank of China; look for the "PICC LIFE" sign. Open M-F 8:30am-12:30pm and 2:30-6:30pm, Sa 10am-4pm. **Jiayuguan Bus Station** (jiāyùguān qìchē zhàn; 嘉峪关汽车站; ☎622 5528), on the corner of Jingtie Xi Lu and Shengli Nan Lu. To: **Dunhuang** (5-8hr., 4 per day 9am-1pm, Y45-66); **Lanzhou** (15hr.; 4 per day 3-6pm; hard seat Y80, sleeper Y130); and **Zhangye** (6hr., 5 per day, Y30.6) via **Xining**.

NORTHWEST

Local Transportation: There are 4 **minibus** routes. Bus fare Y0.5-1. Minibuses **#1** and **#2** run along Xinhua Lu, from the train station to the center of town; **#3** runs west from the Jiayuguan Hotel along the Gansu Highway; **#4** runs southeast-northwest.

Taxis: Base fare Y4-6 (should be metered within the city). **Pedicabs** cost about Y3 around town.

Bike Rental: A stand outside Great Wall Hotel rents bikes for Y3 per hr., deposit Y40. The **Xiongguan Hotel** also rents bikes. Y1 per hr., deposit Y10 or a student ID.

ORIENTATION AND PRACTICAL INFORMATION

The small city of Jiayuguan lies on a tilted grid sliced horizontally by the **Gansu Highway** (National Route 312; sānyāoèr guódào; 312国道), also called **Lanxin Lu** (兰新路), which heads to Jiayuguan Fort in the west. **Xinhua Lu** (新华路) runs from northwest to southeast, meeting **Xiongguan Lu** (雄馆路) at the main traffic circle. The road proceeds south to intersect **Jingtie Lu** (镜铁路), **Jianshe Lu** (建设路), and **Yingbin Lu** (迎宾路) at another small traffic circle. The bus station is at the intersection of Route 312, **Jingtie Xi Lu,** and **Shengli Lu** (胜利路). The train station is in the southwest corner of town, at the west end of Yingbin Xi Lu. Almost all services are within a 10-minute walk of the hotels; none of the far-flung sights are accessible by public transportation.

Travel Agencies: Tours are offered through two formal travel agencies, most large hotels, and any taxi driver; ask at your hotel for the best rates. **Great Wall Travel Service** (gānsū jiāyùguān chángchéng læxíngshè; 甘肃嘉峪关长城旅行社), has branches at the Xiongguan (☎628 2226) and Great Wall Hotels (☎622 6568). Friendly, English-speaking staff arranges one-day tours of Jiayuguan's sights, including a stop in nearby Jiuquan, for Y80 per person, and one-day trips to the July 1st Glacier (Y150 plus, depending on demand). Open daily 8:30am-10pm; off-season 8:30am-6pm. **Gansu Jiayuguan International Travel Service (JIT)** (gānsù jiāyùguān guójì læxíngshè; 甘肃嘉峪关国际旅行社, ☎622 6598), 2 Shengli Bei Lu, 2nd fl., a 5min. walk west of the Jiayuguan Hotel. Pass the government building on Xiongguan Xi Lu and turn right on Shengli Bei Lu; it's to the right of the CITS restaurant. Knowledgeable, multilingual staff is used to dealing with individual travelers. Arranges one-day tours of local sights (Y40) and trips to the July 1st Glacier (Y300, with at least 5 participants). Open 24hr.

Bank of China: On Xinhua Nan Lu, just south of the PICC building. The center counter exchanges traveler's checks. Open M-F 9:30am-5:30pm, Sa-Su 10am-4pm.

PSB: On the corner of Qilian Xi Lu and Shengli Nan Lu, in the south of town (☎631 1043). Visa extensions available. Open M-F 8:30am-12:30pm and 2:30-6:30pm.

Internet Access: In the **China Telecom** building to the left of the post office. Y5 per hr. Open daily 10am-10pm.

Post and Telecommunications: The **post office** (☎622 6255) is opposite Jiayuguan Hotel, on the central traffic circle. EMS and Poste Restante. Open daily 8:30am-7pm. IDD service to left of post office counters. **Postal Code:** 735100.

ACCOMMODATIONS

As of July 2001, only a few relatively high-end hotels accept foreigners; those still offering budget rooms are busy making renovations that will push up their prices. Per city regulations, hotels charge an extra service fee of Y1 per person per day.

Xiongguan Hotel (xióngguān bīnguân; 雄关宾馆; ☎622 5115), at the intersection of Xinhua Nan Lu and the Gansu Highway, near the Traffic Hotel. Accommodating staff (some speak English) and an excellent Sichuanese restaurant in back. Average rooms have cement floors and sparkling common baths. Single travelers can pay by the bed. Hot water 7-10am, 1-3pm, and 8pm-1am. Deposit Y100. 4-bed dorms Y18; 3-bed dorms Y20; doubles with bath Y120-380. ❶

Jiugang Hotel (jiûgāng bīnguân; 酒钢宾馆; front building ☎671 3662; back building ☎671 4425), around the corner from the Jiayuguan Hotel. The Jiugang's front building has doubles and triples with sparkling tile floors and hot water 7:30-9am, noon-2:30pm, and 9pm-midnight. The back building has upscale rooms with tubs, 24hr. hot water, and IDD service. Deposit is twice room rate. Front building: 3-bed dorms without shower Y15; 2-bed dorms with bath Y30; singles with bath Y60. Back building: singles and doubles with bath Y220-360. Tour groups get Y40 discounts on back building rooms, so bargain. ❶

Railway Guesthouse (tiêdào bīnguân; 铁道宾馆; ☎631 1234), 1 Yingbin Xi Lu, across from train station. Out of the way, but 10min. from the city center by minibus. Great rooms reminiscent of Western-style motels. Singles Y120, doubles (individuals may pay by bed) Y180-280, all with clean but small attached baths. ❷

Great Wall Hotel (chángchéng bīnguân; 长城宾馆,☎622 5288), 6 Jianshe Xi Lu. A luxury fortress equipped with business center, sauna, massage parlor, and more. Make reservations a few days in advance. Deposit 20% room rate. Doubles Y280-980; triples Y240. 10-20% discounts possible for students, the elderly, and groups. ❹

Jiayuguan Hotel (jiāyùguān bīnguân; 嘉峪关宾馆; ☎622 6231), on the corner of Xiongguan Xi Lu and Xinhua Bei Lu, kitty-corner from the post office. The "old" building used to house cheap dorms and rooms, but will soon be the "new" building with luxurious Y400 rooms. The old "new" building has rooms starting at Y380. ❺

FOOD

Restaurants and vendors serve up Han and Hui foods at **Jingtie Market** (jìngtiê shìchâng; 镜铁市场) and its larger counterpart, **Fuqiang Market** (fùqiáng shìchâng; 富强市场), above the post office off Xinhua Bei Lu. Fill your belly with 10 different parts of lamb, seasoned and skewered to perfection over an open grill. Sample everything from hot noodles to excellent roast meat (Y8-10) to seasoned and roasted round breads (kâobîngzi; 烤饼子; Y1).

Li Yuan Restaurant (línyuán jiûdiàn; 林苑酒店; ☎628 6918), 34 Xinhua Nan Lu, next to the PICC building. Great food, efficient service, and big windows that overlook the street. Most dishes Y15 and up. ❷

Beijing Dumpling Restaurant (bêijīng jiâozi guân; 北京饺子馆), at the intersection of Xinhua Nan Lu and Jianshe Lu. This little spot, part of a local chain, serves up 30 choices of delicious dumplings at dirt cheap prices—most cost Y1-2 per liâng (half-dozen), one person can eat about 3-6 liâng. ❶

Xiongguan Hotel Restaurant, in the back of the hotel. Top-notch Sichuanese fare for reasonable prices (most dishes Y10-25). Entertainment comes in the form of the myriad Chinese businessmen going wild with the karaoke machine. ❷

SIGHTS

Most visit the sights by pedicab or taxi. For a three-hour excursion to the Jiayuguan Fort and Overhanging Great Wall, expect to pay about Y60 round-trip. In general, use the standard of Y20 per hour. It's best to negotiate the price in advance.

JIAYUGUAN FORT (jiāyùguān chénglóu; 嘉峪关城楼). One of the most photographed spots in northwest China, Jiayuguan Fort stands in a desert against a backdrop of snow-capped peaks and awe-inspiring sunset views. Built in 1372, the fort is traditionally considered to be the end of the 2000km Great Wall, although at various times the wall extended several hundred kilometers farther west. Jiayuguan consists of a 10m-high, 733m-long outer wall. After entering a small gate in the east, visitors find a set of inner walls guarded by watch towers. Here, an "entrapping rampart" once trapped and annihilated raiders. Today, those who force their way into the inner stronghold find a large open square with camel rides and snack stands. The ramps on the north side of each gate once allowed teams of horses onto the wall, enabling mounted archers to speed about. It is said that the masons who were conscripted to build the fort were of such high caliber that they calculated in advance the exact number of bricks needed for the entire structure. Somehow, one brick was left unused. The odd-brick-out still rests on the ledge, taunting the math whiz who forgot to carry the 1. *(Although you can bike here in 30-45min. on the Gansu Highway (turn right at the posted sign and then left at the next posted sign), the 6km trip is best accomplished by pedicab or taxi (one-way Y15-20, round-trip Y30-35). The ticket office is to the right. Open daily 9am-9pm; in winter 8am-7pm. Y40, students with valid ID Y20.)*

OVERHANGING GREAT WALL (xuánbì chángchéng; 悬壁长城). To fill up a day in the area, take a taxi (round-trip Y15) or a 30-minute bike ride to the Overhanging Great Wall, a 750m peripheral defense wall extending from Jiayuguan Fort along the cliffs of the Heishan "Black Mountains" Gorge. Consisting of two main lookout towers, this section of the wall offers a panoramic view of surreal black wasteland and lifeless mountains extending hundreds of kilometers to the northwest. *(From the Jiayuguan Fort parking lot, exit left; make your first left onto a small paved road. You should see the wall to your left as you bike toward the entrance. Open daily 8:30am-8pm. Y8.)*

FIRST BEACON TOWER (dìyī fēnghuǒ tái; 第一烽火台). The only surviving portion of the original Jiayuguan Fort is the beacon tower, once used to relay warnings with windborne smoke signals. Fragments of the wall are scattered in the surrounding area, including the First Beacon Tower. The walk from the main complex to the tower entails crossing a main road and provides not-so-stunning views of Jiayuguan's industrial center. *(7km southwest of Jiayuguan Fort.)*

WEI AND JIN TOMBS (wèijìn mù; 魏晋墓). Thousands of these tombs, dating from AD 220-420, dot the desert surrounding Jiayuguan. Only one is open to the public, but it is quite interesting. There are three chambers inside the tomb, each progressively smaller than the last. The first is meant to serve as an "office" for the tomb's occupants; paintings of hunting scenes adorn the walls. The second chamber represents domestic life, with one side devoted to male images and the other to female ones. The final chamber holds the coffins themselves. While the ouside of the tomb has been slightly fixed up, the paintings are untouched and remain remarkably vibrant. A small museum by the ticket office displays items excavated from the site. *(20km east of Jiayuguan. A taxi costs Y50-60 round-trip or Y35 each way by meter. The folks living in the ticket office claim to welcome visitors 24hr. a day, but you might want to visit during daylight hours. Admission Y30, guides Y25.)*

DAYTRIP FROM JIAYUGUAN: JULY 1ST GLACIER

The July 1st Glacier (qīyī bīngchuān; 七一冰川), 120 km south of Jiayuguan in the Qilian Mountains, boasts impressive 65m-high ice walls, caves, and views of the snowy mountains. Generally accessible from April to September, the glacier is best visited from June to August (when clouds are least likely to obscure the peak). The cheapest way to go is to take a tour (Y150-300 per person for a one-day trip, depending on the size of the group). The drive is at least two hours, which leaves about 5-6 hours at the glacier. It's also possible to go by taxi, although many drivers are unwilling to go. The asking price for daytrips (approx. 3-4hr. of driving) is Y600 for taxis with good clearance and power, and Y800 for 10-person minibuses; this allows for a good 6 hours of climbing or hiking. The best option is to arrange a driver through your hotel, which can refer you to someone experienced in making trips out to the glacier. Even in the summer, take warm clothes and some food, as both hiking and road conditions can change quickly.

ZHANGYE 张掖

☎0936

Zhangye was once one of the most important Silk Road outposts along the Hexi Corridor, a narrow strip of fertile land running between the Qilian Mountains to the south and the Gobi and Budain Jaran Deserts to the north. However, the relics of Zhangye's rich history have been for the most part swallowed up by monotonous block housing, commercial centers, and industrial smokestacks that crowd a skyline once dominated by pagodas and towers. Part of a day, however, can be easily spent at a few sites within the city, most notably the giant reclining Buddha at Big Buddha Temple; Zhangye serves best as a transportation hub for the gorgeous temple town of Matisi, set in the foothills of the Tibetan Plateau.

TRANSPORTATION

Trains: Zhangye Train Station (zhāngyē huǒchē zhàn; 张掖火车站; ☎822 6749), 8km northwest of the town center, is accessible by bus #1. Open 24hr. All trains running between **Lanzhou** and **Ürümqi** stop here. Trains heading westward are mostly in the early evening with a few in the morning; eastbound trains depart throughout the day.

Buses: South Bus Station (nánguān qìchē zhàn; 南关汽车站; ☎821 3554 or 821 3449), on Huancheng Nan Lu, a 5min. walk from the Zhangye Hotel. Open daily 6:30am-7:30pm. To: **Dunhuang** (10hr., 5:30pm, Y76); **Jiayuguan** (4hr., 4 per day 8-11am, Y31); **Lanzhou** (10hr., 8am, Y80); **Matisi** (2hr., 8am and 3pm, Y8.5); **Xining** (12hr., 7:30am and 5:30pm, Y45.5). **East Bus Station** (qìchē dōng zhàn; 汽车东站; ☎821 4073) is accessible via bus #9. Open daily 7am-8:30pm. To **Dunhuang** (10hr.; 5:30pm; hard seat Y76, hard sleeper Y123) and **Lanzhou** (11hr., 7:20am and 8:20am, Y70). Both stations clearly service more buses than the official schedule claims.

Local Buses: Bus #1 connects the South Bus Station, Zhangye Hotel, Drum Tower, and train station; **#9** circles the south and east bus stations as well as the Drum Tower.

NORTHWEST

ORIENTATION AND PRACTICAL INFORMATION

The city is centered around its **Drum Tower** (zhōnggǔ lóu; 钟鼓楼). From here, **Bei** (北), **Nan** (南), **Dong** (东), and **Xi** (西) **Dajie** (大街)—or, North, South, East, and West Street—emanate. **Xianfu Nan Jie** (xiànfǔ nán jiē; 县府南街), home to the Zhangye Hotel, provides access to the city's major sights, running north from **Huancheng Nan Lu** (环城南路) to **Xi Dajie.**

Travel Agency: CITS, 56 Xianfu Nan Jie (☎821 3505), in the lobby of the Zhangye Hotel.

Bank of China: On Dong Dajie, a 5min. walk from the Drum Tower, on the left side of the street. Exchanges traveler's checks. Open M-F 8am-noon and 2:30-6pm. A more convenient option is a smaller branch on Xianfu Nan Jie, just north of the Zhangye Hotel. Exchanges currency. Open daily 8am-6pm.

Internet Access: Century Internet Bar (shìjì wǎngbā; 世纪网吧), on Dong Dajie, just past the Bank of China. Y3 per hr. Open daily 8am-midnight.

Post Office: On Xi Dajie, a 3min. walk west of the Drum Tower, on the right side of the street. Open daily 8am-8pm. **Postal code**: 734000.

ACCOMMODATIONS AND FOOD

Zhangye has fairly limited but decent budget accommodations for foreigners. For food, head to the **pedestrian mall,** north of the intersection between Xianfu Nanjie and Xi Dajie, where small restaurants and vendors serve up tasty treats.

Zhangye Hotel (zhāngyē bīnguân; 张掖宾馆, ☎821 2601, ext. 6289), 56 Xianfu Nan Jie. From the South Bus Station, turn right on Huancheng Nan Lu; take the first right onto Xianfu Nan Jie; the lobby is 2min. ahead on the right. Bright, clean dorms with mopped linoleum floors that overlook a garden. Rear building has more luxurious rooms and a CITS office. 3-bed dorms Y18; singles with bath Y160; doubles with bath Y90-480. ❶

Ganzhou Hotel (gānzhōu bīnguân; 甘州宾馆), 11 Nan Dajie, south of the Drum Tower, on the right. The North Building (bêilóu; 北楼) has cheaper rooms, freshly painted and pretty clean. Shiny attached baths. 3-bed dorms Y25; doubles Y90-380; quads Y160. ❶

SIGHTS

BIG BUDDHA TEMPLE (dàfó sì; 大佛寺). Built in 1098 and restored during the Qing dynasty, this temple houses China's largest reclining Buddha (over 34m tall). The temple also includes an array of guardian arhats surrounding the torpedo-like shape of the Holy One. Several small art galleries and a mediocre archaeological survey of Zhangye's past are behind the temple. The **Earth Pavilion** (tû tâ; 土塔) behind the complex is worth a peek, with an interesting mix of Indo-Tibetan *stupa* forms and traditional flying-eave Chinese pagoda styles. *(On Minzhu Xi Jie, behind the Zhangye Hotel. Open daily 7:30am-6:30pm. Y20.)*

WOOD PAGODA (mù tǎ; 木塔). This 31m-tall, nine-story pagoda makes for a pleasant climb to the top. Built in the 6th century and restored in 1925, the pagoda now competes with a high-rise building just behind. The small **Wanshou Temple** (wànshòu sì; 万寿寺) is also part of the complex. *(On Xianfu Nan Jie, just north of the Zhangye Hotel. Open daily 8am-6pm. Y5.)*

XILAI TEMPLE (xīlái sì; 西来寺). The tiny temple is perhaps more interesting for the throngs of old people who come to pray and socialize than for its interior. Several old monks will certainly offer to show you around the various nooks and crannies. *(From the Wooden Pagoda complex, turn right on Minzhu Xi Jie; make the first left onto a small umarked alley called Xilaisi Jie; the temple is on the right. Open daily sunrise-sunset. Free.)*

NEAR ZHANGYE: MATISI

Matisi (literally "Horse Hoof Temple"; mâtí sì; 马蹄寺) boasts the area's main attraction, the 33rd Heaven Grottoes, and other smaller temples. The temples are built into a vein of sheer cliffs at the foothills of the 2300m-high **Qilian Mountains.** The surrounding landscape is breathtaking; several large waterfalls cascade from the ice-capped peaks above, winding down through cool pine forests and expanses of valley wildflowers. The hike along the ridge above the 33rd Heaven Grottoes ends at the largest waterfall in the area. Many of the Tibetan villagers in the area rent horses and will gladly guide visitors to the most beautiful spots.

The **33rd Heaven Grottoes** (sānshísān tiān shíkū; 三十三天石窟) are fine examples of Tibetan art. Richly detailed tapestries and sculptures depict peaceful, smiling Buddhas and the frightening guardians of the Southern Sea Realm. The name of the grottoes refers to the highest level of heavenly existence short of enlightenment and Buddhahood (see **Tibetan Buddhism,** p. 801). Narrow, tunnel-like passages through the rock give access to the five levels of caves, which overlook two white *stupas* to the west. Look for the horse hoof imprint in stone that gives the temple its name, proudly displayed in a glass case on the floor of the first temple.

Small hostels of comparable price and quality line the main road just after the 33rd Heaven Temple complex. A good bet is the **Golden Horse Hostel** (jīnmâ læshè; 金马旅社), just across from the two *stupas* up on the hill. Rooms have clean sheets and nice brick floors (4-bed dorms Y15). Several **encampments** at the top of the road provide accommodation and entertainment in Tibetan-style tents at the foot of the mountains. This is a good way to experience a bit of Tibetan culture, even if the area has a touristy feel. (Accommodation and food Y50-100 per person.)

Buses (2hr., 8am and 3pm, Y8.5) go from Zhangye South Station to Matisi. Buses run more frequently to **Nangu** (nángû; 南古; every 30-45min. 7am-3pm) and stop near Matisi. Regardless, you're likely to be let off in Mati town, 9km from the temple. Taxi vans cost about Y10-15 to go the rest of the way, kindly stopping to let you pay a Y15 area admission fee. Return buses stop back in town about every 30 minutes until 5:30pm. Taxi vans back to Zhangye cost about Y80. The temple is open daily from 8am to 6pm. Admission is Y4 to the site and Y4 to climb the caves.

DUNHUANG 敦煌 ☎0937

The junction of the southern and northern trade routes that curve around the arid Tarim Basin, Dunhuang was one of ancient China's major trading posts. In the 2nd century BC, the ambitious Han Emperor Wudi incorporated the city into China's empire. Hungry for more territory, he sent General Zhang Qian west to exploit tribal rivalries and forge allies for his next offensive. After eight years, the general returned and reported that local leaders were reluctant to make war but eager to trade. So, caravans laden with precious silk plodded from the oasis of Dunhuang across the trans-Eurasian Silk Road. Dunhuang's location on this route made it attractive to up-and-coming tribes; the Huns, Jie, Xianbei, Qiang, Tubo (Tibetan), Tangut, Mongols, and Uighurs all tried wresting the outpost from Han control.

Lately, Dunhuang has profited from its past by promoting its fantastic desert scenery and the Mogao Grottoes' unparalleled Buddhist cave art. Dunhuang is a relaxing, beautiful area that easily merits a stay of three or four days. Excellent beer gardens, restaurants, and night markets abound, and the surrounding dunes and Crescent Lake are simply stunning.

TRANSPORTATION

Flights: Dunhuang Airport (dünhuáng fēijīchâng; 敦煌飞机场), 13km east of the city. An unreliable shuttle service is offered by a private contractor, but CAAC advises travelers to take a taxi (20min., Y20-30) instead. **CAAC ticket office** (☎882 2389), on Yangguan Dong Lu, near Xinhua Bookstore. Open daily 8-11:30am and 3-6pm. Beware that many Dunhuang hotels pay drivers to bring them potential guests. To: **Beijing** (daily July-Aug., otherwise Su-M, W, and F; Y1650) via **Lanzhou** (Y940); **Ürümqi** (M-Sa, Y650); **Xi'an** (daily, Y1360).

Trains: Dunhuang Train Station (dünhuáng huōchē zhàn; 敦煌火车站; ☎(0937) 557 2995), 2½hr. north of Dunhuang. Frequent buses, taxis, and minibuses to **Liuyuan** leave from the Dunhuang Bus Station. It's usually more difficult to book tickets for trains heading east. For longer trips, make arrangements 2-3 days in advance. Schedules change seasonally; check with John's Cafe, CITS, or Charley at Charley John's Cafe for up-to-date information. Y30 "station fee" for hard sleepers, Y50 for soft sleepers. The ticket office is on Yangguan Dong Lu, past the CAAC office, on the right (look for the Chinese sign 火车站). They also charge the station fee, but you avoid the commission you

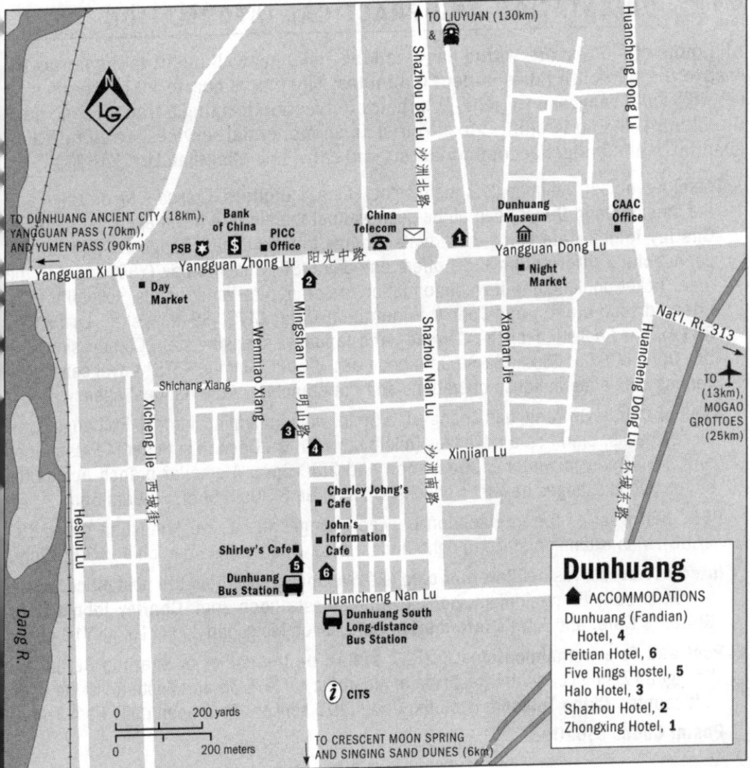

would pay Charley's, John's, or CITS. Open daily 8am-noon and 3:30-5:30pm. To: **Beijing** (40hr., 9:58am, Y544); **Lanzhou** (20hr., 11 per day, Y149-257); **Ürümqi** (13-15hr., 9 per day, Y181) via **Turpan** (12hr.); **Xi'an** (36hr., 4 per day, Y212-301).

Buses: For long-distance travel beyond Liuyuan, most foreigners need a Gansu Insurance Ticket (Y30), available at the **PICC office** (zhōngguó rénmín bǎoxiǎn gōngsī; 中国人民保险公司), 12 Yangguan Zhong Lu (☎882 7469), near the Bank of China. Open M-F 8:30am-noon and 3-6:30pm. Most buses have a side luggage compartment; be prepared to have a wet pack if you leave it on the roof; short but furious rainstorms are frequent in the summer. There are 2 bus stations diagonally across from each other on Mingshan Lu. The **Dunhuang Bus Station** (dūnhuáng qìchē zhàn; 敦煌汽车站; ☎882 2174), on the west side of the intersection, is open daily 6:30am-10:30pm. To: **Golmud** (10hr., 2 per day, Y60-98); **Jiayuguan** (5hr., 2 per day, Y44-71); **Lanzhou** (22hr.; 2 per day; hard seat Y132, sleeper Y191); **Liuyuan** (2½hr., 8 per day, Y15); **Xining** (22hr., daily, Y112-181); **Zhangye** (10hr., daily, Y73-118). **Dunhuang Long-distance Bus Station** (dūnhuáng chángtú qìchē zhàn; 敦煌长途汽车站; ☎882 3072, ext. 8115), on the east side of the road, has slower buses. Open daily 6am-10pm. Buses to **Lanzhou** make frequent stops in all major towns along the way.

Local Transportation: Taxis are not metered. Pedicabs, minibuses, and motorbikes abound, but walking or renting a bike is easier. Most hotels offer **bike rental,** Y1 per hr.

ORIENTATION AND PRACTICAL INFORMATION

All points of interest are within easy walking distance; walking from the far northeast to the far south takes under 20 minutes. The city is quartered by **Shazhou Lu** (沙州路) and **Yangguan Lu** (阳关路), their intersection forming a traffic circle near the China Telecom building. Most tourist and commercial services are along Yangguan Lu, while budget accommodations and cafes line **Mingshan Lu** (鸣山路).

Travel Agencies: Dunhuang's 3 main sights (Mogao Grottoes, Crescent Moon Lake, and the Singing Sand Dunes) can all be seen without the aid of a travel agency. Charley at **Charley John's Cafe** helps individuals arrange trips to distant Yangguan and Yumenguan. **John's Information Cafe** offers one-day (Y30) and two-day (Y80) tours of the area. Ticket booking and travel information are offered at larger hotels, several tourist-oriented restaurants, and John's Information Cafe. **CITS,** 39 Mingshan Lu (☎882 3312), has English-, French-, German-, and Japanese-speaking staff. Commission Y30-50. Open M-F 8am-6pm, Sa-Su 9am-noon and 3-5pm. Similar "CITS" travel services in various hotels are in-house operations and not branches of the national agency.

Bank of China: On Yangguan Zhong Lu, a 5min. walk from Mingshan Lu. Exchanges traveler's checks. Credit card advances (minimum Y1000). Open in summer M-F 8am-noon and 3-6:30pm; in winter 8:30am-noon and 2:30-6pm. A smaller branch across the street also exchanges traveler's checks. Open M-Sa 8:30am-6pm, Su 9am-5pm.

PSB: Just west of the intersection between Yangguan Lu and Mingshan Lu (☎882 2660). Visa extension office to right of main gate. Open M-F 8am-noon and 3-6:30pm.

Internet Access: A small **Internet cafe** is a few doors down from the post office. Y6 per hr. Open daily 8am-midnight, but they often siesta noon-3pm. **Charley John's Cafe, Shirley's Cafe,** and **John's Information Cafe,** all on Mingshan Zhong Lu, all Y10 per hr.

Post and Telecommunications: (☎882 1204), on the corner of Shazhou Bei Lu and Yangguan Zhong Lu, on the west side of the traffic circle. EMS and Poste Restante at the left counter. **China Telecom** is on the 2nd fl. IDD service. Both open daily 8am-7pm.

Postal Code: 736200.

NORTHWEST

ACCOMMODATIONS

Most affordable hotels here are on **Mingshan Lu.** Like almost everything here, accommodation costs are inflated. Prices are negotiable when visitors are rare.

Dunhuang (Fandian) Hotel (dūnhuáng fàndiàn; 敦煌饭店), 16 Mingshan Lu (☎882 7588), not to be confused with the expensive Dunhuang (Binguan) Hotel. Newly renovated, friendly service, breezy rooms, and clean baths. 24hr. hot water. Deposit Y200. 3-5 bed dorms with fan Y25-40; communal doubles with A/C and bath Y320-360. ❶

Five Rings Hostel (wǔhuán bīnguǎn;五环宾馆; ☎882 2620), on Mingshan Lu, across from the Feitian Hotel. Enthusiastic staff, pleasant rooms, and great prices. Dorms Y12-25; doubles Y60, with bath Y140; triples with bath Y150. ❶

Feitian Hotel (fēitiān bīnguǎn; 飞天宾馆; ☎882 2337), on Mingshan Lu, behind John's Information Cafe. Friendly staff. Pricey rooms with huge baths. Clean dorms are basic. 8-bed dorms Y20; 3-bed dorms Y30; doubles Y320-480. Discounts possible. ❶

Halo Hotel (fóguāng dàjiǔdiàn; 佛光大酒店), 15 Mingshan Lu (☎882 5040), opposite the Dunhuang Hotel. English-speaking staff members and great service. Deposit Y50. Doubles Y70-180; triples Y75; quads Y80. Discounts possible. ❶

Shazhou Hotel (shāzhōu fàndiàn; 沙洲饭店; ☎882 2380), on Mingshan Bei Lu. Bright, airy, and well-maintained rooms. Deposit Y100. Doubles Y60; with bath Y280-380. ❶

Zhongxing Hotel (zhōngxīng bīnguǎn; 中兴宾馆), 2 Yangguan Dong Lu (☎882 6488), opposite the post office, in the east end of town. Wide range of rooms, 24hr. hot water, and prompt service. Deposit Y100. Doubles Y60, with bath and A/C Y240-380. ❶

FOOD

Chinese, Muslim, Western, and fusion restaurants are everywhere in Dunhuang. The town is starting to resemble Yangshuo, the backpacker mecca outside Guilin, and signs indicating "cafes" are ubiquitous. Fruit pancakes (Y3), chilled yogurt (Y2.5), fresh fruit juices, and attempts at chocolate soufflé are the norm.

Perhaps the liveliest center for eats is the **night market** to the south of Yangguan Dong Lu, in a rather grand open-air courtyard roughly opposite the museum. The market brims with stalls selling roasted chickens (dàpán jī; 大盘鸡; Y40-45), Chinese-style hamburgers, dumplings, hotpot, pastries, beer, and assorted teas. Market activity peaks around 7:30pm and lasts until 12:30am, but some stalls are open during the day as well. For an interesting culinary experience, try the **donkey meat yellow noodles** (lǘròu huángmiàn; 驴肉黄面; Y4), a local specialty.

Charley John's Cafe (☎883 3039), a 5min. walk from the post office, on the left side of the street. Owner Charley is affable and serves up excellent Chinese and fusion food at excellent prices. Try the "Pakistan Sandwich" (Y6). Internet Y10 per hr., bike rental Y1 per hr. Charley also books train and bus tickets (Y30 commission). His sister runs **Shirley's Cafe** across the street (☎882 6387). Same prices, hours, and services. Both places have a considerable local following. Open daily 7:30am-midnight. ❶

John's Information Cafe (☎282 4816), next to the Feitian Hotel. A modern Silk Road refueling stop for travelers, with franchises in Kashgar, Ürümqi, and Turpan. The food is acceptable though a bit overpriced; the sandwiches are unimpressive, but the fries are mighty good (Y6). Manager Jian Jun Wang can procure bus tickets for no commission, and air and train tickets for Y40 per ticket. IDD calls cost a one-time Y2 fee. Internet Y20 per hr., bike rental Y2 per hr. Open daily 7:30am-midnight. ❶

SIGHTS

There is little to see in Dunhuang itself. The dilapidated **Dunhuang Museum** (dūnhuáng bówùguǎn; 敦煌博物馆; ☎882 2981), on Yangguang Dong Lu, is not the most exciting place in the world and could probably do with a little dusting. Nonetheless, it has some interesting exhibits—the ones on the Jade Gate Pass, Sun Pass, and the Han Dynasty Great Wall are worth a peek if you can't make it to the actual sites. The MIG-15 fighter jet sitting in the parking lot is apparently something of an unwanted gift from the city government. *(Open daily 8am-6:30pm. Y10.)*

MOGAO GROTTOES (mògāo shíkū; 莫高石窟)

25km southeast of Dunhuang. ***Minibuses*** *cruise to the grottoes along Mingshan Lu (daily 7:30-10:30am, Y45). For the return trip, the same men wait around the parking lot area next to the hotel until 6pm or so. John's Cafe has a daily bus (8am, returns at noon, Y10 one-way), but this may arrive too late for the English tour. Open daily 8am-5pm. The most well-preserved* ***caves*** *require a Y60-240 per person surcharge to enter. Caves open to the public are rotated periodically so as to minimize exposure. The most worthwhile are caves #45 and 57, which drip with colors, amazingly bright after hundreds of years (Y60 per person per cave). Arrange at the front ticket office for access and a guide. Arrive at 8am and keep pressing the ticket office to get a guide and tour; many tourists complain of having been told to wait, only to discover that the English tour had already left.* ***Guides*** *are available 8:30-9:30am and 2-4:30pm, but the tours only cover 10-15 caves. The quality of the guides varies widely; some know neither English nor the history of the grottoes. French-, German-, Russian-, and Japanese-speaking guides are also available. Chinese-speaking* ***tours*** *Y66. Because the morning tours end at*

NORTHWEST

noon and the guides siesta until 2pm, it is best not to wait around too long for a tour; otherwise, guides might limit the number of caves visited. ***Tour-hopping*** *to spend more time at your favorite caves is also an option.* ***Photography*** *is prohibited; cameras and bags must be stored to the right of the entrance for Y4. Light in the caves is poor at times.* ***Flashlights*** *are available for rent for Y13, with a Y10 deposit; weak and heavy, these ancient tubes are ineffective; bring your own with fresh batteries (available in town at many small vendors and at an electronics store on Mingshan Lu, near John's Information Cafe; Y1.5-6 per battery).* ***Admission*** *to grottoes Y100, students Y50; Chinese tour Y80/40.*

According to legend, in AD 366 an Eastern Jin dynasty monk Le Zun saw thousands of Buddhas—manifested as rays of light—glimmering from the cliff shafts of the Sanwei Mountain gully one night. He immediately decided to use a cave in the cliffs to honor the Buddhas. A few years later, another monk passed by and, seeing the first monk hard at work, began a second cave. Eventually, everyone joined in.

The clay of Mogao, unlike the cliff boulders of grottoes farther east, is ill-suited to large carvings, so artists created stucco figurines and frescoes. Over the next 11 dynasties, more than a thousand niches were created; nearly 500 remain, containing an astounding 2150 statues and 43,000 murals. Most of the original reds, greens, ochres, and blues have ionized to a dark black, lending the murals an austere appearance. The themes are overwhelmingly Buddhist, but scenes also illustrate Confucian virtues, historical events, landscapes, and daily life. In addition to its endless numbers of Buddhas, *arhats*, and *bodhisattvas*, Mogao is unique for its "flying *apsaras*," hovering angelic Buddhas with fluttering drapery. This trademark has even made its way onto the tails of China Northwest Airlines' jets. During the Cultural Revolution, the caves escaped unharmed, thanks to the protection of Premier Zhou Enlai. In 1987, Mogao was named a UNESCO World Heritage Site.

Today, Dunhuang artwork in China and around the world (one archaeologist donated his "findings" to Harvard University's Fogg Museum) has created a field in art history and religion known as Dunhuangology. The **Dunhuang Research Institute,** to the left of the caves, presents eight hand-painted, professionally-replicated caves, brightly lit to give a much more detailed study of the art than in the originals. Photographs of the various explorers who traveled through the caves and an impressive collection of Tibetan Buddhist bronze art are displayed on the second floor. *(☎886 9050. Open daily 8:20am-5:30pm. Free with Mogao Grottoes ticket.)*

NORTHWEST

CRESCENT MOON SPRING AND SINGING SAND DUNES (yuèyā quán; 月牙泉; and mínshā shān; 鸣沙山). One of the most stunning vistas in northwest China, this shimmering crescent-shaped pool is surrounded by golden sand dunes. Legend has it that the pool, fed by an eternal spring, has been in the same location for 2000 years. Dunhuang's fantastic sand dunes, surging up from the oasis frontier, are visible from the center of town. The highest dunes rise from a series of wind-brushed sand valleys that stretch for kilometers. Even the lesser peaks, best scaled on a wooden "ladder" (Y5-10) pressed into the slope, reward climbers with enchanting views of a vast, barren expanse interrupted only by the remarkable green of Dunhuang's fields and orchards. Although the sands are scalding before 5:30 or 6pm, the earlier you arrive, the farther away you can get from the hordes of tourists that flood the area in the evenings. Fewer people have been coming recently, however, due to the outlandish admission price. You can also join them in "sand surfing" on a primitive sled (Y5), paragliding (Y20), or camel-riding (Y30-40). In the summer, the sun sets around 9 or 9:30pm, and is a prime photo-op. *(An easy 30min. bike ride from Dunhuang. Ride south on Mingshan Lu, turn left at the Jinye Hotel, and follow the road for 6km to the gate. Due to the intense summer heat, departing Dunhuang around 5:30pm is best. Y50.)*

JADE GATE PASS AND SUN PASS (yùmén guān; 玉门关; and yángguān; 阳关). The ruins of Jade Gate Pass and Sun Pass would likely interest history buffs more for their historical import than for their current state. Quickly deteriorating under the relentless heat and wind, these once-great gateways are nothing more than fading mounds in the desert, although the surrounding scenery isn't bad. A trip consumes the better part of a day, costs Y300, and should probably by considered only by those who have time (and money) to burn. For better ruins, head west to Turpan. *(80km west of Dunhuang. Organized tours generally also include a military storage facility (hé cān chéng; 河仓城) and the Han dynasty Great Wall relics (hàn cháng héng; 汉长城). Jade Gate Pass Y30; Sun Pass Y10.)*

DUNHUANG ANCIENT CITY (dūnhuáng gǔchéng; 敦煌古城). This "ancient city" is a bit peculiar, even for China. It's actually a movie set built in 1987 to resemble a Song dynasty village. The price is hardly worth it. (*18km southwest of Dunhuang. Taxis cost Y60; tours also leave from CITS and John's Cafe. Y20.)*

XINJIANG 新疆

Covering a sixth of China's landmass with its deep basins (Tarim and Dzungar) and titanic mountain ranges (Altay, Tianshan, and Kunlun), the Xinjiang Uighur Autonomous Region stretches over an area ten times the size of England. In this land of extremes, freezing peaks rise 7600m while depressions plunge well below sea level, and luscious melons ripen in oasis orchards while ancient ruins languish in parched deserts. The people who make the region their home are just as varied as Xinjiang's terrain, counting Uighurs, Kazakhs, Uzbeks, Mongols, Hui, and Han among their ranks. A world unto itself, Xinjiang has a little of everything, including unspoiled wilderness, well-preserved ruins, and a fascinating cultural landscape.

The first half of the 20th century however, saw Xinjiang running for shelter from a series of military coups, political backstabbings, makeshift coalitions, assassinations, and mysterious disappearances. Only the arrival of the PLA in 1949 imposed some stability on the region, but the Cultural Revolution ushered in a new age of chaos. Heavy state-sponsored Han immigration in past decades has dramatically altered Xinjiang's ethnic composition and animosity between Han Chinese and Uighurs flares up from time to time, spurred by legal injustices, unequal opportunities, and mutual distrust. Ethnic riots rocked Kashgar in 1992 and 1997, while car bombs set by Uighur extremists shook Ürümqi and Beijing. A September 2000 bombing in Ürümqi, allegedly the act of Islamic fundamentalists, killed over 100 people. Although things have calmed down since, hope for autonomy from China lives on in the Uighur population.

In Xinjiang, time is generally told in **Beijing time** (bêijīng shíjiān; 北京时间). However, informally, many people go according to Xinjiang time (xīnjiāng shíjiān; 新疆时间), two or three hours behind Beijing time. Anything official like trains, planes, banks, etc., operates under Beijing time (buses, however, often run by Xinjiang time). Many government offices compensate by opening as late as 10am and staying open until 8pm. Some hotels push back their check-out time to 2pm. In Xinjiang more so than in many other parts of China, **money** can be an issue. Do not pay for tours before you return and are satisfied that the conditions have been met. If you charter a taxi or minibus, do not pay in advance. Many men in Xinjiang carry knives, so above all, handle disagreements as calmly as possible.

THE MAKING OF MINZU

Minority culture in mainland China

Racial thinking is pervasive in China. The notion of a primordial and homogenous "Han ethnic nationality," bordered by underdeveloped or uncivilized "ethnic minorities," is often taken for granted by the general public both inside and outside of China. Yet contrary to this widespread, official ideology, the development of the Han ethnic nationality was one of the most pro-active, politically motivated efforts to create a human community in history.

Dr. Sun Yat-Sen, president of the Nationalist Party from 1912 to 1925, desperately sought to unify the Chinese against the incursions of the Japanese and other foreign nations. Yet, Sun faced what he and other observers noted as a particularly strong bias toward familialism and clanism among the Chinese people. They were as difficult to combine as "a sheet of loose sand." Sun Yat-Sen had been educated in Japan, and he decided to borrow the Japanese term *minzoku*, or ethnic nation, which was a driving concept in Japan's imperialist expansion. Sun created a wholly new term in Mandarin – *minzu*, or ethnic nationality.

In particular, Sun Yat-Sen had to unify the warlords of the Chinese North with the rich merchants of the South in order to create a formidable military. Sun himself was Southern and spoke Mandarin with a thick accent, thus facing traditional Northern suspicions of Southern rebellion. He therefore borrowed the terminology of the northern Han Empire (206BCE – 220CE) and created the term *Han minzu* (*Hanzu*), or the Han ethnic nationality. The *Hanzu* were part of Sun's larger philosophy of *wuzu* – five ethnic nationalities of China. Within the five groups, the *Hanzu* were considered culturally dominant, accompanied by the Manchu, Tibetan, Mongolian, and Mohammedan (Hui and Uighur). According to Sun Yat-Sen's theories, the Han ethnic nation stood against both "external barbarians" (foreign nations), and "internal barbarians" (ethnic minorities). To counter the Japanese, Sun's *wuzu* philosophy essentially formalized China's internal racial opposition.

When the Chinese Communist Party came to power in 1949, they adopted Sun Yat-Sen's race theory. The *Han minzu* was the demographic body that theoretically legitimated the government; moreover, the *Hanzu* became the "vanguard" of progress for all Chinese ethnic groups through phases of Marxist class history. Yet there were no longer merely five ethnicities. In the early 1950's, the Party invited ethnic groups to apply for minority status. They received over 400 requests! A potential nightmare for central planning was mitigated by sending several waves of social scientists and linguists all over China to classify these *xiaoshu minzu* (ethnic minorities). Many distinct groups were merged together until arriving at an official number of 51 in 1976, which later acquired four more to become the present 55.

These groups were supposedly clustered according to language, geography, and customs. Yet none of these requirements were applied to the Han, who remained a political construction. The *Han minzu* still contain eight "dialects," which are in reality mutually unintelligible languages: Cantonese, Hakka, Xiang (or "Hunanese," which lost a close vote to becoming the national language), Mandarin, Kan, Northern Min, Southern Min, and Wu.

Most "Han" encounter their own supposed identity through government channels. School matriculation, census forms, and job applications all require self-identification as Han. Many Han Chinese, according to ethnologist Dru Gladney, are actually unaware of their status until such time. News media, schools, and public propaganda, however, constantly strive to reinforce the idea of China's family of *minzu* and the dominant Han role therein.

Many *xiaoshu minzu*, have also energetically maintained their ethnic classifications to reap benefits within the Communist system. If an ethnic group can prove its distinct identity and its sufficient numbers, it can be granted an "autonomous" region or county with limited political and religious privileges. Many individuals also strive to prove their ethnic minority status to avoid the one-child policy, or, under China's affirmative action program, in order to only compete with other "minorities" as they apply to China's top universities. Ethnic minority classifications have also provided an important tool for unified resistance against Chinese rule. The Tibetan and Uighur ethnic groups, for example, contain many internal, regional differences. Yet they are oppressed and discriminated against uniformly within the Chinese system. Individuals therefore cling to their identities as "ethnic nationals" in order to make unified claims for national sovereignty in opposition to the Han.

But, whereas most ethnic minority groups share a language and many cultural similarities, the Han ethnicity remains highly contrived, and schisms are beginning to arise. In China's southeast, many ethnic communities *within* the Han block, such as the Hakka, South Fujianese Min, and Swatow, are agitating for greater autonomy. People within these groups are re-associating themselves with the southern Tang Dynasty (AD 618 – 907). They have taken advantage of China's "opening up" since 1979 to resurrect regional customs. The trend was generated by these communities' tremendous success in the new economy and their reluctance to share with Beijing. Some counties have avoided paying federal taxes, and they have created trade tariffs across borders with culturally disparate communities now seen as rivals. The recent proliferation of toll roads in southern China has been a result of these areas striving for greater economic autonomy. If the Chinese economy continues to grow, such regional agitation is certain to follow suit.

Minzu served Sun Yat-Sen as a useful paradigm for resistance against the Japanese. Yet, the implicit Han chauvinism quickly turned against ethnic minorities, fueling discriminatory policies and forming barriers to economic entry throughout Communist rule. Ironically, while the Chinese turned this Japanese concept against their invaders, ethnic minorities utilized the category of ethnic nation to unify their own resistance against Chinese imperialism. Meanwhile, economic decentralization has begun to internally erode the notion of *Hanzu*. If tourists, scholars, journalists, or activists visiting China are to understand these evolving allegiances within the new China, the "primordial" *minzu* must be historically contextualized as a politically motivated tool of collective action.

Josh Levin is a Harvard graduate and Let's Go veteran. He has traveled extensively throughout China and has spent much time researching Chinese minority issues.

ÜRÜMQI 乌鲁木齐 ☎0991

Ürümqi is an expansive industriopolis of over 1.4 million inhabitants. Ironically, the capital of the Xinjiang Uighur Autonomous Region is very much a Han city, in both urban appearance and racial composition. Only small numbers of Uighur, Xibo, Hui, and Kazakh people continue to make a living here, creating a strange and fascinating mix. The flashing stripes of color in Uighur skirts, the bob of the *fez* in a thick crowd, and the rich tapestry of Uighur, Cyrillic, and Chinese scripts adorning virtually every street facade impart a sense of a 21st-century Silk Road, an exciting confluence of people and cultures on the move. Ürümqi comes alive after sunset, disregarding the cues of Beijing time as it pulses deep into the night. While you're in the city, enjoy the rich food by strolling through night bazaars and smoky, vibrant back alleys where the scent of freshly baked bread and roasting meat wafts through the streets.

Occupying a strategic point in the Tianshan mountain range, Ürümqi has seen its share of power struggles. The 1955 discovery of oil in nearby Karamay kick-started the economy, and now Ürümqi oil executives are competing with those in Texas and Tokyo in the rush to cash in on the petroleum reserves around the Caspian Sea. Ürümqi offers travelers a magnificent museum, transportation links to China, Russia, and Central Asia, and a network of backpackers and travel agencies from which to glean advice about further travel in Xinjiang.

EARNESTLY STUDY...WHAT AGAIN? In an effort to put himself on an equal theoretical plane with Mao Zedong (Mao Zedong Thought) and Deng Xiaoping (Deng Xiaoping Theory), current president Jiang Zemin has come up with the "Three Representatives of Important Thought" (sāngè dàibiǎo zhòngyào sīxiǎng; 三个代表重要思想), which the Xinjiang Communist Party Committee has zealously promoted with huge red and white banners on every government building. Government employees are required to attend marathon four-hour meetings to listen to speeches by President Jiang and the Xinjiang district and local party secretaries on the theory. Afterwards, each worker must give a 30-minute presentation on his or her reflections on the "Three Representatives." School children, meanwhile, devote a full day to studying the theory, after which they must submit their opinions (which must be approved by the school principal). The odd thing is, despite the endless study and reflection, hardly anyone has the slightest idea what the "Three Representatives" are. One rural party official suggested that it had something to do with relying on oneself. A particularly well-informed Uighur man explained (before snorting derisively) that the "representatives" are 1) the people, 2) the nation's resources, and 3) the leadership of the party. Given all the confusion, one can only wonder what civil servants, teachers, and doctors find to talk about for 30 minutes each at their mandatory "Three Representatives" meetings.

TRANSPORTATION

Flights: Ürümqi Airport (wūlǔmùqí jīchǎng; 乌鲁木齐机场; ☎371 9511, ext. 113) is 20km from town. Shuttle buses (40min., Y8) leave the **Xinjiang Airlines ticket office** (xīnjiāng hángkōng shòupiào chù; 新疆航空售票处), 62 Youhao Nan Lu (☎264 1826, 24hr. ☎265 2826), 2hr. before departure. Taxis from the city center cost about Y50. Xinjiang destinations to: **Hotan** (4 per week, Y1000); **Kashgar** (3 per day, Y980); and **Yining** (1-3 per day, Y590). Other domestic flights to: **Beijing** (4 per day 8:30am-3pm, Y2080); **Dunhuang** (daily, Y650); **Guangzhou** (1-2 per day Su-F, Y2420); **Lanzhou** (1-2 per day, Y1190); **Shanghai** (daily, Y2390); **Xi'an** (several flights daily,

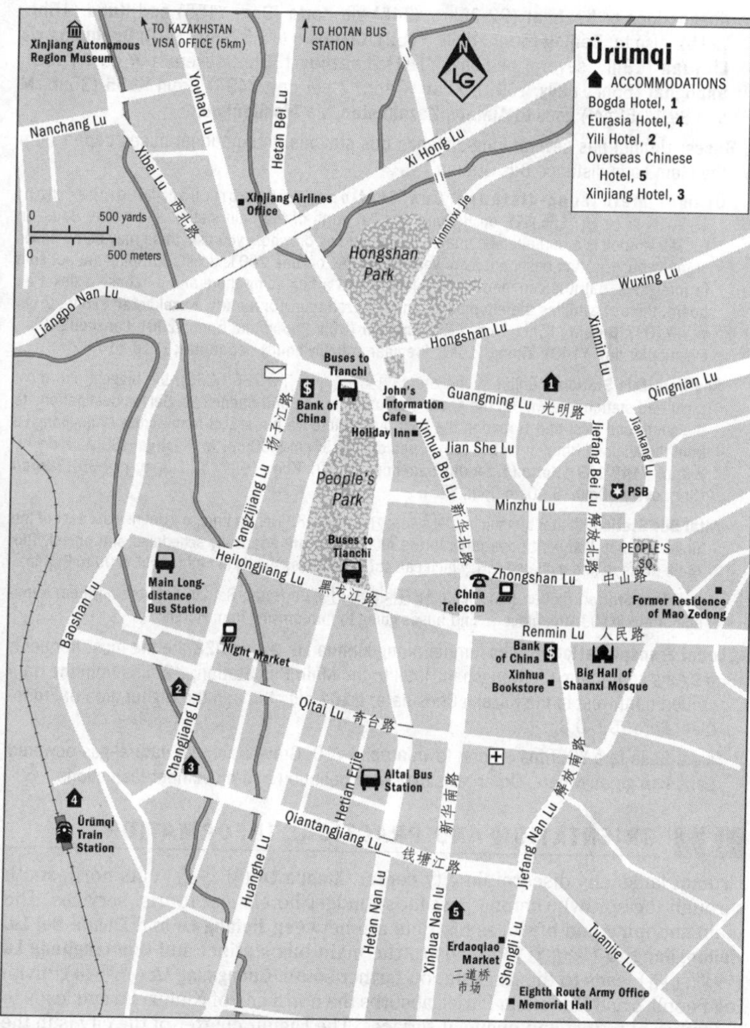

Y1330); **Xining** (5 per week, Y1030). International flights to: **Almaty, Kazakhstan** (M and F, Y1660); **Islamabad, Pakistan** (W and Su, Y2270); **Moscow, Russia** (Tu and F, Y2490) via **Yekaterinburg**; **Novosibirsk, Russia** (M and F, Y1300). **Siberian Air,** 51 Xinhua Nan Lu (☎286 4327), in the Overseas Chinese Hotel compound has flights to **Moscow** (Tu and Sa 3pm, US$200) via **Novosibirsk** (US$150). Open Su- M and W-F noon-7pm.

Trains: Ürümqi Train Station (wūlǔmùqí huǒchē zhàn; 乌鲁木齐火车站; ☎344 5222), in the southwest part of town off the Ürümqi-Turpan highway. Take bus #2 or 10 or a taxi (Y6-9) from Xinhua Lu. Scalpers sell tickets to popular destinations; to avoid a Y30-40 commission, buy tickets 2-4 days in advance. For destinations such as Kashgar or Lanzhou, you can save up to Y100 by going on a slow (pǔkuài; 普快) train. Xinjiang destinations to **Kashgar** (22-26hr., Y345) via **Korla** (9hr., Y155) and **Kuqa** (15hr., Y215). Also to: **Beijing** (59hr., daily, Y652); **Chengdu** (11:52am, Y340); **Dunhuang** via **Liuyuan** (13hr., several per day, Y181); **Lanzhou** (33hr., several per day, Y365); **Shanghai** (65hr., daily, Y699); **Xi'an** (34hr., 7 per day, Y434). Train K895 (30hr., M and Sa 11:58pm) goes to **Almaty, Kazakhstan,** via **Alashankou.**

Buses: Ürümqi has several long-distance bus stations. International buses depart from the Main Long-distance Bus Station.

Ürümqi Main Long-distance Bus Station (wūlǔmùqí chángtú qìchē zhàn; 乌鲁木齐长途汽车站), on Heilongjiang Lu, north of the train station and before Baoshan Lu. This station is a bureaucratic quagmire—depending on whom you ask, there may be no buses or many buses to the destinations of your choice. As of June 2001, tickets to Yining are not sold to foreigners, but it is common for travelers to find a bus going there and purchase a ticket on board, thereby avoiding the alternative, an organized tour. To: **Almaty, Kazakhstan** (16hr., 2 per day, Y104); **Burqin** (15hr., 7pm, Y95); **Kashgar** (30hr., noon and 5pm, Y200); **Lanzhou** (40hr., every other day, Y140); **Yining** (16hr.; irregular, roughly hourly departures; Y110-114).

Southern Bus Station (nánjiāo qìchē zhàn; 南郊汽车站; ☎286 6635), the biggest and most organized station in town, on the south side of Xinhua Lu and Shengli Lu. Serves destinations to the south and west and Turpan in the east. Accessible via bus #109 from across Changjiang Lu from the Xinjiang Hotel or by taxi (Y8). Open daily 8:30am-8:30pm. To: **Kashgar** (30hr., every hr. 2-8pm, Y140-159); **Korla** (5 per day 6am-noon, Y110); **Kuqa** (every hr. 2-8pm, Y74-85); **Turpan** (3hr., every 30min. 8:40am-8pm, Y25).

Altai Bus Station (ālèitài bànshìchù; 阿勒泰办事处), 89 Hetian Erjie, a 10min. walk east of the Xinjiang Hotel. Frequent departures to the Altai region are erratically scheduled and priced. This is the place to find a shared taxi, which can cut travel times nearly in half (about Y200 to Burqin).

Hotan Bus Station (hétián bànshìchù; 和田办事处), on Hetan Bei Lu, near the northern terminus of bus #109. The place to find buses going to and arriving from Hotan.

Local Transportation: Buses lumber along Xinhua Lu: **#7** and **28** are the most frequent; **#1** runs south from the Hongshan Hotel to the Main Bus Station; **#2** runs from the train station northwest to the Kazakh Consulate; **#101** cuts through the Uighur area of Erdaoqiao. Fare Y0.5-0.8.

Taxis: Base fare Y6. Trips around town around Y10. Gray-bottomed, natural-gas-powered cabs can go anywhere. Other taxis may face pollution and movement restrictions.

NORTHWEST

ORIENTATION AND PRACTICAL INFORMATION

Ürümqi lacks any discernible city center. **Xinhua Lu** (新华路) cuts north-south through the sprawl, running past most budget hotels and tourist services. The main shopping and business districts are between **Jiefang Lu** and **Xinhua Bei Lu. Heilongjiang Lu** (黑龙江路) leads to the main bus station, and **Qiantangjiang Lu** (钱塘江路) leads to the train station farther south. **Guangming Lu** (光明路), dividing People's and Hongshan Parks, absorbs the north end of Xinhua Lu and leads to a number of tourist and financial services. The Uighur quarter of the city is in the southern neighborhood of **Erdaoqiao** (二道桥).

Travel Agencies: Tianshan Tianchi International Travel Service (tiānshān tiānchí guójì læxíngshè; 天山天池国际旅行社; ☎281 6018), in the lobby of the Eurasia Hotel, is Kazakh-owned and specializes in trips to Tianchi (Y140) and Hanas Lake in Altai Prefecture (4 days, Y980). Also arranges treks in more remote Kazakh-populated areas. Open 24hr. **Xinjiang Xuelian Travel Service** (xīnjiāng xuēlián læxíngshè; 新疆雪莲旅行社; ☎585 2511, ext. 5138), in the lobby of the Xinjiang Hotel. One-day Y180 tours to Tianchi include meals, tolls, and admission. Also sells tickets on tourist buses to Tianchi (Y20-50, depending on bus quality). Open 24hr. **John's Information Cafe** also runs trips to Tianchi (Y160) and Hanas (Y800).

Adventure Travel: Some agencies offer more rigorous mountain climbing, wilderness backpacking tours, and guided excursions into the desert. **Ürümqi Mountain Climbing Club** leads one of the most reputable and hard-core guided trips, a 1- to 2-week ascent of 5445m Bogda Peak near Tianchi. Contact Wang Tienan, the head of the club (☎(130) 0968 1695; pager ☎(127) 103 1177). Other guided trips cost US$40-50 per day, which includes tents, gear, cooks, and pack animals. **Xinjiang Golden Bridge Folklore International Travel Service** (xīnjiāng jīnqiáo míngsú guójì lǜxíngshè; 新疆金桥民俗国际旅行社), in the Holiday Inn, Rm. 404 (☎284 7605; cgbtxj@xj.cninfo.net), on Xinhua Bei Lu, runs trekking tours (about US$60 per day) of Altai and the Taklimakan Desert, and a 17-day ascent of Mt. Muztaghata (4450m) on the Panir Plateau near Kashgar. A 4-day tour to Hanas costs Y1640 (using cheaper accommodation cuts this cost in half).

Bank of China: 1 Yangzijiang Lu, opposite the post office. Open M-F 10am-6pm, Sa-Su 11am-2:30pm. Exchanges traveler's checks. Credit card advances at counters #4-7. Also at 343 Jiefang Nan Lu, at Renmin Lu, just west of the Xinhua Bookstore. Open M-F 9:30am-1:30pm and 4-7pm, Sa-Su 11am-3pm.

Bookstore: Xinhua Bookstore (☎281 8136). A good selection of English-Uighur phrasebooks and maps of Xinjiang. Open daily 10am-8pm.

PSB: Foreigner Reception Office (wàiguórén jiēdàishì; 外国人接待室; ☎281 0452, ext. 3646), on the corner of Minzhu Lu and Jiankang Lu. Processes visa extensions (US citizens Y186). Open M-F 9:30am-1pm and 4-8pm.

Internet Access: Qisheng Internet Cafe (qíshēng wângbā; 奇声网吧), 39 Changjiang Lu, just past the night market. Y5 per hr. Open 24hr. **New Silk Road Internet Cafe** (xīnsīlù wângbā; 新丝路网吧), 105 Zhongshan Lu, 4th fl. A large, spiffy joint run by China Telecom. Y4 per hr., students Y3. Open daily 10am-2am.

Telecommunications: China Telecom, 157 Zhongshan Lu, at Xinhua Bei Lu. Sells a mind-boggling array of mobile phones. IDD service. Open daily 9:30am-8pm.

Post Office: (☎585 7329), on Yangzijiang Lu, opposite the Bank of China, a 10min. walk west of the Hongshan Hotel. Descend the underground walkway in front of the bank, and re-emerge at the post office entrance. EMS and Poste Restante in the room to the right. Open daily 9:30am-10pm. **Postal Code:** 830000.

ACCOMMODATIONS AND FOOD

Budget accommodations are clustered around the train station to the southeast; staying here is not so convenient for explorations of the city, but it's relatively safe and cheap. Somewhat new buildings are being torn down to make way for newer and better versions. Although this is good from an economic development standpoint, it means that budget options for foreigners are dwindling fast.

Ürümqi has a distinct lack of must-try restaurants. Still, the thousands of little eateries along **Xinhua Lu** and in the **Erdaoqiao Muslim** district always satisfy. **Night markets** abound in the train station area; the best is on Changjiang Lu, about a five-minute walk from the Xinjiang Hotel. Most night markets open around 8:30pm. Try the lamb kebabs (yángròu chuàn; 羊肉串), usually Y1 each. Cold Xinjiang beer is served up at nearly every stand (Y2.5-3 per bottle). **John's Information Cafe** ❷ on Xinhua Bei Lu, about 100m to the right of the Holiday Inn, offers travel advice and ambitiously priced pizzas, steaks (Y25+), and cheap Chinese food.

Xinjiang Hotel (xīnjiāng fàndiàn; 新疆饭店), 107 Changjiang Lu (☎585 2511, ext. 2000), facing the traffic circle at Qiantangjiang Lu and Changjiang Lu, a 10min. walk from the train station. Rooms have clean sheets, phone, and TV. Deposit Y20-200. 3- to 6-bed dorms Y17-24; 2-bed dorms Y35; doubles with bath Y220-888; quads Y80. ❶

Eurasia Hotel (yà'ōu bīnguǎn; 亚欧宾馆; ☎585 6699), in the train station area. The reception desk can handle all your transportation needs. Well-maintained rooms. Cheaper dorms have bunkbeds and thin mattresses. Shower use in the nicer dorms 8-9pm only. Key deposit Y20. Deposit Y50-100 per person. 5-bed dorms with bath Y20; 4-bed dorms with bath Y38; 3-bed dorms with bath Y50; doubles with bath Y280-388. ❶

Bogda Hotel (bógédá bīnguǎn; 博格达宾馆), 10 Guangming Lu (☎282 3910, ext. 2119), a 10min. walk east of the Hongshan Hotel, in the "First Guesthouse of the Xinjiang Military Region" compound. This privatized ex-military hostel has bargain dorms (without showers) but pricey rooms. 4- to 5-bed dorms Y25; doubles with bath Y288-388. Off-season discounts possible. ❶

Overseas Chinese Hotel (huáqiáo bīnguǎn; 华侨宾馆), 51 Xinhua Nan Lu (☎286 0793), in the south of town, past Qiantangjiang Lu. A favorite among visiting Russian merchants, this hotel offers a variety of pleasant rooms. Those in the east building are cheaper. Hotel is attached to Troika Restaurant/Disco. Deposit Y100. 3-bed dorms Y60; singles Y100; doubles Y158-300. Traveler's checks accepted. ❶

Yili Hotel (yīlí dàjiǔdiàn; 伊犁大酒店; www.yilihotel.com), 80 Changjiang Lu (☎585 6888), near the night market. Everything is shiny—almost painfully so. Shiny, new and very fancy rooms. Also has shiny gym, shiny sauna, and shiny karaoke lounge. Doubles Y298-688; triples Y240, but inquire about shiny discounts. ❹

SIGHTS

XINJIANG UIGHUR AUTONOMOUS REGION MUSEUM (xīnjiāng wéiwūěrzú zìzhì qū bówùguǎn; 新疆维吾尔族自治区博物馆). Like many things in Ürümqi, the highly-regarded Xinjiang Museum was recently torn down to make way for a bigger, better, and glitzier version, expected to open in 2003. Still, the museum is worth a visit; many of the best exhibits are on display in a temporary building. Particularly noteworthy is a creepy but fantastic collection of mummies, including an infant who died about 3800 years ago and the "Loulan Beauty," the corpse of a 45-year-old woman of Indo-European ethnicity, reputed to be 4000 years old. The gift shop sells spectacular Uighur rugs. *(In the north part of town, a 25min. walk along Xibei Lu from the post office, or a 5min. ride on bus #7. Bus #2 runs from in front of the Xinjiang Hotel to just across from the museum. Free tours in Mandarin; most exhibits have English captions. Open M-F 9:30am-7:30pm, last admission 6pm; Sa-Su 10:30am-5pm. Y25, students Y12.)*

AQUATIC PARADISE (shǔishàng lèyuán; 水上乐园). Ürümqi's fame as the farthest inland city in the world explains this bizarre amusement park. The main attraction is the city reservoir, where you can ride speedboats (Y10). *(Next to the South Bus Station. Take bus #7 or #109. Y5. Rollercoasters and ferris wheel Y20 each.)*

ERDAOQIAO MARKET (èrdàoqiáo shìchǎng; 二道桥市场). One of the best stops in town, this market sits in the heart of Ürümqi's Uighur quarter. On weekends, shops selling textiles and crafts spread out over an area almost one-fourth the size of Kashgar's famous Sunday bazaar (see p. 780). The main market is on Shengli Lu, stretching for several blocks south of where it turns into Jiefang Lu. A large gateway leads to a back alley full of rugs, silk, and food.

NEAR ÜRÜMQI

TIANCHI LAKE

***Buses** (2-2½hr., same-day round-trip Y23, with A/C Y33) leave for Tianchi daily from the south and north ends of People's Park. Buy tickets the day before or the morning of; buses leave 9-*

9:30am. Be sure to ask whether your ticket includes a highway toll fee, which is tacked on at the last minute by the drivers. If you plan to spend the night at Tianchi, buy another ticket the next day. Buses return to Ürümqi daily 4:30-5:30pm, stopping mid-mountain as well as at the bottom parking lot before heading back to Ürümqi. ***Public buses*** *leave Tianchi every 30min. 8:30-10:30am; you will need to change buses at Fukang (Y10) and Ermao (Y1.5-5), and delays and complications are common. We recommend that you not take the small mini-buses back to Ürümqi; instead, take one of the large* ***tourist buses*** *(running in the afternoon only). Bring warm clothes, especially for overnight stays.*

Nestled high in the Tianshan mountain range, 115km east of Ürümqi, the charming mountain lake of Tianchi (tiānchí; 天池) lies 1950m above sea level, guarded by the stately 6000m Bogda peak. Tianchi rewards visitors with unforgettable experiences, including alpine hiking, star-gazing, and camping in Kazakh yurts. According to myth, the Mother of the Western Skies would hold a feast at this lake whenever a local peach tree bore fruit. As this only happened about once every 3000 years, the banquets were understandably grand affairs. All the immortals would gather together for this long-awaited festival, converting the lake area into something of a Little Heaven—hence its name, the "Heavenly Pool."

While immortals are hard to come by these days, Tianchi's natural beauty attracts hordes of worldly Chinese tourists. Breaking away from the paved lakeside paths and up into the surrounding hills will put plenty of distance between you and them. Several horse trails will take you to the high ridges that overlook snow-capped mountains in the distance; small Kazakh encampments are scattered in pockets of grassland at high altitudes. At the lake, swimming is a great summer activity.

Overnight stays are highly recommended, as the lake regains its heavenly tranquility only after the majority of daytrippers leave around 5pm. Finding lodging in the many lakeside yurts is simple. Just ask; or more likely, you will be asked. Three meals and lodging cost about Y40; agree on the price early on. **Rashit,** an endearing Kazakh guide, has been hosting guests in his nine-yurt camp on the southwest bank of the lake for over 12 years. He speaks Mandarin and English, and is a great cook. While many backpackers go to Tianchi in search of solitude, they usually find their way to Rashit's, attracted by the warm food and convivial atmosphere.

NO. 1 GLACIER AND WHITE POPLAR GULLY

A 3hr. drive south of Ürümqi. Tourist buses (or cars, for smaller groups) leave from the same spots as the Tianchi buses; buy tickets from the same booth (Y160-180, includes lunch). Buses leave at 9:30am, but departures are only guaranteed on weekends; during the week, buses leave only when enough people go, so check the day before. Buses to White Poplar Gully are more frequent and much cheaper than those to No. 1 Glacier. Admission to No. 1 Glacier Y15, White Poplar Gully Y10.

High up in the Tianshan Mountains, the **No. 1 Glacier** (yīhào bīngchuān; 一号冰川) is Ürümqi's second-most famous natural wonder after Tianchi; its isn't all that big, but it's still pretty impressive. The glacier is a 45-minute hike from the parking lot; local Kazakhs rent horses (Y20 per hr.) to speed things up. The nearby **No. 3 Glacier** (sānhào bīngchuān; 三号冰川), right next to the road from and a bit larger than No. 1, is not quite as scenic but also merits a look.

The **White Poplar Gully** (báiyáng gōu; 白杨沟), also known as **Nanshan** (南山), is the usual post-lunch stop after visiting the glacier. From the parking lot, a path leads through a thickly wooded valley up to a lovely waterfall, a 45-minute walk each way. Horse rides are commmon. All in all, these two spots are not must-sees, but they do make for a pleasant and fun trip if you have an extra day in Ürümqi.

ALTAI PREFECTURE 阿勒泰地区

Nestled up in the northernmost corner of Xinjiang, near the Kazakh, Mongolian, and Russian borders, Altai is a sharp contrast to the deserts of the south. Here, thick pine and birch forests lay alongside thundering rivers, while Kazakh and Mongol herders tend their sheep and cattle on fertile grasslands beneath rocky peaks. The weather is never warm, and snow falls regularly nine months out of the year; the main river in the region, the Ertix, is the only one in China to empty into the Arctic Ocean. Altai's main attraction is the lovely Hanas Lake, but the pristine wilderness and remote villages that make up much of the area are equally, if not more, interesting to explore.

BORDER CROSSINGS INTO KAZAKHSTAN AND MONGOLIA

For those looking to skip the country, Altai is fertile ground for border crossings. To Kazakhstan, the main crossing is at **Jimunai** (吉木乃), near Burqin. To Mongolia, there are crossings at **Hongshanzui** (红山嘴) and **Takeshiken** (塔克什肯), both accessible from Altai City. Traveling to any of those border towns requires a permit from the PSB. There is currently no legal way to cross into Russia from Altai. Visas for travel to Kazakhstan are now handled in the **Kazakh Airlines Visa Office** (hāsàkèsītǎn mínhánggōngsī zhùwū bàqiānzhèngchù; 哈萨克斯坦民航公司驻乌办签证处), 31 Kunming Lu (☎383 2324), off Beijing Lu, behind the Torch Mansions (huǒjù dàshà; 火炬大厦); look for the flame sign on Beijing Lu. Accessible by bus #2 or hard-to-find taxis (Y20). Applications require a letter of invitation approved by the Foreign Ministry, available from Kazakh travel agencies (in Kazakhstan). The visa office has a list of such agencies; try the **Otrar Travel Group**, ul. Gogolya 73 (☎588202; fax 331234; s-otrar@mail.group.kz) in Almaty. Visas cost Y85 plus a processing fee (7-day US$30, 3-day US$60). The helpful visa officer speaks fluent English. Open M-Th 10:30am-2:30pm, new applications accepted before 1pm.

BURQIN 布尔津 ☎0906

A sleepy town with mostly Kazakh residents, Burqin is named for the Burqin River, a vast, lazy stream that empties into the Ertix. Apart from the pretty river, there's not much to see in town, but Burqin makes for a convenient base from which to explore Hanas Lake and the rugged wilderness of northern Altai. While Burqin is officially in a county closed to foreigners, the local PSB doesn't mind if you come directly here to arrange permits for Hanas Lake and other parts of Altai.

ORIENTATION AND PRACTICAL INFORMATION

Burqin is small enough to navigate on foot. The main road, **Wenming Lu** (文明路), runs roughly north to south through town, and is home to the bus station, main square, and several night markets. Taking a left out of the bus station on Wenming Lu brings you to **Xingfu Lu** (幸福路), where you can find the PSB and the Jinhe Hotel. Wenming Lu runs past **Huancheng Nan Lu** (环城南路) before exiting town, crossing the Ertix River, and extending toward Ürümqi.

Buses: The **Passenger Terminal** (kèyùnzhàn; 客运站) is on Wenming Lu in the northern part of town. To **Altai City** (1½hr., frequent buses 9am-8pm, Y12) and **Ürümqi** (12hr., at least 1 bus daily 6-8pm, Y92-104). In July and August, **tourist buses** often, but not always, run to Hanas Lake.

Travel Agency: Kanas International Travel Service (kānàsī guójì lǚxíngshè; 喀纳斯国际旅行社), in the Gongxiao Hotel (gōngxiāo bīnguǎn; 供销宾馆), across Wenming Lu from the Tourist Hotel. Helps with travel arrangements to Hanas Lake, though it might be simpler to find a driver at the bus station.

PSB: On the corner of Xingfu Lu and Xiangyang Lu, west of Wenming Lu (☎652 2161, ext. 2009, beeper ☎(0126) 837 7212). Traveling beyond the town of Burqin requires an Alien Travel Permit (lǚxíngzhèng; 旅行证; Y50), easily obtainable here. The officer is quite affable, offering advice on how to get to Hanas and showing off pictures of his own jaunts to the lake with his PSB buddies. Open M-F 9:30am-1:30pm and 4-8pm.

Post and Telecommunications: On Huancheng Nan Lu, near Wenming Lu. Open daily 9:30am-7:30pm.

ACCOMMODATIONS

Jinhe Hotel (jīnhé bīnguǎn; 金河宾馆; ☎652 3170), on Xingfu Lu next to the PSB; from the bus station, turn left on Wenming Lu, then right onto Xingfu Lu. 24hr. hot water. 3-4 bed dorms Y20-25; doubles with bath Y100; suite Y180. ❶

Traffic Hotel (jiāotōng bīnguǎn; 交通宾馆; ☎652 2643), at the bus station. Conveniently located. 2-4 bed dorms Y10-30; singles Y80. ❶

Burqin Tourist Hotel (bù'ěrjīn lǚyóu bīnguǎn; 布尔津旅游宾馆; ☎652 1325), on Huancheng Nan Lu; near the intersection with Wenming Lu. A large, fairly fancy complex in the south of town. 24hr. hot water. 3-bed dorms Y30; doubles in pleasant wooden cottages Y120, ritzier doubles Y320. ❶

SIGHTS

Northwest of town, the **Burqin River** (bù'ěrjīnhé; 布尔津河) is worth a look—especially after a big rainfall (frequent during the summer), when the river can swell to a width of 100m. The banks are lined with birch trees that, combined with the slowly moving water and gentle breeze, make for a very relaxing setting. A bit upstream from the road bridge is an island park where locals hang out and where visitors can sample the fare at a number of yurt-restaurants. *(Round-trip taxi should cost about Y10. Don't get lost and end up in the wrong place: the river on the southern edge of town is the Ertix, not the Burqin, and is decidedly un-scenic.)*

DAYTRIPS FROM BURQIN

HANAS LAKE 哈纳斯湖

*About 150km north of Burqin (a 5hr. drive). As of July 2001, the main access road was closed for construction, requiring a lengthy detour through Habahe River (哈巴河). When the new road is finished, transportation should be much easier, and scheduled **tourist buses** will likely resume operation in July-Aug. Until then, renting a **jeep** is the best option (about Y600 for a 2-day round-trip, less on the new road). Drivers and prospective passengers alike hang out at the Burqin bus station; this is an excellent time to make some new Chinese friends, who provide good company, share the cost of the jeep, and bargain far better than you do. Arrive by 8am for the best chance of meeting other passengers; or come in the evening to arrange transport for the next day. An **Alien Travel Permit,** available from Burqin or Altai City PSB, is required to visit Hanas; numerous border patrol checkpoints dot the area. **Entry** to Hanas Lake area Y100.*

Set in a beautiful alpine valley, Hanas Lake (hānàsī hú; 哈纳斯湖) is the crown jewel of Altai's tourist attractions. Long and narrow, the lake winds through forests of tall pines and steep, rocky mountains. To the north is the icy 4374m crag called **Friendship Peak** (yôuyí fëng; 友谊峰), where the borders of China, Kazakhastan, Mongolia, and Russia meet. From ground level, views of the lake are obstructed; hike up one of the neighboring hills for a better look. A popular day hike leads to **Observing Fish Pavilion** (guãyú tíng; 观鱼亭) up a short, steep trail on the west bank. From the top of the pavilion, you can see the lake, Friendship Peak, the valley behind, and eagles circling overhead. Keep an eye out for the **giant lake monster** (húguài; 湖怪) rumored to live in the depths below. The best time to hike is in the early morning, when the still water reflects brilliantly and mist hangs over the ground. In July and August, wildflowers blanket the area and by September the leaves change into vibrant reds and yellows.

Spending at least one night at Hanas is necessary due to the long drive from Burqin. A **tourist village** has sprung up about 2km south of the lake, where you will likely get dropped off. Foreigners are required to stay at one of the tourist bureau's guesthouses, which, while not as homey as a family yurt, are pretty nice. A good bet is the brand-new **Linhai Mountain Villa** ❶ (lïnhâi shãnzhuãng; 林海山庄), which has pleasant 3-bed dorms for Y30 per person and doubles with bath for Y200, all in wood houses alongside the Hanas River. Take the first—and only—left off the main road and cross the river; the Linhai is the second guesthouse on the left.

So far, the area's designation as a national-level nature reserve and the Y100 admission tickets have yet to mar the isolated beauty of the lake, which remains untouched by pollution. Boardwalks and well-groomed trails are the only evidence of a tourism industry.

HEMU KANAS 禾木喀纳斯

About 30km southeast of Hanas Lake. Accessible only by jeep (about Y1000) over a very bumpy road in poor condition. Best visited as part of a 3-day trip with overnight stops here and at Hanas Lake. A valid Alien Travel Permit for Hanas Lake is the only permit required.

The tiny village of Hemu Kanas (hémù kãnàsï; 禾木喀纳斯), home to mostly Mongol residents, is idyllic almost beyond imagination. A few hundred families reside here, living in log cabins surrounded by towering, mist-enshrouded peaks. Cows lazily wander about the river in search of prime grazing opportunities. Snow lingers on parts of the ground throughout the summer. In July and August, the grass can reach a meter high, and wildflowers of every type and color blanket the hills and valleys outside of town. The best place to see flowers is along the main road, about 10 minutes before reaching the village, where the colorful fields stretch for miles in all directions. The local tourist industry is almost nonexistent, as the muddy, bumpy road keeps most visitors away. Foreigners are required to stay at a simple guesthouse run by the village government (about Y20 per person, with bargaining); your driver will most likely drop you off there.

ALTAI CITY 阿勒泰市 ☎0906

Altai City (ãlètàishì; 阿勒泰市), the prefectural capital, has the feel of a booming frontier town. Set amid gentle, rolling green hills and bisected by the roaring Kelan River, a tributary of the Ertix, the town is also quite a scenic spot. "Altai" means "gold" in Kazakh and Mongolian, and Altai City is renowned for its jewelry industry. An interesting sight is the lovely Birch Forest Park alongside the river. It may not be a must-see city, but Altai City is a relaxing spot to visit for a day or two to arrange permits and explore.

ORIENTATION AND PRACTICAL INFORMATION

Altai City is built up along the banks of the Kelan River, which runs north-south through the city. There are two main roads, also running north-south: **Tuanjie Lu**

(团结路) runs from the bus station in the far south before becoming **Gongyuan Lu** (公园路) and winding northward out of town; **Jiefang Lu** (解放路) branches off Tuanjie Lu near the bus station and is home to the Bank of China, Xinhua Bookstore, and Golden Bridge Hotel. The center of the city is at Golden Mountain Square on Jiefang Lu, where the **Camel Hump Bridge** (tuófēngqiáo; 驼峰桥) connects the two main roads.

Flights: The Altai City Airport (ãlètàishì jĭchâng; 阿勒泰市机场) is 17km from the city. A 20min. taxi from the city costs about Y15-20. The **CAAC Ticket Office** (☎212 8686; beeper ☎(126) 8374094), in the Xinhua Bookstore building, is a few doors to the right of the bookstore. Open M-F 10am-1:30pm and 4-7pm, Sa 11am-1:30pm and 4-6pm. To **Ürümqi** (Tu, Th, and Su 11:30pm; Y400, with 3-day advance purchase Y320).

Buses: Altai Passenger Station (ãlètàishì kèyùnzhàn; 阿勒泰市客运站), on Tuanjie Lu, a 25min. walk south of the city center, accessible by bus #1 or 101. Sleeper buses arriving in Altai tend to continue north into town and should be happy to drop you off wherever you're staying. To: **Burqin** (1½hr., frequent buses approx. 9am-8pm, Y12); **Ürümqi** (13hr., 5 and 7pm, Y100-114); and **Yining** (2 days, 11am and 7pm, Y142-162).

Travel Agencies: Kanas International Travel Agency (kãnàsī guóji læxíngshè; 喀纳斯国际旅行社), in Room 105 of the Tourist Hotel (☎212 0271). Offers 2-3 day tours to Hanas Lake (Y200-400). Open 8:30am-9pm. **Golden Bridge Travel Service** (jĭnqiáo læxíngshè; 金桥旅行社), in the Golden Bridge Hotel, has the same hours and similar services (☎212 0093).

Bank of China: On Jiefang Nan Lu, a 10min. walk south of Golden Mountain Square (☎212 1032). Exchanges traveler's checks. Open M-F 9:30am-1pm and 4-8pm, Sa-Su 11am-2:30pm.

PSB: To the right of the Xinhua Bookstore, at the end of the dead-end road. Permit and visa section on the 2nd fl. Issues 4-5 day Alien Travel Permits (læxíngzhèng; 旅行证; Y50) for Burqin and Hanas Lake, but is reluctant to give out permits for longer durations or for other areas. Open M-F 9:30am-1:30pm and 4-8pm.

Bookstore: Xinhua Bookstore, on Jiefang Lu (☎212 2032), north of Golden Mountain Square. Handy city and regional maps (Y3) on the 3rd fl. Open daily 9:30am-8pm.

Post and Telecommunications: On Jiefang Lu, across from the Xinhua Bookstore. China Telecom is on the 2nd fl. Open daily 9:30am-8pm. **Postal Code:** 836500.

ACCOMMODATIONS AND FOOD

Budget accommodations for foreigners, like the foreigners themselves, are pretty scarce. Still, the **Altai Tourist Hotel** has reasonably priced rooms and, like the Golden Bridge, is conveniently located.

As in most of Xinjiang, lamb is the staple around here. Lamb kebabs (Y0.5), lamb pastries (Y0.5), and lamb dumplings (Y0.2) abound at the **night market** next to the Golden Bridge Hotel. Small but enticing restaurants line **Gongyuan Lu** near the Tourist Hotel and **Jiefang Lu** south of the Golden Mountain Square.

Altai Tourist Hotel (ãlètàidìqū læyóu bĭnguân; 阿勒泰地区旅游宾馆; ☎212 3804), on Gongyuan Lu, just across the Camel Hump Bridge from Golden Mountain Square. A large, pleasant complex replete with trees and even some token goats grazing on the lawn. Rooms have slightly dingy carpets but clean sheets, big windows, nice TVs, and miniature spring-water dispensers. Attached baths are basic but functional. 24hr. hot water. Doubles Y100, triples Y135. Individual beds available. ❷

Golden Bridge Hotel (jĭqiáo dàjiūdiàn; 金桥大酒店), 1 Jiefang Lu (☎212 7566), opposite Golden Mountain Square. Foreign tour groups usually stay at the Golden Bridge, which has the amenities to cater to their rarefied tastes, with the high prices to match. Doubles Y200-260; triples Y230. ❸

SIGHTS

ALTAI JEWELRY COMPANY (ālètài dìqū bǎoshí gōngsī; 阿勒泰地区宝石公司). The delapidated exterior masks the gold and precious stones within. This is where all of the region's jewelry is produced, and a large showroom offers very reasonable prices. Altai is especially well-known for its blue hailan (hǎilán; 海兰) stones. Individual unset stones cost Y5-30, jewelry runs Y200-3000. Prices, as always, are negotiable. *(On Tuajie Lu, midway between the bus station and the center–take bus #1 or 101. Open M-F 10am-noon and 4-7pm, Sa-Su 10am-6pm.)*

BIRCH FOREST PARK (huálín gōngyuán; 桦林公园). Altai City's most famous sight is this vast, thick birch grove along the Kelan River, north of town. Known among Chinese tourists as a prime bird-watching spot, it's well-endowed with wildflowers. A paved road circumnavigates the park, with countless small dirt paths leading into the woods and along the river; one could easily spend the better part of a day exploring or just taking in the sights and smells. A few scattered tea houses serve up snacks and Kazakh milk tea. *(At the northern terminus of bus #101. Open daily sunrise-s unset. Y5.)*

YINING 伊宁 ☎0999

Nestled in a beautiful valley and surrounded by flower-covered grasslands and the towering Tianshan mountain range, Yining is very much on the fringes of China. Strategically located and populated by an eclectic mix of Kazakhs, Uighurs, Xibo, and Han Chinese, Yining has often been a focal point for conflict, most recently in 1997, when the city was rocked by violent riots started by Uighur separatists. Although the city itself has little of interest, the surrounding area is home to some of Xinjiang's most pristine wilderness areas, the most accessible of which is the breathtaking Sayram Lake, 180km east of Yining, where you can easily find yurt accommodation. The bus routes to Yining from both Ürümqi and Korla are spectacular, offering magnificent views of snow-capped mountains, barren deserts, and alpine river valleys. Stopping along the way between Yining and Ürümqi is quite feasible; buses are frequent and often pick up passengers along the way.

TRANSPORTATION

Flights: The **airport** is a 15min. taxi ride north of the city (Y10; drivers might try to charge Y20). **CAAC ticket office** (☎804 4328; 24hr. ☎803 2332), in the Yilite Hotel. Cancellations and delays are extremely common; check in advance with the CAAC ticket office or the travel agency. To **Ürümqi** (1-3 per day, Y590).

Buses: Yining Long-distance Bus Station (yīníng chángtú qìchē zhàn; 伊宁长途汽车站; ☎802 3413), on the northwest end of Jiefang Lu, near Ahemaitijiang Lu. Open daily 8am-8pm. To: **Almaty, Kazakhstan** (Su-M, W, F, US$30); **Altai City,** via Burqin (2 days, daily, Y150); **Kashgar** (48hr.; daily; hardseat Y103, sleeper Y215); **Korla** (18-30hr., daily, Y99); **Ürümqi** (17hr., every hr. 2-9pm, Y101-115). There is also a private company that advertises a 9hr. service to **Ürümqi** for Y175; buy tickets at the service counter across from the main ticket hall. Visas are not available locally.

Local Transportation: Bus #1 (Y0.5) runs along Jiefang Lu from the bus station to Qingnian Square in the east. Bus **#2** runs from the northwest end of Qingnian Square

west along Sidalin Jie before heading south to the Yili River Park (Y1.2) along Yili He Lu. **Pedicabs** cost Y3 within the city.

ORIENTATION AND PRACTICAL INFORMATION

Jiefang Lu (解放路) runs from the bus station in the northwest down to the post office near the southern limits of the city. **Sidalin Jie** (斯大林街) runs east-west, crossing **Qingnian Square** (qīngnián guǎngchǎng; 青年广场) and Jiefang Lu at the post office. Hotels are clustered near the bus station in the west and around Qingnian Square in the southeast.

Travel Agencies: Yili International Travel Agency (yīlí guójì lǚxíngshè; 伊犁国际旅行社; ☎802 4939), on Xinhua Lu, near Ahemaitijiang Lu, in the southeast part of town. Accessible by pedicab (Y3) from the bus station or downtown. Open daily 9:30am-1:30pm and 4-8pm. **Yining International Travel Agency** (yīníng guójì lǚxíng shè; 伊宁国际旅行社; ☎812 0298), on Ahemaitijiang Lu, in Jianyin Mansion (jiànyín dàshà; 建银大厦), a 5min. walk south from Jiefang Lu. Both agencies offer 1- to 3-day package tours of Sayram Lake, Nalati Grasslands, and other Yili Valley sites (about Y50 per day), although single travelers may have to wait to tag along with a larger tour group. Ticket commission Y20 at both agencies.

NORTHWEST

Bank of China: On Jiefang Lu, just east of and across the street from the bus station. Exchange traveler's checks (counters #2, 3, 4). Open in summer M-F 9:30am-1:30pm and 4-8pm; in winter 10am-2pm and 3:30-7:30pm; year-round Sa-Su 11am-5pm.

PSB: (☎802 2491, ext. 3026). On Sidalin Jie, across from Qingnian Park. The unhelpful visa office is in the squat building on the left side of the complex. Staff are a bit secretive—office is appropriately located on Stalin St. Open M-F 9:30am-1:30pm and 4-8pm.

China Telecom: On the corner of Sidalin Lu and Jiefang Lu. IDD. Open daily in summer 9:30am-10pm; in winter 10am-7:30pm.

Post Office: On Xinhua Lu, near Qingnian Lu. EMS and Poste Restante. Open daily in summer 9:30am-10pm; in winter 10am-7:30pm. **Postal Code:** 835000.

ACCOMMODATIONS

Yining has limited budget options; dorm beds are rarely open to foreigners. Many hotels require single travelers to pay for an entire room, a policy that is almost impossible to get around. Luckily, mid-range singles are available in the gorgeous Yili Hotel and, with some haggling, in the conveniently located Yaxiya Hotel.

Yili Hotel (yīlí bīnguân; 伊犁宾馆), 22 Yingbin Lu (☎802 2794 or 802 3799), a 5min. walk north of Qingnian Square, at the end of Hongqi Lu. A beige gate leads to the forest-like grounds of the complex, housing several unassuming buildings and a few old Russian-style restaurants and conference centers. Evening music and dance performances are frequent. Rooms in the beautiful west wing (building #4) have large breezy baths. The main building is more modern and sterile. All rooms have private baths. Singles Y120; standard doubles Y120, nicer ones Y160-300. 30% discounts possible. ❷

Post and Telecommunications Guesthouse (yóudiàn bīnguân; 邮电宾馆), 162 Jiefang Lu (☎822 3844), a short walk east of the Bank of China. Many of the bright, cheery rooms look out onto the trash-strewn roof of the building next door. As an added bonus, this hotel is the "Home of God" (at least according to the enormous, gold-lettered English sign behind the reception). Front building: singles Y158, doubles Y158-300, all with bath. Back building: doubles Y44-54, with bath Y100; triples with bath Y105. ❶

Asia Hotel (yàxìyà bīnguân; 亚细亚宾馆; ☎803 1800, ext. 5100). From the bus station, turn right on Jiefang Lu, then turn right on the street directly across from the Bank of China; the Asia is on the left. The friendly staff speaks a bit of English and is happy to bargain, although you forfeit your free breakfast if you get a discount. Singles with large bed Y98; doubles Y100; triples Y108. ❷

Huacheng Hotel (huāchéng bīnguân; 花城宾馆; ☎812 5050, ext. 828). Veer east on Junmin Lu, a slight left off Jiefang Lu at the trisection just west of the bus station; the hotel is about 100m ahead on the left. This hotel was in the midst of an upgrade from 2 stars to 3 in June 2001, when delapidated dorms were still available for rockbottom prices; whether these will survive the wrecking ball is unclear. 3-bed dorms Y11-25; doubles with bath Y80-180. ❶

SIGHTS

People's Park (rénmín gōngyuán; 人民公园), on Ahetoutijiang Lu, about 10 minutes south of the Huacheng Hotel, is nothing much in itself, but it's still a nice place to walk around. There are some great outdoor restaurants nearby where you can enjoy noodles, lamb kebabs (or lamb's head, if you want), and a cold beer while sitting among the trees. In the back of the park, a mini-park dedicated to the Communist Revolution has several martyrs' tombs and a small photo gallery. (Open daily sunrise-sunset. Park Y3; museum Y2.)

NORTHWEST

Another nice spot is the **Yili River Park** (yīlíjiāng gōngyuán; 伊犁江公园), 6km south of the city, centered around the Yili River Bridge. From the Yili Hotel, take either bus #2 to the bridge (Y1.2) or a taxi (Y7). Buses run every 20 minutes or so in both directions. Although the scenery here is less than astounding, a walk along the far bank takes you through some picturesque farmland along grassy poplar-lined dirt paths. The bank is full of hawkers selling speed boat rides and instant photos.

For the anthropologically inclined, the nearby town of **Qapqal** (pronounced tshap-tshael, in Chinese chábùcháêr; 察布查尔), is home to the tiny Xibo minority, descendents of the Manchu garrisons that were sent to guard the frontier during the Qing dynasty. The Xibo zealously maintain their own spoken language, script (featured on the back of Chinese money—it's the vertically written one), and archery prowess. The town itself is pretty sleepy, but the surrounding countryside is pleasant. There's a tourist village about 6km from town where you can witness an archery display and see traditional life up close. (20km southwest of Yining. Buses leave from in front of the long-distance bus station whenever full (Y3). A permit, available from Yining PSB, is required to visit Qapqal county. Foreigners lacking permits will be fined Y500 and sternly lectured by the Qapqal PSB.)

NEAR YINING: SAYRAM LAKE

Just off the main Ürümqi-Yining highway, 135km north of Yining. If you are coming from the east, take a long-distance ***bus*** *from Ürümqi; the road is in decent condition and buses are fairly reliable. Most buses will stop at the lakeside town, but ask beforehand just to be sure. Heading back to Yining, frequent buses run approx. 8am-5pm; be prepared to hail them down. To go from Yining to the lake, take a bus to* ***Bole*** *(博乐) (2hr., every hr. starting at 11:50am, Y25). Going directly to Ürümqi from Sayram Lake is not advised; sleeper buses are often full and ticket prices are inflated.*

The beauty and isolation of Sayram Lake (sàilǐmù hú; 赛里木湖) make this one of the best options for exploring nature in northwestern Xinjiang. This huge lake surrounded by snow-capped mountains is one of Xinjiang's most awe-inspiring sites. While Tianchi's small size encourages hiking forays up into the surrounding alpine cliffs, Sayram Lake has the relaxing feel of a small ocean, with pebble beaches bleeding out of the lowland pastures and the quiet sound of the tides lapping at the shore. Although the stretch of highway running alongside the lake has become a nauseating tourist center (complete with food stands, trashy cinder block housing, and even a go-cart track), you have only to walk along a small dirt road clockwise around the lake from the bus stop to enjoy the lakeside wildflower meadows and grazing pastures. The lake's pristine grasslands and wildflower coves are home to a few hundred scattered Mongol and Kazakh family yurts; many offer a night's lodging with meals (Y30; more if you want to eat meat—i.e. lamb). Although more isolated yurts may take you in if you offer a simple gift (and payment), yurts with Chinese characters written on their sides are more accustomed to hosting guests. Bring warm clothes, as evenings are downright cold, even in the summer. Indeed, visiting anytime other than June to September is not advised as most local families spend the off season in the Yili Valley, making it difficult to find accommodation.

NORTHWEST

TURPAN 吐鲁番 ☎0995

Turpan is a stunning introduction to the inhospitable, rugged, and inspiring terrain of the Xinjiang region. Nicknamed "The Oven," the town is located in the Turpan Depression, a stifling hot 50,000km^2 desert. Summer temperatures hover around 40°C (100°F), but can sometimes reach as high as 48°C (118°F). Things are hotter still in the nearby Flaming Mountains. Most of the cloud moisture evaporates before it reaches the ground, and the region receives a whopping 1-2cm of rain per year. Despite its hellish climate, however, Turpan, and the neighboring town of Hami have their charms: they are famous for their grapes, multicolored melons, cantaloupes, apricots, and sun-dried raisins. Public transport is still dominated by donkey carts that patrol the shaded, grapevine-covered thoroughfares. Tombs and ruins in the nearby valleys have kept archaeologists occupied for decades, but two days in the stifling heat is more than enough for most visitors. Of course, visitors can always avoid the heat by coming during winter months, when Turpan's extreme temperatures drop to around -25°C (-13°F).

TRANSPORTATION

Trains: Turpan Train Station (tûlûfān zhàn; 吐鲁番站) is actually in the town of **Daheyan** (大河沿), 50km northwest of Turpan. Minibuses go to Daheyan every 30min. or when full. The cheapest transport is by public bus (1-2hr., every 30min. 7am-7pm, Y6), but taxi drivers may make the trip for the same price. To: **Dunhuang/Liuyuan** (11hr., several evening trains, Y151); **Kashgar** (27hr., daily, Y333); **Korla** (9hr., 2 per day, Y120); **Xi'an** (40-45hr., 2 per day, Y305) via **Lanzhou** (32hr., Y242).

Bus: The **long-distance bus station** (☎852 2325) on Laocheng Lu resembles a white- and green-tiled mosque. Open daily 6:30am-8pm. Roads to Hami aren't great; take the train instead. To: **Kashgar** (24hr., daily, Y126) via **Korla** (6-7hr., Y38); **Kuga** (14-15hr., Y61); **Ürümqi** (2½hr., every 30min. 7:30am-7:30pm, Y24).

Local Transportation: Minibus fare Y4. **#1** travels east-west along Xincheng Lu, Laocheng Lu, and Muna'er Lu; **#2** runs north-south along Gaocheng Lu; **#5** goes north on Gaocheng Lu before heading east; **#6** runs south on Gaocheng Lu, before heading east (in front of the Turpan Hotel) and continuing out to Emin Minaret. **Donkey-pulled wagons** and **taxis** also help beat the heat. Fare about Y2-4 within the city.

ORIENTATION AND PRACTICAL INFORMATION

This oasis town is just big enough to have two major streets: **Gaochang Lu** (高昌路), which runs north-south, and **Xincheng Lu** (新城路), which intersects Gaochang Lu, becomes **Laocheng Lu** (老城路), and eventually turns into **Munaer Lu** (木纳尔路) to the east. The long-distance bus station and many tourist offices are along Laocheng Lu; the Turpan Museum is on Gaochang Lu. Hotels are spread rather evenly throughout the area. The center for nightlife and entertainment is the **Cultural Square** (wénhuà yóu guângchâng; 文化游广场), sandwiched between Qingnian Lu and Gaochang Lu, just north of John's Information Cafe.

Travel Agency: CITS (☎852 1352 or 852 2491, ext. 2443), in the Oasis Hotel to the right of the gated entrance. A second branch in the Turpan Hotel is open only during the summer. Commission Y30-60. The employees at the main office are more efficient and speak English, but both offices provide tours of Turpan for Y40-50. The better (and cheaper) bet is to bargain for a tour of the surrounding sights (usually 8 in all) with the Uighur taxi drivers who hang out at John's Information Cafe; the full-day affair costs Y200-300 and can be split among 4-5 people. Mamat, a guide at John's, runs trips out to the Gobi Desert for Y400-500 per car.

Bank of China: 18 Laocheng Lu (☎852 3067), across from the bus station. Exchanges traveler's checks. Open in summer M-F 9am-2pm and 4-8pm; in winter 9:30am-7:30pm.

Bookstore: Xinhua Bookstore (☎852 6644), on the north side of Laocheng Lu, diagonally opposite the Bank of China. No English novels. Helpful bilingual maps (Y2.5) and locally published guidebooks in English and Chinese about Xinjiang (Y28 and up).

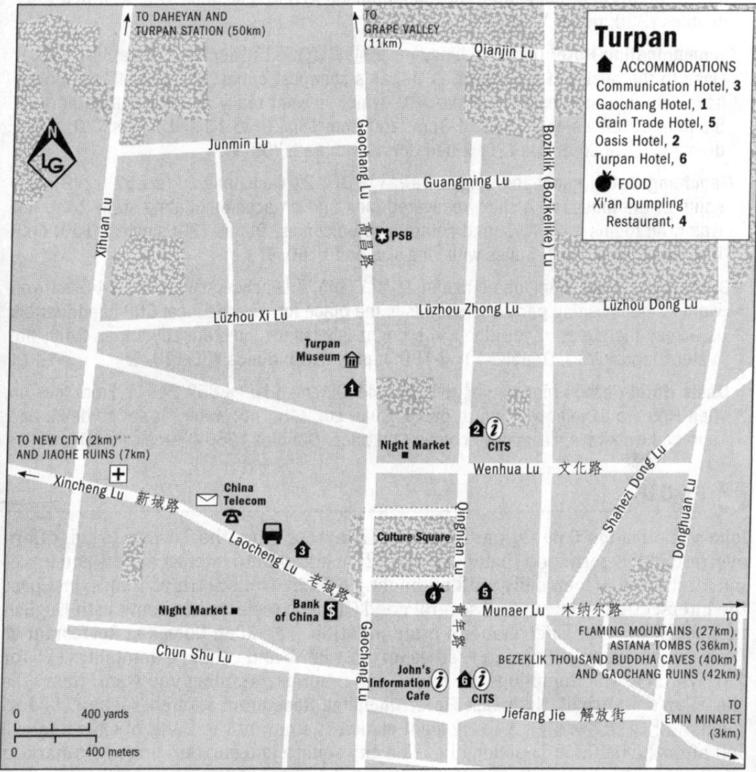

PSB: 47 Gaochang Lu (☎098-9975 3512), opposite the Victory Hotel, in the north part of town. The **Foreign Affairs Office** for visa extensions is on the 2nd fl. of the building, to the right inside the compound gate. Open M-F 9am-noon and 5-8pm.

Telecommunications and Internet Access: China Telecom (☎852 3070), in a small building down an alley 50m past the post office. Y10 per hr. Open daily 9am-midnight. **John's Information Cafe** has IDD service and Internet access (Y10 per hr.).

Post Office: China Post (☎852 2731), on Laocheng Lu, west of the bus station. EMS and Poste Restante. Open daily 9am-8pm. **Postal Code:** 838000.

ACCOMMODATIONS

Almost all hotel rooms in Turpan, except for some of the cheap dorms, have air-conditioning. All are within walking distance of the central square and the night bazaar, although the Turpan Hotel is closest.

Turpan Hotel (tûlûfān bīnguǎn; 吐鲁番宾馆), 2 Qingnian Lu (☎852 2301; fax 852 3262), across from John's Cafe. A swimming pool, massage/sauna center, and a billiard hall are in the nearby building. In the summer, there are nightly Uighur song and dance. Hot water 7am-2am, common showers 3-9pm. Deposit Y50; no deposit on

NORTHWEST

dorms. Dorms in a remarkably cool subterranean A/C-less location Y22, with A/C Y27; doubles Y380; triples Y300. AmEx/MC/V. ❶

Communication Hotel (jiāotōng bīnguân; 交通宾馆), 125 Laocheng Lu (☎853 1320), close to the bustle of downtown, is Turpan's cheapest option. Clean, well-kept dorms have very thin mattresses, but the A/C—which is what really matters around here—is brand-new. Hot water 7-10am, 1-3pm, and 8pm-1am. 6- to 10-bed dorms Y20; 4-bed dorms Y20; 3-bed dorms Y25; 2-bed dorms with bath Y60. ❶

Gaochang Hotel (gāochāng bīnguân; 高昌宾馆), 22 Gaochang Lu (☎852 3229), just south of the museum. A slick, renovated look and an accommodating staff. 24hr. hot water. All rooms have A/C, and some have balconies. Dorms Y20; singles Y100; doubles and triples Y120. Suites with king-size bed Y160. ❶

Grain Trade Hotel (liángmào bīnguân; 粮贸宾馆), 7 Laocheng Lu (☎856 7449). If you want to meet visiting party cadres, this is the place for you; the local CCP headquarters is across the street. If you don't, the bright, pleasant rooms are still super. 24hr. hot water. Deposit Y30. Doubles Y168-180; triples Y150; quads Y80-170. ❸

Oasis Hotel (lǜzhōu bīnguân; 绿洲宾馆), 41 Qingnian Lu (☎852 2491). From the Turpan Hotel, a 10min. walk north on Qingnian Lu. 24hr. hot water, flower gardens, and terraced walkways. Loveliness comes at a price. Doubles Y280-680. MC/V. ❹

FOOD

John's Information Cafe ❷, on Gaochang Lu across from the Turpan Hotel, offers overpriced Western food (hamburgers Y22) in addition to **Internet** access and travel info and tours. (Open daily until midnight.) A 5min. walk north of John's, just past the intersection, you can find several good Chinese restaurants, some with English menus. Beware of English-menu price inflation. The **Xi'an Dumpling Restaurant ❶** (xīān jiâozi guân; 西安饺子馆) serves up tasty lamb and cabbage dumplings (Y6 for 20). Watch as the dumplings are made, and point at the filling you want. Nearby is the Xi'an's archrival, **Northeast Flavor Dumpling Restaurant** (dōngbêi fēngwèi jiâozi guân; 东北风味饺子馆). A lively **night market** is south of the Bank of China; take a left after the bank on Laocheng Lu. The city square and surrounding night markets are perhaps the best options for a cheap meal and cold beer.

SIGHTS

Turpan's sights are best visited in one busy day, especially during the blistering summer months. Taxis average Y250-300 for the day; admission is extra. Although there is no need to hire a guide to the sights in and around Turpan, they can help you make arrangements for further travel within Xinjiang. Most private Uighur guides speak fluent Japanese and excellent English; drivers usually speak Uighur and Mandarin only. For a local tour, go to John's Information Cafe, across from Turpan Hotel; guides and drivers congregate here at all times, and they each offer a similar one-day tour (about Y50 per person). It's cheapest to join a group and hire a guide, but you might have little say in the schedule then.

TURPAN CITY

EMIN MINARET (émĭn tă; 额敏塔). Also known as **Sugong Minaret** (sūgōng tâ 苏公塔), this active mosque was built by Emin Hoja in 1778 and has an impressive tower rising over 43m. In June 2001, the interior was being rebuilt; if renovations aren't complete by the time you visit, it's not worth the admission fee. A climb up the smaller structure to the right provides an excellent view of the surrounding vineyards. *(2km east of town center. Included in most tours. Open daily sunrise-sunset. Y20.)*

TURPAN MUSEUM (tǔlǔfān bówùguǎn; 吐鲁番博物馆). This recently renovated complex is well-lit and well-financed, but the lack of English captions may deter those who don't speak Chinese. Stroll through the displays on human evolution and learn about the incredible variety of prehistoric animals and dinosaurs that roamed Xinjiang in times past. Colorful models, fossilized remains, and reconstructed skeletons offer a glimpse of landscape before the desert took over. The second floor contains an eerie collection of 1500-year-old preserved mummies. *(On Gaochang Lu, just north of the Gaochang Hotel. ☎852 3774. Open daily 9am-8pm. Y20.)*

NEAR TURPAN

JIAOHE RUINS (jiāohé gǔchéng; 交河古城). Built atop a 30m cliff carved out by two rivers, the once-flourishing city of Jiaohe has a 2000-year history. Han records indicate that in 109 BC, the city contained 700 families, 6050 citizens, and 1856 soldiers. It served as the capital of the Kingdom of Jushi in AD 450 but was eventually abandoned, probably due to a lack of water. You can still find the small rooms, temples, courtyards, and streets sculpted out of sun-baked earth. In 1994, archaeologists found the graves of more than 200 infants northwest of the site. The reason for their burial is still a mystery. During the summer, try to visit at sunset, if possible, when the heat lets up a little. *(7km west of town. Open daily sunrise-sunset. Y30.)*

BOZIKELIKE CAVE (bózīkèlǐkè qiānfó dòng; 柏孜克里克千佛洞). Fortunately, Bozikelike has stunning parched mountain scenery, which alone makes the trip worthwhile. Otherwise many of the area's grottoes, stripped of their contents during the early 20th century, can be a big let-down. Prestige-hungry foreign archaeologists (read: art thieves) like Aurel Stein and Albert von Le Coq took much of the art; what remained was heavily vandalized by Islamic fundamentalists who scratched out the eyes of the Buddhist images. Many of the caves open to the public date to the Buddhist kingdom of Gaochang.

GAOCHANG RUINS (gāochāng gǔchéng; 高昌古城). The center of the Uighur empire in the 9th century, Gaochang has largely crumbled away and is a lesser cousin to the impressive Jiaohe Ruins. Founded in the Liang dynasty (397-439), Gaochang was conquered by Tang Emperor Taizong in 640. Later, the famous monk Xuan Zang taught Buddhism here during his 18-year epic journey to obtain Indian scriptures. The only visible structure left is the city's massive outer wall. The many windows and doorways reveal views of the Flaming Mountains beyond. *(A good 40km east of Turpan. Those wary of the oppressive heat can take a donkey cart (Y7-10 round-trip) from the entrance to the main temple site. Open daily sunrise-sunset. Y20.)*

GRAPE VALLEY (pútáo gōu; 葡萄沟). Although your driver will undoubtedly try to take you here for a midday rest, the area boasts little more than some nice walks and a steep admission price. Food options are also limited; two or three vendors inside sell noodles and wine. Be sure to try the tasty raisins, or go to the strip of restaurants just along the cliff edge bearing the huge characters 葡萄沟. And for about Y15 per person, you can sample *laghman* (the local noodle specialty), lamb kebabs, and fresh grapes. The wide variety of fresh and dried fruits is delicious and cheap; the wine, however, is not impressive. The cheaper wine tastes remarkably like bad cough medicine; higher-quality wine costs Y30-40 per bottle. After lunch, most guides take visitors swimming in the irrigation canals just up the hill, a popular leisure spot for local youngsters. *(Open daily sunrise-sunset. Y20.)*

FLAMING MOUNTAINS (huǒyán shān; 火焰山). Aptly named the Flaming Mountains, the midday temperatures on these reddish slopes can top 55°C. According to the famous novel *Journey to the West*, when the Tang dynasty monk Xuan Zang came here, fires raged for hundreds of miles. His companion, the Monkey King, had to extinguish the flames with a magical palm fan whisked from the throat of the ever-protective Iron Fan Princess. *(Free.)*

KAREZ IRRIGATION SYSTEM. An exposed 10m section of the ancient Persian-style underground irrigation tunnels, Karez is visible elsewhere in Turpan and offers essentially the same attractions as the Grape Valley. Hordes of tourists and more trinket vendors than you can count crowd into a tiny section of the original baked earthen wall canals. *(Open daily sunrise-sunset. Y20.)*

KORLA 库尔勒

☎0996

This predominantly Han Chinese city is one of Xinjiang's most important economic centers; sight-seeking tourists who can't tell their supply from their demand will probably find little of interest in Korla. In fact, the most enlightening experience for many who travel here may be the bus ride into the city which features incredible views of the desert's barren canyons and black and red rock formations. Korla's oppressively bleak skyline, crammed full of industrial factories and office towers, is not exactly inspiring after the amazing bus ride. The city does have a few charms; at night the streets teem with food bazaars, live music performances, and fashionable young women. But still, most of Korla's sights—including the largest lake in Xinjiang and a handful of ruins—are unimpressive, with the exception of the Ancient Poplar Forest, a spectacular grove of two- to three-thousand-year-old trees growing in rippling white sand dunes.

TRANSPORTATION

Flights: As of July 2001, the **Korla Airport** (kùěrlè fēijīchǎng; 库尔勒飞机场) had suspended service; if it resumes, there will likely be flights to **Ürümqi.**

Trains: Korla Train Station (kùěrlè huǒchē zhàn; 库尔勒火车站), in the southeast corner of the city. Accessible by bus #1 from People's Square or by taxi (Y10). Booking sleeper tickets to **Kashgar** is virtually impossible here, but you may be able to upgrade to a sleeper once onboard. To **Kashgar** (13hr.; 3 per day; hard seat Y100-130, hard sleeper Y196-239) and **Ürümqi** (11hr., 3 per day, Y155).

Buses: The **bus station** (kèyùn zhōngxīn; 客运中心; ☎207 6390) is on Beishan Lu, in the north of the city. Accessible by bus #2 from People's Square. Although roads are often in terrible condition (especially those heading west), buses are the most convenient way to travel to Kuqa and Ürümqi. To: **Hotan** (26hr., 2 per day, Y130-207); **Kashgar** (24hr., 3 per day, Y102-162); **Kuqa** (7hr., 6 per day, Y28-45); **Ruoqiang** (12hr., daily, Y59-83); **Ürümqi** (12hr., 2 per day, Y65-110); **Yining** (30hr., daily, Y70-102).

Shuttle Taxis: Immediately to the right of the bus station, a stand sells tickets on high speed transport; these shuttles travel about twice as fast as buses. The rates apply to full cars (4 passengers); else, you must either wait or pay for the empty seats. To: **Kuqa** (Y85); **Lotus Lake** or **Western Bosten Lake** (Y15); **Luntai** (Y30); **Ürümqi** (Y150).

Local Transportation: Fare Y0.5-1. **Bus #1** runs along Renmin Lu; **#2** runs north to the long-distance bus station and west to the Bosten Hotel. **Taxi** base fare is Y5. From People's Square to the train station Y10, to most other points Y5.

ORIENTATION AND PRACTICAL INFORMATION

The downtown area clusters around **People's Square** (rénmín guǎngchǎng 人民广场). Most tourist services and accommodations are within a 20-minute walk of the square. **Renmin Lu** (人民路) runs east-west, south of the square. The bus station is to the north on **Beishan Lu** (北山路), which runs south into **Jiaotong**

Lu (交通路). **Jianshe Lu** (建设路) passes People's Square and connects Renmin Lu and Beishan Lu.

Travel Agencies: The Kaide and Bosten hotels both have travel agencies. The **Gongnaisi Travel Service** (gôngnâisī lǚxíngshè; 巩乃斯旅行社; ☎203 2858), Kaide Hotel, 5th fl. Good rates for tours to the Poplar Forest (Y360 includes car, driver, and guide).

Bank of China: On Renmin Lu (☎202 5086), a 10min. walk east of People's Square, on the left. Exchanges traveler's checks. Open daily 9:30am-1:30pm and 4-8pm.

Internet Access: In the China Telecom building in People's Square. Y5 per hr. Open daily past midnight.

Post Office: Post and Telecom Office (☎202 3788), just off People's Square on Renmin Lu, has a large neon sign visible from the street; the sign only says "China Telecom," but the post office is also inside. Open daily 9:30am-1:30pm and 4:30-7:30pm. **Postal Code:** 841000.

ACCOMMODATIONS

Korla's fledgling tourism industry is not taking its first steps in a budget-friendly direction. Only a handful of luxury hotels can take foreigners and, of these, only the Bayinguoleng Hotel has cheap dorm beds.

Kaide Hotel (kâidè jiǔdiàn; 凯德酒店), 12 Renmin Dong Lu (☎209 2188), a 15min. walk east of People's Square. The rooms in this modern glass tower are a relatively good bargain despite the high prices. Business center, travel agency, and excellent restaurant on-site. Singles Y188; doubles Y236; triples Y180. MC/V. ❸

Bayinguoleng Hotel (bāyīnguōlèng bīnguân; 巴音郭愣宾馆; ☎202 4441), also known as the Bazhou Hotel (bāzhōu bīnguân; 巴州宾馆), on Renmin Dong Lu, a 15min. walk east of People's Square. Dorms have the same luxury feel as main tower rooms, with A/C, TV, wooden decor, and sparkling tile floors. 24hr. hot water. Dorms Y30; singles Y188; doubles Y218. ❶

Bosten Hotel (bósīténg bīnguân; 博斯腾宾馆; ☎202 2118), on Renmin Lu, pretty far west from People's Square and the night bazaars. English speaker and on-site travel agency (☎203 3444). Decent singles and doubles Y168; triples Y50 per person. ❷

SIGHTS

Korla's biggest tourist draw is the nearby Bosten Lake, but the best reason to come to Korla is to see the northern border of the **Taklimakan Desert** (tâkèlāmâgān shāmò; 塔克拉玛干沙漠), a fabulous ecosystem filled with flowering bushes, white sands, and ancient poplar trees. The tiny streams and rivulets of the **Tarim River** (tâlîmù hé; 塔里木河) branch through the desert during brief rainy periods.

POPLAR FOREST PARK (húyáng sēnlín gōngyuán; 胡杨森林公园). About 120km south of **Luntai** (轮台), the highway winding through the Taklimakan Desert en route to Hotan encounters a surreal landscape of ancient poplar trees. Gnarled and weathered trunks emerge from seemingly barren white sands that rest high above basins of water. A quiet, solemn feel pervades this exotic forest. The park itself is of little interest and is 15 minutes from the roadside groves that feature the older, more impressive spots. To simplify things, tell the driver that you want to go to the park; have him stop at the roadside groves along the way. Hiking the dunes can easily fill an entire afternoon. *(Take an early morning taxi shuttle (2hr., Y40 per person) from Korla to Luntai; you may have to wait for other people to fill the car's 4 seats. From Luntai, hire a taxi to take you to the forest (Y100 round-trip, more if you want to do some hiking). Make sure the driver understands that you will be gone a long time; pay him once you return to Luntai.*

To return to Korla, take the bus (4-5hr., Y20) or a shuttle taxi. With careful planning and a light pack, you could take the train directly to Luntai from Ürümqi, skipping a potentially expensive night in Korla. After seeing the forest, take a taxi or bus back to Korla. Park admission Y8.)

BOSTEN LAKE (bósīténg hú; 博斯腾湖). Although it is touted as Korla's premier tourist attraction, Bosten Lake is a resounding disappointment. Only two spots on the lake are accessible by public transportation: the Golden Sands Resort and the Lotus Pond. The **Golden Sands** (jīn shātān; 金沙滩) is a tacky beach resort with inflatable air mattresses and plastic umbrellas to spare. If you are willing to shell out Y200-250 for a regretful, bitter afternoon, you can hire a boat to explore the reed-covered marshes and small fishing towns nearby. If you really want to see the lake, a better option is to visit **Lotus Pond** (liánhuā chí; 莲花池), where you can spend a few hours strolling next to thickly growing lotuses and water lilies. In summer months, however, you may not be able to see anything more than the tips of rushes peeking out through the seasonally high water. *(Buses to the Golden Sands Resort (2hr., Y50 round-trip) leave daily at 9-10am from the south side of People's Square, across from the PICC Building; return trip at 6pm. Y20. Lotus Pond is best reached by shuttle taxi (Y12 per person in a 4-person car) from Korla Bus Station.)*

KUQA 库车 ☎0996

Present-day Kuqa is probably the most interesting stop on the way to Kashgar from Ürümqi. This area, nestled in the foothills of the Tianshan mountain range, helped to spread Buddhism into China via the Northern Silk Road. Grottoes and ancient ruins are scattered to the north of the city, a testament to the area's rich, 1500-year history that has been so well-preserved by the the remarkable desert climate. Today, the compact New Town quickly fades into an entrancing network of small dirt roads that weave through traditional mud-brick Uighur architecture, revealing colorful archways, shady grape trellises, mosques, and food markets. Taking a stroll through this area is a great way to immerse yourself in Uighur culture and traditional living without the glare of tour bus glass.

ORIENTATION AND PRACTICAL INFORMATION

Kuqa is divided into two sections. To the east is the predominantly Han Chinese **New Town** (xīn chéng; 新城), a relatively modern area containing foreigner-friendly hotels, tourist services, and the bus and train stations. To the west is the predominantly Uighur section of the city known as the **Old Town** (lǎo chéng; 老城), which contains bustling market streets in the south and residential areas in the north that are connected by small farm plots and poplar-lined dirt roads. **Wenhua Lu** (文化路) runs through the center of town, parallel to **Tianshan Lu** (天山路), which passes the bus station and the Jiaotong and Kuqa Hotels before intersecting with the two main north-south thoroughfares: **Youyi Lu** (友谊路) and **Jiefang Lu** (解放路). Tianshan Lu branches north just past the western limits of the new city before it enters the Uighur residential district. The southern fork becomes **Linji Lu** (林基路), which crosses a large bridge, the effective center of the Friday bazaar, and heads into the heart of the Old Town, passing the Kuqa Mosque on the right.

Trains: Kuqa Train Station (kùchē huǒchē zhàn; 库车火车站; ☎293 6462), 7km southeast of New Town, accessible by taxi (Y10) or bus #2 or 6. As of July 2001, tickets for westbound trains could only be purchased at the station no more than 1hr. before departure. To **Kashgar** (8-9hr., 3 per day, Y48) and **Ürümqi** (15hr., 2 per day, Y57).

Buses: Kuqa Long-distance Bus Station (kùchē chángtú qìchē zhàn; 库车长途汽车站; ☎712 2379), in the southeast of New Town. Take any bus running east on

Tianshan Lu or a Y6 taxi from most hotels. Open daily 8am-8:30pm. Buses to Kashgar originate in Korla or Ürümqi; departure times from Kuqa are irregular, and seats or sleepers are not guaranteed. To: **Kashgar** (20hr., morning and afternoon departures, Y75-110); **Korla** (8hr., every hr. 9:30am-2:30pm, Y25); **Ürümqi** (20hr., 2 per day, sleeper Y80-90); **Yining** (2 days, 8:00am, Y77).

Travel Agency: Kuqa's only travel agency is on Tianshan Lu, in the main lobby of the Qiuci Hotel (☎/fax 712 2524). Although their rates for private tours of the Kuqa area are slightly more expensive than arrangements made with drivers associated with hotels, the staff is friendly and accommodating, and can help single travelers link up with others in order to share expenses. Be sure to specify which of Kuqa's sites you want to see, as there are too many to see in a day. Standard 1-day tours of Kuqa Y250 per car, with A/C Y300. 1-day tours to Big Dragon Lake (dàlóng chí; 大龙池), 140km to the north, Y380 per car. Open daily 9:30am-1:30pm and 4-8pm.

Bank of China: On Tianshan Lu, a 10min. walk west of the bus station. Exchanges traveler's checks. Credit card advances at the counter on the far right. Open daily 9:30am-1:30pm and 4-8pm; in winter 10am-1:30pm and 4-7pm.

PSB: On Tianshan Lu, to the right of the Qiuci Hotel.

Hospital: Kuqa County People's Hospital (kùchēxiàn rénmín yīyuàn; 库车县人民医院), 36 Jiefang Lu. Open 24hr.

Bookstore: Xinhua Bookstore, on the corner of Youyi Lu and Wenhua Lu, in the center of New Town. Sells maps of Kuqa and surrounding tourist sights for Y3.

Post and Telecommunications: On the central downtown corner of Wenhua Lu and Youyi Lu. The **post office** is on the left; **China Telecom** is a few doors down on the right. IDD service. Both open in summer daily 9:30am-8pm; in winter 10am-7:30pm.

ACCOMMODATIONS AND FOOD

When staying in Kuqa, decide how much you care about being in the center of town; the out-of-the-way Traffic and Kuqa Hotels are great values.

The best night markets are in the Uighur quarter. If you're out east, a gaggle of Han and Uighur noodle shops across from the bus station serve up tasty *bàn miàn* (拌面) noodles for Y7. The Kuqa Hotel has top-notch Sichuanese and Muslim restaurants.

Minmao Hotel (mínmào bīnguǎn; 民贸宾馆), 16 Wenhua Lu (☎712 2999), at Jiefang Lu, in the heart of New Town. This small 2-story hotel has a nice surprise inside: doubles are well-lit with new carpets and tiled baths. Doubles Y100, with A/C Y120; triples with A/C Y165. ❷

Kuqa Hotel (kùchē fàndiàn; 库车饭店; ☎713 1156), on Tianshan Lu. From the bus station, take a left and walk 10min.; the hotel is on the right side. The reception area is just off the parking lot to the rear. The location isn't superb, but this hotel offers big rooms with A/C, bath, a spring water dispenser, and TV. 24hr. hot water. Breakfast included. Front desk books eastbound train tickets. Singles Y140; doubles Y160; triples Y120. ❷

Traffic Hotel (jiāotōng bīnguǎn; 交通宾馆; ☎712 2682), facing the parking lot on the right side as you exit the bus station. The cheaper doubles have decent sheets, concrete floors, a new coat of hostel-green paint, and sometimes even a TV. Hot water 6pm-10am. 3-bed dorms Y15; singles Y150; doubles Y20, with bath Y100-120. ❶

Guici Hotel (guīcí bīnguǎn; 龟兹宾馆), 93 Tianshan Lu (☎712 2005), a good 3km west of the bus station. The closest hotel to the Uighur Old Town is also Kuqa's most expensive option. Most rooms have views of the lush arbors and flower gardens, and all have sparkling tile floors, new A/C, phone, and TV. Kuqa's only travel service is near the main lobby. Doubles Y250. ❹

SIGHTS

The mountains around Kuqa are filled with Buddhist grottoes and remnants of Silk Road-era cities, but there is no public transportation available and roads are often in poor condition. The travel agency in the Guici Hotel is a good source for information; check with them to plan out your day in advance. If you have time and money, you can charter a taxi to take you to some of the lesser-known, but much more interesting nearby areas. Normally, a standard one-day tour (Y300) includes the Kizil Grottoes, the Kizilgaha Beacon Tower, the Subashi Temple Ruins, and the Kuqa Mosque. Perhaps the best part of the tour is the ride to the Kizil Grottoes on a desolate highway that winds through the red canyons of the Tianshan foothills. Known as **Tianshanmai** (literally, "the veins of the Tianshan mountains"; tiānshānmài; 天山脉), this amazing area is a great place to stop and take some photos, although the rough terrain makes hiking extremely difficult. Independent taxi drivers charge the lowest prices, often Y50-100 less than hotel travel agencies.

KIZIL GROTTOES (kèzēěr qiān fó dòng; 克孜尔千佛洞). Even though it's supposedly the richest and best-preserved Buddhist grotto site in the Kuqa area, this cliff-side network of caves is actually in rather poor condition. Dating from the 3rd through 9th centuries AD, the caves have been vandalized several times by Islamic fundamentalists who liked to gouge out the painted eyes of the Buddhas and scrape away their hand *mudras* (teaching gestures). To top it off, the caves were also looted by German archaeologist Albert Von Le Coq in the beginning of the 20th century; today, few murals and no sculptures remain intact. Le Coq gave his collection to the Berlin Museum, where most everything was destroyed in WWII by Allied bombing. Many of the caves included in the 10-cave tour are sadly bare, with only a few holes in the walls and a story of what once was. Foreigners will likely be shown cave #110, which is entirely bare except for an inscription describing the plundering of the area by Le Coq and Hungarian Aurel Stein. Moral of the story: don't be a dirty imperialist art thief.

Like those at Dunhuang's Mogao Grottoes, the best preserved caves require a special ticket (Y100 and up). But many visitors feel that these are not worth the extra cash. Photos of caves #38 and 67 grace the gate's tourist board, but don't indicate what you'll actually be seeing in either section. Before leaving, check out the **Gurgling Spring** (gûquán; 汩泉), a 20-minute walk past the caves through a shallow, reed-covered canyon. *(At the main gate, you must buy a ticket for either the slightly closer west caves or the east caves, which are very similar in content. Guides are fairly useless and expensive at Y30-100.)*

SUBASHI TEMPLE RUINS (sūbāshí gǔchéng; 苏巴什古城). This is the post-lunch destination for most tours, as there are no roads connecting the site to the nearby Beacon Tower. These ruins are of a Buddhist temple complex dating back to the Wei and Jin period (3rd century AD). Set against the backdrop of the 2000m Tianshan Mountains, the amorphous mud brick shapes rising from the barren scrubland hint at the scope of the original construction while still remaining hauntingly similar to the textures of the surrounding landscape. This is quite a spectacular spot to see the sun set if you can convince the driver to head out in the late afternoon. *(50km north of the old city, accessible only by a small dirt road.)*

KIZILGAHA BEACON TOWER (kèzēěrgǎhā fēnghuǒ tái; 克孜尔烽尕哈火台). During the Han dynasty, this 13m-high watchtower made of packed earth used to light signal fires when an enemy approached; similar beacon towers along the ancient Silk Road would transmit the signal over great distances of inhospitable desert. *(13km from Kuqa. Y8.)* You may want to ask the driver to take you to the nearby **Kizilgaha Grottoes** (kèzēěrgâhã qiān fó dòng; 克孜尔尕哈千佛洞).

KUQA OLD TOWN MOSQUE (kùchē dàsì; 库车大寺). In the old Uighur quarter, the mosque's intricately masoned brick dome and minaret-flanked facade overlook a bustling neighborhood of grape-covered courtyards and trodding donkey carts full of fruits and breads. *(4km northwest of New Town. You may have to yell for the gatekeeper to let you in. Y5.)*

OTHER SIGHTS. After Kizil, the most famous grottoes in the area are at **Kumtura** (kùmùtǔlā; 库木吐拉) and **Simsem** (sēnmùsāimǔ; 森木塞姆); locals particuarly recommend Simsem, which is about 80km to the east of Kuqa. To the north, deep in the Tianshan Mountain Range, you can find **Big Dragon Lake** (dàlóng chí; 大龙池) and **Small Dragon Lake** (xiǎolóng chí; 小龙池), which feature scenery similar to that of Tianchi (see p. 759), but attract fewer tourists. On the way, you'll pass through the **Kiziliya Grand Canyon** (kèzīlìyà dà xiágǔ; 克孜力亚大峡谷), another spot about which locals rave.

KASHGAR 喀什 ☎0998

Kashgar's relative inaccessibility has had a potent effect on its character, setting it a world apart from China and even Xinjiang province. This predominantly Uighur city has developed rapidly over the past 10 years but still retains hints of its Silk Road trading post character. Bustling markets are full of wizened Uighurs, animated Central Asian traders, and veiled Muslim women. Mosques rise above mud-thatched houses, and donkey carts trundle down small alleys. The completion of the Ürümqi-Kashgar rail line in late 1999 has increased Han Chinese influence over the area, breaching the expanse of Taklimakan Desert that has long protected Kashgar from the whims of the CCP. Since then, Kashgar's Han population has steadily increased, although, like most of Xinjiang's cities, there continues to be a severe polarization of Uighur and Han. Kashgar, today more than ever, is a truly international city and an important nexus for travelers headed for the even more remote regions of Pakistan and Central Asia.

TRANSPORTATION

Flights: Kashgar Airport (kāshí jīchǎng; 喀什机场), 18km north of the city. Take a taxi (25min., Y20) or bus #2 from People's Square. **CAAC ticket office** (mínháng shòupiàochù; 民航售票处), 95 Jiefang Nan Lu (☎282 2113). Open daily in summer 9:30am-8pm; in winter 10am-7:20pm. **Xinjiang Airlines** (xīnjiāng hángkōng gōngsī; 新疆航空公司; ☎283 7998), on the right side of the People's Hotel lobby. Open daily 9:30am-8pm. All flights out of Kashgar go through Ürümqi. To **Ürümqi** (in summer 2 per day, in winter daily; Y980).

Trains: The new **Kashgar Train Station** (kāshí huǒchē zhàn; 喀什火车站) is on Renmin Dong Lu, about 15km east of the city. Accessible by bus (Y0.5) from Renmin Dong Lu, or by taxi (Y10). Tickets can be difficult to book on short notice; CITS, John's Cafe, and most hotels have connections with the station and charge about Y50 commission for sleeper tickets. The Ürümqi express uses double-decker sleeper cars. To: **Ürümqi** (28hr., 2 per day, hard sleeper Y340) via **Kuqa** (9hr.; hard seat Y75, hard sleeper Y125) and **Korla** (14hr.; hard seat Y82, hard sleeper Y155).

Buses: Buses leave from the **International Bus Station** (kāshí guójì qìchē zhàn; 喀什国际汽车站), 5 Jichang Lu. Follow Jiefang Lu north across the river; the ticket office is to the right of the Tuman River Hotel, in the same building. Open daily 8:30am-9pm. Buses run to **Sost, Pakistan** on the Karakorum Highway, via **Tashkurgan** (Y62) and the **Khunjerab Pass** (16hr. plus overnight stop in Tashkurgan, daily in summer only, Y270). Buy tickets at 11am; buses leave around noon. Buses also run to **Bishkek, Kyrgyzstan** via the **Torugut Pass** (16hr., M, US$50). To take the bus, you need a transit permit (pīzhào; 批照) to cross the border; only a travel agency can obtain this permit, and most require you to take their tour in return. For the permit, most agencies charge Y300-350 (for groups of 2-5). Make sure you have a valid entry visa to Kyrgyzstan; they can only be obtained in Beijing or Hong Kong (see **Consulate Services in China,** see p. 48). The International Bus Station also has buses to **Korla** (25hr., 4 per day, sleeper Y163) via **Kuqa** (20hr., sleeper Y117), and **Ürümqi** (40hr., 5 per day, Y129-235). The **Kashgar Main Bus Station** (kèyùn zǒngzhàn; 客运总站), on Tiannan Lu, off Renmin Dong Lu. Open daily 7:30am-8pm. To: **Hotan** (10hr., every 1½hr. 9:30am-9pm, Y50); **Yecheng** (4hr., every hr. 9am-8pm, Y25); and **Tashkurgan** (8hr., 9:30am, Y32).

Local Transportation: Kashgar is best seen on foot or by bike. Local **buses** are unreliable; **#9** goes from the Seman Lu area to the Mosque area and **#10** runs east toward the Abokh Hoja Tomb. The **Oasis Cafe, Qinibagh Hotel,** and **John's Information Cafe** all have **bike rentals** for Y2 per hr.

ORIENTATION AND PRACTICAL INFORMATION

The geographical and commercial center of Kashgar is the intersection of **Jiefang Lu** (解放路) and **Renmin Lu** (人民路); the religious, cultural, and culinary center is the **Id Kah Mosque** and **Id Kah Square,** which lie on Jiefang Bei Lu, north of Renmin Lu. The long-distance bus station is on Jiefang Bei Lu, just across the **Tuman River** (tǔmàn hé; 吐曼河) in the far north of town. The Great Sunday Bazaar is west of the Tuman River, on the south side of **Yizirete Lu** (艾孜热特路). The area of most use to foreigners is in the far west, near the Seman Hotel off **Seman Lu** (色满路).

Travel Agencies:

John's Information Cafe (☎/fax 255 1059; mobile ☎(139) 0998 1722; johncafe@hotmail.com), opposite the Seman Hotel. John speaks fluent English and organizes trips around **Kashgar** (1 day, Y200 per car); **Lake Karakul** (1 day, Y800-1000 per car); **Taklimakan Desert** (1 day, Y1000 per car). For trips to the **Torugut Pass** (4-5 people max., US$200-240 total), fax or email your name, passport number, nationality, and itinerary, and John will obtain the border patrol permit, jeep, and driver. He can also arrange transport to **Bishkek** from the border (US$260).

CITS main branch is to the left of the Qinibagh Hotel with unreliable hours. A smaller, more helpful branch at the hotel gate has regular hours, with a manager who speaks excellent English (☎282 5576; fax 282 3087; wcits-ks@mail.xj.cninfo.net). Tours include: **Lake Karakul trek** (4-5 days; Y800 per car, Y500 per day for trekking guide); **Kashgar** (Y250 per car, English-speaking guide Y100); **Taklimakan Desert** (1 day, Y800); **Torugut Pass** (1-2 days; Y350 permit for 1-5 people, Y1000 transport, Y200 guide). To **Bishkek** from the border is an extra US$280. Sleeper ticket commission Y50, 3 days in advance in summer. Open daily 9:30am-1:30pm and 3:30-8pm.

Kashgar Mountaineering Association (kāshídēngshān xiéhùi; 喀什登山协会; ☎252 3680; mobile ☎(126) 818 2746), 45 Tiyu Lu, near the Yusup Khass Hajib Tomb. Experienced and reputable folks can take you to the top of **K2** (8611m), the world's second-tallest and most dangerous peak (60 days, including one week of camel-trekking each way to reach the base camp). More manageable is the ascent of the 7546m **Mt. Muztagata** (20 days, US$1250 per person), near Lake Karakul. If near-death experiences on icy crags aren't your cup of tea, the Association also arranges all sorts of guided trekking in the remote areas of the **Pamirs,** the **Karakorum Range,** and the **Taklimakan Desert.**

Bookstore: The **Xinhua Bookstore,** 21 Jiefang Bei Lu, sells local and regional tourist maps (Y5) on the 2nd fl. Open daily 8am-8pm.

Bank of China: 239 Renmin Xi Lu (☎282 3562). Exchanges traveler's checks. Credit card advances (M-F). Open daily 9:30am-1:30pm and 4-8pm.

PSB: 139 Yunmulakexia Lu (☎282 2064, ext. 3041), just south of Seman Lu, with an entrance at the far right. Issues visa extensions (UK Y160, US citizens Y125). Open M-F 9:30am-1:30pm and 4-8pm.

Hospital: No. 1 People's Hospital (dìyī rénmín yīyuàn; 第一人民医院), on Jichong Lu, just north of the International Bus Station.

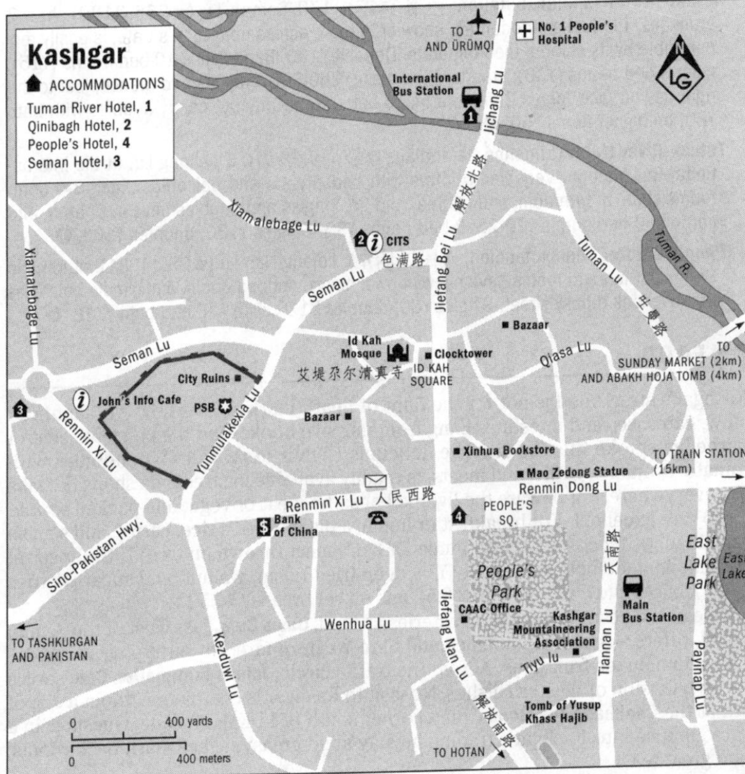

Telephones: China Telecom, across from the post office. IDD service. Open daily 9am-2pm and 4-8pm. Plenty of street booths with English signs reading "IDD" or "long-distance calls" open until around 2am.

Internet Access: China Telecom, next to the main China Telecom building, across the street from the post office. Y8 per hr. Open daily 8am-midnight. The business center of the **Qinibagh Hotel** has Y10 per hr. access, but only 1 computer. **John's Information Cafe** is the most convenient, even though it only has 2 computers. Y15 per hr.

Post Office: 7 Renmin Xi Lu (☎282 7336), 3min. east of the bank. EMS and Poste Restante on the 2nd fl. (M-F only). Open daily 10am-7pm. **Postal Code:** 844000.

ACCOMMODATIONS

Kashgar is a great place to kick back for a week; budget rooms are easy to find. On summer days, the area around the Qinibagh and Seman Hotels becomes a bizarre foreigner's village, as backpackers and package-tour types converge on the city.

Qinibagh Hotel (qíníwâkè bīnguân; 其尼瓦克宾馆), 93 Seman Lu (☎284 2299). There's no better deal in town. Clean rooms and dorms have fans and attached bath; more expensive rooms are newly renovated. Laundry service, IDD service, Internet access, English-speaking staff, and 2 travel agencies right outside. Breakfast included. 4-bed dorms Y20; 3-bed dorms Y25. Singles Y120; doubles Y160-260. ❶

Seman Hotel (sèmân bīnguân; 色满宾馆), 170 Seman Lu (☎255 2129), has 2 branches. The foreigner-oriented, showier branch, across from John's Cafe, is easily recognizable by its colorful tiled minarets. Deposit Y100. Barrack-like 10-bed dorms (Y15); nicer 2-bed dorms (Y30); standard doubles (Y260-380). The second branch, just to the right as you face John's Cafe, is a much better deal. Tiny but comfy doubles with bath Y80, on higher floors Y60. ❶

Tuman River Hotel (tûmànhé dàfàndiàn; 吐曼河大饭店), 5 Jichang Lu, at the International Bus Station. Very clean dorms with bedspreads and balconies. Each 3-4 dorm rooms share a bathroom, sitting area, and TV. Singles and doubles have A/C, bath, and carpets. 4-bed dorms Y20-25; 3-bed dorms Y35. Singles Y180; doubles Y160. ❶

People's Hotel (rénmín fàndiàn; 人民饭店), 1 Jiefang Nan Lu (☎282 4681), at Renmin Dong Lu. Standard rooms have big windows, heavy, padded doors, and simple balconies that overlook a busy street. Singles Y80; doubles Y120, with A/C and bath Y218. ❷

FOOD

Kashgar's street food is not for the faint of heart; markets overflow with ant-head stew, carcasses and intestines hang from massive hooks, and the pungent scent of barbecue smoke fills the air. The delicious Uighur *laghman* (Y3), noodles with tomatoes, onions, garlic, and meats, is readily available in streetside shops. Kebabs are everywhere, but beware the liver kebabs; the meat or vegetable-packed *samsa* (Y0.5) are excellent. For breakfast or lunch, a big bowl of a rice, carrot, and squash (zhuā fàn; 抓饭) costs Y2, with hunks of lamb meat thrown on top Y7. Other street delights include hot sweet milk (Y1), deep-fried raisin, walnut, and sugar pastries (Y0.5), bagel-like creations (Y0.2-0.5), and sweet breads (Y0.5-1).

One of the best Western-style eateries around, **Oasis Cafe,** just west of the Seman Hotel, offers a relaxing ambience and Sino-Western fare. Be sure to try their delicious homemade fruit jams. Across the traffic circle, **John's Information Cafe** serves its own version of Western dishes. No visit to Kashgar is complete without a cup of tea at the **Chakhana Tea House,** on a corner south of Id Kah Mosque. Guests gain a rare glimpse into Kashgar's trading heyday amid greasy dishes, dark back rooms, and great tea.

A KEBAB PRIMER Anyone who has traveled in China for at least two hours is likely to have come across at least a few hardy entrepreneurs hard at work cooking up lamb kebabs (yángròu chuàn; 羊肉串) on a small charcoal fire, carefully sprinkling on spices and handling the skewers with amazing dexterity. While kebabs have become a nationwide craze, the birthplace of the kebab—and still home to the tastiest ones around—is the Northwest. Within this region, *Let's Go* has searched long and hard for the perfect kebab and has determined with scientific certainty that the best ones are found in predominantly Muslim areas adjacent to large grasslands. Of particular note are the Hui communities in Lanzhou, Linxia, and Xining, near the grasslands of the Tibetan Plateau and Uighur areas of northern Xinjiang, especially by Yining and the Nalati and Zhaosu grasslands.

SIGHTS

SUNDAY BAZAAR (kāshí xīngqī tiān shìchǎng; 喀什星期天市场). Nothing can prepare visitors for the grandeur and exoticism of Kashgar's Sunday Bazaar. With an impressive green-tiled dome and a multilingual sign proclaiming "Kashgar

International Trade Market of Central and Western Asia," the bazaar is hard to miss. Every Sunday, the lot is transformed into a bubbling cauldron of human activity. The bazaar, a wild reminder of the days when Kashgar was a major crossroads on the Silk Road, hosts a diverse ethnic mix of Uighurs, Tajiks, Kyrgyz, Uzbeks, Han Chinese, Russians, and tourists. Livestock and other creatures are contained within what looks like the holding pen for Noah's ark; vegetables and other foodstuffs are sequestered in a separate section. The market tantalizes passersby with silks, knives, clothes, and more; bargain for 60-70% off the stated price. All sorts of tasty treats are also available in the alleys: just point and you shall receive. *(On Yizirete Lu, northeast of town. Guard your cash and belongings carefully. The bazaar begins about 9am, peaks at noon-2pm, and ends around 6pm.)*

TOMB OF YUSUP KHASS HAJIP (yùsùfū hāsīhājífū mù; 玉素甫哈斯哈吉甫墓). Here lies the tomb of a much-beloved 11th-century Uighur poet who was also a prolific philosopher. Locals love the fact that visitors stop by to see the city's favorite poet. The tomb is a beautifully detailed structure with a main dome that contains intricate lattices and high minarets. *(From Id Kah Square, follow Jiefang Bei Lu through the main intersection until it turns into Jiefang Nan Lu; after about 1.8km, take a left on the small Tiyu Lu (体育路), just after the stadium. Y10.)*

TOMB OF ABOKH HOJA (ābākèhuòjiā mù; 阿巴克霍加墓). Built around 1635, this unexciting tomb houses Abokh, who is blamed for increasing the tides of Han people to the west. The tomb is also known as the **Tomb of Xiangfei** (xiāngfēi mù; 香妃墓), named for **Ikparhan** (Xiangfei in Mandarin), the Uighur concubine of Emperor Qianlong. *(About 2km northeast of town on a road off Yizirete Lu, a 45min. bike ride along Yizirete Lu. A small, white English sign on the left will mark a turn-off; continue 700m ahead, through an alley on the right. Bike parking Y0.5. Open daily 8am-8pm. Y15.)*

OTHER SIGHTS. Id Kah Mosque (àitígâêr qīngzhēn sì; 艾提尕尔清真寺), on Jiefang Bei Lu north of Renmin Lu, was constructed in 1442. The religious epicenter of the Xinjiang Uighur community, it boasts a crowd of 21,000 on festival days. Please respect local worshipers by covering your arms and legs and remaining silent. *(Free.)* The **Kashgar Museum** (kāshí bówùguân; 喀什博物馆) is not terribly thrilling, especially if you've already seen Ürümqi's museum—the Early Iron Age corpses may be of some interest, though. *(Returning to town along Yizirete Lu from the Tomb of Abokh Hoja, take a left onto Taukuz Lu and continue for 1km; the museum is on the right before Renmin Dong Lu. Open daily 9:30am-1:30pm and 4-8pm. Y6, students Y3.)*

NORTHWEST

THE KARAKORUM HIGHWAY

Running near some of the highest mountains in the world and connecting Kashgar to **Sost, Pakistan** via the 4700m **Khunjerab Pass** (hóngqílāfu dápō; 红其拉甫达坡), the **Karkorum Highway** (zhōngbā yôuyí gōnglù; 中巴友谊公路) has long appealed to backpackers, adventure-seekers, and Pakistani traders who regularly ply the route. Even if you're not going to Pakistan, the highway makes for a fascinating trip to the border at **Tashkurgan** (tâshíkùêrgān; 塔什库尔干), especially if you stop at the breathtaking **Karakul Lake.** Buses run daily May-October; otherwise, transportation options are limited and the road often impassable. Even during the summer, closures are common, as mudslides can demolish the road in seconds. These happen most frequently in warm weather, when the sun melts the snow that then rudely flows down the mountain, picking up rocks and boulders along the way. Generally, buses eventually find some way through or travelers can walk across the obstacle and switch buses; regardless, be prepared for long delays.

KARAKUL LAKE (kālākùlè hú; 喀拉库勒湖)

(200km south of Kashgar, a 6hr. drive along the Karakorum Highway. Buses between Kashgar and Tashkurgan all pass by the lake. The bus from the Kashgar main bus station (9:30am, Y32) is often full; buy your tickets the day before. The Pakistan-bound bus from the International Bus Station (noon, Y43 to Karakul) is easier to book at short notice. There are buses from Tashkurgan to Lake Kashgar (2½hr., 9:30am). To leave the lake, buses to Kashgar pass by at about noon, to Tashkurgan at about 3 and 6pm. It is often possible to catch a ride with travel agency buses that stop at Karakul. Admission to lake Y20.)

With towering glaciers and the "Father of Ice Mountains" itself, **Mt. Muztagata** (7546m), looming on the far side, Karakul has by far the most dramatic scenery of Xinjiang's alpine lakes. It's an ideal spot for hiking and trekking. Give yourself a day to acclimate if you're coming from Kashgar; the lake is 3900m, high enough that many travelers experience mild headaches and shortness of breath upon arrival. The area immediately around the lake is pretty dusty and drab, but there are lots of friendly Kyrgyz yurt dwellers around who are happy to invite you in for a cup of tea and to sell you a neat Kyrgyz-style hat made of camel hair (about Y20), but regulations forbid them from hosting foreigners for the night (the local PSB has been known to raid yurts suspected of harboring foreigners). Instead, tent-less backpackers must resort to the **"Karakul Resort"** ❷ next to the highway. There are standard doubles (Y100 per person) available in the trashy cinderblock building, but more appealing are their nice (if overpriced) yurts, with great views and warm bedding (Y40 per person). Ask for one away from the parking lot and be sure to close the door when you leave or else a local goat might wander in to investigate and leave you a "gift." The **"resort" restaurant** ❷ has big windows and a panoramic view, and serves up noodles (Y10), quasi-Western breakfasts (Y25).

NORTHWEST

TASHKURGAN 塔什库尔干 ☎0998

The small, mostly Tajik town of Tashkurgan plays much the same role today as it did 1500 years ago during the Tang dynasty—namely, that of the forlorn, final outpost of Chinese rule before the big, bad Western world. Travelers going to or coming from Pakistan will have to spend the night here. Even if a border crossing isn't in your future, Tashkurgan makes for a pleasant one-day visit, with its ancient Stone City, fascinating Tajik neighborhood, and awesome mountain scenery.

ORIENTATION AND PRACTICAL INFORMATION. The Karakorum Highway runs south along the western edge of town. Most travelers will never need to leave **Kashigale Lu** (喀什尕勒路), which runs east from the highway. Here, you'll find the bus station, Stone City, hotels, and restaurants. **Maixiawa'er Lu** (买夏瓦尔路) runs parallel to Kashigale Lu to the south; **Nawabati Lu** (那瓦巴提路) is the only major cross street. The **Tashkurgan Bus Station** (tâshíkùĕrgān chángtú qìchēzhàn; 塔什库尔干长途气车站) is on the west end of Kashigale Lu, near the highway. Buses run to **Kashgar** (8hr.; 2 buses at 9:30am; local service Y36, Pakistan bus Y62) and **Sost, Pakistan** (8hr., 9:30am, Y225). The **PSB** is at 5 Maixiawa'er Lu. **Post and Telecom,** on the corner of Maixiawa'er Lu and Nawabati Lu, offers IDD service but operates at irregular hours. There are no banks in town that exchange traveler's checks or provide credit card advances. The **Traffic Hotel** can exchange US dollars and Pakistani rupees.

ACCOMMODATIONS AND FOOD. Both of Tashkurgan's foreigner-friendly budget hotels are good values and conveniently located on Kashigale Lu, near the bus station. The **Traffic Hotel** ❶ (jiāotōng bīnguǎn; 交通宾馆), 50 Kashigale Lu (☎342 1192), has a super-friendly, eager-to-help staff. All doubles are newly renovated and feature warm, colorful comforters. Dorms have concrete floors and exposed pipes, but are clean and comfortable, with common bathrooms. (4-bed dorms Y10 per person; doubles Y60, with bath Y100-120.) **Ice Mountain Hotel ❶** (bīngshān bīnguǎn; 冰山宾馆), 77 Kashigale Lu (☎342 2668), is just down the street from the bus station, on the left. This joint is a bit older and more casual than the Traffic, but is still pretty nice. (3-4 bed dorms Y15-20; slightly small doubles with bath Y30 per person, fancier doubles Y100.)

Restaurants cluster on **Kashigale Lu,** just like everything else. Tons of small and enticing Muslim establishments abound here. The **Ayiguli Restaurant ❶** (āyīgǔlì cāntīng; 阿依古丽餐厅), across from the Traffic Hotel, has noodles (Y5) and Pakistani dishes. The restaurant on the third floor of the Traffic Hotel serves Western-style dishes.

SIGHTS. Tashkurgan's major tourist attraction is **Stone City** (shítóuchéng; 石头城), which is more of a large, mud-brick fort. First built during the Northern and Southern dynasty (AD 502-557), the better-preserved inner castle dates from the Qing dynasty (AD 1644-1911). From the inner fort, the view of the surrounding mountains and yurt-dotted grasslands is stunning. The entrance to Stone City is at the far end of Kashigale Lu, on the left opposite the **Postal Hotel** (yóudiàn bīnguǎn; 邮电宾馆). Whenever the ticket taker is around, admission is Y8; otherwise the gate remains open. To visit the Tajik residential section, with its lovely stone courtyard houses, continue to the end of Kashigale Lu and follow the dirt path to the left. From here, a road runs north along the grassland.

BORDER CROSSING INTO PAKISTAN: KHUNJERAB PASS

The Chinese border post is at the southern edge of Tashkurgan; the Pakistani border post is at Sost, 220km away. The actual border is at the Khunjerab Pass, 126km from Tashkurgan. When going over the 4900m-high pass, many travelers experience mild effects of altitude sickness, including headaches and nausea. Travelers coming **from Pakistan** should bring enough cash to get them to Kashgar; traveler's checks and credit cards are not accepted in Tashkurgan. You can exchange Chinese, Pakistani, and US currency at both border check points (travelers report slightly better rates at the Pakistani post) and at the Traffic Hotel in Tashkurgan. You'll need to buy a new ticket for transport from Tashkurgan to Kashgar (Y62). In the other direction, one ticket is good all the way from Kashgar to Sost. Heading **to Pakistan,** you will likely need to spend the night in Sost. From here, there are frequent connections to Gilgit, where buses run to Islamabad.

NORTHWEST

BEYOND YECHENG

From **Yecheng** (叶城), the road splits: one way links Kashgar and Hotan via **Shache,** the other is an illegal overland route to **Ali** (阿里) in western Tibet (near Kailash, see **Travel Agencies,** p. 804). Drivers will approach foreigners in Yecheng and offer to take them to Ali (3-5 days, Y300). Neither the PSB nor *Let's Go* approves of this method—nonetheless, be sure to take food and warm clothes for the long trip. From Ali to Lhasa, the roads are poor and the trip takes at least a week. This requires hitching a ride in a truck, also not recommended by *Let's Go.* Furthermore, temperatures are often below freezing, and many of the mountain passes are over 5000m. After reaching the Tibetan border, some travelers report being fined Y300 but still allowed to continue into Tibet; as always, regulations, enforcement, and penalties are subject to change. Late summer is not a good time to go, as melting snow can wash away mountain roads.

HOTAN 和田

☎0903

One of the most isolated cities in all of China, Hotan is connected only to Kashgar and, via the new Desert Highway, to Korla. Brought to life by the Karakash (Black Jade) and Yorungkash (White Jade) Rivers, this town has long been a spiritual and commercial center on the Southern Silk Road. City ruins and Buddhist temples stand amidst the gorgeous desert scenery. Hotan's flourishing silk and carpet industry is an impressive reminder of the city's rich history. The incredible variety of patterns and colors that adorns every market stall and drapes from the backs of veiled Uighur women adds to the magical feel of this remote desert oasis.

TRANSPORTATION

Flights: Hotan Airport (hétián fēijīchǎng; 和田飞机场), a Y15-20 taxi ride south of the city. **CAAC ticket office** (☎251 2178), on Wulumuqi Lu, a 5min. walk south of Beijing Lu. Open daily 9:30am-1pm and 4-7:30pm. To **Ürümqi** (daily July-Sept., else Su-M, W, and F; Y1070).

Buses: Hotan Long-distance Bus Station (hétián chángtú qìchē zhàn; 和田长途汽车站; ☎203 2700, ext. 8874), on the highway, in the north part of town. Exit to the right, walk 5min. to the first intersection, and turn right onto Beijing Lu; it's a 10min. walk to the city center. Open daily 8am-8:30pm. To: **Kashgar** (10hr.; 7 per day; hard seat Y37-44, sleeper Y87); **Qiemo** (2 days, 9am, Y52); **Ürümqi** (25hr., 6 afternoon and evening buses, Y233-367) via **Korla** (19hr.) and the **Desert Highway** (the best desert scenery can be seen from the 1pm bus); **Yecheng** (4hr.; 2 per day, or any Kashgar bus; Y20); **Yining** (at least 40hr., 3 per week, Y161).

Local Transportation: All points of interest in the city are within a 15min. walk. **Taxis** are unmetered and cost a flat Y5 to destinations within the city center.

NORTHWEST

ORIENTATION AND PRACTICAL INFORMATION

Beijing Lu (北京路) runs from **Wulumuqi Lu** (乌鲁木齐路) in the west to the **White Jade River** (báiyù hé; 白玉河) 5km east of town. In the town center, Beijing Lu intersects **Hetian Lu** (和田路) to the east and **Tanaiyi Lu** (塔乃依路) to the west. The long-distance bus station is on **Highway 315,** which runs along the north edge of town and becomes **Aiyitika'er Lu** (艾依题卡尔路) after passing a small park that leads east to the bazaar.

Travel Agency: Hotan International Travel Service (hétián guójì lǚxíngshè; 和田国际旅行社; ☎202 6850), at the Yiyuan Hotel gate. Tours around town and to more distant sites like the Rewak Buddhist Temple ruins, Keriya, and Melikawat. English-speaking guide Y100, transport Y100-200. Less-popular ruins often have exorbitant admission prices (Rewak charges Y380 per person).

Bank of China: On Beijing Lu, next to Xinhua Bookstore. Exchanges traveler's checks. Credit card advances. Open in summer M-F 9:30am-1:30pm and 4-8pm; in winter 10am-2pm and 3:30-7:30pm; Sa-Su year-round 11am-6pm.

Bookstore: Xinhua Bookstore, on Beijing Lu between Hetian Lu and Youyi Lu. City maps on 2nd fl. Open daily 9:30am-9pm.

Internet Access: Sanlian Internet Bar (sānlián wǎngbā; 三联网吧), a few doors to the left of the Hotan Guesthouse gate, has painfully slow connections. Y4 per hr.

Post and Telecommunications: On Beijing Lu, across the street from Xinhua Bookstore. EMS, IDD service (no calling cards calls), and Poste Restante. Open daily 9:30am-8:30pm. **Postal Code:** 848000.

ACCOMMODATIONS

All three accommodations listed are conveniently located in the city center within walking distance of the bus station and the old city.

Hotan Guesthouse (hétián yíngbīnguǎn; 和田迎宾馆; ☎202 2824), on Tanaiyi Lu. From the bus station, turn left onto the highway and make a sharp left on Yanaiyi Lu, the first major crossstreet. The hotel is a 10min. walk ahead on the left. Set in a pleasant poplar tree courtyard. Dorms have sparkling common baths, fans, TVs, and wood decor. 24hr. hot water. 3-bed dorms Y20; 2-bed dorms with bath Y45. ❶

Tiancheng City Hotel (tiānchéng bīnguǎn; 天盛宾馆; ☎202 8809), on the corner of Beijing Xi Lu and Tanaiyi Lu. The rooms with baths are fairly new. Hot water 9am-11pm. 4-bed dorms Y15; 3-bed dorms Y20, with bath Y40; 2-bed dorms with bath Y55-75. ❶

Yiyuan Hotel (yíyuàn bīnguǎn; 怡苑宾馆; ☎202 5631), on Tanaiyi Lu, just south of the Hotan Guesthouse. The cheapest dorms are ridiculously tiny, but others are spacious and comfortable. 24hr. hot water. 4-bed dorms Y20; 3-bed dorms with A/C and bath Y45; 2-bed dorms Y30, with A/C and bath Y55. ❶

FOOD

The best Uighur food is found in the east of town, in the **bazaar** area. Most restaurants downtown are Chinese, with a number of tasty cheapies. **Friend Restaurant** ❶ (péngyǒu jiǔjiā; 朋友酒家), on Tanaiyi Lu just south of Beijing Lu, serves up a delicious twice-cooked pork (húiguō ròu; 回锅肉; Y10); most dishes are even cheaper. At **6 Yuan Fast Food** ❶ (liùyuán kuàicān; 6元快餐), on Beijing Lu, five minutes west of Tanaiyi Lu, all dishes are Y6 or less. The service, ironically, is pretty slow, but the food tastes great and the price is right.

SIGHTS

Hotan's Silk Road-era ruins offer little for the casual observer; most relics have been carted off to local or Ürümqi museums, and today these ancient structures are merely eroded mounds of rubble surrounded by vast stretches of sand dunes. If you cross the Taklimakan Desert between Korla and Ürümqi via the Desert Highway, these sights aren't hard to miss. Check with a travel agency if you're really interested in the ruins; you'll have to hire a vehicle (Y100-400, guide Y100 per day). A trip to the closest ruin, **Melikawat,** can also be included in a standard one-day Hotan tour. There are a number of grape vineyards and fruit orchards nearby, but visiting the silk, jade, and carpet factories is more interesting, as each offers an amazing perspective on the skill, coordination, and sheer volume of labor that goes into the production of Hotan's specialty items.

HOTAN CARPET FACTORY (hétián dìtǎn chǎng; 和田地毯厂). Check out the amazing process of carpet-weaving, which often involves complex symmetrical patterns and cutting and tying hundreds of thousands of pieces of yarn or silk into a massive foundation grid. The history of Hotan's carpet industry is said to date back over 2000 years; more recently, in 1992, the factory wove a carpet for Beijing's Great Hall of the People (see p. 132). A large shop features the factory's creations, including custom-made oddities. Most carpets are wool, but lightweight silk rugs (favored by travelers) are also available. Small (0.5m×0.5m) wool carpets start at about Y200. Prices are better at the bazaar, but non-experts might find it safer to shop here, where high quality is guaranteed. (*From in front of the Hotan City Hotel, take east-bound bus #2 to the last stop. From here, take bus #3 to its last stop; the factory is just ahead on the right. Open daily 9:30am-5:30pm; avoid midday rest hours.*)

NORTHWEST

HOTAN BAZAAR (hétiān dà bāzhá; 和田大巴札). The bazaar is best visited on Sundays. Many disappointed by the Kashgar market's touristy feel enjoy this market much more; it is almost as large, has fewer tourists, and is far more chaotic and free-spirited. During the week, hundreds of permanent shops line the market's covered alleyways and sell silk, carpet, and clothing. The **carpet bazaar** is inside the main gate, to the left. Examine carpets carefully before buying; quality varies greatly. The sellers here are notoriously tough hagglers, with some bargain showdowns lasting 30 to 40 minutes. Few carpets should cost more than Y1200, but those with 800 to 1200 knots per inch will cost much more than ordinary silk carpets (0.5m×1m about Y150, 1.5m×3m about Y600). *(Walk north on Hetian Lu from the post office; turn right on Aiyitika'er Lu after the small park. Walk 10min. down the dirt road; the market branches off this main street.)*

WHITE JADE RIVER (bái yù hé; 白玉河). This river, known as the **Yorungkash,** is the area's primary source for white jade; in the late afternoon, locals rake through piles of stones at the river's edge in search of precious stones. Although real jade is scarce, the incredible beauty and variety of stones scattered about the banks is reason enough to visit the area. In the hot afternoon, you can also take a refreshing swim in the fast current. *(About 6km east of the city center. Take bus #2 from in front of the Hotan City Hotel to its last stop, then walk 10min. or take bus #3 east to the river.)*

SILK FACTORY (sīchóu chǎng; 丝绸厂). The most impressive part of this factory is a huge room where cocoons are boiled in long troughs and almost invisible strands of silk are wrapped around thousands of spinning reels. Hundreds of electric looms crank out a ceaseless flow of silk sheets ready to be dyed in the silk-weaving room. It may be difficult to wander around on your own; the security guards are a suspicious lot. If you arrive in the late morning or afternoon, head to the second floor of the office building opposite the main gate. Someone there will often arrange a tour. *(From the bus stop on Hetian Lu just south of Aiyitika'er Lu, take bus #1 (Y0.8) to the last stop; the factory, with a white tile gate and tan office building, is about 200m back toward town on the right.)* About 1.5km south of the silk factory, the **Hotan Winery** (hétiān zhìjiû chǎng; 和田制酒厂) produces specialty pomegranate and rice wines. Bottles can be purchased here at factory prices (Y20-120 per bottle). The security guard at the gate will call to arrange a guide.

HOTAN CITY MUSEUM (hétiān bówùguǎn; 和田博物馆). This small, one-room exhibit is quite impressive, housing relics of the Buddhist-era Uighur culture excavated from the local city ruins. Pottery, sculpture, and a preserved body make this museum a must-see while in Hotan. An excellent guide speaks Uighur and Mandarin. *(On Tanaiyi Lu, about 2min. from the Hotan City Hotel; look for a small white building with blue windows. Open daily 9:30am-1:30pm and 4-8pm. Y7.)*

SOUTHERN SILK ROAD: BEYOND HOTAN

Beyond Hotan, the towns may appear progressively more dusty and drab, but the journey, which circumnavigates the Taklimakan Desert, passes through some of the most untouched and isolated Uighur towns in all of Xinjiang. The route affords direct access to Golmud and Tibet and puts travelers close to Dunhuang. The bus ride to **Qiemo** (且末) involves at least two days of rough travel along poor roads and generally includes a stop in **Minfeng** (民丰) along the way. From Qiemo, take the bus to **Ruoqiang** (若羌); in theory, the area around Ruoqiang is rich in historical and natural treasures. Unfortunately, little remains of the ancient ruins at **Milan** (mǐlán; 米兰) and **Loulan** (lóulán; 楼兰), and reaching either is expensive and perilous (both lie near Lop Nur, the dry lake bed where China conducts nuclear weapons tests). Also nearby is the **Altun Mountain Nature Preserve** (ā ěr jīnshān zìrán bǎohùqū; 阿尔金山自然保护区), China's largest preserve and home to diverse species like black-neck cranes, antelope, wild yaks, camels, and donkeys. Perhaps puzzled by the presence of so much wildlife, the government has set up an International Hunting Ground within the preserve. The preserve, which lies on the Xinjiang-Tibet border in a closed area (make sure you have a permit), is likely to be difficult and costly to reach, as no roads connect it to other towns.

QINGHAI 青海

An enormous salt lake and an acclaimed herbal fungus are Qinghai's only claims to fame. More a political construct than a separate geographical entity, Qinghai province (*Amdo* in Tibetan) has traditionally been a part of Eastern Tibet. Qinghai occupies the northern half of the Tibetan Plateau and is home to many Tibetans, Hui, Mongols, and Kazakhs, and a majority of Han Chinese. But most of the province is uninhabitable due to severe winds and freezing winter temperatures.

With a history as harsh as its climate, the Qinghai region has seen a massive influx of Han Chinese since 1717. In 1928, it was made a province of the Republic of China, even though it continued to be ruled by Hui warlords. Later on, the PLA easily drove out the local strongmen and solidified control over the region. Qinghai quickly became a prime spot for penal colonies, most of which were closed in the 1980s due to high operating costs.

In the eyes of travelers, Qaidam Basin in the northwest offers little more than desert and the occasional salt marsh, but the vast herds tended by Amdowa nomads, sketched onto the backdrop of Qinghai Lake, are a fascinating living portrait of Tibetan life. The central-east Bayan Har mountain range is the source of the Yellow River, while the southern Tanggula Mountains give birth to both the Yangzi and the Mekong. The combination of high altitude (3600m), towering glaciers, and thundering gorges attract daredevils, nature documentary crews, and local tour groups, but transportation is difficult and conditions uncompromising.

NORTHWEST

XINING 西宁 ☎0971

Guarding the overland route to Tibet at 2200m above sea level, Xining occupies a strategic position on the edge of the Tibetan Plateau. During the Song dynasty, the area earned its current name of Xining, or "Western Peace." It was granted the status of provincial capital in 1928. Xining has a diverse populace of Han, Hui, Tibetan, and even a handful of Chinese Christians. Although the city itself has no distinctive sights, it is nonetheless a pleasurable point from which to venture out to the Kumbum Monastery and Qinghai Lake.

TRANSPORTATION

Flights: Xining Airport (xīníng jīchǎng; 西宁机场), 30km east of the city. Buses (30min., Y10) run from the **CAAC ticket office,** 34 Bayi Xi Lu (☎817 4616), accessible by local bus #28. Open daily 8am-6:30pm. To: **Beijing** (daily, Y1310); **Chengdu** (Tu, F, Su; Y900); **Guangzhou** (Tu, Th, Sa; Y1450); **Lhasa** (Su-M, W, F; Y1390); **Shanghai** (M, Tu, Th-Sa; Y1630); **Ürümqi** (Tu, Th, Sa; Y900); **Xi'an** (daily, Y590).

Trains: Xining Train Station (xīníng huǒchē zhàn; 西宁火车站; ☎(09851) 819 2262), on Qilian Lu. Tickets are easy to procure. To: **Beijing** (32hr., daily, Y430); **Golmud** (12-16hr., 3 per day, Y55-122); **Lanzhou** (3hr., 5 per day, Y22-33); **Qingdao** (39hr., daily, Y227); **Shanghai** (38hr., daily, Y437).

Buses: Xining Long-distance Bus Station (xīníng qìchē zhàn; 西宁汽车站; ☎814 9611), on Jianguo Lu, across the river from the train station. Open daily 6am-6pm. To:

Dunhuang (24hr., daily, Y185); **Golmud** (18hr., daily, Y75); **Heimahe** (6hr., 9 per day 7:30am-5pm, Y27) via **Qinghai Lake; Lanzhou** (5hr., every 25min. 7am-5pm, Y31); **Linxia** (8hr., 4 per day, Y22-43); **Zhangye** (12hr., 3 per day, Y39-43).

Local Transportation: Buses cost Y0.5. Bus **#1** runs from the station area to the Great Mosque, Da Shizi, and Xi Men; **#2** goes east from the station area; and **#11** goes to Chengjiang Lu, near the North Temple.

ORIENTATION AND PRACTICAL INFORMATION

The city is centered around **Da Shizi** ("Big Cross"; 大十字) and **Xi Men** ("West Gate"; 西门), about a five-minute walk from one another. The city's main road begins at Xi Men as **Xi Dajie** (西大街), and runs eastward through town, becoming **Dong Dajie** (东大街), **Dongguan Dajie** (东关大街), **Dazhong Jie** (大众街), and, finally, **Bayi Lu** (八一路), which runs east out of the city. **Jianguo Lu** (建国路) runs south from the train and bus stations to **Dazhong Jie.**

Travel Agencies: Spring and Autumn Travel Service (chūnqiū læxíngshè; 春秋旅行社; ☎814 9484, ext. 2752), on the 4th fl. of the Postal Condominium Hotel. English-speaking staff. Offers trips to Qinghai Lake and Bird Island. Open 24hr. **Nationality Travel Service** (mínzú læxíng shè; 民族旅行社; ☎822 4774 or 822 5951, ext. 2227), in the back of the Nationality Hotel, has decent deals on trips to Bird Island. Open daily 9am-6:30pm. **Science and Technology Travel Service** (kējì læxíngshè; 科技旅行社; ☎814 0954), in the Railway Hotel (tiědào bīngguǎn; 铁道宾馆) on Jianguo Lu, with another branch in the lobby of the Kunlun Hotel, offers pricey trips to Bird Island (about Y120) but has a reputation for great service. Open 24hr.

Bank of China: 218 Dongguan Jie, a 2min. walk east of Da Shizi (☎822 7193). Exchanges traveler's checks (1st fl., counter #8) and issues credit card advances (2nd fl., counter #8). Open M-F 8:30am-noon and 2:30-5:30pm, Sa-Su 10am-4:30pm.

Bookstore: Foreign Language Bookstore (wàiwén shūdiàn; 外文书店), 7 Xiguan Dajie, a 10min. walk west of Xi Men on the left. Open daily 9:30am-5:45pm.

Hospital: People's Hospital of Qinghai (qīnghǎishěn rénmín yīyuàn; 青海人民医院), 5 Gonghe Lu (☎817 7911 or 817 7981), near the train and bus stations.

PSB: 35 Bei Dajie (☎824 8190), a 5min. walk north of Da Shizi. Friendly and knowledgeable. Visa extensions available daily 8:30am-noon and 2:30-6pm. Open 24hr.

Internet Access: Wangdian Internet Bar (wǎngdiǎn wǎngbā; 网点网吧), on Weiming Xiang, to the left of the Railway Hotel. The bar is on the left. Open daily 8am until the last person leaves. Y3 per hr.

Post Office: On Da Shizi (☎824 7584), diagonally opposite the Xinhua Bookstore. EMS and Poste Restante (in a small glass door) to the right; IDD service to the left and on the 2nd fl. (open 24hr.). Open daily 8:30am-6pm. **Postal Code:** 810000.

ACCOMMODATIONS

Jiangzhe Hotel (jiāngzhé bīnguǎn; 江浙宾馆; ☎814 9385), across from the train station. Rooms and dorms are new, clean, comfortable, and cheap. Single travelers may pay for individual beds. 3-6 bed dorms Y12-16; very nice 3-bed dorms with TV and attached bath Y30; doubles Y36, with bath Y80-Y120. ❶

Post Hotel (yóuzhèng bīnguǎn; 邮政宾馆), 138 Huzhu Lu (☎814 9484, ext. 2751), near the train station. You might get a bit winded after climbing 6 flights of stairs to get to your room, but this is still a pretty good deal. The rooms are spartan but clean, with nice showers and baths. Hot water 9-11pm. 4-bed dorms Y12; singles with bath Y46, with phone Y50; doubles Y48, with bath Y80 (or pay by the bed). ❶

NORTHWEST

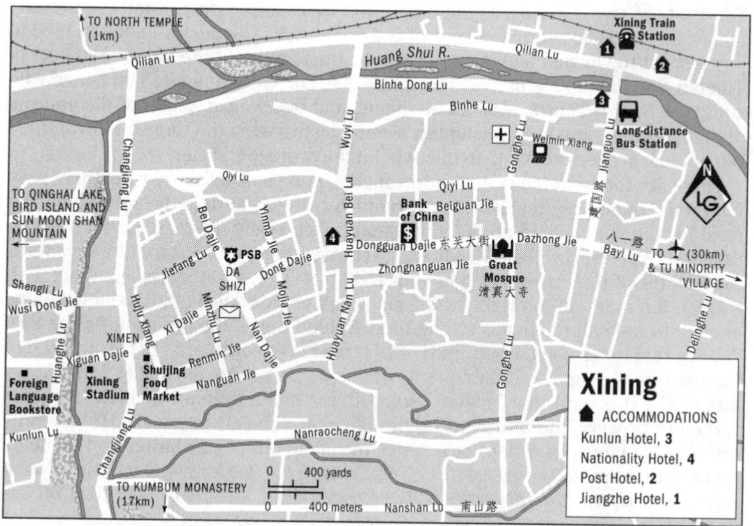

Kunlun Hotel (kūnlún bīnguân; 昆仑宾馆), 2 Jianguo Lu (☎813 3890, ext. 2065), directly across from the long-distance bus station. The 1st and 2nd floors are old military supply and hardware department outlets, perfect for picking up a cheap army parka. Rooms are a bit small but have big windows and red carpets. Hot water 9pm-midnight. Lockout at midnight; knock and someone should let you in. Deposit Y20. Singles Y60-80; doubles Y50-60; triples Y75. ❶

Nationality Hotel (mínzú bīnguân; 民族宾馆), 1 Huayuan Bei Jie (☎822 5951), at Dong Dajie, a 3min. walk east of Da Shizi. Mini-balconies have great views and spacious rooms. No public showers. 24hr. hot water. Reservations recommended. Deposit Y20. Singles with bath Y110; doubles Y130-150; triples Y90, with bath Y180. ❷

NORTHWEST

FOOD

Xining is a market town of magnificent variety. The **Traffic Market** along Huzhu Lu and east of the train station is the largest in Xining, followed by **Da Shizi Market** on Nan Dajie. The best place to feast is at the giant night market on **Yinma Jie,** near Da Shizi. You can buy all types of food here, especially the "small eats" (*xiâochī*; 小吃) of noodles and dumplings. Xining's most famous *xiâochī* are the savory beef noodles (niúròu miàn; 牛肉面) and the often garlicky chopped noodles (miàn piàn; 面片), both around Y4. The **Shuijing food market,** opposite Huju Xiang and east of Xi Men, sells mostly fruit and candy, but there are also some places that cook up Xining's famous *shãguõ* (沙锅), a delicious hotpot of meat, vegetables, and tofu (dòufû; 豆腐; Y5-9). Don't miss the mouth-watering bowls of sugar-topped yogurt (suãnnâi; 酸奶; Y1). **Dicos** ❷ (dékèshì zhájī; 迪克士炸鸡), at Xi Men, serves up McDonald's and KFC-style fast food combos (Y13-25).

SIGHTS

KUMBUM LAMASERY (tǎěr sì; 塔尔寺). Kumbum Lamasery and Labrang Lamasery (see p. 732) are the two most important Tibetan Buddhist lamaseries outside

Tibet; of the two, Labrang is the larger and more impressive. Kumbum literally means the "100,000 roaring images of the Buddha" in Tibetan. Founded in 1560 to pay respect to Qinghai native Tsong Khapa, the founder of the Yellow Hat sect of Tibetan Buddhism (see p. 29), the lamasery is currently home to 600 lamas who study the *Sutra*, Tantra, Tibetan Medicine, and the *chakra*. Many of the embroideries, frescoes, and butter sculptures were destroyed in the Cultural Revolution, but enough artwork remains to overwhelm the average traveler.

There are tours available, but unfortunately none in English. The numbers written on the buildings themselves are completely different than the set of numbers used for the map legend on the admission ticket. Using the map legend numeration, you will see the **Eight Stupas** (#2), representing the life story of Sakyamuni, the Buddha of the Present; it's on your right just upon entering the complex. Farther up the road, on the right, is the giant **Hall of Meditation** (#20), which is large enough to hold all the lamas at one time. Behind this is the beautiful **Golden Roof Pavilion** (#18) with a giant puti (pútí; 菩提) tree in the courtyard (Y3). At the end of the road, on the right, is Kumbum's most unique attraction, the **Hall of Butter Sculpture** (#27). It is said that Master Tsong Khapa had a dream in which the grass turned to flowers, the thorns to bright lights, and the air to jewels. He naturally ordered the lamas to construct a series of reliefs out of yak butter and dedicate them to Buddha. *(27km southeast of Xining. Buses go from the left side of the Xining Gymnasium, west of Xi Men, to the tiny village of Huangzhong (45min., every 30min. 7am-6pm, Y4). The monastery is a 3min. walk up the main road. Open daily 9am-6pm. Y11.)*

OTHER SIGHTS. The **Great Mosque** (qīngzhēn dà sì; 清真大寺) is on Dongguan Jie, a 10- to 15-minute walk east of Da Shizi. Built in 1380, it is now a spiritual center for Xining's Hui residents. Non-Muslims can only peek into the Great Prayer Hall through bars, but the experience may be enlivened by visiting during a prayer service. *(Prayer service daily 5:15am, 1:15, 5:30, 8:45, and 9:45pm; largest service F 1:15pm. Open daily 6am-9pm. Y5.)* **The North Temple** (bêi shān sì; 北山寺) is at the end of a good one-hour hike to the northwest of Xining along Changjiang Lu, and offers fresh air and rolling hills. *(Open daily sunrise-sunset. Y6.)*

NORTHWEST

DAYTRIPS FROM XINING

QINGHAI LAKE (青海)

155km west of Xining. It's possible to make the trip using public transportation, but it is more reliable and hassle-free if arranged through a travel agency. Long-distance ***buses*** *go several times daily from Xining to Heimahe (4hr.), roughly 1hr. from Bird Island. There are no public buses going to the island itself; travelers have been known to hike or thumb a ride the rest of the way. Return buses can be very crowded and you may end up without a seat.* ***Tours*** *should cost about Y100-150, depending on volume (12-13hr. total, departing at 6:30am).* ***Admission*** *to Bird Island Y45, Sun Moon Mountain Y10. If you just want to see the lake and have the time and the patience, take the bus to Heimahe and get off at a random spot along the water to walk around, or you can visit Heimahe, a small lakeside settlement on the south shore. The Xining-Golmud railway line runs along the north shore of the lake.*

Qinghai means "green sea" in Chinese, in Mongolian its name, *Koko Nor* means "blue ocean," and in Tibetan, *Tso Ngonpo* means "turquoise sea." Whatever the name and whatever the hue, this enormous lake, China's largest, sprawls across the Tibetan Plateau at an elevation of 3250m, surrounded by rolling grasslands dotted with vast herds of sheep and yak. In addition to its seemingly unending horizon and abundant supply of fish, the lake is a summer nesting ground for hundreds of thousands of migratory birds. From April until July, flocks of gulls, terns, geese, swans, and cranes arrive on **Bird Island** (niâo dâo; 鸟岛), a peninsula on the south side of the lake, to mate before heading to the plains of India for the winter. From a tourist's vantage point, however, Bird Island appears to be more of a "bird rock," and even avid birdlovers may return disgruntled by the tour buses, the long drive, and the overpriced admission. The tour may also stop on Egg Island nearby, where you can buy caterpillar-infested grass (chóngcâo; 虫草) for medicinal uses.

Even though the road to Qinghai Lake offers expansive views of plateau and open stretches of sky, tour buses here often don't allow visitors to linger for as long as may be hoped. Most tours do, however, make a pleasant first stop at **Sun Moon Mountain** (rìyuèshān; 日月山), a beautiful mountain pass separating the grasslands from the plateau. There is typically a lunch stop; then it's off to view birds. All in all, you must be an ornithologist and not mind long drives for this trip to be worthwhile.

TU MINORITY VILLAGE

In Huzhu Tu Autonomous County near Xining. Frequent buses (45min., Y6) run from the long-distance bus station to Huzhu (互助); ask to be let out at Weiyuanzhen Old Village (wēiyuânzhèn gûchéngcūn; 威远镇古城村). Niu Xiaojun (niú xiâo jūn; 牛晓军), the helpful English translator at the Jiangzhe Hotel in Xining (see p. 788), can help tourists.

The tiny Tu minority of Mandarin-speaking Tibetan Buddhists numbers just 70,000 in total, almost all of whom live in Huzhu county. Weiyuanzhen (pop 700), is 90% Tu. Walking around the village, checking out the traditional mud-brick courtyard houses, and seeing rural life up close is interesting in itself, but be sure to stop by the mayor's house at #47, a short walk up the dirt track from the highway. The mayor runs a self-styled tourist office and gift shop out of his home, and is happy to arrange all sorts of activities, generally charging about Y100 per person for a rather elaborate small-group program, consisting of a one-hour dance performance followed by a huge traditional feast. More modest programs are available, however, as is bargaining. The dance, performed by village girls dressed in traditional costume, is both elaborate and impressive—but be warned that some dances require guests to drink multiple shots of rice wine. Before you leave, be sure to check out the tiny Tibetan Buddhist Bo'er Temple (bóér sì; 伯尔寺), on the hill overlooking the village. (Open during daylight hours. Free.)

GOLMUD 格尔木

☎0979

Golmud, Qinghai's second largest city, is a coal-mining, oil-drilling industrial giant. Virtually all overland traffic into Tibet goes through Golmud, bringing in a constant stream of goods, traders, and travelers that will likely increase once the Golmud-Lhasa train line opens in 2009. Most visitors only come to Golmud to arrange permits and transportation to Lhasa, which can take up to three days, time that is usually whiled away at the city's numerous pool tables. Golmud sits isolated on the edge of vast tracts of salt flats and arid desert, which bring hot summers and frigid winters for the primarily Han Chinese residents; most locals have migrated here from Sichuan, Gansu, and eastern Qinghai provinces, scraping out a living along one of China's last frontiers.

ORIENTATION AND PRACTICAL INFORMATION

Golmud is arranged in a small grid. The bus and train stations are in the south, connected to the north of the city by **Jiangyuan Lu** (江源路). One block west of Jiangyuan Lu is **Kunlun Lu** (昆仑路), home to hotels, the bank, and restaurants.

The bus ride into the city from Xining is full of magnificent scenery ranging from lush terraces to salt flats to lunar landscapes. In contrast, the bus ride from Golmud to Lhasa is cramped and bumpy, often taking 1-2 full days on poor roads with numerous breakdowns. Although the price is not significantly lower than flying from Xining to Lhasa, taking the bus allows for greater freedom from the tight watch of your travel agency in Lhasa, and it also offers a fascinating insight into the stark differences between Western China and the Himalayan culture of Tibet.

Trains: Road quality is poor around Golmud; traveling by train is safer, more reliable, and faster. **Qinghai Train Station** (qīnghǎi huǒchē zhàn; 青海火车站; ☎423 591, ext. 2222), on Jiangyuan Lu, in the south part of town. Open 24hr. To: **Lanzhou** (24hr., daily, Y78-156) and **Xining** (19hr., 3 per day, Y46-122).

Buses: Qinghai Bus Station (qīnghǎi qìchē zhàn; 青海火汽车站; ☎423 688), north of the train station. Open daily 7:30am-10pm. To **Dunhuang** (11hr., 2 per day, Y50-84) and **Lhasa** (at least 30hr., daily, Y180). Officially, you need a Y150 permit, available from the PSB, to travel to Dunhuang; some travelers have reported being able to buy tickets regardless. **Tibet Bus Station** (xīzàng qìchē zhàn; 西藏火汽车站) in northwest Golmud has one bus to **Lhasa** (at least 30hr., 4:30pm, Y200).

Travel Agencies: CITS (☎412 764), on the 2nd fl. of the Golmud Hotel, is the only travel agency in town. You *must* pay Y1660 for a bus and permit into **Lhasa;** this fee includes Y1380 for bus, the permit, and a 3-day "tour" of Lhasa that does not include admission fees. CITS also charges an extra Y280 for your means of departure from Lhasa. If you want to see your Y280 again, you must book through **CITS** in the Tibet Hotel in western Lhasa, and you have only 4 return options: Lhasa to Kathmandu by air; Lhasa to Chengdu by air; Lhasa to Zhangmu by land cruiser with guide; and Lhasa to Golmud by sleeper bus. Arranging tours during the weekend is difficult. Open daily 8:30am-12:30pm and 3-6:30pm.

Bank of China: 19 Taidamu Lu (☎413 727), at Kunlun Lu, a block south of the Golmud Hotel. Exchanges traveler's checks. Open daily 8:30am-noon and 3-6pm.

PSB: In the eastern part of the city (☎412 375). Will not grant Tibet travel permits. Same-day visa extensions. Open daily 8:30am-noon and 3-6pm.

Post Office: On Jiangyuan Lu (☎413 094), a 5min. walk east from the Bank of China. EMS and IDD service. Open daily 8am-6pm. **Postal Code:** 816000.

ACCOMMODATIONS AND FOOD

Only two hotels accept foreigners. The more costly **Qinggang Hotel ❸** (qīnggǎng bīnguǎn; 青港宾馆; ☎421 808), 108 Kunlun Lu boasts a swimming pool and a bowling alley. Doubles have attached bath (Y168). Most travelers opt instead for the **Golmud Hotel ❶** (géěrmù bīnguǎn; 格尔木宾馆), 219 Kunlun Lu, across the street from the Qinggang. Clean dorms are spacious, and CITS is on the second floor. (☎412 061. 3-bed dorms Y22; singles Y30; doubles with bath Y77.)

Along **Kunlun Lu,** near the Golmud Hotel, many small restaurants offer cheap Sichuanese food (Y6-20 per dish). A **street market,** on the right after exiting the Golmud Hotel, sells fruit, nuts, and sweets, perfect for the long bus ride ahead. Next to the street market, a **supermarket** sells dried meat and other packaged foods.

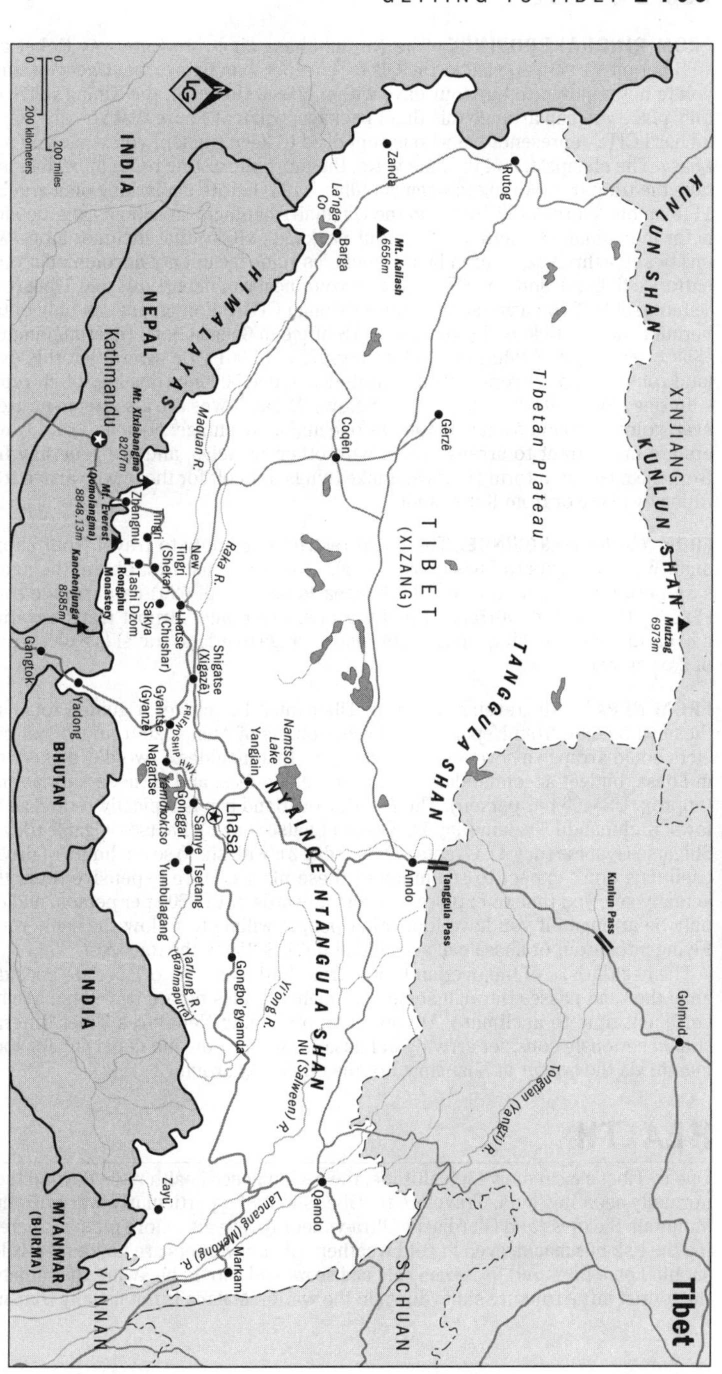
Tibet
XINJIANG
KUNLUN SHAN
KUNLUN SHAN
Mutzag
6973m
Rutog
Zanda
La'nga Co
Barga
Mt. Kailash
6656m
Tibetan Plateau
Gêrzê
Coqên
TIBET
(XIZANG)
TANGGULA SHAN
Kunlun Pass
Golmud
Tongtian (Yangzi) R.
Tanggula Pass
Amdo
Namtso Lake
Yangjain
NYAINQENTANGULA SHAN
Nu (Salween) R.
Yi'ong R.
Qamdo
Lancang (Mekong) R.
Markam
SICHUAN
YUNNAN
MYANMAR
(BURMA)
Zayü
INDIA
Gongbo'gyamda
Yarlung R.
(Brahmaputra)
Lhasa
Samye
Tsetang
Yumbulagang
Gonggar
Yamdroktso
Nagartse
Gyantse
(Gyanzê)
FRIENDSHIP HWY
Shigatse
(Xigazê)
Lhatse
(Chushar)
Sakya
Tashi Dzom
Rongphu Monastery
New Tingri
(Shekar)
Tingri
Zhangmu
Raka R.
Maquan R.
Mt. Everest
(Qomolangma)
8848.13m
Kanchenjunga
8585m
Mt. Xixiabangma
8207m
Kathmandu
NEPAL
HIMALAYAS
INDIA
BHUTAN
Yadong
Gangtok
0
0
200 miles
200 kilometers

FROM QINGHAI PROVINCE. The Xining-Lhasa air route (one-way ticket and TTB permit Y1950), opened in 1999, is far cheaper than flying from Chengdu, since you're not required to buy tour days within Lhasa. However, the Xining CITS, the only place you can arrange this flight package, will make sure that you are met by a Lhasa CITS representative who is supposed to keep track of you while you're in Lhasa. The cheapest, and in some ways, the most interesting route into Tibet is to take the train from Xining to **Golmud** (10hr., Y122) before embarking on a grueling 1115km bus journey (30-50hr.) on the Qinghai-Tibet highway. Standard procedure is for individual travelers to buy a tour package (Y1660) that includes a one-way bus ticket, a three-day tour in Lhasa (includes guide fee but not accommodation or entrance tickets), and a Y280 deposit on your means of departure from Tibet (only reimbursable if you arrange this travel through CITS). Foreigners can only obtain permits and bus tickets through the CITS office in **Golmud Hotel** (géěrmù bīnguǎn; 格尔木宾馆), 219 Kunlun Lu, 2nd fl. (☎(0979) 412 061). Be aware that this overland route spends several hours at altitudes above 5000m; travelers often report suffering from altitude sickness (see below). Breakdowns are also frequent. However, going overland from Golmud has one major advantage: once in Lhasa, travelers are much freer to arrange tours with other agencies, and are generally free from the close monitoring that can make things difficult for those who arrive from China by plane or from Kathmandu.

FROM YUNNAN PROVINCE. The usual restrictions apply to travel from Zhongdian. Weekly flights to Lhasa cost Y1250. Travelers must first obtain the necessary permits and join a tour. The **Kangba Hotel** (see p. 620) can arrange tours (Y2500) that include airfare, travel permits, insurance, airport transportation, and an English-speaking guide. They also arrange overland travel (Y5100, groups of 2 or more).

FROM NEPAL. All travelers entering Tibet must be part of a guided tour, and those who come from Nepal are no exception. As of August 2001, individual travelers could arrange a seven- to eight-day tour that includes a two-day guided tour in Lhasa, budget accommodations, car and guide fees, and all necessary permits (approx. US$400 per person). The five-day overland trip is typically routed as follows: Kathmandu-Nyalam (day 1), Nyalam-Lhatse (day 2), Lhatse-Shigatse (day 3), Shigatse-Gyantse (day 4), Gyantse-Lhasa (day 5); with six to seven hours of driving each day, don't expect to see much of these places. More expensive tours that actually give you time to explore can cost upwards of US$600 per person, and can only be arranged if you have four other people willing to follow the same route. Flying into or out of Lhasa can also add about US$250 to the tour cost.

The health risks of the overland route from Kathmandu into Tibet are considerable; the road passes through some very high altitudes before travelers have had sufficient time to acclimate. Anyone bent on adding Nepal to a Tibet itinerary should seriously consider arriving in Lhasa from Chengdu and departing for Kathmandu via the border at Zhangmu, not the other way around.

HEALTH

Due to Tibet's extremely high altitude, the region poses health risks beyond those normally seen in China. Travelers to Tibet should be particularly wary of Acute Mountain Sickness and Giardiasis. Ultra-violet rays are also more intense, increasing the risk of **sunburn,** even in cold weather. Tibetan winters are no joke; travelers should come prepared for **severe cold and snow,** and should be aware that much of the tourist infrastructure shuts down in the winter. **Malaria** is not usually transmitted at altitudes above 2000m. Those taking an anti-malarial drug like mefloquine may want to consider not taking their doses until after the descent; some of the drug's side effects are similar to those of AMS. For more information on **sunburn** and **hypothermia,** see p. 64; for general advice about health concerns, see p. 62.

ACUTE MOUNTAIN SICKNESS (AMS). Many parts of the Tibetan Plateau sit more than 4000m above sea level. At this altitude, many travelers feel the effects of decreased air pressure and lower oxygen levels. Acute Mountain Sickness (AMS), also known as altitude sickness, typically appears about twelve hours after arrival and lasts three or four days before the body adjusts. **Rate of ascent** affects the risk, duration, and severity of AMS; risk is greatest at altitudes above 3000m if you ascend more than 300m a day. The most common symptoms of AMS are headache, insomnia, fatigue, shortness of breath, dizziness, and nausea. AMS is aggravated by dehydration, alcohol and other depressants, and overexertion.

The best way to alleviate mild AMS (headache, vomiting, fatigue) is to stay hydrated, avoid sedatives (including alcohol), and take it easy. Travelers should consider budgeting a few days in Lhasa in order to get used to the altitude. Mild symptoms of AMS can be treated by normal over-the-counter pain relievers; some physicians prescribe **Diamox** (acetazolamide) to stimulate respiration. Moderate AMS (persistent vomiting and severe headache) is sometimes treated with supplemental oxygen and steroids. Those with moderate AMS also suffer from ataxia, or decreased coordination. If you can't walk a straight line, heel to toe, an immediate descent of 300-700m is recommended to ensure that symptoms don't get worse.

Severe AMS is a life-threatening condition. There are two types of severe AMS: **High Altitude Pulmonary Edema** (HAPE) and **High Altitude Cerebral Edema** (HACE). HAPE is caused by fluid build-up in the lungs; symptoms include blue or pale lips and face and a cough or gurgling respiration. HACE is caused by swelling in the brain; symptoms include disorientation, memory loss, ataxia, and hallucination. Severe fatigue and shortness of breath are symptoms of both. Travelers with severe AMS can slip into comas or even die; those who suspect that they may have it should descend 600-1300m and seek immediate medical assistance.

GIARDIASIS. Commonly called **giardia,** giardiasis is caused by the protozoan parasite *giardia lamblia.* This parasite is present in untreated water, particularly in cold and mountainous regions. Travelers should avoid unboiled tap water and raw food washed with unboiled tap water. Swimming in lakes and streams can also lead to infection. Symptoms of giardiasis include diarrhea, abdominal cramps, and nausea; they usually appear one to two weeks after infection and last for four to six weeks. Giardia is treatable by an anti-amoebic drug such as **Flagyl** (metronizade), which is usually available by prescription only.

HISTORY

EARLY HISTORY

According to legend, the Tibetan people are descended from the Bodhisattva of compassion, Avalokiteshvara, who took the form of a monkey demon and proceeded to have "relations" with an ogress (the Goddess Tara). Fossils and records, however, hold that they were descended from the Qiang people, who were mentioned in Chinese records as early as 200 BC. A Tibetan state didn't emerge until sometime around 127 BC, when an Indian king came to Tibet. Twelve Bön priests, obviously never having been to India, thought that he came from heaven and named him king. For the next few centuries, Tibet was fairly uninteresting, home to squabbling princedoms and little else.

In the 7th century AD, a boy of thirteen named **Songtsen Gampo** became king of Tibet. He is widely known as the man who unified Tibet; his empire extended far past the boundaries of modern Tibet, and included parts of Xinjiang, Gansu, Qinghai, Sichuan, and Yunnan provices. He is also the man who established diplomatic relations with China; he married a Chinese princess in exchange for diplomatic ties with the Tang court. This is not to say, of course, that China and Tibet became fast friends. In the 8th century, China stopped paying tribute to Tibet; in return, the Tibetans sacked Chang'an (modern-day Xi'an).

In the 9th century, struggles over succession to the throne and religion once again divided Tibet. Buddhism, which was introduced to Tibet in AD 173, was steadily gaining in popularity, but many of Tibet's ruling elite were practitioners of the indigenous religion, Bön. The dynasty was destroyed when a Buddhist monk assassinated the Buddhist-persecuting king. For the next 200 years, political authority languished as religious strength flourished. Missionaries flooded in from India, monasteries, including the one at **Sakya** (see p. 827), were founded, and Tibetan priests (**lamas**) began to consolidate political power.

COMING OF THE YELLOW HAT SECT

In the early 15th century, **Tsong Khapa,** disillusioned with the infighting and mysticism that characterized Tibetan Buddhism under the Sakya lamas, founded a new sect that emphasized study and monastic discipline. His sect, named "Gelug," or "the system of virtue," attracted a wide range of followers; they wore yellow hats to distinguish themselves from the other, red-hat-wearing sects of Tibetan Buddhism—the Gelug sect is often known as the "Yellow Hat" sect. The popularity of the sect did not engender affection in the other sects of Tibetan Buddhism, who happened at the time to be allied with Tibet's political rulers. As a result, the next two centuries were consumed by sectarian violence.

The Gelug sect had been using the concept of reincarnation as a method of succession since the late 15th century, when the founder of Tashilhunpo Monastery (see p. 826) prophesied that he would be reincarnated in the form of a young boy. The third in this line, Sonam Gyatso, was granted the title of Dalai Lama by the Mongolian leader Altyn Khan. In Mongolian, *dalai* means "oceanic," or "ocean-wide"; the title refers to the scope of the Dalai Lama's knowledge. The Gelug sect further cemented its relationship with the Mongols when the next Dalai Lama was discovered in the grandson of Altyn Khan.

Over time, the Gelug sect and the Mongols developed a fairly co-dependent relationship. The Mongols had already cultivated a relationship with the Sakye, another Buddhist sect, in which the monks provided religious instruction while the Mongols provided military protection. The Sakye sect did not, however, count a Mongol as one of its religous leaders. So when the Gelug sect faced increasing aggression from other Buddhist sects, they went to the Mongols for help. In the mid-17th century, the Mongols, with the help of Gelug monks, gained military control of Tibet, and executed the king. The Mongols then gave supreme authority of all Tibet to the Dalai Lama and his chief steward, who went about persecuting their main religious rivals and consolidating their land, resources, and influence. The Mongols decided that they liked their new home; their leader, Gushri Khan, declared himself king. The Dalai Lama, however, still held the real reins of power.

In 1717, Tibet and the Gelug sect were again in disarray. The 6th Dalai Lama had renounced his monastic vows, preferring instead to be the Frank Sinatra of the religious world, writing love poems and fooling around with young girls. The Mongolian king, Lhabsang Khan, decided that maybe he'd like to have some real power. He allied with some Tibetan aristocrats, executed the regent, and took control of Tibet. The Gelug sect, opting for the tried-and-true strategy, went again to the Mongols for help; but this time they approached a different tribe. It just so happened that this tribe, the Dzungars, were not on the best of terms with the Qing dynasty. So when the Dzungars took Lhasa, the Qing reacted quickly to curb Mongolian influence in the area. In 1720 they invaded, kicked out the Mongols, and established an overlordship that would last until the fall of the Qing in 1911. Under **Chinese "suzerainty,"** the Tibetans were left to govern internal affairs on their own, the Dalai Lama's government maintained peaceful relations with China, and Tibetan culture absorbed little Chinese influence.

CHINESE SUZERAINTY AND TIBETAN AUTONOMY

In the mid 1800s, Tibet, like much of China, was closed to Western trade, presenting an irresistible challenge to the inimitable British. Their first attempts to enter the region were repelled by the Tibetans, but in 1904, the British military adventurer Younghusband marched into Lhasa, slapped indemnities on the Tibetans, and forced the 13th Dalai Lama to flee to Mongolia to seek support from the Russian czar. Britain and Tibet then signed the Anglo-Tibetan Convention of 1904, which declared Tibet a British protectorate. However, Britain's ministers of trade reminded the government of the importance of Chinese trade relations, and so the British drew up the Anglo-Chinese Convention in 1906 and reaffirmed China's control over Tibet. Qing reaction in Tibet was severe. They turned previously autonomous Tibetan areas into Chinese states and sent several thousand troops to Lhasa, forcing the 13th Dalai Lama once more into exile.

After the Chinese revolution of 1911, the indignant Tibetans (led by the newly returned Dalai Lama) declared independence and expelled Chinese residents. Over the next forty years, Tibet enjoyed complete sovereignty, even though one of the goals of the Chinese nationalists was to "liberate" Tibet from the British and reinstate Tibet as a part of China. In 1912, the ROC declared that Tibet (along with Mongolia and Xinjiang) was an important part of China, nominally reincorparting it into political China. Meanwhile, the 13th Dalai Lama's attempts at reform and modernization were rejected by the conservative aristocracy, and Tibet remained a pious but impoverished theocracy. Tibet's neutrality during WWII did not help it gain international recognition; when Chiang Kai-shek declared Tibet a province of Nationalist China, victorious allied powers didn't protest. After the PRC victory in 1949, however, Tibet began to face real problems—Mao had set his sights on Tibet and was not to be dissuaded.

UNDER CHINESE RULE (1949-PRESENT)

In October 1950, PLA troops invaded Tibet and routed the Tibetan army. In 1951, Tibet buckled under the military pressure and signed the Seventeen-Point Agreement, acknowledging Chinese sovereignty while effectively retaining cultural and religious autonomy. The CCP collectivized Tibetan areas of western Sichuan and Qinghai, but for the most part left Tibet alone. In the mid 1950s, Tibetan rebels engaged the Chinese in a guerrilla war in southern Tibet. The US Central Intelligence Agency (CIA), in an attempt to undermine the power of the CCP, covertly supplied the Tibetan rebels with arms and training. By 1959, the rebels had sparked a mass rebellion. It failed, however, and the Dalai Lama was forced to flee to India (accompanied by relatives, ministers, supporters, CIA-trained rebels, and much of the country's gold reserves). In turn, China renounced the Seventeen-Point Agreement and declared martial law in Tibet.

The CCP moved quickly to consolidate power in Tibet, replacing the traditional ruling class with Beijing-appointed officials and Tibetan Communist cadres. After 1959, the Chinese government pursued the same economic programs in Tibet as it did in the rest of China. The results were disastrous. The standard of living in Tibet fell sharply, and thousands became victims of religious persecution. During the Cultural Revolution, Chinese Red Guards demolished monasteries and religious relics, nuns and monks were forced to marry, and thousands of people were sent to prison camps. Although there are no exact figures, it is estimated that well over a million Tibetans died in the turmoil.

After the rise of Deng Xiaoping in 1979, liberal officials acknowledged past mistakes in Tibet and urged "ethnic sensitivity." Monasteries were rebuilt, economic activity was normalized, and the region was opened to tightly regulated tourism. Nominal religious practice was permitted so long as religious leaders stayed out of politics. In the 1980s, Tibetans, supported by the Dharmasala Tibetan government-in-exile, began to demand greater political and religious freedom. While the 14th Dalai Lama visited the US to state his case and win support, Tibetans in Lhasa followed his activities. On October 1, 1987, a group of monks demonstrated in Lhasa to show their support; the police responded by apprehending the monks and beating them—it was not long before full-scale riots broke out. Over the next two years, Lhasa would see three more riots before the Chinese government declared martial law in 1989.

Today, monasteries are tightly monitored, and monks are required to undergo political education and swear allegiance to the Chinese state. As China struggles to bring Tibet to heel, the **Tibetan Government-in-Exile,** based in Dharamsala, India, works to rally support for a free Tibet from abroad. The government-in-exile is a democratic, constitutional body that rules over the 131,000 Tibetans currently in exile. In the past decade the Dalai Lama has succeeded in drawing world attention to his homeland, but, sadly, the pleas of American celebrities have done little to effect real change. The Chinese government has not backed down from its hard-line policies; indeed, in some ways the restrictions in Tibet are more severe than they ever have been. The display of Dalai Lama photographs has not been allowed since 1994; in June 2001 a woman was sentenced to six years in prison for watching a video of the Dalai Lama. The situation is still tense—staggering numbers of PSB officers are posted in Lhasa, and the Chinese government is suspicious of everyone, including tourists.

PEOPLE

ETHNIC COMPOSITION. About 4.6 million Tibetans live in the Tibet Autonomous Region and in the ethnically Tibetan areas of Qinghai, Gansu, Sichuan, and Yunnan. Since the 1950s, however, these regions have seen an influx of Han and Hui Chinese, mainly merchants and government-sponsored cadres. Most Tibetans support themselves through agriculture, nomadic herding, or small-scale commerce.

LANGUAGE. Tibetan is related to Chinese (both are members of the Sino-Tibetan language family), but the two languages are wholly distinct. The Tibetan script, introduced around AD 600, is derived from and similar to Indian writing systems, and is read from right to left. Regional dialects vary widely; the Lhasa dialect is regarded as the standard. For useful phrases in Tibetan, see p. 844.

FOOD. Tibetan **cuisine,** likewise, would never be mistaken for Chinese. The staple is barley flour (*tsampa*), which is mixed with water to form a porridge that is the foundation of most Tibetan diets. The yak, a pungent, hairy creature well-suited to high altitudes, is also essential to Tibetan cuisine, which uses yak butter, yak meat, yak milk—basically any yak part or derivation thereof. A slaughtered yak is bound to be a well-utilized one. Regional beverages include yak-butter tea and barley beer, known as *chang*. Wheat, mutton, and pork are also widely consumed; favorite dishes include *thukpa* (noodle soups) and *momos* (fried dumplings).

The cheapest restaurants in Lhasa (see p. 803) and—to a lesser extent—along the Friendship Highway (see p. 818) are Tibetan establishments with neither English nor Chinese menus. Communication can sometimes be difficult; the following chart lists some of the most popular dishes along with approximate prices.

DISH	TIBETAN NAME	TIBETAN SCRIPT	PRICE
sweet tea	*cha ngamo*	ཇ་མངར་མོ་	Y1 per glass; Y4 for a small thermos
Tibetan home-brewed beer	*chang*	ཆང་	Y2 per liter
yak-butter tea	*poja*	བོད་ཇ་	Y1 per glass; Y3 for a small thermos
Tibetan noodles	*thug pa*	ཐུག་པ་	Y3-5 per bowl
fried potatoes	*shawgaw ngöbâ*	ཞོག་ཁོག་རྔོས་པ་	Y7-10 per plate
rice	*dray*	འབྲས་	Y1-3 per bowl
fried yak meat	*yag-sha ngöbâ*	གཡག་ཤ་བརྔོས་པ་	Y5-8; Y10 with rice and potatoes
yogurt	*sho*	ཞོ་	Y1-2 per bowl

RELIGION

Few cultures on earth invest as much in religion as the Tibetans do. In Tibet, politics, art, science, and literature all derive from and support spiritual faith. Prior to the Cultural Revolution, many Tibetans based their livelihoods around Buddhist monasteries or nunneries. Chinese intervention and policy, however, are slowly turning Tibetans away from their traditional lifestyle.

BÖN

Before Buddhism, there was Bön. According to legend, Bön was founded by Tönpa Shenrab, an enlightened teacher who studied in heaven. Believed to be the first religion of Tibet, Bön was a highly magical religion that incorporated exorcisms, sacrifice, and demon lore into its mythology. Although most practioners of Bön were persecuted and eliminated in the 8th century AD, many aspects of this ancient religion have been incorporated into Tibetan Buddhism. In Bön, kings were believed to be divine rulers descended from the god of the sky; the Tibetan Buddhist concept of the reincarnated lama, a leader of both the political and the spiritual realms, originated here. Many of Tibetan Buddhism's minor deities and its tradition of religious oracles were also adopted from Bön. Today, Bön is still practiced by a handful of devotees in Tibet and abroad; the Dalai Lama considers it to be the fifth school of Tibetan Buddhism.

TIBETAN BUDDHISM

The Tibetan school of Buddhism integrates what it views as the three schools of Indian Buddhism: **Hinayana,** or individual practice; **Mahayana,** the ethical practice;

and **Vairayana,** or "thunderbolt vehicle." A monk usually studies one of the deities from India's **Tantric Sect** until he can exist as this Buddha in meditation. Then, the monk manipulates his physical energies in order to exist in the foundation of all being, what is known as "clear light." In Tibetan Buddhiam, the key to enlightenment is to use emotional energy in the quest for sacred consciousness.

Tibetan Buddhism is comprised of four **sects.** The oldest, the **Nyingma** ("old ones") sect dates back to the 8th century AD, and is responsible for penning the Tibetan Book of the Dead. For Nyingma adherants, magical spells and diagrams are important tools with which to attain enlightenment. The **Kagyu** ("new translation") sect was founded in the 10th century by two Tibetan masters and has since shattered into several sub-sects. The **Sakya** ("gray earth") sect was founded in the 11th century, and was the sect that brought Buddhism to Mongolia. *Sakya* means "gray earth"; the monastery where the sect was founded had gray earth walls. The **Gelug** sect (see p. 798), to which the Dalai Lama adheres, is the youngest.

Monastic life generally involved years of grueling, intensive study and meditation. Tibetan monasteries are headed by teachers called **lamas,** who are distinct from ordinary monks and nuns. Each living lama is said to be the reincarnation of an earlier lama. Monks consult astrological charts and other oracles; the candidates they find are then typically asked to prove their legitimacy by identifying the former lama's possessions. The **Dalai Lama** and his traditional second-in-command, the **Panchen Lama,** are the most highly honored lamas.

While monks and nuns engage in theological argument and meditation, most Tibetans worship a number of *bodhisattvas*, deities, and demons. Among the most revered of these is **Avalokiteshvara,** represented as both the monkey demon and as the *bodhisattva* of compassion. **Circumambulating** (taking walks along designated sacred paths), the burning of yak-butter lamps (to represent the triumph of enlightenment over ignorance), the offering of bowls of water (to represent one's pure essence), and the **turning of prayer wheels** play an important role in popular practice.

FESTIVALS AND HOLIDAYS

Most Tibetan festivals are local affairs, unique to a village or region and buoyed by strong community spirit. Exact festival dates vary annually based on the local calendar. National festivals are mostly Buddhist holidays, but a few are the lingering remains of Tibet's distant past.

MONTH	FESTIVAL	DETAILS
mid-February, 2003	**Ghost-exorcising Festival**	Tibetans carry burning straw into each room of their houses in order to cast out evil spirits.
mid-February, 2003	**Tibetan New Year**	Liquor and lamb heads are prepared in the pre-dawn hours; at daybreak, families visit temples and shines.
late-February, 2003	**Monlam (Great Prayer) Festival**	This traditional festival celebrated the submission of the state to religion; lamas from Lhasa's three major temples would gather and hold services. The Chinese government has placed significant restrictions on the celebration of this festival.
late-February, 2003	**Butter Oil Lantern Festival**	Held to celebrate Buddha's victory in a religious debate. Tibetans celebrate this festival by making and displaying butter lamp scultures.
May 26, 2003	**The Birth of Buddha**	A celebration of the day when Buddha was born, died, and became enlightened.
June, 2003	**Horse Racing Festival**	Held in Gyantse since 1408, this festival features horse races and archery contests.

MONTH	FESTIVAL	DETAILS
late-July, 2003	**Yalong Cultural Festival**	A festival initiated by the Chinese government to celebrate Tibetan culture. It includes sports events, dancing, opera, and plenty of pro-China propaganda.
mid-August, 2003	**Shoton Festival**	Originally, this was the day on the Tibetan calendar when meditating monks would emerge from the monasteries to receive gifts of yogurt (in Tibetan, *sho*). Since the 17th century, however, this festival has also been known as the Tibetan Opera Festival; each year, opera troupes perform in Norbulingka, in Lhasa.
September, 2003	**Bathing Festival**	Tibetans, believing the water is at its purest during this week, bathe in rivers or creeks to stave off illness.
December 25, 2003	**Death of Tsong Khapa**	Tibetans honor the founder of the Yellow Hat sect by lighting yak-butter lamps and saying prayers.

ལྷ་ས་ LHASA 拉萨 ☎0891

Sillhouetted by layers of mountains, the Potala Palace sits on a hill in the center of Lhasa, the spiritual and political center of the Tibetan Autonomous Region. Narrow gray and maroon alleyways stretch throughout the city, opening onto courtyards, and heading for the Jokhang Temple, the heart of the city, where prayer wheels never cease to turn and the sun sets with a golden shudder under deep blue skies. Despite political machinations and economic development, Lhasa has somehow managed to retain its identity as a spiritual center, evident by the hillside temples of Ganden, Sera, and Drepung, which lie unimpeded by the cement block roads, commercial districts, and neon TV towers. Under the watchful eyes of the PSB, Lhasa treads precariously into an uncertain future, holding onto an intense devotional energy that hopefully will see Han-Tibetan cultural and political tensions through to a happy resolution.

ORIENTATION

At 3700m above sea level, Lhasa sits on the lowland northern bank of the **Lhasa** or **Kyichu River.** Lhasa's jurisdiction extends over 29,052km^2 of terrain, but its city center spans a mere 20km^2, an area visitors can easily navigate with a map and their own two feet. The city center is bounded to the north by **Linkuo Bei Lu** (林廓北路) and to the south by **Jinzhu (Chingdol) Lu** (金珠路). **Beijing Lu** (北京路), Lhasa's main east-west axis, runs from the Potala Palace in the west past most tourist services in the heart of the city, a predominantly Tibetan area that surrounds **Jokhang Temple** and the **Barkhor Market.** Most tourists head to this lively, colorful quarter in search of travel agencies, Western-style restaurants, and cheap accommodations.

TRANSPORTATION

Flights: Lhasa Gonggar Airport (lāsà gònggā jīchǎng; 拉萨贡嘎机场; ☎618 2221), is 95km to the southwest, the greatest distance between a city and its municipal airport in the world. An **airport bus** runs from Gonggar Airport to Lhasa (1½hr., departure times dependent on daily arrival times, Y30). **Land cruisers** (1½hr., Y400-500) ferry passengers between the airport and the city center. Passengers looking to share a taxi or land cruiser to the airport often post notices on the boards at the Yak, Banak Shol, Pentoc, and Kirey Hotels. Buses also run to Gonggar (1½hr.; 6, 10am, and 3pm; Y30) from the Lhasa **CAAC Ticket Office,** 1 Niangre Lu (☎683 3446; fax 683 8609). CAAC can also book flights 15 days in advance. Open daily 9am-8:30pm. **China Southwest Airlines,**

a subsidiary of CAAC, has direct flights to and from Tibet. To: **Beijing** (daily, Y2040) **Chengdu** (3-4 per day, Y1270); **Chongqing** (M, Y1400); **Kathmandu** (Tu, Th, Sa Y2290); **Xi'an** (Su-M, W, F; Y1420); **Xining** (Su-M, W, F; Y1390).

Buses: Lhasa Long-distance Bus Station (☎682 4469), on the corner of Jinzhu (Ching dol) Lu and Minzhu Lu, in the southwestern section of Lhasa. A smaller bus station eas of the Kirey Hotel has the same schedule and prices. Undercover PSB officers check fo permits at both stations. To: **Chengdu** (4 days, 3 per day, Y500); **Gyantse** (3 pe month, Y230); **Naqn** via **Damxung** (6hr., 8:30 and 9am, Y68); **Shigatse** (5hr., 7:30am Y38); **Tsetang** (4hr.; 9, 10, and 11am; Y27) via the **Samye Monastery ferry crossing.**

Local Transportation: Minibuses run 7am-9pm. Fare Y2. Minibus **#5** runs from Ramo che Temple to Sera Lamasery; **#3** runs the length of Linkuo Lu.

Taxis: Taxis to anywhere in the city Y10 (north of the Kyichu River, excluding Sera an Drepung monasteries); bargain for destinations beyond city limits. **Tricycles** transport passengers, but are prohibited from passing the square in front of the Potala Palac before 7:30pm. From the end of Beijing Dong Lu to the Potala Palace (3-4km) Y3-4.

Bike Rental: The **Snowland** and **Yak Hotels** rent bikes for Y3 per hr.

PRACTICAL INFORMATION

TOURIST AND FINANCIAL SERVICES

Tourist Offices: Lhasa Tourism Bureau (lāsàshì lǚyóu jú; 拉萨市旅游局), 33 Jiangsh Lu (☎632 3632, English ☎632 4097; fax 633 1175), does not process visas or entr permits, but arbitrates between tourists and travel agencies or hotels when necessar Open daily 9:30am-12:30pm and 3:30-6pm.

Travel Agencies:

CITS, 208 Beijing Xi Lu (☎683 6626; fax 683 6315), next to the Lhasa Hotel in the far west c town. Open daily 9:30am-1pm and 3:30-6:30pm. **Shigatse Travel** (rìkāzé guójì lǚxíngsh 日喀则国际旅行社; ☎633 0489), a subsidiary branch of CITS in the Yak Hotel, can reliab arrange visas, permits, guides, and jeeps to local destinations like Namtso and Samye. They on arrange trips out west or to the Nepalese border for travelers who arrive in Tibet on a Shigats Travel tour. Open daily 9am-1pm and 3-6:30pm. Both of these CITS branches may charge muc more than other travel agencies.

The **Barkhor Market area** has many agencies, most of which are based in local hotels and ca arrange trips, short ones in particular. Price varies more than quality; shop around. Anyone ren ing a land cruiser should look at the vehicle beforehand.

F.I.T. Travel Agency (☎634 4397), next to Tashi Restaurant on Zangiyuan Dong Lu. Open dai 9am-midnight. They also have a branch (☎634 9239) in the Snowland Hotel with the sam hours. These 2 offices are the most common agents for trips to Namtso, Samye, and spots alor the Friendship Highway. As of July 2001, F.I.T. was the only travel agency that can arrange tou for individuals or small groups heading west to the Nepalese border or to Everest Base Camp.

Tibet International Sports Travel (☎633 4082), in the Himalaya Hotel (xǐmǎlāyǎ fàndià 喜马拉雅饭店), on 6 Lingkuo Dong Lu, is considerably more expensive and caters to thos interested in hard-core, action-packed vacations.

Consulate: Nepal, 13 Luobulinka (Norbulingka) Lu (☎682 2881; fax 683 6890), clos to the Lhasa Hotel; take bus #3. 60-day Nepalese visas Y230; overnight processin Instant processing at the border crossing to Kathmandu (same price, US currency only The consulate closes at 6pm; arrive in the morning for visa applications.

Bank of China: Main branch at 28 Lingkuo Xi Lu. Exchanges currency and traveler checks. Credit card advances. Another branch on Beijing Dong Lu, between the Kir and Banak Shol hotels, only exchanges currency and traveler's checks. Both branches open M-F 9am-1pm and 3:30-6:30pm, Sa-Su 10am-3pm. Authorized hotels also exchange foreign currency for a fee. There are no **ATMs** in Lhasa.

LOCAL SERVICES

Bookstore: Xinhua Bookstore, 45 Renmin Lu, with branches in Barkhor Market and next to the Tibet Hotel. Mainly Chinese and Tibetan books; some English maps of Lhasa and Tibet. Open M-F 9:30am-8pm, Sa-Su 6:30am-7pm.

Library: Lhasa City Library (xīzàngshì túshūguǎn; 西藏市图书馆; ☎683 2954), on Luobulinka (Norbulingka) Lu. Foreign reference books on the 2nd fl., including 2000 English books and 1000 books in Japanese, Spanish, French, and German. Check out a book with deposit and ID. Open M-F 9am-12:30pm and 3:30-6pm, Sa-Su 10am-5pm.

Outdoor and Trekking Gear: North Col Outdoor Equipment Shop (☎681 6379), on the left side of the square that faces the Potala Palace. Rents, buys, and sells the best quality gear (Ozark, Mt. Hardward, and North Face) in Lhasa. Prices are high, but still lower than prices abroad. **Outlook Outdoor Equipment Shop** (☎634 5589), on Beijing Lu, 3min. east of the Yak Hotel, buys, sells, and rents gear and clothes. They plan to distribute maps of local trekking routes (i.e. Ganden to Samye) and can help plan local trips. **Polarfleece,** west of the Kirey Hotel, has cheap imitation North Face and fleece layers.

EMERGENCY AND COMMUNICATIONS

PSB: Lhasa City Office, 8 Lingkuo Bei Lu (☎632 5312, 24hr. ☎632 4422). Another branch at 1 Barkhor Xi Lu (☎632 3393). The main office for travel permit processing is at 157 Beijing Dong Lu (☎682 3809). The PSB doesn't issue travel permits or visa extensions; do this before entering Tibet. The travel agency that brought you to Tibet can also arrange extensions for further travel (see p. 50 for info on travel permits and visas).

Pharmacy: Shengjie Pharmacy (shèngjié yàodiàn; 圣洁药店), 2 Beijing Zhong Lu, Diguang Ju Hostel. Open daily 8am-midnight. Bang on the door if there is an emergency; the proprietors live right behind the drug counter.

Hospital: People's Hospital of the Tibet Autonomous Region (xīzàng zìzhìqū rénmín yīyuàn; 西藏自治区人民医院), 18 Lingkuo Bei Lu (☎633 2462, emergency ☎632 2200). Specializes in treating altitude sickness. Many doctors speak English. Open daily 9am-12:30pm and 3:30-6pm. 24hr. emergency care.

Telephones: Lhasa City Telecommunications Office, 64 Beijing Zhong Lu. From the post office, walk a few doors down the street, away from the Potala. 13 phone booths with IDD service for Y8.2 per min. Purchasing an IC card can get you cheaper rates. Open daily 8:30am-10pm. The main **Lhasa City Telecommunications Office** is on 59 Lingkuo Dong Lu. IDD service. Open daily 9am-12:30pm and 3:30-6:30pm.

Internet Access: Dozens of small Internet cafes have sprung up around the major guesthouses in the Barkhor Lu and Beijing Lu areas. Don't pay more than Y5 per hr. **Boiling Point Cafe** (fèi diǎn; 沸点), on Zangyiyuan Dong Lu, down the street from Tashi restaurant. The biggest and most popular place in town. Y20 per hr. Open daily 9am-midnight.

Post Office: Lhasa City Post Office, on Beijing Zhong Lu, just before the Potala Palace. EMS and Poste Restante. Open daily in summer 9am-8pm; in winter 9:30am-7pm.

ACCOMMODATIONS

Intense competition for foreign business has driven rates down to Y20-25. Most hotels have roof decks, balconies, and similar room quality; the quality of attached restaurants is one way to distinguish the six guesthouses that line **Beijing Dong Lu** and **Zangyiyuan Dong Lu,** near the Barkhor Market. Unless otherwise stated, all listings have IDD service at the reception, 24-hour hot water, and luggage storage.

Eight Auspicious Hotel, also known as the **Tashi Tagel Hotel** (zāxī dájíe bīnguǎn; 扎西达杰宾馆), 8 Zangyiyuan Dong Lu (☎632 5804 or 632 3271). Rooms and hallways are bright and airy. Communal showers and toilets are cleaner than those at most other local hotels. Spectacular roof-top view of the Potala Palace. The popular Tashi 1 restaurant is a 2min. walk away. 3-bed dorms Y15; doubles Y50, with bath Y250. ❶

Pentoc Guesthouse (pānduō lǚguǎn; 攀多旅馆), 5 Zangyiyuan Dong Lu (☎632 6686), a few doors down from Tashi 1 Restaurant. With its outdoor staircases and balconies, this bright, airy guesthouse is often packed with Western travelers of all ages. Rooms are clean with soft beds. Immaculate communal baths. 1-day film processing. English movies nightly. 3-bed dorms Y30; singles Y50; doubles Y80. ❶

Kirey Hotel (jírì bīnguǎn; 吉日宾馆), 105 Beijing Dong Lu (☎632 3462). Throngs of backpackers and tour groups come for the Tibetan-style rooms, a large courtyard, and a view of the mountains. Mad Yak Restaurant and Tashi 2 Restaurant onsite. Gates close at midnight. Somewhat inconveniently located communal showers have hot water 9am-9pm. Free laundry service. 3- to 4-bed dorms Y20; doubles Y50, with bath Y260. ❶

Lhasa Yak Hotel (lāsàyà bīnguǎn; 拉萨亚宾馆), 100 Beijing Dong Lu (☎632 3496). Clean, tiled rooms facing a pleasant courtyard are some of the best Lhasa has to offer in this price range. Friendly staff and in-house Shigatse Travel Agency. Bike rental Y3 per hr. Internet access Y10 per hr. 6- to 10-bed dorms Y20; doubles with bath Y260. ❶

Snowland Hotel (xuěyù bīnguǎn; 雪域宾馆), 4 Zangyiyuan Dong Lu (☎632 3687). Walk for 7min. on Zangiyuan Dong Lu toward Barkhor Market; it's on the left. Well-equipped and conveniently located. Clean, small rooms have thin mattresses. Bike rental Y2 per hr. Hotel restaurant open daily 7am-11pm. F.I.T. Travel Service on 2nd fl. 5- to 10-bed dorms Y25; doubles Y40 per bed, with bath Y260; triples Y30 per bed. ❶

Banak Shol Hotel (bāxuě bīnguǎn; 八雪宾馆), 43 Beijing Dong Lu (☎632 3829), a 20min. walk up Beijing Dong Lu from Zangyiyuan Dong Lu. The oldest (opened in 1985) and most distant of Lhasa's 6 main guesthouses. Popular with Chinese and Tibetan youth, the huge hotel has a large courtyard. Steep stairs are ladder-like. Communal toilets on every floor, showers on 1st fl. Free safety deposit boxes. F.I.T. office on 1st fl. 4- to 5-bed dorms Y25; 2-bed dorms Y60; singles Y30; clean and pleasant doubles with bath Y150. ❶

Mandala Hotel (mǎnzhài jiǔdiàn; 满斋酒店), 31 Bakuo Nan Jie (☎632 4783 or 633 8940), on the right side of Barkhor Market when you face the Jokhang Temple. Its lack of dorm options results in fewer opportunities for backpacker information exchange. Bright, shiny, wood-paneled rooms have A/C, heaters, and TV. On-site restaurant (dishes Y12-25) open 24hr. The nearby Makye Ame Restaurant (see **Food,** below) lures many a guest away. Singles Y180; doubles with bath Y260. ❸

FOOD

The "Land of Yaks" even extends onto your dinner plate; but after you catch a whiff of your entree, it may just stay there. Adventurous travelers can try a variety of yak dishes and products in Lhasa, including yak *momos* (dumplings), stewed yak, stir-fried yak, barbecued yak, and, of course, the wildly popular Tibetan equivalent to coffee, yak-butter tea. Used in numerous dishes, *tsampa* (barley flour) is a staple of the local diet, and *tsampa* beer is a must on festive occasions. The universal staple, wide-cut french fries (Y1 for a small bag), is also available.

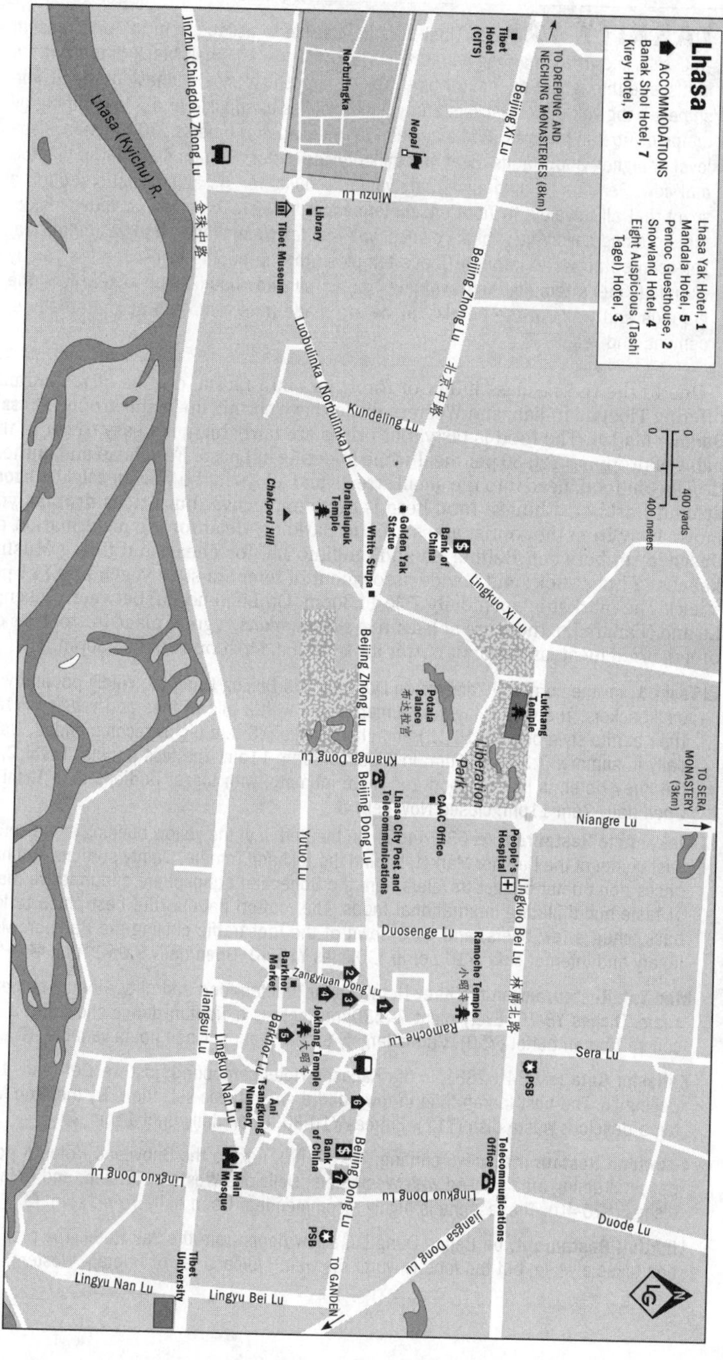

Lhasa

ACCOMMODATIONS
Banak Shol Hotel, **7**
Kirey Hotel, **6**
Lhasa Yak Hotel, **1**
Mandala Hotel, **5**
Pentoc Guesthouse, **2**
Snowland Hotel, **4**
Eight Auspicious (Tashi Tagel) Hotel, **3**

0 400 yards
0 400 meters

TO DREPUNG AND NECHUNG MONASTERIES (8km)
TO SERA MONASTERY (3km)
TO GANDEN
Tibet Hotel (CITS)
Beijing Xi Lu
Beijing Zhong Lu 北京中路
Lingkuo Xi Lu
Bank of China
Nepal
Norbulingka
Minzu Lu
Library
Tibet Museum
Kundeling Lu
Golden Yak Statue
White Stupa
Luobulinka (Norbulinka) Lu
Dralhalupuk Temple
Chakpori Hill
Lukhang Temple
Liberation Park
Potala Palace 布达拉宫
Kharnga Dong Lu
Beijing Zhong Lu
Beijing Dong Lu
Niangre Lu
People's Hospital
CAAC Office
Lhasa City Post and Telecommunications
Yutuo Lu
Lingkuo Bei Lu 林廓北路
Sera Lu
PSB
Duode Lu
Telecommunications Office
Ramoche Temple 小昭寺
Ramoche Lu
Duosenge Lu
Zangyiuan Dong Lu
Jokhang Temple 大昭寺
Barkhor Market
Barkhor Lu
Ani Tsangkung Nunnery
Bank of China
PSB
Main Mosque
Lingkuo Nan Lu
Lingkuo Dong Lu
Jiangsa Dong Lu
Jiangsui Lu
Lingyu Bei Lu
Lingyu Nan Lu
Tibet University
Jinzhu (Chingdol) Zhong Lu 金珠中路
Lhasa (Kyichu) R.

YAKKITY YAK In Tibet, it is impossible to escape from the omnipresent yak, also known as the long-haired cow (máo niú; 毛牛). Their black backs dot the landscape throughout the countryside. Yak oil lamps light most monasteries, and worshipers bring yak butter packets and yak oil candles to sprinkle or dip into the big oil lamps of Tibetan temples. Tibetans claim the yak can only breed at 3000m above sea level or higher, and that its meat and milk provide better nutrition than that of the normal cow. Perhaps its high alimentary value accounts for the animal's strong odor, a scent that all travelers to Tibet encounter sooner or later. The smell pervades restaurants offering savory yak "beef" dishes, yak *momos* (dumplings), and yak-butter tea. Yak-scented air wafts through Tibet's temples. Anyone hoping to escape the yak by skipping Tibet's temples and avoiding Tibetan cuisine should think again. Even the grounds and walls of the Potala Palace are made from a mixture of ground stone, cement, and yak oil.

Due to the recent mass influx of foreigners into Lhasa, dozens of restaurants offering Tibetan, Indian, and Western dishes have sprung up in and around **Lhasa's Barkhor Market.** The food is tasty, but prices are fairly high; it's easy to get in the habit of dropping Y20-30 per meal while lingering in Lhasa. For cheap and authentic Tibetan food, head into the small streets and alleys in the **Tibetan neighborhoods** around Barkhor. Chinese food here is quite expensive, but prices drop as you move away from the tourist areas around Barkhor. Head for the night market on **Dosenge Lu,** between Beijing Lu and Lingkuo Lu, for cheap and filling Muslim kebabs (Y1 per stick) and a wide assortment of tempura-style vegetables (Y1 per stick). The market is open daily 7:30-11:30pm. On Lingkuo Lu, between Dosenge Lu and Niangre Lu, there are at least five **supermarkets,** a great place to stock up on bread, dried meat, and peanut butter for trekking. Most open 9am-7:30pm.

Tashi 1, on the corner of Zangyiyuan Dong Lu and Beijing Dong Lu. Wildly popular with backpackers. The very filling yak burger comes with a pile of fries and veggies (Y18). Their burrito-style *bobis* (Y10-13) and cheesecake (Y6) are highly recommended. Open daily in summer 7:30am-11pm; in winter 8:30am-11pm. The less popular **Tashi 2,** in the Kirey Hotel, is just as good and more intimate, with bigger portions than Tashi 1. Open daily 7am-11pm; closed Nov.-Feb. ❶

Makye Ame Restaurant (☎632 4455), on the 2nd fl. of the yellow building in the southeast corner of the Barkhor Market, behind the Jokhang Temple. Dainty portions and high prices don't deter budget travelers from the Bohemian atmosphere and massive menu of taste-bud-titillating international foods. The rooftop patio is the best place to kick back, chug a few beers, and gaze down at the foot traffic circling the Barkhor. Mini-library and Internet cafe (Y10 per hr.). Dishes Y15-40. Open daily 9am-11pm. ❷

Mad Yak Restaurant, in the Kirey Hotel. Cheap Tibetan food and nifty, Tibetan-carpeted seats. Dishes Y8-25. Every night 7-8:30pm, there is a Tibetan dance show and a 25-course Tibetan buffet (Y50). Caters largely to tour groups. Open hours variable. ❸

Kailasha Cafe (☎634 6288), in the Kailasha Hotel compound, just west of Tashi 1 on Beijing Lu. The best Indian food in town and a great music selection. Try the Aloo Mutter, a delicious pasta dish (Y12). Entrees Y10-30. Open daily until 11pm. ❶

Snowland Restaurant (xuěyù cāntīng; 雪域餐厅), next to the Snowland Hotel. A posh peaceful dining area packed with Westerners. Delicious Western, Tibetan, and Chinese dishes (Y20-40). The lasagna is highly recommended. Open daily 7am-11pm. ❷

Lightfull Restaurant, on Bejing Dong Lu, a few doors from the Yak Hotel. The preparation takes a while, but the food is worth the wait. Typical array of Tibetan, Western, and

TIBET

BEHOLD, THE MAGIC OF SAND Known as *jinkor* or tánchéng (坛城) in Chinese, sand mandalas, typically 4-6 ft. in diameter but historically as large as 35 ft. across, are traditionally constructed during a Kalachakra initiation ceremony. Participants are given instructions for visualizing the abode of the powerful deity Kalachakra (Dukhor); this palace radiates out in the four cardinal directions, with lesser protector deities positioned in various rooms corresponding to the domain of their power. Four monks work with small tapered wooden tubes with a corrugated edge; by rubbing another piece of wood along this edge, they release single grains of sand from the end of the tube. Each of the four monks alternates in their use of different colored sand corresponding to the successive layers of palace architecture. The four principle colors are red, black, green, and yellow. The mandala is complete after the radiating layers of squares and circles have reached the final boundary edges, which symbolize earth and heaven. Initiates are then allowed to view the mandala for two to three days before the deconstruction ceremony takes place, when a high lama takes a **vaira** (thunderbolt) and cuts through the mandala; this severs the lines of power radiating out in geometric order from the center point. The sand is then swept up and taken to a nearby body of water where it is scattered and dispersed. Like many other facets of Tibetan Buddhist culture, the sand mandala signifies the impermanence of life, which is assembled and then destroyed. The devotional act of constructing the mandala is an exercise in perfecting compassionate intention, and is independent of material accomplishment.

Chinese dishes (Y15-25) served in a cozy Tibetan atmosphere. The authentic omelettes (Y10-12) are particularly de-lightfull. Open daily 9am-10pm. ❷

Xinjiang Roast Chicken (xīnjiāng dàpānjī; 新疆大盘鸡), 16 Linkuo Bei Lu (☎(139) 0890 5340), west of Dosenge Lu. Standard Chinese food Y6-20. Try their famous roast chicken and potatoes (pānjī; 盘鸡; Y50-80, serves 2 or more). Open daily 10am-10pm. ❶

SIGHTS

Lhasa's most well-visited and famous sights are its monasteries. Pilgrims used to travel over horrendous roads to pay respects to the Karmapa (Living Buddha), the most highly regarded religious figure currently residing in Tibet, housed in the remote **Tsurphu Monastery** (楚布寺). Although the monastery, where the Karma (Black Cap) sect originated, has been closed indefinitely by the Chinese government, there are still numerous visit-worthy sights to explore.

པོ་ཏ་ལ· POTALA PALACE

New arrivals to Tibet should not visit until after the initial effects of altitude sickness have passed. The best time to go is in late morning; by midday, tourists leave for lunch. The ticket office (open M-F 9am-12:30pm and 3:30-5:30pm, Sa-Su 10am-noon and 3:30-5pm) is at the western end of Beijing Dong Lu. Admission Y70, students with ID Y50, children under 1.2m free; extra fee for pictures. Relics Museum and the Roof of Gold Y10 each.

The Potala Palace (bùdálā gōng; 布达拉宫) has long been a symbol of Lhasa. Although the Dalai Lama's court no longer inhabits the Potala's 1000 rooms, the palace still possesses a somber and awe-inspiring grandeur. During the Cultural Revolution, Premier Zhou Enlai used his personal unit of the PLA to protect the Potala from rioting Red Guards, saving the palace from the destruction that befell so many of Tibet's other religious sites.

King Songtsen Gampo, the same ruler who built the Jokhang, chose the Potala's Red Hill as the site for his palace in the 7th century. Long after his death, politica and military officials continued to mingle with scholarly priests in the court Today, his "likeness" (the statue with two heads) stands in **Dharmraja's Cave.** Wher the Great 5th Dalai Lama, Lobsang Gyatso, united Tibet in the 17th century, he for mally recognized the Dalai Lama's dual role as the religious and political leader o the nation by rebuilding and dividing the palace into the **White Palace** (for oversee ing political matters) and the **Red Palace** (for dealing with religious issues).

RED PALACE. The remains of past Dalai Lamas rest in the western part of this pal ace in jewel-encrusted gold **stupas.** The 12.6m *stupa* of Lobsang Gyatso, the 5tl Dalai Lama, is gilded with 3721kg of gold foil, 10,000 pearls, and precious stones The only Dalai Lama not entombed in the Potala Palace is the 6th, who was drive into exile by Mongolian conquerors. This section of the palace also houses th **Dharmraja's Cave** and some marvelous Buddha and *bodhisattva* statues. The pal ace treasures include the **Wheel of Time,** an exquisite 200,000-pearl mandala mad of coral, turquoise, and gold thread (see p. 801). The **Kalachakra Mandala,** on th east side of the third floor, is a model of the palace paradise of Kalachakr (Dukhor). There are also **sand mandalas** (*jinkor;* see above), two-dimensiona depictions of the same Kalachakra Mandala seen in three-dimensions here.

WHITE PALACE. The White Palace was the abode of the 13th and 14th Dala Lamas; the 14th Dalai Lama's chambers, including his study, meeting rooms, an meditation chambers, are open to visitors. The balcony from which the Dalai Lam made infrequent contact with the Tibetan people overlooks the palace square. A the Dalai Lamas were crowned in the **Great Eastern Assembly Hall.**

DRALHALUPUK TEMPLE AND CHAKPORI HILL

Across from the left foot of the Potala, on the other side of Beijing Dong Lu. A road runs along the side of Chakpori Hill; the entrance is near the white stupa at the site of the old West Gate to the city. Follow the road until you see stairs leading up to 2 temples on the right, about half-way up the hill. Open daily 9:30am-7pm. Y15.

Dralhalupuk Temple served as a cave temple and private retreat for King Songtse Gampo. Although many of the 1000-year-old rock carvings were damaged durin the Cultural Revolution, extensive renovation has restored some of them to the original splendor. Over 60 *bodhisattva* carvings decorate the cliffside temple. second temple, a few meters above Dralhalupuk, was a meditation cave fo Bhrikuti, King Songtsen Gampo's Nepali queen. From the entrance to the two ten ples, a path (15min.) leads to the top of Chakpori Hill, whose southwest face fea tures a colorful collection of 9000 Buddhas, the oldest dating back to the reign c King Gampo. *(Walk down Norbulingka Lu from Potala Square. When you see the Xin Xin Eate (鑫鑫小吃), turn left down the dirt path and continue for 6min. past a military station.)*

ཇོ་ཁང· JOKHANG TEMPLE

Open daily 8am-midnight. Y25 for non-Tibetans.

The Jokhang (dàzhāo sì; 大昭寺) fuses Nepali, Indian, Buddhist, and Tang dynast architectural elements, but most visitors are ultimately captivated by the mystic spirit of this active place of worship. Oil candles illuminate mural-lined corridoı that depict tales from the temple's past, and the hum of devotees outside echoe off the walls. The Jokhang **Lingkhor** (circumambulatory circuit) is one of the mos fervent and energetic of all the Lhasa area temples, drawing both travelers an local Tibetans into its hypnotic revolutions.

Nearly every night at 7:30pm, monks congregate in the main assembly hall to chant. Filtered with bells, drumming, and horn blowing, this, along with the view from the rooftop, is the true highlight of the Jokhang. Head up top after the chanting to catch the sunset, or come anytime for a stunning panorama of the city.

A rich mosaic of myth surrounds the 7th-century temple. Legend holds that King Gampo's Nepali bride believed that the Tibetan Plateau was a demon that could be subdued only by building Buddhist temples on its key body parts. The king's Chinese wife, Princess Wencheng, used divinination and astrological calculation to select the temple site. Jokhang was thus built on Lake Wothang, thought to be the heart of the demon. The **Golden Buddha,** an image of Sakyamuni as a 12-year-old boy, was brought by Princess Wencheng and now resides at the back of the Jokhang's great prayer hall; believers claim that the statue was consecrated by Sakyamuni himself while he lived in India. Other notable figures in the temple include the 1000-arm statue of **Avalokiteshvara** (Guanyin, Goddess of Mercy) and various statues of the **Maitreya Buddha.**

བར་སྐོར· BARKHOR MARKET

The market usually begins in the wee hours of the morning and shuts down at about 7:30pm.

The area around Jokhang's Barkhor Market (bājiǎo shìchǎng; 八角市场), also known as **Chongsaikang Market,** has managed to flourish without becoming excessively commercialized. The scent of burning incense mingles with the odor of yak, and monks interrupt their daily circumambulatory routine around the Jokhang to bargain for prayer beads. The market is a good place to buy Tibetan trinkets, with myriad stalls displaying everything from *hadas* (ceremonial scarves) and prayer wheels to lamb skulls and photographs of religious figures. The entire Barkhor circuit proceeds in a clockwise direction, encircling the Jokhang and branching off into various side streets. Be sure to inspect the goods carefully, but don't touch if you're not going to buy. Hard bargaining can usually bring the price down 40-50% from the original quote; be respectful in your haggling. Check out the **Thanka Mandala Gallery and Workshop,** just to the left when facing the Makye Ame Restaurant. This is one of the only places in Lhasa where you can see *thanka* painters at work and learn about the intricate layering process that goes into their construction.

ནོར་བུ་གླིང་ཁ· NORBULINGKA

On Norbulingka Nan Lu, a 10min. walk south of the Lhasa Hotel. Take bus #2 (Y2). Open M-Sa 9:30am-noon and 3:30-6pm, Su 10am-12:30pm and 4-5:30pm. Y35, Chinese students Y25, gardens only Y5.

A refreshing contrast to the barren Tibetan landscape, the Norbulingka's (luōbùlínkǎ; 罗布林卡) beautifully manicured grounds consist of three main palaces that house a total of 370 rooms. This "Jeweled Garden" served as the summer residence for several Dalai Lamas. The **Daktonmiju Palace** was built in 1956 by the 14th Dalai Lama; however, the Dalai lived here for only two summers before fleeing to India in 1959. Visitors are greeted by two gigantic paintings of a lion and tiger. On the second floor, an elaborate mural traces Tibetan history from monkey-mating (see p. 797) to the 14th Dalai Lama sitting with Chairman Mao. His Holiness's private living quarters, a radio sent as a housewarming gift by the Prime Minister of India, and a richly decorated throne made of solid gold are all on display. **Gesang Palace,** the oldest of the three palaces, served as the main summer residence of the 7th to the 12th Dalai Lamas. Various *tangkas* (painted scrolls) and Eight Medicine Buddhas adorn the walls of the main assembly hall. The two-story **Jianse Palace,** the summer home of the 13th Dalai Lama, is closed to the public periodically.

TIBET MUSEUM 西藏博物馆

Across from the Lhasa Library, on the corner of Norbulinka Lu and Minzu Lu, just north of the bus station. Open daily 9am-6pm. Y30, students with ID Y5.

This museum is not worth the full admission price, but if you're in the area and can snag a student rate, a pleasant hour or two can be spent wandering through the exhibits. The most interesting parts of the collection include a series of medical *thankas* (painted scrolls) that depict Tibetan acupuncture practices and *chakra* energy points. The museum also houses stuffed Tibetan animals, Neolithic tools, pottery, and cave paintings, and pictures of rocks and natural patterns.

RAMOCHE TEMPLE

500m north of the Jokhang Temple, on Ramoche Lu, off Beijing Dong Lu. Open W-M 8am-5pm. Y20.

It may not be the grandest of Lhasa's temples, but Ramoche is still greatly loved: 115 monks and countless pilgrims circumambulate the $4000m^2$ complex, which also houses the Upper Tantric College. Ramoche Temple was built in the 7th century, when Princess Wencheng of the Tang court married King Songtsen Gampo of Tibet. On her journey to Tibet, the princess brought with her the gold statue of the Sakyamuni Buddha (now in the Jokhang Temple) as part of her dowry. When Princess Wencheng's carriage wheels got stuck in the mud and her attendants could not budge the statue from its position at Lhasa's north gate, four pillars were placed around the statue and a brocade draped over it to protect it from harm. Princess Wencheng decided that the gods intended the statue to remain there, so King Songtsen Gampo built Ramoche Temple around it. The princess, either homesick or to make a political statement, decreed that all the gates and doors of the temple face east toward Chang'an (modern-day Xi'an), China's ancient capital.

འབྲས་སྤུངས་ DREPUNG MONASTERY

About 10km from Lhasa. Frequent morning buses leave from the Jokhang Temple parking lot for Drepung (Y3). When returning, especially late in the afternoon, you may have to walk the 1.5km from the monastery to the main road to Lhasa. Often, tractors or cars are willing to give a ride (Y1). For the return trip to Lhasa, take bus #3 or 4 (Y2) from the main road, usually at the entrance to Drepung. Open daily 9am-5pm. Y35, students Y25.

Nicknamed "rice pile" because of its white, heap-like appearance, Drepung (zhébàng sì; 哲蚌寺) is the largest monastery in Tibet, covering over $20,000m^2$ and housing 600 monks. The gargantuan monastery was built in 1416 by Jamygang Choje, fourth disciple of Tsong Khapa (see p. 801), after a dream in which he envisioned the site. Until the 5th Dalai Lama moved the court to the Potala Palace, Drepung's Ganden Palace served as the seat of the Dalai Lamas.

The traditional pilgrimage route through Drepung begins at the Ganden Palace, the first building to the left of the main road, passing a large prayer wheel spinning in a stream. Walk uphill to the Ngagpa College, or "Tratsang," which specializes in tantric Buddhist studies; to the right, three other colleges specialize in logic, medicine, and general studies. From the Ngagpa, cross a small path east to the **Tshomchen,** Drepung's most important and imposing structure; its assembly hall houses a chapel dedicated to **Manjushri,** one of the great *bodhisattvas* of wisdom. It is said that the discovery of a rock bearing Manjushri's likeness determined the exact site of Drepung; the revered rock now serves as one of the chapel's three walls. Set in gold on the roof is a pair of deer (representing Sakyamuni's disciples) holding a wheel (representing Sakyamuni and his success).

སེ་ར་ SERA MONASTERY

At the foot of Phurpa Chokri Mountain, 3km northeast of Lhasa. Take bus #5 (Y2) from the Ramoche Temple or Linkuo Bei Lu. Alternatively, rent a bike or take a long walk: go west on Beijing Lu and turn right just before the Post and Telecom complex on Niangre Lu; follow Niangre Lu for 2-3km; a small road before the General Military Hospital leads to the monastery. Open daily 9am-5pm. Y30, students Y25.

Sera was established in 1419 by Sakya Yeshe, a disciple of the prodigious lama Tsong Khapa, who founded Ganden Monastery, the first and most important of the Yellow Hat institutions. In its heyday, Sera was home to over 5000 monks. Sera's numbers have dwindled to 500, but its spirit remains; debates held in the **Sera Je Tratsang** courtyard (daily 3-5pm) offer an opportunity to observe theological discourse as it's been practiced since the 14th century Yellow Hat renaissance. Here, monks argue loudly over interpretations of the Buddha's teaching. Movement of the left hand represents the relief of suffering, and the right, the destruction of evils, so participants slap their hands together to build confidence while making a point; consistently successful debators are raised in rank.

Sera's three colleges are **Sera Me,** the novice school, **Sera Je,** which orignally taught wandering monks, and **Ngagpa,** the tantric college. The traditional pilgrimage circuit through Sea begins to the left of the main road and bisects the monastic compound, passing Sera Me, Ngagpa, Sera Je, and the Hamdong complex across the main road before reaching Sera's largest building and administrative center, the Tsokchen. After completing this circuit (3hr.), pilgrims often climb the ridge behind Sera to Tsong Khapa's Hermitage (1-5hr.).

དགའ་ལྡན་དགོན་པ་GANDEN MONASTERY

From Lhasa, 45km east along the main road, on the south bank of the Lhasa (Kyichu) River. Pilgrim buses depart from Lhasa's Jokhang Temple parking lot (2-2½hr.; 6:30am departure, 2pm return; round-trip Y16, one-way Y9). Y35, students Y25.

Ganden Monastery straddles the high, grassy ridge of Gokpo Ri, about 1500m above the Kyichu river valley, its 15 major buildings sprawling down the mountainside. Fantastic views of rocky peaks and lush, terraced farmlands greet visitors to Ganden, the foremost monastery of the Yellow Hat sect. Ganden was also the most heavily damaged during the Cultural Revolution; the top third of the monastery is almost entirely in ruins, but nonetheless offers intriguing spaces to explore. Ganden's **lingkhor** (circumambulatory circuit) is hands-down the most impressive feature of the complex. Beginning with a dense mass of prayer flags that creates a small passageway through the rocks above the parking lot, the *lingkhor* descends about 20m down the opposite side of the ridge, passing a dozen or so small shrines built into the rocks and strewn with prayer flags. A well-defined path skirts the ridge, revealing breathtaking views of the flat valley below. Just before you complete the circuit to the east side of the monastery, descend a small path to a **sky burial** site still in use today. If a burial is taking place, it is best to retreat to a more respectful distance in the cliffs above. It is also possible to **trek** from Ganden to Samye, crossing four major passes in four to five strenuous days. Consult the Outlook Outdoor Equipment Shop in Lhasa (see p. 805) for a map and up-to-date info.

ENTERTAINMENT

Most tourists are so worn out after hours of hiking and temple-visiting that the most popular evening activity tends to be sitting around a table and chatting or playing cards over a few beers. In the Barkhor Market area, there are dozens of pool halls and outdoor tables of various qualities (Y1-2 per game). Make sure to ask for 15 balls; most Tibetans play with 6. There are also places to go for song, dance, and comedy performances by local troupes. An excellent troupe performs nightly at the **Gediga** on Lingkuo Lu. (☎633 2571. Open nightly 8:30pm-midnight.)

NORTH OF LHASA: NAMTSO LAKE

200km northwest of Lhasa. No additional ***Alien Travel Permit*** *needed. There is no public transportation to the lake. Most tourists hire a* ***land cruiser*** *to take them directly to the Tashi Dorje Monastery (Y1500-2000 per car for a 3-day, 2-night tour; cars seat 6 passengers, but you may be able to arrange for a 7th person to sit in back with the luggage). Check the boards at the Lhasa Yak, Banak Shol, Pentoc, Snowland, Tashi Tagel, and Kirey Hotels (see* ***Accommodations,*** *p. 805). The trip between Lhasa and the Tashi Dorje Monastery, depending on road conditions, can take anywhere from 6 to 12hr., so plan on spending only a full day at the lake. Extra days typically cost Y150-200 per car. The other option is to take the* ***bus*** *(Y20) from the Lhasa Bus Station headed for Naqu, get off at Damshung, and trek the remaining 40km; foreigners may have difficulty obtaining a ticket to Damshung from the Lhasa Bus Station, but you can try again at the* ***East Suburb Bus Station*** *(dōngqū kèyùn zhàn; 东区客运站). From Damshung, look for the main road that crosses a bridge just west of a strip of restaurants and the Damshung Binguan. North of this bridge, a dirt road runs north to the Namtso Ticket Office (7km) and then to the 5500m* ***Lhachen La Pass*** *(25km), following a rushing stream up the mountain and passing construction crews working on the new road and several nomad camps. Some travelers choose to hitchhike this portion of the journey on tractors or construction trucks. It takes a full day to trek from the pass to the monastery, and hitching will probably be difficult. And regardless of difficulty,* Let's Go *never recommends hitching.* ***Admission*** *to grasslands Y35, plus Y5 to enter monastery and guesthouse area.*

At 4627m above sea level, Namtso (nàmù cuò; 纳木错) is the highest lake in the world. Namtso's name, "Sky Lake," only hints at what appears to be a piece of brilliant blue heaven fallen to earth. Bordered to the south by the **Nyanchen Thanglha** mountain range and surrounded by desolate grassy plains, this vast lake, China's second largest (70km long, 30km wide), lies in one of Tibet's coldest and most unpredictable climates. Even in the summer, frequent storms and high winds sweep down from the mountains and drench the area with rain and hail, leaving visitors dazzled by misty rainbows and the sound of thousands of prayer flags fluttering against silver gray skies. Countless rock cairns, *lapsi* flag pyramids, and *mani* prayer stones that demarcate energy centers and sacred spaces lend a sense of Tibetan's strong spiritual culture to Namtso's astounding natural beauty.

Although the entire lake circuit, one of Tibet's holiest pilgrimages, takes 14-18 days to complete and is extremely difficult, it also contains some lovely, shorter hikes. One of the best **day hikes** around the Tashi Dorje monastery area is a circumambulation of the two main hills that form a peninsula that juts out into the lake. The route encounters several small temples built into the cliffs and about 30 major caves, most of which were once used as meditation hermitages and are filled with Buddhist carvings. Hiking to the top of the two cliff formations is also stunning, offering expansive views of the lake and revealing an amazing diversity of plant and animal life as well as a fragrant spectrum of wildflowers, sage, and juniper.

Spending the night by Namtso is highly recommended. Bring your own tent, or find **accommodations** near the **Tashi Dorje Monastery** (3- to 4-bed dorms Y20-35). Two

> **TIBETAN BURIAL RITUALS** The traditional Tibetan "sky burial" involves burning the hair of the deceased and feeding the rest of the body to birds of prey. When a commoner dies, the corpse is bound up in white twine for the three- to five-day mourning period. The body is then transported by special porters to a flat platform in the mountains, where eagles and vultures devour the remains. Everything has to go if the person is to go to heaven; when the bones are left, they are crushed, dipped in the brain, and offered again to the raptors. If anything remains unconsumed at the end, monks are invited to meditate and chant *sutras* in order to atone for the misdeeds of the dead. Anyone who has committed grievous sins in their lifetime cannot receive a sky burial, nor can those who died of an infectious disease. The latter have their limbs torn off and cast into lakes instead. The bodies of living Buddhas, noblemen, and others destined for reincarnation are either cremated or, as in the case of religious holy men, preserved and placed in bejeweled *stupas* for all to view and worship.

small **restaurants** next to the guesthouses, both labeled "canteen," serve overpriced Chinese and Tibetan food (noodles Y10; fried rice Y15); try to bring your own food.

SOUTH OF LHASA: བསམ་ཡས་ SAMYE MONASTERY

***Buses** between Lhasa and Tsetang pass the pier for boats to Samye Monastery (3hr., 3 per day, Y25-30). Required **travel permits** are granted only for groups traveling in a car with a guide, and you may only be allowed to arrange a tour with the agency that brought you to Lhasa (3-day **tour** typically costs Y2500). There is a **checkpoint** at the ferry crossing; some travelers report having taken the ferry during busy morning hours without being checked. Permits are not checked on the return ferry trip. **Entrance fee** to ferry crossing, Y10. **Motorboat** ride to south shore (45min.; Y3, foreigners usually charged Y10). After they arrive at the island, passengers typically ride on the back of a **truck** or **tractor** (30min., Y5-10) to Samye. Samye can also be approached from Ganden Monastery by **hiking** over two mountain passes (4-5 days); travelers report being able to rent a guide and yaks at the town of Hepu, a 2-3hr. hike from Ganden. The manager at the Outlook Outdoor Equipment Store in Lhasa* *(see p. 805)* *can give you up-to-date info and a good map of the trek. There is no official checkpoint at Samye, so permits technically should not be needed if trekking from Ganden; but the PSB has been known to raid hotels and check for permits at Samye Monastery. A safer bet is **camping** at one of the beautiful spots southwest or northeast of the monastery. Monastery open daily 8am-6pm. Admission Y25.*

Samye Monastery (sāngmùyē sì; 桑木耶寺), with its sparkling golden roof, is surrounded by sand dunes and rocky ridges covered with small shrubs and fragrant herbs. Thought to be Tibet's first monastery, Samye was built in the 8th century by King Trisong Detsen of the Yarlung dynasty, who drew heavily upon Indian architectural styles when designing Samye. Like many Indian temples, Samye was constructed according to the design of **mandala,** with a circular bounding wall and cardinal orientation of the compound's structures around a central sacred space. The main temple, or *utse*, signifies **Mount Sumeru,** the center of the universe in Tibetan and Indian cosmology, and is surrounded by four small temples called *lings*, representing the four continents. Each *ling* is straddled by two smaller ones, representing the eight sub-continents. There is also a **moon chapel,** where a giant Sakyamuni statue stares into the heavens, and a now-destroyed **sun chapel.**

The three floors of Samye's *utse* are said to have been constructed according to Tibetan (first floor), Chinese (middle), and Indian (top floor) design styles. Be sure to check out the murals decorating the internal **kora** (circumambulatory passageway) around the central chapel devoted to Sakyamuni. The second floor houses the monks' dormitories as well as a few small chapels. The impressive top level is comprised of a large, open chapel devoted to Vairocana, with a mandala design on the ceiling that is situated at the very center of the entire Samye compound. A small ladder in the rear climbs to a strange unfurnished attic-like level.

The **Monastery Guesthouse** provides basic facilities for Y20-30 per bed; bargain. The **Monastery Restaurant** is cheap and convenient (fried rice Y5, noodles Y6, yak and vegetables Y10, small thermos of sweet tea Y4); there are also several restaurants outside the east gate, the best being **Friends Snowland Restaurant.**

DAYTRIPS FROM SAMYE: CHIMPU HERMITAGE

A 13km, 4hr. ***hike*** *from Samye Monastery. Exit the monastery's north gate and follow the main road east. As soon as you cross the river, turn left (north) onto a gravel road that heads up the valley toward a high ridge. On a clear day, you should be able to see the white dots of Chimpu's temples on the deepest ridge overlooking the valley. The gravel road soon becomes a dirt road, which winds through dozens of switchbacks as it climbs up the valley. Cutting straight up the valley instead of following the winding road is quicker; follow the main river that flows down from the Chimpu area and you should have no problem finding your way. After approx. 2½hr. of hiking from Samye, you'll pass a series of ruins on your left; continue ascending until you arrive at the main Chimpu temple (30min.). Or, from the Samye Monastery, you can also take a* ***truck*** *to the end of the dirt road that leads to Chimpu (around 6am). From here, it's about a 30min. hike to the Chimpu Guesthouse. A truck returns in the mid-afternoon. Check with your guide or the Samye Monastery Restaurant manager for departure and return times (Y10-15 round-trip).*

One of Tibet's most active hermitage centers, Chimpu is a collection of several dozen high caves and small temples built into a ridge overlooking the Samye Valley. Over 100 practitioners reside in this lushly vegetated mountain area, where crystal-clear streams and winding dirt paths crisscross through fields of wildflowers and fragrant herbs. At the temple, there is a guesthouse (Y10 per bed). A snack shop sells instant noodles and bottled water. From here, the pilgrimage **kora** heads up the mountain on the left (western) path; it passes the **Zangdhok Pelri,** Guru Rimpoche's retreat cave, before reaching the **Drakmar Keutsang,** Chimpu's principle meditation cave, which sits behind a two-story temple and houses a cave shrine. The path then descends to the east and returns to the Chimpu Guesthouse. Above Drakmar Keutsang, near the ridge, are more cave hermitages and many great camp sites. Staying the night in a tent or cave is highly recommended.

TIBET

རྩེ་ཐང་ TSETANG 泽当 ☎0893

Although Tsetang, 185km southeast of Lhasa, is Tibet's third largest city, most visitors just pass through on their way from Lhasa to the ancient sites of Chongye and Yumbulagang in the Yarlung Valley. The uninspiring town, full of Han influence, offers little more than a couple of exorbitantly priced hotels. If it is at all possible, try to avoid spending the night here.

PRACTICAL INFORMATION AND ACCOMMODATIONS

Travel permits (Y150 per person) are required for Tsetang. Individual travelers are rarely given permits; it is best to travel in a group with a guide. Lhasa travel agencies will arrange for land cruiser rentals and all necessary permits to take groups of travelers to Tsetang, Samye, and Yumbulagang (Y2500-3000 for 3 days).

Naidong Lu (乃东路), Tsetang's main road, leads out of Tsetang toward Tranduk Monastery and Yumbulagang Palace. The **Shannan Prefecture PSB** (☎782 0359), on Naidong Lu near the edge of town, is open 24hr. The **People's Hospital of Tsetang Town,** 4 Gesang Lu, has no English-speaking staff members. (☎782 0289. Open daily 9am-12:30pm and 3:30-6:30pm.) Several Internet bars line Naidong Lu across from the Postal Hotel. The cheapest is the **Huanyou Web Cafe** (huányǒu wǎngbā; 环友网吧), which offers Y6 per hour connections. The **Post and Telecommunications Office,** 12 Naidong Lu, opposite the Shannan Prefecture Government building, has IDD service. (Open daily 9am-7:30pm.) The **postal code** is 856000.

According to strict government regulations, only three hotels in Tsetang are allowed to take foreigners. The cheapest of the three is the **Postal Hotel** ❸ (yóuzhèng gōngyù; 邮政公寓), 10 Naidong Lu (☎7812 1888), which has luxurious doubles for Y250 (bargain to Y220) and 24hr. hot water. The **Regional Guesthouse** ❹ (shānnán dìqū zhāodàisuǒ; 山南地区招待所), on Naidong Lu, has musty rooms and hot water from 9am to midnight. (☎782 7984. Y280 per person.) The **Tsetang Hotel** ❺ (zédāng bīnguǎn; 泽当宾馆), also on Naidong Lu, provides somewhat luxurious but ludicrously priced rooms. (☎782 1899. Doubles Y550.) There are several cheap restaurants scattered around town.

DAYTRIPS FROM TSETANG

ཡུམ་བུ་བླ་སྒང་ YUMBULAGANG PALACE

15km south of Tsetang, past Tranduk Monastery, on the left as you come from Tsetang. A separate Alien Travel Permit is not needed for Yumbulagang (but is for Tsetang). Yumbulagang can be reached on foot or by taxi (Y80) from Tsetang. Open daily 9am-5pm. Y15.

Yumbulagang (yōngbùlākāng; 雍布拉康) is awe-inspiring, even from a distance, a thin but imposing structure jutting out of the mountain like a sword stuck in stone. The photogenic palace, which subscribes to the teachings of the Yellow Hat sect, was built more than 2000 years ago as a castle for King Nyatre Tsanpo, the first ruler of the Yarlung dynasty; but after an explosive Red Guard rampage during the Cultural Revolution, only a fragmented stump remained. The present structure was built in 1982, when the original castle was turned into the temple seen today. Perhaps inspired by the shape of the mountain, Yumbulagang means "palace on the hind of a female deer." The palace itself has three floors: the first contains statues of Sakyamuni, the main object of worship, and Yarlung monarchs; the second contains more bronze statues, including one of Tsong Khapa, and murals of Nyatre Tsanpo and Yumbulagang; and the roof offers a picturesque panoramic view of the Yarlungzanbo (Brahmaputra) River Valley, with burnt umber mountains and mud houses in one direction and verdant fields in the other. For a good view of Yumbulagang, go around the back, climb over a low stone wall, and walk up the slope to the flag pyramid or **lapsi** at the crest of the first ridge.

ཁྲ་འབྲུག་ TRANDRUK MONASTERY

5km southwest of Tsetang, on the way to Yumbulagang. A separate Alien Travel Permit is not needed for Tranduk (but is for Tsetang). Easily accessible on foot or by taxi (Y50). Open daily 7am-7pm. Admission for foreigners Y25.

One of Tibet's oldest monasteries, Trandruk Monastery (chāngzhū sì; 昌珠寺) was built in the 8th century by King Songtsen Gampo. The king was persuaded by his Nepalese wife to build Tranduk and other temples at critical geomantic points on the Tibetan Plateau in order to subdue its powerful destructive forces; the king and his Chinese wife used it as their winter palace. The monastery was designed as a miniature version of Lhasa's Jokhang temple. Both have interior **kora** lined with prayer wheels, and a central **dukhang** (assembly hall). The murals that line the *dukhang*'s back wall are breathtaking. Upstairs, the monastery's main attraction is a rare pearl **tangka,** colored in shades of silver, turquoise, and coral.

FRIENDSHIP HIGHWAY

The week-long journey from Lhasa to Nepal over the 920km Friendship Highway strings together some of the region's most impressive attractions: the turquoise Yamdroktso Lake, the gleaming glaciers near Gyantse, the Panchen Lama's capital of Shigatse, the rustic monastery at Sakya, the world's highest temple at Rongphu, Everest Base Camp, the Himalayan town of Tingri, and the subtropical border post of Zhangmu. Most areas of the highway are very well traveled, and road conditions are decent. Travel permits are required to make stops at any of the sights listed above. In the past, some travelers have managed to hitchhike the entire distance on the Friendship Highway illegally, without permits. However, at the time of writing, travel restrictions, random PSB checkpoints, and heavy fines for helping foreigners have all increased, making it virtually impossible to attempt this route without being a part of a government-approved tour. (Besides, *Let's Go* never recommends hitchhiking.) Travelers can hire a **land cruiser** (Y6000-8000 per vehicle for a 6- to 8-day trip, not including the Y350 entrance fee to Everest Base Camp).

If you are on a tight budget or prefer to explore at your own pace without the burden of a guide and driver, free travel, at least for now, is possible to a limited degree. (Don't be surprised if the situation changes, as it often does in Tibet.) However, individual travelers may miss out on several key sites like Everest and Samye. Base yourself in the cities of Lhasa and Shigatse, which don't require permits. Individual travelers can also arrange permits without a car and at a low cost for the cities of Sakya and Lhatse, which are farther west on the Nepal-bound road; from these cities, trekking and hitching into the surrounding area is quite feasible, and you can make it to Nepal at your own pace.

ཡར་འབྲོག་མཚོ YAMDROKTSO LAKE

100km southwest of Lhasa along the Friendship Highway's southern branch. 50km from Nagartse, the Khambala Pass (4900m) provides an incredible view of the lake. No public buses travel to the area; Yamdroktso is usually visited by land cruiser en route to Gyantse and Shigatse from Lhasa. Some travelers have succeeded in taking public transportation to Gyantse and then hitchhiking to Yamdroktso. An Alien Travel Permit is required.

Yamdroktso is one of Tibet's largest and holiest lakes, covering an area of more than 600km^2 at an altitude of 4500m. The name Yamdroktso (Scorpion Lake; yángzhuō yōng hú; 羊卓雍湖) derives from the unique curves and curls of the lake's outline. Surrounded by distant snow-capped mountains, the colorful salt waters of the lake become bright sapphire at some times and an exquisite aquamarine at others. Its depths are home to plenty of fish, and its islands shelter wild ducks and green vegetation. Although a hydroelectric power plant has diminished the vibrancy of the lake's waters in recent years, Yamdroktso remains beautiful.

Most travelers base themselves in the town of **Nagartse** (làngkǎzé; 浪卡子), 2km west of the lake, and either hike or drive to the nearby mountains. One of the best viewpoints of the lake and surrounding snowcaps is from the summit of a small mountain; northwest of Nagartse, this mountain divides the northern branch of Yamdroktso Lake from Lake Dumo Tso to the south. From Nagartse, walk west out of town on a dirt tractor road. After 3km, you'll reach the base of the mountain;

SPORTS UTILITY VEHICLES

Those gas-guzzling, road-hogging beasts that annoy the living daylights out of so many drivers on well-paved Western roads are a lifesaver for travelers in rural Tibet. Due to rugged terrain and frequent mud slides, most attractions are inaccessible by public transportation; only 4-wheel-drive jeeps can conquer washed-out highways, tackle Himalayan inclines, and ford glacier streams. Since visitors in Tibet spend most of their money on transportation, it's worthwhile to be an informed consumer.

1. Hire only imported vehicles—the newer the model, the better. Check out the car (and the driver) the night before your trip, especially for longer journeys. If the jeep breaks down frequently along the way, demand that the driver change jeeps in the next town; companies usually keep vehicles in several towns.
2. Some travelers choose to pick up stragglers along the way. They claim that standard practice is for the stragglers to pay them, and they recommend giving a share to the driver. *Let's Go* does not recommend picking up hitchhikers.
3. Plan your itinerary to allow plenty of travel time during daylight hours at reasonable speeds. **Accidents are frequent** and are usually the result of daredevil drivers or impatient passengers.
4. Arrange with your tour manager beforehand that if days are wasted due to bad roads, accidents, problems with guide or driver, etc., the days will be reimbursed or your tour extended.

then, walk counterclockwise for 7km until you reach the partially ruined **Samding Monastery,** which sits on a low ridge facing the valley. Or, hike to the summit (4900m, 2hr.) for a view of the lake.

Nagartse has two main roads: one that runs east-west; and the main strip, lined with cheap hotels and small restaurants, that runs north-south. The two best and cheapest places to stay are on opposite sides of the north-south road, about 200m from the south end of town. The **Nagartse Guesthouse** ❶ (làngkăzixiàn zhāodàisuǒ; 浪卡子县招待所) has the slight edge in comfort, with thicker mattresses in its 4-bed dorms (Y10-15). Across the street, the **Grain Guesthouse** ❶ (rìguāng liángshí lǚdiàn; 日光粮食旅店) is marked by a red, yellow, and green sign that reads "Guest House." (Dorms Y10-15.) None of the hotels in town has bath or shower facilities; a **public shower** (Y5) is across from the Grain Guesthouse. There are also several decent Chinese restaurants along the street. The **Sichuan Village Restaurant** ❷ (shǔcūntáng cāntīng; 蜀村堂餐厅), right under the Grain Guesthouse's sign, serves some tasty dishes for Y15-30. (Open daily 8am-11:30pm.) The **post office** at the end of the street has IDD service. (Open daily 9:30am-1pm and 3:30-5:30pm.)

RALUNG MONASTERY

About 60km from Gyantse. Ralung Monastery is on the way from Yamdroktso to Gyantse; a red sign on the left indicates the direction. Travel down the track for about 10km. ***Beware the ferocious sheep dogs;*** *wait for the monks to tie them up before entering. Open 24hr.; ask the monks to let you in. Y15.*

Situated at the foot of a range of snow-capped mountains (7191m), Ralung is surrounded by vast empty grasslands and fields of yellow flowers. It is one of the most isolated monasteries in central Tibet and was once a sprawling complex that housed a famous *chorten* and over 500 monks. During the Cultural Revolution, Chinese dynamite leveled most of the temple buildings, leaving saddening, albeit gorgeous ruins scattered across the hillside. A new monastery is undergoing slow reconstruction in the old style, and houses a few interesting rooms that may not be worth the Y15 admission fee for those on a tight budget. Several hours can easily be spent exploring the ruins surrounding and uphill from the new monastery. The ruins of the *chorten* are clearly visible across a small stream.

རྒྱལ་རྩེ་ GYANTSE 江孜 ☎0892

Apart from a small cluster of Han Chinese restaurants and shops around the main crossroads, Gyantse—more than any other Tibetan city of similar size—retains a distinctly Tibetan character. Fanning out between the cliff-top Dzong Fort and the Palkhor Chode Monastery complex are thousands of traditional Tibetan houses, woven together through an entrancing network of winding alleys and sunny courtyards. A stroll through the city's dirt and cobblestone streets reveals packs of wandering dogs and meanderings cows, mellow tea houses, and outdoor pool tables. Gyantse's surrounding farmlands are the most fertile in Tibet; from June 8 to 14, they come alive for the traditional horse-racing festivals. Due to its location at the intersection of several important trade routes connecting Nepal and Bhutan with Central and Eastern Tibet, Gyantse has had a history of military conflicts. Both the Dzong Fort and the Palkhor Chode Monastery's cliff-top walls are lasting monuments of the "Great Game," when British and Russian imperialists competed to fill the power vacuum left in Tibet by the decline of the Qing in the late 19th century.

ORIENTATION AND PRACTICAL INFORMATION

The crossroads serve as the heart of compact Gyantse. Travelers arriving from Yamdroktso enter the city from the east on **Weiguo Lu** (卫国路), which becomes **Baiju (Palchoi) Lu** (白居路) west of the crossroads. Baiju (Palchoi) Lu, as the name indicates, leads to Palkhor Chode Monastery. **Yingxiong Lu** (英雄路) runs north-south through the crossroads, passing the entrance to Dzong Fort and running to Shigatse north of the crossroads. There is no long-distance bus station in Gyantse; **taxis** (Y200) and **minibuses** (Y25) depart for Shigatse from the crossroads.

Travel Permits: An **Alien Travel Permit** is required for Gyantse and all of its sights. Permits are no longer available through the Shigatse PSB or CITS. The only legal way to get to Gyantse is to organize a tour with a Lhasa travel agency.

Bike Rental: Gyantse Hotel, on Yingxiong Nan Lu, rents to hotel guests (Y5 per hr.).

PSB: Gyantse County (24hr. ☎817 2032), on Weiguo Lu, behind the Gyantse cinema. **Gyantse town** (☎817 2084), on Baiju (Palchoi) Lu. Open daily 9am-1pm and 4-7pm.

Pharmacy: Tongji Drugstore, on Weiguo Lu, opposite Gyantse County Hotel. Open daily 8am-10pm.

Hospital: People's Hospital of Gyantse County (☎817 2003), on Yingxiong Bei Lu. Ambulance service. Open daily 9:30am-12:30pm and 3:30-6:30pm.

Post and Telecommunications: On 17 Weiguo Lu. IDD service. Open daily 9am-12:30pm and 4-7pm. **Postal Code:** 857400.

ACCOMMODATIONS

Several decent budget options cluster around the central crossroads. **Public showers** (Y5) are available on Yingxiong Lu, across from the Canda Hotel.

Hotel of Gyantse Town Furniture Factory (tiánmù jiājùchǎng zhāodàisuǒ; 田牧家具场招待所; ☎817 2254), on Baiju (Palchoi) Lu, facing the crossroads. Clean dorms, have a fabulous deck view of the Dzong but face a noisy major street. Public showers (7-11pm) Y5 if you stay in the dorms. 4-bed dorms Y25; Tibetan-style rooms Y40 per bed. ❶

Wutse Hotel (wūzī fàndiàn; 乌孜饭店; ☎817 2880), on Yingxiong Lu, 100m from the crossroads. The sterile dorms have tile floors and TV, and doubles have absolutely beautiful private showers. 24hr. hot water. 4-bed dorms Y40; doubles Y300. ❶

Gyantse Foodstuff Storage Hotel (jiāngzī guójiā liángshì chǔbèi zhāodàisuǒ; 江孜国家粮食储备招待所; ☎817 2873), just east of the crossroads. Look for the red and blue "Hotel" sign. Clean, carpeted rooms and not-so-clean public toilets. 3-bed dorms Y30; doubles with bath Y45. ❶

Canda Hotel (càndá bīnguǎn; 灿达宾馆; ☎817 2573), on Yingxiong Lu, next to the Wutse Hotel. Look for the tinted blue windows. Cramped, unventilated dorms are the cheapest in town. Slightly musty standard doubles are noisy, with sub-par private baths. Dorms Y20; doubles Y50 per bed. ❶

FOOD

Gyantse's cheapest eats can be found in any small Chinese or Tibetan restaurant that doesn't offer an English menu. Many such places line Yingxiong Lu past the Wutse Hotel; a few small Tibetan spots lie along Palchoi Lu just west of the crossroads. For Y25-45, you can treat yourself to Western or sub-par Indian food in one of the foreigner-oriented restaurants around the crossroads.

Wutse Restaurant (wūzī cāntīng; 乌孜餐厅; ☎817 2880), in the Wutse Hotel. Wutse Restaurant has Gyantse's cheapest menu and a cozy Tibetan feel. A wide selection of Western, Chinese, Tibetan, Nepali, and Indian foods. The deep dish cheese pizza (Y20) is delicious but not filling. Try their stacked plate of fries (Y6). Open M-F 6:30am-8pm, Sa-Su 6:30am until the last customer leaves. ❷

Dongpo Restaurant (dōngpō cāntīng; 东坡餐厅), across the street from the Jianzang Hotel, 3min. south of the crossroads on Yingxiong Nan Lu. Cheap Chinese food with some dynamite dishes. Try the fish-flavored pork (yúxiāng ròusī; 鱼香肉丝; Y12) and the sweet and sour pork (tángcù lǐjí; 糖醋里脊; Y25). English menu. Open early for breakfast and until 10pm. ❷

Tashi Restaurant (☎817 2793), on Baiju (Palchoi) Lu, facing the crossroads at the mouth of Palchoi Lu. For some reason, most foreigners eat here despite inflated prices, perhaps because of the Western music and atmosphere. Entrees Y15-45; pastas Y25-30. Open daily 8am until the last customer leaves. ❷

SIGHTS

PALKHOR CHODE MONASTERY

From Gyantse's main crossroads, walk 10min. northwest on Baiju (Palchoi) Lu. Open daily 9am-1:30pm and 3-6pm. Y30. Y10 to take photographs inside.

Founded in 1418 by Rapdan Gunsang and the first Panchen Lama, Keldrup Je, the Palkhor Chode (also known as Palchoi) Monastery is where the Gelug, Sakya, and Bönpa sects of Tibetan Buddhism are said to coexist peacefully. The throne in the main assembly hall was once occupied by the Dalai Lama; now a photograph of the 10th Panchen Lama occupies the seat. In the center chapel, **Sakyamuni** (Buddha of the present age) is flanked by **Dipamkara** (Buddha of the past) on the left and **Maitreya** (Buddha of the future) on the right; Sakyamuni is surrounded by the ministers and messengers responsible for bringing his knowledge to mankind. Upstairs, the main chapel houses an intricate bronze **mandala** capped by a crystal orb. The solitary figure clothed in blue is **Vajrapani,** the *bodhisattva* of energy and power. Statues depicting lamas, teachers, and famous ascetics of the Sakyapa School line the walls surrounding the mandala.

Palkhor Chode Kumbum (qiānfó tǎ; 千佛塔) surpasses the monastery in both age and fame. The pagoda is one of the world's most famous *stupas*, built almost 800 years ago. It is 32m high and has 108 doors, 77 chapels, and at least 100,000 images of Buddhist deities (the name Kumbum itself means 100,000 images). The cardinally-oriented chapels on the first four floors each represent the particular realm of a deity, with a focal sculpture and a series of murals covering the cave-like space. The fifth and top floors house four Buddhas facing north (green), south (red), east (blue), and west (yellow).

DZONG FORT

From Gyantse's main crossroads, walk south for 3min. on Yingxiong Nan Lu; turn left down a small alleyway marked by a sign in English. It's a 10min. walk up a paved slope to the fort entrance. Open daily 8am-8pm. Y25.

Flanked by crumbling auburn walls, this imposing and handsome citadel overlooks the Palkhor Chode Monastery to the south and affords views of the dense Gyantse neighborhoods and surrounding green and yellow farmlands. Here, Tibetan defenders fought to the bitter end in a losing cause against the British Younghusband's "Expedition." (See **The Empire Strikes,** below).

Built in AD 967 by the grandson of Tibet's last *Tsanpo*, Dzong Fort (quán shān kàngyīng yízhǐ; 泉山抗英遗址) was expanded and used by various regimes, dynasties, and religious sects (Sakya, Padru, Gadan, and Podrang in particular) to defend Gyantse from separatist regimes. Gyantse occupies a crossroads linking Lhasa with Shigatse and Yadong; until Younghusband and his troops marched into this crucial juncture, the fortress was long considered impregnable. The **"Anti-British Museum"** commemorates the bloody aftermath in an exhibition that describes the British invasion. While the aerial view of Gyantse is indeed superb, the fort itself is quite uninteresting and best-appreciated from the city below.

PALA MANOR HOUSE

About 3km from Gyantse's city center. Walk down Yingxiong Nan Lu and turn right after the big "A" structure. A sign indicating the direction of the house is on the left, past the cement factory; the entrance is about 1km down a dirt road. Open daily 8am-8pm. Y20.

Pala Manor House (pàlā zhuāngyuán; 帕拉庄园; in Tibetan, *Pachou Lakang*) once belonged to a wealthy aristocrat, and was rebuilt in 1937. The original Pala Manor House, in Gyanka village, about 1km from Gyantse, was destroyed during the British invasion of Tibet. Reputedly the best-preserved manor house in all of Tibet, Pala Manor escaped the ravages of the Cultural Revolution by acting as the PLA's regional headquarters. A visit to this three-story house can be the perfect antidote to an overdose on monasteries. The third floor once served as the nobleman's private living quarters, and now contains a winter solarium and a private prayer hall. During important religious days and festivals, lamas were invited here to pray and meditate. The second floor holds the manor's eclectic assortment of historical and religious items, including turn-of-the-century *tangkas*, old Tibetan stamps (of

THE EMPIRE STRIKES In early 1903, a British adventurer named Younghusband led a Sepoy army from India to "check out" suspected Russian activity in Lhasa. After mowing down 1400 bewildered Tibetan troops with hill-top machine guns south of Gyantse, Younghusband marched into the city, expecting little resistance. A wave of reinforcements from Lhasa nearly captured Younghusband, but British firepower eventually prevailed.

Younghusband lured the Tibetan leadership into a "peaceful meeting." His troops then opened fire, killing the two main Tibetan generals, the heads of Tibet's three largest monasteries, the Panchen Lama's chief representative, and 500 Tibetan soldiers. A hero was created, however, when the Panchen Lama's bodyguard managed to kill 10 Englishmen with his knife before being shot down. The Tibetan defenders withdrew to Palkhor Chode Monastery and then to Dzong Fort. As the battle dragged on into July, Tibetans resorted to drinking out of mud pools and hurling boulders after they ran out of ammunition. The fort finally fell to a barrage of artillery fire, and the survivors retreated through hidden tunnels. According to British accounts, some 300 Tibetans lay dead while the British suffered only four dead and 30 wounded. A smug Younghusband marched into Lhasa, the first foreigner ever to do so.

which only 13 remain in the world), the master's alcohol collection, and a human skull that was made into a bowl to hold wine for the gods.

གཞིས་ཀ་རྩེ SHIGATSE 日喀则 ☎0892

Tibet's second largest city, Shigatse, is most famous as the seat of the Panchen Lama, who is traditionally regarded by Tibetans (discounting those in Lhasa) to be on equal footing with the Dalai Lama. A visit to Shigatse requires a stop at Tashilhunpo Monastery, where all of the Panchen Lamas since the 4th have lived (including the controversial 11th, who was chosen by the Chinese government to replace the imprisoned six-year-old). While much of Shigatse is dominated by Han Chinese businesses and modern architecture, there are pockets of traditional Tibetan neighborhoods, largely clustered in the north around the Tenzin Hotel. These areas offer interesting flea markets and countless Tibetan-style tea houses; the Chinese areas provide a wide selection of dining options and most of the resources of a larger city. Cheap, comfortable accommodations make the city a good stop on the way from Lhasa to Sakya and on to the border with Nepal.

TRANSPORTATION

Buses: Passengers Transportation Co. (☎882 6070), on Shanghai Lu and Zhufeng Dong Lu. Open daily 9:30am-9pm. There are 2 roads from Lhasa to Shigatse: the more scenic dirt road passes through Yamdroktso and Gyantse; the new paved highway winds along Yarlungzanbo River. Bus traffic runs only along the new one, which is 2-3hr. faster. All buses leave Shigatse at 8am; buses to Lhasa and other destinations may have additional morning departure times on demand. Travel time depends on road conditions. To: **Gyantse** (100km, Y25); **Lhasa** (280km, Y37); **Sakya** (150km, Y27); **Yadong** (300km, Y50). A single bus route runs from the main crossroads just east of the Tenzin Hotel, past the Tashilhunpo gates and ends near the bus station (Y0.5-1).

Local Transportation: Tricycle and **motorcycle** rides cost about Y3 to destinations within the city. **Taxis** are easy to come by, even after dark (Y10).

Bike Rental: Tenzin Hotel has 2 bikes to rent to hotel guests for Y3 per hr.

PRACTICAL INFORMATION

An **Alien Travel Permit** is not necessary for Shigatse. The Shigatse PSB, however, only issues travel permits for individuals heading west to Nepal; these permits are typically only for three to four days of travel. They will no longer issue permits for Gyantse, Yamdroktso, or Yadong; you can only get a permit for Sakya, Lhatse, and Zhangmu—essentially a direct route out of Tibet. Keep in mind that the permit situation is in constant flux. The **Shigatse PSB** has been, in the past, one of the most lenient offices, a helpful place for foreigners in Tibet. Ask around in Lhasa for the most current information if you are planning to travel out of Shigatse.

Travel Agency: The **CITS** in Shigatse is really just one man, Bakee (cell ☎(139) 0892 1189), who has a small office in the back of the Tashi 1 Restaurant. He arranges PSB permits for **Sakya, Lhatse,** and **Zhanmu** (3-4 days max., Y100 per person) without a tour. 4-day tours stopping at **Everest** and **Sakya** (Y4500, including permits) can be split between a max. of 6 people. Direct rides to the **Nepalese border** (1½ days) cost Y2700 (max. 6 people). If you obtain permits through CITS or the Shigatse PSB without a tour, Bakee can offer advice on taking a bus from Shigatse to Sakya, then a minibus from Sakya to Lhatse, and then hitching from Lhatse to the Nepal border. *Let's Go,* however, never recommends hitchhiking.

Bank of China: 7 Jiefang Zhong Lu. Exchanges traveler's checks. Open M-F 9am-1pm and 4-7pm, Sa-Su 10am-4pm.

Markets: There are 2 major flea markets in the northwest part of the city. The **Antique Market,** on Bangjia Gonglu opposite the Tenzin Hotel, sells mostly bead necklaces and other handicrafts. The market across the road sells mainly clothing and essentials.

Department Store: Shigatse Commercial City (☎882 3674), on the corner of Beijing Lu and Gongjiu Lin Lu. Used mainly by locals. Karaoke facilities, a tea garden, and restaurants on the 3rd and 4th fl. Open daily 9am-7pm.

PSB: 4 Jiji Langka Lu (24hr. ☎882 2241). The **Foreign Affairs Office** (☎882 2240), to the right of the main entrance, is the place to obtain travel permits. Visa extensions are no longer possible in Shigatse, or anywhere else in Tibet. On weekends, foreigners can contact Mr. Laba Ciren (☎882 3268) at his home. Other local branches on Renbu Lu; behind the Sanzuzi Hotel, on Gangjielin Lu; on Xin Gonglu; and on Yanhe Lu, near the river. All PSB offices open daily 9am-1pm and 4-7pm.

Hospitals: People's Hospital of Shigatse Prefecture (dìqū rénmín yīyuàn; 地区人民医院), 5 Shanghai Zhong Lu (emergency ☎882 2650). Ambulance service. Open daily 9am-12:30pm and 4-6:30pm. **Zang (Tibetan) Hospital** (zàng yīyuàn; 藏医院), 3 Shanghai Zhong Lu (☎882 2654). Tibetan and Western medicine. Open M-Sa 9am-12:30pm and 4-6:30pm. Emergency ward open until 9pm.

Pharmacy: Shigatse New and Special Medicines, 8 Shanghai Zhong Lu (24hr. ☎882 3101). Open daily 9am-9pm.

Internet Access: The **Telecom Internet Bar,** next to the main post and telecommunications office, has the fastest connection in town. Y10 per hr. Several cheaper Internet bars are along Beijing Lu, across the street from the Telecom bar. Y5 per hr.

Post and Telecommunications: Main Post and Telecommunications Office, 2 Beijing Bei Lu. Post office open daily 9am-7pm; **China Telecom** open daily 9:30am-midnight. IDD service also at Shigatse Commercial City (see **Department Store,** above). Open daily 9am-8pm. **Postal Code:** 857000.

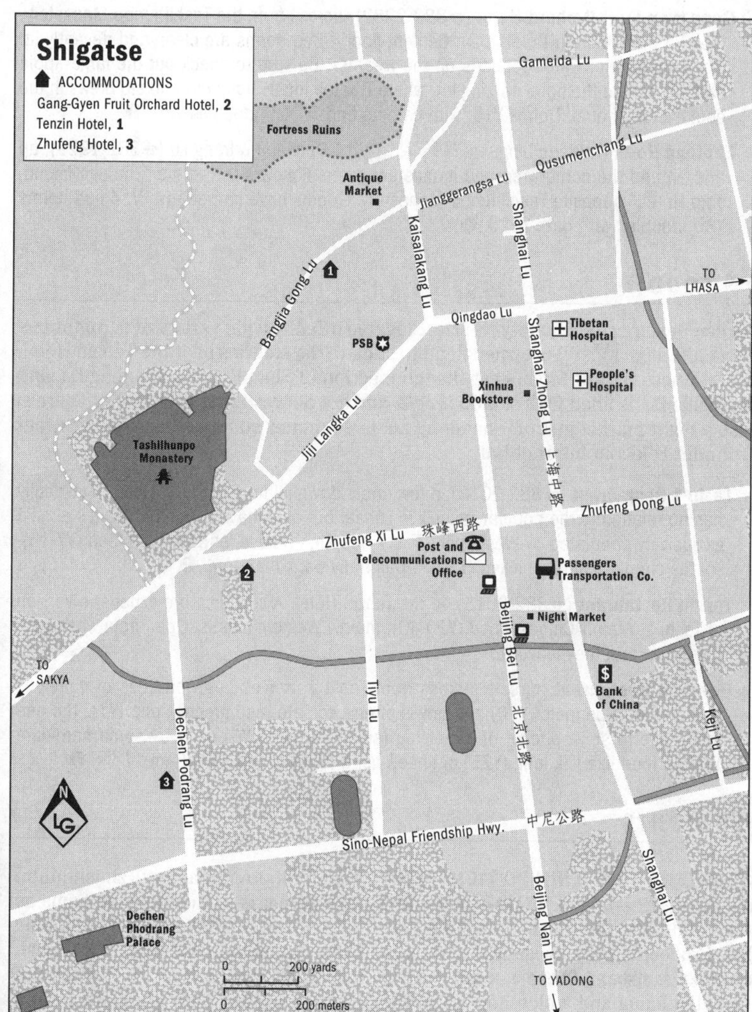

ACCOMMODATIONS

Although not as backpacker-friendly as Lhasa, Shigatse offers a handful of excellent budget hotels.

Tenzin Hotel, 10 Banjia Gonglu (☎882 2018). The destination of choice for backpackers. Tenzin's bulletin board is virtually the only place in Shigatse to find other travelers with whom to share Nepal-bound tours. This clean and convenient hotel has a nice patio area and rooms with Tibetan decor. Hot water 8:30am-10:30pm. Large dorms Y25; 3-bed dorms Y30; 2-bed dorms Y40; singles Y60-80. ❶

Gang-gyen Fruit Orchard Hotel (☎882 2282), across from the Tashilhunpo Monastery; look for the "Orchard Hotel" sign. Cement-floor 4-bed dorms are clean and decently lit. Solar-heated hot water depends on the weather. Be sure to check out the large apple orchard behind the hotel parking lot, where Tibetan locals hang out and sip brews in the cool evening hours. Dorms Y15, with carpets and TV Y25; doubles Y80. ❶

Zhufeng Hotel (zhūfēng bīnguǎn; 珠峰宾馆), 14 Dechen Podrang Lu (☎882 1929), up and around the corner from the monastery gates. Follow signs to the "Zhufeng Friendship Hotel," opposite Tashilhunpo Monastery. Rooms have carpet and TV. 4-bed dorms Y30; doubles with bath Y120. ❶

FOOD

As can be expected of a city its size, Shigatse offers a wide variety of scrumptious food, although most Westerners tend to stick to the eateries near the Tenzin Hotel. The Chinese part of town, near the intersection of Shandong Lu, Zhufeng Lu, and Shanghai Lu, is lined with small *xiǎochī* and hot pot restaurants (Y15-20). There is also a night market just off Shandong Lu, five minutes south and across the street from the Telecom Internet Bar.

Tashi 1 Restaurant (☎882 2018), a few doors downhill from the Fruit Hotel, technically has no relation to the popular Tashi 1 in Lhasa, but does have a similar feel; it's almost exclusively populated by Westerners. Tasty Tibetan, Chinese, and Western food (Y7-15). Try the chunky walnut chicken (Y20). Open daily 6am-11:30pm. ❶

Tenzin Restaurant (☎882 2018), in the Tenzin Hotel. A slightly more expensive version of Tashi 1. Mainly Chinese food (Y10-40), mainly Western clients. Open from when people arrive until they leave. ❷

Gangyen Restaurant, directly across from Tashi 1, serves large portions of delicious fried rice with peppers (Y10) and bowls of egg, tomato, and greens soup (Y1). The perfect place to sip a pitcher of sweet tea (small Y4, large Y6) or to try some hard-core Tibetan food like yak lung (Y25) or sheep head (Y20). Open daily 8am-11pm. ❶

SIGHTS

བཀྲ་ཤིས་ལྷུན་པོ་ **TASHILHUNPO MONASTERY.** Tashilhunpo Monastery (zhāshílúnbù sì; 扎什伦布寺), built in 1447 by the first Dalai Lama, is to the Panchen Lama as the Potala is to the Dalai Lama. Four main buildings sit on the monastery's sloping hill. Proceeding clockwise in the traditional **kora** circuit, one encounters the westernmost **Jamkhang Chenmo,** a tall red building which was built in 1914 by the 9th Panchen Lama and which houses a 26m-tall statue of the Maitreya Buddha. Continuing along a stone path eastward, the next building is the **Labrang Gyaltsen Thonpo,** the palace of the Panchen Lamas; it's usually closed to visitors. Farther east along the main path on your left is the **Kudhung Lhakhang,** built in 1662 out of 547kg of gold and 75kg of silver. It contains the impressive 11m *chorten*-tomb of the 4th Panchen Lama. The final and easternmost building in the *kora* circuit is the **Kesang Lhakhang,** Tashilhunpo's largest building complex, at the center of a stone-paved courtyard lined with painted murals. This courtyard is used for all-important monastic dances, debates, and festivals, as well as daily teachings. Up the stairs behind the balcony is a large **dukhang** assembly hall, where in the late afternoon visitors can often immerse themselves in a sea of chanting monks. *(Open M-Sa 9am-12:30pm and 4-6pm. Y35.)*

FOUR'S A CROWD As you visit monasteries across Tibet, you will notice frequent depictions of an elephant with a monkey, a hare, and a bird piled upon each others' backs. This description is not born of an incredibly simplistic view of the animal food chain, but rather of an ancient Tibetan fable known as the "The Union of the Four Brethren." Once upon a time, on a hot sunny day, these four creatures decided to seek shelter under the same tree. The elephant exclaimed: "The tree is only big enough to shade me!" "No, no, there is only room for me," said the monkey. The rabbit also made the same claim. It is only when the tiny little bird squeaked, "I planted the seed for that tree," that they realized they were all being a bit selfish, so the four animals piled onto each others' backs and spent the afternoon together in the shade. The moral of the story is known as "friendship."

ས་སྐྱ་ SAKYA 萨迦

☎08024

The town of Sakya, 150km west of Shigatse, shows few signs of Chinese influence, save the PSB checkpoint and military base at the edge of town. In the city center, a fortress-like monastery rises above a dense network of traditional mud-wall housing. One of the first cityscapes travelers encounter when heading westward toward Nepal is that of Sakya. The characteristic blue, red-, and white-striped patterns are a sacred configuration of colors derived from the early Vinaya Buddhist sect. Not many travelers spend the night in Sakya, but the feel of this quiet monastery town merits what time you can afford.

ORIENTATION AND PRACTICAL INFORMATION. An **Alien Travel Permit** is required; travelers must stop at the PSB checkpoint at the town entrance. The enormous **Sakya Monastery** serves as the town center; a handful of hotels, shops, and eateries are clustered east of the monastery walls. **Buses** (Y15) depart for Lhatse daily. From Sakya, Shigatse-bound buses depart every other day from the Sakya County Guesthouse. There is a **post office** across the street from the County Guesthouse. (Open daily 9:30am-12:30pm and 4-7pm.) The **postal code** is 857800.

ACCOMMODATIONS AND FOOD. Of the extremely limited accommodation options in Sakya, the most passable one is the **Sakya Hotel ❶**, just outside the monastery's northeast corner. Enter through the gates just to the right of the **Sakya Monastery Restaurant and Tea House.** Dorm beds (Y10) have communal toilets. Most travelers to Sakya stay in nearby **Lhatse** (30km west of the Sakya turn-off), where creature comforts are more plentiful. The **Lhatse Hotel ❶** has musty, crowded dorms and fancier Tibetan-style rooms with carpets and TV. Be sure to ask for a room facing the inner courtyard or you'll incur the wrath of karaoke for the duration of the night. (☎(08032) 2208. Showers Y5. Dorms Y20-40; doubles Y90.) **Farmer's Hotel ❶** (nóngmíng yúlè lǚguǎn; 农民娱乐旅馆), on the right as you enter town from the east, is often cheaper and quieter. (Dorms Y20; pricier doubles.)

Several restaurants with names involving "Sakya," "monastery," and "Tibetan" all offer similarly over-priced Chinese and Tibetan food. Don't pay more than Y10 for rice, potatoes, and meat, or Y5 for a small thermos of sweet tea. The **Tashi 2** restaurant, next to the Lhatse Hotel, serves tasty but overpriced Chinese dishes (Y18-30). A row of cheaper Sichuanese restaurants lines the other side of the street.

SIGHTS. Sakya Monastery (sàjiā sì; 萨迦寺) is comprised of two parts. The northern complex across the river is mostly ruins, with two small, but interesting temples still in use. The southern, castle-like complex is nestled within the town. Originally containing 108 structures, the northern complex was laid out according to variations in terrain rather than the strict geometry and cardinal relationships that dominated the earlier planning scheme seen in the southern complex. The Sakya Monastery, completed in 1268, is home to the Red Hat (Sakyapa) sect of Tibetan Buddhism (see p. 801). Climbing the monastery walls and walking along the top ridge affords incredible views of the monastery and the surrounding valley. Be careful; there are no side railings. A ground floor entrance is via the east wall, which leads to the central courtyard.

To the left is the **Purkhang Chapel,** which houses the 700-year-old figure of Sakyamuni, 7000 glass-encased *bodhisattvas*, and other relics. The central figure is Manjushri, the Bodhisattva of Wisdom; Sakyamuni is a few paces to the left. The temple across from the chapel contains the *stupas* of 11 Sakya abbots, a dusty *mandala*, and hundreds of ancient scripts. Directly opposite the main entrance is the cavernous **assembly hall,** where the familiar figure of Sakyamuni is flanked by a symmetrical arrangement of statues. The remains of the founder of Sakya Monastery, Kon Konchog Gyelpo, are preserved inside the enormous central Buddha. The remarkable assortment of figures on display includes Manjushri, Maitreya, and Kunga Nyingpo (the center figure of the trio to the right of Sakyamuni), a famous abbot of Sakya. The pillars themselves are single tree trunks, brought from India. Bring a flashlight to observe the mesmerizing murals on the walls. *(Open daily 8am-5pm; closed for a 1hr. lunch break. Y35; Y20 fee for photos taken inside the monastery.*

ཇམ་གླང་མ་ MT. EVEREST 珠穆朗马峰

The approach to Mt. Everest via **Pangla Pass** is one of the most beautiful and stunning routes in the world. After hours zigzagging across the plateau, the majestic Himalayas unfold in full force, with four of the six highest peaks in the world—Cho Oyu (8201m), Malaku (8463m), Lhotse (8516m), and Qomolangma (Everest, 8848.13m)—looming before the awestruck traveler. The most magnificent view of the "Third Pole of the World," however, is from Rongphu Monastery. On the rare clear day, lucky visitors can clamber up to base camp and watch the sun's rays slowly illuminate the mountain.

From Lhatse, the Friendship Highway continues for three hours, past **Shegar** (New Tingri) to the 65km **Everest access road.** After the turn-off, the bumpy and windy access road winds up for one-and-a-half hours, passing Pangla Pass, 5220m above sea level, before descending to the village of **Tashi Dzom.** Most visitors stop here for lunch or stay the night. After crossing a large valley and several tiny villages, the road ends up at **Rongphu Monastery. Base camp** is a few kilometers up the Rongphu glacier bed. The Everest access road trip takes about five hours; a new road that was being constructed at the time of writing could, by the summer of 2002, cut several hours off this time.

PRACTICAL INFORMATION AND ACCOMMODATIONS

An **Alien Travel Permit** is required for Rongphu Monastery and Everest Base Camp, and there is a checkpoint at the beginning of the Everest access road. At the time of writing, the Shigatse PSB would not issue EBC permits to individual travelers, but you may have better luck going through the Shigatse CITS. EBC permits are easily obtained in **Chasa** if you book a car and guide. There is a Y65 per person **admission** fee to enter the Everest region, as well as a hefty Y405 vehicle fee (some travel agencies include this fee in land cruiser packages). These fees are collected at **New Tingri (Shekar),** about 5km from the turn-off; there is also a checkpoint just after the turn-off. Several restaurant/guesthouses lining the main road in Tashi Dzom offer very similar accommodations for Y25 per night, as well as over-priced Tibetan food (Y10-15). **Tashi Dzom,** two hours away, has cheaper and often warmer rooms than those at **Rongphu,** making this town a good place to spend the night before heading back to the Friendship Highway. The **Qomolangma Sunlight Guesthouse** has a slight edge in terms of room quality, and may offer you a Y20-per-bed rate. All three hotels have concrete floors, pit toilets, and no showers.

SIGHTS

The unbeatable views from the Rongphu Monastery and the Everest Base Camp are the only reason to come all this way—enjoy.

RONGPHU MONASTERY (róngbù sì; 绒布寺). Rongphu Monastery, two hours farther up the Everest access road from Tashi Dzom, is the small and run-down home of 21 nuns and nine monks. At 4980m, Rongphu has basic accommodations in cold rooms (dorms Y25), but at least you can brag that you've slept in the world's highest temple. An incredible view makes up for the lack of electricity and door locks. Camping on the grounds costs Y10-15. Next to the monastery, a guesthouse offers nice dorm rooms (Y40 per bed) and a lodge where visitors can warm up by the stove, eat noodles (Y10) or fried rice (Y10), and drink sweet tea (Y5-8).

EVEREST BASE CAMP (zhūfēng dàběnyíng; 珠峰大本营). For centuries, the sight of Everest's peak has taken many a breath away. From 5000m above sea level, the grandeur of the mighty peak may not be apparent at first glance, but the shimmering beauty of the pyramidal north face quickly dissipates any initial disappointment. The best time to view it is in the early morning, when the chances of a cloudless sky are highest and the sun's first rays glint off the perpetually snow-clad peak. During summer months, clouds from Nepal can enshroud the Himalayas for up to a week; only the lucky may catch a glimpse of the peak.

For the intrepid, a hike from Rongphu Monastery to Everest Base Camp takes about two hours. For the faint-hearted, a 20-minute ride in a land cruiser will do the trick. Although there isn't that much to do at Base Camp, the "Mt. Qomolangma Base Camp" marker provides an unbeatable photo-op. One word of caution: do not attempt to hike to Base Camp if you have just arrived in Tibet via Kathmandu. Acute Mountain Sickness (see p. 797) can strike without warning and debilitate even the fittest trekker. Spend a few days getting acclimated before setting out on any long hikes. Also note that several PSB tents set up at base camp, waiting to hand out US$100 fines to anyone who tries to continue up the path to Camp 1; if you are planning to hike in the area, avoid problems with the PSB by heading east up a canyon to the Qianjing Glacier rather than toward Camp 1.

TIBET

TINGRI 定日

The small village of Tingri is little more than a few houses along the Friendship Highway. Foreigners need an **Alien Travel Permit** (although only an individual one), to get there. Tingri is where most travelers spend either their last night (if heading to Kathmandu) or first night (if coming from Kathmandu) in Tibet. There is little to do in the town except admire the wonderful view of the Himalayan Range in the gorgeous natural backdrop to the town.

Himalaya Hotel (xǐmǎlāyǎ lǚguǎn; 喜玛拉雅旅馆), on the Friendship Highway, a few hundred meters before the center of town, is the cheapest place around town. There are communal toilets but no showers; plenty of hot boiled water is available for rinsing. (2- to 4-bed dorms Y15. ❶) In the center of town, the **Amdo Hotel** has a nice shower and outdoor pit toilets with great views of the surrounding valley. (Showers Y10, non-guests Y15. 3- to 4-bed dorms Y20. ❶)

There are a bunch of eateries lining the Friendship Highway, each rehashing the same pricey menu. On the Nepal-bound side of town, the **Amdo Restaurant** is about as cheap and good as it gets (Tibetan dishes Y10-20). If you're looking for more variety, be patient; you'll probably be in Kathmandu soon.

གཉའ་ལམ་ NYALAM

The small but modern town of Nyalam, 40km from Zhanmu and the Nepalese border, clusters around a strip of the Friendship Highway; travelers from Kathmandu often spend the night here. If you are coming from Lhasa, Nyalam's green slopes and beautiful trees give a tantalizing hint of the lush and vibrant ecosystem into which you are about to descend. A **PSB checkpoint,** next to the prison at the northern end of town, will check for permits. Accommodations are cheap and plentiful in Nyalam; the cheapest is probably the **Snowlands Guesthouse** ❶ (xuěyù lǔguǎn; 雪域旅馆), near the north end of town. (Dorms Y15-20; doubles with no showers Y25-30.) The larger and slightly higher-quality **Nyalam Hotel** ❶, at the southern end of town past the basketball courts, has bright, clean cement-floored dorms (Y30) and doubles (Y30-35). Showers are across the lot (Y10). The cheapest place to eat is the **Nepali Restaurant** ❷, next to the basketball courts at the center of town. They insistently refill plates of lentils, rice, and curry (vegetables Y15, chicken Y18). The **Snowlands Restaurant** ❶, across from the Snowlands Hotel, serves the best breakfast, with a great deal on thick pancakes, eggs, peanut butter, jam, and coffee or tea (Y15). If you have a few free hours, visit the small **Nyalam Temple** and relax on the surrounding grassy hillside, up the main hall behind the town.

འགྲམ་ ZHANGMU 樟木 ☎08704

The lush green cliffs sloping above the border town of Zhangmu are a dead give-away that Nepal is near, and many travelers consider it to be the most spectacular scenery in either Tibet or Nepal. Beautiful waterfalls splash down thousands of feet, sometimes drenching passing cars in the process. The entire town lies along the Friendship Highway as it curves and descends into Nepal. The population, a curious mix of Tibetan, Nepalese, and Chinese, is growing at a rapid rate, in large part due to brisk border trade.

An **Alien Travel Permit** is technically required for Zhangmu—there is a PSB checkpoint at the entrance to town. There is a **post office** near the top of town; **Bank of China** is opposite the Zhangmu Hotel. Money changers also work the streets in front of the bank, offering better rates than in Kathmandu.

The most luxurious accommodation in town is the **Zhangmu Hotel** ❶, at the base of town near the border post. This two-star behemoth's restaurant serves excellent buffets. (☎2221. Breakfast buffet Y60, lunch and dinner Y90. 4-bed dorms Y50.) Across the street, the **Gang-gyen Hotel** ❶ has bright and airy dorms with communal toilets and nice views of the valley below. (☎2188. 24hr. hot water. 5-bed dorms Y50.) Uphill from here, on the left, the **Zhangmu Friendship Guesthouse** ❶ (zhāngmù yǒuyí lǔguǎn; 樟木友谊旅馆) is of similar quality to the Gang-gyen Hotel but may not always take foreigners. (☎2261. Dorms Y20.) The Chinese-Tibetan restaurant next door to the Gang-gyen Hotel, **Gang-gyen Restaurant,** is over-priced but popular with the backpacking crowd. (Open daily 8am-10:30pm.) The cheapest place to eat is the **Kelsang Restaurant** ❶, five minutes uphill from the Lhasa Restaurant, with delicious, all-you-can-eat Nepali *dal*, rice, and potatoes for Y8.

BORDER CROSSING INTO NEPAL: ZHANGMU

The customs checkpoint for China is at Zhangmu, at the bottom of town. From Zhangmu, most travelers pay for a ride on a truck (US$5-7) or walk the remaining 8km to **Kodari** (about 2hr.) and the Friendship Bridge, where the customs checkpoint for Nepal is located. With a light pack, you may want to take a small rocky path that descends steeply to the Friendship Bridge, shortcutting the main road's many switchbacks, though it may be very slippery in the rain; walking the trail (2km) takes about 1½hr. from the Zhanmu border. Nepali **visas** are available at the border (1st entry to Nepal US$30, subsequent entries US$50), or from the Nepalese consulate in Lhasa (see p. 804). From Kodari, two buses depart in the morning for Kathmandu, leaving from the Friendship Bridge when full (150Rs). A taxi to Kathmandu costs 2500Rs for four people. Cheaper minibuses or large vans charge 500Rs per person. Set your clocks back 2hr. and 15min. when entering. Barring landslides and other delays, the trip from Kodari to Kathmandu takes about five hours.

APPENDIX

GLOSSARY

apsara: Buddhist angel
arhat: one who has attained spiritual enlightenment
avos: the smallest denomination of Mecanese currency; 1/100th of a pataca
bāozi: steamed, stuffed buns
batik: hand-dyed textiles
bei: north
binguan: hotel
bodhisattva: a devout Buddhist who has attained enlightenment but remained on earth to help others
CAAC: Civil Aviation Administration of China
CCP: Chinese Communist Party
CITS: China International Travel Service
CTS: China Travel Service
dadao: boulevard
dagoba: a bell-shaped Buddhist commemorative shine
dajie: avenue
dasha: mansions
DDD phones: Domestic Direct Dial phones; telephones from which domestic long-distance numbers can be dialed directly
dim sum: Cantonese bite-sized dumplings and buns usually eaten for breakfast or lunch
dong: east
fandian: hotel or restaurant
fēn: the smallest denomination of Chinese currency; 1/100th of a *yuán*
feng: peak
feng shui: literally "wind and water"; a system of geomancy used to determine auspicious locations or positions for buildings or other structures
GMD: Guomindang; the Nationalist People's Party led by Chiang Kai-shek that lost to the Communists in 1949 and fled to Taiwan; also called KMT (Kuomintang)
Guanyin: Buddhist goddess of mercy
gŭlóu: drum tower
gwailo: Cantonese slang for foreigner
hai: sea
Han Chinese: China's ethnic majority; comprises 91% of the population
he: river
hu: lake
hútòng: an alley
IDD phones: International Direct Dial phones; telephones from which international long-distance numbers can be dialed directly
jiang: river
jie: street
jiudian: a hotel or restaurant; more upscale than a *fandian* or *binguan*
jiăo: 10 *fēn;* also called *"máo"*
jiăozi: dumplings
karst: eroded limestone formation
kitsch: something that is tacky; especially prevalent at Chinese tourist spots
lama: spiritual leader in Tibetan Buddhism
lăowài: Mandarin slang term for "foreigner"
lingkor: a Buddhist pilgrimage cirucuit around select holy sites
loess: fine, yellowish silt
lohan: an enlightened being similar to an *arhat*
lu: road
mahjong: popular Chinese game that resembles gin played with tiles
men: gate or door
miàndí: yellow mini-van taxis that are shaped like loaves of bread
nan: south
pataca: unit of currency of Macau
PLA: People's Liberation Army
PSB: Public Security Bureau; the police
pagoda: an elongated, multi-story tower which tapers at the top
PRC: People's Republic of China
qiao: bridge
rénmínbì: the official name for Chinese currency; literally, "people's money"
sampan: small, motorized boat
SEZ: Special Economic Zone
shan: hill or mountain
si: temple
shui: water
stele: an upright stone tablet with carvings or inscriptions
stupa: Buddhist monument which often houses sacred relics
sutra: sacred Buddhist text
ta: pagoda
tai chi: slow speed martial art generally practiced as a form of early morning exercise
taipan: a 19th-century term for a powerful foreign businessman in Hong Kong
tian: heaven or sky
tratsang: Buddhist college
Uighur: Turkic-speaking Muslim minority group living primarily in Xinjiang; also spelled Uygur
via ferrata: literally "iron way"; a mountain path equipped with ladders, metal handholds, and cables.
xi: west
xiăochī: literally "small eats"; Chinese snacks
yuán: unit of Chinese currency
yurt: circular tent used by Central Asian nomads
zhan: station
zhaodaisuo: hostel
zhong: middle
zhōngguó: China; literally "Middle Kingdom"

PINYIN PRONUNCIATION GUIDE

The most difficult aspect of the Chinese language for foreigners is the **tone system.** Do not let the challenge posed by tones prevent you from trying out a few Chinese phrases; even with no grasp of them, you should be able to make yourself understood. Most letters used in the pinyin system are pronounced just as they are in English. The exceptions are the following:

a	as in f**a**ther
ai	"i" as in **eye**
ao	"ow" as in all**ow**
ang	"on" as in d**awn**
e	"uh" as in d**uh**
ei	"ay" as in w**ay** or s**ay**
i	"ee" as in f**ee**t after most consonants "rih" sound after "ch," "sh," "zh," and "r" "ih" after "c," "s," and "z"
ia	"ya" as in **ya**hoo
ie	"ye" as in **ye**s
iu	"eo" as in L**eo** or **"yo, watup?"**
ong	"oan" as in l**oan**
ou	"o" as in **o**cean
o	"wo" as in m**o**re
u	after l or n, "oo" as in b**oo**t; else "u" as in c**u**te or m**u**te
ü	"u" as in c**u**te or m**u**te
ui	"way" as in a**way**
uo	"wo" as in **war**
un	"wen" as in **Wen**dy
c	"ts" as in ca**ts**
ch	as in **ch**urn
q	"ch" as in **ch**eat; an airy sound produced by pushing short burst of air while the tongue is pressed against the palate
r	as in **r**ain
sh	as in **sh**op
x	"sh" as in **sh**eet
z	"ds" as in rea**ds**
zh	"dj" as in **Dj**ibouti; pronounced like "j" but with the tongue rolled back

MANDARIN PHRASEBOOK

NUMBERS	PINYIN	CHINESE
0	líng	零
½	yíbàn	一半
1	yī or yāo	一
2	èr or liǎng	二 or 两
3	sān	三
4	sì	四
5	wǔ	五
6	liù	六
7	qī	七
8	bā	八

NUMBERS	PINYIN	CHINESE
9	jiǔ	九
10	shí	十
11	shíyī	十一
12	shíèr	十二
20	èrshí	二十
21	èrshíyī	二十一
100	yìbǎi	一百
200	liǎngbǎi	两百
1000	yìqiān	一千
10,000	yíwàn	一万

THE BASICS	PINYIN	CHINESE
Hello	nǐhǎo	你好
Good bye	zài jiàn	再见
How are you?	nǐ hǎo ma?	你好吗?
Please	qǐng	请
Thank you	xièxiè	谢谢
You're welcome	bùkèqi or bùxiè	不客气 or 不谢
Help!	jiùmìng!	救命!
I'm sorry	duìbùqǐ	对不起

THE BASICS	PINYIN	CHINESE
It doesn't matter (when asked to make a choice)	dōu kěyǐ or méi guānxī	都可以
It doesn't matter (don't worry about it)	wú suǒwèi	没关系
Forget about it	suàn le ba	算了吧
What's your name?	nǐ jiào shénme míngzi?	你叫什么名子?
My name is...	wǒ jiào...	我叫...
I	wǒ	我
you	nǐ (standard) or nín (formal)	你, 您
he, she, it	tā	他, 她, 它
plural: we, you, they	add mén to singular: wǒmén, nǐmén, tāmén	我们, 你们, 他们
to be	shì (invariable)	是
Yes	shì	是
No	búshì	不是
to have	yǒu (invariable)	有
to not have	méiyǒu	没有
okay	kéyǐ or xíng	可以 or 行
not okay	bùxíng or bùkéyǐ	不可以 or 不行
to want, would like	yào	要
to not want	búyào	不要
Do you have...?	yǒu méiyǒu...?	有没有...?
I want ...	wǒ yào...	我要...
I don't speak Chinese	wǒ bú huì shuō zhōngwén	我不会说中文
Do you speak English?	nǐ huì shuō yīngwén ma?	您会说中文吗?
I can't hear you	wǒ tīng bú jiàn	我听不见
Speak more slowly	màn yī diǎr	慢一点儿
Repeat that	chóngfù yíbiàn/zài shuō yī cì	重复一便 or 再说一次
I don't understand	wǒ bù míngbái/wǒ bù dǒng	我不明白/我不懂
I need help	wǒ xūyào bāngzhù	我需要帮助
You are cheating me	nǐ zài piàn wǒ	你在骗我
What time do you open?	nǐ jǐdiǎn kāi mén/nǐ jǐdiǎn shàng bān?	你几点开门/你几点上班?
What time do you close?	nǐ jǐdiǎn guān mén/nǐ jǐdiǎn xià bān?	你几点关门/你几点下班?
restroom	cèsuǒ	厕所
man	nán	男
woman	nǚ	女
toilet paper	wèishēng zhǐ	卫生纸
Western toilet	mǎtǒng	马桶
squat toilet	dūnkēng	蹲坑
big	dà	大
small	xiǎo	小

DIRECTIONS	PINYIN	CHINESE
Where is...?	...zài nǎr/...zài nǎlǐ	...在哪儿/...在哪里?
How do I get to ...?	qù...zěnme zǒu?	去...怎么走?
I want to go to...	wǒ yào qù...	我要去...

APPENDIX

DIRECTIONS	PINYIN	CHINESE
How far is...from here?	...yǒu duō yuǎn?	有多远?
How long does it take to get to...?	qù...děi huā duōcháng shíjiān?	去...得花多长时间?
north	běi	北
south	nán	南
east	dōng	东
west	xī	西
left	zuǒ	左
right	yòu	右
front, forward /in the front	qián/qiánmiàn	前/前面
back, rear/behind	hòu/hòumiàn	后/后面
center, middle	zhōng	中
upper, above, ascend	shàng	上
lower, below, descend	xià	下
between...and...	zài...hé...zhījiān	在...和...之间
to enter/entrance	jìn/jìnkǒu	进/进口
to exit/exit	chū/chūkǒu	出/出口
far, distant	yǔan	远
close, near/nearby	jìn/fùjìn	近/附近
next to...	zài...pángbiān	在...旁边

TRANSPORTATION	PINYIN	CHINESE
passenger (adj.)	kèyùn	客运
insurance	bǎoxiǎn	保险
People's Insurance Company of China (PICC)	zhōngguó rénmín bǎoxiǎn gōngsī	中国人民保险公司
I want to take [a plane, train, bus] to...	wǒ yào zuò [fēijī, huǒchē, qìchē] qù...	我要坐飞机,火车,汽车] 去...
ticket office	shòupiào chù	售票处
ticket	piào	票
I want to reserve a ticket	wǒ xiǎng dìng piào	我想订票
I want to buy a ticket to...	wǒ xiǎng mǎi qù...de piào	我想买去...的票
one-way ticket	dānchéng piào	单程票
round-trip ticket	wǎngfǎn piào	往反票
Can I cancel my ticket?	kěyǐ tuì piào ma?	可以退票吗?
Can I change my ticket?	kěyǐ huànpiào ma?	可以还票吗?
There are no seats (sleepers)	méi yǒu zuòwèi (pùwèi)	没有座位 (铺位)
commission	shǒuxù fèi	手续费
schedule	shíkèbiǎo	时刻表
What time does it leave?	jǐ diǎn chūfā?	几点出发?
What time does it arrive?	jǐ diǎn dào?	几点到?
How long does it take?	yàohuā duōshǎo shíjiān?	要花多少时间?
Check (verify) ticket	chá piào	查票
waiting room	hòuchē shì	候车室
luggage storage	jìcùn chù	寄存处
airplane	fēijī	飞机

APPENDIX

TRANSPORTATION	PINYIN	CHINESE
airport	fēijīchǎng	飞机场
CAAC office	zhōngguó mínháng shòupiào chù	中国民航售票处
train	huǒchē	火车
train station	huǒchē zhàn	火车站
hard/soft seat	yìng zuò/ruǎn zuò	硬座/软座
hard/soft sleeper	yìng wò/ruǎn wò	硬卧/软卧
upper/middle/lower bunk	shàng pù/zhōng pù/xià pù	上铺/中铺/下铺
platform	zhàntái	站台
long-distance bus	chángtú qìchē	长途汽车
bus station	qìchē zhàn	汽车站
sleeper bus	wòpù chē	卧铺车
boat	chuán	船
docks	mǎtóu	码头
1st, 2nd,...class cabin	yī, èr,...děng cāng	一, 二,...等舱
city bus	gōnggòng qìchē	公共汽车
minibus	zhōngbā	中巴
I want to get off (the bus, etc.)	wǒ yào xià chē	我要下车
subway	dìtiě	地铁
taxi	chūzū chē	出租车
breadbox *(miandi)* taxi	miàndī	面的
To request a cab, say: get a cab	dǎ ge dì	打个的
Turn on the meter	dǎ biǎo	打表
bicycle	zìxíngchē	自行车
I want to rent a bicycle	wǒ xiǎng zū zìxíngchē	我想租自行车

MONEY	PINYIN	CHINESE
money	qián	钱
Chinese currency	rénmínbì	人民币
one (two, three) yuan	yī (èr, sān) kuài	一(二,三)块
1/10th of one yuan	máo	毛
1/100th of one yuan	fēn	分
cash	xiànjīn	现金
US dollars	měi yuán	美元
traveler's checks	lǚxíng zhīpiào	旅行支票
credit card	xìnyòng kǎ	信用卡
Can I use a foreign credit card?	kěyǐ yòng wàiguó de xìnyòng kǎ ma?	可以用外国的信用卡吗?
bank	yínháng	银行
Bank of China	zhōngguó yínháng	中国银行
change money	huàn qián	换钱
Can I exchange money (traveler's checks) here?	zhèr kěyǐ huàn qián (lǚxíng zhīpiào) ma?	这儿可以换钱(旅行支票)吗?
ATM	zìdòng qǔ kuǎn/zìdòng yínháng	自动取款/自动银行
price	jiàqián/jiàgé	价钱/价格

MONEY	PINYIN	CHINESE
pay/pay for	fù qián	付钱
spend money	huā qián	花钱
give change	zhǎo qián	找钱
bargain	tǎojià huànjià	讨价还价
How much does it cost?	duōshǎo qián?	多少钱?
inexpensive	piányì	便宜
most inexpensive	zuì piányì	最便宜
expensive	guì	贵
too expensive	tài guìle	太贵了
This is fake	zhè shì jiǎ de	这是假的
Can I have a discount/do you give discounts?	kēyǐ piányì yīdiǎn ma/nǐ dǎ bù dǎ zhé?	可以便宜一点吗/你打不打折?
Write a receipt	kāi piào	开票
I want a receipt	wǒ yào fāpiào	我要发票

HEALTH & EMERGENCY	PINYIN	CHINESE
sick/disease	bìng	病
Western medicine	xī yī	西医
Chinese medicine	zhōng yī	中医
I am sick	wǒ bìng le	我病了
I don't feel well	wǒ bù shūfu	我不舒服
I am injured	wǒ shòushāngle	我受伤了
hurt/pain	téng	疼
My head hurts	wǒ tóu téng	我头疼
My stomach hurts	wǒ dùzi téng	我肚子疼
I'm allergic to...	wǒ duì...guòmǐn	我对...过敏
I feel nauseous	wǒ ěxīn	我恶心
I've caught a cold	wǒ gǎnmào le	我感冒了
I have a fever	wǒ fāshāo le	我发烧了
AIDS	àizībìng	艾兹病
altitude sickness	gāoshān fǎnyìng	高山反应
diarrhea	lā dùzi	拉肚子
hepatitis	gānyán	肝炎
malaria	nüèjí	疟疾
rabies	kuángquǎnbìng	狂犬病
tetanus	pòshāngfēng	破伤风
hospital	yīyuàn	医院
Where is the hospital?	yīyuàn zài nǎr?	医院在那儿?
doctor	dàifu	大夫
Please use sterilized equipment	qǐng yòng yīcìxìng yíqì	请用一次性仪器
I do not want a blood transfusion	wǒ bù yào shū xuè	我不要输血
shot/injection	zhùshè	注射
Please use my own syringe	qǐng yòng wǒ zìjǐ de zhùshèqì	请用我自已的注射器
pharmacy	yàodiàn/yàofáng	药店/药房

HEALTH & EMERGENCY	PINYIN	CHINESE
medicine	yàopiàn	药片
antibiotic	kàngshēngsù/kàngjùnsù	抗生素/抗菌素
aspirin/painkiller	āsīpīlín	阿斯匹林
condom	bìyùntào	避孕套
contraceptive	bìyùnyào	避孕药
rehydration salts	fùshuǐ yán	复水盐
Fire!	zháo huǒ lā!	着火啦!
police	jǐngchá	警察
Thief (pickpocket)!	xiǎotōu!	小偷!
My money/passport has been stolen.	yǒurén tōu le wǒde qián/hùzhào	有人偷了我的钱/护照
I've lost my money/passport.	wǒ bǎ wǒ de qián/hùzhào diu le	我把我的钱/护照丢了
danger/dangerous	wéixiǎn	危险
Go away!	zǒukāi	走开

ACCOMMODATIONS	PINYIN	CHINESE
hotel	bīnguǎn/fàndiàn/jiǔdiàn/lǚguǎn	宾馆/饭店/酒店/旅馆
hostel	zhāodàisuǒ/lǚshè	招待所/旅社
yurt	ménggǔ bāo	蒙古包
room	fángjiān	房间
dormitory	duōrén fáng/jiān	多人房/间
single room	dānrén fáng/jiān	单人房/间
double room	shuāngrén fáng/jiān	双人房/间
triple room	sānrén fáng/jiān	三人房/间
economy room	jīngjì fáng/jiān	经济房/间
standard room	biāozhǔn fáng/jiān	标准房/间
luxury room	háohúa tàofáng/jiān	豪华套房/间
bed	chuángwèi	床位
You must pay for the entire room	nǐ xūyào bāofáng	你需要包房
check-out	tuìfáng	退房
key	yàoshí	钥匙
deposit	yājīn	押金
attendant	fúwùyuán	服务员
Can I look at the room?	wǒ kěyǐ kànkan fángjiān ma?	我可以看看房间吗?
Is it okay for men and women to stay together?	néng nánnǚ tóngjū ma?	能男女同居吗?
We are a married couple	wǒmen jiéhūnle	我们结婚了
(24hr.) hot water	(èrshísì gè xiǎoshí) rèshuǐ	24个小时热水
When is hot water available?	shénme shíhoù yǒu rèshuǐ?	什么时候有热水?
air-conditioning	kōngtiáo	空调
free breakfast	miǎnfèi zǎocān	免费早餐
Please wash these clothes	qǐng bǎ zhè xiē yīfu xǐ hǎo	请把这些衣服洗好

COMMUNICATIONS	PINYIN	CHINESE
post office	yóujú	邮局
letter	xìn	信
envelope	xìnfēng	信封
postcard	míngxìnpiàn	明信片
stamp	yóupiào	邮票
package	bāoguǒ	包裹
Express Mail International Service (EMS)	guójì tèkuài zhuāndì	国际特快专递
air mail	hángkōng xìn	航空信
surface mail	píngyóu	平邮
registered mail	guà hàoxìn	挂号信
Poste Restante	cúnjú hòulǐng	存局候领
telephone office	diànxùn dàlóu	电讯大楼
China Telecom	zhōngguó diànxìn	中国电信
telephone	diànhuà	电话
phone card	diànhuà kǎ	电话卡
long-distance call	chángtú diànhuà	长途电话
international call	guójì chángtú diànhuà	国际长途电话
collect call	duìfāng fùqián diànhuà	对方付钱电话
I want to make a long-distance phone call	wǒ yào dǎ chángtú diànhuà	我要打长途电话
What is the number for...?	...de diànhuà hàomǎ shì duōshǎo ?	...的电话号码是多少?
First dial "0"	xiān bō líng	先拨零
I want to [send/receive] a fax	wǒ yào [fā/shōu] chuánzhēn	我要[发/收] 传真
Internet bar	wǎngbā	网吧
computer	diànnǎo	电脑
I want to get on the Internet	wǒ yào shàng wǎng	我要上网
I want to send an email	wǒ yào fā diànzi yóujiàn	我要发电子邮件
How much is it per hour?	yī ge xiǎoshí duōshǎo qián?	一个小时多少钱?

PASSPORT & VISA	PINYIN	CHINESE
passport	hùzhào	护照
visa	qiānzhèng	签证
I need to extend my visa	wǒ xūyào yáncháng wǒ de qiānzhèng	我需要延长我的签证
PSB Division of Exit and Entry	gōng ān jú chūrù jìng guǎnlǐ chù	公安局出入境管理处
PSB Foreign Affairs Branch	gōng ān jú wàishì kē	公安局外事科
embassy	dàshǐguǎn	大使馆
consulate	língshìguǎn	领事馆

LEISURE	PINYIN	CHINESE
film	diànyǐng	电影
I want to watch a film	wǒ xiǎng kàn diànyǐng	我想看电影
movie theater	diànyǐng yuàn	电影院

APPENDIX

LEISURE	PINYIN	CHINESE
music	yīnyuè	音乐
music concert	yīnyuè huì	音乐会
opera	xìjù	戏剧
sports	tǐyù	体育
stadium	tǐyùchǎng	体育场
to play (a sport)	dǎ	打
soccer	zúqiú	足球
table tennis	pīngpāng qiú	乒乓球
basketball	lánqiú	篮球
swimming (pool)	yóuyǒng (chí)	游泳(池)
martial arts	wǔshù	武术
tai chi	tàijí quán	太极拳
mahjong	májiàng	麻将
I am here strictly to travel	wǒ shì zhuānmén lái lǚyóu de	我是专门来旅游的
How old are you?	nǐ duō dà/nǐ duō dà niánlíng?	你多大/你多大年龄?
I am 20 (30, ...) years old	wǒ (èrshí, sānshí...) suì	我(20, 30, ...) 岁
What do you do (what is your occupation)?	nǐ shì zuò shénme de?	你是作什么的?
I am a student/I go to school	wǒ shì xuéshēng/wǒ zài shàng xué	我是学生/我在上学
I am a teacher/I teach school	wǒ shì lǎoshī/wǒ zài jiàoshū	我是老师/我在教书
I work	wǒ shàngbān	我上班
I am retired	wǒ tuìxiú le	我退休了
I (don't) have any children	wǒ (méi) yǒu háizi	我(没) 有孩子
bar	jiǔbā	酒吧
nightclub	jùlèbù	俱乐部
cover	ménpiào	门票
entertainment center	yúlè chǎng	娱乐场
massage	àn mó	按摩
sauna	sāngná	桑拿
karaoke	kǎlā OK	卡拉OK
You are very pretty/handsome	nǐ hěn piàoliang/hǎokàn	你很漂亮/好看
You are truly remarkable	nǐ zhēn liǎo bù qǐ	你真了不起
I love you	wǒ ài nǐ	我爱你
to make love	zuò ài [colloquial: qí mǎ]	做爱[骑马]
I am not that casual	wǒ bù nàme suíbiàn	我不那么随便

TIME	PINYIN	CHINESE
minutes	fēnzhōng	分钟
hour	xiǎoshí	小时
...o'clock	...diǎn	...点
What time is now?	xiànzài jǐ diǎn?	现在几点?
morning	zǎochén	早晨
noon	zhōngwǔ	中午
afternoon	xiàwǔ	下午

TIME	PINYIN	CHINESE
week	xīngqī/lǐbài	星期/礼拜
Monday	xīngqī yī	星期一
Tuesday	xīngqī èr	星期二
Wednesday	xīngqī sān	星期三
Thursday	xīngqī sì	星期四
Friday	xīngqī wǔ	星期五
Saturday	xīngqī liù	星期六

TIME	PINYIN	CHINESE
evening	bāngwǎn	傍晚
night	wǎnshàng	晚上
midnight	bànyè	半夜
daytime	báitiān	白天
nighttime	wǎnshàng	晚上
now	xiànzài	现在
day	tiān or rì	天 or 日
today	jīn tiān	今天
yesterday	zuó tiān	昨天
tomorrow	míngtiān	明天

FOOD	PINYIN	CHINESE
to eat	chīfàn	吃饭
supermarket	chāoshì	超市
restaurant	cānguǎn	餐馆
street stall	dài pái dàng	大排挡
to go	dàizǒu	带走
delivery	sòng	送
waitstaff/ waitress	fúwùyuán/ xiǎojiē	服务员/小姐
how many people are in your party?	nǐ jǐ wèi?	你几位?
menu	càidān	菜单
check/bill	zhàngdān	账单
chopsticks	kuàizi	筷子
napkin	cānjīnzhǐ	餐巾纸
fork	chāzi	叉子
knife	dàozi	刀子
spoon	sháozi	勺子
bowl	wǎn	碗
plate	pánzi	盘子
Is the food ready yet?	fàn zuò hǎo le ma?	饭做好了吗?
delicious	hǎochī	好吃
This has no flavor	zhè méi yǒu wèidào	这没有味道
hot (temp.)	rè	热
cold	liáng	凉
Not too much...	bùyào tài duō	不要太多
spicy	là	辣
garlic	dàsuàn	大蒜
MSG	wèijīng	味精

TIME	PINYIN	CHINESE
Sunday	xīngqī rì/tiān	星期日/天
month (moon)	yuè	月
Months are referred to numerically starting with Jan.:		
January	yīyuè	一月
February	èryuè	二月
year	nián	年
last year	qù nián	去年
1978	yī jiu qī bā nián	一九七八年
past	yǐqián	以前
future	jiānglái, weìlái	将来, 未来

FOOD	PINYIN	CHINESE
I am vegetarian	wǒ chī sù	我吃素
I don't eat meat	wǒ bù chī ròu	我不吃肉
I am on a diet	wǒ jiǎnféi	我减肥
buffet	zìzhù cān	自助餐
dim sum	diǎnxīn	点心
snacks	xiǎochī	小吃
Muslim	qīngzhēn	清真
fast food	kuài cān	快餐
McDonald's	màidāngláo	麦当劳
hamburger	hànbǎobāo	汉堡包
white rice	mǐfàn	米饭
fried rice	chǎofàn	炒饭
noodles	miàntiáo	面条
Northwest noodles	xīběi lāmián	西北拉面
mixed noodles	bàn miàn	半面
kebab	ròu chuān	肉串
bean curd/ tofu	dòufǔ	豆腐
soup	miàntāng	面汤
noodle soup	shāguǒ	沙锅
beef noodle soup	niúròu miàn	牛肉面
hotpot	shuàn yángròu	涮羊肉
hotpot (Sichuan)	huǒguō	火锅
curry	gālí	咖喱
wontons	húndùn	馄饨
dumplings	jiǎozi	饺子
steamed dumplings	bāozi	包子

FOOD	PINYIN	CHINESE
oil	yóu	油
pepper	làjiāo	辣椒
salt (salty)	yán (xián)	盐(咸)
soy sauce	jiàng yóu	酱油
sugar (sweet)	táng (tián)	塘(甜)
vinegar	cù	醋
vegetables	shūcài	蔬菜
Chinese cabbage	báicài	白菜
corn	yùmǐ	玉米
cucumber	huángguā	黄瓜
green vegetables	qīngcài	青菜
mushrooms	xiānggū/mógū	香菇/蘑菇
peas	wāndòu	豌豆
fruit	shuǐguǒ	水果
apple	píngguǒ	苹果
banana	xiāngjiāo	香蕉
grape	pútáo	葡萄
lychee	lìzhī	荔枝
mango	mángguǒ	芒果
peach	táozi	桃子
pineapple	bōluó	菠萝
watermelon	xīguā	西瓜
ice cream	bīngqílín	冰淇淋
shake	nǎixī	奶昔
sweet soy milk	dòujiāng	豆浆
yogurt	suānnǎi	酸奶
moon cake	yuè bǐng	月饼
sweet bean paste rolls	dòushā(gāo/bāo)	豆沙(糕/包)
soft drinks	qìshuǐ	汽水
Coke	kěkǒu kělè	可口可乐

PLACES	PINYIN	CHINESE
sea	hǎi	海
river	jiāng or hé	江 or 河
lake	hú	湖
pond	chí	池

FOOD	PINYIN	CHINESE
Shanghai-style dumplings	xiǎolóng bāo	小龙包
egg	jīdàn	鸡蛋
steamed buns	mántóu	馒头
bread	miànbāo	面包
fried bread sticks	yóutiáo	油条
beef	niúròu	牛肉
chicken	jī	鸡
dog	gǒu	狗
Beijing duck	kǎoyā	烤鸭
fish	yú	鱼
frog	qīngwā	青蛙
lamb	yángròu	羊肉
pork	zhūròu	猪肉
seafood	hǎixiān	海鲜
shrimp	xiā	虾
snake	shé	蛇
to drink	hē	喝
beverage	yínliào	饮料
water	shuǐ	水
bottle	píng	瓶
cup	bēi	杯
hot water	bái kāi shuǐ	白开水
tea house	chá guǎn/chá fáng	茶馆/茶房
cafe	kāfeiguǎn	咖啡馆
tea	chá	茶
eight-treasure tea	bā bǎo chá	八宝茶
milk pearl tea	zhēnzhū nǎi chá	珍珠奶茶
coffee	kāfēi	咖啡
beer	píjiǔ	啤酒
Tsingtao beer	qīngdǎo píjiǔ	青岛啤酒

PLACES	PINYIN	CHINESE
What country are you from?	nǐ shì nǎguó rén? or nǐ shì nǎlǐ lái de?	你是哪国人? or 你是哪里来的?
I am a native of (country).	wǒ shì...rén.	我是...人
Chinese	zhōngguó rén	中国人
foreigner	wàiguó rén	外国人

PLACES	PINYIN	CHINESE
stream	xī	溪
waterfall	pùbù	瀑布
island	dǎo	岛
peninsula	bàndǎo	半岛
beach	hǎitān (shātān)	海滩(沙滩)
forest	sēnlín	森林
grasslands	cǎoyuán	草原
desert	shāmò	沙漠
plateau	gāoyuán	高原
mountain	shān	山
glacier	bīngchuān	冰川
cave	dòng	洞
grotto	shíkū	石窟
hot springs	wēnquán	温泉
countryside	nóngcūn	农村
downtown	shì zhōngxīn	市中心
city	chéngshì	城市
county	xiàn	县
square	guǎngchǎng	广场
temple	sì	寺
park	gōngyuán	公园
museum	bówùguǎn	博物馆
road	lù	路
street	jiē	街
boulevard or avenue	dàjiē or dàdào	大街 or 大道

PLACES	PINYIN	CHINESE
Where are you going?	nǐ qù nǎ gè guójiā?	你去哪个国家?
border crossing	jièxiàn	界线
Australia	aōdàlìyà	澳大利亚
Canada	jiānádà	加拿大
France	fǎguó	法国
India	yìndù	印度
Ireland	āiěrlán	爱尔兰
Japan	rìběn	日本
Kazakhstan	hāsàkèsītǎn	哈萨克斯坦
Kyrgyzstan	jíěrjísītǎn	吉尔吉斯斯坦
Laos	lǎowō	老挝
Mongolia	ménggǔ	蒙古
Myanmar	miǎndiàn	缅甸
Nepal	níbóěr	尼泊尔
New Zealand	xīn xīlán	新西兰
North Korea	běi cháoxiān	北朝鲜
Pakistan	bājīsítǎn	巴基斯坦
Russia	éluósí	俄罗斯
South Africa	nánfēi	南非
South Korea	hánguó	韩国
Taiwan	táiwān	台湾
Thailand	tàiguó	泰国
UK	yīngguó	英国
US	měiguó	美国
Vietnam	yuènán	越南

WEATHER	PINYIN	CHINESE
weather	tiānqì	天气
How's the weather?	tiānqì zěnmè yàng?	天气怎么样?
weather forecast	tiānqì yùbào	天气预报
°C	shèshí wēndù	摄氏温度
clear	tiānqíng	天晴
sun	tàiyáng	太阳
cloudy	duōyún	多云
windy	guāfēng	刮风
hot and humid	mēnrè	闷热
extremely hot	rè sǐ le	热死了

WEATHER	PINYIN	CHINESE
Is it going to rain?	huì xiàyǔ ma?	会下雨吗?
rain	xiàyǔ	下雨
thunderstorms	léizhènyǔ	雷阵雨
hail	bīngbáo	冰雹
typhoon	táifēng	台风
flood	shuǐzāi	水灾
raincoat	yǔyī	雨衣
umbrella	yǔsǎn	雨伞
snow	xiàxuě	下雪
extremely cold	lěng sǐ le	冷死了

CANTONESE PHRASEBOOK

NUMBERS					
0	ling	**6**	luk	**12**	sap yee

APPENDIX

NUMBERS					
1	yat	**7**	chat	**20**	yee sap
2	yee	**8**	pak	**21**	yee sap yat
3	sam	**9**	gau	**100**	yat pak
4	sei	**10**	sap	**10,000**	yat man
5	mm	**11**	sap yat	**100,000**	sap man

USEFUL PHRASES			
Hello	nei hou	**Goodbye**	bai bai
How are you?	nei hou ma?	**I'm sorry**	doi mm chi
Thank you	do je/mm goi	**You're welcome**	mm sai mm goi
What's your name?	nei giu meh meng?	**My name is ...**	ngo giu ...?
yes	hai	**no**	mm hai
I don't speak Chinese.	ngo mm sek kong kong tong wa.	**Do you speak English?**	nei kong ying man ma?
I don't understand.	ngo mm meng.	**Where is ... ?**	... hai bin tou?
How much does it cost?	gei chin ah?	**too expensive**	tai gwai lah

TIBETAN PHRASEBOOK

USEFUL PHRASES			
Hello	Tah-shi de-lah	**Goodbye (to the person leaving)**	Kah-leh phe
How are you?	Keh-rahng ku-su de-bo yin-peh?	**Goodbye (to the person staying behind)**	Kah-leh shoo
Please have some	shey shey	**No thank you**	La meh
What's your name?	Keh-rahng gi ming la kah-rey yin?	**My name is ...**	Ngah...yin.
Go away!	gyu!	**Don't do that!**	mah che!
I don't speak Tibetan.	Ngah Phö-keh shing-gi-meh	**Do you speak English?**	Dhey In-jee-keh shing-ken yo-ray-peh?
I don't understand.	Ha-kho-mah-song	**Where is ... ?**	...kah-bah yo-ray?
How much does it cost?	...gi kong kah-tsö ray?	**Please help me.**	Ngah la

UIGHUR PHRASEBOOK

USEFUL PHRASES			
Hello, how are you?	yak-shimi-sis	**to eat**	tam-ak
Okay	yak-shi	**invite to eat**	tam-ak yang
Goodbye	hara-hosh	**lamb kebab**	kawap
What are you doing?	azer ne-mar-ish ka-li-sis	**My name is...**	lagh-man
How much does	nai-chi po	**lamb and vegetable pita pocket**	sam-sa
Out of the way!	bosh, bosh!	**hami melon**	how-hun
Thank you	rah-mat siz-ga	**tea**	chai

USEFUL CONVERSIONS

DISTANCE CONVERSIONS							
Meters	1	15	50	100	200	500	1000
Feet	3.281	50	164	328	656	1640	3280

APPENDIX

TEMPERATURE CONVERSIONS

°Celsius	-40	-20	-18	0	15	25	35
°Fahrenheit	-40	-4	0	32	59	77	95

MEASUREMENT CONVERSIONS

1 inch (in.) = 25.4 millimeters (mm)	1 millimeter (mm) = 0.039 in.
1 foot (ft.) = 0.30 m	1 meter (m) = 3.28 ft.
1 yard (yd.) = 0.914m	1 meter (m) = 1.09 yd.
1 mile = 1.61km	1 kilometer (km) = 0.62 mi.
1 ounce (oz.) = 28.35g	1 gram (g) = 0.035 oz.
1 pound (lb.) = 0.454kg	1 kilogram (kg) = 2.202 lb.
1 fluid ounce (fl. oz.) = 29.57ml	1 milliliter (ml) = 0.034 fl. oz.
1 gallon (gal.) = 3.785L	1 liter (L) = 0.264 gal.
1 acre (ac.) = 0.405ha	1 hectare (ha) = 2.47 ac.
1 square mile (sq. mi.) = 2.59km²	1 square kilometer (km²) = 0.386 sq. mi.

CLIMATE

To convert from °C to °F, multiply by 1.8 and add 32. For a rough approximation, double the Celsius and add 25. To convert from °F to °C, subtract 32 and multiply by 0.55 (approx. 5/9). For a rough approximation, subtract 25 and cut it in half.

Avg. Temp. (low/high)	January		April		July		October	
	°C	°F	°C	°F	°C	°F	°C	°F
Beijing	-10/1	14/34	7/21	45/70	21/31	70/88	6/20	43/68
Chongqing	5/9	41/49	16/23	60/73	24/34	76/93	16/22	61/71
Harbin	-24/-5	-5/14	0/13	32/54	18/26	65/83	0/12	32/53
Hong Kong	13/18	56/64	19/24	67/75	26/31	78/87	23/27	73/81
Lhasa	-10/7	14/44	1/16	33/60	9/23	49/74	1/17	34/62
Shanghai	1/8	33/46	10/19	50/66	23/32	74/90	14/23	57/74
Ürümqi	-22/-11	-7/13	2/16	36/60	14/28	58/82	-1/10	31/50

Avg. Rain (mm)	Jan	Feb	Mar	Apr	May	Jun	july	Aug	Sep	Oct	Nov	Dec
Beijing	4	5	8	17	35	78	196	244	58	16	11	3
Chongqing	15	20	38	99	142	180	142	122	150	112	48	20
Harbin	5	5	15	20	35	90	150	110	40	25	10	5
Hong Kong	33	46	74	137	292	394	381	367	257	114	43	31
Lhasa	0	13	8	5	25	64	122	89	66	13	3	0
Shanghai	48	58	84	94	94	180	147	142	130	71	51	36
Ürümqi	15	8	13	38	28	38	18	25	15	43	41	10

INDEX

A

B

INDEX

C

INDEX

D

E

F

G

INDEX

INDEX

N

O

P

Q

R

S

T

Y

Z

Book your air, hotel, and transportation all in one place.
Hotel or hostel? Cruise or canoe? Car? Plane? Camel? Wherever you're going, visit Yahoo! Travel and get total control over your arrangements. Even choose your seat assignment. So. One hump or two? travel.yahoo.com

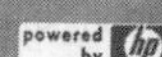
powered by hp

YAHOO!
Travel

Do You Yahoo!?

MAP INDEX

MAP LEGEND

Hospital
Police
Post Office
Tourist Office
Bank
Embassy/Consulate
Site or Point of Interest
Telephone Office
Theater
Airport
Bus Station
Train Station
METRO STATION
Ferry Landing
Church
Synagogue
Mosque
Mountain
Museum
Hotel/Hostel
Camping
Food & Drink
Shopping
Entertainment
Nightlife
Cafe
Internet Café
Park
Beach
Water

The Let's Go compass always points NORTH.

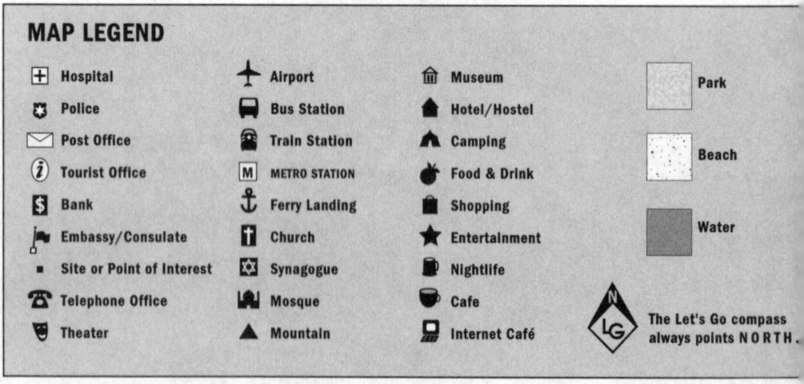